Pro ASP.NET Core 3

Develop Cloud-Ready Web Applications Using MVC,
Blazor, and Razor Pages

Eighth Edition

Adam Freeman

D1294346

Apress®

Pro ASP.NET Core 3: Develop Cloud-Ready Web Applications Using MVC, Blazor, and Razor Pages

Adam Freeman
London, UK

ISBN-13 (pbk): 978-1-4842-5439-4   ISBN-13 (electronic): 978-1-4842-5440-0
https://doi.org/10.1007/978-1-4842-5440-0

Managing Director, Apress Media LLC: Welmoed Spahr
Acquisitions Editor: Joan Murray
Development Editor: Laura Berendson
Editorial Operations Manager: Mark Powers

Cover designed by eStudioCalamar

Cover image designed by Freepik (www.freepik.com)

Distributed to the book trade worldwide by Apress Media, LLC, 1 New York Plaza, New York, NY 10004, U.S.A. Phone 1-800-SPRINGER, fax (201) 348-4505, e-mail orders-ny@springer-sbm.com, or visit www.springeronline.com. Apress Media, LLC is a California LLC and the sole member (owner) is Springer Science + Business Media Finance Inc (SSBM Finance Inc). SSBM Finance Inc is a **Delaware** corporation.

For information on translations, please e-mail editorial@apress.com; for reprint, paperback, or audio rights, please email bookpermissions@springernature.com.

Apress titles may be purchased in bulk for academic, corporate, or promotional use. eBook versions and licenses are also available for most titles. For more information, reference our Print and eBook Bulk Sales web page at www.apress.com/bulk-sales.

Any source code or other supplementary material referenced by the author in this book is available to readers on GitHub via the book's product page, located at www.apress.com/9781484254394. For more detailed information, please visit www.apress.com/source-code.

Printed on acid-free paper

Dedicated to my lovely wife, Jacqui Griffyth.
(And also to Peanut.)

Table of Contents

About the Author

Adam Freeman is an experienced IT professional who has held senior positions in a range of companies, most recently serving as chief technology officer and chief operating officer of a global bank. Now retired, he spends his time writing and long-distance running.

About the Technical Reviewer

Fabio Claudio Ferracchiati is a senior consultant and a senior analyst/developer using Microsoft technologies. He works for BluArancio (www.bluarancio.com). He is a Microsoft Certified Solution Developer for .NET, a Microsoft Certified Application Developer for .NET, a Microsoft Certified Professional, and a prolific author and technical reviewer. Over the past ten years, he's written articles for Italian and international magazines and coauthored more than ten books on a variety of computer topics.

Introducing ASP.NET Core

CHAPTER 1

■ ■ ■

Putting ASP.NET Core in Context

Understanding ASP.NET Core

ASP.NET Core is Microsoft's web development platform. The original ASP.NET was introduced in 2002, and it has been through several reinventions and reincarnations to become ASP.NET Core 3, which is the topic of this book.

ASP.NET Core consists of a platform for processing HTTP requests, a series of principal frameworks for creating applications, and secondary utility frameworks that provide supporting features, as illustrated by Figure 1-1.

Figure 1-1. *The structure of ASP.NET Core*

Understanding the Application Frameworks

When you start using ASP.NET Core, it can be confusing to find that there are different application frameworks available. As you will learn, these frameworks are complementary and solve different problems, or, for some features, solve the same problems in different ways. Understanding the relationship between these frameworks means understanding the changing design patterns that Microsoft has supported, as I explain in the sections that follow.

Understanding the MVC Framework

The MVC Framework was introduced in the pre-Core days of ASP.NET. The original ASP.NET relied on a development model called Web Pages, which re-created the experience of writing desktop applications but resulted in unwieldy web projects that did not scale well. The MVC Framework was introduced alongside Web Pages with a development model that embraced the character of HTTP and HTML, rather than trying to hide it.

© Adam Freeman 2020

A. Freeman, *Pro ASP.NET Core 3*, https://doi.org/10.1007/978-1-4842-5440-0_1

MVC stands for Model-View-Controller, which is a design pattern that describes the shape of an application. The MVC pattern emphasizes *separation of concerns*, where areas of functionality are defined independently, which was an effective antidote to the indistinct architectures that Web Pages led to.

Early versions of the MVC Framework were built on the ASP.NET foundations that were originally designed for Web Pages, which led to some awkward features and workarounds. With the move to .NET Core, ASP.NET became ASP.NET Core, and the MVC Framework was rebuilt on an open, extensible, and cross-platform foundation.

The MVC Framework remains an important part of ASP.NET Core, but the way it is commonly used has changed with the rise of single-page applications (SPAs). In an SPA, the browser makes a single HTTP request and receives an HTML document that delivers a rich client, typically written in a JavaScript client such as Angular or React. The shift to SPAs means that the clean separation that the MVC Framework was originally intended for is not as important, and the emphasis placed on following the MVC pattern is no longer essential, even though the MVC Framework remains useful (and is used to support SPAs through web services, as described in Chapter 19).

PUTTING PATTERNS IN THEIR PLACE

Design patterns provoke strong reactions, as the emails I receive from readers will testify. A substantial proportion of the messages I receive are complaints that I have not applied a pattern correctly.

Patterns are just other people's solutions to the problems they encountered in other projects. If you find yourself facing the same problem, understanding how it has been solved before can be helpful. But that doesn't mean you have to follow the pattern exactly, or at all, as long as you understand the consequences. If a pattern is intended to make projects manageable, for example, and you choose to deviate from that pattern, then you must accept that your project may be more difficult to manage. But a pattern followed slavishly can be worse than no pattern at all, and no pattern is suited to every project.

My advice is to use patterns freely, adapt them as necessary, and ignore zealots who confuse patterns with commandments.

Understanding Razor Pages

One drawback of the MVC Framework is that it can require a lot of preparatory work before an application can start producing content. Despite its structural problems, one advantage of Web Pages was that simple applications could be created in a couple of hours.

Razor Pages takes the development ethos of Web Pages and implements it using the platform features originally developed for the MVC Framework. Code and content are mixed to form self-contained pages; this re-creates the speed of Web Pages development without some of the underlying technical problems (although the issue of scaling up complex projects can still be an issue).

Razor Pages can be used alongside the MVC Framework, which is how I tend to use them. I write the main parts of the application using the MVC Framework and use Razor Pages for the secondary features, such as administration and reporting tools. You can see this approach in Chapters 7–11, where I develop a realistic ASP.NET Core application called SportsStore.

Understanding Blazor

The rise of JavaScript client-side frameworks can be a barrier for C# developers, who must learn a different—and somewhat idiosyncratic—programming language. I have come to love JavaScript, which is as fluid and expressive as C#. But it takes time and commitment to become proficient in a new programming language, especially one that has fundamental differences from C#.

Blazor attempts to bridge this gap by allowing C# to be used to write client-side applications. There are two versions of Blazor: Blazor Server and Blazor WebAssembly. Blazor Server is a stable and supported part of ASP.NET Core, and it works by using a persistent HTTP connection to the ASP.NET Core server, where the application's C# code is executed. Blazor WebAssembly is an experimental release that goes one step further and executes the application's C# code in the browser. Neither version of Blazor is suited for all situations, as I explain in Chapter 33, but they both give a sense of direction for the future of ASP.NET Core development.

Understanding the Utility Frameworks

Two frameworks are closely associated with ASP.NET Core but are not used directly to generate HTML content or data. Entity Framework Core is Microsoft's object-relational mapping (ORM) framework, which represents data stored in a relational database as .NET objects. Entity Framework Core can be used in any .NET Core application, and it is commonly used to access databases in ASP.NET Core applications.

ASP.NET Core Identity is Microsoft's authentication and authorization framework, and it is used to validate user credentials in ASP.NET Core applications and restrict access to application features.

I describe only the basic features of both frameworks in this book, focusing on the capabilities required by most ASP.NET Core applications. But these are both complex frameworks that are too large to describe in detail in what is already a large book about ASP.NET Core.

TOPICS FOR FUTURE EDITIONS

I don't have space in this book to cover every Entity Framework Core and ASP.NET Core Identity feature, so I have focused on those aspects that most projects require. If there are topics you think I should include in the next edition or in new deep-dive books, then please send me your suggestions at adam@adam-freeman.com.

Understanding the ASP.NET Core Platform

The ASP.NET Core platform contains the low-level features required to receive and process HTTP requests and create responses. There is an integrated HTTP server, a system of middleware components to handle requests, and core features that the application frameworks depend on, such as URL routing and the Razor view engine.

Most of your development time will be spent with the application frameworks, but effective ASP.NET Core use requires an understanding of the powerful capabilities that the platform provides, without which the higher-level frameworks could not function. I demonstrate how the ASP.NET Core platform works in detail in Part 2 of this book and explain how the features it provides underpin every aspect of ASP.NET Core development.

I have not described two notable platform features in this book: SignalR and gRPC. SignalR is used to create low-latency communication channels between applications. It provides the foundation for the Blazor Server framework that I describe in Part 4 of this book, but SignalR is rarely used directly, and there are better alternatives for those few projects that need low-latency messaging, such as Azure Event Grid or Azure Service Bus.

gRPC is an emerging standard for cross-platform remote procedure calls (RPCs) over HTTP that was originally created by Google (the g in gRPC) and offers efficiency and scalability benefits. gRPC may be the future standard for web services, but it cannot be used in web applications because it requires low-level control of the HTTP messages that it sends, which browsers do not allow. (There is a browser library that allows gRPC to be used via a proxy server, but that undermines the benefits of using gRPC.) Until gRPC can be used in the browser, its inclusion in ASP.NET Core is of interest only for projects that use it for communication between back-end servers, for which many alternative protocols exist. I may cover gRPC in future editions of this book but not until it can be used in the browser or becomes the dominant data-center protocol.

Understanding This Book

To get the most from this book, you should be familiar with the basics of web development, understand how HTML and CSS work, and have a working knowledge of C#. Don't worry if you haven't done any client-side development, such as JavaScript. The emphasis in this book is on C# and ASP.NET Core, and you will be able to pick up everything you need to know as you progress through the chapters. In Chapter 5, I summarize the most important C# features for ASP.NET Core development, which you will find useful if you are coming to ASP.NET Core from earlier versions of .NET Core or the .NET Framework.

What Software Do I Need to Follow the Examples?

You need a code editor (either Visual Studio or Visual Studio Code), the .NET Core Software Development Kit, and SQL Server LocalDB. All are available for use from Microsoft without charge, and Chapter 2 contains instructions for installing everything you need.

What Platform Do I Need to Follow the Examples?

This book is written for Windows. I used Windows 10 Pro, but any version of Windows supported by Visual Studio, Visual Studio Code, and .NET Core should work. ASP.NET Core is supported on other platforms, but the examples in this book rely on the SQL Server LocalDB feature, which is specific to Windows. You can contact me at adam@adam-freeman.com if you are trying to use another platform, and I will give you some general pointers for adapting the examples, albeit with the caveat that I won't be able to provide detailed help if you get stuck.

What If I Have Problems Following the Examples?

The first thing to do is to go back to the start of the chapter and begin again. Most problems are caused by missing a step or not fully following a listing. Pay close attention to the emphasis in code listings, which highlights the changes that are required.

Next, check the errata/corrections list, which is included in the book's GitHub repository. Technical books are complex, and mistakes are inevitable, despite my best efforts and those of my editors. Check the errata list for the list of known errors and instructions to resolve them.

If you still have problems, then download the project for the chapter you are reading from the book's GitHub repository, `https://github.com/apress/pro-asp.net-core-3`, and compare it to your project. I create the code for the GitHub repository by working through each chapter, so you should have the same files with the same contents in your project.

If you still can't get the examples working, then you can contact me at `adam@adam-freeman.com` for help. Please make it clear in your email which book you are reading and which chapter/example is causing the problem. Please remember that I get a lot of emails and that I may not respond immediately.

What If I Find an Error in the Book?

You can report errors to me by email at `adam@adam-freeman.com`, although I ask that you first check the errata/corrections list for this book, which you can find in the book's GitHub repository at `https://github.com/apress/pro-asp.net-core-3`, in case it has already been reported.

I add errors that are likely to cause confusion to readers, especially problems with example code, to the errata/corrections file on the GitHub repository, with a grateful acknowledgment to the first reader who reported them. I keep a list of less serious issues, which usually means errors in the text surrounding examples, and I fix them when I write a new edition.

What Does This Book Cover?

I have tried to cover the features that will be required by most ASP.NET Core projects. This book is split into four parts, each of which covers a set of related topics.

Part 1: Introducing ASP.NET Core

This part of the book—which includes this chapter—introduces ASP.NET Core. In addition to setting up your development environment and creating your first application, you'll learn about the most important C# features for ASP.NET Core development and how to use the ASP.NET Core development tools. But most of Part 1 is given over to the development of a project called SportsStore, through which I show you a realistic development process from inception to deployment, touching on all the main features of ASP.NET Core and showing how they fit together—something that can be lost in the deep-dive chapters in the rest of the book.

Part 2: The ASP.NET Core Platform

The chapters in this part of the book describe the key features of the ASP.NET Core platform. I explain how HTTP requests are processed, how to create and use middleware components, how to create routes, how to define and consume services, and how to work with Entity Framework Core. These chapters explain the foundations of ASP.NET Core, and understanding them is essential for effective ASP.NET Core development.

Part 3: ASP.NET Core Applications

The chapters in this part of the book explain how to create different types of applications, including RESTful web services and HTML applications using controllers and Razor Pages. These chapters also describe the features that make it easy to generate HTML, including the views, view components, and tag helpers.

Part 4: Advanced ASP.NET Core Features

The final part of the book explains how to create applications using Blazor Server, how to use the experimental Blazor WebAssembly, and how to authenticate users and authorize access using ASP.NET Core Identity.

What Doesn't This Book Cover?

This book doesn't cover basic web development topics, such as HTML and CSS, and doesn't teach basic C# (although Chapter 5 does describe C# features useful for ASP.NET Core development that may not be familiar to developers using older versions of .NET).

As much as I like to dive into the details in my books, not every ASP.NET Core feature is useful in mainstream development, and I have to keep my books to a printable size. When I decide to omit a feature, it is because I don't think it is important or because the same outcome can be achieved using a technique that I do cover.

As noted earlier, I have not described the ASP.NET Core support for SignalR and gRPC, and I note other features in later chapters that I don't describe, either because they are not broadly applicable or because there are better alternatives available. In each case, I explain why I have omitted a description and provide a reference to the Microsoft documentation for that topic.

How Do I Contact the Author?

You can email me at adam@adam-freeman.com. It has been a few years since I first published an email address in my books. I wasn't entirely sure that it was a good idea, but I am glad that I did it. I have received emails from around the world, from readers working or studying in every industry, and—for the most part anyway—the emails are positive, polite, and a pleasure to receive.

I try to reply promptly, but I get a lot of email, and sometimes I get a backlog, especially when I have my head down trying to finish writing a book. I always try to help readers who are stuck with an example in the book, although I ask that you follow the steps described earlier in this chapter before contacting me.

While I welcome reader emails, there are some common questions for which the answers will always be no. I am afraid that I won't write the code for your new startup, help you with your college assignment, get involved in your development team's design dispute, or teach you how to program.

What If I Really Enjoyed This Book?

Please email me at adam@adam-freeman.com and let me know. It is always a delight to hear from a happy reader, and I appreciate the time it takes to send those emails. Writing these books can be difficult, and those emails provide essential motivation to persist at an activity that can sometimes feel impossible.

What If This Book Has Made Me Angry and I Want to Complain?

You can still email me at adam@adam-freeman.com, and I will still try to help you. Bear in mind that I can only help if you explain what the problem is and what you would like me to do about it. You should understand that sometimes the only outcome is to accept I am not the writer for you and that we will have closure only when you return this book and select another. I'll give careful thought to whatever has upset you, but after 25 years of writing books, I have come to understand that not everyone enjoys reading the books I like to write.

Summary

In this chapter, I set the scene for the rest of the book. I provided a brief overview of ASP.NET Core, explained the requirements for and the content of this book, and explained how you can contact me. In the next chapter, I show you how to prepare for ASP.NET Core development.

CHAPTER 2

Getting Started

The best way to appreciate a software development framework is to jump right in and use it. In this chapter, I explain how to prepare for ASP.NET Core development and how to create and run an ASP.NET Core application.

UPDATES TO THIS BOOK

Microsoft has an active development schedule for .NET Core and ASP.NET Core, which means that there may be new releases available by the time you read this book. It doesn't seem fair to expect readers to buy a new book every few months, especially since most changes are relatively minor. Instead, I will post free updates to the GitHub repository for this book (https://github.com/apress/pro-asp.net-core-3) for breaking changes.

This kind of update is an ongoing experiment for me (and for Apress), and it continues to evolve—not least because I don't know what the future major releases of ASP.NET Core will contain—but the goal is to extend the life of this book by supplementing the examples it contains.

I am not making any promises about what the updates will be like, what form they will take, or how long I will produce them before folding them into a new edition of this book. Please keep an open mind and check the repository for this book when new ASP.NET Core versions are released. If you have ideas about how the updates could be improved, then email me at adam@adam-freeman.com and let me know.

Choosing a Code Editor

Microsoft provides a choice of tools for ASP.NET Core development: Visual Studio and Visual Studio Code. Visual Studio is the traditional development environment for .NET applications, and it offers an enormous range of tools and features for developing all sorts of applications. But it can be resource-hungry and slow, and some of the features are so determined to be helpful they get in the way of development.

Visual Studio Code is a light-weight alternative that doesn't have the bells and whistles of Visual Studio but is perfectly capable of handling ASP.NET Core development.

All the examples in this book include instructions for both editors, and both Visual Studio and Visual Studio Code can be used without charge, so you can use whichever suits your development style.

If you are new to .NET Core development, then start with Visual Studio. It provides more structured support for creating the different types of files used in ASP.NET Core development, which will help ensure you get the expected results from the code examples.

Note This book describes ASP.NET Core development for Windows. It is possible to develop and run ASP.NET Core applications on Linux and macOS, but most readers use Windows, and that is what I have chosen to focus on. Almost all the examples in this book rely on LocalDB, which is a Windows-only feature provided by SQL Server that is not available on other platforms. If you want to follow this book on another platform, then you can contact me using the email address in Chapter 1, and I will try to help you get started.

A. Freeman, *Pro ASP.NET Core 3*, https://doi.org/10.1007/978-1-4842-5440-0_2

Installing Visual Studio

ASP.NET Core 3 requires Visual Studio 2019. I use the free Visual Studio 2019 Community Edition, which can be downloaded from www.visualstudio.com. Run the installer, and you will see the prompt shown in Figure 2-1.

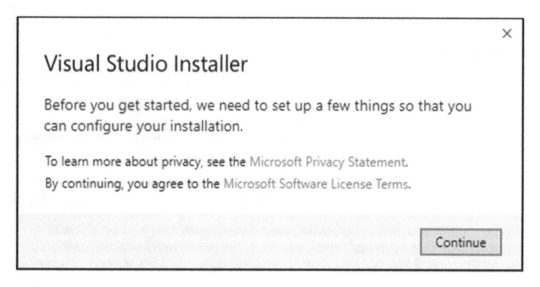

Figure 2-1. *Starting the Visual Studio installer*

Click the Continue button, and the installer will download the installation files, as shown in Figure 2-2.

Figure 2-2. *Downloading the Visual Studio installer files*

When the installer files have been downloaded, you will be presented with a set of installation options, grouped into workloads. Ensure that the "ASP.NET and web development" workload is checked, as shown in Figure 2-3.

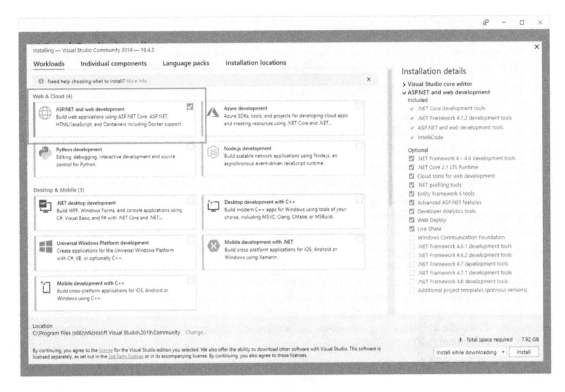

Figure 2-3. *Selecting the workload*

Select the "Individual components" section at the top of the window and ensure the SQL Server Express 2016 LocalDB option is checked, as shown in Figure 2-4. This is the database component that I will be using to store data in later chapters.

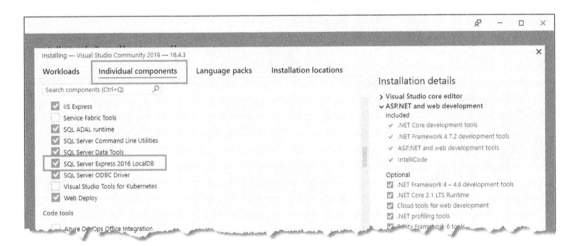

Figure 2-4. *Ensuring LocalDB is installed*

Click the Install button, and the files required for the selected workload will be downloaded and installed. To complete the installation, a reboot is required, as shown in Figure 2-5.

Reboot required

Success! One more step to go. Please restart your computer before you start Visual Studio
Community 2019.

Get troubleshooting tips   Restart   Not now

Figure 2-5. *Completing the installation*

Installing the .NET Core SDK

The Visual Studio installer will install the .NET Core Software Development Kit (SDK), but it may not install the version required for the examples in this book. Go to `https://dotnet.microsoft.com/download/dotnet-core/3.1` and download the installer for version 3.1.1 of the .NET Core SDK, which is the long-term support release at the time of writing. Run the installer; once the installation is complete, open a new PowerShell command prompt from the Windows Start menu and run the command shown in Listing 2-1, which displays a list of the installed .NET Core SDKs.

Listing 2-1. Listing the Installed SDKs

```
dotnet --list-sdks
```

Here is the output from a fresh installation on a Windows machine that has not been used for .NET Core:

```
3.1.101 [C:\Program Files\dotnet\sdk]
```

If you have been working with different versions of .NET Core, you may see a longer list, like this one:

```
2.1.401 [C:\Program Files\dotnet\sdk]
2.1.502 [C:\Program Files\dotnet\sdk]
2.1.505 [C:\Program Files\dotnet\sdk]
2.1.602 [C:\Program Files\dotnet\sdk]
2.1.802 [C:\Program Files\dotnet\sdk]
3.0.100 [C:\Program Files\dotnet\sdk]
3.1.100 [C:\Program Files\dotnet\sdk]
3.1.101 [C:\Program Files\dotnet\sdk]
```

Regardless of how many entries there are, you must ensure there is one for the 3.1.1xx version, where the last two digits may differ.

Installing Visual Studio Code

If you have chosen to use Visual Studio Code, download the installer from `https://code.visualstudio.com`. No specific version is required, and you should select the current stable build. Run the installer and ensure you check the Add to PATH option, as shown in Figure 2-6.

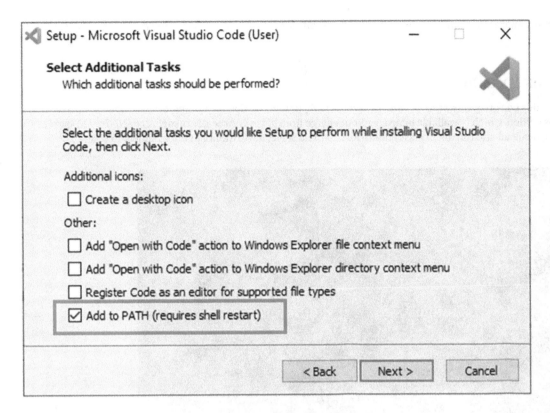

Figure 2-6. *Configuring the Visual Studio Code installation*

Installing the .NET Core SDK

The Visual Studio installer does not include the .NET Core SDK, which must be installed separately. Go to https://dotnet.microsoft.com/download/dotnet-core/3.1 and download the installer for version 3.1.1 of the .NET Core SDK, which is the long-term support release at the time of writing. Run the installer; once the installation is complete, open a new PowerShell command prompt from the Windows Start menu and run the command shown in Listing 2-2, which displays a list of the installed .NET Core SDKs.

Listing 2-2. Listing the Installed SDKs

```
dotnet --list-sdks
```

Here is the output from a fresh installation on a Windows machine that has not been used for .NET Core:

```
3.1.101 [C:\Program Files\dotnet\sdk]
```

If you have been working with different versions of .NET Core, you may see a longer list, like this one:

```
2.1.401 [C:\Program Files\dotnet\sdk]
2.1.502 [C:\Program Files\dotnet\sdk]
2.1.505 [C:\Program Files\dotnet\sdk]
2.1.602 [C:\Program Files\dotnet\sdk]
2.1.802 [C:\Program Files\dotnet\sdk]
3.0.100 [C:\Program Files\dotnet\sdk]
3.1.100 [C:\Program Files\dotnet\sdk]
3.1.101 [C:\Program Files\dotnet\sdk]
```

Regardless of how many entries there are, you must ensure there is one for the 3.1.1xx version, where the last two digits may differ.

Installing SQL Server LocalDB

The database examples in this book require LocalDB, which is a zero-configuration version of SQL Server that can be installed as part of the SQL Server Express edition, which is available for use without charge from `https://www.microsoft.com/en-in/sql-server/sql-server-downloads`. Download and run the Express edition installer and select the Custom option, as shown in Figure 2-7.

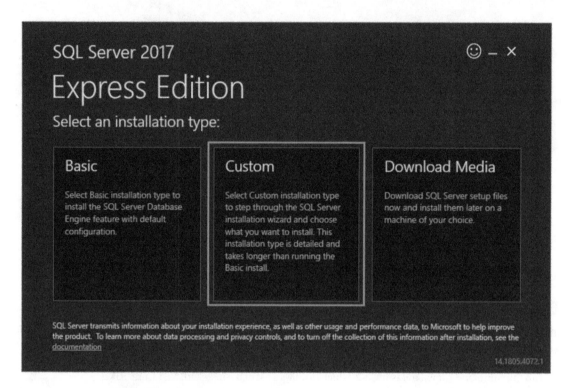

Figure 2-7. *Selecting the installation option for SQL Server*

Once you have selected the Custom option, you will be prompted to select a download location for the installation files. Click the Install button, and the download will begin.

When prompted, select the option to create a new SQL Server installation, as shown in Figure 2-8.

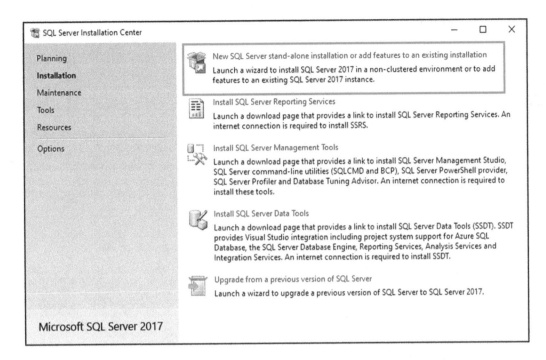

Figure 2-8. *Selecting an installation option*

Work through the installation process, selecting the default options as they are presented. When you reach the Feature Selection page, ensure that the LocalDB option is checked, as shown in Figure 2-9. (You may want to uncheck the options for R and Python, which are not used in this book and take a long time to download and install.)

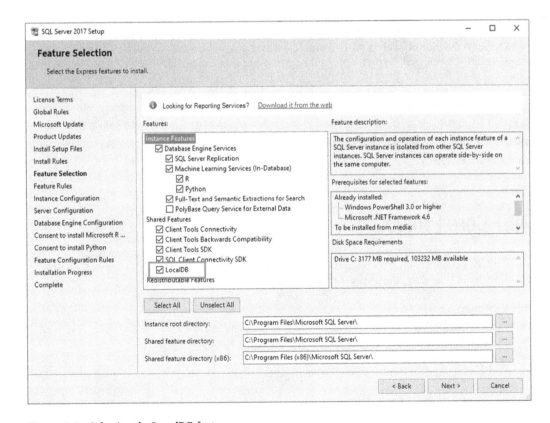

Figure 2-9. *Selecting the LocalDB feature*

On the Instance Configuration page, select the "Default instance" option, as shown in Figure 2-10.

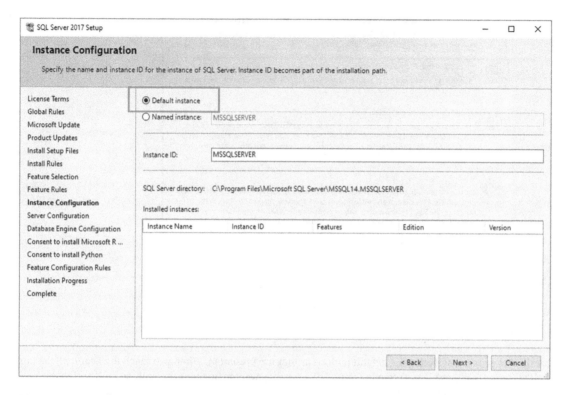

Figure 2-10. *Configuring the database*

Continue to work through the installation process, selecting the default values. Once the installation is complete, install the latest cumulative update for SQL Server. At the time of writing, the latest update is available at `https://support.microsoft.com/en-us/help/4527377/cumulative-update-18-for-sql-server-2017`, although newer updates may have been released by the time you read this chapter.

■ **Caution** It can be tempting to skip the update stage, but it is important to perform this step to get the expected results from the examples in this book. As an example, the base installation of SQL Server has a bug that prevents LocalDB from creating database files, which will cause problems when you reach Chapter 7.

Creating an ASP.NET Core Project

The most direct way to create a project is to use the command line, although Visual Studio provides a wizard system that I demonstrate in Chapter 4. Open a new PowerShell command prompt from the Windows Start menu, navigate to the folder where you want to create your ASP.NET Core projects, and run the commands shown in Listing 2-3.

■ **Tip** You can download the example project for this chapter—and for all the other chapters in this book—from `https://github.com/apress/pro-asp.net-core-3`. See Chapter 1 for how to get help if you have problems running the examples.

Listing 2-3. Creating a New Project

```
dotnet new globaljson --sdk-version 3.1.101 --output FirstProject
dotnet new mvc --no-https --output FirstProject --framework netcoreapp3.1
```

The first command creates a folder named `FirstProject` and adds to it a file named `global.json`, which specifies the version of .NET Core that the project will use; this ensures you get the expected results when following the examples. The second command creates a new ASP.NET Core project. The .NET Core SDK includes a range of templates for starting new projects, and the `mvc` template is one of the options available for ASP.NET Core applications. This project template creates a project that is configured for the MVC Framework, which is one of the application types supported by ASP.NET Core. Don't be intimidated by the idea of choosing a framework, and don't worry if you have not heard of MVC—by the end of the book, you will understand the features that each offers and how they fit together.

▪ **Note** This is one of a small number of chapters in which I use a project template that contains placeholder content. I don't like using predefined project templates because they encourage developers to treat important features, such as authentication, as black boxes. My goal in this book is to give you the knowledge to understand and manage every aspect of your ASP.NET Core applications, and that's why I start with an empty ASP.NET Core project. This chapter is about getting started quickly, for which the `mvc` template is well-suited.

Opening the Project Using Visual Studio

Start Visual Studio and click the "Open a project or solution" button, as shown in Figure 2-11.

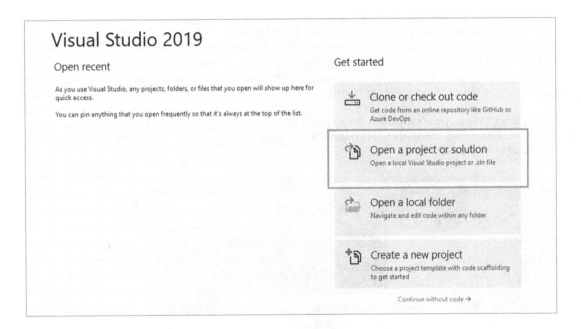

Figure 2-11. *Opening the ASP.NET Core project*

Navigate to the `FirstProject` folder, select the `FirstProject.csproj` file, and click the Open button. Visual Studio will open the project and display its contents in the Solution Explorer window, as shown in Figure 2-12. The files in the project were created by the project template.

Figure 2-12. Opening the project in Visual Studio

Choosing a Browser

Visual Studio will open a browser window automatically when the project is run. To select the browser that is used, click the small arrow to the right of the IIS Express drop-down and select your preferred browser from the Web Browser menu, as shown in Figure 2-13. I use Google Chrome throughout this book.

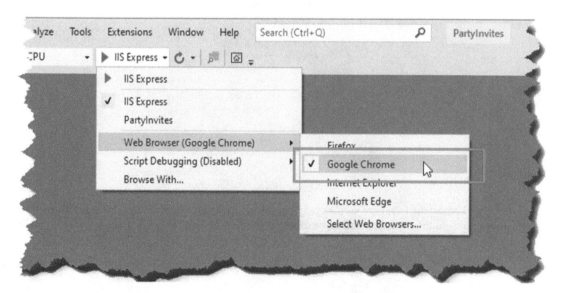

Figure 2-13. Selecting the browser

Opening the Project with Visual Studio Code

Start Visual Studio Code and select FIle ➤ Open Folder. Navigate to the FirstProject folder and click the Select Folder button. Visual Studio Code will open the project and display its contents in the Explorer pane, as shown in Figure 2-14. (The default dark theme used in Visual Studio Code doesn't show well on the page, so I have changed to the light theme for the screenshots in this book.)

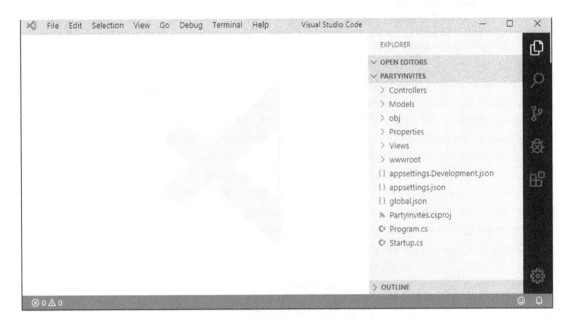

Figure 2-14. *Opening the project in Visual Studio Code*

Additional configuration is required the first time you open a .NET Core project in Visual Studio Code. The first step is to click the Startup.cs file in the Explorer pane. This will trigger a prompt from Visual Studio Code to install the features required for C# development, as shown in Figure 2-15. If you have opened a C# project before, you will see a prompt that offers to install the required assets, also shown in Figure 2-15.

Figure 2-15. *Installing Visual Studio Code C# features*

Click the Install or Yes button, as appropriate, and Visual Studio Code will download and install the features required for .NET Core projects.

Running the ASP.NET Core Application

The template creates a project that contains everything needed to build and run the application. Select Start Without Debugging from the Debug menu, and Visual Studio will compile and start the example application and then open a new browser window to send the application an HTTP request, as shown in Figure 2-17. (If you don't see the Start Without Debugging item in the Debug menu, then click the Startup.cs file in the Solution Explorer window and check the menu again.)

If you are using Visual Studio Code, select Run Without Debugging in the Debug menu. Since this is the first time the project has been started, you will be prompted to select an execution environment. Select the .NET Core option, as shown in Figure 2-16.

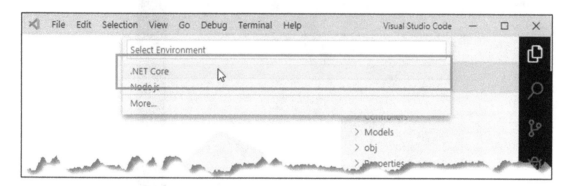

Figure 2-16. *Selecting an execution environment*

Visual Studio Code will create a launch.json file that contains the startup settings for the project and that you can ignore for this book. Select Run Without Debugging from the Debug menu again, and Visual Studio Code will compile the project, start executing the application, and open a new browser window, as shown in Figure 2-17.

You can also start the application from the command line. Open a new PowerShell command prompt from the Windows Start menu; navigate to the FirstProject project folder, which is the folder that contains the FirstProject.csproj file; and run the command shown in Listing 2-4.

Listing 2-4. Starting the Example Application

```
dotnet run
```

Once the application has started, you will need to open a new browser window and request http://localhost:5000, which will produce the response shown in Figure 2-17.

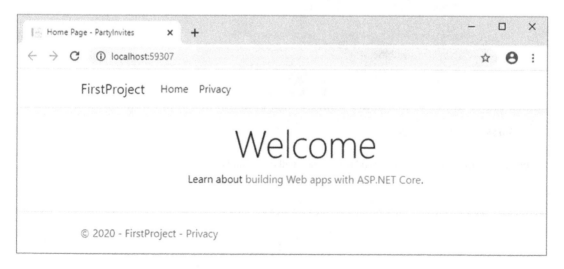

Figure 2-17. *Running the example project*

■ **Tip** If you are using Visual Studio Code or running the application from the command line, then ASP.NET Core listens for HTTP requests on port 5000. If you are using Visual Studio, you will notice that the browser requests a different port, which is chosen when the project is created. If you look in the Windows taskbar notification area, you will find an icon for IIS Express. This is a cut-down version of the full IIS application server that is included with Visual Studio and is used to deliver ASP.NET Core content and services during development. In later chapters, I show you how to change the project configuration to use the same HTTP port as Visual Studio Code.

When you are finished, close the browser window that Visual Studio opened. If you are using Visual Studio Code, you click the stop button displayed in the window that pops up over the code editor. If you started the application from the command line, then use Control+C to stop execution.

Understanding Endpoints

In an ASP.NET Core application, incoming requests are handled by *endpoints*. The endpoint that produced the response in Figure 2-17 is an *action*, which is a method that is written in C#. An action is defined in a *controller*, which is a C# class that is derived from the `Microsoft.AspNetCore.Mvc.Controller` class, the built-in controller base class.

Each public method defined by a controller is an action, which means you can invoke the action method to handle an HTTP request. The convention in ASP.NET Core projects is to put controller classes in a folder named `Controllers`, which was created by the template used to set up the project in Listing 2-3.

The project template added a controller to the `Controllers` folder to help jump-start development. The controller is defined in the class file named `HomeController.cs`. Controller classes contain a name followed by the word `Controller`, which means that when you see a file called `HomeController.cs`, you know that it contains a controller called Home, which is the default controller that is used in ASP.NET Core applications.

■ **Tip** Don't worry if the terms *controller* and *action* don't make immediate sense. Just keep following the example, and you will see how the HTTP request sent by the browser is handled by C# code.

Find the `HomeController.cs` file in the Solution Explorer or Explorer pane and click it to open it for editing. You will see the following code:

```
using System;
using System.Collections.Generic;
using System.Diagnostics;
using System.Linq;
using System.Threading.Tasks;
using Microsoft.AspNetCore.Mvc;
using Microsoft.Extensions.Logging;
using FirstProject.Models;

namespace FirstProject.Controllers {
    public class HomeController : Controller {
        private readonly ILogger<HomeController> _logger;

        public HomeController(ILogger<HomeController> logger) {
            _logger = logger;
        }

        public IActionResult Index() {
            return View();
        }

        public IActionResult Privacy() {
            return View();
        }
```

```
    [ResponseCache(Duration = 0, Location = ResponseCacheLocation.None,
        NoStore = true)]
    public IActionResult Error() {
        return View(new ErrorViewModel { RequestId = Activity.Current?.Id
            ?? HttpContext.TraceIdentifier });
    }
  }
}
```

Using the code editor, replace the contents of the HomeController.cs file so that it matches Listing 2-5. I have removed all but one of the methods, changed the result type and its implementation, and removed the using statements for unused namespaces.

Listing 2-5. Changing the HomeController.cs File in the Controllers Folder

```
using Microsoft.AspNetCore.Mvc;

namespace FirstProject.Controllers {

    public class HomeController : Controller {

        public string Index() {
            return "Hello World";
        }
    }
}
```

The result is that the Home controller defines a single action, named Index. These changes don't produce a dramatic effect, but they make for a nice demonstration. I have changed the method named Index so that it returns the string Hello World. Run the project again by selecting Start Without Debugging or Run Without Debugging from the Debug menu.

The browser will make an HTTP request to the ASP.NET Core server. The configuration of the project created by the template in Listing 2-5 means the HTTP request will be processed by the Index action defined by the Home controller. Put another way, the request will be processed by the Index method defined by the HomeController class. The string produced by the Index method is used as the response to the browser's HTTP request, as shown in Figure 2-18.

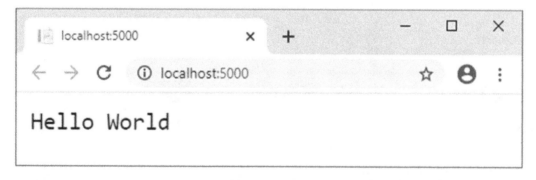

Figure 2-18. *The output from the action method*

Understanding Routes

The ASP.NET Core *routing* system is responsible for selecting the endpoint that will handle an HTTP request. A *route* is a rule that is used to decide how a request is handled. When the project was created, a default rule was created to get started. You can request any of the following URLs, and they will be dispatched to the Index action defined by the Home controller:

- /
- /Home
- /Home/Index

So, when a browser requests `http://yoursite/` or `http://yoursite/Home`, it gets back the output from `HomeController`'s `Index` method. You can try this yourself by changing the URL in the browser. At the moment, it will be `http://localhost:5000/`, except that the port part may be different if you are using Visual Studio. If you append `/Home` or `/Home/Index` to the URL and press Return, you will see the same `Hello World` result from the application.

Understanding HTML Rendering

The output from the previous example wasn't HTML—it was just the string `Hello World`. To produce an HTML response to a browser request, I need a *view*, which tells ASP.NET Core how to process the result produced by the `Index` method into an HTML response that can be sent to the browser.

Creating and Rendering a View

The first thing I need to do is modify my `Index` action method, as shown in Listing 2-6. The changes are shown in bold, which is a convention I follow throughout this book to make the examples easier to follow.

Listing 2-6. Rendering a View in the HomeController.cs File in the Controllers Folder

```
using Microsoft.AspNetCore.Mvc;

namespace FirstProject.Controllers {

    public class HomeController : Controller {

        public ViewResult Index() {
            return View("MyView");
        }
    }
}
```

When I return a `ViewResult` object from an action method, I am instructing ASP.NET Core to *render* a view. I create the `ViewResult` by calling the `View` method, specifying the name of the view that I want to use, which is `MyView`. If you run the application, you can see ASP.NET Core trying to find the view, as shown by the error message displayed in Figure 2-19.

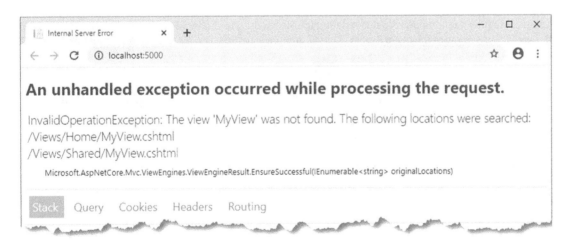

Figure 2-19. *Ttrying to find a view*

This is a helpful error message. It explains that ASP.NET Core could not find the view I specified for the action method and explains where it looked. Views are stored in the Views folder, organized into subfolders. Views that are associated with the Home controller, for example, are stored in a folder called Views/Home. Views that are not specific to a single controller are stored in a folder called Views/Shared. The template used to create the project added the Home and Shared folders automatically and added some placeholder views to get the project started.

If you are using Visual Studio, right-click the Views/Home folder in the Solution Explorer and select Add ➤ New Item from the popup menu. Visual Studio will present you with a list of templates for adding items to the project. Locate the Razor View item, which can be found in the ASP.NET Core ➤ Web ➤ ASP.NET section, as shown in Figure 2-20. Set the name of the new file to MyView.cshtml and click the Add button. Visual Studio will add a file named MyView.cshtml to the Views/Home folder and will open it for editing. Replace the contents of the file with those shown in Listing 2-7.

Figure 2-20. *Selecting a Visual Studio item template*

Visual Studio Code doesn't provide item templates. Instead, right-click the Views/Home folder in the file explorer pane and select New File from the popup menu. Set the name of the file to MyView.cshtml and press Return. The file will be created and opened for editing. Add the content shown in Listing 2-7.

■ **Tip**　It is easy to end up creating the view file in the wrong folder. If you didn't end up with a file called MyView.cshtml in the Views/Home folder, then either drag the file into the correct folder or delete the file and try again.

Listing 2-7.　The Contents of the MyView.cshtml File in the Views/Home Folder

```
@{
    Layout = null;
}

<!DOCTYPE html>

<html>
<head>
    <meta name="viewport" content="width=device-width" />
    <title>Index</title>
</head>
```

```
<body>
    <div>
        Hello World (from the view)
    </div>
</body>
</html>
```

The new contents of the view file are mostly HTML. The exception is the part that looks like this:

```
...
@{
    Layout = null;
}
...
```

This is an expression that will be interpreted by Razor, which is the component that processes the contents of views and generates HTML that is sent to the browser. Razor is a *view engine*, and the expressions in views are known as *Razor expressions*.

The Razor expression in Listing 2-7 tells Razor that I chose not to use a layout, which is like a template for the HTML that will be sent to the browser (and which I describe in Chapter 22). To see the effect of creating the view, stop ASP.NET Core if it is running and select Start Without Debugging (for Visual Studio) or Run Without Debugging (for Visual Studio Code) from the Debug menu. A new browser window will open and produce the response shown in Figure 2-21.

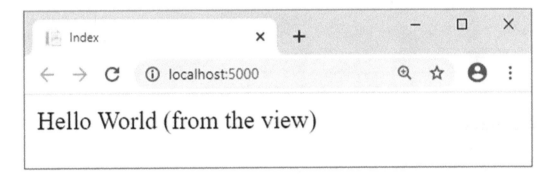

Figure 2-21. *Rendering a view*

When I first edited the Index action method, it returned a string value. This meant that ASP.NET Core did nothing except pass the string value as is to the browser. Now that the Index method returns a ViewResult, Razor is used to process a view and render an HTML response. Razor was able to locate the view because I followed the standard naming convention, which is to put view files in a folder whose name matched the controller that contains the action method. In this case, this meant putting the view file in the Views/Home folder, since the action method is defined by the Home controller.

I can return other results from action methods besides strings and ViewResult objects. For example, if I return a RedirectResult, the browser will be redirected to another URL. If I return an HttpUnauthorizedResult, I can prompt the user to log in. These objects are collectively known as *action results*. The action result system lets you encapsulate and reuse common responses in actions. I'll tell you more about them and explain the different ways they can be used in Chapter 19.

Adding Dynamic Output

The whole point of a web application is to construct and display *dynamic* output. The job of the action method is to construct data and pass it to the view so it can be used to create HTML content based on the data values. Action methods provide data to views by passing arguments to the View method, as shown in Listing 2-8. The data provided to the view is known as the *view model*.

Listing 2-8. Providing a View Model in the HomeController.cs File in the Controllers Folder

```
using Microsoft.AspNetCore.Mvc;
using System;

namespace FirstProject.Controllers {

    public class HomeController : Controller {

        public ViewResult Index() {
            int hour = DateTime.Now.Hour;
            string viewModel = hour < 12 ? "Good Morning" : "Good Afternoon";
            return View("MyView", viewModel);
        }
    }
}
```

The view model in this example is a `string`, and it is provided to the view as the second argument to the `View` method. Listing 2-9 updates the view so that it receives and uses the view model in the HTML it generates.

Listing 2-9. Using a View Model in the MyView.cshtml File in the Views/Home Folder

```
@model string
@{
    Layout = null;
}

<!DOCTYPE html>

<html>
<head>
    <meta name="viewport" content="width=device-width" />
    <title>Index</title>
</head>
<body>
    <div>
        @Model World (from the view)
    </div>
</body>
</html>
```

The type of the view model is specified using the `@model` expression, with a lowercase *m*. The view model value is included in the HTML output using the `@Model` expression, with an uppercase *M*. (It can be difficult at first to remember which is lowercase and which is uppercase, but it soon becomes second nature.)

When the view is rendered, the view model data provided by the action method is inserted into the HTML response. Select Start Without Debugging (using Visual Studio) or Run Without Debugging (using Visual Studio Code), and you will see the output shown in Figure 2-22 (although you may see the afternoon greeting if you are following this example after midday).

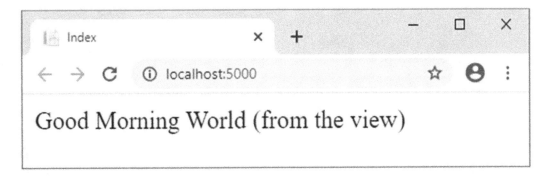

Figure 2-22. *Generating dynamic content*

Putting the Pieces Together

It is a simple result, but this example reveals all the building blocks you need to create a simple ASP.NET Core web application and to generate a dynamic response. The ASP.NET Core platform receives an HTTP request and uses the routing system to match the request URL to an endpoint. The endpoint, in this case, is the Index action method defined by the Home controller. The method is invoked and produces a ViewResult object that contains the name of a view and a view model object. The Razor view engine locates and processes the view, evaluating the @Model expression to insert the data provided by the action method into the response, which is returned to the browser and displayed to the user. There are, of course, many other features available, but this is the essence of ASP.NET Core, and it is worth bearing this simple sequence in mind as you read the rest of the book.

Summary

In this chapter, I explained how to get set up for ASP.NET Core development by installing Visual Studio or Visual Studio Code and the .NET Core SDK. I showed you how to create a simple project and briefly explained how the endpoint, the view, and the URL routing system work together. In the next chapter, I show you how to create a simple data-entry application.

CHAPTER 3

Your First ASP.NET Core Application

Now that you are set up for ASP.NET Core development, it is time to create a simple application. In this chapter, you'll create a data-entry application using ASP.NET Core. My goal is to demonstrate ASP.NET Core in action, so I will pick up the pace a little and skip over some of the explanations as to how things work behind the scenes. But don't worry; I'll revisit these topics in depth in later chapters.

Setting the Scene

Imagine that a friend has decided to host a New Year's Eve party and that she has asked me to create a web app that allows her invitees to electronically RSVP. She has asked for these four key features:

- A home page that shows information about the party

- A form that can be used to RSVP

- Validation for the RSVP form, which will display a thank-you page

- A summary page that shows who is coming to the party

In this chapter, I create an ASP.NET Core project and use it to create a simple application that contains these features; once everything works, I'll apply some styling to improve the appearance of the finished application.

Creating the Project

Open a PowerShell command prompt from the Windows Start menu, navigate to a convenient location, and run the commands in Listing 3-1 to create a project named PartyInvites.

■ **Tip** You can download the example project for this chapter—and for all the other chapters in this book—from https://github. com/apress/pro-asp.net-core-3. See Chapter 1 for how to get help if you have problems running the examples.

Listing 3-1. Creating a New Project

```
dotnet new globaljson --sdk-version 3.1.101 --output PartyInvites
dotnet new mvc --no-https --output PartyInvites --framework netcoreapp3.1
```

These are the same commands I used to create the project in Chapter 2. If you are a Visual Studio user, I explain how you can use a wizard to create a project in Chapter 4, but these commands are simple and will ensure you get the right project starting point that uses the required version of .NET Core.

Open the project and edit the HomeController.cs file in the Controllers folder, replacing the contents with the code shown in Listing 3-2.

Listing 3-2. Replacing the Contents of the HomeController.cs File in the Controllers Folder

```
using Microsoft.AspNetCore.Mvc;

namespace PartyInvites.Controllers {
    public class HomeController : Controller {

        public IActionResult Index() {
            return View();
        }
    }
}
```

The provides a clean starting point for the new application, defining a single action method that selects the default view for rendering. To provide a welcome message to party invitees, open the Index.cshtml file in the Views/Home folder and replace the contents with those shown in Listing 3-3.

Listing 3-3. Replacing the Contents of the Index.cshtml File in the Views/Home Folder

```
@{
    Layout = null;
}

<!DOCTYPE html>
<html>
<head>
    <meta name="viewport" content="width=device-width" />
    <title>Party!</title>
</head>
<body>
    <div>
        <div>
            We're going to have an exciting party.<br />
            (To do: sell it better. Add pictures or something.)
        </div>
    </div>
</body>
</html>
```

Start the application by selecting Start Without Debugging (for Visual Studio) or Run Without Debugging (for Visual Studio Code), and you will see the details of the party (well, the placeholder for the details, but you get the idea), as shown in Figure 3-1.

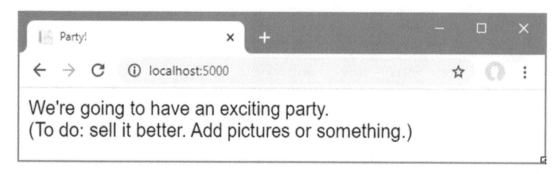

Figure 3-1. Adding to the view HTML

Adding a Data Model

The data model is the most important part of any ASP.NET Core application. The model is the representation of the real-world objects, processes, and rules that define the subject, known as the *domain*, of the application. The model, often referred to as a *domain model*, contains the C# objects (known as *domain objects*) that make up the universe of the application and the methods that manipulate them. In most projects, the job of the ASP.NET Core application is to provide the user with access to the data model and the features that allow the user to interact with it.

The convention for an ASP.NET Core application is that the data model classes are defined in a folder named Models, which was added to the project by the template used in Listing 3-1.

I don't need a complex model for the PartyInvites project because it is such a simple application. In fact, I need just one domain class that I will call GuestResponse. This object will represent an RSVP from an invitee.

If you are using Visual Studio, right-click the Models folder and select Add ➤ Class from the popup menu. Set the name of the class to GuestResponse.cs and click the Add button. If you are using Visual Studio Code, right-click the Models folder, select New File, and enter GuestResponse.cs as the file name. Use the new file to define the class shown in Listing 3-4.

Listing 3-4. The Contents of the GuestResponse.cs File in the Models Folder

```
namespace PartyInvites.Models {

    public class GuestResponse {

        public string Name { get; set; }
        public string Email { get; set; }
        public string Phone { get; set; }
        public bool? WillAttend { get; set; }
    }
}
```

▪ **Tip** You may have noticed that the WillAttend property is a nullable bool, which means that it can be true, false, or null. I explain the rationale for this in the "Adding Validation" section later in the chapter.

Creating a Second Action and View

One of my application goals is to include an RSVP form, which means I need to define an action method that can receive requests for that form. A single controller class can define multiple action methods, and the convention is to group related actions together in the same controller. Listing 3-5 adds a new action method to the Home controller.

Listing 3-5. Adding an Action Method in the HomeController.cs File in the Controllers Folder

```
using Microsoft.AspNetCore.Mvc;

namespace PartyInvites.Controllers {
    public class HomeController : Controller {

        public IActionResult Index() {
            return View();
        }

        public ViewResult RsvpForm() {
            return View();
        }
    }
}
```

Both action methods invoke the View method without arguments, which may seem odd, but remember that the Razor view engine will use the name of the action method when looking for a view file. That means the result from the Index action method tells Razor to look for a view called Index.cshtml, while the result from the RsvpForm action method tells Razor to look for a view called RsvpForm.cshtml.

If you are using Visual Studio, right-click the Views/Home folder and select Add ➤ New Item from the popup menu. Select the Razor View item, set the name to RsvpForm.cshtml, and click the Add button to create the file. Replace the contents with those shown in Listing 3-6.

If you are using Visual Studio Code, right-click the Views/Home folder and select New File from the popup menu. Set the name of the file to RsvpForm.cshtml and add the contents shown in Listing 3-6.

Listing 3-6. The Contents of the RsvpForm.cshtml File in the Views/Home Folder

```
@{
    Layout = null;
}

<!DOCTYPE html>

<html>
<head>
    <meta name="viewport" content="width=device-width" />
    <title>RsvpForm</title>
</head>
<body>
    <div>
        This is the RsvpForm.cshtml View
    </div>
</body>
</html>
```

This content is just static HTML for the moment. To test the new action method and view, start the application by selecting Start Without Debugging or Run Without Debugging from the Debug menu.

Using the browser window that is opened, request http://localhost:5000/home/rsvpform. (If you are using Visual Studio, you will have to change the port to the one assigned when the project was created.) The Razor view engine locates the RsvpForm.cshtml file and uses it to produce a response, as shown in Figure 3-2.

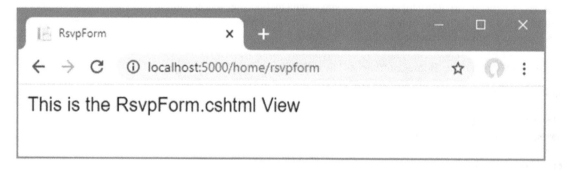

Figure 3-2. *Rendering a second view*

Linking Action Methods

I want to be able to create a link from the Index view so that guests can see the RsvpForm view without having to know the URL that targets a specific action method, as shown in Listing 3-7.

Listing 3-7. Adding a Link in the Index.cshtml File in the Views/Home Folder

```
@{
    Layout = null;
}

<!DOCTYPE html>
<html>
<head>
    <meta name="viewport" content="width=device-width" />
    <title>Party!</title>
</head>
<body>
    <div>
        <div>
            We're going to have an exciting party.<br />
            (To do: sell it better. Add pictures or something.)
        </div>
        <a asp-action="RsvpForm">RSVP Now</a>
    </div>
</body>
</html>
```

The addition to the listing is an a element that has an `asp-action` attribute. The attribute is an example of a *tag helper* attribute, which is an instruction for Razor that will be performed when the view is rendered. The `asp-action` attribute is an instruction to add an `href` attribute to the a element that contains a URL for an action method. I explain how tag helpers work in Chapters 25–27, but this tag helper tells Razor to insert a URL for an action method defined by the same controller for which the current view is being rendered. You can see the link that the helper creates by running the project, as shown in Figure 3-3.

Figure 3-3. *Linking between action methods*

Roll the mouse over the RSVP Now link in the browser. You will see that the link points to the following URL (allowing for the different port number that Visual Studio will have assigned to your project):

```
http://localhost:5000/Home/RsvpForm
```

There is an important principle at work here, which is that you should use the features provided by ASP.NET Core to generate URLs, rather than hard-code them into your views. When the tag helper created the `href` attribute for the a element, it inspected the configuration of the application to figure out what the URL should be. This allows the configuration of the application to be changed to support different URL formats without needing to update any views.

Building the Form

Now that I have created the view and can reach it from the Index view, I am going to build out the contents of the RsvpForm.cshtml file to turn it into an HTML form for editing GuestResponse objects, as shown in Listing 3-8.

Listing 3-8. Creating a Form View in the RsvpForm.cshtml File in the Views/Home Folder

```
@model PartyInvites.Models.GuestResponse
@{
    Layout = null;
}

<!DOCTYPE html>

<html>
<head>
    <meta name="viewport" content="width=device-width" />
    <title>RsvpForm</title>
</head>
<body>
    <form asp-action="RsvpForm" method="post">
        <div>
            <label asp-for="Name">Your name:</label>
            <input asp-for="Name" />
        </div>
        <div>
            <label asp-for="Email">Your email:</label>
            <input asp-for="Email" />
        </div>
        <div>
            <label asp-for="Phone">Your phone:</label>
            <input asp-for="Phone" />
        </div>
        <div>
            <label>Will you attend?</label>
            <select asp-for="WillAttend">
                <option value="">Choose an option</option>
                <option value="true">Yes, I'll be there</option>
                <option value="false">No, I can't come</option>
            </select>
        </div>
        <button type="submit">Submit RSVP</button>
    </form>
</body>
</html>
```

The @model expression specifies that the view expects to receive a GuestResponse object as its view model. I have defined a label and input element for each property of the GuestResponse model class (or, in the case of the WillAttend property, a select element). Each element is associated with the model property using the asp-for attribute, which is another tag helper attribute. The tag helper attributes configure the elements to tie them to the view model object. Here is an example of the HTML that the tag helpers produce:

```
<p>
    <label for="Name">Your name:</label>
    <input type="text" id="Name" name="Name" value="">
</p>
```

The asp-for attribute on the label element sets the value of the for attribute. The asp-for attribute on the input element sets the id and name elements. This may not look especially useful, but you will see that associating elements with a model property offers additional advantages as the application functionality is defined.

Of more immediate use is the asp-action attribute applied to the form element, which uses the application's URL routing configuration to set the action attribute to a URL that will target a specific action method, like this:

```
<form method="post" action="/Home/RsvpForm">
```

As with the helper attribute I applied to the a element, the benefit of this approach is that you can change the system of URLs that the application uses, and the content generated by the tag helpers will reflect the changes automatically.

You can see the form by running the application and clicking the RSVP Now link, as shown in Figure 3-4.

Figure 3-4. *Adding an HTML form to the application*

Receiving Form Data

I have not yet told ASP.NET Core what I want to do when the form is posted to the server. As things stand, clicking the Submit RSVP button just clears any values you have entered in the form. That is because the form posts back to the RsvpForm action method in the Home controller, which just renders the view again. To receive and process submitted form data, I am going to use an important feature of controllers. I will add a second RsvpForm action method to create the following:

- *A method that responds to HTTP GET requests*: A GET request is what a browser issues normally each time someone clicks a link. This version of the action will be responsible for displaying the initial blank form when someone first visits /Home/RsvpForm.

- *A method that responds to HTTP POST requests*: By default, forms rendered using Html.BeginForm() are submitted by the browser as a POST request. This version of the action will be responsible for receiving submitted data and deciding what to do with it.

Handing GET and POST requests in separate C# methods helps to keep my controller code tidy since the two methods have different responsibilities. Both action methods are invoked by the same URL, but ASP.NET Core makes sure that the appropriate method is called, based on whether I am dealing with a GET or POST request. Listing 3-9 shows the changes to the HomeController class.

Listing 3-9. Adding a Method in the HomeController.cs File in the Controllers Folder

```
using Microsoft.AspNetCore.Mvc;
using PartyInvites.Models;

namespace PartyInvites.Controllers {
    public class HomeController : Controller {

        public IActionResult Index() {
            return View();
        }

        [HttpGet]
        public ViewResult RsvpForm() {
            return View();
        }
    }
```

```
    [HttpPost]
    public ViewResult RsvpForm(GuestResponse guestResponse) {
        // TODO: store response from guest
        return View();
    }
    }
}
```

I have added the HttpGet attribute to the existing RsvpForm action method, which declares that this method should be used only for GET requests. I then added an overloaded version of the RsvpForm method, which accepts a GuestResponse object. I applied the HttpPost attribute to this method, which declares that the new method will deal with POST requests. I explain how these additions to the listing work in the following sections. I also imported the PartyInvites.Models namespace—this is just so I can refer to the GuestResponse model type without needing to qualify the class name.

Understanding Model Binding

The first overload of the RsvpForm action method renders the same view as before—the RsvpForm.cshtml file—to generate the form shown in Figure 3-4. The second overload is more interesting because of the parameter, but given that the action method will be invoked in response to an HTTP POST request and that the GuestResponse type is a C# class, how are the two connected?

The answer is *model binding*, a useful ASP.NET Core feature whereby incoming data is parsed and the key/value pairs in the HTTP request are used to populate properties of domain model types.

Model binding is a powerful and customizable feature that eliminates the grind of dealing with HTTP requests directly and lets you work with C# objects rather than dealing with individual data values sent by the browser. The GuestResponse object that is passed as the parameter to the action method is automatically populated with the data from the form fields. I dive into the details of model binding in Chapter 28.

To demonstrate how model binding works, I need to do some preparatory work. One of the application goals is to present a summary page with details of who is attending the party, which means that I need to keep track of the responses that I receive. I am going to do this by creating an in-memory collection of objects. This isn't useful in a real application because the response data will be lost when the application is stopped or restarted, but this approach will allow me to keep the focus on ASP.NET Core and create an application that can easily be reset to its initial state. Later chapters will demonstrate persistent data storage.

Add a class file named Repository.cs to the Models folder and use it to define the class shown in Listing 3-10.

Listing 3-10. The Contents of the Repository.cs File in the Models Folder

```
using System.Collections.Generic;

namespace PartyInvites.Models {
    public static class Repository {
        private static List<GuestResponse> responses = new List<GuestResponse>();

        public static IEnumerable<GuestResponse> Responses => responses;

        public static void AddResponse(GuestResponse response) {
            responses.Add(response);
        }
    }
}
```

The Repository class and its members are static, which will make it easy for me to store and retrieve data from different places in the application. ASP.NET Core provides a more sophisticated approach for defining common functionality, called *dependency injection*, which I describe in Chapter 14, but a static class is a good way to get started for a simple application like this one.

Storing Responses

Now that I have somewhere to store the data, I can update the action method that receives the HTTP POST requests, as shown in Listing 3-11.

Listing 3-11. Updating an Action Method in the HomeController.cs File in the Controllers Folder

```
using Microsoft.AspNetCore.Mvc;
using PartyInvites.Models;

namespace PartyInvites.Controllers {
    public class HomeController : Controller {

        public IActionResult Index() {
            return View();
        }

        [HttpGet]
        public ViewResult RsvpForm() {
            return View();
        }

        [HttpPost]
        public ViewResult RsvpForm(GuestResponse guestResponse) {
            Repository.AddResponse(guestResponse);
            return View("Thanks", guestResponse);
        }
    }
}
```

Before the POST version of the RsvpForm method is invoked, the ASP.NET Core model binding feature extracts values from the HTML form and assigns them to the properties of the GuestResponse object. The result is used as the argument when the method is invoked to handle the HTTP request, and all I have to do to deal with the form data sent in a request is to work with the GuestResponse object that is passed to the action method—in this case, to pass it as an argument to the Repository.AddResponse method so that the response can be stored.

Adding the Thanks View

The call to the View method in the RsvpForm action method creates a ViewResult that selects a view called Thanks and uses the GuestResponse object created by the model binder as the view model. Add a Razor View named Thanks.cshtml to the Views/Home folder with the content shown in Listing 3-12 to present a response to the user.

Listing 3-12. The Contents of the Thanks.cshtml File in the Views/Home Folder

```
@model PartyInvites.Models.GuestResponse
@{
    Layout = null;
}

<!DOCTYPE html>

<html>
<head>
    <meta name="viewport" content="width=device-width" />
    <title>Thanks</title>
</head>
<body>
    <div>
        <h1>Thank you, @Model.Name!</h1>
        @if (Model.WillAttend == true) {
            @:It's great that you're coming. The drinks are already in the fridge!
        } else {
```

```
                    @:Sorry to hear that you can't make it, but thanks for letting us know.
        }
    </div>
    Click <a asp-action="ListResponses">here</a> to see who is coming.
</body>
</html>
```

The HTML produced by the Thanks.cshtml view depends on the values assigned to the GuestResponse view model provided by the RsvpForm action method. To access the value of a property in the domain object, I use an @Model.<PropertyName> expression. So, for example, to get the value of the Name property, I use the @Model.Name expression. Don't worry if the Razor syntax doesn't make sense—I explain it in more detail in Chapter 21.

Now that I have created the Thanks view, I have a basic working example of handling a form. Start the application, click the RSVP Now link, add some data to the form, and click the Submit RSVP button. You will see the response shown in Figure 3-5 (although it will differ if your name is not Joe or you said you could not attend).

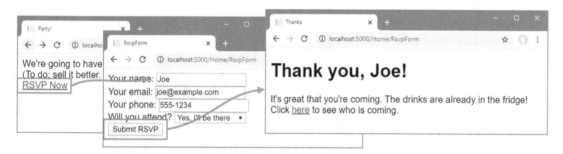

Figure 3-5. *The Thanks view*

Displaying the Responses

At the end of the Thanks.cshtml view, I added an a element to create a link to display the list of people who are coming to the party. I used the asp-action tag helper attribute to create a URL that targets an action method called ListResponses, like this:

```
...
<div>Click <a asp-action="ListResponses">here</a> to see who is coming.</div>
...
```

If you hover the mouse over the link that is displayed by the browser, you will see that it targets the /Home/ListResponses URL. This doesn't correspond to any of the action methods in the Home controller, and if you click the link, you will see a 404 Not Found error response.

To add an endpoint that will handle the URL, I need to add another action method to the Home controller, as shown in Listing 3-13.

Listing 3-13. Adding an Action Method in the HomeController.cs File in the Controllers Folder

```
using Microsoft.AspNetCore.Mvc;
using PartyInvites.Models;
using System.Linq;

namespace PartyInvites.Controllers {
    public class HomeController : Controller {

        public IActionResult Index() {
            return View();
        }
```

```
        [HttpGet]
        public ViewResult RsvpForm() {
            return View();
        }

        [HttpPost]
        public ViewResult RsvpForm(GuestResponse guestResponse) {
            Repository.AddResponse(guestResponse);
            return View("Thanks", guestResponse);
        }

        public ViewResult ListResponses() {
            return View(Repository.Responses.Where(r => r.WillAttend == true));
        }
    }
}
```

The new action method is called `ListResponses`, and it calls the `View` method, using the `Repository.Responses` property as the argument. This will cause Razor to render the default view, using the action method name as the name of the view file, and to use the data from the repository as the view model. The view model data is filtered using LINQ so that only positive responses are provided to the view.

Add a Razor View named `ListResponses.cshtml` to the `Views/Home` folder with the content shown in Listing 3-14.

Listing 3-14. Displaying Acceptances in the ListResponses.cshtml File in the Views/Home Folder

```
@model IEnumerable<PartyInvites.Models.GuestResponse>
@{
    Layout = null;
}

<!DOCTYPE html>

<html>
<head>
    <meta name="viewport" content="width=device-width" />
    <title>Responses</title>
</head>
<body>
    <h2>Here is the list of people attending the party</h2>
    <table>
        <thead>
            <tr><th>Name</th><th>Email</th><th>Phone</th></tr>
        </thead>
        <tbody>
            @foreach (PartyInvites.Models.GuestResponse r in Model) {
                <tr>
                    <td>@r.Name</td>
                    <td>@r.Email</td>
                    <td>@r.Phone</td>
                </tr>
            }
        </tbody>
    </table>
</body>
</html>
```

Razor view files have the .cshtml file extension because they are a mix of C# code and HTML elements. You can see this in Listing 3-14 where I have used a @foreach expression to process each of the GuestResponse objects that the action method passes to the view using the View method. Unlike a normal C# foreach loop, the body of a Razor @foreach expression contains HTML elements that are added to the response that will be sent back to the browser. In this view, each GuestResponse object generates a tr element that contains td elements populated with the value of an object property.

Start the application, submit some form data, and click the link to see the list of responses. You will see a summary of the data you have entered since the application was started, as shown in Figure 3-6. The view does not present the data in an appealing way, but it is enough for the moment, and I will address the styling of the application later in this chapter.

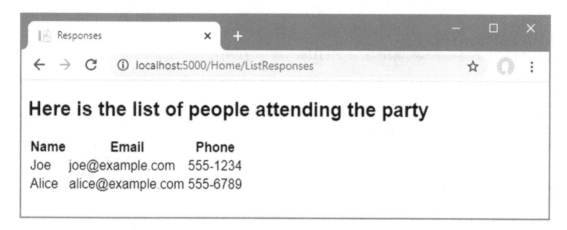

Figure 3-6. *Showing a list of party attendees*

Adding Validation

I can now add data validation to the application. Without validation, users could enter nonsense data or even submit an empty form. In an ASP.NET Core application, validation rules are defined by applying attributes to model classes, which means the same validation rules can be applied in any form that uses that class. ASP.NET Core relies on attributes from the System.ComponentModel. DataAnnotations namespace, which I have applied to the GuestResponse class in Listing 3-15.

Listing 3-15. Applying Validation in the GuestResponse.cs File in the Models Folder

```
using System.ComponentModel.DataAnnotations;

namespace PartyInvites.Models {

    public class GuestResponse {

        [Required(ErrorMessage = "Please enter your name")]
        public string Name { get; set; }

        [Required(ErrorMessage = "Please enter your email address")]
        [EmailAddress]
        public string Email { get; set; }

        [Required(ErrorMessage = "Please enter your phone number")]
        public string Phone { get; set; }

        [Required(ErrorMessage = "Please specify whether you'll attend")]
        public bool? WillAttend { get; set; }
    }
}
```

ASP.NET Core detects the attributes and uses them to validate data during the model-binding process.

■ **Tip**   As noted earlier, I used a nullable bool for the WillAttend property. I did this so that I could apply the Required validation attribute. If I had used a regular bool, the value I received through model binding could be only true or false, and I would not be able to tell whether the user had selected a value. A nullable bool has three possible values: true, false, and null. The browser sends a null value if the user has not selected a value, and this causes the Required attribute to report a validation error. This is a nice example of how ASP.NET Core elegantly blends C# features with HTML and HTTP.

I check to see whether there has been a validation problem using the ModelState.IsValid property in the action method that receives the form data, as shown in Listing 3-16.

Listing 3-16. Checking for Validation Errors in the HomeController.cs File in the Controllers Folder

```
using Microsoft.AspNetCore.Mvc;
using PartyInvites.Models;
using System.Linq;

namespace PartyInvites.Controllers {
    public class HomeController : Controller {

        public IActionResult Index() {
            return View();
        }

        [HttpGet]
        public ViewResult RsvpForm() {
            return View();
        }

        [HttpPost]
        public ViewResult RsvpForm(GuestResponse guestResponse) {
            if (ModelState.IsValid) {
                Repository.AddResponse(guestResponse);
                return View("Thanks", guestResponse);
            } else {
                return View();
            }
        }

        public ViewResult ListResponses() {
            return View(Repository.Responses.Where(r => r.WillAttend == true));
        }
    }
}
```

The Controller base class provides a property called ModelState that provides details of the outcome of the model binding process. If the ModelState.IsValid property returns true, then I know that the model binder has been able to satisfy the validation constraints I specified through the attributes on the GuestResponse class. When this happens, I render the Thanks view, just as I did previously.

If the ModelState.IsValid property returns false, then I know that there are validation errors. The object returned by the ModelState property provides details of each problem that has been encountered, but I don't need to get into that level of detail because I can rely on a useful feature that automates the process of asking the user to address any problems by calling the View method without any parameters.

When it renders a view, Razor has access to the details of any validation errors associated with the request, and tag helpers can access the details to display validation errors to the user. Listing 3-17 shows the addition of validation tag helper attributes to the RsvpForm view.

Listing 3-17. Adding a Validation Summary to the RsvpForm.cshtml File in the Views/Home Folder

```
@model PartyInvites.Models.GuestResponse
@{
    Layout = null;
}

<!DOCTYPE html>

<html>
<head>
    <meta name="viewport" content="width=device-width" />
    <title>RsvpForm</title>
</head>
<body>
    <form asp-action="RsvpForm" method="post">
        <div asp-validation-summary="All"></div>
        <div>
            <label asp-for="Name">Your name:</label>
            <input asp-for="Name" />
        </div>
        <div>
            <label asp-for="Email">Your email:</label>
            <input asp-for="Email" />
        </div>
        <div>
            <label asp-for="Phone">Your phone:</label>
            <input asp-for="Phone" />
        </div>
        <div>
            <label>Will you attend?</label>
            <select asp-for="WillAttend">
                <option value="">Choose an option</option>
                <option value="true">Yes, I'll be there</option>
                <option value="false">No, I can't come</option>
            </select>
        </div>
        <button type="submit">Submit RSVP</button>
    </form>
</body>
</html>
```

The asp-validation-summary attribute is applied to a div element, and it displays a list of validation errors when the view is rendered. The value for the asp-validation-summary attribute is a value from an enumeration called ValidationSummary, which specifies what types of validation errors the summary will contain. I specified All, which is a good starting point for most applications, and I describe the other values and explain how they work in Chapter 29.

To see how the validation summary works, run the application, fill out the Name field, and submit the form without entering any other data. You will see a summary of validation errors, as shown in Figure 3-7.

Figure 3-7. Displaying validation errors

The RsvpForm action method will not render the Thanks view until all the validation constraints applied to the GuestResponse class have been satisfied. Notice that the data entered in the Name field was preserved and displayed again when Razor rendered the view with the validation summary. This is another benefit of model binding, and it simplifies working with form data.

Highlighting Invalid Fields

The tag helper attributes that associate model properties with elements have a handy feature that can be used in conjunction with model binding. When a model class property has failed validation, the helper attributes will generate slightly different HTML. Here is the input element that is generated for the Phone field when there is no validation error:

```
<input type="text" data-val="true" data-val-required="Please enter your phone number" id="Phone" name="Phone"
value="">
```

For comparison, here is the same HTML element after the user has submitted the form without entering data into the text field (which is a validation error because I applied the Required attribute to the Phone property of the GuestResponse class):

```
<input type="text" class="input-validation-error" data-val="true"
    data-val-required="Please enter your phone number" id="Phone"
    name="Phone" value="">
```

I have highlighted the difference: the asp-for tag helper attribute added the input element to a class called input-validation-error. I can take advantage of this feature by creating a stylesheet that contains CSS styles for this class and the others that different HTML helper attributes use.

The convention in ASP.NET Core projects is that static content delivered to clients is placed into the wwwroot folder and organized by content type so that CSS stylesheets go into the wwwroot/css folder, JavaScript files go into the wwwroot/js folder, and so on.

■ **Tip** Visual Studio creates a site.css file in the wwwroot/css folder when a project is created using the Web Application template. You can ignore this file, which I don't use in this chapter.

If you are using Visual Studio, right-click the wwwroot/css folder and select Add ➤ New Item from the popup menu. Locate the Style Sheet item template, as shown in Figure 3-8; set the name of the file to styles.css; and click the Add button.

Figure 3-8. *Creating a CSS stylesheet*

If you are using Visual Studio Code, right-click the `wwwroot/css` folder, select New File from the popup menu, and use `styles.css` as the file name. Regardless of which editor you use, replace the contents of the file with the styles shown in Listing 3-18.

Listing 3-18. The Contents of the styles.css File in the wwwroot/css Folder

```
.field-validation-error    {color: #f00;}
.field-validation-valid    { display: none;}
.input-validation-error    { border: 1px solid #f00; background-color: #fee; }
.validation-summary-errors { font-weight: bold; color: #f00;}
.validation-summary-valid  { display: none;}
```

To apply this stylesheet, I added a `link` element to the `head` section of the `RsvpForm` view, as shown in Listing 3-19.

Listing 3-19. Applying a Stylesheet in the RsvpForm.cshtml File in the Views/Home Folder

```
...
<head>
    <meta name="viewport" content="width=device-width" />
    <title>RsvpForm</title>
    <link rel="stylesheet" href="/css/styles.css" />
</head>
...
```

The `link` element uses the `href` attribute to specify the location of the stylesheet. Notice that the `wwwroot` folder is omitted from the URL. The default configuration for ASP.NET includes support for serving static content, such as images, CSS stylesheets, and JavaScript files, and it maps requests to the `wwwroot` folder automatically. With the application of the stylesheet, a more obvious validation error will be displayed when data is submitted that causes a validation error, as shown in Figure 3-9.

Figure 3-9. *Automatically highlighted validation errors*

Styling the Content

All the functional goals for the application are complete, but the overall appearance of the application is poor. When you create a project using the mvc template, as I did for the example in this chapter, some common client-side development packages are installed. While I am not a fan of using template projects, I do like the client-side libraries that Microsoft has chosen. One of them is called Bootstrap, which is a good CSS framework originally developed by Twitter that has become a major open source project and a mainstay of web application development.

Styling the Welcome View

The basic Bootstrap features work by applying classes to elements that correspond to CSS selectors defined in the files added to the wwwroot/lib/bootstrap folder. You can get full details of the classes that Bootstrap defines from http://getbootstrap.com, but you can see how I have applied some basic styling to the Index.cshtml view file in Listing 3-20.

Listing 3-20. Adding Bootstrap to the Index.cshtml File in the Views/Home Folder

```
@{
    Layout = null;
}

<!DOCTYPE html>

<html>
<head>
    <meta name="viewport" content="width=device-width" />
    <link rel="stylesheet" href="/lib/bootstrap/dist/css/bootstrap.css" />
    <title>Index</title>
</head>
<body>
    <div class="text-center">
        <h3> We're going to have an exciting party!</h3>
        <h4>And YOU are invited!</h4>
        <a class="btn btn-primary" asp-action="RsvpForm">RSVP Now</a>
    </div>
</body>
</html>
```

I have added a link element whose href attribute loads the bootstrap.css file from the wwwroot/lib/bootstrap/dist/css folder. The convention is that third-party CSS and JavaScript packages are installed into the wwwroot/lib folder, and I describe the tool that is used to manage these packages in Chapter 12.

Having imported the Bootstrap stylesheets, I need to style my elements. This is a simple example, so I need to use only a small number of Bootstrap CSS classes: text-center, btn, and btn-primary.

The text-center class centers the content of an element and its children. The btn class styles a button, input, or a element as a pretty button, and the btn-primary class specifies which of a range of colors I want the button to be. You can see the effect by running the application, as shown in Figure 3-10.

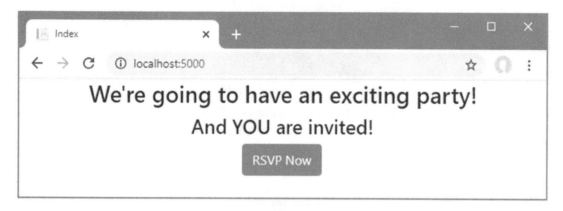

Figure 3-10. *Styling a view*

It will be obvious to you that I am not a web designer. In fact, as a child, I was excused from art lessons on the basis that I had absolutely no talent whatsoever. This had the happy result of making more time for math lessons but meant that my artistic skills have not developed beyond those of the average 10-year-old. For a real project, I would seek a professional to help design and style the content, but for this example, I am going it alone, and that means applying Bootstrap with as much restraint and consistency as I can muster.

Styling the Form View

Bootstrap defines classes that can be used to style forms. I am not going to go into detail, but you can see how I have applied these classes in Listing 3-21.

Listing 3-21. Adding Bootstrap to the RsvpForm.cshtml File in the Views/Home Folder

```
@model PartyInvites.Models.GuestResponse
@{
    Layout = null;
}

<!DOCTYPE html>

<html>
<head>
    <meta name="viewport" content="width=device-width" />
    <title>RsvpForm</title>
    <link rel="stylesheet" href="/css/styles.css" />
    <link rel="stylesheet" href="/lib/bootstrap/dist/css/bootstrap.css" />
</head>
<body>
    <h5 class="bg-primary text-white text-center m-2 p-2">RSVP</h5>
    <form asp-action="RsvpForm" method="post" class="m-2">
        <div asp-validation-summary="All"></div>
```

```
<div class="form-group">
    <label asp-for="Name">Your name:</label>
    <input asp-for="Name" class="form-control" />
</div>
<div class="form-group">
    <label asp-for="Email">Your email:</label>
    <input asp-for="Email" class="form-control" />
</div>
<div class="form-group">
    <label asp-for="Phone">Your phone:</label>
    <input asp-for="Phone" class="form-control" />
</div>
<div class="form-group">
    <label>Will you attend?</label>
    <select asp-for="WillAttend" class="form-control">
        <option value="">Choose an option</option>
        <option value="true">Yes, I'll be there</option>
        <option value="false">No, I can't come</option>
    </select>
</div>
<button type="submit" class="btn btn-primary">Submit RSVP</button>
</form>
</body>
</html>
```

The Bootstrap classes in this example create a header, just to give structure to the layout. To style the form, I have used the form-group class, which is used to style the element that contains the label and the associated input or select element, which is assigned to the form-control class. You can see the effect of the styles in Figure 3-11.

Figure 3-11. *Styling the RsvpForm view*

Styling the Thanks View

The next view file to style is Thanks.cshtml, and you can see how I have done this in Listing 3-22, using CSS classes that are similar to the ones I used for the other views. To make an application easier to manage, it is a good principle to avoid duplicating code and markup wherever possible. ASP.NET Core provides several features to help reduce duplication, which I describe in later chapters. These features include Razor layouts (Chapter 22), partial views (Chapter 22), and view components (Chapter 24).

Listing 3-22. Applying Bootstrap to the Thanks.cshtml File in the Views/Home Folder

```
@model PartyInvites.Models.GuestResponse
@{
    Layout = null;
}

<!DOCTYPE html>

<html>
<head>
    <meta name="viewport" content="width=device-width" />
    <title>Thanks</title>
    <link rel="stylesheet" href="/lib/bootstrap/dist/css/bootstrap.css" />
</head>
<body class="text-center">
    <div>
        <h1>Thank you, @Model.Name!</h1>
        @if (Model.WillAttend == true) {
            @:It's great that you're coming. The drinks are already in the fridge!
        } else {
            @:Sorry to hear that you can't make it, but thanks for letting us know.
        }
    </div>
    Click <a asp-action="ListResponses">here</a> to see who is coming.</div>
</body>
</html>
```

Figure 3-12 shows the effect of the styles.

Figure 3-12. *Styling the Thanks view*

Styling the List View

The final view to style is `ListResponses`, which presents the list of attendees. Styling the content follows the same approach as used for the other views, as shown in Listing 3-23.

Listing 3-23. Adding Bootstrap to the ListResponses.cshtml File in the Views/Home Folder

```
@model IEnumerable<PartyInvites.Models.GuestResponse>
@{
    Layout = null;
}

<!DOCTYPE html>

<html>
<head>
    <meta name="viewport" content="width=device-width" />
    <title>Responses</title>
    <link rel="stylesheet" href="/lib/bootstrap/dist/css/bootstrap.css" />
</head>
<body>
    <div class="text-center p-2">
        <h2>Here is the list of people attending the party</h2>
        <table class="table table-bordered table-striped table-sm">
            <thead>
                <tr><th>Name</th><th>Email</th><th>Phone</th></tr>
            </thead>
            <tbody>
                @foreach (PartyInvites.Models.GuestResponse r in Model) {
                    <tr>
                        <td>@r.Name</td>
                        <td>@r.Email</td>
                        <td>@r.Phone</td>
                    </tr>
                }
            </tbody>
        </table>
    </div>
</body>
</html>
```

Figure 3-13 shows the way that the table of attendees is presented. Adding these styles to the view completes the example application, which now meets all the development goals and has an improved appearance.

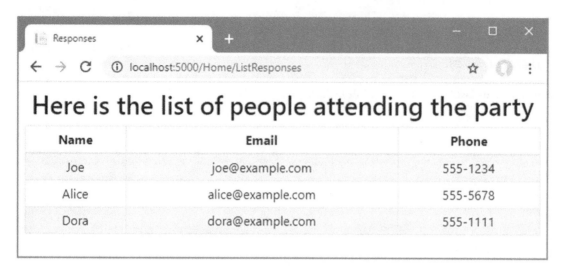

Figure 3-13. *Styling the ListResponses view*

Summary

In this chapter, I created a new ASP.NET Core project and used it to construct a simple data-entry application, giving you a first glimpse of important ASP.NET features, such as tag helpers, model binding, and data validation. In the next chapter, I describe the development tools that are used for ASP.NET Core development.

CHAPTER 4

Using the Development Tools

In this chapter, I introduce the tools that Microsoft provides for ASP.NET Core development and that are used throughout this book.

Unlike earlier editions of this book, I rely on the command-line tools provided by the .NET Core SDK and additional tool packages that Microsoft publishes. In part, I have done this to help ensure you get the expected results from the examples but also because the command-line tools provide access to all the features required for ASP.NET Core development, regardless of which editor/IDE you have chosen.

Visual Studio—and, to a lesser extent, Visual Studio Code—offers access to some of the tools through user interfaces, which I describe in this chapter, but Visual Studio and Visual Studio Code don't support all the features that are required for ASP.NET Core development, so there are times that using the command line is inevitable.

As ASP.NET Core has evolved, I have gradually moved to using just the command-line tools, except for when I need to use a debugger (although, as I explain later in the chapter, this is a rare requirement). Your preferences may differ, especially if you are used to working entirely within an IDE, but my suggestion is to give the command-line tools a go. They are simple, concise, and predictable, which cannot be said for all the equivalent functionality provided by Visual Studio and Visual Studio Code. Table 4-1 summarizes the chapter.

Table 4-1. *Chapter Summary*

Problem	Solution	Listing
Creating a project	Use the `dotnet new` commands or the Visual Studio wizard	1–4
Building and running projects	Use the `dotnet build` and `dotnet run` commands or use the menus provided by Visual Studio and Visual Studio Code	5–7
Adding packages to a project	Use the `dotnet add package` command or use the Visual Studio package manager	8–10
Installing tool commands	Use the `dotnet tool` command	11, 12
Managing client-side packages	Use the `libman` command or the Visual Studio client-side package manager	13–16

Creating ASP.NET Core Projects

The .NET Core SDK includes a set of command-line tools for creating, managing, building, and running projects. Visual Studio provides integrated support for some of these tasks, but if you are using Visual Studio Code, then the command line is the only option.

I use the command-line tools even when working with Visual Studio because they are simple and concise, while the Visual Studio features tend to require more effort to locate the templates or settings I require. In the sections that follow, I show you how to create and use both sets of tools. The results are the same whichever approach you choose, and you can freely switch between Visual Studio and the command-line tools.

Tip You can download the example project for this chapter—and for all the other chapters in this book—from `https://github.com/apress/pro-asp.net-core-3`. See Chapter 1 for how to get help if you have problems running the examples.

© Adam Freeman 2020
A. Freeman, *Pro ASP.NET Core 3*, https://doi.org/10.1007/978-1-4842-5440-0_4

Creating a Project Using the Command Line

The dotnet command provides access to the .NET Core command-line features. The dotnet new command is used to create a new project, configuration file, or solution file. To see the list of templates available for creating new items, open a PowerShell command prompt and run the command shown in Listing 4-1.

Listing 4-1. Listing the .NET Core Templates

```
dotnet new
```

Each template has a short name that makes it easier to use. There are a lot of templates available, but Table 4-2 describes the ones that are most useful for creating ASP.NET Core projects.

Table 4-2. *Useful ASP.NET Core Project Templates*

Name	Description
web	This template creates a project that is set up with the minimum code and content required for ASP.NET Core development. This is the template I use for most of the chapters in this book.
mvc	This template creates an ASP.NET Core project configured to use the MVC Framework.
webapp	This template creates an ASP.NET Core project configured to use Razor Pages.
blazorserver	This template creates an ASP.NET Core project configured to use Blazor Server.
angular	This template creates an ASP.NET Core project that contains client-side features using the Angular JavaScript framework.
react	This template creates an ASP.NET Core project that contains client-side features using the React JavaScript framework.
reactredux	This template creates an ASP.NET Core project that contains client-side features using the React JavaScript framework and the popular Redux library.

There are also templates that create commonly required files used to configure projects, as described in Table 4-3.

UNDERSTANDING THE LIMITATIONS OF PROJECT TEMPLATES

The project templates described in Table 4-2 are intended to help jump-start development by taking care of basic configuration settings and adding placeholder content.

These templates can give you a sense of rapid progress, but they contain assumptions about how a project should be configured and developed. If you don't understand the impact of those assumptions, you won't be able to get the results you require for the specific demands of your project.

The web template creates a project with the minimum configuration required for ASP.NET Core development. This is the project template I use for most of the examples in this book so that I can explain how each feature is configured and how the features can be used together.

Once you understand how ASP.NET Core works, the other project templates can be useful because you will know how to adapt them to your needs. But, while you are learning, I recommend sticking to the web template, even though it can take a little more effort to get results.

Table 4-3. *The Configuration Item Templates*

Name	Description
globaljson	This template adds a global.json file to a project, specifying the version of .NET Core that will be used.
sln	This template creates a solution file, which is used to group multiple projects and is commonly used by Visual Studio. The solution file is populated with the dotnet sln add command, as shown in the following listing.
gitignore	This template creates a .gitignore file that excludes unwanted items from Git source control.

To create a project, open a new PowerShell command prompt and run the commands shown in Listing 4-2.

Listing 4-2. Creating a New Project

```
dotnet new globaljson --sdk-version 3.1.101 --output MySolution/MyProject
dotnet new web --no-https --output MySolution/MyProject --framework netcoreapp3.1
dotnet new sln -o MySolution

dotnet sln MySolution add MySolution/MyProject
```

The first command creates a MySolution/MyProject folder that contains a global.json file, which specifies that the project will use .NET Core version 3.1.1. The top-level folder, named MySolution, is used to group multiple projects together. The nested MyProject folder will contain a single project.

I use the globaljson template to help ensure you get the expected results when following the examples in this book. Microsoft is good at ensuring backward compatibility with .NET Core releases, but breaking changes do occur, and it is a good idea to add a global.json file to projects so that everyone in the development team is using the same version.

The second command creates the project using the web template, which I use for most of the examples in this book. As noted in Table 4-3, this template creates a project with the minimum content required for ASP.NET Core development. Each template has its own set of arguments that influence the project that is created. The --no-https argument creates a project without support for HTTPS. (I explain how to use HTTPS in Chapter 16.) The --framework argument selects the .NET Core runtime that will be used for the project.

The other commands create a solution file that references the new project. Solution files are a convenient way of opening multiple related files at the same time. A MySolution.sln file is created in the MySolution folder, and opening this file in Visual Studio will load the project created with the web template. This is not essential, but it stops Visual Studio from prompting you to create the file when you exit the code editor.

Opening the Project

To open the project, start Visual Studio, select "Open a Project or Solution," and open the MySolution.sln file in the MySolution folder. Visual Studio will open the solution file, discover the reference to the project that was added by the final command in Listing 4-2, and open the project as well.

Visual Studio Code works differently. Start Visual Studio Code, select File ➤ Open Folder, and navigate to the MySolution folder. Click Select Folder, and Visual Studio Code will open the project.

Although Visual Studio Code and Visual Studio are working with the same project, each displays the contents differently. Visual Studio Code shows you a simple list of files, ordered alphabetically, as shown on the left of Figure 4-1. Visual Studio hides some files and nests others within related file items, as shown on the right of Figure 4-1.

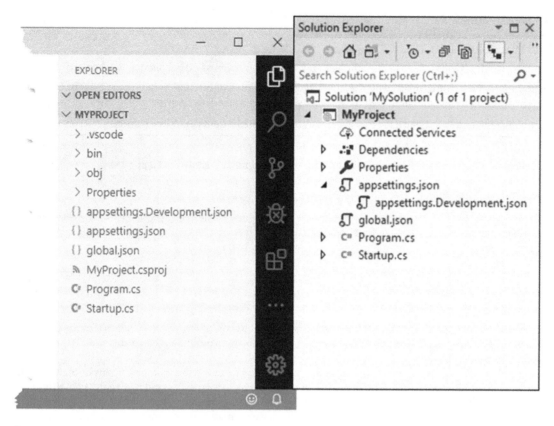

Figure 4-1. *Opening a project in Visual Studio Code and Visual Studio*

There are buttons at the top of the Visual Studio Solution Explorer that disable file nesting and show the hidden items in the project. When you open a project for the first time in Visual Studio Code, you may be prompted to add assets for building and debugging the project, as shown in Figure 4-2. Click the Yes button.

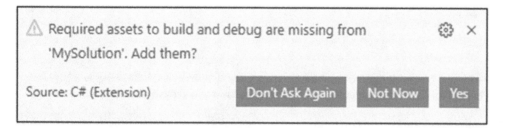

Figure 4-2. *Adding assets in Visual Studio Code*

Creating a Project Using Visual Studio

Visual Studio creates projects in the same way, using the same templates, but provides a wizard. Although my preference is to use the command line, the result is the same if you pay close attention to the options you choose along the way. Start Visual Studio and click "Create a New Project," Then select the ASP.NET Core Web Application category, as shown in Figure 4-3, and click the Next button.

Figure 4-3. *Creating a new project in Visual Studio*

Enter My**Project** in the "Project name" field and My**Solution** in the "Solution name" field, as shown in Figure 4-4. Use the Location field to select a convenient folder in which to create the project and click the Create button.

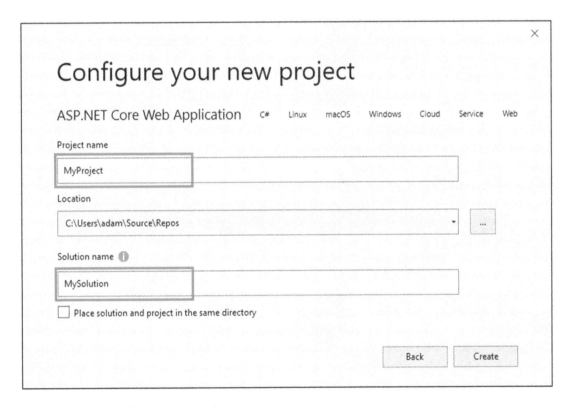

Figure 4-4. *Selecting the project and solution names*

The next step requires close attention, and because it is so prone to errors, I have used the command-line tools for the examples in this book. First, use the drop-downs at the top of the window to select .NET Core and ASP.NET Core 3.1. Next, select the Empty template from the list. Even though the name *Empty* is used, the content added to the project corresponds to the web template.

Uncheck the Configure for HTTPS option—which is equivalent to the `--no-https` command-line argument—and ensure the Enable Docker Support option is unchecked that the Authentication option is set to No Authentication, as shown in Figure 4-5.

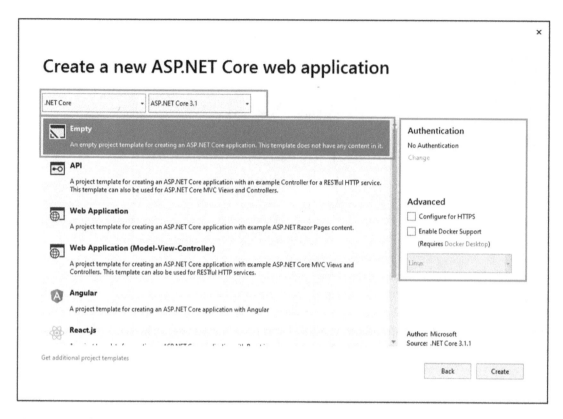

Figure 4-5. *Selecting and configuring the project template*

Click the Create button, and Visual Studio will create the project and the solution file and then open them for editing, as shown in Figure 4-6.

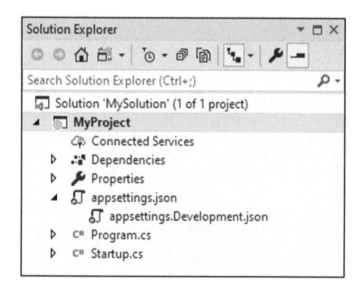

Figure 4-6. *The new project in the Visual Studio Solution Explorer*

Once the project has been opened, right-click the MyProject item in the Solution Explorer window and select Add ➤ New Item from the popup menu. Locate the JSON File item from the list of templates and set the Name field to global.json. Click the Add button to create the file and replace its contents with those shown in Listing 4-3.

Listing 4-3. The Contents of the global.json File in the MyProject Folder

```
{
    "sdk": {
        "version": "3.1.101"
    }
}
```

Adding the `global.json` file ensures the right version of the .NET Core SDK will be used by the project.

Adding Code and Content to Projects

If you are using Visual Studio Code, then you add items to the project by right-clicking the folder that should contain the file and selecting New File from the popup menu (or selecting New Folder if you are adding a folder).

■ **Note** You are responsible for ensuring that the file extension matches the type of item you want to add; for example, an HTML file must be added with the `.html` extension. I give the complete file name and the name of the containing folder for every item added to a project throughout this book, so you will always know exactly what files you need to add.

Right-click the `MyProject` item in the file explorer page, select New Folder, and set the name to wwwroot, which is where static content is stored in ASP.NET Core projects. Press Enter, and a folder named wwwroot will be added to the project. Right-click the new wwwroot folder, select New Item, and set the name to demo.html. Press Enter to create the HTML file and add the content shown in Listing 4-4.

Listing 4-4. The Contents of the demo.html File in the wwwroot Folder

```
<!DOCTYPE html>
<html>
<head>
    <meta charset="utf-8" />
    <title></title>
</head>
<body>
    <h3>HTML File from MyProject</h3>
</body>
</html>
```

Visual Studio provides a more comprehensive approach that can be helpful but only when used selectively. To create a folder, right-click the `MyProject` item in the Solution Explorer and select Add ➤ New Folder from the popup menu. Set the name of the new item to wwwroot and press Enter; Visual Studio will create the folder.

Right-click the new wwwroot item in the Solution Explorer and select Add ➤ New Item from the popup menu. Visual Studio will present you with an extensive selection of templates for adding items to the project. These templates can be searched using the text field in the top-right corner of the window or filtered using the categories on the left of the window. The item template for an HTML file is named HTML Page, as shown in Figure 4-7.

Figure 4-7. *Adding an item to the example project*

Enter **demo.html** in the Name field, click the Add button to create the new file, and replace the contents with the element shown in Listing 4-4. (If you omit the file extension, Visual Studio will add it for you based on the item template you have selected. If you entered just **demo** into the Name field when you created the file, Visual Studio would have created a file with the .html extension because you had selected the HTML Page item template.)

Understanding Item Scaffolding

The item templates presented by Visual Studio can be useful, especially for C# classes where it sets the namespace and class name automatically. But Visual Studio also provides *scaffolded items*, which I recommend against using. The Add ➤ New Scaffolded Item leads to a selection of items that guide you through a process to add more complex items. Visual Studio will also offer individual scaffolded items based on the name of the folder that you are adding an item to. For example, if you right-click a folder named Views, Visual Studio will helpfully add scaffolded items to the top of the menu, as shown in Figure 4-8.

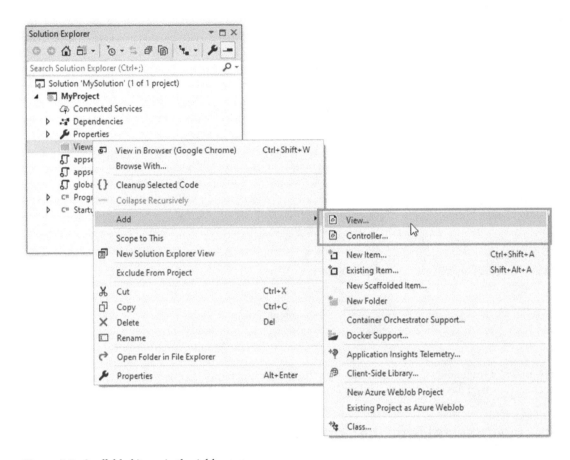

Figure 4-8. *Scaffolded items in the Add menu*

The View and Controller items are scaffolded, and selecting them will present you with choices that determine the content of the items you create.

Just like the project templates, I recommend against using scaffolded items, at least until you understand the content they create. In this book, I use only the Add ➤ New Item menu for the examples and change the placeholder content immediately.

Building and Running Projects

You can build and run projects from the command line or from within Visual Studio and Visual Studio Code. To prepare, add the statement shown in Listing 4-5 to the Startup.cs class file in the MyProject folder.

Listing 4-5. Adding a Statement in the Startup.cs File in the MyProject Folder

```
using System;
using System.Collections.Generic;
using System.Linq;
using System.Threading.Tasks;
using Microsoft.AspNetCore.Builder;
using Microsoft.AspNetCore.Hosting;
using Microsoft.AspNetCore.Http;
using Microsoft.Extensions.DependencyInjection;
using Microsoft.Extensions.Hosting;
```

```
namespace MyProject {
    public class Startup {

        public void ConfigureServices(IServiceCollection services) {
        }

        public void Configure(IApplicationBuilder app, IWebHostEnvironment env) {

            if (env.IsDevelopment()) {
                app.UseDeveloperExceptionPage();
            }

            app.UseStaticFiles();
            app.UseRouting();

            app.UseEndpoints(endpoints => {
                endpoints.MapGet("/", async context => {
                    await context.Response.WriteAsync("Hello World!");
                });
            });
        }
    }
}
```

This statement adds support for responding to HTTP requests with static content in the wwwroot folder, such as the HTML file created in the previous section. (I explain this feature in more detail in Chapter 15.)

Building and Running Projects Using the Command Line

To build the example project, run the command shown in Listing 4-6 in the MyProject or MySolution folder.

Listing 4-6. Building the Project

```
dotnet build
```

You can build and run the project in a single step by running the command shown in Listing 4-7 in the MyProject folder.

Listing 4-7. Building and Running the Project

```
dotnet run
```

The compiler will build the project and then start the integrated ASP.NET Core HTTP server to listen for HTTP requests on port 5000. You can see the contents of the static HTML file added to the project earlier in the chapter by opening a new browser window and requesting http://localhost:5000/demo.html, which produces the response shown in Figure 4-9.

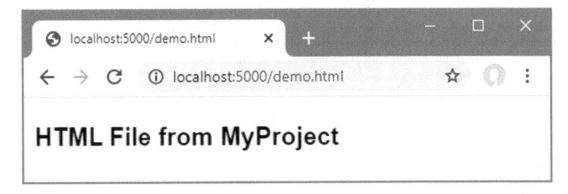

Figure 4-9. *Running the example application*

Building and Running Projects Using Visual Studio Code

Visual Studio Code can build and execute the project for you if you prefer not to use the command line. Select Terminal ➤ Run Build Task, and Visual Studio Code will compile the project.

To build and run the project in a single step, select Debug Run ➤ Without Debugging. Visual Studio Code will compile and run the project and open a new browser window that will send an HTTP request to the ASP.NET Core server and produce the placeholder response. Request `http://localhost:5000/demo.html`, and you will receive the response shown in Figure 4-9.

Building and Running Projects Using Visual Studio

Visual Studio uses IIS Express as a reverse proxy for the built-in ASP.NET Core HTTP server that is used directly when you use the `dotnet run` command. When the project is created, an HTTP port is picked for IIS Express to use. To change the HTTP port to the one used throughout this book, select Project ➤ MyProject Properties and select the Debug section. Locate the App URL field and change the port number in the URL to 5000, as shown in Figure 4-10.

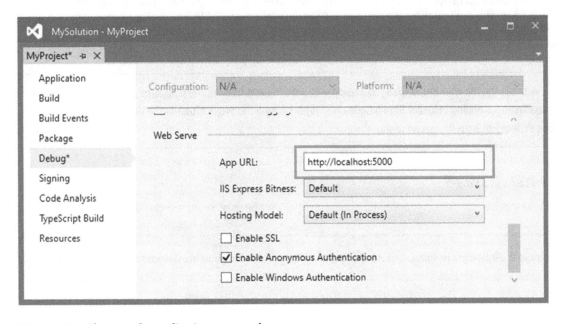

Figure 4-10. *Changing the application port number*

Select File ➤ Save All to apply the changes. To build the project, select Build Solution or Build MyProject from the Build menu. To build and run the project, select Debug ➤ Start Without Debugging. Once the project has been compiled, Visual Studio will open a new browser window, which sends an HTTP request that is received by IIS Express and passes it to the ASP.NET Core HTTP server, producing a placeholder response set up by the template used to create the project. Request `http://localhost:5000/demo.html`, and you will see the response shown in Figure 4-9.

■ **Tip** IIS Express is generally reliable, but if you have problems, right-click the IIS Express icon in the Windows taskbar's System Tray and select Exit from the popup menu.

Managing Packages

Most projects require additional features beyond those set up by the project templates, such as support for accessing databases or for making HTTP requests, neither of which is included in the standard ASP.NET Core packages added to the project by the template used to create the example project. In the sections that follow, I describe the tools available to manage the different types of packages that are used in ASP.NET Core development.

Managing NuGet Packages

.NET packages are added to a project with the `dotnet add package` command. Use a PowerShell command prompt to run the command shown in Listing 4-8 in the MyProject folder to add a package to the example project.

Listing 4-8. Adding a Package to the Example Project

```
dotnet add package Microsoft.EntityFrameworkCore.SqlServer --version 3.1.1
```

This command installs version 3.1.1 of the `Microsoft.EntityFrameworkCore.SqlServer` package. The package repository for .NET projects is `nuget.org`, where you can search for the package and see the versions available. The package installed in Listing 4-8, for example, is described at `https://www.nuget.org/packages/Microsoft.EntityFrameworkCore.SqlServer/3.1.1`.

You can see the packages installed in a project by running the command shown in Listing 4-9.

■ **Tip** The project file—which is the file with the `.csproj` extension—is used to keep track of the packages added to a project. You can examine this file by opening it for editing in Visual Studio Code or by right-clicking the project item in the Visual Studio Solution Explorer and selecting Edit Project File from the popup menu.

Listing 4-9. Listing the Packages in a Project

```
dotnet list package
```

This command produces the following output when it is run in the MyProject folder, showing the package added in Listing 4-8:

```
[netcoreapp3.1]:
Top-level Package                              Requested   Resolved
> Microsoft.EntityFrameworkCore.SqlServer      3.1.1       3.1.1
```

Packages are removed with the `dotnet remove package` command. To remove the package from the example project, run the command shown in Listing 4-10 in the MyProject folder.

Listing 4-10. Removing a Package from the Example Project

```
dotnet remove package Microsoft.EntityFrameworkCore.SqlServer
```

Managing Tool Packages

Tool packages install commands that can be used from the command line to perform operations on .NET Core projects. One common example is the Entity Framework Core tools package that installs commands that are used to manage databases in ASP. NET Core projects. Tool packages are managed using the dotnet tool command. To install the Entity Framework Core tools package, run the commands shown in Listing 4-11.

Listing 4-11. Installing a Tool Package

```
dotnet tool uninstall --global dotnet-ef
dotnet tool install --global dotnet-ef --version 3.1.1
```

The first command removes the dotnet-ef package, which is named dotnet-ef. This command will produce an error if the package has not already been installed, but it is a good idea to remove existing versions before installing a package. The dotnet tool install command installs version 3.1.1 of the dotnet-ef package, which is the version I use in this book. The commands installed by tool packages are used through the dotnet command. To test the package installed in Listing 4-11, run the command shown in Listing 4-12 in the MyProject folder.

■ **Tip** The --global arguments in Listing 4-11 mean the package is installed for global use and not just for a specific project. You can install tool packages into just one project, in which case the command is accessed with dotnet tool run <command>. The tools I use in this book are all installed globally.

Listing 4-12. Running a Tool Package Command

```
dotnet ef --help
```

The commands added by this tool package are accessed using dotnet ef, and you will see examples in later chapters that rely on these commands.

Managing Client-Side Packages

Client-side packages contain content that is delivered to the client, such as images, CSS stylesheets, JavaScript files, and static HTML. Client-side packages are added to ASP.NET Core using the Library Manager (LibMan) tool. To install the LibMan tool package, run the commands shown in Listing 4-13.

Listing 4-13. Installing the LibMan Tool Package

```
dotnet tool uninstall --global Microsoft.Web.LibraryManager.Cli
dotnet tool install --global Microsoft.Web.LibraryManager.Cli --version 2.0.96
```

These commands remove any existing LibMan package and install the version that is used throughout this book. The next step is to initialize the project, which creates the file that LibMan uses to keep track of the client packages it installs. Run the command shown in Listing 4-14 in the MyProject folder to initialize the example project.

Listing 4-14. Initializing the Example Project

```
libman init -p cdnjs
```

LibMan can download packages from different repositories. The -p argument in Listing 4-14 specifies the repository at https://cdnjs.com, which is the most widely used. Once the project is initialized, client-side packages can be installed. To install the Bootstrap CSS framework that I use to style HTML content throughout this book, run the command shown in Listing 4-15 in the MyProject folder.

Listing 4-15. Installing the Bootstrap CSS Framework

```
libman install twitter-bootstrap@4.3.1 -d wwwroot/lib/twitter-bootstrap
```

The command installs version 4.3.1 of the Bootstrap package, which is known by the name twitter-bootstrap on the CDNJS repository. There is some inconsistency in the way that popular packages are named on different repositories, and it is worth checking that you are getting the package you expect before adding to your project. The -d argument specifies the location into which the package is installed. The convention in ASP.NET Core projects is to install client-side packages into the wwwroot/lib folder.

Once the package has been installed, add the classes shown in Listing 4-16 to the elements in the demo.html file. This is how the features provided by the Bootstrap package are applied.

■ **Note** I don't get into the details of using the Bootstrap CSS framework in this book. See https://getbootstrap.com for the Bootstrap documentation.

Listing 4-16. Applying Bootstrap Classes in the demo.html File in the wwwroot Folder

```
<!DOCTYPE html>
<html>
<head>
    <meta charset="utf-8" />
    <title></title>
    <link href="/lib/twitter-bootstrap/css/bootstrap.min.css" rel="stylesheet" />
</head>
<body>
    <h3 class="bg-primary text-white text-center p-2">
        HTML File from MyProject
    </h3>
</body>
</html>
```

Start ASP.NET Core and request http://localhost:5000/demo.html, and you will see the styled content shown in Figure 4-11.

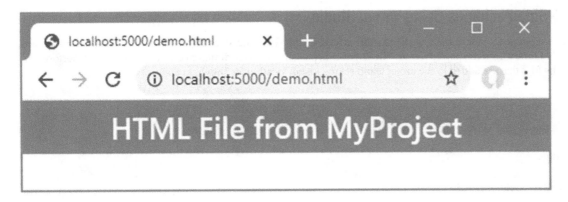

Figure 4-11. *Using a client-side package*

Managing Packages Using Visual Studio

Visual Studio provides tools for managing packages without using the command line. Select Project ➤ Manage NuGet Packages, and Visual Studio will open the NuGet package manager tool. Click Browse and enter **Microsoft.EntityFrameworkCore.SqlServer** into the search box to search for matching packages. Click the `Microsoft.EntityFrameworkCore.SqlServer` entry, which should be at the top of the list, and you will be able to choose a version and install the package, as shown in Figure 4-12.

■ **Caution**   The Visual Studio NuGet package manager cannot be used to install global tool packages, which can be installed only from the command line.

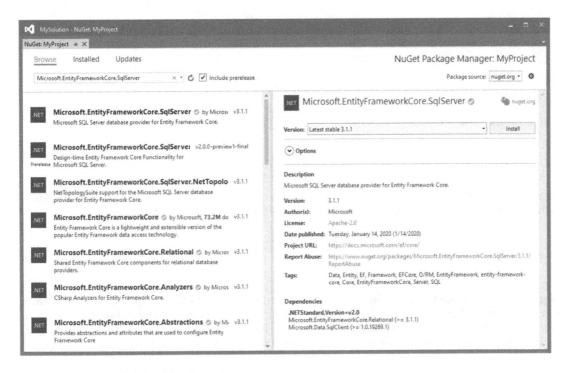

Figure 4-12. *Using the Visual Studio package manager*

The Visual Studio NuGet package manager can also be used to inspect the packages that have been installed in the project and check whether new versions of packages are available.

Managing Client-Side Packages Using Visual Studio

Visual Studio provides a separate tool for managing client-side packages. Right-click the MyProject item in the Solution Explorer and select Add ➤ Client Side Library from the popup menu. The client-side package tool is rudimentary, but it allows you to perform basic searches, select the files that are added to the project, and set the install location, as shown in Figure 4-13.

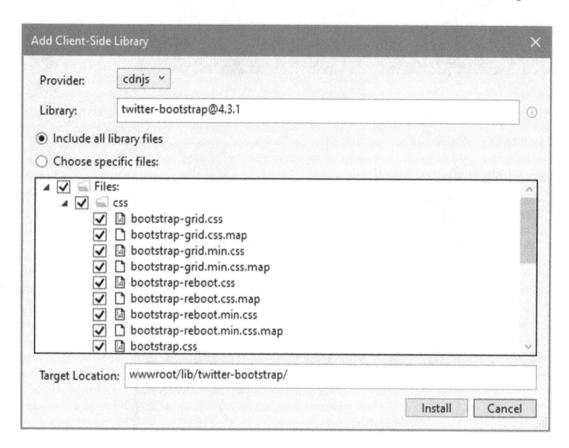

Figure 4-13. *Using the Visual Studio client-side package manager*

Debugging Projects

Visual Studio and Visual Studio Code both provide debuggers that can be used to control and inspect the execution of an ASP.NET Core application. Open the Startup.cs file in the MyProject folder, and click this statement in the code editor:

```
...
await context.Response.WriteAsync("Hello World!");
...
```

Select Debug ➤ Toggle Breakpoint, which is available in both Visual Studio and Visual Studio Code. A breakpoint is shown as a red dot alongside the code statement, as shown in Figure 4-14, and will interrupt execution and pass control to the user.

Start the project by selecting Debug ➤ Start Debugging, which is available in both Visual Studio and Visual Studio Code. (Choose .NET Core if Visual Studio Code prompts you to select an environment and then select the Start Debugging menu item again.)

Figure 4-14. *Setting a breakpoint*

The application will be started and continue normally until the statement to which the breakpoint is reached, at which point execution is halted. Execution can be controlled using the Debug menu or the controls that Visual Studio and Visual Studio Code display. Both debuggers are packed with features—more so if you have a paid-for version of Visual Studio—and I don't describe them in depth in this book. The Visual Studio 2019 debugger is described at https://docs.microsoft.com/en-us/visualstudio/debugger/?view=vs-2019, and the Visual Studio Code debugger is described at https://code.visualstudio.com/docs/editor/debugging.

HOW I DEBUG MY CODE

Debuggers are powerful tools, but I rarely use them. In most situations, I prefer to add System.Console.WriteLine statements to my code to figure out what is going on, which I can easily do because I tend to use the dotnet run command to run my projects from the command line. This is a rudimentary approach that works for me, not least because most of the errors in my code tend to be where statements are not being called because a condition in an if statement isn't effective. If I want to examine an object in detail, I tend to serialize it to JSON and pass the result to the WriteLine method.

This may seem like madness if you are a dedicated user of the debugger, but it has the advantage of being quick and simple. When I am trying to figure out why code isn't working, I want to explore and iterate quickly, and I find the amount of time taken to start the debugger to be a barrier. My approach is also reliable. The Visual Studio and Visual Studio Code debuggers are sophisticated, but they are not always entirely predictable, and .NET Core and ASP.NET Core change too quickly for the debugger features to have entirely settled down. When I am utterly confused by the behavior of some code, I want the simplest possible diagnostic tool, and that, for me, is a message written to the console.

I am not suggesting that this is the approach you should use, but it can be a good place to start when you are not getting the results you expect and you don't want to battle with the debugger to figure out why.

Summary

In this chapter, I described the tools used for ASP.NET Core development. I explained that the command-line tools are the most concise and reliable way to work with ASP.NET Core projects, which is why I have used them in the examples in this book. I also demonstrated the alternative user interfaces that Visual Studio and Visual Studio Code provide, which can be a useful alternative for some—but not all—of the command-line tools. In the next chapter, I describe the C# feature that are essential for effective ASP.NET Core development.

CHAPTER 5

Essential C# Features

In this chapter, I describe C# features used in web application development that are not widely understood or that often cause confusion. This is not a book about C#, however, so I provide only a brief example for each feature so that you can follow the examples in the rest of the book and take advantage of these features in your own projects. Table 5-1 summarizes this chapter.

Table 5-1. *Chapter Summary*

Problem	Solution	Listing
Managing null values	Use the null conditional and null coalescing operators	7, 10
Creating properties with getters and setters	Define automatically implemented properties	11–13
Mixing static and dynamic values in strings	Use string interpolation	14
Initializing and populate objects	Use the object and collection initializers	15–18
Assigning a value for specific types	Use pattern matching	19, 20
Extending the functionality of a class without modifying it	Define an extension method	21–28
Expressing functions and methods concisely	Use lambda expressions	29–36
Defining a variable without explicitly declaring its type	Use the var keyword	37–39
Modifying an interface without requiring changes in its implementation classes	Define a default implementation	40–44
Performing work asynchronously	Use tasks or the async/await keywords	45–47
Producing a sequence of values over time	Use an asynchronous enumerable	48–51
Getting the name of a class or member	Use a nameof expression	52, 53

Preparing for This Chapter

To create the example project for this chapter, open a new PowerShell command prompt and run the commands shown in Listing 5-1. If you are using Visual Studio and prefer not to use the command line, you can create the project using the process described in Chapter 4.

Tip You can download the example project for this chapter—and for all the other chapters in this book—from https://github.com/apress/pro-asp.net-core-3. See Chapter 1 for how to get help if you have problems running the examples.

Listing 5-1. Creating the Example Project

```
dotnet new globaljson --sdk-version 3.1.101 --output LanguageFeatures
dotnet new web --no-https --output LanguageFeatures --framework netcoreapp3.1
dotnet new sln -o LanguageFeatures

dotnet sln LanguageFeatures add LanguageFeatures
```

Opening the Project

If you are using Visual Studio, select File ➤ Open ➤ Project/Solution, select the LanguageFeatures.sln file in the LanguageFeatures folder, and click the Open button to open the solution file and the project it references. If you are using Visual Studio Code, select File ➤ Open Folder, navigate to the LanguageFeatures folder, and click the Select Folder button.

Enabling the MVC Framework

The web project template creates a project that contains a minimal ASP.NET Core configuration. This means the placeholder content that is added by the mvc template used in Chapter 3 is not available and that extra steps are required to reach the point where the application can produce useful output. In this section, I make the changes required to set up the MVC Framework, which is one of the application frameworks supported by ASP.NET Core, as I explained in Chapter 1. First, to enable the MVC framework, make the changes shown in Listing 5-2 to the Startup class.

Listing 5-2. Enabling MVC in the Startup.cs File in the LanguageFeatures Folder

```
using System;
using System.Collections.Generic;
using System.Linq;
using System.Threading.Tasks;
using Microsoft.AspNetCore.Builder;
using Microsoft.AspNetCore.Hosting;
using Microsoft.AspNetCore.Http;
using Microsoft.Extensions.DependencyInjection;
using Microsoft.Extensions.Hosting;

namespace LanguageFeatures {
    public class Startup {
        public void ConfigureServices(IServiceCollection services) {
            services.AddControllersWithViews();
        }

        public void Configure(IApplicationBuilder app, IWebHostEnvironment env) {
            if (env.IsDevelopment()) {
                app.UseDeveloperExceptionPage();
            }

            app.UseRouting();

            app.UseEndpoints(endpoints => {
                //endpoints.MapGet("/", async context => {
                //    await context.Response.WriteAsync("Hello World!");
                //});
                endpoints.MapDefaultControllerRoute();
            });
        }
    }
}
```

I explain how to configure ASP.NET Core applications in Part 2, but the two statements added in Listing 5-2 provide a basic MVC framework setup using a default configuration.

Creating the Application Components

Now that the MVC framework is set up, I can add the application components that I will use to demonstrate important C# language features.

Creating the Data Model

I started by creating a simple model class so that I can have some data to work with. I added a folder called Models and created a class file called Product.cs within it, which I used to define the class shown in Listing 5-3.

Listing 5-3. The Contents of the Product.cs File in the Models Folder

```
namespace LanguageFeatures.Models {
    public class Product {

        public string Name { get; set; }
        public decimal? Price { get; set; }

        public static Product[] GetProducts() {

            Product kayak = new Product {
                Name = "Kayak", Price = 275M
            };

            Product lifejacket = new Product {
                Name = "Lifejacket", Price = 48.95M
            };

            return new Product[] { kayak, lifejacket, null };
        }
    }
}
```

The Product class defines Name and Price properties, and there is a static method called GetProducts that returns a Product array. One of the elements contained in the array returned by the GetProducts method is set to null, which I will use to demonstrate some useful language features later in the chapter.

Creating the Controller and View

For the examples in this chapter, I use a simple controller class to demonstrate different language features. I created a Controllers folder and added to it a class file called HomeController.cs, the contents of which are shown in Listing 5-4.

Listing 5-4. The Contents of the HomeController.cs File in the Controllers Folder

```
using Microsoft.AspNetCore.Mvc;

namespace LanguageFeatures.Controllers {
    public class HomeController : Controller {

        public ViewResult Index() {
            return View(new string[] { "C#", "Language", "Features" });
        }
    }
}
```

The Index action method tells ASP.NET Core to render the default view and provides it with an array of strings as its view model, which will be included in the HTML sent to the client. To create the view, I added a Views/Home folder (by creating a Views folder and then adding a Home folder within it) and added a Razor View called Index.cshtml, the contents of which are shown in Listing 5-5.

Listing 5-5. The Contents of the Index.cshtml File in the Views/Home Folder

```
@model IEnumerable<string>
@{ Layout = null; }

<!DOCTYPE html>
<html>
<head>
    <meta name="viewport" content="width=device-width" />
    <title>Language Features</title>
</head>
<body>
    <ul>
        @foreach (string s in Model) {
            <li>@s</li>
        }
    </ul>
</body>
</html>
```

Selecting the HTTP Port

If you are using Visual Studio, select Project ➤ LanguageFeatures Properties, select the Debug section, and change the HTTP port to 5000 in the App URL field, as shown in Figure 5-1. Select File ➤ Save All to save the new port. (This change is not required if you are using Visual Studio Code.)

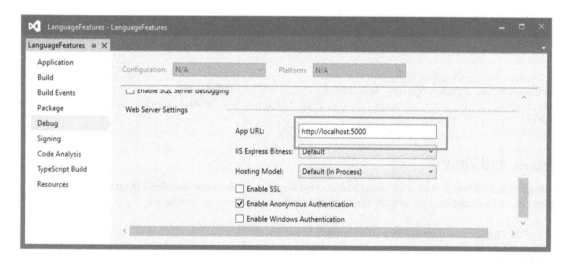

Figure 5-1. Setting the HTTP port

Running the Example Application

Start ASP.NET Core by selecting Start Without Debugging (Visual Studio) or Run Without Debugging (Visual Studio Code) from the Debug menu or by running the command shown in Listing 5-6 in the LanguageFeatures folder.

Listing 5-6. Running the Example Application

```
dotnet run
```

Request `http://localhost:5000`, and you will see the output shown in Figure 5-2.

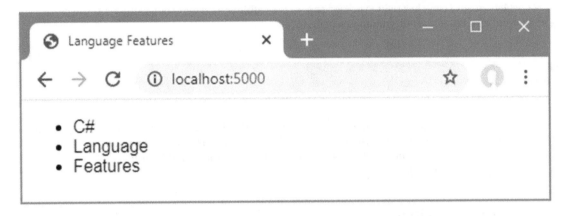

Figure 5-2. *Running the example application*

Since the output from all the examples in this chapter is text, I will show the messages displayed by the browser like this:

```
C#
Language
Features
```

Using the Null Conditional Operator

The null conditional operator allows for `null` values to be detected more elegantly. There can be a lot of checking for nulls in ASP.NET Core development as you work out whether a request contains a specific header or value or whether the model contains a specific data item. Traditionally, dealing with `null` values requires making an explicit check, which can become tedious and error-prone when both an object and its properties need to be inspected. The null conditional operator makes this process simpler and more concise, as shown in Listing 5-7.

Listing 5-7. Detecting null Values in the HomeController.cs File in the Controllers Folder

```
using Microsoft.AspNetCore.Mvc;
using System.Collections.Generic;
using LanguageFeatures.Models;

namespace LanguageFeatures.Controllers {
    public class HomeController : Controller {

        public ViewResult Index() {

            List<string> results = new List<string>();

            foreach (Product p in Product.GetProducts()) {
                string name = p?.Name;
                decimal? price = p?.Price;
                results.Add(string.Format("Name: {0}, Price: {1}", name, price));
            }
```

```
        return View(results);
    }
  }
}
```

The static GetProducts method defined by the Product class returns an array of objects that I inspect in the Index action method to get a list of the Name and Price values. The problem is that both the object in the array and the value of the properties could be null, which means I can't just refer to p.Name or p.Price within the foreach loop without causing a NullReferenceException. To avoid this, I used the null conditional operator, like this:

```
...
string name = p?.Name;
decimal? price = p?.Price;
...
```

The null conditional operator is a single question mark (the ? character). If p is null, then name will be set to null as well. If p is not null, then name will be set to the value of the Person.Name property. The Price property is subject to the same test. Notice that the variable you assign to when using the null conditional operator must be able to be assigned null, which is why the price variable is declared as a nullable decimal (decimal?).

Chaining the Null Conditional Operator

The null conditional operator can be chained to navigate through a hierarchy of objects, which is where it becomes an effective tool for simplifying code and allowing safe navigation. In Listing 5-8, I have added a property to the Product class that creates a more complex object hierarchy.

Listing 5-8. Adding a Property in the Product.cs File in the Models Folder

```
namespace LanguageFeatures.Models {
    public class Product {

        public string Name { get; set; }
        public decimal? Price { get; set; }
        public Product Related { get; set; }

        public static Product[] GetProducts() {

            Product kayak = new Product {
                Name = "Kayak", Price = 275M
            };
            Product lifejacket = new Product {
                Name = "Lifejacket", Price = 48.95M
            };

            kayak.Related = lifejacket;

            return new Product[] { kayak, lifejacket, null };
        }
    }
}
```

Each Product object has a Related property that can refer to another Product object. In the GetProducts method, I set the Related property for the Product object that represents a kayak. Listing 5-9 shows how I can chain the null conditional operator to navigate through the object properties without causing an exception.

Listing 5-9. Detecting Nested null Values in the HomeController.cs File in the Controllers Folder

```
using Microsoft.AspNetCore.Mvc;
using System.Collections.Generic;
using LanguageFeatures.Models;

namespace LanguageFeatures.Controllers {
    public class HomeController : Controller {

        public ViewResult Index() {

            List<string> results = new List<string>();

            foreach (Product p in Product.GetProducts()) {
                string name = p?.Name;
                decimal? price = p?.Price;
                string relatedName = p?.Related?.Name;
                results.Add(string.Format("Name: {0}, Price: {1}, Related: {2}",
                    name, price, relatedName));
            }

            return View(results);
        }
    }
}
```

The null conditional operator can be applied to each part of a chain of properties, like this:

```
...
string relatedName = p?.Related?.Name;
...
```

The result is that the relatedName variable will be null when p is null or when p.Related is null. Otherwise, the variable will be assigned the value of the p.Related.Name property. Restart ASP.NET Core and request http://localhost:5000, and you will see the following output in the browser window:

```
Name: Kayak, Price: 275, Related: Lifejacket
Name: Lifejacket, Price: 48.95, Related:
Name: , Price: , Related:
```

Combining the Conditional and Coalescing Operators

It can be useful to combine the null conditional operator (a single question mark) with the null coalescing operator (two question marks) to set a fallback value to prevent null values being used in the application, as shown in Listing 5-10.

Listing 5-10. Combining Null Operators in the HomeController.cs File in the Controllers Folder

```
using Microsoft.AspNetCore.Mvc;
using System.Collections.Generic;
using LanguageFeatures.Models;

namespace LanguageFeatures.Controllers {
    public class HomeController : Controller {
```

```
        public ViewResult Index() {

            List<string> results = new List<string>();

            foreach (Product p in Product.GetProducts()) {
                string name = p?.Name ?? "<No Name>";
                decimal? price = p?.Price ?? 0;
                string relatedName = p?.Related?.Name ?? "<None>";
                results.Add(string.Format("Name: {0}, Price: {1}, Related: {2}",
                    name, price, relatedName));
            }

            return View(results);
        }
    }
}
```

The null conditional operator ensures that I don't get a NullReferenceException when navigating through the object properties, and the null coalescing operator ensures that I don't include null values in the results displayed in the browser. If you run the example, you will see the following results displayed in the browser window:

```
Name: Kayak, Price: 275, Related: Lifejacket
Name: Lifejacket, Price: 48.95, Related: <None>
Name: <No Name>, Price: 0, Related: <None>
```

NULLABLE AND NON-NULLABLE REFERENCE TYPES

Encountering unexpected null values is one of the most common causes of bugs. By default, C# treats null as a valid value for all types, which means that I can assign null to a string variable, like this:

```
...
string product = null;
...
```

It is the responsibility of the code that uses the variable to check for null values, which can be especially problematic when the same variable is in multiple places. It is easy to omit one of the checks or assume that a value won't be null, producing an error at runtime.

Nullable reference types shift responsibility for null checking to the code that assigns the value to a variable. When the nullable reference feature is enabled, regular reference types cannot be assigned null values, such as assigning null to a string, for example. Instead, nullable reference types must be used if null values are possible, like this:

```
...
string product = null; // compiler error - this is a non-nullable type
string? product = null; // no error - this is a nullable type
...
```

The string? type is nullable, while string is not, which means that the code that consumes a variable doesn't have to worry about null values unless it is dealing with a nullable type. To enable nullable reference types, an element must be added to the csproj file, like this:

```
...
<Project Sdk="Microsoft.NET.Sdk.Web">

  <PropertyGroup>
    <TargetFramework>netcoreapp3.1</TargetFramework>
    <Nullable>enable</Nullable>
  </PropertyGroup>
```

```
</Project>
...
```

If you are using Visual Studio, you can open the project file by right-clicking the project item in the Solution Explorer and selecting Edit Project File from the popup menu.

I like this feature, but it is not yet used widely enough for me to use it in this book, especially since it can make some complex topics even more difficult to follow. But, once the rest of .NET Core catches up with this feature, I expect it to be embraced in ASP.NET Core by default, and you can expect to see nullable reference types used in future editions of this book.

Using Automatically Implemented Properties

C# supports automatically implemented properties, and I used them when defining properties for the Person class in the previous section, like this:

```
namespace LanguageFeatures.Models {
    public class Product {

        public string Name { get; set; }
        public decimal? Price { get; set; }
        public Product Related { get; set; }

        public static Product[] GetProducts() {

            Product kayak = new Product {
                Name = "Kayak", Price = 275M
            };
            Product lifejacket = new Product {
                Name = "Lifejacket", Price = 48.95M
            };

            kayak.Related = lifejacket;

            return new Product[] { kayak, lifejacket, null };
        }
    }
}
```

This feature allows me to define properties without having to implement the get and set bodies. Using the auto-implemented property feature means I can define a property like this:

```
...
public string Name { get; set; }
...
is equivalent to the following code:
...
public string Name {
    get { return name; }
    set { name = value; }
}
...
```

This type of feature is known as *syntactic sugar*, which means that it makes C# more pleasant to use—in this case by eliminating redundant code that ends up being duplicated for every property—without substantially altering the way that the language behaves. The term *sugar* may seem pejorative, but any enhancements that make code easier to write and maintain can be beneficial, especially in large and complex projects.

Using Auto-implemented Property Initializers

Automatically implemented properties have been supported since C# 3.0. The latest version of C# supports initializers for automatically implemented properties, which allows an initial value to be set without having to use the constructor, as shown in Listing 5-11.

Listing 5-11. Using an Auto-implemented Property Initializer in the Product.cs File in the Models Folder

```
namespace LanguageFeatures.Models {
    public class Product {

        public string Name { get; set; }
        public string Category { get; set; } = "Watersports";
        public decimal? Price { get; set; }
        public Product Related { get; set; }

        public static Product[] GetProducts() {
            Product kayak = new Product {
                Name = "Kayak",
                Category = "Water Craft",
                Price = 275M
            };
            Product lifejacket = new Product {
                Name = "Lifejacket", Price = 48.95M
            };

            kayak.Related = lifejacket;

            return new Product[] { kayak, lifejacket, null };
        }
    }
}
```

Assigning a value to an auto-implemented property doesn't prevent the setter from being used to change the property later and just tidies up the code for simple types that ended up with a constructor that contained a list of property assignments to provide default values. In the example, the initializer assigns a value of Watersports to the Category property. The initial value can be changed, which I do when I create the kayak object and specify a value of Water Craft instead.

Creating Read-Only Automatically Implemented Properties

You can create a read-only property by using an initializer and omitting the set keyword from an auto-implemented property that has an initializer, as shown in Listing 5-12.

Listing 5-12. Creating a Read-Only Property in the Product.cs File in the Models Folder

```
namespace LanguageFeatures.Models {
    public class Product {

        public string Name { get; set; }
        public string Category { get; set; } = "Watersports";
        public decimal? Price { get; set; }
```

```
        public Product Related { get; set; }
        public bool InStock { get; } = true;

        public static Product[] GetProducts() {

            Product kayak = new Product {
                Name = "Kayak",
                Category = "Water Craft",
                Price = 275M
            };
            Product lifejacket = new Product {
                Name = "Lifejacket", Price = 48.95M
            };

            kayak.Related = lifejacket;

            return new Product[] { kayak, lifejacket, null };
        }
    }
}
```

The InStock property is initialized to true and cannot be changed; however, the value can be assigned to in the type's constructor, as shown in Listing 5-13.

Listing 5-13. Assigning a Value to a Read-Only Property in the Product.cs File in the Models Folder

```
namespace LanguageFeatures.Models {
    public class Product {

        public Product(bool stock = true) {
            InStock = stock;
        }

        public string Name { get; set; }
        public string Category { get; set; } = "Watersports";
        public decimal? Price { get; set; }
        public Product Related { get; set; }
        public bool InStock { get; }

        public static Product[] GetProducts() {
            Product kayak = new Product {
                Name = "Kayak",
                Category = "Water Craft",
                Price = 275M
            };

            Product lifejacket = new Product(false) {
                Name = "Lifejacket",
                Price = 48.95M
            };

            kayak.Related = lifejacket;

            return new Product[] { kayak, lifejacket, null };
        }
    }
}
```

The constructor allows the value for the read-only property to be specified as an argument and defaults to true if no value is provided. The property value cannot be changed once set by the constructor.

Using String Interpolation

The string.Format method is the traditional C# tool for composing strings that contain data values. Here is an example of this technique from the Home controller:

```
...
results.Add(string.Format("Name: {0}, Price: {1}, Related: {2}",
                    name, price, relatedName));
...
```

C# also supports a different approach, known as *string interpolation*, that avoids the need to ensure that the {0} references in the string template match up with the variables specified as arguments. Instead, string interpolation uses the variable names directly, as shown in Listing 5-14.

Listing 5-14. Using String Interpolation in the HomeController.cs File in the Controllers Folder

```
using Microsoft.AspNetCore.Mvc;
using System.Collections.Generic;
using LanguageFeatures.Models;

namespace LanguageFeatures.Controllers {
    public class HomeController : Controller {

        public ViewResult Index() {

            List<string> results = new List<string>();

            foreach (Product p in Product.GetProducts()) {
                string name = p?.Name ?? "<No Name>";
                decimal? price = p?.Price ?? 0;
                string relatedName = p?.Related?.Name ?? "<None>";
                results.Add($"Name: {name}, Price: {price}, Related: {relatedName}");
            }

            return View(results);
        }
    }
}
```

Interpolated strings are prefixed with the $ character and contain *holes*, which are references to values contained within the { and } characters. When the string is evaluated, the holes are filled in with the current values of the variables or constants that are specified.

■ **Tip** String interpolation supports all the format specifiers that are available with the string.Format method. The format specifics are included as part of the hole, so $"Price: {price:C2}" would format the price value as a currency value with two decimal digits.

Using Object and Collection Initializers

When I create an object in the static GetProducts method of the Product class, I use an *object initializer*, which allows me to create an object and specify its property values in a single step, like this:

```
...
Product kayak = new Product {
    Name = "Kayak",
    Category = "Water Craft",
    Price = 275M
};
...
```

This is another syntactic sugar feature that makes C# easier to use. Without this feature, I would have to call the Product constructor and then use the newly created object to set each of the properties, like this:

```
...
Product kayak = new Product();
kayak.Name = "Kayak";
kayak.Category = "Water Craft";
kayak.Price = 275M;
...
```

A related feature is the *collection initializer*, which allows the creation of a collection and its contents to be specified in a single step. Without an initializer, creating a string array, for example, requires the size of the array and the array elements to be specified separately, as shown in Listing 5-15.

Listing 5-15. Initializing an Object in the HomeController.cs File in the Controllers Folder

```
using Microsoft.AspNetCore.Mvc;
using System.Collections.Generic;
using LanguageFeatures.Models;

namespace LanguageFeatures.Controllers {
    public class HomeController : Controller {

        public ViewResult Index() {
            string[] names = new string[3];
            names[0] = "Bob";
            names[1] = "Joe";
            names[2] = "Alice";
            return View("Index", names);
        }
    }
}
```

Using a collection initializer allows the contents of the array to be specified as part of the construction, which implicitly provides the compiler with the size of the array, as shown in Listing 5-16.

Listing 5-16. Using a Collection Initializer in the HomeController.cs File in the Controllers Folder

```
using Microsoft.AspNetCore.Mvc;
using System.Collections.Generic;
using LanguageFeatures.Models;

namespace LanguageFeatures.Controllers {
    public class HomeController : Controller {
```

```
    public ViewResult Index() {
        return View("Index", new string[] { "Bob", "Joe", "Alice" });
    }
}
}
```

The array elements are specified between the { and } characters, which allows for a more concise definition of the collection and makes it possible to define a collection inline within a method call. The code in Listing 5-16 has the same effect as the code in Listing 5-15. Restart ASP.NET Core and request http://localhost:5000, and you will see the following output in the browser window:

```
Bob
Joe
Alice
```

Using an Index Initializer

Recent versions of C# tidy up the way collections that use indexes, such as dictionaries, are initialized. Listing 5-17 shows the Index action rewritten to define a collection using the traditional C# approach to initializing a dictionary.

Listing 5-17. Initializing a Dictionary in the HomeController.cs File in the Controllers Folder

```
using Microsoft.AspNetCore.Mvc;
using System.Collections.Generic;
using LanguageFeatures.Models;

namespace LanguageFeatures.Controllers {
    public class HomeController : Controller {

        public ViewResult Index() {
            Dictionary<string, Product> products = new Dictionary<string, Product> {
                { "Kayak", new Product { Name = "Kayak", Price = 275M } },
                { "Lifejacket",  new Product{ Name = "Lifejacket", Price = 48.95M } }
            };
            return View("Index", products.Keys);
        }
    }
}
```

The syntax for initializing this type of collection relies too much on the { and } characters, especially when the collection values are created using object initializers. The latest versions of C# support a more natural approach to initializing indexed collections that is consistent with the way that values are retrieved or modified once the collection has been initialized, as shown in Listing 5-18.

Listing 5-18. Using Collection Initializer Syntax in the HomeController.cs File in the Controllers Folder

```
using Microsoft.AspNetCore.Mvc;
using System.Collections.Generic;
using LanguageFeatures.Models;

namespace LanguageFeatures.Controllers {
    public class HomeController : Controller {

        public ViewResult Index() {
            Dictionary<string, Product> products = new Dictionary<string, Product> {
                ["Kayak"] = new Product { Name = "Kayak", Price = 275M },
```

```
        ["Lifejacket"] = new Product { Name = "Lifejacket", Price = 48.95M }
    };

    return View("Index", products.Keys);
    }
  }
}
```

The effect is the same—to create a dictionary whose keys are Kayak and Lifejacket and whose values are Product objects—but the elements are created using the index notation that is used for other collection operations. Restart ASP.NET Core and request http://localhost:5000, and you will see the following results in the browser:

```
Kayak
Lifejacket
```

Pattern Matching

One of the most useful recent additions to C# is support for pattern matching, which can be used to test that an object is of a specific type or has specific characteristics. This is another form of syntactic sugar, and it can dramatically simplify complex blocks of conditional statements. The is keyword is used to perform a type test, as demonstrated in Listing 5-19.

Listing 5-19. Performing a Type Test in the HomeController.cs File in the Controllers Folder

```
using Microsoft.AspNetCore.Mvc;
using System.Collections.Generic;
using LanguageFeatures.Models;

namespace LanguageFeatures.Controllers {
    public class HomeController : Controller {

        public ViewResult Index() {

            object[] data = new object[] { 275M, 29.95M,
                "apple", "orange", 100, 10 };
            decimal total = 0;
            for (int i = 0; i < data.Length; i++) {
                if (data[i] is decimal d) {
                    total += d;
                }
            }

            return View("Index", new string[] { $"Total: {total:C2}" });
        }
    }
}
```

The is keyword performs a type check and, if a value is of the specified type, will assign the value to a new variable, like this:

```
...
if (data[i] is decimal d) {
...
```

This expression evaluates as true if the value stored in data[i] is a decimal. The value of data[i] will be assigned to the variable d, which allows it to be used in subsequent statements without needing to perform any type conversions. The is keyword will match only the specified type, which means that only two of the values in the data array will be processed (the other items in the array are string and int values). If you run the application, you will see the following output in the browser window:

```
Total: $304.95
```

Pattern Matching in switch Statements

Pattern matching can also be used in switch statements, which support the when keyword for restricting when a value is matched by a case statement, as shown in Listing 5-20.

Listing 5-20. Pattern Matching in the HomeController.cs File in the Controllers Folder

```
using Microsoft.AspNetCore.Mvc;
using System.Collections.Generic;
using LanguageFeatures.Models;

namespace LanguageFeatures.Controllers {
    public class HomeController : Controller {

        public ViewResult Index() {

            object[] data = new object[] { 275M, 29.95M,
                "apple", "orange", 100, 10 };
            decimal total = 0;
            for (int i = 0; i < data.Length; i++) {
                switch (data[i]) {
                    case decimal decimalValue:
                        total += decimalValue;
                        break;
                    case int intValue when intValue > 50:
                        total += intValue;
                        break;
                }
            }

            return View("Index", new string[] { $"Total: {total:C2}" });
        }
    }
}
```

To match any value of a specific type, use the type and variable name in the case statement, like this:

```
...
case decimal decimalValue:
...
```

This case statement matches any decimal value and assigns it to a new variable called decimalValue. To be more selective, the when keyword can be included, like this:

```
...
case int intValue when intValue > 50:
...
```

This case statement matches int values and assigns them to a variable called intValue, but only when the value is greater than 50. Restart ASP.NET Core and request http://localhost:5000, and you will see the following output in the browser window:

```
Total: $404.95
```

Using Extension Methods

Extension methods are a convenient way of adding methods to classes that you cannot modify directly, typically because they are provided by Microsoft or a third-party package. Listing 5-21 shows the definition of the ShoppingCart class, which I added to the Models folder in a class file called ShoppingCart.cs file and which represents a collection of Product objects.

Listing 5-21. The Contents of the ShoppingCart.cs File in the Models Folder

```csharp
using System.Collections.Generic;

namespace LanguageFeatures.Models {

    public class ShoppingCart {
        public IEnumerable<Product> Products { get; set; }
    }
}
```

This is a simple class that acts as a wrapper around a sequence of Product objects (I only need a basic class for this example). Suppose I need to be able to determine the total value of the Product objects in the ShoppingCart class, but I cannot modify the class because it comes from a third party, and I do not have the source code. I can use an extension method to add the functionality I need.

Add a class file named MyExtensionMethods.cs in the Models folder and use it to define the class shown in Listing 5-22.

Listing 5-22. The Contents of the MyExtensionMethods.cs File in the Models Folder

```csharp
namespace LanguageFeatures.Models {

    public static class MyExtensionMethods {

        public static decimal TotalPrices(this ShoppingCart cartParam) {
            decimal total = 0;
            foreach (Product prod in cartParam.Products) {
                total += prod?.Price ?? 0;
            }
            return total;
        }
    }
}
```

Extension methods are defined in static classes within the same namespace as the class the extension methods applies to. In this case, the static MyExtensionMethods class is in the LanguageFeatures.Models namespace, which means that it can contain extension methods for classes in that namespace.

Extension methods are also static, and Listing 5-22 defines a single extension method named TotalPrices. The this keyword in front of the first parameter marks TotalPrices as an extension method. The first parameter tells .NET which class the extension method can be applied to—ShoppingCart in this case. I can refer to the instance of the ShoppingCart that the extension method has been applied to by using the cartParam parameter. This extension method enumerates the Product objects in the ShoppingCart and returns the sum of the Product.Price property values. Listing 5-23 shows how I apply the extension method in the Home controller's action method.

■ **Note** Extension methods do not let you break through the access rules that classes define for methods, fields, and properties. You can extend the functionality of a class by using an extension method but only using the class members that you had access to anyway.

Listing 5-23. Applying an Extension Method in the HomeController.cs File in the Controllers Folder

```
using Microsoft.AspNetCore.Mvc;
using System.Collections.Generic;
using LanguageFeatures.Models;

namespace LanguageFeatures.Controllers {
    public class HomeController : Controller {

        public ViewResult Index() {
            ShoppingCart cart
                = new ShoppingCart { Products = Product.GetProducts() };
            decimal cartTotal = cart.TotalPrices();
            return View("Index", new string[] { $"Total: {cartTotal:C2}" });
        }
    }
}
```

The key statement is this one:

```
...
decimal cartTotal = cart.TotalPrices();
...
```

I call the TotalPrices method on a ShoppingCart object as though it were part of the ShoppingCart class, even though it is an extension method defined by a different class altogether. .NET will find extension classes if they are in the scope of the current class, meaning that they are part of the same namespace or in a namespace that is the subject of a using statement. Restart ASP.NET Core and request http://localhost:5000, which will produce the following output in the browser window:

```
Total: $323.95
```

Applying Extension Methods to an Interface

Extension methods can also be applied to an interface, which allows me to call the extension method on all the classes that implement the interface. Listing 5-24 shows the ShoppingCart class updated to implement the IEnumerable<Product> interface.

Listing 5-24. Implementing an Interface in the ShoppingCart.cs File in the Models Folder

```
using System.Collections;
using System.Collections.Generic;

namespace LanguageFeatures.Models {

    public class ShoppingCart : IEnumerable<Product> {
        public IEnumerable<Product> Products { get; set; }

        public IEnumerator<Product> GetEnumerator() {
            return Products.GetEnumerator();
        }
```

```
        IEnumerator IEnumerable.GetEnumerator() {
            return GetEnumerator();
        }
    }
}
```

I can now update the extension method so that it deals with IEnumerable<Product>, as shown in Listing 5-25.

Listing 5-25. Updating an Extension Method in the MyExtensionMethods.cs File in the Models Folder

```
using System.Collections.Generic;

namespace LanguageFeatures.Models {

    public static class MyExtensionMethods {

        public static decimal TotalPrices(this IEnumerable<Product> products) {
            decimal total = 0;
            foreach (Product prod in products) {
                total += prod?.Price ?? 0;
            }
            return total;
        }
    }
}
```

The first parameter type has changed to IEnumerable<Product>, which means that the foreach loop in the method body works directly on Product objects. The change to using the interface means that I can calculate the total value of the Product objects enumerated by any IEnumerable<Product>, which includes instances of ShoppingCart but also arrays of Product objects, as shown in Listing 5-26.

Listing 5-26. Applying an Extension Method in the HomeController.cs File in the Controllers Folder

```
using Microsoft.AspNetCore.Mvc;
using System.Collections.Generic;
using LanguageFeatures.Models;

namespace LanguageFeatures.Controllers {
    public class HomeController : Controller {

        public ViewResult Index() {

            ShoppingCart cart
                = new ShoppingCart { Products = Product.GetProducts() };

            Product[] productArray = {
                new Product {Name = "Kayak", Price = 275M},
                new Product {Name = "Lifejacket", Price = 48.95M}
            };

            decimal cartTotal = cart.TotalPrices();
            decimal arrayTotal = productArray.TotalPrices();

            return View("Index", new string[] {
                $"Cart Total: {cartTotal:C2}",
                $"Array Total: {arrayTotal:C2}" });
        }
    }
}
```

Restart ASP.NET Core and request http://localhost:5000, which will produce the following output in the browser, demonstrating that I get the same result from the extension method, irrespective of how the Product objects are collected:

```
Cart Total: $323.95
Array Total: $323.95
```

Creating Filtering Extension Methods

The last thing I want to show you about extension methods is that they can be used to filter collections of objects. An extension method that operates on an IEnumerable<T> and that also returns an IEnumerable<T> can use the yield keyword to apply selection criteria to items in the source data to produce a reduced set of results. Listing 5-27 demonstrates such a method, which I have added to the MyExtensionMethods class.

Listing 5-27. A Filtering Extension Method in the MyExtensionMethods.cs File in the Models Folder

```
using System.Collections.Generic;

namespace LanguageFeatures.Models {

    public static class MyExtensionMethods {

        public static decimal TotalPrices(this IEnumerable<Product> products) {
            decimal total = 0;
            foreach (Product prod in products) {
                total += prod?.Price ?? 0;
            }
            return total;
        }

        public static IEnumerable<Product> FilterByPrice(
                this IEnumerable<Product> productEnum, decimal minimumPrice) {

            foreach (Product prod in productEnum) {
                if ((prod?.Price ?? 0) >= minimumPrice) {
                    yield return prod;
                }
            }
        }
    }
}
```

This extension method, called FilterByPrice, takes an additional parameter that allows me to filter products so that Product objects whose Price property matches or exceeds the parameter are returned in the result. Listing 5-28 shows this method being used.

Listing 5-28. Using the Filtering Extension Method in the HomeController.cs File in the Controllers Folder

```
using Microsoft.AspNetCore.Mvc;
using System.Collections.Generic;
using LanguageFeatures.Models;

namespace LanguageFeatures.Controllers {
    public class HomeController : Controller {
```

```
public ViewResult Index() {

    Product[] productArray = {
        new Product {Name = "Kayak", Price = 275M},
        new Product {Name = "Lifejacket", Price = 48.95M},
        new Product {Name = "Soccer ball", Price = 19.50M},
        new Product {Name = "Corner flag", Price = 34.95M}
    };

    decimal arrayTotal = productArray.FilterByPrice(20).TotalPrices();

    return View("Index", new string[] { $"Array Total: {arrayTotal:C2}" });
}
    }
}
```

When I call the FilterByPrice method on the array of Product objects, only those that cost more than $20 are received by the TotalPrices method and used to calculate the total. If you run the application, you will see the following output in the browser window:

```
Total: $358.90
```

Using Lambda Expressions

Lambda expressions are a feature that causes a lot of confusion, not least because the feature they simplify is also confusing. To understand the problem that is being solved, consider the FilterByPrice extension method that I defined in the previous section. This method is written so that it can filter Product objects by price, which means I must create a second method I want to filter by name, as shown in Listing 5-29.

Listing 5-29. Adding a Filter Method in the MyExtensionMethods.cs File in the Models Folder

```
using System.Collections.Generic;

namespace LanguageFeatures.Models {

    public static class MyExtensionMethods {

        public static decimal TotalPrices(this IEnumerable<Product> products) {
            decimal total = 0;
            foreach (Product prod in products) {
                total += prod?.Price ?? 0;
            }
            return total;
        }

        public static IEnumerable<Product> FilterByPrice(
                this IEnumerable<Product> productEnum, decimal minimumPrice) {

            foreach (Product prod in productEnum) {
                if ((prod?.Price ?? 0) >= minimumPrice) {
                    yield return prod;
                }
            }
        }
```

```
        public static IEnumerable<Product> FilterByName(
                this IEnumerable<Product> productEnum, char firstLetter) {

            foreach (Product prod in productEnum) {
                if (prod?.Name?[0] == firstLetter) {
                    yield return prod;
                }
            }
        }
    }
}
```

Listing 5-30 shows the use of both filter methods applied in the controller to create two different totals.

Listing 5-30. Using Two Filter Methods in the HomeController.cs File in the Controllers Folder

```
using Microsoft.AspNetCore.Mvc;
using System.Collections.Generic;
using LanguageFeatures.Models;

namespace LanguageFeatures.Controllers {
    public class HomeController : Controller {

        public ViewResult Index() {

            Product[] productArray = {
                new Product {Name = "Kayak", Price = 275M},
                new Product {Name = "Lifejacket", Price = 48.95M},
                new Product {Name = "Soccer ball", Price = 19.50M},
                new Product {Name = "Corner flag", Price = 34.95M}
            };

            decimal priceFilterTotal = productArray.FilterByPrice(20).TotalPrices();
            decimal nameFilterTotal = productArray.FilterByName('S').TotalPrices();

            return View("Index", new string[] {
                $"Price Total: {priceFilterTotal:C2}",
                $"Name Total: {nameFilterTotal:C2}" });
        }
    }
}
```

The first filter selects all the products with a price of $20 or more, and the second filter selects products whose name starts with the letter *S*. You will see the following output in the browser window if you run the example application:

```
Price Total: $358.90
Name Total: $19.50
```

Defining Functions

I can repeat this process indefinitely to create filter methods for every property and every combination of properties that I am interested in. A more elegant approach is to separate the code that processes the enumeration from the selection criteria. C# makes this easy by allowing functions to be passed around as objects. Listing 5-31 shows a single extension method that filters an enumeration of Product objects but that delegates the decision about which ones are included in the results to a separate function.

Listing 5-31. Creating a General Filter Method in the MyExtensionMethods.cs File in the Models Folder

```
using System.Collections.Generic;
using System;

namespace LanguageFeatures.Models {

    public static class MyExtensionMethods {

        public static decimal TotalPrices(this IEnumerable<Product> products) {
            decimal total = 0;
            foreach (Product prod in products) {
                total += prod?.Price ?? 0;
            }
            return total;
        }

        public static IEnumerable<Product> Filter(
                this IEnumerable<Product> productEnum,
                Func<Product, bool> selector) {

            foreach (Product prod in productEnum) {
                if (selector(prod)) {
                    yield return prod;
                }
            }
        }
    }
}
```

The second argument to the `Filter` method is a function that accepts a `Product` object and that returns a `bool` value. The `Filter` method calls the function for each `Product` object and includes it in the result if the function returns `true`. To use the `Filter` method, I can specify a method or create a stand-alone function, as shown in Listing 5-32.

Listing 5-32. Using a Function to Filter Objects in the HomeController.cs File in the Controllers Folder

```
using Microsoft.AspNetCore.Mvc;
using System.Collections.Generic;
using LanguageFeatures.Models;
using System;

namespace LanguageFeatures.Controllers {
    public class HomeController : Controller {

        bool FilterByPrice(Product p) {
            return (p?.Price ?? 0) >= 20;
        }

        public ViewResult Index() {

            Product[] productArray = {
                new Product {Name = "Kayak", Price = 275M},
                new Product {Name = "Lifejacket", Price = 48.95M},
                new Product {Name = "Soccer ball", Price = 19.50M},
                new Product {Name = "Corner flag", Price = 34.95M}
            };
```

```
        Func<Product, bool> nameFilter = delegate (Product prod) {
            return prod?.Name?[0] == 'S';
        };

        decimal priceFilterTotal = productArray
            .Filter(FilterByPrice)
            .TotalPrices();
        decimal nameFilterTotal = productArray
            .Filter(nameFilter)
            .TotalPrices();

        return View("Index", new string[] {
            $"Price Total: {priceFilterTotal:C2}",
            $"Name Total: {nameFilterTotal:C2}" });
    }
}
}
```

Neither approach is ideal. Defining methods like FilterByPrice clutters up a class definition. Creating a Func<Product, bool> object avoids this problem but uses an awkward syntax that is hard to read and hard to maintain. It is this issue that lambda expressions address by allowing functions to be defined in a more elegant and expressive way, as shown in Listing 5-33.

Listing 5-33. Using a Lambda Expression in the HomeController.cs File in the Controllers Folder

```
using Microsoft.AspNetCore.Mvc;
using System.Collections.Generic;
using LanguageFeatures.Models;
using System;

namespace LanguageFeatures.Controllers {
    public class HomeController : Controller {

        public ViewResult Index() {

            Product[] productArray = {
                new Product {Name = "Kayak", Price = 275M},
                new Product {Name = "Lifejacket", Price = 48.95M},
                new Product {Name = "Soccer ball", Price = 19.50M},
                new Product {Name = "Corner flag", Price = 34.95M}
            };

            decimal priceFilterTotal = productArray
                .Filter(p => (p?.Price ?? 0) >= 20)
                .TotalPrices();
            decimal nameFilterTotal = productArray
                .Filter(p => p?.Name?[0] == 'S')
                .TotalPrices();

            return View("Index", new string[] {
                $"Price Total: {priceFilterTotal:C2}",
                $"Name Total: {nameFilterTotal:C2}" });
        }
    }
}
```

The lambda expressions are shown in bold. The parameters are expressed without specifying a type, which will be inferred automatically. The => characters are read aloud as "goes to" and link the parameter to the result of the lambda expression. In my examples, a Product parameter called p goes to a bool result, which will be true if the Price property is equal or greater than 20 in the first expression or if the Name property starts with *S* in the second expression. This code works in the same way as the separate method and the function delegate but is more concise and is—for most people—easier to read.

OTHER FORMS FOR LAMBDA EXPRESSIONS

I don't need to express the logic of my delegate in the lambda expression. I can as easily call a method, like this:

```
...
prod => EvaluateProduct(prod)
...
```

If I need a lambda expression for a delegate that has multiple parameters, I must wrap the parameters in parentheses, like this:

```
...
(prod, count) => prod.Price > 20 && count > 0
...
```

Finally, if I need logic in the lambda expression that requires more than one statement, I can do so by using braces ({}) and finishing with a return statement, like this:

```
...
(prod, count) => {
    // ...multiple code statements...
    return result;
}
...
```

You do not need to use lambda expressions in your code, but they are a neat way of expressing complex functions simply and in a manner that is readable and clear. I like them a lot, and you will see them used throughout this book.

Using Lambda Expression Methods and Properties

Lambda expressions can be used to implement constructors, methods, and properties. In ASP.NET Core development, you will often end up with methods that contain a single statement that selects the data to display and the view to render. In Listing 5-34, I have rewritten the Index action method so that it follows this common pattern.

Listing 5-34. Creating a Common Action Pattern in the HomeController.cs File in the Controllers Folder

```
using Microsoft.AspNetCore.Mvc;
using System.Collections.Generic;
using LanguageFeatures.Models;
using System;
using System.Linq;

namespace LanguageFeatures.Controllers {
    public class HomeController : Controller {

        public ViewResult Index() {
            return View(Product.GetProducts().Select(p => p?.Name));
        }
    }
}
```

The action method gets a collection of Product objects from the static Product.GetProducts method and uses LINQ to project the values of the Name properties, which are then used as the view model for the default view. If you run the application, you will see the following output displayed in the browser window:

```
Kayak
Lifejacket
```

There will be an empty list item in the browser window as well because the GetProducts method includes a null reference in its results, but that doesn't matter for this section of the chapter.

When a constructor or method body consists of a single statement, it can be rewritten as a lambda expression, as shown in Listing 5-35.

Listing 5-35. A Lambda Action Method in the HomeController.cs File in the Controllers Folder

```csharp
using Microsoft.AspNetCore.Mvc;
using System.Collections.Generic;
using LanguageFeatures.Models;
using System;
using System.Linq;

namespace LanguageFeatures.Controllers {
    public class HomeController : Controller {

        public ViewResult Index() =>
            View(Product.GetProducts().Select(p => p?.Name));
    }
}
```

Lambda expressions for methods omit the return keyword and use => (goes to) to associate the method signature (including its arguments) with its implementation. The Index method shown in Listing 5-35 works in the same way as the one shown in Listing 5-34 but is expressed more concisely. The same basic approach can also be used to define properties. Listing 5-36 shows the addition of a property that uses a lambda expression to the Product class.

Listing 5-36. A Lambda Property in the Product.cs File in the Models Folder

```csharp
namespace LanguageFeatures.Models {
    public class Product {

        public Product(bool stock = true) {
            InStock = stock;
        }

        public string Name { get; set; }
        public string Category { get; set; } = "Watersports";
        public decimal? Price { get; set; }
        public Product Related { get; set; }
        public bool InStock { get; }
        public bool NameBeginsWithS => Name?[0] == 'S';

        public static Product[] GetProducts() {

            Product kayak = new Product {
                Name = "Kayak",
                Category = "Water Craft",
                Price = 275M
            };
```

```
        Product lifejacket = new Product(false) {
            Name = "Lifejacket",
            Price = 48.95M
        };

        kayak.Related = lifejacket;

        return new Product[] { kayak, lifejacket, null };
    }
  }
}
```

Using Type Inference and Anonymous Types

The var keyword allows you to define a local variable without explicitly specifying the variable type, as demonstrated by Listing 5-37. This is called *type inference*, or *implicit typing*.

Listing 5-37. Using Type Inference in the HomeController.cs File in the Controllers Folder

```
using Microsoft.AspNetCore.Mvc;
using System.Collections.Generic;
using LanguageFeatures.Models;
using System;
using System.Linq;

namespace LanguageFeatures.Controllers {
    public class HomeController : Controller {

        public ViewResult Index() {
            var names = new [] { "Kayak", "Lifejacket", "Soccer ball" };
            return View(names);
        }
    }
}
```

It is not that the names variable does not have a type; instead, I am asking the compiler to infer the type from the code. The compiler examines the array declaration and works out that it is a string array. Running the example produces the following output:

```
Kayak
Lifejacket
Soccer ball
```

Using Anonymous Types

By combining object initializers and type inference, I can create simple view model objects that are useful for transferring data between a controller and a view without having to define a class or struct, as shown in Listing 5-38.

Listing 5-38. Creating an Anonymous Type in the HomeController.cs File in the Controllers Folder

```
using Microsoft.AspNetCore.Mvc;
using System.Collections.Generic;
using LanguageFeatures.Models;
using System;
using System.Linq;
```

```
namespace LanguageFeatures.Controllers {
    public class HomeController : Controller {

        public ViewResult Index() {
            var products = new [] {
                new { Name = "Kayak", Price = 275M },
                new { Name = "Lifejacket", Price = 48.95M },
                new { Name = "Soccer ball", Price = 19.50M },
                new { Name = "Corner flag", Price = 34.95M }
            };

            return View(products.Select(p => p.Name));
        }
    }
}
```

Each of the objects in the products array is an anonymously typed object. This does not mean that it is dynamic in the sense that JavaScript variables are dynamic. It just means that the type definition will be created automatically by the compiler. Strong typing is still enforced. You can get and set only the properties that have been defined in the initializer, for example. Restart ASP.NET Core and request http://localhost:5000, and you will see the following output in the browser window:

```
Kayak
Lifejacket
Soccer ball
Corner flag
```

The C# compiler generates the class based on the name and type of the parameters in the initializer. Two anonymously typed objects that have the same property names and types will be assigned to the same automatically generated class. This means that all the objects in the products array will have the same type because they define the same properties.

■ **Tip** I have to use the var keyword to define the array of anonymously typed objects because the type isn't created until the code is compiled, so I don't know the name of the type to use. The elements in an array of anonymously typed objects must all define the same properties; otherwise, the compiler can't work out what the array type should be.

To demonstrate this, I have changed the output from the example in Listing 5-39 so that it shows the type name rather than the value of the Name property.

Listing 5-39. Displaying the Type Name in the HomeController.cs File in the Controllers Folder

```
using Microsoft.AspNetCore.Mvc;
using System.Collections.Generic;
using LanguageFeatures.Models;
using System;
using System.Linq;

namespace LanguageFeatures.Controllers {
    public class HomeController : Controller {

        public ViewResult Index() {
            var products = new [] {
                new { Name = "Kayak", Price = 275M },
                new { Name = "Lifejacket", Price = 48.95M },
```

```
            new { Name = "Soccer ball", Price = 19.50M },
            new { Name = "Corner flag", Price = 34.95M }
        };

        return View(products.Select(p => p.GetType().Name));
    }
  }
}
```

All the objects in the array have been assigned the same type, which you can see if you run the example. The type name isn't user-friendly but isn't intended to be used directly, and you may see a different name than the one shown in the following output:

```
<>f__AnonymousType0`2
<>f__AnonymousType0`2
<>f__AnonymousType0`2
<>f__AnonymousType0`2
```

Using Default Implementations in Interfaces

C# 8.0 introduces the ability to define default implementations for properties and methods defined by interfaces. This may seem like an odd feature because interfaces are intended to be a description of features without specifying an implementation, but this addition to C# makes it possible to update interfaces without breaking the existing implementations of them.

Add a class file named IProductSelection.cs to the Models folder and use it to define the interface shown in Listing 5-40.

Listing 5-40. The Contents of the IProductSelection.cs File in the Models Folder

```
using System.Collections.Generic;

namespace LanguageFeatures.Models {
    public interface IProductSelection {

        IEnumerable<Product> Products { get; }
    }
}
```

Update the ShoppingCart class to implement the new interface, as shown in Listing 5-41.

Listing 5-41. Implementing an Interface in the ShoppingCart.cs File in the Models Folder

```
using System.Collections;
using System.Collections.Generic;

namespace LanguageFeatures.Models {

    public class ShoppingCart : IProductSelection {
        private List<Product> products = new List<Product>();

        public ShoppingCart(params Product[] prods) {
            products.AddRange(prods);
        }

        public IEnumerable<Product> Products { get => products; }
    }
}
```

Listing 5-42 updates the Home controller so that it uses the ShoppingCart class.

Listing 5-42. Using an Interface in the HomeController.cs File in the Controllers Folder

```
using Microsoft.AspNetCore.Mvc;
using System.Collections.Generic;
using LanguageFeatures.Models;
using System;
using System.Linq;

namespace LanguageFeatures.Controllers {
    public class HomeController : Controller {

        public ViewResult Index() {
            IProductSelection cart = new ShoppingCart(
                new Product { Name = "Kayak", Price = 275M },
                new Product { Name = "Lifejacket", Price = 48.95M },
                new Product { Name = "Soccer ball", Price = 19.50M },
                new Product { Name = "Corner flag", Price = 34.95M }
            );
            return View(cart.Products.Select(p => p.Name));
        }
    }
}
```

This is the familiar use of an interface, and if you restart ASP.NET Core and request http://localhost:5000, you will see the following output in the browser:

```
Kayak
Lifejacket
Soccer ball
Corner flag
```

If I want to add a new feature to the interface, I must locate and update all the classes that implement it, which can be difficult, especially if an interface is used by other development teams in their projects. This is where the default implementation feature can be used, allowing new features to be added to an interface, as shown in Listing 5-43.

Listing 5-43. Adding a Feature in the IProductSelection.cs File in the Models Folder

```
using System.Collections.Generic;
using System.Linq;

namespace LanguageFeatures.Models {
    public interface IProductSelection {

        IEnumerable<Product> Products { get; }

        IEnumerable<string> Names => Products.Select(p => p.Name);
    }
}
```

The listing defines a Names property and provides a default implementation, which means that consumers of the IProductSelection interface can use the Total property even if it isn't defined by implementation classes, as shown in Listing 5-44.

Listing 5-44. Using a Default Implementation in the HomeController.cs File in the Controllers Folder

```
using Microsoft.AspNetCore.Mvc;
using System.Collections.Generic;
using LanguageFeatures.Models;
using System;
using System.Linq;

namespace LanguageFeatures.Controllers {
    public class HomeController : Controller {

        public ViewResult Index() {

            IProductSelection cart = new ShoppingCart(
                new Product { Name = "Kayak", Price = 275M },
                new Product { Name = "Lifejacket", Price = 48.95M },
                new Product { Name = "Soccer ball", Price = 19.50M },
                new Product { Name = "Corner flag", Price = 34.95M }
            );
            return View(cart.Names);
        }
    }
}
```

The ShoppingCart class has not been modified, but the Index method is able to use the default implementation of the Names property. Restart ASP.NET Core and request `http://localhost:5000`, and you will see the following output in the browser:

```
Kayak
Lifejacket
Soccer ball
Corner flag
```

Using Asynchronous Methods

Asynchronous methods perform work in the background and notify you when they are complete, allowing your code to take care of other business while the background work is performed. Asynchronous methods are an important tool in removing bottlenecks from code and allow applications to take advantage of multiple processors and processor cores to perform work in parallel.

In ASP.NET Core, asynchronous methods can be used to improve the overall performance of an application by allowing the server more flexibility in the way that requests are scheduled and executed. Two C# keywords—`async` and `await`—are used to perform work asynchronously.

Working with Tasks Directly

C# and .NET have excellent support for asynchronous methods, but the code has tended to be verbose, and developers who are not used to parallel programming often get bogged down by the unusual syntax. To create an example, add a class file called `MyAsyncMethods.cs` to the Models folder and add the code shown in Listing 5-45.

Listing 5-45. The Contents of the MyAsyncMethods.cs File in the Models Folder

```
using System.Net.Http;
using System.Threading.Tasks;

namespace LanguageFeatures.Models {
```

```
public class MyAsyncMethods {

    public static Task<long?> GetPageLength() {
        HttpClient client = new HttpClient();
        var httpTask = client.GetAsync("http://apress.com");
        return httpTask.ContinueWith((Task<HttpResponseMessage> antecedent) => {
            return antecedent.Result.Content.Headers.ContentLength;
        });
    }
}
}
```

This method uses a `System.Net.Http.HttpClient` object to request the contents of the Apress home page and returns its length. .NET represents work that will be done asynchronously as a Task. Task objects are strongly typed based on the result that the background work produces. So, when I call the `HttpClient.GetAsync` method, what I get back is a `Task<HttpResponseMessage>`. This tells me that the request will be performed in the background and that the result of the request will be an `HttpResponseMessage` object.

■ **Tip**   When I use words like *background*, I am skipping over a lot of detail to make just the key points that are important to the world of ASP.NET Core. The .NET support for asynchronous methods and parallel programming is excellent, and I encourage you to learn more about it if you want to create truly high-performing applications that can take advantage of multicore and multiprocessor hardware. You will see how ASP.NET Core makes it easy to create asynchronous web applications throughout this book as I introduce different features.

The part that most programmers get bogged down with is the *continuation*, which is the mechanism by which you specify what you want to happen when the task is complete. In the example, I have used the `ContinueWith` method to process the `HttpResponseMessage` object I get from the `HttpClient.GetAsync` method, which I do with a lambda expression that returns the value of a property that contains the length of the content I get from the Apress web server. Here is the continuation code:

```
...
return httpTask.ContinueWith((Task<HttpResponseMessage> antecedent) => {
    return antecedent.Result.Content.Headers.ContentLength;
});
...
```

Notice that I use the `return` keyword twice. This is the part that causes confusion. The first use of the `return` keyword specifies that I am returning a `Task<HttpResponseMessage>` object, which, when the task is complete, will `return` the length of the `ContentLength` header. The `ContentLength` header returns a `long?` result (a nullable long value), and this means that the result of my `GetPageLength` method is `Task<long?>`, like this:

```
...
public static Task<long?> GetPageLength() {
...
```

Do not worry if this does not make sense—you are not alone in your confusion. It is for this reason that Microsoft added keywords to C# to simplify asynchronous methods.

Applying the async and await Keywords

Microsoft introduced two keywords to C# that simplify using asynchronous methods like `HttpClient.GetAsync`. The keywords are `async` and `await`, and you can see how I have used them to simplify my example method in Listing 5-46.

Listing 5-46. Using the async and await Keywords in the MyAsyncMethods.cs File in the Models Folder

```
using System.Net.Http;
using System.Threading.Tasks;

namespace LanguageFeatures.Models {

    public class MyAsyncMethods {

        public async static Task<long?> GetPageLength() {
            HttpClient client = new HttpClient();
            var httpMessage = await client.GetAsync("http://apress.com");
            return httpMessage.Content.Headers.ContentLength;
        }
    }
}
```

I used the await keyword when calling the asynchronous method. This tells the C# compiler that I want to wait for the result of the Task that the GetAsync method returns and then carry on executing other statements in the same method.

Applying the await keyword means I can treat the result from the GetAsync method as though it were a regular method and just assign the HttpResponseMessage object that it returns to a variable. Even better, I can then use the return keyword in the normal way to produce a result from another method—in this case, the value of the ContentLength property. This is a much more natural technique, and it means I do not have to worry about the ContinueWith method and multiple uses of the return keyword.

When you use the await keyword, you must also add the async keyword to the method signature, as I have done in the example. The method result type does not change—my example GetPageLength method still returns a Task<long?>. This is because await and async are implemented using some clever compiler tricks, meaning that they allow a more natural syntax, but they do not change what is happening in the methods to which they are applied. Someone who is calling my GetPageLength method still has to deal with a Task<long?> result because there is still a background operation that produces a nullable long—although, of course, that programmer can also choose to use the await and async keywords as well.

This pattern follows through into the controller, which makes it easy to write asynchronous action methods, as shown in Listing 5-47.

■ **Note** You can also use the async and await keywords in lambda expressions, which I demonstrate in later chapters.

Listing 5-47. An Asynchronous Action Methods in the HomeController.cs File in the Controllers Folder

```
using Microsoft.AspNetCore.Mvc;
using System.Collections.Generic;
using LanguageFeatures.Models;
using System;
using System.Linq;
using System.Threading.Tasks;

namespace LanguageFeatures.Controllers {
    public class HomeController : Controller {

        public async Task<ViewResult> Index() {
            long? length = await MyAsyncMethods.GetPageLength();
            return View(new string[] { $"Length: {length}" });
        }
    }
}
```

I have changed the result of the Index action method to Task<ViewResult>, which declares that the action method will return a Task that will produce a ViewResult object when it completes, which will provide details of the view that should be rendered and the data that it requires. I have added the async keyword to the method's definition, which allows me to use the await keyword when calling the MyAsyncMethods.GetPathLength method. .NET takes care of dealing with the continuations, and the result is asynchronous code that is easy to write, easy to read, and easy to maintain. Restart ASP.NET Core and request http://localhost:5000, and you will see output similar to the following (although with a different length since the content of the Apress web site changes often):

```
Length: 101868
```

Using an Asynchronous Enumerable

An asynchronous enumerable describes a sequence of values that will be generated over time. To demonstrate the issue that this feature addresses, Listing 5-48 adds a method to the MyAsyncMethods class.

Listing 5-48. Adding a Method in the MyAsyncMethods.cs File in the Models Folder

```
using System.Net.Http;
using System.Threading.Tasks;
using System.Collections.Generic;

namespace LanguageFeatures.Models {

    public class MyAsyncMethods {

        public async static Task<long?> GetPageLength() {
            HttpClient client = new HttpClient();
            var httpMessage = await client.GetAsync("http://apress.com");
            return httpMessage.Content.Headers.ContentLength;
        }

        public static async Task<IEnumerable<long?>>
                GetPageLengths(List<string> output, params string[] urls) {
            List<long?> results = new List<long?>();
            HttpClient client = new HttpClient();
            foreach (string url in urls) {
                output.Add($"Started request for {url}");
                var httpMessage = await client.GetAsync($"http://{url}");
                results.Add(httpMessage.Content.Headers.ContentLength);
                output.Add($"Completed request for {url}");
            }
            return results;
        }
    }
}
```

The GetPageLengths method makes HTTP requests to a series of web sites and gets their length. The requests are performed asynchronously, but there is no way to feed the results back to the method's caller as they arrive. Instead, the method waits until all the requests are complete and then returns all of the results in one go. In addition to the URLs that will be requested, this method accepts a List<string> to which I add messages in order to highlight how the code works. Listing 5-49 updates the Index action method of the Home controller to use the new method.

Listing 5-49. Using the New Method in the HomeController.cs File in the Controllers Folder

```
using Microsoft.AspNetCore.Mvc;
using System.Collections.Generic;
using LanguageFeatures.Models;
using System;
using System.Linq;
using System.Threading.Tasks;

namespace LanguageFeatures.Controllers {
    public class HomeController : Controller {

        public async Task<ViewResult> Index() {
            List<string> output = new List<string>();
            foreach(long? len in await MyAsyncMethods.GetPageLengths(output,
                    "apress.com", "microsoft.com", "amazon.com")) {
                output.Add($"Page length: { len}");
            }
            return View(output);
        }
    }
}
```

The action method enumerates the sequence produced by the GetPageLengths method and adds each result to the List<string> object, which produces an ordered sequence of messages showing the interaction between the foreach loop in the Index method that processes the results and the foreach loop in the GetPageLengths method that generates them. Restart ASP.NET Core and request http://localhost:5000, and you will see the following output in the browser (which may take several seconds to appear and may have different page lengths):

```
Started request for apress.com
Completed request for apress.com
Started request for microsoft.com
Completed request for microsoft.com
Started request for amazon.com
Completed request for amazon.com
Page length: 101868
Page length: 159158
Page length: 91879
```

You can see that the Index action method doesn't receive the results until all the HTTP requests have been completed. This is the problem that the asynchronous enumerable feature solves, as shown in Listing 5-50.

Listing 5-50. Using an Asynchronous Enumerable in the MyAsyncMethods.cs File in the Models Folder

```
using System.Net.Http;
using System.Threading.Tasks;
using System.Collections.Generic;

namespace LanguageFeatures.Models {

    public class MyAsyncMethods {

        public async static Task<long?> GetPageLength() {
            HttpClient client = new HttpClient();
            var httpMessage = await client.GetAsync("http://apress.com");
            return httpMessage.Content.Headers.ContentLength;
        }
```

```
    public static async IAsyncEnumerable<long?>
            GetPageLengths(List<string> output, params string[] urls) {
        HttpClient client = new HttpClient();
        foreach (string url in urls) {
            output.Add($"Started request for {url}");
            var httpMessage = await client.GetAsync($"http://{url}");
            output.Add($"Completed request for {url}");
            yield return httpMessage.Content.Headers.ContentLength;
        }
    }
}
}
```

The methods result is IAsyncEnumerable<long?>, which denotes an asynchronous sequence of nullable long values. This result type has special support in .NET Core and works with standard yield return statements, which isn't otherwise possible because the result constraints for asynchronous methods conflict with the yield keyword. Listing 5-51 updates the controller to use the revised method.

Listing 5-51. Using an Asynchronous Enumerable in the HomeController.cs File in the Controllers Folder

```
using Microsoft.AspNetCore.Mvc;
using System.Collections.Generic;
using LanguageFeatures.Models;
using System;
using System.Linq;
using System.Threading.Tasks;

namespace LanguageFeatures.Controllers {
    public class HomeController : Controller {

        public async Task<ViewResult> Index() {
            List<string> output = new List<string>();
            await foreach(long? len in MyAsyncMethods.GetPageLengths(output,
                    "apress.com", "microsoft.com", "amazon.com")) {
                output.Add($"Page length: { len}");
            }
            return View(output);
        }
    }
}
```

The difference is that the await keyword is applied before the foreach keyword and not before the call to the async method. Restart ASP.NET Core and request http://localhost:5000; once the HTTP requests are complete, you will see that the order of the response messages has changed, like this:

```
Started request for apress.com
Completed request for apress.com
Page length: 101868
Started request for microsoft.com
Completed request for microsoft.com
Page length: 159160
Started request for amazon.com
Completed request for amazon.com
Page length: 91674
```

The controller receives the next result in the sequence as it is produced. As I explain in Chapter 19, ASP.NET Core has special support for using IAsyncEnumerable<T> results in web services, allowing data values to be serialized as the values in the sequence are generated.

Getting Names

There are many tasks in web application development in which you need to refer to the name of an argument, variable, method, or class. Common examples include when you throw an exception or create a validation error when processing input from the user. The traditional approach has been to use a string value hard-coded with the name, as shown in Listing 5-52.

Listing 5-52. Hard-Coding a Name in the HomeController.cs File in the Controllers Folder

```
using Microsoft.AspNetCore.Mvc;
using System.Collections.Generic;
using LanguageFeatures.Models;
using System;
using System.Linq;
using System.Threading.Tasks;

namespace LanguageFeatures.Controllers {
    public class HomeController : Controller {

        public ViewResult Index() {
            var products = new[] {
                new { Name = "Kayak", Price = 275M },
                new { Name = "Lifejacket", Price = 48.95M },
                new { Name = "Soccer ball", Price = 19.50M },
                new { Name = "Corner flag", Price = 34.95M }
            };
            return View(products.Select(p => $"Name: {p.Name}, Price: {p.Price}"));
        }
    }
}
```

The call to the LINQ Select method generates a sequence of strings, each of which contains a hard-coded reference to the Name and Price properties. Restart ASP.NET Core and request http://localhost:5000, and you will see the following output in the browser window:

```
Name: Kayak, Price: 275
Name: Lifejacket, Price: 48.95
Name: Soccer ball, Price: 19.50
Name: Corner flag, Price: 34.95
```

This approach is prone to errors, either because the name was mistyped or because the code was refactored and the name in the string isn't correctly updated. C# supports the nameof expression, in which the compiler takes responsibility for producing a name string, as shown in Listing 5-53.

Listing 5-53. Using nameof Expressions in the HomeController.cs File in the Controllers Folder

```
using Microsoft.AspNetCore.Mvc;
using System.Collections.Generic;
using LanguageFeatures.Models;
using System;
using System.Linq;
using System.Threading.Tasks;
```

```
namespace LanguageFeatures.Controllers {
    public class HomeController : Controller {

        public ViewResult Index() {
            var products = new[] {
                new { Name = "Kayak", Price = 275M },
                new { Name = "Lifejacket", Price = 48.95M },
                new { Name = "Soccer ball", Price = 19.50M },
                new { Name = "Corner flag", Price = 34.95M }
            };
            return View(products.Select(p =>
                $"{nameof(p.Name)}: {p.Name}, {nameof(p.Price)}: {p.Price}"));
        }
    }
}
```

The compiler processes a reference such as p.Name so that only the last part is included in the string, producing the same output as in previous examples. There is IntelliSense support for nameof expressions, so you will be prompted to select references, and expressions will be correctly updated when you refactor code. Since the compiler is responsible for dealing with nameof, using an invalid reference causes a compiler error, which prevents incorrect or outdated references from escaping notice.

Summary

In this chapter, I gave you an overview of the key C# language features that an effective ASP.NET Core programmer needs to know. C# is a sufficiently flexible language that there are usually different ways to approach any problem, but these are the features that you will encounter most often during web application development and that you will see throughout the examples in this book. In the next chapter, I explain how to set up a unit test project for ASP.NET Core.

CHAPTER 6

Testing ASP.NET Core Applications

In this chapter, I demonstrate how to unit test ASP.NET Core applications. Unit testing is a form of testing in which individual components are isolated from the rest of the application so their behavior can be thoroughly validated. ASP.NET Core has been designed to make it easy to create unit tests, and there is support for a wide range of unit testing frameworks. I show you how to set up a unit test project and describe the process for writing and running tests. Table 6-1 summarizes the chapter.

DECIDING WHETHER TO UNIT TEST

Being able to easily perform unit testing is one of the benefits of using ASP.NET Core, but it isn't for everyone, and I have no intention of pretending otherwise.

I like unit testing, and I use it in my own projects, but not all of them and not as consistently as you might expect. I tend to focus on writing unit tests for features and functions that I know will be hard to write and likely to be the source of bugs in deployment. In these situations, unit testing helps structure my thoughts about how to best implement what I need. I find that just thinking about what I need to test helps produce ideas about potential problems, and that's before I start dealing with actual bugs and defects.

That said, unit testing is a tool and not a religion, and only you know how much testing you require. If you don't find unit testing useful or if you have a different methodology that suits you better, then don't feel you need to unit test just because it is fashionable. (However, if you *don't* have a better methodology and you are not testing at all, then you are probably letting users find your bugs, which is rarely ideal. You don't *have* to unit test, but you really should consider doing *some* testing of *some* kind.)

If you have not encountered unit testing before, then I encourage you to give it a try to see how it works. If you are not a fan of unit testing, then you can skip this chapter and move on to Chapter 7, where I start to build a more realistic ASP.NET Core application.

Table 6-1. *Chapter Summary*

Problem	Solution	Listing
Creating a unit test project	Use the dotnet new command with the project template for your preferred test framework	7
Creating an XUnit test	Create a class with methods decorated with the Fact attribute and use the Assert class to inspect the test results	9
Running unit tests	Use the Visual Studio or Visual Studio Code test runners or use the dotnet test command	11
Isolating a component for testing	Create mock implementations of the objects that the component under test requires	12–19

Preparing for This Chapter

To prepare for this chapter, I need to create a simple ASP.NET Core project. Open a new PowerShell command prompt using the Windows Start menu, navigate to a convenient location, and run the commands shown in Listing 6-1.

© Adam Freeman 2020
A. Freeman, *Pro ASP.NET Core 3*, https://doi.org/10.1007/978-1-4842-5440-0_6

■ **Tip** You can download the example project for this chapter—and for all the other chapters in this book—from `https://github.com/apress/pro-asp.net-core-3`. See Chapter 1 for how to get help if you have problems running the examples.

Listing 6-1. Creating the Example Project

```
dotnet new globaljson --sdk-version 3.1.101 --output Testing/SimpleApp
dotnet new web --no-https --output Testing/SimpleApp --framework netcoreapp3.1
dotnet new sln -o Testing

dotnet sln Testing add Testing/SimpleApp
```

These commands create a new project named `SimpleApp` using the web template, which contains the minimal configuration for ASP.NET Core applications. The project folder is contained within a solution folder also called `Testing`.

Opening the Project

If you are using Visual Studio, select File ➤ Open ➤ Project/Solution, select the `Testing.sln` file in the `Testing` folder, and click the Open button to open the solution file and the project it references. If you are using Visual Studio Code, select File ➤ Open Folder, navigate to the `Testing` folder, and click the Select Folder button.

Selecting the HTTP Port

If you are using Visual Studio, select Project ➤ SimpleApp Properties, select the Debug section, and change the HTTP port to 5000 in the App URL field, as shown in Figure 6-1. Select File ➤ Save All to save the new port. (This change is not required if you are using Visual Studio Code.)

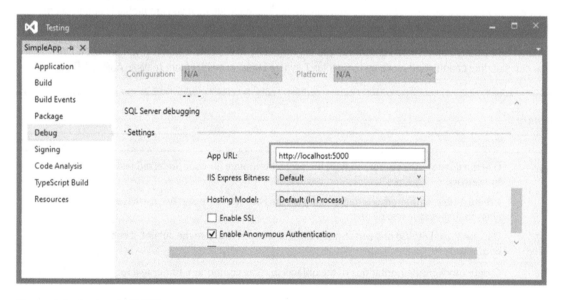

Figure 6-1. Setting the HTTP port

Enabling the MVC Framework

As I explained in Chapter 1, ASP.NET Core supports different application frameworks, but I am going to continue using the MVC Framework in this chapter. I introduce the other frameworks in the SportsStore application that I start to build in Chapter 7, but for the moment, the MVC Framework gives me a foundation for demonstrating how to perform unit testing that is familiar from earlier examples. Add the statements shown in Listing 6-2 to the Startup.cs file in the SimpleApp folder.

Listing 6-2. Enabling the MVC Framework in the Startup.cs File in the SimpleApp Folder

```
using System;
using System.Collections.Generic;
using System.Linq;
using System.Threading.Tasks;
using Microsoft.AspNetCore.Builder;
using Microsoft.AspNetCore.Hosting;
using Microsoft.AspNetCore.Http;
using Microsoft.Extensions.DependencyInjection;
using Microsoft.Extensions.Hosting;

namespace SimpleApp {
    public class Startup {

        public void ConfigureServices(IServiceCollection services) {
            services.AddControllersWithViews();
        }

        public void Configure(IApplicationBuilder app, IWebHostEnvironment env) {
            if (env.IsDevelopment()) {
                app.UseDeveloperExceptionPage();
            }

            app.UseRouting();

            app.UseEndpoints(endpoints => {
                endpoints.MapDefaultControllerRoute();
                //endpoints.MapGet("/", async context => {
                //    await context.Response.WriteAsync("Hello World!");
                //});
            });
        }
    }
}
```

Creating the Application Components

Now that the MVC Framework is set up, I can add the application components that I will use to demonstrate important C# language features.

Creating the Data Model

I started by creating a simple model class so that I can have some data to work with. I added a folder called Models and created a class file called Product.cs within it, which I used to define the class shown in Listing 6-3.

Listing 6-3. The Contents of the Product.cs File in the SimpleApp/Models Folder

```
namespace SimpleApp.Models {
    public class Product {

        public string Name { get; set; }
        public decimal? Price { get; set; }
```

```
    public static Product[] GetProducts() {

        Product kayak = new Product {
            Name = "Kayak", Price = 275M
        };

        Product lifejacket = new Product {
            Name = "Lifejacket", Price = 48.95M
        };

        return new Product[] { kayak, lifejacket };
    }
}
}
```

The Product class defines Name and Price properties, and there is a static method called GetProducts that returns a Products array.

Creating the Controller and View

For the examples in this chapter, I use a simple controller class to demonstrate different language features. I created a Controllers folder and added to it a class file called HomeController.cs, the contents of which are shown in Listing 6-4.

Listing 6-4. The Contents of the HomeController.cs File in the SimpleApp/Controllers Folder

```
using Microsoft.AspNetCore.Mvc;
using SimpleApp.Models;

namespace SimpleApp.Controllers {
    public class HomeController : Controller {

        public ViewResult Index() {
            return View(Product.GetProducts());
        }
    }
}
```

The Index action method tells ASP.NET Core to render the default view and provides it with the Product objects obtained from the static Product.GetProducts method. To create the view for the action method, I added a Views/Home folder (by creating a Views folder and then adding a Home folder within it) and added a Razor View called Index.cshtml, with the contents shown in Listing 6-5.

Listing 6-5. The Contents of the Index.cshtml File in the SimpleApp/Views/Home Folder

```
@using SimpleApp.Models
@model IEnumerable<Product>
@{ Layout = null; }

<!DOCTYPE html>
<html>
<head>
    <meta name="viewport" content="width=device-width" />
    <title>Simple App</title>
</head>
```

```
<body>
    <ul>
        @foreach (Product p in Model) {
            <li>Name: @p.Name, Price: @p.Price</li>
        }
    </ul>
</body>
</html>
```

Running the Example Application

Start ASP.NET Core by selecting Start Without Debugging (Visual Studio) or Run Without Debugging (Visual Studio Code) from the Debug menu or by running the command shown in Listing 6-6 in the SimpleApp folder.

Listing 6-6. Running the Example Application

```
dotnet run
```

Request http://localhost:5000, and you will see the output shown in Figure 6-2.

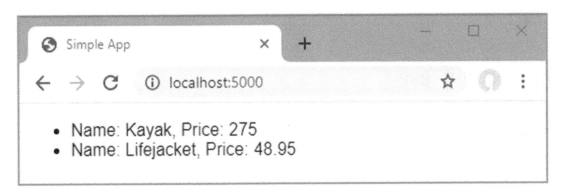

Figure 6-2. Running the example application

Creating a Unit Test Project

For ASP.NET Core applications, you generally create a separate Visual Studio project to hold the unit tests, each of which is defined as a method in a C# class. Using a separate project means you can deploy your application without also deploying the tests. The .NET Core SDK includes templates for unit test projects using three popular test tools, as described in Table 6-2.

Table 6-2. The Unit Test Project Tools

Name	Description
mstest	This template creates a project configured for the MS Test framework, which is produced by Microsoft.
nunit	This template creates a project configured for the NUnit framework.
xunit	This template creates a project configured for the XUnit framework.

These testing frameworks have largely the same feature set and differ only in how they are implemented and how they integrate into third-party testing environments. I recommend starting with XUnit If you do not have an established preference, largely because it is the test framework that I find easiest to work with.

The convention is to name the unit test project <ApplicationName>.Tests. Run the commands shown in Listing 6-7 in the Testing folder to create the XUnit test project named SimpleApp.Tests, add it to the solution file, and create a reference between projects so the unit tests can be applied to the classes defined in the SimpleApp project.

Listing 6-7. Creating the Unit Test Project

```
dotnet new xunit -o SimpleApp.Tests --framework netcoreapp3.1
dotnet sln add SimpleApp.Tests
dotnet add SimpleApp.Tests reference SimpleApp
```

If you are using Visual Studio, you will be prompted to reload the solution, which will cause the new unit test project to be displayed in the Solution Explorer, alongside the existing project. You may find that Visual Studio Code doesn't build the new project. If that happens, select Terminal ➤ Configure Default Build Task, select "build" from the list, and, if prompted, select .NET Core from the list of environments.

Removing the Default Test Class

The project template adds a C# class file to the test project, which will confuse the results of later examples. Either delete the UnitTest1.cs file from the SimpleApp.Tests folder using the Solution Explorer or File Explorer pane or run the command shown in Listing 6-8 in the Testing folder.

Listing 6-8. Removing the Default Test Class File

```
Remove-Item SimpleApp.Tests/UnitTest1.cs
```

Writing and Running Unit Tests

Now that all the preparation is complete, I can write some tests. To get started, I added a class file called ProductTests.cs to the SimpleApp.Tests project and used it to define the class shown in Listing 6-9. This is a simple class, but it contains everything required to get started with unit testing.

■ **Note** The CanChangeProductPrice method contains a deliberate error that I resolve later in this section.

Listing 6-9. The Contents of the ProductTests.cs File in the SimpleApp.Tests Folder

```
using SimpleApp.Models;
using Xunit;

namespace SimpleApp.Tests {

    public class ProductTests {

        [Fact]
        public void CanChangeProductName() {

            // Arrange
            var p = new Product { Name = "Test", Price = 100M };

            // Act
            p.Name = "New Name";

            //Assert
            Assert.Equal("New Name", p.Name);
        }
```

```
[Fact]
public void CanChangeProductPrice() {

    // Arrange
    var p = new Product { Name = "Test", Price = 100M };

    // Act
    p.Price = 200M;

    //Assert
    Assert.Equal(100M, p.Price);
  }
 }
}
```

There are two unit tests in the `ProductTests` class, each of which tests a behavior of the `Product` model class from the `SimpleApp` project. A test project can contain many classes, each of which can contain many unit tests.

Conventionally, the name of the test methods describes what the test does, and the name of the class describes what is being tested. This makes it easier to structure the tests in a project and to understand what the results of all the tests are when they are run by Visual Studio. The name `ProductTests` indicates that the class contains tests for the `Product` class, and the method names indicate that they test the ability to change the name and price of a `Product` object.

The `Fact` attribute is applied to each method to indicate that it is a test. Within the method body, a unit test follows a pattern called *arrange, act, assert* (A/A/A). *Arrange* refers to setting up the conditions for the test, *act* refers to performing the test, and *assert* refers to verifying that the result was the one that was expected.

The arrange and act sections of these tests are regular C# code, but the assert section is handled by xUnit.net, which provides a class called `Assert`, whose methods are used to check that the outcome of an action is the one that is expected.

■ **Tip** The `Fact` attribute and the `Asset` class are defined in the `Xunit` namespace, for which there must be a `using` statement in every test class.

The methods of the `Assert` class are static and are used to perform different kinds of comparison between the expected and actual results. Table 6-3 shows the commonly used `Assert` methods.

Table 6-3. *Commonly Used xUnit.net Assert Methods*

Name	Description
`Equal(expected, result)`	This method asserts that the result is equal to the expected outcome. There are overloaded versions of this method for comparing different types and for comparing collections. There is also a version of this method that accepts an additional argument of an object that implements the `IEqualityComparer<T>` interface for comparing objects.
`NotEqual(expected, result)`	This method asserts that the result is not equal to the expected outcome.
`True(result)`	This method asserts that the result is `true`.
`False(result)`	This method asserts that the result is `false`.
`IsType(expected, result)`	This method asserts that the result is of a specific type.
`IsNotType(expected, result)`	This method asserts that the result is not a specific type.
`IsNull(result)`	This method asserts that the result is `null`.
`IsNotNull(result)`	This method asserts that the result is not `null`.
`InRange(result, low, high)`	This method asserts that the result falls between `low` and `high`.
`NotInRange(result, low, high)`	This method asserts that the result falls outside `low` and `high`.
`Throws(exception, expression)`	This method asserts that the specified expression throws a specific exception type.

Each `Assert` method allows different types of comparison to be made and throws an exception if the result is not what was expected. The exception is used to indicate that a test has failed. In the tests in Listing 6-9, I used the `Equal` method to determine whether the value of a property has been changed correctly.

```
...
Assert.Equal("New Name", p.Name);
...
```

Running Tests with the Visual Studio Test Explorer

Visual Studio includes support for finding and running unit tests through the Test Explorer window, which is available through the Test ➤ Test Explorer menu and is shown in Figure 6-3.

■ **Tip** Build the solution if you don't see the unit tests in the Test Explorer window. Compilation triggers the process by which unit tests are discovered.

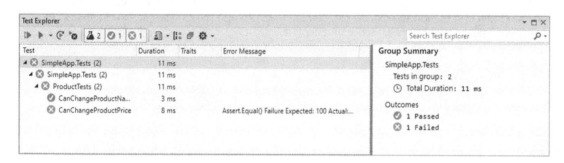

Figure 6-3. *The Visual Studio Test Explorer*

Run the tests by clicking the Run All Tests button in the Test Explorer window (it is the button that shows two arrows and is the first button in the row at the top of the window). As noted, the `CanChangeProductPrice` test contains an error that causes the test to fail, which is clearly indicated in the test results shown in the figure.

Running Tests with Visual Studio Code

Visual Studio Code detects tests and allows them to be run using the code lens feature, which displays details about code features in the editor. To run all the tests in the `ProductTests` class, click Run All Tests in the code editor when the unit test class is open, as shown in Figure 6-4.

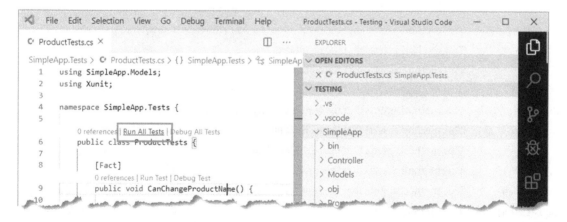

Figure 6-4. *Running tests with the Visual Studio Code code lens feature*

■ **Tip** Close and reopen the Testing folder in Visual Studio Code if you don't see the code lens test features.

Visual Studio Code runs the tests using the command-line tools that I describe in the following section, and the results are displayed as text in a terminal window.

Running Tests from the Command Line

To run the tests in the project, run the command shown in Listing 6-10 in the Testing folder.

Listing 6-10. Running Unit Tests

```
dotnet test
```

The tests are discovered and executed, producing the following results, which show the deliberate error that I introduced earlier:

```
Test run for C:\Users\adam\SimpleApp.Tests.dll(.NETCoreApp,Version=v3.1)
Microsoft (R) Test Execution Command Line Tool Version 16.3.0
Copyright (c) Microsoft Corporation.  All rights reserved.

  Starting test execution, please wait...

A total of 1 test files matched the specified pattern.
[xUnit.net 00:00:00.83]     SimpleApp.Tests.ProductTests.CanChangeProductPrice [FAIL]
  X SimpleApp.Tests.ProductTests.CanChangeProductPrice [6ms]
  Error Message:
   Assert.Equal() Failure
Expected: 100
Actual:   200
  Stack Trace:
     at SimpleApp.Tests.ProductTests.CanChangeProductPrice() in C:\Users\adam\Documents\Books\Pro ASP.NET Core
     MVC 3\Source Code\Current\Testin
g\SimpleApp.Tests\ProductTests.cs:line 31

Test Run Failed.
Total tests: 2
     Passed: 1
     Failed: 1
 Total time: 1.7201 Seconds
```

Correcting the Unit Test

The problem with the unit test is with the arguments to the Assert.Equal method, which compares the test result to the original Price property value rather than the value it has been changed to. Listing 6-11 corrects the problem.

■ **Tip** When a test fails, it is always a good idea to check the accuracy of the test before looking at the component it targets, especially if the test is new or has been recently modified.

Listing 6-11. Correcting a Test in the ProductTests.cs File in the SimpleApp.Tests Folder

```
using SimpleApp.Models;
using Xunit;

namespace SimpleApp.Tests {

    public class ProductTests {

        [Fact]
        public void CanChangeProductName() {

            // Arrange
            var p = new Product { Name = "Test", Price = 100M };

            // Act
            p.Name = "New Name";

            //Assert
            Assert.Equal("New Name", p.Name);
        }

        [Fact]
        public void CanChangeProductPrice() {

            // Arrange
            var p = new Product { Name = "Test", Price = 100M };

            // Act
            p.Price = 200M;

            //Assert
            Assert.Equal(200M, p.Price);
        }
    }
}
```

Run the tests again, and you will see they all pass. If you are using Visual Studio, you can click the Run Failed Tests button, which will execute only the tests that failed, as shown in Figure 6-5.

Figure 6-5. *Running only failed tests*

Isolating Components for Unit Testing

Writing unit tests for model classes like Product is easy. Not only is the Product class simple, but it is self-contained, which means that when I perform an action on a Product object, I can be confident that I am testing the functionality provided by the Product class.

The situation is more complicated with other components in an ASP.NET Core application because there are dependencies between them. The next set of tests that I define will operate on the controller, examining the sequence of Product objects that are passed between the controller and the view.

When comparing objects instantiated from custom classes, you will need to use the xUnit.net Assert.Equal method that accepts an argument that implements the IEqualityComparer<T> interface so that the objects can be compared. My first step is to add a class file called Comparer.cs to the unit test project and use it to define the helper classes shown in Listing 6-12.

Listing 6-12. The Contents of the Comparer.cs File in the SimpleApp.Tests Folder

```
using System;
using System.Collections.Generic;

namespace SimpleApp.Tests {

    public class Comparer {

        public static Comparer<U> Get<U>(Func<U, U, bool> func) {
            return new Comparer<U>(func);
        }
    }

    public class Comparer<T> : Comparer, IEqualityComparer<T> {
        private Func<T, T, bool> comparisonFunction;

        public Comparer(Func<T, T, bool> func) {
            comparisonFunction = func;
        }

        public bool Equals(T x, T y) {
            return comparisonFunction(x, y);
        }

        public int GetHashCode(T obj) {
            return obj.GetHashCode();
        }
    }
}
```

These classes will allow me to create IEqualityComparer<T> objects using lambda expressions rather than having to define a new class for each type of comparison that I want to make. This isn't essential, but it will simplify the code in my unit test classes and make them easier to read and maintain.

Now that I can easily make comparisons, I can illustrate the problem of dependencies between components in the application. I added a new class called HomeControllerTests.cs to the SimpleApp.Tests folder and used it to define the unit test shown in Listing 6-13.

Listing 6-13. The HomeControllerTests.cs File in the SimpleApp.Tests Folder

```
using Microsoft.AspNetCore.Mvc;
using System.Collections.Generic;
using SimpleApp.Controllers;
using SimpleApp.Models;
using Xunit;

namespace SimpleApp.Tests {
    public class HomeControllerTests {

        [Fact]
        public void IndexActionModelIsComplete() {
            // Arrange
```

```
            var controller = new HomeController();
            Product[] products = new Product[] {
                new Product { Name = "Kayak", Price = 275M },
                new Product { Name = "Lifejacket", Price = 48.95M}
            };

            // Act
            var model = (controller.Index() as ViewResult)?.ViewData.Model
                as IEnumerable<Product>;

            // Assert
            Assert.Equal(products, model,
                Comparer.Get<Product>((p1, p2) => p1.Name == p2.Name
                    && p1.Price == p2.Price));
        }
    }
}
```

The unit test creates an array of Product objects and checks that they correspond to the ones the Index action method provides as the view model. (Ignore the act section of the test for the moment; I explain the ViewResult class in Chapters 21 and 22. For the moment, it is enough to know that I am getting the model data returned by the Index action method.)

The test passes, but it isn't a useful result because the Product data that I am testing is coming from the hardwired objects' Product class. I can't write a test to make sure that the controller behaves correctly when there are more than two Product objects, for example, or if the Price property of the first object has a decimal fraction. The overall effect is that I am testing the combined behavior of the HomeController and Product classes and only for the specific hardwired objects.

Unit tests are effective when they target small parts of an application, such as an individual method or class. What I need is the ability to isolate the Home controller from the rest of the application so that I can limit the scope of the test and rule out any impact caused by the repository.

Isolating a Component

The key to isolating components is to use C# interfaces. To separate the controller from the repository, I added a new class file called IDataSource.cs to the Models folder and used it to define the interface shown in Listing 6-14.

Listing 6-14. The Contents of the IDataSource.cs File in the SimpleApp/Models Folder

```
using System.Collections.Generic;

namespace SimpleApp.Models {
    public interface IDataSource {

        IEnumerable<Product> Products { get; }
    }
}
```

In Listing 6-15, I have removed the static method from the Product class and created a new class that implements the IDataSource interface.

Listing 6-15. Creating a Data Source in the Product.cs File in the SimpleApp/Models Folder

```
using System.Collections.Generic;

namespace SimpleApp.Models {

    public class Product {
        public string Name { get; set; }
        public decimal? Price { get; set; }
    }
```

```
public class ProductDataSource : IDataSource {
    public IEnumerable<Product> Products =>
        new Product[] {
            new Product { Name = "Kayak", Price = 275M },
            new Product { Name = "Lifejacket", Price = 48.95M }
        };
}
}
```

The next step is to modify the controller so that it uses the `ProductDataSource` class as the source for its data, as shown in Listing 6-16.

■ **Tip** ASP.NET Core supports a more elegant approach for solving this problem, known as *dependency injection*, which I describe in Chapter 14. Dependency injection often causes confusion, so I isolate components in a simpler and more manual way in this chapter.

Listing 6-16. Adding a Property in the HomeController.cs File in the SimpleApp/Controllers Folder

```
using Microsoft.AspNetCore.Mvc;
using SimpleApp.Models;

namespace SimpleApp.Controllers {
    public class HomeController : Controller {
        public IDataSource dataSource = new ProductDataSource();

        public ViewResult Index() {
            return View(dataSource.Products);
        }
    }
}
```

This may not seem like a significant change, but it allows me to change the data source the controller uses during testing, which is how I can isolate the controller. In Listing 6-17, I have updated the controller unit tests so they use a special version of the repository.

Listing 6-17. Isolating the Controller in the HomeControllerTests.cs File in the SimpleApp.Tests Folder

```
using Microsoft.AspNetCore.Mvc;
using System.Collections.Generic;
using SimpleApp.Controllers;
using SimpleApp.Models;
using Xunit;

namespace SimpleApp.Tests {
    public class HomeControllerTests {

        class FakeDataSource : IDataSource {
            public FakeDataSource(Product[] data) => Products = data;
            public IEnumerable<Product> Products { get; set; }
        }

        [Fact]
        public void IndexActionModelIsComplete() {
            // Arrange
            Product[] testData = new Product[] {
                new Product { Name = "P1", Price = 75.10M },
```

```
                new Product { Name = "P2", Price = 120M },
                new Product { Name = "P3", Price = 110M }
            };
            IDataSource data = new FakeDataSource(testData);
            var controller = new HomeController();
            controller.dataSource = data;

            // Act
            var model = (controller.Index() as ViewResult)?.ViewData.Model
                as IEnumerable<Product>;

            // Assert
            Assert.Equal(data.Products, model,
                Comparer.Get<Product>((p1, p2) => p1.Name == p2.Name
                    && p1.Price == p2.Price));
        }
    }
}
```

I have defined a fake implementation of the IDataSource interface that lets me use any test data with the controller.

UNDERSTANDING TEST-DRIVEN DEVELOPMENT

I have followed the most commonly used unit testing style in this chapter, in which an application feature is written and then tested to make sure it works as required. This is popular because most developers think about application code first and testing comes second (this is certainly the category that I fall into).

This approach is that it tends to produce unit tests that focus only on the parts of the application code that were difficult to write or that needed some serious debugging, leaving some aspects of a feature only partially tested or untested altogether.

An alternative approach is *Test-Driven Development* (TDD). There are lots of variations on TDD, but the core idea is that you write the tests for a feature before implementing the feature itself. Writing the tests first makes you think more carefully about the specification you are implementing and how you will know that a feature has been implemented correctly. Rather than diving into the implementation detail, TDD makes you consider what the measures of success or failure will be in advance.

The tests that you write will all fail initially because your new feature will not be implemented. But as you add code to the application, your tests will gradually move from red to green, and all your tests will pass by the time that the feature is complete. TDD requires discipline, but it does produce a more comprehensive set of tests and can lead to more robust and reliable code.

Using a Mocking Package

It was easy to create a fake implementation for the IDataSource interface, but most classes for which fake implementations are required are more complex and cannot be handled as easily.

A better approach is to use a mocking package, which makes it easy to create fake—or mock—objects for tests. There are many mocking packages available, but the one I use (and have for years) is called Moq. To add Moq to the unit test project, run the command shown in Listing 6-18 in the Testing folder.

▪ **Note**   The Moq package is added to the unit testing project and not the project that contains the application to be tested.

Listing 6-18. Installing the Mocking Package

```
dotnet add SimpleApp.Tests package Moq --version 4.13.1
```

Creating a Mock Object

I can use the Moq framework to create a fake IDataSource object without having to define a custom test class, as shown in Listing 6-19.

Listing 6-19. Creating a Mock Object in the HomeControllerTests.cs File in the SimpleApp.Tests Folder

```
using Microsoft.AspNetCore.Mvc;
using System.Collections.Generic;
using SimpleApp.Controllers;
using SimpleApp.Models;
using Xunit;
using Moq;

namespace SimpleApp.Tests {
    public class HomeControllerTests {

        //class FakeDataSource : IDataSource {
        //    public FakeDataSource(params Product[] data) => Products = data;
        //    public IEnumerable<Product> Products { get; set; }
        //}

        [Fact]
        public void IndexActionModelIsComplete() {

            // Arrange
            Product[] testData = new Product[] {
                new Product { Name = "P1", Price = 75.10M },
                new Product { Name = "P2", Price = 120M },
                new Product { Name = "P3", Price = 110M }
            };
            var mock = new Mock<IDataSource>();
            mock.SetupGet(m => m.Products).Returns(testData);
            var controller = new HomeController();
            controller.dataSource = mock.Object;

            // Act
            var model = (controller.Index() as ViewResult)?.ViewData.Model
                as IEnumerable<Product>;

            // Assert
            Assert.Equal(testData, model,
                Comparer.Get<Product>((p1, p2) => p1.Name == p2.Name
                    && p1.Price == p2.Price));
            mock.VerifyGet(m => m.Products, Times.Once);
        }
    }
}
```

The use of Moq has allowed me to remove the fake implementation of the IDataSource interface and replace it with a few lines of code. I am not going to go into detail about the different features that Moq supports, but I will explain the way that I used Moq in the examples. (See https://github.com/Moq/moq4 for examples and documentation for Moq. There are also examples in later chapters as I explain how to unit test different types of components.)

The first step is to create a new instance of the Mock object, specifying the interface that should be implemented, like this:

```
...
var mock = new Mock<IDataSource>();
...
```

The Mock object I created will fake the IDataSource interface. To create an implementation of the Product property, I use the SetUpGet method, like this:

```
...
mock.SetupGet(m => m.Products).Returns(testData);
...
```

The SetupGet method is used to implement the getter for a property. The argument to this method is a lambda expression that specifies the property to be implemented, which is Products in this example. The Returns method is called on the result of the SetupGet method to specify the result that will be returned when the property value is read.

The Mock class defines an Object property, which returns the object that implements the specified interface with the behaviors that have been defined. I used the Object property to set the dataSource field defined by the HomeController, like this:

```
...
controller.dataSource = mock.Object;
...
```

The final Moq feature I used was to check that the Products property was called once, like this:

```
...
mock.VerifyGet(m => m.Products, Times.Once);
...
```

The VerifyGet method is one of the methods defined by the Mock class to inspect the state of the mock object when the test has completed. In this case, the VerifyGet method allows me to check the number of times that the Products property method has been read. The Times.Once value specifies that the VerifyGet method should throw an exception if the property has not been read exactly once, which will cause the test to fail. (The Assert methods usually used in tests work by throwing an exception when a test fails, which is why the VerifyGet method can be used to replace an Assert method when working with mock objects.)

The overall effect is the same as my fake interface implementation, but mocking is more flexible and more concise and can provide more insight into the behavior of the components under test.

Summary

This chapter focused on unit testing, which can be a powerful tool for improving the quality of code. Unit testing doesn't suit every developer, but it is worth experimenting with and can be useful even if used only for complex features or problem diagnosis. I described the use of the xUnit.net test framework, explained the importance of isolating components for testing, and demonstrated some tools and techniques for simplifying unit test code. In the next chapter, I start the development of a more realistic project, named SportsStore.

CHAPTER 7

SportsStore: A Real Application

In the previous chapters, I built quick and simple ASP.NET Core applications. I described ASP.NET Core patterns, the essential C# features, and the tools that good ASP.NET Core developers require. Now it is time to put everything together and build a simple but realistic e-commerce application.

My application, called SportsStore, will follow the classic approach taken by online stores everywhere. I will create an online product catalog that customers can browse by category and page, a shopping cart where users can add and remove products, and a checkout where customers can enter their shipping details. I will also create an administration area that includes create, read, update, and delete (CRUD) facilities for managing the catalog, and I will protect it so that only logged-in administrators can make changes.

My goal in this chapter and those that follow is to give you a sense of what real ASP.NET Core development is by creating as realistic an example as possible. I want to focus on ASP.NET Core, of course, so I have simplified the integration with external systems, such as the database, and omitted others entirely, such as payment processing.

You might find the going a little slow as I build up the levels of infrastructure I need, but the initial investment will result in maintainable, extensible, well-structured code with excellent support for unit testing.

UNIT TESTING

I include sections on unit testing different components in the SportsStore application throughout the development process, demonstrating how to isolate and test different ASP.NET Core components.

I know that unit testing is not embraced by everyone. If you do not want to unit test, that is fine with me. To that end, when I have something to say that is purely about testing, I put it in a sidebar like this one. If you are not interested in unit testing, you can skip right over these sections, and the SportsStore application will work just fine. You do not need to do any kind of unit testing to get the technology benefits of ASP.NET Core, although, of course, support for testing is a key reason for adopting ASP.NET Core in many projects.

Most of the features I use for the SportsStore application have their own chapters later in the book. Rather than duplicate everything here, I tell you just enough to make sense of the example application and point you to another chapter for in-depth information.

I will call out each step needed to build the application so that you can see how the ASP.NET Core features fit together. You should pay particular attention when I create views. You will get some odd results if you do not follow the examples closely.

Creating the Projects

I am going to start with a minimal ASP.NET Core project and add the features I require as they are needed. Open a new PowerShell command prompt from the Windows Start menu and run the commands shown in Listing 7-1 to get started.

■ **Tip** You can download the example project for this chapter—and for all the other chapters in this book—from `https://github.com/apress/pro-asp.net-core-3`. See Chapter 1 for how to get help if you have problems running the examples.

Listing 7-1. Creating the SportsStore Project

```
dotnet new globaljson --sdk-version 3.1.101 --output SportsSln/SportsStore
dotnet new web --no-https --output SportsSln/SportsStore --framework netcoreapp3.1
dotnet new sln -o SportsSln

dotnet sln SportsSln add SportsSln/SportsStore
```

These commands create a SportsSln solution folder that contains a SportsStore project folder created with the web project template. The SportsSln folder also contains a solution file, to which the SportsStore project is added.

I am using different names for the solution and project folders to make the examples easier to follow, but if you create a project with Visual Studio, the default is to use the same name for both folders. There is no "right" approach, and you can use whatever names suit your project.

Creating the Unit Test Project

To create the unit test project, run the commands shown in Listing 7-2 in the same location you used for the commands shown in Listing 7-1.

Listing 7-2. Creating the Unit Test Project

```
dotnet new xunit -o SportsSln/SportsStore.Tests --framework netcoreapp3.1
dotnet sln SportsSln add SportsSln/SportsStore.Tests
dotnet add SportsSln/SportsStore.Tests reference SportsSln/SportsStore
```

I am going to use the Moq package to create mock objects. Run the command shown in Listing 7-3 to install the Moq package into the unit testing project. Run this command from the same location as the commands in Listings 7-1 and 7-2.

Listing 7-3. Installing the Moq Package

```
dotnet add SportsSln/SportsStore.Tests package Moq --version 4.13.1
```

Creating the Application Project Folders

The next step is to create folders that will contain the application's components. Right-click the SportsStore item in the Visual Studio Solution Explorer or Visual Studio Code Explorer pane and select Add ➤ New Folder or New Folder to create the set of folders described in Table 7-1.

Table 7-1. *The Folders Created in Listing 7-3*

Name	Description
Models	This folder will contain the data model and the classes that provide access to the data in the application's database.
Controllers	This folder will contain the controller classes that handle HTTP requests.
Views	This folder will contain all the Razor files, grouped into separate subfolders.
Views/Home	This folder will contain Razor files that are specific to the Home controller, which I create in the "Creating the Controller and View" section.
Views/Shared	This folder will contain Razor files that are common to all controllers.

Opening the Projects

If you are using Visual Studio Code, select File ➤ Open Folder, navigate to the SportsSln folder, and click the Select Folder button. Visual Studio Code will open the folder and discover the solution and project files. When prompted, as shown in Figure 7-1, click Yes to install the assets required to build the projects. Select SportsStore if Visual Studio Code prompts you to select the project to run.

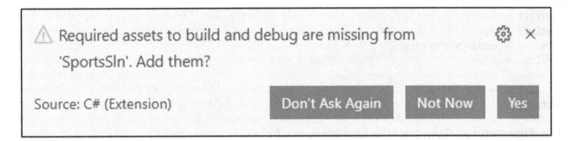

Figure 7-1. *Adding assets in Visual Studio Code*

If you are using Visual Studio, click the "Open a project or solution" button on the splash screen or select File ➤ Open ➤ Project/Solution. Select the SportsSln.sln file in the SportsSln folder and click the Open button to open the project. Once the projects have been opened, select Project ➤ SportsStore Properties, select the Debug section, and change the port for the URL in the App URL field to 5000, as shown in Figure 7-2. Select File ➤ Save All to save the new URL.

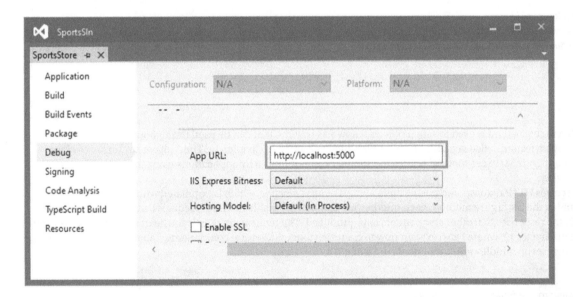

Figure 7-2. *Changing the HTTP port in Visual Studio*

Preparing the Application Services and the Request Pipeline

The Startup class is responsible for configuring the ASP.NET Core application. Apply the changes shown in Listing 7-4 to the Startup class in the SportsStore project to configure the basic application features.

■ **Note** The Startup class is an important ASP.NET Core feature. I describe it in detail in Chapter 12.

Listing 7-4 Configuring the Application in the Startup.cs File in the SportsStore Folder

```
using System;
using System.Collections.Generic;
using System.Linq;
using System.Threading.Tasks;
using Microsoft.AspNetCore.Builder;
using Microsoft.AspNetCore.Hosting;
using Microsoft.AspNetCore.Http;
using Microsoft.Extensions.DependencyInjection;
using Microsoft.Extensions.Hosting;

namespace SportsStore {
    public class Startup {

        public void ConfigureServices(IServiceCollection services) {
            services.AddControllersWithViews();
        }

        public void Configure(IApplicationBuilder app, IWebHostEnvironment env) {

            app.UseDeveloperExceptionPage();
            app.UseStatusCodePages();
            app.UseStaticFiles();

            app.UseRouting();
            app.UseEndpoints(endpoints => {
                endpoints.MapDefaultControllerRoute();
            });
        }
    }
}
```

The ConfigureServices method is used to set up objects, known as *services*, that can be used throughout the application and that are accessed through a feature called *dependency injection*, which I describe in Chapter 14. The AddControllersWithViews method called in the ConfigureServices method sets up the shared objects required by applications using the MVC Framework and the Razor view engine.

ASP.NET Core receives HTTP requests and passes them along a *request pipeline*, which is populated with middleware components registered in the Configure method. Each middleware component is able to inspect requests, modify them, generate a response, or modify the responses that other components have produced. The request pipeline is the heart of ASP.NET Core, and I describe it in detail in Chapter 12, where I also explain how to create custom middleware components. Table 7-2 describes the methods that are used to set up middleware components in Listing 7-4.

Table 7-2. *The Middleware Methods Used in Listing 7-4*

Name	Description
UseDeveloperExceptionPage()	This extension method displays details of exceptions that occur in the application, which is useful during the development process, as described in Chapter 16. It should not be enabled in deployed applications, and I disable this feature when I prepare the SportsStore application for deployment in Chapter 11.
UseStatusCodePages()	This extension method adds a simple message to HTTP responses that would not otherwise have a body, such as 404 - Not Found responses. This feature is described in Chapter 16.
UseStaticFiles()	This extension method enables support for serving static content from the wwwroot folder. I describe the support for static content in Chapter 15.

One especially important middleware component provides the endpoint routing feature, which matches HTTP requests to the application features - known as endpoints - able to produce responses for them, a process I describe in detail in Chapter 13. The endpoint routing feature is added to the request pipeline with the `UseRouting` and `UseEndpoints` methods. To register the MVC Framework as a source of endpoints, Listing 7-4 calls the `MapDefaultControllerRoute` method.

Configuring the Razor View Engine

The Razor view engine is responsible for processing view files, which have the `.cshtml` extension, to generate HTML responses. Some initial preparation is required to configure Razor to make it easier to create views for the application.

Add a Razor View Imports file named _ViewImports.cshtml in the Views folder with the content shown in Listing 7-5.

■ **Caution**   Pay close attention to the contents of this file. It is easy to make a mistake that causes the application to generate incorrect HTML content.

Listing 7-5. The Contents of the _ViewImports.cshtml File in the SportsStore/Views Folder

```
@using SportsStore.Models
@addTagHelper *, Microsoft.AspNetCore.Mvc.TagHelpers
```

The `@using` statement will allow me to use the types in the `SportsStore.Models` namespace in views without needing to refer to the namespace. The `@addTagHelper` statement enables the built-in tag helpers, which I use later to create HTML elements that reflect the configuration of the SportsStore application and which I describe in detail in Chapter 15.

Add a Razor View Start file named _ViewStart.cshtml to the SportsStore/Views folder with the content shown in Listing 7-6. (The file will already contain this expression if you create the file using the Visual Studio item template.)

Listing 7-6. The Contents of the _ViewStart.cshtml File in the SportsStore/Views Folder

```
@{
    Layout = "_Layout";
}
```

The view start file tells Razor to use a layout file in the HTML that it generates, reducing the amount of duplication in views. To create the view, add a Razor layout named _Layout.cshtml to the Views/Shared folder, with the content shown in Listing 7-7.

Listing 7-7. The Contents of the _Layout.cshtml File in the SportsStore/Views/Shared Folder

```
<!DOCTYPE html>
<html>
<head>
    <meta name="viewport" content="width=device-width" />
    <title>SportsStore</title>
</head>
<body>
    <div>
        @RenderBody()
    </div>
</body>
</html>
```

This file defines a simple HTML document into which the contents of other views will be inserted by the @RenderBody expression. I explain how Razor expressions work in detail in Chapter 21.

Creating the Controller and View

Add a class file named HomeController.cs in the SportsStore/Controllers folder and use it to define the class shown in Listing 7-8. This is a minimal controller that contains just enough functionality to produce a response.

Listing 7-8. The Contents of the HomeController.cs File in the SportsStore/Controllers Folder

```
using Microsoft.AspNetCore.Mvc;

namespace SportsStore.Controllers {
    public class HomeController: Controller {

        public IActionResult Index() => View();

    }
}
```

The MapDefaultControllerRoute method used in Listing 7-4 tells ASP.NET Core how to match URLs to controller classes. The configuration applied by that method declares that the Index action method defined by the Home controller will be used to handle requests.

The Index action method doesn't do anything useful yet and just returns the result of calling the View method, which is inherited from the Controller base class. This result tells ASP.NET Core to render the default view associated with the action method. To create the view, add a Razor View file named Index.cshtml to the Views/Home folder with the content shown in Listing 7-9.

Listing 7-9. The Contents of the Index.cshtml File in the SportsStore/Views/Home Folder

```
<h4>Welcome to SportsStore</h4>
```

Starting the Data Model

Almost all projects have a data model of some sort. Since this is an e-commerce application, the most obvious model I need is for a product. Add a class file named Product.cs to the Models folder and use it to define the class shown in Listing 7-10.

Listing 7-10. The Contents of the Product.cs File in the SportsStore/Models Folder

```
using System.ComponentModel.DataAnnotations.Schema;

namespace SportsStore.Models {

    public class Product {

        public long ProductID { get; set; }

        public string Name { get; set; }

        public string Description { get; set; }

        [Column(TypeName = "decimal(8, 2)")]
        public decimal Price { get; set; }

        public string Category { get; set; }
    }
}
```

The Price property has been decorated with the Column attribute to specify the SQL data type that will be used to store values for this property. Not all C# types map neatly onto SQL types, and this attribute ensures the database uses an appropriate type for the application data.

Checking and Running the Application

Before going any further, it is a good idea to make sure the application builds and runs as expected. Select Start Without Debugging or Run Without Debugging from the Debug menu or run the command shown in Listing 7-11 in the SportsStore folder.

Listing 7-11 Running the Example Application

```
dotnet run
```

Request http://localhost:5000, and you will see the response shown in Figure 7-3.

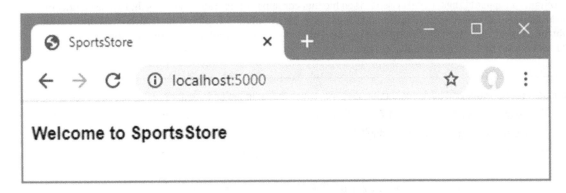

Figure 7-3. *Running the example application*

Adding Data to the Application

Now that the SportsStore contains some basic setup and can produce a simple response, it is time to add some data so that the application has something more useful to display. The SportsStore application will store its data in a SQL Server LocalDB database, which is accessed using Entity Framework Core. Entity Framework Core is the Microsoft object-to-relational mapping (ORM) framework, and it is the most widely used method of accessing databases in ASP.NET Core projects.

■ **Caution**   If you did not install LocalDB when you prepared your development environment in Chapter 2, you must do so now. The SportsStore application will not work without its database.

Installing the Entity Framework Core Packages

The first step is to add Entity Framework Core to the project. Use a PowerShell command prompt to run the command shown in Listing 7-12 in the SportsStore folder.

Listing 7-12. Adding the Entity Framework Core Packages to the SportsStore Project

```
dotnet add package Microsoft.EntityFrameworkCore.Design --version 3.1.1
dotnet add package Microsoft.EntityFrameworkCore.SqlServer --version 3.1.1
```

These packages install Entity Framework Core and the support for using SQL Server. Entity Framework Core also requires a tools package, which includes the command-line tools required to prepare and create databases for ASP.NET Core applications. Run the commands shown in Listing 7-13 to remove any existing version of the tools package, if there is one, and install the version used in this book. (Since this package is installed globally, you can run these commands in any folder.)

Listing 7-13. Installing the Entity Framework Core Tool Package

```
dotnet tool uninstall --global dotnet-ef
dotnet tool install --global dotnet-ef --version 3.1.1
```

Defining the Connection String

Configuration settings, such as database connection strings, are stored in JSON configuration files. To describe the connection to the database that will be used for the SportsStore data, add the entries shown in Listing 7-14 to the appsettings.json file in the SportsStore folder.

The project also contains an appsettings.Development.json file that contains configuration settings that are used only in development. This file is displayed as nested within the appsettings.json file by Solution Explorer but is always visible in Visual Studio Code. I use only the appsettings.json file for the development of the SportsStore project, but I explain the relationship between the files and how they are both used in detail in Chapter 15.

■ **Tip** Connection strings must be expressed as a single unbroken line, which is fine in the code editor but doesn't fit on the printed page and is the cause of the awkward formatting in Listing 7-14. When you define the connection string in your own project, make sure that the value of the SportsStoreConnection item is on a single line.

Listing 7-14. Adding a Configuration Setting in the appsettings.json File in the SportsStore Folder

```
{
  "Logging": {
    "LogLevel": {
      "Default": "Information",
      "Microsoft": "Warning",
      "Microsoft.Hosting.Lifetime": "Information"
    }
  },
  "AllowedHosts": "*",
  "ConnectionStrings": {
    "SportsStoreConnection": "Server=(localdb)\\MSSQLLocalDB;Database=SportsStore;MultipleActiveResultSets=true"
  }
}
```

This configuration string specifies a LocalDB database called SportsStore and enables the multiple active result set feature (MARS), which is required for some of the database queries that will be made by the SportsStore application using Entity Framework Core.

Pay close attention when you add the configuration setting. JSON data must be expressed exactly as shown in the listing, which means you must ensure you correctly quote the property names and values. You can download the configuration file from the GitHub repository if you have difficulty.

■ **Tip** Each database server requires its own connection string format. A helpful site for formulating connection strings is www.connectionstrings.com.

Creating the Database Context Class

Entity Framework Core provides access to the database through a context class. Add a class file named StoreDbContext.cs to the Models folder and use it to define the class shown in Listing 7-15.

Listing 7-15. The Contents of the StoreDbContext.cs File in the SportsStore/Models Folder

```
using Microsoft.EntityFrameworkCore;

namespace SportsStore.Models {
    public class StoreDbContext: DbContext {

        public StoreDbContext(DbContextOptions<StoreDbContext> options)
            : base(options) { }

        public DbSet<Product> Products { get; set; }
    }
}
```

The DbContext base class provides access to the Entity Framework Core's underlying functionality, and the Products property will provide access to the Product objects in the database. The StoreDbContext class is derived from DbContext and adds the properties that will be used to read and write the application's data. There is only one property for now, which will provide access to Product objects.

Configuring Entity Framework Core

Entity Framework Core must be configured so that it knows the type of database to which it will connect, which connection string describes that connection, and which context class will present the data in the database. Listing 7-16 shows the required changes to the Startup class.

Listing 7-16. Configuring Entity Framework Core in the Startup.cs File in the SportsStore Folder

```
using System;
using System.Collections.Generic;
using System.Linq;
using System.Threading.Tasks;
using Microsoft.AspNetCore.Builder;
using Microsoft.AspNetCore.Hosting;
using Microsoft.AspNetCore.Http;
using Microsoft.Extensions.DependencyInjection;
using Microsoft.Extensions.Hosting;
using Microsoft.Extensions.Configuration;
using Microsoft.EntityFrameworkCore;
using SportsStore.Models;

namespace SportsStore {
    public class Startup {

        public Startup(IConfiguration config) {
            Configuration = config;
        }

        private IConfiguration Configuration { get; set; }

        public void ConfigureServices(IServiceCollection services) {
            services.AddControllersWithViews();
            services.AddDbContext<StoreDbContext>(opts => {
                opts.UseSqlServer(
                    Configuration["ConnectionStrings:SportsStoreConnection"]);
            });
        }

        public void Configure(IApplicationBuilder app, IWebHostEnvironment env) {
```

```
            app.UseDeveloperExceptionPage();
            app.UseStatusCodePages();
            app.UseStaticFiles();

            app.UseRouting();
            app.UseEndpoints(endpoints => {
                endpoints.MapDefaultControllerRoute();
            });
        }
    }
}
```

The IConfiguration interface provides access to the ASP.NET Core configuration system, which includes the contents of the appsettings.json file and which I describe in detail in Chapter 15. The constructor receives an IConfiguration object through its constructor and assigns it to the Configuration property, which is used to access the connection string.

Entity Framework Core is configured with the AddDbContext method, which registers the database context class and configures the relationship with the database. The UseSQLServer method declares that SQL Server is being used and the connection string is read via the IConfiguration object.

Creating a Repository

The next step is to create a repository interface and implementation class. The repository pattern is one of the most widely used, and it provides a consistent way to access the features presented by the database context class. Not everyone finds a repository useful, but my experience is that it can reduce duplication and ensures that operations on the database are performed consistently. Add a class file named IStoreRepository.cs to the Models folder and use it to define the interface shown in Listing 7-17.

Listing 7-17. The Contents of the IStoreRepository.cs File in the SportsStore/Models Folder

```
using System.Linq;

namespace SportsStore.Models {
    public interface IStoreRepository {

        IQueryable<Product> Products { get; }
    }
}
```

This interface uses IQueryable<T> to allow a caller to obtain a sequence of Product objects. The IQueryable<T> interface is derived from the more familiar IEnumerable<T> interface and represents a collection of objects that can be queried, such as those managed by a database.

A class that depends on the IProductRepository interface can obtain Product objects without needing to know the details of how they are stored or how the implementation class will deliver them.

UNDERSTANDING IENUMERABLE<T> AND IQUERYABLE<T> INTERFACES

The IQueryable<T> interface is useful because it allows a collection of objects to be queried efficiently. Later in this chapter, I add support for retrieving a subset of Product objects from a database, and using the IQueryable<T> interface allows me to ask the database for just the objects that I require using standard LINQ statements and without needing to know what database server stores the data or how it processes the query. Without the IQueryable<T> interface, I would have to retrieve all of the Product objects from the database and then discard the ones that I don't want, which becomes an expensive operation as the amount of data used by an application increases. It is for this reason that the IQueryable<T> interface is typically used instead of IEnumerable<T> in database repository interfaces and classes.

However, care must be taken with the IQueryable<T> interface because each time the collection of objects is enumerated, the query will be evaluated again, which means that a new query will be sent to the database. This can undermine the efficiency gains of using IQueryable<T>. In such situations, you can convert the IQueryable<T> interface to a more predictable form using the ToList or ToArray extension method.

To create an implementation of the repository interface, add a class file named EFStoreRepository.cs in the Models folder and use it to define the class shown in Listing 7-18.

Listing 7-18. The Contents of the EFStoreRepository.cs File in the SportsStore/Models Folder

```
using System.Linq;

namespace SportsStore.Models {
    public class EFStoreRepository : IStoreRepository {
        private StoreDbContext context;

        public EFStoreRepository(StoreDbContext ctx) {
            context = ctx;
        }

        public IQueryable<Product> Products => context.Products;
    }
}
```

I'll add additional functionality as I add features to the application, but for the moment, the repository implementation just maps the Products property defined by the IStoreRepository interface onto the Products property defined by the StoreDbContext class. The Products property in the context class returns a DbSet<Product> object, which implements the IQueryable<T> interface and makes it easy to implement the repository interface when using Entity Framework Core.

Earlier in the chapter, I explained that ASP.NET Core supports services that allow objects to be accessed throughout the application. One benefit of services is they allow classes to use interfaces without needing to know which implementation class is being used. I explain this in detail in Chapter 14, but for the SportsStore chapters, it means that application components can access objects that implement the IStoreRepository interface without knowing that it is the EFStoreRepository implementation class they are using. This makes it easy to change the implementation class the application uses without needing to make changes to the individual components. Add the statement shown in Listing 7-19 to the Startup class to create a service for the IStoreRepository interface that uses EFStoreRepository as the implementation class.

■ **Tip** Don't worry if this doesn't make sense right now. This topic is one of the most confusing aspects of working with ASP.NET Core, and it can take a while to understand.

Listing 7-19. Creating the Repository Service in the Startup.cs File in the SportsStore Folder

```
using System;
using System.Collections.Generic;
using System.Linq;
using System.Threading.Tasks;
using Microsoft.AspNetCore.Builder;
using Microsoft.AspNetCore.Hosting;
using Microsoft.AspNetCore.Http;
using Microsoft.Extensions.DependencyInjection;
using Microsoft.Extensions.Hosting;
using Microsoft.Extensions.Configuration;
using Microsoft.EntityFrameworkCore;
using SportsStore.Models;

namespace SportsStore {
    public class Startup {
```

```
public Startup(IConfiguration config) {
    Configuration = config;
}

private IConfiguration Configuration { get; set; }

public void ConfigureServices(IServiceCollection services) {
    services.AddControllersWithViews();

    services.AddDbContext<StoreDbContext>(opts => {
        opts.UseSqlServer(
            Configuration["ConnectionStrings:SportsStoreConnection"]);
    });
    services.AddScoped<IStoreRepository, EFStoreRepository>();
}

public void Configure(IApplicationBuilder app, IWebHostEnvironment env) {

    app.UseDeveloperExceptionPage();
    app.UseStatusCodePages();
    app.UseStaticFiles();

    app.UseRouting();
    app.UseEndpoints(endpoints => {
        endpoints.MapDefaultControllerRoute();
    });
}
    }
}
```

The AddScoped method creates a service where each HTTP request gets its own repository object, which is the way that Entity Framework Core is typically used.

Creating the Database Migration

Entity Framework Core is able to generate the schema for the database using the data model classes through a feature called *migrations*. When you prepare a migration, Entity Framework Core creates a C# class that contains the SQL commands required to prepare the database. If you need to modify your model classes, then you can create a new migration that contains the SQL commands required to reflect the changes. In this way, you don't have to worry about manually writing and testing SQL commands and can just focus on the C# model classes in the application.

Entity Framework Core commands are performed from the command line. Open a PowerShell command prompt and run the command shown in Listing 7-20 in the SportsStore folder to create the migration class that will prepare the database for its first use.

Listing 7-20. Creating the Database Migration

```
dotnet ef migrations add Initial
```

When this command has finished, the SportsStore project will contain a Migrations folder. This is where Entity Framework Core stores its migration classes. One of the file names will be a timestamp followed by _Initial.cs, and this is the class that will be used to create the initial schema for the database. If you examine the contents of this file, you can see how the Product model class has been used to create the schema.

```
┌─────────────────────────────────────────────────────────────────────────────┐
│      WHAT ABOUT THE ADD-MIGRATION AND UPDATE-DATABASE COMMANDS?              │
└─────────────────────────────────────────────────────────────────────────────┘
```

If you are an experienced Entity Framework developer, you may be used to using the `Add-Migration` command to create a database migration and to using the `Update-Database` command to apply it to a database.

With the introduction of .NET Core, Entity Framework Core has added commands that are integrated into the `dotnet` command-line tool, using the commands added by the `Microsoft.EntityFrameworkCore.Tools.DotNet` package. These are the commands that I have used because they are consistent with other .NET commands and they can be used in any command prompt or PowerShell window, unlike the `Add-Migration` and `Update-Database` commands, which work only in a specific Visual Studio window.

Creating Seed Data

To populate the database and provide some sample data, I added a class file called `SeedData.cs` to the `Models` folder and defined the class shown in Listing 7-21.

Listing 7-21. The Contents of the SeedData.cs File in the SportsStore/Models Folder

```csharp
using System.Linq;
using Microsoft.AspNetCore.Builder;
using Microsoft.Extensions.DependencyInjection;
using Microsoft.EntityFrameworkCore;

namespace SportsStore.Models {

    public static class SeedData {

        public static void EnsurePopulated(IApplicationBuilder app) {
            StoreDbContext context = app.ApplicationServices
                .CreateScope().ServiceProvider.GetRequiredService<StoreDbContext>();

            if (context.Database.GetPendingMigrations().Any()) {
                context.Database.Migrate();
            }

            if (!context.Products.Any()) {
                context.Products.AddRange(
                    new Product {
                        Name = "Kayak", Description = "A boat for one person",
                        Category = "Watersports", Price = 275
                    },
                    new Product {
                        Name = "Lifejacket",
                        Description = "Protective and fashionable",
                        Category = "Watersports", Price = 48.95m
                    },
                    new Product {
                        Name = "Soccer Ball",
                        Description = "FIFA-approved size and weight",
                        Category = "Soccer", Price = 19.50m
                    },
                    new Product {
                        Name = "Corner Flags",
                        Description = "Give your playing field a professional touch",
                        Category = "Soccer", Price = 34.95m
                    },
```

```
                new Product {
                    Name = "Stadium",
                    Description = "Flat-packed 35,000-seat stadium",
                    Category = "Soccer", Price = 79500
                },
                new Product {
                    Name = "Thinking Cap",
                    Description = "Improve brain efficiency by 75%",
                    Category = "Chess", Price = 16
                },
                new Product {
                    Name = "Unsteady Chair",
                    Description = "Secretly give your opponent a disadvantage",
                    Category = "Chess", Price = 29.95m
                },
                new Product {
                    Name = "Human Chess Board",
                    Description = "A fun game for the family",
                    Category = "Chess", Price = 75
                },
                new Product {
                    Name = "Bling-Bling King",
                    Description = "Gold-plated, diamond-studded King",
                    Category = "Chess", Price = 1200
                }
            );
            context.SaveChanges();
        }
    }
}
}
```

The static EnsurePopulated method receives an IApplicationBuilder argument, which is the interface used in the Configure method of the Startup class to register middleware components to handle HTTP requests. IApplicationBuilder also provides access to the application's services, including the Entity Framework Core database context service.

The EnsurePopulated method obtains a StoreDbContext object through the IApplicationBuilder interface and calls the Database.Migrate method if there are any pending migrations, which means that the database will be created and prepared so that it can store Product objects. Next, the number of Product objects in the database is checked. If there are no objects in the database, then the database is populated using a collection of Product objects using the AddRange method and then written to the database using the SaveChanges method.

The final change is to seed the database when the application starts, which I have done by adding a call to the EnsurePopulated method from the Startup class, as shown in Listing 7-22.

Listing 7-22. Seeding the Database in the Startup.cs File in the SportsStore Folder

```
using System;
using System.Collections.Generic;
using System.Linq;
using System.Threading.Tasks;
using Microsoft.AspNetCore.Builder;
using Microsoft.AspNetCore.Hosting;
using Microsoft.AspNetCore.Http;
using Microsoft.Extensions.DependencyInjection;
using Microsoft.Extensions.Hosting;
using Microsoft.Extensions.Configuration;
using Microsoft.EntityFrameworkCore;
using SportsStore.Models;
```

```
namespace SportsStore {
    public class Startup {

        public Startup(IConfiguration config) {
            Configuration = config;
        }

        private IConfiguration Configuration { get; set; }

        public void ConfigureServices(IServiceCollection services) {
            services.AddControllersWithViews();

            services.AddDbContext<StoreDbContext>(opts => {
                opts.UseSqlServer(
                    Configuration["ConnectionStrings:SportsStoreConnection"]);
            });
            services.AddScoped<IStoreRepository, EFStoreRepository>();
        }

        public void Configure(IApplicationBuilder app, IWebHostEnvironment env) {

            app.UseDeveloperExceptionPage();
            app.UseStatusCodePages();
            app.UseStaticFiles();

            app.UseRouting();
            app.UseEndpoints(endpoints => {
                endpoints.MapDefaultControllerRoute();
            });
            SeedData.EnsurePopulated(app);
        }
    }
}
```

RESETTING THE DATABASE

If you need to reset the database, then run this command in the SportsStore folder:

```
...
dotnet ef database drop --force --context StoreDbContext
...
```

Start ASP.NET Core, and the database will be re-created and seeded with data.

Displaying a List of Products

As you have seen, the initial preparation work for an ASP.NET Core project can take some time. But the good news is that once the foundation is in place, the pace improves, and features are added more rapidly. In this section, I am going to create a controller and an action method that can display details of the products in the repository.

USING THE VISUAL STUDIO SCAFFOLDING

As I noted in Chapter 4, Visual Studio supports scaffolding to add items to a project.

I don't use the scaffolding in this book. The code and markup that the scaffolding generates are so generic as to be all but useless, and the scenarios that are supported are narrow and don't address common development problems. My goal in this book is not only to make sure you know how to create ASP.NET Core applications but also to explain how everything works behind the scenes, and that is harder to do when responsibility for creating components is handed to the scaffolding.

If you are using Visual Scer in the Solution Explorer, selecting Add ➤ New Item from the pop-up menu, and then choosing an item template from the Add New Item window.

You may find your development style to be different from mine, and you may find that you prefer working with the scaffolding in your own projects. That's perfectly reasonable, although I recommend you take the time to understand what the scaffolding does so you know where to look if you don't get the results you expect.

Preparing the Controller

Add the statements shown in Listing 7-23 to prepare the controller to display the list of products.

Listing 7-23. Preparing the Controller in the HomeController.cs File in the SportsStore/Controllers Folder

```
using Microsoft.AspNetCore.Mvc;
using SportsStore.Models;

namespace SportsStore.Controllers {
    public class HomeController : Controller {
        private IStoreRepository repository;

        public HomeController(IStoreRepository repo) {
            repository = repo;
        }

        public IActionResult Index() => View(repository.Products);
    }
}
```

When ASP.NET Core needs to create a new instance of the HomeController class to handle an HTTP request, it will inspect the constructor and see that it requires an object that implements the IStoreRepository interface. To determine what implementation class should be used, ASP.NET Core consults the configuration in the Startup class, which tells it that EFStoreRepository should be used and that a new instance should be created for every request. ASP.NET Core creates a new EFStoreRepository object and uses it to invoke the HomeController constructor to create the controller object that will process the HTTP request.

This is known as *dependency injection,* and its approach allows the HomeController object to access the application's repository through the IStoreRepository interface without knowing which implementation class has been configured. I could reconfigure the service to use a different implementation class—one that doesn't use Entity Framework Core, for example—and dependency injection means that the controller will continue to work without changes.

■ **Note** Some developers don't like dependency injection and believe it makes applications more complicated. That's not my view, but if you are new to dependency injection, then I recommend you wait until you have read Chapter 14 before you make up your mind.

```
╔══════════════════════════════════════════════════════════════════════╗
║                   UNIT TEST: REPOSITORY ACCESS                         ║
╚══════════════════════════════════════════════════════════════════════╝
```

I can unit test that the controller is accessing the repository correctly by creating a mock repository, injecting it into the constructor of the HomeController class, and then calling the Index method to get the response that contains the list of products. I then compare the Product objects I get to what I would expect from the test data in the mock implementation. See Chapter 6 for details of how to set up unit tests. Here is the unit test I created for this purpose, in a class file called HomeControllerTests.cs that I added to the SportsStore.Tests project:

```
using System.Collections.Generic;
using System.Linq;
using Microsoft.AspNetCore.Mvc;
```

```
using Moq;
using SportsStore.Controllers;
using SportsStore.Models;
using Xunit;

namespace SportsStore.Tests {

    public class ProductControllerTests {

        [Fact]
        public void Can_Use_Repository() {
            // Arrange
            Mock<IStoreRepository> mock = new Mock<IStoreRepository>();
            mock.Setup(m => m.Products).Returns((new Product[] {
                new Product {ProductID = 1, Name = "P1"},
                new Product {ProductID = 2, Name = "P2"}
            }).AsQueryable<Product>());

            HomeController controller = new HomeController(mock.Object);

            // Act
            IEnumerable<Product> result =
                (controller.Index() as ViewResult).ViewData.Model
                    as IEnumerable<Product>;

            // Assert
            Product[] prodArray = result.ToArray();
            Assert.True(prodArray.Length == 2);
            Assert.Equal("P1", prodArray[0].Name);
            Assert.Equal("P2", prodArray[1].Name);
        }
    }
}
```

It is a little awkward to get the data returned from the action method. The result is a ViewResult object, and I have to cast the value of its ViewData.Model property to the expected data type. I explain the different result types that can be returned by action methods and how to work with them in Part 2.

Updating the View

The Index action method in Listing 7-23 passes the collection of Product objects from the repository to the View method, which means these objects will be the view model that Razor uses when it generates HTML content from the view. Make the changes to the view shown in Listing 7-24 to generate content using the Product view model objects.

Listing 7-24. Using the Product Data in the Index.cshtml File in the SportsStore/Views/Home Folder

```
@model IQueryable<Product>

@foreach (var p in Model) {
    <div>
        <h3>@p.Name</h3>
        @p.Description
        <h4>@p.Price.ToString("c")</h4>
    </div>
}
```

The @model expression at the top of the file specifies that the view expects to receive a sequence of Product objects from the action method as its model data. I use an @foreach expression to work through the sequence and generate a simple set of HTML elements for each Product object that is received.

The view doesn't know where the Product objects came from, how they were obtained, or whether they represent all the products known to the application. Instead, the view deals only with how details of each Product are displayed using HTML elements.

■ **Tip**   I converted the Price property to a string using the ToString("c") method, which renders numerical values as currency according to the culture settings that are in effect on your server. For example, if the server is set up as en-US, then (1002.3). ToString("c") will return $1,002.30, but if the server is set to en-GB, then the same method will return £1,002.30.

Running the Application

Start ASP.NET Core and request http://localhost:5000 to see the list of products, which is shown in Figure 7-4. This is the typical pattern of development for ASP.NET Core. An initial investment of time setting everything up is necessary, and then the basic features of the application snap together quickly.

Figure 7-4. *Displaying a list of products*

Adding Pagination

You can see from Figure 7-4 that the Index.cshtml view displays the products in the database on a single page. In this section, I will add support for pagination so that the view displays a smaller number of products on a page, and the user can move from page to page to view the overall catalog. To do this, I am going to add a parameter to the Index method in the Home controller, as shown in Listing 7-25.

Listing 7-25. Adding Pagination in the HomeController.cs File in the SportsStore/Controllers Folder

```
using Microsoft.AspNetCore.Mvc;
using SportsStore.Models;
using System.Linq;

namespace SportsStore.Controllers {
    public class HomeController : Controller {
        private IStoreRepository repository;
        public int PageSize = 4;
```

```
public HomeController(IStoreRepository repo) {
    repository = repo;
}

public ViewResult Index(int productPage = 1)
    => View(repository.Products
        .OrderBy(p => p.ProductID)
        .Skip((productPage - 1) * PageSize)
        .Take(PageSize));
    }
}
```

The PageSize field specifies that I want four products per page. I have added an optional parameter to the Index method, which means that if the method is called without a parameter, the call is treated as though I had supplied the value specified in the parameter definition, with the effect that the action method displays the first page of products when it is invoked without an argument. Within the body of the action method, I get the Product objects, order them by the primary key, skip over the products that occur before the start of the current page, and take the number of products specified by the PageSize field.

UNIT TEST: PAGINATION

I can unit test the pagination feature by mocking the repository, requesting a specific page from the controller, and making sure I get the expected subset of the data. Here is the unit test I created for this purpose and added to the HomeControllerTests.cs file in the SportsStore.Tests project:

```
using System.Collections.Generic;
using System.Linq;
using Microsoft.AspNetCore.Mvc;
using Moq;
using SportsStore.Controllers;
using SportsStore.Models;
using Xunit;

namespace SportsStore.Tests {

    public class ProductControllerTests {

        [Fact]
        public void Can_Use_Repository() {
            // ...statements omitted for brevity...
        }

        [Fact]
        public void Can_Paginate() {
            // Arrange
            Mock<IStoreRepository> mock = new Mock<IStoreRepository>();
            mock.Setup(m => m.Products).Returns((new Product[] {
                new Product {ProductID = 1, Name = "P1"},
                new Product {ProductID = 2, Name = "P2"},
                new Product {ProductID = 3, Name = "P3"},
                new Product {ProductID = 4, Name = "P4"},
                new Product {ProductID = 5, Name = "P5"}
            }).AsQueryable<Product>());

            HomeController controller = new HomeController(mock.Object);
            controller.PageSize = 3;

            // Act
            IEnumerable<Product> result =
                (controller.Index(2) as ViewResult).ViewData.Model
                    as IEnumerable<Product>;
```

```
            // Assert
            Product[] prodArray = result.ToArray();
            Assert.True(prodArray.Length == 2);
            Assert.Equal("P4", prodArray[0].Name);
            Assert.Equal("P5", prodArray[1].Name);
        }
    }
}
```

You can see the new test follows the pattern of the existing one, relying on Moq to provide a known set of data with which to work.

Displaying Page Links

Restart ASP.NET Core and request `http://localhost:5000`, and you will see that there are now four items shown on the page, as shown in Figure 7-5. If you want to view another page, you can append query string parameters to the end of the URL, like this:

```
http://localhost:5000/?productPage=2
```

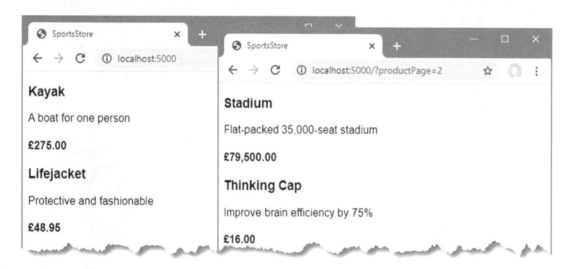

Figure 7-5. *Paging through data*

Using these query strings, you can navigate through the catalog of products. There is no way for customers to figure out that these query string parameters exist, and even if there were, customers are not going to want to navigate this way. Instead, I need to render some page links at the bottom of each list of products so that customers can navigate between pages. To do this, I am going to create a *tag helper*, which generates the HTML markup for the links I require.

Adding the View Model

To support the tag helper, I am going to pass information to the view about the number of pages available, the current page, and the total number of products in the repository. The easiest way to do this is to create a view model class, which is used specifically to pass data between a controller and a view. Create a `Models/ViewModels` folder in the `SportsStore` project, add to it a class file named `PagingInfo.cs`, and define the class shown in Listing 7-26.

Listing 7-26. The Contents of the PagingInfo.cs File in the SportsStore/Models/ViewModels Folder

```
using System;

namespace SportsStore.Models.ViewModels {

    public class PagingInfo {
        public int TotalItems { get; set; }
        public int ItemsPerPage { get; set; }
        public int CurrentPage { get; set; }

        public int TotalPages =>
            (int)Math.Ceiling((decimal)TotalItems / ItemsPerPage);
    }
}
```

Adding the Tag Helper Class

Now that I have a view model, it is time to create a tag helper class. Create a folder named `Infrastructure` in the `SportsStore` project and add to it a class file called `PageLinkTagHelper.cs`, with the code shown in Listing 7-27. Tag helpers are a big part of ASP. NET Core development, and I explain how they work and how to use and create them in Chapters 25–27.

■ **Tip** The `Infrastructure` folder is where I put classes that deliver the plumbing for an application but that are not related to the application's main functionality. You don't have to follow this convention in your own projects.

Listing 7-27. The Contents of the PageLinkTagHelper.cs File in the SportsStore/Infrastructure Folder

```
using Microsoft.AspNetCore.Mvc;
using Microsoft.AspNetCore.Mvc.Rendering;
using Microsoft.AspNetCore.Mvc.Routing;
using Microsoft.AspNetCore.Mvc.ViewFeatures;
using Microsoft.AspNetCore.Razor.TagHelpers;
using SportsStore.Models.ViewModels;

namespace SportsStore.Infrastructure {

    [HtmlTargetElement("div", Attributes = "page-model")]
    public class PageLinkTagHelper : TagHelper {
        private IUrlHelperFactory urlHelperFactory;

        public PageLinkTagHelper(IUrlHelperFactory helperFactory) {
            urlHelperFactory = helperFactory;
        }

        [ViewContext]
        [HtmlAttributeNotBound]
        public ViewContext ViewContext { get; set; }

        public PagingInfo PageModel { get; set; }

        public string PageAction { get; set; }

        public override void Process(TagHelperContext context,
                TagHelperOutput output) {
            IUrlHelper urlHelper = urlHelperFactory.GetUrlHelper(ViewContext);
```

```
            TagBuilder result = new TagBuilder("div");
            for (int i = 1; i <= PageModel.TotalPages; i++) {
                TagBuilder tag = new TagBuilder("a");
                tag.Attributes["href"] = urlHelper.Action(PageAction,
                    new { productPage = i });
                tag.InnerHtml.Append(i.ToString());
                result.InnerHtml.AppendHtml(tag);
            }
            output.Content.AppendHtml(result.InnerHtml);
        }
    }
}
```

This tag helper populates a div element with a elements that correspond to pages of products. I am not going to go into detail about tag helpers now; it is enough to know that they are one of the most useful ways that you can introduce C# logic into your views. The code for a tag helper can look tortured because C# and HTML don't mix easily. But using tag helpers is preferable to including blocks of C# code in a view because a tag helper can be easily unit tested.

Most ASP.NET Core components, such as controllers and views, are discovered automatically, but tag helpers have to be registered. In Listing 7-28, I have added a statement to the _ViewImports.cshtml file in the Views folder that tells ASP.NET Core to look for tag helper classes in the SportsStore project. I also added an @using expression so that I can refer to the view model classes in views without having to qualify their names with the namespace.

Listing 7-28. Registering a Tag Helper in the _ViewImports.cshtml File in the SportsStore/Views Folder

```
@using SportsStore.Models
@using SportsStore.Models.ViewModels
@addTagHelper *, Microsoft.AspNetCore.Mvc.TagHelpers
@addTagHelper *, SportsStore
```

UNIT TEST: CREATING PAGE LINKS

To test the PageLinkTagHelper tag helper class, I call the Process method with test data and provide a TagHelperOutput object that I inspect to see the HTML that is generated, as follows, which I defined in a new PageLinkTagHelperTests.cs file in the SportsStore.Tests project:

```
using System.Collections.Generic;
using System.Threading.Tasks;
using Microsoft.AspNetCore.Mvc;
using Microsoft.AspNetCore.Mvc.Routing;
using Microsoft.AspNetCore.Razor.TagHelpers;
using Moq;
using SportsStore.Infrastructure;
using SportsStore.Models.ViewModels;
using Xunit;

namespace SportsStore.Tests {

    public class PageLinkTagHelperTests {

        [Fact]
        public void Can_Generate_Page_Links() {
            // Arrange
            var urlHelper = new Mock<IUrlHelper>();
            urlHelper.SetupSequence(x => x.Action(It.IsAny<UrlActionContext>()))
                .Returns("Test/Page1")
                .Returns("Test/Page2")
                .Returns("Test/Page3");
```

```
            var urlHelperFactory = new Mock<IUrlHelperFactory>();
            urlHelperFactory.Setup(f =>
                    f.GetUrlHelper(It.IsAny<ActionContext>()))
                        .Returns(urlHelper.Object);

            PageLinkTagHelper helper =
                    new PageLinkTagHelper(urlHelperFactory.Object) {
                PageModel = new PagingInfo {
                    CurrentPage = 2,
                    TotalItems = 28,
                    ItemsPerPage = 10
                },
                PageAction = "Test"
            };

            TagHelperContext ctx = new TagHelperContext(
                new TagHelperAttributeList(),
                new Dictionary<object, object>(), "");

            var content = new Mock<TagHelperContent>();
            TagHelperOutput output = new TagHelperOutput("div",
                new TagHelperAttributeList(),
                (cache, encoder) => Task.FromResult(content.Object));

            // Act
            helper.Process(ctx, output);

            // Assert
            Assert.Equal(@"<a href=""Test/Page1"">1</a>"
                + @"<a href=""Test/Page2"">2</a>"
                + @"<a href=""Test/Page3"">3</a>",
                  output.Content.GetContent());
        }
    }
}
```

The complexity in this test is in creating the objects that are required to create and use a tag helper. Tag helpers use IUrlHelperFactory objects to generate URLs that target different parts of the application, and I have used Moq to create an implementation of this interface and the related IUrlHelper interface that provides test data.

The core part of the test verifies the tag helper output by using a literal string value that contains double quotes. C# is perfectly capable of working with such strings, as long as the string is prefixed with @ and uses two sets of double quotes ("") in place of one set of double quotes. You must remember not to break the literal string into separate lines unless the string you are comparing to is similarly broken. For example, the literal I use in the test method has wrapped onto several lines because the width of a printed page is narrow. I have not added a newline character; if I did, the test would fail.

Adding the View Model Data

I am not quite ready to use the tag helper because I have yet to provide an instance of the PagingInfo view model class to the view. To do this, I added a class file called ProductsListViewModel.cs to the Models/ViewModels folder of the SportsStore project with the content shown in Listing 7-29.

Listing 7-29. The Contents of the ProductsListViewModel.cs File in the SportsStore/Models/ViewModels Folder

```
using System.Collections.Generic;
using SportsStore.Models;

namespace SportsStore.Models.ViewModels {
```

```
        public class ProductsListViewModel {
            public IEnumerable<Product> Products { get; set; }
            public PagingInfo PagingInfo { get; set; }
        }
}
```

I can update the Index action method in the HomeController class to use the ProductsListViewModel class to provide the view with details of the products to display on the page and with details of the pagination, as shown in Listing 7-30.

Listing 7-30. Updating the Action Method in the HomeController.cs File in the SportsStore/Controllers Folder

```
using Microsoft.AspNetCore.Mvc;
using SportsStore.Models;
using System.Linq;
using SportsStore.Models.ViewModels;

namespace SportsStore.Controllers {
    public class HomeController : Controller {
        private IStoreRepository repository;
        public int PageSize = 4;

        public HomeController(IStoreRepository repo) {
            repository = repo;
        }

        public ViewResult Index(int productPage = 1)
            => View(new ProductsListViewModel {
                Products = repository.Products
                    .OrderBy(p => p.ProductID)
                    .Skip((productPage - 1) * PageSize)
                    .Take(PageSize),
                PagingInfo = new PagingInfo {
                    CurrentPage = productPage,
                    ItemsPerPage = PageSize,
                    TotalItems = repository.Products.Count()
                }
            });
    }
}
```

These changes pass a ProductsListViewModel object as the model data to the view.

UNIT TEST: PAGE MODEL VIEW DATA

I need to ensure that the controller sends the correct pagination data to the view. Here is the unit test I added to the HomeControllerTests class in the test project to make sure:

```
...
[Fact]
public void Can_Send_Pagination_View_Model() {

    // Arrange
    Mock<IStoreRepository> mock = new Mock<IStoreRepository>();
    mock.Setup(m => m.Products).Returns((new Product[] {
        new Product {ProductID = 1, Name = "P1"},
        new Product {ProductID = 2, Name = "P2"},
        new Product {ProductID = 3, Name = "P3"},
```

```
        new Product {ProductID = 4, Name = "P4"},
        new Product {ProductID = 5, Name = "P5"}
    }).AsQueryable<Product>());

    // Arrange
    HomeController controller =
        new HomeController(mock.Object) { PageSize = 3 };

    // Act
    ProductsListViewModel result =
        controller.Index(2).ViewData.Model as ProductsListViewModel;

    // Assert
    PagingInfo pageInfo = result.PagingInfo;
    Assert.Equal(2, pageInfo.CurrentPage);
    Assert.Equal(3, pageInfo.ItemsPerPage);
    Assert.Equal(5, pageInfo.TotalItems);
    Assert.Equal(2, pageInfo.TotalPages);
}
...
```

I also need to modify the earlier unit tests to reflect the new result from the `Index` action method. Here are the revised tests:

```
...
[Fact]
public void Can_Use_Repository() {
    // Arrange
    Mock<IStoreRepository> mock = new Mock<IStoreRepository>();
    mock.Setup(m => m.Products).Returns((new Product[] {
        new Product {ProductID = 1, Name = "P1"},
        new Product {ProductID = 2, Name = "P2"}
    }).AsQueryable<Product>());

    HomeController controller = new HomeController(mock.Object);

    // Act
    ProductsListViewModel result =
        controller.Index().ViewData.Model as ProductsListViewModel;

    // Assert
    Product[] prodArray = result.Products.ToArray();
    Assert.True(prodArray.Length == 2);
    Assert.Equal("P1", prodArray[0].Name);
    Assert.Equal("P2", prodArray[1].Name);
}
[Fact]
public void Can_Paginate() {
    // Arrange
    Mock<IStoreRepository> mock = new Mock<IStoreRepository>();
    mock.Setup(m => m.Products).Returns((new Product[] {
        new Product {ProductID = 1, Name = "P1"},
        new Product {ProductID = 2, Name = "P2"},
        new Product {ProductID = 3, Name = "P3"},
        new Product {ProductID = 4, Name = "P4"},
        new Product {ProductID = 5, Name = "P5"}
    }).AsQueryable<Product>());

    HomeController controller = new HomeController(mock.Object);
    controller.PageSize = 3;

    // Act
    ProductsListViewModel result =
        controller.Index(2).ViewData.Model as ProductsListViewModel;
```

```
        // Assert
        Product[] prodArray = result.Products.ToArray();
        Assert.True(prodArray.Length == 2);
        Assert.Equal("P4", prodArray[0].Name);
        Assert.Equal("P5", prodArray[1].Name);
    }
    ...
```

I would usually create a common setup method, given the degree of duplication between these two test methods. However, since I am delivering the unit tests in individual sidebars like this one, I am going to keep everything separate so you can see each test on its own.

The view is currently expecting a sequence of Product objects, so I need to update the Index.cshtml file, as shown in Listing 7-31, to deal with the new view model type.

Listing 7-31. Updating the Index.cshtml File in the SportsStore/Views/Home Folder

```
@model ProductsListViewModel

@foreach (var p in Model.Products) {
    <div>
        <h3>@p.Name</h3>
        @p.Description
        <h4>@p.Price.ToString("c")</h4>
    </div>
}
```

I have changed the @model directive to tell Razor that I am now working with a different data type. I updated the foreach loop so that the data source is the Products property of the model data.

Displaying the Page Links

I have everything in place to add the page links to the Index view. I created the view model that contains the paging information, updated the controller so that it passes this information to the view, and changed the @model directive to match the new model view type. All that remains is to add an HTML element that the tag helper will process to create the page links, as shown in Listing 7-32.

Listing 7-32. Adding the Pagination Links in the Index.cshtml File in the SportsStore/Views/Home Folder

```
@model ProductsListViewModel

@foreach (var p in Model.Products) {
    <div>
        <h3>@p.Name</h3>
        @p.Description
        <h4>@p.Price.ToString("c")</h4>
    </div>
}

<div page-model="@Model.PagingInfo" page-action="Index"></div>
```

Restart ASP.NET Core and request http://localhost:5000, and you will see the new page links, as shown in Figure 7-6. The style is still basic, which I will fix later in the chapter. What is important for the moment is that the links take the user from page to page in the catalog and allow for exploration of the products for sale. When Razor finds the page-model attribute on the div element, it asks the PageLinkTagHelper class to transform the element, which produces the set of links shown in the figure.

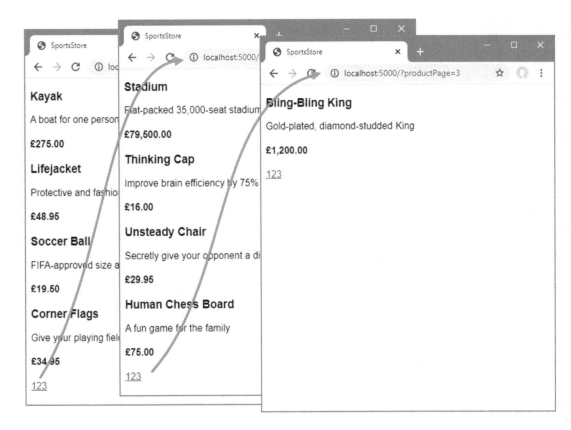

Figure 7-6. *Displaying page navigation links*

Improving the URLs

I have the page links working, but they still use the query string to pass page information to the server, like this:

```
http://localhost/?productPage=2
```

I can create URLs that are more appealing by creating a scheme that follows the pattern of *composable URLs*. A composable URL is one that makes sense to the user, like this one:

```
http://localhost/Page2
```

The ASP.NET Core routing feature makes it easy to change the URL scheme in an application. All I need to do is add a new route in the Startup class, as shown in Listing 7-33.

Listing 7-33. Adding a New Route in the Startup.cs File in the SportsStore Folder

```
using System;
using System.Collections.Generic;
using System.Linq;
using System.Threading.Tasks;
using Microsoft.AspNetCore.Builder;
using Microsoft.AspNetCore.Hosting;
using Microsoft.AspNetCore.Http;
using Microsoft.Extensions.DependencyInjection;
using Microsoft.Extensions.Hosting;
```

```
using Microsoft.Extensions.Configuration;
using Microsoft.EntityFrameworkCore;
using SportsStore.Models;

namespace SportsStore {
    public class Startup {

        public Startup(IConfiguration config) {
            Configuration = config;
        }

        private IConfiguration Configuration { get; set; }

        public void ConfigureServices(IServiceCollection services) {
            services.AddControllersWithViews();

            services.AddDbContext<StoreDbContext>(opts => {
                opts.UseSqlServer(
                    Configuration["ConnectionStrings:SportsStoreConnection"]);
            });
            services.AddScoped<IStoreRepository, EFStoreRepository>();
        }

        public void Configure(IApplicationBuilder app, IWebHostEnvironment env) {

            app.UseDeveloperExceptionPage();
            app.UseStatusCodePages();
            app.UseStaticFiles();

            app.UseRouting();
            app.UseEndpoints(endpoints => {
                endpoints.MapControllerRoute("pagination",
                    "Products/Page{productPage}",
                    new { Controller = "Home", action = "Index" });
                endpoints.MapDefaultControllerRoute();
            });

            SeedData.EnsurePopulated(app);
        }
    }
}
```

It is important that you add the new route before the call to the MapDefaultControllerRoute method. As you will learn in Chapter 13, the routing system processes routes in the order they are listed, and I need the new route to take precedence over the existing one.

This is the only alteration required to change the URL scheme for product pagination. ASP.NET Core and the routing function are tightly integrated, so the application automatically reflects a change like this in the URLs used by the application, including those generated by tag helpers like the one I use to generate the page navigation links.

Restart ASP.NET Core, request http://localhost:5000, and click one of the pagination links. The browser will navigate to a URL that uses the new URL scheme, as shown in Figure 7-7.

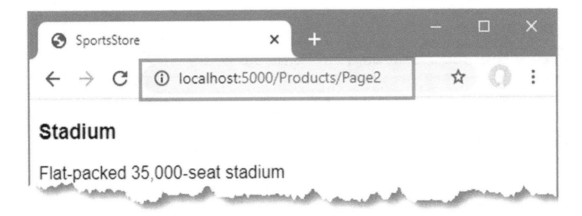

Figure 7-7. *The new URL scheme displayed in the browser*

Styling the Content

I have built a great deal of infrastructure, and the basic features of the application are starting to come together, but I have not paid any attention to appearance. Even though this book is not about design or CSS, the SportsStore application design is so miserably plain that it undermines its technical strengths. In this section, I will put some of that right. I am going to implement a classic two-column layout with a header, as shown in Figure 7-8.

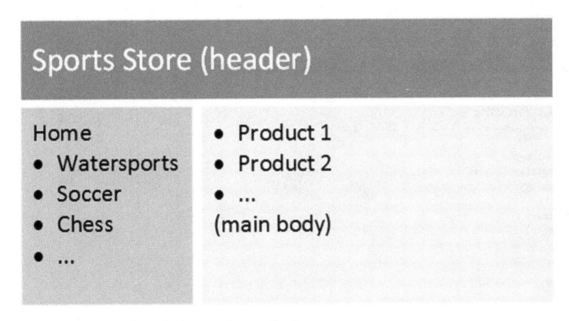

Figure 7-8. *The design goal for the SportsStore application*

Installing the Bootstrap Package

I am going to use the Bootstrap package to provide the CSS styles I will apply to the application. As explained in Chapter 4, client-side packages are installed using LibMan. If you did not install the LibMan package when following the examples in Chapter 4, use a PowerShell command prompt to run the commands shown in Listing 7-34, which remove any existing LibMan package and install the version required for this book.

Listing 7-34. Installing the LibMan Tool Package

```
dotnet tool uninstall --global Microsoft.Web.LibraryManager.Cli
dotnet tool install --global Microsoft.Web.LibraryManager.Cli --version 2.0.96
```

Once you have installed LibMan, run the commands shown in Listing 7-35 in the SportsStore folder to initialize the example project and install the Bootstrap package.

Listing 7-35. Initializing the Example Project

```
libman init -p cdnjs
libman install twitter-bootstrap@4.3.1 -d wwwroot/lib/twitter-bootstrap
```

Applying Bootstrap Styles

Razor layouts provide common content so that it doesn't have to be repeated in multiple views. Add the elements shown in Listing 7-36 to the _Layout.cshtml file in the Views/Shared folder to include the Bootstrap CSS stylesheet in the content sent to the browser and define a common header that will be used throughout the SportsStore application.

Listing 7-36. Applying Bootstrap CSS to the _Layout.cshtml File in the SportsStore/Views/Shared Folder

```
<!DOCTYPE html>
<html>
<head>
    <meta name="viewport" content="width=device-width" />
    <title>SportsStore</title>
    <link href="/lib/twitter-bootstrap/css/bootstrap.min.css" rel="stylesheet" />
</head>
<body>
    <div class="bg-dark text-white p-2">
        <span class="navbar-brand ml-2">SPORTS STORE</span>
    </div>
    <div class="row m-1 p-1">
        <div id="categories" class="col-3">
            Put something useful here later
        </div>
        <div class="col-9">
            @RenderBody()
        </div>
    </div>
</body>
</html>
```

Adding the Bootstrap CSS stylesheet to the layout means that I can use the styles it defines in any of the views that rely on the layout. Listing 7-37 shows the styling I applied to the Index.cshtml file.

Listing 7-37. Styling Content in the Index.cshtml File in the SportsStore/Views/HomeFolder

```
@model ProductsListViewModel

@foreach (var p in Model.Products) {
    <div class="card card-outline-primary m-1 p-1">
        <div class="bg-faded p-1">
            <h4>
                @p.Name
```

```
                <span class="badge badge-pill badge-primary" style="float:right">
                    <small>@p.Price.ToString("c")</small>
                </span>
            </h4>
        </div>
        <div class="card-text p-1">@p.Description</div>
    </div>
}


<div page-model="@Model.PagingInfo" page-action="Index" page-classes-enabled="true"
     page-class="btn" page-class-normal="btn-outline-dark"
     page-class-selected="btn-primary" class="btn-group pull-right m-1">
</div>
```

I need to style the buttons generated by the PageLinkTagHelper class, but I don't want to hardwire the Bootstrap classes into the C# code because it makes it harder to reuse the tag helper elsewhere in the application or change the appearance of the buttons. Instead, I have defined custom attributes on the div element that specify the classes that I require, and these correspond to properties I added to the tag helper class, which are then used to style the a elements that are produced, as shown in Listing 7-38.

Listing 7-38. Adding Classes to Elements in the PageLinkTagHelper.cs File in the SportsStore/Infrastructure Folder

```
using Microsoft.AspNetCore.Mvc;
using Microsoft.AspNetCore.Mvc.Rendering;
using Microsoft.AspNetCore.Mvc.Routing;
using Microsoft.AspNetCore.Mvc.ViewFeatures;
using Microsoft.AspNetCore.Razor.TagHelpers;
using SportsStore.Models.ViewModels;

namespace SportsStore.Infrastructure {

    [HtmlTargetElement("div", Attributes = "page-model")]
    public class PageLinkTagHelper : TagHelper {
        private IUrlHelperFactory urlHelperFactory;

        public PageLinkTagHelper(IUrlHelperFactory helperFactory) {
            urlHelperFactory = helperFactory;
        }

        [ViewContext]
        [HtmlAttributeNotBound]
        public ViewContext ViewContext { get; set; }

        public PagingInfo PageModel { get; set; }

        public string PageAction { get; set; }

        public bool PageClassesEnabled { get; set; } = false;
        public string PageClass { get; set; }
        public string PageClassNormal { get; set; }
        public string PageClassSelected { get; set; }

        public override void Process(TagHelperContext context,
                TagHelperOutput output) {
            IUrlHelper urlHelper = urlHelperFactory.GetUrlHelper(ViewContext);
            TagBuilder result = new TagBuilder("div");
            for (int i = 1; i <= PageModel.TotalPages; i++) {
                TagBuilder tag = new TagBuilder("a");
```

```
                tag.Attributes["href"] = urlHelper.Action(PageAction,
                    new { productPage = i });
                if (PageClassesEnabled) {
                    tag.AddCssClass(PageClass);
                    tag.AddCssClass(i == PageModel.CurrentPage
                        ? PageClassSelected : PageClassNormal);
                }
                tag.InnerHtml.Append(i.ToString());
                result.InnerHtml.AppendHtml(tag);
            }
            output.Content.AppendHtml(result.InnerHtml);
        }
    }
}
```

The values of the attributes are automatically used to set the tag helper property values, with the mapping between the HTML attribute name format (page-class-normal) and the C# property name format (PageClassNormal) taken into account. This allows tag helpers to respond differently based on the attributes of an HTML element, creating a more flexible way to generate content in an ASP.NET Core application.

Restart ASP.NET Core and request http://localhost:5000, and you will see the appearance of the application has been improved—at least a little, anyway—as illustrated by Figure 7-9.

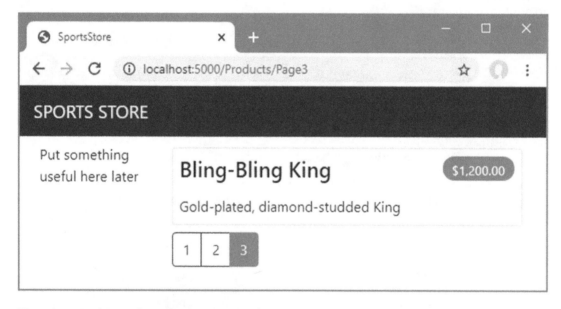

Figure 7-9. *Applying styles to the SportsStore application*

Creating a Partial View

As a finishing flourish for this chapter, I am going to refactor the application to simplify the Index.cshtml view. I am going to create a *partial view*, which is a fragment of content that you can embed into another view, rather like a template. I describe partial views in detail in Chapter 22, and they help reduce duplication when you need the same content to appear in different places in an application. Rather than copy and paste the same Razor markup into multiple views, you can define it once in a partial view. To create the partial view, I added a Razor View called ProductSummary.cshtml to the Views/Shared folder and added the markup shown in Listing 7-39.

Listing 7-39. The Contents of the ProductSummary.cshtml File in the SportsStore/Views/Shared Folder

```
@model Product

<div class="card card-outline-primary m-1 p-1">
    <div class="bg-faded p-1">
        <h4>
            @Model.Name
            <span class="badge badge-pill badge-primary" style="float:right">
                <small>@Model.Price.ToString("c")</small>
            </span>
        </h4>
    </div>
    <div class="card-text p-1">@Model.Description</div>
</div>
```

Now I need to update the Index.cshtml file in the Views/Home folder so that it uses the partial view, as shown in Listing 7-40.

Listing 7-40. Using a Partial View in the Index.cshtml File in the SportsStore/Views/Home Folder

```
@model ProductsListViewModel

@foreach (var p in Model.Products) {
    <partial name="ProductSummary" model="p" />
}

<div page-model="@Model.PagingInfo" page-action="Index" page-classes-enabled="true"
    page-class="btn" page-class-normal="btn-outline-dark"
    page-class-selected="btn-primary" class="btn-group pull-right m-1">
</div>
```

I have taken the markup that was previously in the @foreach expression in the Index.cshtml view and moved it to the new partial view. I call the partial view using a partial element, using the name and model attributes to specify the name of the partial view and its view model. Using a partial view allows the same markup to be inserted into any view that needs to display a summary of a product.

Restart ASP.NET Core and request http://localhost:5000, and you will see that introducing the partial view doesn't change the appearance of the application; it just changes where Razor finds the content that is used to generate the response sent to the browser.

Summary

In this chapter, I built the core infrastructure for the SportsStore application. It does not have many features that you could demonstrate to a client at this point, but behind the scenes, there are the beginnings of a domain model with a product repository backed by SQL Server and Entity Framework Core. There is a single controller, HomeController, that can produce paginated lists of products, and I have set up a clean and friendly URL scheme.

If this chapter felt like a lot of setup for little benefit, then the next chapter will balance the equation. Now that the fundamental structure is in place, we can forge ahead and add all the customer-facing features: navigation by category and the start of a shopping cart.

CHAPTER 8

SportsStore: Navigation and Cart

In this chapter, I continue to build out the SportsStore example app. I add support for navigating around the application and start building a shopping cart.

█ Tip You can download the example project for this chapter—and for all the other chapters in this book—from `https://github.com/apress/pro-asp.net-core-3`. See Chapter 1 for how to get help if you have problems running the examples.

Adding Navigation Controls

The SportsStore application will be more useful if customers can navigate products by category. I will do this in three phases.

- Enhance the `Index` action method in the `HomeController` class so that it can filter the `Product` objects in the repository

- Revisit and enhance the URL scheme

- Create a category list that will go into the sidebar of the site, highlighting the current category and linking to others

Filtering the Product List

I am going to start by enhancing the view model class, `ProductsListViewModel`, which I added to the `SportsStore` project in the previous chapter. I need to communicate the current category to the view to render the sidebar, and this is as good a place to start as any. Listing 8-1 shows the changes I made to the `ProductsListViewModel.cs` file in the `Models/ViewModels` folder.

Listing 8-1. Modifying the ProductsListViewModel.cs File in the SportsStore/Models/ViewModels Folder

```
using System.Collections.Generic;
using SportsStore.Models;

namespace SportsStore.Models.ViewModels {

    public class ProductsListViewModel {
        public IEnumerable<Product> Products { get; set; }
        public PagingInfo PagingInfo { get; set; }
        public string CurrentCategory { get; set; }
    }
}
```

I added a property called `CurrentCategory`. The next step is to update the `Home` controller so that the `Index` action method will filter `Product` objects by category and use the property I added to the view model to indicate which category has been selected, as shown in Listing 8-2.

Listing 8-2. Adding Category Support in the HomeController.cs File in the SportsStore/Controllers Folder

```csharp
using Microsoft.AspNetCore.Mvc;
using SportsStore.Models;
using System.Linq;
using SportsStore.Models.ViewModels;

namespace SportsStore.Controllers {
    public class HomeController : Controller {
        private IStoreRepository repository;
        public int PageSize = 4;

        public HomeController(IStoreRepository repo) {
            repository = repo;
        }

        public ViewResult Index(string category, int productPage = 1)
            => View(new ProductsListViewModel {
                Products = repository.Products
                    .Where(p => category == null || p.Category == category)
                    .OrderBy(p => p.ProductID)
                    .Skip((productPage - 1) * PageSize)
                    .Take(PageSize),
                PagingInfo = new PagingInfo {
                    CurrentPage = productPage,
                    ItemsPerPage = PageSize,
                    TotalItems = repository.Products.Count()
                },
                CurrentCategory = category
            });
    }
}
```

I made three changes to the action method. First, I added a parameter called category. This category parameter is used by the second change in the listing, which is an enhancement to the LINQ query: if category is not null, only those Product objects with a matching Category property are selected. The last change is to set the value of the CurrentCategory property I added to the ProductsListViewModel class. However, these changes mean that the value of PagingInfo.TotalItems is incorrectly calculated because it doesn't take the category filter into account. I will fix this in a while.

UNIT TEST: UPDATING EXISTING UNIT TESTS

I changed the signature of the Index action method, which will prevent some of the existing unit test methods from compiling. To address this, I need to pass null as the first parameter to the Index method in those unit tests that work with the controller. For example, in the Can_Use_Repository test in the HomeControllerTests.cs file, the action section of the unit test becomes as follows:

```csharp
...
[Fact]
public void Can_Use_Repository() {
    // Arrange
    Mock<IStoreRepository> mock = new Mock<IStoreRepository>();
    mock.Setup(m => m.Products).Returns((new Product[] {
        new Product {ProductID = 1, Name = "P1"},
        new Product {ProductID = 2, Name = "P2"}
    }).AsQueryable<Product>());

    HomeController controller = new HomeController(mock.Object);
```

```
    // Act
    ProductsListViewModel result =
        controller.Index(null).ViewData.Model as ProductsListViewModel;

    // Assert
    Product[] prodArray = result.Products.ToArray();
    Assert.True(prodArray.Length == 2);
    Assert.Equal("P1", prodArray[0].Name);
    Assert.Equal("P2", prodArray[1].Name);
}
...
```

By using null for the category argument, I receive all the Product objects that the controller gets from the repository, which is the same situation I had before adding the new parameter. I need to make the same change to the Can_Paginate and Can_Send_Pagination_View_Model tests as well.

```
...
[Fact]
public void Can_Paginate() {
    // Arrange
    Mock<IStoreRepository> mock = new Mock<IStoreRepository>();
    mock.Setup(m => m.Products).Returns((new Product[] {
        new Product {ProductID = 1, Name = "P1"},
        new Product {ProductID = 2, Name = "P2"},
        new Product {ProductID = 3, Name = "P3"},
        new Product {ProductID = 4, Name = "P4"},
        new Product {ProductID = 5, Name = "P5"}
    }).AsQueryable<Product>());

    HomeController controller = new HomeController(mock.Object);
    controller.PageSize = 3;

    // Act
    ProductsListViewModel result =
        controller.Index(null, 2).ViewData.Model as ProductsListViewModel;

    // Assert
    Product[] prodArray = result.Products.ToArray();

    Assert.True(prodArray.Length == 2);
    Assert.Equal("P4", prodArray[0].Name);
    Assert.Equal("P5", prodArray[1].Name);
}

[Fact]
public void Can_Send_Pagination_View_Model() {

    // Arrange
    Mock<IStoreRepository> mock = new Mock<IStoreRepository>();
    mock.Setup(m => m.Products).Returns((new Product[] {
        new Product {ProductID = 1, Name = "P1"},
        new Product {ProductID = 2, Name = "P2"},
        new Product {ProductID = 3, Name = "P3"},
        new Product {ProductID = 4, Name = "P4"},
        new Product {ProductID = 5, Name = "P5"}
    }).AsQueryable<Product>());

    // Arrange
    HomeController controller =
        new HomeController(mock.Object) { PageSize = 3 };
```

```
    // Act
    ProductsListViewModel result =
        controller.Index(null, 2).ViewData.Model as ProductsListViewModel;

    // Assert
    PagingInfo pageInfo = result.PagingInfo;
    Assert.Equal(2, pageInfo.CurrentPage);
    Assert.Equal(3, pageInfo.ItemsPerPage);
    Assert.Equal(5, pageInfo.TotalItems);
    Assert.Equal(2, pageInfo.TotalPages);
}
...
```

Keeping your unit tests synchronized with your code changes quickly becomes second nature when you get into the testing mindset.

To see the effect of the category filtering, start ASP.NET Core and select a category using the following URL, taking care to use an uppercase S for Soccer:

```
http://localhost:5000/?category=Soccer
```

You will see only the products in the Soccer category, as shown in Figure 8-1.

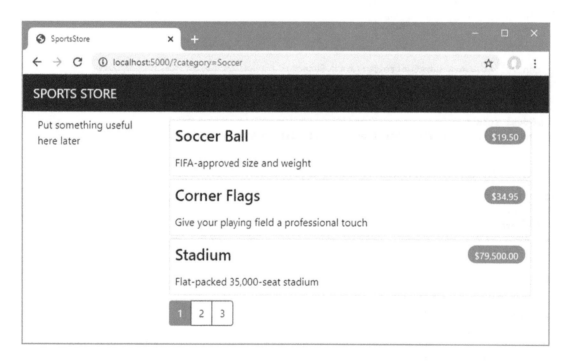

Figure 8-1. *Using the query string to filter by category*

Obviously, users won't want to navigate to categories using URLs, but you can see how small changes can have a big impact once the basic structure of an ASP.NET Core application is in place.

```
┌─────────────────────────────────────────────────────────────────────────┐
│                    UNIT TEST: CATEGORY FILTERING                          │
└─────────────────────────────────────────────────────────────────────────┘
```

I need a unit test to properly test the category filtering function to ensure that the filter can correctly generate products in a specified category. Here is the test method I added to the `ProductControllerTests` class:

```csharp
...
[Fact]
public void Can_Filter_Products() {

    // Arrange
    // - create the mock repository
    Mock<IStoreRepository> mock = new Mock<IStoreRepository>();
    mock.Setup(m => m.Products).Returns((new Product[] {
        new Product {ProductID = 1, Name = "P1", Category = "Cat1"},
        new Product {ProductID = 2, Name = "P2", Category = "Cat2"},
        new Product {ProductID = 3, Name = "P3", Category = "Cat1"},
        new Product {ProductID = 4, Name = "P4", Category = "Cat2"},
        new Product {ProductID = 5, Name = "P5", Category = "Cat3"}
    }).AsQueryable<Product>());

    // Arrange - create a controller and make the page size 3 items
    HomeController controller = new HomeController(mock.Object);
    controller.PageSize = 3;

    // Action
    Product[] result =
        (controller.Index("Cat2", 1).ViewData.Model as ProductsListViewModel)
            .Products.ToArray();

    // Assert
    Assert.Equal(2, result.Length);
    Assert.True(result[0].Name == "P2" && result[0].Category == "Cat2");
    Assert.True(result[1].Name == "P4" && result[1].Category == "Cat2");
}
...
```

This test creates a mock repository containing `Product` objects that belong to a range of categories. One specific category is requested using the action method, and the results are checked to ensure that the results are the right objects in the right order.

Refining the URL Scheme

No one wants to see or use ugly URLs such as /?category=Soccer. To address this, I am going to change the routing configuration in the Configure method of the Startup class to create a more useful set of URLs, as shown in Listing 8-3.

■ **Caution**   It is important to add the new routes in Listing 8-3 in the order they are shown. Routes are applied in the order in which they are defined, and you will get some odd effects if you change the order.

Listing 8-3. Changing the Routing Schema in the Startup.cs File in the SportsStore Folder

```csharp
using System;
using System.Collections.Generic;
using System.Linq;
using System.Threading.Tasks;
using Microsoft.AspNetCore.Builder;
using Microsoft.AspNetCore.Hosting;
```

```
using Microsoft.AspNetCore.Http;
using Microsoft.Extensions.DependencyInjection;
using Microsoft.Extensions.Hosting;
using Microsoft.Extensions.Configuration;
using Microsoft.EntityFrameworkCore;
using SportsStore.Models;

namespace SportsStore {
    public class Startup {

        public Startup(IConfiguration config) {
            Configuration = config;
        }

        private IConfiguration Configuration { get; set; }

        public void ConfigureServices(IServiceCollection services) {
            services.AddControllersWithViews();

            services.AddDbContext<StoreDbContext>(opts => {
                opts.UseSqlServer(
                    Configuration["ConnectionStrings:SportsStoreConnection"]);
            });
            services.AddScoped<IStoreRepository, EFStoreRepository>();
        }

        public void Configure(IApplicationBuilder app, IWebHostEnvironment env) {
            app.UseDeveloperExceptionPage();
            app.UseStatusCodePages();
            app.UseStaticFiles();

            app.UseRouting();
            app.UseEndpoints(endpoints => {
                endpoints.MapControllerRoute("catpage",
                    "{category}/Page{productPage:int}",
                    new { Controller = "Home", action = "Index" });

                endpoints.MapControllerRoute("page", "Page{productPage:int}",
                    new { Controller = "Home", action = "Index", productPage = 1 });

                endpoints.MapControllerRoute("category", "{category}",
                    new { Controller = "Home", action = "Index", productPage = 1 });

                endpoints.MapControllerRoute("pagination",
                    "Products/Page{productPage}",
                    new { Controller = "Home", action = "Index", productPage = 1 });
                endpoints.MapDefaultControllerRoute();
            });

            SeedData.EnsurePopulated(app);
        }
    }
}
```

Table 8-1 describes the URL scheme that these routes represent. I explain the routing system in detail in Chapter 13.

Table 8-1. *Route Summary*

URL	Leads To
/	Lists the first page of products from all categories
/Page2	Lists the specified page (in this case, page 2), showing items from all categories
/Soccer	Shows the first page of items from a specific category (in this case, the Soccer category)
/Soccer/Page2	Shows the specified page (in this case, page 2) of items from the specified category (in this case, Soccer)

The ASP.NET Core routing system handles *incoming* requests from clients, but it also generates *outgoing* URLs that conform to the URL scheme and that can be embedded in web pages. By using the routing system both to handle incoming requests and to generate outgoing URLs, I can ensure that all the URLs in the application are consistent.

The IUrlHelper interface provides access to URL-generating functionality. I used this interface and the Action method it defines in the tag helper I created in the previous chapter. Now that I want to start generating more complex URLs, I need a way to receive additional information from the view without having to add extra properties to the tag helper class. Fortunately, tag helpers have a nice feature that allows properties with a common prefix to be received all together in a single collection, as shown in Listing 8-4.

Listing 8-4. Prefixed Values in the PageLinkTagHelper.cs File in the SportsStore/Infrastructure Folder

```
using Microsoft.AspNetCore.Mvc;
using Microsoft.AspNetCore.Mvc.Rendering;
using Microsoft.AspNetCore.Mvc.Routing;
using Microsoft.AspNetCore.Mvc.ViewFeatures;
using Microsoft.AspNetCore.Razor.TagHelpers;
using SportsStore.Models.ViewModels;
using System.Collections.Generic;

namespace SportsStore.Infrastructure {

    [HtmlTargetElement("div", Attributes = "page-model")]
    public class PageLinkTagHelper : TagHelper {
        private IUrlHelperFactory urlHelperFactory;

        public PageLinkTagHelper(IUrlHelperFactory helperFactory) {
            urlHelperFactory = helperFactory;
        }

        [ViewContext]
        [HtmlAttributeNotBound]
        public ViewContext ViewContext { get; set; }

        public PagingInfo PageModel { get; set; }

        public string PageAction { get; set; }

        [HtmlAttributeName(DictionaryAttributePrefix = "page-url-")]
        public Dictionary<string, object> PageUrlValues { get; set; }
            = new Dictionary<string, object>();

        public bool PageClassesEnabled { get; set; } = false;
        public string PageClass { get; set; }
        public string PageClassNormal { get; set; }
        public string PageClassSelected { get; set; }

        public override void Process(TagHelperContext context,
                TagHelperOutput output) {
            IUrlHelper urlHelper = urlHelperFactory.GetUrlHelper(ViewContext);
```

163

```
            TagBuilder result = new TagBuilder("div");
            for (int i = 1; i <= PageModel.TotalPages; i++) {
                TagBuilder tag = new TagBuilder("a");
                PageUrlValues["productPage"] = i;
                tag.Attributes["href"] = urlHelper.Action(PageAction, PageUrlValues);
                if (PageClassesEnabled) {
                    tag.AddCssClass(PageClass);
                    tag.AddCssClass(i == PageModel.CurrentPage
                        ? PageClassSelected : PageClassNormal);
                }
                tag.InnerHtml.Append(i.ToString());
                result.InnerHtml.AppendHtml(tag);
            }
            output.Content.AppendHtml(result.InnerHtml);
        }
    }
}
```

Decorating a tag helper property with the HtmlAttributeName attribute allows me to specify a prefix for attribute names on the element, which in this case will be page-url-. The value of any attribute whose name begins with this prefix will be added to the dictionary that is assigned to the PageUrlValues property, which is then passed to the IUrlHelper.Action method to generate the URL for the href attribute of the a elements that the tag helper produces.

In Listing 8-5, I have added a new attribute to the div element that is processed by the tag helper, specifying the category that will be used to generate the URL. I have added only one new attribute to the view, but any attribute with the same prefix would be added to the dictionary.

Listing 8-5. Adding a New Attribute in the Index.cshtml File in the SportsStore/Views/Home Folder

```
@model ProductsListViewModel

@foreach (var p in Model.Products) {
    <partial name="ProductSummary" model="p" />
}

<div page-model="@Model.PagingInfo" page-action="Index" page-classes-enabled="true"
    page-class="btn" page-class-normal="btn-outline-dark"
    page-class-selected="btn-primary" page-url-category="@Model.CurrentCategory"
    class="btn-group pull-right m-1">
</div>
```

Prior to this change, the links generated for the pagination links looked like this:

```
http://localhost:5000/Page1
```

If the user clicked a page link like this, the category filter would be lost, and the application would present a page containing products from all categories. By adding the current category, taken from the view model, I generate URLs like this instead:

```
http://localhost:5000/Chess/Page1
```

When the user clicks this kind of link, the current category will be passed to the Index action method, and the filtering will be preserved. To see the effect of this change, start ASP.NET Core and request http://localhost:5000/Chess, which will display just the products in the Chess category, as shown in Figure 8-2.

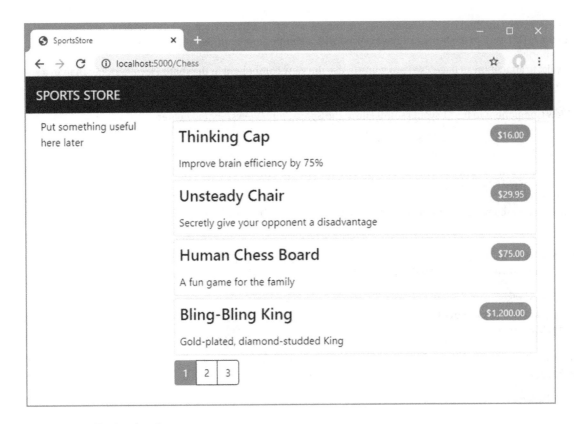

Figure 8-2. *Filtering data by category*

Building a Category Navigation Menu

I need to provide users with a way to select a category that does not involve typing in URLs. This means presenting a list of the available categories and indicating which, if any, is currently selected.

ASP.NET Core has the concept of *view components*, which are perfect for creating items such as reusable navigation controls. A view component is a C# class that provides a small amount of reusable application logic with the ability to select and display Razor partial views. I describe view components in detail in Chapter 24.

In this case, I will create a view component that renders the navigation menu and integrate it into the application by invoking the component from the shared layout. This approach gives me a regular C# class that can contain whatever application logic I need and that can be unit tested like any other class.

Creating the Navigation View Component

I created a folder called Components, which is the conventional home of view components, in the SportsStore project and added to it a class file named NavigationMenuViewComponent.cs, which I used to define the class shown in Listing 8-6.

Listing 8-6. The Contents of the NavigationMenuViewComponent.cs File in the SportsStore/Components Folder

```
using Microsoft.AspNetCore.Mvc;

namespace SportsStore.Components {

    public class NavigationMenuViewComponent : ViewComponent {

        public string Invoke() {
            return "Hello from the Nav View Component";
        }
    }
}
```

The view component's Invoke method is called when the component is used in a Razor view, and the result of the Invoke method is inserted into the HTML sent to the browser. I have started with a simple view component that returns a string, but I'll replace this with HTML shortly.

I want the category list to appear on all pages, so I am going to use the view component in the shared layout, rather than in a specific view. Within a view, view components are applied using a tag helper, as shown in Listing 8-7.

Listing 8-7. Using a View Component in the _Layout.cshtml File in the SportsStore/Views/Shared Folder

```html
<!DOCTYPE html>
<html>
<head>
    <meta name="viewport" content="width=device-width" />
    <title>SportsStore</title>
    <link href="/lib/twitter-bootstrap/css/bootstrap.min.css" rel="stylesheet" />
</head>
<body>
    <div class="bg-dark text-white p-2">
        <span class="navbar-brand ml-2">SPORTS STORE</span>
    </div>
    <div class="row m-1 p-1">
        <div id="categories" class="col-3">
            <vc:navigation-menu />
        </div>
        <div class="col-9">
            @RenderBody()
        </div>
    </div>
</body>
</html>
```

I removed the placeholder text and replaced it with the vc:navigation-menu element, which inserts the view component. The element omits the ViewComponent part of the class name and hyphenates it, such that vc:navigation-menu specifies the NavigationMenuViewComponent class.

Restart ASP.NET Core and request http://localhost:5000, and you will see that the output from the Invoke method is included in the HTML sent to the browser, as shown in Figure 8-3.

Figure 8-3. Using a view component

Generating Category Lists

I can now return to the navigation view component and generate a real set of categories. I could build the HTML for the categories programmatically, as I did for the page tag helper, but one of the benefits of working with view components is they can render Razor partial views. That means I can use the view component to generate the list of components and then use the more expressive Razor syntax to render the HTML that will display them. The first step is to update the view component, as shown in Listing 8-8.

Listing 8-8. Adding Categories in the NavigationMenuViewComponent.cs File in the SportsStore/Components Folder

```
using Microsoft.AspNetCore.Mvc;
using System.Linq;
using SportsStore.Models;

namespace SportsStore.Components {

    public class NavigationMenuViewComponent : ViewComponent {
        private IStoreRepository  repository;

        public NavigationMenuViewComponent(IStoreRepository repo) {
            repository = repo;
        }

        public IViewComponentResult Invoke() {
            return View(repository.Products
                .Select(x => x.Category)
                .Distinct()
                .OrderBy(x => x));
        }
    }
}
```

The constructor defined in Listing 8-8 defines an IStoreRepository parameter. When ASP.NET Core needs to create an instance of the view component class, it will note the need to provide a value for this parameter and inspect the configuration in the Startup class to determine which implementation object should be used. This is the same dependency injection feature that I used in the controller in Chapter 7, and it has the same effect, which is to allow the view component to access data without knowing which repository implementation will be used, a feature I describe in detail in Chapter 14.

In the Invoke method, I use LINQ to select and order the set of categories in the repository and pass them as the argument to the View method, which renders the default Razor partial view, details of which are returned from the method using an IViewComponentResult object, a process I describe in more detail in Chapter 24.

UNIT TEST: GENERATING THE CATEGORY LIST

The unit test for my ability to produce a category list is relatively simple. The goal is to create a list that is sorted in alphabetical order and contains no duplicates, and the simplest way to do this is to supply some test data that *does* have duplicate categories and that is *not* in order, pass this to the tag helper class, and assert that the data has been properly cleaned up. Here is the unit test, which I defined in a new class file called NavigationMenuViewComponentTests.cs in the SportsStore.Tests project:

```
using System.Collections.Generic;
using System.Linq;
using Microsoft.AspNetCore.Components;
using Microsoft.AspNetCore.Mvc.Rendering;
using Microsoft.AspNetCore.Mvc.ViewComponents;
using Moq;
using SportsStore.Components;
using SportsStore.Models;
using Xunit;
```

```
namespace SportsStore.Tests {

    public class NavigationMenuViewComponentTests {

        [Fact]
        public void Can_Select_Categories() {
            // Arrange
            Mock<IStoreRepository> mock = new Mock<IStoreRepository>();
            mock.Setup(m => m.Products).Returns((new Product[] {
                new Product {ProductID = 1, Name = "P1", Category = "Apples"},
                new Product {ProductID = 2, Name = "P2", Category = "Apples"},
                new Product {ProductID = 3, Name = "P3", Category = "Plums"},
                new Product {ProductID = 4, Name = "P4", Category = "Oranges"},
            }).AsQueryable<Product>());

            NavigationMenuViewComponent target =
                new NavigationMenuViewComponent(mock.Object);

            // Act = get the set of categories
            string[] results = ((IEnumerable<string>)(target.Invoke()
                as ViewViewComponentResult).ViewData.Model).ToArray();

            // Assert
            Assert.True(Enumerable.SequenceEqual(new string[] { "Apples",
                "Oranges", "Plums" }, results));
        }
    }
}
```

I created a mock repository implementation that contains repeating categories and categories that are not in order. I assert that the duplicates are removed and that alphabetical ordering is imposed.

Creating the View

Razor uses different conventions for locating with views that are selected by view components. Both the default name of the view and the locations that are searched for the view are different from those used for controllers. To that end, I created the Views/Shared/Components/NavigationMenu folder in the SportsStore project and added to it a Razor view named Default.cshtml, to which I added the content shown in Listing 8-9.

Listing 8-9. The Contents of the Default.cshtml File in the SportsStore/Views/Shared/Components/NavigationMenu Folder

```
@model IEnumerable<string>

<a class="btn btn-block btn-outline-secondary"asp-action="Index"
    asp-controller="Home" asp-route-category="">
    Home
</a>

@foreach (string category in Model) {
    <a class="btn btn-block btn-outline-secondary"
        asp-action="Index" asp-controller="Home"
        asp-route-category="@category"
        asp-route-productPage="1">
        @category
    </a>
}
```

This view uses one of the built-in tag helpers, which I describe in Chapters 25–27, to create anchor elements whose href attribute contains a URL that selects a different product category.

Restart ASP.NET Core and request `http://localhost:5000` to see the category navigation buttons. If you click a button, the list of items is updated to show only items from the selected category, as shown in Figure 8-4.

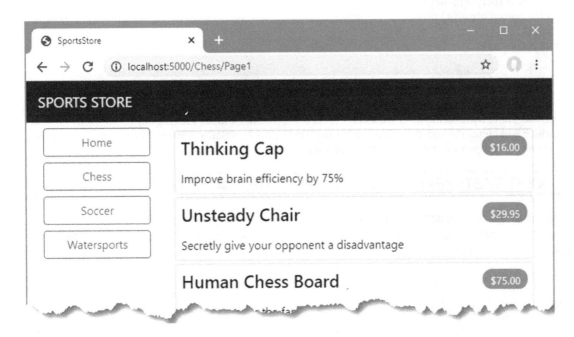

Figure 8-4. *Generating category links with a view component*

Highlighting the Current Category

There is no feedback to the user to indicate which category has been selected. It might be possible to infer the category from the items in the list, but some clear visual feedback seems like a good idea. ASP.NET Core components such as controllers and view components can receive information about the current request by asking for a context object. Most of the time, you can rely on the base classes that you use to create components to take care of getting the context object for you, such as when you use the `Controller` base class to create controllers.

The `ViewComponent` base class is no exception and provides access to context objects through a set of properties. One of the properties is called `RouteData`, which provides information about how the request URL was handled by the routing system.

In Listing 8-10, I use the `RouteData` property to access the request data in order to get the value for the currently selected category. I could pass the category to the view by creating another view model class (and that's what I would do in a real project), but for variety, I am going to use the view bag feature, which allows unstructured data to be passed to a view alongside the view model object. I describe how this feature works in detail in Chapter 22.

Listing 8-10. Passing the Selected Category in the NavigationMenuViewComponent.cs File in the SportsStore/Components Folder

```
using Microsoft.AspNetCore.Mvc;
using System.Linq;
using SportsStore.Models;

namespace SportsStore.Components {

    public class NavigationMenuViewComponent : ViewComponent {
        private IStoreRepository  repository;

        public NavigationMenuViewComponent(IStoreRepository repo) {
            repository = repo;
        }
```

```
        public IViewComponentResult Invoke() {
            ViewBag.SelectedCategory = RouteData?.Values["category"];
            return View(repository.Products
                .Select(x => x.Category)
                .Distinct()
                .OrderBy(x => x));
        }
    }
}
```

Inside the Invoke method, I have dynamically assigned a SelectedCategory property to the ViewBag object and set its value to be the current category, which is obtained through the context object returned by the RouteData property. The ViewBag is a dynamic object that allows me to define new properties simply by assigning values to them.

UNIT TEST: REPORTING THE SELECTED CATEGORY

I can test that the view component correctly adds details of the selected category by reading the value of the ViewBag property in a unit test, which is available through the ViewViewComponentResult class. Here is the test, which I added to the NavigatioMenuViewComponentTests class:

```
...
[Fact]
public void Indicates_Selected_Category() {
    // Arrange
    string categoryToSelect = "Apples";
    Mock<IStoreRepository> mock = new Mock<IStoreRepository>();
    mock.Setup(m => m.Products).Returns((new Product[] {
        new Product {ProductID = 1, Name = "P1", Category = "Apples"},
        new Product {ProductID = 4, Name = "P2", Category = "Oranges"},
    }).AsQueryable<Product>());

    NavigationMenuViewComponent target =
        new NavigationMenuViewComponent(mock.Object);
    target.ViewComponentContext = new ViewComponentContext {
        ViewContext = new ViewContext {
            RouteData = new Microsoft.AspNetCore.Routing.RouteData()
        }
    };
    target.RouteData.Values["category"] = categoryToSelect;

    // Action
    string result = (string)(target.Invoke() as
        ViewViewComponentResult).ViewData["SelectedCategory"];

    // Assert
    Assert.Equal(categoryToSelect, result);
}
...
```

This unit test provides the view component with routing data through the ViewComponentContext property, which is how view components receive all their context data. The ViewComponentContext property provides access to view-specific context data through its ViewContext property, which in turn provides access to the routing information through its RouteData property. Most of the code in the unit test goes into creating the context objects that will provide the selected category in the same way that it would be presented when the application is running and the context data is provided by ASP.NET Core MVC.

Now that I am providing information about which category is selected, I can update the view selected by the view component and vary the CSS classes used to style the links so that the one representing the current category is distinct. Listing 8-11 shows the change I made to the Default.cshtml file.

Listing 8-11. Highlighting in the Default.cshtml File in the SportsStore/Views/Shared/Components/NavigationMenu Folder

```
@model IEnumerable<string>

<a class="btn btn-block btn-outline-secondary"asp-action="Index"
   asp-controller="Home" asp-route-category="">
   Home
</a>

@foreach (string category in Model) {
    <a class="btn btn-block
       @(category == ViewBag.SelectedCategory
           ? "btn-primary": "btn-outline-secondary")"
       asp-action="Index" asp-controller="Home"
       asp-route-category="@category"
       asp-route-productPage="1">
         @category
    </a>
}
```

I have used a Razor expression within the `class` attribute to apply the `btn-primary` class to the element that represents the selected category and the `btn-secondary` class otherwise. These classes apply different Bootstrap styles and make the active button obvious, which you can see by restarting ASP.NET Core, requesting `http://localhost:5000`, and clicking one of the category buttons, as shown in Figure 8-5.

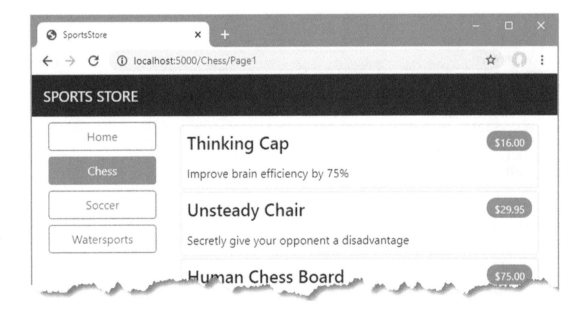

Figure 8-5. *Highlighting the selected category*

Correcting the Page Count

I need to correct the page links so that they work correctly when a category is selected. Currently, the number of page links is determined by the total number of products in the repository and not the number of products in the selected category. This means that the customer can click the link for page 2 of the Chess category and end up with an empty page because there are not enough chess products to fill two pages. You can see the problem in Figure 8-6.

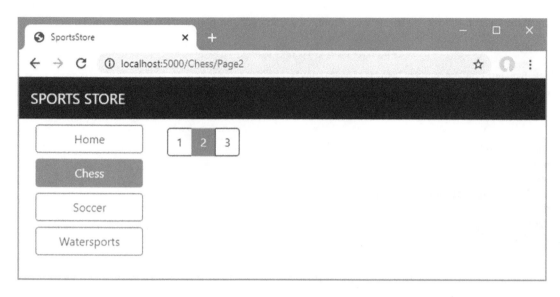

Figure 8-6. *Displaying the wrong page links when a category is selected*

I can fix this by updating the Index action method in the Home controller so that the pagination information takes the categories into account, as shown in Listing 8-12.

Listing 8-12. Creating Category Pagination Data in the HomeController.cs File in the SportsStore/Controllers Folder

```
using Microsoft.AspNetCore.Mvc;
using SportsStore.Models;
using System.Linq;
using SportsStore.Models.ViewModels;

namespace SportsStore.Controllers {
    public class HomeController : Controller {
        private IStoreRepository repository;
        public int PageSize = 4;

        public HomeController(IStoreRepository repo) {
            repository = repo;
        }

        public ViewResult Index(string category, int productPage = 1)
            => View(new ProductsListViewModel {
                Products = repository.Products
                    .Where(p => category == null || p.Category == category)
                    .OrderBy(p => p.ProductID)
                    .Skip((productPage - 1) * PageSize)
                    .Take(PageSize),
                PagingInfo = new PagingInfo {
                    CurrentPage = productPage,
                    ItemsPerPage = PageSize,
                    TotalItems = category == null ?
                        repository.Products.Count() :
                        repository.Products.Where(e =>
                            e.Category == category).Count()
                },
                CurrentCategory = category
            });
    }
}
```

If a category has been selected, I return the number of items in that category; if not, I return the total number of products. Restart ASP.NET Core and request http://localhost:5000 to see the changes when a category is selected, as shown in Figure 8-7.

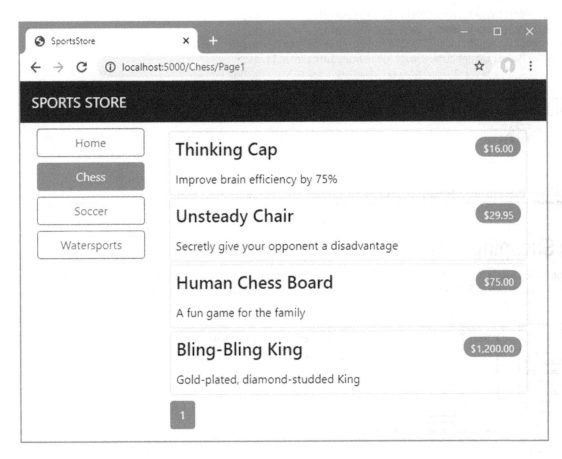

Figure 8-7. *Displaying category-specific page counts*

UNIT TEST: CATEGORY-SPECIFIC PRODUCT COUNTS

Testing that I am able to generate the current product count for different categories is simple. I create a mock repository that contains known data in a range of categories and then call the List action method requesting each category in turn. Here is the unit test method that I added to the HomeControllerTests class (you will need to import the System namespace for this test):

```
...
[Fact]
public void Generate_Category_Specific_Product_Count() {
    // Arrange
    Mock<IStoreRepository> mock = new Mock<IStoreRepository>();
    mock.Setup(m => m.Products).Returns((new Product[] {
        new Product {ProductID = 1, Name = "P1", Category = "Cat1"},
        new Product {ProductID = 2, Name = "P2", Category = "Cat2"},
        new Product {ProductID = 3, Name = "P3", Category = "Cat1"},
        new Product {ProductID = 4, Name = "P4", Category = "Cat2"},
        new Product {ProductID = 5, Name = "P5", Category = "Cat3"}
    }).AsQueryable<Product>());

    HomeController target = new HomeController(mock.Object);
    target.PageSize = 3;
```

```
        Func<ViewResult, ProductsListViewModel> GetModel = result =>
            result?.ViewData?.Model as ProductsListViewModel;

        // Action
        int? res1 = GetModel(target.Index("Cat1"))?.PagingInfo.TotalItems;
        int? res2 = GetModel(target.Index("Cat2"))?.PagingInfo.TotalItems;
        int? res3 = GetModel(target.Index("Cat3"))?.PagingInfo.TotalItems;
        int? resAll = GetModel(target.Index(null))?.PagingInfo.TotalItems;

        // Assert
        Assert.Equal(2, res1);
        Assert.Equal(2, res2);
        Assert.Equal(1, res3);
        Assert.Equal(5, resAll);
    }
    ...
```

Notice that I also call the Index method, specifying no category, to make sure I get the correct total count as well.

Building the Shopping Cart

The application is progressing nicely, but I cannot sell any products until I implement a shopping cart. In this section, I will create the shopping cart experience shown in Figure 8-8. This will be familiar to anyone who has ever made a purchase online.

Figure 8-8. The basic shopping cart flow

An Add To Cart button will be displayed alongside each of the products in the catalog. Clicking this button will show a summary of the products the customer has selected so far, including the total cost. At this point, the user can click the Continue Shopping button to return to the product catalog or click the Checkout Now button to complete the order and finish the shopping session.

Configuring Razor Pages

So far, I have used the MVC Framework to define the SportsStore project features. For variety, I am going to use Razor Pages—another application framework supported by ASP.NET Core—to implement the shopping cart. Listing 8-13 configures the Startup class to enable Razor Pages in the SportsStore application.

Listing 8-13. Enabling Razor Pages in the Startup.cs File in the SportsStore Folder

```
using System;
using System.Collections.Generic;
using System.Linq;
using System.Threading.Tasks;
using Microsoft.AspNetCore.Builder;
using Microsoft.AspNetCore.Hosting;
using Microsoft.AspNetCore.Http;
using Microsoft.Extensions.DependencyInjection;
```

```
using Microsoft.Extensions.Hosting;
using Microsoft.Extensions.Configuration;
using Microsoft.EntityFrameworkCore;
using SportsStore.Models;

namespace SportsStore {
    public class Startup {

        public Startup(IConfiguration config) {
            Configuration = config;
        }

        private IConfiguration Configuration { get; set; }

        public void ConfigureServices(IServiceCollection services) {
            services.AddControllersWithViews();
            services.AddDbContext<StoreDbContext>(opts => {
                opts.UseSqlServer(
                    Configuration["ConnectionStrings:SportsStoreConnection"]);
            });
            services.AddScoped<IStoreRepository, EFStoreRepository>();
            services.AddRazorPages();
        }

        public void Configure(IApplicationBuilder app, IWebHostEnvironment env) {
            app.UseDeveloperExceptionPage();
            app.UseStatusCodePages();
            app.UseStaticFiles();

            app.UseRouting();
            app.UseEndpoints(endpoints => {
                endpoints.MapControllerRoute("catpage",
                    "{category}/Page{productPage:int}",
                    new { Controller = "Home", action = "Index" });

                endpoints.MapControllerRoute("page", "Page{productPage:int}",
                    new { Controller = "Home", action = "Index", productPage = 1 });

                endpoints.MapControllerRoute("category", "{category}",
                    new { Controller = "Home", action = "Index", productPage = 1 });

                endpoints.MapControllerRoute("pagination",
                    "Products/Page{productPage}",
                    new { Controller = "Home", action = "Index", productPage = 1 });
                endpoints.MapDefaultControllerRoute();
                endpoints.MapRazorPages();
            });

            SeedData.EnsurePopulated(app);
        }
    }
}
```

The AddRazorPages method sets up the services used by Razor Pages, and the MapRazorPages method registers Razor Pages as endpoints that the URL routing system can use to handle requests.

Add a folder named Pages, which is the conventional location for Razor Pages, to the SportsStore project. Add a Razor View Imports file named _ViewImports.cshtml to the Pages folder with the content shown in Listing 8-14. These expressions set the namespace that the Razor Pages will belong to and allow the SportsStore classes to be used in Razor Pages without needing to specify their namespace.

Listing 8-14. The Contents of the _ViewImports.cshtml File in the SportsStore/Pages Folder

```
@namespace SportsStore.Pages
@using Microsoft.AspNetCore.Mvc.RazorPages
@using SportsStore.Models
@using SportsStore.Infrastructure
@addTagHelper *, Microsoft.AspNetCore.Mvc.TagHelpers
```

Next, add a Razor View Start file named `_ViewStart.cshtml` to the Pages folder, with the content shown in Listing 8-15. Razor Pages have their own configuration files, and this one specifies that the Razor Pages in the SportsStore project will use a layout file named `_CartLayout` by default.

Listing 8-15. The Contents of the _ViewStart.cshtml File in the SportsStore/Pages Folder

```
@{
    Layout = "_CartLayout";
}
```

Finally, to provide the layout the Razor Pages will use, add a Razor View named `_CartLayout.cshtml` to the Pages folder with the content shown in Listing 8-16.

Listing 8-16. The Contents of the _CartLayout.cshtml File in the SportsStore/Pages Folder

```
<!DOCTYPE html>
<html>
<head>
    <meta name="viewport" content="width=device-width" />
    <title>SportsStore</title>
    <link href="/lib/twitter-bootstrap/css/bootstrap.min.css" rel="stylesheet" />
</head>
<body>
    <div class="bg-dark text-white p-2">
        <span class="navbar-brand ml-2">SPORTS STORE</span>
    </div>
    <div class="m-1 p-1">
            @RenderBody()
    </div>
</body>
</html>
```

Creating a Razor Page

If you are using Visual Studio, use the Razor Page template item and set the item name to `Cart.cshtml`. This will create a `Cart.cshtml` file and a `Cart.cshtml.cs` class file. Replace the contents of the file with those shown in Listing 8-17. If you are using Visual Studio Code, just create a `Cart.cshtml` file with the content shown in Listing 8-17.

Listing 8-17. The Contents of the Cart.cshtml File in the SportsStore/Pages Folder

```
@page

<h4>This is the Cart Page</h4>
```

Restart ASP.NET Core and request `http://localhost:5000/cart` to see the placeholder content from Listing 8-17, which is shown in Figure 8-9. Notice that I have not had to register the page and that the mapping between the `/cart` URL path and the Razor Page has been handled automatically.

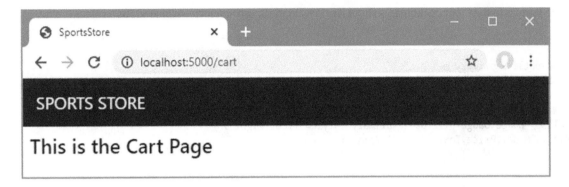

Figure 8-9. *Placeholder content from a Razor Page*

Creating the Add To Cart Buttons

I have some preparation to do before I can implement the cart feature. First, I need to create the buttons that will add products to the cart. To prepare for this, I added a class file called UrlExtensions.cs to the Infrastructure folder and defined the extension method shown in Listing 8-18.

Listing 8-18. The Contents of the UrlExtensions.cs File in the SportsStore/Infrastructure Folder

```
using Microsoft.AspNetCore.Http;

namespace SportsStore.Infrastructure {

    public static class UrlExtensions {

        public static string PathAndQuery(this HttpRequest request) =>
            request.QueryString.HasValue
                ? $"{request.Path}{request.QueryString}"
                : request.Path.ToString();
    }
}
```

The PathAndQuery extension method operates on the HttpRequest class, which ASP.NET Core uses to describe an HTTP request. The extension method generates a URL that the browser will be returned to after the cart has been updated, taking into account the query string, if there is one. In Listing 8-19, I have added the namespace that contains the extension method to the view imports file so that I can use it in the partial view.

■ **Note** This is the view imports file in the Views folder and not the one added to the Pages folder.

Listing 8-19. Adding a Namespace in the _ViewImports.cshtml File in the SportsStore/Views Folder

```
@using SportsStore.Models
@using SportsStore.Models.ViewModels
@using SportsStore.Infrastructure
@addTagHelper *, Microsoft.AspNetCore.Mvc.TagHelpers
@addTagHelper *, SportsStore
```

In Listing 8-20, I have updated the partial view that describes each product so that it contains an Add to Cart button.

Listing 8-20. Adding the Buttons to the ProductSummary.cshtml File View in the SportsStore/Views/Shared Folder

```
@model Product

<div class="card card-outline-primary m-1 p-1">
    <div class="bg-faded p-1">
        <h4>
            @Model.Name
            <span class="badge badge-pill badge-primary" style="float:right">
                <small>@Model.Price.ToString("c")</small>
            </span>
        </h4>
    </div>
    <form id="@Model.ProductID" asp-page="/Cart" method="post">
        <input type="hidden" asp-for="ProductID" />
        <input type="hidden" name="returnUrl"
            value="@ViewContext.HttpContext.Request.PathAndQuery()" />
        <span class="card-text p-1">
            @Model.Description
            <button type="submit"
                class="btn btn-success btn-sm pull-right" style="float:right">
                Add To Cart
            </button>
        </span>
    </form>
</div>
```

I have added a form element that contains hidden input elements specifying the ProductID value from the view model and the URL that the browser should be returned to after the cart has been updated. The form element and one of the input elements are configured using built-in tag helpers, which are a useful way of generating forms that contain model values and that target controllers or Razor Pages, as described in Chapter 27. The other input element uses the extension method I created to set the return URL. I also added a button element that will submit the form to the application.

▪ **Note**   Notice that I have set the method attribute on the form element to post, which instructs the browser to submit the form data using an HTTP POST request. You can change this so that forms use the GET method, but you should think carefully about doing so. The HTTP specification requires that GET requests must be *idempotent*, meaning that they must not cause changes, and adding a product to a cart is definitely a change.

Enabling Sessions

I am going to store details of a user's cart using *session state*, which is data associated with a series of requests made by a user. ASP. NET provides a range of different ways to store session state, including storing it in memory, which is the approach that I am going to use. This has the advantage of simplicity, but it means that the session data is lost when the application is stopped or restarted. Enabling sessions requires adding services and middleware in the Startup class, as shown in Listing 8-21.

Listing 8-21. Enabling Sessions in the Startup.cs File in the SportsStore Folder

```
using System;
using System.Collections.Generic;
using System.Linq;
using System.Threading.Tasks;
using Microsoft.AspNetCore.Builder;
using Microsoft.AspNetCore.Hosting;
using Microsoft.AspNetCore.Http;
using Microsoft.Extensions.DependencyInjection;
```

```
using Microsoft.Extensions.Hosting;
using Microsoft.Extensions.Configuration;
using Microsoft.EntityFrameworkCore;
using SportsStore.Models;

namespace SportsStore {
    public class Startup {

        public Startup(IConfiguration config) {
            Configuration = config;
        }

        private IConfiguration Configuration { get; set; }

        public void ConfigureServices(IServiceCollection services) {
            services.AddControllersWithViews();
            services.AddDbContext<StoreDbContext>(opts => {
                opts.UseSqlServer(
                    Configuration["ConnectionStrings:SportsStoreConnection"]);
            });
            services.AddScoped<IStoreRepository, EFStoreRepository>();
            services.AddRazorPages();
            services.AddDistributedMemoryCache();
            services.AddSession();
        }

        public void Configure(IApplicationBuilder app, IWebHostEnvironment env) {
            app.UseDeveloperExceptionPage();
            app.UseStatusCodePages();
            app.UseStaticFiles();
            app.UseSession();
            app.UseRouting();
            app.UseEndpoints(endpoints => {
                endpoints.MapControllerRoute("catpage",
                    "{category}/Page{productPage:int}",
                    new { Controller = "Home", action = "Index" });

                endpoints.MapControllerRoute("page", "Page{productPage:int}",
                    new { Controller = "Home", action = "Index", productPage = 1 });

                endpoints.MapControllerRoute("category", "{category}",
                    new { Controller = "Home", action = "Index", productPage = 1 });

                endpoints.MapControllerRoute("pagination",
                    "Products/Page{productPage}",
                    new { Controller = "Home", action = "Index", productPage = 1 });
                endpoints.MapDefaultControllerRoute();
                endpoints.MapRazorPages();
            });

            SeedData.EnsurePopulated(app);
        }
    }
}
```

The AddDistributedMemoryCache method call sets up the in-memory data store. The AddSession method registers the services used to access session data, and the UseSession method allows the session system to automatically associate requests with sessions when they arrive from the client.

Implementing the Cart Feature

Now that the preparations are complete, I can implement the cart features. I started by adding a class file called Cart.cs to the Models folder in the SportsStore project and used it to define the classes shown in Listing 8-22.

Listing 8-22. The Contents of the Cart.cs File in the SportsStore/Models Folder

```
using System.Collections.Generic;
using System.Linq;

namespace SportsStore.Models {

    public class Cart {

        public List<CartLine> Lines { get; set; } = new List<CartLine>();

        public void AddItem(Product product, int quantity) {
            CartLine line = Lines
                .Where(p => p.Product.ProductID == product.ProductID)
                .FirstOrDefault();

            if (line == null) {
                Lines.Add(new CartLine {
                    Product = product,
                    Quantity = quantity
                });
            } else {
                line.Quantity += quantity;
            }
        }

        public void RemoveLine(Product product) =>
            Lines.RemoveAll(l => l.Product.ProductID == product.ProductID);

        public decimal ComputeTotalValue() =>
            Lines.Sum(e => e.Product.Price * e.Quantity);

        public void Clear() => Lines.Clear();
    }

    public class CartLine {
        public int CartLineID { get; set; }
        public Product Product { get; set; }
        public int Quantity { get; set; }
    }
}
```

The Cart class uses the CartLine class, defined in the same file, to represent a product selected by the customer and the quantity the user wants to buy. I defined methods to add an item to the cart, remove a previously added item from the cart, calculate the total cost of the items in the cart, and reset the cart by removing all the items.

UNIT TEST: TESTING THE CART

The Cart class is relatively simple, but it has a range of important behaviors that must work properly. A poorly functioning cart would undermine the entire SportsStore application. I have broken down the features and tested them individually. I created a new unit test file called CartTests.cs in the SportsStore.Tests project to contain these tests.

The first behavior relates to when I add an item to the cart. If this is the first time that a given `Product` has been added to the cart, I want a new `CartLine` to be added. Here is the test, including the unit test class definition:

```
using System.Linq;
using SportsStore.Models;
using Xunit;

namespace SportsStore.Tests {

    public class CartTests {

        [Fact]
        public void Can_Add_New_Lines() {

            // Arrange - create some test products
            Product p1 = new Product { ProductID = 1, Name = "P1" };
            Product p2 = new Product { ProductID = 2, Name = "P2" };

            // Arrange - create a new cart
            Cart target = new Cart();

            // Act
            target.AddItem(p1, 1);
            target.AddItem(p2, 1);
            CartLine[] results = target.Lines.ToArray();

            // Assert
            Assert.Equal(2, results.Length);
            Assert.Equal(p1, results[0].Product);
            Assert.Equal(p2, results[1].Product);
        }
    }
}
```

However, if the customer has already added a `Product` to the cart, I want to increment the quantity of the corresponding `CartLine` and not create a new one. Here is the test:

```
...
[Fact]
public void Can_Add_Quantity_For_Existing_Lines() {
    // Arrange - create some test products
    Product p1 = new Product { ProductID = 1, Name = "P1" };
    Product p2 = new Product { ProductID = 2, Name = "P2" };

    // Arrange - create a new cart
    Cart target = new Cart();

    // Act
    target.AddItem(p1, 1);
    target.AddItem(p2, 1);
    target.AddItem(p1, 10);
    CartLine[] results = target.Lines
        .OrderBy(c => c.Product.ProductID).ToArray();

    // Assert
    Assert.Equal(2, results.Length);
    Assert.Equal(11, results[0].Quantity);
    Assert.Equal(1, results[1].Quantity);
}
...
```

I also need to check that users can change their mind and remove products from the cart. This feature is implemented by the RemoveLine method. Here is the test:

```
...
[Fact]
public void Can_Remove_Line() {
    // Arrange - create some test products
    Product p1 = new Product { ProductID = 1, Name = "P1" };
    Product p2 = new Product { ProductID = 2, Name = "P2" };
    Product p3 = new Product { ProductID = 3, Name = "P3" };

    // Arrange - create a new cart
    Cart target = new Cart();
    // Arrange - add some products to the cart
    target.AddItem(p1, 1);
    target.AddItem(p2, 3);
    target.AddItem(p3, 5);
    target.AddItem(p2, 1);

    // Act
    target.RemoveLine(p2);

    // Assert
    Assert.Empty(target.Lines.Where(c => c.Product == p2));
    Assert.Equal(2, target.Lines.Count());
}
...
```

The next behavior I want to test is the ability to calculate the total cost of the items in the cart. Here's the test for this behavior:

```
...
[Fact]
public void Calculate_Cart_Total() {
    // Arrange - create some test products
    Product p1 = new Product { ProductID = 1, Name = "P1", Price = 100M };
    Product p2 = new Product { ProductID = 2, Name = "P2", Price = 50M };

    // Arrange - create a new cart
    Cart target = new Cart();

    // Act
    target.AddItem(p1, 1);
    target.AddItem(p2, 1);
    target.AddItem(p1, 3);
    decimal result = target.ComputeTotalValue();

    // Assert
    Assert.Equal(450M, result);
}
...
```

The final test is simple. I want to ensure that the contents of the cart are properly removed when reset. Here is the test:

```
...
[Fact]
public void Can_Clear_Contents() {
    // Arrange - create some test products
    Product p1 = new Product { ProductID = 1, Name = "P1", Price = 100M };
    Product p2 = new Product { ProductID = 2, Name = "P2", Price = 50M };

    // Arrange - create a new cart
    Cart target = new Cart();
```

```
    // Arrange - add some items
    target.AddItem(p1, 1);
    target.AddItem(p2, 1);

    // Act - reset the cart
    target.Clear();

    // Assert
    Assert.Empty(target.Lines);
}
...
```

Sometimes, as in this case, the code required to test the functionality of a class is longer and more complex than the class itself. Do not let that put you off writing the unit tests. Defects in simple classes can have huge impacts, especially ones that play such an important role as Cart does in the example application.

Defining Session State Extension Methods

The session state feature in ASP.NET Core stores only int, string, and byte[ ] values. Since I want to store a Cart object, I need to define extension methods to the ISession interface, which provides access to the session state data to serialize Cart objects into JSON and convert them back. I added a class file called SessionExtensions.cs to the Infrastructure folder and defined the extension methods shown in Listing 8-23.

Listing 8-23. The Contents of the SessionExtensions.cs File in the SportsStore/Infrastructure Folder

```
using Microsoft.AspNetCore.Http;
using System.Text.Json;

namespace SportsStore.Infrastructure {

    public static class SessionExtensions {

        public static void SetJson(this ISession session, string key, object value) {
            session.SetString(key, JsonSerializer.Serialize(value));
        }

        public static T GetJson<T>(this ISession session, string key) {
            var sessionData = session.GetString(key);
            return sessionData == null
                ? default(T) : JsonSerializer.Deserialize<T>(sessionData);
        }
    }
}
```

These methods serialize objects into the JavaScript Object Notation format, making it easy to store and retrieve Cart objects.

Completing the Razor Page

The Cart Razor Page will receive the HTTP POST request that the browser sends when the user clicks an Add To Cart button. It will use the request form data to get the Product object from the database and use it to update the user's cart, which will be stored as session data for use by future requests. Listing 8-24 implements these features.

Listing 8-24. Handling Requests in the Cart.cshtml File in the SportsStore/Pages Folder

```
@page
@model CartModel

<h2>Your cart</h2>
<table class="table table-bordered table-striped">
    <thead>
        <tr>
            <th>Quantity</th>
            <th>Item</th>
            <th class="text-right">Price</th>
            <th class="text-right">Subtotal</th>
        </tr>
    </thead>
    <tbody>
        @foreach (var line in Model.Cart.Lines) {
            <tr>
                <td class="text-center">@line.Quantity</td>
                <td class="text-left">@line.Product.Name</td>
                <td class="text-right">@line.Product.Price.ToString("c")</td>
                <td class="text-right">
                    @((line.Quantity * line.Product.Price).ToString("c"))
                </td>
            </tr>
        }
    </tbody>
    <tfoot>
        <tr>
            <td colspan="3" class="text-right">Total:</td>
            <td class="text-right">
                @Model.Cart.ComputeTotalValue().ToString("c")
            </td>
        </tr>
    </tfoot>
</table>

<div class="text-center">
    <a class="btn btn-primary" href="@Model.ReturnUrl">Continue shopping</a>
</div>
```

Razor Pages allow HTML content, Razor expressions, and code to be combined in a single file, as I explain in Chapter 23, but if you want to unit test a Razor Page, then you need to use a separate class file. If you are using Visual Studio, there will already be a class file named Cart.cshtml.cs in the Pages folder, which was created by the Razor Page template item. If you are using Visual Studio Code, you will need to create the class file separately. Use the class file, however it has been created, to define the class shown in Listing 8-25.

Listing 8-25. The Contents of the Cart.cshtml.cs File in the SportsStore/Pages Folder

```
using Microsoft.AspNetCore.Mvc;
using Microsoft.AspNetCore.Mvc.RazorPages;
using SportsStore.Infrastructure;
using SportsStore.Models;
using System.Linq;

namespace SportsStore.Pages {
```

```
public class CartModel : PageModel {
    private IStoreRepository repository;

    public CartModel(IStoreRepository repo) {
        repository = repo;
    }

    public Cart Cart { get; set; }
    public string ReturnUrl { get; set; }

    public void OnGet(string returnUrl) {
        ReturnUrl = returnUrl ?? "/";
        Cart = HttpContext.Session.GetJson<Cart>("cart") ?? new Cart();
    }

    public IActionResult OnPost(long productId, string returnUrl) {
        Product product = repository.Products
            .FirstOrDefault(p => p.ProductID == productId);
        Cart = HttpContext.Session.GetJson<Cart>("cart") ?? new Cart();
        Cart.AddItem(product, 1);
        HttpContext.Session.SetJson("cart", Cart);
        return RedirectToPage(new { returnUrl = returnUrl });
    }
}
```

}

The class associated with a Razor Page is known as its page model class, and it defines handler methods that are invoked for different types of HTTP requests, which update state before rendering the view. The page model class in Listing 8-25, which is named CartModel, defines an OnPost hander method, which is invoked to handle HTTP POST requests. It does this by retrieving a Product from the database, retrieving the user's Cart from the session data, and updating its content using the Product. The modified Cart is stored, and the browser is redirected to the same Razor Page, which it will do using a GET request (which prevents reloading the browser from triggering a duplicate POST request).

The GET request is handled by the OnGet handler method, which sets the values of the ReturnUrl and Cart properties, after which the Razor content section of the page is rendered. The expressions in the HTML content are evaluated using the CartModel as the view model object, which means that the values assigned to the ReturnUrl and Cart properties can be accessed within the expressions. The content generated by the Razor Page details the products added to the user's cart and provides a button to navigate back to the point where the product was added to the cart.

The handler methods use parameter names that match the input elements in the HTML forms produced by the ProductSummary.cshtml view. This allows ASP.NET Core to associate incoming form POST variables with those parameters, meaning I do not need to process the form directly. This is known as *model binding* and is a powerful tool for simplifying development, as I explain in detail in Chapter 28.

UNDERSTANDING RAZOR PAGES

Razor Pages can feel a little odd when you first start using them, especially if you have previous experience with the MVC Framework features provided by ASP.NET Core. But Razor Pages are complementary to the MVC Framework, and I find myself using them alongside controllers and views because they are well-suited to self-contained features that don't require the complexity of the MVC Framework. I describe Razor Pages in Chapter 23 and show their use alongside controllers throughout Part 3 and Part 4 of this book.

The result is that the basic functions of the shopping cart are in place. First, products are listed along with a button to add them to the cart, which you can see by restarting ASP.NET Core and requesting http://localhost:5000, as shown in Figure 8-10.

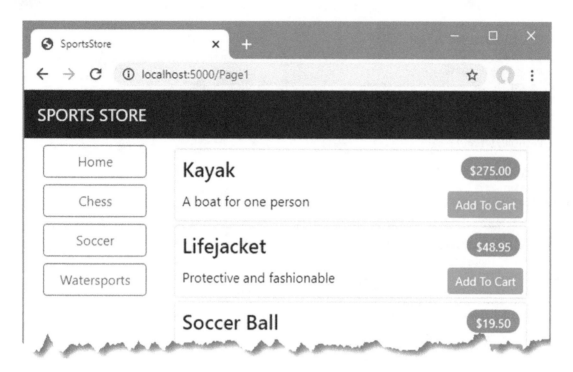

Figure 8-10. *The Add To Cart buttons*

Second, when the user clicks an Add To Cart button, the appropriate product is added to their cart, and a summary of the cart is displayed, as shown in Figure 8-11. Clicking the Continue Shopping button returns the user to the product page they came from.

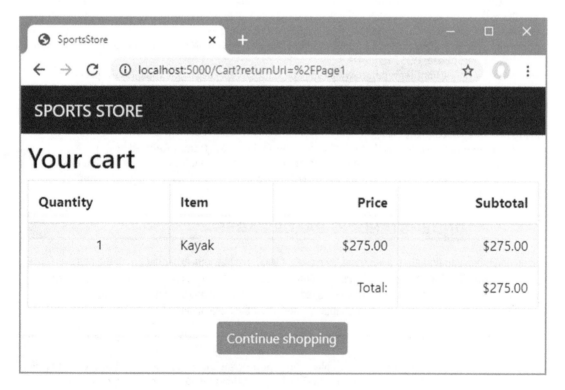

Figure 8-11. *Displaying the contents of the shopping cart*

UNIT TESTING: RAZOR PAGES

Testing Razor Pages can require a lot of mocking to create the context objects that the page model class requires. To test the behavior of the OnGet method defined by the CartModel class, I added a class file named CartPageTests.cs to the SportsStore.Tests project and defined this test:

```
using Microsoft.AspNetCore.Http;
using Microsoft.AspNetCore.Mvc;
using Microsoft.AspNetCore.Mvc.RazorPages;
using Microsoft.AspNetCore.Routing;
using Moq;
using SportsStore.Models;
using SportsStore.Pages;
using System.Linq;
using System.Text;
using System.Text.Json;
using Xunit;

namespace SportsStore.Tests {

    public class CartPageTests {

        [Fact]
        public void Can_Load_Cart() {

            // Arrange
            // - create a mock repository
            Product p1 = new Product { ProductID = 1, Name = "P1" };
            Product p2 = new Product { ProductID = 2, Name = "P2" };
            Mock<IStoreRepository> mockRepo = new Mock<IStoreRepository>();
            mockRepo.Setup(m => m.Products).Returns((new Product[] {
                p1, p2
            }).AsQueryable<Product>());

            // - create a cart
            Cart testCart = new Cart();
            testCart.AddItem(p1, 2);
            testCart.AddItem(p2, 1);
            // - create a mock page context and session
            Mock<ISession> mockSession = new Mock<ISession>();
            byte[] data =
                Encoding.UTF8.GetBytes(JsonSerializer.Serialize(testCart));
            mockSession.Setup(c => c.TryGetValue(It.IsAny<string>(), out data));
            Mock<HttpContext> mockContext = new Mock<HttpContext>();
            mockContext.SetupGet(c => c.Session).Returns(mockSession.Object);

            // Action
            CartModel cartModel = new CartModel(mockRepo.Object) {
                PageContext = new PageContext(new ActionContext {
                    HttpContext = mockContext.Object,
                    RouteData = new RouteData(),
                    ActionDescriptor = new PageActionDescriptor()
                })
            };
            cartModel.OnGet("myUrl");

            //Assert
            Assert.Equal(2, cartModel.Cart.Lines.Count());
            Assert.Equal("myUrl", cartModel.ReturnUrl);
        }
    }
}
```

I am not going to describe these unit tests in detail because there is a simpler way to perform these tests, which I explain in the next chapter. The complexity in this test is mocking the ISession interface so that the page model class can use extension methods to retrieve a JSON representation of a Cart object. The ISession interface only stored byte arrays, and getting and deserializing a string is performed by extension methods. Once the mock objects are defined, they can be wrapped in context objects and used to configure an instance of the page model class, which can be subjected to tests.

The process of testing the OnPost method of the page model class means capturing the byte array that is passed to the ISession interface mock and then deserializing it to ensure that it contains the expected content. Here is the unit test I added to the CartTestsPage class:

```
...
[Fact]
public void Can_Update_Cart() {
    // Arrange
    // - create a mock repository
    Mock<IStoreRepository> mockRepo = new Mock<IStoreRepository>();
    mockRepo.Setup(m => m.Products).Returns((new Product[] {
        new Product { ProductID = 1, Name = "P1" }
    }).AsQueryable<Product>());

    Cart testCart = new Cart();

    Mock<ISession> mockSession = new Mock<ISession>();
    mockSession.Setup(s => s.Set(It.IsAny<string>(), It.IsAny<byte[]>()))
        .Callback<string, byte[]>((key, val) => {
            testCart =
                JsonSerializer.Deserialize<Cart>(Encoding.UTF8.GetString(val));
        });

    Mock<HttpContext> mockContext = new Mock<HttpContext>();
    mockContext.SetupGet(c => c.Session).Returns(mockSession.Object);

    // Action
    CartModel cartModel = new CartModel(mockRepo.Object) {
        PageContext = new PageContext(new ActionContext {
            HttpContext = mockContext.Object,
            RouteData = new RouteData(),
            ActionDescriptor = new PageActionDescriptor()
        })
    };
    cartModel.OnPost(1, "myUrl");

    //Assert
    Assert.Single(testCart.Lines);
    Assert.Equal("P1", testCart.Lines.First().Product.Name);
    Assert.Equal(1, testCart.Lines.First().Quantity);
}
...
```

Patience and a little experimentation are required to write effective unit tests, especially when the feature you are testing operates on the context objects that ASP.NET Core provides.

Summary

In this chapter, I started to flesh out the customer-facing parts of the SportsStore app. I provided the means by which the user can navigate by category and put the basic building blocks in place for adding items to a shopping cart. I have more work to do, and I continue the development of the application in the next chapter.

CHAPTER 9

SportsStore: Completing the Cart

In this chapter, I continue to build the SportsStore example app. In the previous chapter, I added the basic support for a shopping cart, and now I am going to improve on and complete that functionality.

■ **Tip** You can download the example project for this chapter—and for all the other chapters in this book—from `https://github.com/apress/pro-asp.net-core-3`. See Chapter 1 for how to get help if you have problems running the examples.

Refining the Cart Model with a Service

I defined a `Cart` model class in the previous chapter and demonstrated how it can be stored using the session feature, allowing the user to build up a set of products for purchase. The responsibility for managing the persistence of the `Cart` class fell to the `Cart` Razor Page, which has to deal with getting and storing `Cart` objects as session data.

The problem with this approach is that I will have to duplicate the code that obtains and stores `Cart` objects in any other Razor Page or controller that uses them. In this section, I am going to use the services feature that sits at the heart of ASP.NET Core to simplify the way that `Cart` objects are managed, freeing individual components such as the `Cart` controller from needing to deal with the details directly.

Services are commonly used to hide details of how interfaces are implemented from the components that depend on them. But services can be used to solve lots of other problems as well and can be used to shape and reshape an application, even when you are working with concrete classes such as `Cart`.

Creating a Storage-Aware Cart Class

The first step in tidying up the way that the `Cart` class is used will be to create a subclass that is aware of how to store itself using session state. To prepare, I apply the `virtual` keyword to the `Cart` class, as shown in Listing 9-1, so that I can override the members.

Listing 9-1. Applying the Virtual Keyword in the Cart.cs File in the SportsStore/Models Folder

```
using System.Collections.Generic;
using System.Linq;

namespace SportsStore.Models {

    public class Cart {

        public List<CartLine> Lines { get; set; } = new List<CartLine>();

        public virtual void AddItem(Product product, int quantity) {
            CartLine line = Lines
                .Where(p => p.Product.ProductID == product.ProductID)
                .FirstOrDefault();
```

```
            if (line == null) {
                Lines.Add(new CartLine {
                    Product = product,
                    Quantity = quantity
                });
            } else {
                line.Quantity += quantity;
            }
        }

        public virtual void RemoveLine(Product product) =>
            Lines.RemoveAll(l => l.Product.ProductID == product.ProductID);

        public decimal ComputeTotalValue() =>
            Lines.Sum(e => e.Product.Price * e.Quantity);

        public virtual void Clear() => Lines.Clear();
    }

    public class CartLine {
        public int CartLineID { get; set; }
        public Product Product { get; set; }
        public int Quantity { get; set; }
    }
}
```

Next, I added a class file called SessionCart.cs to the Models folder and used it to define the class shown in Listing 9-2.

Listing 9-2. The Contents of the SessionCart.cs File in the SportsStore/Models Folder

```
using System;
using System.Text.Json.Serialization;
using Microsoft.AspNetCore.Http;
using Microsoft.Extensions.DependencyInjection;
using SportsStore.Infrastructure;

namespace SportsStore.Models {

    public class SessionCart : Cart {

        public static Cart GetCart(IServiceProvider services) {
            ISession session = services.GetRequiredService<IHttpContextAccessor>()?
                .HttpContext.Session;
            SessionCart cart = session?.GetJson<SessionCart>("Cart")
                ?? new SessionCart();
            cart.Session = session;
            return cart;
        }

        [JsonIgnore]
        public ISession Session { get; set; }

        public override void AddItem(Product product, int quantity) {
            base.AddItem(product, quantity);
            Session.SetJson("Cart", this);
        }
```

```
public override void RemoveLine(Product product) {
    base.RemoveLine(product);
    Session.SetJson("Cart", this);
}

public override void Clear() {
    base.Clear();
    Session.Remove("Cart");
}
    }
}
```

The SessionCart class subclasses the Cart class and overrides the AddItem, RemoveLine, and Clear methods so they call the base implementations and then store the updated state in the session using the extension methods on the ISession interface. The static GetCart method is a factory for creating SessionCart objects and providing them with an ISession object so they can store themselves.

Getting hold of the ISession object is a little complicated. I obtain an instance of the IHttpContextAccessor service, which provides me with access to an HttpContext object that, in turn, provides me with the ISession. This indirect approach is required because the session isn't provided as a regular service.

Registering the Service

The next step is to create a service for the Cart class. My goal is to satisfy requests for Cart objects with SessionCart objects that will seamlessly store themselves. You can see how I created the service in Listing 9-3.

Listing 9-3. Creating the Cart Service in the Startup.cs File in the SportsStore Folder

```
using System;
using System.Collections.Generic;
using System.Linq;
using System.Threading.Tasks;
using Microsoft.AspNetCore.Builder;
using Microsoft.AspNetCore.Hosting;
using Microsoft.AspNetCore.Http;
using Microsoft.Extensions.DependencyInjection;
using Microsoft.Extensions.Hosting;
using Microsoft.Extensions.Configuration;
using Microsoft.EntityFrameworkCore;
using SportsStore.Models;

namespace SportsStore {
    public class Startup {

        public Startup(IConfiguration config) {
            Configuration = config;
        }

        private IConfiguration Configuration { get; set; }

        public void ConfigureServices(IServiceCollection services) {
            services.AddControllersWithViews();
            services.AddDbContext<StoreDbContext>(opts => {
                opts.UseSqlServer(
                    Configuration["ConnectionStrings:SportsStoreConnection"]);
            });
            services.AddScoped<IStoreRepository, EFStoreRepository>();
            services.AddRazorPages();
```

```
            services.AddDistributedMemoryCache();
            services.AddSession();
            services.AddScoped<Cart>(sp => SessionCart.GetCart(sp));
            services.AddSingleton<IHttpContextAccessor, HttpContextAccessor>();
        }

        public void Configure(IApplicationBuilder app, IWebHostEnvironment env) {
            app.UseDeveloperExceptionPage();
            app.UseStatusCodePages();
            app.UseStaticFiles();
            app.UseSession();
            app.UseRouting();
            app.UseEndpoints(endpoints => {
                endpoints.MapControllerRoute("catpage",
                    "{category}/Page{productPage:int}",
                    new { Controller = "Home", action = "Index" });

                endpoints.MapControllerRoute("page", "Page{productPage:int}",
                    new { Controller = "Home", action = "Index", productPage = 1 });

                endpoints.MapControllerRoute("category", "{category}",
                    new { Controller = "Home", action = "Index", productPage = 1 });

                endpoints.MapControllerRoute("pagination",
                    "Products/Page{productPage}",
                    new { Controller = "Home", action = "Index", productPage = 1 });
                endpoints.MapDefaultControllerRoute();
                endpoints.MapRazorPages();
            });

            SeedData.EnsurePopulated(app);
        }
    }
}
```

The AddScoped method specifies that the same object should be used to satisfy related requests for Cart instances. How requests are related can be configured, but by default, it means that any Cart required by components handling the same HTTP request will receive the same object.

Rather than provide the AddScoped method with a type mapping, as I did for the repository, I have specified a lambda expression that will be invoked to satisfy Cart requests. The expression receives the collection of services that have been registered and passes the collection to the GetCart method of the SessionCart class. The result is that requests for the Cart service will be handled by creating SessionCart objects, which will serialize themselves as session data when they are modified.

I also added a service using the AddSingleton method, which specifies that the same object should always be used. The service I created tells ASP.NET Core to use the HttpContextAccessor class when implementations of the IHttpContextAccessor interface are required. This service is required so I can access the current session in the SessionCart class.

Simplifying the Cart Razor Page

The benefit of creating this kind of service is that it allows me to simplify the code where Cart objects are used. In Listing 9-4, I have reworked the page model class for the Cart Razor Page to take advantage of the new service.

Listing 9-4. Using the Cart Service in the Cart.cshtml.cs File in the SportsStore/Pages Folder

```
using Microsoft.AspNetCore.Mvc;
using Microsoft.AspNetCore.Mvc.RazorPages;
using SportsStore.Infrastructure;
using SportsStore.Models;
using System.Linq;
```

```
namespace SportsStore.Pages {

    public class CartModel : PageModel {
        private IStoreRepository repository;

        public CartModel(IStoreRepository repo, Cart cartService) {
            repository = repo;
            Cart = cartService;
        }

        public Cart Cart { get; set; }
        public string ReturnUrl { get; set; }

        public void OnGet(string returnUrl) {
            ReturnUrl = returnUrl ?? "/";
        }

        public IActionResult OnPost(long productId, string returnUrl) {
            Product product = repository.Products
                .FirstOrDefault(p => p.ProductID == productId);
            Cart.AddItem(product, 1);
            return RedirectToPage(new { returnUrl = returnUrl });
        }
    }
}
```

The page model class indicates that it needs a Cart object by declaring a constructor argument, which has allowed me to remove the statements that load and store sessions from the handler methods. The result is a simpler page model class that focuses on its role in the application without having to worry about how Cart objects are created or persisted. And, since services are available throughout the application, any component can get hold of the user's cart using the same technique.

UPDATING THE UNIT TESTS

The simplification of the CartModel class in Listing 9-4 requires a corresponding change to the unit tests in the CartPageTests.cs file in the unit test project so that the Cart is provided as a constructor argument and not accessed through the context objects. Here is the change to the test for reading the cart:

```
...
[Fact]
public void Can_Load_Cart() {

    // Arrange
    // - create a mock repository
    Product p1 = new Product { ProductID = 1, Name = "P1" };
    Product p2 = new Product { ProductID = 2, Name = "P2" };
    Mock<IStoreRepository> mockRepo = new Mock<IStoreRepository>();
    mockRepo.Setup(m => m.Products).Returns((new Product[] {
        p1, p2
    }).AsQueryable<Product>());

    // - create a cart
    Cart testCart = new Cart();
    testCart.AddItem(p1, 2);
    testCart.AddItem(p2, 1);

    // Action
    CartModel cartModel = new CartModel(mockRepo.Object, testCart);
    cartModel.OnGet("myUrl");
```

```
    //Assert
    Assert.Equal(2, cartModel.Cart.Lines.Count());
    Assert.Equal("myUrl", cartModel.ReturnUrl);
}
...
```

I applied the same change to the unit test that checks changes to the cart:

```
...
[Fact]
public void Can_Update_Cart() {
    // Arrange
    // - create a mock repository
    Mock<IStoreRepository> mockRepo = new Mock<IStoreRepository>();
    mockRepo.Setup(m => m.Products).Returns((new Product[] {
        new Product { ProductID = 1, Name = "P1" }
    }).AsQueryable<Product>());

    Cart testCart = new Cart();

    // Action
    CartModel cartModel = new CartModel(mockRepo.Object, testCart);
    cartModel.OnPost(1, "myUrl");

    //Assert
    Assert.Single(testCart.Lines);
    Assert.Equal("P1", testCart.Lines.First().Product.Name);
    Assert.Equal(1, testCart.Lines.First().Quantity);
}
...
```

Using services simplifies the testing process and makes it much easier to provide the class being tested with its dependencies.

Completing the Cart Functionality

Now that I have introduced the Cart service, it is time to complete the cart functionality by adding two new features. The first will allow the customer to remove an item from the cart. The second feature will display a summary of the cart at the top of the page.

Removing Items from the Cart

To remove items from the cart, I need to add a Remove button to the content rendered by the Cart Razor Page that will submit an HTTP POST request. The changes are shown in Listing 9-5.

Listing 9-5. Removing Cart Items in the Cart.cshtml File in the SportsStore/Pages Folder

```
@page
@model CartModel

<h2>Your cart</h2>
<table class="table table-bordered table-striped">
    <thead>
        <tr>
            <th>Quantity</th>
            <th>Item</th>
            <th class="text-right">Price</th>
            <th class="text-right">Subtotal</th>
            <th></th>
        </tr>
    </thead>
```

```
<tbody>
    @foreach (var line in Model.Cart.Lines) {
        <tr>
            <td class="text-center">@line.Quantity</td>
            <td class="text-left">@line.Product.Name</td>
            <td class="text-right">@line.Product.Price.ToString("c")</td>
            <td class="text-right">
                @((line.Quantity * line.Product.Price).ToString("c"))
            </td>
            <td class="text-center">
                <form asp-page-handler="Remove" method="post">
                    <input type="hidden" name="ProductID"
                            value="@line.Product.ProductID" />
                    <input type="hidden" name="returnUrl"
                            value="@Model.ReturnUrl" />
                    <button type="submit" class="btn btn-sm btn-danger">
                        Remove
                    </button>
                </form>
            </td>
        </tr>
    }
</tbody>
<tfoot>
    <tr>
        <td colspan="3" class="text-right">Total:</td>
        <td class="text-right">
            @Model.Cart.ComputeTotalValue().ToString("c")
        </td>
    </tr>
</tfoot>
</table>

<div class="text-center">
    <a class="btn btn-primary" href="@Model.ReturnUrl">Continue shopping</a>
</div>
```

The button requires a new handler method in the page model class that will receive the request and modify the cart, as shown in Listing 9-6.

Listing 9-6. Removing an Item in the Cart.cshtml.cs File in the SportsStore/Pages Folder

```
using Microsoft.AspNetCore.Mvc;
using Microsoft.AspNetCore.Mvc.RazorPages;
using SportsStore.Infrastructure;
using SportsStore.Models;
using System.Linq;

namespace SportsStore.Pages {

    public class CartModel : PageModel {
        private IStoreRepository repository;

        public CartModel(IStoreRepository repo, Cart cartService) {
            repository = repo;
            Cart = cartService;
        }
```

```
        public Cart Cart { get; set; }
        public string ReturnUrl { get; set; }

        public void OnGet(string returnUrl) {
            ReturnUrl = returnUrl ?? "/";
        }

        public IActionResult OnPost(long productId, string returnUrl) {
            Product product = repository.Products
                .FirstOrDefault(p => p.ProductID == productId);
            Cart.AddItem(product, 1);
            return RedirectToPage(new { returnUrl = returnUrl });
        }

        public IActionResult OnPostRemove(long productId, string returnUrl) {
            Cart.RemoveLine(Cart.Lines.First(cl =>
                cl.Product.ProductID == productId).Product);
            return RedirectToPage(new { returnUrl = returnUrl });
        }
    }
}
```

The new HTML content defines an HTML form. The handler method that will receive the request is specified with the asp-page-handler tag helper attribute, like this:

```
...
<form asp-page-handler="Remove" method="post">
...
```

The specified name is prefixed with On and given a suffix that matches the request type so that a value of Remove selects the OnRemovePost handler method. The handler method uses the value it receives to locate the item in the cart and remove it.

Restart ASP.NET Core and request http://localhost:5000. Click the Add To Cart buttons to add items to the cart and then click a Remove button. The cart will be updated to remove the item you specified, as shown in Figure 9-1.

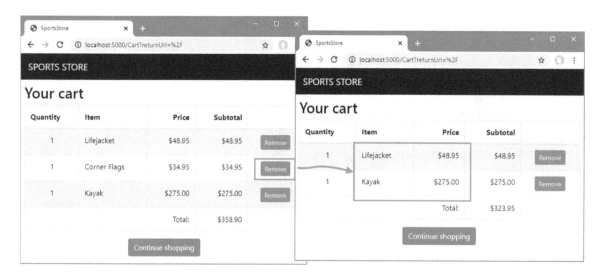

Figure 9-1. *Removing items from the shopping cart*

Adding the Cart Summary Widget

I may have a functioning cart, but there is an issue with the way it is integrated into the interface. Customers can tell what is in their cart only by viewing the cart summary screen. And they can view the cart summary screen only by adding a new item to the cart.

To solve this problem, I am going to add a widget that summarizes the contents of the cart and that can be clicked to display the cart contents throughout the application. I will do this in much the same way that I added the navigation widget—as a view component whose output I can include in a Razor layout.

Adding the Font Awesome Package

As part of the cart summary, I am going to display a button that allows the user to check out. Rather than display the word *checkout* in the button, I want to use a cart symbol. Since I have no artistic skills, I am going to use the Font Awesome package, which is an excellent set of open source icons that are integrated into applications as fonts, where each character in the font is a different image. You can learn more about Font Awesome, including inspecting the icons it contains, at http://fortawesome.github.io/Font-Awesome.

To install the client-side package, use a PowerShell command prompt to run the command shown in Listing 9-7 in the SportsStore project.

Listing 9-7. Installing the Icon Package

```
libman install font-awesome@5.12.0 -d wwwroot/lib/font-awesome
```

Creating the View Component Class and View

I added a class file called CartSummaryViewComponent.cs in the Components folder and used it to define the view component shown in Listing 9-8.

Listing 9-8. The Contents of the CartSummaryViewComponent.cs File in the SportsStore/Components Folder

```
using Microsoft.AspNetCore.Mvc;
using SportsStore.Models;

namespace SportsStore.Components {

    public class CartSummaryViewComponent : ViewComponent {
        private Cart cart;

        public CartSummaryViewComponent(Cart cartService) {
            cart = cartService;
        }

        public IViewComponentResult Invoke() {
            return View(cart);
        }
    }
}
```

This view component is able to take advantage of the service that I created earlier in the chapter to receive a Cart object as a constructor argument. The result is a simple view component class that passes on the Cart to the View method to generate the fragment of HTML that will be included in the layout. To create the view for the component, I created the Views/Shared/Components/CartSummary folder and added to it a Razor View named Default.cshtml with the content shown in Listing 9-9.

Listing 9-9. The Default.cshtml File in the Views/Shared/Components/CartSummary Folder

```
@model Cart

<div class="">
    @if (Model.Lines.Count() > 0) {
        <small class="navbar-text">
            <b>Your cart:</b>
```

```
                @Model.Lines.Sum(x => x.Quantity) item(s)
                @Model.ComputeTotalValue().ToString("c")
            </small>
    }
    <a class="btn btn-sm btn-secondary navbar-btn" asp-page="/Cart"
        asp-route-returnurl="@ViewContext.HttpContext.Request.PathAndQuery()">
        <i class="fa fa-shopping-cart"></i>
    </a>
</div>
```

The view displays a button with the Font Awesome cart icon and, if there are items in the cart, provides a snapshot that details the number of items and their total value. Now that I have a view component and a view, I can modify the layout so that the cart summary is included in the responses generated by the Home controller, as shown in Listing 9-10.

Listing 9-10. Adding the Cart Summary in the _Layout.cshtml File in the Views/Shared Folder

```
<!DOCTYPE html>
<html>
<head>
    <meta name="viewport" content="width=device-width" />
    <title>SportsStore</title>
    <link href="/lib/twitter-bootstrap/css/bootstrap.min.css" rel="stylesheet" />
    <link href="/lib/font-awesome/css/all.min.css" rel="stylesheet" />
</head>
<body>
    <div class="bg-dark text-white p-2">
        <div class="container-fluid">
            <div class="row">
                <div class="col navbar-brand">SPORTS STORE</div>
                <div class="col-6 text-right">
                    <vc:cart-summary />
                </div>
            </div>
        </div>
    </div>
    <div class="row m-1 p-1">
        <div id="categories" class="col-3">
            <vc:navigation-menu />
        </div>
        <div class="col-9">
            @RenderBody()
        </div>
    </div>
</body>
</html>
```

You can see the cart summary by starting the application. When the cart is empty, only the checkout button is shown. If you add items to the cart, then the number of items and their combined cost are shown, as illustrated in Figure 9-2. With this addition, customers know what is in their cart and have an obvious way to check out from the store.

Figure 9-2. *Displaying a summary of the cart*

Submitting Orders

I have now reached the final customer feature in SportsStore: the ability to check out and complete an order. In the following sections, I will extend the data model to provide support for capturing the shipping details from a user and add the application support to process those details.

Creating the Model Class

I added a class file called Order.cs to the Models folder and used it to define the class shown in Listing 9-11. This is the class I will use to represent the shipping details for a customer.

Listing 9-11. The Contents of the Order.cs File in the SportsStore/Models Folder

```csharp
using System.Collections.Generic;
using System.ComponentModel.DataAnnotations;
using Microsoft.AspNetCore.Mvc.ModelBinding;

namespace SportsStore.Models {

    public class Order {

        [BindNever]
        public int OrderID { get; set; }
        [BindNever]
        public ICollection<CartLine> Lines { get; set; }

        [Required(ErrorMessage = "Please enter a name")]
        public string Name { get; set; }

        [Required(ErrorMessage = "Please enter the first address line")]
        public string Line1 { get; set; }
        public string Line2 { get; set; }
        public string Line3 { get; set; }

        [Required(ErrorMessage = "Please enter a city name")]
        public string City { get; set; }
```

```
        [Required(ErrorMessage = "Please enter a state name")]
        public string State { get; set; }

        public string Zip { get; set; }

        [Required(ErrorMessage = "Please enter a country name")]
        public string Country { get; set; }

        public bool GiftWrap { get; set; }
    }
}
```

I am using the validation attributes from the `System.ComponentModel.DataAnnotations` namespace, just as I did in Chapter 3. I describe validation further in Chapter 29.

I also use the `BindNever` attribute, which prevents the user from supplying values for these properties in an HTTP request. This is a feature of the model binding system, which I describe in Chapter 28, and it stops ASP.NET Core using values from the HTTP request to populate sensitive or important model properties.

Adding the Checkout Process

The goal is to reach the point where users are able to enter their shipping details and submit an order. To start, I need to add a Checkout button to the cart view, as shown in Listing 9-12.

Listing 9-12. Adding a Button in the Cart.cshtml File in the SportsStore/Pages Folder

```
...
<div class="text-center">
    <a class="btn btn-primary" href="@Model.ReturnUrl">Continue shopping</a>
    <a class="btn btn-primary" asp-action="Checkout" asp-controller="Order">
        Checkout
    </a>
</div>
...
```

This change generates a link that I have styled as a button and that, when clicked, calls the `Checkout` action method of the `Order` controller, which I create in the following section. To show how Razor Pages and controllers can work together, I am going to handle the order processing in a controller and then return to a Razor Page at the end of the process. To see the Checkout button, restart ASP.NET Core, request `http://localhost:5000`, and click one of the Add To Cart buttons. The new button is shown as part of the cart summary, as shown in Figure 9-3.

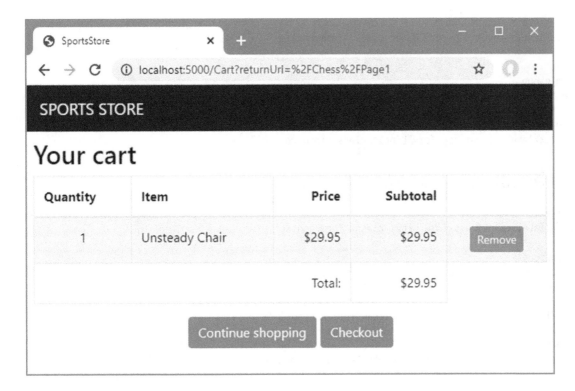

Figure 9-3. *The Checkout button*

Creating the Controller and View

I now need to define the controller that will deal with the order. I added a class file called OrderController.cs to the Controllers folder and used it to define the class shown in Listing 9-13.

Listing 9-13. The Contents of the OrderController.cs File in the SportsStore/Controllers Folder

```
using Microsoft.AspNetCore.Mvc;
using SportsStore.Models;

namespace SportsStore.Controllers {

    public class OrderController : Controller {

        public ViewResult Checkout() => View(new Order());
    }
}
```

The Checkout method returns the default view and passes a new Order object as the view model. To create the view, I created the Views/Order folder and added to it a Razor View called Checkout.cshtml with the markup shown in Listing 9-14.

Listing 9-14. The Contents of the Checkout.cshtml File in the SportsStore/Views/Order Folder

```
@model Order

<h2>Check out now</h2>
<p>Please enter your details, and we'll ship your goods right away!</p>

<form asp-action="Checkout" method="post">
    <h3>Ship to</h3>
```

```
    <div class="form-group">
        <label>Name:</label><input asp-for="Name" class="form-control" />
    </div>
    <h3>Address</h3>
    <div class="form-group">
        <label>Line 1:</label><input asp-for="Line1" class="form-control" />
    </div>
    <div class="form-group">
        <label>Line 2:</label><input asp-for="Line2" class="form-control" />
    </div>
    <div class="form-group">
        <label>Line 3:</label><input asp-for="Line3" class="form-control" />
    </div>
    <div class="form-group">
        <label>City:</label><input asp-for="City" class="form-control" />
    </div>
    <div class="form-group">
        <label>State:</label><input asp-for="State" class="form-control" />
    </div>
    <div class="form-group">
        <label>Zip:</label><input asp-for="Zip" class="form-control" />
    </div>
    <div class="form-group">
        <label>Country:</label><input asp-for="Country" class="form-control" />
    </div>
    <h3>Options</h3>
    <div class="checkbox">
        <label>
            <input asp-for="GiftWrap" /> Gift wrap these items
        </label>
    </div>
    <div class="text-center">
        <input class="btn btn-primary" type="submit" value="Complete Order" />
    </div>
</form>
```

For each of the properties in the model, I have created a label and input elements to capture the user input, styled with Bootstrap and configured using a tag helper. The asp-for attribute on the input elements is handled by a built-in tag helper that generates the type, id, name, and value attributes based on the specified model property, as described in Chapter 27.

You can see the form, shown in Figure 9-4, by restarting ASP.NET Core, requesting http://localhost:5000, adding an item to the basket, and clicking the Checkout button. Or, more directly, you can request http://localhost:5000/order/checkout.

Figure 9-4. *The shipping details form*

Implementing Order Processing

I will process orders by writing them to the database. Most e-commerce sites would not simply stop there, of course, and I have not provided support for processing credit cards or other forms of payment. But I want to keep things focused on ASP.NET Core, so a simple database entry will do.

Extending the Database

Adding a new kind of model to the database is simple because of the initial setup I went through in Chapter 7. First, I added a new property to the database context class, as shown in Listing 9-15.

Listing 9-15. Adding a Property in the StoreDbContext.cs File in the SportsStore/Models Folder

```
using Microsoft.EntityFrameworkCore;

namespace SportsStore.Models {
    public class StoreDbContext: DbContext {

        public StoreDbContext(DbContextOptions<StoreDbContext> options)
            : base(options) { }

        public DbSet<Product> Products { get; set; }
        public DbSet<Order> Orders { get; set; }
    }
}
```

This change is enough for Entity Framework Core to create a database migration that will allow Order objects to be stored in the database. To create the migration, use a PowerShell command prompt to run the command shown in Listing 9-16 in the SportsStore folder.

Listing 9-16. Creating a Migration

```
dotnet ef migrations add Orders
```

This command tells Entity Framework Core to take a new snapshot of the application data model, work out how it differs from the previous database version, and generate a new migration called Orders. The new migration will be applied automatically when the application starts because the SeedData calls the Migrate method provided by Entity Framework Core.

RESETTING THE DATABASE

When you are making frequent changes to the model, there will come a point when your migrations and your database schema get out of sync. The easiest thing to do is delete the database and start over. However, this applies only during development, of course, because you will lose any data you have stored. Run this command to delete the database:

```
dotnet ef database drop --force --context StoreDbContext
```

Once the database has been removed, run the following command from the SportsStore folder to re-create the database and apply the migrations you have created by running the following command:

```
dotnet ef database update --context StoreDbContext
```

The migrations will also be applied by the SeedData class if you just start the application. Either way, the database will be reset so that it accurately reflects your data model and allows you to return to developing your application.

Creating the Order Repository

I am going to follow the same pattern I used for the product repository to provide access to the Order objects. I added a class file called IOrderRepository.cs to the Models folder and used it to define the interface shown in Listing 9-17.

Listing 9-17. The Contents of the IOrderRepository.cs File in the SportsStore/Models Folder

```
using System.Linq;

namespace SportsStore.Models {

    public interface IOrderRepository {

        IQueryable<Order> Orders { get; }
        void SaveOrder(Order order);
    }
}
```

To implement the order repository interface, I added a class file called EFOrderRepository.cs to the Models folder and defined the class shown in Listing 9-18.

Listing 9-18. The Contents of the EFOrderRepository.cs File in the SportsStore/Models Folder

```
using Microsoft.EntityFrameworkCore;
using System.Linq;

namespace SportsStore.Models {

    public class EFOrderRepository : IOrderRepository {
        private StoreDbContext context;

        public EFOrderRepository(StoreDbContext ctx) {
            context = ctx;
        }

        public IQueryable<Order> Orders => context.Orders
                        .Include(o => o.Lines)
                        .ThenInclude(l => l.Product);

        public void SaveOrder(Order order) {
            context.AttachRange(order.Lines.Select(l => l.Product));
            if (order.OrderID == 0) {
                context.Orders.Add(order);
            }
            context.SaveChanges();
        }
    }
}
```

This class implements the IOrderRepository interface using Entity Framework Core, allowing the set of Order objects that have been stored to be retrieved and allowing for orders to be created or changed.

UNDERSTANDING THE ORDER REPOSITORY

Entity Framework Core requires instruction to load related data if it spans multiple tables. In Listing 9-18, I used the Include and ThenInclude methods to specify that when an Order object is read from the database, the collection associated with the Lines property should also be loaded along with each Product object associated with each collection object.

```
...
public IQueryable<Order> Orders => context.Orders
    .Include(o => o.Lines)
    .ThenInclude(l => l.Product);
...
```

This ensures that I receive all the data objects that I need without having to perform separate queries and then assemble the data myself.

An additional step is also required when I store an Order object in the database. When the user's cart data is de-serialized from the session store, new objects are created that are not known to Entity Framework Core, which then tries to write all the objects into the database. For the Product objects associated with an Order, this means that Entity Framework Core tries to write objects that have already been stored, which causes an error. To avoid this problem, I notify Entity Framework Core that the objects exist and shouldn't be stored in the database unless they are modified, as follows:

```
...
context.AttachRange(order.Lines.Select(l => l.Product));
...
```

This ensures that Entity Framework Core won't try to write the de-serialized Product objects that are associated with the Order object.

In Listing 9-19, I have registered the order repository as a service in the ConfigureServices method of the Startup class.

Listing 9-19. Registering the Order Repository Service in the Startup.cs File in the SportsStore Folder

```
...
public void ConfigureServices(IServiceCollection services) {
    services.AddControllersWithViews();
    services.AddDbContext<StoreDbContext>(opts => {
        opts.UseSqlServer(
            Configuration["ConnectionStrings:SportsStoreConnection"]);
    });
    services.AddScoped<IStoreRepository, EFStoreRepository>();
    services.AddScoped<IOrderRepository, EFOrderRepository>();
    services.AddRazorPages();
    services.AddDistributedMemoryCache();
    services.AddSession();
    services.AddScoped<Cart>(sp => SessionCart.GetCart(sp));
    services.AddSingleton<IHttpContextAccessor, HttpContextAccessor>();
}
...
```

Completing the Order Controller

To complete the OrderController class, I need to modify the constructor so that it receives the services it requires to process an order and add an action method that will handle the HTTP form POST request when the user clicks the Complete Order button. Listing 9-20 shows both changes.

Listing 9-20. Completing the Controller in the OrderController.cs File in the SportsStore/Controllers Folder

```
using Microsoft.AspNetCore.Mvc;
using SportsStore.Models;
using System.Linq;

namespace SportsStore.Controllers {
```

```
public class OrderController : Controller {
    private IOrderRepository repository;
    private Cart cart;

    public OrderController(IOrderRepository repoService, Cart cartService) {
        repository = repoService;
        cart = cartService;
    }

    public ViewResult Checkout() => View(new Order());

    [HttpPost]
    public IActionResult Checkout(Order order) {
        if (cart.Lines.Count() == 0) {
            ModelState.AddModelError("", "Sorry, your cart is empty!");
        }
        if (ModelState.IsValid) {
            order.Lines = cart.Lines.ToArray();
            repository.SaveOrder(order);
            cart.Clear();
            return RedirectToPage("/Completed", new { orderId = order.OrderID });
        } else {
            return View();
        }
    }
}
```

The Checkout action method is decorated with the HttpPost attribute, which means that it will be used to handle POST requests—in this case, when the user submits the form.

In Chapter 8, I use the ASP.NET Core model binding feature to receive simple data values from the request. This same feature is used in the new action method to receive a completed Order object. When a request is processed, the model binding system tries to find values for the properties defined by the Order class. This works on a best-effort basis, which means I may receive an Order object lacking property values if there is no corresponding data item in the request.

To ensure I have the data I require, I applied validation attributes to the Order class. ASP.NET Core checks the validation constraints that I applied to the Order class and provides details of the result through the ModelState property. I can see whether there are any problems by checking the ModelState.IsValid property. I call the ModelState.AddModelError method to register an error message if there are no items in the cart. I will explain how to display such errors shortly, and I have much more to say about model binding and validation in Chapters 28 and 29.

UNIT TEST: ORDER PROCESSING

To perform unit testing for the OrderController class, I need to test the behavior of the POST version of the Checkout method. Although the method looks short and simple, the use of model binding means that there is a lot going on behind the scenes that needs to be tested.

I want to process an order only if there are items in the cart *and* the customer has provided valid shipping details. Under all other circumstances, the customer should be shown an error. Here is the first test method, which I defined in a class file called OrderControllerTests.cs in the SportsStore.Tests project:

```
using Microsoft.AspNetCore.Mvc;
using Moq;
using SportsStore.Controllers;
using SportsStore.Models;
using Xunit;

namespace SportsStore.Tests {
```

```
public class OrderControllerTests {

    [Fact]
    public void Cannot_Checkout_Empty_Cart() {
        // Arrange - create a mock repository
        Mock<IOrderRepository> mock = new Mock<IOrderRepository>();
        // Arrange - create an empty cart
        Cart cart = new Cart();
        // Arrange - create the order
        Order order = new Order();
        // Arrange - create an instance of the controller
        OrderController target = new OrderController(mock.Object, cart);

        // Act
        ViewResult result = target.Checkout(order) as ViewResult;

        // Assert - check that the order hasn't been stored
        mock.Verify(m => m.SaveOrder(It.IsAny<Order>()), Times.Never);
        // Assert - check that the method is returning the default view
        Assert.True(string.IsNullOrEmpty(result.ViewName));
        // Assert - check that I am passing an invalid model to the view
        Assert.False(result.ViewData.ModelState.IsValid);
    }
}
```

This test ensures that I cannot check out with an empty cart. I check this by ensuring that the SaveOrder of the mock IOrderRepository implementation is never called, that the view the method returns is the default view (which will redisplay the data entered by customers and give them a chance to correct it), and that the model state being passed to the view has been marked as invalid. This may seem like a belt-and-braces set of assertions, but I need all three to be sure that I have the right behavior. The next test method works in much the same way but injects an error into the view model to simulate a problem reported by the model binder (which would happen in production when the customer enters invalid shipping data):

```
...
[Fact]
public void Cannot_Checkout_Invalid_ShippingDetails() {

    // Arrange - create a mock order repository
    Mock<IOrderRepository> mock = new Mock<IOrderRepository>();
    // Arrange - create a cart with one item
    Cart cart = new Cart();
    cart.AddItem(new Product(), 1);
    // Arrange - create an instance of the controller
    OrderController target = new OrderController(mock.Object, cart);
    // Arrange - add an error to the model
    target.ModelState.AddModelError("error", "error");

    // Act - try to checkout
    ViewResult result = target.Checkout(new Order()) as ViewResult;

    // Assert - check that the order hasn't been passed stored
    mock.Verify(m => m.SaveOrder(It.IsAny<Order>()), Times.Never);
    // Assert - check that the method is returning the default view
    Assert.True(string.IsNullOrEmpty(result.ViewName));
    // Assert - check that I am passing an invalid model to the view
    Assert.False(result.ViewData.ModelState.IsValid);
}
...
```

Having established that an empty cart or invalid details will prevent an order from being processed, I need to ensure that I process orders when appropriate. Here is the test:

```
...
[Fact]
public void Can_Checkout_And_Submit_Order() {
    // Arrange - create a mock order repository
    Mock<IOrderRepository> mock = new Mock<IOrderRepository>();
    // Arrange - create a cart with one item
    Cart cart = new Cart();
    cart.AddItem(new Product(), 1);
    // Arrange - create an instance of the controller
    OrderController target = new OrderController(mock.Object, cart);

    // Act - try to checkout
    RedirectToPageResult result =
            target.Checkout(new Order()) as RedirectToPageResult;

    // Assert - check that the order has been stored
    mock.Verify(m => m.SaveOrder(It.IsAny<Order>()), Times.Once);
    // Assert - check that the method is redirecting to the Completed action
    Assert.Equal("/Completed", result.PageName);
}
...
```

I did not need to test that I can identify valid shipping details. This is handled for me automatically by the model binder using the attributes applied to the properties of the Order class.

Displaying Validation Errors

ASP.NET Core uses the validation attributes applied to the Order class to validate user data, but I need to make a simple change to display any problems. This relies on another built-in tag helper that inspects the validation state of the data provided by the user and adds warning messages for each problem that has been discovered. Listing 9-21 shows the addition of an HTML element that will be processed by the tag helper to the Checkout.cshtml file.

Listing 9-21. Adding a Validation Summary to the Checkout.cshtml File in the SportsStore/Views/Order Folder

```
@model Order

<h2>Check out now</h2>
<p>Please enter your details, and we'll ship your goods right away!</p>

<div asp-validation-summary="All" class="text-danger"></div>

<form asp-action="Checkout" method="post">
    <h3>Ship to</h3>
    <div class="form-group">
        <label>Name:</label><input asp-for="Name" class="form-control" />
    </div>
    <h3>Address</h3>
    <div class="form-group">
        <label>Line 1:</label><input asp-for="Line1" class="form-control" />
    </div>
    <div class="form-group">
        <label>Line 2:</label><input asp-for="Line2" class="form-control" />
    </div>
    <div class="form-group">
        <label>Line 3:</label><input asp-for="Line3" class="form-control" />
    </div>
```

```
<div class="form-group">
    <label>City:</label><input asp-for="City" class="form-control" />
</div>
<div class="form-group">
    <label>State:</label><input asp-for="State" class="form-control" />
</div>
<div class="form-group">
    <label>Zip:</label><input asp-for="Zip" class="form-control" />
</div>
<div class="form-group">
    <label>Country:</label><input asp-for="Country" class="form-control" />
</div>
<h3>Options</h3>
<div class="checkbox">
    <label>
        <input asp-for="GiftWrap" /> Gift wrap these items
    </label>
</div>
<div class="text-center">
    <input class="btn btn-primary" type="submit" value="Complete Order" />
</div>
</form>
```

With this simple change, validation errors are reported to the user. To see the effect, restart ASP.NET Core, request http://localhost:5000/Order/Checkout, and click the Complete Order button without filling out the form. ASP.NET Core will process the form data, detect that the required values were not found, and generate the validation errors shown in Figure 9-5.

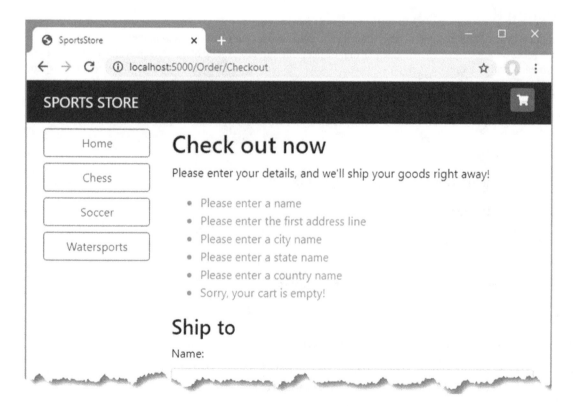

Figure 9-5. *Displaying validation messages*

■ **Tip** The data submitted by the user is sent to the server before it is validated, which is known as *server-side validation* and for which ASP.NET Core has excellent support. The problem with server-side validation is that the user isn't told about errors until after the data has been sent to the server and processed and the result page has been generated—something that can take a few seconds on a busy server. For this reason, server-side validation is usually complemented by *client-side validation*, where JavaScript is used to check the values that the user has entered before the form data is sent to the server. I describe client-side validation in Chapter 29.

Displaying a Summary Page

To complete the checkout process, I am going to create a Razor Page that displays a thank-you message with a summary of the order. Add a Razor Page named Completed.cshtml to the Pages folder with the contents shown in Listing 9-22.

Listing 9-22. The Contents of the Completed.cshtml File in the SportsStore/Pages Folder

```
@page

<div class="text-center">
    <h2>Thanks!</h2>
    <p>Thanks for placing order #@OrderId</p>
    <p>We'll ship your goods as soon as possible.</p>
    <a class="btn btn-primary" asp-controller="Home">Return to Store</a>
</div>

@functions {

    [BindProperty(SupportsGet = true)]
    public string OrderId { get; set; }
}
```

Although Razor Pages usually have page model classes, they are not a requirement, and simple features can be developed without them. In this example, I have defined a property named OrderId and decorated it with the BindProperty attribute, which specifies that a value for this property should be obtained from the request by the model binding system

Now customers can go through the entire process, from selecting products to checking out. If they provide valid shipping details (and have items in their cart), they will see the summary page when they click the Complete Order button, as shown in Figure 9-6.

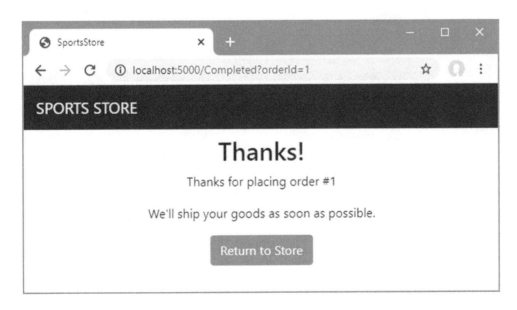

Figure 9-6. The completed order summary view

Notice the way the application moves between controllers and Razor Pages. The application features that ASP.NET Core provides are complementary and can be mixed freely in projects.

Summary

I have completed all the major parts of the customer-facing portion of SportsStore. It might not be enough to worry Amazon, but I have a product catalog that can be browsed by category and page, a neat shopping cart, and a simple checkout process.

The approach I have taken means I can easily change the behavior of any piece of the application without causing problems or inconsistencies elsewhere. For example, I could change the way that orders are stored, and it would not have any impact on the shopping cart, the product catalog, or any other area of the application. In the next chapter, I add the features required to administer the SportsStore application.

CHAPTER 10

SportsStore: Administration

In this chapter, I continue to build the SportsStore application in order to give the site administrator a way to manage orders and products. In this chapter, I use Blazor to create administration features. Blazor is a new addition to ASP.NET Core, and it combines client-side JavaScript code with server-side code executed by ASP.NET Core, connected by a persistent HTTP connection. I describe Blazor in detail in Chapters 32–35, but it is important to understand that the Blazor model is not suited to all projects. (I use Blazor Server in this chapter, which is a supported part of the ASP.NET Core platform. There is also Blazor WebAssembly, which is, at the time of writing, experimental and runs entirely in the browser. I describe Blazor WebAssembly in Chapter 36.)

■ **Tip** You can download the example project for this chapter—and for all the other chapters in this book—from `https://github.com/apress/pro-asp.net-core-3`. See Chapter 1 for how to get help if you have problems running the examples.

Preparing Blazor Server

The first step is to enable the services and middleware for Blazor, as shown in Listing 10-1.

Listing 10-1. Enabling Blazor in the Startup.cs File in the SportsStore Folder

```
using System;
using System.Collections.Generic;
using System.Linq;
using System.Threading.Tasks;
using Microsoft.AspNetCore.Builder;
using Microsoft.AspNetCore.Hosting;
using Microsoft.AspNetCore.Http;
using Microsoft.Extensions.DependencyInjection;
using Microsoft.Extensions.Hosting;
using Microsoft.Extensions.Configuration;
using Microsoft.EntityFrameworkCore;
using SportsStore.Models;

namespace SportsStore {
    public class Startup {

        public Startup(IConfiguration config) {
            Configuration = config;
        }

        private IConfiguration Configuration { get; set; }

        public void ConfigureServices(IServiceCollection services) {
            services.AddControllersWithViews();
            services.AddDbContext<StoreDbContext>(opts => {
```

```
        opts.UseSqlServer(
            Configuration["ConnectionStrings:SportsStoreConnection"]);
    });
    services.AddScoped<IStoreRepository, EFStoreRepository>();
    services.AddScoped<IOrderRepository, EFOrderRepository>();
    services.AddRazorPages();
    services.AddDistributedMemoryCache();
    services.AddSession();
    services.AddScoped<Cart>(sp => SessionCart.GetCart(sp));
    services.AddSingleton<IHttpContextAccessor, HttpContextAccessor>();
    services.AddServerSideBlazor();
}

public void Configure(IApplicationBuilder app, IWebHostEnvironment env) {
    app.UseDeveloperExceptionPage();
    app.UseStatusCodePages();
    app.UseStaticFiles();
    app.UseSession();
    app.UseRouting();

    app.UseEndpoints(endpoints => {
        endpoints.MapControllerRoute("catpage",
            "{category}/Page{productPage:int}",
            new { Controller = "Home", action = "Index" });

        endpoints.MapControllerRoute("page", "Page{productPage:int}",
            new { Controller = "Home", action = "Index", productPage = 1 });

        endpoints.MapControllerRoute("category", "{category}",
            new { Controller = "Home", action = "Index", productPage = 1 });

        endpoints.MapControllerRoute("pagination",
            "Products/Page{productPage}",
            new { Controller = "Home", action = "Index", productPage = 1 });
        endpoints.MapDefaultControllerRoute();
        endpoints.MapRazorPages();
        endpoints.MapBlazorHub();
        endpoints.MapFallbackToPage("/admin/{*catchall}", "/Admin/Index");
    });

    SeedData.EnsurePopulated(app);
}
  }
}
```

The AddServerSideBlazor method creates the services that Blazor uses, and the MapBlazorHub method registers the Blazor middleware components. The final addition is to finesse the routing system to ensure that Blazor works seamlessly with the rest of the application.

Creating the Imports File

Blazor requires its own imports file to specify the namespaces that it uses. Create the Pages/Admin folder and add to it a file named _Imports.razor with the content shown in Listing 10-2. (If you are using Visual Studio, you can use the Razor Components template to create this file.)

■ **Note**   The conventional location for Blazor files is within the Pages folder, but Blazor files can be defined anywhere in the project. In Part 4, for example, I used a folder named Blazor to help emphasize which features were provided by Blazor and which by Razor Pages.

Listing 10-2. The Contents of the _Imports.razor File in the SportsStore/Pages/Admin Folder

```
@using Microsoft.AspNetCore.Components
@using Microsoft.AspNetCore.Components.Forms
@using Microsoft.AspNetCore.Components.Routing
@using Microsoft.AspNetCore.Components.Web
@using Microsoft.EntityFrameworkCore
@using SportsStore.Models
```

The first four @using expressions are for the namespaces required for Blazor. The last two expressions are for convenience in the examples that follow because they will allow me to use Entity Framework Core and the classes in the Models namespace.

Creating the Startup Razor Page

Blazor relies on a Razor Page to provide the initial content to the browser, which includes the JavaScript code that connects to the server and renders the Blazor HTML content. Add a Razor Page named Index.cshtml to the Pages/Admin folder with the contents shown in Listing 10-3.

Listing 10-3. The Contents of the Index.cshtml File in the SportsStore/Pages/Admin Folder

```
@page "/admin"
@{ Layout = null; }

<!DOCTYPE html>
<html>
<head>
    <title>SportsStore Admin</title>
    <link href="/lib/twitter-bootstrap/css/bootstrap.min.css" rel="stylesheet" />
    <base href="/" />
</head>
<body>
    <component type="typeof(Routed)" render-mode="Server" />
    <script src="/_framework/blazor.server.js"></script>
</body>
</html>
```

The component element is used to insert a Razor Component in the output from the Razor Page. Razor Components are the confusingly named Blazor building blocks, and the component element applied in Listing 10-3 is named Routed and will be created shortly. The Razor Page also contains a script element that tells the browser to load the JavaScript file that Blazor Server uses. Requests for this file are intercepted by the Blazor Server middleware, and you don't need to explicitly add the JavaScript file to the project.

Creating the Routing and Layout Components

Add a Razor Component named Routed.razor to the Pages/Admin folder and add the content shown in Listing 10-4.

Listing 10-4. The Contents of the Routed.razor File in the SportsStore/Pages/Admin Folder

```
<Router AppAssembly="typeof(Startup).Assembly">
    <Found>
        <RouteView RouteData="@context" DefaultLayout="typeof(AdminLayout)" />
    </Found>
    <NotFound>
        <h4 class="bg-danger text-white text-center p-2">
            No Matching Route Found
        </h4>
    </NotFound>
</Router>
```

The content of this component is described in detail in Part 4 of this book, but, for this chapter, it is enough to know that the component will use the browser's current URL to locate a Razor Component that can be displayed to the user. If no matching component can be found, then an error message is displayed.

Blazor has its own system of layouts. To create the layout for the administration tools, add a Razor Component named AdminLayout.razor to the Pages/Admin folder with the content shown in Listing 10-5.

Listing 10-5. The Contents of the AdminLayout.razor File in the SportsStore/Pages/Admin Folder

```
@inherits LayoutComponentBase

<div class="bg-info text-white p-2">
    <span class="navbar-brand ml-2">SPORTS STORE Administration</span>
</div>
<div class="container-fluid">
    <div class="row p-2">
        <div class="col-3">
            <NavLink class="btn btn-outline-primary btn-block"
                        href="/admin/products"
                        ActiveClass="btn-primary text-white"
                        Match="NavLinkMatch.Prefix">
                Products
            </NavLink>
            <NavLink class="btn btn-outline-primary btn-block"
                        href="/admin/orders"
                        ActiveClass="btn-primary text-white"
                        Match="NavLinkMatch.Prefix">
                Orders
            </NavLink>
        </div>
        <div class="col">
            @Body
        </div>
    </div>
</div>
```

Blazor uses Razor syntax to generate HTML but introduces its own directives and features. This layout renders a two-column display with Product and Order navigation buttons, which are created using NavLink elements. These elements apply a built-in Razor Component that changes the URL without triggering a new HTTP request, which allows Blazor to respond to user interaction without losing the application state.

Creating the Razor Components

To complete the initial setup, I need to add the components that will provide the administration tools, although they will contain placeholder messages at first. Add a Razor Component named Products.razor to the Pages/Admin folder with the content shown in Listing 10-6.

Listing 10-6. The Contents of the Products.razor File in the SportsStore/Pages/Admin Folder

```
@page "/admin/products"
@page "/admin"

<h4>This is the products component</h4>
```

The @page directives specify the URLs for which this component will be displayed, which is /admin/products and /admin. Next, add a Razor Component named Orders.razor to the Pages/Admin folder with the content shown in Listing 10-7.

Listing 10-7. The Contents of the Orders.razor File in the SportsStore/Pages/Admin Folder

```
@page "/admin/orders"

<h4>This is the orders component</h4>
```

Checking the Blazor Setup

To make sure that Blazor is working correctly, start ASP.NET Core and request `http://localhost:5000/admin`. This request will be handled by the `Index` Razor Page in the `Pages/Admin` folder, which will include the Blazor JavaScript file in the content it sends to the browser. The JavaScript code will open a persistent HTTP connection to the ASP.NET Core server, and the initial Blazor content will be rendered, as shown in Figure 10-1.

■ **Note** Microsoft has not yet released the tools required to test Razor Components, which is why there are no unit testing examples in this chapter.

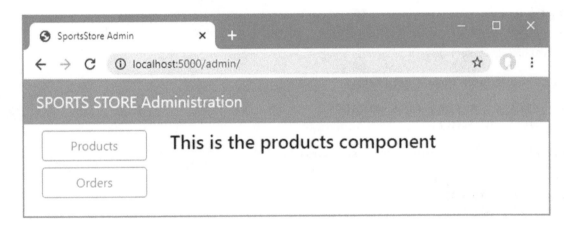

Figure 10-1. The Blazor application

Click the Orders button, and content generated by the Orders Razor Component will be displayed, as shown in Figure 10-2. Unlike the other ASP.NET Core application frameworks I used in earlier chapters, the new content is displayed without a new HTTP request being sent, even though the URL displayed by the browser changes.

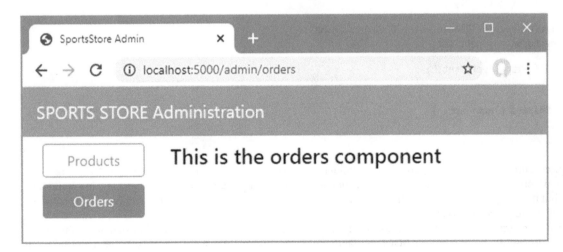

Figure 10-2. Navigating in the Blazor application

Managing Orders

Now that Blazor has been set up and tested, I am going to start implementing administration features. In the previous chapter, I added support for receiving orders from customers and storing them in a database. In this section, I am going to create a simple administration tool that will let me view the orders that have been received and mark them as shipped.

Enhancing the Model

The first change I need to make is to enhance the data model so that I can record which orders have been shipped. Listing 10-8 shows the addition of a new property to the Order class, which is defined in the Order.cs file in the Models folder.

Listing 10-8. Adding a Property in the Order.cs File in the SportsStore/Models Folder

```
using System.Collections.Generic;
using System.ComponentModel.DataAnnotations;
using Microsoft.AspNetCore.Mvc.ModelBinding;

namespace SportsStore.Models {

    public class Order {

        [BindNever]
        public int OrderID { get; set; }
        [BindNever]
        public ICollection<CartLine> Lines { get; set; }

        [Required(ErrorMessage = "Please enter a name")]
        public string Name { get; set; }

        [Required(ErrorMessage = "Please enter the first address line")]

        public string Line1 { get; set; }
        public string Line2 { get; set; }
        public string Line3 { get; set; }

        [Required(ErrorMessage = "Please enter a city name")]
        public string City { get; set; }

        [Required(ErrorMessage = "Please enter a state name")]
        public string State { get; set; }

        public string Zip { get; set; }

        [Required(ErrorMessage = "Please enter a country name")]
        public string Country { get; set; }

        public bool GiftWrap { get; set; }

        [BindNever]
        public bool Shipped { get; set; }
    }
}
```

This iterative approach of extending and adapting the data model to support different features is typical of ASP.NET Core development. In an ideal world, you would be able to completely define the data model at the start of the project and just build the application around it, but that happens only for the simplest of projects, and, in practice, iterative development is to be expected as the understanding of what is required develops and evolves.

Entity Framework Core migrations make this process easier because you don't have to manually keep the database schema synchronized to the model class by writing your own SQL commands. To update the database to reflect the addition of the Shipped property to the Order class, open a new PowerShell window and run the command shown in Listing 10-9 in the SportsStore project.

Listing 10-9. Creating a New Migration

```
dotnet ef migrations add ShippedOrders
```

The migration will be applied automatically when the application is started and the SeedData class calls the Migrate method provided by Entity Framework Core.

Displaying Orders to the Administrator

I am going to display two tables, one of which shows the orders waiting to be shipped and the other the shipped orders. Each order will be presented with a button that changes the shipping state. This is not entirely realistic because orders processing is typically more complex than simply updating a field in the database, but integration with warehouse and fulfillment systems is well beyond the scope of this book.

To avoid duplicating code and content, I am going to create a Razor Component that displays a table without knowing which category of order it is dealing with. Add a Razor Component named OrderTable.razor to the Pages/Admin folder with the content shown in Listing 10-10.

Listing 10-10. The Contents of the OrderTable.razor File in the SportsStore/Pages/Admin Folder

```
<table class="table table-sm table-striped table-bordered">
    <thead>
        <tr><th colspan="5" class="text-center">@TableTitle</th></tr>
    </thead>
    <tbody>
        @if (Orders?.Count() > 0) {
            @foreach (Order o in Orders) {
                <tr>
                    <td>@o.Name</td><td>@o.Zip</td><th>Product</th><th>Quantity</th>
                    <td>
                        <button class="btn btn-sm btn-danger"
                                @onclick="@(e => OrderSelected.InvokeAsync(o.OrderID))">
                            @ButtonLabel
                        </button>
                    </td>
                </tr>
                @foreach (CartLine line in o.Lines) {
                    <tr>
                        <td colspan="2"></td>
                        <td>@line.Product.Name</td><td>@line.Quantity</td>
                        <td></td>
                    </tr>
                }
            }
        } else {
            <tr><td colspan="5" class="text-center">No Orders</td></tr>
        }
    </tbody>
</table>

@code {

    [Parameter]
    public string TableTitle { get; set; } = "Orders";

    [Parameter]
    public IEnumerable<Order> Orders { get; set; }
```

```
    [Parameter]
    public string ButtonLabel { get; set; } = "Ship";

    [Parameter]
    public EventCallback<int> OrderSelected{ get; set; }
}
```

Razor Components, as the name suggests, rely on the Razor approach to annotated HTML elements. The view part of the component is supported by the statements in the @code section. The @code section in this component defines four properties that are decorated with the Parameter attribute, which means the values will be provided at runtime by the parent component, which I will create shortly. The values provided for the parameters are used in the view section of the component to display details of a sequence of Order objects.

Blazor adds expressions to the Razor syntax. The view section of this component includes this button element, which has an @onclick attribute.

```
...
<button class="btn btn-sm btn-danger"
        @onclick="@(e => OrderSelected.InvokeAsync(o.OrderID))">
    @ButtonLabel
</button>
...
```

This tells Blazor how to react when the user clicks the button. In this case, the expression tells Razor to call the InvokeAsync method of the OrderSelected property. This is how the table will communicate with the rest of the Blazor application and will become clearer as I build out additional features.

■ **Tip**   I describe Blazor in-depth in Part 4 of this book, so don't worry if the Razor Components in this chapter do not make immediate sense. The purpose of the SportsStore example is to show the overall development process, even if individual features are not understood.

The next step is to create a component that will get the Order data from the database and use the OrderTable component to display it to the user. Remove the placeholder content in the Orders component and replace it with the code and content shown in Listing 10-11.

Listing 10-11. The Revised Contents of the Orders.razor File in the SportsStore/Pages/Admin Folder

```
@page "/admin/orders"
@inherits OwningComponentBase<IOrderRepository>

<OrderTable TableTitle="Unshipped Orders"
        Orders="UnshippedOrders" ButtonLabel="Ship" OrderSelected="ShipOrder" />
<OrderTable TableTitle="Shipped Orders"
        Orders="ShippedOrders" ButtonLabel="Reset" OrderSelected="ResetOrder" />
<button class="btn btn-info" @onclick="@(e => UpdateData())">Refresh Data</button>

@code {

    public IOrderRepository Repository => Service;

    public IEnumerable<Order> AllOrders { get; set; }
    public IEnumerable<Order> UnshippedOrders { get; set; }
    public IEnumerable<Order> ShippedOrders { get; set; }

    protected async override Task OnInitializedAsync() {
        await UpdateData();
    }
```

```
public async Task UpdateData() {
    AllOrders = await Repository.Orders.ToListAsync();
    UnshippedOrders = AllOrders.Where(o => !o.Shipped);
    ShippedOrders = AllOrders.Where(o => o.Shipped);
}

public void ShipOrder(int id) => UpdateOrder(id, true);
public void ResetOrder(int id) => UpdateOrder(id, false);

private void UpdateOrder(int id, bool shipValue) {
    Order o = Repository.Orders.FirstOrDefault(o => o.OrderID == id);
    o.Shipped = shipValue;
    Repository.SaveOrder(o);
}
}
```

Blazor Components are not like the other application framework building blocks used for the user-facing sections of the SportsStore application. Instead of dealing with individual requests, components can be long-lived and deal with multiple user interactions over a longer period. This requires a different style of development, especially when it comes to dealing with data using Entity Framework Core. The @inherits expression ensures that this component gets its own repository object, which ensures its operations are separate from those performed by other components displayed to the same user. And to avoid repeatedly querying the database—which can be a serious problem in Blazor, as I explain in Part 4—the repository is used only when the component is initialized, when Blazor invokes the OnInitializedAsync method, or when the user clicks a Refresh Data button.

To display its data to the user, the OrderTable component is used, which is applied as an HTML element, like this:

```
...
<OrderTable TableTitle="Unshipped Orders"
        Orders="UnshippedOrders" ButtonLabel="Ship" OrderSelected="ShipOrder" />
...
```

The values assigned to the OrderTable element's attributes are used to set the properties decorated with the Parameter attribute in Listing 10-10. In this way, a single component can be configured to present two different sets of data without the need to duplicate code and content.

The ShipOrder and ResetOrder methods are used as the values for the OrderSelected attributes, which means they are invoked when the user clicks one of the buttons presented by the OrderTable component, updating the data in the database through the repository.

To see the new features, restart ASP.NET Core, request http://localhost:5000, and create an order. Once you have at least one order in the database, request http://localhost:5000/admin/orders, and you will see a summary of the order you created displayed in the Unshipped Orders table. Click the Ship button, and the order will be updated and moved to the Shipped Orders table, as shown in Figure 10-3.

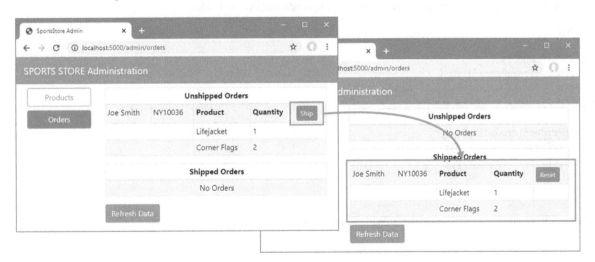

Figure 10-3. *Administering orders*

Adding Catalog Management

The convention for managing more complex collections of items is to present the user with two interfaces: a *list* interface and an *edit* interface, as shown in Figure 10-4.

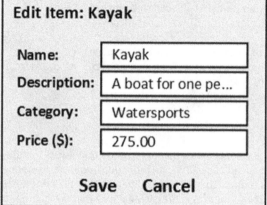

Figure 10-4. *Sketch of a CRUD UI for the product catalog*

Together, these interfaces allow a user to create, read, update, and delete items in the collection. Collectively, these actions are known as *CRUD*. In this section, I will implement these interfaces using Blazor.

■ **Tip**   Developers need to implement CRUD so often that Visual Studio scaffolding includes scenarios for creating CRUD controllers or Razor Pages. But, like all Visual Studio scaffolding, I think it is better to learn how to create these features directly, which is why I demonstrate CRUD operations for all the ASP.NET Core application frameworks in later chapters.

Expanding the Repository

The first step is to add features to the repository that will allow Product objects to be created, modified, and deleted. Listing 10-12 adds new methods to the IStoreRepository interface.

Listing 10-12. Adding Methods in the IStoreRepository.cs File in the SportsStore/Models Folder

```
using System.Linq;

namespace SportsStore.Models {
    public interface IStoreRepository {

        IQueryable<Product> Products { get; }

        void SaveProduct(Product p);
        void CreateProduct(Product p);
        void DeleteProduct(Product p);
    }
}
```

Listing 10-13 adds implementations of these methods to the Entity Framework Core repository class.

Listing 10-13. Implementing Methods in the EFStoreRepository.cs File in the SportsStore/Models Folder

```
using System.Linq;

namespace SportsStore.Models {
    public class EFStoreRepository : IStoreRepository {
        private StoreDbContext context;

        public EFStoreRepository(StoreDbContext ctx) {
            context = ctx;
        }

        public IQueryable<Product> Products => context.Products;

        public void CreateProduct(Product p) {
            context.Add(p);
            context.SaveChanges();
        }

        public void DeleteProduct(Product p) {
            context.Remove(p);
            context.SaveChanges();
        }

        public void SaveProduct(Product p) {
            context.SaveChanges();
        }
    }
}
```

Applying Validation Attributes to the Data Model

I want to validate the values the user provides when editing or creating Product objects, just as I did for the customer checkout process. In Listing 10-14, I have added validation attributes to the Product data model class.

Listing 10-14. Adding Validation Attributes in the Product.cs File in the SportsStore/Models Folder

```
using System.ComponentModel.DataAnnotations.Schema;
using System.ComponentModel.DataAnnotations;

namespace SportsStore.Models {

    public class Product {
        public long ProductID { get; set; }

        [Required(ErrorMessage = "Please enter a product name")]
        public string Name { get; set; }

        [Required(ErrorMessage = "Please enter a description")]
        public string Description { get; set; }

        [Required]
        [Range(0.01, double.MaxValue,
            ErrorMessage = "Please enter a positive price")]
        [Column(TypeName = "decimal(8, 2)")]
        public decimal Price { get; set; }
```

```
        [Required(ErrorMessage = "Please specify a category")]
        public string Category { get; set; }
    }
}
```

Blazor uses the same approach to validation as the rest of ASP.NET Core but, as you will see, applies it a different way to deal with the more interactive nature of Razor Components.

Creating the List Component

I am going to start by creating the table that will present the user with a table of products and the links that will allow them to be inspected and edited. Replace the contents of the Products.razor file with those shown in Listing 10-15.

Listing 10-15. The Revised Contents of the Products.razor File in the SportsStore/Pages/Admin Folder

```
@page "/admin/products"
@page "/admin"
@inherits OwningComponentBase<IStoreRepository>

<table class="table table-sm table-striped table-bordered">
    <thead>
        <tr>
            <th>ID</th><th>Name</th>
            <th>Category</th><th>Price</th><td/>
        </tr>
    </thead>
    <tbody>
        @if (ProductData?.Count() > 0) {
            @foreach (Product p in ProductData) {
                <tr>
                    <td>@p.ProductID</td>
                    <td>@p.Name</td>
                    <td>@p.Category</td>
                    <td>@p.Price.ToString("c")</td>
                    <td>
                        <NavLink class="btn btn-info btn-sm"
                                 href="@GetDetailsUrl(p.ProductID)">
                            Details
                        </NavLink>
                        <NavLink class="btn btn-warning btn-sm"
                                 href="@GetEditUrl(p.ProductID)">
                            Edit
                        </NavLink>
                    </td>
                </tr>
            }
        } else {
            <tr>
                <td colspan="5" class="text-center">No Products</td>
            </tr>
        }
    </tbody>
</table>

<NavLink class="btn btn-primary" href="/admin/products/create">Create</NavLink>
```

```
@code {

    public IStoreRepository Repository => Service;

    public IEnumerable<Product> ProductData { get; set; }

    protected async override Task OnInitializedAsync() {
        await UpdateData();
    }

    public async Task UpdateData() {
        ProductData = await Repository.Products.ToListAsync();
    }

    public string GetDetailsUrl(long id) => $"/admin/products/details/{id}";
    public string GetEditUrl(long id) => $"/admin/products/edit/{id}";
}
```

The component presents each Product object in the repository in a table row with NavLink components that will navigate to the components that will provide a detailed view and an editor. There is also a button that navigates to the component that will allow new Product objects to be created and stored in the database. Restart ASP.NET Core and request http://localhost:5000/admin/ products, and you will see the content shown in Figure 10-5, although none of the buttons presented by the Products component work currently because I have yet to create the components they target.

Figure 10-5. *Presenting a list of products*

Creating the Detail Component

The job of the detail component is to display all the fields for a single Product object. Add a Razor Component named Details.razor to the Pages/Admin folder with the content shown in Listing 10-16.

Listing 10-16. The Contents of the Details.razor File in the SportsStore/Pages/Admin Folder

```
@page "/admin/products/details/{id:long}"

<h3 class="bg-info text-white text-center p-1">Details</h3>

<table class="table table-sm table-bordered table-striped">
    <tbody>
        <tr><th>ID</th><td>@Product.ProductID</td></tr>
        <tr><th>Name</th><td>@Product.Name</td></tr>
        <tr><th>Description</th><td>@Product.Description</td></tr>
        <tr><th>Category</th><td>@Product.Category</td></tr>
        <tr><th>Price</th><td>@Product.Price.ToString("C")</td></tr>
    </tbody>
</table>

<NavLink class="btn btn-warning" href="@EditUrl">Edit</NavLink>
<NavLink class="btn btn-secondary" href="/admin/products">Back</NavLink>

@code {

    [Inject]
    public IStoreRepository Repository { get; set; }

    [Parameter]
    public long Id { get; set; }

    public Product Product { get; set; }

    protected override void OnParametersSet() {
        Product = Repository.Products.FirstOrDefault(p => p.ProductID == Id);
    }

    public string EditUrl => $"/admin/products/edit/{Product.ProductID}";
}
```

The component uses the Inject attribute to declare that it requires an implementation of the IStoreRepository interface, which is one of the ways that Blazor provides access to the application's services. The value of the Id property will be populated from the URL that has been used to navigate to the component, which is used to retrieve the Product object from the database. To see the detail view, restart ASP.NET Core, request http://localhost:5000/admin/products, and click one of the Details buttons, as shown in Figure 10-6.

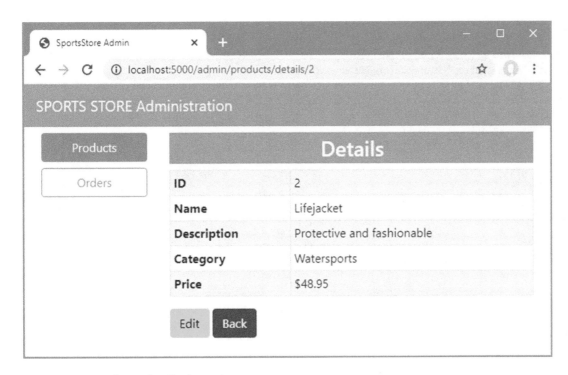

Figure 10-6. *Displaying details of a product*

Creating the Editor Component

The operations to create and edit data will be handled by the same component. Add a Razor Component named Editor.razor to the Pages/Admin folder with the content shown in Listing 10-17.

Listing 10-17. The Contents of the Editor.razor File in the SportsStore/Pages/Admin Folder

```
@page "/admin/products/edit/{id:long}"
@page "/admin/products/create"
@inherits OwningComponentBase<IStoreRepository>

<style>
    div.validation-message { color: rgb(220, 53, 69); font-weight: 500 }
</style>

<h3 class="bg-@ThemeColor text-white text-center p-1">@TitleText a Product</h3>
<EditForm Model="Product" OnValidSubmit="SaveProduct">
    <DataAnnotationsValidator />
    @if(Product.ProductID != 0) {
        <div class="form-group">
            <label>ID</label>
            <input class="form-control" disabled value="@Product.ProductID" />
        </div>
    }
    <div class="form-group">
        <label>Name</label>
        <ValidationMessage For="@(() => Product.Name)" />
        <InputText class="form-control" @bind-Value="Product.Name" />
    </div>
```

```
    <div class="form-group">
        <label>Description</label>
        <ValidationMessage For="@(() => Product.Description)" />
        <InputText class="form-control" @bind-Value="Product.Description" />
    </div>
    <div class="form-group">
        <label>Category</label>
        <ValidationMessage For="@(() => Product.Category)" />
        <InputText class="form-control" @bind-Value="Product.Category" />
    </div>
    <div class="form-group">
        <label>Price</label>
        <ValidationMessage For="@(() => Product.Price)" />
        <InputNumber class="form-control" @bind-Value="Product.Price" />
    </div>
    <button type="submit" class="btn btn-@ThemeColor">Save</button>
    <NavLink class="btn btn-secondary" href="/admin/products">Cancel</NavLink>
</EditForm>

@code {

    public IStoreRepository Repository => Service;

    [Inject]
    public NavigationManager NavManager { get; set; }

    [Parameter]
    public long Id { get; set; } = 0;

    public Product Product { get; set; } = new Product();

    protected override void OnParametersSet() {
        if (Id != 0) {
            Product = Repository.Products.FirstOrDefault(p => p.ProductID == Id);
        }
    }

    public void SaveProduct() {
        if (Id == 0) {
            Repository.CreateProduct(Product);
        } else {
            Repository.SaveProduct(Product);
        }
        NavManager.NavigateTo("/admin/products");
    }

    public string ThemeColor => Id == 0 ? "primary" : "warning";
    public string TitleText => Id == 0 ? "Create" : "Edit";
}
```

Blazor provides a set of built-in Razor Components that are used to display and validate forms, which is important because the browser can't submit data using a POST request in a Blazor Component. The EditForm component is used to render a Blazor-friendly form, and the InputText and InputNumber components render input elements that accept string and number values and that automatically update a model property when the user makes a change.

Data validation is integrated into these built-in components, and the OnValidSubmit attribute on the EditForm component is used to specify a method that is invoked only if the data entered into the form conforms to the rules defined by the validation attributes.

Blazor also provides the `NavigationManager` class, which is used to programmatically navigate between components without triggering a new HTTP request. The `Editor` component uses `NavigationManager`, which is obtained as a service, to return to the `Products` component after the database has been updated.

To see the editor, restart ASP.NET Core, request `http://localhost:5000/admin`, and click the Create button. Click the Save button without filling out the form fields, and you will see the validation errors that Blazor produces automatically, as shown in Figure 10-7. Fill out the form and click Save again, and you will see the product you created displayed in the table, also as shown in Figure 10-7.

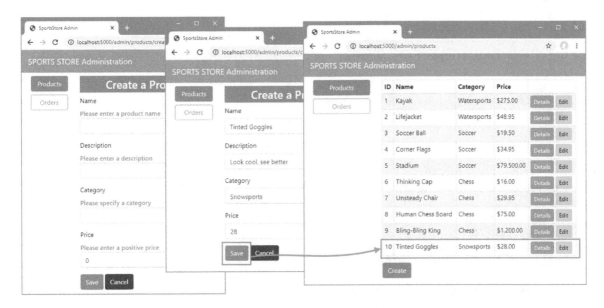

Figure 10-7. *Using the Editor component*

Click the Edit button for one of the products, and the same component will be used to edit the selected `Product` object's properties. Click the Save button, and any changes you made—if they pass validation—will be stored in the database, as shown in Figure 10-8.

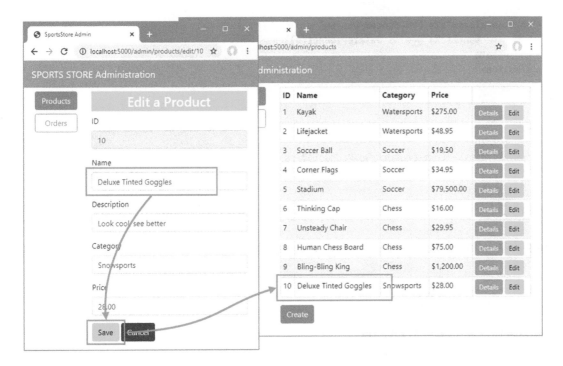

Figure 10-8. *Editing products*

Deleting Products

The final CRUD feature is deleting products, which is easily implemented in the Products component, as shown in Listing 10-18.

Listing 10-18. Adding Delete Support in the Products.razor File in the SportsStore/Pages/Admin Folder

```
@page "/admin/products"
@page "/admin"
@inherits OwningComponentBase<IStoreRepository>

<table class="table table-sm table-striped table-bordered">
    <thead>
        <tr>
            <th>ID</th><th>Name</th>
            <th>Category</th><th>Price</th><td/>
        </tr>
    </thead>
    <tbody>
        @if (ProductData?.Count() > 0) {
            @foreach (Product p in ProductData) {
                <tr>
                    <td>@p.ProductID</td>
                    <td>@p.Name</td>
                    <td>@p.Category</td>
                    <td>@p.Price.ToString("c")</td>
                    <td>
                        <NavLink class="btn btn-info btn-sm"
                                 href="@GetDetailsUrl(p.ProductID)">
                            Details
                        </NavLink>
                        <NavLink class="btn btn-warning btn-sm"
                                 href="@GetEditUrl(p.ProductID)">
                            Edit
                        </NavLink>
                        <button class="btn btn-danger btn-sm"
                                @onclick="@(e => DeleteProduct(p))">
                            Delete
                        </button>
                    </td>
                </tr>
            }
        } else {
            <tr>
                <td colspan="5" class="text-center">No Products</td>
            </tr>
        }
    </tbody>
</table>

<NavLink class="btn btn-primary" href="/admin/products/create">Create</NavLink>

@code {

    public IStoreRepository Repository => Service;

    public IEnumerable<Product> ProductData { get; set; }
```

```
protected async override Task OnInitializedAsync() {
    await UpdateData();
}

public async Task UpdateData() {
    ProductData = await Repository.Products.ToListAsync();
}

public async Task DeleteProduct(Product p) {
    Repository.DeleteProduct(p);
    await UpdateData();
}

public string GetDetailsUrl(long id) => $"/admin/products/details/{id}";
public string GetEditUrl(long id) => $"/admin/products/edit/{id}";
}
```

The new button element is configured with the @onclick attribute, which invokes the DeleteProduct method. The selected Product object is removed from the database, and the data displayed by the component is updated. Restart ASP.NET Core, request http://localhost:5000/admin/products, and click a Delete button to remove an object from the database, as shown in Figure 10-9.

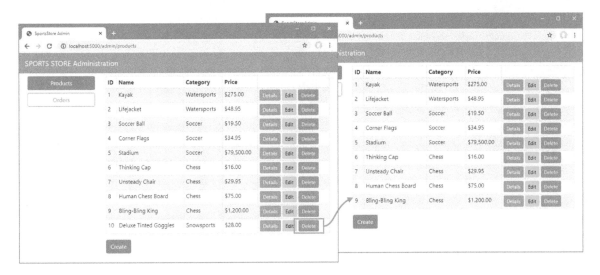

Figure 10-9. *Deleting objects from the database*

Summary

In this chapter, I introduced the administration capability and showed you how to use Blazor Server to implement CRUD operations that allow the administrator to create, read, update, and delete products from the repository and mark orders as shipped. In the next chapter, I show you how to secure the administration functions so that they are not available to all users, and I prepare the SportsStore application for deployment into production.

CHAPTER 11

SportsStore: Security and Deployment

Securing the Administration Features

Authentication and authorization are provided by the ASP.NET Core Identity system, which integrates neatly into the ASP.NET Core platform and the individual application frameworks. In the sections that follow, I will create a basic security setup that allows one user, called Admin, to authenticate and access the administration features in the application. ASP.NET Core Identity provides many more features for authenticating users and authorizing access to application features and data, and you can find more information in Chapters 37 and 38, where I show you how to create and manage user accounts and how to perform authorization using roles. But, as I noted previously, ASP.NET Core Identity is a large framework in its own right, and I cover only the basic features in this book.

My goal in this chapter is just to get enough functionality in place to prevent customers from being able to access the sensitive parts of the SportsStore application and, in doing so, give you a flavor of how authentication and authorization fit into an ASP.NET Core application.

■ **Tip** You can download the example project for this chapter—and for all the other chapters in this book—from `https://github.com/apress/pro-asp.net-core-3`. See Chapter 1 for how to get help if you have problems running the examples.

Creating the Identity Database

The ASP.NET Identity system is endlessly configurable and extensible and supports lots of options for how its user data is stored. I am going to use the most common, which is to store the data using Microsoft SQL Server accessed using Entity Framework Core.

Installing the Identity Package for Entity Framework Core

To add the package that contains the ASPASP.NET Core Identity support for Entity Framework Core, use a PowerShell command prompt to run the command shown in Listing 11-1 in the SportsStore folder.

Listing 11-1. Installing the Entity Framework Core Package

```
dotnet add package Microsoft.AspNetCore.Identity.EntityFrameworkCore --version 3.1.0
```

Creating the Context Class

I need to create a database context file that will act as the bridge between the database and the Identity model objects it provides access to. I added a class file called AppIdentityDbContext.cs to the Models folder and used it to define the class shown in Listing 11-2.

Listing 11-2. The Contents of the AppIdentityDbContext.cs File in the SportsStore/Models Folder

```
using Microsoft.AspNetCore.Identity;
using Microsoft.AspNetCore.Identity.EntityFrameworkCore;
using Microsoft.EntityFrameworkCore;
```

© Adam Freeman 2020   233
A. Freeman, *Pro ASP.NET Core 3*, https://doi.org/10.1007/978-1-4842-5440-0_11

```
namespace SportsStore.Models {

    public class AppIdentityDbContext : IdentityDbContext<IdentityUser> {

        public AppIdentityDbContext(DbContextOptions<AppIdentityDbContext> options)
            : base(options) { }
    }
}
```

The AppIdentityDbContext class is derived from IdentityDbContext, which provides Identity-specific features for Entity Framework Core. For the type parameter, I used the IdentityUser class, which is the built-in class used to represent users.

Defining the Connection String

The next step is to define the connection string that will be for the database. Listing 11-3 shows the connection string to the appsettings.json file of the SportsStore project, which follows the same format as the connection string that I defined for the product database.

Listing 11-3. Defining a Connection String in the appsettings.json File in the SportsStore Folder

```
{
  "Logging": {
    "LogLevel": {
      "Default": "Information",
      "Microsoft": "Warning",
      "Microsoft.Hosting.Lifetime": "Information"
    }
  },
  "AllowedHosts": "*",
  "ConnectionStrings": {
    "SportsStoreConnection": "Server=(localdb)\\MSSQLLocalDB;Database=SportsStore;MultipleActiveResultSets=tr
ue",
    "IdentityConnection": "Server=(localdb)\\MSSQLLocalDB;Database=Identity;MultipleActiveResultSets=true"
  }
}
```

Remember that the connection string has to be defined in a single unbroken line in the appsettings.json file and is shown across multiple lines in the listing only because of the fixed width of a book page. The addition in the listing defines a connection string called IdentityConnection that specifies a LocalDB database called Identity.

Configuring the Application

Like other ASP.NET Core features, Identity is configured in the Startup class. Listing 11-4 shows the additions I made to set up Identity in the SportsStore project, using the context class and connection string defined previously.

Listing 11-4. Configuring Identity in the Startup.cs File in the SportsStore Folder

```
using System;
using System.Collections.Generic;
using System.Linq;
using System.Threading.Tasks;
using Microsoft.AspNetCore.Builder;
using Microsoft.AspNetCore.Hosting;
using Microsoft.AspNetCore.Http;
using Microsoft.Extensions.DependencyInjection;
using Microsoft.Extensions.Hosting;
using Microsoft.Extensions.Configuration;
```

```
using Microsoft.EntityFrameworkCore;
using SportsStore.Models;
using Microsoft.AspNetCore.Identity;

namespace SportsStore {
    public class Startup {

        public Startup(IConfiguration config) {
            Configuration = config;
        }

        private IConfiguration Configuration { get; set; }

        public void ConfigureServices(IServiceCollection services) {
            services.AddControllersWithViews();
            services.AddDbContext<StoreDbContext>(opts => {
                opts.UseSqlServer(
                    Configuration["ConnectionStrings:SportsStoreConnection"]);
            });
            services.AddScoped<IStoreRepository, EFStoreRepository>();
            services.AddScoped<IOrderRepository, EFOrderRepository>();
            services.AddRazorPages();
            services.AddDistributedMemoryCache();
            services.AddSession();
            services.AddScoped<Cart>(sp => SessionCart.GetCart(sp));
            services.AddSingleton<IHttpContextAccessor, HttpContextAccessor>();
            services.AddServerSideBlazor();

            services.AddDbContext<AppIdentityDbContext>(options =>
                options.UseSqlServer(
                    Configuration["ConnectionStrings:IdentityConnection"]));

            services.AddIdentity<IdentityUser, IdentityRole>()
                .AddEntityFrameworkStores<AppIdentityDbContext>();
        }

        public void Configure(IApplicationBuilder app, IWebHostEnvironment env) {
            app.UseDeveloperExceptionPage();
            app.UseStatusCodePages();
            app.UseStaticFiles();
            app.UseSession();
            app.UseRouting();

            app.UseAuthentication();
            app.UseAuthorization();

            app.UseEndpoints(endpoints => {
                endpoints.MapControllerRoute("catpage",
                    "{category}/Page{productPage:int}",
                    new { Controller = "Home", action = "Index" });

                endpoints.MapControllerRoute("page", "Page{productPage:int}",
                    new { Controller = "Home", action = "Index", productPage = 1 });

                endpoints.MapControllerRoute("category", "{category}",
                    new { Controller = "Home", action = "Index", productPage = 1 });
```

```
            endpoints.MapControllerRoute("pagination",
                "Products/Page{productPage}",
                new { Controller = "Home", action = "Index", productPage = 1 });
            endpoints.MapDefaultControllerRoute();
            endpoints.MapRazorPages();
            endpoints.MapBlazorHub();
            endpoints.MapFallbackToPage("/admin/{*catchall}", "/Admin/Index");
        });

        SeedData.EnsurePopulated(app);
    }
  }
}
```

In the ConfigureServices method, I extended the Entity Framework Core configuration to register the context class and used the AddIdentity method to set up the Identity services using the built-in classes to represent users and roles.

In the Configure method, I called the UseAuthentication and UseAuthorization methods to set up the middleware components that implement the security policy. These methods must appear between the UseRouting and UseEndpoints methods.

Creating and Applying the Database Migration

The basic configuration is in place, and it is time to use the Entity Framework Core migrations feature to define the schema and apply it to the database. Open a new command prompt or PowerShell window and run the command shown in Listing 11-5 in the SportsStore folder to create a new migration for the Identity database.

Listing 11-5. Creating the Identity Migration

```
dotnet ef migrations add Initial --context AppIdentityDbContext
```

The important difference from previous database commands is that I have used the -context argument to specify the name of the context class associated with the database that I want to work with, which is AppIdentityDbContext. When you have multiple databases in the application, it is important to ensure that you are working with the right context class.

Once Entity Framework Core has generated the initial migration, run the command shown in Listing 11-6 in the SportsStore folder to create the database and apply the migration.

Listing 11-6. Applying the Identity Migration

```
dotnet ef database update --context AppIdentityDbContext
```

The result is a new LocalDB database called Identity that you can inspect using the Visual Studio SQL Server Object Explorer.

Defining the Seed Data

I am going to explicitly create the Admin user by seeding the database when the application starts. I added a class file called IdentitySeedData.cs to the Models folder and defined the static class shown in Listing 11-7.

Listing 11-7. The Contents of the IdentitySeedData.cs File in the SportsStore/Models Folder

```
using Microsoft.AspNetCore.Builder;
using Microsoft.AspNetCore.Identity;
using Microsoft.Extensions.DependencyInjection;
using Microsoft.EntityFrameworkCore;
using System.Linq;
```

```
namespace SportsStore.Models {

    public static class IdentitySeedData {
        private const string adminUser = "Admin";
        private const string adminPassword = "Secret123$";

        public static async void EnsurePopulated(IApplicationBuilder app) {

            AppIdentityDbContext context = app.ApplicationServices
                .CreateScope().ServiceProvider
                .GetRequiredService<AppIdentityDbContext>();
            if (context.Database.GetPendingMigrations().Any()) {
                context.Database.Migrate();
            }

            UserManager<IdentityUser> userManager = app.ApplicationServices
                .CreateScope().ServiceProvider
                .GetRequiredService<UserManager<IdentityUser>>();

            IdentityUser user = await userManager.FindByIdAsync(adminUser);
            if (user == null) {
                user = new IdentityUser("Admin");
                user.Email = "admin@example.com";
                user.PhoneNumber = "555-1234";
                await userManager.CreateAsync(user, adminPassword);
            }
        }
    }
}
```

This code ensures the database is created and up-to-date and uses the UserManager<T> class, which is provided as a service by ASP.NET Core Identity for managing users, as described in Chapter 38. The database is searched for the Admin user account, which is created—with a password of Secret123$—if it is not present. Do not change the hard-coded password in this example because Identity has a validation policy that requires passwords to contain a number and range of characters. See Chapter 38 for details of how to change the validation settings.

■ **Caution**   Hard-coding the details of an administrator account is often required so that you can log into an application once it has been deployed and start administering it. When you do this, you must remember to change the password for the account you have created. See Chapter 38 for details of how to change passwords using Identity. See Chapter 15 for how to keep sensitive data, such as default passwords, out of source code control.

To ensure that the Identity database is seeded when the application starts, I added the statement shown in Listing 11-8 to the Configure method of the Startup class.

Listing 11-8. Seeding the Identity Database in the Startup.cs File in the SportsStore Folder

```
...
public void Configure(IApplicationBuilder app, IWebHostEnvironment env) {
    app.UseDeveloperExceptionPage();
    app.UseStatusCodePages();
    app.UseStaticFiles();
    app.UseSession();
    app.UseAuthentication();
    app.UseRouting();
```

```
    app.UseEndpoints(endpoints => {
        endpoints.MapControllerRoute("catpage",
            "{category}/Page{productPage:int}",
            new { Controller = "Home", action = "Index" });

        endpoints.MapControllerRoute("page", "Page{productPage:int}",
            new { Controller = "Home", action = "Index", productPage = 1 });

        endpoints.MapControllerRoute("category", "{category}",
            new { Controller = "Home", action = "Index", productPage = 1 });

        endpoints.MapControllerRoute("pagination",
            "Products/Page{productPage}",
            new { Controller = "Home", action = "Index", productPage = 1 });
        endpoints.MapDefaultControllerRoute();
        endpoints.MapRazorPages();
        endpoints.MapBlazorHub();
        endpoints.MapFallbackToPage("/admin/{*catchall}", "/Admin/Index");
    });

    SeedData.EnsurePopulated(app);
    IdentitySeedData.EnsurePopulated(app);
}
...
```

DELETING AND RE-CREATING THE ASP.NET CORE IDENTITY DATABASE

If you need to reset the Identity database, then run the following command:

```
dotnet ef database drop --force --context AppIdentityDbContext
```

Restart the application, and the database will be re-created and populated with seed data.

Adding a Conventional Administration Feature

In Listing 11-9, I used Blazor to create the administration features so that I could demonstrate a wide range of ASP.NET Core features in the SportsStore project. Although Blazor is useful, it is not suitable for all projects—as I explain in Part 4—and most projects are likely to use controllers or Razor Pages for their administration features. I describe the way that ASP.NET Core Identity works with all the application frameworks in Chapter 38, but just to provide a balance to the all-Blazor tools created in Chapter 10, I am going to create a Razor Page that will display the list of users in the ASP.NET Core Identity database. I describe how to manage the Identity database in more detail in Chapter 38, and this Razor Page is just to add a sensitive feature to the SportsStore application that isn't created with Blazor. Add a Razor Page named IdentityUsers.cshtml to the SportsStore/Pages/Admin folder with the contents shown in Listing 11-9.

Listing 11-9. The Contents of the IdentityUsers.cshtml File in the SportsStore/Pages/Admin Folder

```
@page
@model IdentityUsersModel
@using Microsoft.AspNetCore.Identity

<h3 class="bg-primary text-white text-center p-2">Admin User</h3>

<table class="table table-sm table-striped table-bordered">
    <tbody>
        <tr><th>User</th><td>@Model.AdminUser.UserName</td></tr>
        <tr><th>Email</th><td>@Model.AdminUser.Email</td></tr>
```

```
        <tr><th>Phone</th><td>@Model.AdminUser.PhoneNumber</td></tr>
    </tbody>
</table>

@functions{

    public class IdentityUsersModel: PageModel {
        private UserManager<IdentityUser> userManager;

        public IdentityUsersModel(UserManager<IdentityUser> mgr) {
            userManager = mgr;
        }

        public IdentityUser AdminUser{ get; set; }

        public async Task OnGetAsync() {
            AdminUser = await userManager.FindByNameAsync("Admin");
        }
    }
}
```

Restart ASP.NET Core and request http://localhost:5000/admin/identityusers to see the content generated by the Razor Page, which is shown in Figure 11-1.

Figure 11-1. *A Razor Page administration feature*

Applying a Basic Authorization Policy

Now that I have configured ASP.NET Core Identity, I can apply an authorization policy to the parts of the application that I want to protect. I am going to use the most basic authorization policy possible, which is to allow access to any authenticated user. Although this can be a useful policy in real applications as well, there are also options for creating finer-grained authorization controls, as described in Chapters 37 and 38, but since the SportsStore application has only one user, distinguishing between anonymous and authenticated requests is sufficient.

For controllers and Razor pages, the Authorize attribute is used to restrict access, as shown in Listing 11-10.

Listing 11-10. Restricting Access in the IdentityUsers.cshtml File in the SportsStore/Pages/Admin Folder

```
@page
@model IdentityUsersModel
@using Microsoft.AspNetCore.Identity
@using Microsoft.AspNetCore.Authorization

<h3 class="bg-primary text-white text-center p-2">Admin User</h3>

<table class="table table-sm table-striped table-bordered">
    <tbody>
        <tr><th>User</th><td>@Model.AdminUser.UserName</td></tr>
        <tr><th>Email</th><td>@Model.AdminUser.Email</td></tr>
        <tr><th>Phone</th><td>@Model.AdminUser.PhoneNumber</td></tr>
    </tbody>
</table>

@functions{

    [Authorize]
    public class IdentityUsersModel: PageModel {
        private UserManager<IdentityUser> userManager;

        public IdentityUsersModel(UserManager<IdentityUser> mgr) {
            userManager = mgr;
        }

        public IdentityUser AdminUser{ get; set; }

        public async Task OnGetAsync() {
            AdminUser = await userManager.FindByNameAsync("Admin");
        }
    }
}
```

When there are only authorized and unauthorized users, the Authorize attribute can be applied to the Razor Page that acts as the entry point for the Blazor part of the application, as shown in Listing 11-11.

Listing 11-11. Applying Authorization in the Index.cshtml File in the SportsStore/Pages/Admin Folder

```
@page "/admin"
@{ Layout = null; }
@using Microsoft.AspNetCore.Authorization
@attribute [Authorize]

<!DOCTYPE html>
<html>
<head>
    <title>SportsStore Admin</title>
    <link href="/lib/twitter-bootstrap/css/bootstrap.min.css" rel="stylesheet" />
    <base href="/" />
</head>
<body>
    <component type="typeof(Routed)" render-mode="Server" />
    <script src="/_framework/blazor.server.js"></script>
</body>
</html>
```

Since this Razor Page has been configured with a page model class, I can apply the attribute with an @attribute expression.

Creating the Account Controller and Views

When an unauthenticated user sends a request that requires authorization, the user is redirected to the /Account/Login URL, which the application can use to prompt the user for their credentials. In Listing 11-12, I show you how to handle authentication using Razor Pages, so, for variety, I am going to use controllers and views for SportsStore. In preparation, I added a view model to represent the user's credentials by adding a class file called LoginModel.cs to the Models/ViewModels folder and using it to define the class shown in Listing 11-12.

Listing 11-12. The Contents of the LoginModel.cs File in the SportsStore/Models/ViewModels Folder

```
using System.ComponentModel.DataAnnotations;

namespace SportsStore.Models.ViewModels {

    public class LoginModel {

        [Required]
        public string Name { get; set; }

        [Required]
        public string Password { get; set; }

        public string ReturnUrl { get; set; } = "/";
    }
}
```

The Name and Password properties have been decorated with the Required attribute, which uses model validation to ensure that values have been provided. Next, I added a class file called AccountController.cs to the Controllers folder and used it to define the controller shown in Listing 11-13. This is the controller that will respond to requests to the /Account/Login URL.

Listing 11-13. The Contents of the AccountController.cs File in the SportsStore/Controllers Folder

```
using System.Threading.Tasks;
using Microsoft.AspNetCore.Authorization;
using Microsoft.AspNetCore.Identity;
using Microsoft.AspNetCore.Mvc;
using SportsStore.Models.ViewModels;

namespace SportsStore.Controllers {

    public class AccountController : Controller {
        private UserManager<IdentityUser> userManager;
        private SignInManager<IdentityUser> signInManager;

        public AccountController(UserManager<IdentityUser> userMgr,
                SignInManager<IdentityUser> signInMgr) {
            userManager = userMgr;
            signInManager = signInMgr;
        }

        public ViewResult Login(string returnUrl) {
            return View(new LoginModel {
                ReturnUrl = returnUrl
            });
        }

        [HttpPost]
        [ValidateAntiForgeryToken]
```

```
        public async Task<IActionResult> Login(LoginModel loginModel) {
            if (ModelState.IsValid) {
                IdentityUser user =
                    await userManager.FindByNameAsync(loginModel.Name);
                if (user != null) {
                    await signInManager.SignOutAsync();
                    if ((await signInManager.PasswordSignInAsync(user,
                            loginModel.Password, false, false)).Succeeded) {
                        return Redirect(loginModel?.ReturnUrl ?? "/Admin");
                    }
                }
            }
            ModelState.AddModelError("", "Invalid name or password");
            return View(loginModel);
        }

        [Authorize]
        public async Task<RedirectResult> Logout(string returnUrl = "/") {
            await signInManager.SignOutAsync();
            return Redirect(returnUrl);
        }
    }
}
```

When the user is redirected to the /Account/Login URL, the GET version of the Login action method renders the default view for the page, providing a view model object that includes the URL that the browser should be redirected to if the authentication request is successful.

Authentication credentials are submitted to the POST version of the Login method, which uses the UserManager<IdentityUser> and SignInManager<IdentityUser> services that have been received through the controller's constructor to authenticate the user and log them into the system. I explain how these classes work in Chapters 37 and 38, but for now, it is enough to know that if there is an authentication failure, then I create a model validation error and render the default view; however, if authentication is successful, then I redirect the user to the URL that they want to access before they are prompted for their credentials.

■ **Caution**   In general, using client-side data validation is a good idea. It offloads some of the work from your server and gives users immediate feedback about the data they are providing. However, you should not be tempted to perform authentication at the client, as this would typically involve sending valid credentials to the client so they can be used to check the username and password that the user has entered, or at least trusting the client's report of whether they have successfully authenticated. Authentication should always be done at the server.

To provide the Login method with a view to render, I created the Views/Account folder and added a Razor View file called Login.cshtml with the contents shown in Listing 11-14.

Listing 11-14. The Contents of the Login.cshtml File in the SportsStore/Views/Account Folder

```
@model LoginModel
@{ Layout = null; }
<!DOCTYPE html>
<html>
<head>
    <meta name="viewport" content="width=device-width" />
    <title>SportsStore</title>
    <link href="/lib/twitter-bootstrap/css/bootstrap.min.css" rel="stylesheet" />
</head>
```

```
<body>
    <div class="bg-dark text-white p-2">
        <span class="navbar-brand ml-2">SPORTS STORE</span>
    </div>
    <div class="m-1 p-1">
        <div class="text-danger" asp-validation-summary="All"></div>

        <form asp-action="Login" asp-controller="Account" method="post">
            <input type="hidden" asp-for="ReturnUrl" />
            <div class="form-group">
                <label asp-for="Name"></label>
                <div asp-validation-for="Name" class="text-danger"></div>
                <input asp-for="Name" class="form-control" />
            </div>
            <div class="form-group">
                <label asp-for="Password"></label>
                <div asp-validation-for="Password" class="text-danger"></div>
                <input asp-for="Password" type="password" class="form-control" />
            </div>
            <button class="btn btn-primary" type="submit">Log In</button>
        </form>
    </div>
</body>
</html>
```

The final step is a change to the shared administration layout to add a button that will log the current user out by sending a request to the Logout action, as shown in Listing 11-15. This is a useful feature that makes it easier to test the application, without which you would need to clear the browser's cookies to return to the unauthenticated state.

Listing 11-15. Adding a Logout Button in the AdminLayout.razor File in the SportsStore/Pages/Admin Folder

```
@inherits LayoutComponentBase

<div class="bg-info text-white p-2">
    <div class="container-fluid">
        <div class="row">
            <div class="col">
                <span class="navbar-brand ml-2">SPORTS STORE Administration</span>
            </div>
            <div class="col-2 text-right">
                <a class="btn btn-sm btn-primary" href="/account/logout">Log Out</a>
            </div>
        </div>
    </div>
</div>
<div class="container-fluid">
    <div class="row p-2">
        <div class="col-3">
            <NavLink class="btn btn-outline-primary btn-block"
                     href="/admin/products"
                     ActiveClass="btn-primary text-white"
                     Match="NavLinkMatch.Prefix">
                Products
            </NavLink>
            <NavLink class="btn btn-outline-primary btn-block"
                     href="/admin/orders"
                     ActiveClass="btn-primary text-white"
                     Match="NavLinkMatch.Prefix">
```

```
                    Orders
                </NavLink>
            </div>
            <div class="col">
                @Body
            </div>
        </div>
    </div>
</div>
```

Testing the Security Policy

Everything is in place, and you can test the security policy by restarting ASP.NET Core and requesting http://localhost:5000/admin or http://localhost:5000/admin/identityusers.

Since you are presently unauthenticated and you are trying to target an action that requires authorization, your browser will be redirected to the /Account/Login URL. Enter **Admin** and **Secret123$** as the name and password and submit the form. The Account controller will check the credentials you provided with the seed data added to the Identity database and—assuming you entered the right details—authenticate you and redirect you to the URL you requested, to which you now have access. Figure 11-2 illustrates the process.

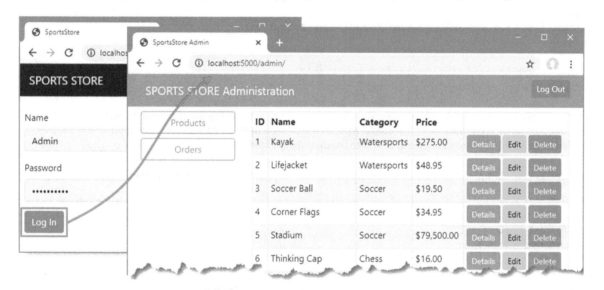

Figure 11-2. *The administration authentication/authorization process*

Preparing ASP.NET Core for Deployment

In this section, I will prepare SportsStore and create a container that can be deployed into production. There is a wide range of deployment models available for ASP.NET Core applications, but I have picked Docker containers because they can be run on most hosting platforms or be deployed into a private data center. This is not a complete guide to deployment, but it will give you a sense of the process to prepare an application.

Configuring Error Handling

At the moment, the application is configured to use the developer-friendly error pages, which provide helpful information when a problem occurs. This is not information that end users should see, so I added a Razor Page named Error.cshtml to the Pages folder with the content shown in Listing 11-16.

Listing 11-16. The Contents of the Error.cshtml File in the Pages Folder

```
@page "/error"
@{ Layout = null; }
<!DOCTYPE html>
```

```html
<html>
<head>
    <meta name="viewport" content="width=device-width" />
    <link href="/lib/twitter-bootstrap/css/bootstrap.min.css" rel="stylesheet" />
    <title>Error</title>
</head>
<body class="text-center">
    <h2 class="text-danger">Error.</h2>
    <h3 class="text-danger">An error occurred while processing your request</h3>
</body>
</html>
```

This kind of error page is the last resort, and it is best to keep it as simple as possible and not to rely on shared views, view components, or other rich features. In this case, I have disabled shared layouts and defined a simple HTML document that explains that there has been an error, without providing any information about what has happened.

In Listing 11-17, I have reconfigured the application so that the Error page is used for unhandled exceptions when the application is in the production environment.

Listing 11-17. Configuring Error Handling in the Startup.cs File in the SportsStore Folder

```csharp
...
public void Configure(IApplicationBuilder app, IWebHostEnvironment env) {

    if (env.IsProduction()) {
        app.UseExceptionHandler("/error");
    } else {
        app.UseDeveloperExceptionPage();
        app.UseStatusCodePages();
    }

    app.UseStaticFiles();
    app.UseSession();

    app.UseRouting();

    app.UseAuthentication();
    app.UseAuthorization();

    app.UseEndpoints(endpoints => {
        endpoints.MapControllerRoute("catpage",
            "{category}/Page{productPage:int}",
            new { Controller = "Home", action = "Index" });

        endpoints.MapControllerRoute("page", "Page{productPage:int}",
            new { Controller = "Home", action = "Index", productPage = 1 });

        endpoints.MapControllerRoute("category", "{category}",
            new { Controller = "Home", action = "Index", productPage = 1 });

        endpoints.MapControllerRoute("pagination",
            "Products/Page{productPage}",
            new { Controller = "Home", action = "Index", productPage = 1 });
        endpoints.MapDefaultControllerRoute();
        endpoints.MapRazorPages();
        endpoints.MapBlazorHub();
        endpoints.MapFallbackToPage("/admin/{*catchall}", "/Admin/Index");
    });
```

```
    SeedData.EnsurePopulated(app);
    IdentitySeedData.EnsurePopulated(app);
}
...
```

As I explain in Chapter 12, the IWebHostEnvironment parameter defined by the Configure method describes the environment in which the application is running. The changes mean that the UseExceptionHandler method is called when the application is in production, but the developer-friendly error pages are used otherwise.

Creating the Production Configuration Settings

The JSON configuration files that are used to define settings such as connection strings can be created so they apply only when the application is in a specific environment, such as development, staging, or production. The template I used to create the SportsStore project in Chapter 7 created the appsettings.json and appsettings.Development.json files, which are intended to be the default settings that are overridden with those that are specific for development. I am going to take the reverse approach for this chapter and define a file that contains just those settings that are specific to production. Add a JSON File named appsettings.Production.json to the SportsStore folder with the content shown in Listing 11-18.

■ **Caution** Do not use these connection strings in real projects. You must correctly describe the connection to your production database, which is unlikely to be the same as the ones in the listing.

Listing 11-18. The Contents of the appsettings.Production.json File in the SportsStore Folder

```
{
  "ConnectionStrings": {
    "SportsStoreConnection": "Server=sqlserver;Database=SportsStore;MultipleActiveResultSets=true;User=sa;
    Password=MyDatabaseSecret123",
    "IdentityConnection": "Server=sqlserver;Database=Identity;MultipleActiveResultSets=true;User=sa;Password=
    MyDatabaseSecret123"
  }
}
```

These connection strings, each of which is defined on a single line, describe connections to SQL Server running on sqlserver, which is another Docker container running SQL Server.

Creating the Docker Image

In the sections that follow, I configure and create the Docker image for the application that can be deployed into a container environment such as Microsoft Azure or Amazon Web Services. Bear in mind that containers are only one style of deployment and there are many others available if this approach does not suit you.

■ **Note** Bear in mind that I am going to connect to a database running on the development machine, which is not how most real applications are configured. Be sure to configure the database connection strings and the container networking settings to match your production environment.

Installing Docker Desktop

Go to Docker.com and download and install the Docker Desktop package. Follow the installation process, reboot your Windows machine, and run the command shown in Listing 11-19 to check that Docker has been installed and is in your path. (The Docker installation process seems to change often, which is why I have not been more specific about the process.)

■ **Note** You will have to create an account on Docker.com to download the installer.

Listing 11-19. Checking the Docker Desktop Installation

```
docker --version
```

Creating the Docker Configuration Files

Docker is configured using a file named Dockerfile. There is no Visual Studio item template for this file, so use the Text File template to add a file named Dockerfile.text to the project and then rename the file to Dockerfile. If you are using Visual Studio Code, you can just create a file named Dockerfile without the extension. Use the configuration settings shown in Listing 11-20 as the contents for the new file.

Listing 11-20. The Contents of the Dockerfile File in the SportsStore Folder

```
FROM mcr.microsoft.com/dotnet/core/aspnet:3.1
FROM mcr.microsoft.com/dotnet/core/sdk:3.1

COPY /bin/Release/netcoreapp3.1/publish/ SportsStore/

ENV ASPNETCORE_ENVIRONMENT Production

EXPOSE 5000
WORKDIR /SportsStore
ENTRYPOINT ["dotnet", "SportsStore.dll",  "--urls=http://0.0.0.0:5000"]
```

These instructions copy the SportsStore application into a Docker image and configure its execution. Next, create a file called docker-compose.yml, with the content shown in Listing 11-21. Visual Studio doesn't have a template for this type of file, but if you select the Text File template and enter the complete filename, it will create the file. Visual Studio Code users can simply create a file named docker-compose.yml.

Listing 11-21. The Contents of the docker-compose.yml File in the SportsStore Folder

```
version: "3"
services:
    sportsstore:
        build: .
        ports:
            - "5000:5000"
        environment:
            - ASPNETCORE_ENVIRONMENT=Production
        depends_on:
            - sqlserver
    sqlserver:
        image: "mcr.microsoft.com/mssql/server"
        environment:
            SA_PASSWORD: "MyDatabaseSecret123"
            ACCEPT_EULA: "Y"
```

The YML files are especially sensitive to formatting and indentation, and it is important to create this file exactly as shown. If you have problems, then use the docker-compose.yml file from the GitHub repository for this book, https://github.com/apress/pro-asp.net-core-3.

Publishing and Imaging the Application

Prepare the SportsStore application by using a PowerShell prompt to run the command shown Listing 11-22 in the SportsStore folder.

Listing 11-22. Preparing the Application

```
dotnet publish -c Release
```

Next, run the command shown in Listing 11-23 to create the Docker image for the SportsStore application. This command will take some time to complete the first time it is run because it will download the Docker images for ASP.NET Core.

Listing 11-23. Performing the Docker Build

```
docker-compose build
```

The first time you run this command, you may be prompted to allow Docker to use the network, as shown in Figure 11-3.

Figure 11-3. *Granting network access*

Click the Allow button, return to the PowerShell prompt, use Control+C to terminate the Docker containers, and run the command in Listing 11-23 again.

Running the Containerized Application

Run the command shown in Listing 11-24 in the SportsStore folder to start the Docker containers for the SportsStore application and SQL Server. This command will take some time to complete the first time it is run because it will download the Docker images for SQL Server.

Listing 11-24. Starting the Containers

```
docker-compose up
```

It can take some time for both containers to start. There is a lot of output, mostly from SQL Server, but the application will be ready when you see output like this:

```
...
sportsstore_1  | info: Microsoft.Hosting.Lifetime[0]
sportsstore_1  |       Now listening on: http://0.0.0.0:5000
sportsstore_1  | info: Microsoft.Hosting.Lifetime[0]
sportsstore_1  |       Application started. Press Ctrl+C to shut down.
sportsstore_1  | info: Microsoft.Hosting.Lifetime[0]
sportsstore_1  |       Hosting environment: Production
sportsstore_1  | info: Microsoft.Hosting.Lifetime[0]
sportsstore_1  |       Content root path: /SportsStore
...
```

Open a new browser window and request http://localhost:5000, and you will receive a response from the containerized version of SportsStore, as shown in Figure 11-4, which is now ready for deployment. Use Control+C at the PowerShell command prompt to terminate the Docker containers.

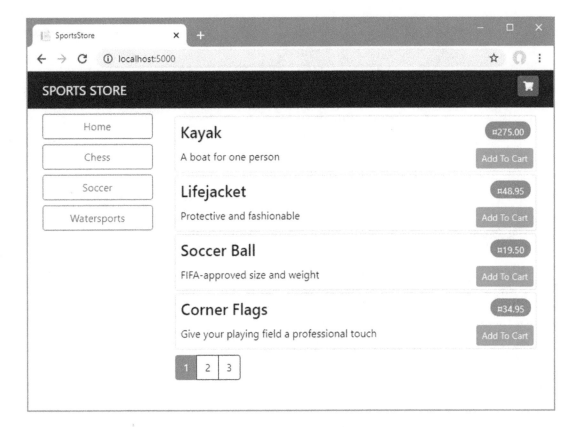

Figure 11-4. *Running the SportsStore application in a container*

Summary

In this and previous chapters, I demonstrated how the ASP.NET Core can be used to create a realistic e-commerce application. This extended example introduced many key features: controllers, action methods, views, Razor Pages, Blazor, routing, validation, authentication, and more. You also saw how some of the key technologies related to how ASP.NET Core can be used. These included the Entity Framework Core, ASP.NET Core Identity, and unit testing. And that's the end of the SportsStore application. In the next part of the book, I start to dig into the details of ASP.NET Core.

PART II

The ASP.NET Core Platform

CHAPTER 12

Understanding the ASP.NET Core Platform

The ASP.NET Core platform is the foundation for creating web applications and provides the features that allow frameworks like MVC and Blazor to be used. In this chapter, I explain how the basic ASP.NET Core features work, describe the purpose of the files in an ASP.NET Core project, and explain how the ASP.NET Core request pipeline is used to process HTTP requests and demonstrate the different ways that it can be customized.

Don't worry if not everything in this chapter makes immediate sense or appears to apply to the applications you intend to create. The features I describe in this chapter are the underpinnings for everything that ASP.NET Core does, and understanding how they work helps provide a context for understanding the features that you will use on a daily basis, as well as giving you the knowledge you need to diagnose problems when you don't get the behavior you expect. Table 12-1 puts the ASP.NET Core platform in context.

Table 12-1. *Putting the ASP.NET Core Platform in Context*

Question	Answer
What is it?	The ASP.NET Core platform is the foundation on which web applications are built and provides features for processing HTTP requests.
Why is it useful?	The ASP.NET Core platform takes care of the low-level details of web applications so that developers can focus on features for the end user.
How is it used?	The key building blocks are services and middleware components, both of which can be created in the Startup class.
Are there any pitfalls or limitations?	The use of the Startup class can be confusing, and close attention must be paid to the order of the statements it contains.
Are there any alternatives?	The ASP.NET Core platform is required for ASP.NET Core applications, but you can choose not to work with the platform directly and rely on just the higher-level ASP.NET Core features, which are described in later chapters.

Table 12-2 summarizes the chapter.

Table 12-2. *Chapter Summary*

Problem	Solution	Listing
Creating a middleware component	Call the Use or UseMiddleware method to add a function or class to the request pipeline	4–6
Modifying a response	Write a middleware component that uses the return pipeline path	7
Preventing other components from processing a request	Short-circuit the request pipeline or create terminal middleware	8, 11, 12
Using different sets of middleware	Create a pipeline branch	9
Configuring middleware components	Use the options pattern	13–16

A. Freeman, *Pro ASP.NET Core 3*, https://doi.org/10.1007/978-1-4842-5440-0_12

Preparing for This Chapter

To prepare for this chapter, I am going to create a new project named Platform, using the template that provides the minimal ASP.NET Core setup. Open a new PowerShell command prompt from the Windows Start menu and run the commands shown in Listing 12-1.

■ **Tip** You can download the example project for this chapter—and for all the other chapters in this book—from `https://github.com/apress/pro-asp.net-core-3`. See Chapter 1 for how to get help if you have problems running the examples.

Listing 12-1. Creating the Project

```
dotnet new globaljson --sdk-version 3.1.101 --output Platform
dotnet new web --no-https --output Platform --framework netcoreapp3.1
dotnet new sln -o Platform

dotnet sln Platform add Platform
```

If you are using Visual Studio, open the Platform.sln file in the Platform folder. Select Project ➤ Platform Properties, navigate to the Debug page, and change the App URL field to **http://localhost:5000**, as shown in Figure 12-1. This changes the port that will be used to receive HTTP requests. Select File ➤ Save All to save the configuration changes.

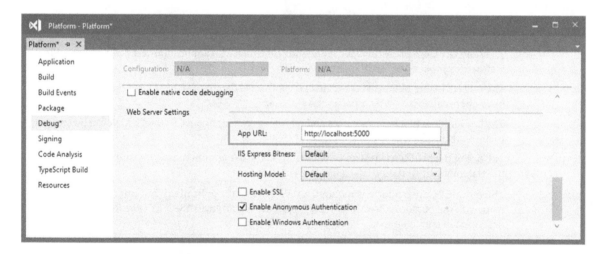

Figure 12-1. Changing the HTTP port

If you are using Visual Studio Code, open the Platform folder. Click the Yes button when prompted to add the assets required for building and debugging the project, as shown in Figure 12-2.

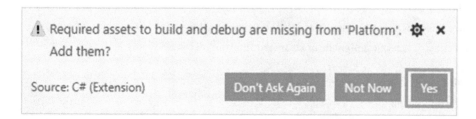

Figure 12-2. Adding project assets

254

Running the Example Application

Start the example application by selecting Start Without Debugging or Run Without Debugging from the Debug menu. If you are using Visual Studio Code, select .NET Core when prompted to select an environment. This is a selection that is made only when the project is first started. A new browser window will be opened, and you will see the output shown in Figure 12-3.

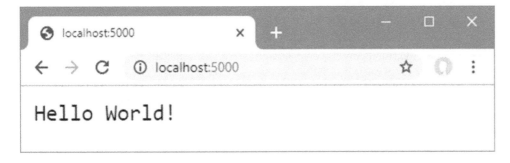

Figure 12-3. *Running the example application*

You can also start the application from the command line by running the command shown in Listing 12-2 in the Platform folder.

Listing 12-2. Starting the Example Application

```
dotnet run
```

This command doesn't open a new browser window, and you will have to manually navigate to http://localhost:5000 to see the output shown in Figure 12-3.

Understanding the ASP.NET Core Platform

To understand ASP.NET Core, it is helpful to focus on just the key features: the request pipeline, middleware, and services. Understanding how these features fit together—even without going into detail—provides useful context for understanding the contents of the ASP.NET Core project and the shape of the ASP.NET Core platform.

Understanding Middleware and the Request Pipeline

The purpose of the ASP.NET Core platform is to receive HTTP requests and send responses to them, which ASP.NET Core delegates to *middleware components*. Middleware components are arranged in a chain, known as the *request pipeline*.

When a new HTTP request arrives, the ASP.NET Core platform creates an object that describes it and a corresponding object that describes the response that will be sent in return. These objects are passed to the first middleware component in the chain, which inspects the request and modifies the response. The request is then passed to the next middleware component in the chain, with each component inspecting the request and adding to the response. Once the request has made its way through the pipeline, the ASP.NET Core platform sends the response, as illustrated in Figure 12-4.

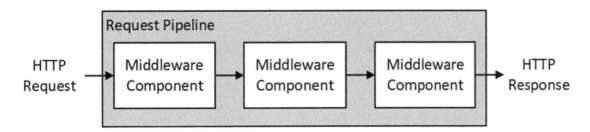

Figure 12-4. *The ASP.NET Core request pipeline*

Some components focus on generating responses for requests, but others are there to provide supporting features, such as formatting specific data types or reading and writing cookies. ASP.NET Core includes middleware components that solve common problems, as described in Chapters 15 and 16, and I show how to create custom middleware components later in this chapter. If no response is generated by the middleware components, then ASP.NET Core will return a response with the HTTP 404 Not Found status code.

Understanding Services

Services are objects that provide features in a web application. Any class can be used as a service, and there are no restrictions on the features that services provide. What makes services special is that they are managed by ASP.NET Core, and a feature called *dependency injection* makes it possible to easily access services anywhere in the application, including middleware components.

Dependency injection can be a difficult topic to understand, and I describe it in detail in Chapter 14. For now, it is enough to know that there are objects that are managed by the ASP.NET Core platform that can be shared by middleware components, either to coordinate between components or to avoid duplicating common features, such as logging or loading configuration data, as shown in Figure 12-5.

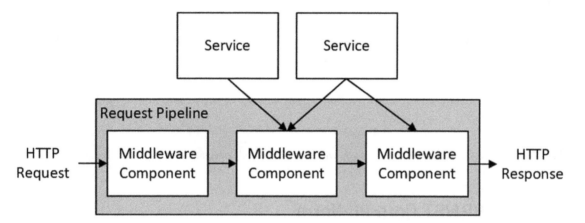

Figure 12-5. *Services in the ASP.NET Core platform*

As the figure shows, middleware components use only the services they require to do their work. As you will learn in later chapters, ASP.NET Core provides some basic services that can be supplemented by additional services that are specific to an application.

Understanding the ASP.NET Core Project

The Empty template produces a project with just enough code and configuration to start the ASP.NET Core runtime with some basic services and middleware components. Figure 12-6 shows the files added to the project by the template.

Figure 12-6. *The files in the example project*

Visual Studio and Visual Studio Code take different approaches to displaying files and folders. Visual Studio hides items that are not commonly used by the development and nests related items together, while Visual Studio Code shows everything.

This is why the two project views shown in the figure are different: Visual Studio has hidden the bin and obj folders and nested the appsettings.Development.json file within the appsettings.json file. The buttons at the top of the Solution Explorer window can be used to prevent nesting and to show all of the files in the project.

Although there are few files in the project, they underpin ASP.NET Core development and are described in Table 12-3.

Table 12-3. *The Files and Folders in the Example Project*

Name	Description
appsettings.json	This file is used to configure the application, as described in Chapter 15.
appsettings.Development.json	This file is used to define configuration settings that are specific to development, as explained in Chapter 15.
bin	This folder contains the compiled application files. Visual Studio hides this folder.
global.json	This file is used to select a specific version of the .NET Core SDK.
Properties/launchSettings.json	This file is used to configure the application when it starts. Visual Studio hides this folder and file.
obj	This folder contains the intermediate output from the compiler. Visual Studio hides this folder.
Platform.csproj	This file describes the project to the .NET Core tools, including the package dependencies and build instructions, as described in the "Understanding the Project File" section. Visual Studio hides this file, but it can be edited by right-clicking the project item in the Solution Explorer and selecting Edit Project File from the pop-up menu.
Program.cs	This file is the entry point for the ASP.NET Core platform.
Startup.cs	This file is used to configure the ASP.NET Core runtime and its associated frameworks, as described in the "Understanding the Startup Class" section.

Understanding the Entry Point

.NET Core applications define a main method, which is invoked when the application is executed and which is known as the application's *entry point*. For ASP.NET Core, the main method is defined by the Program class in the Program.cs file. Here is the content of the Program.cs in the example project:

```
using System;
using System.Collections.Generic;
using System.Linq;
using System.Threading.Tasks;
using Microsoft.AspNetCore.Hosting;
using Microsoft.Extensions.Configuration;
using Microsoft.Extensions.Hosting;
using Microsoft.Extensions.Logging;

namespace Platform {
    public class Program {

        public static void Main(string[] args) {
            CreateHostBuilder(args).Build().Run();
        }

        public static IHostBuilder CreateHostBuilder(string[] args) =>
            Host.CreateDefaultBuilder(args)
                .ConfigureWebHostDefaults(webBuilder => {
                    webBuilder.UseStartup<Startup>();
                });
    }
}
```

The .NET Core runtime invokes the Main method, which calls the CreateHostBuilder method. The first step in the setup process is the call to the Host.CreateDefaultBuilder method.

```
...
public static IHostBuilder CreateHostBuilder(string[] args) =>
    Host.CreateDefaultBuilder(args)
        .ConfigureWebHostDefaults(webBuilder => {
            webBuilder.UseStartup<Startup>();
        });
...
```

This method is responsible for setting up the basic features of the ASP.NET Core platform, including creating services responsible for configuration data and logging, both of which are described in Chapter 15. This method also sets up the HTTP server, named Kestrel, that is used to receive HTTP requests and adds support for working with Internet Information Services (IIS).

The result from the CreateDefaultBuilder method is passed to the ConfigureWebHostDefaults method, which selects the Startup class as the next step in the startup process.

```
...
public static IHostBuilder CreateHostBuilder(string[] args) =>
    Host.CreateDefaultBuilder(args)
        .ConfigureWebHostDefaults(webBuilder => {
            webBuilder.UseStartup<Startup>();
        });
...
```

The statements added to the Program class by the Empty template are suitable for most ASP.NET Core projects, but you can change them if an application has specific requirements.

Understanding the Startup Class

The Startup class is where most of the setup required by an application is performed, using the two methods that are added to the class when the project is created.

```
using System;
using System.Collections.Generic;
using System.Linq;
using System.Threading.Tasks;
using Microsoft.AspNetCore.Builder;
using Microsoft.AspNetCore.Hosting;
using Microsoft.AspNetCore.Http;
using Microsoft.Extensions.DependencyInjection;
using Microsoft.Extensions.Hosting;

namespace Platform {
    public class Startup {

        public void ConfigureServices(IServiceCollection services) {
        }

        public void Configure(IApplicationBuilder app, IWebHostEnvironment env) {

            if (env.IsDevelopment()) {
                app.UseDeveloperExceptionPage();
            }

            app.UseRouting();

            app.UseEndpoints(endpoints => {
                endpoints.MapGet("/", async context => {
                    await context.Response.WriteAsync("Hello World!");
                });
            });
        }
    }
}
```

The ConfigureServices method is used to define the services that the application requires. By default, only the services created by the Program class are available, but you will see examples of different types of service used in later chapters, and Chapter 14 describes in detail the mechanism for using services.

The Configure method is used to register the middleware components for the request pipeline. Three middleware components are added to the pipeline by default when a project is created using the Empty template, each of which is described in Table 12-4.

Table 12-4. *The Middleware Added to the Pipeline by the Empty Template*

Middleware Method	Description
UseDeveloperExceptionPage	This method adds a middleware component that includes details of unhandled exceptions. The IsDevelopment method is used to ensure this information isn't presented to users, as described in Chapter 16.
UseRouting	This method adds the endpoint routing middleware component to the pipeline, which is responsible for determining how some requests are handled and is used with other parts of ASP.NET Core such as the MVC Framework. Routing is described in detail in Chapter 13.
UseEndpoints	This method provides the configuration for the endpoint routing middleware added by the UseRouting method. The configuration is described in Chapter 13.

Microsoft provides other middleware as part of ASP.NET Core that deals with the most common features required by web applications, which I describe in Chapters 15 and 16. You can also create your own middleware, as described in the "Creating Custom Middleware" section, when the built-in features don't suit your requirements.

Understanding the Project File

The `Platform.csproj` file, known as the *project file*, contains the information that .NET Core uses to build the project and keep track of dependencies. Here is the content that was added to the file by the Empty template when the project was created:

```
<Project Sdk="Microsoft.NET.Sdk.Web">

  <PropertyGroup>
    <TargetFramework>netcoreapp3.1</TargetFramework>
  </PropertyGroup>

</Project>
```

The `csproj` file is hidden when using Visual Studio; you can edit it by right-clicking the Platform project item in the Solution Explorer and selecting Edit Project File from the popup menu.

The project file contains XML elements that describe the project to MSBuild, the Microsoft build engine. MSBuild can be used to create complex build processes and is described in detail at `https://docs.microsoft.com/en-gb/visualstudio/msbuild/msbuild`.

There is no need to edit the project file directly in most projects. The most common change to the file is to add dependencies on other .NET packages, but these are typically added using the command-line tools or through the interface provided by Visual Studio.

To add a package to the project using the command line, open a new PowerShell command prompt, navigate to the `Platform` project folder (the one that contains the `csproj` file), and run the command shown in Listing 12-3.

Listing 12-3. Adding a Package to the Project

```
dotnet add package Swashbuckle.AspNetCore --version 5.0.0-rc2
```

This command adds the `Swashbuckle.AspNetCore` package to the project. You will see this package used in Chapter 20, but for now, it is the effect of the `dotnet add package` command that is important.

If you are using Visual Studio, you can add the package by right-clicking the Platform item in the Solution Explorer and selecting Manage NuGet packages from the popup menu. Click Browse and enter **Swashbuckle.AspNetCore** into the search text box. Select the Swashbuckle.AspNetCore package from the list, choose the 5.0.0-rc2 version from the Version drop-down list, and click the Install button, as shown in Figure 12-7. You will be prompted to accept the license of the package and its dependencies.

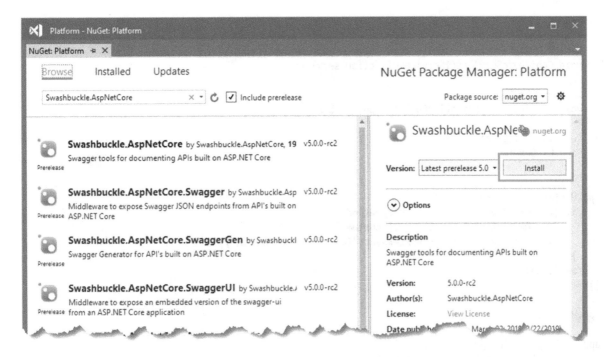

Figure 12-7. *Installing a package in Visual Studio*

The new dependency will be shown in the Platform.csproj file, regardless of which approach you use to install the package.

```
<Project Sdk="Microsoft.NET.Sdk.Web">

  <PropertyGroup>
    <TargetFramework>netcoreapp3.1</TargetFramework>
  </PropertyGroup>

  <ItemGroup>
    <PackageReference Include="Swashbuckle.AspNetCore" Version="5.0.0-rc2" />
  </ItemGroup>

</Project>
```

Creating Custom Middleware

As mentioned, Microsoft provides various middleware components for ASP.NET Core that handle the features most commonly required by web applications. You can also create your own middleware, which is a useful way to understand how ASP.NET Core works, even if you use only the standard components in your projects. The key method for creating middleware is Use, as shown in Listing 12-4.

Listing 12-4. Creating Custom Middleware in the Startup.cs File in the Platform Folder

```
using System;
using System.Collections.Generic;
using System.Linq;
using System.Threading.Tasks;
using Microsoft.AspNetCore.Builder;
using Microsoft.AspNetCore.Hosting;
using Microsoft.AspNetCore.Http;
using Microsoft.Extensions.DependencyInjection;
using Microsoft.Extensions.Hosting;
```

```
namespace Platform {
    public class Startup {

        public void ConfigureServices(IServiceCollection services) {
        }

        public void Configure(IApplicationBuilder app, IWebHostEnvironment env) {

            if (env.IsDevelopment()) {
                app.UseDeveloperExceptionPage();
            }

            app.Use(async (context, next) => {
                if (context.Request.Method == HttpMethods.Get
                        && context.Request.Query["custom"] == "true") {
                    await context.Response.WriteAsync("Custom Middleware \n");
                }
                await next();
            });

            app.UseRouting();

            app.UseEndpoints(endpoints => {
                endpoints.MapGet("/", async context => {
                    await context.Response.WriteAsync("Hello World!");
                });
            });
        }
    }
}
```

The Use method registers a middleware component that is typically expressed as a lambda function that receives each request as it passes through the pipeline (there is another method used for classes, as described in the next section).

The arguments to the lambda function are an HttpContext object and a function that is invoked to tell ASP.NET Core to pass the request to the next middleware component in the pipeline.

The HttpContext object describes the HTTP request and the HTTP response and provides additional context, including details of the user associated with the request. Table 12-5 describes the most useful members provided by the HttpContext class, which is defined in the Microsoft.AspNetCore.Http namespace.

Table 12-5. *Useful HttpContext Members*

Name	Description
Connection	This property returns a ConnectionInfo object that provides information about the network connection underlying the HTTP request, including details of local and remote IP addresses and ports.
Request	This property returns an HttpRequest object that describes the HTTP request being processed.
RequestServices	This property provides access to the services available for the request, as described in Chapter 14.
Response	This property returns an HttpResponse object that is used to create a response to the HTTP request.
Session	This property returns the session data associated with the request. The session data feature is described in Chapter 16.
User	This property returns details of the user associated with the request, as described in Chapters 37 and 38.
Features	This property provides access to request features, which allow access to the low-level aspects of request handling. See Chapter 16 for an example of using a request feature.

The ASP.NET Core platform is responsible for processing the HTTP request to create the HttpRequest object, which means that middleware and endpoints don't have to worry about the raw request data. Table 12-6 describes the most useful members of the HttpRequest class.

Table 12-6. *Useful HttpRequest Members*

Name	Description
Body	This property returns a stream that can be used to read the request body.
ContentLength	This property returns the value of the Content-Length header.
ContentType	This property returns the value of the Content-Type header.
Cookies	This property returns the request cookies.
Form	This property returns a representation of the request body as a form.
Headers	This property returns the request headers.
IsHttps	This property returns true if the request was made using HTTPS.
Method	This property returns the HTTP verb used for the request.
Path	This property returns the path section of the request URL.
Query	This property returns the query string section of the request URL as key/value pairs.

The HttpResponse object describes the HTTP response that will be sent back to the client when the request has made its way through the pipeline. Table 12-7 describes the most useful members of the HttpResponse class. The ASP.NET Core platform makes dealing with responses as easy as possible, sets headers automatically, and makes it easy to send content to the client.

Table 12-7. *Useful HttpResponse Members*

Name	Description
ContentLength	This property sets the value of the Content-Length header.
ContentType	This property sets the value of the Content-Type header.
Cookies	This property allows cookies to be associated with the request.
HasStarted	This property returns true if ASP.NET Core has started to send the response headers to the client, after which it is not possible to make changes.
Headers	This property allows the response headers to be set.
StatusCode	This property sets the status code for the response.
WriteAsync(data)	This asynchronous method writes a data string to the response body.
Redirect(url)	This method sends a redirection response.

When creating custom middleware, the HttpContext, HttpRequest, and HttpResponse objects are used directly, but, as you will learn in later chapters, this isn't usually required when using the higher-level ASP.NET Core features such as the MVC Framework and Razor Pages.

The middleware function I defined in Listing 12-4 uses the HttpRequest object to check the HTTP method and query string to identify GET requests that have a custom parameter in the query string whose value is true, like this:

```
...
if (context.Request.Method == HttpMethods.Get
    && context.Request.Query["custom"] == "true") {
...
```

The HttpMethods class defines static strings for each HTTP method. For GET requests with the expected query string, the middleware function uses the WriteAsync method to add a string to the body of the response.

```
...
await context.Response.WriteAsync("Custom Middleware \n");
...
```

Note In this part of the book, all the examples send simple string results to the browser. In Part 3, I show you how to create web services that return JSON data and introduce the different ways that ASP.NET Core can produce HTML results.

The second argument to the middleware is the function conventionally named next that tells ASP.NET Core to pass the request to the next component in the request pipeline.

```
...
if (context.Request.Method == HttpMethods.Get
        && context.Request.Query["custom"] == "true") {
    await context.Response.WriteAsync("Custom Middleware \n");
}
await next();
...
```

No arguments are required when invoking the next middleware component because ASP.NET Core takes care of providing the component with the HttpContext object and its own next function so that it can process the request. The next function is asynchronous, which is why the await keyword is used and why the lambda function is defined with the async keyword.

Tip You may encounter middleware that calls next.Invoke() instead of next(). These are equivalent, and next() is provided as a convenience by the compiler to produce concise code.

Restart ASP.NET Core and navigate to http://localhost:5000/?custom=true. You will see that the new middleware function appends its message to the response body before passing on the request to the next middleware component, as shown in Figure 12-8. Remove the query string, or change true to false, and the middleware component will pass on the request without adding to the response.

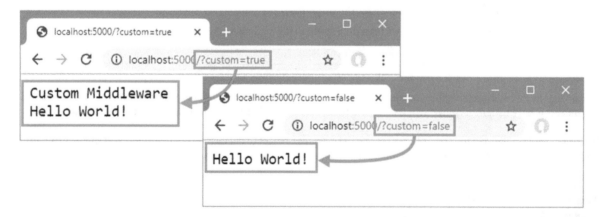

Figure 12-8. Creating custom middleware

Defining Middleware Using a Class

Defining middleware using lambda functions is convenient, but it can lead to a long and complex Configure method in the Startup class and makes it hard to reuse middleware in different projects. Middleware can also be defined using classes. Add a class file named Middleware.cs to the Platform folder and add the code shown in Listing 12-5.

Listing 12-5. The Contents of the Middleware.cs File in the Platform Folder

```
using Microsoft.AspNetCore.Http;
using System.Threading.Tasks;

namespace Platform {

    public class QueryStringMiddleWare {
        private RequestDelegate next;

        public QueryStringMiddleWare(RequestDelegate nextDelegate) {
            next = nextDelegate;
        }

        public async Task Invoke(HttpContext context) {
            if (context.Request.Method == HttpMethods.Get
                        && context.Request.Query["custom"] == "true") {
                await context.Response.WriteAsync("Class-based Middleware \n");
            }
            await next(context);
        }
    }
}
```

Middleware classes receive a RequestDelegate as a constructor parameter, which is used to forward the request to the next component in the pipeline. The Invoke method is called by ASP.NET Core when a request is received and receives an HttpContext object that provides access to the request and response, using the same classes that lambda function middleware receives. The RequestDelegate returns a Task, which allows it to work asynchronously.

One important difference in class-based middleware is that the HttpContext object must be used as an argument when invoking the RequestDelete to forward the request, like this:

```
...
await next(context);
...
```

Class-based middleware components are added to the pipeline with the UseMiddleware method, which accepts the middleware as a type argument, as shown in Listing 12-6.

Listing 12-6. Adding a Class-Based Middleware Component in the Startup.cs File in the Platform Folder

```
using System;
using System.Collections.Generic;
using System.Linq;
using System.Threading.Tasks;
using Microsoft.AspNetCore.Builder;
using Microsoft.AspNetCore.Hosting;
using Microsoft.AspNetCore.Http;
using Microsoft.Extensions.DependencyInjection;
using Microsoft.Extensions.Hosting;
```

```
namespace Platform {
    public class Startup {

        public void ConfigureServices(IServiceCollection services) {
        }

        public void Configure(IApplicationBuilder app, IWebHostEnvironment env) {

            if (env.IsDevelopment()) {
                app.UseDeveloperExceptionPage();
            }

            app.Use(async (context, next) => {
                if (context.Request.Method == HttpMethods.Get
                        && context.Request.Query["custom"] == "true") {
                    await context.Response.WriteAsync("Custom Middleware \n");
                }
                await next();
            });

            app.UseMiddleware<QueryStringMiddleWare>();

            app.UseRouting();

            app.UseEndpoints(endpoints => {
                endpoints.MapGet("/", async context => {
                    await context.Response.WriteAsync("Hello World!");
                });
            });
        }
    }
}
```

When the ASP.NET Core is started, the QueryStringMiddleware class will be instantiated, and its Invoke method will be called to process requests as they are received.

■ **Caution**   A single middleware object is used to handle all requests, which means that the code in the Invoke method must be thread-safe.

Select Start Without Debugging from the Debug menu or restart ASP.NET Core using the dotnet run command. Navigate to http://localhost:5000?custom=true, and you will see the output from both middleware components, as shown in Figure 12-9.

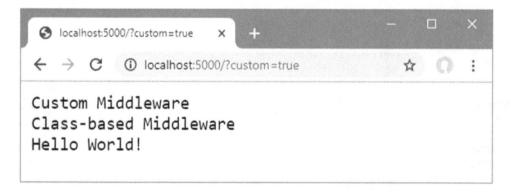

Figure 12-9. Using a class-based middleware component

Understanding the Return Pipeline Path

Middleware components can modify the HTTPResponse object after the next function has been called, as shown by the new middleware in Listing 12-7.

Listing 12-7. Adding New Middleware in the Startup.cs File in the Platform Folder

```csharp
using System;
using System.Collections.Generic;
using System.Linq;
using System.Threading.Tasks;
using Microsoft.AspNetCore.Builder;
using Microsoft.AspNetCore.Hosting;
using Microsoft.AspNetCore.Http;
using Microsoft.Extensions.DependencyInjection;
using Microsoft.Extensions.Hosting;

namespace Platform {
    public class Startup {

        public void ConfigureServices(IServiceCollection services) {
        }

        public void Configure(IApplicationBuilder app, IWebHostEnvironment env) {

            if (env.IsDevelopment()) {
                app.UseDeveloperExceptionPage();
            }

            app.Use(async (context, next) => {
                await next();
                await context.Response
                    .WriteAsync($"\nStatus Code: { context.Response.StatusCode}");
            });

            app.Use(async (context, next) => {
                if (context.Request.Method == HttpMethods.Get
                        && context.Request.Query["custom"] == "true") {
                    await context.Response.WriteAsync("Custom Middleware \n");
                }
                await next();
            });

            app.UseMiddleware<QueryStringMiddleWare>();

            app.UseRouting();

            app.UseEndpoints(endpoints => {
                endpoints.MapGet("/", async context => {
                    await context.Response.WriteAsync("Hello World!");
                });
            });
        }
    }
}
```

The new middleware immediately calls the next method to pass the request along the pipeline and then uses the WriteAsync method to add a string to the response body. This may seem like an odd approach, but it allows middleware to make changes to the response before and after it is passed along the request pipeline by defining statements before and after the next function is invoked, as illustrated by Figure 12-10.

Figure 12-10. *Passing request and responses through the ASP.NET Core pipeline*

Middleware can operate before the request is passed on, after the request has been processed by other components, or both. The result is that several middleware components collectively contribute to the response that is produced, each providing some aspect of the response or providing some feature or data that is used later in the pipeline.

Select Start Without Debugging from the Debug menu or use dotnet to see the effect of the middleware defined in Listing 12-7, as shown in Figure 12-11. If you are using the command line, start ASP.NET Core using the dotnet run command and navigate to http://localhost:5000.

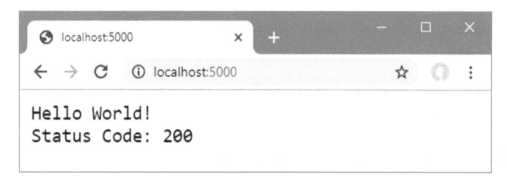

Figure 12-11. *Modifying a response in the return path*

■ **Note** Middleware components must not make changes to the HttpResponse object after ASP.NET Core has started to send the response to the client. The HasStarted property, described in Table 12-7, can be checked to avoid exceptions.

Short-Circuiting the Request Pipeline

Components that generate complete responses can choose not to call the next function so that the request isn't passed on. Components that don't pass on requests are said to *short-circuit* the pipeline, which is what the new middleware component shown in Listing 12-8 does for requests that target the /short URL.

Listing 12-8. Short-Circuiting the Request Pipeline in the Startup.cs File in the Platform Folder

```
using System;
using System.Collections.Generic;
using System.Linq;
using System.Threading.Tasks;
using Microsoft.AspNetCore.Builder;
using Microsoft.AspNetCore.Hosting;
using Microsoft.AspNetCore.Http;
```

```
using Microsoft.Extensions.DependencyInjection;
using Microsoft.Extensions.Hosting;

namespace Platform {
    public class Startup {

        public void ConfigureServices(IServiceCollection services) {
        }

        public void Configure(IApplicationBuilder app, IWebHostEnvironment env) {

            if (env.IsDevelopment()) {
                app.UseDeveloperExceptionPage();
            }

            app.Use(async (context, next) => {
                await next();
                await context.Response
                    .WriteAsync($"\nStatus Code: { context.Response.StatusCode}");
            });

            app.Use(async (context, next) => {
                if (context.Request.Path == "/short") {
                    await context.Response
                        .WriteAsync($"Request Short Circuited");
                } else {
                    await next();
                }
            });

            app.Use(async (context, next) => {
                if (context.Request.Method == HttpMethods.Get
                        && context.Request.Query["custom"] == "true") {
                    await context.Response.WriteAsync("Custom Middleware \n");
                }
                await next();
            });

            app.UseMiddleware<QueryStringMiddleWare>();

            app.UseRouting();

            app.UseEndpoints(endpoints => {
                endpoints.MapGet("/", async context => {
                    await context.Response.WriteAsync("Hello World!");
                });
            });
        }
    }
}
```

The new middleware checks the Path property of the HttpRequest object to see whether the request is for the /short URL; if it is, it calls the WriteAsync method without calling the next function. To see the effect, restart ASP.NET Core and navigate to the http://localhost:5000/short?custom=true URL, which will produce the output shown in Figure 12-12.

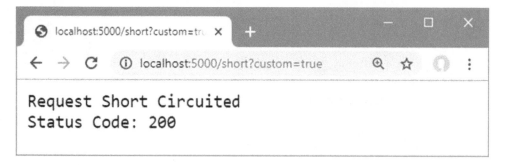

Figure 12-12. *Short-circuiting the request pipeline*

Even though the URL has the query string parameter that is expected by the next component in the pipeline, the request isn't forwarded, so that middleware doesn't get used. Notice, however, that the previous component in the pipeline has added its message to the response. That's because the short-circuiting only prevents components further along the pipeline from being used and doesn't affect earlier components, as illustrated in Figure 12-13.

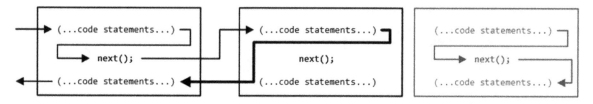

Figure 12-13. *Short-circuiting the request pipeline*

Creating Pipeline Branches

The Map method is used to create a section of pipeline that is used to process requests for specific URLs, creating a separate sequence of middleware components, as shown in Listing 12-9.

Listing 12-9. Creating a Pipeline Branch

```
using System;
using System.Collections.Generic;
using System.Linq;
using System.Threading.Tasks;
using Microsoft.AspNetCore.Builder;
using Microsoft.AspNetCore.Hosting;
using Microsoft.AspNetCore.Http;
using Microsoft.Extensions.DependencyInjection;
using Microsoft.Extensions.Hosting;

namespace Platform {
    public class Startup {

        public void ConfigureServices(IServiceCollection services) {
        }

        public void Configure(IApplicationBuilder app, IWebHostEnvironment env) {

            if (env.IsDevelopment()) {
                app.UseDeveloperExceptionPage();
            }
```

```
app.Map("/branch", branch => {

    branch.UseMiddleware<QueryStringMiddleWare>();

    branch.Use(async (context, next) => {
        await context.Response.WriteAsync($"Branch Middleware");
    });
});

app.UseMiddleware<QueryStringMiddleWare>();

app.UseRouting();

app.UseEndpoints(endpoints => {
    endpoints.MapGet("/", async context => {
        await context.Response.WriteAsync("Hello World!");
    });
});
    }
  }
}
```

The first argument to the Map method specifies the string that will be used to match URLs. The second argument is the branch of the pipeline, to which middleware components are added with the Use and UseMiddleware methods. The statements in Listing 12-9 create a branch that is used for URLs that start with /branch and that pass requests through the QueryStringMiddleware class defined in Listing 12-9, and the statements define a middleware lambda expression that adds a message to the response. Figure 12-14 shows the effect of the branch on the request pipeline.

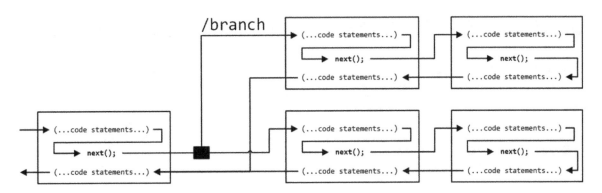

Figure 12-14. *Adding a branch to the request pipeline*

When a URL is matched by the Map method, it follows the branch and no longer passes through the middleware components on the main path through the pipeline. The same middleware can be used in different parts of the pipeline, which can be seen in Listing 12-9, where the QueryStringMiddleWare class is used in both the main part of the pipeline and the branch.

To see the different ways that requests are handled, restart ASP.NET Core and request the http://localhost:5000?custom=true URL, which will be handled on the main part of the pipeline and will produce the output shown on the left of Figure 12-15. Navigate to http://localhost:5000/branch?custom=true, and the request will be forwarded to the middleware in the branch, producing the output shown on the right in Figure 12-15.

Figure 12-15. *The effect of branching the request pipeline*

BRANCHING WITH A PREDICATE

ASP.NET Core also supports the MapWhen method, which can be used to match requests using a predicate, allowing requests to be selected for a pipeline branch on criteria other than just URLs.

The arguments to the MapWhen method are a predicate function that receives an HttpContext and that returns true for requests that should follow the branch, and a function that receives an IApplicationBuilder object representing the pipeline branch, to which middleware is added. Here is an example of using the MapWhen method to branch the pipeline:

```
...
app.MapWhen(context => context.Request.Query.Keys.Contains("branch"),
    branch => {
        // ...add middleware components here...
    });
...
```

The predicate function returns true to branch for requests whose query string contains a parameter named branch.

Creating Terminal Middleware

Terminal middleware never forwards requests to other components and always marks the end of the request pipeline. There is a terminal middleware component in the Startup class, as shown here:

```
...
branch.Use(async (context, next) => {
    await context.Response.WriteAsync($"Branch Middleware");
});
...
```

ASP.NET Core supports the Run method as a convenience feature for creating terminal middleware, which makes it obvious that a middleware component won't forward requests and that a deliberate decision has been made not to call the next function. In Listing 12-10, I have used the Run method for the terminal middleware in the pipeline branch.

Listing 12-10. Using the Run Method in the Startup.cs File in the Platform Folder

```
...
app.Map("/branch", branch => {

    branch.UseMiddleware<QueryStringMiddleWare>();

    branch.Run(async (context) => {
        await context.Response.WriteAsync($"Branch Middleware");
    });
});
...
```

The middleware function passed to the Run method receives only an HttpContext object and doesn't have to define a parameter that isn't used. Behind the scenes, the Run method is implemented through the Use method, and this feature is provided only as a convenience.

■ **Caution**   Middleware added to the pipeline after a terminal component will never receive requests. ASP.NET Core won't warn you if you add a terminal component before the end of the pipeline.

Class-based components can be written so they can be used as both regular and terminal middleware, as shown in Listing 12-11.

Listing 12-11. Adding Terminal Support in the Middleware.cs File in the Platform Folder

```
using Microsoft.AspNetCore.Http;
using System.Threading.Tasks;

namespace Platform {

    public class QueryStringMiddleWare {
        private RequestDelegate next;

        public QueryStringMiddleWare() {
            // do nothing
        }

        public QueryStringMiddleWare(RequestDelegate nextDelegate) {
            next = nextDelegate;
        }

        public async Task Invoke(HttpContext context) {
            if (context.Request.Method == HttpMethods.Get
                        && context.Request.Query["custom"] == "true") {
                await context.Response.WriteAsync("Class-based Middleware \n");
            }
            if (next != null) {
                await next(context);
            }
        }
    }
}
```

The component will forward requests only when the constructor has been provided with a non-null value for the nextDelegate parameter. Listing 12-12 shows the application of the component in both standard and terminal forms.

Listing 12-12. Applying Class-Based Middleware in the Startup.cs File in the Platform Folder

```
using System;
using System.Collections.Generic;
using System.Linq;
using System.Threading.Tasks;
using Microsoft.AspNetCore.Builder;
using Microsoft.AspNetCore.Hosting;
using Microsoft.AspNetCore.Http;
using Microsoft.Extensions.DependencyInjection;
using Microsoft.Extensions.Hosting;
```

```
namespace Platform {
    public class Startup {

        public void ConfigureServices(IServiceCollection services) {
        }

        public void Configure(IApplicationBuilder app, IWebHostEnvironment env) {

            if (env.IsDevelopment()) {
                app.UseDeveloperExceptionPage();
            }

            app.Map("/branch", branch => {
                branch.Run(new QueryStringMiddleWare().Invoke);
            });

            app.UseMiddleware<QueryStringMiddleWare>();

            app.UseRouting();

            app.UseEndpoints(endpoints => {
                endpoints.MapGet("/", async context => {
                    await context.Response.WriteAsync("Hello World!");
                });
            });
        }
    }
}
```

There is no equivalent to the UseMiddleware method for terminal middleware, so the Run method must be used by creating a new instance of the middleware class and selecting its Invoke method. Using the Run method doesn't alter the output from the middleware, which you can see by restarting ASP.NET Core and navigating to the http://localhost:5000/branch?custom=true URL, which produces the content shown in Figure 12-16.

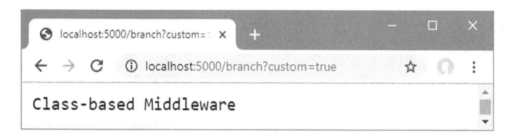

Figure 12-16. *Using the Run method to create terminal middleware*

Configuring Middleware

There is a common pattern for configuring middleware that is known as the *options pattern* and that is used by some of the built-in middleware components described in later chapters.

The starting point is to define a class that contains the configuration options for a middleware component. Add a class file named MessageOptions.cs to the Platform folder with the code shown in Listing 12-13.

Listing 12-13. The Contents of the MessageOptions.cs File in the Platform Folder

```
namespace Platform {

    public class MessageOptions {

        public string CityName { get; set; } = "New York";
        public string CountryName{ get; set; } = "USA";
    }
}
```

The MessageOptions class defines properties that detail a city and a country. In Listing 12-14, I have used the options pattern to create a custom middleware component that relies on the MessageOptions class for its configuration. I have also removed some of the middleware from previous examples for brevity.

Listing 12-14. Using the Options Pattern in the Startup.cs File in the Platform Folder

```
using System;
using System.Collections.Generic;
using System.Linq;
using System.Threading.Tasks;
using Microsoft.AspNetCore.Builder;
using Microsoft.AspNetCore.Hosting;
using Microsoft.AspNetCore.Http;
using Microsoft.Extensions.DependencyInjection;
using Microsoft.Extensions.Hosting;
using Microsoft.Extensions.Options;

namespace Platform {
    public class Startup {

        public void ConfigureServices(IServiceCollection services) {
            services.Configure<MessageOptions>(options => {
                options.CityName= "Albany";
            });
        }

        public void Configure(IApplicationBuilder app, IWebHostEnvironment env,
                IOptions<MessageOptions> msgOptions) {

            if (env.IsDevelopment()) {
                app.UseDeveloperExceptionPage();
            }

            app.Use(async (context, next) => {
                if (context.Request.Path == "/location") {
                    MessageOptions opts = msgOptions.Value;
                    await context.Response
                        .WriteAsync($"{opts.CityName}, {opts.CountryName}");
                } else {
                    await next();
                }
            });

            app.UseRouting();

            app.UseEndpoints(endpoints => {
                endpoints.MapGet("/", async context => {
                    await context.Response.WriteAsync("Hello World!");
```

```
            });
        });
    }
}
}
```

The options are set up using `IServiceCollection.Configure` in the `ConfigureServices` method. The generic type parameter is used to specify the `options` class, like this:

```
...
services.Configure<MessageOptions>(options => {
    options.CityName= "Albany";
});
...
```

This statement creates options using the `MessageOptions` class and changes the value of the `CityName` property. When the application starts, the ASP.NET Core platform will create a new instance of the `options` class and pass it to the function supplied as the argument to the `Configure` method, allowing the default option values to be changed.

The options are accessed by adding an `IOptions<T>` parameter to the `Startup.Configure` method, where the generic type argument specifies the `options` class, like this:

```
...
public void Configure(IApplicationBuilder app,IWebHostEnvironment env,
    CounterService counter, IOptions<MessageOptions> msgOptions) {
...
```

The `IOptions<T>` interface defines a `Value` property that returns the `options` object created by the ASP.NET Core platform, allowing middleware components and endpoints to use the options, like this:

```
...
app.Use(async (context, next) => {
    if (context.Request.Path == "/location") {
        MessageOptions opts = msgOptions.Value;
        await context.Response.WriteAsync($"{opts.CityName}, {opts.CountryName}");
    } else {
        await next();
    }
});
...
```

You can see the result by restarting ASP.NET Core and using the browser to navigate to `http://localhost:5000/location`. The middleware component uses the options to produce the output shown in Figure 12-17.

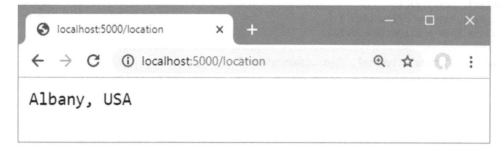

Figure 12-17. *Using the options pattern*

Using the Options Pattern with Class-Based Middleware

Although the options pattern can be used with lambda function middleware, you will usually see it applied to class-based middleware, such as the built-in features described in Chapters 15 and 16. When used with class-based middleware, the configuration options don't have to be accessed through a Startup.Configure method parameter, which produces a more elegant result.

Add the statements shown in Listing 12-15 to the Middleware.cs file to define a class-based middleware component that uses the MessageOptions class for configuration.

Listing 12-15. Defining a Middleware Component in the Middleware.cs File in the Platform Folder

```
using Microsoft.AspNetCore.Http;
using System.Threading.Tasks;
using Microsoft.Extensions.Options;

namespace Platform {

    public class QueryStringMiddleWare {
        private RequestDelegate? next;

        // ...statements omitted for brevity...
    }

    public class LocationMiddleware {
        private RequestDelegate next;
        private MessageOptions options;

        public LocationMiddleware(RequestDelegate nextDelegate,
                IOptions<MessageOptions> opts) {
            next = nextDelegate;
            options = opts.Value;
        }

        public async Task Invoke(HttpContext context) {
            if (context.Request.Path == "/location") {
                await context.Response
                    .WriteAsync($"{options.CityName}, {options.CountryName}");
            } else {
                await next(context);
            }
        }
    }
}
```

The LocationMiddleware class defines an IOptions<MessageOptions> constructor parameter. In Listing 12-16, I have replaced the lambda function middleware component with the class from Listing 12-15 and removed the IOptions<MessageOptions> parameter.

Listing 12-16. Using Class-Based Middleware in the Startup.cs File in the Platform Folder

```
using System;
using System.Collections.Generic;
using System.Linq;
using System.Threading.Tasks;
using Microsoft.AspNetCore.Builder;
using Microsoft.AspNetCore.Hosting;
using Microsoft.AspNetCore.Http;
using Microsoft.Extensions.DependencyInjection;
using Microsoft.Extensions.Hosting;
```

```
using Microsoft.Extensions.Options;

namespace Platform {
    public class Startup {

        public void ConfigureServices(IServiceCollection services) {
            services.Configure<MessageOptions>(options => {
                options.CityName= "Albany";
            });
        }

        public void Configure(IApplicationBuilder app, IWebHostEnvironment env) {

            if (env.IsDevelopment()) {
                app.UseDeveloperExceptionPage();
            }

            app.UseMiddleware<LocationMiddleware>();

            app.UseRouting();

            app.UseEndpoints(endpoints => {
                endpoints.MapGet("/", async context => {
                    await context.Response.WriteAsync("Hello World!");
                });
            });
        }
    }
}
```

When the UseMiddleware statement is executed, the LocationMiddleware constructor is inspected, and its IOptions<MessageOptions> parameter will be resolved using the object created in the ConfigureServices method. This is done using the dependency injection feature that is described in Chapter 14, but the immediate effect is that the options pattern can be used to easily configure class-based middleware. Restart ASP.NET Core and request http://localhost:5000/location to test the new middleware, which will produce the same output as shown in Figure 12-17.

Summary

In this chapter, I focused on the ASP.NET Core platform, introducing the request pipeline, middleware components, and, briefly, services. I described the files added to the project when the Empty template is used and explained the role of the Program and Startup classes. In the next chapter, I describe the ASP.NET Core URL routing feature.

CHAPTER 13

Using URL Routing

The URL routing feature is provided by a pair of middleware components that make it easier to generate responses by consolidating the processing and matching of request URLs. In this chapter, I explain how the ASP.NET Core platform supports URL routing, show its use, and explain why it can be preferable to creating your own custom middleware components. Table 13-1 puts URL routing in context.

> **Note** This chapter focuses on URL routing for the ASP.NET Core platform. See Part 3 for details of how the higher-level parts of ASP.NET Core build on the features described in this chapter.

Table 13-1. *Putting URL Routing in Context*

Question	Answer
What is it?	URL routing consolidates the processing and matching of URLs, allowing components known as *endpoints* to generate responses.
Why is it useful?	URL routing obviates the need for each middleware component to process the URL to see whether the request will be handled or passed along the pipeline. The result is more efficient and easier to maintain.
How is it used?	The URL routing middleware components are added to the request pipeline and configured with a set of routes. Each route contains a URL path and a delegate that will generate a response when a request with the matching path is received.
Are there any pitfalls or limitations?	It can be difficult to define the set of routes matching all the URLs supported by a complex application.
Are there any alternatives?	URL routing is optional, and custom middleware components can be used instead.

Table 13-2 summarizes the chapter.

Table 13-2. *Chapter Summary*

Problem	Solution	Listing
Handling requests for a specific set of URLs	Define a route with a pattern that matches the required URLs	1–6
Extracting values from URLs	Use segment variables	7–10, 14
Generating URLs	Use the link generator to produce URLs from routes	11–13, 15
Matching URLs with different numbers of segments	Use optional segments or catchall segments in the URL routing pattern	16–18
Restricting matches	Use constraints in the URL routing pattern	19–21, 23–26
Matching requests that are not otherwise handled	Define fallback routes	22
Seeing which endpoint will handle a request	Use the routing context data	27

© Adam Freeman 2020

A. Freeman, *Pro ASP.NET Core 3*, https://doi.org/10.1007/978-1-4842-5440-0_13

Preparing for This Chapter

In this chapter, I continue to use the Platform project from Chapter 12. To prepare for this chapter, add a file called Population.cs to the Platform folder with the code shown in Listing 13-1.

▊ **Tip**   You can download the example project for this chapter—and for all the other chapters in this book—from https://github.com/apress/pro-asp.net-core-3. See Chapter 1 for how to get help if you have problems running the examples.

Listing 13-1. The Contents of the Population.cs File in the Platform Folder

```
using Microsoft.AspNetCore.Http;
using System;
using System.Threading.Tasks;

namespace Platform {
    public class Population {
        private RequestDelegate next;

        public Population() { }

        public Population(RequestDelegate nextDelegate) {
            next = nextDelegate;
        }

        public async Task Invoke(HttpContext context) {
            string[] parts = context.Request.Path.ToString()
                .Split("/", StringSplitOptions.RemoveEmptyEntries);
            if (parts.Length == 2 && parts[0] == "population") {
                string city = parts[1];
                int? pop = null;
                switch (city.ToLower()) {
                    case "london":
                        pop = 8_136_000;
                        break;
                    case "paris":
                        pop = 2_141_000;
                        break;
                    case "monaco":
                        pop = 39_000;
                        break;
                }
                if (pop.HasValue) {
                    await context.Response
                        .WriteAsync($"City: {city}, Population: {pop}");
                    return;
                }
            }
            if (next != null) {
                await next(context);
            }
        }
    }
}
```

This middleware component responds to requests for /population/<city> where <city> is london, paris, or monaco. The middleware component splits up the URL path string, checks that it has the expected length, and uses a switch statement to determine it is a request for a URL that it can respond to. If the URL matches the pattern the middleware is looking for, then a response is generated; otherwise, the request is passed along the pipeline.

Add a class file named Capital.cs to the Platform folder with the code shown in Listing 13-2.

Listing 13-2. The Contents of the Capital.cs File in the Platform Folder

```
using Microsoft.AspNetCore.Http;
using System;
using System.Threading.Tasks;

namespace Platform {
    public class Capital {
        private RequestDelegate next;

        public Capital() { }

        public Capital(RequestDelegate nextDelegate) {
            next = nextDelegate;
        }

        public async Task Invoke(HttpContext context) {
            string[] parts = context.Request.Path.ToString()
                .Split("/", StringSplitOptions.RemoveEmptyEntries);
            if (parts.Length == 2 && parts[0] == "capital") {
                string capital = null;
                string country = parts[1];
                switch (country.ToLower()) {
                    case "uk":
                        capital= "London";
                        break;
                    case "france":
                        capital = "Paris";
                        break;
                    case "monaco":
                        context.Response.Redirect($"/population/{country}");
                        return;
                }
                if (capital != null) {
                    await context.Response
                        .WriteAsync($"{capital} is the capital of {country}");
                    return;
                }
            }
            if (next != null) {
                await next(context);
            }
        }
    }
}
```

This middleware component is looking for requests for /capital/<country>, where <country> is uk, france, or monaco. The capital cities of the United Kingdom and France are displayed, but requests for Monaco, which is a city and a state, are redirected to /population/monaco.

Listing 13-3 replaces the middleware examples from the previous chapter and adds the new middleware components to the request pipeline.

Listing 13-3. Replacing the Contents of the Startup.cs File in the Platform Folder

```
using Microsoft.AspNetCore.Builder;
using Microsoft.AspNetCore.Hosting;
using Microsoft.AspNetCore.Http;
using Microsoft.Extensions.DependencyInjection;

namespace Platform {
    public class Startup {

        public void ConfigureServices(IServiceCollection services) {
        }

        public void Configure(IApplicationBuilder app, IWebHostEnvironment env) {
            app.UseDeveloperExceptionPage();
            app.UseMiddleware<Population>();
            app.UseMiddleware<Capital>();
            app.Use(async (context, next) => {
                await context.Response.WriteAsync("Terminal Middleware Reached");
            });
        }
    }
}
```

Start the application by selecting Start Without Debugging or Run Without Debugging from the Debug menu or by opening a new PowerShell command prompt, navigating to the Platform project folder (which contains the Platform.csproj file), and running the command shown in Listing 13-4.

Listing 13-4. Starting the ASP.NET Core Runtime

```
dotnet run
```

Navigate to http://localhost:5000/population/london, and you will see the output on the left side of Figure 13-1. Navigate to http://localhost:5000/capital/France to see the output from the other middleware component, which is shown on the right side of Figure 13-1.

Figure 13-1. Running the example application

Understanding URL Routing

Each middleware component decides whether to act on a request as it passes along the pipeline. Some components are looking for a specific header or query string value, but most components—especially terminal and short-circuiting components—are trying to match URLs.

Each middleware component has to repeat the same set of steps as the request works its way along the pipeline. You can see this in the middleware defined in the prevision section, where both components go through the same process: split up the URL, check the number of parts, inspect the first part, and so on.

This approach is inefficient, it is difficult to maintain, and it breaks easily when changed. It is inefficient because the same set of operations is repeated to process the URL. It is difficult to maintain because the URL that each component is looking for is hidden in its code. It breaks easily because changes must be carefully worked through in multiple places. For example, the Capital component redirects requests to a URL whose path starts with /population, which is handled by the Population component. If the Population component is revised to support the /size URL instead, then this change must also be reflected in the Capital component. Real applications can support complex sets of URLs, and working changes fully through individual middleware components can be difficult.

URL routing solves these problems by introducing middleware that takes care of matching request URLs so that components, called *endpoints*, can focus on responses. The mapping between endpoints and the URLs they require is expressed in a *route*. The routing middleware processes the URL, inspects the set of routes and finds the endpoint to handle the request, a process known as *routing*.

Adding the Routing Middleware and Defining an Endpoint

The routing middleware is added using two separate methods: UseRouting and UseEndpoints. The UseRouting method adds the middleware responsible for processing requests to the pipeline. The UseEndpoints method is used to define the routes that match URLs to endpoints. URLs are matched using patterns that are compared to the path of request URLs, and each route creates a relationship between one URL pattern and one endpoint. Listing 13-5 shows the use of the routing middleware and contains a simple route.

■ **Tip** I explain why there are two methods for routing in the "Accessing the Endpoint in a Middleware Component" section.

Listing 13-5. Using the Routing Middleware in the Startup.cs File in the Platform Folder

```
using Microsoft.AspNetCore.Builder;
using Microsoft.AspNetCore.Hosting;
using Microsoft.AspNetCore.Http;
using Microsoft.Extensions.DependencyInjection;

namespace Platform {
    public class Startup {

        public void ConfigureServices(IServiceCollection services) {
        }

        public void Configure(IApplicationBuilder app, IWebHostEnvironment env) {
            app.UseDeveloperExceptionPage();
            app.UseMiddleware<Population>();
            app.UseMiddleware<Capital>();

            app.UseRouting();

            app.UseEndpoints(endpoints => {
                endpoints.MapGet("routing", async context => {
                    await context.Response.WriteAsync("Request Was Routed");
                });
            });

            app.Use(async (context, next) => {
                await context.Response.WriteAsync("Terminal Middleware Reached");
            });
        }
    }
}
```

There are no arguments to the UseRouting method. The UseEndpoints method receives a function that accepts an IEndpointRouteBuilder object and uses it to create routes using the extension methods described in Table 13-3.

■ **Tip** There are also extension methods that set up endpoints for other parts of ASP.NET Core, such as the MVC Framework, as explained in Part 3.

Table 13-3. *The IEndpointRouteBuilder Extension Methods*

Name	Description
MapGet(pattern, endpoint)	This method routes HTTP GET requests that match the URL pattern to the endpoint.
MapPost(pattern, endpoint)	This method routes HTTP POST requests that match to the URL pattern to the endpoint.
MapPut(pattern, endpoint)	This method routes HTTP PUT requests that match the URL pattern to the endpoint.
MapDelete(pattern, endpoint)	This method routes HTTP DELETE requests that match the URL pattern to the endpoint.
MapMethods(pattern, methods, endpoint)	This method routes requests made with one of the specified HTTP methods that match the URL pattern to the endpoint.
Map(pattern, endpoint)	This method routes all HTTP requests that match the URL pattern to the endpoint.

Endpoints are defined using RequestDelegate, which is the same delegate used by conventional middleware, so endpoints are asynchronous methods that receive an HttpContext object and use it to generate a response. This means that all the features described in earlier chapters for middleware components can also be used in endpoints.

Restart ASP.NET Core and navigate to http://localhost:5000/routing to test the new route. When matching a request, the routing middleware applies the route's URL pattern to the path section of the URL. The path is separated from the hostname by the / character, as shown in Figure 13-2.

Figure 13-2. *The URL path*

The path in the URL matches the pattern specified in the route.

```
...
endpoints.MapGet("routing", async context => {
...
```

URL patterns are expressed without a leading / character, which isn't part of the URL path. When the request URL path matches the URL pattern, the request will be forwarded to the endpoint function, which generates the response shown in Figure 13-3.

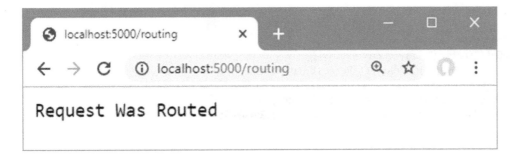

Figure 13-3. *Using an endpoint to generate a response*

The routing middleware short-circuits the pipeline when a route matches a URL so that the response is generated only by the route's endpoint. The request isn't forwarded to other endpoints or middleware components that appear later in the request pipeline.

If the request URL isn't matched by any route, then the routing middleware passes the request to the next middleware component in the request pipeline. To test this behavior, request the http://localhost:5000/notrouted URL, whose path doesn't match the pattern in the route defined in Listing 13-5.

The routing middleware can't match the URL path to a route and forwards the request, which reaches the terminal middleware, producing the response shown in Figure 13-4.

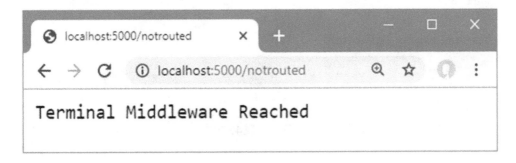

Figure 13-4. *Requesting a URL for which there is no matching route*

Endpoints generate responses in the same way as the middleware components demonstrated in earlier chapters: they receive an HttpContext object that provides access to the request and response through HttpRequest and HttpResponse objects. This means that any middleware component can also be used as an endpoint. Listing 13-6 adds a route that uses the Capital and Population middleware components as endpoints.

Listing 13-6. Using Middleware Components as Endpoints in the Startup.cs File in the Platform Folder

```
using Microsoft.AspNetCore.Builder;
using Microsoft.AspNetCore.Hosting;
using Microsoft.AspNetCore.Http;
using Microsoft.Extensions.DependencyInjection;

namespace Platform {
    public class Startup {

        public void ConfigureServices(IServiceCollection services) {
        }

        public void Configure(IApplicationBuilder app, IWebHostEnvironment env) {
            app.UseDeveloperExceptionPage();
            // app.UseMiddleware<Population>();
            // app.UseMiddleware<Capital>();
```

```
        app.UseRouting();

        app.UseEndpoints(endpoints => {
            endpoints.MapGet("routing", async context => {
                await context.Response.WriteAsync("Request Was Routed");
            });
            endpoints.MapGet("capital/uk", new Capital().Invoke);
            endpoints.MapGet("population/paris", new Population().Invoke);
        });

        app.Use(async (context, next) => {
            await context.Response.WriteAsync("Terminal Middleware Reached");
        });
    }
  }
}
```

Using middleware components like this is awkward because I need to create new instances of the classes to select the Invoke method as the endpoint. The URL patterns used by the routes support only some of the URLs that the middleware components support, but it is useful to understand that endpoints rely on features that are familiar from earlier chapters. To test the new routes, restart ASP.NET Core and navigate to http://localhost:5000/capital/uk and http://localhost:5000/population/paris, which will produce the results shown in Figure 13-5.

Figure 13-5. *Using middleware components as endpoints*

Understanding URL Patterns

Using middleware components as endpoints shows that the URL routing feature builds on the standard ASP.NET Core platform. Although the URLs that the application handles can be seen by examining the routes, not all of the URLs understood by the Capital and Population classes are routed, and there have been no efficiency gains since the URL is processed once by the routing middleware to select the route and again by the Capital or Population class in order to extract the data values they require.

Making improvements requires understanding more about how URL patterns are used. When a request arrives, the routing middleware processes the URL to extract the segments from its path, which are the sections of the path separated by the / character, as shown in Figure 13-6.

Figure 13-6. *The URL segments*

The routing middleware also extracts the segments from the URL routing pattern, as shown in Figure 13-7.

Figure 13-7. *The URL pattern segments*

To route a request, the segments from the URL pattern are compared to those from the request to see whether they match. The request is routed to the endpoint if its path contains the same number of segments and each segment has the same content as those in the URL pattern, as summarized in Table 13-4.

Table 13-4. *Matching URL Segments*

URL Path	Description
/capital	No match—too few segments
/capital/europe/uk	No match—too many segments
/name/uk	No match—first segment is not capital
/capital/uk	Matches

Using Segment Variables in URL Patterns

The URL pattern used in Listing 13-6 uses *literal segments*, also known as *static segments*, which match requests using fixed strings. The first segment in the pattern will match only those requests whose path has capital as the first segment, for example, and the second segment in the pattern will match only those requests whose second segment is uk. Put these together and you can see why the route matches only those requests whose path is /capital/uk.

Segment variables, also known as *route parameters*, expand the range of path segments that a pattern segment will match, allowing more flexible routing. Segment variables are given a name and are denoted by curly braces (the { and } characters), as shown in Listing 13-7.

Listing 13-7. Using Segment Variables in the Startup.cs File in the Platform Folder

```
using Microsoft.AspNetCore.Builder;
using Microsoft.AspNetCore.Hosting;
using Microsoft.AspNetCore.Http;
using Microsoft.Extensions.DependencyInjection;

namespace Platform {
    public class Startup {

        public void ConfigureServices(IServiceCollection services) {
        }

        public void Configure(IApplicationBuilder app, IWebHostEnvironment env) {
            app.UseDeveloperExceptionPage();
            app.UseRouting();

            app.UseEndpoints(endpoints => {
                endpoints.MapGet("{first}/{second}/{third}", async context => {
                    await context.Response.WriteAsync("Request Was Routed\n");
```

```
                foreach (var kvp in context.Request.RouteValues) {
                    await context.Response
                        .WriteAsync($"{kvp.Key}: {kvp.Value}\n");
                }
            });
            endpoints.MapGet("capital/uk", new Capital().Invoke);
            endpoints.MapGet("population/paris", new Population().Invoke);
        });

        app.Use(async (context, next) => {
            await context.Response.WriteAsync("Terminal Middleware Reached");
        });
    }
  }
}
```

The URL pattern {first}/{second}/{third} matches URLs whose path contains three segments, regardless of what those segments contain. When a segment variable is used, the routing middleware provides the endpoint with the contents of the URL path segment they have matched. This content is available through the HttpRequest.RouteValues property, which returns a RouteValuesDictionary object. Table 13-5 describes the most useful RouteValuesDictionary members.

■ **Tip** There are some reserved words that cannot be used as the names for segment variables: action, area, controller, handler, and page.

Table 13-5. *Useful RouteValuesDictionary Members*

Name	Description
[key]	The class defines an indexer that allows values to be retrieved by key.
Keys	This property returns the collection of segment variable names.
Values	This property returns the collection of segment variable values.
Count	This property returns the number of segment variables.
ContainsKey(key)	This method returns true if the route data contains a value for the specified key.

The RouteValuesDictionary class is enumerable, which means that it can be used in a foreach loop to generate a sequence of KeyValuePair<string, object> objects, each of which corresponds to the name of a segment variable and the corresponding value extracted from the request URL. The endpoint in Listing 13-7 enumerates the HttpRequest.RouteValues property to generate a response that lists the names and value of the segment variables matched by the URL pattern.

The names of the segment variables are first, second, and third, and you can see the values extracted from the URL by restarting ASP.NET Core and requesting any three-segment URL, such as http://localhost:5000/apples/oranges/cherries, which produces the response shown in Figure 13-8.

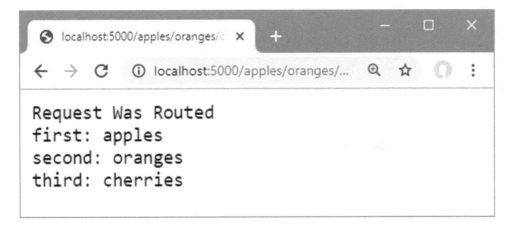

Figure 13-8. *Using segment variables*

UNDERSTANDING ROUTE SELECTION

When processing a request, the middleware finds all the routes that can match the request and gives each a score, and the route with the lowest score is selected to handle the route. The scoring process is complex, but the effect is that the most specific route receives the request. This means that literal segments are given preference over segment variables and that segment variables with constraints are given preference over those without (constraints are described in the "Constraining Segment Matching" section later in this chapter). The scoring system can produce surprising results, and you should check to make sure that the URLs supported by your application are matched by the routes you expect.

If two routes have the same score, meaning they are equally suited to routing the request, then an exception will be thrown, indicating an ambiguous routing selection. See the "Avoiding Ambiguous Route Exceptions" section later in the chapter for details of how to avoid ambiguous routes.

Refactoring Middleware into an Endpoint

Endpoints usually rely on the routing middleware to provide specific segment variables, rather than enumerating all the segment variables. By relying on the URL pattern to provide a specific value, I can refactor the Capital and Population classes to depend on the route data, as shown in Listing 13-8.

Listing 13-8. Depending on the Route Data in the Capital.cs File in the Platform Folder

```
using Microsoft.AspNetCore.Http;
using System;
using System.Threading.Tasks;
using Microsoft.AspNetCore.Routing;

namespace Platform {
    public static class Capital {

        public static async Task Endpoint(HttpContext context) {
            string capital = null;
            string country = context.Request.RouteValues["country"] as string;
            switch ((country ?? "").ToLower()) {
                case "uk":
                    capital = "London";
                    break;
                case "france":
                    capital = "Paris";
```

CHAPTER 13 ■ USING URL ROUTING

```
                    break;
                case "monaco":
                    context.Response.Redirect($"/population/{country}");
                    return;
            }
            if (capital != null) {
                await context.Response
                    .WriteAsync($"{capital} is the capital of {country}");
            } else {
                context.Response.StatusCode = StatusCodes.Status404NotFound;
            }
        }
    }
}
```

Middleware components can be used as endpoints, but the opposite isn't true once there is a dependency on the data provided by the routing middleware. In Listing 13-8, I used the route data to get the value of a segment variable named country through the indexer defined by the RouteValuesDictionary class.

```
...
string country = context.Request.RouteValues["country"] as string;
...
```

The indexer returns an object value that is cast to a string using the as keyword. The listing removes the statements that pass the request along the pipeline, which the routing middleware handles on behalf of endpoints.

The use of the segment variable means that requests may be routed to the endpoint with values that are not supported, so I added a statement that returns a 404 status code for countries the endpoint doesn't understand.

I also removed the constructors and replaced the Invoke instance method with a static method named Endpoint, which better fits with the way that endpoints are used in routes. Listing 13-9 applies the same set of changes to the Population class, transforming it from a standard middleware component into an endpoint that depends on the routing middleware to process URLs.

Listing 13-9. Depending on Route Data in the Population.cs File in the Platform Folder

```
using Microsoft.AspNetCore.Http;
using System;
using System.Threading.Tasks;

namespace Platform {
    public class Population {

        public static async Task Endpoint(HttpContext context) {
            string city = context.Request.RouteValues["city"] as string;
            int? pop = null;
            switch ((city ?? "").ToLower()) {
                case "london":
                    pop = 8_136_000;
                    break;
                case "paris":
                    pop = 2_141_000;
                    break;
                case "monaco":
                    pop = 39_000;
                    break;
            }
            if (pop.HasValue) {
                await context.Response
                    .WriteAsync($"City: {city}, Population: {pop}");
            } else {
```

```
                context.Response.StatusCode = StatusCodes.Status404NotFound;
            }
        }
    }
}
```

The change to static methods tidies up the use of the endpoints when defining routes, as shown in Listing 13-10.

Listing 13-10. Updating Routes in the Startup.cs File in the Platform Folder

```
...
app.UseEndpoints(endpoints => {
    endpoints.MapGet("{first}/{second}/{third}", async context => {
        await context.Response.WriteAsync("Request Was Routed\n");
        foreach (var kvp in context.Request.RouteValues) {
            await context.Response.WriteAsync($"{kvp.Key}: {kvp.Value}\n");
        }
    });
    endpoints.MapGet("capital/{country}", Capital.Endpoint);
    endpoints.MapGet("population/{city}", Population.Endpoint);
});
...
```

The new routes match URLs whose path has two segments, the first of which is capital or population. The contents of the second segment are assigned to the segment variables named country and city, allowing the endpoints to support the full set of URLs that were handled at the start of the chapter, without the need to process the URL directly. To test the new routes, restart ASP. NET Core and request http://localhost:5000/capital/uk and http://localhost:5000/population/london, which will produce the responses shown in Figure 13-9.

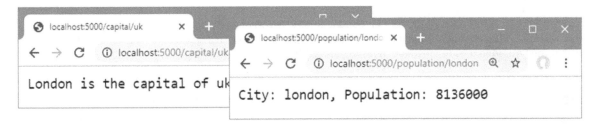

Figure 13-9. *Using segment variables in endpoints*

These changes address two of the problems I described at the start of the chapter. Efficiency has improved because the URL is processed only once by the routing middleware and not by multiple components. And it is easier to see the URLs that each endpoint supports because the URL patterns show how requests will be matched.

Generating URLs from Routes

The final problem was the difficulty in making changes. The Capital endpoint still has a hardwired dependency on the URL that the Population endpoint supports. To break this dependency, the routing system allows URLs to be generated by supplying data values for segment variables. The first step is to assign a name to the route that will be the target of the URL that is generated, as shown in Listing 13-11.

Listing 13-11. Naming a Route in the Startup.cs File in the Platform Folder

```
using Microsoft.AspNetCore.Builder;
using Microsoft.AspNetCore.Hosting;
using Microsoft.AspNetCore.Http;
using Microsoft.Extensions.DependencyInjection;
using Microsoft.AspNetCore.Routing;
```

```
namespace Platform {
    public class Startup {

        public void ConfigureServices(IServiceCollection services) {
        }

        public void Configure(IApplicationBuilder app, IWebHostEnvironment env) {
            app.UseDeveloperExceptionPage();
            app.UseRouting();

            app.UseEndpoints(endpoints => {
                endpoints.MapGet("{first}/{second}/{third}", async context => {
                    await context.Response.WriteAsync("Request Was Routed\n");
                    foreach (var kvp in context.Request.RouteValues) {
                        await context.Response
                            .WriteAsync($"{kvp.Key}: {kvp.Value}\n");
                    }
                });
                endpoints.MapGet("capital/{country}", Capital.Endpoint);
                endpoints.MapGet("population/{city}", Population.Endpoint)
                    .WithMetadata(new RouteNameMetadata("population"));
            });

            app.Use(async (context, next) => {
                await context.Response.WriteAsync("Terminal Middleware Reached");
            });
        }
    }
}
```

The WithMetadata method is used on the result from the MapGet method to assign metadata to the route. The only metadata required for generating URLs is a name, which is assigned by passing a new RouteNameMetadata object, whose constructor argument specifies the name that will be used to refer to the route. In Listing 13-11, I have named the route population.

■ **Tip** Naming routes helps to avoid links being generated that target a route other than the one you expect, but they can be omitted, in which case the routing system will try to find the best matching route. You can see an example of this approach in Chapter 17.

In Listing 13-12, I have revised the Capital endpoint to remove the direct dependency on the /population URL and rely on the routing features to generate a URL.

Listing 13-12. Generating a URL in the Capital.cs File in the Platform Folder

```
using Microsoft.AspNetCore.Http;
using System;
using System.Threading.Tasks;
using Microsoft.AspNetCore.Routing;
using Microsoft.Extensions.DependencyInjection;

namespace Platform {
    public static class Capital {
        public static async Task Endpoint(HttpContext context) {
            string capital = null;
            string country = context.Request.RouteValues["country"] as string;
            switch ((country ?? "").ToLower()) {
                case "uk":
```

```
                    capital= "London";
                    break;
                case "france":
                    capital = "Paris";
                    break;
                case "monaco":
                    LinkGenerator generator =
                        context.RequestServices.GetService<LinkGenerator>();
                    string url = generator.GetPathByRouteValues(context,
                        "population", new { city = country });
                    context.Response.Redirect(url);
                    return;
            }
            if (capital != null) {
                await context.Response
                    .WriteAsync($"{capital} is the capital of {country}");
            } else {
                context.Response.StatusCode = StatusCodes.Status404NotFound;
            }
        }
    }
}
```

URLs are generated using the LinkGenerator class. You can't just create a new LinkGenerator instance; one must be obtained using the dependency injection feature that is described in Chapter 14. For the purposes of this chapter, it is enough to know that this statement obtains the LinkGenerator object that the endpoint will use:

```
...
LinkGenerator generator = context.RequestServices.GetService<LinkGenerator>();
...
```

The LinkGenerator class provides the GetPathByRouteValues method, which is used to generate the URL that will be used in the redirection.

```
...
generator.GetPathByRouteValues(context, "population", new { city = country });
...
```

The arguments to the GetPathByRouteValues method are the endpoint's HttpContext object, the name of the route that will be used to generate the link, and an object that is used to provide values for the segment variables. The GetPathByRouteValues method returns a URL that will be routed to the Population endpoint, which can be confirmed by restarting ASP.NET Core and requesting the http://localhost:5000/capital/monaco URL. The request will be routed to the Capital endpoint, which will generate the URL and use it to redirect the browser, producing the result shown in Figure 13-10.

Figure 13-10. *Generating a URL*

The benefit of this approach is that the URL is generated from the URL pattern in the named route, which means a change in the URL pattern is reflected in the generated URLs, without the need to make changes to endpoints. To demonstrate, Listing 13-13 changes the URL pattern.

Listing 13-13. Changing a URL Pattern in the Startup.cs File in the Platform Folder

```
...
app.UseEndpoints(endpoints => {
    endpoints.MapGet("{first}/{second}/{third}", async context => {
        await context.Response.WriteAsync("Request Was Routed\n");
        foreach (var kvp in context.Request.RouteValues) {
            await context.Response.WriteAsync($"{kvp.Key}: {kvp.Value}\n");
        }
    });
    endpoints.MapGet("capital/{country}", Capital.Endpoint);
    endpoints.MapGet("size/{city}", Population.Endpoint)
        .WithMetadata(new RouteNameMetadata("population"));
});
...
```

The name assigned to the route is unchanged, which ensures that the same endpoint is targeted by the generated URL. To see the effect of the new pattern, restart ASP.NET Core and request the http://localhost:5000/capital/monaco URL again. The redirection is to a URL that is matched by the modified pattern, as shown in Figure 13-11. This feature addresses the final problem that I described at the start of the chapter, making it easy to change the URLs that an application supports.

Figure 13-11. Changing the URL pattern

URL ROUTING AND AREAS

The URL routing system supports a feature called *areas*, which allows separate sections of the application to have their own controllers, views, and Razor Pages. I have not described the areas feature in this book because it is not widely used and, when it is used, it tends to cause more problems than it solves. If you want to break up an application, then I recommend creating separate projects.

Managing URL Matching

The previous section introduced the basic URL routing features, but most applications require more work to ensure that URLs are routed correctly, either to increase or to restrict the range of URLs that are matched by a route. In the sections that follow, I show you the different ways that URL patterns can be adjusted to fine-tune the matching process.

Matching Multiple Values from a Single URL Segment

Most segment variables correspond directly to a segment in the URL path, but the routing middleware is able to perform more complex matches, allowing a single segment to be matched to a variable while discarding unwanted characters. Listing 13-14 defines a route that matches only part of a URL segment to a variable.

Listing 13-14. Matching Part of a Segment in the Startup.cs File in the Platform Folder

```
...
app.UseEndpoints(endpoints => {
    endpoints.MapGet("files/{filename}.{ext}", async context => {
        await context.Response.WriteAsync("Request Was Routed\n");
        foreach (var kvp in context.Request.RouteValues) {
            await context.Response.WriteAsync($"{kvp.Key}: {kvp.Value}\n");
        }
    });
    endpoints.MapGet("capital/{country}", Capital.Endpoint);
    endpoints.MapGet("size/{city}", Population.Endpoint)
        .WithMetadata(new RouteNameMetadata("population"));
});
...
```

A URL pattern can contain as many segment variables as you need, as long as they are separated by a static string. The requirement for a static separator is so the routing middleware knows where the content for one variable ends and content for the next starts. The pattern in Listing 13-14 matches segment variables named `filename` and `ext`, which are separated by a period; this pattern is often used by process file names. To see how the pattern matches URLs, restart ASP.NET Core and request the `http://localhost:5000/files/myfile.txt` URL, which will produce the response shown in Figure 13-12.

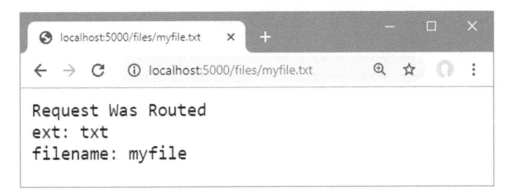

Figure 13-12. *Matching multiple values from a single path segment*

AVOIDING THE COMPLEX PATTERN MISMATCHING PITFALL

The order of the segment variables shown in Figure 13-12 shows that pattern segments that contain multiple variables are matched from right to left. This isn't important most of the time, because endpoints can't rely on a specific key order, but it does show that complex URL patterns are handled differently, which reflects the difficulty in matching them.

In fact, the matching process is so diffiscult that there can be unexpected matching failures. The specific failures change with each release of ASP.NET Core as the matching process is adjusted to address problems, but the adjustments often introduce new issues. At the time of writing, there is a problem with URL patterns where the content that should be matched by the first variable also appears as a literal string at the start of a segment. This is easier to understand with an example, as shown here:

```
...
endpoints.MapGet("example/red{color}", async context => {
...
```

This pattern has a segment that begins with the literal string `red`, followed by a segment variable named `color`. The routing middleware will correctly match the pattern against the URL path `example/redgreen`, and the value of the `color` route variable will be `green`. However, the URL path `example/redredgreen` won't match because the matching process confuses the position of the literal content with the first part of the content that should be assigned to the `color` variable. This problem may be fixed by the time you read this book, but there will be other issues with complex patterns. It is a good idea to keep URL patterns as simple as possible and make sure you get the matching results you expect.

Using Default Values for Segment Variables

Patterns can be defined with default values that are used when the URL doesn't contain a value for the corresponding segment, increasing the range of URLs that a route can match. Listing 13-15 shows the use of default values in a pattern.

Listing 13-15. Using Default Values in the Startup.cs File in the Platform Folder

```
...
app.UseEndpoints(endpoints => {
    endpoints.MapGet("files/{filename}.{ext}", async context => {
        await context.Response.WriteAsync("Request Was Routed\n");
        foreach (var kvp in context.Request.RouteValues) {
            await context.Response.WriteAsync($"{kvp.Key}: {kvp.Value}\n");
        }
    });
    endpoints.MapGet("capital/{country=France}", Capital.Endpoint);
    endpoints.MapGet("size/{city}", Population.Endpoint)
        .WithMetadata(new RouteNameMetadata("population"));
});
...
```

Default values are defined using an equal sign and the value to be used. The default value in the listing uses the value `France` when there is no second segment in the URL path. The result is that the range of URLs that can be matched by the route increases, as described in Table 13-6.

Table 13-6. *Matching URLs*

URL Path	Description
/	No match—too few segments
/city	No match—first segment isn't `capital`
/capital	Matches, country variable is `France`
/capital/uk	Matches, country variable is `uk`
/capital/europe/italy	No match—too many segments

To test the default value, restart ASP.NET Core and navigate to `http://localhost:5000/capital`, which will produce the result shown in Figure 13-13.

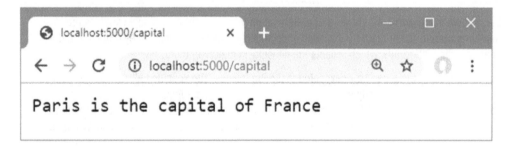

Figure 13-13. *Using a default value for a segment variable*

Using Optional Segments in a URL Pattern

Default values allow URLs to be matched with fewer segments, but the use of the default value isn't obvious to the endpoint. Some endpoints define their own responses to deal with URLs that omit segments, for which *optional segments* are used. To prepare, Listing 13-16 updates the `Population` endpoint so that it uses a default value when no `city` value is available in the routing data.

Listing 13-16. Using a Default Value in the Population.cs File in the Platform Folder

```
using Microsoft.AspNetCore.Http;
using System;
using System.Threading.Tasks;

namespace Platform {
    public class Population {

        public static async Task Endpoint(HttpContext context) {
            string city = context.Request.RouteValues["city"] as string ?? "london";
            int? pop = null;
            switch (city.ToLower()) {
                case "london":
                    pop = 8_136_000;
                    break;
                case "paris":
                    pop = 2_141_000;
                    break;
                case "monaco":
                    pop = 39_000;
                    break;
            }
            if (pop.HasValue) {
                await context.Response
                    .WriteAsync($"City: {city}, Population: {pop}");
            } else {
                context.Response.StatusCode = StatusCodes.Status404NotFound;
            }
        }
    }
}
```

The change uses london as the default value because there is no city segment variable available. Listing 13-17 updates the route for the Population endpoint to make the second segment optional.

Listing 13-17. Using an Optional Segment in the Startup.cs File in the Platform Folder

```
...
app.UseEndpoints(endpoints => {
    endpoints.MapGet("files/{filename}.{ext}", async context => {
        await context.Response.WriteAsync("Request Was Routed\n");
        foreach (var kvp in context.Request.RouteValues) {
            await context.Response.WriteAsync($"{kvp.Key}: {kvp.Value}\n");
        }
    });
    endpoints.MapGet("capital/{country=France}", Capital.Endpoint);
    endpoints.MapGet("size/{city?}", Population.Endpoint)
        .WithMetadata(new RouteNameMetadata("population"));
});
...
```

Optional segments are denoted with a question mark (the ? character) after the variable name and allow the route to match URLs that don't have a corresponding path segment, as described in Table 13-7.

Table 13-7. *Matching URLs*

URL Path	Description
/	No match—too few segments.
/city	No match—first segment isn't size.
/size	Matches. No value for the city variable is provided to the endpoint.
/size/paris	Matches, city variable is paris.
/size/europe/italy	No match—too many segments.

To test the optional segment, restart ASP.NET Core and navigate to http://localhost:5000/size, which will produce the response shown in Figure 13-14.

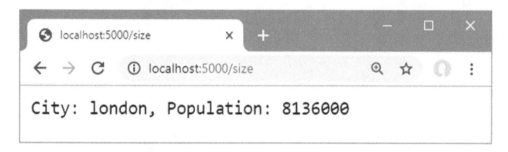

Figure 13-14. *Using an optional segment*

Using a catchall Segment Variable

Optional segments allow a pattern to match shorter URL paths. A *catchall* segment does the opposite and allows routes to match URLs that contain more segments than the pattern. A catchall segment is denoted with an asterisk before the variable name, as shown in Listing 13-18.

Listing 13-18. Using a Catchall Segment in the Startup.cs File in the Platform Folder

```
...
app.UseEndpoints(endpoints => {
    endpoints.MapGet("{first}/{second}/{*catchall}", async context => {
        await context.Response.WriteAsync("Request Was Routed\n");
        foreach (var kvp in context.Request.RouteValues) {
            await context.Response.WriteAsync($"{kvp.Key}: {kvp.Value}\n");
        }
    });
    endpoints.MapGet("capital/{country=France}", Capital.Endpoint);
    endpoints.MapGet("size/{city?}", Population.Endpoint)
        .WithMetadata(new RouteNameMetadata("population"));
});
...
```

The new pattern contains two-segment variables and a catchall, and the result is that the route will match any URL whose path contains two or more segments. There is no upper limit to the number of segments that the URL pattern in this route will match, and the contents of any additional segments are assigned to the segment variable named catchall. Restart ASP.NET Core and navigate to http://localhost:5000/one/two/three/four, which produces the response shown in Figure 13-15.

■ **Tip** Notice that the segments captured by the catchall are presented in the form *segment/segment/segment* and that the endpoint is responsible for processing the string to break out the individual segments.

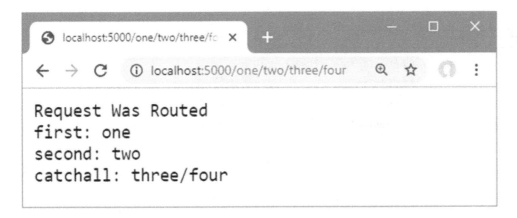

Figure 13-15. *Using a catchall segment variable*

Constraining Segment Matching

Default values, optional segments, and catchall segments all increase the range of URLs that a route will match. Constraints have the opposite effect and restrict matches. This can be useful if an endpoint can deal only with specific segment contents or if you want to differentiate matching closely related URLs for different endpoints. Constraints are applied by a colon (the : character) and a constraint type after a segment variable name, as shown in Listing 13-19.

Listing 13-19. Applying Constraints in the Startup.cs File in the Platform Folder

```
...
app.UseEndpoints(endpoints => {
    endpoints.MapGet("{first:int}/{second:bool}", async context => {
        await context.Response.WriteAsync("Request Was Routed\n");
        foreach (var kvp in context.Request.RouteValues) {
            await context.Response.WriteAsync($"{kvp.Key}: {kvp.Value}\n");
        }
    });
    endpoints.MapGet("capital/{country=France}", Capital.Endpoint);
    endpoints.MapGet("size/{city?}", Population.Endpoint)
        .WithMetadata(new RouteNameMetadata("population"));
});
...
```

This example constrains the first segment variable so it will match only the path segments that can be parsed to an int value, and it constrains the second segment so it will match only the path segments that can be parsed to a bool. Values that don't match the constraints won't be matched by the route. Table 13-8 describes the URL pattern constraints.

■ **Note**   Some of the constraints match types whose format can differ based on locale. The routing middleware doesn't handle localized formats and will match only those values that are expressed in the invariant culture format.

Table 13-8. *The URL Pattern Constraints*

Constraint	Description
alpha	This constraint matches the letters *a* to *z* (and is case-insensitive).
bool	This constraint matches true and false (and is case-insensitive).
datetime	This constraint matches DateTime values, expressed in the nonlocalized invariant culture format.
decimal	This constraint matches decimal values, formatted in the nonlocalized invariant culture.
double	This constraint matches double values, formatted in the nonlocalized invariant culture.
file	This constraint matches segments whose content represents a file name, in the form name.ext. The existence of the file is not validated.
float	This constraint matches float values, formatted in the nonlocalized invariant culture.
guid	This constraint matches GUID values.
int	This constraint matches int values.
length(len)	This constraint matches path segments that have the specified number of characters.
length(min, max)	This constraint matches path segments whose length falls between the lower and upper values specified.
long	This constraint matches long values.
max(val)	This constraint matches path segments that can be parsed to an int value that is less than or equal to the specified value.
maxlength(len)	This constraint matches path segments whose length is equal to or less than the specified value.
min(val)	This constraint matches path segments that can be parsed to an int value that is more than or equal to the specified value.
minlength(len)	This constraint matches path segments whose length is equal to or more than the specified value.
nonfile	This constraint matches segments that do not represent a file name, i.e., values that would not be matched by the file constraint.
range(min, max)	This constraint matches path segments that can be parsed to an int value that falls between the inclusive range specified.
regex(expression)	This constraint applies a regular expression to match path segments.

To test the constraints, restart ASP.NET Core and request http://localhost:5000/100/true, which is a URL whose path segments conform to the constraints in Listing 13-19 and that produces the result shown on the left side of Figure 13-16. Request http://localhost:5000/apples/oranges, which has the right number of segments but contains values that don't conform to the constraints. None of the routes matches the request, which is forwarded to the terminal middleware, as shown on the right of Figure 13-16.

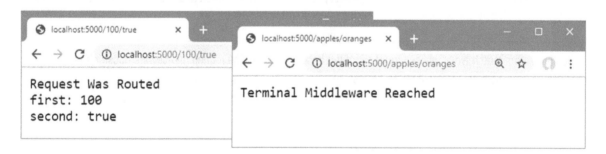

Figure 13-16. *Testing constraints*

Constraints can be combined to further restrict matching, as shown in Listing 13-20.

Listing 13-20. Combining URL Pattern Constraints in the Startup.cs File in the Platform Folder

```
...
app.UseEndpoints(endpoints => {
    endpoints.MapGet("{first:alpha:length(3)}/{second:bool}", async context => {
        await context.Response.WriteAsync("Request Was Routed\n");
        foreach (var kvp in context.Request.RouteValues) {
            await context.Response.WriteAsync($"{kvp.Key}: {kvp.Value}\n");
        }
    });
    endpoints.MapGet("capital/{country=France}", Capital.Endpoint);
    endpoints.MapGet("size/{city?}", Population.Endpoint)
        .WithMetadata(new RouteNameMetadata("population"));
});
...
```

The constraints are combined, and only path segments that can satisfy all the constraints will be matched. The combination in Listing 13-20 constrains the URL pattern so that the first segment will match only three alphabetic characters. To test the pattern, restart ASP.NET Core and request http://localhost:5000/dog/true, which will produce the output shown in Figure 13-17. Requesting the URL http://localhost:5000/dogs/true won't match the route because the first segment contains four characters.

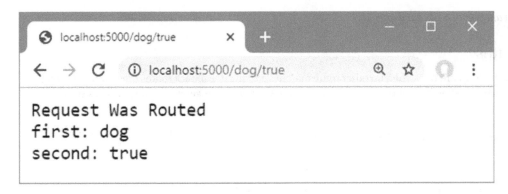

Figure 13-17. Combining constraints

Constraining Matching to a Specific Set of Values

The regex constraint applies a regular expression, which provides the basis for one of the most commonly required restrictions: matching only a specific set of values. In Listing 13-21, I have applied the regex constraint to the routes for the Capital endpoint, so it will receive requests only for the values it is able to process.

Listing 13-21. Matching Specific Values in the Startup.cs File in the Platform Folder

```
...
app.UseEndpoints(endpoints => {
    endpoints.MapGet("{first:alpha:length(3)}/{second:bool}", async context => {
        await context.Response.WriteAsync("Request Was Routed\n");
        foreach (var kvp in context.Request.RouteValues) {
            await context.Response.WriteAsync($"{kvp.Key}: {kvp.Value}\n");
        }
    });

    endpoints.MapGet("capital/{country:regex(^uk|france|monaco$)}",
        Capital.Endpoint);
    endpoints.MapGet("size/{city?}", Population.Endpoint)
        .WithMetadata(new RouteNameMetadata("population"));
});
...
```

The route will match only those URLs with two segments. The first segment must be capital, and the second segment must be uk, france, or monaco. Regular expressions are case-insensitive, which you can confirm by restarting ASP.NET Core and requesting http://localhost:5000/capital/UK, which will produce the result shown in Figure 13-18.

■ **Tip** You may find that your browser requests /capital/uk, with a lowercase uk. If this happens, clear your browser history and try again.

Figure 13-18. *Matching specific values with a regular expression*

Defining Fallback Routes

Fallback routes direct a request to an endpoint only when no other route matches a request. Fallback routes prevent requests from being passed further along the request pipeline by ensuring that the routing system will always generate a response, as shown in Listing 13-22.

Listing 13-22. Using a Fallback Route in the Startup.cs File in the Platform Folder

```
...
app.UseEndpoints(endpoints => {
    endpoints.MapGet("{first:alpha:length(3)}/{second:bool}", async context => {
        await context.Response.WriteAsync("Request Was Routed\n");
        foreach (var kvp in context.Request.RouteValues) {
            await context.Response.WriteAsync($"{kvp.Key}: {kvp.Value}\n");
        }
    });

    endpoints.MapGet("capital/{country:regex(^uk|france|monaco$)}",
        Capital.Endpoint);
    endpoints.MapGet("size/{city?}", Population.Endpoint)
        .WithMetadata(new RouteNameMetadata("population"));

    endpoints.MapFallback(async context => {
        await context.Response.WriteAsync("Routed to fallback endpoint");
    });
});
...
```

The MapFallback method creates a route that will be used as a last resort and that will match any request. The methods for creating fallback routes are described in Table 13-9. (There are also methods for creating fallback routes that are specific to other parts of ASP.NET Core and that are described in Part 3.)

Table 13-9. *The Methods for Creating Fallback Routes*

Name	Description
MapFallback(endpoint)	This method creates a fallback that routes requests to an endpoint.
MapFallbackToFile(path)	This method creates a fallback that routes requests to a file.

With the addition of the route in Listing 13-22, the routing middleware with handle all requests, including those that match none of the regular routes. Restart ASP.NET Core and navigate to a URL that won't be matched by any of the routes, such as http://localhost:5000/notmatched, and you will see the response shown in Figure 13-19.

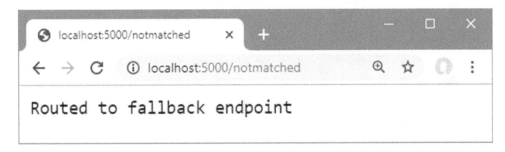

Figure 13-19. *Using a fallback route*

There is no magic to fallback routes. The URL pattern used by fallbacks is {path:nofile}, and they rely on the Order property to ensure that the route is used only if there are no other suitable routes, which is a feature described in the "Avoiding Ambiguous Route Exceptions" section.

Advanced Routing Features

The routing features described in the previous sections address the needs of most projects, especially since they are usually accessed through higher-level features such as the MVC Framework, described in Part 3. There are some advanced features for projects that have unusual routing requirements, which I describe in the following sections.

Creating Custom Constraints

If the constraints described in Table 13-8 are not sufficient, you can define your own custom constraints by implementing the IRouteConstraint interface. To create a custom constraint, add a file named CountryRouteConstraint.cs to the Platform folder and add the code shown in Listing 13-23.

Listing 13-23. The Contents of the CountryRouteConstraint.cs File in the Platform Folder

```
using System;
using Microsoft.AspNetCore.Http;
using Microsoft.AspNetCore.Routing;

namespace Platform {

    public class CountryRouteConstraint: IRouteConstraint {
        private static string[] countries = { "uk", "france", "monaco" };

        public bool Match(HttpContext httpContext, IRouter route, string routeKey,
                RouteValueDictionary values, RouteDirection routeDirection) {
            string segmentValue = values[routeKey] as string ?? "";
            return Array.IndexOf(countries, segmentValue.ToLower()) > -1;
        }
    }
}
```

The IRouteConstraint interface defines the Match method, which is called to allow a constraint to decide whether a request should be matched by the route. The parameters for the Match method provide the HttpContext object for the request, the route, the name of the segment, the segment variables extracted from the URL, and whether the request is to check for an incoming or outgoing URL. The Match method returns true if the constraint is satisfied by the request and false if it is not. The constraint in Listing 13-23 defines a set of countries that are compared to the value of the segment variable to which the constraint has been applied. The constraint is satisfied if the segment matches one of the countries. Custom constraints are set up using the options pattern, as shown in Listing 13-24. (The options pattern is described in Chapter 12.)

Listing 13-24. Using a Custom Constraint in the Startup.cs File in the Platform Folder

```
using Microsoft.AspNetCore.Builder;
using Microsoft.AspNetCore.Hosting;
using Microsoft.AspNetCore.Http;
using Microsoft.Extensions.DependencyInjection;
using Microsoft.AspNetCore.Routing;

namespace Platform {
    public class Startup {

        public void ConfigureServices(IServiceCollection services) {
            services.Configure<RouteOptions>(opts => {
                opts.ConstraintMap.Add("countryName",
                    typeof(CountryRouteConstraint));
            });
        }

        public void Configure(IApplicationBuilder app, IWebHostEnvironment env) {
            app.UseDeveloperExceptionPage();
            app.UseRouting();

            app.UseEndpoints(endpoints => {
                endpoints.MapGet("{first:alpha:length(3)}/{second:bool}",
                    async context => {
                        await context.Response.WriteAsync("Request Was Routed\n");
                        foreach (var kvp in context.Request.RouteValues) {
                            await context.Response
                                .WriteAsync($"{kvp.Key}: {kvp.Value}\n");
                        }
                    });

                endpoints.MapGet("capital/{country:countryName}", Capital.Endpoint);

                endpoints.MapGet("size/{city?}", Population.Endpoint)
                    .WithMetadata(new RouteNameMetadata("population"));

                endpoints.MapFallback(async context => {
                    await context.Response.WriteAsync("Routed to fallback endpoint");
                });
            });

            app.Use(async (context, next) => {
                await context.Response.WriteAsync("Terminal Middleware Reached");
            });
        }
    }
}
```

The options pattern is applied to the RouteOptions class, which defines the ConstraintMap property. Each constraint is registered with a key that allows it to be applied in URL patterns. In Listing 13-24, the key for the CountryRouteConstraint class is countyName, which allows me to constraint a route like this:

```
...
endpoints.MapGet("capital/{country:countryName}", Capital.Endpoint);
...
```

Requests will be matched by this route only when the first segment of the URL is capital and the second segment is one of the countries defined in Listing 13-23.

Avoiding Ambiguous Route Exceptions

When trying to route a request, the routing middleware assigns each route a score. As explained earlier in the chapter, precedence is given to more specific routes, and route selection is usually a straightforward process that behaves predictably, albeit with the occasional surprise if you don't think through and test the full range of URLs the application will support.

If two routes have the same score, the routing system can't choose between them and throws an exception, indicating that the routes are ambiguous. In most cases, the best approach is to modify the ambiguous routes to increase specificity by introducing literal segments or a constraint. There are some situations where that won't be possible, and some extra work is required to get the routing system to work as intended. Listing 13-25 replaces the routes from the previous example with two new routes that are ambiguous, but only for some requests.

Listing 13-25. Defining Ambiguous Routes in the Startup.cs File in the Platform Folder

```
using Microsoft.AspNetCore.Builder;
using Microsoft.AspNetCore.Hosting;
using Microsoft.AspNetCore.Http;
using Microsoft.Extensions.DependencyInjection;
using Microsoft.AspNetCore.Routing;

namespace Platform {
    public class Startup {

        public void ConfigureServices(IServiceCollection services) {
            services.Configure<RouteOptions>(opts => {
                opts.ConstraintMap.Add("countryName",
                    typeof(CountryRouteConstraint));
            });
        }

        public void Configure(IApplicationBuilder app, IWebHostEnvironment env) {
            app.UseDeveloperExceptionPage();
            app.UseRouting();

            app.UseEndpoints(endpoints => {
                endpoints.Map("{number:int}", async context => {
                    await context.Response.WriteAsync("Routed to the int endpoint");
                });
                endpoints.Map("{number:double}", async context => {
                    await context.Response
                        .WriteAsync("Routed to the double endpoint");
                });
            });

            app.Use(async (context, next) => {
                await context.Response.WriteAsync("Terminal Middleware Reached");
            });
        }
    }
}
```

These routes are ambiguous only for some values. Only one route matches URLs where the first path segment can be parsed to a double, but both routes match for where the segment can be parsed as an int or a double. To see the issue, restart ASP.NET Core and request http://localhost:5000/23.5. The path segment 23.5 can be parsed to a double and produces the response shown on the left side of Figure 13-20. Request http://localhost:5000/23, and you will see the exception shown on the right of Figure 13-20. The segment 23 can be parsed as both an int and a double, which means that the routing system cannot identify a single route to handle the request.

Figure 13-20. *An occasionally ambiguous routing configuration*

For these situations, preference can be given to a route by defining its order relative to other matching routes, as shown in Listing 13-26.

Listing 13-26. Breaking Route Ambiguity in the Startup.cs File in the Platform Folder

```
...
app.UseEndpoints(endpoints => {
    endpoints.Map("{number:int}", async context => {
        await context.Response.WriteAsync("Routed to the int endpoint");
    }).Add(b => ((RouteEndpointBuilder)b).Order = 1);

    endpoints.Map("{number:double}", async context => {
        await context.Response.WriteAsync("Routed to the double endpoint");
    }).Add(b => ((RouteEndpointBuilder)b).Order = 2);
});
...
```

The process is awkward and requires a call to the Add method, casting to a RouteEndpointBuilder and setting the value of the Order property. Precedence is given to the route with the lowest Order value, which means that the changes in Listing 13-26 tell the routing system to use the first route for URLs that both routes can handle. Restart ASP.NET Core and request the http://localhost:5000/23 URL again, and you will see that the first route handles the request, as shown in Figure 13-21.

Figure 13-21. *Avoiding ambiguous routes*

Accessing the Endpoint in a Middleware Component

As earlier chapters demonstrated, not all middleware generates responses. Some components provide features used later in the request pipeline, such as the session middleware, or enhance the response in some way, such as status code middleware.

One limitation of the normal request pipeline is that a middleware component at the start of the pipeline can't tell which of the later components will generate a response. The routing middleware does something different. Although routes are registered in the UseEndpoints method, the selection of a route is done in the UseRouting method, and the endpoint is executed to generate a response in the UseEndpoints method. Any middleware component that is added to the request pipeline between the UseRouting method and the UseEndpoints method can see which endpoint has been selected before the response is generated and alter its behavior accordingly.

In Listing 13-27, I have added a middleware component that adds different messages to the response based on the route that has been selected to handle the request.

Listing 13-27. Adding a Middleware Component in the Startup.cs File in the Platform Folder

```
using Microsoft.AspNetCore.Builder;
using Microsoft.AspNetCore.Hosting;
using Microsoft.AspNetCore.Http;
using Microsoft.Extensions.DependencyInjection;
using Microsoft.AspNetCore.Routing;

namespace Platform {
    public class Startup {

        public void ConfigureServices(IServiceCollection services) {
            services.Configure<RouteOptions>(opts => {
                opts.ConstraintMap.Add("countryName",
                    typeof(CountryRouteConstraint));
            });
        }

        public void Configure(IApplicationBuilder app, IWebHostEnvironment env) {
            app.UseDeveloperExceptionPage();
            app.UseRouting();

            app.Use(async (context, next) => {
                Endpoint end = context.GetEndpoint();
                if (end != null) {
                    await context.Response
                        .WriteAsync($"{end.DisplayName} Selected \n");
                } else {
                    await context.Response.WriteAsync("No Endpoint Selected \n");
                }
                await next();
            });

            app.UseEndpoints(endpoints => {
                endpoints.Map("{number:int}", async context => {
                    await context.Response.WriteAsync("Routed to the int endpoint");
                })
                .WithDisplayName("Int Endpoint")
                .Add(b => ((RouteEndpointBuilder)b).Order = 1);

                endpoints.Map("{number:double}", async context => {
                    await context.Response
                        .WriteAsync("Routed to the double endpoint");
                })
                .WithDisplayName("Double Endpoint")
```

```
                    .Add(b => ((RouteEndpointBuilder)b).Order = 2);
            });

            app.Use(async (context, next) => {
                await context.Response.WriteAsync("Terminal Middleware Reached");
            });
        }
    }
}
```

The GetEndpoint extension method on the HttpContext class returns the endpoint that has been selected to handle the request, described through an Endpoint object. The Endpoint class defines the properties described in Table 13-10.

■ **Caution**   There is also a SetEndpoint method that allows the endpoint chosen by the routing middleware to be changed before the response is generated. This should be used with caution and only when there is a compelling need to interfere with the normal route selection process.

Table 13-10. *The Properties Defined by the Endpoint Class*

Name	Description
DisplayName	This property returns the display name associated with the endpoint, which can be set using the WithDisplayName method when creating a route.
Metadata	This property returns the collection of metadata associated with the endpoint.
RequestDelegate	This property returns the delegate that will be used to generate the response.

To make it easier to identify the endpoint that the routing middleware has selected, I used the WithDisplayName method to assign names to the routes in Listing 13-27. The new middleware component adds a message to the response reporting the endpoint that has been selected. Restart ASP.NET Core and request the http://localhost:5000/23 URL to see the output from the middleware that shows the endpoint has been selected between the two methods that add the routing middleware to the request pipeline, as shown in Figure 13-22.

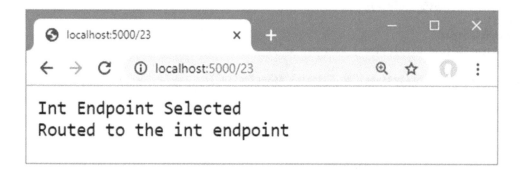

Figure 13-22. *Determining the endpoint*

Summary

In this chapter, I introduced the endpoint routing system and explained how it deals with some common problems arising in regular middleware. I showed you how to define routes, how to match and generate URLs, and how to use constraints to restrict the use of routes. I also showed you some of the advanced uses of the routing system, including custom constraints and avoiding route ambiguity. In the next chapter, I explain how ASP.NET Core services work.

CHAPTER 14

Using Dependency Injection

Services are objects that are shared between middleware components and endpoints. There are no restrictions on the features that services can provide, but they are usually used for tasks that are needed in multiple parts of the application, such as logging or database access.

The ASP.NET Core *dependency injection* feature is used to create and consume services. This is a topic that causes confusion and can be difficult to understand. In this chapter, I describe the problems that dependency injection solves and explain how dependency injection is supported by the ASP.NET Core platform. Table 14-1 puts dependency injection in context.

Table 14-1. *Putting Dependency Injection in Context*

Question	Answer
What is it?	Dependency Injection makes it easy to create loosely coupled components, which typically means that components consume functionality defined by interfaces without having any firsthand knowledge of which implementation classes are being used.
Why is it useful?	Dependency injection makes it easier to change the behavior of an application by changing the components that implement the interfaces that define application features. It also results in components that are easier to isolate for unit testing.
How is it used?	The Startup class is used to specify which implementation classes are used to deliver the functionality specified by the interfaces used by the application. Services can be explicitly requested through the IServiceProvider interface or by declaring constructor or method parameters.
Are there any pitfalls or limitations?	There are some differences in the way that middleware components and endpoints are handled and the way that services with different lifecycles are accessed.
Are there any alternatives?	You don't have to use dependency injection in your own code, but it is helpful to know how it works because it is used by the ASP.NET Core platform to provide features to developers.

Table 14-2 summarizes the chapter.

Table 14-2. *Chapter Summary*

Problem	Solution	Listing
Obtaining a service in the Startup class	Add a parameter to the Configure method	13
Obtaining a service in a middleware component	Define a constructor parameter	14, 33–35
Obtaining a service in an endpoint	Get an IServiceProvider object through the context objects	15–18
Instantiating a class that has constructor dependencies	Use the ActivatorUtilities class	19–21
Defining services that are instantiated for every dependency	Define transient services	22–27
Defining services that are instantiated for every request	Define scoped services	28–32
Accessing services in the Startup.ConfigureServices method	Define a Startup constructor parameter and assign the value to the property	36

© Adam Freeman 2020

A. Freeman, *Pro ASP.NET Core 3*, https://doi.org/10.1007/978-1-4842-5440-0_14

Table 14-2. (*continued*)

Problem	Solution	Listing
Managing service instantiation	Use a service factory	37, 38
Defining multiple implementations for a service	Define multiple services with the same scope and consume them through the GetServices method	39–41
Using services that support generic type parameters	Use a service with an unbound type	42

Preparing for This Chapter

In this chapter, I continue to use the Platform project from Chapter 13. New classes are required to prepare for this chapter. Start by creating the Platform/Services folder and add to it a class file named IResponseFormatter.cs, with the code shown in Listing 14-1.

■ **Tip** You can download the example project for this chapter—and for all the other chapters in this book—from https://github.com/apress/pro-asp.net-core-3. See Chapter 1 for how to get help if you have problems running the examples.

Listing 14-1. The Contents of the IResponseFormatter.cs File in the Services Folder

```
using Microsoft.AspNetCore.Http;
using System.Threading.Tasks;

namespace Platform.Services {
    public interface IResponseFormatter {

        Task Format(HttpContext context, string content);
    }
}
```

The IResponseFormatter interface defines a single method that receives an HttpContext object and a string. To create an implementation of the interface, add a class called TextResponseFormatter.cs to the Platform/Services folder with the code shown in Listing 14-2.

Listing 14-2. The Contents of the TextResponseFormatter.cs File in the Services Folder

```
using System.Threading.Tasks;
using Microsoft.AspNetCore.Http;

namespace Platform.Services {
    public class TextResponseFormatter : IResponseFormatter {
        private int responseCounter = 0;

        public async Task Format(HttpContext context, string content) {
            await context.Response.
                WriteAsync($"Response {++responseCounter}:\n{content}");
        }
    }
}
```

The TextResponseFormatter class implements the interface and writes the content to the response as a simple string with a prefix to make it obvious when the class is used.

Creating a Middleware Component and an Endpoint

Some of the examples in this chapter show how features are applied differently when using middleware and endpoints. Add a file called WeatherMiddleware.cs to the Platform folder with the code shown in Listing 14-3.

Listing 14-3. The Contents of the WeatherMiddleware.cs File in the Platform Folder

```
using Microsoft.AspNetCore.Http;
using System.Threading.Tasks;

namespace Platform {
    public class WeatherMiddleware {
        private RequestDelegate next;

        public WeatherMiddleware(RequestDelegate nextDelegate) {
            next = nextDelegate;
        }

        public async Task Invoke(HttpContext context) {
            if (context.Request.Path == "/middleware/class") {
                await context.Response
                    .WriteAsync("Middleware Class: It is raining in London");
            } else {
                await next(context);
            }
        }
    }
}
```

To create an endpoint that produces a similar result to the middleware component, add a file called WeatherEndpoint.cs to the Platform folder with the code shown in Listing 14-4.

Listing 14-4. The Contents of the WeatherEndpoint.cs File in the Platform Folder

```
using Microsoft.AspNetCore.Http;
using System.Threading.Tasks;

namespace Platform {
    public class WeatherEndpoint {

        public static async Task Endpoint(HttpContext context) {
            await context.Response
                .WriteAsync("Endpoint Class: It is cloudy in Milan");
        }
    }
}
```

Configuring the Request Pipeline

Replace the contents of the Startup.cs file with those shown in Listing 14-5. The classes defined in the previous section are applied alongside lambda functions that produce similar results.

Listing 14-5. Replacing the Contents of the Startup.cs File in the Platform Folder

```
using Microsoft.AspNetCore.Builder;
using Microsoft.AspNetCore.Hosting;
using Microsoft.AspNetCore.Http;
using Microsoft.Extensions.DependencyInjection;
using Microsoft.AspNetCore.Routing;
```

```
using Platform.Services;

namespace Platform {
    public class Startup {

        public void ConfigureServices(IServiceCollection services) {
        }

        public void Configure(IApplicationBuilder app, IWebHostEnvironment env) {
            app.UseDeveloperExceptionPage();
            app.UseRouting();
            app.UseMiddleware<WeatherMiddleware>();

            IResponseFormatter formatter = new TextResponseFormatter();
            app.Use(async (context, next) => {
                if (context.Request.Path == "/middleware/function") {
                    await formatter.Format(context,
                        "Middleware Function: It is snowing in Chicago");
                } else {
                    await next();
                }
            });

            app.UseEndpoints(endpoints => {

                endpoints.MapGet("/endpoint/class", WeatherEndpoint.Endpoint);

                endpoints.MapGet("/endpoint/function", async context => {
                    await context.Response
                        .WriteAsync("Endpoint Function: It is sunny in LA");
                });
            });
        }
    }
}
```

Start the application by selecting Start Without Debugging or Run Without Debugging from the Debug menu or by opening a new PowerShell command prompt, navigating to the Platform project folder (which contains the Platform.csproj file, and running the command shown in Listing 14-6.

Listing 14-6. Starting the ASP.NET Core Runtime

```
dotnet run
```

Use a browser to request http://localhost:5000/middleware/function, and you will see the response shown in Figure 14-1. Each time you reload the browser, the counter shown in the response will be incremented.

Figure 14-1. *Running the example application*

Understanding Service Location and Tight Coupling

To understand dependency injection, it is important to start with the two problems it solves. In the sections that follow, I describe both problems addressed by dependency injection.

TAKING A VIEW ON DEPENDENCY INJECTION

Dependency injection is one of the topics that readers contact me about most often. About half of the emails complain that I am "forcing" DI upon them. Oddly, the other half are complaints that I did not emphasize the benefits of DI strongly enough and other readers may not have realized how useful it can be.

Dependency injection can be a difficult topic to understand, and its value is contentious. DI can be a useful tool, but not everyone likes it—or needs it.

DI offers limited benefit if you are not doing unit testing or if you are working on a small, self-contained and stable project. It is still helpful to understand how DI works because DI is used to access some important ASP.NET Core features described in earlier chapters, but you don't always need to embrace DI in the custom classes you write. There are alternative ways of creating shared features—two of which I describe in the following sections—and using these is perfectly acceptable if you don't like DI.

I rely on DI in my own applications because I find that projects often go in unexpected directions, and being able to easily replace a component with a new implementation can save me a lot of tedious and error-prone changes. I'd rather put in some effort at the start of the project than do a complex set of edits later.

But I am not dogmatic about dependency injection and nor should you be. Dependency injection solves a problem that doesn't arise in every project, and only you can determine whether you need DI for your project.

Understanding the Service Location Problem

Most projects have features that need to be used in different parts of the application, which are known as *services*. Common examples include logging tools and configuration settings but can extend to any shared feature, including the TextResponseFormatter class that is defined in Listing 14-2 and used by one of the middleware components.

Each TextResponseFormatter object maintains a counter that is included in the response sent to the browser, and if I want to incorporate the same counter into the responses generated by other endpoints, I need to have a way to make a single TextResponseFormatter object available in such a way that it can be easily found and consumed at every point where responses are generated.

There are many ways to make services locatable, but there are two main approaches, aside from the one that is the main topic of this chapter. The first approach is to create an object and use it as a constructor or method argument to pass it to the part of the application where it is required. The other approach is to add a static property to the service class that provides direct access to the shared instance, as shown in Listing 14-7. This is known as the *singleton pattern*, and it was a common approach before the widespread use of dependency injection.

Listing 14-7. Creating a Singleton in the TextResponseFormatter.cs File in the Services Folder

```
using System.Threading.Tasks;
using Microsoft.AspNetCore.Http;

namespace Platform.Services {
    public class TextResponseFormatter : IResponseFormatter {
        private int responseCounter = 0;
        private static TextResponseFormatter shared;

        public async Task Format(HttpContext context, string content) {
            await context.Response.
                WriteAsync($"Response {++responseCounter}:\n{content}");
        }
```

```
        public static TextResponseFormatter Singleton {
            get {
                if (shared == null) {
                    shared = new TextResponseFormatter();
                }
                return shared;
            }
        }
    }
}
```

This is a basic implementation of the singleton pattern, and there are many variations that pay closer attention to issues such as safe concurrent access. What's important for this chapter is that the changes in Listing 14-7 rely on the consumers of the TextResponseFormatter service obtaining a shared object through the static Singleton property, as shown in Listing 14-8.

Listing 14-8. Using a Service in the Startup.cs File in the Platform Folder

```
using Microsoft.AspNetCore.Builder;
using Microsoft.AspNetCore.Hosting;
using Microsoft.AspNetCore.Http;
using Microsoft.Extensions.DependencyInjection;
using Microsoft.AspNetCore.Routing;
using Platform.Services;

namespace Platform {
    public class Startup {

        public void ConfigureServices(IServiceCollection services) {
        }

        public void Configure(IApplicationBuilder app, IWebHostEnvironment env) {
            app.UseDeveloperExceptionPage();
            app.UseRouting();
            app.UseMiddleware<WeatherMiddleware>();

            app.Use(async (context, next) => {
                if (context.Request.Path == "/middleware/function") {
                    await TextResponseFormatter.Singleton.Format(context,
                        "Middleware Function: It is snowing in Chicago");
                } else {
                    await next();
                }
            });

            app.UseEndpoints(endpoints => {

                endpoints.MapGet("/endpoint/class", WeatherEndpoint.Endpoint);

                endpoints.MapGet("/endpoint/function", async context => {
                    await TextResponseFormatter.Singleton.Format(context,
                        "Endpoint Function: It is sunny in LA");
                });
            });
        }
    }
}
```

The singleton pattern allows me to share a single TextResponseFormatter so it is used by a middleware component and an endpoint, with the effect that a single counter is incremented by requests for two different URLs. To see the effect of the singleton pattern, restart ASP.NET Core and request the http://localhost:5000/middleware/function and http://localhost:5000/endpoint/function URLs. A single counter is updated for both URLs, as shown in Figure 14-2.

Figure 14-2. *Implementing the singleton pattern to create a shared service*

The singleton pattern is simple to understand and easy to use, but the knowledge of how services are located is spread throughout the application, and every service class and every service consumer needs to understand how to access the shared object. This can lead to variations in the singleton pattern as new services are created and creates many points in the code that must be updated when there is a change. This pattern can also be rigid and doesn't allow any flexibility in how services are managed because every consumer always shares a single service object.

Understanding the Tightly Coupled Components Problem

Although I defined an interface in Listing 14-1, the way that I have used the singleton pattern means that consumers are always aware of the implementation class they are using because that's the class whose static property is used to get the shared object. If I want to switch to a different implementation of the IResponseFormatter interface, I must locate every use of the service and replace the existing implementation class with the new one. There are patterns to solve this problem, too, such as the *type broker* pattern, in which a class provides access to singleton objects through their interfaces. Add a class file called TypeBroker.cs to the Platform/Services folder and use it to define the code shown in Listing 14-9.

Listing 14-9. The Contents of the TypeBroker.cs File in the Services Folder

```
namespace Platform.Services {
    public static class TypeBroker {
        private static IResponseFormatter formatter = new TextResponseFormatter();

        public static IResponseFormatter Formatter => formatter;
    }
}
```

The Formatter property provides access to a shared service object that implements the IResponseFormatter interface. Consumers of the service need to know that the TypeBroker class is responsible for selecting the implementation that will be used, but this pattern means that service consumers can work through interfaces rather than concrete classes, as shown in Listing 14-10.

Listing 14-10. Using a TypeBroker in the Startup.cs File in the Platform Folder

```
using Microsoft.AspNetCore.Builder;
using Microsoft.AspNetCore.Hosting;
using Microsoft.AspNetCore.Http;
using Microsoft.Extensions.DependencyInjection;
using Microsoft.AspNetCore.Routing;
using Platform.Services;

namespace Platform {
    public class Startup {

        public void ConfigureServices(IServiceCollection services) {
        }
```

```
    public void Configure(IApplicationBuilder app, IWebHostEnvironment env) {
        app.UseDeveloperExceptionPage();
        app.UseRouting();
        app.UseMiddleware<WeatherMiddleware>();

        app.Use(async (context, next) => {
            if (context.Request.Path == "/middleware/function") {
                await TypeBroker.Formatter.Format(context,
                    "Middleware Function: It is snowing in Chicago");
            } else {
                await next();
            }
        });

        app.UseEndpoints(endpoints => {

            endpoints.MapGet("/endpoint/class", WeatherEndpoint.Endpoint);

            endpoints.MapGet("/endpoint/function", async context => {
                await TypeBroker.Formatter.Format(context,
                    "Endpoint Function: It is sunny in LA");
            });
        });
    }
}
}
```

This approach makes it easy to switch to a different implementation class by altering just the TypeBroker class and prevents service consumers from creating dependencies on a specific implementation. It also means that service classes can focus on the features they provide without having to deal with how those features will be located. To demonstrate, add a class file called HtmlResponseFormatter.cs to the Platform/Services folder with the code shown in Listing 14-11.

Listing 14-11. The Contents of the HtmlResponseFormatter.cs File in the Services Folder

```
using System.Threading.Tasks;
using Microsoft.AspNetCore.Http;

namespace Platform.Services {
    public class HtmlResponseFormatter : IResponseFormatter {

        public async Task Format(HttpContext context, string content) {
            context.Response.ContentType = "text/html";
            await context.Response.WriteAsync($@"
                <!DOCTYPE html>
                <html lang=""en"">
                <head><title>Response</title></head>
                <body>
                    <h2>Formatted Response</h2>
                    <span>{content}</span>
                </body>
                </html>");
        }
    }
}
```

This implementation of the IResponseFormatter sets the ContentType property of the HttpResponse object and inserts the content into an HTML template string. To use the new formatter class, I only need to change the TypeBroker, as shown in Listing 14-12.

Listing 14-12. Changing Implementation in the TypeBroker.cs File in the Platform/Services Folder

```
namespace Platform.Services {
    public static class TypeBroker {
        private static IResponseFormatter formatter = new HtmlResponseFormatter();

        public static IResponseFormatter Formatter => formatter;
    }
}
```

To make sure the new formatter works, restart ASP.NET Core and request `http://localhost:5000/endpoint/function`, which will produce the result shown in Figure 14-3.

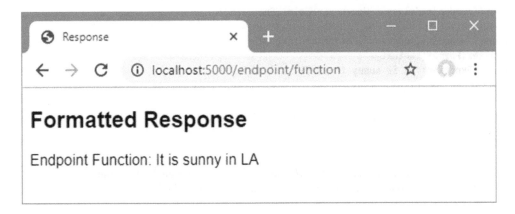

Figure 14-3. Using a different service implementation class

Using Dependency Injection

Dependency injection provides an alternative approach to providing services that tidy up the rough edges that arise in the singleton and type broker pattern, and it is integrated with other ASP.NET Core features. Listing 14-13 shows the use of ASP.NET Core dependency injection to replace the type broker from the previous section.

Listing 14-13. Using Dependency Injection in the Startup.cs File in the Platform Folder

```
using Microsoft.AspNetCore.Builder;
using Microsoft.AspNetCore.Hosting;
using Microsoft.AspNetCore.Http;
using Microsoft.Extensions.DependencyInjection;
using Microsoft.AspNetCore.Routing;
using Platform.Services;

namespace Platform {
    public class Startup {

        public void ConfigureServices(IServiceCollection services) {
            services.AddSingleton<IResponseFormatter, HtmlResponseFormatter>();
        }

        public void Configure(IApplicationBuilder app, IWebHostEnvironment env,
                IResponseFormatter formatter) {

            app.UseDeveloperExceptionPage();
            app.UseRouting();
```

317

```
        app.UseMiddleware<WeatherMiddleware>();

        app.Use(async (context, next) => {
            if (context.Request.Path == "/middleware/function") {
                await formatter.Format(context,
                    "Middleware Function: It is snowing in Chicago");
            } else {
                await next();
            }
        });

        app.UseEndpoints(endpoints => {

            endpoints.MapGet("/endpoint/class", WeatherEndpoint.Endpoint);

            endpoints.MapGet("/endpoint/function", async context => {
                await formatter.Format(context,
                    "Endpoint Function: It is sunny in LA");
            });
        });
    }
  }
}
```

Services are registered in the ConfigureServices method of the Startup class, using extensions methods on the IServiceCollection parameter. In Listing 14-13, I used an extension method to create a service for the IResponseFormatter interface.

```
...
public void ConfigureServices(IServiceCollection services) {
    services.AddSingleton<IResponseFormatter, HtmlResponseFormatter>();
}
...
```

The AddSingleton method is one of the extension methods available for services and tells ASP.NET Core that a single object should be used to satisfy demands for the service (the other extension methods are described in the "Using Service Lifecycles" section). The interface and the implementation class are specified as generic type arguments. To consume the service, I added a parameter to the Configure method.

```
...
public void Configure(IApplicationBuilder app, IWebHostEnvironment env,
    IResponseFormatter formatter) {
...
```

The new parameter declares a dependency on the IResponseFormatter interface, and the method is said to depend on the interface. Before the Configure method is invoked, its parameters are inspected, the dependency is detected, and the application's services are inspected to determine whether it is possible to resolve the dependency. The statement in the ConfigureServices method tells the dependency injection system that a dependency on the IResponseFormatter interface can be resolved with an HtmlResponseFormatter object. The object is created and used as an argument to invoke the method. Because the object that resolves the dependency is provided from outside the class or function that uses it, it is said to have been injected, which is why the process is known as *dependency injection*.

Using a Service in a Middleware Class

Defining a service in the ConfigureServices method and consuming it in the Configure method may not seem impressive, but once a service is defined, it can be used almost anywhere in an ASP.NET Core application. Listing 14-14 declares a dependency on the IResponseFormatter interface in the middleware class defined at the start of the chapter.

Listing 14-14. Declaring a Dependency in the WeatherMiddleware.cs File in the Services Folder

```
using Microsoft.AspNetCore.Http;
using System.Threading.Tasks;
using Platform.Services;

namespace Platform {
    public class WeatherMiddleware {
        private RequestDelegate next;
        private IResponseFormatter formatter;

        public WeatherMiddleware(RequestDelegate nextDelegate,
                IResponseFormatter respFormatter) {
            next = nextDelegate;
            formatter = respFormatter;
        }

        public async Task Invoke(HttpContext context) {
            if (context.Request.Path == "/middleware/class") {
                await formatter.Format(context,
                    "Middleware Class: It is raining in London");
            } else {
                await next(context);
            }
        }
    }
}
```

To declare the dependency, I added a constructor parameter. To see the result, restart ASP.NET Core and request the http://localhost:5000/middleware/class URL, which will produce the response shown in Figure 14-4.

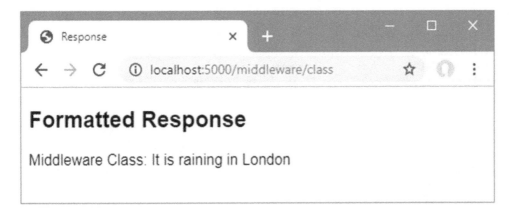

Figure 14-4. Declaring a dependency in a middleware class

When the request pipeline is being set up, the ASP.NET Core platform reaches the statement in the Configure method that adds the WeatherMiddleware class as a component.

```
...
app.UseMiddleware<WeatherMiddleware>();
...
```

The platform understands it needs to create an instance of the WeatherMiddleware class and inspects the constructor. The dependency on the IResponseFormatter interface is detected, the services are inspected to see if the dependency can be resolved, and the shared service object is used when the constructor is invoked.

There are two important points to understand about this example. The first is that WeatherMiddleware doesn't know which implementation class will be used to resolve its dependency on the IResponseFormatter interface—it just knows that it will receive an object that conforms to the interface through its constructor parameter. Second, the WeatherMiddleware class doesn't know how the dependency is resolved—it just declares a constructor parameter. This is a more elegant approach than my implementations of the singleton and type broker patterns earlier in the chapter, and I can change the implementation class used to resolve the service by changing the generic type parameters used in the Startup.ConfigureServices method.

Using a Service in an Endpoint

The situation is more complicated in the WeatherEndpoint class, which is static and doesn't have a constructor through which dependencies can be declared. There are several approaches available to resolve dependencies for an endpoint class, which are described in the sections that follow.

Getting Services from the HttpContext Object

Services can be accessed through the HttpContext object that is received when a request is routed to an endpoint, as shown in Listing 14-15.

Listing 14-15. Using a Service in the WeatherEndpoint.cs File in the Platform Folder

```
using Microsoft.AspNetCore.Http;
using System.Threading.Tasks;
using Platform.Services;
using Microsoft.Extensions.DependencyInjection;

namespace Platform {
    public class WeatherEndpoint {

        public static async Task Endpoint(HttpContext context) {
            IResponseFormatter formatter =
                context.RequestServices.GetRequiredService<IResponseFormatter>();
            await formatter.Format(context, "Endpoint Class: It is cloudy in Milan");
        }
    }
}
```

The HttpContext.RequestServices property returns an object that implements the IServiceProvider interfaces, which provides access to the services that have been configured in the application's Start.ConfigureServices method. The Microsoft. Extensions.DependencyInjection namespace used in Listing 14-15 contains extension methods for the IServiceProvider interface that allow individual services to be obtained, as described in Table 14-3.

Table 14-3. The IServiceProvider Extension Methods for Obtaining Services

Name	Description
GetService<T>()	This method returns a service for the type specified by the generic type parameter or null if no such service has been defined.
GetService(type)	This method returns a service for the type specified or null if no such service has been defined.
GetRequiredService<T>()	This method returns a service specified by the generic type parameter and throws an exception if a service isn't available.
GetRequiredService(type)	This method returns a service for the type specified and throws an exception if a service isn't available.

When the Endpoint method is invoked, the GetRequiredService<T> method is used to obtain an IResponseFormatter object, which is used to format the response. To see the effect, restart ASP.NET Core and use the browser to request http://localhost:5000/endpoint/class, which will produce the formatted response shown in Figure 14-5.

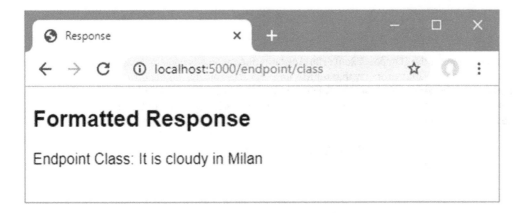

Figure 14-5. *Using a service in an endpoint class*

Using an Adapter Function

The drawback of using the HttpContext.RequestServices method is that the service must be resolved for every request that is routed to the endpoints. As you will learn later in the chapter, there are some services for which this is required because they provide features that are specific to a single request or response. This isn't the case for the IResponseFormatter service, where a single object can be used to format multiple responses.

A more elegant approach is to get the service when the endpoint's route is created and not for each request. Listing 14-16 changes the static Endpoint method so that it declares a dependency on the IResponseFormatter interface.

Listing 14-16. Defining an Adapter Function in the WeatherEndpoint.cs File in the Platform Folder

```
using Microsoft.AspNetCore.Http;
using System.Threading.Tasks;
using Platform.Services;

namespace Platform {
    public class WeatherEndpoint {

        public static async Task Endpoint(HttpContext context,
                IResponseFormatter formatter) {
            await formatter.Format(context, "Endpoint Class: It is cloudy in Milan");
        }
    }
}
```

Add a file called EndPointExtensions.cs to the Platform/Services folder and add the code shown in Listing 14-17.

Listing 14-17. The Contents of the EndpointExtensions.cs File in the Services Folder

```
using Microsoft.AspNetCore.Routing;
using Microsoft.Extensions.DependencyInjection;
using Platform.Services;

namespace Microsoft.AspNetCore.Builder {

    public static class EndpointExtensions {
        public static void MapWeather(this IEndpointRouteBuilder app, string path) {
```

```
        IResponseFormatter formatter =
            app.ServiceProvider.GetService<IResponseFormatter>();
        app.MapGet(path, context => Platform.WeatherEndpoint
            .Endpoint(context, formatter));
    }
  }
}
```

The new file creates an extension method for the IEndpointRouterBuilder interface, which is used to create routes in the Startup class. The interface defines a ServiceProvider property that returns an IServiceProvider object through which services can be obtained. The extension method gets the service and uses the MapGet method to register a RequestDelegate that passes on the HttpContext object and the IResponseFormatter object to the WeatherEndpoint.Endpoint method. In Listing 14-18, I have used the extension method to create the route for the endpoint.

Listing 14-18. Creating a Route in the Startup.cs File in the Platform Folder

```
...
app.UseEndpoints(endpoints => {

    //endpoints.MapGet("/endpoint/class", WeatherEndpoint.Endpoint);
    endpoints.MapWeather("/endpoint/class");

    endpoints.MapGet("/endpoint/function", async context => {
        await formatter.Format(context,
            "Endpoint Function: It is sunny in LA");
    });
});
...
```

The MapWeather extension method sets up the route and creates the adapter around the endpoint class. To see the result, restart ASP.NET Core and request the http://localhost:5000/endpoint/class URL, which will produce the same result as the previous example, shown in Figure 14-5.

Using the Activation Utility Class

I used static methods for endpoint classes in Chapter 13 because it makes them easier to use when creating routes. But for endpoints that require services, it can often be easier to use a class that can be instantiated because it allows for a more generalized approach to handling services. Listing 14-19 revises the endpoint with a constructor and removes the static keyword from the Endpoint method.

Listing 14-19. Revising the Endpoint in the WeatherEndpoint.cs File in the Platform Folder

```
using Microsoft.AspNetCore.Http;
using System.Threading.Tasks;
using Platform.Services;

namespace Platform {
    public class WeatherEndpoint {
        private IResponseFormatter formatter;

        public WeatherEndpoint(IResponseFormatter responseFormatter) {
            formatter = responseFormatter;
        }

        public async Task Endpoint(HttpContext context) {
            await formatter.Format(context, "Endpoint Class: It is cloudy in Milan");
        }
    }
}
```

The most common use of dependency injection in ASP.NET Core applications is in class constructors. Injection through methods, such as performed for middleware classes, is a complex process to re-create, but there are some useful built-in tools that take care of inspecting constructors and resolving dependencies using services, as shown in Listing 14-20.

Listing 14-20. Resolving Dependencies in the EndpointExtensions.cs File in the Services Folder

```
using Microsoft.AspNetCore.Http;
using Microsoft.AspNetCore.Routing;
using Microsoft.Extensions.DependencyInjection;
using Platform.Services;
using System.Reflection;
using System.Threading.Tasks;

namespace Microsoft.AspNetCore.Builder {

    public static class EndpointExtensions {

        public static void MapEndpoint<T> (this IEndpointRouteBuilder app,
                string path, string methodName = "Endpoint") {

            MethodInfo methodInfo = typeof(T).GetMethod(methodName);
            if (methodInfo == null || methodInfo.ReturnType != typeof(Task)) {
                throw new System.Exception("Method cannot be used");
            }
            T endpointInstance =
                ActivatorUtilities.CreateInstance<T>(app.ServiceProvider);
            app.MapGet(path,  (RequestDelegate)methodInfo
                .CreateDelegate(typeof(RequestDelegate), endpointInstance));
        }
    }
}
```

The extension method accepts a generic type parameter that specifies the endpoint class that will be used. The other arguments are the path that will be used to create the route and the name of the endpoint class method that processes requests.

A new instance of the endpoint class is created, and a delegate to the specified method is used to create a route. Like any code that uses .NET reflection, the extension method in Listing 14-20 can be difficult to read, but the key statement for the purposes of this chapter is this one:

```
...
T endpointInstance = ActivatorUtilities.CreateInstance<T>(app.ServiceProvider);
...
```

The ActivatorUtilities class, defined in the Microsoft.Extensions.DependencyInjection namespace, provides methods for instantiating classes that have dependencies declared through their constructor. Table 14-4 shows the most useful ActivatorUtilities methods.

Table 14-4. *The ActivatorUtilities Methods*

Name	Description
CreateInstance<T>(services, args)	This method creates a new instance of the class specified by the type parameter, resolving dependencies using the services and additional (optional) arguments.
CreateInstance(services, type, args)	This method creates a new instance of the class specified by the parameter, resolving dependencies using the services and additional (optional) arguments.
GetServiceOrCreateInstance<T>(services, args)	This method returns a service of the specified type, if one is available, or creates a new instance if there is no service.
GetServiceOrCreateInstance(services, type, args)	This method returns a service of the specified type, if one is available, or creates a new instance if there is no service.

Both methods resolve constructor dependencies using services through an ISserviceProvider object and an optional array of arguments that are used for dependencies that are not services. These methods make it easy to apply dependency injection to custom classes, and the use of the CreateInstance method results in an extension method that can create routes with endpoint classes that consume services. Listing 14-21 uses the new extension method to create a route.

Listing 14-21. Creating a Route Using an Extension Method in the Startup.cs File in the Platform Folder

```
...
app.UseEndpoints(endpoints => {

    endpoints.MapEndpoint<WeatherEndpoint>("/endpoint/class");

    endpoints.MapGet("/endpoint/function", async context => {
        await formatter.Format(context,
            "Endpoint Function: It is sunny in LA");
    });
});
...
```

This type of extension method makes it easy to work with endpoint classes and provides a similar experience to the UseMiddleware method described in Chapter 12. To make sure that requests are routed to the endpoint, restart ASP.NET Core and request the http://localhost:5000/endpoint/class URL, which should produce the same response as shown in Figure 14-5.

Using Service Lifecycles

When I created the service in the previous section, I used the AddSingleton extension method, like this:

```
...
public void ConfigureServices(IServiceCollection services) {
    services.AddSingleton<IResponseFormatter, HtmlResponseFormatter>();
}
...
```

The AddSingleton method produces a service that is instantiated the first time it is used to resolve a dependency and is then reused for each subsequent dependency. This means that any dependency on the IResponseFormatter object will be resolved using the same HtmlResponseFormatter object.

Singletons are a good way to get started with services, but there are some problems for which they are not suited, so ASP.NET Core supports *scoped services*, which give a lifecycle for the objects that are created to resolve dependencies. Table 14-5 describes the set of methods used to create services. There are versions of these methods that accept types as conventional arguments, as demonstrated in the "Using Unbound Types in Services" section, later in this chapter.

There are versions of the methods in Table 14-5 that have a single type argument, which allows a service to be created that solves the service location problem without addressing the tightly coupled issue. You can see an example of this type of service in Chapter 24, where I share a simple data source that isn't accessed through an interface.

Table 14-5. *The Extension Methods for Creating Services*

Name	Description
AddSingleton<T, U>()	This method creates a single object of type U that is used to resolve all dependencies on type T.
AddTransient<T, U>()	This method creates a new object of type U to resolve each dependency on type T.
AddScoped<T, U>()	This method creates a new object of type U that is used to resolve dependencies on T within a single scope, such as request.

Creating Transient Services

The AddTransient method does the opposite of the AddSingleton method and creates a new instance of the implementation class for every dependency that is resolved. To create a service that will demonstrate the use of service lifecycles, add a file called GuidService.cs to the Platform/Services folder with the code shown in Listing 14-22.

Listing 14-22. The Contents of the GuidService.cs File in the Services Folder

```
using System;
using System.Threading.Tasks;
using Microsoft.AspNetCore.Http;

namespace Platform.Services {

    public class GuidService : IResponseFormatter {
        private Guid guid = Guid.NewGuid();

        public async Task Format(HttpContext context, string content) {
            await context.Response.WriteAsync($"Guid: {guid}\n{content}");
        }
    }
}
```

The Guid struct generates a unique identifier, which will make it obvious when a different instance is used to resolve a dependency on the IResponseFormatter interface. In Listing 14-23, I have changed the statement that creates the IResponseFormatter service to use the AddTransient method and the GuidService implementation class.

Listing 14-23. Creating a Transient Service in the Startup.cs File in the Platform Folder

```
...
public void ConfigureServices(IServiceCollection services) {
    services.AddTransient<IResponseFormatter, GuidService>();
}
...
```

If you restart ASP.NET Core and request the http://localhost:5000/endpoint/class and http://localhost:5000/middleware/class URLs, you will receive the responses shown in Figure 14-6. Each response will be shown with a different GUID value, confirming that transient service objects have been used to resolve the dependencies on the IResponseFormatter service for the endpoint and the middleware component. (The nature of GUIDs means you will see different values in your responses. What is important is that you don't see the same value used for both responses.)

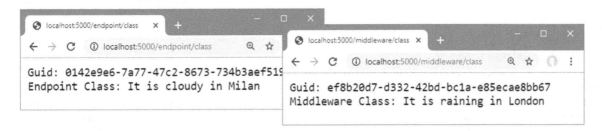

Figure 14-6. Using transient services

Avoiding the Transient Service Reuse Pitfall

The previous example demonstrated that when different service objects are created, the effect is not quite as you might expect, which you can see by clicking the reload buttons. Rather than seeing new GUID values, responses contain the same value, as shown in Figure 14-7.

Figure 14-7. *The same GUID values appearing in responses*

New service objects are created only when dependencies are resolved, not when services are used. The components and endpoints in the example application have their dependencies resolved only when the application starts and the Startup. Configure method is invoked. Each receives a separate service object, which is then reused for every request that is processed.

To solve this problem for the middleware component, the dependency for the service can be moved to the Invoke method, as shown in Listing 14-24.

Listing 14-24. Moving a Dependency in the WeatherMiddleware.cs File in the Platform Folder

```
using Microsoft.AspNetCore.Http;
using System.Threading.Tasks;
using Platform.Services;

namespace Platform {
    public class WeatherMiddleware {
        private RequestDelegate next;
        //private IResponseFormatter formatter;

        public WeatherMiddleware(RequestDelegate nextDelegate) {
            next = nextDelegate;
            //formatter = respFormatter;
        }

        public async Task Invoke(HttpContext context, IResponseFormatter formatter) {
            if (context.Request.Path == "/middleware/class") {
                await formatter.Format(context,
                    "Middleware Class: It is raining in London");
            } else {
                await next(context);
            }
        }
    }
}
```

The ASP.NET Core platform will resolve dependencies declared by the Invoke method every time a request is processed, which ensures that a new transient service object is created.

The ActivatorUtilities class doesn't deal with resolving dependencies for methods, and ASP.NET Core includes this feature only for middleware components. The simplest way of solving this issue for endpoints is to explicitly request services when each request is handled, which is the approach I used earlier when showing how services are used. It is also possible to enhance the extension method to request services on behalf of an endpoint, as shown in Listing 14-25.

Listing 14-25. Requesting Services in the EndpointExtensions.cs File in the Services Folder

```
using Microsoft.AspNetCore.Http;
using Microsoft.AspNetCore.Routing;
using Microsoft.Extensions.DependencyInjection;
using Platform.Services;
```

```
using System.Reflection;
using System.Threading.Tasks;
using System.Linq;

namespace Microsoft.AspNetCore.Builder {

    public static class EndpointExtensions {

        public static void MapEndpoint<T>(this IEndpointRouteBuilder app,
                string path, string methodName = "Endpoint") {

            MethodInfo methodInfo = typeof(T).GetMethod(methodName);
            if (methodInfo == null || methodInfo.ReturnType != typeof(Task)) {
                throw new System.Exception("Method cannot be used");
            }

            T endpointInstance =
                ActivatorUtilities.CreateInstance<T>(app.ServiceProvider);

            ParameterInfo[] methodParams = methodInfo.GetParameters();
            app.MapGet(path, context => (Task)methodInfo.Invoke(endpointInstance,
                methodParams.Select(p => p.ParameterType == typeof(HttpContext)
                ? context
                : app.ServiceProvider.GetService(p.ParameterType)).ToArray()));
        }
    }
}
```

The code in Listing 14-25 isn't as efficient as the approach taken by the ASP.NET Core platform for middleware components. All the parameters defined by the method that handles requests are treated as services to be resolved, except for the HttpContext parameter. A route is created with a delegate that resolves the services for every request and invokes the method that handles the request. Listing 14-26 revises the WeatherEndpoint class to move the dependency on IResponseFormatter to the Endpoint method so that a new service object will be received for every request.

Listing 14-26. Moving the Dependency in the WeatherEndpoint.cs File in the Platform Folder

```
using Microsoft.AspNetCore.Http;
using System.Threading.Tasks;
using Platform.Services;

namespace Platform {
    public class WeatherEndpoint {
        //private IResponseFormatter formatter;

        //public WeatherEndpoint(IResponseFormatter responseFormatter) {
        //    formatter = responseFormatter;
        //}

        public async Task Endpoint(HttpContext context,
                IResponseFormatter formatter) {
            await formatter.Format(context, "Endpoint Class: It is cloudy in Milan");
        }
    }
}
```

The changes in Listing 14-24 to Listing 14-26 ensure that the transient service is resolved for every request, which means that a new GuidService object is created and every response contains a unique ID.

For the middleware and endpoint defined as lambda expressions, the service must be obtained as each request is handled because the dependency declared by the Configure method parameter is resolved only once, when the request pipeline is configured. Listing 14-27 shows the changes required to get a new service object.

Listing 14-27. Using a Transient Service in the Startup.cs File in the Platform Folder

```
using Microsoft.AspNetCore.Builder;
using Microsoft.AspNetCore.Hosting;
using Microsoft.AspNetCore.Http;
using Microsoft.Extensions.DependencyInjection;
using Microsoft.AspNetCore.Routing;
using Platform.Services;

namespace Platform {
    public class Startup {

        public void ConfigureServices(IServiceCollection services) {
            services.AddTransient<IResponseFormatter, GuidService>();
        }

        public void Configure(IApplicationBuilder app, IWebHostEnvironment env) {
            app.UseDeveloperExceptionPage();
            app.UseRouting();
            app.UseMiddleware<WeatherMiddleware>();

            app.Use(async (context, next) => {
                if (context.Request.Path == "/middleware/function") {
                    IResponseFormatter formatter
                        = app.ApplicationServices.GetService<IResponseFormatter>();
                    await formatter.Format(context,
                        "Middleware Function: It is snowing in Chicago");
                } else {
                    await next();
                }
            });

            app.UseEndpoints(endpoints => {

                endpoints.MapEndpoint<WeatherEndpoint>("/endpoint/class");

                endpoints.MapGet("/endpoint/function", async context => {
                    IResponseFormatter formatter
                        = app.ApplicationServices.GetService<IResponseFormatter>();
                    await formatter.Format(context,
                        "Endpoint Function: It is sunny in LA");
                });
            });
        }
    }
}
```

Restart ASP.NET Core, navigate to any of the four URLs supported by the application (http://localhost:5000/middleware/class, /middleware/function, /endpoint/class, and /endpoint/function), and click the browser's reload button. Each time you reload, a new request is sent to ASP.NET Core, and the component or endpoint that handles the request receives a new service object, such that a different GUID is shown in each response, as shown in Figure 14-8.

Figure 14-8. *Using a transient service*

Using Scoped Services

Scoped services strike a balance between singleton and transient services. Within a scope, dependencies are resolved with the same object. A new scope is started for each HTTP request, which means that a service object will be shared by all the components that handle that request. To prepare for a scoped service, Listing 14-28 changes the WeatherMiddleware class to declare three dependencies on the same service.

Listing 14-28. Adding Dependencies in the WeatherMiddleware.cs File in the Platform Folder

```
using Microsoft.AspNetCore.Http;
using System.Threading.Tasks;
using Platform.Services;

namespace Platform {
    public class WeatherMiddleware {
        private RequestDelegate next;

        public WeatherMiddleware(RequestDelegate nextDelegate) {
            next = nextDelegate;
        }

        public async Task Invoke(HttpContext context, IResponseFormatter formatter1,
                IResponseFormatter formatter2, IResponseFormatter formatter3) {
            if (context.Request.Path == "/middleware/class") {
                await formatter1.Format(context, string.Empty);
                await formatter2.Format(context, string.Empty);
                await formatter3.Format(context, string.Empty);
            } else {
                await next(context);
            }
        }
    }
}
```

Declaring several dependencies on the same service isn't required in real projects, but it is useful for this example because each dependency is resolved independently. Since the IResponseFormatter service was created with the AddTransient method, each dependency is resolved with a different object. Restart ASP.NET Core and request http://localhost:5000/middleware/class, and you will see that a different GUID is used for each of the three messages written to the response, as shown in Figure 14-9. When you reload the browser, a new set of three GUIDs is displayed.

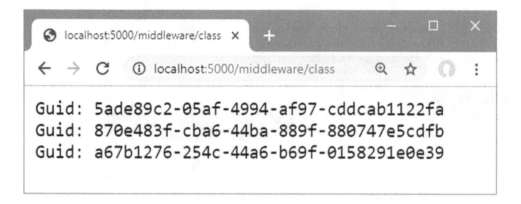

Figure 14-9. *Resolving dependencies on a transient service*

Listing 14-29 changes the IResponseFormatter service to use the scoped lifecycle with the AddScoped method.

■ **Tip**   You can create your own scopes through the CreateScope extension method for the IServiceProvider interface. The result is an IServiceProvider that is associated with a new scope and that will have its own implementation objects for scoped services.

Listing 14-29. Using a Scoped Service in the Startup.cs File in the Platform Folder

```
...
public void ConfigureServices(IServiceCollection services) {
    services.AddScoped<IResponseFormatter, GuidService>();
}
...
```

Restart ASP.NET Core and request http://localhost:5000/middleware/class again, and you will see that the same GUID is used to resolve all three dependencies declared by the middleware component, as shown in Figure 14-10. When the browser is reloaded, the HTTP request sent to ASP.NET Core creates a new scope and a new service object.

Figure 14-10. *Using a scoped service*

Avoiding the Scoped Service Validation Pitfall

Service consumers are unaware of the lifecycle that has been selected for singleton and transient services: they declare a dependency or request a service and get the object they require.

Scoped services can be used only within a scope. A new scope is created automatically for each request that was received. Requesting a scoped service outside of a scope causes an exception. To see the problem, request http://localhost:5000/endpoint/class, which will generate the exception response shown in Figure 14-11.

Figure 14-11. *Requesting a scoped service*

The extension method that configures the endpoint resolves services through an ISeviceProvider object obtained from the routing middleware, like this:

```
...
app.MapGet(path, context => (Task)methodInfo.Invoke(endpointInstance,
    methodParams.Select(p => p.ParameterType == typeof(HttpContext)
    ? context : app.ServiceProvider.GetService(p.ParameterType)).ToArray()));
...
```

This is known as the *root provider*, and it does not provide access to scoped services to prevent the accidental use of services that are not intended for use outside of a scope.

Accessing Scoped Services Through the Context Object

The HttpContext class defines a RequestServices property that returns an IServiceProvider object that allows access to scoped services, as well as singleton and transient services. This fits well with the most common use of scoped services, which is to use a single service object for each HTTP request. Listing 14-30 revises the endpoint extension method so that dependencies are resolved using the services provided through the HttpContext.

Listing 14-30. Using a Scoped Service in the EndpointExtensions.cs File in the Services Folder

```
using Microsoft.AspNetCore.Http;
using Microsoft.AspNetCore.Routing;
using Microsoft.Extensions.DependencyInjection;
using Platform.Services;
using System.Reflection;
using System.Threading.Tasks;
using System.Linq;

namespace Microsoft.AspNetCore.Builder {

    public static class EndpointExtensions {

        public static void MapEndpoint<T>(this IEndpointRouteBuilder app,
                string path, string methodName = "Endpoint") {
```

```
        MethodInfo methodInfo = typeof(T).GetMethod(methodName);
        if (methodInfo == null || methodInfo.ReturnType != typeof(Task)) {
            throw new System.Exception("Method cannot be used");
        }

        T endpointInstance =
            ActivatorUtilities.CreateInstance<T>(app.ServiceProvider);

        ParameterInfo[] methodParams = methodInfo.GetParameters();
        app.MapGet(path, context => (Task)methodInfo.Invoke(endpointInstance,
            methodParams.Select(p => p.ParameterType == typeof(HttpContext)
            ? context
            : context.RequestServices.GetService(p.ParameterType)).ToArray()));
    }
  }
}
```

Only dependencies that are declared by the method that handles the request are resolved using the HttpContext. RequestServices property. Services that are declared by an endpoint class constructor are still resolved using the IEndpointRouteBuilder.ServiceProvider property, which ensures that endpoints don't use scoped services inappropriately.

Creating New Handlers for Each Request

The problem with the extension method is that it requires endpoint classes to know the lifecycles for the services they depend on. The WeatherEndpoint class depends on the IResponseFormatter service and must know that a dependency can be declared only through the Endpoint method and not the constructor.

To remove the need for this knowledge, a new instance of the endpoint class can be created to handle each request, as shown in Listing 14-31, which allows constructor and method dependencies to be resolved without needing to know which services are scoped.

Listing 14-31. Instantiating Endpoints in the EndpointExtensions.cs File in the Services Folder

```
using Microsoft.AspNetCore.Http;
using Microsoft.AspNetCore.Routing;
using Microsoft.Extensions.DependencyInjection;
using Platform.Services;
using System.Reflection;
using System.Threading.Tasks;
using System.Linq;

namespace Microsoft.AspNetCore.Builder {

    public static class EndpointExtensions {

        public static void MapEndpoint<T>(this IEndpointRouteBuilder app,
                string path, string methodName = "Endpoint") {

            MethodInfo methodInfo = typeof(T).GetMethod(methodName);
            if (methodInfo == null || methodInfo.ReturnType != typeof(Task)) {
                throw new System.Exception("Method cannot be used");
            }

            ParameterInfo[] methodParams = methodInfo.GetParameters();
            app.MapGet(path, context => {
                T endpointInstance =
                    ActivatorUtilities.CreateInstance<T>(context.RequestServices);
```

```
            return (Task)methodInfo.Invoke(endpointInstance,
                methodParams.Select(p =>
                 p.ParameterType == typeof(HttpContext) ? context :
                  context.RequestServices.GetService(p.ParameterType)).ToArray());
        });
    }
  }
}
```

This approach requires a new instance of the endpoint class to handle each request, but it ensures that no knowledge of service lifecycles is required.

Using Scoped Services in Lambda Expressions

The HttpContext class can also be used in middleware components and endpoints that are defined as lambda expressions, as shown in Listing 14-32.

Listing 14-32. Using a Scoped Service in the Startup.cs File in the Platform Folder

```
using Microsoft.AspNetCore.Builder;
using Microsoft.AspNetCore.Hosting;
using Microsoft.AspNetCore.Http;
using Microsoft.Extensions.DependencyInjection;
using Microsoft.AspNetCore.Routing;
using Platform.Services;

namespace Platform {
    public class Startup {

        public void ConfigureServices(IServiceCollection services) {
            services.AddScoped<IResponseFormatter, GuidService>();
        }

        public void Configure(IApplicationBuilder app, IWebHostEnvironment env) {
            app.UseDeveloperExceptionPage();
            app.UseRouting();
            app.UseMiddleware<WeatherMiddleware>();

            app.Use(async (context, next) => {
                if (context.Request.Path == "/middleware/function") {
                    IResponseFormatter formatter
                        = context.RequestServices.GetService<IResponseFormatter>();
                    await formatter.Format(context,
                        "Middleware Function: It is snowing in Chicago");
                } else {
                    await next();
                }
            });

            app.UseEndpoints(endpoints => {

                endpoints.MapEndpoint<WeatherEndpoint>("/endpoint/class");

                endpoints.MapGet("/endpoint/function", async context => {
                    IResponseFormatter formatter
                        = context.RequestServices.GetService<IResponseFormatter>();
                    await formatter.Format(context,
                        "Endpoint Function: It is sunny in LA");
```

```
            });
        });
    }
  }
}
```

Restart ASP.NET Core and request the URLs that target the lambda functions: `http://localhost:5000/endpoint/function` and `/middleware/function`. The scoped service will be obtained without an exception, producing the responses shown in Figure 14-12.

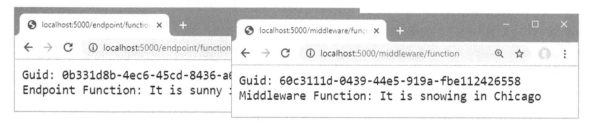

Figure 14-12. *Using scoped services in lambda functions*

Other Dependency Injection Features

In the sections that follow, I describe some additional features available when using dependency injection. These are not required for all projects, but they are worth understanding because they provide context for how dependency injection works and can be helpful when the standard features are not quite what a project requires.

Creating Dependency Chains

When a class is instantiated to resolve a service dependency, its constructor is inspected, and any dependencies on services are resolved. This allows one service to declare a dependency on another service, creating a chain that is resolved automatically. To demonstrate, add a class file called `TimeStamping.cs` to the `Platform/Services` folder with the code shown in Listing 14-33.

Listing 14-33. The Contents of the TimeStamping.cs File in the Services Folder

```
using System;

namespace Platform.Services {

    public interface ITimeStamper {
        string TimeStamp { get; }
    }

    public class DefaultTimeStamper : ITimeStamper {

        public string TimeStamp {
            get => DateTime.Now.ToShortTimeString();
        }
    }
}
```

The class file defines an interface named `ITimeStamper` and an implementation class named `DefaultTimeStamper`. Next, add a file called `TimeResponseFormatter.cs` to the `Platform/Services` folder with the code shown in Listing 14-34.

Listing 14-34. The Contents of the TimeResponseFormatter.cs File in the Services Folder

```
using System.Threading.Tasks;
using Microsoft.AspNetCore.Http;

namespace Platform.Services {
    public class TimeResponseFormatter : IResponseFormatter {
        private ITimeStamper stamper;

        public TimeResponseFormatter(ITimeStamper timeStamper) {
            stamper = timeStamper;
        }

        public async Task Format(HttpContext context, string content) {
            await context.Response.WriteAsync($"{stamper.TimeStamp}: {content}");
        }
    }
}
```

The TimeResponseFormatter class is an implementation of the IResponseFormatter interface that declares a dependency on the ITimeStamper interface with a constructor parameter. Listing 14-35 defines services for both interfaces in the ConfigureServices method of the Startup class.

■ **Note**   Services don't need to have the same lifecycle as their dependencies, but you can end up with odd effects if you mix lifecycles. Lifecycles are applied only when a dependency is resolved, which means that if a scoped service depends on a transient service, for example, then the transient object will behave as though it was assigned the scoped lifecycle.

Listing 14-35. Configuring Services in the Startup.cs File in the Platform Folder

```
...
public void ConfigureServices(IServiceCollection services) {
    services.AddScoped<IResponseFormatter, TimeResponseFormatter>();
    services.AddScoped<ITimeStamper, DefaultTimeStamper>();
}
...
```

When a dependency on the IResponseFormatter service is resolved, the TimeResponseFormatter constructor will be inspected, and its dependency on the ITimeStamper service will be detected. A DefaultTimeStamper object will be created and injected into the TimeResponseFormatter constructor, which allows the original dependency to be resolved. To see the dependency chain in action, restart ASP.NET Core and request http://localhost:5000/middleware/function, and you will see the timestamp generated by the DefaultTimeStamper class included in the response produced by the TimeResponseFormatter class, as shown in Figure 14-13.

Figure 14-13. *Creating a chain of dependencies*

Accessing Services in the ConfigureServices Method

The dependency injection feature is set up by the Platform class before the Startup class is instantiated and the ConfigureServices method is invoked. During the setup process, the services required by the ASP.NET Core platform are created, as well as the basic services provided to applications, such as configuration data, logging, and the environment setting, all of which are described in earlier chapters.

The Startup class can declare dependencies on these services by defining a constructor. When the Startup class is instantiated during application startup, the constructor is inspected, and the dependencies it declares are resolved. The objects injected into the constructor can be assigned to properties and accessed in the ConfigureService method, which adds the services that are specific to the application. The combined set of services is then available to the Configure method and to the middleware components and endpoints that process requests.

■ **Note** The methods defined by the Startup class are not treated the same way. The Configure method can declare dependencies using parameters, but you will receive an exception if you add parameters to the ConfigureServices method. The technique described in this section is the only way to declare dependencies on services for use in the ConfigureServices method.

The most common use of the Startup constructor is to declare a dependency on the IConfiguration service, which provides access to the application's configuration data, as shown in Listing 14-36. The configuration data is described in detail in Chapter 15.

Listing 14-36. Declaring a Dependency in the Startup.cs File in the Platform Folder

```
using Microsoft.AspNetCore.Builder;
using Microsoft.AspNetCore.Hosting;
using Microsoft.AspNetCore.Routing;
using Microsoft.Extensions.DependencyInjection;
using Platform.Services;
using Microsoft.Extensions.Configuration;

namespace Platform {

    public class Startup {

        public Startup(IConfiguration config) {
            Configuration = config;
        }

        private IConfiguration Configuration;

        public void ConfigureServices(IServiceCollection services) {
            services.AddScoped<IResponseFormatter, TimeResponseFormatter>();
            services.AddScoped<ITimeStamper, DefaultTimeStamper>();
        }

        public void Configure(IApplicationBuilder app, IWebHostEnvironment env) {

            // ...statements omitted for brevity...
        }
    }
}
```

The IConfiguration service is received through the constructor and assigned to a property named Configuration, which can then be used by the ConfigureServices method. This example doesn't change the responses produced by the application, but you can see how configuration data can be used to configure services in the next section.

Using Service Factory Functions

Factory functions allow you to take control of the way that service implementation objects are created, rather than relying on ASP.
NET Core to create instances for you. There are factory versions of the AddSingleton, AddTransient, and AddScoped methods, all of
which are used with a function that receives an IServiceProvider object and returns an implementation object for the service.

One use for factory functions is to define the implementation class for a service as a configuration setting, which is read
through the IConfguration service. This requires the pattern described in the previous section so that the configuration data is
accessible in the ConfigureServices method. Listing 14-37 adds a factory function for the IResponseFormatter service that gets the
implementation class from the configuration data.

Listing 14-37. Using a Factory Function in the Startup.cs File in the Platform Folder

```
using Microsoft.AspNetCore.Builder;
using Microsoft.AspNetCore.Hosting;
using Microsoft.AspNetCore.Http;
using Microsoft.Extensions.DependencyInjection;
using Microsoft.AspNetCore.Routing;
using Platform.Services;
using Microsoft.Extensions.Configuration;
using System;

namespace Platform {
    public class Startup {

        public Startup(IConfiguration config) {
            Configuration = config;
        }

        private IConfiguration Configuration;

        public void ConfigureServices(IServiceCollection services) {
            services.AddScoped<IResponseFormatter>(serviceProvider => {
                string typeName = Configuration["services:IResponseFormatter"];
                return (IResponseFormatter)ActivatorUtilities
                    .CreateInstance(serviceProvider, typeName == null
                        ? typeof(GuidService) : Type.GetType(typeName, true));
            });
            services.AddScoped<ITimeStamper, DefaultTimeStamper>();
        }

        public void Configure(IApplicationBuilder app, IWebHostEnvironment env) {

            // ...statements omitted for brevity...
        }
    }
}
```

The factory function reads a value from the configuration data, which is converted into a type and passed to the
ActivatorUtilities.CreateInstance method. Listing 14-38 adds a configuration setting to the appsettings.Development.
json file that selects the HtmlResponseFormatter class as the implementation for the IResponseFormatter service. The JSON
configuration file is described in detail in Chapter 15.

Listing 14-38. Defining a Setting in the appsettings.Development.json File in the Platform Folder

```
{
  "Logging": {
    "LogLevel": {
      "Default": "Information",
      "Microsoft": "Warning",
      "Microsoft.Hosting.Lifetime": "Information"
    }
  },
  "services": {
    "IResponseFormatter": "Platform.Services.HtmlResponseFormatter"
  }
}
```

When a dependency on the IResponseFormatter service is resolved, the factory function creates an instance of the type specified in the configuration file. Restart ASP.NET Core and request the http://localhost:5000/middleware/function URL, which will produce the response shown in Figure 14-14.

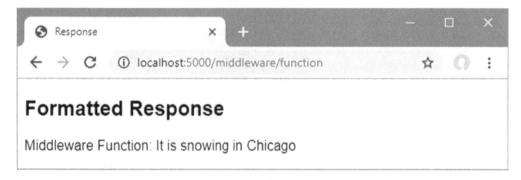

Figure 14-14. *Using a service factory*

Creating Services with Multiple Implementations

Services can be defined with multiple implementations, which allows a consumer to select an implementation that best suits a specific problem. This is a feature that works best when the service interface provides insight into the capabilities of each implementation class. To provide information about the capabilities of the IResponseFormatter implementation classes, add the default property shown in Listing 14-39 to the interface.

Listing 14-39. Adding a Property in the IResponseFormatter.cs File in the Services Folder

```
using Microsoft.AspNetCore.Http;
using System.Threading.Tasks;

namespace Platform.Services {
    public interface IResponseFormatter {

        Task Format(HttpContext context, string content);

        public bool RichOutput => false;
    }
}
```

This RichOutput property will be false for implementation classes that don't override the default value. To ensure there is one implementation that returns true, add the property shown in Listing 14-40 to the HtmlResponseFormatter class.

Listing 14-40. Overriding a Property in the HtmlResponseFormatter.cs File in the Services Folder

```
using System.Threading.Tasks;
using Microsoft.AspNetCore.Http;

namespace Platform.Services {
    public class HtmlResponseFormatter : IResponseFormatter {

        public async Task Format(HttpContext context, string content) {
            context.Response.ContentType = "text/html";
            await context.Response.WriteAsync($@"
                <!DOCTYPE html>
                <html lang=""en"">
                <head><title>Response</title></head>
                <body>
                    <h2>Formatted Response</h2>
                    <span>{content}</span>
                </body>
                </html>");
        }

        public bool RichOutput => true;
    }
}
```

Listing 14-41 registers multiple implementations for the IResponseFormatter service, which is done by making repeated calls to the Add<lifecycle> method. The listing also replaces the existing request pipeline with two routes that demonstrate how the service can be used.

Listing 14-41. Defining and Using a Service in the Startup.cs File in the Platform Folder

```
using Microsoft.AspNetCore.Builder;
using Microsoft.AspNetCore.Hosting;
using Microsoft.AspNetCore.Http;
using Microsoft.Extensions.DependencyInjection;
using Microsoft.AspNetCore.Routing;
using Platform.Services;
using Microsoft.Extensions.Configuration;
using System;
using System.Linq;

namespace Platform {
    public class Startup {

        public Startup(IConfiguration config) {
            Configuration = config;
        }

        private IConfiguration Configuration;

        public void ConfigureServices(IServiceCollection services) {
            services.AddScoped<ITimeStamper, DefaultTimeStamper>();
            services.AddScoped<IResponseFormatter, TextResponseFormatter>();
            services.AddScoped<IResponseFormatter, HtmlResponseFormatter>();
            services.AddScoped<IResponseFormatter, GuidService>();
        }
```

```
        public void Configure(IApplicationBuilder app, IWebHostEnvironment env) {
            app.UseDeveloperExceptionPage();
            app.UseRouting();
            app.UseEndpoints(endpoints => {
                endpoints.MapGet("/single", async context => {
                    IResponseFormatter formatter = context.RequestServices
                        .GetService<IResponseFormatter>();
                    await formatter.Format(context, "Single service");
                });

                endpoints.MapGet("/", async context => {
                    IResponseFormatter formatter = context.RequestServices
                        .GetServices<IResponseFormatter>().First(f => f.RichOutput);
                    await formatter.Format(context, "Multiple services");
                });
            });
        }
    }
}
```

The AddScoped statements register three services for the IResponseFormatter interface, each with a different implementation class. The route for the /single URL uses the IServiceProvider.GetService<T> method to request a service, like this:

```
...
context.RequestServices.GetService<IResponseFormatter>();
...
```

This is a service consumer that is unaware that there are multiple implementations available. The service is resolved using the most recently registered implementation, which is the GuidService class. Restart ASP.NET Core and request http://localhost:5000/single, and you will see the output on the left side of Figure 14-15.

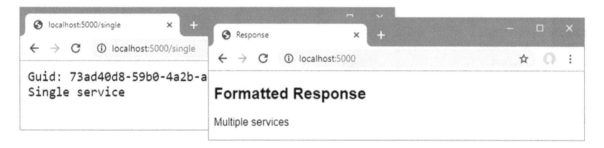

Figure 14-15. *Using multiple service implementations*

The other endpoint is a service consumer that is aware that multiple implementations may be available and that requests the service using the IServiceProvider.GetServices<T> method.

```
...
context.RequestServices.GetServices<IResponseFormatter>().First(f => f.RichOutput);
...
```

This method returns an IEnumerable<IResponseFormatter> that enumerates the implementations that are available. These are filtered using the LINQ First method to select an implementation whose RichOutput property returns true. If you request http://localhost:5000, you will see the output on the right of Figure 14-15, showing that the endpoint has selected the service implementation that best suits its needs.

Using Unbound Types in Services

Services can be defined with generic type parameters that are bound to specific types when the service is requested, as shown in Listing 14-42.

Listing 14-42. Using an Unbound Type in the Startup.cs File in the Platform Folder

```
using Microsoft.AspNetCore.Builder;
using Microsoft.AspNetCore.Hosting;
using Microsoft.AspNetCore.Http;
using Microsoft.Extensions.DependencyInjection;
using Microsoft.AspNetCore.Routing;
using Platform.Services;
using Microsoft.Extensions.Configuration;
using System;
using System.Linq;
using System.Collections.Generic;

namespace Platform {
    public class Startup {

        public Startup(IConfiguration config) {
            Configuration = config;
        }

        private IConfiguration Configuration;

        public void ConfigureServices(IServiceCollection services) {
            services.AddSingleton(typeof(ICollection<>), typeof(List<>));
        }

        public void Configure(IApplicationBuilder app, IWebHostEnvironment env) {
            app.UseDeveloperExceptionPage();
            app.UseRouting();
            app.UseEndpoints(endpoints => {
                endpoints.MapGet("/string", async context => {
                    ICollection<string> collection
                        = context.RequestServices.GetService<ICollection<string>>();
                    collection.Add($"Request: { DateTime.Now.ToLongTimeString() }");
                    foreach (string str in collection) {
                        await context.Response.WriteAsync($"String: {str}\n");
                    }
                });

                endpoints.MapGet("/int", async context => {
                    ICollection<int> collection
                        = context.RequestServices.GetService<ICollection<int>>();
                    collection.Add(collection.Count() + 1);
                    foreach (int val in collection) {
                        await context.Response.WriteAsync($"Int: {val}\n");
                    }
                });
            });
        }
    }
}
```

This feature relies on the versions of the AddSIngleton, AddScoped, and AddTransient methods that accept types as conventional arguments and cannot be performed using generic type arguments. The service in Listing 14-42 is created with unbound types, like this:

```
...
services.AddSingleton(typeof(ICollection<>), typeof(List<>));
...
```

When a dependency on an ICollection<T> service is resolved, a List<T> object will be created so that a dependency on ICollection<string>, for example, will be resolved using a List<string> object. Rather than require separate services for each type, the unbound service allows mappings for all generic types to be created.

The two endpoints in Listing 14-42 request ICollection<string> and ICollection<int> services, each of which will be resolved with a different List<T> object. To target the endpoints, restart ASP.NET Core and request http://localhost:5000/string and http://localhost:5000/int. The service has been defined as a singleton, which means that the same List<string> and List<int> objects will be used to resolve all requests for ICollection<string> and ICollection<int>. Each request adds a new item to the collection, which you can see by reloading the web browser, as shown in Figure 14-16.

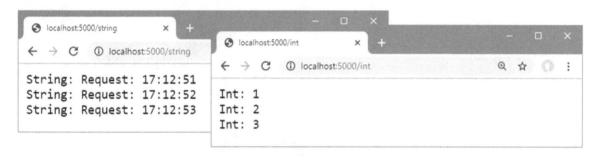

Figure 14-16. *Using a singleton service with an unbound type*

Summary

In this chapter, I described dependency injection, which is used to define services that are easy to use, easy to change, and easy to consume. I showed you the different ways that services are consumed, explained the different lifecycles that services can be given, and explained some of the less frequently used features such as dependency chains and unbound service types. In the next chapter, I describe the built-in features provided by the ASP.NET Core platform.

CHAPTER 15

Using the Platform Features, Part 1

ASP.NET Core includes a set of built-in services and middleware components that provide features that are commonly required by web applications. In this chapter, I describe three of the most important and widely used features: application configuration, logging, and serving static content. In Chapter 16, I continue to describe the platform features, focusing on the more advanced built-in services and middleware. Table 15-1 puts the chapter in context.

Table 15-1. *Putting Platform Features in Context*

Question	Answer
What are they?	The platform features deal with common web application requirements, such as configuration, logging, static files, sessions, authentication, and database access.
Why are they useful?	Using these features means you don't have to re-create their functionality in your own projects.
How are they used?	The built-in middleware components are added to the request pipeline in the Startup. Configure method using extension methods whose name starts with Use. Services are set up in the Startup.ConfigureServices method using methods that start with Add.
Are there any pitfalls or limitations?	The most common problems relate to the order in which middleware components are added to the request pipeline. Remember that middleware components form a chain along which requests pass, as described in Chapter 12.
Are there any alternatives?	You don't have to use any of the services or middleware components that ASP.NET Core provides.

Table 15-2 summarizes the chapter.

Table 15-2. *Chapter Summary*

Problem	Solution	Listing
Accessing the configuration data	Use the IConfiguration service	4–7
Setting the application environment	Use the launch settings file	11
Determining the application environment	Use the IWebHostEnvironment service	12
Keeping sensitive data outside of the project	Create user secrets	13–19
Logging messages	Use the ILogger<T> service	20–22
Delivering static content	Enable the static content middleware	23–26
Delivering client-side packages	Install the package with LibMan and deliver it with the static content middleware	27–30

© Adam Freeman 2020
A. Freeman, *Pro ASP.NET Core 3*, https://doi.org/10.1007/978-1-4842-5440-0_15

Preparing for This Chapter

In this chapter, I continue to use the Platform project created in Chapter 14. To prepare for this chapter, update the Startup class to remove middleware and services, as shown in Listing 15-1.

Listing 15-1. Removing Middleware and Services in the Startup.cs File in the Platform Folder

```
using System;
using System.Collections.Generic;
using System.Linq;
using System.Threading.Tasks;
using Microsoft.AspNetCore.Builder;
using Microsoft.AspNetCore.Hosting;
using Microsoft.AspNetCore.Http;
using Microsoft.Extensions.DependencyInjection;
using Microsoft.Extensions.Hosting;
using Microsoft.Extensions.Options;

namespace Platform {
    public class Startup {

        public void ConfigureServices(IServiceCollection services) {
        }

        public void Configure(IApplicationBuilder app, IWebHostEnvironment env) {
            app.UseDeveloperExceptionPage();
            app.UseRouting();
            app.UseEndpoints(endpoints => {
                endpoints.MapGet("/", async context => {
                    await context.Response.WriteAsync("Hello World!");
                });
            });
        }
    }
}
```

One of the main topics in this chapter is configuration data. Replace the contents of the appsettings.Development.json file with the contents of Listing 15-2 to remove the setting added in Chapter 14.

Listing 15-2. Replacing the Contents of the appsettings.Development.json File in the Platform Folder

```
{
  "Logging": {
    "LogLevel": {
      "Default": "Debug",
      "System": "Information",
      "Microsoft": "Information"
    }
  }
}
```

Start the application by selecting Start Without Debugging or Run Without Debugging from the Debug menu or by opening a new PowerShell command prompt, navigating to the Platform project folder (which contains the Platform.csproj file), and running the command shown in Listing 15-3.

■ **Tip** You can download the example project for this chapter—and for all the other chapters in this book—from `https://github.com/apress/pro-asp.net-core-3`. See Chapter 1 for how to get help if you have problems running the examples.

Listing 15-3. Starting the ASP.NET Core Runtime

```
dotnet run
```

If the application was started using Visual Studio or Visual Studio Code, a new browser window will open and display the content shown in Figure 15-1. If the application was started from the command line, open a new browser tab and navigate to `http://localhost:5000`; you will see the content shown in Figure 15-1.

Figure 15-1. *Running the example application*

Using the Configuration Service

One of the built-in features provided by ASP.NET Core is access to the application's configuration settings, which is then presented as a service.

The main source of configuration data is the `appsettings.json` file. The `appsettings.json` file created by the Empty template contains the following settings:

```
{
  "Logging": {
    "LogLevel": {
      "Default": "Information",
      "Microsoft": "Warning",
      "Microsoft.Hosting.Lifetime": "Information"
    }
  },
  "AllowedHosts": "*"
}
```

The configuration service will process the JSON configuration file and create nested configuration sections that contain individual settings. For the `appsettings.json` file in the example application, the configuration service will create a `Logging` configuration section that contains a `LogLevel` section. The `LogLevel` section will contain settings for `Default`, `Microsoft`, and `Microsoft.Hosting.Lifetime` settings. There will also be an `AllowedHosts` setting that isn't part of a configuration section and whose value is an asterisk (the * character).

The configuration service doesn't understand the meaning of the configuration sections or settings in the `appsettings.json` file and is just responsible for processing the JSON data file and merging the configuration settings with the values obtained from other sources, such as environment variables or command-line arguments. The result is a hierarchical set of configuration properties, as shown in Figure 15-2.

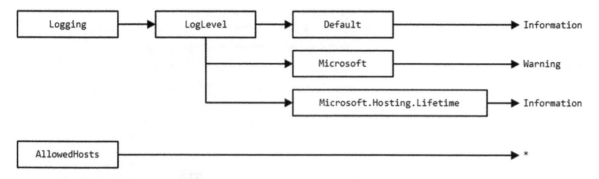

Figure 15-2. *The hierarchy of configuration properties in the appsettings.json File*

Understanding the Environment-Specific Configuration File

Most projects contain more than one JSON configuration file, allowing different settings to be defined for different parts of the development cycle. There are three predefined environments, named Development, Staging, and Production, each of which corresponds to a commonly used phase of development. During startup, the configuration service looks for a JSON file whose name includes the current environment. The default environment is Development, which means the configuration service will load the appsettings.Development.json file and use its contents to supplement the contents of the main appsettings.json file.

■ **Note**   The Visual Studio Solution Explorer nests the appsettings.Development.json file in the appsettings.json item. You can expand the appsettings.json file to see and edit the nested entries or click the button at the top of the Solution Explorer that disables the nesting feature.

Here are the configuration settings added to the appsettings.Development.json file in Listing 15-2:

```
{
  "Logging": {
    "LogLevel": {
      "Default": "Debug",
      "System": "Information",
      "Microsoft": "Information"
    }
  }
}
```

Where the same setting is defined in both files, the value in the appsettings.Development.json file will replace the one in the appsettings.json file, which means that the contents of the two JSON files will produce the hierarchy of configuration settings shown in Figure 15-3.

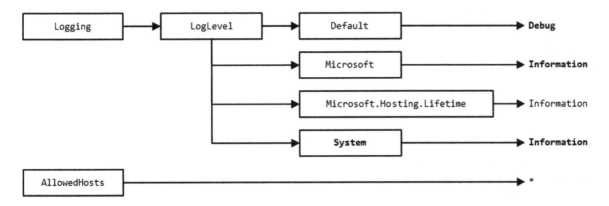

Figure 15-3. *Merging JSON configuration settings*

The effect of the additional configuration settings is to increase the detail level of logging messages, which I describe in more detail in the "Using the Logging Service" section.

Accessing Configuration Settings

The configuration data is accessed through a service. If you only require the configuration data to configure middleware, then the dependency on the configuration service can be declared using a parameter of the Configure method, as shown in Listing 15-4.

Listing 15-4. Accessing Configuration Data in the Startup.cs File in the Platform Folder

```
using System;
using System.Collections.Generic;
using System.Linq;
using System.Threading.Tasks;
using Microsoft.AspNetCore.Builder;
using Microsoft.AspNetCore.Hosting;
using Microsoft.AspNetCore.Http;
using Microsoft.Extensions.DependencyInjection;
using Microsoft.Extensions.Hosting;
using Microsoft.Extensions.Options;
using Microsoft.Extensions.Configuration;

namespace Platform {
    public class Startup {

        public void ConfigureServices(IServiceCollection services) {
        }

        public void Configure(IApplicationBuilder app, IWebHostEnvironment env,
                IConfiguration config ) {

            app.UseDeveloperExceptionPage();
            app.UseRouting();

            app.Use(async (context, next) => {
                string defaultDebug = config["Logging:LogLevel:Default"];
                await context.Response
                    .WriteAsync($"The config setting is: {defaultDebug}");
            });
```

```
        app.UseEndpoints(endpoints => {
            endpoints.MapGet("/", async context => {
                await context.Response.WriteAsync("Hello World!");
            });
        });
    }
}
}
```

Configuration data is provided through the IConfiguration interface; this interface is defined in the Microsoft.Extensions.Configuration namespace and provides an API for navigating through the configuration hierarchy and reading configuration settings. To receive the configuration data in the Startup class, an IConfiguration parameter is added to the Configure method. Configuration settings can be read by specifying the path through the configuration sections, like this:

```
...
string defaultDebug = config["Logging:LogLevel:Default"];
...
```

This statement reads the value of the Default setting, which is defined in the LogLevel section of the Logging part of the configuration. The names of the configuration sections and the configuration settings are separated by colons (the : character).

The value of the configuration setting read in Listing 15-4 is used to provide a result for a middleware component that handles the /config URL. Restart the ASP.NET Core platform by selecting Degug ➤ Start Without Debugging or by using Control+C at the command prompt and running the command shown in Listing 15-5 in the Platform folder.

Listing 15-5. Starting the ASP.NET Core Platform

```
dotnet run
```

Once the runtime has restarted, navigate to the http://localhost:5000/config URL, and you will see the value of the configuration setting displayed in the browser tab, as shown in Figure 15-4.

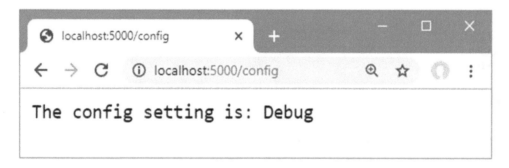

Figure 15-4. *Reading configuration data*

Using the Configuration Data in Services

A slightly different approach is required to access configuration data in the ConfigureServices method, where adding parameters to receive the IConfiguration object isn't supported. As explained in Chapter 14, some services are created before the Startup class is instantiated, which allows dependencies on them to be declared using a constructor parameter. Listing 15-6 adds a constructor parameter to the Startup class that declares a dependency on the IConfiguration service and assigns the object used to resolve the dependency to a property that can be accessed in both the ConfigureServices and Configure methods.

Listing 15-6. Using Configuration Data in the Startup.cs File in the Platform Folder

```csharp
using System;
using System.Collections.Generic;
using System.Linq;
using System.Threading.Tasks;
using Microsoft.AspNetCore.Builder;
using Microsoft.AspNetCore.Hosting;
using Microsoft.AspNetCore.Http;
using Microsoft.Extensions.DependencyInjection;
using Microsoft.Extensions.Hosting;
using Microsoft.Extensions.Options;
using Microsoft.Extensions.Configuration;

namespace Platform {
    public class Startup {

        public Startup(IConfiguration configService) {
            Configuration = configService;
        }

        private IConfiguration Configuration { get; set; }

        public void ConfigureServices(IServiceCollection services) {

            // configuration data can be accessed here
        }

        public void Configure(IApplicationBuilder app, IWebHostEnvironment env) {
            app.UseDeveloperExceptionPage();
            app.UseRouting();

            app.Use(async (context, next) => {
                string defaultDebug = Configuration["Logging:LogLevel:Default"];
                await context.Response
                    .WriteAsync($"The config setting is: {defaultDebug}");
            });

            app.UseEndpoints(endpoints => {
                endpoints.MapGet("/", async context => {
                    await context.Response.WriteAsync("Hello World!");
                });
            });
        }
    }
}
```

The constructor assigns the object received through the IConfiguration parameter to the property named Configuration, which allows the access to the configuration data in both the Configure and ConfigureServices methods.

Using Configuration Data with the Options Pattern

Configuration data in the ConfigureServices method is used with the options pattern that I described in Chapter 14. In that chapter, I showed you how default option values can be changed using a lambda function. An alternative approach is to use configuration settings to set options.

To prepare, add the configuration settings shown in Listing 15-7 to the appsettings.json file.

Listing 15-7. Adding Configuration Data in the appsettings.json File in the Platform Folder

```
{
  "Location": {
      "CityName": "Buffalo"
  },
  "Logging": {
    "LogLevel": {
      "Default": "Information",
      "Microsoft": "Warning",
      "Microsoft.Hosting.Lifetime": "Information"
    }
  },
  "AllowedHosts": "*"
}
```

In Listing 15-8, I have used the options pattern to configure the LocationMiddleware component created in Chapter 14, using the configuration data defined in Listing 15-7.

Listing 15-8. Using Configuration Data in the Startup.cs File in the Platform Folder

```
using System;
using System.Collections.Generic;
using System.Linq;
using System.Threading.Tasks;
using Microsoft.AspNetCore.Builder;
using Microsoft.AspNetCore.Hosting;
using Microsoft.AspNetCore.Http;
using Microsoft.Extensions.DependencyInjection;
using Microsoft.Extensions.Hosting;
using Microsoft.Extensions.Options;
using Microsoft.Extensions.Configuration;

namespace Platform {
    public class Startup {

        public Startup(IConfiguration configService) {
            Configuration = configService;
        }

        private IConfiguration Configuration { get; set; }

        public void ConfigureServices(IServiceCollection services) {
            services.Configure<MessageOptions>(Configuration.GetSection("Location"));
        }

        public void Configure(IApplicationBuilder app, IWebHostEnvironment env) {
            app.UseDeveloperExceptionPage();
            app.UseRouting();

            app.UseMiddleware<LocationMiddleware>();

            app.Use(async (context, next) => {
                string defaultDebug = Configuration["Logging:LogLevel:Default"];
                await context.Response
                    .WriteAsync($"The config setting is: {defaultDebug}");
            });
```

```
        app.UseEndpoints(endpoints => {
            endpoints.MapGet("/", async context => {
                await context.Response.WriteAsync("Hello World!");
            });
        });
    }
  }
}
```

The section of the configuration data is obtained using the GetSection method and passed to the Configure method when the options are created. The configuration values in the selected section are inspected and used to replace the default values with the same names in the options class. To see the effect, restart ASP.NET Core and use the browser to navigate to the http://localhost:5000/location URL. You will see the results shown in Figure 15-5, where the CityName option is taken from the configuration data and the CountryName option is taken from the default value in the options class.

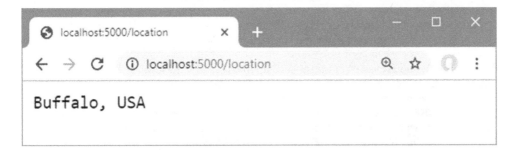

Figure 15-5. *Using configuration data in the options pattern*

Understanding the Launch Settings File

The launchSettings.json file in the Properties folder contains the configuration settings for starting the ASP.NET Core platform, including the TCP ports that are used to listen for HTTP and HTTPS requests and the environment used to select the additional JSON configuration files.

■ **Tip**   Visual Studio often hides the Properties folder by default. Click the Show All Files button at the top of the Solution Explorer to reveal the folder and the launchSettings.json file.

Here is the content added to the launchSettings.json file when the Empty template is used to create a project:

```
{
  "iisSettings": {
    "windowsAuthentication": false,
    "anonymousAuthentication": true,
    "iisExpress": {
      "applicationUrl": "http://localhost:5000",
      "sslPort": 0
    }
  },
  "profiles": {
    "IIS Express": {
      "commandName": "IISExpress",
      "launchBrowser": true,
      "environmentVariables": {
        "ASPNETCORE_ENVIRONMENT": "Development"
      }
    },
```

```
    "Platform": {
      "commandName": "Project",
      "launchBrowser": true,
      "applicationUrl": "http://localhost:5000",
      "environmentVariables": {
        "ASPNETCORE_ENVIRONMENT": "Development"
      }
    }
  }
}
```

The iisSettings section is used to configure the HTTP and HTTPS ports used when the ASP.NET Core platform is started through IIS Express, which happens when Visual Studio is used.

These settings are supplemented by the IIS Express section, which specifies whether a new browser window should be opened when the application starts and which contains environmentVariables, which is used to define environment variables that are added to the application's configuration data.

The Platform section contains the configuration that is used when the application is started using Visual Studio Code or directly using the dotnet run command at the command prompt, and the section specifies the settings for the ASP.NET Core Kestrel HTTP server.

The most important part of both sections is the environmentVariables section, which defines the ASPNETCORE_ENVIRONMENT setting. During startup, the value of the ASPNETCORE_ENVIRONMENT setting is used to select the additional JSON configuration file so that a value of Development, for example, will cause the appsettings.Development.json file to be loaded.

If you are using Visual Studio Code, ASPNETCORE_ENVIRONMENT is set in a different file. Select Debug ➤ Open Configurations to open the launch.json file in the .vscode folder, which is created when a project is edited with Visual Studio Code. Here is the default configuration for the example project, showing the current ASPNETCORE_ENVIRONMENT value:

```
{
    "version": "0.2.0",
    "configurations": [
        {
            "name": ".NET Core Launch (web)",
            "type": "coreclr",
            "request": "launch",
            "preLaunchTask": "build",
            "program": "${workspaceFolder}/bin/Debug/netcoreapp3.0/Platform.dll",
            "args": [],
            "cwd": "${workspaceFolder}",
            "stopAtEntry": false,
            "serverReadyAction": {
                "action": "openExternally",
                "pattern": "^\\s*Now listening on:\\s+(https?://\\S+)"
            },
            "env": {
                "ASPNETCORE_ENVIRONMENT": "Development"
            },
            "sourceFileMap": {
                "/Views": "${workspaceFolder}/Views"
            }
        },
        {
            "name": ".NET Core Attach",
            "type": "coreclr",
            "request": "attach",
            "processId": "${command:pickProcess}"
        }
    ]
}
```

To display the value of the ASPNETCORE_ENVIRONMENT setting, add the statements to the middleware component that responds to the /config URL, as shown in Listing 15-9.

Listing 15-9. Displaying the Configuration Setting in the Startup.cs File in the Platform Folder

```
using System;
using System.Collections.Generic;
using System.Linq;
using System.Threading.Tasks;
using Microsoft.AspNetCore.Builder;
using Microsoft.AspNetCore.Hosting;
using Microsoft.AspNetCore.Http;
using Microsoft.Extensions.DependencyInjection;
using Microsoft.Extensions.Hosting;
using Microsoft.Extensions.Options;
using Microsoft.Extensions.Configuration;

namespace Platform {
    public class Startup {

        public Startup(IConfiguration configService) {
            Configuration = configService;
        }

        private IConfiguration Configuration { get; set; }

        public void ConfigureServices(IServiceCollection services) {
            services.Configure<MessageOptions>(Configuration.GetSection("Location"));
        }

        public void Configure(IApplicationBuilder app, IWebHostEnvironment env) {
            app.UseDeveloperExceptionPage();
            app.UseRouting();

            app.UseMiddleware<LocationMiddleware>();

            app.Use(async (context, next) => {
                string defaultDebug = Configuration["Logging:LogLevel:Default"];
                await context.Response
                    .WriteAsync($"The config setting is: {defaultDebug}");
                string environ = Configuration["ASPNETCORE_ENVIRONMENT"];
                await context.Response
                    .WriteAsync($"\nThe env setting is: {environ}");
            });

            app.UseEndpoints(endpoints => {
                endpoints.MapGet("/", async context => {
                    await context.Response.WriteAsync("Hello World!");
                });
            });
        }
    }
}
```

Restart ASP.NET Core and navigate to http://localhost:5000/config, and you will see the value of the ASPNETCORE_ENVIRONMENT setting, as shown in Figure 15-6.

Figure 15-6. *Displaying the environment configuration setting*

To see the effect that the ASPNETCORE_ENVIRONMENT setting has on the overall configuration, change the value in the launchSettings.json file, as shown in Listing 15-10.

Listing 15-10. Changing the Environment in the launchSettings.json File in the Platform/Properties Folder

```
{
  "iisSettings": {
    "windowsAuthentication": false,
    "anonymousAuthentication": true,
    "iisExpress": {
      "applicationUrl": "http://localhost:5000",
      "sslPort": 0
    }
  },
  "profiles": {
    "IIS Express": {
      "commandName": "IISExpress",
      "launchBrowser": true,
      "environmentVariables": {
        "ASPNETCORE_ENVIRONMENT": "Production"
      }
    },
    "Platform": {
      "commandName": "Project",
      "launchBrowser": true,
      "applicationUrl": "http://localhost:5000",
      "environmentVariables": {
        "ASPNETCORE_ENVIRONMENT": "Production"
      }
    }
  }
}
```

If you are using Visual Studio, you can change the environment variables by selecting Project ➤ Platform Properties and navigating to the Debug tab. Double-click the value for the ASPNETCORE_ENVIRONMENT variable, and you will be able to change the value to **Production**, as shown in Figure 15-7.

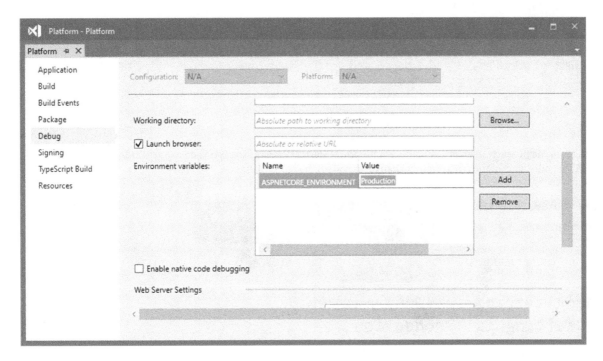

Figure 15-7. *Changing an environment variable using Visual Studio*

If you are using Visual Studio Code, select Debug ➤ Open Configurations and change the value in the env section, as shown in Listing 15-11.

Listing 15-11. Changing the Environment in the launch.json File in the Platform/.vscode Folder

```
{
    "version": "0.2.0",
    "configurations": [
        {
            "name": ".NET Core Launch (web)",
            "type": "coreclr",
            "request": "launch",
            "preLaunchTask": "build",
            "program": "${workspaceFolder}/bin/Debug/netcoreapp3.0/Platform.dll",
            "args": [],
            "cwd": "${workspaceFolder}",
            "stopAtEntry": false,
            "serverReadyAction": {
                "action": "openExternally",
                "pattern": "^\\s*Now listening on:\\s+(https?://\\S+)"
            },
            "env": {
                "ASPNETCORE_ENVIRONMENT": "Production"
            },
            "sourceFileMap": {
                "/Views": "${workspaceFolder}/Views"
            }
        },
```

```
    {
        "name": ".NET Core Attach",
        "type": "coreclr",
        "request": "attach",
        "processId": "${command:pickProcess}"
    }
  ]
}
```

Save the changes to the property page or configuration file and restart ASP.NET Core. Navigate to `http://localhost:5000/config`, and you will see the effect of the environment change, as shown in Figure 15-8.

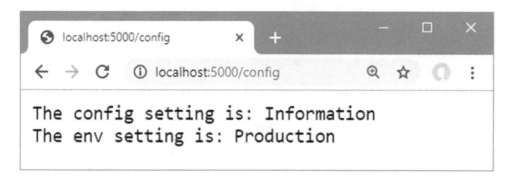

Figure 15-8. *The effect of changing the environment configuration setting*

Notice that both configuration values displayed in the browser have changed. The `appsettings.Development.json` file is no longer loaded, and there is no `appsettings.Production.json` file in the project, so only the configuration settings in the `appsettings.json` file are used.

Determining the Environment in the Startup Class

The ASP.NET Core platform provides the `IWebHostEnvironment` service for determining the current environment, which avoids the need to get the configuration setting manually. The `IWebHostEnvironment` service defines the methods shown in Table 15-3. These methods are extension methods that are defined in the `Microsoft.Extensions.Hosting` namespace, which must be imported with a `using` statement before they can be used.

Table 15-3. *The IWebHostEnvironment Extension Methods*

Name	Description
IsDevelopment()	This method returns `true` when the `Development` environment has been selected.
IsStaging()	This method returns `true` when the `Staging` environment has been selected.
IsProduction()	This method returns `true` when the `Production` environment has been selected.
IsEnvironment(env)	This method returns `true` when the environment specified by the argument has been selected.

The `Configure` method in the `Startup` class already has an `IWebHostEnvironment` parameter, which was added when the project was created using the Empty template in Chapter 14. This is often used with the methods described in Table 15-3 to select the middleware components that are added to the request pipeline. The most common example is to determine whether the `UseDeveloperExceptionPage` method is used, because `UseDeveloperExceptionPage` adds middleware that generates responses that should be used only in development. To ensure that the middleware is used only during development, Listing 15-12 uses the `IWebHostEnvironment` service and the `IsDevelopment` method.

Listing 15-12. Selecting Middleware in the Startup.cs File in the Platform Folder

```
...
public void Configure(IApplicationBuilder app, IWebHostEnvironment env) {

    if (env.IsDevelopment()) {
        app.UseDeveloperExceptionPage();
    }
    app.UseRouting();

    app.UseMiddleware<LocationMiddleware>();

    app.Use(async (context, next) => {
        string defaultDebug = Configuration["Logging:LogLevel:Default"];
        await context.Response
            .WriteAsync($"The config setting is: {defaultDebug}");
        string environ = Configuration["ASPNETCORE_ENVIRONMENT"];
        await context.Response
            .WriteAsync($"\nThe env setting is: {environ}");
    });

    app.UseEndpoints(endpoints => {
        endpoints.MapGet("/", async context => {
            await context.Response.WriteAsync("Hello World!");
        });
    });
}
...
```

This middleware catches exceptions thrown when a request is processed and displays a detailed stack trace, which is something that should not be seen once the application has been deployed. I demonstrate the error handling middleware in Chapter 16.

■ **Tip**　The IWebHostEnvironment service also defines properties that can be used to get details of the file location for the application, as demonstrated in Chapter 16.

Storing User Secrets

During development, it is often necessary to use sensitive data to work with the services that an application depends on. This data can include API keys, database connection passwords, or default administration accounts, and it is used both to access services and to reinitialize them to test application changes with a fresh database or user configuration.

If the sensitive data is included in the C# classes or JSON configuration files, it will be checked into the source code version control repository and become visible to all developers and to anyone else who can see the code—which may mean visible to the world for projects that have open repositories or repositories that are poorly secured.

The user secrets service allows sensitive data to be stored in a file that isn't part of the project and won't be checked in to version control, allowing each developer to have their own sensitive data that won't be accidentally exposed through a version control check-in.

Storing User Secrets

The first step is to prepare the file that will be used to store sensitive data. Open a new PowerShell command prompt and run the commands shown in Listing 15-13 in the Platform folder (the folder that contains the Platform.csproj file).

Listing 15-13. Installing the User Secrets Tool Package

```
dotnet tool uninstall  --global dotnet-user-secrets
dotnet tool install --global dotnet-user-secrets --version 3.0.0-preview-18579-0056
```

These commands remove the package if it has been installed previously and install the version required by this chapter. Next, run the command shown in Listing 15-14 in the Platform folder.

■ **Note**   If you have problems running the commands in this section, then close the PowerShell prompt and open a new one after installing the global tools package.

Listing 15-14. Initializing User Secrets

```
dotnet user-secrets init
```

This command adds an element to the Platform.csproj project file that contains a unique ID for the project that will be associated with the secrets on each developer machine. Next, run the commands shown in Listing 15-15 in the Platform folder.

Listing 15-15. Storing a User Secret

```
dotnet user-secrets set "WebService:Id" "MyAccount"

dotnet user-secrets set "WebService:Key" "MySecret123$"
```

Each secret has a key and a value, and related secrets can be grouped together by using a common prefix, followed by a colon (the : character), followed by the secret name. The commands in Listing 15-15 create related Id and Key secrets that have the WebService prefix.

After each command, you will see a message confirming that a secret has been added to the secret store. To check the secrets for the project, use the command prompt to run the command shown in Listing 15-16 in the Platform folder.

Listing 15-16. Listing the User Secrets

```
dotnet user-secrets list
```

This command produces the following output:

```
WebService:Key = MySecret123$
WebService:Id = MyAccount
```

Behind the scenes, a JSON file has been created in the %APPDATA%\Microsoft\UserSecrets folder (or the ~/.microsoft/usersecrets folder for Linux) to store the secrets. Each project its own folder (whose name corresponds to the unique ID created by the init command in Listing 15-14).

■ **Tip**   If you are using Visual Studio, you can create and edit the JSON file directly by right-clicking the project in the Solution Explorer and selecting Manage User Secrets from the popup menu.

Reading User Secrets

User secrets are merged with the normal configuration settings and accessed in the same way. In Listing 15-17, I have added a statement that displays the secrets to the middleware component that handles the /config URL.

Listing 15-17. Using User Secrets in the Startup.cs File in the Platform Folder

```
...
app.Use(async (context, next) => {
    string defaultDebug = Configuration["Logging:LogLevel:Default"];
    await context.Response
        .WriteAsync($"The config setting is: {defaultDebug}");
    string environ = Configuration["ASPNETCORE_ENVIRONMENT"];
    await context.Response
        .WriteAsync($"\nThe env setting is: {environ}");
    string wsID = Configuration["WebService:Id"];
    string wsKey = Configuration["WebService:Key"];
    await context.Response.WriteAsync($"\nThe secret ID is: {wsID}");
    await context.Response.WriteAsync($"\nThe secret Key is: {wsKey}");
});
...
```

User secrets are loaded only when the application is set to the Development environment. Edit the launchSettings.json file to change the environment to Development, as shown in Listing 15-18. (If you prefer, you can use the Visual Studio interface by selecting Project ➤ Platform Properties.)

Listing 15-18. Changing the Environment in the launchSettings.json File in the Platform/Properties Folder

```
{
  "iisSettings": {
    "windowsAuthentication": false,
    "anonymousAuthentication": true,
    "iisExpress": {
      "applicationUrl": "http://localhost:5000",
      "sslPort": 0
    }
  },
  "profiles": {
    "IIS Express": {
      "commandName": "IISExpress",
      "launchBrowser": true,
      "environmentVariables": {
        "ASPNETCORE_ENVIRONMENT": "Development"
      }
    },
    "Platform": {
      "commandName": "Project",
      "launchBrowser": true,
      "applicationUrl": "http://localhost:5000",
      "environmentVariables": {
        "ASPNETCORE_ENVIRONMENT": "Development"
      }
    }
  }
}
```

If you are launching the application from within Visual Studio Code, you must also edit the environment by selecting Debug ➤ Open Configurations and changing the value in the env section, as shown in Listing 15-19.

Listing 15-19. Changing the Environment in the launch.json File in the .vscode Folder

```
{
    "version": "0.2.0",
    "configurations": [
        {
            "name": ".NET Core Launch (web)",
            "type": "coreclr",
            "request": "launch",
            "preLaunchTask": "build",
            "program": "${workspaceFolder}/bin/Debug/netcoreapp3.0/Platform.dll",
            "args": [],
            "cwd": "${workspaceFolder}",
            "stopAtEntry": false,
            "serverReadyAction": {
                "action": "openExternally",
                "pattern": "^\\s*Now listening on:\\s+(https?://\\S+)"
            },
            "env": {
                "ASPNETCORE_ENVIRONMENT": "Development"
            },
            "sourceFileMap": {
                "/Views": "${workspaceFolder}/Views"
            }
        },
        {
            "name": ".NET Core Attach",
            "type": "coreclr",
            "request": "attach",
            "processId": "${command:pickProcess}"
        }
    ]
}
```

Save the changes, restart the ASP.NET Core runtime, and request the `http://localhost:5000/config` URL to see the user secrets, as shown in Figure 15-9.

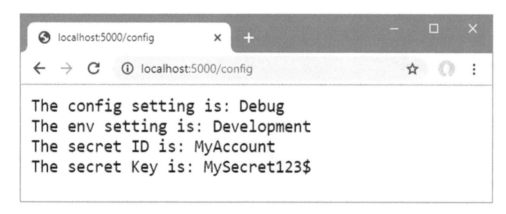

Figure 15-9. *Displaying user secrets*

Using the Logging Service

ASP.NET Core provides a logging service that can be used to record messages that describe the state of the application to track errors, monitor performance, and help diagnose problems.

Log messages are sent to logging providers, which are responsible for forwarding messages to where they can be seen, stored, and processed. There are built-in providers for basic logging, and there is a range of third-party providers available for feeding messages into logging frameworks that allow messages to be collated and analyzed.

Three of the built-in providers are enabled by default: the console provider, the debug provider, and the EventSource provider. The debug provider forwards messages so they can be processed through the System.Diagnostics.Debug class, and the EventSource provider forwards messages for event tracing tools, such as PerfView (https://github.com/Microsoft/perfview). I use the console provider in this chapter because it is simple and doesn't require any additional configuration to display logging messages.

■ **Tip** You can see the list of providers available and instructions for enabling them at https://docs.microsoft.com/en-gb/aspnet/core/fundamentals/logging.

Generating Logging Messages

Logging messages are generated using the unbounded ILogger<T> service. Listing 15-20 declares a dependency on the service in the Startup.Configure method and removes the middleware from the previous examples for brevity.

Listing 15-20. Generating a Logging Message in the Startup.cs File in the Platform Folder

```
using System;
using System.Collections.Generic;
using System.Linq;
using System.Threading.Tasks;
using Microsoft.AspNetCore.Builder;
using Microsoft.AspNetCore.Hosting;
using Microsoft.AspNetCore.Http;
using Microsoft.Extensions.DependencyInjection;
using Microsoft.Extensions.Hosting;
using Microsoft.Extensions.Options;
using Microsoft.Extensions.Configuration;
using Microsoft.Extensions.Logging;

namespace Platform {
    public class Startup {

        public Startup(IConfiguration configService) {
            Configuration = configService;
        }

        private IConfiguration Configuration { get; set; }

        public void ConfigureServices(IServiceCollection services) {
            services.Configure<MessageOptions>(Configuration.GetSection("Location"));
        }

        public void Configure(IApplicationBuilder app,
                IWebHostEnvironment env, ILogger<Startup> logger) {

            if (env.IsDevelopment()) {
                app.UseDeveloperExceptionPage();
            }
```

361

```
        app.UseRouting();

        app.UseMiddleware<LocationMiddleware>();

        app.UseEndpoints(endpoints => {
            endpoints.MapGet("/", async context => {
                logger.LogDebug("Response for / started");
                await context.Response.WriteAsync("Hello World!");
                logger.LogDebug("Response for / completed");
            });
        });
    }
  }
}
```

The logging service groups log messages together based on the category assigned to messages. Log messages are written using the ILogger<T> interface, where the generic parameter T is used to specify the category. The convention is to use the type of the class that generates the messages as the category type, which is why Listing 15-20 declares a dependency on the unbound service using Startup for the type argument, like this:

```
...
public void Configure(IApplicationBuilder app,
            IWebHostEnvironment env, ILogger<Startup> logger) {
...
```

This ensures that log messages generated in the Configure method will be assigned the category Startup. Log messages are created using the extension methods shown in Table 15-4.

Table 15-4. *The ILogger<T> Extension Methods*

Name	Description
LogTrace	This method generates a Trace-level message, used for low-level debugging during development.
LogDebug	This method generates a Debug-level message, used for low-level debugging during development or production problem resolution.
LogInformation	This method generates an Information-level message, used to provide information about the general state of the application.
LogError	This method generates an Error-level message, used to record exceptions or errors that are not handled by the application.
LogCritical	This method generates a Critical-level message, used to record serious failures.

Log messages are assigned a level that reflects their importance and detail. The levels range from Trace, for detailed diagnostics, to Critical, for the most important information that requires an immediate response. There are overloaded versions of each method that allow log messages to be generated using strings or exceptions. In Listing 15-20, I used the LogDebug method to generate logging messages when a request is handled.

```
...
logger.LogDebug("Response for / started");
...
```

The result is log messages at the Debug level that are generated when the response is started and completed. To see the log messages, select Debug ➤ Start Without Debugging. If you are using the command line, use Control+C to stop the ASP.NET Core runtime and use the command shown in Listing 15-21 in the Platform folder to start it again.

Listing 15-21. Starting the Example Application

```
dotnet run
```

Once the application has started, use a browser tab to request the http://localhost:5000 URL. If you are using the command line, you will see the logging messages displayed in the output from the application, like this:

```
...
info: Microsoft.AspNetCore.Hosting.Diagnostics[1]
      Request starting HTTP/1.1 GET http://localhost:5000/
info: Microsoft.AspNetCore.Routing.EndpointMiddleware[0]
      Executing endpoint '/ HTTP: GET'
dbug: Platform.Startup[0]
      Response for / started
dbug: Platform.Startup[0]
      Response for / completed
info: Microsoft.AspNetCore.Routing.EndpointMiddleware[1]
      Executed endpoint '/ HTTP: GET'
info: Microsoft.AspNetCore.Hosting.Diagnostics[2]
      Request finished in 23.022100000000002ms 200
...
```

If you are using Visual Studio, the output from the application is shown in the Output window, which can be selected from the View menu. Select ASP.NET Core Web Server from the drop-down menu to see the output, as shown in Figure 15-10.

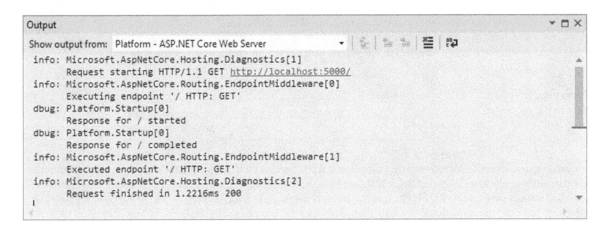

Figure 15-10. *Selecting the logging messages in the Visual Studio Output window*

If you are using Visual Studio Code, the log messages will be displayed in the Debug Console window, as shown in Figure 15-11, which can be selected from the View menu.

Figure 15-11. *Viewing logging messages in the Visual Studio Code Debug Console window*

Configuring Minimum Logging Levels

In Chapter 14, I showed you the default contents of the appsettings.json and appsettings.Development.json files and explained how they are merged to create the application's configuration settings. The settings in the JSON file are used to configure the logging service, which ASP.NET Core provides to record messages about the state of the application.

The Logging:LogLevel section of the appsettings.json file is used to set the minimum level for logging messages. Log messages that are below the minimum level are discarded. The appsettings.json file contains the following levels:

```
...
"Default": "Information",
"Microsoft": "Warning",
"Microsoft.Hosting.Lifetime": "Information",
...
```

The category for the log messages—which is set using the generic type argument in Listing 15-20—is used to select a minimum filter level. For the log messages generated by the startup class, for example, the category will be Platform.Startup, which means that they can be matched directly by adding a Platform.Startup entry to the appsettings.json file or indirectly by specifying just the Platform namespace. Any category for which there is no minimum log level is matched by the Default entry, which is set to Information.

It is common to increase the detail of the log messages displayed during development, which is why the levels in the appsettings.Development.json file specify more detailed logging levels, like this:

```
...
"Default": "Debug",
"System": "Information",
"Microsoft": "Information"
...
```

When the application is configured for the Development environment, the default logging level is Debug. The levels for the System and Microsoft categories are set to Information, which affects the logging messages generated by ASP.NET Core and the other packages and frameworks provided by Microsoft.

You can tailor the logging levels to focus the log on those parts of the application that are of interest by setting a level to Trace, Debug, Information, Error, or Critical. Logging messages can be disabled for a category using the None value.

In Listing 15-22, I added a new logging level to the appsettings.Development.json file that will disable the messages that report the time taken to respond to requests. I also increased the level to Trace for the Microsoft setting, which will increase the detail displayed for the classes in the ASP.NET Core platform.

■ **Tip** If you are using Visual Studio, you may have to expand the appsettings.json item in the Solution Explorer to see the appsettings.Development.json file.

Listing 15-22. Selecting a Log Level in the appsettings.Development.json File in the Platform Folder

```
{
  "Logging": {
    "LogLevel": {
      "Default": "Debug",
      "System": "Information",
      "Microsoft": "Trace",
      "Microsoft.AspnetCore.Hosting.Diagnostics": "None"
    }
  }
}
```

Restart ASP.NET Core and request the http://localhost:5000 URL, and you will see that the amount of detail displayed for each request has changed. The amount of detail will depend on how the application is run. If you are using Visual Studio Code or using the dotnet run command, you may see additional details about the generation of HTTP/2 responses. You won't see these messages if you use Visual Studio because the application will be run using IIS Express, which handles the incoming HTTP requests on behalf of the ASP.NET Core platform. There are some messages that will always be seen, however:

```
...
dbug: Microsoft.AspNetCore.HostFiltering.HostFilteringMiddleware[0]
      Wildcard detected, all requests with hosts will be allowed.
trce: Microsoft.AspNetCore.HostFiltering.HostFilteringMiddleware[2]
      All hosts are allowed.
...
```

These messages are generated by the Host Filter middleware, which is used to restrict requests based on the Hosts header, as described in Chapter 16.

Using Static Content and Client-Side Packages

Most web applications rely on a mix of dynamically generated and static content. The dynamic content is generated by the application based on the user's identity and actions, such as the contents of a shopping cart or the detail of a specific product and is generated fresh for each request. I describe the different ways that dynamic content can be created using ASP.NET Core in Part 3.

Static content doesn't change and is used to provide images, CSS stylesheets, JavaScript files, and anything else on which the application relies but which doesn't have to be generated for every request. The conventional location for static content in an ASP.NET Core project is the wwwroot folder.

To prepare static content to use in the examples for this section, create the Platform/wwwroot folder and add to it a file called static.html, with the content shown in Listing 15-23. You can create the file with the HTML Page template if you are using Visual Studio.

Listing 15-23. The Contents of the static.html File in the wwwroot Folder

```html
<!DOCTYPE html>
<html lang="en">
<head>
    <title>Static Content</title>
</head>
<body>
    <h3>This is static content</h3>
</body>
</html>
```

The file contains a basic HTML document with just the basic elements required to display a message in the browser.

Adding the Static Content Middleware

ASP.NET Core provides a middleware component that handles requests for static content, which is added to the request pipeline in Listing 15-24.

Listing 15-24. Adding Middleware in the Startup.cs File in the Platform Folder

```csharp
using System;
using System.Collections.Generic;
using System.Linq;
using System.Threading.Tasks;
using Microsoft.AspNetCore.Builder;
using Microsoft.AspNetCore.Hosting;
using Microsoft.AspNetCore.Http;
using Microsoft.Extensions.DependencyInjection;
using Microsoft.Extensions.Hosting;
using Microsoft.Extensions.Options;
using Microsoft.Extensions.Configuration;
using Microsoft.Extensions.Logging;

namespace Platform {
    public class Startup {

        public Startup(IConfiguration configService) {
            Configuration = configService;
        }

        private IConfiguration Configuration { get; set; }

        public void ConfigureServices(IServiceCollection services) {
            services.Configure<MessageOptions>(Configuration.GetSection("Location"));
        }

        public void Configure(IApplicationBuilder app,
                IWebHostEnvironment env, ILogger<Startup> logger) {

            if (env.IsDevelopment()) {
                app.UseDeveloperExceptionPage();
            }
            app.UseStaticFiles();
            app.UseRouting();

            app.UseMiddleware<LocationMiddleware>();
```

```
app.UseEndpoints(endpoints => {
    endpoints.MapGet("/", async context => {
        logger.LogDebug("Response for / started");
        await context.Response.WriteAsync("Hello World!");
        logger.LogDebug("Response for / completed");
    });
});
        }
    }
}
```

The UseStaticFiles extension method adds the static file middleware to the request pipeline. This middleware responds to requests that correspond to the names of disk files and passes on all other requests to the next component in the pipeline. This middleware is usually added close to the start of the request pipeline so that other components don't handle requests that are for static files.

Restart ASP.NET Core and navigate to http://localhost:5000/static.html. The static file middleware will receive the request and respond with the contents of the static.html file in the wwwroot folder, as shown in Figure 15-12.

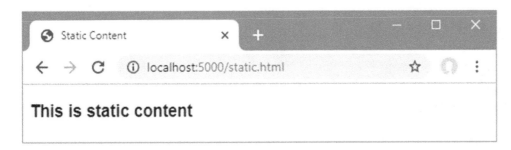

Figure 15-12. *Serving static content*

The middleware component returns the content of the requested file and sets the response headers, such as Content-Type and Content-Length, that describe the content to the browser.

Changing the Default Options for the Static Content Middleware

When the UseStaticFiles method is invoked without arguments, the middleware will use the wwwroot folder to locate files that match the path of the requested URL.

This behavior can be adjusted by passing a StaticFileOptions object to the UseStaticFiles method. Table 15-5 describes the properties defined by the StaticFileOptions class.

Table 15-5. *The Properties Defined by the StaticFileOptions Class*

Name	Description
ContentTypeProvider	This property is used to get or set the IContentTypeProvider object that is responsible for producing the MIME type for a file. The default implementation of the interface uses the file extension to determine the content type and supports the most common file types.
DefaultContentType	This property is used to set the default content type if the IContentTypeProvider cannot determine the type of the file.
FileProvider	This property is used to locate the content for requests, as shown below.
OnPrepareResponse	This property can be used to register an action that will be invoked before the static content response is generated.
RequestPath	This property is used to specify the URL path that the middleware will respond to, as shown below.
ServeUnknownFileTypes	By default, the static content middleware will not serve files whose content type cannot be determined by the IContentTypeProvider. This behavior is changed by setting this property to true.

The FileProvider and RequestPath properties are the most commonly used. The FileProvider property is used to select a different location for static content, and the RequestPath property is used to specify a URL prefix that denotes requests for static context. Listing 15-25 uses both properties to configure the static file middleware in the Startup class.

■ **Tip** There is also a version of the UseStaticFiles method that accepts a single string argument, which is used to set the RequestPath configuration property. This is a convenient way of adding support for URLs without needing to create an options object.

Listing 15-25. Configuring the Static File Middleware in the Startup.cs File in the Platform Folder

```
using System;
using System.Collections.Generic;
using System.Linq;
using System.Threading.Tasks;
using Microsoft.AspNetCore.Builder;
using Microsoft.AspNetCore.Hosting;
using Microsoft.AspNetCore.Http;
using Microsoft.Extensions.DependencyInjection;
using Microsoft.Extensions.Hosting;
using Microsoft.Extensions.Options;
using Microsoft.Extensions.Configuration;
using Microsoft.Extensions.Logging;
using Microsoft.Extensions.FileProviders;

namespace Platform {
    public class Startup {

        public Startup(IConfiguration configService) {
            Configuration = configService;
        }

        private IConfiguration Configuration { get; set; }

        public void ConfigureServices(IServiceCollection services) {
            services.Configure<MessageOptions>(Configuration.GetSection("Location"));
        }

        public void Configure(IApplicationBuilder app,
                IWebHostEnvironment env, ILogger<Startup> logger) {

            if (env.IsDevelopment()) {
                app.UseDeveloperExceptionPage();
            }
            app.UseStaticFiles();

            app.UseStaticFiles(new StaticFileOptions {
                FileProvider = new
                    PhysicalFileProvider($"{env.ContentRootPath}/staticfiles"),
                RequestPath = "/files"
            });

            app.UseRouting();

            app.UseMiddleware<LocationMiddleware>();
```

```
    app.UseEndpoints(endpoints => {
        endpoints.MapGet("/", async context => {
            logger.LogDebug("Response for / started");
            await context.Response.WriteAsync("Hello World!");
            logger.LogDebug("Response for / completed");
        });
    });
  }
 }
}
```

Multiple instances of the middleware component can be added to the pipeline, each of which handles a separate mapping between URLs and file locations. In the listing, a second instance of the static files middleware is added to the request pipeline so that requests for URLs that start with /files will be handled using files from a folder named staticfiles. Reading files from the folder is done with an instance of the PhysicalFileProvider class, which is responsible for reading disk files. The PhysicalFileProvider class requires an absolute path to work with, which I based on the value of the ContentRootPath property defined by the IWebHostEnvironment interface, which is the same interface used to determine whether the application is running in the Development or Production environment.

To provide content for the new middleware component to use, create the Platform/staticfiles folder and add to it an HTML file named hello.html with the content shown in Listing 15-26.

Listing 15-26. The Contents of the hello.html File in the Platform/staticfiles Folder

```
<!DOCTYPE html>
<html lang="en">
<head>
    <title>Static Content</title>
</head>
<body>
    <h3>This is additional static content</h3>
</body>
</html>
```

Restart ASP.NET Core and use the browser to request the http://localhost:5000/files/hello.html URL. Requests for URLs that begin with /files and that correspond to files in the staticfiles folder are handled by the new middleware, as shown in Figure 15-13.

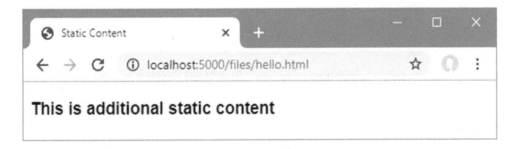

Figure 15-13. *Configuring the static files middleware*

Using Client-Side Packages

Most web applications rely on client-side packages to support the content they generate, using CSS frameworks to style content or JavaScript packages to create rich functionality in the browser. Microsoft provides the Library Manager tool, known as LibMan, for downloading and managing client-side packages.

WHAT HAPPENED TO BOWER?

Earlier versions of ASP.NET Core relied on a tool named Bower to manage client-side packages. Bower was widely used in JavaScript development until its creator retired the project and recommended migration to other tools. Microsoft's introduction of Library Manager, which is a .NET Core application, should help provide a consistent experience for dealing with client-side packages and avoid the turbulence that can arise around tools in the dynamic (and sometimes chaotic) world of JavaScript development.

Preparing the Project for Client-Side Packages

Use the command prompt to run the command shown in Listing 15-27, which installs LibMan as a global .NET Core tool (although you may find that LibMan has already been installed).

Listing 15-27. Installing LibMan

```
dotnet tool install --global Microsoft.Web.LibraryManager.Cli --version 2.0.96
```

The next step is to create the LibMan configuration file, which specifies the repository that will be used to get client-side packages and the directory into which packages will be downloaded. Open a PowerShell command prompt and run the command shown in Listing 15-28 in the Platform folder.

Listing 15-28. Initialzing LibMan

```
libman init -p cdnjs
```

The -p argument specifies the provider that will get packages. I have used cdnjs, which selects cdnjs.com. The other option is unpkg, which selects unpkg.com. If you don't have existing experience with package repositories, then you should start with the cdnjs option.

The command in Listing 15-28 creates a file named libman.json in the Platform folder; the file contains the following settings:

```
...
{
  "version": "1.0",
  "defaultProvider": "cdnjs",
  "libraries": []
}
...
```

If you are using Visual Studio, you can create and edit the libman.json file directly by selecting Project ➤ Manage Client-Side Libraries.

Installing Client-Side Packages

If you are using Visual Studio, you can install client-side packages by right-clicking the Platform project item in the Solution Explorer and selecting Add ➤ Client-Side Library from the popup menu. Visual Studio will present a simple user interface that allows packages to be located in the repository and installed into the project. As you type into the Library text field, the repository is queried for packages with matching names. Enter **twitter-bootstrap** into the text field, and the popular Bootstrap CSS framework will be selected, as shown in Figure 15-14.

Figure 15-14. *Selecting a client-side package in Visual Studio*

The latest version of the package is selected, which is 4.3.1 at the time of writing. Click the Install button to download and install the Bootstrap package.

PACKAGE NAMES AND REPOSITORIES

The same package may be known by different names in different repositories. If you are accustomed to using Bower or the Node Package Manager tool (NPM) to install packages, then you may be used to referring to the Bootstrap CSS framework as just bootstrap. The CDNJS repository refers to the same package as twitter-bootstrap, even though the package and its contents are the same. The best way to figure out what package you require is to go to the repository website and perform a search directly. For the LibMan configuration I use in this chapter, that means going to cdnjs.com.

Packages can also be installed from the command line. If you are using Visual Studio Code (or simply prefer the command line, as I do), then run the command shown in Listing 15-29 in the Platform folder to install the Bootstrap package.

Listing 15-29. Installing the Bootstrap Package

```
libman install twitter-bootstrap@4.3.1 -d wwwroot/lib/twitter-bootstrap
```

The required version is separated from the package name by the @ character, and the -d argument is used to specify where the package will be installed. The wwwroot/lib folder is the conventional location for installing client-side packages in ASP.NET Core projects.

Regardless of which approach you take to install the client-side package, the result will be the wwwroot/lib/twitter-boostrap folder that contains the CSS stylesheets and JavaScript files that are provided by the Bootstrap CSS framework.

Using a Client-Side Package

Once a client-side package has been installed, its files can be referenced by script or link HTML elements or by using the features provided by the higher-level ASP.NET Core features described in later chapters.

For simplicity in this chapter, Listing 15-30 adds a link element to the static HTML file created earlier in this section.

Listing 15-30. Using a Client-Side Package in the static.html File in the Platform/wwwroot Folder

```
<!DOCTYPE html>
<html lang="en">
<head>
    <link rel="stylesheet" href="/lib/twitter-bootstrap/css/bootstrap.min.css" />
    <title>Static Content</title>
</head>
<body>
    <h3 class="p-2 bg-primary text-white">This is static content</h3>
</body>
</html>
```

Restart ASP.NET Core and request http://localhost:5000/static.html. When the browser receives and processes the contents of the static.html file, it will encounter the link element and send an HTTP request to the ASP.NET Core runtime for the /lib/twitter-bootstrap/css/bootstrap.min.css URL. The original static file middleware component added in Listing 15-24 will receive this request, determine that it corresponds to a file in the wwwroot folder, and return its contents, providing the browser with the Bootstrap CSS stylesheet. The Bootstrap styles are applied through the classes to which the h3 element has been assigned, producing the result shown in Figure 15-15.

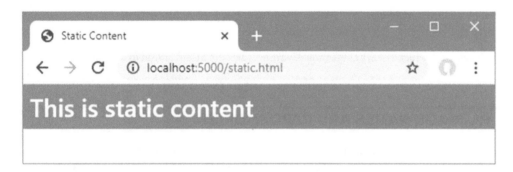

Figure 15-15. *Using a client-side package*

Summary

In this chapter, I described some of the most important and useful features that ASP.NET Core provides for web applications. I showed you how ASP.NET Core applications are configured, how logging messages are generated and managed, and how to serve static content, including the contents of client-side packages. In the next chapter, I continue to describe the ASP.NET Core platform features.

CHAPTER 16

■ ■ ■

Using the Platform Features, Part 2

In this chapter, I continue to describe the basic features provided by the ASP.NET Core platform. I explain how cookies are used and how the user's consent for tracking cookies is managed. I describe how sessions provide a robust alternative to basic cookies, how to use and enforce HTTPS requests, how to deal with errors, and how to filter requests based on the Host header. Table 16-1 summarizes the chapter.

Table 16-1. *Chapter Summary*

Problem	Solution	Listing
Using cookies	Use the context objects to read and write cookies	1–3
Managing cookie consent	Use the consent middleware	4–6
Storing data across requests	Use sessions	7, 8
Securing HTTP requests	Use the HTTPS middleware	9–13
Handling errors	Use the error and status code middleware	14–19
Restricting a request with the host header	Set the AllowedHosts configuration setting	20

Preparing for This Chapter

In this chapter, I continue to use the Platform project from Chapter 15. To prepare for this chapter, replace the contents of the Startup.cs file with the contents of Listing 16-1, which remove the middleware and services from the previous chapter.

Listing 16-1. Replacing the Contents of the Startup.cs File in the Platform Folder

```
using Microsoft.AspNetCore.Builder;
using Microsoft.AspNetCore.Http;
using Microsoft.Extensions.DependencyInjection;

namespace Platform {
    public class Startup {

        public void ConfigureServices(IServiceCollection services) {
        }

        public void Configure(IApplicationBuilder app) {
            app.UseDeveloperExceptionPage();
            app.UseRouting();
```

© Adam Freeman 2020
A. Freeman, *Pro ASP.NET Core 3*, https://doi.org/10.1007/978-1-4842-5440-0_16

```
        app.UseEndpoints(endpoints => {
            endpoints.MapFallback(async context =>
                await context.Response.WriteAsync("Hello World!"));
        });
    }
  }
}
```

Start the application by selecting Start Without Debugging or Run Without Debugging from the Debug menu or by opening a new PowerShell command prompt, navigating to the folder that contains the Platform.csproj file, and running the command shown in Listing 16-2.

■ **Tip** You can download the example project for this chapter—and for all the other chapters in this book—from https://github.com/apress/pro-asp.net-core-3. See Chapter 1 for how to get help if you have problems running the examples.

Listing 16-2. Starting the ASP.NET Core Runtime

```
dotnet run
```

If the application was started using Visual Studio or Visual Studio Code, a new browser window will open and display the content shown in Figure 16-1. If the application was started from the command line, open a new browser tab and navigate to http://localhost:5000; you will see the content shown in Figure 16-1.

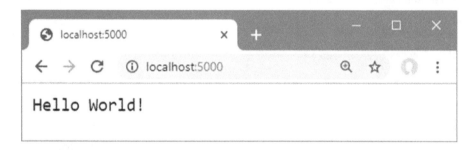

Figure 16-1. *Running the example application*

Using Cookies

Cookies are small amounts of text added to responses that the browser includes in subsequent requests. Cookies are important for web applications because they allow features to be developed that span a series of HTTP requests, each of which can be identified by the cookies that the browser sends to the server.

ASP.NET Core provides support for working with cookies through the HttpRequest and HttpResponse objects that are provided to middleware components. To demonstrate, Listing 16-3 changes the routing configuration in the example application to add endpoints that implement a counter.

Listing 16-3. Using Cookies in the Startup.cs File in the Platform Folder

```
using Microsoft.AspNetCore.Builder;
using Microsoft.AspNetCore.Http;
using Microsoft.Extensions.DependencyInjection;
using System;
using System.Threading.Tasks;
```

```
namespace Platform {
    public class Startup {

        public void ConfigureServices(IServiceCollection services) {
        }

        public void Configure(IApplicationBuilder app) {
            app.UseDeveloperExceptionPage();
            app.UseRouting();

            app.UseEndpoints(endpoints => {

                endpoints.MapGet("/cookie", async context => {
                    int counter1 =
                        int.Parse(context.Request.Cookies["counter1"] ?? "0") + 1;
                    context.Response.Cookies.Append("counter1", counter1.ToString(),
                        new CookieOptions {
                            MaxAge = TimeSpan.FromMinutes(30)
                        });
                    int counter2 =
                        int.Parse(context.Request.Cookies["counter2"] ?? "0") + 1;
                    context.Response.Cookies.Append("counter2", counter1.ToString(),
                        new CookieOptions {
                            MaxAge = TimeSpan.FromMinutes(30)
                        });
                    await context.Response
                        .WriteAsync($"Counter1: {counter1}, Counter2: {counter2}");
                });

                endpoints.MapGet("clear", context => {
                    context.Response.Cookies.Delete("counter1");
                    context.Response.Cookies.Delete("counter2");
                    context.Response.Redirect("/");
                    return Task.CompletedTask;
                });

                endpoints.MapFallback(async context =>
                    await context.Response.WriteAsync("Hello World!"));
            });
        }
    }
}
```

The new endpoints rely on cookies called counter1 and counter2. When the /cookie URL is requested, the middleware looks for the cookies and parses the values to an int. If there is no cookie, a fallback zero is used.

```
...
int counter1 = int.Parse(context.Request.Cookies["counter1"] ?? "0") + 1;
...
```

Cookies are accessed through the HttpRequest.Cookies property, where the name of the cookie is used as the key. The value retrieved from the cookie is incremented and used to set a cookie in the response, like this:

```
...
context.Response.Cookies.Append("counter1", counter1.ToString(),
    new CookieOptions {
        MaxAge = TimeSpan.FromMinutes(30)
    });
...
```

Cookies are set through the HttpResponse.Cookies property, and the Append method creates or replaces a cookie in the response. The arguments to the Append method are the name of the cookie, its value, and a CookieOptions object, which is used to configure the cookie. The CookieOptions class defines the properties described in Table 16-2, each of which corresponds to a cookie field.

Table 16-2. *The CookieOptions Properties*

Name	Description
Domain	This property specifies the hosts to which the browser will send the cookie. By default, the cookie will be sent only to the host that created the cookie.
Expires	This property sets the expiry for the cookie.
HttpOnly	When true, this property tells the browser not to include the cookie in requests made by JavaScript code.
IsEssential	This property is used to indicate that a cookie is essential, as described in the "Managing Cookie Consent" section.
MaxAge	This property specifies the number of seconds until the cookie expires. Older browsers do not support cookies with this setting.
Path	This property is used to set a URL path that must be present in the request before the cookie will be sent by the browser.
SameSite	This property is used to specify whether the cookie should be included in cross-site requests. The values are Lax, Strict, and None (which is the default value).
Secure	When true, this property tells the browser to send the cookie using HTTPS only.

The only cookie option set in Listing 16-3 is MaxAge, which tells the browser that the cookies expire after 30 minutes. The middleware in Listing 16-3 deletes the cookies when the /clear URL is requested, which is done using the HttpResponse.Cookie. Delete method, after which the browser is redirected to the / URL.

```
...
} else if (context.Request.Path == "/clear") {
    context.Response.Cookies.Delete("counter1");
    context.Response.Cookies.Delete("counter2");
    context.Response.Redirect("/");
}
...
```

Restart ASP.NET Core and navigate to http://localhost:5000/cookie. The response will contain cookies that are included in subsequent requests, and the counters will be incremented each time the browser is reloaded, as shown in Figure 16-2. A request for http://localhost:5000/clear will delete the cookies, and the counters will be reset.

Figure 16-2. *Using a cookie*

Enabling Cookie Consent Checking

The EU General Data Protection Regulation (GDPR) requires the user's consent before nonessential cookies can be used. ASP.NET Core provides support for obtaining consent and preventing nonessential cookies being sent to the browser when consent has not been granted. The options pattern is used to create a policy for cookies, which is applied by a middleware component, as shown in Listing 16-4.

■ **Caution**   Cookie consent is only one part of GDPR. See https://en.wikipedia.org/wiki/General_Data_Protection_ Regulation for a good overview of the regulations.

Listing 16-4. Enabling Cookie Consent in the Startup.cs File in the Platform Folder

```
using Microsoft.AspNetCore.Builder;
using Microsoft.AspNetCore.Http;
using Microsoft.Extensions.DependencyInjection;
using System;
using System.Threading.Tasks;

namespace Platform {
    public class Startup {

        public void ConfigureServices(IServiceCollection services) {
            services.Configure<CookiePolicyOptions>(opts => {
                opts.CheckConsentNeeded = context => true;
            });
        }

        public void Configure(IApplicationBuilder app) {
            app.UseDeveloperExceptionPage();
            app.UseCookiePolicy();
            app.UseRouting();

            app.UseEndpoints(endpoints => {

                endpoints.MapGet("/cookie", async context => {
                    int counter1 =
                        int.Parse(context.Request.Cookies["counter1"] ?? "0") + 1;
                    context.Response.Cookies.Append("counter1", counter1.ToString(),
                        new CookieOptions {
                            MaxAge = TimeSpan.FromMinutes(30),
                            IsEssential = true
                        });
                    int counter2 =
                        int.Parse(context.Request.Cookies["counter2"] ?? "0") + 1;
                    context.Response.Cookies.Append("counter2", counter1.ToString(),
                        new CookieOptions {
                            MaxAge = TimeSpan.FromMinutes(30)
                        });
                    await context.Response
                        .WriteAsync($"Counter1: {counter1}, Counter2: {counter2}");
                });

                endpoints.MapGet("clear", context => {
                    context.Response.Cookies.Delete("counter1");
                    context.Response.Cookies.Delete("counter2");
                    context.Response.Redirect("/");
                    return Task.CompletedTask;
                });

                endpoints.MapFallback(async context =>
                    await context.Response.WriteAsync("Hello World!"));
            });
```

```
        }
    }
}
}
```

The options pattern is used to configure a CookiePolicyOptions object, which sets the overall policy for cookies in the application using the properties described in Table 16-3.

Table 16-3. *The CookiePolicyOptions Properties*

Name	Description
CheckConsentNeeded	This property is assigned a function that receives an HttpContext object and returns true if it represents a request for which cookie consent is required. The function is called for every request, and the default function always returns false.
ConsentCookie	This property returns an object that is used to configure the cookie sent to the browser to record the user's cookie consent.
HttpOnly	This property sets the default value for the HttpOnly property, as described in Table 16-2.
MinimumSameSitePolicy	This property sets the lowest level of security for the SameSite property, as described in Table 16-2.
Secure	This property sets the default value for the Secure property, as described in Table 16-2.

To enable consent checking, I assigned a new function to the CheckConsentNeeded property that always returns true. The function is called for every request that ASP.NET Core receives, which means that sophisticated rules can be defined to select the requests for which consent is required. For this application, I have taken the most cautious approach and required consent for all requests.

The middleware that enforces the cookie policy is added to the request pipeline using the UseCookiePolicy method. The result is that only cookies whose IsEssential property is true will be added to responses. Listing 16-4 sets the IsEssential property on cookie1 only, and you can see the effect by restarting ASP.NET Core, requesting http://localhost:5000/cookie, and reloading the browser. Only the counter whose cookie is marked as essential updates, as shown in Figure 16-3.

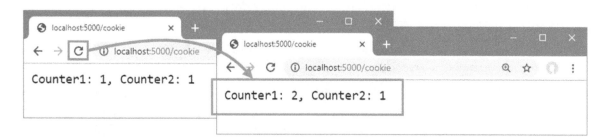

Figure 16-3. *Using cookie consent*

Managing Cookie Consent

Unless the user has given consent, only cookies that are essential to the core features of the web application are allowed. Consent is managed through a *request feature*, which provides middleware components with access to the implementation details of how requests and responses are handled by ASP.NET Core. Features are accessed through the HttpRequest.Features property, and each feature is represented by an interface whose properties and methods deal with one aspect of low-level request handling.

Features deal with aspects of request handling that rarely need to be altered, such as the structure of responses. The exception is the management of cookie consent, which is handled through the ITrackingConsentFeature interface, which defines the methods and properties described in Table 16-4.

Table 16-4. *The ITrackingConsentFeature Members*

Name	Description
CanTrack	This property returns true if nonessential cookies can be added to the current request, either because the user has given consent or because consent is not required.
CreateConsentCookie()	This method returns a cookie that can be used by JavaScript clients to indicate consent.
GrantConsent()	Calling this method adds a cookie to the response that grants consent for nonessential cookies.
HasConsent	This property returns true if the user has given consent for nonessential cookies.
IsConsentNeeded	This property returns true if consent for nonessential cookies is required for the current request.
WithdrawConsent()	This method deletes the consent cookie.

To deal with consent, add a class file named ConsentMiddleware.cs to the Platform folder and the code shown in Listing 16-5. Managing cookie consent can be done using lambda expressions, but I have used a class in this example to keep the Configure method uncluttered.

Listing 16-5. The Contents of the ConsentMiddleware.cs File in the Platform Folder

```
using Microsoft.AspNetCore.Http;
using Microsoft.AspNetCore.Http.Features;
using System.Threading.Tasks;

namespace Platform {
    public class ConsentMiddleware {
        private RequestDelegate next;

        public ConsentMiddleware(RequestDelegate nextDelgate) {
            next = nextDelgate;
        }

        public async Task Invoke(HttpContext context) {
            if (context.Request.Path == "/consent") {
                ITrackingConsentFeature consentFeature
                    = context.Features.Get<ITrackingConsentFeature>();
                if (!consentFeature.HasConsent) {
                    consentFeature.GrantConsent();
                } else {
                    consentFeature.WithdrawConsent();
                }
                await context.Response.WriteAsync(consentFeature.HasConsent
                    ? "Consent Granted \n" : "Consent Withdrawn\n");
            }
            await next(context);
        }
    }
}
```

Request features are obtained using the Get method, where the generic type argument specifies the feature interface that is required, like this:

```
...
ITrackingConsentFeature consentFeature
    = context.Features.Get<ITrackingConsentFeature>();
...
```

Using the properties and methods described in Table 16-4, the new middleware component responds to the /consent URL to determine and change the cookie consent. Listing 16-6 adds the new middleware to the request pipeline.

Listing 16-6. Adding Middleware in the Startup.cs File in the Platform Folder

```
...
public void Configure(IApplicationBuilder app) {
    app.UseDeveloperExceptionPage();
    app.UseCookiePolicy();
    app.UseMiddleware<ConsentMiddleware>();
    app.UseRouting();

    // ...statments omitted for brevity...
}
...
```

To see the effect, restart ASP.NET Core and request http://localhost:5000/consent and then http://localhost:5000/cookie. When consent is granted, nonessential cookies are allowed, and both the counters in the example will work, as shown in Figure 16-4. Repeat the process to withdraw consent, and you will find that only the counter whose cookie has been denoted as essential works.

Figure 16-4. *Managing cookie consent*

Using Sessions

The example in the previous section used cookies to store the application's state data, providing the middleware component with the data required. The problem with this approach is that the contents of the cookie are stored at the client, where it can be manipulated and used to alter the behavior of the application.

A better approach is to use the ASP.NET Core session feature. The session middleware adds a cookie to responses, which allows related requests to be identified and which is also associated with data stored at the server.

When a request containing the session cookie is received, the session middleware component retrieves the server-side data associated with the session and makes it available to other middleware components through the HttpContext object. Using sessions means that the application's data remains at the server and only the identifier for the session is sent to the browser.

Configuring the Session Service and Middleware

Setting up sessions requires configuring services and adding a middleware component to the request pipeline. Listing 16-7 adds the statements to the Startup class to set up sessions for the example application and removes the endpoints from the previous section.

Listing 16-7. Configuring Sessions in the Startup.cs File in the Platform Folder

```
using Microsoft.AspNetCore.Builder;
using Microsoft.AspNetCore.Http;
using Microsoft.Extensions.DependencyInjection;
using System;
using System.Threading.Tasks;
```

```
namespace Platform {
    public class Startup {

        public void ConfigureServices(IServiceCollection services) {
            services.Configure<CookiePolicyOptions>(opts => {
                opts.CheckConsentNeeded = context => true;
            });

            services.AddDistributedMemoryCache();

            services.AddSession(options => {
                options.IdleTimeout = TimeSpan.FromMinutes(30);
                options.Cookie.IsEssential = true;
            });
        }

        public void Configure(IApplicationBuilder app) {
            app.UseDeveloperExceptionPage();
            app.UseCookiePolicy();
            app.UseMiddleware<ConsentMiddleware>();
            app.UseSession();
            app.UseRouting();

            app.UseEndpoints(endpoints => {
                endpoints.MapFallback(async context =>
                    await context.Response.WriteAsync("Hello World!"));
            });
        }
    }
}
```

When you use sessions, you must decide how to store the associated data. ASP.NET Core provides three options for session data storage, each of which has its own method to register a service in the ConfigureServices method of the Startup class, as described in Table 16-5.

Table 16-5. *The Session Storage Methods*

Name	Description
AddDistributedMemoryCache	This method sets up an in-memory cache. Despite the name, the cache is not distributed and is responsible only for storing data for the instance of the ASP.NET Core runtime where it is created.
AddDistributedSqlServerCache	This method sets up a cache that stores data in SQL Server and is available when the Microsoft.Extensions.Caching.SqlServer package is installed. This cache is used in Chapter 17.
AddStackExchangeRedisCache	This method sets up a Redis cache and is available when the Microsoft.Extensions.Caching.Redis package is installed.

Caching is described in detail in Chapter 17, but for this chapter, I used the in-memory cache, which is set up in the ConfigureServices method:

```
...
services.AddDistributedMemoryCache();
...
```

Despite its name, the cache service created by the AddDistributedMemoryCache method isn't distributed and stores the session data for a single instance of the ASP.NET Core runtime. If you scale an application by deploying multiple instances of the runtime, then you should use one of the other caches, such as the SQL Server cache, which is demonstrated in Chapter 17.

The next step is to use the options pattern to configure the session middleware, like this:

```
...
services.AddSession(options => {
    options.IdleTimeout = TimeSpan.FromMinutes(30);
    options.Cookie.IsEssential = true;
});
...
```

Table 16-6 shows that the options class for sessions is SessionOptions and describes the key properties it defines.

Table 16-6. *Properties Defined by the SessionOptions Class*

Name	Description
Cookie	This property is used to configure the session cookie.
IdleTimeout	This property is used to configure the time span after which a session expires.

The Cookie property returns an object that can be used to configure the session cookie. Table 16-7 describes the most useful cookie configuration properties for session data.

Table 16-7. *Cookie Configuration Properties*

Name	Description
HttpOnly	This property specifies whether the browser will prevent the cookie from being included in HTTP requests sent by JavaScript code. This property should be set to true for projects that use a JavaScript application whose requests should be included in the session. The default value is true.
IsEssential	This property specifies whether the cookie is required for the application to function and should be used even when the user has specified that they don't want the application to use cookies. The default value is false. See the "Managing Cookie Consent" section for more details.
SecurityPolicy	This property sets the security policy for the cookie, using a value from the CookieSecurePolicy enum. The values are Always (which restricts the cookie to HTTPS requests), SameAsRequest (which restricts the cookie to HTTPS if the original request was made using HTTPS) and None (which allows the cookie to be used on HTTP and HTTPS requests). The default value is None.

The options set in Listing 16-7 allow the session cookie to be included in requests started by JavaScript and flag the cookie as essential so that it will be used even when the user has expressed a preference not to use cookies (see the "Managing Cookie Consent" section for more details about essential cookies). The IdleTimeout option has been set so that sessions expire if no request containing the sessions cookie is received for 30 minutes.

■ **Caution** The session cookie isn't denoted as essential by default, which can cause problems when cookie consent is used. Listing 16-7 sets the IsEssential property to true to ensure that sessions always work. If you find sessions don't work as expected, then this is the likely cause, and you must either set IsEssential to true or adapt your application to deal with users who don't grant consent and won't accept session cookies.

The final step is to add the session middleware component to the request pipeline, which is done with the UseSession method. When the middleware processes a request that contains a session cookie, it retrieves the session data from the cache and makes it available through the HttpContext object, before passing the request along the request pipeline and providing it to other middleware components. When a request arrives without a session cookie, a new session is started, and a cookie is added to the response so that subsequent requests can be identified as being part of the session.

Using Session Data

The session middleware provides access to details of the session associated with a request through the Session property of the HttpContext object. The Session property returns an object that implements the ISession interface, which provides the methods shown in Table 16-8 for accessing session data.

Table 16-8. *Useful ISession Methods and Extension Methods*

Name	Description
Clear()	This method removes all the data in the session.
CommitAsync()	This asynchronous method commits changed session data to the cache.
GetString(key)	This method retrieves a string value using the specified key.
GetInt32(key)	This method retrieves an integer value using the specified key.
Id	This property returns the unique identifier for the session.
IsAvailable	This returns true when the session data has been loaded.
Keys	This enumerates the keys for the session data items.
Remove(key)	This method removes the value associated with the specified key.
SetString(key, val)	This method stores a string using the specified key.
SetInt32(key, val)	This method stores an integer using the specified key.

Session data is stored in key/value pairs, where the keys are strings and the values are strings or integers. This simple data structure allows session data to be stored easily by each of the caches listed in Table 16-6. Applications that need to store more complex data can use serialization, which is the approach I took for the SportsStore. Listing 16-8 uses session data to re-create the counter example.

Listing 16-8. Using Session Data in the Startup.cs File in the Platform Folder

```
...
public void Configure(IApplicationBuilder app) {
    app.UseDeveloperExceptionPage();
    app.UseCookiePolicy();
    app.UseMiddleware<ConsentMiddleware>();
    app.UseSession();
    app.UseRouting();

    app.UseEndpoints(endpoints => {

        endpoints.MapGet("/cookie", async context => {
            int counter1 = (context.Session.GetInt32("counter1") ?? 0) + 1;
            int counter2 = (context.Session.GetInt32("counter2") ?? 0) + 1;
            context.Session.SetInt32("counter1", counter1);
            context.Session.SetInt32("counter2", counter2);
            await context.Session.CommitAsync();
            await context.Response
                .WriteAsync($"Counter1: {counter1}, Counter2: {counter2}");
        });

        endpoints.MapFallback(async context =>
            await context.Response.WriteAsync("Hello World!"));
    });
}
...
```

The GetInt32 method is used to read the values associated with the keys counter1 and counter2. If this is the first request in a session, no value will be available, and the null coalescing operator is used to provide an initial value. The value is incremented and then stored using the SetInt32 method and used to generate a simple result for the client.

The use of the CommitAsync method is optional, but it is good practice to use it because it will throw an exception if the session data can't be stored in the cache. By default, no error is reported if there are caching problems, which can lead to unpredictable and confusing behavior.

All changes to the session data must be made before the response is sent to the client, which is why I read, update, and store the session data before calling the Response.WriteAsync method in Listing 16-8.

Notice that the new statements in Listing 16-8 do not have to deal with the session cookie, detect expired sessions, or load the session data from the cache. All this work is done automatically by the session middleware, which presents the results through the HttpContext.Session property. One consequence of this approach is that the HttpContext.Session property is not populated with data until after the session middleware has processed a request, which means that you should attempt to access session data only in middleware or endpoints that are added to the request pipeline after the UseSession method is called.

Restart ASP.NET Core and navigate to the http://localhost:5000/cookie URL, and you will see the value of the counter. Reload the browser, and the counter values will be incremented, as shown in Figure 16-5. The sessions and session data will be lost when ASP.NET Core is stopped because I chose the in-memory cache. The other storage options operate outside of the ASP.NET Core runtime and survive application restarts.

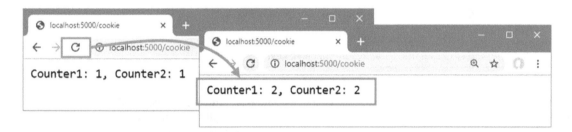

Figure 16-5. *Using session data*

Working with HTTPS Connections

Users increasingly expect web applications to use HTTPS connections, even for requests that don't contain or return sensitive data. ASP.NET Core supports both HTTP and HTTPS connections and provides middleware that can force HTTP clients to use HTTPS.

HTTPS VS SSL VS TLS

HTTPS is the combination of HTTP and the Transport Layer Security (TLS) or Secure Sockets Layer (SSL). TLS has replaced the obsolete SSL protocol, but the term SSL has become synonymous with secure networking and is often used when TLS is actually being used. If you are interested in security and cryptography, then the details of HTTPS are worth exploring, and https://en.wikipedia.org/wiki/HTTPS is a good place to start.

Enabling HTTP Connections

If you are using Visual Studio, select Project ➤ Platform Properties, navigate to the Debug section, and check the Enable SSL option, as shown in Figure 16-6. Once you have checked the option, select File ➤ Save All to save the configuration change.

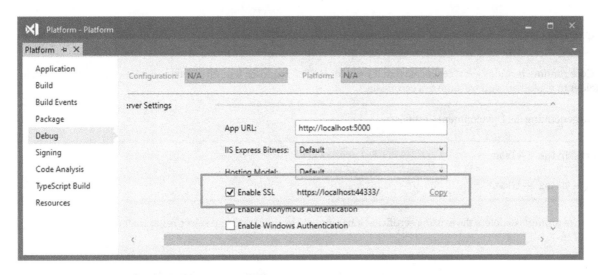

Figure 16-6. *Enabling HTTPS in Visual Studio*

The port used to receive HTTPS is assigned randomly. To change the port, click the Show All button at the top of the Solution Explorer to reveal the Properties folder and the launchSettings.json file if they are not already visible. Edit the file to change the HTTPS port that is used by the application, as shown in Listing 16-9.

Listing 16-9. Changing the HTTPS Port in the launchSettings.json File in the Platform/Properties Folder

```
{
  "iisSettings": {
    "windowsAuthentication": false,
    "anonymousAuthentication": true,
    "iisExpress": {
      "applicationUrl": "http://localhost:5000",
      "sslPort": 44350
    }
  },
  "profiles": {
    "IIS Express": {
      "commandName": "IISExpress",
      "launchBrowser": true,
      "environmentVariables": {
        "ASPNETCORE_ENVIRONMENT": "Development"
      }
    },
    "Platform": {
      "commandName": "Project",
      "launchBrowser": true,
      "environmentVariables": {
        "ASPNETCORE_ENVIRONMENT": "Development"
      },
      "applicationUrl": "https://localhost:44350;http://localhost:5000"
    }
  }
}
```

The new value for the sslPort setting changes the port used when the application is started within Visual Studio. The new applicationUrl setting sets the port used when the application is started from the command line or with Visual Studio.

■ **Note**   IIS Express supports HTTPS only on port numbers between 4400 and 44399.

The .NET Core runtime includes a test certificate that is used for HTTPS requests. Run the commands shown in Listing 16-10 in the Platform folder to regenerate and trust the test certificate.

Listing 16-10. Regenerating the Development Certificates

```
dotnet dev-certs https --clean

dotnet dev-certs https --trust
```

Select Yes to the prompts to delete the existing certificate it has already been trusted and select Yes to trust the new certificate, as shown in Figure 16-7.

Figure 16-7. *Regenerating the HTTPS certificate*

Detecting HTTPS Requests

Requests made using HTTPS can be detected through the HttpRequest.IsHttps property. In Listing 16-11, I added a new middleware component to the request pipeline that adds a message to the response when a request is made using HTTPS.

Listing 16-11. Detecting HTTPS in the Startup.cs File in the Platform Folder

```
...
public void Configure(IApplicationBuilder app) {
    app.UseDeveloperExceptionPage();
    app.UseCookiePolicy();
    app.UseMiddleware<ConsentMiddleware>();
    app.UseSession();
    app.UseRouting();

    app.Use(async (context, next) => {
        await context.Response
            .WriteAsync($"HTTPS Request: {context.Request.IsHttps} \n");
```

```
        await next();
    });

    app.UseEndpoints(endpoints => {

        endpoints.MapGet("/cookie", async context => {
            int counter1 = (context.Session.GetInt32("counter1") ?? 0) + 1;
            int counter2 = (context.Session.GetInt32("counter2") ?? 0) + 1;
            context.Session.SetInt32("counter1", counter1);
            context.Session.SetInt32("counter2", counter2);
            await context.Session.CommitAsync();
            await context.Response
                .WriteAsync($"Counter1: {counter1}, Counter2: {counter2}");
        });

        endpoints.MapFallback(async context =>
            await context.Response.WriteAsync("Hello World!"));
    });
}
...
```

To test HTTPS, restart ASP.NET Core and navigate to http://localhost:5000. This is a regular HTTP request and will produce the result shown on the left of Figure 16-8. Next, navigate to https://localhost:44350, paying close attention to the URL scheme, which is https and not http, as it has been in previous examples. The new middleware will detect the HTTPS connection and produce the output on the right of Figure 16-8.

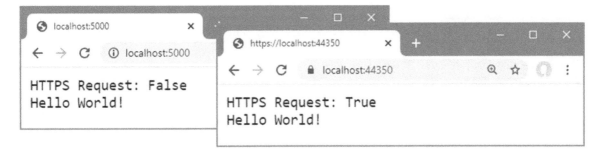

Figure 16-8. *Making an HTTPS request*

Enforcing HTTPS Requests

ASP.NET Core provides a middleware component that enforces the use of HTTPS by sending a redirection response for requests that arrive over HTTP. Listing 16-12 adds this middleware to the request pipeline.

Listing 16-12. Enforcing HTTPS in the Startup.cs File in the Platform Folder

```
...
public void Configure(IApplicationBuilder app) {
    app.UseDeveloperExceptionPage();
    app.UseHttpsRedirection();
    app.UseCookiePolicy();
    app.UseMiddleware<ConsentMiddleware>();
    app.UseSession();
    app.UseRouting();
```

```
app.Use(async (context, next) => {
    await context.Response
        .WriteAsync($"HTTPS Request: {context.Request.IsHttps} \n");
    await next();
});

app.UseEndpoints(endpoints => {

    endpoints.MapGet("/cookie", async context => {
        int counter1 = (context.Session.GetInt32("counter1") ?? 0) + 1;
        int counter2 = (context.Session.GetInt32("counter2") ?? 0) + 1;
        context.Session.SetInt32("counter1", counter1);
        context.Session.SetInt32("counter2", counter2);
        await context.Session.CommitAsync();
        await context.Response
            .WriteAsync($"Counter1: {counter1}, Counter2: {counter2}");
    });

    endpoints.MapFallback(async context =>
        await context.Response.WriteAsync("Hello World!"));
});
}
...
```

The UseHttpsRedirection method adds the middleware component, which appears at the start of the request pipeline so that the redirection to HTTPS occurs before any other component can short-circuit the pipeline and produce a response using regular HTTP.

CONFIGURING HTTPS REDIRECTION

The options pattern can be used configure the HTTPS redirection middleware, by calling the AddHttpsRedirection method in the ConfigureServices method, like this:

```
...
services.AddHttpsRedirection(opts => {
    opts.RedirectStatusCode = StatusCodes.Status307TemporaryRedirect;
    opts.HttpsPort = 443;
});
...
```

The only two configuration options are shown in this fragment, which sets the status code used in the redirection responses the port to which the client is redirected, overriding the value that is loaded from the configuration files. Specifying the HTTPS port can be useful when deploying the application, but care should be taken when changing the redirection status code.

Restart ASP.NET Core and request http://localhost:5000, which is the HTTP URL for the application. The HTTPS redirection middleware will intercept the request and redirect the browser to the HTTPS URL, as shown in Figure 16-9.

■ **Tip** Modern browsers often hide the URL scheme, which is why you should pay attention to the port number that is displayed. To display the URL scheme in the figure, I had to click the URL bar so the browser would display the full URL.

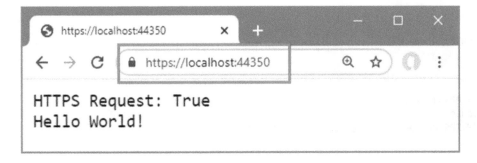

Figure 16-9. *Forcing HTTPS requests*

Enabling HTTP Strict Transport Security

One limitation of HTTPS redirection is that the user can make an initial request using HTTP before being redirected to a secure connection, presenting a security risk.

The HTTP Strict Transport Security (HSTS) protocol is intended to help mitigate this risk and works by including a header in responses that tells browsers to use HTTPS only when sending requests to the web application's host. After an HSTS header has been received, browsers that support HSTS will send requests to the application using HTTPS even if the user specifies an HTTP URL. Listing 16-13 shows the addition of the HSTS middleware to the request pipeline.

Listing 16-13. Enabling HSTS in the Startup.cs File in the Platform Folder

```
using Microsoft.AspNetCore.Builder;
using Microsoft.AspNetCore.Http;
using Microsoft.Extensions.DependencyInjection;
using System;
using System.Threading.Tasks;
using Microsoft.AspNetCore.Hosting;
using Microsoft.Extensions.Hosting;

namespace Platform {
    public class Startup {

        public void ConfigureServices(IServiceCollection services) {
            services.Configure<CookiePolicyOptions>(opts => {
                opts.CheckConsentNeeded = context => true;
            });

            services.AddDistributedMemoryCache();

            services.AddSession(options => {
                options.IdleTimeout = TimeSpan.FromMinutes(30);
                options.Cookie.IsEssential = true;
            });

            services.AddHsts(opts => {
                opts.MaxAge = TimeSpan.FromDays(1);
                opts.IncludeSubDomains = true;
            });
        }

        public void Configure(IApplicationBuilder app, IWebHostEnvironment env) {
            app.UseDeveloperExceptionPage();
            if (env.IsProduction()) {
                app.UseHsts();
            }
```

```
        app.UseHttpsRedirection();
        app.UseCookiePolicy();
        app.UseMiddleware<ConsentMiddleware>();
        app.UseSession();
        app.UseRouting();

        app.Use(async (context, next) => {
            await context.Response
                .WriteAsync($"HTTPS Request: {context.Request.IsHttps} \n");
            await next();
        });

        app.UseEndpoints(endpoints => {

            endpoints.MapGet("/cookie", async context => {
                int counter1 = (context.Session.GetInt32("counter1") ?? 0) + 1;
                int counter2 = (context.Session.GetInt32("counter2") ?? 0) + 1;
                context.Session.SetInt32("counter1", counter1);
                context.Session.SetInt32("counter2", counter2);
                await context.Session.CommitAsync();
                await context.Response
                    .WriteAsync($"Counter1: {counter1}, Counter2: {counter2}");
            });

            endpoints.MapFallback(async context =>
                await context.Response.WriteAsync("Hello World!"));
        });
    }
  }
}
```

The middleware is added to the request pipeline using the UseHsts method. The HSTS middleware can be configured with the AddHsts method, using the properties described in Table 16-9.

Table 16-9. *The HSTS Configuration Properties*

Name	Description
ExcludeHosts	This property returns a List<string> that contains the hosts for which the middleware won't send an HSTS header. The defaults exclude localhost and the loopback addresses for IP version 4 and version 6.
IncludeSubDomains	When true, the browser will apply the HSTS setting to subdomains. The default value is false.
MaxAge	This property specifies the time period for which the browser should make only HTTPS requests. The default value is 30 days.
Preload	This property is set to true for domains that are part of the HSTS preload scheme. The domains are hard-coded into the browser, which avoids the initial insecure request and ensures that only HTTPS is used. See hstspreload.org for more details.

HSTS is disabled during development and enabled only in production, which is why the UseHsts method is called only for that environment.

```
...
if (env.IsProduction()) {
    app.UseHsts();
}
...
```

HSTS must be used with care because it is easy to create a situation where clients cannot access the application, especially when nonstandard ports are used for HTTP and HTTPS.

If the example application is deployed to a server named myhost, for example, and the user requests http://myhost:5000, the browser will be sent the HSTS header and redirected to https://myhost:5001, and the application will work as expected. But the next time the user requests http://myhost:5000, they will receive an error stating that a secure connection cannot be established.

This problem arises because browsers take a simplistic approach to HSTS and assume that HTTP requests are handled on port 80 and HTTPS requests on port 443.

When the user requests http://myhost:5000, the browser checks its HSTS data and sees that it previously received an HSTS header for myhost. Instead of the HTTP URL that the user entered, the browser sends a request to https://myhost:5000. ASP.NET Core doesn't handle HTTPS on the port it uses for HTTP, and the request fails. The browser doesn't remember or understand the redirection it previously received for port 5001.

This isn't an issue where port 80 is used for HTTP and 443 is used for HTTPS. The URL http://myhost is equivalent to http://myhost:80, and https://myhost is equivalent to https://myhost:443, which means that changing the scheme targets the right port.

Once a browser has received an HSTS header, it will continue to honor it for the duration of the header's MaxAge property. When you first deploy an application, it is a good idea to set the HSTS MaxAge property to a relatively short duration until you are confident that your HTTPS infrastructure is working correctly, which is why I have set MaxAge to one day in Listing 16-13. Once you are sure that clients will not need to make HTTP requests, you can increase the MaxAge property. A MaxAge value of one year is commonly used.

■ **Tip** If you are testing HSTS with Google Chrome, you can inspect and edit the list of domains to which HSTS is applied by navigating to chrome://net-internals/#hsts.

Handling Exceptions and Errors

If an exception occurs when processing a request, the ASP.NET Core will return a response using the status code 500, which tells the browser that something has gone wrong.

A plain 500 result isn't useful during development because it reveals nothing about the case of the problem. The UseDeveloperExceptionPage method adds a middleware component that intercepts exceptions and presents a more useful response.

To demonstrate the way that exceptions are handled, Listing 16-14 replaces the middleware and endpoints used in earlier examples with a new component that deliberately throws an exception.

Listing 16-14. Adding a Middleware Component in the Startup.cs File in the Platform Folder

```
using Microsoft.AspNetCore.Builder;
using Microsoft.AspNetCore.Http;
using Microsoft.Extensions.DependencyInjection;
using System;
using System.Threading.Tasks;
using Microsoft.AspNetCore.Hosting;
using Microsoft.Extensions.Hosting;

namespace Platform {
    public class Startup {

        public void ConfigureServices(IServiceCollection services) {
            services.Configure<CookiePolicyOptions>(opts => {
                opts.CheckConsentNeeded = context => true;
            });

            services.AddDistributedMemoryCache();

            services.AddSession(options => {
                options.IdleTimeout = TimeSpan.FromMinutes(30);
                options.Cookie.IsEssential = true;
            });
```

```
            services.AddHsts(opts => {
                opts.MaxAge = TimeSpan.FromDays(1);
                opts.IncludeSubDomains = true;
            });
        }

        public void Configure(IApplicationBuilder app, IWebHostEnvironment env) {
            app.UseDeveloperExceptionPage();
            if (env.IsProduction()) {
                app.UseHsts();
            }
            app.UseHttpsRedirection();
            app.UseCookiePolicy();
            app.UseMiddleware<ConsentMiddleware>();
            app.UseSession();

            app.Run(context => {
                throw new Exception("Something has gone wrong");
            });
        }
    }
}
```

Restart ASP.NET Core and navigate to https://localhost:44350 to see the response that the middleware component generates, which is shown in Figure 16-10. The page presents a stack trace and details about the request, including details of the headers and cookies it contained.

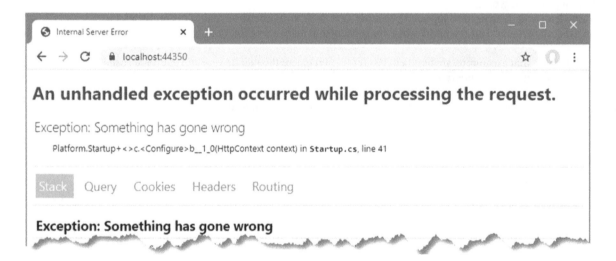

Figure 16-10. *The developer exception page*

MANAGING DEVELOPMENT AND PRODUCTION MIDDLEWARE

The details shown in Figure 16-10 should be revealed only to developers, which is why the middleware is added to the pipeline only during development. A common pattern is to use the IWebHostEnvironment service to check the environment, calling the UseDeveloperExceptionPage method in Development and the UseHsts method in the other environments, like this:

```
...
public void Configure(IApplicationBuilder app, IWebHostEnvironment env) {
    if (env.IsDevelopment()) {
        app.UseDeveloperExceptionPage();
    } else {
        app.UseHsts();
    }
    app.UseHttpsRedirection();
    app.UseCookiePolicy();
    app.UseMiddleware<ConsentMiddleware>();
    app.UseSession();

     app.Run(context => {
        throw new Exception("Something has gone wrong");
    });
}
...
```

This combination ensures that the exception handling middleware is added only in development and the HSTS middleware is added only outside of development.

Returning an HTML Error Response

When the developer exception middleware is disabled, as it should be when the application is in production, ASP.NET Core deals with unhandled exceptions by sending a response that contains just an error code. Listing 16-15 disables the development exception middleware so that the default behavior can be seen.

Listing 16-15. Disabling Middleware in the Startup.cs File in the Platform Folder

```
...
public void Configure(IApplicationBuilder app, IWebHostEnvironment env) {
    //app.UseDeveloperExceptionPage();
    if (env.IsProduction()) {
        app.UseHsts();
    }
    app.UseHttpsRedirection();
    app.UseCookiePolicy();
    app.UseMiddleware<ConsentMiddleware>();
    app.UseSession();

     app.Run(context => {
        throw new Exception("Something has gone wrong");
    });
}
...
```

Restart ASP.NET Core and navigate to https://localhost:44350. The response you see will depend on your browser because ASP.NET Core has only provided it with a response containing status code 500, without any content to display. Figure 16-11 shows how this is handled by Google Chrome.

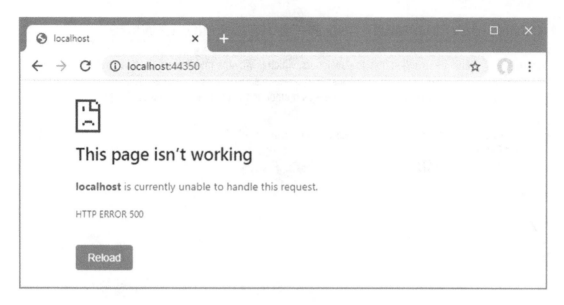

Figure 16-11. *Returning an error response*

As an alternative to returning just status codes, ASP.NET Core provides middleware that intercepts unhandled exceptions and sends a redirection to the browser instead, which can be used to show a friendlier response than the raw status code. The exception redirection middleware is added with the UseExceptionHandler method, as shown in Listing 16-16.

Listing 16-16. Returning an HTML Error Response in the Startup.cs File in the Platform Folder

```
...
public void Configure(IApplicationBuilder app, IWebHostEnvironment env) {
    //app.UseDeveloperExceptionPage();
    app.UseExceptionHandler("/error.html");
    if (env.IsProduction()) {
        app.UseHsts();
    }
    app.UseHttpsRedirection();
    app.UseCookiePolicy();
    app.UseStaticFiles();
    app.UseMiddleware<ConsentMiddleware>();
    app.UseSession();

     app.Run(context => {
        throw new Exception("Something has gone wrong");
    });
}
...
```

When an exception is thrown, the exception handler middleware will intercept the response and redirect the browser to the URL provided as the argument to the UseExceptionHandler method. For this example, the redirection is to a URL that will be handled by a static file, so the UseStaticFiles middleware has also been added to the pipeline.

To add the file that the browser will receive, create an HTML file named error.html in the wwwroot folder and add the content shown in Listing 16-17.

Listing 16-17. The Contents of the error.html File in the Platform/wwwroot Folder

```
<!DOCTYPE html>
<html lang="en">
```

```
<head>
    <link rel="stylesheet" href="/lib/twitter-bootstrap/css/bootstrap.min.css" />
    <title>Error</title>
</head>
<body class="text-center">
    <h3 class="p-2">Something went wrong...</h3>
    <h6>You can go back to the <a href="/">homepage</a> and try again</h6>
</body>
</html>
```

Restart ASP.NET Core and navigate to `https://localhost:44350` to see the effect of the new middleware. Instead of the raw status code, the browser will be sent a redirection to the `/error.html` URL, as shown in Figure 16-12.

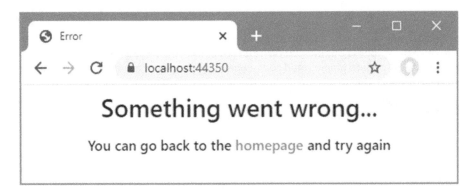

Figure 16-12. *Displaying an HTML error*

There are versions of the `UseExceptionHandler` method that allow more complex responses to be composed, but my advice is to keep error handling as simple as possible because you can't anticipate all of the problems an application may encounter, and you run the risk of encountering another exception when trying to handle the one that triggered the handler, resulting in a confusing response or no response at all.

Enriching Status Code Responses

Not all error responses will be the result of uncaught exceptions. Some requests cannot be processed for reasons other than software defects, such as requests for URLs that are not supported or that require authentication. For this type of problem, redirecting the client to a different URL can be problematic because some clients rely on the error code to detect problems. You will see examples of this in later chapters when I show you how to create and consume RESTful web applications.

ASP.NET Core provides middleware that adds user-friendly content to error responses without requiring redirection. This preserves the error status code while providing a human-readable message that helps users make sense of the problem.

The simplest approach is to define a string that will be used as the body for the response. This is more awkward than simply pointing at a file, but it is a more reliable technique and, as a rule, simple and reliable techniques are preferable when handling errors. To create the string response for the example project, add a class file named `ResponseStrings.cs` to the `Platform` folder with the code shown in Listing 16-18.

Listing 16-18. The Contents of the ResponseStrings.cs File in the Platform Folder

```
namespace Platform {

public static class Responses {

    public static string DefaultResponse = @"
        <!DOCTYPE html>
            <html lang=""en"">
```

```
        <head>
            <link rel=""stylesheet""
                href=""/lib/twitter-bootstrap/css/bootstrap.min.css"" />
            <title>Error</title>
        </head>
        <body class=""text-center"">
            <h3 class=""p-2"">Error {0}</h3>
            <h6>
                You can go back to the <a href=""/"">homepage</a> and try again
            </h6>
        </body>
    </html>";
    }
}
```

The Responses class defines a DefaultResponse property to which I have assigned a multiline string containing a simple HTML document. There is a placeholder—{0}—into which the response status code will be inserted when the response is sent to the client.

Listing 16-19 adds the status code middleware to the request pipeline and adds a new middleware component that will return a 404 status code, indicating that the requested URL was not found.

Listing 16-19. Adding Status Code Middleware in the Startup.cs File in the Platform Folder

```
...
public void Configure(IApplicationBuilder app, IWebHostEnvironment env) {
    //app.UseDeveloperExceptionPage();
    app.UseExceptionHandler("/error.html");
    if (env.IsProduction()) {
        app.UseHsts();
    }
    app.UseStaticFiles();
    app.UseHttpsRedirection();
    app.UseStatusCodePages("text/html", Responses.DefaultResponse);
    app.UseCookiePolicy();
    app.UseMiddleware<ConsentMiddleware>();
    app.UseSession();

    app.Use(async (context, next) => {
        if (context.Request.Path == "/error") {
            context.Response.StatusCode = StatusCodes.Status404NotFound;
            await Task.CompletedTask;
        } else {
            await next();
        }
    });

     app.Run(context => {
        throw new Exception("Something has gone wrong");
    });
}
...
```

The UseStatusCodePages method adds the response-enriching middleware to the request pipeline. The first argument is the value that will be used for the response's Content-Type header, which is text/html in this example. The second argument is the string that will be used as the body of the response, which is the HTML string from Listing 16-18.

The custom middleware component sets the HttpResponse.StatusCode property to specify the status code for the response, using a value defined by the StatusCode class. Middleware components are required to return a Task, so I have used the Task.CompletedTask property because there is no work for this middleware component to do.

To see how the 404 status code is handled, restart ASP.NET Core and request `https://localhost:44350/error`. The status code middleware will intercept the result and add the content shown in Figure 16-13 to the response. The string used as the second argument to `UseStatusCodePages` is interpolated using the status code to resolve the placeholder.

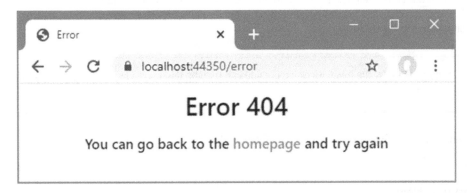

Figure 16-13. *Using the status code middleware*

The status code middleware responds only to status codes between 400 and 600 and doesn't alter responses that already contain content, which means you won't see the response in the figure if an error occurs after another middleware component has started to generate a response. The status code middleware won't respond to unhandled exceptions because exceptions disrupt the flow of a request through the pipeline, meaning that the status code middleware isn't given the opportunity to inspect the response before it is sent to the client. As a result, the `UseStatusCodePages` method is typically used in conjunction with the `UseExceptionHandler` or `UseDeveloperExceptionPage` method.

■ **Note**   There are two related methods, `UseStatusCodePagesWithRedirects` and `UseStatusCodePagesWithReExecute`, which work by redirecting the client to a different URL or by rerunning the request through the pipeline with a different URL. In both cases, the original status code may be lost.

Filtering Requests Using the Host Header

The HTTP specification requires requests to include a `Host` header that specifies the hostname the request is intended for, which makes it possible to support virtual servers where one HTTP server receives requests on a single port and handles them differently based on the hostname that was requested.

The default set of middleware that is added to the request pipeline by the `Program` class includes middleware that filters requests based on the `Host` header so that only requests that target a list of approved hostnames are handled and all other requests are rejected.

The default configuration for the `Hosts` header middleware is included in the `appsettings.json` file, as follows:

```
...
{
  "Location": {
      "CityName": "Buffalo"
  },
  "Logging": {
    "LogLevel": {
      "Default": "Information",
      "Microsoft": "Warning",
      "Microsoft.Hosting.Lifetime": "Information"
    }
  },
```

```
  "AllowedHosts": "*"
}
...
```

The AllowedHosts configuration property is added to the JSON file when the project is created, and the default value accepts requests regardless of the Host header value. You can change the configuration by editing the JSON file. The configuration can also be changed using the options pattern, as shown in Listing 16-20.

■ **Note** The middleware is already added to the pipeline by the Program class, but you can use the UseHostFiltering method if you need to add the middleware explicitly.

Listing 16-20. Configuring Host Header Filtering in the Startup.cs File in the Platform Folder

```
using Microsoft.AspNetCore.Builder;
using Microsoft.AspNetCore.Http;
using Microsoft.Extensions.DependencyInjection;
using System;
using System.Threading.Tasks;
using Microsoft.AspNetCore.Hosting;
using Microsoft.Extensions.Hosting;
using Microsoft.AspNetCore.HostFiltering;

namespace Platform {
    public class Startup {

        public void ConfigureServices(IServiceCollection services) {
            services.Configure<CookiePolicyOptions>(opts => {
                opts.CheckConsentNeeded = context => true;
            });

            services.AddDistributedMemoryCache();

            services.AddSession(options => {
                options.IdleTimeout = TimeSpan.FromMinutes(30);
                options.Cookie.IsEssential = true;
            });

            services.AddHsts(opts => {
                opts.MaxAge = TimeSpan.FromDays(1);
                opts.IncludeSubDomains = true;
            });

            services.Configure<HostFilteringOptions>(opts => {
                opts.AllowedHosts.Clear();
                opts.AllowedHosts.Add("*.example.com");
            });
        }

        public void Configure(IApplicationBuilder app, IWebHostEnvironment env) {

            // ...statements omitted for brevity...
        }
    }
}
```

The HostFilteringOptions class is used to configure the host filtering middleware using the properties described in Table 16-10.

Table 16-10. *The HostFilteringOptions Properties*

Name	Description
AllowedHosts	This property returns a List<string> that contains the domains for which requests are allowed. Wildcards are allowed so that *.example.com accepts all names in the example.com domain and * accepts all header values.
AllowEmptyHosts	When false, this property tells the middleware to reject requests that do not contain a Host header. The default value is true.
IncludeFailureMessage	When true, this property includes a message in the response that indicates the reason for the error. The default value is true.

In Listing 16-20, I called the Clear method to remove the wildcard entry that has been loaded from the appsettings.json file and then called the Add method to accept all hosts in the example.com domain. Requests sent from the browser to localhost will no longer contain an acceptable Host header. You can see what happens by restarting ASP.NET Core and using the browser to request http://localhost:5000. The Host header middleware checks the Host header in the request determines that the request hostname doesn't match the AllowedHosts list and terminates the request with the 400 status code, which indicates a bad request. Figure 16-14 shows the error message.

░ **Tip** Notice that the browser isn't redirected to use HTTPS because the Host header middleware is added to the request pipeline before the HTTPS redirection middleware.

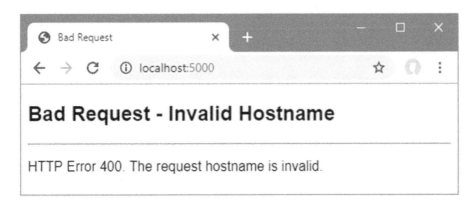

Figure 16-14. *A request rejected based on the Host header*

Summary

In this chapter, I continued to describe the basic features provided by the ASP.NET Core platform. I showed you how to manage cookies and track cookie consent, how to use sessions, how to use and enforce HTTPS, how to deal with unhandled exceptions and status code responses, and, finally, how to filter requests based on the Host header. In the next chapter, I explain how ASP.NET Core supports working with data.

CHAPTER 17

Working with Data

All the examples in the earlier chapters in this part of the book have generated fresh responses for each request, which is easy to do when dealing with simple strings or small fragments of HTML. Most real projects deal with data that is expensive to produce and needs to be used as efficiently as possible. In this chapter, I describe the features that ASP.NET Core provides for caching data and caching entire responses. I also show you how to create and configure the services required to access data in a database using Entity Framework Core. Table 17-1 puts the ASP.NET Core features for working with data in context.

> **Note** The examples in this chapter rely on the SQL Server LocalDB feature that was installed in Chapter 2. You will encounter errors if you have not installed LocalDB and the required updates.

Table 17-1. *Putting the ASP.NET Core Data Features in Context*

Question	Answer
What are they?	The features described in this chapter allow responses to be produced using data that has been previously created, either because it was created for an earlier request or because it has been stored in a database.
Why are they useful?	Most web applications deal with data that is expensive to re-create for every request. The features in this chapter allow responses to be produced more efficiently and with fewer resources.
How are they used?	Data values are cached using a service. Responses are cached by a middleware component based on the Cache-Control header. Databases are accessed through a service that translates LINQ queries into SQL statements.
Are there any pitfalls or limitations?	For caching, it is important to test the effect of your cache policy before deploying the application to ensure you have found the right balance between efficiency and responsiveness. For Entity Framework Core, it is important to pay attention to the queries sent to the database to ensure that they are not retrieving large amounts of data that is processed and then discarded by the application.
Are there any alternatives?	All the features described in this chapter are optional. You can elect not to cache data or responses or to use an external cache. You can choose not to use a database or to access a database using a framework other than Entity Framework Core.

© Adam Freeman 2020
A. Freeman, *Pro ASP.NET Core 3*, https://doi.org/10.1007/978-1-4842-5440-0_17

Table 17-2 summarizes the chapter.

Table 17-2. *Chapter Summary*

Problem	Solution	Listing
Caching data values	Set up a cache service and use it in endpoints and middleware components to store data values	7, 8
Creating a persistent cache	Use the database-backed cache	9–14
Caching entire responses	Enable the caching middleware and set the Cache-Control header in responses	15, 16
Storing application data	Use Entity Framework Core	17–23, 26–28
Creating a database schema	Create and apply migrations	24, 25
Accessing data in endpoints	Consume the database context service	29
Including all request details in logging messages	Enable the sensitive data logging feature	30

Preparing for This Chapter

In this chapter, I continue to use the Platform project from Chapter 16. To prepare for this chapter, replace the contents of the Startup.cs file with the code shown in Listing 17-1.

■ **Tip** You can download the example project for this chapter—and for all the other chapters in this book—from https://github. com/apress/pro-asp.net-core-3. See Chapter 1 for how to get help if you have problems running the examples.

Listing 17-1. Replacing the Contents of the Startup.cs File in the Platform Folder

```
using Microsoft.AspNetCore.Builder;
using Microsoft.AspNetCore.Http;
using Microsoft.Extensions.DependencyInjection;

namespace Platform {
    public class Startup {

        public void ConfigureServices(IServiceCollection services) {
        }

        public void Configure(IApplicationBuilder app) {
            app.UseDeveloperExceptionPage();
            app.UseStaticFiles();
            app.UseRouting();
            app.UseEndpoints(endpoints => {
                endpoints.MapGet("/", async context => {
                    await context.Response.WriteAsync("Hello World!");
                });
            });
        }
    }
}
```

To reduce the detail level of the logging messages displayed by the application, make the changes shown in Listing 17-2 to the appsettings.Development.json file.

Listing 17-2. Changing the Log Detail in the appsettings.Development.json File in the Platform Folder

```
{
    "Logging": {
      "LogLevel": {
        "Default": "Debug",
        "System": "Information",
        "Microsoft": "Information",
        "Microsoft.AspnetCore.Hosting.Diagnostics": "None"
      }
    }
}
```

If you are using Visual Studio, select Project ➤ Platform Properties, navigate to the Debug tab, uncheck the Enable SSL option (as shown in Figure 17-1), and select File ➤ Save All.

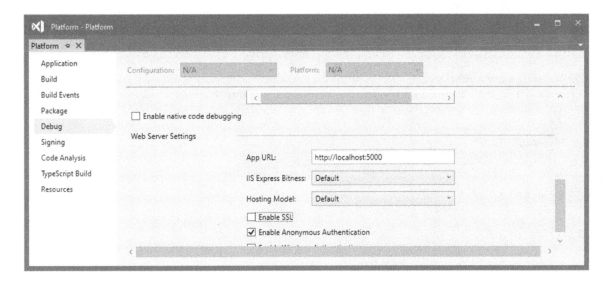

Figure 17-1. *Disabling HTTPS*

If you are using Visual Studio Code, open the `Properties/launchSettings.json` file to remove the HTTPS URL, as shown in Listing 17-3.

Listing 17-3. Disabling SSL in the launchSettings.json File in the Platform/Properties Folder

```
{
  "iisSettings": {
    "windowsAuthentication": false,
    "anonymousAuthentication": true,
    "iisExpress": {
      "applicationUrl": "http://localhost:5000",
      "sslPort": 0
    }
  },
  "profiles": {
    "IIS Express": {
      "commandName": "IISExpress",
      "launchBrowser": true,
      "environmentVariables": {
        "ASPNETCORE_ENVIRONMENT": "Development"
      }
    },
```

```
  "Platform": {
    "commandName": "Project",
    "launchBrowser": true,
    "environmentVariables": {
      "ASPNETCORE_ENVIRONMENT": "Development"
    },
    "applicationUrl": "http://localhost:5000"
  }
 }
}
```

Start the application by selecting Start Without Debugging or Run Without Debugging from the Debug menu or by opening a new PowerShell command prompt, navigating to the Platform project folder (which contains the Platform.csproj file), and running the command shown in Listing 17-4.

Listing 17-4. Starting the ASP.NET Core Runtime

```
dotnet run
```

If the application was started using Visual Studio or Visual Studio Code, a new browser window will open and display the content shown in Figure 17-2. If the application was started from the command line, open a new browser tab and navigate to https://localhost:5000; you will see the content shown in Figure 17-2.

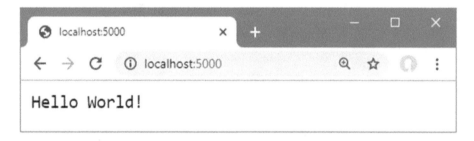

Figure 17-2. *Running the example application*

Caching Data

In most web applications, there will be some items of data that are relatively expensive to generate but are required repeatedly. The exact nature of the data is specific to each project, but repeatedly performing the same set of calculations can increase the resources required to host the application and drive up hosting costs. To represent an expensive response, add a class file called SumEndpoint.cs to the Platform folder with the code shown in Listing 17-5.

Listing 17-5. The Contents of the SumEndpoint.cs File in the Platform Folder

```
using Microsoft.AspNetCore.Http;
using System;
using System.Threading.Tasks;

namespace Platform {

    public class SumEndpoint {

        public async Task Endpoint(HttpContext context) {
            int count = int.Parse((string)context.Request.RouteValues["count"]);
            long total = 0;
```

```
            for (int i = 1; i <= count; i++) {
                total += i;
            }
            string totalString = $"({ DateTime.Now.ToLongTimeString() }) {total}";
            await context.Response.WriteAsync(
                $"({DateTime.Now.ToLongTimeString()}) Total for {count}"
                + $" values:\n{totalString}\n");
        }
    }
}
```

Listing 17-6 creates a route that uses the endpoint, which is applied using the MapEndpoint extension methods created in Chapter 13.

Listing 17-6. Adding an Endpoint in the Startup.cs File in the Platform Folder

```
using Microsoft.AspNetCore.Builder;
using Microsoft.AspNetCore.Http;
using Microsoft.Extensions.DependencyInjection;

namespace Platform {
    public class Startup {

        public void ConfigureServices(IServiceCollection services) {
        }

        public void Configure(IApplicationBuilder app) {
            app.UseDeveloperExceptionPage();
            app.UseStaticFiles();
            app.UseRouting();
            app.UseEndpoints(endpoints => {

                endpoints.MapEndpoint<SumEndpoint>("/sum/{count:int=1000000000}");

                endpoints.MapGet("/", async context => {
                    await context.Response.WriteAsync("Hello World!");
                });
            });
        }
    }
}
```

Restart ASP.NET Core and use a browser to request https://localhost:5000/sum. The endpoint will sum 1,000,000,000 integer values and produce the result shown in Figure 17-3.

Reload the browser window, and the endpoint will repeat the calculation. Both the timestamps in the response change, as shown in the figure, indicating that every part of the response was produced fresh for each request.

■ **Tip** You may need to increase or decrease the default value for the route parameter based on the capabilities of your machine. Try to find a value that takes two or three seconds to produce the result—just long enough that you can tell when the calculation is being performed but not so long that you can step out for coffee while it happens.

Figure 17-3. *An expensive response*

Caching Data Values

ASP.NET Core provides a service that can be used to cache data values through the IDistributedCache interface. Listing 17-7 revises the endpoint to declare a dependency on the service and use it to cache calculated values.

Listing 17-7. Using the Cache Service in the SumEndpoint.cs File in the Platform Folder

```
using Microsoft.AspNetCore.Http;
using System;
using System.Threading.Tasks;
using Microsoft.Extensions.Caching.Distributed;

namespace Platform {

    public class SumEndpoint {

        public async Task Endpoint(HttpContext context, IDistributedCache cache) {
            int count = int.Parse((string)context.Request.RouteValues["count"]);
            string cacheKey = $"sum_{count}";
            string totalString = await cache.GetStringAsync(cacheKey);
            if (totalString == null) {
                long total = 0;
                for (int i = 1; i <= count; i++) {
                    total += i;
                }
                totalString = $"({ DateTime.Now.ToLongTimeString() }) {total}";
                await cache.SetStringAsync(cacheKey, totalString,
                    new DistributedCacheEntryOptions {
                        AbsoluteExpirationRelativeToNow = TimeSpan.FromMinutes(2)
                    });
            }
            await context.Response.WriteAsync(
                $"({DateTime.Now.ToLongTimeString()}) Total for {count}"
                + $" values:\n{totalString}\n");
        }
    }
}
```

The cache service can store only byte arrays, which can be restrictive but allows for a range of IDistributedCache implementations to be used. There are extension methods available that allow strings to be used, which is a more convenient way of caching most data. Table 17-3 describes the most useful methods for using the cache.

Table 17-3. *Useful IDistributedCache Methods*

Name	Description
GetString(key)	This method returns the cached string associated with the specified key, or null if there is no such item.
GetStringAsync(key)	This method returns a Task<string> that produces the cached string associated with the key, or null if there is no such item.
SetString(key, value, options)	This method stores a string in the cache using the specified key. The cache entry can be configured with an optional DistributedCacheEntryOptions object.
SetStringAsync(key, value, options)	This method asynchronously stores a string in the cache using the specified key. The cache entry can be configured with an optional DistributedCacheEntryOptions object.
Refresh(key)	This method resets the expiry interval for the value associated with the key, preventing it from being flushed from the cache.
RefreshAsync(key)	This method asynchronously resets the expiry interval for the value associated with the key, preventing it from being flushed from the cache.
Remove(key)	This method removes the cached item associated with the key.
RemoveAsync(key)	This method asynchronously removes the cached item associated with the key.

By default, entries remain in the cache indefinitely, but the SetString and SetStringAsync methods accept an optional DistributedCacheEntryOptions argument that is used to set an expiry policy, which tells the cache when to eject the item. Table 17-4 shows the properties defined by the DistributedCacheEntryOptions class.

Table 17-4. *The DistributedCacheEntryOptions Properties*

Name	Description
AbsoluteExpiration	This property is used to specify an absolute expiry date.
AbsoluteExpirationRelativeToNow	This property is used to specify a relative expiry date.
SlidingExpiration	This property is used to specify a period of inactivity, after which the item will be ejected from the cache if it hasn't been read.

In Listing 17-7, the endpoint uses the GetStringAsync to see whether there is a cached result available from a previous request. If there is no cached value, the endpoint performs the calculation and caches the result using SetStringAsync method, with the AbsoluteExpirationRelativeToNow property to tell the cache to eject the item after two minutes.

```
...
await cache.SetStringAsync(cacheKey, totalStr,
    new DistributedCacheEntryOptions {
        AbsoluteExpirationRelativeToNow = TimeSpan.FromMinutes(2)
    });
...
```

The next step is to set up the cache service in the Startup class, as shown in Listing 17-8.

Listing 17-8. Adding a Service in the Startup.cs File in the Platform Folder

```
using Microsoft.AspNetCore.Builder;
using Microsoft.AspNetCore.Http;
using Microsoft.Extensions.DependencyInjection;

namespace Platform {
    public class Startup {
```

```
        public void ConfigureServices(IServiceCollection services) {
            services.AddDistributedMemoryCache(opts => {
                opts.SizeLimit = 200;
            });
        }

        public void Configure(IApplicationBuilder app) {
            app.UseDeveloperExceptionPage();
            app.UseStaticFiles();
            app.UseRouting();
            app.UseEndpoints(endpoints => {

                endpoints.MapEndpoint<SumEndpoint>("/sum/{count:int=1000000000}");

                endpoints.MapGet("/", async context => {
                    await context.Response.WriteAsync("Hello World!");
                });
            });
        }
    }
}
```

AddDistributedMemoryCache is the same method I used in Chapter 16 to provide the data store for session data. This is one of the three methods used to select an implementation for the IDistributedCache service, as described in Table 17-5.

Table 17-5. *The Cache Service Implementation Methods*

Name	Description
AddDistributedMemoryCache	This method sets up an in-memory cache.
AddDistributedSqlServerCache	This method sets up a cache that stores data in SQL Server and is available when the Microsoft.Extensions.Caching.SqlServer package is installed. See the "Caching Responses" section for details.
AddStackExchangeRedisCache	This method sets up a Redis cache and is available when the Microsoft.Extensions.Caching.Redis package is installed.

Listing 17-8 uses the AddDistributedMemoryCache method to create an in-memory cache as the implementation for the IDistributedCache service. This cache is configured using the MemoryCacheOptions class, whose most useful properties are described in Table 17-6.

Table 17-6. *Useful MemoryCacheOptions Properties*

Name	Description
ExpirationScanFrequency	This property is used to set a TimeSpan that determines how often the cache scans for expired items.
SizeLimit	This property specifies the maximum number of items in the cache. When the size is reached, the cache will eject items.
CompactionPercentage	This property specifies the percentage by which the size of the cache is reduced when SizeLimit is reached.

The statement in Listing 17-8 uses the SizeLimit property to restrict the cache to 200 items. Care must be taken when using an in-memory cache to find the right balance between allocating enough memory for the cache to be effective without exhausting server resources.

To see the effect of the cache, restart ASP.NET Core and request the http://localhost:5000/sum URL. Reload the browser, and you will see that only one of the timestamps will change, as shown in Figure 17-4. This is because the cache has provided the calculation response, which allows the endpoint to produce the result without having to repeat the calculation.

Figure 17-4. *Caching data values*

If you wait for two minutes and then reload the browser, then both timestamps will change because the cached result will have been ejected, and the endpoint will have to perform the calculation to produce the result.

Using a Shared and Persistent Data Cache

The cache created by the AddDistributedMemoryCache method isn't distributed, despite the name. The items are stored in memory as part of the ASP.NET Core process, which means that applications that run on multiple servers or containers don't share cached data. It also means that the contents of the cache are lost when ASP.NET Core is stopped.

The AddDistributedSqlServerCache method stores the cache data in a SQL Server database, which can be shared between multiple ASP.NET Core servers and which stores the data persistently.

The first step is to create a database that will be used to store the cached data. You can store the cached data alongside the application's other data, but for this chapter, I am going to use a separate database, which will be named CacheDb. You can create the database using Azure Data Studio or SQL Server Management Studio, both of which are available for free from Microsoft. Databases can also be created from the command line using sqlcmd. Open a new PowerShell command prompt and run the command shown in Listing 17-9 to connect to the LocalDB server.

■ **Tip**   The sqlcmd tool should have been installed as part of the Visual Studio workload or as part of the SQL Server Express installation. If it has not been installed, then you can download an installer from https://docs.microsoft.com/en-us/sql/tools/sqlcmd-utility?view=sql-server-2017.

Listing 17-9. Connecting to the Database

```
sqlcmd -S "(localdb)\MSSQLLocalDB"
```

Pay close attention to the argument that specifies the database. There is one backslash, which is followed by MSSQLLocalDB. It can be hard to spot the repeated letters: **MS-SQL-L**ocalDB (but without the hyphens).

When the connection has been established, you will see a 1> prompt. Enter the commands shown in Listing 17-10 and press the Enter key after each command.

■ **Caution**   If you are using Visual Studio, you must apply the updates for SQL Server described in Chapter 2. The version of SQL Server that is installed by default when you install Visual Studio cannot create LocalDB databases.

Listing 17-10. Creating the Database

```
CREATE DATABASE CacheDb
GO
```

If no errors are reported, then enter exit and press Enter to terminate the connection. The next step is to run the command shown in Listing 17-11 to create a table in the new database, which uses a global .NET Core tool to prepare the database.

■ **Tip** If you need to reset the cache database, use the command in Listing 17-9 to open a connection and use the command DROP DATABASE CacheDB. You can then re-create the database using the commands in Listing 17-10.

Listing 17-11. Creating the Cache Database Table

```
dotnet sql-cache create "Server=(localdb)\MSSQLLocalDB;Database=CacheDb" dbo DataCache
```

The arguments for this command are the connection string that specifies the database, the schema, and the name of the table that will be used to store the cached data. Enter the command on a single line and press Enter. It will take a few seconds for the tool to connect to the database. If the process is successful, you will see the following message:

```
Table and index were created successfully.
```

Creating the Persistent Cache Service

Now that the database is ready, I can create the service that will use it to store cached data. To add the NuGet package required for SQL Server caching support, open a new PowerShell command prompt, navigate to the Platform project folder, and run the command shown in Listing 17-12. (If you are using Visual Studio, you can add the package by selecting Project ➤ Manage Nuget Packages.)

Listing 17-12. Adding a Package to the Project

```
dotnet add package Microsoft.Extensions.Caching.SqlServer --version 3.1.1
```

The next step is to define a connection string, which describes the database connection in the JSON configuration file, as shown in Listing 17-13.

■ **Note** The cache created by the AddDistributedSqlServerCache method is distributed, meaning that multiple applications can use the same database and share cache data. If you are deploying the same application to multiple servers or containers, all instances will be able to share cached data. If you are sharing a cache between different applications, then you should pay close attention to the keys you use to ensure that applications receive the data types they expect.

Listing 17-13. Defining a Connection String in the appsettings.json File in the Platform Folder

```
{
    "Location": {
        "CityName": "Buffalo"
    },
```

```
  "Logging": {
    "LogLevel": {
      "Default": "Information",
      "Microsoft": "Warning",
      "Microsoft.Hosting.Lifetime": "Information"
    }
  },
  "AllowedHosts": "*",
  "ConnectionStrings": {
    "CacheConnection": "Server=(localdb)\\MSSQLLocalDB;Database=CacheDb"
  }
}
```

Notice that the connection string uses two backslash characters (\\) to escape the character in the JSON file. Listing 17-14 change the implementation for the cache service in the Startup class to use SQL Server with the connection string from Listing 17-13.

Listing 17-14. Using a Persistent Data Cache in the Startup.cs File in the Platform Folder

```csharp
using Microsoft.AspNetCore.Builder;
using Microsoft.AspNetCore.Http;
using Microsoft.Extensions.DependencyInjection;
using Microsoft.Extensions.Configuration;

namespace Platform {
    public class Startup {

        public Startup(IConfiguration config) {
            Configuration = config;
        }

        private IConfiguration Configuration {get; set;}

        public void ConfigureServices(IServiceCollection services) {

            services.AddDistributedSqlServerCache(opts => {
                opts.ConnectionString
                    = Configuration["ConnectionStrings:CacheConnection"];
                opts.SchemaName = "dbo";
                opts.TableName = "DataCache";
            });
        }

        public void Configure(IApplicationBuilder app) {
            app.UseDeveloperExceptionPage();
            app.UseStaticFiles();
            app.UseRouting();
            app.UseEndpoints(endpoints => {

                endpoints.MapEndpoint<SumEndpoint>("/sum/{count:int=1000000000}");

                endpoints.MapGet("/", async context => {
                    await context.Response.WriteAsync("Hello World!");
                });
            });
        }
    }
}
```

411

The IConfiguration service is used to access the connection string from the application's configuration data. The cache service is created using the AddDistributedSqlServerCache method and is configured using an instance of the SqlServerCacheOptions class, whose most useful properties are described in Table 17-7.

Table 17-7. *Useful SqlServerCacheOptions Properties*

Name	Description
ConnectionString	This property specifies the connection string, which is conventionally stored in the JSON configuration file and accessed through the IConfguration service.
SchemaName	This property specifies the schema name for the cache table.
TableName	This property specifies the name of the cache table.
ExpiredItemsDeletionInterval	This property specifies how often the table is scanned for expired items. The default is 30 minutes.
DefaultSlidingExpiration	This property specifies how long an item remains unread in the cache before it expires. The default is 20 minutes.

The listing uses the ConnectionString, SchemaName, and TableName properties to configure the cache middleware to use the database table. Restart ASP.NET Core and use a browser to request the http://localhost:5000/sum URL. There is no change in the response produced by the application, which is shown in Figure 17-4, but you will find that the cached responses are persistent and will be used even when you restart ASP.NET Core.

CACHING SESSION-SPECIFIC DATA VALUES

When you use the IDistributedCache service, the data values are shared between all requests. If you want to cache different data values for each user, then you can use the session middleware described in Chapter 16. The session middleware relies on the IDistributedCache service to store its data, which means that session data will be stored persistently and be available to a distributed application when the AddDistributedSqlServerCache method is used.

Caching Responses

An alternative to caching individual data items is to cache entire responses, which can be a useful approach if a response is expensive to compose and is likely to be repeated. Caching responses requires the addition of a service and a middleware component, as shown in Listing 17-15.

Listing 17-15. Configuring Response Caching in the Startup.cs File in the Platform Folder

```
using Microsoft.AspNetCore.Builder;
using Microsoft.AspNetCore.Http;
using Microsoft.Extensions.DependencyInjection;
using Microsoft.Extensions.Configuration;
using Platform.Services;

namespace Platform {
    public class Startup {

        public Startup(IConfiguration config) {
            Configuration = config;
        }

        private IConfiguration Configuration {get; set;}
```

```
        public void ConfigureServices(IServiceCollection services) {
            services.AddDistributedSqlServerCache(opts => {
                opts.ConnectionString
                    = Configuration["ConnectionStrings:CacheConnection"];
                opts.SchemaName = "dbo";
                opts.TableName = "DataCache";
            });
            services.AddResponseCaching();
            services.AddSingleton<IResponseFormatter, HtmlResponseFormatter>();
        }

        public void Configure(IApplicationBuilder app) {
            app.UseDeveloperExceptionPage();
            app.UseResponseCaching();
            app.UseStaticFiles();
            app.UseRouting();
            app.UseEndpoints(endpoints => {

                endpoints.MapEndpoint<SumEndpoint>("/sum/{count:int=1000000000}");

                endpoints.MapGet("/", async context => {
                    await context.Response.WriteAsync("Hello World!");
                });
            });
        }
    }
}
```

The AddResponseCaching method is used in the ConfigureServices method to set up the service used by the cache. The middleware component is added with the UseResponseCaching method, which should be called before any endpoint or middleware that needs its responses cached.

I have also defined the IResponseFormatter service, which I used to explain how dependency injection works in Chapter 14. Response caching is used only in certain circumstances, and, as I explain shortly, demonstrating the feature requires an HTML response.

■ **Note**   The response caching feature does not use the IDistributedCache service. Responses are cached in memory and are not distributed.

In Listing 17-16, I have updated the SumEndpoint class so that it requests response caching instead of caching just a data value.

Listing 17-16. Using Response Caching in the SumEndpoint.cs File in the Platform Folder

```
using Microsoft.AspNetCore.Http;
using System;
using System.Threading.Tasks;
using Microsoft.Extensions.Caching.Distributed;
using Microsoft.AspNetCore.Routing;
using Platform.Services;

namespace Platform {

    public class SumEndpoint {

        public async Task Endpoint(HttpContext context, IDistributedCache cache,
                IResponseFormatter formatter, LinkGenerator generator) {
```

413

```
        int count = int.Parse((string)context.Request.RouteValues["count"]);
        long total = 0;
        for (int i = 1; i <= count; i++) {
            total += i;
        }
        string totalString = $"({ DateTime.Now.ToLongTimeString() }) {total}";

        context.Response.Headers["Cache-Control"] = "public, max-age=120";

        string url = generator.GetPathByRouteValues(context, null,
            new { count = count });

        await formatter.Format(context,
            $"<div>({DateTime.Now.ToLongTimeString()}) Total for {count}"
            + $" values:</div><div>{totalString}</div>"
            + $"<a href={url}>Reload</a>");
    }
  }
}
```

Some of the changes to the endpoint enable response caching, but others are just to demonstrate that it is working. For enabling response caching, the important statement is the one that adds a header to the response, like this:

```
...
context.Response.Headers["Cache-Control"] = "public, max-age=120";
...
```

The Cache-Control header is used to control response caching. The middleware will only cache responses that have a Cache-Control header that contains the public directive. The max-age directive is used to specify the period that the response can be cached for, expressed in seconds. The Cache-Control header used in Listing 17-16 enables caching and specifies that responses can be cached for two minutes.

Enabling response caching is simple, but checking that it is working requires care. When you reload the browser window or press Return in the URL bar, browsers will include a Cache-Control header in the request that sets the max-age directive to zero, which bypasses the response cache and causes a new response to be generated by the endpoint. The only reliable way to request a URL without the Cache-Control header is to navigate using an HTML anchor element, which is why the endpoint in Listing 17-16 uses the IResponseFormatter service to generate an HTML response and uses the LinkGenerator service to create a URL that can be used in the anchor element's href attribute.

To check the response cache, restart ASP.NET Core and use the browser to request http://localhost:5000/sum. Once the response has been generated, click the Reload link to request the same URL. You will see that neither of the timestamps in the response change, indicating that the entire response has been cached, as shown in Figure 17-5.

Figure 17-5. *Caching responses*

The Cache-Control header can be combined with the Vary header to provide fine-grained control over which requests are cached. See https://developer.mozilla.org/en-US/docs/Web/HTTP/Headers/Cache-Control and https://developer.mozilla.org/en-US/docs/Web/HTTP/Headers/Vary for details of the features provided by both headers.

COMPRESSING RESPONSES

ASP.NET Core includes middleware that will compress responses for browsers that have indicated they can handle compressed data. The middleware is added to the pipeline with the UseResponseCompression method. Compression is a trade-off between the server resources required for compression and the bandwidth required to deliver content to the client, and it should not be switched on without testing to determine the performance impact.

Using Entity Framework Core

Not all data values are produced directly by the application, and most projects will need to access data in a database. Entity Framework Core is well-integrated into the ASP.NET Core platform, with good support for creating a database from C# classes and for creating C# classes to represent an existing database. In the sections that follow, I demonstrate the process for creating a simple data model, using it to create a database, and querying that database in an endpoint.

WORKING WITH ENTITY FRAMEWORK CORE

The most common complaint about Entity Framework Core is poor performance. When I review projects that have Entity Framework Core performance issues, the problem is almost always because the development team has treated Entity Framework Core as a black box and not paid attention to the SQL queries that are sent to the database. Not all LINQ features can be translated into SQL, and the most common problem is a query that retrieves large amounts of data from the database, which is then discarded after it has been reduced to produce a single value.

Using Entity Framework Core requires a good understanding of SQL and ensuring that the LINQ queries made by the application are translated into efficient SQL queries. There are rare applications that have high-performance data requirements that cannot be met by Entity Framework Core, but that isn't the case for most typical web applications.

That is not to say that Entity Framework Core is perfect. It has its quirks and requires an investment in time to become proficient. If you don't like the way that Entity Framework Core works, then you may prefer to use an alternative, such as Dapper (https://github.com/StackExchange/Dapper). But if your issue is that queries are not being performed fast enough, then you should spend some time exploring how those queries are being processed, which you can do using the techniques described in the remainder of the chapter.

Installing Entity Framework Core

Entity Framework Core requires a global tool package that is used to manage databases from the command line and to manage packages for the project that provide data access. To install the tools package, open a new PowerShell command prompt and run the commands shown in Listing 17-17.

Listing 17-17. Installing the Entity Framework Core Global Tool Package

```
dotnet tool uninstall --global dotnet-ef
dotnet tool install --global dotnet-ef --version 3.1.1
```

The first command removes any existing version of the dotnet-ef package, and the second command installs the version required for the examples in this book. This package provides the dotnet ef commands that you will see in later examples. To ensure the package is working as expected, run the command shown in Listing 17-18.

Listing 17-18. Testing the Entity Framework Core Global Tool

```
dotnet ef --help
```

This command shows the help message for the global tool and produces the following output:

```
Entity Framework Core .NET Command-line Tools 3.1.1
Usage: dotnet ef [options] [command]
Options:
  --version       Show version information
  -h|--help       Show help information
  -v|--verbose    Show verbose output.
  --no-color      Don't colorize output.
  --prefix-output Prefix output with level.
Commands:
  database   Commands to manage the database.
  dbcontext  Commands to manage DbContext types.
  migrations Commands to manage migrations.
Use "dotnet ef [command] --help" for more information about a command.
```

Entity Framework Core also requires packages to be added to the project. If you are using Visual Studio Code or prefer working from the command line, navigate to the Platform project folder (the folder that contains the Platform.csproj file) and run the commands shown in Listing 17-19.

Listing 17-19. Adding Entity Framework Core Packages to the Project

```
dotnet add package Microsoft.EntityFrameworkCore.Design --version 3.1.1
dotnet add package Microsoft.EntityFrameworkCore.SqlServer --version 3.1.1
```

Creating the Data Model

For this chapter, I am going to define the data model using C# classes and use Entity Framework Core to create the database and schema. Create the Platform/Models folder and add to it a class file called Calculation.cs with the contents shown in Listing 17-20.

Listing 17-20. The Contents of the Calculation.cs File in the Platform/Models Folder

```
namespace Platform.Models {

    public class Calculaton {
        public long Id { get; set; }
        public int Count { get; set; }
        public long Result { get; set; }
    }
}
```

You can see more complex data models in other chapters, but for this example, I am going to keep with the theme of this chapter and model the calculation performed in earlier examples. The Id property will be used to create a unique key for each object stored in the database, and the Count and Result properties will describe a calculation and its result.

Entity Framework Core uses a context class that provides access to the database. Add a file called CalculationContext.cs to the Platform/Models folder with the content shown in Listing 17-21.

Listing 17-21. The Contents of the CalculationContext.cs File in the Platform/Models Folder

```
using Microsoft.EntityFrameworkCore;

namespace Platform.Models {

    public class CalculationContext: DbContext {

        public CalculationContext(DbContextOptions<CalculationContext> opts)
            : base(opts) {}

        public DbSet<Calculaton> Calculations { get; set; }
    }
}
```

The CalculationContext class defines a constructor that is used to receive an options object that is passed on to the base constructor. The Calculations property provides access to the Calculation objects that Entity Framework Core will retrieve from the database.

Configuring the Database Service

Access to the database is provided through a service that is configured in the Startup class, as shown in Listing 17-22.

Listing 17-22. Configuring the Data Service in the Startup.cs File in the Platform Folder

```
using Microsoft.AspNetCore.Builder;
using Microsoft.AspNetCore.Http;
using Microsoft.Extensions.DependencyInjection;
using Microsoft.Extensions.Configuration;
using Platform.Services;
using Microsoft.EntityFrameworkCore;
using Platform.Models;

namespace Platform {
    public class Startup {

        public Startup(IConfiguration config) {
            Configuration = config;
        }

        private IConfiguration Configuration {get; set;}

        public void ConfigureServices(IServiceCollection services) {
            services.AddDistributedSqlServerCache(opts => {
                opts.ConnectionString
                    = Configuration["ConnectionStrings:CacheConnection"];
                opts.SchemaName = "dbo";
                opts.TableName = "DataCache";
            });
            services.AddResponseCaching();
            services.AddSingleton<IResponseFormatter, HtmlResponseFormatter>();

            services.AddDbContext<CalculationContext>(opts => {
                opts.UseSqlServer(Configuration["ConnectionStrings:CalcConnection"]);
            });
        }
```

```
    public void Configure(IApplicationBuilder app) {
        app.UseDeveloperExceptionPage();
        app.UseResponseCaching();
        app.UseStaticFiles();
        app.UseRouting();
        app.UseEndpoints(endpoints => {

            endpoints.MapEndpoint<SumEndpoint>("/sum/{count:int=1000000000}");

            endpoints.MapGet("/", async context => {
                await context.Response.WriteAsync("Hello World!");
            });
        });
    }
}
}
```

The AddDbContext method creates a service for an Entity Framework Core context class. The method receives an options object that is used to select the database provider, which is done with the UseSqlServer method. The IConfiguration service is used to get the connection string for the database, which is defined in Listing 17-23.

Listing 17-23. Defining a Connection String in the appsettings.json File in the Platform Folder

```
{
    "Location": {
        "CityName": "Buffalo"
    },
    "Logging": {
      "LogLevel": {
        "Default": "Information",
        "Microsoft": "Warning",
        "Microsoft.Hosting.Lifetime": "Information",
        "Microsoft.EntityFrameworkCore": "Information"
      }
    },
    "AllowedHosts": "*",
    "ConnectionStrings": {
        "CacheConnection": "Server=(localdb)\\MSSQLLocalDB;Database=CacheDb",
        "CalcConnection": "Server=(localdb)\\MSSQLLocalDB;Database=CalcDb"
    }
}
```

The listing also sets the logging level for the Microsoft.EntityFrameworkCore category, which will show the SQL statements that are used by Entity Framework Core to query the database.

■ **Tip** Set the MultipleActiveResultSets option to True for connection strings that will be used to make queries with multiple result sets. You can see an example of this option set in the connection strings for the SportsStore project in Chapter 7.

Creating and Applying the Database Migration

Entity Framework Core manages the relationship between data model classes and the database using a feature called *migrations*. When changes are made to the model classes, a new migration is created that modifies the database to match those changes. To create the initial migration, which will create a new database and prepare it to store Calculation objects, open a new PowerShell command prompt, navigate to the folder that contains the Platform.csproj file, and run the command shown in Listing 17-24.

Listing 17-24. Creating a Migration

```
dotnet ef migrations add Initial
```

The dotnet ef commands relate to Entity Framework Core. The command in Listing 17-24 creates a new migration named Initial, which is the name conventionally given to the first migration for a project. You will see that a Migrations folder has been added to the project and that it contains class files whose statements prepare the database so that it can store the objects in the data model. To apply the migration, run the command shown in Listing 17-25 in the Platform project folder.

Listing 17-25. Applying a Migration

```
dotnet ef database update
```

This command executes the commands in the migration created in Listing 17-24 and uses them to prepare the database, which you can see in the SQL statements written to the command prompt.

Seeding the Database

Most applications require some seed data, especially during development. Entity Framework Core does provide a database seeding feature, but it is of limited use for most projects because it doesn't allow data to be seeded where the database allocates unique keys to the objects it stores. This is an important feature in most data models because it means the application doesn't have to worry about allocating unique key values.

A more flexible approach is to use the regular Entity Framework Core features to add seed data to the database. Create a file called SeedData.cs in the Platform/Models folder with the code shown in Listing 17-26.

Listing 17-26. The Contents of the SeedData.cs File in the Platform/Models Folder

```
using Microsoft.EntityFrameworkCore;
using Microsoft.Extensions.Logging;
using System.Collections.Generic;
using System.Linq;

namespace Platform.Models {
    public class SeedData {
        private CalculationContext context;
        private ILogger<SeedData> logger;

        private static Dictionary<int, long> data
            = new Dictionary<int, long>() {
                {1, 1}, {2, 3}, {3, 6}, {4, 10}, {5, 15},
                {6, 21}, {7, 28}, {8, 36}, {9, 45}, {10, 55}
            };

        public SeedData(CalculationContext dataContext, ILogger<SeedData> log) {
            context = dataContext;
            logger = log;
        }

        public void SeedDatabase() {
            context.Database.Migrate();
            if (context.Calculations.Count() == 0) {
                logger.LogInformation("Preparing to seed database");
                context.Calculations!.AddRange(data.Select(kvp => new Calculaton() {
                    Count = kvp.Key, Result = kvp.Value
                }));
```

```
                context.SaveChanges();
                logger.LogInformation("Database seeded");
            } else {
                logger.LogInformation("Database not seeded");
            }
        }
    }
}
```

The SeedData class declares constructor dependencies on the CalculationContext and ILogger<T> types, which are used in the SeedDatabase method to prepare the database. The context's Database.Migrate method is used to apply any pending migrations to the database, and the Calculations property is used to store new data using the AddRange method, which accepts a sequence of Calculation objects.

The new objects are stored in the database using the SaveChanges method. To use the SeedData class, make the changes shown in Listing 17-27 to the Startup class.

Listing 17-27. Enabling Database Seeding in the Startup.cs File in the Platform Folder

```
using Microsoft.AspNetCore.Builder;
using Microsoft.AspNetCore.Http;
using Microsoft.Extensions.DependencyInjection;
using Microsoft.Extensions.Configuration;
using Platform.Services;
using Microsoft.EntityFrameworkCore;
using Platform.Models;
using Microsoft.Extensions.Hosting;
using Microsoft.AspNetCore.Hosting;

namespace Platform {
    public class Startup {

        public Startup(IConfiguration config) {
            Configuration = config;
        }

        private IConfiguration Configuration {get; set;}

        public void ConfigureServices(IServiceCollection services) {
            services.AddDistributedSqlServerCache(opts => {
                opts.ConnectionString
                    = Configuration["ConnectionStrings:CacheConnection"];
                opts.SchemaName = "dbo";
                opts.TableName = "DataCache";
            });
            services.AddResponseCaching();
            services.AddSingleton<IResponseFormatter, HtmlResponseFormatter>();

            services.AddDbContext<CalculationContext>(opts => {
                opts.UseSqlServer(Configuration["ConnectionStrings:CalcConnection"]);
            });
            services.AddTransient<SeedData>();
        }

        public void Configure(IApplicationBuilder app,
                IHostApplicationLifetime lifetime, IWebHostEnvironment env,
                SeedData seedData) {
            app.UseDeveloperExceptionPage();
            app.UseResponseCaching();
```

```
        app.UseStaticFiles();
        app.UseRouting();
        app.UseEndpoints(endpoints => {

            endpoints.MapEndpoint<SumEndpoint>("/sum/{count:int=1000000000}");

            endpoints.MapGet("/", async context => {
                await context.Response.WriteAsync("Hello World!");
            });
        });

        bool cmdLineInit = (Configuration["INITDB"] ?? "false") == "true";
        if (env.IsDevelopment() || cmdLineInit) {
            seedData.SeedDatabase();
            if (cmdLineInit) {
                lifetime.StopApplication();
            }
        }
    }
  }
 }
}
```

The statement in the ConfigureServices method creates a SeedData service. Although services are generally defined using interfaces, as described in Chapter 14, there are versions of the AddSingleton, AddScoped, and AddTransient methods that create a service using a single type argument. This makes it easy to instantiate a class that has constructor dependencies and allows the use of the service lifecycles. The statement in Listing 17-27 creates a transient service, which means that a new SeedData object will be created to resolve each dependency on the service.

The additions to the Configure method allow the database to be seeded in two situations. If the hosting environment is Development, the database will be seeded automatically as the application starts. It can also be useful to seed the database explicitly, especially when setting up the application for staging or production testing. This statement checks for a configuration setting named INITDB:

```
...
bool cmdLineInit = (Configuration["INITDB"] ?? "false") == "true";
...
```

This setting can be supplied on the command line to seed the database, after which the application is terminated using the IHostApplicationLifetime service. This is one of the less-used services, but it provides events that are triggered when the application is started and stopped, and it provides the StopApplication method, which terminates the application. To see the database, open a new PowerShell command prompt, navigate to the project folder, and run the command shown in Listing 17-28.

Listing 17-28. Seeding the Database

```
dotnet run INITDB=true
```

The application will start, and the database will be seeded with the results for the ten calculations defined by the SeedData class, after which the application will be terminated. During the seeding process, you will see the SQL statements that are sent to the database, which check to see whether there are any pending migrations, count the number of rows in the table used to store Calculation data, and, if the table is empty, add the seed data.

If you prefer not to use the command line, then you can seed the database by selecting Debug ➤ Start Without Debugging. As long as the environment is Development, the database will be seeded as part of the normal ASP.NET Core start sequence.

■ **Note** If you need to reset the database, you can use the dotnet ef database drop --force command. You can then use dotnet run INITDB=true to re-create and seed the database again.

Using Data in an Endpoint

Endpoints and middleware components access Entity Framework Core data by declaring a dependency on the context class and using its DbSet<T> properties to perform LINQ queries. The LINQ queries are translated into SQL and sent to the database. The tabular data received from the database is used to create data model objects that are used to produce responses. Listing 17-29 updates the SumEndpoint class to use Entity Framework Core.

Listing 17-29. Using a Database in the SumEndpoint.cs File in the Platform Folder

```
using Microsoft.AspNetCore.Http;
using System;
using System.Threading.Tasks;
using Microsoft.Extensions.Caching.Distributed;
using Microsoft.AspNetCore.Routing;
using Platform.Services;
using Platform.Models;
using System.Linq;

namespace Platform {

    public class SumEndpoint {

        public async Task Endpoint(HttpContext context,
                CalculationContext dataContext) {
            int count = int.Parse((string)context.Request.RouteValues["count"]);
            long total = dataContext.Calculations
                .FirstOrDefault(c => c.Count == count)?.Result ?? 0;
            if (total == 0) {
                for (int i = 1; i <= count; i++) {
                    total += i;
                }
                dataContext.Calculations!
                    .Add(new Calculaton() { Count = count, Result = total});
                await dataContext.SaveChangesAsync();
            }
            string totalString = $"({ DateTime.Now.ToLongTimeString() }) {total}";
            await context.Response.WriteAsync(
                $"({DateTime.Now.ToLongTimeString()}) Total for {count}"
                + $" values:\n{totalString}\n");
        }
    }
}
```

The endpoint uses the LINQ FirstOrDefault to search for a stored Calculation object for the calculation that has been requested like this:

```
...
dataContext.Calculations.FirstOrDefault(c => c.Count == count)?.Result ?? 0;
...
```

If an object has been stored, it is used to prepare the response. If not, then the calculation is performed, and a new Calculation object is stored by these statements:

```
...
dataContext.Calculations!.Add(new Calculaton() { Count = count, Result = total});
await dataContext.SaveChangesAsync();
...
```

The Add method is used to tell Entity Framework Core that the object should be stored, but the update isn't performed until the SaveChangesAsync method is called. To see the effect of the changes, restart ASP.NET Core MVC (without the INITDB argument if you are using the command line) and request the http://localhost:5000/sum/10 URL. This is one of the calculations with which the database has been seeded, and you will be able to see the query sent to the database in the logging messages produced by the application.

```
...
Executing DbCommand [Parameters=[@__count_0='?' (DbType = Int32)],
    CommandType='Text', CommandTimeout='30']
SELECT TOP(1) [c].[Id], [c].[Count], [c].[Result]
FROM [Calculations] AS [c]
WHERE ([c].[Count] = @__count_0) AND @__count_0 IS NOT NULL
...
```

If you request http://localhost:5000/sum/100, the database will be queried, but no result will be found. The endpoint performs the calculation and stores the result in the database before producing the result shown in Figure 17-6.

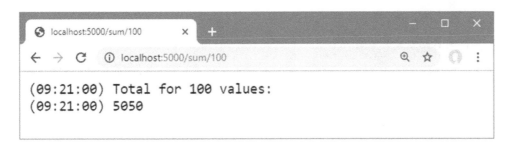

Figure 17-6. *Performing a calculation*

Once a result has been stored in the database, subsequent requests for the same URL will be satisfied using the stored data. You can see the SQL statement used to store the data in the logging output produced by Entity Framework Core.

```
...
Executing DbCommand [Parameters=[@p0='?' (DbType = Int32), @p1='?' (DbType = Int64)],
    CommandType='Text', CommandTimeout='30']
SET NOCOUNT ON;
INSERT INTO [Calculations] ([Count], [Result])
VALUES (@p0, @p1);
SELECT [Id]
FROM [Calculations]
WHERE @@ROWCOUNT = 1 AND [Id] = scope_identity();
...
```

▨ **Note** Notice that the data retrieved from the database is not cached and that each request leads to a new SQL query. Depending on the frequency and complexity of the queries you require, you may want to cache data values or responses using the techniques described earlier in the chapter.

Enabling Sensitive Data Logging

Entity Framework Core doesn't include parameter values in the logging messages it produces, which is why the logging output contains question marks, like this:

```
...
Executing DbCommand [Parameters=[@__count_0='?' (DbType = Int32)], CommandType='Text', CommandTimeout='30']
...
```

The data is omitted as a precaution to prevent sensitive data from being stored in logs. If you are having problems with queries and need to see the values sent to the database, then you can use the EnableSensitiveDataLogging method when configuring the database context, as shown in Listing 17-30.

Listing 17-30. Enabling Sensitive Data Logging in the Startup.cs File in the Platform Folder

```
...
services.AddDbContext<CalculationContext>(opts => {
    opts.UseSqlServer(Configuration["ConnectionStrings:CalcConnection"]);
    opts.EnableSensitiveDataLogging(true);
});
...
```

Restart ASP.NET Core MVC and request the http://localhost:5000/sum/100 URL again. When the request is handled, Entity Framework Core will include parameter values in the logging message it creates to show the SQL query, like this:

```
...
Executing DbCommand [Parameters=[@__count_0='100'], CommandType='Text',
    CommandTimeout='30']
SELECT TOP(1) [c].[Id], [c].[Count], [c].[Result]
FROM [Calculations] AS [c]
WHERE ([c].[Count] = @__count_0) AND @__count_0 IS NOT NULL
...
```

This is a feature that should be used with caution because logs are often accessible by people who would not usually have access to the sensitive data that applications handle, such as credit card numbers and account details.

Summary

In this chapter, I demonstrated the ASP.NET Core platform features that are useful for working with data. I showed you how to cache individual data values, both locally and in a shared database. I also showed you how to cache responses and how to read and write data in a database using Entity Framework Core. In Part 3 of this book, I explain how to build on the ASP.NET Core platform to create web applications.

PART III

ASP.NET Core Applications

CHAPTER 18

Creating the Example Project

In this chapter, you will create the example project used throughout this part of the book. The project contains a simple data model, a client-side package for formatting HTML content, and a simple request pipeline.

Creating the Project

Open a new PowerShell command prompt from the Windows Start menu and run the commands shown in Listing 18-1.

Tip You can download the example project for this chapter—and for all the other chapters in this book—from `https://github.com/apress/pro-asp.net-core-3`. See Chapter 1 for how to get help if you have problems running the examples.

Listing 18-1. Creating the Project

```
dotnet new globaljson --sdk-version 3.1.101 --output WebApp
dotnet new web --no-https --output WebApp --framework netcoreapp3.1
dotnet new sln -o WebApp

dotnet sln WebApp add WebApp
```

If you are using Visual Studio, open the WebApp.sln file in the WebApp folder. Select Project ➤ Platform Properties, navigate to the Debug page, and change the App URL field to `http://localhost:5000`, as shown in Figure 18-1. This changes the port that will be used to receive HTTP requests. Select File ➤ Save All to save the configuration changes.

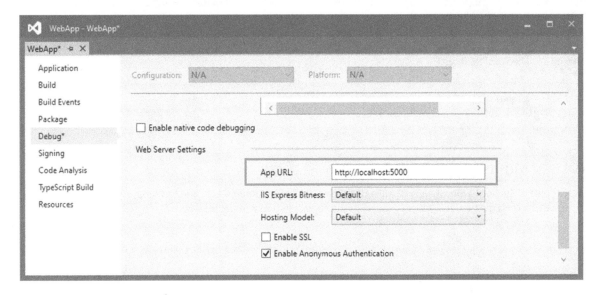

Figure 18-1. *Changing the HTTP port*

© Adam Freeman 2020

A. Freeman, *Pro ASP.NET Core 3*, https://doi.org/10.1007/978-1-4842-5440-0_18

If you are using Visual Studio Code, open the WebApp folder. Click the Yes button when prompted to add the assets required for building and debugging the project, as shown in Figure 18-2.

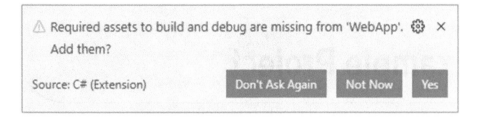

Figure 18-2. Adding project assets

Adding a Data Model

A data model helps demonstrate the different ways that web applications can be built using ASP.NET Core, showing how complex responses can be composed and how data can be submitted by the user. In the sections that follow, I create a simple data model and use it to create the database schema that will be used to store the application's data.

Adding NuGet Packages to the Project

The data model will use Entity Framework Core to store and query data in a SQL Server LocalDB database. To add the NuGet packages for Entity Framework Core, use a PowerShell command prompt to run the commands shown in Listing 18-2 in the WebApp project folder.

Listing 18-2. Adding Packages to the Project

```
dotnet add package Microsoft.EntityFrameworkCore.Design --version 3.1.1
dotnet add package Microsoft.EntityFrameworkCore.SqlServer --version 3.1.1
```

If you are using Visual Studio, you can add the packages by selecting Project ➤ Manage NuGet Packages. Take care to choose the correct version of the packages to add to the project.

If you have not followed the examples in earlier chapters, you will need to install the global tool package that is used to create and manage Entity Framework Core migrations. Run the commands shown in Listing 18-3 to remove any existing version of the package and install the version required for this book. (You can skip these commands if you installed this version of the tools package in earlier chapters.)

Listing 18-3. Installing a Global Tool Package

```
dotnet tool uninstall --global dotnet-ef
dotnet tool install --global dotnet-ef --version 3.1.1
```

Creating the Data Model

The data model for this part of the book will consist of three related classes: Product, Supplier, and Category. Create a new folder named Models and add to it a class file named Category.cs, with the contents shown in Listing 18-4.

Listing 18-4. The Contents of the Category.cs File in the Models Folder

```
using System.Collections.Generic;

namespace WebApp.Models {
    public class Category {

        public long CategoryId { get; set; }
        public string Name { get; set; }

        public IEnumerable<Product> Products { get; set; }
    }
}
```

Add a class called `Supplier.cs` to the `Models` folder and use it to define the class shown in Listing 18-5.

Listing 18-5. The Contents of the Supplier.cs File in the Models Folder

```
using System.Collections.Generic;

namespace WebApp.Models {
    public class Supplier {

        public long SupplierId { get; set; }
        public string Name { get; set; }
        public string City { get; set; }

        public IEnumerable<Product> Products { get; set; }
    }
}
```

Next, add a class named `Product.cs` to the `Models` folder and use it to define the class shown in Listing 18-6.

Listing 18-6. The Contents of the Product.cs File in the Models Folder

```
using System.ComponentModel.DataAnnotations.Schema;

namespace WebApp.Models {
    public class Product {

        public long ProductId { get; set; }

        public string Name { get; set; }
        [Column(TypeName = "decimal(8, 2)")]
        public decimal Price { get; set; }

        public long CategoryId { get; set; }
        public Category Category { get; set; }

        public long SupplierId { get; set; }
        public Supplier Supplier { get; set; }
    }
}
```

Each of the three data model classes defines a key property whose value will be allocated by the database when new objects are stored. There are also navigation properties that will be used to query for related data so that it will be possible to query for all the products in a specific category, for example.

The Price property has been decorated with the Column attribute, which specifies the precision of the values that will be stored in the database. There isn't a one-to-one mapping between C# and SQL numeric types, and the Column attribute tells Entity Framework Core which SQL type should be used in the database to store Price values. In this case, the decimal(8, 2) type will allow a total of eight digits, including two following the decimal point.

To create the Entity Framework Core context class that will provide access to the database, add a file called DataContext.cs to the Models folder and add the code shown in Listing 18-7.

Listing 18-7. The Contents of the DataContext.cs File in the Models Folder

```
using Microsoft.EntityFrameworkCore;

namespace WebApp.Models {
    public class DataContext: DbContext {

        public DataContext(DbContextOptions<DataContext> opts)
            : base(opts) { }

        public DbSet<Product> Products { get; set; }
        public DbSet<Category> Categories { get; set; }
        public DbSet<Supplier> Suppliers { get; set; }
    }
}
```

The context class defines properties that will be used to query the database for Product, Category, and Supplier data.

Preparing the Seed Data

Add a class called SeedData.cs to the Models folder and add the code shown in Listing 18-8 to define the seed data that will be used to populate the database.

Listing 18-8. The Contents of the SeedData.cs File in the Models Folder

```
using Microsoft.EntityFrameworkCore;
using System.Linq;

namespace WebApp.Models {
    public static class SeedData {

        public static void SeedDatabase(DataContext context) {
            context.Database.Migrate();
            if (context.Products.Count() == 0 && context.Suppliers.Count() == 0
                    && context.Categories.Count() == 0) {

                Supplier s1 = new Supplier
                    { Name = "Splash Dudes", City = "San Jose"};
                Supplier s2 = new Supplier
                    { Name = "Soccer Town", City = "Chicago"};
                Supplier s3 = new Supplier
                    { Name = "Chess Co", City = "New York"};

                Category c1 = new Category { Name = "Watersports" };
                Category c2 = new Category { Name = "Soccer" };
                Category c3 = new Category { Name = "Chess" };

                context.Products.AddRange(
                    new Product {  Name = "Kayak", Price = 275,
                        Category = c1, Supplier = s1},
```

```
                new Product {  Name = "Lifejacket", Price = 48.95m,
                    Category = c1, Supplier = s1},
                new Product {  Name = "Soccer Ball", Price = 19.50m,
                    Category = c2, Supplier = s2},
                new Product {  Name = "Corner Flags", Price = 34.95m,
                    Category = c2, Supplier = s2},
                new Product {  Name = "Stadium", Price = 79500,
                    Category = c2, Supplier = s2},
                new Product {  Name = "Thinking Cap", Price = 16,
                    Category = c3, Supplier = s3},
                new Product {  Name = "Unsteady Chair", Price = 29.95m,
                    Category = c3, Supplier = s3},
                new Product {  Name = "Human Chess Board", Price = 75,
                    Category = c3, Supplier = s3},
                new Product {  Name = "Bling-Bling King", Price = 1200,
                    Category = c3, Supplier = s3}
            );
            context.SaveChanges();
        }
    }
  }
}
```

The static SeedDatabase method ensures that all pending migrations have been applied to the database. If the database is empty, it is seeded with categories, suppliers, and products. Entity Framework Core will take care of mapping the objects into the tables in the database, and the key properties will be assigned automatically when the data is stored.

Configuring Entity Framework Core Services and Middleware

Make the changes to the Startup class shown in Listing 18-9, which configure Entity Framework Core and set up the DataContext services that will be used throughout this part of the book to access the database.

Listing 18-9. Preparing Services and Middleware in the Startup.cs File in the WebApp Folder

```
using System;
using System.Collections.Generic;
using System.Linq;
using System.Threading.Tasks;
using Microsoft.AspNetCore.Builder;
using Microsoft.AspNetCore.Hosting;
using Microsoft.AspNetCore.Http;
using Microsoft.Extensions.DependencyInjection;
using Microsoft.Extensions.Hosting;
using Microsoft.Extensions.Configuration;
using Microsoft.EntityFrameworkCore;
using WebApp.Models;

namespace WebApp {
    public class Startup {

        public Startup(IConfiguration config) {
            Configuration = config;
        }

        public IConfiguration Configuration { get; set; }
```

```
        public void ConfigureServices(IServiceCollection services) {
            services.AddDbContext<DataContext>(opts => {
                opts.UseSqlServer(Configuration[
                    "ConnectionStrings:ProductConnection"]);
                opts.EnableSensitiveDataLogging(true);
            });
        }

        public void Configure(IApplicationBuilder app, DataContext context) {

            app.UseDeveloperExceptionPage();
            app.UseRouting();

            app.UseEndpoints(endpoints => {
                endpoints.MapGet("/", async context => {
                    await context.Response.WriteAsync("Hello World!");
                });
            });

            SeedData.SeedDatabase(context);
        }
    }
}
```

To define the connection string that will be used for the application's data, add the configuration settings shown in Listing 18-10 in the appsettings.json file. The connection string should be entered on a single line.

Listing 18-10. Defining a Connection String in the appsettings.json File in the WebApp Folder

```
{
  "Logging": {
    "LogLevel": {
      "Default": "Information",
      "Microsoft": "Warning",
      "Microsoft.Hosting.Lifetime": "Information",
      "Microsoft.EntityFrameworkCore": "Information"
    }
  },
  "AllowedHosts": "*",
  "ConnectionStrings": {
    "ProductConnection": "Server=(localdb)\\MSSQLLocalDB;Database=Products;MultipleActiveResultSets=True"
  }
}
```

In addition to the connection string, Listing 18-10 increases the logging detail for Entity Framework Core so that the SQL queries sent to the database are logged.

Creating and Applying the Migration

To create the migration that will set up the database schema, use a PowerShell command prompt to run the command shown in Listing 18-11 in the WebApp project folder.

Listing 18-11. Creating an Entity Framework Core Migration

```
dotnet ef migrations add Initial
```

Once the migration has been created, apply it to the database using the command shown in Listing 18-12.

Listing 18-12. Applying the Migration to the Database

```
dotnet ef database update
```

The logging messages displayed by the application will show the SQL commands that are sent to the database.

■ **Note** If you need to reset the database, then run the `dotnet ef database drop --force` command and then the command in Listing 18-12.

Adding the CSS Framework

Later chapters will demonstrate the different ways that HTML responses can be generated. Run the commands shown in Listing 18-13 to remove any existing version of the LibMan package and install the version used in this book. (You can skip these commands if you installed this version of LibMan in earlier chapters.)

Listing 18-13. Installing the LibMan Tool Package

```
dotnet tool uninstall --global Microsoft.Web.LibraryManager.Cli
dotnet tool install --global Microsoft.Web.LibraryManager.Cli --version 2.0.96
```

To add the Bootstrap CSS framework so that the HTML responses can be styled, run the commands shown in Listing 18-14 in the WebApp project folder.

Listing 18-14. Installing the Bootstrap CSS Framework

```
libman init -p cdnjs
libman install twitter-bootstrap@4.3.1 -d wwwroot/lib/twitter-bootstrap
```

Configuring the Request Pipeline

To define a simple middleware component that will be used to make sure the example project has been set up correctly, add a class file called TestMiddleware.cs to the WebApp folder and add the code shown in Listing 18-15.

Listing 18-15. The Contents of the TestMiddleware.cs File in the WebApp Folder

```
using Microsoft.AspNetCore.Http;
using System.Linq;
using System.Threading.Tasks;
using WebApp.Models;

namespace WebApp {
    public class TestMiddleware {
        private RequestDelegate nextDelegate;

        public TestMiddleware(RequestDelegate next) {
            nextDelegate = next;
        }
```

```
        public async Task Invoke(HttpContext context, DataContext dataContext) {
            if (context.Request.Path == "/test") {
                await context.Response.WriteAsync(
                    $"There are {dataContext.Products.Count()} products\n");
                await context.Response.WriteAsync(
                    $"There are {dataContext.Categories.Count()} categories\n");
                await context.Response.WriteAsync(
                    $"There are {dataContext.Suppliers.Count()} suppliers\n");
            } else {
                await nextDelegate(context);
            }
        }
    }
}
```

Add the middleware component to the request pipeline in the Startup class, as shown in Listing 18-16.

Listing 18-16. Adding a Middleware Component in the Startup.cs File in the WebApp Folder

```
using System;
using System.Collections.Generic;
using System.Linq;
using System.Threading.Tasks;
using Microsoft.AspNetCore.Builder;
using Microsoft.AspNetCore.Hosting;
using Microsoft.AspNetCore.Http;
using Microsoft.Extensions.DependencyInjection;
using Microsoft.Extensions.Hosting;
using Microsoft.Extensions.Configuration;
using Microsoft.EntityFrameworkCore;
using WebApp.Models;

namespace WebApp {
    public class Startup {

        public Startup(IConfiguration config) {
            Configuration = config;
        }

        public IConfiguration Configuration { get; set; }

        public void ConfigureServices(IServiceCollection services) {
            services.AddDbContext<DataContext>(opts => {
                opts.UseSqlServer(Configuration[
                    "ConnectionStrings:ProductConnection"]);
                opts.EnableSensitiveDataLogging(true);
            });
        }

        public void Configure(IApplicationBuilder app, DataContext context) {

            app.UseDeveloperExceptionPage();
            app.UseStaticFiles();
            app.UseRouting();
            app.UseMiddleware<TestMiddleware>();
            app.UseEndpoints(endpoints => {
                endpoints.MapGet("/", async context => {
                    await context.Response.WriteAsync("Hello World!");
```

```
            });
        });

        SeedData.SeedDatabase(context);
    }
}
}
```

Running the Example Application

Start the application, either by selecting Start Without Debugging or Run Without Debugging from the Debug menu or by running the command shown in Listing 18-17 in the WebApp project folder.

Listing 18-17. Running the Example Application

```
dotnet run
```

Use a new browser tab and request http://localhost:5000/test, and you will see the response shown in Figure 18-3.

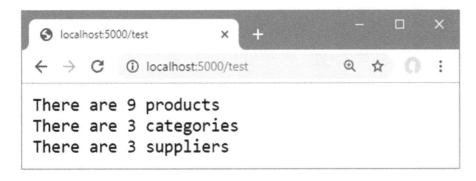

Figure 18-3. Running the example application

Summary

In this chapter, I created the example application that is used throughout this part of the book. The project was created with the Empty template, contains a data model that relies on Entity Framework Core, and is configured with a request pipeline that contains a simple test middleware component. In the next chapter, I show you how to create web services using ASP.NET Core.

CHAPTER 19

■ ■ ■

Creating RESTful Web Services

Web services accept HTTP requests and generate responses that contain data. In this chapter, I explain how the features provided by the MVC Framework, which is an integral part of ASP.NET Core, can be used to build on the capabilities described in Part 2 to create web services.

The nature of web services means that some of the examples in this chapter are tested using command-line tools provided by PowerShell, and it is important to enter the commands exactly as shown. Chapter 20 introduces more sophisticated tools for working with web services, but the command-line approach is better suited to following examples in a book chapter, even if they can feel a little awkward as you type them in. Table 19-1 puts RESTful web services in context.

Table 19-1. *Putting RESTful Web Services in Context*

Question	Answer
What are they?	Web services provide access to an application's data, typically expressed in the JSON format.
Why are they useful?	Web services are most often used to provide rich client-side applications with data.
How are they used?	The combination of the URL and an HTTP method describes an operation that is handled by an action method defined by an ASP.NET Core controller.
Are there any pitfalls or limitations?	There is no widespread agreement about how web services should be implemented, and care must be taken to produce just the data the client expects.
Are there any alternatives?	There are a number of different approaches to providing clients with data, although RESTful web services are the most common.

Table 19-2 summarizes the chapter.

Table 19-2. *Chapter Summary*

Problem	Solution	Listing
Defining a web service	Create a controller with action methods that correspond to the operations that you require	1–14
Generating data sequences over time	Use the IAsyncEnumerable<T> response, which will prevent the request thread from blocking while results are generated.	15
Preventing request values being used for sensitive data properties	Use a binding target to restrict the model binding process to only safe properties	16–18
Expressing nondata outcomes	Use action results to describe the response that ASP.NET Core should send	19–24
Validating data	Use the ASP.NET Core model binding and model validation features	25–27
Automatically validating requests	Use the ApiController attribute	28
Omitting null values from data responses	Map the data objects to filter out properties or configure the JSON serializer to ignore null properties	29–31

© Adam Freeman 2020

A. Freeman, *Pro ASP.NET Core 3*, https://doi.org/10.1007/978-1-4842-5440-0_19

Preparing for This Chapter

In this chapter, I continue to use the WebApp project created in Chapter 18. To prepare for this chapter, drop the database by opening a new PowerShell command prompt, navigating to the folder that contains the WebApp.csproj file, and running the command shown in Listing 19-1.

■ **Tip** You can download the example project for this chapter—and for all the other chapters in this book—from https://github. com/apress/pro-asp.net-core-3. See Chapter 1 for how to get help if you have problems running the examples.

Listing 19-1. Dropping the Database

```
dotnet ef database drop --force
```

Start the application by selecting Start Without Debugging or Run Without Debugging from the Debug menu or by running the command shown in Listing 19-2 in the project folder.

Listing 19-2. Starting the Example Application

```
dotnet run
```

Request the URL http://localhost:5000/test once ASP.NET Core has started, and you will see the response shown in Figure 19-1.

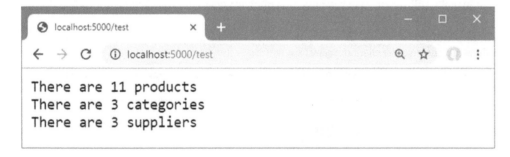

Figure 19-1. *Running the example application*

Understanding RESTful Web Services

Web services respond to HTTP requests with data that can be consumed by clients, such as JavaScript applications. There are no hard-and-fast rules for how web services should work, but the most common approach is to adopt the Representational State Transfer (REST) pattern. There is no authoritative specification for REST, and there is no consensus about what constitutes a RESTful web service, but there are some common themes that are widely used for web services. The lack of a detailed specification leads to endless disagreement about what REST means and how RESTful web services should be created, all of which can be safely ignored if the web services you create work for your projects.

Understanding Request URLs and Methods

The core premise of REST—and the only aspect for which there is broad agreement—is that a web service defines an API through a combination of URLs and HTTP methods such as GET and POST, which are also known as the HTTP *verbs*. The method specifies the type of operation, while the URL specifies the data object or objects that the operation applies to.

As an example, here is a URL that might identify a `Product` object in the example application:

```
/api/products/1
```

This URL may identify the `Product` object that has a value of 1 for its `ProductId` property. The URL identifies the `Product`, but it is the HTTP method that specifies what should be done with it. Table 19-3 lists the HTTP methods that are commonly used in web services and the operations they conventionally represent.

Table 19-3. *HTTP Methods and Operations*

HTTP Method	Description
GET	This method is used to retrieve one or more data objects.
POST	This method is used to create a new object.
PUT	This method is used to update an existing object.
PATCH	This method is used to update part of an existing object.
DELETE	This method is used to delete an object.

Understanding JSON

Most RESTful web services format the response data using the JavaScript Object Notation (JSON) format. JSON has become popular because it is simple and easily consumed by JavaScript clients. JSON is described in detail at `www.json.org`, but you don't need to understand every aspect of JSON to create web services because ASP.NET Core provides all the features required to create JSON responses.

UNDERSTANDING THE ALTERNATIVES TO RESTFUL WEB SERVICES

REST isn't the only way to design web services, and there are some popular alternatives. *GraphQL* is most closely associated with the React JavaScript framework, but it can be used more widely. Unlike REST web services, which provide specific queries through individual combinations of a URL and an HTTP method, GraphQL provides access to all an application's data and lets clients query for just the data they require in the format they require. GraphQL can be complex to set up—and can require more sophisticated clients—but the result is a more flexible web service that puts the developers of the client in control of the data they consume. GraphQL isn't supported directly by ASP.NET Core, but there are .NET implementations available. See `https://graphql.org` for more detail.

A new alternative is gRPC, a full remote procedure call framework that focuses on speed and efficiency. At the time of writing, gRPC cannot be used in web browsers, such as by the Angular or React framework, because browsers don't provide the fine-grained access that gRPC requires to formulate its HTTP requests.

Creating a Web Service Using a Custom Endpoint

As you learn about the facilities that ASP.NET Core provides for web services, it can be easy to forget they are built on the features described in Part 2. To create a simple web service, add a file named WebServiceEndpoint.cs to the WebApp folder and use it to define the class shown in Listing 19-3.

Listing 19-3. The Contents of the WebServiceEndpoint.cs File in the WebApp Folder

```
using Microsoft.AspNetCore.Http;
using Microsoft.AspNetCore.Routing;
using Microsoft.Extensions.DependencyInjection;
using System.Collections.Generic;
```

```
using System.Text.Json;
using WebApp.Models;

namespace Microsoft.AspNetCore.Builder {

    public static class WebServiceEndpoint {
        private static string BASEURL = "api/products";

        public static void MapWebService(this IEndpointRouteBuilder app) {

            app.MapGet($"{BASEURL}/{{id}}", async context => {
                long key = long.Parse(context.Request.RouteValues["id"] as string);
                DataContext data = context.RequestServices.GetService<DataContext>();
                Product p = data.Products.Find(key);
                if (p == null) {
                    context.Response.StatusCode = StatusCodes.Status404NotFound;
                } else {
                    context.Response.ContentType = "application/json";
                    await context.Response
                        .WriteAsync(JsonSerializer.Serialize<Product>(p));
                }
            });

            app.MapGet(BASEURL, async context => {
                DataContext data = context.RequestServices.GetService<DataContext>();
                context.Response.ContentType = "application/json";
                await context.Response.WriteAsync(JsonSerializer
                    .Serialize<IEnumerable<Product>>(data.Products));
            });

            app.MapPost(BASEURL, async context => {
                DataContext data = context.RequestServices.GetService<DataContext>();
                Product p = await
                    JsonSerializer.DeserializeAsync<Product>(context.Request.Body);
                await data.AddAsync(p);
                await data.SaveChangesAsync();
                context.Response.StatusCode = StatusCodes.Status200OK;
            });
        }
    }
}
```

The MapWebService extension method creates three routes that form a basic web service using only the features that have been described in earlier chapters. The routes match URLs that start with /api, which is the conventional URL prefix for web services. The endpoint for the first route receives a value from a segment variable that is used to locate a single Product object in the database. The endpoint for the second route retrieves all the Product objects in the database. The third endpoint handles POST requests and reads the request body to get a JSON representation of a new object to add to the database.

There are better ASP.NET Core features for creating web services, which you will see shortly, but the code in Listing 19-3 shows how the HTTP method and the URL can be combined to describe an operation. Listing 19-4 uses the MapWebService extension method to add the endpoints to the example application's routing configuration.

Listing 19-4. Adding Routes in the Startup.cs File in the WebApp Folder

```
...
public void Configure(IApplicationBuilder app, DataContext context) {
    app.UseDeveloperExceptionPage();
    app.UseRouting();
    app.UseMiddleware<TestMiddleware>();
```

```
app.UseEndpoints(endpoints => {
    endpoints.MapGet("/", async context => {
        await context.Response.WriteAsync("Hello World!");
    });
    endpoints.MapWebService();
});
    SeedData.SeedDatabase(context);
}
...
```

To test the web service, restart ASP.NET Core and request http://localhost:5000/api/products/1. The request will be matched by the first route defined in Listing 19-4 and will produce the response shown on the left of Figure 19-2. Next, request http://localhost:5000/api/products, which will be matched by the second route and produce the response shown on the right of Figure 19-2.

■ **Note**   The responses shown in the figure contain null values for the Supplier and Category properties because the LINQ queries do not include related data. See Chapter 20 for details.

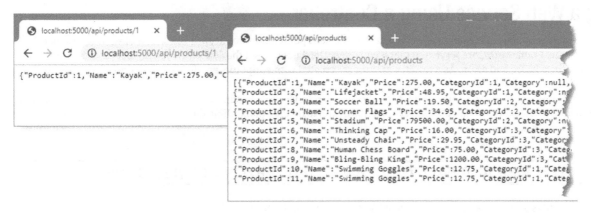

Figure 19-2. *Web service response*

Testing the third route requires a different approach because it isn't possible to send HTTP POST requests using the browser. Open a new PowerShell command prompt and run the command shown in Listing 19-5. It is important to enter the command exactly as shown because the Invoke-RestMethod command is fussy about the syntax of its arguments.

■ **Tip**   You may receive an error when you use the Invoke-RestMethod or Invoke-WebRequest command to test the examples in this chapter if you have not performed the initial setup for Microsoft Edge or Internet Explorer. The problem can be fixed by running IE and selecting the initial configurations you require.

Listing 19-5. Sending a POST Request

```
Invoke-RestMethod http://localhost:5000/api/products -Method POST -Body  (@{ Name="Swimming Goggles";
Price=12.75; CategoryId=1; SupplierId=1} | ConvertTo-Json) -ContentType "application/json"
```

The command sends an HTTP POST command that is matched by the third route defined in Listing 19-5. The body of the request is a JSON-formatted object that is parsed to create a Product, which is then stored in the database. The JSON object included in the request contains values for the Name, Price, CategoryId, and SupplierId properties. The unique key for the object, which is associated with the ProductId property, is assigned by the database when the object is stored. Use the browser to request the http://localhost:5000/api/products URL again, and you will see that the JSON response contains the new object, as shown in Figure 19-3.

Figure 19-3. *Storing new data using the web service*

Creating a Web Service Using a Controller

The drawback of using endpoints to create a web service is that each endpoint has to duplicate a similar set of steps to produce a response: get the Entity Framework Core service so that it can query the database, set the Content-Type header for the response, serialize the objects into JSON, and so on. As a result, web services created with endpoints are difficult to understand and awkward to maintain.

A more elegant approach is to use a *controller*, which allows a web service to be defined in a single class. Controllers are part of the MVC Framework, which builds on the ASP.NET Core platform and takes care of handling data in the same way that endpoints take care of processing URLs.

THE RISE AND FALL OF THE MVC PATTERN IN ASP.NET CORE

The MVC Framework is an implementation of the Model-View-Controller pattern, which describes one way to structure an application. The examples in this chapter use two of the three pillars of the pattern: a data model (the *M* in MVC) and controllers (the *C* in MVC). Chapter 21 provides the missing piece and explains how views can be used to create HTML responses using Razor.

The MVC pattern was an important step in the evolution of ASP.NET and allowed the platform to break away from the Web Forms model that predated it. Web Forms applications were easy to start but quickly became difficult to manage and hid details of HTTP requests and responses from the developer. By contrast, the adherence to the MVC pattern provided a strong and scalable structure for applications written with the MVC Framework and hid nothing from the developer. The MVC Framework revitalized ASP.NET and provided the foundation for what became ASP.NET Core, which dropped support for Web Forms and focused solely on using the MVC pattern.

As ASP.NET Core evolved, other styles of web application have been embraced, and the MVC Framework is only one of the ways that applications can be created. That doesn't undermine the utility of the MVC pattern, but it doesn't have the central role that it used to in ASP.NET Core development, and the features that used to be unique to the MVC Framework can now be accessed through other approaches, such as Razor Pages and Blazor.

A consequence of this evolution is that understanding the MVC pattern is no longer a prerequisite for effective ASP.NET Core development. If you are interested in understanding the MVC pattern, then https://en.wikipedia.org/wiki/Model-view-controller is a good place to start. But for this book, understanding how the features provided by the MVC Framework build on the ASP.NET Core platform is all the context that is required.

Enabling the MVC Framework

The first step to creating a web service using a controller is to configure the MVC framework, which requires a service and an endpoint, as shown in Listing 19-6.

Listing 19-6. Enabling the MVC Framework in the Startup.cs File in the WebApp Folder

```
using System;
using System.Collections.Generic;
using System.Linq;
using System.Threading.Tasks;
using Microsoft.AspNetCore.Builder;
using Microsoft.AspNetCore.Hosting;
using Microsoft.AspNetCore.Http;
using Microsoft.Extensions.DependencyInjection;
using Microsoft.Extensions.Hosting;
using Microsoft.Extensions.Configuration;
using Microsoft.EntityFrameworkCore;
using WebApp.Models;

namespace WebApp {
    public class Startup {

        public Startup(IConfiguration config) {
            Configuration = config;
        }

        public IConfiguration Configuration { get; set; }

        public void ConfigureServices(IServiceCollection services) {
            services.AddDbContext<DataContext>(opts => {
                opts.UseSqlServer(Configuration[
                    "ConnectionStrings:ProductConnection"]);
                opts.EnableSensitiveDataLogging(true);
            });

            services.AddControllers();
        }

        public void Configure(IApplicationBuilder app, DataContext context) {
            app.UseDeveloperExceptionPage();
            app.UseRouting();
            app.UseMiddleware<TestMiddleware>();
            app.UseEndpoints(endpoints => {
                endpoints.MapGet("/", async context => {
                    await context.Response.WriteAsync("Hello World!");
                });
                //endpoints.MapWebService();
                endpoints.MapControllers();
            });
            SeedData.SeedDatabase(context);
        }
    }
}
```

The `AddControllers` method defines the services that are required by the MVC framework, and the `MapControllers` method defines routes that will allow controllers to handle requests. You will see other methods used to configure the MVC framework used in later chapters, which provide access to different features, but the methods used in Listing 19-6 are the ones that configure the MVC framework for web services.

Creating a Controller

Controllers are classes whose methods, known as *actions,* can process HTTP requests. Controllers are discovered automatically when the application is started. The basic discovery process is simple: any public class whose name ends with `Controller` is a controller, and any `public` method a controller defines is an action. To demonstrate how simple a controller can be, create the `WebApp/Controllers` folder and add to it a file named `ProductsController.cs` with the code shown in Listing 19-7.

■ **Tip** Controllers are conventionally defined in the `Controllers` folder, but they can be defined anywhere in the project, and they will still be discovered.

Listing 19-7. The Contents of the ProductsController.cs File in the Controllers Folder

```
using Microsoft.AspNetCore.Mvc;
using System.Collections.Generic;
using WebApp.Models;

namespace WebApp.Controllers {

    [Route("api/[controller]")]
    public class ProductsController: ControllerBase {

        [HttpGet]
        public IEnumerable<Product> GetProducts() {
            return new Product[] {
                new Product() { Name = "Product #1" },
                new Product() { Name = "Product #2" },
            };
        }

        [HttpGet("{id}")]
        public Product GetProduct() {
            return new Product() {
                ProductId = 1, Name = "Test Product"
            };
        }
    }
}
```

The `ProductsController` class meets the criteria that the MVC framework looks for in a controller. It defines public methods named `GetProducts` and `GetProduct`, which will be treated as actions.

Understanding the Base Class

Controllers are derived from the `ControllerBase` class, which provides access to features provided by the MVC Framework and the underlying ASP.NET Core platform. Table 19-4 describes the most useful properties provided by the `ControllerBase` class.

■ **Note** Although controllers are typically derived from the `ControllerBase` or `Controller` classes (described in Chapter 21), this is just convention, and the MVC Framework will accept any class whose name ends with `Controller`, that is derived from a class whose name ends with `Controller`, or that has been decorated with the `Controller` attribute. Apply the `NonController` attribute to classes that meet these criteria but that should not receive HTTP requests.

Table 19-4. Useful ControllerBase Properties

Name	Description
HttpContext	This property returns the HttpContext object for the current request.
ModelState	This property returns details of the data validation process, as demonstrated in the "Validating Data" section later in the chapter and described in detail in Chapter 29.
Request	This property returns the HttpRequest object for the current request.
Response	This property returns the HttpResponse object for the current response.
RouteData	This property returns the data extracted from the request URL by the routing middleware, as described in Chapter 13.
User	This property returns an object that describes the user associated with the current request, as described in Chapter 38.

A new instance of the controller class is created each time one of its actions is used to handle a request, which means the properties in Table 19-4 describe only the current request.

Understanding the Controller Attributes

The HTTP methods and URLs supported by the action methods are determined by the combination of attributes that are applied to the controller. The URL for the controller is specified by the Route attribute, which is applied to the class, like this:

```
...
[Route("api/[controller]")]
public class ProductsController: ControllerBase {
...
```

The [controller] part of the attribute argument is used to derive the URL from the name of the controller class. The Controller part of the class name is dropped, which means that the attribute in Listing 19-7 sets the URL for the controller to /api/products.

Each action is decorated with an attribute that specifies the HTTP method that it supports, like this:

```
...
[HttpGet]
public Product[] GetProducts() {
...
```

The name given to action methods doesn't matter in controllers used for web services. There are other uses for controllers, described in Chapter 21, where the name does matter, but for web services, it is the HTTP method attributes and the route patterns that are important.

The HttpGet attribute tells the MVC framework that the GetProducts action method will handle HTTP GET requests. Table 19-5 describes the full set of attributes that can be applied to actions to specify HTTP methods.

Table 19-5. The HTTP Method Attributes

Name	Description
HttpGet	This attribute specifies that the action can be invoked only by HTTP requests that use the GET verb.
HttpPost	This attribute specifies that the action can be invoked only by HTTP requests that use the POST verb.
HttpDelete	This attribute specifies that the action can be invoked only by HTTP requests that use the DELETE verb.
HttpPut	This attribute specifies that the action can be invoked only by HTTP requests that use the PUT verb.
HttpPatch	This attribute specifies that the action can be invoked only by HTTP requests that use the PATCH verb.
HttpHead	This attribute specifies that the action can be invoked only by HTTP requests that use the HEAD verb.
AcceptVerbs	This attribute is used to specify multiple HTTP verbs.

The attributes applied to actions to specify HTTP methods can also be used to build on the controller's base URL.

```
...
[HttpGet("{id}")]
public Product GetProduct() {
...
```

This attribute tells the MVC framework that the GetProduct action method handles GET requests for the URL pattern api/products/{id}. During the discovery process, the attributes applied to the controller are used to build the set of URL patterns that the controller can handle, summarized in Table 19-6.

■ **Tip**   When writing a controller, it is important to ensure that each combination of the HTTP method and URL pattern that the controller supports is mapped to only one action method. An exception will be thrown when a request can be handled by multiple actions because the MVC Framework is unable to decide which to use.

Table 19-6. *The URL Patterns*

HTTP Method	URL Pattern	Action Method Name
GET	api/products	GetProducts
GET	api/products/{id}	GetProduct

You can see how the combination of attributes is equivalent to the MapGet methods I used for the same URL patterns when I used endpoints to create a web service earlier in the chapter.

GET AND POST: PICK THE RIGHT ONE

The rule of thumb is that GET requests should be used for all read-only information retrieval, while POST requests should be used for any operation that changes the application state. In standards-compliance terms, GET requests are for *safe* interactions (having no side effects besides information retrieval), and POST requests are for *unsafe* interactions (making a decision or changing something). These conventions are set by the World Wide Web Consortium (W3C), at www.w3.org/Protocols/rfc2616/rfc2616-sec9.html.

GET requests are *addressable*: all the information is contained in the URL, so it's possible to bookmark and link to these addresses. Do not use GET requests for operations that change state. Many web developers learned this the hard way in 2005 when Google Web Accelerator was released to the public. This application prefetched all the content linked from each page, which is legal within the HTTP because GET requests should be safe. Unfortunately, many web developers had ignored the HTTP conventions and placed simple links to "delete item" or "add to shopping cart" in their applications. Chaos ensued.

Understanding Action Method Results

One of the main benefits provided by controllers is that the MVC Framework takes care of setting the response headers and serializing the data objects that are sent to the client. You can see this in the results defined by the action methods, like this:

```
...
[HttpGet("{id}")]
public Product GetProduct() {
...
```

When I used an endpoint, I had to work directly with the JSON serializer to create a string that can be written to the response and set the Content-Type header to tell the client that the response contained JSON data. The action method returns a Product object, which is processed automatically.

To see how the results from the action methods are handled, restart ASP.NET Core and request `http://localhost:5000/api/products`, which will produce the response shown on the left of Figure 19-4, which is produced by the `GetProducts` action method. Next, request `http://localhost:5000/api/products/1`, which will be handled by the `GetProduct` method and produce the result shown on the right side of Figure 19-4.

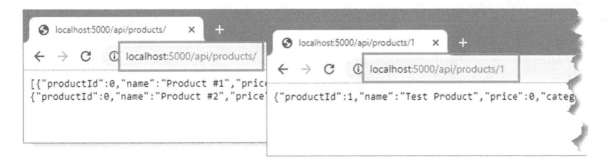

Figure 19-4. *Using a controller*

Using Dependency Injection in Controllers

A new instance of the controller class is created each time one of its actions is used to handle a request. The application's services are used to resolve any dependencies the controller declares through its constructor and any dependencies that the action method defines. This allows services that are required by all actions to be handled through the constructor while still allowing individual actions to declare their own dependencies, as shown in Listing 19-8.

Listing 19-8. Using Services in the ProductsController.cs File in the Controllers Folder

```
using Microsoft.AspNetCore.Mvc;
using WebApp.Models;
using System.Collections.Generic;
using Microsoft.Extensions.Logging;
using System.Linq;

namespace WebApp.Controllers {

    [Route("api/[controller]")]
    public class ProductsController: ControllerBase {
        private DataContext context;

        public ProductsController(DataContext ctx) {
            context = ctx;
        }

        [HttpGet]
        public IEnumerable<Product> GetProducts() {
            return context.Products;
        }

        [HttpGet("{id}")]
        public Product GetProduct([FromServices]
                ILogger<ProductsController> logger) {
            logger.LogDebug("GetProduct Action Invoked");
            return context.Products.FirstOrDefault();
        }
    }
}
```

The constructor declares a dependency on the DataContext service, which provides access to the application's data. The services are resolved using the request scope, which means that a controller can request all services, without needing to understand their lifecycle.

THE ENTITY FRAMEWORK CORE CONTEXT SERVICE LIFECYCLE

A new Entity Framework Core context object is created for each controller. Some developers will try to refuse context objects as a perceived performance improvement, but this causes problems because data from one query can affect subsequent queries, as described in Chapter 20. Behind the scenes, Entity Framework Core efficiently manages the connections to the database, and you should not try to store or reuse context objects outside of the controller for which they are created.

The GetProducts action method uses the DataContext to request all the Product objects in the database. The GetProduct method also uses the DataContext service, but it declares a dependency on ILogger<T>, which is the logging service described in Chapter 15. Dependencies that are declared by action methods must be decorated with the FromServices attribute, like this:

```
...
public Product GetProduct([FromServices] ILogger<ProductsController> logger) {
...
```

By default, the MVC Framework attempts to find values for action method parameters from the request URL, and the FromServices attribute overrides this behavior. To see the use of the services in the controller, restart ASP.NET Core and request http://localhost:5000/api/products/1, which will produce the response shown in Figure 19-5. You will also see the following logging message in the application's output:

```
...
dbug: WebApp.Controllers.ProductsController[0]
      GetProduct Action Invoked
...
```

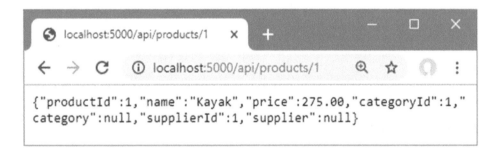

Figure 19-5. *Using services in a controller*

■ **Caution**   One consequence of the controller lifecycle is that you can't rely on side effects caused by methods being called in a specific sequence. So, for example, I can't assign the ILogger<T> object received by the GetProduct method in Listing 19-8 to a property that can be read by the GetProducts action in later requests. Each controller object is used to handle one request, and only one action method will be invoked by the MVC Framework for each object.

Using Model Binding to Access Route Data

In the previous section, I noted that the MVC Framework uses the request URL to find values for action method parameters, a process known as *model binding*. Model binding is described in detail in Chapter 28, but Listing 19-9 shows a simple example.

Listing 19-9. Using Model Binding in the ProductsController.cs File in the Controllers Folder

```
using Microsoft.AspNetCore.Mvc;
using WebApp.Models;
using System.Collections.Generic;
using Microsoft.Extensions.Logging;
using System.Linq;

namespace WebApp.Controllers {

    [Route("api/[controller]")]
    public class ProductsController: ControllerBase {
        private DataContext context;

        public ProductsController(DataContext ctx) {
            context = ctx;
        }

        [HttpGet]
        public IEnumerable<Product> GetProducts() {
            return context.Products;
        }

        [HttpGet("{id}")]
        public Product GetProduct(long id,
                [FromServices] ILogger<ProductsController> logger) {
            logger.LogDebug("GetProduct Action Invoked");
            return context.Products.Find(id);
        }
    }
}
```

The listing adds a `long` parameter named `id` to the `GetProduct` method. When the action method is invoked, the MVC Framework injects the value with the same name from the routing data, automatically converting it to a `long` value, which is used by the action to query the database using the LINQ `Find` method. The result is that the action method responds to the URL, which you can see by restarting ASP.NET Core and requesting `http://localhost:5000/api/products/5`, which will produce the response shown in Figure 19-6.

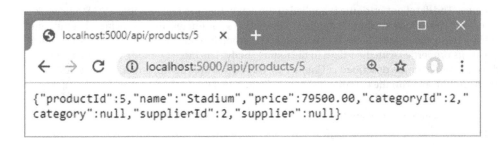

Figure 19-6. *Using model binding in an action*

Model Binding from the Request Body

The model binding feature can also be used on the data in the request body, which allows clients to send data that is easily received by an action method. Listing 19-10 adds a new action method that responds to POST requests and allows clients to provide a JSON representation of the `Product` object in the request body.

Listing 19-10. Adding an Action in the ProductsController.cs File in the Controllers Folder

```
using Microsoft.AspNetCore.Mvc;
using WebApp.Models;
using System.Collections.Generic;
using Microsoft.Extensions.Logging;
using System.Linq;

namespace WebApp.Controllers {

    [Route("api/[controller]")]
    public class ProductsController: ControllerBase {
        private DataContext context;

        public ProductsController(DataContext ctx) {
            context = ctx;
        }

        [HttpGet]
        public IEnumerable<Product> GetProducts() {
            return context.Products;
        }

        [HttpGet("{id}")]
        public Product GetProduct(long id,
                [FromServices] ILogger<ProductsController> logger) {
            logger.LogDebug("GetProduct Action Invoked");
            return context.Products.Find(id);
        }

        [HttpPost]
        public void SaveProduct([FromBody]Product product) {
            context.Products.Add(product);
            context.SaveChanges();
        }
    }
}
```

The new action relies on two attributes. The HttpPost attribute is applied to the action method and tells the MVC Framework that the action can process POST requests. The FromBody attribute is applied to the action's parameter, and it specifies that the value for this parameter should be obtained by parsing the request body. When the action method is invoked, the MVC Framework will create a new Product object and populate its properties with the values in the request body. The model binding process can be complex and is usually combined with data validation, as described in Chapter 29, but for a simple demonstration, restart ASP.NET Core, open a new PowerShell command prompt, and run the command shown in Listing 19-11.

Listing 19-11. Sending a POST Request to the Example Application

```
Invoke-RestMethod http://localhost:5000/api/products -Method POST -Body  (@{ Name="Soccer Boots"; Price=89.99;
CategoryId=2; SupplierId=2} | ConvertTo-Json) -ContentType "application/json"
```

Once the command has executed, use a web browser to request http://localhost:5000/api/products, and you will see the new object that has been stored in the database, as shown in Figure 19-7.

```
[{"productId":1,"name":"Kayak","price":275.00,"categoryId":1,"category":
{"productId":2,"name":"Lifejacket","price":48.95,"categoryId":1,"category
{"productId":3,"name":"Soccer Ball","price":19.50,"categoryId":2,"categor
{"productId":4,"name":"Corner Flags","price":34.95,"categoryId":2,"catego
{"productId":5,"name":"Stadium","price":79500.00,"categoryId":2,"categor
{"productId":6,"name":"Thinking Cap","price":16.00,"categoryId":3,"categ
{"productId":7,"name":"Unsteady Chair","price":29.95,"categoryId":3,"cate
{"productId":8,"name":"Human Chess Board","price":75.00,"categoryId":3,"
{"productId":9,"name":"Bling-Bling King","price":1200.00,"categoryId":3,"
{"productId":10,"name":"Swimming Goggles","price":12.75,"categoryId":1,"c
{"productId":11,"name":"Soccer Boots","price":89.99,"categoryId":2,"cate
```

Figure 19-7. *Storing new data using a controller*

Adding Additional Actions

Now that the basic features are in place, I can add actions that allow clients to replace and delete Product objects using the HTTP PUT and DELETE methods, as shown in Listing 19-12.

Listing 19-12. Adding Actions in the ProductsController.cs File in the Controllers Folder

```csharp
using Microsoft.AspNetCore.Mvc;
using WebApp.Models;
using System.Collections.Generic;
using Microsoft.Extensions.Logging;
using System.Linq;

namespace WebApp.Controllers {

    [Route("api/[controller]")]
    public class ProductsController: ControllerBase {
        private DataContext context;

        public ProductsController(DataContext ctx) {
            context = ctx;
        }

        [HttpGet]
        public IEnumerable<Product> GetProducts() {
            return context.Products;
        }

        [HttpGet("{id}")]
        public Product GetProduct(long id,
                [FromServices] ILogger<ProductsController> logger) {
            logger.LogDebug("GetProduct Action Invoked");
            return context.Products.Find(id);
        }
```

```
        [HttpPost]
        public void SaveProduct([FromBody]Product product) {
            context.Products.Add(product);
            context.SaveChanges();
        }

        [HttpPut]
        public void UpdateProduct([FromBody]Product product) {
            context.Products.Update(product);
            context.SaveChanges();
        }

        [HttpDelete("{id}")]
        public void DeleteProduct(long id) {
            context.Products.Remove(new Product() { ProductId = id });
            context.SaveChanges();
        }
    }
}
```

The UpdateProduct action is similar to the SaveProduct action and uses model binding to receive a Product object from the request body. The DeleteProduct action receives a primary key value from the URL and uses it to create a Product that has a value only for the ProductId property, which is required because Entity Framework Core works only with objects, but web service clients typically expect to be able to delete objects using just a key value.

Restart ASP.NET Core and then use a different PowerShell command prompt to run the command shown in Listing 19-13, which tests the UpdateProduct action.

Listing 19-13. Updating an Object

```
Invoke-RestMethod http://localhost:5000/api/products -Method PUT -Body  (@{ ProductId=1; Name="Green Kayak";
Price=275; CategoryId=1; SupplierId=1} | ConvertTo-Json) -ContentType "application/json"
```

The command sends an HTTP PUT request whose body contains a replacement object. The action method receives the object through the model binding feature and updates the database. Next, run the command shown in Listing 19-14 to test the DeleteProduct action.

Listing 19-14. Deleting an Object

```
Invoke-RestMethod http://localhost:5000/api/products/2 -Method DELETE
```

This command sends an HTTP DELETE request, which will delete the object whose ProductId property is 2. To see the effect of the changes, use the browser to request http://localhost:5000/api/products, which will send a GET request that is handled by the GetProducts action and produce the response shown in Figure 19-8.

```
[{"productId":1,"name":"Green Kayak","price":275.00,"categoryId":1,"category":
{"productId":3,"name":"Soccer Ball","price":19.50,"categoryId":2,"category":nul
 productId :4, name : Corner Flags , price :34.95, categoryId :2, category :n
{"productId":5,"name":"Stadium","price":79500.00,"categoryId":2,"category":nul
{"productId":6,"name":"Thinking Cap","price":16.00,"categoryId":3,"category":nu
{"product  :7,"na       hoodue Chair" price 29.95,"category d" 3,"category" 
```

Figure 19-8. *Updating and deleting objects*

Improving the Web Service

The controller in Listing 19-14 re-creates all the functionality provided by the separate endpoints, but there are still improvements that can be made, as described in the following sections.

SUPPORTING CROSS-ORIGIN REQUESTS

If you are supporting third-party JavaScript clients, you may need to enable support for cross-origin requests (CORS). Browsers protect users by only allowing JavaScript code to make HTTP requests within the same origin, which means to URLs that have the same scheme, host, and port as the URL used to load the JavaScript code. CORS loosens this restriction by performing an initial HTTP request to check that the server will allow requests originating from a specific URL, helping prevent malicious code using your service without the user's consent.

ASP.NET Core provides a built-in service that handles CORS, which is enabled by adding the following statement to the ConfigureServices method in the Startup class:

```
...
Services.AddCors();
...
```

The options pattern is used to configure CORS with the CorsOptions class defined in the Microsoft.AspNetCore.Cors.Infrastructure namespace. See https://docs.microsoft.com/en-gb/aspnet/core/security/cors?view=aspnetcore-3.1 for details.

Using Asynchronous Actions

The ASP.NET Core platform processes each request by assigning a thread from a pool. The number of requests that can be processed concurrently is limited to the size of the pool, and a thread can't be used to process any other request while it is waiting for an action to produce a result.

Actions that depend on external resources can cause a request thread to wait for an extended period. A database server, for example, may have its own concurrency limits and may queue up queries until they can be executed. The ASP.NET Core request thread is unavailable to process any other requests until the database produces a result for the action, which then produces a response that can be sent to the HTTP client.

This problem can be addressed by defining asynchronous actions, which allow ASP.NET Core threads to process other requests when they would otherwise be blocked, increasing the number of HTTP requests that the application can process simultaneously. Listing 19-15 revises the controller to use asynchronous actions.

453

■ **Note**   Asynchronous actions don't produce responses any quicker, and the benefit is only to increase the number of requests that can be processed concurrently.

Listing 19-15. Asynchronous Actions in the ProductsController.cs File in the Controllers Folder

```
using Microsoft.AspNetCore.Mvc;
using WebApp.Models;
using System.Collections.Generic;
using Microsoft.Extensions.Logging;
using System.Linq;
using System.Threading.Tasks;

namespace WebApp.Controllers {

    [Route("api/[controller]")]
    public class ProductsController: ControllerBase {
        private DataContext context;

        public ProductsController(DataContext ctx) {
            context = ctx;
        }

        [HttpGet]
        public IAsyncEnumerable<Product> GetProducts() {
            return context.Products;
        }

        [HttpGet("{id}")]
        public async Task<Product> GetProduct(long id) {
            return await context.Products.FindAsync(id);
        }

        [HttpPost]
        public async Task SaveProduct([FromBody]Product product) {
            await context.Products.AddAsync(product);
            await context.SaveChangesAsync();
        }

        [HttpPut]
        public async Task UpdateProduct([FromBody]Product product) {
            context.Update(product);
            await context.SaveChangesAsync();
        }

        [HttpDelete("{id}")]
        public async Task DeleteProduct(long id) {
            context.Products.Remove(new Product() { ProductId = id });
            await context.SaveChangesAsync();
        }
    }
}
```

Entity Framework Core provides asynchronous versions of some methods, such as FindAsync, AdddAsync, and SaveChangesAsync, and I have used these with the await keyword. Not all operations can be performed asynchronously, which is why the Update and Remove methods are unchanged.

For some operations—including LINQ queries to the database—the IAsyncEnumerable<T> interface can be used, which denotes a sequence of objects that should be enumerated asynchronously and prevents the ASP.NET Core request thread from waiting for each object to be produced by the database, as explained in Chapter 5.

There is no change to the responses produced by the controller, but the threads that ASP.NET Core assigns to process each request are not necessarily blocked by the action methods.

Preventing Over-Binding

Some of the action methods use the model binding feature to get data from the response body so that it can be used to perform database operations. There is a problem with the SaveProduct action, which can be seen by using a PowerShell prompt to run the command shown in Listing 19-16.

Listing 19-16. Saving a Product

```
Invoke-RestMethod http://localhost:5000/api/products -Method POST -Body  (@{ ProductId=100; Name="Swim Buoy";
Price=19.99; CategoryId=1; SupplierId=1} | ConvertTo-Json) -ContentType "application/json"
```

Unlike the command that was used to test the POST method in Listing 19-11, this command includes a value for the ProductId property. When Entity Framework Core sends the data to the database, the following exception is thrown:

```
...
Microsoft.Data.SqlClient.SqlException (0x80131904): Cannot insert explicit value for identity column in table
'Products' when IDENTITY_INSERT is set to OFF.
...
```

By default, Entity Framework Core configures the database to assign primary key values when new objects are stored. This means the application doesn't have to worry about keeping track of which key values have already been assigned and allows multiple applications to share the same database without the need to coordinate key allocation. The Product data model class needs a ProductId property, but the model binding process doesn't understand the significance of the property and adds any values that the client provides to the objects it creates, which causes the exception in the SaveProduct action method.

This is known as *over-binding*, and it can cause serious problems when a client provides values that the developer wasn't expecting. At best, the application will behave unexpectedly, but this technique has been used to subvert application security and grant users more access than they should have.

The safest way to prevent over-binding is to create separate data model classes that are used only for receiving data through the model binding process. Add a class file named ProductBindingTarget.cs to the WebApp/Models folder and use it to define the class shown in Listing 19-17.

Listing 19-17. The Contents of the ProductBindingTarget.cs File in the WebApp/Models Folder

```
namespace WebApp.Models {
    public class ProductBindingTarget {

        public string Name { get; set; }

        public decimal Price { get; set; }

        public long CategoryId { get; set; }

        public long SupplierId { get; set; }

        public Product ToProduct() => new Product() {
            Name = this.Name, Price = this.Price,
            CategoryId = this.CategoryId, SupplierId = this.SupplierId
        };
    }
}
```

The ProductBindingTarget class defines only the properties that the application wants to receive from the client when storing a new object. The ToProduct method creates a Product that can be used with the rest of the application, ensuring that the client can only provide properties for the Name, Price, CategoryId, and SupplierId properties. Listing 19-18 uses the binding target class in the SaveProduct action to prevent over-binding.

Listing 19-18. Using a Binding Target in the ProductsController.cs File in the Controllers Folder

```
...
[HttpPost]
public async Task SaveProduct([FromBody]ProductBindingTarget target) {
    await context.Products.AddAsync(target.ToProduct());
    await context.SaveChangesAsync();
}
...
```

Restart ASP.NET Core and repeat the command from Listing 19-16, and you will see the response shown in Figure 19-9. The client has included the ProductId value, but it is ignored by the model binding process, which discards values for read-only properties. (You may see a different value for the ProductId property when you run this example depending on the changes you made to the database before running the command.)

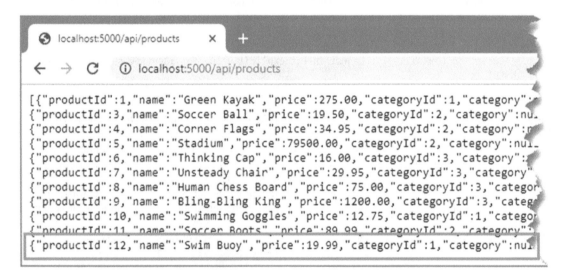

Figure 19-9. *Discarding unwanted data values*

Using Action Results

The MVC Framework sets the status code for responses automatically, but you won't always get the result you desire, in part because there are no firm rules for RESTful web services, and the assumptions that Microsoft makes may not match your expectations. To see an example, use a PowerShell command prompt to run the command shown in Listing 19-19, which sends a GET request to the web service.

Listing 19-19. Sending a GET Request

```
Invoke-WebRequest http://localhost:5000/api/products/1000 |Select-Object StatusCode
```

The Invoke-WebRequest command is similar to the Invoke-RestMethod command used in earlier examples but makes it easier to get the status code from the response. The URL requested in Listing 19-19 will be handled by the GetProduct action method, which will query the database for an object whose ProductId value is 1000, and the command produces the following output:

```
StatusCode
----------
       204
```

There is no matching object in the database, which means that the GetProduct action method returns null. When the MVC Framework receives null from an action method, it returns the 204 status code, which indicates a successful request that has produced no data. Not all web services behave this way, and a common alternative is to return a 404 response, indicating not found.

Similarly, the SaveProducts action will return a 200 response when it stores an object, but since the primary key isn't generated until the data is stored, the client doesn't know what key value was assigned.

■ **Note** There is no right or wrong when it comes to these kinds of web service implementation details, and you should pick the approaches that best suit your project and personal preferences. This section is an example of how to change the default behavior and not a direction to follow any specific style of web service.

Action methods can direct the MVC Framework to send a specific response by returning an object that implements the IActionResult interface, which is known as an *action result*. This allows the action method to specify the type of response that is required without having to produce it directly using the HttpResponse object.

The ControllerBase class provides a set of methods that are used to create action result objects, which can be returned from action methods. Table 19-7 describes the most useful action result methods.

Table 19-7. *Useful ControllerBase Action Result Methods*

Name	Description
Ok	The IActionResult returned by this method produces a 200 OK status code and sends an optional data object in the response body.
NoContent	The IActionResult returned by this method produces a 204 NO CONTENT status code.
BadRequest	The IActionResult returned by this method produces a 400 BAD REQUEST status code. The method accepts an optional model state object that describes the problem to the client, as demonstrated in the "Validating Data" section.
File	The IActionResult returned by this method produces a 200 OK response, sets the Content-Type header to the specified type, and sends the specified file to the client.
NotFound	The IActionResult returned by this method produces a 404 NOT FOUND status code.
RedirectRedirectPermanent	The IActionResult returned by these methods redirects the client to a specified URL.
RedirectToRoute RedirectToRoutePermanent	The IActionResult returned by these methods redirects the client to the specified URL that is created using the routing system, using convention routing, as described in the "Redirecting Using Route Values" sidebar.
LocalRedirectLocal RedirectPermanent	The IActionResult returned by these methods redirects the client to the specified URL that is local to the application.
RedirectToActionRedirect ToActionPermanent	The IActionResult returned by these methods redirects the client to an action method. The URL for the redirection is created using the URL routing system.
RedirectToPageRedirect ToPagePermanent	The IActionResult returned by these methods redirects the client to a Razor Page, described in Chapter 23.
StatusCode	The IActionResult returned by this method produces a response with a specific status code.

When an action method returns an object, it is equivalent to passing the object to the Ok method and returning the result. When an action returns null, it is equivalent to returning the result from the NoContent method. Listing 19-20 revises the behavior of the GetProduct and SaveProduct actions so they use the methods from Table 19-7 to override the default behavior for web service controllers.

Listing 19-20. Using Action Results in the ProductsController.cs File in the Controllers Folder

```
using Microsoft.AspNetCore.Mvc;
using WebApp.Models;
using System.Collections.Generic;
using Microsoft.Extensions.Logging;
using System.Linq;
using System.Threading.Tasks;

namespace WebApp.Controllers {

    [Route("api/[controller]")]
    public class ProductsController : ControllerBase {
        private DataContext context;

        public ProductsController(DataContext ctx) {
            context = ctx;
        }

        [HttpGet]
        public IAsyncEnumerable<Product> GetProducts() {
            return context.Products;
        }

        [HttpGet("{id}")]
        public async Task<IActionResult> GetProduct(long id) {
            Product p = await context.Products.FindAsync(id);
            if (p == null) {
                return NotFound();

            }
            return Ok(p);
        }

        [HttpPost]
        public async Task<IActionResult>
                SaveProduct([FromBody]ProductBindingTarget target) {
            Product p = target.ToProduct();
            await context.Products.AddAsync(p);
            await context.SaveChangesAsync();
            return Ok(p);
        }

        [HttpPut]
        public async Task UpdateProduct([FromBody]Product product) {
            context.Update(product);
            await context.SaveChangesAsync();
        }
```

```
        [HttpDelete("{id}")]
        public async Task DeleteProduct(long id) {
            context.Products.Remove(new Product() { ProductId = id });
            await context.SaveChangesAsync();
        }
    }
}
```

Restart ASP.NET Core and repeat the command from Listing 19-19, and you will see an exception, which is how the Invoke-WebRequest command responds to error status codes, such as the 404 Not Found returned by the GetProduct action method.

To see the effect of the change to the SaveProduct action method, use a PowerShell command prompt to run the command shown in Listing 19-21, which sends a POST request to the web service.

Listing 19-21. Sending a POST Request

```
Invoke-RestMethod http://localhost:5000/api/products -Method POST -Body  (@{Name="Boot Laces"; Price=19.99;
CategoryId=2; SupplierId=2} | ConvertTo-Json) -ContentType "application/json"
```

The command will produce the following output, showing the values that were parsed from the JSON data received from the web service:

```
productId  : 13
name       : Boot Laces
price      : 19.99
categoryId : 2
category   :
supplierId : 2
supplier   :
```

Performing Redirections

Many of the action result methods in Table 19-7 relate to redirections, which direct the client to another URL. The most basic way to perform a direction is to call the Redirect method, as shown in Listing 19-22.

■ **Tip** The LocalRedirect and LocalRedirectPermanent methods throw an exception if a controller tries to perform a redirection to any URL that is not local. This is useful when you are redirecting to URLs provided by users, where an *open redirection attack* is attempted to redirect another user to an untrusted site.

Listing 19-22. Redirecting in the ProductsController.cs File in the Controllers Folder

```
using Microsoft.AspNetCore.Mvc;
using WebApp.Models;
using System.Collections.Generic;
using Microsoft.Extensions.Logging;
using System.Linq;
using System.Threading.Tasks;

namespace WebApp.Controllers {

    [Route("api/[controller]")]
    public class ProductsController : ControllerBase {
        private DataContext context;
```

```
        public ProductsController(DataContext ctx) {
            context = ctx;
        }

        // ...other action methods omitted for brevity...

        [HttpGet("redirect")]
        public IActionResult Redirect() {
            return Redirect("/api/products/1");
        }
    }
}
```

The redirection URL is expressed as a string argument to the Redirect method, which produces a temporary redirection. Restart ASP.NET Core and use a PowerShell command prompt to run the command shown in Listing 19-23, which sends a GET request that will be handled by the new action method.

Listing 19-23. Testing Redirection

```
Invoke-RestMethod http://localhost:5000/api/products/redirect
```

The Invoke-RestMethod command will receive the redirection response from the web service and send a new request to the URL it is given, producing the following response:

```
productId  : 1
name       : GreenKayak
price      : 275.00
categoryId : 1
category   :
supplierId : 1
supplier   :
```

Redirecting to an Action Method

You can redirect to another action method using the RedirectToAction method (for temporary redirections) or the RedirectToActionPermanent method (for permanent redirections). Listing 19-24 changes the Redirect action method so that the client will be redirected to another action method defined by the controller.

Listing 19-24. Redirecting to an Action the ProductsController.cs File in the Controllers Folder

```
using Microsoft.AspNetCore.Mvc;
using WebApp.Models;
using System.Collections.Generic;
using Microsoft.Extensions.Logging;
using System.Linq;
using System.Threading.Tasks;

namespace WebApp.Controllers {

    [Route("api/[controller]")]
    public class ProductsController : ControllerBase {
        private DataContext context;

        public ProductsController(DataContext ctx) {
            context = ctx;
        }
```

```
        // ...other action methods omitted for brevity...

        [HttpGet("redirect")]
        public IActionResult Redirect() {
            return RedirectToAction(nameof(GetProduct), new { Id = 1 });
        }
    }
}
```

The action method is specified as a string, although the nameof expression can be used to select an action method without the risk of a typo. Any additional values required to create the route are supplied using an anonymous object. Restart ASP.NET Core and use a PowerShell command prompt to repeat the command in Listing 19-23. The routing system will be used to create a URL that targets the specified action method, producing the following response:

```
productId   : 1
name        : Kayak
price       : 100.00
categoryId  : 1
category    :
supplierId  : 1
supplier    :
```

If you specify only an action method name, then the redirection will target the current controller. There is an overload of the RedirectToAction method that accepts action and controller names.

REDIRECTING USING ROUTE VALUES

The RedirectToRoute and RedirectToRoutePermanent methods redirect the client to a URL that is created by providing the routing system with values for segment variables and allowing it to select a route to use. This can be useful for applications with complex routing configurations, and caution should be used because it is easy to create a redirection to the wrong URL. Here is an example of redirection with the RedirectToRoute method:

```
...
[HttpGet("redirect")]
public IActionResult Redirect() {
    return RedirectToRoute(new {
        controller = "Products", action = "GetProduct", Id = 1
    });
}
...
```

The set of values in this redirection relies on convention routing to select the controller and action method. Convention routing is typically used with controllers that produce HTML responses, as described in Chapter 21.

Validating Data

When you accept data from clients, you must assume that a lot of the data will be invalid and be prepared to filter out values that the application can't use. The data validation features provided for MVC Framework controllers are described in detail in Chapter 29, but for this chapter, I am going to focus on only one problem: ensuring that the client provides values for the properties that are required to store data in the database. The first step in model binding is to apply attributes to the properties of the data model class, as shown in Listing 19-25.

Listing 19-25. Applying Attributes in the ProductBindingTarget.cs File in the Models Folder

```
using System.ComponentModel.DataAnnotations;

namespace WebApp.Models {
    public class ProductBindingTarget {

        [Required]
        public string Name { get; set; }

        [Range(1, 1000)]
        public decimal Price { get; set; }

        [Range(1, long.MaxValue)]
        public long CategoryId { get; set; }

        [Range(1, long.MaxValue)]
        public long SupplierId { get; set; }

        public Product ToProduct() => new Product() {
            Name = this.Name, Price = this.Price,
            CategoryId = this.CategoryId, SupplierId = this.SupplierId
        };
    }
}
```

The Required attribute denotes properties for which the client must provide a value and can be applied to properties that are assigned null when there is no value in the request. The Range attribute requires a value between upper and lower limits and is used for primitive types that will default to zero when there is no value in the request.

Listing 19-26 updates the SaveProduct action to perform validation before storing the object that is created by the model binding process, ensuring that only objects that contain values for all four properties are decorated with the validation attributes.

Listing 19-26. Applying Validation in the ProductsController.cs File in the Controllers Folder

```
...
[HttpPost]
public async Task<IActionResult> SaveProduct([FromBody]ProductBindingTarget target) {
    if (ModelState.IsValid) {
        Product p = target.ToProduct();
        await context.Products.AddAsync(p);
        await context.SaveChangesAsync();
        return Ok(p);
    }
    return BadRequest(ModelState);
}
...
```

The ModelState property is inherited from the ControllerBase class, and the IsValid property returns true if the model binding process has produced data that meets the validation criteria. If the data received from the client is valid, then the action result from the Ok method is returned. If the data sent by the client fails the validation check, then the IsValid property will be false, and the action result from the BadRequest method is used instead. The BadRequest method accepts the object returned by the ModelState property, which is used to describe the validation errors to the client. (There is no standard way to describe validation errors, so the client may rely only on the 400 status code to determine that there is a problem.)

To test the validation, restart ASP.NET Core and use a new PowerShell command prompt to run the command shown in Listing 19-27.

Listing 19-27. Testing Validation

```
Invoke-WebRequest http://localhost:5000/api/products -Method POST -Body  (@{Name="Boot Laces"} |
ConvertTo-Json) -ContentType "application/json"
```

The command will throw an exception that shows the web service has returned a 400 Bad Request response. Details of the validation errors are not shown because neither the Invoke-WebRequest command nor the Invoke-RestMethod command provides access to error response bodies. Although you can't see it, the body contains a JSON object that has properties for each data property that has failed validation, like this:

```
{
 "Price":["The field Price must be between 1 and 1000."],
  "CategoryId":["The field CategoryId must be between 1 and 9.223372036854776E+18."],
  "SupplierId":["The field SupplierId must be between 1 and 9.223372036854776E+18."]
}
```

You can see examples of working with validation messages in Chapter 29 where the validation feature is described in detail.

Applying the API Controller Attribute

The ApiController attribute can be applied to web service controller classes to change the behavior of the model binding and validation features. The use of the FromBody attribute to select data from the request body and explicitly checking the ModelState. IsValid property is not required in controllers that have been decorated with the ApiController attribute. Getting data from the body and validating data are required so commonly in web services that they are applied automatically when the attribute is used, restoring the focus of the code in the controller's action to dealing with the application features, as shown in Listing 19-28.

Listing 19-28. Using ApiController in the ProductsController.cs File in the Controllers Folder

```
using Microsoft.AspNetCore.Mvc;
using WebApp.Models;
using System.Collections.Generic;
using Microsoft.Extensions.Logging;
using System.Linq;
using System.Threading.Tasks;

namespace WebApp.Controllers {

    [ApiController]
    [Route("api/[controller]")]
    public class ProductsController : ControllerBase {
        private DataContext context;

        public ProductsController(DataContext ctx) {
            context = ctx;
        }

        [HttpGet]
        public IAsyncEnumerable<Product> GetProducts() {
            return context.Products;
        }

        [HttpGet("{id}")]
        public async Task<IActionResult> GetProduct(long id) {
            Product p = await context.Products.FindAsync(id);
            if (p == null) {
```

```
            return NotFound();
        }
        return Ok(p);
    }

    [HttpPost]
    public async Task<IActionResult> SaveProduct(ProductBindingTarget target) {
        Product p = target.ToProduct();
        await context.Products.AddAsync(p);
        await context.SaveChangesAsync();
        return Ok(p);
    }

    [HttpPut]
    public async Task UpdateProduct(Product product) {
        context.Update(product);
        await context.SaveChangesAsync();
    }

    [HttpDelete("{id}")]
    public async Task DeleteProduct(long id) {
        context.Products.Remove(new Product() { ProductId = id });
        await context.SaveChangesAsync();
    }

    [HttpGet("redirect")]
    public IActionResult Redirect() {
        return RedirectToAction(nameof(GetProduct), new { Id = 1 });
    }
    }
}
```

Using the ApiController attribute is optional, but it helps produce concise web service controllers.

Omitting Null Properties

The final change I am going to make in this chapter is to remove the null values from the data returned by the web service. The data model classes contain navigation properties that are used by Entity Framework Core to associate related data in complex queries, as explained in Chapter 20. For the simple queries that are performed in this chapter, no values are assigned to these navigation properties, which means that the client receives properties for which values are never going to be available. To see the problem, use a PowerShell command prompt to run the command shown in Listing 19-29.

Listing 19-29. Sending a GET Request

```
Invoke-WebRequest http://localhost:5000/api/products/1 | Select-Object Content
```

The command sends a GET request and displays the body of the response from the web service, producing the following output:

```
Content
-------
{"productId":1,"name":"Green Kayak","price":275.00,"categoryId":1,"category":null,"supplierId":1,"supplier":null}
```

The request was handled by the GetProduct action method, and the category and supplier values in the response will always be null because the action doesn't ask Entity Framework Core to populate these properties.

Projecting Selected Properties

The first approach is to return just the properties that the client requires. This gives you complete control over each response, but it can become difficult to manage and confusing for client developers if each action returns a different set of values. Listing 19-30 shows how the Product object obtained from the database can be projected so that the navigation properties are omitted.

Listing 19-30. Omitting Properties in the ProductsController.cs File in the Controllers Folder

```
...
[HttpGet("{id}")]
public async Task<IActionResult> GetProduct(long id) {
    Product p = await context.Products.FindAsync(id);
    if (p == null) {
        return NotFound();
    }
    return Ok(new {
        ProductId = p.ProductId, Name = p.Name,
        Price = p.Price, CategoryId = p.CategoryId,
        SupplierId = p.SupplierId
    });
}
...
```

The properties that the client requires are selected and added to an object that is passed to the Ok method. Restart ASP.NET Core and run the command from Listing 19-30, and you will receive a response that omits the navigation properties and their null values, like this:

```
Content
-------
{"productId":1,"name":"Green Kayak","price":275.00,"categoryId":1,"supplierId":1}
```

Configuring the JSON Serializer

The JSON serializer can be configured to omit properties whose value is null when it serializes objects. The serializer is configured using the options pattern in the Startup class, as shown in Listing 19-31.

Listing 19-31. Configuring the JSON Serializer in the Startup.cs File in the WebApp Folder

```
using System;
using System.Collections.Generic;
using System.Linq;
using System.Threading.Tasks;
using Microsoft.AspNetCore.Builder;
using Microsoft.AspNetCore.Hosting;
using Microsoft.AspNetCore.Http;
using Microsoft.Extensions.DependencyInjection;
using Microsoft.Extensions.Hosting;
using Microsoft.Extensions.Configuration;
using Microsoft.EntityFrameworkCore;
using WebApp.Models;
using Microsoft.AspNetCore.Mvc;
```

```
namespace WebApp {
    public class Startup {

        public Startup(IConfiguration config) {
            Configuration = config;
        }

        public IConfiguration Configuration { get; set; }

        public void ConfigureServices(IServiceCollection services) {
            services.AddDbContext<DataContext>(opts => {
                opts.UseSqlServer(Configuration[
                    "ConnectionStrings:ProductConnection"]);
                opts.EnableSensitiveDataLogging(true);
            });

            services.AddControllers();
            services.Configure<JsonOptions>(opts => {
                opts.JsonSerializerOptions.IgnoreNullValues = true;
            });
        }

        public void Configure(IApplicationBuilder app, DataContext context) {
            app.UseDeveloperExceptionPage();
            app.UseRouting();
            app.UseMiddleware<TestMiddleware>();
            app.UseEndpoints(endpoints => {
                endpoints.MapGet("/", async context => {
                    await context.Response.WriteAsync("Hello World!");
                });
                endpoints.MapControllers();
            });
            SeedData.SeedDatabase(context);
        }
    }
}
```

The JSON serializer is configured using the JsonSerializerOptions property of the JsonOptions class, and null values are discarded when the IgnoreNullValues property is true.

This configuration change affects all JSON responses and should be used with caution, especially if any of your data model classes use null values to impart information to the client. To see the effect of the change, restart ASP.NET Core and use a browser to request http://localhost:5000/api/products, which will produce the response shown in Figure 19-10.

Figure 19-10. *Configuring the JSON serializer*

Summary

In this chapter, I showed you how to use the MVC Framework to create RESTful web services. I explained that the MVC Framework is built on top of the ASP.NET Core platform and showed you how a single controller class can define multiple action methods, each of which can process a different combination of URL and HTTP method. I showed you how to use dependency injection to consume services, how to use model binding to access request data, how to validate request data, and how to take control of the responses that are returned to the client. In the next chapter, I describe the advanced features that ASP.NET Core provides for web services.

CHAPTER 20

Advanced Web Service Features

In this chapter, I describe advanced features that can be used to create RESTful web services. I explain how to deal with related data in Entity Framework Core queries, how to add support for the HTTP PATCH method, how to use content negations, and how to use OpenAPI to describe your web services. Table 20-1 puts this chapter in context.

Table 20-1. *Putting Advanced Web Service Features in Context*

Question	Answer
What are they?	The features described in this chapter provide greater control over how ASP.NET Core web services work, including managing the data sent to the client and the format used for that data.
Why are they useful?	The default behaviors provided by ASP.NET Core don't meet the needs of every project, and the features described in this chapter allow web services to be reshaped to fit specific requirements.
How are they used?	The common theme for the features in this chapter is altering the responses produced by action methods.
Are there any pitfalls or limitations?	It can be hard to decide how to implement web services, especially if they are consumed by third-party clients. The behavior of a web service becomes fixed as soon as clients start using a web service, which means that careful thought is required when using the features described in this chapter.
Are there any alternatives?	The features described in this chapter are optional, and you can rely on the default behaviors of ASP.NET Core web services.

Table 20-2 summarizes the chapter.

Table 20-2. *Chapter Summary*

Problem	Solution	Listing
Using relational data	Use the Include and ThenInclude methods in LINQ queries	4
Breaking circular references	Explicitly set navigation properties to null	5
Allowing clients to selectively update data	Support the HTTP PATCH method	6–9
Supporting a range of response data types	Support content formatting and negotiation	10–24
Documenting a web service	Use OpenAPI to describe the web service	25–29

Preparing for This Chapter

This chapter uses the WebApp project created in Chapter 18 and modified in Chapter 19. To prepare for this chapter, add a file named SuppliersController.cs to the WebApp/Controllers folder with the content shown in Listing 20-1.

© Adam Freeman 2020
A. Freeman, *Pro ASP.NET Core 3*, https://doi.org/10.1007/978-1-4842-5440-0_20

Listing 20-1. The Contents of the SuppliersController.cs File in the Controllers Folder

```
using Microsoft.AspNetCore.Mvc;
using WebApp.Models;
using System.Threading.Tasks;

namespace WebApp.Controllers {

    [ApiController]
    [Route("api/[controller]")]
    public class SuppliersController: ControllerBase {
        private DataContext context;

        public SuppliersController(DataContext ctx) {
            context = ctx;
        }

        [HttpGet("{id}")]
        public async Task<Supplier> GetSupplier(long id) {
            return await context.Suppliers.FindAsync(id);
        }
    }
}
```

The controller extends the ControllerBase class, declares a dependency on the DataContext service, and defines an action named GetSupplier that handles GET requests for the /api/[controller]/{id} URL pattern.

Dropping the Database

Open a new PowerShell command prompt, navigate to the folder that contains the WebApp.csproj file, and run the command shown in Listing 20-2 to drop the database.

■ **Tip** You can download the example project for this chapter—and for all the other chapters in this book—from https://github.com/apress/pro-asp.net-core-3. See Chapter 1 for how to get help if you have problems running the examples.

Listing 20-2. Dropping the Database

```
dotnet ef database drop --force
```

Running the Example Application

Once the database has been dropped, select Start Without Debugging or Run Without Debugging from the Debug menu or use the PowerShell command prompt to run the command shown in Listing 20-3.

Listing 20-3. Running the Example Application

```
dotnet run
```

The database will be seeded as part of the application startup. Once ASP.NET Core is running, use a web browser to request http://localhost:5000/api/suppliers/1, which will produce the response shown in Figure 20-1.

Figure 20-1. Running the example application

The response shows the Supplier object whose primary key matches the last segment of the request URL. In Chapter 19, the JSON serializer was configured to ignore properties with null values, which is why the response doesn't include the navigation property defined by the Supplier data model class.

Dealing with Related Data

Although this isn't a book about Entity Framework Core, there is one aspect of querying for data that most web services encounter. The data model classes defined in Chapter 18 include navigation properties, which Entity Framework Core can populate by following relationships in the database when the Include method is used, as shown in Listing 20-4.

Listing 20-4. Requesting Related Data in the SuppliersController.cs File in the Controllers Folder

```
using Microsoft.AspNetCore.Mvc;
using WebApp.Models;
using System.Threading.Tasks;
using Microsoft.EntityFrameworkCore;

namespace WebApp.Controllers {

    [ApiController]
    [Route("api/[controller]")]
    public class SuppliersController: ControllerBase {
        private DataContext context;

        public SuppliersController(DataContext ctx) {
            context = ctx;
        }

        [HttpGet("{id}")]
        public async Task<Supplier> GetSupplier(long id) {
            return await context.Suppliers
                .Include(s => s.Products)
                .FirstAsync(s => s.SupplierId == id);
        }
    }
}
```

The Include method tells Entity Framework Core to follow a relationship in the database and load the related data. In this case, the Include method selects the Products navigation property defined by the Supplier class, which causes Entity Framework Core to load the Product objects associated with the selected Supplier and assign them to the Products property.

Restart ASP.NET Core and use a browser to request http://localhost:5000/api/suppliers/1, which will target the GetSupplier action method. The request fails, and you will see the exception shown in Figure 20-2.

Figure 20-2. *An exception caused by querying for related data*

The JSON serializer has reported an "object cycle," which means there is a circular reference in the data that is being serialized for the response.

Looking at the code in Listing 20-4, you might struggle to see why using the Include method has created a circular reference. The problem is caused by an Entity Framework Core feature that attempts to minimize the amount of data read from the database but that causes problems in ASP.NET Core applications.

When Entity Framework Core creates objects, it populates navigation properties with objects that have already been created by the same database context. This can be a useful feature in some kinds of applications, such as desktop apps, where a database context object has a long life and is used to make many requests over time. It isn't useful for ASP.NET Core applications, where a new context object is created for each HTTP request.

Entity Framework Core queries the database for the Product objects associated with the selected Supplier and assigns them to the Supplier.Products navigation property. The problem is that Entity Framework Core then looks at each Product object it has created and uses the query response to populate the Product.Supplier navigation property as well. For an ASP.NET Core application, this is an unhelpful step to take because it creates a circular reference between the navigation properties of the Supplier and Product objects, as shown in Figure 20-3.

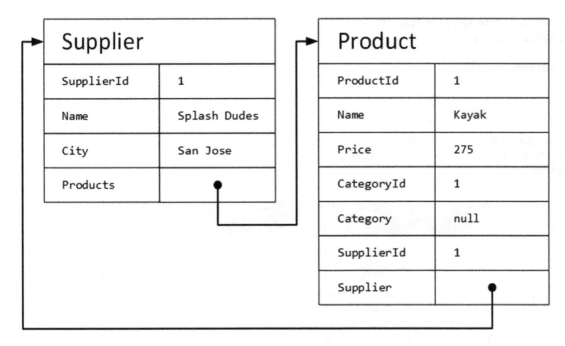

Figure 20-3. *Understanding how Entity Framework Core uses related data*

When the Supplier object is returned by the controller's action method, the JSON serializer works its way through the properties and follows the references to the Product objects, each of which has a reference back to the Supplier object, which it follows in a loop until the maximum depth is reached and the exception shown in Figure 20-2 is thrown.

Breaking Circular References in Related Data

There is no way to stop Entity Framework Core from creating circular references in the data it loads in the database. Preventing the exception means presenting the JSON serializer with data that doesn't contain circular references, which is most easily done by altering the objects after they have been created by Entity Framework Core and before they are serialized, as shown in Listing 20-5.

Listing 20-5. Breaking References in the SuppliersController.cs File in the Controllers Folder

```
using Microsoft.AspNetCore.Mvc;
using WebApp.Models;
using System.Threading.Tasks;
using Microsoft.EntityFrameworkCore;

namespace WebApp.Controllers {

    [ApiController]
    [Route("api/[controller]")]
    public class SuppliersController: ControllerBase {
        private DataContext context;

        public SuppliersController(DataContext ctx) {
            context = ctx;
        }

        [HttpGet("{id}")]
        public async Task<Supplier> GetSupplier(long id) {
            Supplier supplier = await context.Suppliers.Include(s => s.Products)
                .FirstAsync(s => s.SupplierId == id);
```

```
        foreach (Product p in supplier.Products) {
            p.Supplier = null;
        };
        return supplier;
    }
  }
}
```

The foreach loop sets the Supplier property of each Product object to null, which breaks the circular references. Restart ASP.NET Core and request http://localhost:5000/api/suppliers/1 to query for a supplier and its related products, which produces the response shown in Figure 20-4.

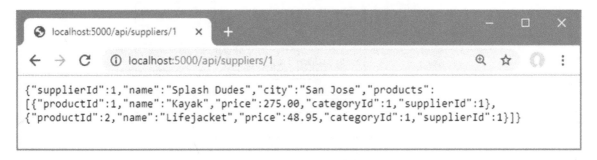

Figure 20-4. *Querying for related data*

Supporting the HTTP PATCH Method

For simple data types, edit operations can be handled by replacing the existing object using the PUT method, which is the approach I took in Chapter 19. Even if you only need to change a single property value in the Product class, for example, it isn't too much trouble to use a PUT method and include the values for all the other Product properties, too.

Not all data types are as easy to work with, either because they define too many properties or because the client has only received values for selected properties. The solution is to use a PATCH request, which sends just the changes to the web service rather than a complete replacement object.

Understanding JSON Patch

ASP.NET Core has support for working with the JSON Patch standard, which allows changes to be specified in a uniform way. The JSON Patch standard allows for a complex set of changes to be described, but for this chapter, I am going to focus on just the ability to change the value of a property.

I am not going to go into the details of the JSON Patch standard, which you can read at https://tools.ietf.org/html/rfc6902, but the client is going to send the web service JSON data like this in its HTTP PATCH requests:

```
[
 { "op": "replace", "path": "Name", "value": "Surf Co"},
 { "op": "replace", "path": "City", "value": "Los Angeles"},
]
```

A JSON Patch document is expressed as an array of operations. Each operation has an op property, which specifies the type of operation, and a path property, which specifies where the operation will be applied.

For the example application—and, in fact, for most applications—only the replace operation is required, which is used to change the value of a property. This JSON Patch document sets new values for the Name and City properties. The properties defined by the Supplier class not mentioned in the JSON Patch document will not be modified.

Installing and Configuring the JSON Patch Package

Support for JSON Patch isn't installed when a project is created with the Empty template. To install the JSON Patch package, open a new PowerShell command prompt, navigate to the folder that contains the WebApp.csproj file, and run the command shown in Listing 20-6. If you are using Visual Studio, you can install the package by selecting Project ➤ Manage NuGet Packages.

Listing 20-6. Installing the JSON Patch Package

```
dotnet add package Microsoft.AspNetCore.Mvc.NewtonsoftJson --version 3.1.1
```

The Microsoft implementation of JSON Patch relies on the third-party Newtonsoft JSON.NET serializer that was used in ASP.NET Core 2.x but that has been replaced with a bespoke JSON serializer in ASP.NET Core 3.x. Add the statement shown in Listing 20-7 to the ConfigureServices method of the Startup class to enable the old serializer.

Listing 20-7. Enabling the JSON.NET Serializer in the Startup.cs File in the WebApp Folder

```
...
public void ConfigureServices(IServiceCollection services) {
    services.AddDbContext<DataContext>(opts => {
        opts.UseSqlServer(Configuration[
            "ConnectionStrings:ProductConnection"]);
        opts.EnableSensitiveDataLogging(true);
    });

    services.AddControllers().AddNewtonsoftJson();

    services.Configure<MvcNewtonsoftJsonOptions>(opts => {
        opts.SerializerSettings.NullValueHandling
            = Newtonsoft.Json.NullValueHandling.Ignore;
    });

    //services.Configure<JsonOptions>(opts => {
    //    opts.JsonSerializerOptions.IgnoreNullValues = true;
    //});
}
...
```

The AddNewtonsoftJson method enables the JSON.NET serializer, which replaces the standard ASP.NET Core serializer. The JSON.NET serializer has its own configuration class, MvcNewtonsoftJsonOptions, which is applied through the options pattern. Listing 20-7 sets the NullValueHandling value, which tells the serializer to discard properties with null values.

■ **Tip** See https://www.newtonsoft.com/json for details of the other configuration options available for the JSON.NET serializer.

Defining the Action Method

To add support for the PATCH method, add the action method shown in Listing 20-8 to the SuppliersController class.

Listing 20-8. Adding an Action in the SuppliersController.cs File in the Controller Folder

```
using Microsoft.AspNetCore.Mvc;
using WebApp.Models;
using System.Threading.Tasks;
using Microsoft.EntityFrameworkCore;
using Microsoft.AspNetCore.JsonPatch;
```

```
namespace WebApp.Controllers {

    [ApiController]
    [Route("api/[controller]")]
    public class SuppliersController : ControllerBase {
        private DataContext context;

        public SuppliersController(DataContext ctx) {
            context = ctx;
        }

        [HttpGet("{id}")]
        public async Task<Supplier> GetSupplier(long id) {
            Supplier supplier = await context.Suppliers.Include(s => s.Products)
                .FirstAsync(s => s.SupplierId == id);
            foreach (Product p in supplier.Products) {
                p.Supplier = null;
            };
            return supplier;
        }

        [HttpPatch("{id}")]
        public async Task<Supplier> PatchSupplier(long id,
                JsonPatchDocument<Supplier> patchDoc) {
            Supplier s = await context.Suppliers.FindAsync(id);
            if (s != null) {
                patchDoc.ApplyTo(s);
                await context.SaveChangesAsync();
            }
            return s;
        }
    }
}
```

The action method is decorated with the HttpPatch attribute, which denotes that it will handle HTTP requests. The model binding feature is used to process the JSON Patch document through a JsonPatchDocument<T> method parameter. The JsonPatchDocument<T> class defines an ApplyTo method, which applies each operation to an object. The action method in Listing 20-8 retrieves a Supplier object from the database, applies the JSON PATCH, and stores the modified object.

Restart ASP.NET Core and use a PowerShell command prompt to run the command shown in Listing 20-9, which sends an HTTP PATCH request with a JSON PATCH document that changes the value of the City property to Los Angeles.

Listing 20-9. Sending an HTTP PATCH Request

```
Invoke-RestMethod http://localhost:5000/api/suppliers/1 -Method PATCH -ContentType "application/json"
-Body '[{"op":"replace","path":"City","value":"Los Angeles"}]'
```

The PatchSupplier action method returns the modified Supplier object as its result, which is serialized and sent to the client in the HTTP response. You can also see the effect of the change by using a web browser to request http://localhost:5000/suppliers/1, which produces the response shown in Figure 20-5.

Figure 20-5. *Updating using a PATCH request*

Understanding Content Formatting

The web service examples so far have produced JSON results, but this is not the only data format that action methods can produce. The content format selected for an action result depends on four factors: the formats that the client will accept, the formats that the application can produce, the content policy specified by the action method, and the type returned by the action method. Figuring out how everything fits together can be daunting, but the good news is that the default policy works just fine for most applications, and you only need to understand what happens behind the scenes when you need to make a change or when you are not getting results in the format that you expect.

Understanding the Default Content Policy

The best way to get acquainted with content formatting is to understand what happens when neither the client nor the action method applies any restrictions to the formats that can be used. In this situation, the outcome is simple and predictable.

1. If the action method returns a string, the string is sent unmodified to the client, and the Content-Type header of the response is set to text/plain.

2. For all other data types, including other simple types such as int, the data is formatted as JSON, and the Content-Type header of the response is set to application/json.

Strings get special treatment because they cause problems when they are encoded as JSON. When you encode other simple types, such as the C# int value 2, then the result is a quoted string, such as "2". When you encode a string, you end up with two sets of quotes so that "Hello" becomes ""Hello"". Not all clients cope well with this double encoding, so it is more reliable to use the text/plain format and sidestep the issue entirely. This is rarely an issue because few applications send string values; it is more common to send objects in the JSON format. To see the default policy, add a class file named ContentController.cs to the WebApps/Controllers folder with the code shown in Listing 20-10.

Listing 20-10. The Contents of the ContentController.cs File in the Controllers Folder

```
using Microsoft.AspNetCore.Mvc;
using Microsoft.EntityFrameworkCore;
using System.Threading.Tasks;
using WebApp.Models;

namespace WebApp.Controllers {

    [ApiController]
    [Route("/api/[controller]")]
    public class ContentController : ControllerBase {
        private DataContext context;

        public ContentController(DataContext dataContext) {
            context = dataContext;
        }
```

```
        [HttpGet("string")]
        public string GetString() => "This is a string response";

        [HttpGet("object")]
        public async Task<Product> GetObject() {
            return await context.Products.FirstAsync();
        }
    }
}
```

The controller defines actions that return string and object results. Restart ASP.NET Core and use a PowerShell prompt to run the command shown in Listing 20-11; this command sends a request that invokes the GetString action method, which returns a string.

Listing 20-11. Requesting a String Response

```
Invoke-WebRequest http://localhost:5000/api/content/string | select @{n='Content-Type';e={ $_.Headers.
"Content-Type" }}, Content
```

This command sends a GET request to the /api/content/string URL and processes the response to display the Content-Type header and the content from the response. The command produces the following output, which shows the Content-Type header for the response:

```
Content-Type                 Content
------------                 -------
text/plain; charset=utf-8 This is a string response
```

Next, run the command shown in Listing 20-12, which sends a request that will be handled by the GetObject action method.

Listing 20-12. Requesting an Object Response

```
Invoke-WebRequest http://localhost:5000/api/content/object | select @{n='Content-Type';e={
$_.Headers."Content-Type" }}, Content
```

This command produces the following output, formatted for clarity, that shows that the response has been encoded as JSON:

```
Content-Type                       Content
------------                       -------
application/json; charset=utf-8 {"productId":1,"name":"Kayak",
                                   "price":275.00,"categoryId":1,"supplierId":1}
```

Understanding Content Negotiation

Most clients include an Accept header in a request, which specifies the set of formats that they are willing to receive in the response, expressed as a set of MIME types. Here is the Accept header that Google Chrome sends in requests:

```
Accept: text/html,application/xhtml+xml,application/xml;q=0.9,image/webp,image/apng,
        */*;q=0.8
```

This header indicates that Chrome can handle the HTML and XHTML formats (XHTML is an XML-compliant dialect of HTML), XML, and the WEBP image format (which is the animated PNG image format).

The q values in the header specify relative preference, where the value is 1.0 by default. Specifying a q value for 0.9 for application/xml tells the server that Chrome will accept XML data but prefers to deal with HTML or XHTML. The */* item tells the server that Chrome will accept any format, but its q value specifies that it is the lowest preference of the specified types. Putting this together means that the Accept header sent by Chrome provides the server with the following information:

1. Chrome prefers to receive HTML or XHTML data or WEBP and APNG images.

2. If those formats are not available, then the next most preferred format is XML.

3. If none of the preferred formats is available, then Chrome will accept any format.

You might assume from this that you can change the format produced by the ASP.NET Core application by setting the Accept header, but it doesn't work that way—or, rather, it doesn't work that way just yet because there is some preparation required.

To see what happens when the Accept header is changed, use a PowerShell prompt to run the command shown in Listing 20-13, which sets the Accept header to tell ASP.NET Core that the client is willing to receive only XML data.

Listing 20-13. Requesting XML Data

```
Invoke-WebRequest http://localhost:5000/api/content/object -Headers @{Accept="application/xml"} | select
@{n='Content-Type';e={ $_.Headers."Content-Type" }}, Content
```

Here are the results, which show that the application has sent an application/json response:

```
Content-Type                    Content
------------                    -------
application/json; charset=utf-8 {"productId":1,"name":"Kayak",
                                 "price":275.00,"categoryId":1,"supplierId":1}
```

Including the Accept header has no effect on the format, even though the ASP.NET Core application sent the client a format that it hasn't specified. The problem is that, by default, the MVC Framework is configured to only use JSON. Rather than return an error, the MVC Framework sends JSON data in the hope that the client can process it, even though it was not one of the formats specified by the request Accept header.

Enabling XML Formatting

For content negotiation to work, the application must be configured so there is some choice in the formats that can be used. Although JSON has become the default format for web applications, the MVC Framework can also support encoding data as XML, as shown in Listing 20-14.

■ **Tip** You can create your own content format by deriving from the Microsoft.AspNetCore.Mvc.Formatters.OutputFormatter class. This is rarely used because creating a custom data format isn't a useful way of exposing the data in your application, and the most common formats—JSON and XML—are already implemented.

Listing 20-14. Enabling XML Formatting in the Startup.cs File in the WebApp Folder

```
...
public void ConfigureServices(IServiceCollection services) {
    services.AddDbContext<DataContext>(opts => {
        opts.UseSqlServer(Configuration[
            "ConnectionStrings:ProductConnection"]);
        opts.EnableSensitiveDataLogging(true);
    });

    services.AddControllers().AddNewtonsoftJson().AddXmlSerializerFormatters();
```

```
    services.Configure<MvcNewtonsoftJsonOptions>(opts => {
        opts.SerializerSettings.NullValueHandling
            = Newtonsoft.Json.NullValueHandling.Ignore;
    });
}
...
```

The XML Serializer has some limitations, including the inability to deal with Entity Framework Core navigation properties because they are defined through an interface. To create an object that can be serialized, Listing 20-15 uses ProductBindingTarget defined in Chapter 19.

Listing 20-15. Creating a Serializable Object in the ContentController.cs File in the Controllers Folder

```
using Microsoft.AspNetCore.Mvc;
using Microsoft.EntityFrameworkCore;
using System.Threading.Tasks;
using WebApp.Models;

namespace WebApp.Controllers {

    [ApiController]
    [Route("/api/[controller]")]
    public class ContentController : ControllerBase {
        private DataContext context;

        public ContentController(DataContext dataContext) {
            context = dataContext;
        }

        [HttpGet("string")]
        public string GetString() => "This is a string response";

        [HttpGet("object")]
        public async Task<ProductBindingTarget> GetObject() {
            Product p = await context.Products.FirstAsync();
            return new ProductBindingTarget() {
                Name = p.Name, Price = p.Price, CategoryId = p.CategoryId,
                SupplierId = p.SupplierId
            };
        }
    }
}
```

When the MVC Framework had only the JSON format available, it had no choice but to encode responses as JSON. Now that there is a choice, you can see the content negotiation process working more fully. Restart ASP.NET Core MVC and run the command in Listing 20-13 again to request XML data, and you will see the following output (from which I have omitted he namespace attributes for brevity):

```
Content-Type                  Content
------------                  -------
application/xml; charset=utf-8 <ProductBindingTarget>
                                  <Name>Kayak</Name>
                                  <Price>275.00</Price>
                                  <CategoryId>1</CategoryId>
                                  <SupplierId>1</SupplierId>
                              </ProductBindingTarget>
```

Fully Respecting Accept Headers

The MVC Framework will always use the JSON format if the Accept header contains */*, indicating any format, even if there are other supported formats with a higher preference. This is an odd feature that is intended to deal with requests from browsers consistently, although it can be a source of confusion. Run the command shown in Listing 20-16 to send a request with an Accept header that requests XML but will accept any other format if XML isn't available.

Listing 20-16. Requesting an XML Response with a Fallback

```
Invoke-WebRequest http://localhost:5000/api/content/object -Headers @{Accept="application/xml,*/*;q=0.8"} |
select @{n='Content-Type';e={ $_.Headers."Content-Type" }}, Content
```

Even though the Accept header tells the MVC Framework that the client prefers XML, the presence of the */* fallback means that a JSON response is sent. A related problem is that a JSON response will be sent when the client requests a format that the MVC Framework hasn't been configured to produce, which you can see by running the command shown in Listing 20-17.

Listing 20-17. Requesting a PNG Response

```
Invoke-WebRequest http://localhost:5000/api/content/object -Headers @{Accept="img/png"} | select @{n='Content-
Type';e={ $_.Headers."Content-Type" }}, Content
```

The commands in Listing 20-16 and Listing 20-17 both produce this response:

```
Content-Type                    Content
------------                    -------
application/json; charset=utf-8 {"name":"Kayak","price":275.00,
                                 "categoryId":1,"supplierId":1}
```

In both cases, the MVC Framework returns JSON data, which may not be what the client is expecting. Two configuration settings are used to tell the MVC Framework to respect the Accept setting sent by the client and not send JSON data by default. To change the configuration, add the statements shown in Listing 20-18 to the Startup class.

Listing 20-18. Configuring Content Negotiation in the Startup.cs File in the WebApp Folder

```
...
public void ConfigureServices(IServiceCollection services) {
    services.AddDbContext<DataContext>(opts => {
        opts.UseSqlServer(Configuration[
            "ConnectionStrings:ProductConnection"]);
        opts.EnableSensitiveDataLogging(true);
    });

    services.AddControllers().AddNewtonsoftJson().AddXmlSerializerFormatters();

    services.Configure<MvcNewtonsoftJsonOptions>(opts => {
        opts.SerializerSettings.NullValueHandling
            = Newtonsoft.Json.NullValueHandling.Ignore;
    });

    services.Configure<MvcOptions>(opts => {
        opts.RespectBrowserAcceptHeader = true;
        opts.ReturnHttpNotAcceptable = true;
    });
}
...
```

The options pattern is used to set the properties of a MvcOptions object. Setting RespectBrowserAcceptHeader to true disables the fallback to JSON when the Accept header contains */*. Setting ReturnHttpNotAcceptable to true disables the fallback to JSON when the client requests an unsupported data format.

Restart ASP.NET Core and repeat the command from Listing 20-16. Instead of a JSON response, the format preferences specified by the Accept header will be respected, and an XML response will be sent. Repeat the command from Listing 20-17, and you will receive a response with the 406 status code.

```
...
Invoke-WebRequest : The remote server returned an error: (406) Not Acceptable.
...
```

Sending a 406 code indicates there is no overlap between the formats the client can handle and the formats that the MVC Framework can produce, ensuring that the client doesn't receive a data format it cannot process.

Specifying an Action Result Format

The data formats that the MVC Framework can use for an action method result can be constrained using the Produces attribute, as shown in Listing 20-19.

■ **Tip** The Produces attribute is an example of a filter, which allows attributes to alter requests and responses. See Chapter 30 for more details.

Listing 20-19. Specifying a Data Format in the ContentController.cs File in the Controllers Folder

```
using Microsoft.AspNetCore.Mvc;
using Microsoft.EntityFrameworkCore;
using System.Threading.Tasks;
using WebApp.Models;

namespace WebApp.Controllers {

    [ApiController]
    [Route("/api/[controller]")]
    public class ContentController : ControllerBase {
        private DataContext context;

        public ContentController(DataContext dataContext) {
            context = dataContext;
        }

        [HttpGet("string")]
        public string GetString() => "This is a string response";

        [HttpGet("object")]
        [Produces("application/json")]
        public async Task<ProductBindingTarget> GetObject() {
            Product p = await context.Products.FirstAsync();
            return new ProductBindingTarget() {
                Name = p.Name, Price = p.Price, CategoryId = p.CategoryId,
                SupplierId = p.SupplierId
            };
        }
    }
}
```

The argument for the attribute specifies the format that will be used for the result from the action, and more than one type can be specified. The Produces attribute restricts the types that the MVC Framework will consider when processing an Accept header. To see the effect of the Produces attribute, use a PowerShell prompt to run the command shown in Listing 20-20.

Listing 20-20. Requesting Data

```
Invoke-WebRequest http://localhost:5000/api/content/object -Headers @{Accept="application/xml,application/
json;q=0.8"} | select @{n='Content-Type';e={ $_.Headers."Content-Type" }}, Content
```

The Accept header tells the MVC Framework that the client prefers XML data but will accept JSON. The Produces attribute means that XML data isn't available as the data format for the GetObject action method and so the JSON serializer is selected, which produces the following response:

```
Content-Type                    Content
------------                    -------
application/json; charset=utf-8 {"name":"Kayak","price":275.00,
                                 "categoryId":1,"supplierId":1}
```

Requesting a Format in the URL

The Accept header isn't always under the control of the programmer who is writing the client. In such situations, it can be helpful to allow the data format for the response to be requested using the URL. This feature is enabled by decorating an action method with the FormatFilter attribute and ensuring there is a format segment variable in the action method's route, as shown in Listing 20-21.

Listing 20-21. Enabling Formatting in the ContentController.cs File in the Controllers Folder

```
using Microsoft.AspNetCore.Mvc;
using Microsoft.EntityFrameworkCore;
using System.Threading.Tasks;
using WebApp.Models;

namespace WebApp.Controllers {

    [ApiController]
    [Route("/api/[controller]")]
    public class ContentController : ControllerBase {
        private DataContext context;

        public ContentController(DataContext dataContext) {
            context = dataContext;
        }

        [HttpGet("string")]
        public string GetString() => "This is a string response";

        [HttpGet("object/{format?}")]
        [FormatFilter]
        [Produces("application/json", "application/xml")]
        public async Task<ProductBindingTarget> GetObject() {
            Product p = await context.Products.FirstAsync();
            return new ProductBindingTarget() {
                Name = p.Name, Price = p.Price, CategoryId = p.CategoryId,
                SupplierId = p.SupplierId
            };
        }
    }
}
```

The FormatFilter attribute is an example of a filter, which is an attribute that can modify requests and responses, as described in Chapter 30. This filter gets the value of the format segment variable from the route that matched the request and uses it to override the Accept header sent by the client. I have also expanded the range of types specified by the Produces attribute so that the action method can return both JSON and XML responses.

Each data format supported by the application has a shorthand: xml for XML data and json for JSON data. When the action method is targeted by a URL that contains one of these shorthand names, the Accept header is ignored, and the specified format is used. To see the effect, restart ASP.NET Core and use the browser to request http://localhost:5000/api/content/object/json and http://localhost:5000/api/content/object/xml, which produce the responses shown in Figure 20-6.

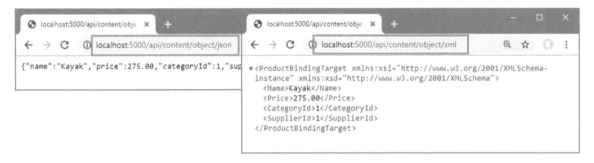

Figure 20-6. *Requesting data formats in the URL*

Restricting the Formats Received by an Action Method

Most content formatting decisions focus on the data formats the ASP.NET Core application sends to the client, but the same serializers that deal with results are used to deserialize the data sent by clients in request bodies. The deserialization process happens automatically, and most applications will be happy to accept data in all the formats they are configured to send. The example application is configured to send JSON and XML data, which means that clients can send JSON and XML data in requests.

The Consumes attribute can be applied to action methods to restrict the data types it will handle, as shown in Listing 20-22.

Listing 20-22. Adding Action Methods in the ContentController.cs File in the Controllers Folder

```
using Microsoft.AspNetCore.Mvc;
using Microsoft.EntityFrameworkCore;
using System.Threading.Tasks;
using WebApp.Models;

namespace WebApp.Controllers {

    [ApiController]
    [Route("/api/[controller]")]
    public class ContentController : ControllerBase {
        private DataContext context;

        public ContentController(DataContext dataContext) {
            context = dataContext;
        }

        [HttpGet("string")]
        public string GetString() => "This is a string response";

        [HttpGet("object/{format?}")]
        [FormatFilter]
        [Produces("application/json", "application/xml")]
```

```
        public async Task<ProductBindingTarget> GetObject() {
            Product p = await context.Products.FirstAsync();
            return new ProductBindingTarget() {
                Name = p.Name, Price = p.Price, CategoryId = p.CategoryId,
                SupplierId = p.SupplierId
            };
        }

        [HttpPost]
        [Consumes("application/json")]
        public string SaveProductJson(ProductBindingTarget product) {
            return $"JSON: {product.Name}";
        }

        [HttpPost]
        [Consumes("application/xml")]
        public string SaveProductXml(ProductBindingTarget product) {
            return $"XML: {product.Name}";
        }
    }
}
```

The new action methods are decorated with the Consumes attribute, restricting the data types that each can handle. The combination of attributes means that HTTP POST attributes whose Content-Type header is application/json will be handled by the SaveProductJson action method. HTTP POST requests whose Content-Type header is application/xml will be handled by the SaveProductXml action method. Restart ASP.NET Core and use a PowerShell command prompt to run the command shown in Listing 20-23 to send JSON data to the example application.

Listing 20-23. Sending JSON Data

```
Invoke-RestMethod http://localhost:5000/api/content -Method POST -Body  (@{ Name="Swimming Goggles";
Price=12.75; CategoryId=1; SupplierId=1} | ConvertTo-Json) -ContentType "application/json"
```

The request is automatically routed to the correct action method, which produces the following response:

```
JSON: Swimming Goggles
```

Run the command shown in Listing 20-24 to send XML data to the example application.

Listing 20-24. Sending XML Data

```
Invoke-RestMethod http://localhost:5000/api/content -Method POST -Body  "<ProductBindingTarget><Name>Kayak
</Name><Price>275.00</Price><CategoryId>1</CategoryId><SupplierId>1</SupplierId></ProductBindingTarget>"
-ContentType "application/xml"
```

The request is routed to the SaveProductXml action method and produces the following response:

```
XML: Kayak
```

The MVC Framework will send a 415 - Unsupported Media Type response if a request is sent with a Content-Type header that doesn't match the data types that the application supports.

Documenting and Exploring Web Services

When you are responsible for developing both the web service and its client, the purpose of each action and its results are obvious and are usually written at the same time. If you are responsible for a web service that is consumed by third-party developers, then you may need to provide documentation that describes how the web service works. The OpenAPI specification, which is also known as Swagger, describes web services in a way that can be understood by other programmers and consumed programmatically. In this section, I demonstrate how to use OpenAPI to describe a web service and show you how to fine-tune that description.

Resolving Action Conflicts

The OpenAPI discovery process requires a unique combination of the HTTP method and URL pattern for each action method. The process doesn't support the Consumes attribute, so a change is required to the ContentController to remove the separate actions for receiving XML and JSON data, as shown in Listing 20-25.

Listing 20-25. Removing an Action in the ContentController.cs File in the Controllers Folder

```
using Microsoft.AspNetCore.Mvc;
using Microsoft.EntityFrameworkCore;
using System.Threading.Tasks;
using WebApp.Models;

namespace WebApp.Controllers {

    [ApiController]
    [Route("/api/[controller]")]
    public class ContentController : ControllerBase {
        private DataContext context;

        public ContentController(DataContext dataContext) {
            context = dataContext;
        }

        [HttpGet("string")]
        public string GetString() => "This is a string response";

        [HttpGet("object/{format?}")]
        [FormatFilter]
        [Produces("application/json", "application/xml")]
        public async Task<ProductBindingTarget> GetObject() {
            Product p = await context.Products.FirstAsync();
            return new ProductBindingTarget() {
                Name = p.Name, Price = p.Price, CategoryId = p.CategoryId,
                SupplierId = p.SupplierId
            };
        }

        [HttpPost]
        [Consumes("application/json")]
        public string SaveProductJson(ProductBindingTarget product) {
            return $"JSON: {product.Name}";
        }
```

```
        //[HttpPost]
        //[Consumes("application/xml")]
        //public string SaveProductXml(ProductBindingTarget product) {
        //    return $"XML: {product.Name}";
        //}
    }
}
```

Commenting out one of the action methods ensures that each remaining action has a unique combination of HTTP method and URL.

Installing and Configuring the Swashbuckle Package

The Swashbuckle package is the most popular ASP.NET Core implementation of the OpenAPI specification and will automatically generate a description for the web services in an ASP.NET Core application. The package also includes tools that consume that description to allow the web service to be inspected and tested.

Open a new PowerShell command prompt, navigate to the folder that contains the WebApp.csproj file, and run the commands shown in Listing 20-26 to install the NuGet package. If you are using Visual Studio, you can select Project ➤ Manage Nuget Packages and install the package through the Visual Studio package user interface.

Listing 20-26. Adding a Package to the Project

```
dotnet add package Swashbuckle.AspNetCore --version 5.0.0-rc2
```

Add the statements shown in Listing 20-27 to the Startup class to add the services and middleware provided by the Swashbuckle package.

Listing 20-27. Configuring Swashbuckle in the Startup.cs File in the WebApp Folder

```
using System;
using System.Collections.Generic;
using System.Linq;
using System.Threading.Tasks;
using Microsoft.AspNetCore.Builder;
using Microsoft.AspNetCore.Hosting;
using Microsoft.AspNetCore.Http;
using Microsoft.Extensions.DependencyInjection;
using Microsoft.Extensions.Hosting;
using Microsoft.Extensions.Configuration;
using Microsoft.EntityFrameworkCore;
using WebApp.Models;
using Microsoft.AspNetCore.Mvc;
using Microsoft.OpenApi.Models;

namespace WebApp {
    public class Startup {

        public Startup(IConfiguration config) {
            Configuration = config;
        }

        public IConfiguration Configuration { get; set; }
```

```
public void ConfigureServices(IServiceCollection services) {
    services.AddDbContext<DataContext>(opts => {
        opts.UseSqlServer(Configuration[
            "ConnectionStrings:ProductConnection"]);
        opts.EnableSensitiveDataLogging(true);
    });

    services.AddControllers()
        .AddNewtonsoftJson().AddXmlSerializerFormatters();

    services.Configure<MvcNewtonsoftJsonOptions>(opts => {
        opts.SerializerSettings.NullValueHandling
            = Newtonsoft.Json.NullValueHandling.Ignore;
    });

    services.Configure<MvcOptions>(opts => {
        opts.RespectBrowserAcceptHeader = true;
        opts.ReturnHttpNotAcceptable = true;
    });

    services.AddSwaggerGen(options => {
        options.SwaggerDoc("v1",
            new OpenApiInfo { Title = "WebApp", Version = "v1" });
    });
}

public void Configure(IApplicationBuilder app, DataContext context) {
    app.UseDeveloperExceptionPage();
    app.UseRouting();
    app.UseMiddleware<TestMiddleware>();
    app.UseEndpoints(endpoints => {
        endpoints.MapGet("/", async context => {
            await context.Response.WriteAsync("Hello World!");
        });;
        endpoints.MapControllers();
    });
    app.UseSwagger();
    app.UseSwaggerUI(options => {
        options.SwaggerEndpoint("/swagger/v1/swagger.json", "WebApp");
    });
    SeedData.SeedDatabase(context);
}
}
}
```

There are two features set up by the statements in Listing 20-27. The feature generates an OpenAPI description of the web services that the application contains. You can see the description by restarting ASP.NET Core and using the browser to request the URL http://localhost:5000/swagger/v1/swagger.json, which produces the response shown in Figure 20-7. The OpenAPI format is verbose, but you can see each URL that the web service controllers support, along with details of the data each expects to receive and the range of responses that it will generate.

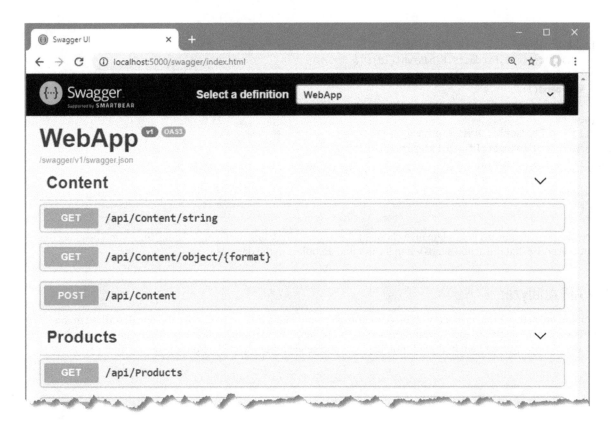

Figure 20-7. The OpenAPI description of the web service

The second feature is a UI that consumes the OpenAPI description of the web service and presents the information in a more easily understood way, along with support for testing each action. Use the browser to request `http://localhost:5000/swagger`, and you will see the interface shown in Figure 20-8. You can expand each action to see details, including the data that is expected in the request and the different responses that the client can expect.

Figure 20-8. The OpenAPI explorer interface

Fine-Tuning the API Description

Relying on the API discovery process can produce a result that doesn't truly capture the web service. You can see this by examining the entry in the Products section that describes GET requests matched by the /api/Product/{id} URL pattern. Expand this item and examine the response section, and you will see there is only one status code response that will be returned, as shown in Figure 20-9.

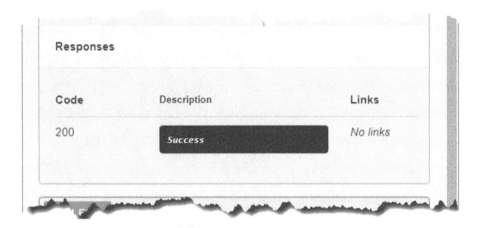

Figure 20-9. *The data formats listed in the OpenAPI web service description*

The API discovery process makes assumptions about the responses produced by an action method and doesn't always reflect what can really happen. In this case, the GetProduct action method in the ProductController class can return another response that the discovery process hasn't detected.

```
...
[HttpGet("{id}")]
public async Task<IActionResult> GetProduct(long id) {
    Product p = await context.Products.FindAsync(id);
    if (p == null) {
        return NotFound();
    }
    return Ok(new {
        ProductId = p.ProductId, Name = p.Name,
        Price = p.Price, CategoryId = p.CategoryId,
        SupplierId = p.SupplierId
    });
}
...
```

If a third-party developer attempts to implement a client for the web service using the OpenAPI data, they won't be expecting the 404 - Not Found response that the action sends when it can't find an object in the database.

Running the API Analyzer

ASP.NET Core includes an analyzer that inspects web service controllers and highlights problems like the one described in the previous section. To enable the analyzer, add the elements shown in Listing 20-28 to the WebApp.cspoj file. (If you are using Visual Studio, right-click the WebApp project item in the Solution Explorer and select Edit Project File from the popup menu.)

Listing 20-28. Enabling the Analyzer in the WebApp.csproj File in the WebApp Folder

```
<Project Sdk="Microsoft.NET.Sdk.Web">

  <PropertyGroup>
    <TargetFramework>netcoreapp3.1</TargetFramework>
  </PropertyGroup>

  <ItemGroup>
    <PackageReference Include="Microsoft.AspNetCore.Mvc.NewtonsoftJson"
        Version="3.1.1" />
    <PackageReference Include="Microsoft.EntityFrameworkCore.Design" Version="3.1.1">
      <IncludeAssets>runtime; build; native; contentfiles; analyzers;
          buildtransitive</IncludeAssets>
      <PrivateAssets>all</PrivateAssets>
    </PackageReference>
    <PackageReference Include="Microsoft.EntityFrameworkCore.SqlServer"
        Version="3.1.1" />
    <PackageReference Include="Swashbuckle.AspNetCore" Version="5.0.0-rc2" />
  </ItemGroup>

  <PropertyGroup>
    <IncludeOpenAPIAnalyzers>true</IncludeOpenAPIAnalyzers>
  </PropertyGroup>

</Project>
```

If you are using Visual Studio, you will see any problems detected by the API analyzer shown in the controller class file, as shown in Figure 20-10.

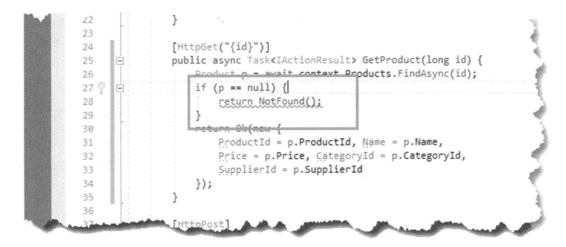

Figure 20-10. *A problem detected by the API analyzer*

If you are using Visual Studio Code, you will see warning messages when the project is compiled, either using the dotnet build command or when it is executed using the dotnet run command. When the project is compiled, you will see this message that describes the issue in the ProductController class:

```
Controllers\ProductsController.cs(28,9): warning API1000: Action method returns undeclared status code '404'.
[C:\WebApp\WebApp.csproj]
    1 Warning(s)
    0 Error(s)
```

Declaring the Action Method Result Type

To fix the problem detected by the analyzer, the ProducesResponseType attribute can be used to declare each of the response types that the action method can produce, as shown in Listing 20-29.

Listing 20-29. Declaring the Result in the ProductsController.cs File in the Controllers Folder

```
using Microsoft.AspNetCore.Mvc;
using WebApp.Models;
using System.Collections.Generic;
using Microsoft.Extensions.Logging;
using System.Linq;
using System.Threading.Tasks;
using Microsoft.AspNetCore.Http;

namespace WebApp.Controllers {

    [ApiController]
    [Route("api/[controller]")]
    public class ProductsController : ControllerBase {
        private DataContext context;

        public ProductsController(DataContext ctx) {
            context = ctx;
        }

        [HttpGet]
        public IAsyncEnumerable<Product> GetProducts() {
            return context.Products;
        }

        [HttpGet("{id}")]
        [ProducesResponseType(StatusCodes.Status200OK)]
        [ProducesResponseType(StatusCodes.Status404NotFound)]
        public async Task<IActionResult> GetProduct(long id) {
            Product p = await context.Products.FindAsync(id);
            if (p == null) {
                return NotFound();
            }
            return Ok(new {
                ProductId = p.ProductId, Name = p.Name,
                Price = p.Price, CategoryId = p.CategoryId,
                SupplierId = p.SupplierId
            });
        }

        // ...action methods omitted for brevity...
    }
}
```

Restart ASP.NET Core and use a browser to request http://localhost:5000/swagger, and you will see the description for the action method has been updated to reflect the 404 response, as shown in Figure 20-11.

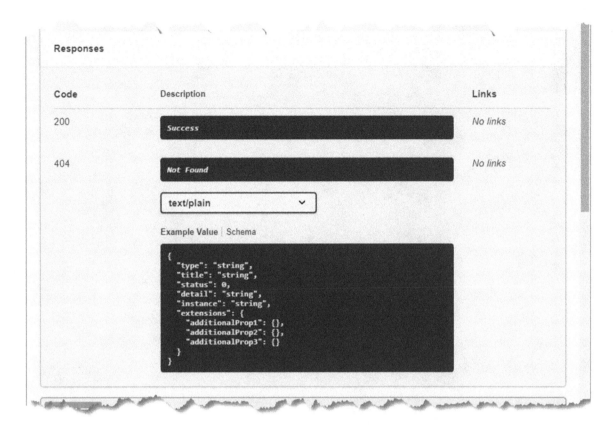

Figure 20-11. *Reflecting all the status codes produced by an action method*

Summary

In this chapter, I described some of the advanced features available for creating web services. I explained how to deal with related data in Entity Framework Core queries, how to support the HTTP PATCH method for handling selective updates, how content negotiation works, and how to use OpenAPI to describe the web services you create. In the next chapter, I describe how controllers can generate HTML responses.

CHAPTER 21

Using Controllers with Views, Part I

In this chapter, I introduce the *Razor view engine*, which is responsible for generating HTML responses that can be displayed directly to the user (as opposed to the JSON and XML responses, which are typically consumed by other applications). *Views* are files that contain C# expressions and HTML fragments that are processed by the view engine to generate HTML responses. I show how views work, explain how they are used in action methods, and describe the different types of C# expression they contain. In Chapter 22, I describe some of the other features that views support. Table 21-1 puts Razor views in context.

Table 21-1. *Putting Razor Views in Context*

Question	Answer
What are they?	Views are files that contain a mix of static HTML content and C# expressions.
Why are they useful?	Views are used to create HTML responses for HTTP requests. The C# expressions are evaluated and combined with the HTML content to create a response.
How are they used?	The View method defined by the Controller class creates an action response that uses a view.
Are there any pitfalls or limitations?	It can take a little time to get used to the syntax of view files and the way they combine code and content.
Are there any alternatives?	There are a number of third-party view engines that can be used in ASP.NET Core MVC, but their use is limited.

Table 21-2 summarizes the chapter.

Table 21-2. *Chapter Summary*

Problem	Solution	Listing
Enabling views	Use the AddControllersWithViews and MapControllerRoute methods to set up the required services and endpoints	1–5
Returning an HTML response from a controller action method	Use the View method to create a ViewResult	6
Creating dynamic HTML content	Create a Razor view that uses expressions for dynamic content	7–9, 20, 21
Selecting a view by name	Provide the view name as an argument to the View method	10, 11
Creating a view that can be used by multiple controllers	Create a shared view	12–14
Specifying a model type for a view	Use an @model expression	15–19
Generating content selectively	Use @if, @switch or @foreach expressions	22–26
Including C# code in a view	Use a code block	27

Preparing for This Chapter

This chapter uses the WebApp project from Chapter 20. To prepare for this chapter, open a new PowerShell command prompt and run the command shown in Listing 21-1 in the WebApp folder to install a new package. If you are using Visual Studio, you can install the package by selecting Project ➤ Manage NuGet Packages.

Listing 21-1. Adding a Package to the Example Project

```
dotnet add package Microsoft.AspNetCore.Mvc.Razor.RuntimeCompilation --version 3.1.1
```

Next, replace the contents of the Startup class with the statements shown in Listing 21-2, which remove some of the services and middleware used in earlier chapters.

▪ **Tip** You can download the example project for this chapter—and for all the other chapters in this book—from https://github. com/apress/pro-asp.net-core-3. See Chapter 1 for how to get help if you have problems running the examples.

Listing 21-2. Replacing the Contents of the Startup.cs File in the WebApp Folder

```
using System;
using System.Collections.Generic;
using System.Linq;
using Microsoft.AspNetCore.Builder;
using Microsoft.Extensions.DependencyInjection;
using Microsoft.Extensions.Configuration;
using Microsoft.EntityFrameworkCore;
using WebApp.Models;

namespace WebApp {
    public class Startup {

        public Startup(IConfiguration config) {
            Configuration = config;
        }

        public IConfiguration Configuration { get; set; }

        public void ConfigureServices(IServiceCollection services) {
            services.AddDbContext<DataContext>(opts => {
                opts.UseSqlServer(Configuration[
                    "ConnectionStrings:ProductConnection"]);
                opts.EnableSensitiveDataLogging(true);
            });
            services.AddControllers();
        }

        public void Configure(IApplicationBuilder app, DataContext context) {
            app.UseDeveloperExceptionPage();
            app.UseStaticFiles();
            app.UseRouting();
            app.UseEndpoints(endpoints => {
                endpoints.MapControllers();
            });
```

```
            SeedData.SeedDatabase(context);
        }
    }
}
```

Dropping the Database

Open a new PowerShell command prompt, navigate to the folder that contains the WebApp.csproj file, and run the command shown in Listing 21-3 to drop the database.

Listing 21-3. Dropping the Database

```
dotnet ef database drop --force
```

Running the Example Application

Select Start Without Debugging or Run Without Debugging from the Debug menu or use the PowerShell command prompt to run the command shown in Listing 21-4.

Listing 21-4. Running the Example Application

```
dotnet run
```

The database will be seeded as part of the application startup. Once ASP.NET Core is running, use a web browser to request http://localhost:5000/api/products, which will produce the response shown in Figure 21-1.

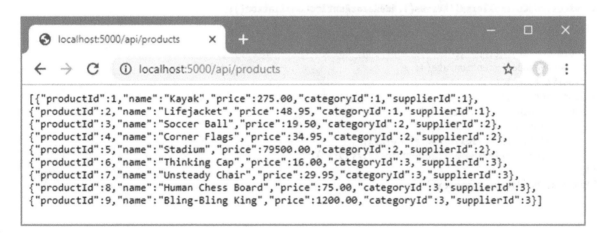

Figure 21-1. Running the example application

Getting Started with Views

I started this chapter with a web service controller to demonstrate the similarity with a controller that uses views. It is easy to think about web service and view controllers as being separate, but it is important to understand that the same underlying features are used for both types of response. In the sections that follow, I configure the application to support HTML applications and repurpose the Home controller so that it produces an HTML response.

Configuring the Application

The first step is to configure ASP.NET Core to enable HTML responses, as shown in Listing 21-5.

Listing 21-5. Changing the Configuration in the Startup.cs File in the WebApp Folder

```
using System;
using System.Collections.Generic;
using System.Linq;
using Microsoft.AspNetCore.Builder;
using Microsoft.Extensions.DependencyInjection;
using Microsoft.Extensions.Configuration;
using Microsoft.EntityFrameworkCore;
using WebApp.Models;

namespace WebApp {
    public class Startup {

        public Startup(IConfiguration config) {
            Configuration = config;
        }

        public IConfiguration Configuration { get; set; }

        public void ConfigureServices(IServiceCollection services) {
            services.AddDbContext<DataContext>(opts => {
                opts.UseSqlServer(Configuration[
                    "ConnectionStrings:ProductConnection"]);
                opts.EnableSensitiveDataLogging(true);
            });
            services.AddControllersWithViews().AddRazorRuntimeCompilation();
        }

        public void Configure(IApplicationBuilder app, DataContext context) {
            app.UseDeveloperExceptionPage();
            app.UseStaticFiles();
            app.UseRouting();
            app.UseEndpoints(endpoints => {
                endpoints.MapControllers();
                endpoints.MapControllerRoute("Default",
                    "{controller=Home}/{action=Index}/{id?}");
            });
            SeedData.SeedDatabase(context);
        }
    }
}
```

HTML responses are created using views, which are files containing a mix of HTML elements and C# expressions. The AddControllers method I used in Chapter 19 to enable the MVC Framework only supports web service controllers. To enable support for views, the AddControllersWithViews method is used. The AddRazorRuntimeCompilation method is used to enable the feature provided by the package installed in Listing 21-1, which makes it easier to work with views during development, as explained shortly.

The second change is the addition of the MapControllerRoute method in the endpoint routing configuration. Controllers that generate HTML responses don't use the same routing attributes that are applied to web service controllers and rely on a feature named *convention routing*, which I describe in the next section.

Creating an HTML Controller

Controllers for HTML applications are similar to those used for web services but with some important differences. To create an HTML controller, add a class file named HomeController.cs to the Controllers folder with the statements shown in Listing 21-6.

Listing 21-6. The Contents of the HomeController.cs File in the Controllers Folder

```
using Microsoft.AspNetCore.Mvc;
using System.Threading.Tasks;
using WebApp.Models;

namespace WebApp.Controllers {

    public class HomeController: Controller {
        private DataContext context;

        public HomeController(DataContext ctx) {
            context = ctx;
        }

        public async Task<IActionResult> Index(long id = 1) {
            return View(await context.Products.FindAsync(id));
        }
    }
}
```

The base class for HTML controllers is Controller, which is derived from the ControllerBase class used for web service controllers and provides additional methods that are specific to working with views.

```
...
public class HomeController:Controller {
...
```

Action methods in HTML controllers return objects that implement the IActionResult interface, which is the same result type used in Chapter 19 to return specific status code responses. The Controller base class provides the View method, which is used to select a view that will be used to create a response.

```
...
return View(await context.Products.FindAsync(id));
...
```

■ **Tip** Notice that the controller in Listing 21-6 hasn't been decorated with attributes. The ApiController attribute is applied only to web service controllers and should not be used for HTML controllers. The Route and HTTP method attributes are not required because HTML controllers rely on convention-based routing, which was configured in Listing 21-5 and which is introduced shortly.

The View method creates an instance of the ViewResult class, which implements the IActonResult interface and tells the MVC Framework that a view should be used to produce the response for the client. The argument to the View method is called the *view model* and provides the view with the data it needs to generate a response.

There are no views for the MVC Framework to use at the moment, but if you restart ASP.NET Core and use a browser to request http://localhost:5000, you will see an error message that shows how the MVC Framework responds to the ViewResult it received from the Index action method, as shown in Figure 21-2.

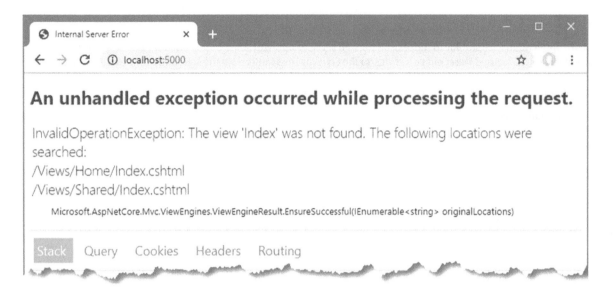

Figure 21-2. *Using a view result*

Behind the scenes, there are two important conventions at work, which are described in the following sections.

___

■ **Note**   There are two features that can expand the range of search locations. The search will include the /Pages/Shared folder if the project uses Razor Pages, as explained in Chapter 23.

___

Understanding Convention Routing

HTML controllers rely on *convention routing* instead of the Route attribute. The convention in this term refers to the use of the controller class name and the action method name used to configure the routing system, which was done in Listing 21-6 by adding this statement to the endpoint routing configuration:

```
...
endpoints.MapControllerRoute("Default", "{controller=Home}/{action=Index}/{id?}");
...
```

The route that this statement sets up matches two- and three-segment URLs. The value of the first segment is used as the name of the controller class, without the Controller suffix, so that Home refers to the HomeController class. The second segment is the name of the action method, and the optional third segment allows action methods to receive a parameter named id. Default values are used to select the Index action method on the Home controller for URLs that do not contain all the segments. This is such a common convention that the same routing configuration can be set up without having to specify the URL pattern, as shown in Listing 21-7.

Listing 21-7. Using the Default Routing Convention in the Startup.cs File in the WebApp Folder

```
...
public void Configure(IApplicationBuilder app, DataContext context) {
    app.UseDeveloperExceptionPage();
    app.UseStaticFiles();
    app.UseRouting();
```

```
    app.UseEndpoints(endpoints => {
        endpoints.MapControllers();
        endpoints.MapDefaultControllerRoute();
    });
    SeedData.SeedDatabase(context);
}
...
```

The MapDefaultControllerRoute method avoids the risk of mistyping the URL pattern and sets up the convention-based routing. I have configured one route in this chapter, but an application can define as many routes as it needs, and later chapters expand the routing configuration to make examples easier to follow.

■ **Tip** The MVC Framework assumes that any public method defined by an HTML controller is an action method and that action methods support all HTTP methods. If you need to define a method in a controller that is not an action, you can make it private or, if that is not possible, decorate the method with the NonAction attribute. You can restrict an action method to support specific HTTP methods by applying attributes so that the HttpGet attribute denotes an action that handles GET requests, the HttpPost method denotes an action that handles POST requests, and so on.

Understanding the Razor View Convention

When the Index action method defined by the Home controller is invoked, it uses the value of the id parameter to retrieve an object from the database and passes it to the View method.

```
...
public async Task<IActionResult> Index(long id = 1) {
    return View(await context.Products.FindAsync(id));
}
...
```

When an action method invokes the View method, it creates a ViewResult that tells the MVC Framework to use the default convention to locate a view. The Razor view engine looks for a view with the same name as the action method, with the addition of the cshtml file extension, which is the file type used by the Razor view engine. Views are stored in the Views folder, grouped by the controller they are associated with. The first location searched is the Views/Home folder, since the action method is defined by the Home controller (the name of which is taken by dropping Controller from the name of the controller class). If the Index.cshtml file cannot be found in the Views/Home folder, then the Views/Shared folder is checked, which is the location where views that are shared between controllers are stored.

While most controllers have their own views, views can also be shared so that common functionality doesn't have to be duplicated, as demonstrated in the "Using Shared Views" section.

The exception response in Figure 21-2 shows the result of both conventions. The routing conventions are used to process the request using the Index action method defined by the Home controller, which tells the Razor view engine to use the view search convention to locate a view. The view engine uses the name of the action method and controller to build its search pattern and checks for the Views/Home/Index.cshtml and Views/Shared/Index.cshtml files.

Creating a Razor View

To provide the MVC Framework with a view to display, create the Views/Home folder and add to it a file named Index.cshtml with the content shown in Listing 21-8. If you are using Visual Studio, create the view by right-clicking the Views/Home folder, selecting Add ➤ New Item from the popup menu, and selecting the Razor View item in the ASP.NET Core ➤ Web category, as shown in Figure 21-3.

■ **Tip** There is a menu item for creating views in the Add popup menu, but this relies on the Visual Studio scaffolding feature, which adds template content to create different types of view. I don't rely on the scaffolding in this book and instead show you how to create views from scratch.

Figure 21-3. *Creating a view using Visual Studio*

Listing 21-8. The Contents of the Index.cshtml File in the Views/Home Folder

```
<!DOCTYPE html>
<html>
<head>
    <link href="/lib/twitter-bootstrap/css/bootstrap.min.css" rel="stylesheet" />
</head>
<body>
    <h6 class="bg-primary text-white text-center m-2 p-2">Product Table</h6>
    <div class="m-2">
        <table class="table table-sm table-striped table-bordered">
            <tbody>
                <tr><th>Name</th><td>@Model.Name</td></tr>
                <tr><th>Price</th><td>@Model.Price.ToString("c")</td></tr>
            </tbody>
        </table>
    </div>
</body>
</html>
```

The view file contains standard HTML elements that are styled using the Bootstrap CSS framework, which is applied through the `class` attribute. The key view feature is the ability to generate content using C# expressions, like this:

```
...
<tr><th>Name</th><td>@Model.Name</td></tr>
<tr><th>Price</th><td>@Model.Price.ToString("c")</td></tr>
...
```

I explain how these expressions work in the "Understanding the Razor Syntax" section, but for now, it is enough to know that these expressions insert the value of the Name and Price properties from the Product view model passed to the View method by the action method in Listing 21-6. Restart ASP.NET Core and use a browser to request http://localhost:5000, and you will see the HTML response shown in Figure 21-4.

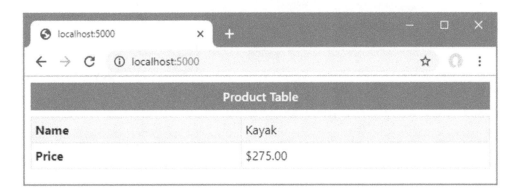

Figure 21-4. *A view response*

Modifying a Razor View

The package I added in Listing 21-1 and configured in Listing 21-5 detects and recompiles Razor views automatically, meaning that the ASP.NET Core runtime doesn't have to be restarted. To demonstrate the recompilation process, Listing 21-9 adds new elements to the Index view.

Listing 21-9. Adding Elements in the Index.cshtml File in the Views/Home Folder

```
<!DOCTYPE html>
<html>
<head>
    <link href="/lib/twitter-bootstrap/css/bootstrap.min.css" rel="stylesheet" />
</head>
<body>
    <h6 class="bg-primary text-white text-center m-2 p-2">Product Table</h6>
    <div class="m-2">
        <table class="table table-sm table-striped table-bordered">
            <tbody>
                <tr><th>Name</th><td>@Model.Name</td></tr>
                <tr><th>Price</th><td>@Model.Price.ToString("c")</td></tr>
                <tr><th>Category ID</th><td>@Model.CategoryId</td></tr>
            </tbody>
        </table>
    </div>
</body>
</html>
```

Save the changes to the view and reload the browser window without restarting ASP.NET Core. The changes to the view will be detected, and there will be a brief pause as the views are compiled, after which the response shown in Figure 21-5 will be displayed.

■ **Note** This feature applies only to views and not the C# classes in a project. If you make a change to a class file, then you will have to restart ASP.NET Core for the change to take effect.

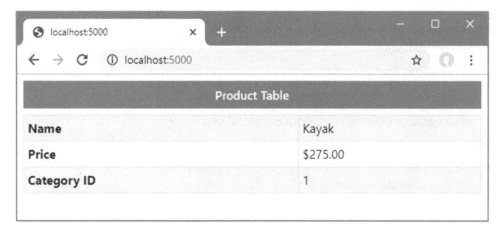

Figure 21-5. *Modifying a Razor view*

Selecting a View by Name

The action method in Listing 21-6 relies entirely on convention, leaving Razor to select the view that is used to generate the response. Action methods can select a view by providing a name as an argument to the View method, as shown in Listing 21-10.

Listing 21-10. Selecting a View in the HomeController.cs File in the Controllers Folder

```
using Microsoft.AspNetCore.Mvc;
using System.Threading.Tasks;
using WebApp.Models;

namespace WebApp.Controllers {

    public class HomeController: Controller {
        private DataContext context;

        public HomeController(DataContext ctx) {
            context = ctx;
        }

        public async Task<IActionResult> Index(long id = 1) {
            Product prod = await context.Products.FindAsync(id);
            if (prod.CategoryId == 1) {
                return View("Watersports", prod);
            } else {
                return View(prod);
            }
        }
    }
}
```

The action method selects the view based on the CategoryId property of the Product object that is retrieved from the database. If the CategoryId is 1, the action method invokes the View method with an additional argument that selects a view named Watersports.

```
...
return View("Watersports", prod);
...
```

Notice that the action method doesn't specify the file extension or the location for the view. It is the job of the view engine to translate Watersports into a view file. To create the view, add a Razor view file named Watersports.cshtml file to the Views/Home folder with the content shown in Listing 21-11.

Listing 21-11. The Contents of the Watersports.cshtml File in the Views/Home Folder

```
<!DOCTYPE html>
<html>
<head>
    <link href="/lib/twitter-bootstrap/css/bootstrap.min.css" rel="stylesheet" />
</head>
<body>
    <h6 class="bg-secondary text-white text-center m-2 p-2">Watersports</h6>
    <div class="m-2">
        <table class="table table-sm table-striped table-bordered">
            <tbody>
                <tr><th>Name</th><td>@Model.Name</td></tr>
                <tr><th>Price</th><td>@Model.Price.ToString("c")</td></tr>
                <tr><th>Category ID</th><td>@Model.CategoryId</td></tr>
            </tbody>
        </table>
    </div>
</body>
</html>
```

The new view follows the same pattern as the Index view but has a different title above the table. Since the HomeController class has been changed, restart ASP.NET Core and request http://localhost:5000/home/index/1 and http://localhost:5000/home/index/4. The action method selects the Watersports view for the first URL and the default view for the second URL, producing the two responses shown in Figure 21-6.

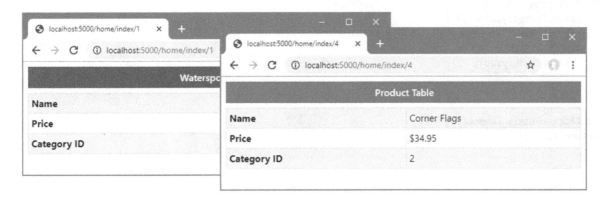

Figure 21-6. *Selecting views*

Using Shared Views

When the Razor view engine locates a view, it looks in the View/[controller] folder and then the Views/Shared folder. This search pattern means that views that contain common content can be shared between controllers, avoiding duplication. To see how this process works, add a Razor view file named Common.cshtml to the Views/Shared folder with the content shown in Listing 21-12.

Listing 21-12. The Contents of the Common.cshtml File in the Views/Shared Folder

```
<!DOCTYPE html>
<html>
<head>
    <link href="/lib/twitter-bootstrap/css/bootstrap.min.css" rel="stylesheet" />
</head>
<body>
    <h6 class="bg-secondary text-white text-center m-2 p-2">Shared View</h6>
</body>
</html>
```

Next, add an action method to the Home controller that uses the new view, as shown in Listing 21-13.

Listing 21-13. Adding an Action in the HomeController.cs File in the Controllers Folder

```
using Microsoft.AspNetCore.Mvc;
using System.Threading.Tasks;
using WebApp.Models;

namespace WebApp.Controllers {

    public class HomeController: Controller {
        private DataContext context;

        public HomeController(DataContext ctx) {
            context = ctx;
        }

        public async Task<IActionResult> Index(long id = 1) {
            Product prod = await context.Products.FindAsync(id);
            if (prod.CategoryId == 1) {
                return View("Watersports", prod);
            } else {
                return View(prod);
            }
        }

        public IActionResult Common() {
            return View();
        }
    }
}
```

The new action relies on the convention of using the method name as the name of the view. When a view doesn't require any data to display to the user, the View method can be called without arguments. Next, create a new controller by adding a class file named SecondController.cs to the Controllers folder, with the code shown in Listing 21-14.

Listing 21-14. The Contents of the SecondController.cs File in the Controllers Folder

```
using Microsoft.AspNetCore.Mvc;

namespace WebApp.Controllers {

    public class SecondController : Controller {
```

```
        public IActionResult Index() {
            return View("Common");
        }
    }
}
```

The new controller defines a single action, named Index, which invokes the View method to select the Common view. Restart ASP. NET Core and navigate to http://localhost:5000/home/common and http://localhost:5000/second, both of which will render the Common view, producing the responses shown in Figure 21-7.

Figure 21-7. *Using a shared view*

SPECIFYING A VIEW LOCATION

The Razor view engine will look for a controller-specific view before a shared view. You can change this behavior by specifying the complete path to a view file, which can be useful if you want to select a shared view that would otherwise be ignored because there is a controller-specific view with the same name.

```
...
public IActionResult Index() {
    return View("/Views/Shared/Common.cshtml");
}
...
```

When specifying the view, the path relative to the project folder must be specified, starting with the / character. Notice that the full name of the file, including the file extension, is used.

This is a technique that should be used sparingly because it creates a dependency on a specific file, rather than allowing the view engine to select the file.

Working with Razor Views

Razor views contain HTML elements and C# expressions. Expressions are mixed in with the HTML elements and denoted with the @ character, like this:

```
...
<tr><th>Name</th><td>@Model.Name</td></tr>
...
```

When the view is used to generate a response, the expressions are evaluated, and the results are included in the content sent to the client. This expression gets the name of the Product view model object provided by the action method and produces output like this:

```
...
<tr><th>Name</th><td>Corner Flags</td></tr>
...
```

This transformation can seem like magic, but Razor is simpler than it first appears. Razor views are converted into C# classes that inherit from the RazorPage class, which are then compiled like any other C# class.

■ **Tip**   You can see the generated view classes by examining the contents of the obj/Debug/netcoreapp3.0/Razor/Views folder with the Windows File Explorer.

The view from Listing 21-11, for example, would be transformed into a class like this:

```
using Microsoft.AspNetCore.Mvc.Razor;
using System.Threading.Tasks;
using Microsoft.AspNetCore.Mvc.Rendering;
using Microsoft.AspNetCore.Mvc;
using Microsoft.AspNetCore.Mvc.ViewFeatures;

namespace AspNetCore {

    public class Views_Home_Watersports : RazorPage<dynamic> {

        public async override Task ExecuteAsync() {
            WriteLiteral("<!DOCTYPE html>\r\n<html>\r\n");
            WriteLiteral("<head>");
            WriteLiteral(@"<link
                href=""/lib/twitter-bootstrap/css/bootstrap.min.css""
                rel=""stylesheet"" />");
            WriteLiteral("</head>");
            WriteLiteral("<body>");
            WriteLiteral(@"<h6 class=""bg-secondary text-white text-center
                m-2 p-2"">Watersports</h6>\r\n<div class=""m-2"">\r\n<table
                class=""table table-sm table-striped table-bordered"">\r\n
                <tbody>\r\n>");
            WriteLiteral("<th>Name</th><td>");
            Write(Model.Name);
            WriteLiteral("</td></tr>");
            WriteLiteral("<tr><th>Price</th><td>");
            Write(Model.Price.ToString("c"));
            WriteLiteral("</td></tr>\r\n<tr><th>Category ID</th><td>");
            Write(Model.CategoryId);
            WriteLiteral("</td></tr>\r\n</tbody>\r\n</table>\r\n</div>");
            WriteLiteral("</body></html>");
        }

        public IUrlHelper Url { get; private set; }
        public IViewComponentHelper Component { get; private set; }
        public IJsonHelper Json { get; private set; }
        public IHtmlHelper<dynamic> Html { get; private set; }
        public IModelExpressionProvider ModelExpressionProvider { get; private set; }
    }
}
```

This class is a simplification of the code that is generated so that I can focus on the features that are most important for this chapter. The first point to note is that the class generated from the view inherits from the RazorPage<T> class.

```
...
public class Views_Home_Watersports : RazorPage<dynamic> {
...
```

Table 21-3 describes the most useful properties and methods defined by RazorPage<T>.

CACHING RESPONSES

Responses from views can be cached by applying the ResponseCache attribute to action methods (or to the controller class, which caches the responses from all the action methods). See Chapter 17 for details of how response caching is enabled.

Table 21-3. *The RazorPage<T> Members*

Name	Description
Context	This property returns the HttpContext object for the current request.
Layout	This property is used to set the view layout, as described in Chapter 22.
Model	This property returns the view model passed to the View method by the action.
RenderBody()	This method is used in layouts to include content from a view, as described in Chapter 22.
RenderSection()	This method is used in layouts to include content from a section in a view, as described in Chapter 22.
TempData	This property is used to access the temp data feature, which is described in Chapter 22.
ViewBag	This property is used to access the view bag, which is described in Chapter 22.
ViewContext	This property returns a ViewContext object that provides context data.
ViewData	This property returns the view data, which I used for unit testing controllers in the SportsStore application.
Write(str)	This method writes a string, which will be safely encoded for use in HTML.
WriteLiteral(str)	This method writes a string without encoding it for safe use in HTML.

The expressions in the view are translated into calls to the Write method, which encodes the result of the expression so that it can be included safely in an HTML document. The WriteLiteral method is used to deal with the static HTML regions of the view, which don't need further encoding.

■ **Tip**   See Chapter 22 for more details about HTML encoding.

The result is a fragment like this from the CSHTML file:

```
...
<tr><th>Name</th><td>@Model.Name</td></tr>
...
```

This is converted into a series of C# statements like these in the ExecuteAsync method:

```
...
WriteLiteral("<th>Name</th><td>");
Write(Model.Name);
WriteLiteral("</td></tr>");
...
```

When the ExecuteAsync method is invoked, the response is generated with a mix of the static HTML and the expressions contained in the view. When the statements in the generated class are executed, the combination of the HTML fragments and the results from evaluating the expressions are written to the response, producing HTML like this:

```
...
<th>Name</th><td>Kayak</td></tr>
...
```

In addition to the properties and methods inherited from the RazorPage<T> class, the generated view class defines the properties described in Table 21-4, some of which are used for features described in later chapters.

Table 21-4. *The Additional View Class Properties*

Name	Description
Component	This property returns a helper for working with view components, which is accessed through the vc tag helper described in Chapter 25.
Html	This property returns an implementation of the IHtmlHelper interface. This property is used to manage HTML encoding, as described in Chapter 22.
Json	This property returns an implementation of the IJsonHelper interface, which is used to encode data as JSON, as described in Chapter 22.
ModelExpressionProvider	This property provides access to expressions that select properties from the model, which is used through tag helpers, described in Chapters 25–27.
Url	This property returns a helper for working with URLs, as described in Chapter 26.

Setting the View Model Type

The generated class for the Watersports.cshtml file is derived from RazorPage<T>, but Razor doesn't know what type will be used by the action method for the view model, so it has selected dynamic as the generic type argument. This means that the @Model expression can be used with any property or method name, which is evaluated at runtime when a response is generated. To demonstrate what happens when a nonexistent member is used in an exception, add the content shown in Listing 21-15 to the Watersports.cshtml file.

Listing 21-15. Adding Content in the Watersports.cshtml File in the Views/Home Folder

```
<!DOCTYPE html>
<html>
<head>
    <link href="/lib/twitter-bootstrap/css/bootstrap.min.css" rel="stylesheet" />
</head>
<body>
    <h6 class="bg-secondary text-white text-center m-2 p-2">Watersports</h6>
    <div class="m-2">
        <table class="table table-sm table-striped table-bordered">
            <tbody>
                <tr><th>Name</th><td>@Model.Name</td></tr>
                <tr><th>Price</th><td>@Model.Price.ToString("c")</td></tr>
                <tr><th>Category ID</th><td>@Model.CategoryId</td></tr>
                <tr><th>Tax Rate</th><td>@Model.TaxRate</td></tr>
            </tbody>
        </table>
    </div>
</body>
</html>
```

Use a browser to request `http://localhost:5000`, and you will see the exception shown in Figure 21-8.

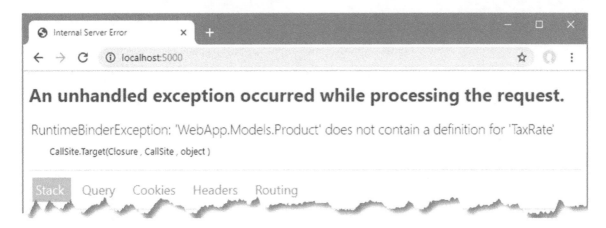

Figure 21-8. *Using a nonexistent property in a view expression*

To check expressions during development, the type of the Model object can be specified using the model keyword, as shown in Listing 21-16.

■ **Tip**   It is easy to get the two terms confused. Model, with an uppercase M, is used in expressions to access the view model object provided by the action method, while model, with a lowercase m, is used to specify the type of the view model.

Listing 21-16. Declaring the Model Type in the Watersports.cshtml File in the Views/Home Folder

```
@model WebApp.Models.Product
<!DOCTYPE html>
<html>
<head>
    <link href="/lib/twitter-bootstrap/css/bootstrap.min.css" rel="stylesheet" />
</head>
<body>
    <h6 class="bg-secondary text-white text-center m-2 p-2">Watersports</h6>
    <div class="m-2">
        <table class="table table-sm table-striped table-bordered">
            <tbody>
                <tr><th>Name</th><td>@Model.Name</td></tr>
                <tr><th>Price</th><td>@Model.Price.ToString("c")</td></tr>
                <tr><th>Category ID</th><td>@Model.CategoryId</td></tr>
                <tr><th>Tax Rate</th><td>@Model.TaxRate</td></tr>
            </tbody>
        </table>
    </div>
</body>
</html>
```

An error warning will appear in the editor after a few seconds, as Visual Studio or Visual Studio Code checks the view in the background, as shown in Figure 21-9. The compiler will also report an error if you build the project or use the dotnet build or dotnet run command.

Figure 21-9. *An error warning in a view file*

When the C# class for the view is generated, the view model type is used as the generic type argument for the base class, like this:

```
...
public class Views_Home_Watersports : RazorPage<Product> {
...
```

Specifying a view model type allows Visual Studio and Visual Studio Code to suggest property and method names as you edit views. Replace the nonexistent property with the one shown in Listing 21-17.

Listing 21-17. Replacing a Property in the Watersports.cshtml File in the Views/Home Folder

```
@model WebApp.Models.Product
<!DOCTYPE html>
<html>
<head>
    <link href="/lib/twitter-bootstrap/css/bootstrap.min.css" rel="stylesheet" />
</head>
<body>
    <h6 class="bg-secondary text-white text-center m-2 p-2">Watersports</h6>
    <div class="m-2">
        <table class="table table-sm table-striped table-bordered">
            <tbody>
                <tr><th>Name</th><td>@Model.Name</td></tr>
                <tr><th>Price</th><td>@Model.Price.ToString("c")</td></tr>
                <tr><th>Category ID</th><td>@Model.CategoryId</td></tr>
                <tr><th>Supplier ID</th><td>@Model.SupplierId</td></tr>
            </tbody>
        </table>
    </div>
</body>
</html>
```

As you type, the editor will prompt you with the possible member names defined by the view model class, as shown in Figure 21-10. This figure shows the Visual Studio code editor, but Visual Studio Code has a comparable feature.

Figure 21-10. *Editor suggestions when using a view model type*

Using a View Imports File

When I declared the view model object at the start of the Watersports.cshtml file, I had to include the namespace that contains the class, like this:

```
...
@model WebApp.Models.Product
...
```

By default, all types that are referenced in a Razor view must be qualified with a namespace. This isn't a big deal when the only type reference is for the model object, but it can make a view more difficult to read when writing more complex Razor expressions such as the ones I describe later in this chapter.

You can specify a set of namespaces that should be searched for types by adding a *view imports* file to the project. The view imports file is placed in the Views folder and is named _ViewImports.cshtml.

■ **Note** Files in the Views folder whose names begin with an underscore (the _ character) are not returned to the user, which allows the file name to differentiate between views that you want to render and the files that support them. View imports files and layouts (which I describe shortly) are prefixed with an underscore.

If you are using Visual Studio, right-click the Views folder in the Solution Explorer, select Add ➤ New Item from the pop-up menu, and select the Razor View Imports template from the ASP.NET Core category, as shown in Figure 21-11.

Figure 21-11. *Creating a view imports file*

Visual Studio will automatically set the name of the file to _ViewImports.cshtml, and clicking the Add button will create the file, which will be empty. If you are using Visual Studio Code, simply select the Views folder and add a new file called _ViewImports. cshtml.

Regardless of which editor you used, add the expression shown Listing 21-18.

Listing 21-18. The Contents of the _ViewImports.cshtml File in the Views Folder

```
@using WebApp.Models
```

The namespaces that should be searched for classes used in Razor views are specified using the @using expression, followed by the namespace. In Listing 21-18, I have added an entry for the WebApp.Models namespace that contains the view model class used in the Watersports.cshtml view.

Now that the namespace is included in the view imports file, I can remove the namespace from the view, as shown in Listing 21-19.

■ **Tip** You can also add an @using expression to individual view files, which allows types to be used without namespaces in a single view.

Listing 21-19. Simplifying the Model Type in the Watersports.cshtml File in the Views/Home Folder

```
@model Product
<!DOCTYPE html>
<html>
<head>
    <link href="/lib/twitter-bootstrap/css/bootstrap.min.css" rel="stylesheet" />
</head>
<body>
```

```
        <h6 class="bg-secondary text-white text-center m-2 p-2">Watersports</h6>
        <div class="m-2">
            <table class="table table-sm table-striped table-bordered">
                <tbody>
                    <tr><th>Name</th><td>@Model.Name</td></tr>
                    <tr><th>Price</th><td>@Model.Price.ToString("c")</td></tr>
                    <tr><th>Category ID</th><td>@Model.CategoryId</td></tr>
                    <tr><th>Supplier ID</th><td>@Model.SupplierId</td></tr>
                </tbody>
            </table>
        </div>
    </body>
</html>
```

Save the view file and use a browser to request http://localhost:5000, and you will see the response shown in Figure 21-12.

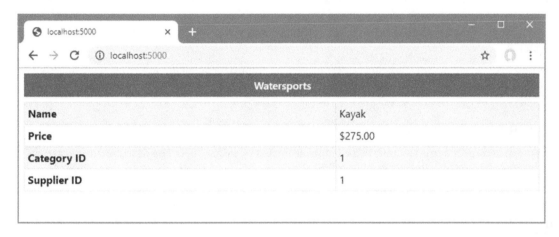

Figure 21-12. *Using a view imports file*

Understanding the Razor Syntax

The Razor compiler separates the static fragments of HTML from the C# expressions, which are then handled separately in the generated class file. There are several types of expression that can be included in views, which I describe in the sections that follow.

Understanding Directives

Directives are expressions that give instructions to the Razor view engine. The @model expression is a directive, for example, that tells the view engine to use a specific type for the view model, while the @using directive tells the view engine to import a namespace. Table 21-5 describes the most useful Razor directives.

Table 21-5. Useful Razor Directives

Name	Description
@model	This directive specifies the type of the view model.
@using	This directive imports a namespace.
@page	This directive denotes a Razor Page, described in Chapter 23.
@section	This directive denotes a layout section, as described In Chapter 22.
@addTagHelper	This directive adds tag helpers to a view, as described in Chapter 25.
@namespace	This directive sets the namespace for the C# class generated from a view.
@functions	This directive adds C# properties and methods to the C# class generated from a view and is commonly used in Razor Pages, as described in Chapter 23.
@attribute	This directive adds an attribute to the C# class generated from a view. I use this feature to apply authorization restrictions in Chapter 38.
@implements	This directive declares that the C# class generated from a view inherits an interface or is derived from a base class. This feature is demonstrated in Chapter 33.
@inherits	This directive sets the base class for the C# class generated from a view. This feature is demonstrated in Chapter 33.
@inject	This directive provides a view with direct access to a service through dependency injection. This feature is demonstrated in Chapter 23.

Understanding Content Expressions

Razor content expressions produce content that is included in the output generated by a view. Table 21-6 describes the most useful content expressions, which are demonstrated in the sections that follow.

Table 21-6. Useful Razor Content Expressions

Name	Description
@<expression>	This is the basic Razor expression, which is evaluated, and the result it produces is inserted into the response.
@if	This expression is used to select regions of content based on the result of an expression. See the "Using Conditional Expressions" section for examples.
@switch	This expression is used to select regions of content based on the result of an expression. See the "Using Conditional Expressions" section for examples.
@foreach	This expression generates the same region of content for each element in a sequence. See the "Enumerating Sequences" for examples.
@{ ... }	This expression defines a code block. See the "Using Razor Code Blocks" section for an example.
@:	This expression denotes a section of content that is not enclosed in HTML elements. See the "Using Conditional Expressions" section for an example.
@try	This expression is used to catch exceptions.
@await	This expression is used to perform an asynchronous operation, the result of which is inserted into the response. See Chapter 24 for examples.

Setting Element Content

The simplest expressions are evaluated to produce a single value that is used as the content for an HTML element in the response sent to the client. The most common type of expression inserts a value from the view model object, like these expressions from the Watersports.cshtml view file:

```
...
<tr><th>Name</th><td>@Model.Name</td></tr>
<tr><th>Price</th><td>@Model.Price.ToString("c")</td></tr>
...
```

This type of expression can read property values or invoke methods, as these examples demonstrate. Views can contain more complex expressions, but these need to be enclosed in parentheses so that the Razor compiler can differentiate between the code and static content, as shown in Listing 21-20.

Listing 21-20. Adding Expressions in the Watersports.cshtml File in the Views/Home Folder

```
@model Product
<!DOCTYPE html>
<html>
<head>
    <link href="/lib/twitter-bootstrap/css/bootstrap.min.css" rel="stylesheet" />
</head>
<body>
    <h6 class="bg-secondary text-white text-center m-2 p-2">Watersports</h6>
    <div class="m-2">
        <table class="table table-sm table-striped table-bordered">
            <tbody>
                <tr><th>Name</th><td>@Model.Name</td></tr>
                <tr><th>Price</th><td>@Model.Price.ToString("c")</td></tr>
                <tr><th>Tax</th><td>@Model.Price * 0.2m</td></tr>
                <tr><th>Tax</th><td>@(Model.Price * 0.2m)</td></tr>
            </tbody>
        </table>
    </div>
</body>
</html>
```

Use a browser to request http://localhost:5000; the response, shown in Figure 21-13, shows why parentheses are important.

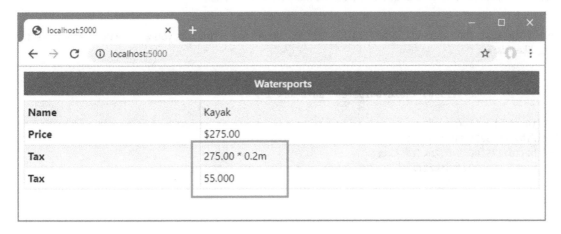

Figure 21-13. *Expressions with and without parentheses*

The Razor view compiler matches expressions conservatively and has assumed that the asterisk and the numeric value in the first expression are static content. This problem is avoided by parentheses for the second expression.

Setting Attribute Values

An expression can be used to set the values of element attributes, as shown in Listing 21-21.

Listing 21-21. Setting an Attribute in the Watersports.cshtml File in the Views/Home Folder

```
@model Product
<!DOCTYPE html>
<html>
<head>
    <link href="/lib/twitter-bootstrap/css/bootstrap.min.css" rel="stylesheet" />
</head>
<body>
    <h6 class="bg-secondary text-white text-center m-2 p-2">Watersports</h6>
    <div class="m-2">
        <table class="table table-sm table-striped table-bordered"
                data-id="@Model.ProductId">
            <tbody>
                <tr><th>Name</th><td>@Model.Name</td></tr>
                <tr><th>Price</th><td>@Model.Price.ToString("c")</td></tr>
                <tr><th>Tax</th><td>@Model.Price * 0.2m</td></tr>
                <tr><th>Tax</th><td>@(Model.Price * 0.2m)</td></tr>
            </tbody>
        </table>
    </div>
</body>
</html>
```

I used the Razor expressions to set the value for some data attributes on the `table` element.

■ **Tip**   Data attributes, which are attributes whose names are prefixed by `data-`, have been an informal way of creating custom attributes for many years and have been made part of the formal standard as part of HTML5. They are most often applied so that JavaScript code can locate specific elements or so that CSS styles can be more narrowly applied.

If you request `http://localhost:5000` and look at the HTML source that is sent to the browser, you will see that Razor has set the values of the attribute, like this:

```
...
<table class="table table-sm table-striped table-bordered" data-id="1">
    <tbody>
        <tr><th>Name</th><td>Kayak</td></tr>
        <tr><th>Price</th><td>$275.00</td></tr>
        <tr><th>Tax</th><td>275.00 * 0.2m</td></tr>
        <tr><th>Tax</th><td>55.000</td></tr>
    </tbody>
</table>
...
```

Using Conditional Expressions

Razor supports conditional expressions, which means that the output can be tailored based on the view model. This technique is at the heart of Razor and allows you to create complex and fluid responses from views that are simple to read and maintain. In Listing 21-22, I have added a conditional statement to the Watersports view.

Listing 21-22. Using an If Expression in the Watersports.cshtml File in the Views/Home Folder

```
@model Product
<!DOCTYPE html>
<html>
<head>
    <link href="/lib/twitter-bootstrap/css/bootstrap.min.css" rel="stylesheet" />
</head>
<body>
    <h6 class="bg-secondary text-white text-center m-2 p-2">Watersports</h6>
    <div class="m-2">
        <table class="table table-sm table-striped table-bordered"
               data-id="@Model.ProductId">
            <tbody>
                @if (Model.Price > 200) {
                    <tr><th>Name</th><td>Luxury @Model.Name</td></tr>
                } else {
                    <tr><th>Name</th><td>Basic @Model.Name</td></tr>
                }
                <tr><th>Price</th><td>@Model.Price.ToString("c")</td></tr>
                <tr><th>Tax</th><td>@Model.Price * 0.2m</td></tr>
                <tr><th>Tax</th><td>@(Model.Price * 0.2m)</td></tr>
            </tbody>
        </table>
    </div>
</body>
</html>
```

The @ character is followed by the if keyword and a condition that will be evaluated at runtime. The if expression supports optional else and elseif clauses and is terminated with a close brace (the } character). If the condition is met, then the content in the if clause is inserted into the response; otherwise, the content in the else clause is used instead.

Notice that the @ prefix isn't required to access a Model property in the condition.

```
...
@if (Model.Price > 200) {
...
```

But the @ prefix is required inside the if and else clauses, like this:

```
...
<tr><th>Name</th><td>Luxury @Model.Name</td></tr>
...
```

To see the effect of the conditional statement, use a browser to request http://localhost:5000/home/index/1 and http://localhost:5000/home/index/2. The conditional statement will produce different HTML elements for these URLs, as shown in Figure 21-14.

Figure 21-14. *Using a conditional statement*

Razor also supports @switch expressions, which can be a more concise way of handling multiple conditions, as shown in Listing 21-23.

Listing 21-23. Using a Switch Expression in the Watersports.cshtml File in the Views/Home Folder

```
@model Product
<!DOCTYPE html>
<html>
<head>
    <link href="/lib/twitter-bootstrap/css/bootstrap.min.css" rel="stylesheet" />
</head>
<body>
    <h6 class="bg-secondary text-white text-center m-2 p-2">Watersports</h6>
    <div class="m-2">
        <table class="table table-sm table-striped table-bordered"
                data-id="@Model.ProductId">
            <tbody>
                @switch (Model.Name) {
                    case "Kayak":
                        <tr><th>Name</th><td>Small Boat</td></tr>
                        break;
                    case "Lifejacket":
                        <tr><th>Name</th><td>Flotation Aid</td></tr>
                        break;
                    default:
                        <tr><th>Name</th><td>@Model.Name</td></tr>
                        break;
                }
                <tr><th>Price</th><td>@Model.Price.ToString("c")</td></tr>
                <tr><th>Tax</th><td>@Model.Price * 0.2m</td></tr>
                <tr><th>Tax</th><td>@(Model.Price * 0.2m)</td></tr>
            </tbody>
        </table>
    </div>
</body>
</html>
```

Conditional expressions can lead to the same blocks of content being duplicated for each result clause. In the switch expression, for example, each case clause differs only in the content of the td element, while the tr and th elements remain the same. To remove this duplication, conditional expressions can be used within an element, as shown in Listing 21-24.

Listing 21-24. Setting Content in the Watersports.cshtml File in the Views/Home Folder

```
@model Product
<!DOCTYPE html>
<html>
<head>
    <link href="/lib/twitter-bootstrap/css/bootstrap.min.css" rel="stylesheet" />
</head>
<body>
    <h6 class="bg-secondary text-white text-center m-2 p-2">Watersports</h6>
    <div class="m-2">
        <table class="table table-sm table-striped table-bordered"
                data-id="@Model.ProductId">
            <tbody>
                <tr><th>Name</th><td>
                @switch (Model.Name) {
                    case "Kayak":
                        @:Small Boat
                        break;
                    case "Lifejacket":
                        @:Flotation Aid
                        break;
                    default:
                        @Model.Name
                        break;
                }
                </td></tr>
                <tr><th>Price</th><td>@Model.Price.ToString("c")</td></tr>
                <tr><th>Tax</th><td>@Model.Price * 0.2m</td></tr>
                <tr><th>Tax</th><td>@(Model.Price * 0.2m)</td></tr>
            </tbody>
        </table>
    </div>
</body>
</html>
```

The Razor compiler needs help with literal values that are not enclosed in HTML elements, requiring the @: prefix, like this:

```
...
@:Small Boat
...
```

The compiler copes with HTML elements because it detects the open tag, but this additional help is required for text content. To see the effect of the switch statement, use a web browser to request http://localhost:5000/home/index/2, which produces the response shown in Figure 21-15.

Watersports	
Name	Flotation Aid
Price	$48.95
Tax	48.95 * 0.2m
Tax	9.790

Figure 21-15. *Using a switch expression with literal content*

Enumerating Sequences

The Razor @foreach expression generates content for each object in an array or a collection, which is a common requirement when processing data. Listing 21-25 adds an action method to the Home controller that produces a sequence of objects.

Listing 21-25. Adding an Action in the HomeController.cs File in the Controllers Folder

```
using Microsoft.AspNetCore.Mvc;
using System.Threading.Tasks;
using WebApp.Models;

namespace WebApp.Controllers {

    public class HomeController : Controller {
        private DataContext context;

        public HomeController(DataContext ctx) {
            context = ctx;
        }

        public async Task<IActionResult> Index(long id = 1) {
            Product prod = await context.Products.FindAsync(id);
            if (prod.CategoryId == 1) {
                return View("Watersports", prod);
            } else {
                return View(prod);
            }
        }

        public IActionResult Common() {
            return View();
        }
```

```
        public IActionResult List() {
            return View(context.Products);
        }
    }
}
```

The new action is called List, and it provides its view with the sequence of Product objects obtained from the Entity Framework Core data context. Add a Razor view file named List.cshtml to the Views/Home folder and add the content shown in Listing 21-26.

Listing 21-26. The Contents of the List.cshtml File in the Views/Home Folder

```
@model IEnumerable<Product>
<!DOCTYPE html>
<html>
<head>
    <link href="/lib/twitter-bootstrap/css/bootstrap.min.css" rel="stylesheet" />
</head>
<body>
    <h6 class="bg-secondary text-white text-center m-2 p-2">Products</h6>
    <div class="m-2">
        <table class="table table-sm table-striped table-bordered">
            <thead>
                <tr><th>Name</th><th>Price</th></tr>
            </thead>
            <tbody>
                @foreach (Product p in Model) {
                    <tr><td>@p.Name</td><td>@p.Price</td></tr>
                }
            </tbody>
        </table>
    </div>
</body>
</html>
```

The foreach expression follows the same format as the C# foreach statement. In the example, the variable p is assigned each object in the sequence provided by the action method. The content within the expression is duplicated for each object and inserted into the response after the expressions it contains are evaluated. In this case, the content in the foreach expression generates a table row with cells that have their own expressions.

```
...
<tr><td>@p.Name</td><td>@p.Price</td></tr>
...
```

Restart ASP.NET Core so that the new action method will be available and use a browser to request http://localhost:5000/home/list, which produces the result shown in Figure 21-16, showing how the foreach expression populates a table body.

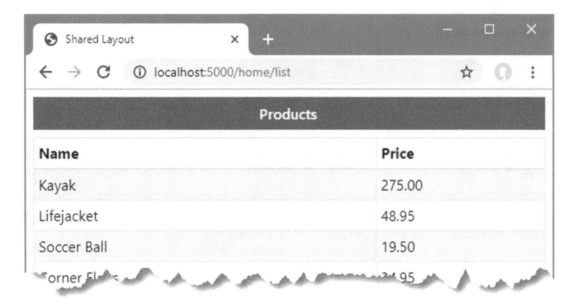

Figure 21-16. *Using a foreach expression*

Using Razor Code Blocks

Code blocks are regions of C# content that do not generate content but that can be useful to perform tasks that support the expressions that do. Listing 21-27 adds a code block that calculates an average value.

■ **Tip** The most common use of code blocks is to select a layout, which is described in Chapter 21.

Listing 21-27. Using a Code Block in the List.cshtml File in the Views/Home Folder

```
@model IEnumerable<Product>
@{
    decimal average = Model.Average(p => p.Price);
}
<!DOCTYPE html>
<html>
<head>
    <link href="/lib/twitter-bootstrap/css/bootstrap.min.css" rel="stylesheet" />
</head>
<body>
    <h6 class="bg-secondary text-white text-center m-2 p-2">Products</h6>
    <div class="m-2">
        <table class="table table-sm table-striped table-bordered">
            <thead>
                <tr><th>Name</th><th>Price</th><th></th></tr>
            </thead>
            <tbody>
                @foreach (Product p in Model) {
                    <tr>
                        <td>@p.Name</td><td>@p.Price</td>
                        <td>@((p.Price / average * 100).ToString("F1"))
                            % of average</td>
                    </tr>
                }
```

```
            </tbody>
          </table>
      </div>
  </body>
</html>
```

The code block is denoted by @{ and } and contains standard C# statements. The code block in Listing 21-27 uses LINQ to calculate a value that is assigned to a variable named average, which is used in an expression to set the contents of a table cell, avoiding the need to repeat the average calculation for each object in the view model sequence. Use a browser to request http://localhost:5000/home/list, and you will see the response shown in Figure 21-17.

▪ **Note**   Code blocks can become difficult to manage if they contain more than a few statements. For more complex tasks, consider using the view bag, described in Chapter 22, or adding a nonaction method to the controller.

Figure 21-17. *Using a code block*

Summary

In this chapter, I introduced Razor views, which are used to create HTML responses from action methods. I explained how views are defined, how they are transformed into C# classes, and how the expressions they contain can be used to generate dynamic content. In the next chapter, I continue to describe how controllers can be used with views.

CHAPTER 22

Using Controllers with Views, Part II

In this chapter, I describe more of the features provided by Razor views. I show you how to pass additional data to a view using the view bang and how to use layouts and layout sections to reduce duplication. I also explain how the results from expressions are encoded and how to disable the encoding process. Table 22-1 summarizes the chapter.

Table 22-1. *Chapter Summary*

Problem	Solution	Listing
Providing unstructured data to a view	Use the view bag	5, 6
Providing temporary data to a view	Use temp data	7, 8
Using the same content in multiple views	Use a layout	9–12, 15–18
Selecting the default layout for views	Use a view start file	13, 14
Interleaving unique and common content	Use layout sections	19–24
Creating reusable sections of content	Use a partial view	25–29
Inserting HTML into a response using a Razor expression	Encode the HTML	30–32
Including JSON in a view	Use the JSON encoder	33

Preparing for This Chapter

This chapter uses the WebApp project from Chapter 21. To prepare for this chapter, replace the contents of the HomeController.cs file with the code shown in Listing 22-1.

Listing 22-1. The Contents of the HomeController.cs File in the Controllers Folder

```
using Microsoft.AspNetCore.Mvc;
using System.Threading.Tasks;
using WebApp.Models;

namespace WebApp.Controllers {

    public class HomeController: Controller {
        private DataContext context;

        public HomeController(DataContext ctx) {
            context = ctx;
        }

        public async Task<IActionResult> Index(long id = 1) {
            return View(await context.Products.FindAsync(id));
        }
    }
```

```
        public IActionResult List() {
            return View(context.Products);
        }
    }
}
```

One of the features used in this chapter requires the session feature, which was described in Chapter 16. To enable sessions, add the statements shown in Listing 22-2 to the Startup class.

Listing 22-2. Enabling Sessions in the Startup.cs File in the WebApp Folder

```
using System;
using System.Collections.Generic;
using System.Linq;
using Microsoft.AspNetCore.Builder;
using Microsoft.Extensions.DependencyInjection;
using Microsoft.Extensions.Configuration;
using Microsoft.EntityFrameworkCore;
using WebApp.Models;

namespace WebApp {
    public class Startup {

        public Startup(IConfiguration config) {
            Configuration = config;
        }

        public IConfiguration Configuration { get; set; }

        public void ConfigureServices(IServiceCollection services) {
            services.AddDbContext<DataContext>(opts => {
                opts.UseSqlServer(Configuration[
                    "ConnectionStrings:ProductConnection"]);
                opts.EnableSensitiveDataLogging(true);
            });
            services.AddControllersWithViews().AddRazorRuntimeCompilation();

            services.AddDistributedMemoryCache();
            services.AddSession(options => {
                options.Cookie.IsEssential = true;
            });
        }

        public void Configure(IApplicationBuilder app, DataContext context) {
            app.UseDeveloperExceptionPage();
            app.UseStaticFiles();
            app.UseSession();
            app.UseRouting();
            app.UseEndpoints(endpoints => {
                endpoints.MapControllers();
                endpoints.MapDefaultControllerRoute();
            });
            SeedData.SeedDatabase(context);
        }
    }
}
```

Dropping the Database

Open a new PowerShell command prompt, navigate to the folder that contains the WebApp.csproj file, and run the command shown in Listing 22-3 to drop the database.

■ **Tip** You can download the example project for this chapter—and for all the other chapters in this book—from https://github. com/apress/pro-asp.net-core-3. See Chapter 1 for how to get help if you have problems running the examples.

Listing 22-3. Dropping the Database

```
dotnet ef database drop --force
```

Running the Example Application

Once the database has been dropped, select Start Without Debugging or Run Without Debugging from the Debug menu, or use the PowerShell command prompt to run the command shown in Listing 22-4.

Listing 22-4. Running the Example Application

```
dotnet run
```

The database will be seeded as part of the application startup. Once ASP.NET Core is running, use a web browser to request http://localhost:5000, which will produce the response shown in Figure 22-1.

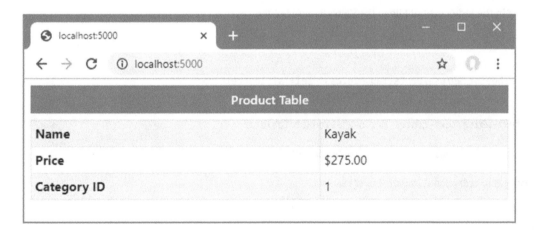

Figure 22-1. Running the example application

Using the View Bag

Action methods provide views with data to display with a view model, but sometimes additional information is required. Action methods can use the *view bag* to provide a view with extra data, as shown in Listing 22-5.

Listing 22-5. Using the View Bag in the HomeController.cs File in the Controllers Folder

```
using Microsoft.AspNetCore.Mvc;
using System.Threading.Tasks;
using WebApp.Models;
using Microsoft.EntityFrameworkCore;

namespace WebApp.Controllers {

    public class HomeController: Controller {
        private DataContext context;

        public HomeController(DataContext ctx) {
            context = ctx;
        }

        public async Task<IActionResult> Index(long id = 1) {
            ViewBag.AveragePrice = await context.Products.AverageAsync(p => p.Price);
            return View(await context.Products.FindAsync(id));
        }

        public IActionResult List() {
            return View(context.Products);
        }
    }
}
```

The ViewBag property is inherited from the Controller base class and returns a dynamic object. This allows action methods to create new properties just by assigning values to them, as shown in the listing. The values assigned to the ViewBag property by the action method are available to the view through a property also called ViewBag, as shown in Listing 22-6.

Listing 22-6. Using the View Bag in the Index.cshtml File in the Views/Home Folder

```
<!DOCTYPE html>
<html>
<head>
    <link href="/lib/twitter-bootstrap/css/bootstrap.min.css" rel="stylesheet" />
</head>
<body>
    <h6 class="bg-primary text-white text-center m-2 p-2">Product Table</h6>
    <div class="m-2">
        <table class="table table-sm table-striped table-bordered">
            <tbody>
                <tr><th>Name</th><td>@Model.Name</td></tr>
                <tr>
                    <th>Price</th>
                    <td>
                        @Model.Price.ToString("c")
                        (@(((Model.Price / ViewBag.AveragePrice)
                            * 100).ToString("F2"))% of average price)
                    </td>
                </tr>
                <tr><th>Category ID</th><td>@Model.CategoryId</td></tr>
            </tbody>
        </table>
    </div>
</body>
</html>
```

The ViewBag property conveys the object from the action to the view, alongside the view model object. In the listing, the action method queries for the average of the Product.Price properties in the database and assigns it to a view bag property named AveragePrice, which the view uses in an expression. Restart ASP.NET Core and use a browser to request http://localhost:5000, which produces the response shown in Figure 22-2.

Figure 22-2. *Using the view bag*

WHEN TO USE THE VIEW BAG

The view bag works best when it is used to provide the view with small amounts of supplementary data without having to create new view model classes for each action method. The problem with the view bag is that the compiler cannot check the use of the properties on dynamic objects, much like views that don't use an @model expression. It can be difficult to judge when a new view model class should be used, and my rule of thumb is to create a new view model class when the same view model property is used by multiple actions or when an action method adds more than two or three properties to the view bag.

Using Temp Data

The temp data feature allows a controller to preserve data from one request to another, which is useful when performing redirections. Temp data is stored using a cookie unless session state is enabled when it is stored as session data. Unlike session data, temp data values are marked for deletion when they are read and removed when the request has been processed.

Add a class file called CubedController.cs to the WebApp/Controllers folder and use it to define the controller shown in Listing 22-7.

Listing 22-7. The Contents of the CubedController.cs File in the Controllers Folder

```
using Microsoft.AspNetCore.Mvc;
using System;

namespace WebApp.Controllers {
    public class CubedController: Controller {

        public IActionResult Index() {
            return View("Cubed");
        }

        public IActionResult Cube(double num) {
            TempData["value"] = num.ToString();
            TempData["result"] = Math.Pow(num, 3).ToString();
```

```
                return RedirectToAction(nameof(Index));
        }
    }
}
```

The Cubed controller defines an Index method that selects a view named Cubed. There is also a Cube action, which relies on the model binding process to obtain a value for its num parameter from the request (a process described in detail in Chapter 28). The Cubed action method performs its calculation and stores the num value and the calculation result using TempData property, which returns a dictionary that is used to store key/value pairs. Since the temp data feature is built on top of the sessions feature, only values that can be serialized to strings can be stored, which is why I convert both double values to strings in Listing 22-7. Once the values are stored as temp data, the Cube method performs a redirection to the Index method. To provide the controller with a view, add a Razor view file named Cubed.cshtml to the WebApp/Views/Shared folder with the content shown in Listing 22-8.

Listing 22-8. The Contents of the Cubed.cshtml File in the Views/Shared Folder

```html
<!DOCTYPE html>
<html>
<head>
    <link href="/lib/twitter-bootstrap/css/bootstrap.min.css" rel="stylesheet" />
</head>
<body>
    <h6 class="bg-secondary text-white text-center m-2 p-2">Cubed</h6>
    <form method="get" action="/cubed/cube" class="m-2">
        <div class="form-group">
            <label>Value</label>
            <input name="num" class="form-control" value="@(TempData["value"])" />
        </div>
        <button class="btn btn-primary" type="submit">Submit</button>
    </form>
    @if (TempData["result"] != null) {
        <div class="bg-info text-white m-2 p-2">
            The cube of @TempData["value"] is @TempData["result"]
        </div>
    }
</body>
</html>
```

The base class used for Razor views provides access to the temp data through a TempData property, allowing values to be read within expressions. In this case, temp data is used to set the content of an input element and display a results summary. Reading a temp data value doesn't remove it immediately, which means that values can be read repeatedly in the same view. It is only once the request has been processed that the marked values are removed.

To see the effect, restart ASP.NET Core, use a browser to navigate to http://localhost:5000/cubed, enter a value into the form field, and click the Submit button. The browser will send a request that will set the temp data and trigger the redirection. The temp data values are preserved for the new request, and the results are displayed to the user. But reading the data values marks them for deletion, and if you reload the browser, the contents of the input element and the results summary are no longer displayed, as shown in Figure 22-3.

■ **Tip** The object returned by the TempData property provides a Peek method, which allows you to get a data value without marking it for deletion, and a Keep method, which can be used to prevent a previously read value from being deleted. The Keep method doesn't protect a value forever. If the value is read again, it will be marked for removal once more. Use session data if you want to store items so that they won't be removed when the request is processed.

Figure 22-3. Using temp data

USING THE TEMP DATA ATTRIBUTE

Controllers can define properties that are decorated with the TempData attribute, which is an alternative to using the TempData property, like this:

```
using Microsoft.AspNetCore.Mvc;
using System;

namespace WebApp.Controllers {
    public class CubedController: Controller {

        public IActionResult Index() {
            return View("Cubed");
        }

        public IActionResult Cube(double num) {
            Value = num.ToString();
            Result = Math.Pow(num, 3).ToString();
            return RedirectToAction(nameof(Index));
        }

        [TempData]
        public string Value { get; set; }

        [TempData]
        public string Result { get; set; }
    }
}
```

The values assigned to these properties are automatically added to the temp data store, and there is no difference in the way they are accessed in the view. My preference is to use the TempData dictionary to store values because it makes the intent of the action method obvious to other developers. However, both approaches are entirely valid, and choosing between them is a matter of preference.

Working with Layouts

The views in the example application contain duplicate elements that deal with setting up the HTML document, defining the head section, loading the Bootstrap CSS file, and so on. Razor supports *layouts*, which avoid this sort of duplication by consolidating common content in a single file that can be used by any view.

Layouts are typically stored in the Views/Shared folder because they are usually used by the action methods of more than one controller. If you are using Visual Studio, right-click the Views/Shared folder, select Add ➤ New Item from the popup menu, and choose the Razor Layout template, as shown in Figure 22-4. Make sure the name of the file is _Layout.cshtml and click the Add button to create the new file. Replace the content added to the file by Visual Studio with the elements shown in Listing 22-9.

Figure 22-4. *Creating a layout*

If you are using Visual Studio Code, create a file named _Layout.cshtml in the Views/Shared folder and add the content shown in Listing 22-9.

Listing 22-9. The Contents of the _Layout.cshtml File in the Views/Shared Folder

```
<!DOCTYPE html>
<html>
<head>
    <link href="/lib/twitter-bootstrap/css/bootstrap.min.css" rel="stylesheet" />
</head>
<body>
    <h6 class="bg-primary text-white text-center m-2 p-2">Shared View</h6>
    @RenderBody()
</body>
</html>
```

The layout contains the common content that will be used by multiple views. The content that is unique to each view is inserted into the response by calling the RenderBody method, which is inherited by the RazorPage<T> class, as described in Chapter 21. Views that use layouts can focus on just their unique content, as shown in Listing 22-10.

Listing 22-10. Using a Layout in the Index.cshtml File in the Views/Home Folder

```
@model Product
@{
    Layout = "_Layout";
}
<div class="m-2">
    <table class="table table-sm table-striped table-bordered">
        <tbody>
            <tr><th>Name</th><td>@Model.Name</td></tr>
            <tr>
                <th>Price</th>
                <td>
                    @Model.Price.ToString("c")
                    (@(((Model.Price / ViewBag.AveragePrice)
                        * 100).ToString("F2"))% of average price)
                </td>
            </tr>
            <tr><th>Category ID</th><td>@Model.CategoryId</td></tr>
        </tbody>
    </table>
</div>
```

The layout is selected by adding a code block, denoted by the @{ and } characters, that sets the Layout property inherited from the RazorPage<T> class. In this case, the Layout property is set to the name of the layout file. As with normal views, the layout is specified without a path or file extension, and the Razor engine will search in the /Views/[controller] and /Views/Shared folders to find a matching file. Use the browser to request http://localhost:5000, and you will see the response shown in Figure 22-5.

Figure 22-5. Using a layout

Configuring Layouts Using the View Bag

The view can provide the layout with data values, allowing the common content provided by the view to be customized. The view bag properties are defined in the code block that selects the layout, as shown in Listing 22-11.

Listing 22-11. Setting a View Bag Property in the Index.cshtml File in the Views/Home Folder

```
@model Product
@{
    Layout = "_Layout";
    ViewBag.Title = "Product Table";
}
```

```
<div class="m-2">
    <table class="table table-sm table-striped table-bordered">
        <tbody>
            <tr><th>Name</th><td>@Model.Name</td></tr>
            <tr>
                <th>Price</th>
                <td>
                    @Model.Price.ToString("c")
                    (@(((Model.Price / ViewBag.AveragePrice)
                        * 100).ToString("F2"))% of average price)
                </td>
            </tr>
            <tr><th>Category ID</th><td>@Model.CategoryId</td></tr>
        </tbody>
    </table>
</div>
```

The view sets a Title property, which can be used in the layout, as shown in Listing 22-12.

Listing 22-12. Using a View Bag Property in the _Layout.cshtml File in the Views/Shared Folder

```
<!DOCTYPE html>
<html>
<head>
    <title>@ViewBag.Title</title>
    <link href="/lib/twitter-bootstrap/css/bootstrap.min.css" rel="stylesheet" />
</head>
<body>
    <h6 class="bg-primary text-white text-center m-2 p-2">
        @(ViewBag.Title ?? "Layout")
    </h6>
    @RenderBody()
</body>
</html>
```

The Title property is used to set the content of the title element and h6 element in the body section. Layouts cannot rely on view bag properties being defined, which is why the expression in the h6 element provides a fallback value if the view doesn't define a Title property. To see the effect of the view bag property, use a browser to request http://localhost:5000, which produces the response shown in Figure 22-6.

UNDERSTANDING VIEW BAG PRECEDENCE

The values defined by the view take precedence if the same view bag property is defined by the view and the action method. If you want to allow the action to override the value defined in the view, then use a statement like this in the view code block:

```
...
@{
    Layout = "_Layout";
    ViewBag.Title = ViewBag.Title ?? "Product Table";
}
...
```

This statement will set the value for the Title property only if it has not already been defined by the action method.

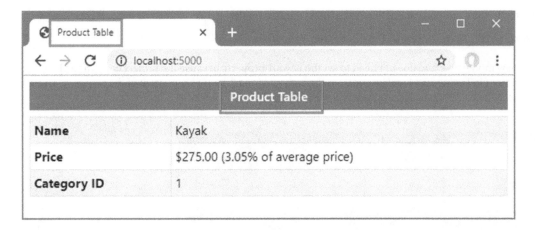

Figure 22-6. *Using a view bag property to configure a layout*

Using a View Start File

Instead of setting the Layout property in every view, you can add a *view start* file to the project that provides a default Layout value. If you are using Visual Studio, right-click the Views folder item in the Solution Explorer, select Add ➤ New Item, and locate the Razor View Start template, as shown in Figure 22-7. Make sure the name of the file is _ViewStart.cshtml and click the Add button to create the file, which will have the content shown in Listing 22-13.

Figure 22-7. *Creating a view start file*

If you are using Visual Studio Code, then add a file named _ViewStart.cshtml to the Views folder and add the content shown in Listing 22-13.

Listing 22-13. The Contents of the _ViewStart.cshtml File in the Views Folder

```
@{
    Layout = "_Layout";
}
```

The file contains sets the Layout property, and the value will be used as the default. Listing 22-14 removes the content from the Common.cshtml file that is contained in the layout.

Listing 22-14. Removing Content in the Common.cshtml File in the Views/Shared Folder

```
<h6 class="bg-secondary text-white text-center m-2 p-2">Shared View</h6>
```

The view doesn't define a view model type and doesn't need to set the Layout property because the project contains a view start file. The result is that the content in Listing 22-14 will be added to the body section of the HTML content of the response. Use a browser to navigate to http://localhost:5000/second, and you will see the response in Figure 22-8.

Figure 22-8. *Using a view start file*

Overriding the Default Layout

There are two situations where you may need to define a Layout property in a view even when there is a view start file in the project. In the first situation, a view requires a different layout from the one specified by the view start file. To demonstrate, add a Razor layout file named _ImportantLayout.cshtml to the Views/Shared folder with the content shown in Listing 22-15.

Listing 22-15. The Contents of the _ImportantLayout.cshtml File in the Views/Shared Folder

```
<!DOCTYPE html>
<html>
<head>
    <title>@ViewBag.Title</title>
    <link href="/lib/twitter-bootstrap/css/bootstrap.min.css" rel="stylesheet" />
</head>
<body>
    <h3 class="bg-warning text-white text-center p-2 m-2">Important</h3>
    @RenderBody()
</body>
</html>
```

In addition to the HTML document structure, this file contains a header element that displays Important in large text. Views can select this layout by assigning its name to the Layout property, as shown in Listing 22-16.

■ **Tip**   If you need to use a different layout for all the actions of a single controller, then add a view start file to the Views/[controller] folder that selects the view you require. The Razor engine will use the layout specified by the controller-specific view start file.

Listing 22-16. Using a Specific Layout in the Index.cshtml File in the Views/Home Folder

```
@model Product
@{
    Layout = "_ImportantLayout";
    ViewBag.Title = ViewBag.Title ?? "Product Table";
}
<div class="m-2">
    <table class="table table-sm table-striped table-bordered">
        <tbody>
            <tr><th>Name</th><td>@Model.Name</td></tr>
            <tr>
                <th>Price</th>
                <td>
                    @Model.Price.ToString("c")
                    (@(((Model.Price / ViewBag.AveragePrice)
                        * 100).ToString("F2"))% of average price)
                </td>
            </tr>
            <tr><th>Category ID</th><td>@Model.CategoryId</td></tr>
        </tbody>
    </table>
</div>
```

The Layout value in the view start file is overridden by the value in the view, allowing different layouts to be applied. Use a browse to request http://localhost:5000, and the response will be produced using the new layout, as shown in Figure 22-9.

SELECTING A LAYOUT PROGRAMMATICALLY

The value that a view assigns to the Layout property can be the result of an expression that allows layouts to be selected by the view, similar to the way that action methods can select views. Here is an example that selects the layout based on a property defined by the view model object:

```
...
@model Product
@{
    Layout = Model.Price > 100 ? "_ImportantLayout" : "_Layout";
    ViewBag.Title = ViewBag.Title ?? "Product Table";
}
...
```

The layout named _ImportantLayout is selected when the value of the view model object's Price property is greater than 100; otherwise, _Layout is used.

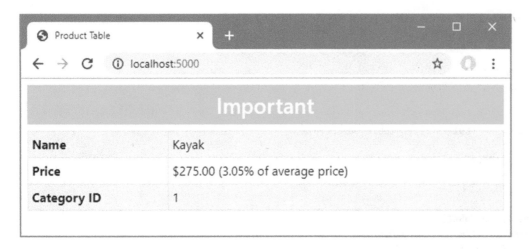

Figure 22-9. *Specifying a layout in a view*

The second situation where a Layout property can be needed is when a view contains a complete HTML document and doesn't require a layout at all. To see the problem, open a new PowerShell command prompt and run the command shown in Listing 22-17.

Listing 22-17. Sending an HTTP Request

```
Invoke-WebRequest http://localhost:5000/home/list | Select-Object  -expand Content
```

This command sends an HTTP GET request whose response will be produced using the List.cshtml file in the Views/Home folder. This view contains a complete HTML document, which is combined with the content in the view specified by the view start file, producing a malformed HTML document, like this:

```
<!DOCTYPE html>
<html>
<head>
    <title></title>
    <link href="/lib/twitter-bootstrap/css/bootstrap.min.css" rel="stylesheet" />
</head>
<body>
    <h6 class="bg-primary text-white text-center m-2 p-2">
        Layout
    </h6>
    <!DOCTYPE html>
<html>
<head>
    <link href="/lib/twitter-bootstrap/css/bootstrap.min.css" rel="stylesheet" />
</head>
<body>
    <h6 class="bg-secondary text-white text-center m-2 p-2">Products</h6>
    <div class="m-2">
        <table class="table table-sm table-striped table-bordered">
            <thead>
                <tr><th>Name</th><th>Price</th></tr>
            </thead>
            <tbody>
                <tr><td>Kayak</td><td>275.00</td></tr>
                <tr><td>Lifejacket</td><td>48.95</td></tr>
                <tr><td>Soccer Ball</td><td>19.50</td></tr>
                <tr><td>Corner Flags</td><td>34.95</td></tr>
```

```
            <tr><td>Stadium</td><td>79500.00</td></tr>
            <tr><td>Thinking Cap</td><td>16.00</td></tr>
            <tr><td>Unsteady Chair</td><td>29.95</td></tr>
            <tr><td>Human Chess Board</td><td>75.00</td></tr>
            <tr><td>Bling-Bling King</td><td>1200.00</td></tr>
        </tbody>
      </table>
    </div>
  </body>
</html>
</body>
</html>
```

The structural elements for the HTML document are duplicated, so there are two html, head, body, and link elements. Browsers are adept at handling malformed HTML but don't always cope with poorly structured content. Where a view contains a complete HTML document, the Layout property can be set to null, as shown in Listing 22-18.

Listing 22-18. Disabling Layouts in the List.cshtml File in the Views/Home Folder

```
@model IEnumerable<Product>
@{
    Layout = null;
}
<!DOCTYPE html>
<html>
<head>
    <link href="/lib/twitter-bootstrap/css/bootstrap.min.css" rel="stylesheet" />
</head>
<body>
    <h6 class="bg-secondary text-white text-center m-2 p-2">Products</h6>
    <div class="m-2">
        <table class="table table-sm table-striped table-bordered">
            <thead>
                <tr><th>Name</th><th>Price</th></tr>
            </thead>
            <tbody>
                @foreach (Product p in Model) {
                    <tr><td>@p.Name</td><td>@p.Price</td></tr>
                }
            </tbody>
        </table>
    </div>
</body>
</html>
```

Save the view and run the command shown in Listing 22-17 again, and you will see that the response contains only the elements in the view and that the layout has been disabled.

```
<!DOCTYPE html>
<html>
<head>
    <link href="/lib/twitter-bootstrap/css/bootstrap.min.css" rel="stylesheet" />
</head>
<body>
    <h6 class="bg-secondary text-white text-center m-2 p-2">Products</h6>
    <div class="m-2">
        <table class="table table-sm table-striped table-bordered">
```

```
            <thead>
                <tr><th>Name</th><th>Price</th></tr>
            </thead>
            <tbody>
                    <tr><td>Kayak</td><td>275.00</td></tr>
                    <tr><td>Lifejacket</td><td>48.95</td></tr>
                    <tr><td>Soccer Ball</td><td>19.50</td></tr>
                    <tr><td>Corner Flags</td><td>34.95</td></tr>
                    <tr><td>Stadium</td><td>79500.00</td></tr>
                    <tr><td>Thinking Cap</td><td>16.00</td></tr>
                    <tr><td>Unsteady Chair</td><td>29.95</td></tr>
                    <tr><td>Human Chess Board</td><td>75.00</td></tr>
                    <tr><td>Bling-Bling King</td><td>1200.00</td></tr>
            </tbody>
        </table>
    </div>
</body>
</html>
```

Using Layout Sections

The Razor view engine supports the concept of *sections*, which allow you to provide regions of content within a layout. Razor sections give greater control over which parts of the view are inserted into the layout and where they are placed. To demonstrate the sections feature, I have edited the /Views/Home/Index.cshtml file, as shown in Listing 22-19.

Listing 22-19. Defining Sections in the Index.cshtml File in the Views/Home Folder

```
@model Product
@{
    Layout = "_Layout";
    ViewBag.Title = ViewBag.Title ?? "Product Table";
}

@section Header {
    Product Information
}

<tr><th>Name</th><td>@Model.Name</td></tr>
<tr>
    <th>Price</th>
    <td>@Model.Price.ToString("c")</td>
</tr>
<tr><th>Category ID</th><td>@Model.CategoryId</td></tr>

@section Footer {
    @(((Model.Price / ViewBag.AveragePrice)
        * 100).ToString("F2"))% of average price
}
```

Sections are defined using the Razor @section expression followed by a name for the section. Listing 22-19 defines sections named Header and Footer, and sections can contain the same mix of HTML content and expressions, just like the main part of the view. Sections are applied in a layout with the @RenderSection expression, as shown in Listing 22-20.

Listing 22-20. Using Sections in the _Layout.cshtml File in the Views/Shared Folder

```
<!DOCTYPE html>
<html>
<head>
    <title>@ViewBag.Title</title>
    <link href="/lib/twitter-bootstrap/css/bootstrap.min.css" rel="stylesheet" />
</head>
<body>
    <div class="bg-info text-white m-2 p-1">
        This is part of the layout
    </div>

    <h6 class="bg-primary text-white text-center m-2 p-2">
        @RenderSection("Header")
    </h6>

    <div class="bg-info text-white m-2 p-1">
        This is part of the layout
    </div>

    <div class="m-2">
        <table class="table table-sm table-striped table-bordered">
            <tbody>
                @RenderBody()
            </tbody>
        </table>
    </div>

    <div class="bg-info text-white m-2 p-1">
        This is part of the layout
    </div>

    <h6 class="bg-primary text-white text-center m-2 p-2">
        @RenderSection("Footer")
    </h6>

    <div class="bg-info text-white m-2 p-1">
        This is part of the layout
    </div>
</body>
</html>
```

When the layout is applied, the RenderSection expression inserts the content of the specified section into the response. The regions of the view that are not contained within a section are inserted into the response by the RenderBody method. To see how the sections are applied, use a browser to request http://localhost:5000, which provides the response shown in Figure 22-10.

■ **Note** A view can define only the sections that are referred to in the layout. The view engine throws an exception if you define sections in the view for which there is no corresponding @RenderSection expression in the layout.

543

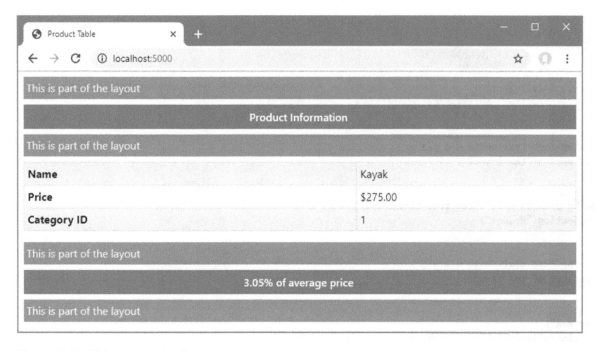

Figure 22-10. *Using sections in a layout*

Sections allow views to provide fragments of content to the layout without specifying how they are used. As an example, Listing 22-21 redefines the layout to consolidate the body and sections into a single HTML table.

Listing 22-21. Using a Table in the _Layout.cshtml File in the Views/Shared Folder

```
<!DOCTYPE html>
<html>
<head>
    <title>@ViewBag.Title</title>
    <link href="/lib/twitter-bootstrap/css/bootstrap.min.css" rel="stylesheet" />
</head>
<body>
    <div class="m-2">
        <table class="table table-sm table-striped table-bordered">
            <thead>
                <tr>
                    <th class="bg-primary text-white text-center" colspan="2">
                        @RenderSection("Header")
                    </th>
                </tr>
            </thead>
            <tbody>
                @RenderBody()
            </tbody>
            <tfoot>
                <tr>
                    <th class="bg-primary text-white text-center" colspan="2">
                        @RenderSection("Footer")
                    </th>
                </tr>
            </tfoot>
```

```
            </table>
        </div>
    </body>
</html>
```

To see the effect of the change to the view, use a browser to request `http://localhost:5000`, which will produce the response shown in Figure 22-11.

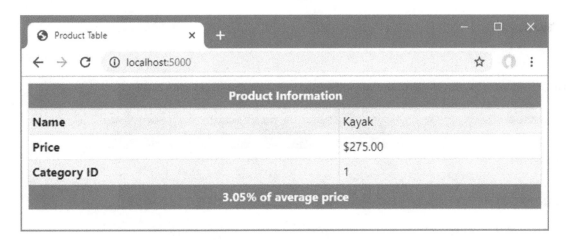

Figure 22-11. *Changing how sections are displayed in a layout*

Using Optional Layout Sections

By default, a view must contain all the sections for which there are RenderSection calls in the layout, and an exception will be thrown if the layout requires a section that the view hasn't defined. Listing 22-22 adds a call to the RenderSection method that requires a section named Summary.

Listing 22-22. Adding a Section in the _Layout.cshtml File in the Views/Shared Folder

```
<!DOCTYPE html>
<html>
<head>
    <title>@ViewBag.Title</title>
    <link href="/lib/twitter-bootstrap/css/bootstrap.min.css" rel="stylesheet" />
</head>
<body>
    <div class="m-2">
        <table class="table table-sm table-striped table-bordered">
            <thead>
                <tr>
                    <th class="bg-primary text-white text-center" colspan="2">
                        @RenderSection("Header")
                    </th>
                </tr>
            </thead>
            <tbody>
                @RenderBody()
            </tbody>
```

```
                <tfoot>
                    <tr>
                        <th class="bg-primary text-white text-center" colspan="2">
                            @RenderSection("Footer")
                        </th>
                    </tr>
                </tfoot>
            </table>
        </div>
        @RenderSection("Summary")
</body>
</html>
```

Use a browser to request `http://localhost:5000`, and you will see the exception shown in Figure 22-12.

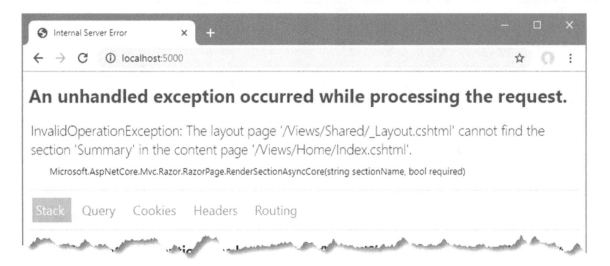

Figure 22-12. *Attempting to render a nonexistent view section*

There are two ways to solve this problem. The first is to create an optional section, which will be rendered only if it is defined by the view. Optional sections are created by passing a second argument to the RenderSection method, as shown in Listing 22-23.

Listing 22-23. Defining an Optional Section in the _Layout.cshtml File in the Views/Shared Folder

```
<!DOCTYPE html>
<html>
<head>
    <title>@ViewBag.Title</title>
    <link href="/lib/twitter-bootstrap/css/bootstrap.min.css" rel="stylesheet" />
</head>
<body>
    <div class="m-2">
        <table class="table table-sm table-striped table-bordered">
            <thead>
                <tr>
                    <th class="bg-primary text-white text-center" colspan="2">
                        @RenderSection("Header", false)
                    </th>
                </tr>
            </thead>
```

```
            <tbody>
                @RenderBody()
            </tbody>
            <tfoot>
                <tr>
                    <th class="bg-primary text-white text-center" colspan="2">
                        @RenderSection("Footer", false)
                    </th>
                </tr>
            </tfoot>
        </table>
    </div>
    @RenderSection("Summary", false)
</body>
</html>
```

The second argument specifies whether a section is required, and using `false` prevents an exception when the view doesn't define the section.

Testing for Layout Sections

The `IsSectionDefined` method is used to determine whether a view defines a specified section and can be used in an `if` expression to render fallback content, as shown in Listing 22-24.

Listing 22-24. Checking for a Section in the _Layout.cshtml File in the Views/Shared Folder

```
<!DOCTYPE html>
<html>
<head>
    <title>@ViewBag.Title</title>
    <link href="/lib/twitter-bootstrap/css/bootstrap.min.css" rel="stylesheet" />
</head>
<body>
    <div class="m-2">
        <table class="table table-sm table-striped table-bordered">
            <thead>
                <tr>
                    <th class="bg-primary text-white text-center" colspan="2">
                        @RenderSection("Header", false)
                    </th>
                </tr>
            </thead>
            <tbody>
                @RenderBody()
            </tbody>
            <tfoot>
                <tr>
                    <th class="bg-primary text-white text-center" colspan="2">
                        @RenderSection("Footer", false)
                    </th>
                </tr>
            </tfoot>
        </table>
    </div>
```

```
@if (IsSectionDefined("Summary")) {
    @RenderSection("Summary", false)
} else {
    <div class="bg-info text-center text-white m-2 p-2">
        This is the default summary
    </div>
}
</body>
</html>
```

The IsSectionDefined method is invoked with the name of the section you want to check and returns true if the view defines that section. In the example, I used this helper to render fallback content when the view does not define the Summary section. To see the fallback content, use a browser to request http://localhost:5000, which produces the response shown in Figure 22-13.

Figure 22-13. *Displaying fallback content for a view section*

Using Partial Views

You will often need to use the same set of HTML elements and expressions in several different places. *Partial views* are views that contain fragments of content that will be included in other views to produce complex responses without duplication.

Enabling Partial Views

Partial views are applied using a feature called *tag helpers*, which are described in detail in Chapter 25; tag helpers are configured in the view imports file, which was added to the project in Chapter 21. To enable the feature required for partial views, add the statement shown in Listing 22-25 to the _ViewImports.cshtml file.

Listing 22-25. Enabling Tag Helpers in the _ViewImports.cshtml File in the Views Folder

```
@using WebApp.Models
@addTagHelper *, Microsoft.AspNetCore.Mvc.TagHelpers
```

Creating a Partial View

Partial views are just regular CSHTML files, and it is only the way they are used that differentiates them from standard views. If you are using Visual Studio, right-click the Views/Home folder, select Add ➤ New Item, and use the Razor View template to create a file named _RowPartial.cshtml. Once the file has been created, replace the contents with those shown in Listing 22-26. If you are using Visual Studio Code, add a file named _RowPartial.cshtml to the Views/Home folder and add to it the content shown in Listing 22-26.

■ **Tip** Visual Studio provides some tooling support for creating prepopulated partial views, but the simplest way to create a partial view is to create a regular view using the Razor View item template.

Listing 22-26. The Contents of the _RowPartial.cshtml File in the Views/Home Folder

```
@model Product

<tr>
    <td>@Model.Name</td>
    <td>@Model.Price</td>
</tr>
```

The model expression is used to define the view model type for the partial view, which contains the same mix of expressions and HTML elements as regular views. The content of this partial view creates a table row, using the Name and Price properties of a Product object to populate the table cells.

Applying a Partial View

Partial views are applied by adding a partial element in another view or layout. In Listing 22-27, I have added the element to the List.cshtml file so the partial view is used to generate the rows in the table.

Listing 22-27. Using a Partial View in the List.cshtml File in the Views/Home Folder

```
@model IEnumerable<Product>
@{
    Layout = null;
}
<!DOCTYPE html>
<html>
<head>
    <link href="/lib/twitter-bootstrap/css/bootstrap.min.css" rel="stylesheet" />
</head>
<body>
    <h6 class="bg-secondary text-white text-center m-2 p-2">Products</h6>
    <div class="m-2">
        <table class="table table-sm table-striped table-bordered">
            <thead>
                <tr><th>Name</th><th>Price</th></tr>
            </thead>
            <tbody>
                @foreach (Product p in Model) {
                    <partial name="_RowPartial" model="p" />
                }
            </tbody>
        </table>
    </div>
</body>
</html>
```

The attributes applied to the partial element control the selection and configuration of the partial view, as described in Table 22-2.

Table 22-2. *The partial Element Attributes*

Name	Description
name	This property specifies the name of the partial view, which is located using the same search process as regular views.
model	This property specifies the value that will be used as the view model object for the partial view.
for	This property is used to define an expression that selects the view model object for the partial view, as explained next.
view-data	This property is used to provide the partial view with additional data.

The partial element in Listing 22-27 uses the name attribute to select the _RowPartial view and the model attribute to select the Product object that will be used as the view model object. The partial element is applied within the @foreach expression, which means that it will be used to generate each row in the table, which you can see by using a browser to request http:// localhost:5000/home/list to produce the response shown in Figure 22-14.

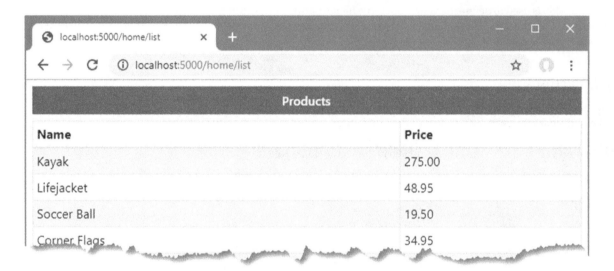

Figure 22-14. *Using a partial view*

USING THE HTML HELPER TO APPLY PARTIAL VIEWS

In earlier versions of ASP.NET Core, partial views were applied using the Html property that is added to the C# class generated from the view, as explained in Chapter 21. The object returned by the Html property implements the IHtmlHelper interface, through which views can be applied, like this:

```
...
@Html.Partial("_RowPartial")
...
```

This type of expression works and is still supported, but the partial element provides a more elegant approach that is consistent with the rest of the HTML elements in the view.

Selecting the Partial View Model Using an Expression

The for attribute is used to set the partial view's model using an expression that is applied to the view's model, which is a feature more easily demonstrated than described. Add a partial view named _CellPartial.cshtml to the Views/Home folder with the content shown in Listing 22-28.

Listing 22-28. The Contents of the _CellPartial.cshtml File in the Views/Home Folder

```
@model string

<td class="bg-info text-white">@Model</td>
```

This partial view has a string view model object, which it uses as the contents of a table cell element; the table cell element is styled using the Bootstrap CSS framework. In Listing 22-29, I have added a partial element to the _RowPartial.cshtml file that uses the _CellPartial partial view to display the table cell for the name of the Product object.

Listing 22-29. Using a Partial View in the _RowPartial.cshtml File in the Views/Home Folder

```
@model Product

<tr>
    <partial name="_CellPartial" for="Name" />
    <td>@Model.Price</td>
</tr>
```

The for attribute selects the Name property as the model for the _CellPartial partial view. To see the effect, use a browser to request http://localhost:5000/home/list, which will produce the response shown in Figure 22-15.

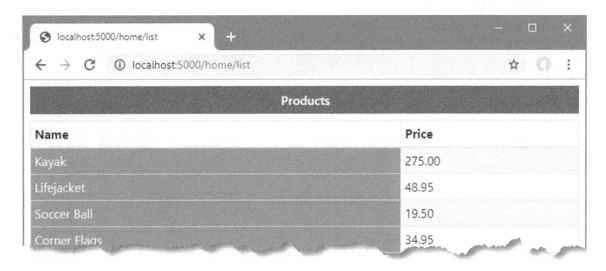

Figure 22-15. *Selecting a model property for use in a partial view*

USING TEMPLATED DELEGATES

Templated delegates are an alternative way of avoiding duplication in a view. Templated delegates are defined in a code block, like this:

```
...
@{
    Func<Product, object> row
        = @<tr><td>@item.Name</td><td>@item.Price</td></tr>;
}
...
```

The template is a function that accepts a Product input object and returns a dynamic result. Within the template expression, the input object is referred to as item in expressions. The templated delegate is invoked as a method expression to generate content.

```
...
<tbody>
    @foreach (Product p in Model) {
        @row(p)
    }
</tbody>
...
```

I find this feature awkward and prefer using partial views, although this is a matter of preference and habit rather than any objective problems with the way that templated delegates work.

Understanding Content-Encoding

Razor views provide two useful features for encoding content. The HTML content-encoding feature ensures that expression responses don't change the structure of the response sent to the browser, which is an important security feature. The JSON encoding feature encodes an object as JSON and inserts it into the response, which can be a useful debugging feature and can also be useful when providing data to JavaScript applications. Both encoding features are described in the following sections.

Understanding HTML Encoding

The Razor view engine encodes expression results to make them safe to include in an HTML document without changing its structure. This is an important feature when dealing with content that is provided by users, who may try to subvert the application or accidentally enter dangerous content. Listing 22-30 adds an action method to the Home controller that passes a fragment of HTML to the View method.

Listing 22-30. Adding an Action in the HomeController.cs File in the Controllers Folder

```
using Microsoft.AspNetCore.Mvc;
using System.Threading.Tasks;
using WebApp.Models;
using Microsoft.EntityFrameworkCore;

namespace WebApp.Controllers {

    public class HomeController: Controller {
        private DataContext context;

        public HomeController(DataContext ctx) {
            context = ctx;
        }

        public async Task<IActionResult> Index(long id = 1) {
            ViewBag.AveragePrice = await context.Products.AverageAsync(p => p.Price);
            return View(await context.Products.FindAsync(id));
        }

        public IActionResult List() {
            return View(context.Products);
        }

        public IActionResult Html() {
            return View((object)"This is a <h3><i>string</i></h3>");
        }
    }
}
```

The new action passes a string that contains HTML elements. To create the view for the new action method, add a Razor view file named Html.cshtml to the Views/Home folder with the content shown in Listing 22-31.

■ **Tip**   Notice that I cast the string passed to the View method as an object, without which the string is assumed to be the name of a view and not the view model object.

Listing 22-31. The Contents of the Html.cshtml File in the Views/Home Folder

```
@model string
@{
    Layout = null;
}
<!DOCTYPE html>
<html>
<head>
    <link href="/lib/twitter-bootstrap/css/bootstrap.min.css" rel="stylesheet" />
</head>
<body>
    <div class="bg-secondary text-white text-center m-2 p-2">@Model</div>
</body>
</html>
```

Restart ASP.NET Core and use a browser to request http://localhost:5000/home/html. The response, which is shown on the left of Figure 22-17, shows how the potentially dangerous characters in the view model string have been escaped.

To include the result of an expression without safe encoding, you can invoke the Html.Raw method. The Html property is one of the properties added to the generated view class, described in Chapter 21, which returns an object that implements the IHtmlHelper interface, as shown in Listing 22-32.

Listing 22-32. Disabling Encoding in the Html.cshtml File in the Views/Home Folder

```
@model string
@{
    Layout = null;
}
<!DOCTYPE html>
<html>
<head>
    <link href="/lib/twitter-bootstrap/css/bootstrap.min.css" rel="stylesheet" />
</head>
<body>
    <div class="bg-secondary text-white text-center m-2 p-2">@Html.Raw(Model)</div>
</body>
</html>
```

Request the http://localhost:5000/home/html URL again, and you will see that the view model string is passed on without being encoded and is then interpreted by the browser as part of the HTML document, as shown on the right of Figure 22-16.

■ **Caution**   Do not disable safe encoding unless you are entirely confident that no malicious content will be passed to the view. Careless use of this feature presents a security risk to your application and your users.

Figure 22-16. *HTML result encoding*

Understanding JSON Encoding

The Json property, which is added to the class generated from the view, as described in Chapter 21, can be used to encode an object as JSON. The most common use for JSON data is in RESTful web services, as described in earlier chapters, but I find the Razor JSON encoding feature useful as a debugging aid when I don't get the output I expect from a view. Listing 22-33 adds a JSON representation of the view model object to the output produced by the Index view.

Listing 22-33. Using JSON Encoding in the Index.cshtml File in the Views/Home Folder

```
@model Product
@{
    Layout = "_Layout";
    ViewBag.Title = ViewBag.Title ?? "Product Table";
}

@section Header {
    Product Information
}

<tr><th>Name</th><td>@Model.Name</td></tr>
<tr>
    <th>Price</th>
    <td>@Model.Price.ToString("c")</td>
</tr>
<tr><th>Category ID</th><td>@Model.CategoryId</td></tr>

@section Footer {
    @(((Model.Price / ViewBag.AveragePrice)
        * 100).ToString("F2"))% of average price
}

@section Summary {
    <div class="bg-info text-white m-2 p-2">
        @Json.Serialize(Model)
    </div>
}
```

The Json property returns an implementation of the IJsonHelper interface, whose Serialize method produces a JSON representation of an object. Use a browser to request http://localhost:5000, and you will see the response shown in Figure 22-17, which includes JSON in the Summary section of the view.

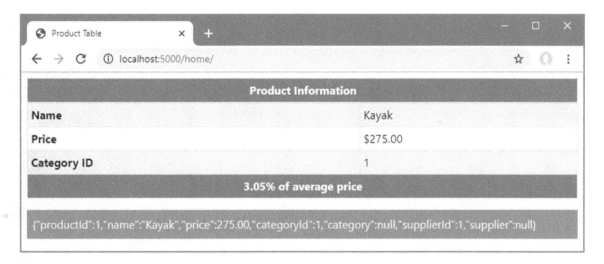

Figure 22-17. *Encoding an expression result as JSON*

Summary

In this chapter, I continued to describe the features available in Razor views. I showed you how to use the view bag, how to use layouts and partial views to deal with common content, and how to manage the encoding process for expression results. In the next chapter, I introduce Razor Pages, which provides an alternative way to generate HTML responses.

CHAPTER 23

Using Razor Pages

In this chapter, I introduce Razor Pages, which is a simpler approach to generating HTML content, intended to capture some of the enthusiasm for the legacy ASP.NET Web Pages framework. I explain how Razor Pages work, explain how they differ from the controllers and views approach taken by the MVC Framework, and show you how they fit into the wider ASP.NET Core platform.

The process of explaining how Razor Pages work can minimize the differences from the controllers and views described in earlier chapters. You might form the impression that Razor Pages are just MVC-lite and dismiss them, which would be a shame. Razor Pages are interesting because of the developer experience and not the way they are implemented.

My advice is to give Razor Pages a chance, especially if you are an experienced MVC developer. Although the technology used will be familiar, the process of creating application features is different and is well-suited to small and tightly focused features that don't require the scale and complexity of controllers and views. I have been using the MVC Framework since it was first introduced, and I admit to ignoring the early releases of Razor Pages. Now, however, I find myself mixing Razor Pages and the MVC Framework in most projects, much as I did in the SportsStore example in Part 1. Table 23-1 puts Razor Pages in context.

Table 23-1. *Putting Razor Pages in Context*

Question	Answer
What are they?	Razor Pages are a simplified way of generating HTML responses.
Why are they useful?	The simplicity of Razor Pages means you can start getting results sooner than with the MVC Framework, which can require a relatively complex preparation process. Razor Pages are also easier for less experienced web developers to understand because the relationship between the code and content is more obvious.
How are they used?	Razor Pages associate a single view with the class that provides it with features and uses a file-based routing system to match URLs.
Are there any pitfalls or limitations?	Razor Pages are less flexible than the MVC Framework, which makes them unsuitable for complex applications. Razor Pages can be used only to generate HTML responses and cannot be used to create RESTful web services.
Are there any alternatives?	The MVC Framework's approach of controllers and views can be used instead of Razor Pages.

Table 23-2 summarizes the chapter.

© Adam Freeman 2020
A. Freeman, *Pro ASP.NET Core 3*, https://doi.org/10.1007/978-1-4842-5440-0_23

Table 23-2. *Chapter Summary*

Problem	Solution	Listing
Enabling Razor Pages	Use AddRazorPages and MapRazorPages to set up the required services and middleware	3
Creating a self-contained endpoint	Create a Razor Page	4, 26, 27
Routing requests to a Razor Page	Use the name of the page or specify a route using the @page directive	5–8
Providing logic to support the view section of a Razor Page	Use a page model class	9–12
Creating results that are not rendered using the view section of a Razor Page	Define a handler method that returns an action result	13–15
Handling multiple HTTP methods	Define handlers in the page model class	16–18
Avoiding duplication of content	Use a layout or a partial view	19–25

Preparing for This Chapter

This chapter uses the WebApp project from Chapter 22. Open a new PowerShell command prompt, navigate to the folder that contains the WebApp.csproj file, and run the command shown in Listing 23-1 to drop the database.

▪ **Tip**   You can download the example project for this chapter—and for all the other chapters in this book—from https://github.com/apress/pro-asp.net-core-3. See Chapter 1 for how to get help if you have problems running the examples.

Listing 23-1. Dropping the Database

```
dotnet ef database drop --force
```

Running the Example Application

Once the database has been dropped, select Start Without Debugging or Run Without Debugging from the Debug menu or use the PowerShell command prompt to run the command shown in Listing 23-2.

Listing 23-2. Running the Example Application

```
dotnet run
```

The database will be seeded as part of the application startup. Once ASP.NET Core is running, use a web browser to request http://localhost:5000, which will produce the response shown in Figure 23-1.

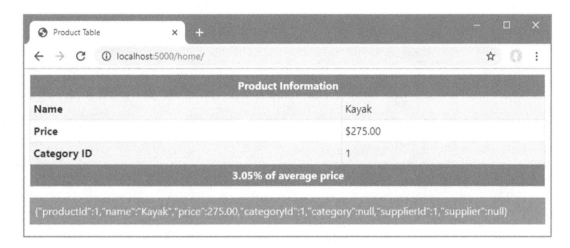

Figure 23-1. *Running the example application*

Understanding Razor Pages

As you learn how Razor Pages work, you will see they share common functionality with the MVC Framework. In fact, Razor Pages are typically described as a simplification of the MVC Framework—which is true—but that doesn't give any sense of why Razor Pages can be useful.

The MVC Framework solves every problem in the same way: a controller defines action methods that select views to produce responses. It is a solution that works because it is so flexible: the controller can define multiple action methods that respond to different requests, the action method can decide which view will be used as the request is being processed, and the view can depend on private or shared partial views to produce its response.

Not every feature in web applications needs the flexibility of the MVC Framework. For many features, a single action method will be used to handle a wide range of requests, all of which are dealt with using the same view. Razor Pages offer a more focused approach that ties together markup and C# code, sacrificing flexibility for focus.

But Razor Pages have limitations. Razor Pages tend to start out focusing on a single feature but slowly grow out of control as enhancements are made. And, unlike MVC controllers, Razor Pages cannot be used to create web services.

You don't have to choose just one model because the MVC Framework and Razor Pages coexist, as demonstrated in this chapter. This means that self-contained features can be easily developed with Razor Pages, leaving the more complex aspects of an application to be implemented using the MVC controllers and actions.

In the sections that follow, I show you how to configure and use Razor pages, and then I explain how they work and demonstrate the common foundation they share with MVC controllers and actions.

Configuring Razor Pages

To prepare the application for Razor Pages, statements must be added to the Startup class to set up services and configure the endpoint routing system, as shown in Listing 23-3.

Listing 23-3. Configuring the Application in the Startup.cs File in the WebApp Folder

```
using System;
using System.Collections.Generic;
using System.Linq;
using Microsoft.AspNetCore.Builder;
using Microsoft.Extensions.DependencyInjection;
using Microsoft.Extensions.Configuration;
using Microsoft.EntityFrameworkCore;
using WebApp.Models;
```

```
namespace WebApp {
    public class Startup {

        public Startup(IConfiguration config) {
            Configuration = config;
        }

        public IConfiguration Configuration { get; set; }

        public void ConfigureServices(IServiceCollection services) {
            services.AddDbContext<DataContext>(opts => {
                opts.UseSqlServer(Configuration[
                    "ConnectionStrings:ProductConnection"]);
                opts.EnableSensitiveDataLogging(true);
            });
            services.AddControllersWithViews().AddRazorRuntimeCompilation();
            services.AddRazorPages().AddRazorRuntimeCompilation();

            services.AddDistributedMemoryCache();
            services.AddSession(options => {
                options.Cookie.IsEssential = true;
            });
        }

        public void Configure(IApplicationBuilder app, DataContext context) {
            app.UseDeveloperExceptionPage();
            app.UseStaticFiles();
            app.UseSession();
            app.UseRouting();
            app.UseEndpoints(endpoints => {
                endpoints.MapControllers();
                endpoints.MapDefaultControllerRoute();
                endpoints.MapRazorPages();
            });
            SeedData.SeedDatabase(context);
        }
    }
}
```

The AddRazorPages method sets up the service that is required to use Razor Pages, while the optional AddRazorRuntimeCompilation method enables runtime recompilation, using the package added to the project in Chapter 21. The MapRazorPages method creates the routing configuration that matches URLs to pages, which is explained later in the chapter.

Creating a Razor Page

Razor Pages are defined in the Pages folder. If you are using Visual Studio, create the WebApp/Pages folder, right-click it in the Solution Explorer, select Add ➤ New Item from the popup menu, and select the Razor Page template, as shown in Figure 23-2. Set the Name field to Index.cshtml and click the Add button to create the file and replace the contents of the file with those shown in Listing 23-4.

Figure 23-2. *Creating a Razor Page*

If you are using Visual Studio Code, create the WebApp/Pages folder and add to it a new file named Index.cshtml with the content shown in Listing 23-4.

Listing 23-4. The Contents of the Index.cshtml File in the Pages Folder

```
@page
@model IndexModel
@using Microsoft.AspNetCore.Mvc.RazorPages
@using WebApp.Models;

<!DOCTYPE html>
<html>
<head>
    <link href="/lib/twitter-bootstrap/css/bootstrap.min.css" rel="stylesheet" />
</head>
<body>
    <div class="bg-primary text-white text-center m-2 p-2">@Model.Product.Name</div>
</body>
</html>

@functions {

    public class IndexModel: PageModel {
        private DataContext context;

        public Product Product { get; set; }

        public IndexModel(DataContext ctx) {
            context = ctx;
        }

        public async Task OnGetAsync(long id = 1) {
            Product = await context.Products.FindAsync(id);
        }
    }
}
```

561

Razor Pages use the Razor syntax that I described in Chapters 21 and 22, and Razor Pages even use the same CSHTML file extension. But there are some important differences.

The @page directive must be the first thing in a Razor Page, which ensures that the file is not mistaken for a view associated with a controller. But the most important difference is that the @functions directive is used to define the C# code that supports the Razor content in the same file. I explain how Razor Pages work shortly, but to see the output generated by the Razor Page, restart ASP.NET Core and use a browser to request http://localhost:5000/index, which produces the response shown in Figure 23-3.

Figure 23-3. *Using a Razor Page*

Understanding the URL Routing Convention

URL routing for Razor Pages is based on the file name and location, relative to the Pages folder. The Razor Page in Listing 23-4 is in a file named Index.cshtml, in the Pages folder, which means that it will handle requests for the /index. The routing convention can be overridden, as described in the "Understanding Razor Pages Routing" section, but, by default, it is the location of the Razor Page file that determines the URLs that it responds to.

Understanding the Page Model

In a Razor Page, the @model directive is used to select a *page model* class, rather than identifying the type of the object provided by an action method. The @model directive in Listing 23-4 selects the IndexModel class.

```
...
@model IndexModel
...
```

The page model is defined within the @functions directive and is derived from the PageModel class, like this:

```
...
@functions {
    public class IndexModel: PageModel {
...
```

When the Razor Page is selected to handle an HTTP request, a new instance of the page model class is created, and dependency injection is used to resolve any dependencies that have been declared using constructor parameters, using the features described in Chapter 14. The IndexModel class declares a dependency on the DataContext service created in Chapter 18, which allows it to access the data in the database.

```
...
public IndexModel(DataContext ctx) {
    context = ctx;
}
...
```

After the page model object has been created, a handler method is invoked. The name of the handler method is On, followed by the HTTP method for the request so that the OnGet method is invoked when the Razor Page is selected to handle an HTTP GET request. Handler methods can be asynchronous, in which case a GET request will invoke the OnGetAsync method, which is the method implemented by the IndexModel class.

```
...
public async Task OnGetAsync(long id = 1) {
    Product = await context.Products.FindAsync(id);
}
...
```

Values for the handler method parameters are obtained from the HTTP request using the model binding process, which is described in detail in Chapter 28. The OnGetAsync method receives the value for its id parameters from the model binder, which it uses to query the database and assign the result to its Product property.

Understanding the Page View

Razor Pages use the same mix of HTML fragments and code expressions to generate content, which defines the view presented to the user. The page model's methods and properties are accessible in the Razor Page through the @Model expression. The Product property defined by the IndexModel class is used to set the content of an HTML element, like this:

```
...
<div class="bg-primary text-white text-center m-2 p-2">@Model.Product.Name</div>
...
```

The @Model expression returns an IndexModel object, and this expression reads the Name property of the object returned by the Product property.

Understanding the Generated C# Class

Behind the scenes, Razor Pages are transformed into C# classes, just like regular Razor views. Here is a simplified version of the C# class that is produced from the Razor Page in Listing 23-4:

```
using System;
using System.Collections.Generic;
using System.Linq;
using System.Threading.Tasks;
using Microsoft.AspNetCore.Mvc;
using Microsoft.AspNetCore.Mvc.Rendering;
using Microsoft.AspNetCore.Mvc.ViewFeatures;
using Microsoft.AspNetCore.Mvc.Razor.TagHelpers;
using Microsoft.AspNetCore.Mvc.ViewFeatures;
using Microsoft.AspNetCore.Mvc.Rendering;
using Microsoft.AspNetCore.Mvc.RazorPages;
using Microsoft.AspNetCore.Razor.Runtime.TagHelpers;
using Microsoft.AspNetCore.Razor.TagHelpers;
using WebApp.Models;

namespace AspNetCore {

    public class Pages_Index : Page {
        public <IndexModel> ViewData => (<IndexModel>)PageContext?.ViewData;
        public IndexModel Model => ViewData.Model;

        public async override Task ExecuteAsync() {
            WriteLiteral("\r\n<!DOCTYPE html>\r\n<html>\r\n");
            WriteLiteral("<head>");
```

```
        WriteLiteral("@<link
            href=\"/lib/twitter-bootstrap/css/bootstrap.min.css\"
            rel=\"stylesheet\" />");
        WriteLiteral("</head>");
        WriteLiteral("<body>");
        WriteLiteral("<div class=\"bg-primary text-white text-center m-2 p-2\">")
        Write(Model.Product.Name);
        WriteLiteral("</div>");
        WriteLiteral("</body></html>\r\n\r\n");
    }

    public class IndexModel: PageModel {
        private DataContext context;
        public Product Product { get; set; }

        public IndexModel(DataContext ctx) {
            context = ctx;
        }

        public async Task OnGetAsync(long id = 1) {
            Product = await context.Products.FindAsync(id);
        }
    }

    public IUrlHelper Url { get; private set; }
    public IViewComponentHelper Component { get; private set; }
    public IJsonHelper Json { get; private set; }
    public IHtmlHelper<IndexModel> Html { get; private set; }
    public IModelExpressionProvider ModelExpressionProvider { get; private set; }
    }
}
```

If you compare this code with the equivalent shown in Chapter 21, you can see how Razor Pages rely on the same features used by the MVC Framework. The HTML fragments and view expressions are transformed into calls to the `WriteLiteral` and `Write` methods.

■ **Tip** You can see the generated classes by examining the contents of the `obj/Debug/netcoreapp3.0/Razor/Pages` folder with the Windows File Explorer.

Understanding Razor Pages Routing

Razor Pages rely on the location of the CSHTML file for routing so that a request for `http://localhost:5000/index` is handled by the `Pages/Index.cshtml` file. Adding a more complex URL structure for an application is done by adding folders whose names represent the segments in the URL you want to support. As an example, create the `WebApp/Pages/Suppliers` folder and add to it a Razor Page named `List.cshtml` with the contents shown in Listing 23-5.

Listing 23-5. The Contents of the List.cshtml File in the Pages/Suppliers Folder

```
@page
@model ListModel
@using Microsoft.AspNetCore.Mvc.RazorPages
@using WebApp.Models;
```

```
<!DOCTYPE html>
<html>
<head>
    <link href="/lib/twitter-bootstrap/css/bootstrap.min.css" rel="stylesheet" />
</head>
<body>
    <h5 class="bg-primary text-white text-center m-2 p-2">Suppliers</h5>
    <ul class="list-group m-2">
        @foreach (string s in Model.Suppliers) {
            <li class="list-group-item">@s</li>
        }
    </ul>
</body>
</html>

@functions {

    public class ListModel : PageModel {
        private DataContext context;

        public IEnumerable<string> Suppliers { get; set; }

        public ListModel(DataContext ctx) {
            context = ctx;
        }

        public void OnGet() {
            Suppliers = context.Suppliers.Select(s => s.Name);
        }
    }
}
```

The new page model class defines a Suppliers property that is set to the sequence of Name values for the Supplier objects in the database. The database operation in this example is synchronous, so the page model class defined the OnGet method, rather than OnGetAsync. The supplier names are displayed in a list using an @foreach expression. To use the new Razor Page, use a browser to request http://localhost:5000/suppliers/list, which produces the response shown in Figure 23-4. The path segments of the request URL correspond to the folder and file name of the List.cshtml Razor Page.

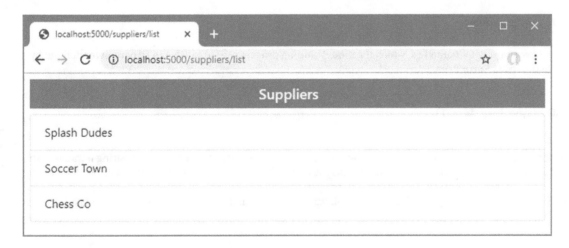

Figure 23-4. *Using a folder structure to route requests*

UNDERSTANDING THE DEFAULT URL HANDLING

The MapRazorPages method sets up a route for the default URL for the Index.cshtml Razor Page, following a similar convention used by the MVC Framework. It is for this reason that the first Razor Page added to a project is usually called Index.cshtml. However, when the application mixes Razor Pages and the MVC Framework together, the default route is set up by whichever is configured first, which is why requests for http://localhost:5000 for the example application are handled by the Index action of the Home MVC controller. If you want the Index.cshtml file to handle the default URL, then you can change the order of the endpoint routing statements so that Razor Pages is set up first, like this:

```
...
app.UseEndpoints(endpoints => {
    endpoints.MapRazorPages();
    endpoints.MapControllers();
    endpoints.MapDefaultControllerRoute();
});
...
```

In my own projects, where I mix Razor Pages and MVC controllers, I tend to rely on the MVC Framework to handle the default URL, and I avoid creating the Index.cshtml Razor Page to avoid confusion.

Specifying a Routing Pattern in a Razor Page

Using the folder and file structure to perform routing means there are no segment variables for the model binding process to use. Instead, values for the request handler methods are obtained from the URL query string, which you can see by using a browser to request http://localhost:5000/index?id=2, which produces the response shown in Figure 23-5.

Figure 23-5. *Using a query string parameter*

The query string provides a parameter named id, which the model binding process uses to satisfy the id parameter defined by the OnGetAsync method in the Index Razor Page.

```
...
public async Task OnGetAsync(long id = 1) {
...
```

I explain how model binding works in detail in Chapter 28, but for now, it is enough to know that the query string parameter in the request URL is used to provide the id argument when the OnGetAsync method is invoked, which is used to query the database for a product.

The @page directive can be used with a routing pattern, which allows segment variables to be defined, as shown in Listing 23-6.

Listing 23-6. Defining a Segment Variable in the Index.cshtml File in the Pages Folder

```
@page "{id:long?}"
@model IndexModel
@using Microsoft.AspNetCore.Mvc.RazorPages
@using WebApp.Models;

<!DOCTYPE html>
<html>
<head>
    <link href="/lib/twitter-bootstrap/css/bootstrap.min.css" rel="stylesheet" />
</head>
<body>
    <div class="bg-primary text-white text-center m-2 p-2">@Model.Product.Name</div>
</body>
</html>

@functions {

    // ...statements omitted for brevity...

}
```

All the URL pattern features that are described in Chapter 13 can be used with the @page directive. The route pattern used in Listing 23-6 adds an optional segment variable named id, which is constrained so that it will match only those segments that can be parsed to a long value. To see the change, restart ASP.NET Core (automatic recompilation doesn't detect routing changes) and use a browser to request http://localhost:5000/index/4, which produces the response shown on the left of Figure 23-6.

The @page directive can also be used to override the file-based routing convention for a Razor Page, as shown in Listing 23-7.

Listing 23-7. Changing the Route in the List.cshtml File in the Pages/Suppliers Folder

```
@page "/lists/suppliers"
@model ListModel
@using Microsoft.AspNetCore.Mvc.RazorPages
@using WebApp.Models;

<!DOCTYPE html>
<html>
<head>
    <link href="/lib/twitter-bootstrap/css/bootstrap.min.css" rel="stylesheet" />
</head>
<body>
    <h5 class="bg-primary text-white text-center m-2 p-2">Suppliers</h5>
    <ul class="list-group m-2">
        @foreach (string s in Model.Suppliers) {
            <li class="list-group-item">@s</li>
        }
    </ul>
</body>
</html>

@functions {

    // ...statements omitted for brevity...

}
```

The directive changes the route for the List page so that it matches URLs whose path is /lists/suppliers. To see the effect of the change, restart ASP.NET Core and request http://localhost:5000/lists/suppliers, which produces the response shown on the right of Figure 23-6.

Figure 23-6. *Changing routes using the @page directive*

Adding Routes for a Razor Page

Using the @page directive replaces the default file-based route for a Razor Page. If you want to define multiple routes for a page, then configuration statements can be added to the Startup class, as shown in Listing 23-8.

Listing 23-8. Adding Razor Page Routes in the Startup.cs File in the WebApp Folder

```
using System;
using System.Collections.Generic;
using System.Linq;
using Microsoft.AspNetCore.Builder;
using Microsoft.Extensions.DependencyInjection;
using Microsoft.Extensions.Configuration;
using Microsoft.EntityFrameworkCore;
using WebApp.Models;
using Microsoft.AspNetCore.Mvc.RazorPages;

namespace WebApp {
    public class Startup {

        public Startup(IConfiguration config) {
            Configuration = config;
        }

        public IConfiguration Configuration { get; set; }

        public void ConfigureServices(IServiceCollection services) {
            services.AddDbContext<DataContext>(opts => {
                opts.UseSqlServer(Configuration[
                    "ConnectionStrings:ProductConnection"]);
                opts.EnableSensitiveDataLogging(true);
            });
            services.AddControllersWithViews().AddRazorRuntimeCompilation();
            services.AddRazorPages().AddRazorRuntimeCompilation();

            services.AddDistributedMemoryCache();
            services.AddSession(options => {
                options.Cookie.IsEssential = true;
            });

            services.Configure<RazorPagesOptions>(opts => {
                opts.Conventions.AddPageRoute("/Index", "/extra/page/{id:long?}");
            });
        }
```

568

```
        public void Configure(IApplicationBuilder app, DataContext context) {
            app.UseDeveloperExceptionPage();
            app.UseStaticFiles();
            app.UseSession();
            app.UseRouting();
            app.UseEndpoints(endpoints => {
                endpoints.MapControllers();
                endpoints.MapDefaultControllerRoute();
                endpoints.MapRazorPages();
            });
            SeedData.SeedDatabase(context);
        }
    }
}
```

The options pattern is used to add additional routes for a Razor Page using the RazorPageOptions class. The AddPageRoute extension method is called on the Conventions property to add a route for a page. The first argument is the path to the page, without the file extension and relative to the Pages folder. The second argument is the URL pattern to add to the routing configuration. To test the new route, restart ASP.NET Core and use a browser to request http://localhost:5000/extra/page/2, which is matched by the URL pattern added in Listing 23-8 and produces the response shown on the left of Figure 23-7. The route added in Listing 23-8 supplements the route defined by the @page attribute, which you can test by requesting http://localhost:5000/index/2, which will produce the response shown on the right of Figure 23-7.

Figure 23-7. *Adding a route for a Razor Page*

Understanding the Page Model Class

Page models are derived from the PageModel class, which provides the link between the rest of ASP.NET Core and the view part of the Razor Page. The PageModel class provides methods for managing how requests are handled and properties that provide context data, the most useful of which are described in Table 23-3. I have listed these properties for completeness, but they are not often required in Razor Page development, which focuses more on selecting the data that is required to render the view part of the page.

Table 23-3. *Selected PageModel Properties for Context Data*

Name	Description
HttpContext	This property returns an HttpContext object, described in Chapter 12.
ModelState	This property provides access to the model binding and validation features described in Chapters 28 and 29.
PageContext	This property returns a PageContext object that provides access to many of the same properties defined by the PageModel class, along with additional information about the current page selection.
Request	This property returns an HttpRequest object that describes the current HTTP request, as described in Chapter 12.
Response	This property returns an HttpResponse object that represents the current response, as described in Chapter 12.
RouteData	This property provides access to the data matched by the routing system, as described in Chapter 13.
TempData	This property provides access to the temp data feature, which is used to store data until it can be read by a subsequent request. See Chapter 22 for details.
User	This property returns an object that describes the user associated with the request, as described in Chapter 38.

Using a Code-Behind Class File

The @function directive allows the page-behind class and the Razor content to be defined in the same file, which is a development approach used by popular client-side frameworks, such as React or Vue.js.

Defining code and markup in the same file is convenient but can become difficult to manage for more complex applications. Razor Pages can also be split into separate view and code files, which is similar to the MVC examples in previous chapters and is reminiscent of ASP.NET Web Pages, which defined C# classes in files known as *code-behind files*. The first step is to remove the page model class from the CSHTML file, as shown in Listing 23-9.

Listing 23-9. Removing the Page Model Class in the Index.cshtml File in the Pages Folder

```
@page "{id:long?}"
@model WebApp.Pages.IndexModel

<!DOCTYPE html>
<html>
<head>
    <link href="/lib/twitter-bootstrap/css/bootstrap.min.css" rel="stylesheet" />
</head>
<body>
    <div class="bg-primary text-white text-center m-2 p-2">@Model.Product.Name</div>
</body>
</html>
```

The convention for naming Razor Pages code-behind files is to append the .cs file extension to the name of the view file. If you are using Visual Studio, the code-behind file was created by the Razor Page template when the Index.cshtml file was added to the project. Expand the Index.cshtml item in the Solution Explorer and you will see the code-behind file, as shown in Figure 23-8. Open the file for editing and replace the contents with the statements shown in Listing 23-10.

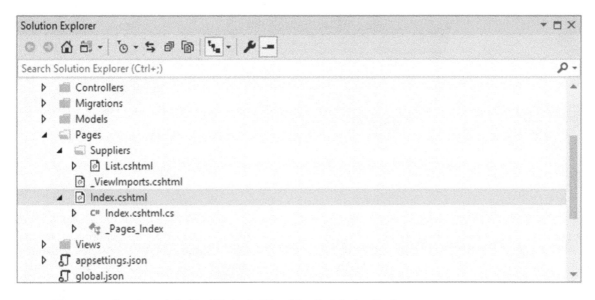

Figure 23-8. Revealing the code-behind file in the Visual Studio Solution Explorer

If you are using Visual Studio Code, add a file named Index.cshtml.cs to the WebApp/Pages folder with the content shown in Listing 23-10.

Listing 23-10. The Contents of the Index.cshtml.cs File in the Pages Folder

```
using System.Threading.Tasks;
using Microsoft.AspNetCore.Mvc.RazorPages;
using WebApp.Models;

namespace WebApp.Pages {

    public class IndexModel: PageModel {
        private DataContext context;

        public Product Product { get; set; }

        public IndexModel(DataContext ctx) {
            context = ctx;
        }

        public async Task OnGetAsync(long id = 1) {
            Product = await context.Products.FindAsync(id);
        }
    }
}
```

When defining the separate page model class, I defined the class in the WebApp.Pages namespace. This isn't a requirement, but it makes the C# class consistent with the rest of the application.

One drawback of using a code-behind file is that automatic recompilation applies only to CSHTML files, which means that changes to the class file are not applied until the application has been restarted. Restart ASP.NET Core and request http://localhost:5000/index to ensure the code-behind file is used, producing the response shown in Figure 23-9.

Figure 23-9. *Using a code-behind file*

Adding a View Imports File

A view imports file can be used to avoid using the fully qualified name for the page model class in the view file, performing the same role as the one I used in Chapter 22 for the MVC Framework. If you are using Visual Studio, use the Razor View Imports template to add a file named _ViewImports.cshtml to the WebApp/Pages folder, with the content shown in Listing 23-11. If you are using Visual Studio Code, add the file directly.

Listing 23-11. The Contents of the _ViewImports.cshtml File in the WebApp/Pages Folder

```
@namespace WebApp.Pages
@using WebApp.Models
```

The @namespace directive sets the namespace for the C# class that is generated by a view, and using the directive in the view imports file sets the default namespace for all the Razor Pages in the application, with the effect that the view and its page model class are in the same namespace and the @model directive does not require a fully qualified type, as shown in Listing 23-12.

Listing 23-12. Removing the Page Model Namespace in the Index.cshtml File in the Pages Folder

```
@page "{id:long?}"
@model IndexModel

<!DOCTYPE html>
<html>
<head>
    <link href="/lib/twitter-bootstrap/css/bootstrap.min.css" rel="stylesheet" />
</head>
<body>
    <div class="bg-primary text-white text-center m-2 p-2">@Model.Product.Name</div>
</body>
</html>
```

Use the browser to request http://localhost:5000/index, which will trigger the recompilation of the views. There is no difference in the response produced by the Razor Page, which is shown in Figure 23-9.

Understanding Action Results in Razor Pages

Although it is not obvious, Razor Page handler methods use the same IActionResult interface to control the responses they generate. To make page model classes easier to develop, handler methods have an implied result that displays the view part of the page. Listing 23-13 makes the result explicit.

Listing 23-13. Using an Explicit Result in the Index.cshtml.cs File in the Pages Folder

```
using System.Threading.Tasks;
using Microsoft.AspNetCore.Mvc.RazorPages;
using WebApp.Models;
using Microsoft.AspNetCore.Mvc;
```

```
namespace WebApp.Pages {

    public class IndexModel : PageModel {
        private DataContext context;

        public Product Product { get; set; }

        public IndexModel(DataContext ctx) {
            context = ctx;
        }

        public async Task<IActionResult> OnGetAsync(long id = 1) {
            Product = await context.Products.FindAsync(id);
            return Page();
        }
    }
}
```

The Page method is inherited from the PageModel class and creates a PageResult object, which tells the framework to render the view part of the page. Unlike the View method used in MVC action methods, the Razor Pages Page method doesn't accept arguments and always renders the view part of the page that has been selected to handle the request.

The PageModel class provides other methods that create different action results to produce different outcomes, as described in Table 23-4.

Table 23-4. *The PageModel Action Result Methods*

Name	Description
Page()	This IActionResult returned by this method produces a 200 OK status code and renders the view part of the Razor Page.
NotFound()	The IActionResult returned by this method produces a 404 NOT FOUND status code.
BadRequest(state)	The IActionResult returned by this method produces a 400 BAD REQUEST status code. The method accepts an optional model state object that describes the problem to the client, as demonstrated in Chapter 19.
File(name, type)	The IActionResult returned by this method produces a 200 OK response, sets the Content-Type header to the specified type, and sends the specified file to the client.
Redirect(path) RedirectPermanent(path)	The IActionResult returned by these methods produces 302 FOUND and 301 MOVED PERMANENTLY responses, which redirect the client to the specified URL.
RedirectToAction(name)RedirectTo ActionPermanent(name)	The IActionResult returned by these methods produces 302 FOUND and 301 MOVED PERMANENTLY responses, which redirect the client to the specified action method. The URL used to redirect the client is produced using the routing features described in Chapter 13.
RedirectToPage(name) RedirectToPagePermanent(name)	The IActionResult returned by these methods produce 302 FOUND and 301 MOVED PERMANENTLY responses that redirect the client to another Razor Page. If no name is supplied, the client is redirected to the current page.
StatusCode(code)	The IActionResult returned by this method produces a response with the specific status code.

Using an Action Result

Except for the Page method, the methods in Table 23-4 are the same as those available in action methods. However, care must be taken with these methods because sending a status code response is unhelpful in Razor Pages because they are used only when a client expects the content of the view.

Instead of using the NotFound method when requested data cannot be found, for example, a better approach is to redirect the client to another URL that can display an HTML message for the user. The redirection can be to a static HTML file, to another Razor Page, or to an action defined by a controller. Add a Razor Page named NotFound.cshtml to the Pages folder and add the content shown in Listing 23-14.

Listing 23-14. The Contents of the NotFound.cshtml File in the Pages Folder

```
@page "/noid"
@model NotFoundModel
@using Microsoft.AspNetCore.Mvc.RazorPages
@using WebApp.Models;

<!DOCTYPE html>
<html>
<head>
    <link href="/lib/twitter-bootstrap/css/bootstrap.min.css" rel="stylesheet" />
    <title>Not Found</title>
</head>
<body>
    <div class="bg-primary text-white text-center m-2 p-2">No Matching ID</div>
    <ul class="list-group m-2">
        @foreach (Product p in Model.Products) {
            <li class="list-group-item">@p.Name (ID: @p.ProductId)</li>
        }
    </ul>
</body>
</html>

@functions {

    public class NotFoundModel: PageModel {
        private DataContext context;

        public IEnumerable<Product> Products { get; set; }

        public NotFoundModel(DataContext ctx) {
            context = ctx;
        }

        public void OnGetAsync(long id = 1) {
            Products = context.Products;
        }
    }
}
```

The @page directive overrides the route convention so that this Razor Page will handle the /noid URL path. The page model class uses an Entity Framework Core context object to query the database and displays a list of the product names and key values that are in the database.

In Listing 23-15, I have updated the handle method of the IndexModel class to redirect the user to the NotFound page when a request is received that doesn't match a Product object in the database.

Listing 23-15. Using a Redirection in the Index.cshtml.cs File in the Pages Folder

```
using System.Threading.Tasks;
using Microsoft.AspNetCore.Mvc.RazorPages;
using WebApp.Models;
using Microsoft.AspNetCore.Mvc;
```

```
namespace WebApp.Pages {

    public class IndexModel : PageModel {
        private DataContext context;

        public Product Product { get; set; }

        public IndexModel(DataContext ctx) {
            context = ctx;
        }

        public async Task<IActionResult> OnGetAsync(long id = 1) {
            Product = await context.Products.FindAsync(id);
            if (Product == null) {
                return RedirectToPage("NotFound");
            }
            return Page();
        }
    }
}
```

The RedirectToPage method produces an action result that redirects the client to a different Razor Page. The name of the target page is specified without the file extension, and any folder structure is specified relative to the Pages folder. To test the redirection, restart ASP.NET Core and request http://localhost:5000/index/500, which provides a value of 500 for the id segment variable and does not match anything in the database. The browser will be redirected and produce the result shown in Figure 23-10.

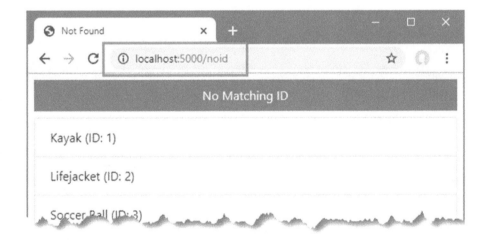

Figure 23-10. *Redirecting to a different Razor Page*

Notice that the routing system is used to produce the URL to which the client is redirected, which uses the routing pattern specified with the @page directive. In this example, the argument to the RedirectToPage method was NotFound, but this has been translated into a redirection to the /noid path specified by the @page directive in Listing 23-14.

Handling Multiple HTTP Methods

Razor Pages can define handler methods that respond to different HTTP methods. The most common combination is to support the GET and POST methods that allow users to view and edit data. To demonstrate, add a Razor Page called Editor.cshtml to the Pages folder and add the content shown in Listing 23-16.

■ **Note**   I have kept this example as simple as possible, but there are excellent ASP.NET Core features for creating HTML forms and for receiving data when it is submitted, as described in Chapter 31.

Listing 23-16. The Contents of the Editor.cshtml File in the WebApps/Pages Folder

```
@page "{id:long}"
@model EditorModel

<!DOCTYPE html>
<html>
<head>
    <link href="/lib/twitter-bootstrap/css/bootstrap.min.css" rel="stylesheet" />
</head>
<body>
    <div class="bg-primary text-white text-center m-2 p-2">Editor</div>
    <div class="m-2">
        <table class="table table-sm table-striped table-bordered">
            <tbody>
                <tr><th>Name</th><td>@Model.Product.Name</td></tr>
                <tr><th>Price</th><td>@Model.Product.Price</td></tr>
            </tbody>
        </table>
        <form method="post">
            @Html.AntiForgeryToken()
            <div class="form-group">
                <label>Price</label>
                <input name="price" class="form-control"
                        value="@Model.Product.Price" />
            </div>
            <button class="btn btn-primary" type="submit">Submit</button>
        </form>
    </div>
</body>
</html>
```

The elements in the Razor Page view create a simple HTML form that presents the user with an input element containing the value of the Price property for a Product object. The form element is defined without an action attribute, which means the browser will send a POST request to the Razor Page's URL when the user clicks the Submit button.

■ **Note**   The @Html.AntiForgeryToken() expression in Listing 23-16 adds a hidden form field to the HTML form that ASP.NET Core uses to guard against cross-site request forgery (CSRF) attacks. I explain how this feature works in Chapter 27, but for this chapter, it is enough to know that POST requests that do not contain this form field will be rejected.

If you are using Visual Studio, expand the Editor.cshtml item in the Solution Explorer to reveal the Editor.cshtml.cs class file and replace its contents with the code shown in Listing 23-17. If you are using Visual Studio Code, add a file named Editor. cshtml.cs to the WebApp/Pages folder and use it to define the class shown in Listing 23-17.

Listing 23-17. The Contents of the Editor.cshtml.cs File in the Pages Folder

```
using System.Threading.Tasks;
using Microsoft.AspNetCore.Mvc;
using Microsoft.AspNetCore.Mvc.RazorPages;
using WebApp.Models;
```

```
namespace WebApp.Pages {
    public class EditorModel : PageModel {
        private DataContext context;

        public Product Product { get; set; }

        public EditorModel(DataContext ctx) {
            context = ctx;
        }

        public async Task OnGetAsync(long id) {
            Product = await context.Products.FindAsync(id);
        }

        public async Task<IActionResult> OnPostAsync(long id, decimal price) {
            Product p = await context.Products.FindAsync(id);
            p.Price = price;
            await context.SaveChangesAsync();
            return RedirectToPage();
        }
    }
}
```

The page model class defines two handler methods, and the name of the method tells the Razor Pages framework which HTTP method each handles. The OnGetAsync method is used to handle GET requests, which it does by locating a Product, whose details are displayed by the view.

The OnPostAsync method is used to handle POST requests, which will be sent by the browser when the user submits the HTML form. The parameters for the OnPostAsync method are obtained from the request so that the id value is obtained from the URL route and the price value is obtained from the form. (The model binding feature that extracts data from forms is described in Chapter 28.)

UNDERSTANDING THE POST REDIRECTION

Notice that the last statement in the OnPostAsync method invokes the RedirectToPage method without an argument, which redirects the client to the URL for the Razor Page. This may seem odd, but the effect is to tell the browser to send a GET request to the URL it used for the POST request. This type of redirection means that the browser won't resubmit the POST request if the user reloads the browser, preventing the same action from being accidentally performed more than once.

To see how the page model class handles different HTTP methods, restart ASP.NET Core and use a browser to navigate to http://localhost:5000/editor/1. Edit the field to set the price to 100 and click the Submit button. The browser will send a POST request that is handled by the OnPostAsync method. The database will be updated, and the browser will be redirected so that the updated data is displayed, as shown in Figure 23-11.

Figure 23-11. *Handling multiple HTTP methods*

Selecting a Handler Method

The page model class can define multiple handler methods, allowing the request to select a method using a `handler` query string parameter or routing segment variable. To demonstrate this feature, add a Razor Page file named `HandlerSelector.cshtml` to the Pages folder with the content shown in Listing 23-18.

Listing 23-18. The Contents of the HandlerSelector.cshtml File in the Pages Folder

```
@page
@model HandlerSelectorModel
@using Microsoft.AspNetCore.Mvc.RazorPages
@using Microsoft.EntityFrameworkCore

<!DOCTYPE html>
<html>
<head>
    <link href="/lib/twitter-bootstrap/css/bootstrap.min.css" rel="stylesheet" />
</head>
<body>
    <div class="bg-primary text-white text-center m-2 p-2">Selector</div>
    <div class="m-2">
        <table class="table table-sm table-striped table-bordered">
            <tbody>
                <tr><th>Name</th><td>@Model.Product.Name</td></tr>
                <tr><th>Price</th><td>@Model.Product.Name</td></tr>
                <tr><th>Category</th><td>@Model.Product.Category?.Name</td></tr>
                <tr><th>Supplier</th><td>@Model.Product.Supplier?.Name</td></tr>
            </tbody>
        </table>
        <a href="/handlerselector" class="btn btn-primary">Standard</a>
        <a href="/handlerselector?handler=related" class="btn btn-primary">
            Related
        </a>
    </div>
</body>
</html>
```

```
@functions{

    public class HandlerSelectorModel: PageModel {
        private DataContext context;

        public Product Product { get; set; }

        public HandlerSelectorModel(DataContext ctx) {
            context = ctx;
        }

        public async Task OnGetAsync(long id = 1) {
            Product = await context.Products.FindAsync(id);
        }

        public async Task OnGetRelatedAsync(long id = 1) {
            Product = await context.Products
                .Include(p => p.Supplier)
                .Include(p => p.Category)
                .FirstOrDefaultAsync(p => p.ProductId == id);
            Product.Supplier.Products = null;
            Product.Category.Products = null;
        }
    }
}
```

The page model class in this example defines two handler methods: OnGetAsync and OnGetRelatedAsync. The OnGetAsync method is used by default, which you can see by using a browser to request http://localhost:5000/handlerselector. The handler method queries the database and presents the result to the user, as shown on the left of Figure 23-12.

One of the anchor elements rendered by the page targets a URL with a handler query string parameter, like this:

```
...
<a href="/handlerselector?handler=related" class="btn btn-primary">Related</a>
...
```

The name of the handler method is specified without the On[method] prefix and without the Async suffix so that the OnGetRelatedAsync method is selected using a handler value of related. This alternative handler method includes related data in its query and presents additional data to the user, as shown on the right of Figure 23-12.

Figure 23-12. *Selecting handler methods*

579

Understanding the Razor Page View

The view part of a Razor Page uses the same syntax and has the same features as the views used with controllers. Razor Pages can use the full range of expressions and features such as sessions, temp data, and layouts. Aside from the use of the @page directive and the page model classes, the only differences are a certain amount of duplication to configure features such as layouts and partial views, as described in the sections that follow.

Creating a Layout for Razor Pages

Layouts for Razor Pages are created in the same way as for controller views but in the Pages/Shared folder. If you are using Visual Studio, create the Pages/Shared folder and add to it a file named _Layout.cshtml using the Razor Layout template with the contents shown in Listing 23-19. If you are using Visual Studio Code, create the Pages/Shared folder, create the _Layout.cshtml file in the new folder, and add the content shown in Listing 23-19.

■ **Note**   Layouts can be created in the same folder as the Razor Pages that use them, in which case they will be used in preference to the files in the Shared folder.

Listing 23-19. The Contents of the _Layout.cshtml File in the Pages/Shared Folder

```
<!DOCTYPE html>
<html>
<head>
    <link href="/lib/twitter-bootstrap/css/bootstrap.min.css" rel="stylesheet" />
    <title>@ViewBag.Title</title>
</head>
<body>
    <h5 class="bg-secondary text-white text-center m-2 p-2">
        Razor Page
    </h5>
    @RenderBody()
</body>
</html>
```

The layout doesn't use any features that are specific to Razor Pages and contains the same elements and expressions used in Chapter 22 when I created a layout for the controller views.

Next, use the Razor View Start template to add a file named _ViewStart.cshtml to the Pages folder. Visual Studio will create the file with the content shown in Listing 23-20. If you are using Visual Studio Code, create the _ViewStart.cshtml file and add the content shown in Listing 23-20.

Listing 23-20. The Contents of the _ViewStart.cshtml File in the Pages Folder

```
@{
    Layout = "_Layout";
}
```

The C# classes generated from Razor Pages are derived from the Page class, which provides the Layout property used by the view start file, which has the same purpose as the one used by controller views. In Listing 23-21, I have updated the Index page to remove the elements that will be provided by the layout.

Listing 23-21. Removing Elements in the Index.cshtml File in the Pages Folder

```
@page "{id:long?}"
@model IndexModel

<div class="bg-primary text-white text-center m-2 p-2">@Model.Product.Name</div>
```

Using a view start file applies the layout to all pages that don't override the value assigned to the Layout property. In Listing 23-22, I have added a code block to the Editor page so that it doesn't use a layout.

Listing 23-22. Disabling Layouts in the Editor.cshtml File in the Pages Folder

```
@page "{id:long}"
@model EditorModel
@{
    Layout = null;
}

<!DOCTYPE html>
<html>
<head>
    <link href="/lib/twitter-bootstrap/css/bootstrap.min.css" rel="stylesheet" />
</head>
<body>

    <! ...elements omitted for brevity ... />

</body>
</html>
```

Use a browser to request http://localhost:5000/index, and you will see the effect of the new layout, which is shown on the left of Figure 23-13. Use the browser to request http://localhost:5000/editor/1, and you will receive content that is generated without the layout, as shown on the right of Figure 23-13.

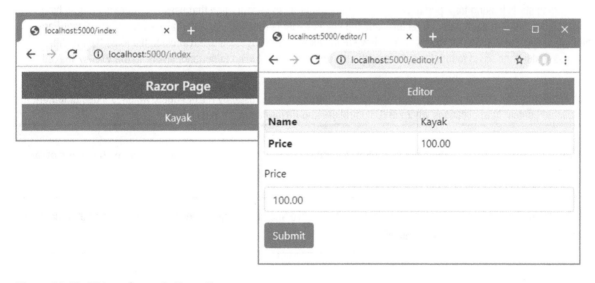

Figure 23-13. *Using a layout in Razor Pages*

Using Partial Views in Razor Pages

Razor Pages can use partial views so that common content isn't duplicated. The example in this section relies on the tag helpers feature, which I describe in detail in Chapter 25. For this chapter, add the directive shown in Listing 23-23 to the view imports file, which enables the custom HTML element used to apply partial views.

Listing 23-23. Enabling Tag Helpers in the _ViewImports.cshtml File in the Pages Folder

```
@namespace WebApp.Pages
@using WebApp.Models
@addTagHelper *, Microsoft.AspNetCore.Mvc.TagHelpers
```

Next, add a Razor view named _ProductPartial.cshtml in the Pages/Shared folder and add the content shown in Listing 23-24.

Listing 23-24. The Contents of the _ProductPartial.cshtml File in the Pages/Shared Folder

```
@model Product

<div class="m-2">
    <table class="table table-sm table-striped table-bordered">
        <tbody>
            <tr><th>Name</th><td>@Model.Name</td></tr>
            <tr><th>Price</th><td>@Model.Price</td></tr>
        </tbody>
    </table>
</div>
```

Notice there is nothing specific to Razor Pages in the partial view. Partial views use the @model directive to receive a view model object and do not use the @page directive or have page models, both of which are specific to Razor Pages. This allows Razor Pages to share partial views with MVC controllers, as described in the sidebar.

UNDERSTANDING THE PARTIAL METHOD SEARCH PATH

The Razor view engine starts looking for a partial view in the same folder as the Razor Page that uses it. If there is no matching file, then the search continues in each parent directory until the Pages folder is reached. For a partial view used by a Razor Page defined in the Pages/App/Data folder, for example, the view engine looks in the Pages/App/Data folder, the Page/App folder, and then the Pages folder. If no file is found, the search continues to the Pages/Shared folder and, finally, to the Views/Shared folder.

The last search location allows partial views defined for use with controllers to be used by Razor Pages, which is a useful feature for avoiding duplicate content in applications where MVC controllers and Razor Pages are both used.

Partial views are applied using partial element, as shown in Listing 23-25, with the name attribute specifying the name of the view and the model attribute providing the view model.

■ **Caution** Partial views receive a view model through their @model directive and not a page model. It is for this reason that the value of the model attribute is Model.Product and not just Model.

Listing 23-25. Using a Partial View in the Index.cshtml File in the Pages Folder

```
@page "{id:long?}"
@model IndexModel

<div class="bg-primary text-white text-center m-2 p-2">@Model.Product.Name</div>
<partial name="_ProductPartial" model="Model.Product" />
```

When the Razor Page is used to handle a response, the contents of the partial view are incorporated into the response. Use a browser to request `http://localhost:5000/index`, and the response includes the table defined in the partial view, as shown in Figure 23-14.

Figure 23-14. *Using a partial view*

Creating Razor Pages Without Page Models

If a Razor Page is simply presenting data to the user, the result can be a page model class that simply declares a constructor dependency to set a property that is consumed in the view. To understand this pattern, add a Razor Page named `Data.cshtml` to the WebApp/Pages folder with the content shown in Listing 23-26.

Listing 23-26. The Contents of the Data.cshtml File in the Pages Folder

```
@page
@model DataPageModel
@using Microsoft.AspNetCore.Mvc.RazorPages

<h5 class="bg-primary text-white text-center m-2 p-2">Categories</h5>
<ul class="list-group m-2">
    @foreach (Category c in Model.Categories) {
        <li class="list-group-item">@c.Name</li>
    }
</ul>

@functions {

    public class DataPageModel : PageModel {
        private DataContext context;

        public IEnumerable<Category> Categories { get; set; }

        public DataPageModel(DataContext ctx) {
            context = ctx;
        }
```

```
        public void OnGet() {
            Categories = context.Categories;
        }
    }
}
```

The page model in this example doesn't transform data, perform calculations, or do anything other than giving the view access to the data through dependency injection. To avoid this pattern, where a page model class is used only to access a service, the @inject directive can be used to obtain the service in the view, without the need for a page model, as shown in Listing 23-27.

■ **Caution**　The @inject directive should be used sparingly and only when the page model class adds no value other than to provide access to services. In all other situations, using a page model class is easier to manage and maintain.

Listing 23-27.　Accessing a Service in the Data.cshtml File in the Pages Folder

```
@page
@inject DataContext context;

<h5 class="bg-primary text-white text-center m-2 p-2">Categories</h5>
<ul class="list-group m-2">
    @foreach (Category c in context.Categories) {
        <li class="list-group-item">@c.Name</li>
    }
</ul>
```

The @inject expression specifies the service type and the name by which the service is accessed. In this example, the service type is DataContext, and the name by which it is accessed is context. Within the view, the @foreach expression generates elements for each object returned by the DataContext.Categories properties. Since there is no page model in this example, I have removed the @page and @using directives. Use a browser to navigate to http://localhost:5000/data, and you will see the response shown in Figure 23-15.

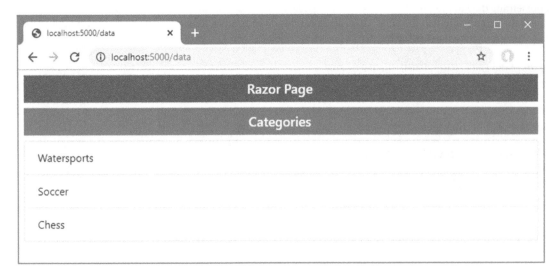

Figure 23-15.　Using a Razor Page without a page model

Summary

In this chapter, I introduced Razor Pages and explained how they differ from the controllers and views. I showed you how to define content and code in the same file, how to use a code-behind file, and how page models provide the underpinnings for the most important Razor Pages features. In the next chapter, I describe the view components feature.

CHAPTER 24

Using View Components

I describe *view components* in this chapter, which are classes that provide action-style logic to support partial views; this means view components provide complex content to be embedded in views while allowing the C# code that supports it to be easily maintained. Table 24-1 puts view components in context.

Table 24-1. *Putting View Components in Context*

Question	Answer
What are they?	View components are classes that provide application logic to support partial views or to inject small fragments of HTML or JSON data into a parent view.
Why are they useful?	Without view components, it is hard to create embedded functionality such as shopping baskets or login panels in a way that is easy to maintain.
How are they used?	View components are typically derived from the ViewComponent class and are applied in a parent view using the custom vc HTML element or the @await Component.InvokeAsync expression.
Are there any pitfalls or limitations?	View components are a simple and predictable feature. The main pitfall is not using them and trying to include application logic within views where it is difficult to test and maintain.
Are there any alternatives?	You could put the data access and processing logic directly in a partial view, but the result is difficult to work with and hard to maintain.

Table 24-2 summarizes the chapter.

Table 24-2. *Chapter Summary*

Problem	Solution	Listing
Creating a reusable unit of code and content	Define a view component	7–13
Creating a response from a view component	Use one of the IViewComponentResult implementation classes	14–18
Getting context data	Use the properties inherited from the base class or use the parameters of the Invoke or InvokeAsync method	19–23
Generating view component responses asynchronously	Override the InvokeAsync method	24–26
Integrating a view component into another endpoint	Create a hybrid controller or Razor Page	27–34

Preparing for This Chapter

This chapter uses the WebApp project from Chapter 23. To prepare for this chapter, add a class file named City.cs to the WebApp/Models folder with the content shown in Listing 24-1.

Tip You can download the example project for this chapter—and for all the other chapters in this book—from https://github.com/apress/pro-asp.net-core-3. See Chapter 1 for how to get help if you have problems running the examples.

© Adam Freeman 2020
A. Freeman, *Pro ASP.NET Core 3*, https://doi.org/10.1007/978-1-4842-5440-0_24

Listing 24-1. The Contents of the City.cs File in the Models Folder

```
namespace WebApp.Models {

    public class City {
        public string Name { get; set; }
        public string Country { get; set; }
        public int Population { get; set; }
    }
}
```

Add a class named CitiesData.cs to the WebApp/Models folder with the content shown in Listing 24-2.

Listing 24-2. The Contents of the CitiesData.cs File in the WebApp/Models Folder

```
using System.Collections.Generic;

namespace WebApp.Models {

    public class CitiesData {

        private List<City> cities = new List<City> {
            new City { Name = "London", Country = "UK", Population = 8539000},
            new City { Name = "New York", Country = "USA", Population = 8406000 },
            new City { Name = "San Jose", Country = "USA", Population = 998537 },
            new City { Name = "Paris", Country = "France", Population = 2244000 }
        };

        public IEnumerable<City> Cities => cities;

        public void AddCity(City newCity) {
            cities.Add(newCity);
        }
    }
}
```

The CitiesData class provides access to a collection of City objects and provides an AddCity method that adds a new object to the collection. Add the statement shown in Listing 24-3 to the ConfigureServices method of the Startup class to create a service for the CitiesData class.

Listing 24-3. Defining a Service in the Startup.cs File in the WebApp Folder

```
using System;
using System.Collections.Generic;
using System.Linq;
using Microsoft.AspNetCore.Builder;
using Microsoft.Extensions.DependencyInjection;
using Microsoft.Extensions.Configuration;
using Microsoft.EntityFrameworkCore;
using WebApp.Models;
using Microsoft.AspNetCore.Mvc.RazorPages;

namespace WebApp {
    public class Startup {

        public Startup(IConfiguration config) {
            Configuration = config;
        }
```

```
    public IConfiguration Configuration { get; set; }

    public void ConfigureServices(IServiceCollection services) {
        services.AddDbContext<DataContext>(opts => {
            opts.UseSqlServer(Configuration[
                "ConnectionStrings:ProductConnection"]);
            opts.EnableSensitiveDataLogging(true);
        });
        services.AddControllersWithViews().AddRazorRuntimeCompilation();
        services.AddRazorPages().AddRazorRuntimeCompilation();

        services.AddDistributedMemoryCache();
        services.AddSession(options => {
            options.Cookie.IsEssential = true;
        });

        services.Configure<RazorPagesOptions>(opts => {
            opts.Conventions.AddPageRoute("/Index", "/extra/page/{id:long?}");
        });

        services.AddSingleton<CitiesData>();
    }

    public void Configure(IApplicationBuilder app, DataContext context) {
        app.UseDeveloperExceptionPage();
        app.UseStaticFiles();
        app.UseSession();
        app.UseRouting();
        app.UseEndpoints(endpoints => {
            endpoints.MapControllers();
            endpoints.MapDefaultControllerRoute();
            endpoints.MapRazorPages();
        });
        SeedData.SeedDatabase(context);
    }
    }
}
```

The new statement uses the AddSingleton method to create a CitiesData service. There is no interface/implementation separation in this service, which I have created to easily distribute a shared CitiesData object. Add a Razor Page named Cities. cshtml to the WebApp/Pages folder and add the content shown in Listing 24-4.

Listing 24-4. The Contents of the Cities.cshtml File in the Pages Folder

```
@page
@inject CitiesData Data

<div class="m-2">
    <table class="table table-sm table-striped table-bordered">
        <tbody>
            @foreach (City c in Data.Cities) {
                <tr>
                    <td>@c.Name</td>
                    <td>@c.Country</td>
                    <td>@c.Population</td>
                </tr>
            }
```

```
        </tbody>
    </table>
</div>
```

Dropping the Database

Open a new PowerShell command prompt, navigate to the folder that contains the WebApp.csproj file, and run the command shown in Listing 24-5 to drop the database.

Listing 24-5. Dropping the Database

```
dotnet ef database drop --force
```

Running the Example Application

Select Start Without Debugging or Run Without Debugging from the Debug menu or use the PowerShell command prompt to run the command shown in Listing 24-6.

Listing 24-6. Running the Example Application

```
dotnet run
```

The database will be seeded as part of the application startup. Once ASP.NET Core is running, use a web browser to request http://localhost:5000/cities, which will produce the response shown in Figure 24-1.

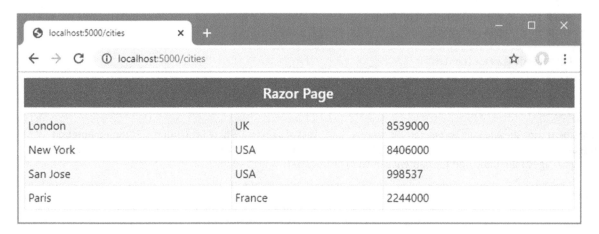

Figure 24-1. *Running the example application*

Understanding View Components

Applications commonly need to embed content in views that isn't related to the main purpose of the application. Common examples include site navigation tools and authentication panels that let the user log in without visiting a separate page.

The data for this type of feature isn't part of the model data passed from the action method or page model to the view. It is for this reason that I have created two sources of data in the example project: I am going to display some content generated using City data, which isn't easily done in a view that receives data from the Entity Framework Core repository and the Product, Category, and Supplier objects it contains.

Partial views are used to create reusable markup that is required in views, avoiding the need to duplicate the same content in multiple places in the application. Partial views are a useful feature, but they just contain fragments of HTML and Razor directives, and the data they operate on is received from the parent view. If you need to display different data, then you run into a problem. You could access the data you need directly from the partial view, but this breaks the development model and produces an application that is difficult to understand and maintain. Alternatively, you could extend the view models used by the application so that it includes the data you require, but this means you have to change every action method, which makes it hard to isolate the functionality of action methods for effective maintenance and testing.

This is where view components come in. A view component is a C# class that provides a partial view with the data that it needs, independently from the action method or Razor Page. In this regard, a view component can be thought of as a specialized action or page, but one that is used only to provide a partial view with data; it cannot receive HTTP requests, and the content that it provides will always be included in the parent view.

Creating and Using a View Component

A view component is any class whose name ends with ViewComponent and that defines an Invoke or InvokeAsync method or any class that is derived from the ViewComponent base class or that has been decorated with the ViewComponent attribute. I demonstrate the use of the attribute in the "Getting Context Data" section, but the other examples in this chapter rely on the base class.

View components can be defined anywhere in a project, but the convention is to group them in a folder named Components. Create the WebApp/Components folder and add to it a class file named CitySummary.cs with the content shown in Listing 24-7.

Listing 24-7. The Contents of the CitySummary.cs File in the Components Folder

```
using Microsoft.AspNetCore.Mvc;
using System.Linq;
using WebApp.Models;

namespace WebApp.Components {

    public class CitySummary: ViewComponent {
        private CitiesData data;

        public CitySummary(CitiesData cdata) {
            data = cdata;
        }

        public string Invoke() {
            return $"{data.Cities.Count()} cities, "
            + $"{data.Cities.Sum(c => c.Population)} people";
        }
    }
}
```

View components can take advantage of dependency injection to receive the services they require. In this example, the view component declares a dependency on the CitiesData class, which is then used in the Invoke method to create a string that contains the number of cities and the population total.

Applying a View Component

View components can be applied in two different ways. The first technique is to use the Component property that is added to the C# classes generated from views and Razor Pages. This property returns an object that implements the IViewComponentHelper interface, which provides the InvokeAsync method. Listing 24-8 uses this technique to apply the view component in the Index.cshtml file in the Views/Home folder.

Listing 24-8. Using a View Component in the Index.cshtml File in the Views/Index Folder

```
@model Product
@{
    Layout = "_Layout";
    ViewBag.Title = ViewBag.Title ?? "Product Table";
}

@section Header { Product Information }

<tr><th>Name</th><td>@Model.Name</td></tr>
<tr>
    <th>Price</th>
    <td>@Model.Price.ToString("c")</td>
</tr>
<tr><th>Category ID</th><td>@Model.CategoryId</td></tr>

@section Footer {
    @(((Model.Price / ViewBag.AveragePrice)
        * 100).ToString("F2"))% of average price
}

@section Summary {
    <div class="bg-info text-white m-2 p-2">
        @await Component.InvokeAsync("CitySummary")
    </div>
}
```

View components are applied using the Component.InvokeAsync method, using the name of the view component class as the argument. The syntax for this technique can be confusing. View component classes define either an Invoke or InvokeAsync method, depending on whether their work is performed synchronously or asynchronously. But the Component.InvokeAsync method is always used, even to apply view components that define the Invoke method and whose operations are entirely synchronous.

To add the namespace for the view components to the list that are included in views, I added the statement shown in Listing 24-9 to the _ViewImports.json file in the Views folder.

Listing 24-9. Adding a Namespace in the _ViewImports.json File in the Views Folder

```
@using WebApp.Models
@addTagHelper *, Microsoft.AspNetCore.Mvc.TagHelpers
@using WebApp.Components
```

Restart ASP.NET Core and use a browser to request http://localhost:5000/home/index/1, which will produce the result shown in Figure 24-2.

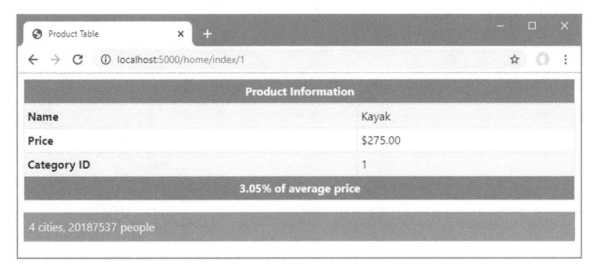

Figure 24-2. *Using a view component*

Applying View Components Using a Tag Helper

Razor views and pages can contain tag helpers, which are custom HTML elements that are managed by C# classes. I explain how tag helpers work in detail in Chapter 25, but view components can be applied using an HTML element that is implemented as a tag helper. To enable this feature, add the directive shown in Listing 24-10 to the _ViewImports.cshtml file in the Views folder.

■ **Note**   View components can be used only in controller views or Razor Pages and cannot be used to handle requests directly.

Listing 24-10.   Configuring a Tag Helper in the _ViewImports.cshtml File in the Views Folder

```
@using WebApp.Models
@addTagHelper *, Microsoft.AspNetCore.Mvc.TagHelpers
@using WebApp.Components
@addTagHelper *, WebApp
```

The new directive adds tag helper support for the example project, which is specified by name. (You must change WebApp to the name of your project.) In Listing 24-11, I have used the custom HTML element to apply the view component.

Listing 24-11.   Applying a View Component in the Index.cshtml File in the Views/Home Folder

```
@model Product
@{
    Layout = "_Layout";
    ViewBag.Title = ViewBag.Title ?? "Product Table";
}

@section Header { Product Information }

<tr><th>Name</th><td>@Model.Name</td></tr>
<tr>
    <th>Price</th>
    <td>@Model.Price.ToString("c")</td>
</tr>
```

```
<tr><th>Category ID</th><td>@Model.CategoryId</td></tr>

@section Footer {
    @(((Model.Price / ViewBag.AveragePrice)
        * 100).ToString("F2"))% of average price
}

@section Summary {
    <div class="bg-info text-white m-2 p-2">
        <vc:city-summary />
    </div>
}
```

The tag for the custom element is vc, followed by a colon, followed by the name of the view component class, which is transformed into kebab-case. Each capitalized word in the class name is converted to lowercase and separated by a hyphen so that CitySummary becomes city-summary, and the CitySummary view component is applied using the vc:city-summary element.

Applying View Components in Razor Pages

Razor Pages use view components in the same way, either through the Component property or through the custom HTML element. Since Razor Pages have their own view imports file, a separate @addTagHelper directive is required, as shown in Listing 24-12.

Listing 24-12. Adding a Directive in the _ViewImports.cshtml File in the Pages Folder

```
@namespace WebApp.Pages
@using WebApp.Models
@addTagHelper *, Microsoft.AspNetCore.Mvc.TagHelpers
@addTagHelper *, WebApp
```

Listing 24-13 applies the CitySummary view component to the Data page.

Listing 24-13. Using a View Component in the Data.cshtml File in the Pages Folder

```
@page
@inject DataContext context;

<h5 class="bg-primary text-white text-center m-2 p-2">Categories</h5>
<ul class="list-group m-2">
    @foreach (Category c in context.Categories) {
        <li class="list-group-item">@c.Name</li>
    }
</ul>

<div class="bg-info text-white m-2 p-2">
    <vc:city-summary />
</div>
```

Use a browser to request http://localhost:5000/data, and you will see the response shown in Figure 24-3, which displays the city data alongside the categories in the database.

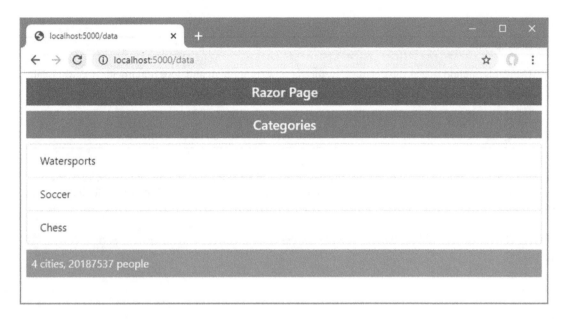

Figure 24-3. *Using a view component in a Razor Page*

Understanding View Component Results

The ability to insert simple string values into a view or page isn't especially useful, but fortunately, view components are capable of much more. More complex effects can be achieved by having the Invoke or InvokeAsync method return an object that implements the IViewComponentResult interface. There are three built-in classes that implement the IViewComponentResult interface, and they are described in Table 24-3, along with the convenience methods for creating them provided by the ViewComponent base class. I describe the use of each result type in the sections that follow.

Table 24-3. *The Built-in IViewComponentResult Implementation Classes*

Name	Description
ViewViewComponentResult	This class is used to specify a Razor view, with optional view model data. Instances of this class are created using the View method.
ContentViewComponentResult	This class is used to specify a text result that will be safely encoded for inclusion in an HTML document. Instances of this class are created using the Content method.
HtmlContentViewComponentResult	This class is used to specify a fragment of HTML that will be included in the HTML document without further encoding. There is no ViewComponent method to create this type of result.

There is special handling for two result types. If a view component returns a string, then it is used to create a ContentViewComponentResult object, which is what I relied on in earlier examples. If a view component returns an IHtmlContent object, then it is used to create an HtmlContentViewComponentResult object.

Returning a Partial View

The most useful response is the awkwardly named ViewViewComponentResult object, which tells Razor to render a partial view and include the result in the parent view. The ViewComponent base class provides the View method for creating ViewViewComponentResult objects, and four versions of the method are available, described in Table 24-4.

Table 24-4. *The ViewComponent.View Methods*

Name	Description
View()	Using this method selects the default view for the view component and does not provide a view model.
View(model)	Using the method selects the default view and uses the specified object as the view model.
View(viewName)	Using this method selects the specified view and does not provide a view model.
View(viewName, model)	Using this method selects the specified view and uses the specified object as the view model.

These methods correspond to those provided by the `Controller` base class and are used in much the same way. To create a view model class that the view component can use, add a class file named `CityViewModel.cs` to the `WebApp/Models` folder and use it to define the class shown in Listing 24-14.

Listing 24-14. The Contents of the CityViewModel.cs File in the Models Folder

```
namespace WebApp.Models {

    public class CityViewModel {
        public int Cities { get; set; }
        public int Population { get; set; }
    }
}
```

Listing 24-15 modifies the `Invoke` method of the `CitySummary` view component so it uses the `View` method to select a partial view and provides view data using a `CityViewModel` object.

Listing 24-15. Selecting a View in the CitySummary.cs File in the Components Folder

```
using Microsoft.AspNetCore.Mvc;
using System.Linq;
using WebApp.Models;

namespace WebApp.Components {

    public class CitySummary: ViewComponent {
        private CitiesData data;

        public CitySummary(CitiesData cdata) {
            data = cdata;
        }

        public IViewComponentResult Invoke() {
            return View(new CityViewModel {
                Cities = data.Cities.Count(),
                Population = data.Cities.Sum(c => c.Population)
            });
        }
    }
}
```

There is no view available for the view component currently, but the error message this produces reveals the locations that are searched. Restart ASP.NET Core and use a browser to request `http://localhost:5000/home/index/1` to see the locations that are searched when the view component is used with a controller. Request `http://localhost:5000/data` to see the locations searched when a view component is used with a Razor Page. Figure 24-4 shows both responses.

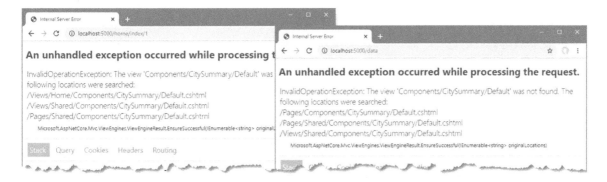

Figure 24-4. *The search locations for view component views*

Razor searches for a view named `Default.cshtml` when a view component invokes the `View` method without specifying a name. If the view component is used with a controller, then the search locations are as follows:

- `/Views/[controller]/Components/[viewcomponent]/Default.cshtml`

- `/Views/Shared/Components/[viewcomponent]/Default.cshtml`

- `/Pages/Shared/Components/[viewcomponent]/Default.cshtml`

When the `CitySummary` component is rendered by a view selected through the `Home` controller, for example, `[controller]` is `Home` and `[viewcomponent]` is `CitySummary`, which means the first search location is `/Views/Home/Components/CitySummary/Default.cshtml`. If the view component is used with a Razor Page, then the search locations are as follows:

- `/Pages/Components/[viewcomponent]/Default.cshtml`

- `/Pages/Shared/Components/[viewcomponent]/Default.cshtml`

- `/Views/Shared/Components/[viewcomponent]/Default.cshtml`

If the search paths for Razor Pages do not include the page name but a Razor Page is defined in a subfolder, then the Razor view engine will look for a view in the `Components/[viewcomponent]` folder, relative to the location in which the Razor Page is defined, working its way up the folder hierarchy until it finds a view or reaches the `Pages` folder.

■ **Tip**   Notice that view components used in Razor Pages will find views defined in the `Views/Shared/Components` folder and that view components defined in controllers will find views in the `Pages/Shared/Components` folder. This means you don't have to duplicate views when a view component is used by controllers and Razor Pages.

Create the `WebApp/Views/Shared/Components/CitySummary` folder and add to it a Razor view named `Default.cshtml` with the content shown in Listing 24-16.

Listing 24-16. The Default.cshtml File in the Views/Shared/Components/CitySummary Folder

```
@model CityViewModel

<table class="table table-sm table-bordered text-white bg-secondary">
    <thead>
        <tr><th colspan="2">Cities Summary</th></tr>
    </thead>
    <tbody>
        <tr>
            <td>Cities:</td>
            <td class="text-right">
                @Model.Cities
            </td>
        </tr>
```

```
        <tr>
            <td>Population:</td>
            <td class="text-right">
                @Model.Population.ToString("#,###")
            </td>
        </tr>
    </tbody>
</table>
```

Views for view components are similar to partial views and use the @model directive to set the type of the view model object. This view receives a CityViewModel object from its view component, which is used to populate the cells in an HTML table. Use a browser to request http://localhost:5000/home/index/1 and http://localhost:5000/data, and you will see the view incorporated into the responses, as shown in Figure 24-5.

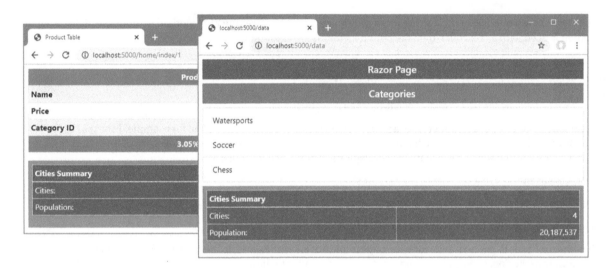

Figure 24-5. *Using a view with a view component*

Returning HTML Fragments

The ContentViewComponentResult class is used to include fragments of HTML in the parent view without using a view. Instances of the ContentViewComponentResult class are created using the Content method inherited from the ViewComponent base class, which accepts a string value. Listing 24-17 demonstrates the use of the Content method.

■ **Tip**   In addition to the Content method, the Invoke method can return a string, which will be automatically converted to a ContentViewComponentResult. This is the approach I took in the view component when it was first defined.

Listing 24-17. Using the Content Method in the CitySummary.cs File in the Components Folder

```
using Microsoft.AspNetCore.Mvc;
using System.Linq;
using WebApp.Models;

namespace WebApp.Components {

    public class CitySummary: ViewComponent {
        private CitiesData data;
```

```
        public CitySummary(CitiesData cdata) {
            data = cdata;
        }

        public IViewComponentResult Invoke() {
            return Content("This is a <h3><i>string</i></h3>");
        }
    }
}
```

The string received by the Content method is encoded to make it safe to include in an HTML document. This is particularly important when dealing with content that has been provided by users or external systems because it prevents JavaScript content from being embedded into the HTML generated by the application.

In this example, the string that I passed to the Content method contains some basic HTML tags. Restart ASP.NET Core and use a browser to request http://localhost:5000/home/index/1. The response will include the encoded HTML fragment, as shown in Figure 24-6.

Figure 24-6. *Returning an encoded HTML fragment using a view component*

If you look at the HTML that the view component produced, you will see that the angle brackets have been replaced so that the browser doesn't interpret the content as HTML elements, as follows:

```
...
<div class="bg-info text-white m-2 p-2">
    This is a <h3><i>string</i></h3>
</div>
...
```

You don't need to encode content if you trust its source and want it to be interpreted as HTML. The Content method always encodes its argument, so you must create the HtmlContentViewComponentResult object directly and provide its constructor with an HtmlString object, which represents a string that you know is safe to display, either because it comes from a source that you trust or because you are confident that it has already been encoded, as shown in Listing 24-18.

Listing 24-18. Returning an HTML Fragment in the CitySummary.cs File in the Components Folder

```
using Microsoft.AspNetCore.Mvc;
using System.Linq;
using WebApp.Models;
using Microsoft.AspNetCore.Mvc.ViewComponents;
using Microsoft.AspNetCore.Html;
```

```
namespace WebApp.Components {

    public class CitySummary: ViewComponent {
        private CitiesData data;

        public CitySummary(CitiesData cdata) {
            data = cdata;
        }

        public IViewComponentResult Invoke() {
            return new HtmlContentViewComponentResult(
                new HtmlString("This is a <h3><i>string</i></h3>"));
        }
    }
}
```

This technique should be used with caution and only with sources of content that cannot be tampered with and that perform their own encoding. Restart ASP.NET Core and use a browser to request http://localhost:5000/home/index/1, and you will see the response isn't encoded and is interpreted as HTML elements, as shown in Figure 24-7.

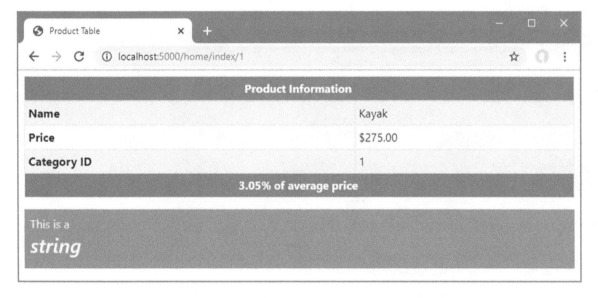

Figure 24-7. *Returning an unencoded HTML fragment using a view component*

Getting Context Data

Details about the current request and the parent view are provided to a view component through properties defined by the ViewComponent base class, as described in Table 24-5.

Table 24-5. *The ViewComponentContext Properties*

Name	Description
HttpContext	This property returns an HttpContext object that describes the current request and the response that is being prepared.
Request	This property returns an HttpRequest object that describes the current HTTP request.
User	This property returns an IPrincipal object that describes the current user, as described in Chapters 37 and 38.
RouteData	This property returns a RouteData object that describes the routing data for the current request.
ViewBag	This property returns the dynamic view bag object, which can be used to pass data between the view component and the view, as described in Chapter 22.
ModelState	This property returns a ModelStateDictionary, which provides details of the model binding process, as described in Chapter 29.
ViewData	This property returns a ViewDataDictionary, which provides access to the view data provided for the view component.

The context data can be used in whatever way helps the view component do its work, including varying the way that data is selected or rendering different content or views. It is hard to devise a representative example of using context data in a view component because the problems it solves are specific to each project. In Listing 24-19, I check the route data for the request to determine whether the routing pattern contains a controller segment variable, which indicates a request that will be handled by a controller and view.

Listing 24-19. Using Request Data in the CitySummary.cs File in the Components Folder

```
using Microsoft.AspNetCore.Mvc;
using System.Linq;
using WebApp.Models;
using Microsoft.AspNetCore.Mvc.ViewComponents;
using Microsoft.AspNetCore.Html;

namespace WebApp.Components {

    public class CitySummary: ViewComponent {
        private CitiesData data;

        public CitySummary(CitiesData cdata) {
            data = cdata;
        }

        public string Invoke() {
            if (RouteData.Values["controller"] != null) {
                return "Controller Request";
            } else {
                return "Razor Page Request";
            }
        }
    }
}
```

Restart ASP.NET Core and use a browser to request http://localhost:5000/home/index/1 and http://localhost:5000/data, and you will see that the view component alters its output, as shown in Figure 24-8.

Figure 24-8. *Using context data in a view component*

Providing Context from the Parent View Using Arguments

Parent views can provide additional context data to view components, providing them with either data or guidance about the content that should be produced. The context data is received through the Invoke or InvokeAsync method, as shown in Listing 24-20.

Listing 24-20. Receiving a Value in the CitySummary.cs File in the Components Folder

```
using Microsoft.AspNetCore.Mvc;
using System.Linq;
using WebApp.Models;
using Microsoft.AspNetCore.Mvc.ViewComponents;
using Microsoft.AspNetCore.Html;

namespace WebApp.Components {

    public class CitySummary: ViewComponent {
        private CitiesData data;

        public CitySummary(CitiesData cdata) {
            data = cdata;
        }

        public IViewComponentResult Invoke(string themeName) {
            ViewBag.Theme = themeName;

            return View(new CityViewModel {
                Cities = data.Cities.Count(),
                Population = data.Cities.Sum(c => c.Population)
            });
        }
    }
}
```

The Invoke method defines a themeName parameter that is passed on to the partial view using the view bag, which was described in Chapter 22. Listing 24-21 updates the Default view to use the received value to style the content it produces.

Listing 24-21. Styling Content in the Default.cshtml File in the Views/Shared/Components/CitySummary Folder

```
@model CityViewModel

<table class="table table-sm table-bordered text-white bg-@ViewBag.Theme">
    <thead>
        <tr><th colspan="2">Cities Summary</th></tr>
    </thead>
    <tbody>
        <tr>
            <td>Cities:</td>
            <td class="text-right">
                @Model.Cities
            </td>
        </tr>
        <tr>
            <td>Population:</td>
            <td class="text-right">
                @Model.Population.ToString("#,###")
            </td>
        </tr>
    </tbody>
</table>
```

A value for all parameters defined by a view component's Invoke or InvokeAsync method must always be provided. Listing 24-22 provides a value for themeName parameter in the view selected by the Home controller.

■ **Tip** The view component will not be used if you do not provide values for all the parameters it defines but no error message is displayed. If you don't see any content from a view component, then the likely cause is a missing parameter value.

Listing 24-22. Supplying a Value in the Index.cshtml File in the Views/Home Folder

```
@model Product
@{
    Layout = "_Layout";
    ViewBag.Title = ViewBag.Title ?? "Product Table";
}

@section Header { Product Information }

<tr><th>Name</th><td>@Model.Name</td></tr>
<tr>
    <th>Price</th>
    <td>@Model.Price.ToString("c")</td>
</tr>
<tr><th>Category ID</th><td>@Model.CategoryId</td></tr>

@section Footer {
    @(((Model.Price / ViewBag.AveragePrice)
        * 100).ToString("F2"))% of average price
}

@section Summary {
    <div class="bg-info text-white m-2 p-2">
        <vc:city-summary theme-name="secondary" />
    </div>
}
```

601

The name of each parameter is expressed an attribute using kebab-case so that the theme-name attribute provides a value for the themeName parameter. Listing 24-23 sets a value in the Data.cshtml Razor Page.

Listing 24-23. Supplying a Value in the Data.cshtml File in the Pages Folder

```
@page
@inject DataContext context;

<h5 class="bg-primary text-white text-center m-2 p-2">Categories</h5>
<ul class="list-group m-2">
    @foreach (Category c in context.Categories) {
        <li class="list-group-item">@c.Name</li>
    }
</ul>

<div class="bg-info text-white m-2 p-2">
    <vc:city-summary theme-name="danger" />
</div>
```

Restart ASP.NET Core and use a browser to request http://localhost:5000/home/index/1 and http://localhost:5000/data. The view component is provided with different values for the themeName parameter, producing the responses shown in Figure 24-9.

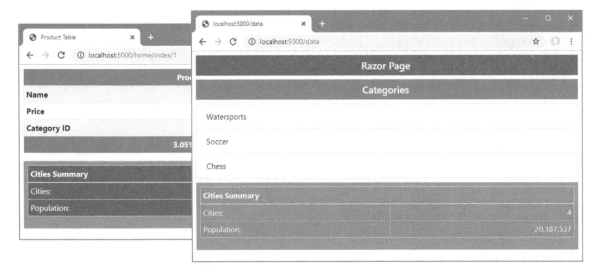

Figure 24-9. *Using context data in a view component*

PROVIDING VALUES USING THE COMPONENT HELPER

If you prefer applying view components using the Component.InvokeAsync helper, then you can provide context using method arguments, like this:

```
...
<div class="bg-info text-white m-2 p-2">
    @await Component.InvokeAsync("CitySummary", new { themeName = "danger" })
</div>
...
```

The first argument to the InvokeAsync method is the name of the view component class. The second argument is an object whose names correspond to the parameters defined by the view component.

Creating Asynchronous View Components

All the examples so far in this chapter have been synchronous view components, which can be recognized because they define the Invoke method. If your view component relies on asynchronous APIs, then you can create an asynchronous view component by defining an InvokeAsync method that returns a Task. When Razor receives the Task from the InvokeAsync method, it will wait for it to complete and then insert the result into the main view. To create a new component, add a class file named PageSize.cs to the Components folder and use it to define the class shown in Listing 24-24.

Listing 24-24. The Contents of the PageSize.cs File in the Components Folder

```
using Microsoft.AspNetCore.Mvc;
using System.Net.Http;
using System.Threading.Tasks;

namespace WebApp.Components {

    public class PageSize : ViewComponent {

        public async Task<IViewComponentResult> InvokeAsync() {
            HttpClient client = new HttpClient();
            HttpResponseMessage response
                = await client.GetAsync("http://apress.com");
            return View(response.Content.Headers.ContentLength);
        }
    }
}
```

The InvokeAsync method uses the async and await keywords to consume the asynchronous API provided by the HttpClient class and get the length of the content returned by sending a GET request to Apress.com. The length is passed to the View method, which selects the default partial view associated with the view component.

Create the Views/Shared/Components/PageSize folder and add to it a Razor view named Default.cshtml with the content shown in Listing 24-25.

Listing 24-25. The Contents of the Default.cshtml File in the Views/Shared/Components/PageSize Folder

```
@model long
<div class="m-1 p-1 bg-light text-dark">Page size: @Model</div>
```

The final step is to use the component, which I have done in the Index view used by the Home controller, as shown in Listing 24-26. No change is required in the way that asynchronous view components are used.

Listing 24-26. Using an Asynchronous Component in the Index.cshtml File in the Views/Home Folder

```
@model Product
@{
    Layout = "_Layout";
    ViewBag.Title = ViewBag.Title ?? "Product Table";
}

@section Header { Product Information }

<tr><th>Name</th><td>@Model.Name</td></tr>
<tr>
    <th>Price</th>
    <td>@Model.Price.ToString("c")</td>
</tr>
<tr><th>Category ID</th><td>@Model.CategoryId</td></tr>
```

```
@section Footer {
    @(((Model.Price / ViewBag.AveragePrice)
        * 100).ToString("F2"))% of average price
}

@section Summary {
    <div class="bg-info text-white m-2 p-2">
        <vc:city-summary theme-name="secondary" />
        <vc:page-size />
    </div>
}
```

Restart ASP.NET Core and use a browser to request http://localhost:5000/home/index/1, which will produce a response that includes the size of the Apress.com home page, as shown in Figure 24-10. You may see a different number displayed since the Apress web site is updated frequently.

■ **Note** Asynchronous view components are useful when there are several different regions of content to be created, each of which can be performed concurrently. The response isn't sent to the browser until all the content is ready. If you want to update the content presented to the user dynamically, then you can use Blazor, as described in Part 4.

Figure 24-10. *Using an asynchronous component*

Creating View Components Classes

View components often provide a summary or snapshot of functionality that is handled in-depth by a controller or Razor Page. For a view component that summarizes a shopping basket, for example, there will often be a link that targets a controller that provides a detailed list of the products in the basket and that can be used to check out and complete the purchase.

In this situation, you can create a class that is a view component as well as a controller or Razor Page. If you are using Visual Studio, expand the Cities.cshtml item in the Solution Explorer to show the Cities.cshtml.cs file and replace its contents with those shown in Listing 24-27. If you are using Visual Studio Code, add a file named Cities.cshtml.cs to the Pages folder with the content shown in Listing 24-27.

Listing 24-27. The Contents of the Cities.cshtml.cs File in the Pages Folder

```
using System.Linq;
using Microsoft.AspNetCore.Mvc;
using Microsoft.AspNetCore.Mvc.RazorPages;
using Microsoft.AspNetCore.Mvc.ViewComponents;
using Microsoft.AspNetCore.Mvc.ViewFeatures;
using WebApp.Models;
```

```
namespace WebApp.Pages {

    [ViewComponent(Name = "CitiesPageHybrid")]
    public class CitiesModel : PageModel {

        public CitiesModel(CitiesData cdata) {
            Data = cdata;
        }

        public CitiesData Data { get; set; }

        [ViewComponentContext]
        public ViewComponentContext Context { get; set; }

        public IViewComponentResult Invoke() {
            return new ViewViewComponentResult() {
                ViewData = new ViewDataDictionary<CityViewModel>(
                    Context.ViewData,
                    new CityViewModel {
                        Cities = Data.Cities.Count(),
                        Population = Data.Cities.Sum(c => c.Population)
                    })
            };
        }
    }
}
```

This page model class is decorated with the ViewComponent attribute, which allows it to be used as a view component.
The Name argument specifies the name by which the view component will be applied. Since a page model cannot inherit from
the ViewComponent base class, a property whose type is ViewComponentContext is decorated with the ViewComponentContext
attribute, which signals that it should be assigned an object that defines the properties described in Table 24-5 before the Invoke
or InvokeAsync method is invoked. The View method isn't available, so I have to create a ViewViewComponentResult object, which
relies on the context object received through the decorated property. Listing 24-28 updates the view part of the page to use the new
page model class.

Listing 24-28. Updating the View in the Cities.cshtml File in the Pages Folder

```
@page
@model WebApp.Pages.CitiesModel

<div class="m-2">
    <table class="table table-sm table-striped table-bordered">
        <tbody>
            @foreach (City c in Model.Data.Cities) {
                <tr>
                    <td>@c.Name</td>
                    <td>@c.Country</td>
                    <td>@c.Population</td>
                </tr>
            }
        </tbody>
    </table>
</div>
```

The changes update the directives to use the page model class. To create the view for the hybrid view component, create the
Pages/Shared/Components/CitiesPageHybrid folder and add to it a Razor view named Default.cshtml with the content shown in
Listing 24-29.

Listing 24-29. The Default.cshtml File in the Pages/Shared/Components/CitiesPageHybrid Folder

```
@model CityViewModel

<table class="table table-sm table-bordered text-white bg-dark">
    <thead><tr><th colspan="2">Hybrid Page Summary</th></tr></thead>
    <tbody>
        <tr>
            <td>Cities:</td>
            <td class="text-right">@Model.Cities</td>
        </tr>
        <tr>
            <td>Population:</td>
            <td class="text-right">
                @Model.Population.ToString("#,###")
            </td>
        </tr>
    </tbody>
</table>
```

Listing 24-30 applies the view component part of the hybrid class in another page.

Listing 24-30. Using a View Component in the Data.cshtml File in the Pages Folder

```
@page
@inject DataContext context;

<h5 class="bg-primary text-white text-center m-2 p-2">Categories</h5>
<ul class="list-group m-2">
    @foreach (Category c in context.Categories) {
        <li class="list-group-item">@c.Name</li>
    }
</ul>

<div class="bg-info text-white m-2 p-2">
    <vc:cities-page-hybrid />
</div>
```

Hybrids are applied just like any other view component. Restart ASP.NET Core and request `http://localhost:5000/cities` and `http://localhost:5000/data`. Both URLs are processed by the same class. For the first URL, the class acts as a page model; for the second URL, the class acts as a view component. Figure 24-11 shows the output for both URLs.

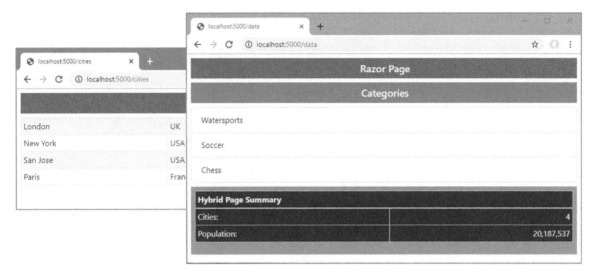

Figure 24-11. *A hybrid page model and view component class*

Creating a Hybrid Controller Class

The same technique can be applied to controllers. Add a class file named `CitiesController.cs` to the `Controllers` folder and add the statements shown in Listing 24-31.

Listing 24-31. The Contents of the CitiesController.cs File in the Controllers Folder

```
using Microsoft.AspNetCore.Mvc;
using Microsoft.AspNetCore.Mvc.ViewComponents;
using Microsoft.AspNetCore.Mvc.ViewFeatures;
using System.Linq;
using WebApp.Models;

namespace WebApp.Controllers {

    [ViewComponent(Name = "CitiesControllerHybrid")]
    public class CitiesController: Controller {
        private CitiesData data;

        public CitiesController(CitiesData cdata) {
            data = cdata;
        }

        public IActionResult Index() {
            return View(data.Cities);
        }

        public IViewComponentResult Invoke() {
            return new ViewViewComponentResult() {
                ViewData = new ViewDataDictionary<CityViewModel>(
                    ViewData,
                    new CityViewModel {
                        Cities = data.Cities.Count(),
                        Population = data.Cities.Sum(c => c.Population)
                    })
            };
        }
    }
}
```

607

A quirk in the way that controllers are instantiated means that a property decorated with the ViewComponentContext attribute isn't required and the ViewData property inherited from the Controller base class can be used to create the view component result.

To provide a view for the action method, create the Views/Cities folder and add to it a file named Index.cshtml with the content shown in Listing 24-32.

Listing 24-32. The Contents of the Index.cshtml File in the Views/Cities Folder

```
@model IEnumerable<City>
@{
    Layout = "_ImportantLayout";
}

<div class="m-2">
    <table class="table table-sm table-striped table-bordered">
        <tbody>
            @foreach (City c in Model) {
                <tr>
                    <td>@c.Name</td>
                    <td>@c.Country</td>
                    <td>@c.Population</td>
                </tr>
            }
        </tbody>
    </table>
</div>
```

To provide a view for the view component, create the Views/Shared/Components/CitiesControllerHybrid folder and add to it a Razor view named Default.cshtml with the content shown in Listing 24-33.

Listing 24-33. The Default.cshtml File in the Views/Shared/Components/CitiesControllerHybrid Folder

```
@model CityViewModel
<table class="table table-sm table-bordered text-white bg-dark">
    <thead><tr><th colspan="2">Hybrid Controller Summary</th></tr></thead>
    <tbody>
        <tr>
            <td>Cities:</td>
            <td class="text-right">@Model.Cities</td>
        </tr>
        <tr>
            <td>Population:</td>
            <td class="text-right">
                @Model.Population.ToString("#,###")
            </td>
        </tr>
    </tbody>
</table>
```

Listing 24-34 applies the hybrid view component in the Data.cshtml Razor Page, replacing the hybrid class created in the previous section.

Listing 24-34. Applying the View Component in the Data.cshtml File in the Pages Folder

```
@page
@inject DataContext context;

<h5 class="bg-primary text-white text-center m-2 p-2">Categories</h5>
<ul class="list-group m-2">
```

```
    @foreach (Category c in context.Categories) {
        <li class="list-group-item">@c.Name</li>
    }
</ul>

<div class="bg-info text-white m-2 p-2">
    <vc:cities-controller-hybrid />
</div>
```

Restart ASP.NET Core and use a browser to request http://localhost:5000/cities/index and http://localhost:5000/
data. For the first URL, the class in Listing 24-34 is used as a controller; for the second URL, the class is used as a view component.
Figure 24-12 shows the responses for both URLs.

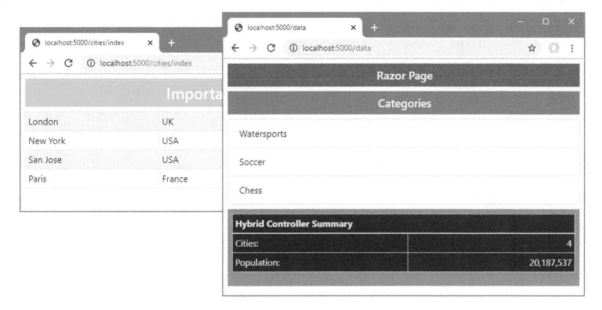

Figure 24-12. *A hybrid controller and view component class*

Summary

In this chapter, I described the view components feature, which allows orthogonal features to be included in views used by
controllers or Razor Pages. I explained how view components work and how they are applied, and I demonstrated the different
types of results they produce. I completed the chapter by showing you how to create classes that are both view components and
controllers or Razor Pages. In the next chapter, I introduce tag helpers. which are used to transform HTML elements.

CHAPTER 25

Using Tag Helpers

Tag helpers are C# classes that transform HTML elements in a view or page. Common uses for tag helpers include generating URLs for forms using the application's routing configuration, ensuring that elements of a specific type are styled consistently, and replacing custom shorthand elements with commonly used fragments of content. In this chapter, I describe how tag helpers work and how custom tag helpers are created and applied. In Chapter 26, I describe the built-in tag helpers, and in Chapter 27, I use tag helpers to explain how HTML forms are created. Table 25-1 puts tag helpers in context.

Table 25-1. *Putting Tag Helpers in Context*

Question	Answer
What are they?	Tag helpers are classes that manipulate HTML elements, either to change them in some way, to supplement them with additional content, or to replace them entirely with new content.
Why are they useful?	Tag helpers allow view content to be generated or transformed using C# logic, ensuring that the HTML sent to the client reflects the state of the application.
How are they used?	The HTML elements to which tag helpers are applied are selected based on the name of the class or with the HTMLTargetElement attribute. When a view is rendered, elements are transformed by tag helpers and included in the HTML sent to the client.
Are there any pitfalls or limitations?	It can be easy to get carried away and generate complex sections of HTML content using tag helpers, which is something that is more readily achieved using view components, described in Chapter 24.
Are there any alternatives?	You don't have to use tag helpers, but they make it easy to generate complex HTML in ASP.NET Core applications.

Table 25-2 summarizes the chapter.

Table 25-2. *Chapter Summary*

Problem	Solution	Listing
Creating a tag helper	Define a class that is derived from the TagHelper class	1–7
Controlling the scope of a tag helper	Alter the range of elements specified by the HtmlTargetElement attribute	8–11
Creating custom HTML elements that are replaced with content	Use shorthand elements	12, 13
Creating elements programmatically	Use the TagBuilder class	14
Controlling where content is inserted	Use the prepend and append features	15–18
Getting context data	Use the context object	19, 20
Operating on the view model or page model	Use a model expression	21–24
Creating coordinating tag helpers	Use the Items property	25–26
Suppressing content	Use the SuppressOutput method	27, 28
Defining tag helper as services	Create tag helper components	29–32

Preparing for This Chapter

This chapter uses the WebApp project from Chapter 24. To prepare for this chapter, replace the contents of the Startup.cs file with those in Listing 25-1, removing some of the configuration statements used in earlier chapters.

■ **Tip** You can download the example project for this chapter—and for all the other chapters in this book—from https://github. com/apress/pro-asp.net-core-3. See Chapter 1 for how to get help if you have problems running the examples.

Listing 25-1. The Contents of the Startup.cs File in the WebApp Folder

```
using Microsoft.AspNetCore.Builder;
using Microsoft.Extensions.DependencyInjection;
using Microsoft.Extensions.Configuration;
using Microsoft.EntityFrameworkCore;
using WebApp.Models;

namespace WebApp {
    public class Startup {

        public Startup(IConfiguration config) {
            Configuration = config;
        }

        public IConfiguration Configuration { get; set; }

        public void ConfigureServices(IServiceCollection services) {
            services.AddDbContext<DataContext>(opts => {
                opts.UseSqlServer(Configuration[
                    "ConnectionStrings:ProductConnection"]);
                opts.EnableSensitiveDataLogging(true);
            });
            services.AddControllersWithViews().AddRazorRuntimeCompilation();
            services.AddRazorPages().AddRazorRuntimeCompilation();
            services.AddSingleton<CitiesData>();
        }

        public void Configure(IApplicationBuilder app, DataContext context) {
            app.UseDeveloperExceptionPage();
            app.UseStaticFiles();
            app.UseRouting();
            app.UseEndpoints(endpoints => {
                endpoints.MapControllers();
                endpoints.MapDefaultControllerRoute();
                endpoints.MapRazorPages();
            });
            SeedData.SeedDatabase(context);
        }
    }
}
```

Next, replace the contents of the Index.cshtml file in the Views/Home folder with the content shown in Listing 25-2.

Listing 25-2. The Contents of the Index.cshtml File in the Views/Home Folder

```
@model Product
@{
    Layout = "_SimpleLayout";
}

<table class="table table-striped table-bordered table-sm">
    <thead>
        <tr>
            <th colspan="2">Product Summary</th>
        </tr>
    </thead>
    <tbody>
        <tr><th>Name</th><td>@Model.Name</td></tr>
        <tr>
            <th>Price</th>
            <td>@Model.Price.ToString("c")</td>
        </tr>
        <tr><th>Category ID</th><td>@Model.CategoryId</td></tr>
    </tbody>
</table>
```

The view in Listing 25-2 relies on a new layout. Add a Razor view file named _SimpleLayout.cshtml in the Views/Shared folder with the content shown in Listing 25-3.

Listing 25-3. The Contents of the _SimpleLayout.cshtml File in the Views/Shared Folder

```
<!DOCTYPE html>
<html>
<head>
    <title>@ViewBag.Title</title>
    <link href="/lib/twitter-bootstrap/css/bootstrap.min.css" rel="stylesheet" />
</head>
<body>
    <div class="m-2">
        @RenderBody()
    </div>
</body>
</html>
```

Dropping the Database

Open a new PowerShell command prompt, navigate to the folder that contains the WebApp.csproj file, and run the command shown in Listing 25-4 to drop the database.

Listing 25-4. Dropping the Database

```
dotnet ef database drop --force
```

Running the Example Application

Select Start Without Debugging or Run Without Debugging from the Debug menu or use the PowerShell command prompt to run the command shown in Listing 25-5.

Listing 25-5. Running the Example Application

```
dotnet run
```

Use a browser to request `http://localhost:5000/home`, which will produce the response shown in Figure 25-1.

Figure 25-1. *Running the example application*

Creating a Tag Helper

The best way to understand tag helpers is to create one, which reveals how they operate and how they fit into an ASP.NET Core application. In the sections that follow, I go through the process of creating and applying a tag helper that will set the Bootstrap CSS classes for a tr element so that an element like this:

```
...
<tr tr-color="primary">
    <th colspan="2">Product Summary</th>
</tr>
...
```

will be transformed into this:

```
...
<tr class="bg-primary text-white text-center">
    <th colspan="2">Product Summary</th>
</tr>
...
```

The tag helper will recognize the `tr-color` attribute and use its value to set the `class` attribute on the element sent to the browser. This isn't the most dramatic—or useful—transformation, but it provides a foundation for explaining how tag helpers work.

Defining the Tag Helper Class

Tag helpers can be defined anywhere in the project, but it helps to keep them together because they need to be registered before they can be used. Create the WebApp/TagHelpers folder and add to it a class file named TrTagHelper.cs with the code shown in Listing 25-6.

Listing 25-6. The Contents of the TrTagHelper.cs File in the TagHelpers Folder

```
using Microsoft.AspNetCore.Razor.TagHelpers;

namespace WebApp.TagHelpers {

    public class TrTagHelper: TagHelper {

        public string BgColor { get; set; } = "dark";
        public string TextColor { get; set; } = "white";

        public override void Process(TagHelperContext context,
                TagHelperOutput output) {
            output.Attributes.SetAttribute("class",
                $"bg-{BgColor} text-center text-{TextColor}");
        }
    }
}
```

Tag helpers are derived from the TagHelper class, which is defined in the Microsoft.AspNetCore.Razor.TagHelpers namespace. The TagHelper class defines a Process method, which is overridden by subclasses to implement the behavior that transforms elements.

The name of the tag helper combines the name of the element it transforms followed by TagHelper. In the case of the example, the class name TrTagHelper indicates this is a tag helper that operates on tr elements. The range of elements to which a tag helper can be applied can be broadened or narrowed using attributes, as described later in this chapter, but the default behavior is defined by the class name.

■ **Tip**   Asynchronous tag helpers can be created by overriding the ProcessAsync method instead of the Process method, but this isn't required for most helpers, which tend to make small and focused changes to HTML elements. You can see an example of an asynchronous tag helper in the "Advanced Tag Helper Features" section.

Receiving Context Data

Tag helpers receive information about the element they are transforming through an instance of the TagHelperContext class, which is received as an argument to the Process method and which defines the properties described in Table 25-3.

Table 25-3. *The TagHelperContext Properties*

Name	Description
AllAttributes	This property returns a read-only dictionary of the attributes applied to the element being transformed, indexed by name and by index.
Items	This property returns a dictionary that is used to coordinate between tag helpers, as described in the "Coordinating Between Tag Helpers" section.
UniqueId	This property returns a unique identifier for the element being transformed.

Although you can access details of the element's attributes through the AllAttributes dictionary, a more convenient approach is to define a property whose name corresponds to the attribute you are interested in, like this:

```
...
public string BgColor { get; set; } = "dark";
public string TextColor { get; set; } = "white";
...
```

When a tag helper is being used, the properties it defines are inspected and assigned the value of any whose name matches attributes applied to the HTML element. As part of this process, the attribute value will be converted to match the type of the C# property so that bool properties can be used to receive true and false attribute values and int properties can be used to receive numeric attribute values such as 1 and 2.

Properties for which there are no corresponding HTML element attributes are not set, which means you should check to ensure that you are not dealing with null or provide default values, which is the approach taken in Listing 25-6.

The name of the attribute is automatically converted from the default HTML style, bg-color, to the C# style, BgColor. You can use any attribute prefix except asp- (which Microsoft uses) and data- (which is reserved for custom attributes that are sent to the client). The example tag helper will be configured using bg-color and text-color attributes, which will provide values for the BgColor and TextColor properties and be used to configure the tr element in the Process method, as follows:

```
...
output.Attributes.SetAttribute("class",
    $"bg-{BgColor} text-center text-{TextColor}");
...
```

■ **Tip** Using the HTML attribute name for tag helper properties doesn't always lead to readable or understandable classes. You can break the link between the name of the property and the attribute it represents using the HtmlAttributeName attribute, which can be used to specify the HTML attribute that the property represents.

Producing Output

The Process method transforms an element by configuring the TagHelperOutput object that is received as an argument. The TagHelperOuput object starts by describing the HTML element as it appears in the view and is modified through the properties and methods described in Table 25-4.

Table 25-4. *The TagHelperOutput Properties and Methods*

Name	Description
TagName	This property is used to get or set the tag name for the output element.
Attributes	This property returns a dictionary containing the attributes for the output element.
Content	This property returns a TagHelperContent object that is used to set the content of the element.
GetChildContentAsync()	This asynchronous method provides access to the content of the element that will be transformed, as demonstrated in the "Creating Shorthand Elements" section.
PreElement	This property returns a TagHelperContext object that is used to insert content in the view before the output element. See the "Prepending and Appending Content and Elements" section.
PostElement	This property returns a TagHelperContext object that is used to insert content in the view after the output element. See the "Prepending and Appending Content and Elements" section.
PreContent	This property returns a TagHelperContext object that is used to insert content before the output element's content. See the "Prepending and Appending Content and Elements" section.
PostContent	This property returns a TagHelperContext object that is used to insert content after the output element's content. See the "Prepending and Appending Content and Elements" section.
TagMode	This property specifies how the output element will be written, using a value from the TagMode enumeration. See the "Creating Shorthand Elements" section.
SupressOuput()	Calling this method excludes an element from the view. See the "Suppressing the Output Element" section.

In the TrTagHelper class, I used the Attributes dictionary to add a class attribute to the HTML element that specifies Bootstrap styles, including the value of the BgColor and TextColor properties. The effect is that the background color for tr elements can be specified by setting bg-color and text-color attributes to Bootstrap names, such as primary, info, and danger.

Registering Tag Helpers

Tag helper classes must be registered with the @addTagHelper directive before they can be used. The set of views or pages to which a tag helper can be applied depends on where the @addTagHelper directive is used.

For a single view or page, the directive appears in the CSHTML file itself. To make a tag helper available more widely, it can be added to the view imports file, which is defined in the Views folder for controllers and the Pages folder for Razor Pages.

I want the tag helpers that I create in this chapter to be available anywhere in the application, which means that the @addTagHelper directive is added to the _ViewImports.cshtml files in the Views and Pages folders. The vc element used in Chapter 24 to apply view components is a tag helper, which is why the directive required to enable tag helpers is already in the _ViewImports.cshtml file.

```
@using WebApp.Models
@addTagHelper *, Microsoft.AspNetCore.Mvc.TagHelpers
@using WebApp.Components
@addTagHelper *, WebApp
```

The first part of the argument specifies the names of the tag helper classes, with support for wildcards, and the second part specifies the name of the assembly in which they are defined. This @addTagHelper directive uses the wildcard to select all namespaces in the WebApp assembly, with the effect that tag helpers defined anywhere in the project can be used in any controller view. There is an identical statement in the Razor Pages _ViewImports.cshtml file in the Pages folder.

```
@namespace WebApp.Pages
@using WebApp.Models
@addTagHelper *, Microsoft.AspNetCore.Mvc.TagHelpers
@addTagHelper *, WebApp
```

The other @addTagHelper directive enables the built-in tag helpers that Microsoft provides, which are described in Chapter 26.

Using a Tag Helper

The final step is to use the tag helper to transform an element. In Listing 25-7, I have added the attribute to the tr element, which will apply the tag helper.

Listing 25-7. Using a Tag Helper in the Index.cshtml File in the Views/Home Folder

```
@model Product
@{
    Layout = "_SimpleLayout";
}

<table class="table table-striped table-bordered table-sm">
    <thead>
        <tr bg-color="info" text-color="white">
            <th colspan="2">Product Summary</th>
        </tr>
    </thead>
    <tbody>
        <tr><th>Name</th><td>@Model.Name</td></tr>
        <tr>
            <th>Price</th>
            <td>@Model.Price.ToString("c")</td>
        </tr>
        <tr><th>Category ID</th><td>@Model.CategoryId</td></tr>
    </tbody>
</table>
```

Restart ASP.NET Core and use a browser to request http://localhost:5000/home, which produces the response shown in Figure 25-2.

Figure 25-2. Using a tag helper

The tr element to which the attributes were applied in Listing 25-7 has been transformed, but that isn't the only change shown in the figure. By default, tag helpers apply to all elements of a specific type, which means that all the tr elements in the view have been transformed using the default values defined in the tag helper class, since no attributes were defined.

In fact, the problem is more serious because the @addTagHelper directives in the view import files mean that the example tag helper is applied to all tr elements used in any view rendered by controllers and Razor Pages. Use a browser to request http://localhost:5000/cities, for example, and you will see the tr elements in the response from Cities Razor Page have also been transformed, as shown in Figure 25-3.

Figure 25-3. *Unexpectedly modifying elements with a tag helper*

Narrowing the Scope of a Tag Helper

The range of elements that are transformed by a tag helper can be controlled using the HtmlTargetElement element, as shown in Listing 25-8.

Listing 25-8. Narrowing Scope in the TrTagHelper.cs File in the TagHelpers Folder

```
using Microsoft.AspNetCore.Razor.TagHelpers;

namespace WebApp.TagHelpers {

    [HtmlTargetElement("tr", Attributes = "bg-color,text-color", ParentTag ="thead")]
    public class TrTagHelper: TagHelper {

        public string BgColor { get; set; } = "dark";
        public string TextColor { get; set; } = "white";

        public override void Process(TagHelperContext context,
                TagHelperOutput output) {
            output.Attributes.SetAttribute("class",
                $"bg-{BgColor} text-center text-{TextColor}");
        }
    }
}
```

The HtmlTargetElement attribute describes the elements to which the tag helper applies. The first argument specifies the element type and supports the additional named properties described in Table 25-5.

Table 25-5. *The HtmlTargetElement Properties*

Name	Description
Attributes	This property is used to specify that a tag helper should be applied only to elements that have a given set of attributes, supplied as a comma-separated list. An attribute name that ends with an asterisk will be treated as a prefix so that bg-* will match bg-color, bg-size, and so on.
ParentTag	This property is used to specify that a tag helper should be applied only to elements that are contained within an element of a given type.
TagStructure	This property is used to specify that a tag helper should be applied only to elements whose tag structure corresponds to the given value from the TagStructure enumeration, which defines Unspecified, NormalOrSelfClosing, and WithoutEndTag.

The Attributes property supports CSS attribute selector syntax so that [bg-color] matches elements that have a bg-color attribute, [bg-color=primary] matches elements that have a bg-color attribute whose value is primary, and [bg-color^=p] matches elements with a bg-color attribute whose value begins with p. The attribute applied to the tag helper in Listing 25-8 matches tr elements with both bg-color and text-color attributes that are children of a thead element. Restart ASP.NET Core and use a browser to request http://localhost:5000/home/index/1, and you will see the scope of the tag helper has been narrowed, as shown in Figure 25-4.

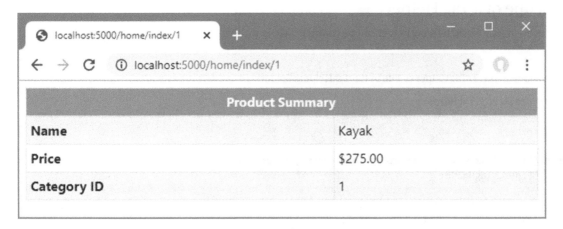

Figure 25-4. *Narrowing the scope of a tag helper*

Widening the Scope of a Tag Helper

The HtmlTargetElement attribute can also be used to widen the scope of a tag helper so that it matches a broader range of elements. This is done by setting the attribute's first argument to an asterisk (the * character), which matches any element. Listing 25-9 changes the attribute applied to the example tag helper so that it matches any element that has bg-color and text-color attributes.

Listing 25-9. Widening Scope in the TrTagHelper.cs File in the TagHelpers Folder

```
using Microsoft.AspNetCore.Razor.TagHelpers;

namespace WebApp.TagHelpers {

    [HtmlTargetElement("*", Attributes = "bg-color,text-color")]
    public class TrTagHelper: TagHelper {

        public string BgColor { get; set; } = "dark";
        public string TextColor { get; set; } = "white";
```

```
        public override void Process(TagHelperContext context,
                TagHelperOutput output) {
            output.Attributes.SetAttribute("class",
                $"bg-{BgColor} text-center text-{TextColor}");
        }
    }
}
```

Care must be taken when using the asterisk because it is easy to match too widely and select elements that should not be transformed. A safer middle ground is to apply the HtmlTargetElement attribute for each type of element, as shown in Listing 25-10.

Listing 25-10. Balancing Scope in the TrTagHelper.cs File in the TagHelpers Folder

```
using Microsoft.AspNetCore.Razor.TagHelpers;

namespace WebApp.TagHelpers {

    [HtmlTargetElement("tr", Attributes = "bg-color,text-color")]
    [HtmlTargetElement("td", Attributes = "bg-color")]
    public class TrTagHelper: TagHelper {

        public string BgColor { get; set; } = "dark";
        public string TextColor { get; set; } = "white";

        public override void Process(TagHelperContext context,
                TagHelperOutput output) {
            output.Attributes.SetAttribute("class",
                $"bg-{BgColor} text-center text-{TextColor}");
        }
    }
}
```

Each instance of the attribute can use different selection criteria. This tag helper matches tr elements with bg-color and text-color attributes and matches td elements with bg-color attributes. Listing 25-11 adds an element to be transformed to the Index view to demonstrate the revised scope.

Listing 25-11. Adding Attributes in the Index.cshtml File in the Views/Home Folder

```
@model Product
@{
    Layout = "_SimpleLayout";
}

<table class="table table-striped table-bordered table-sm">
    <thead>
        <tr bg-color="info" text-color="white">
            <th colspan="2">Product Summary</th>
        </tr>
    </thead>
    <tbody>
        <tr><th>Name</th><td>@Model.Name</td></tr>
        <tr>
            <th>Price</th>
            <td bg-color="dark">@Model.Price.ToString("c")</td>
        </tr>
        <tr><th>Category ID</th><td>@Model.CategoryId</td></tr>
    </tbody>
</table>
```

Restart ASP.NET Core and use a browser to request `http://localhost:5000/home/index/1`. The response will contain two transformed elements, as shown in Figure 25-5.

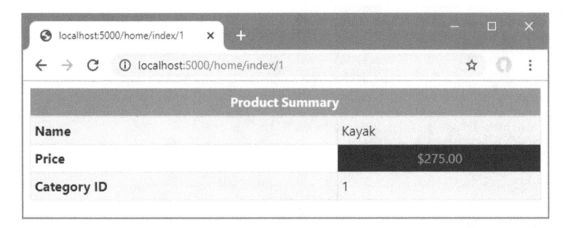

Figure 25-5. *Managing the scope of a tag helper*

ORDERING TAG HELPER EXECUTION

If you need to apply multiple tag helpers to an element, you can control the sequence in which they execute by setting the `Order` property, which is inherited from the `TagHelper` base class. Managing the sequence can help minimize the conflicts between tag helpers, although it is still easy to encounter problems.

Advanced Tag Helper Features

The previous section demonstrated how to create a basic tag helper, but that just scratches the surface of what's possible. In the sections that follow, I show more advanced uses for tag helpers and the features they provide.

Creating Shorthand Elements

Tag helpers are not restricted to transforming the standard HTML elements and can also be used to replace custom elements with commonly used content. This can be a useful feature for making views more concise and making their intent more obvious. To demonstrate, Listing 25-12 replaces the `thead` element in the `Index` view with a custom HTML element.

Listing 25-12. Adding a Custom HTML Element in the Index.cshtml File in the Views/Home Folder

```
@model Product
@{
    Layout = "_SimpleLayout";
}

<table class="table table-striped table-bordered table-sm">
    <tablehead bg-color="dark">Product Summary</tablehead>
    <tbody>
        <tr><th>Name</th><td>@Model.Name</td></tr>
        <tr>
            <th>Price</th>
            <td bg-color="dark">@Model.Price.ToString("c")</td>
        </tr>
```

```
            <tr><th>Category ID</th><td>@Model.CategoryId</td></tr>
        </tbody>
</table>
```

The tablehead element isn't part of the HTML specification and won't be understood by browsers. Instead, I am going to use this element as shorthand for generating the thead element and its content for the HTML table. Add a class named TableHeadTagHelper.cs to the TagHelpers folder and use it to define the class shown in Listing 25-13.

■ **Tip** When dealing with custom elements that are not part of the HTML specification, you must apply the HtmlTargetElement attribute and specify the element name, as shown in Listing 25-13. The convention of applying tag helpers to elements based on the class name works only for standard element names.

Listing 25-13. The Contents of TableHeadTagHelper.cs in the TagHelpers Folder

```
using Microsoft.AspNetCore.Razor.TagHelpers;
using System.Threading.Tasks;

namespace WebApp.TagHelpers {

    [HtmlTargetElement("tablehead")]
    public class TableHeadTagHelper: TagHelper {

        public string BgColor { get; set; } = "light";

        public override async Task ProcessAsync(TagHelperContext context,
                TagHelperOutput output) {

            output.TagName = "thead";
            output.TagMode = TagMode.StartTagAndEndTag;
            output.Attributes.SetAttribute("class",
                $"bg-{BgColor} text-white text-center");

            string content = (await output.GetChildContentAsync()).GetContent();
            output.Content
                .SetHtmlContent($"<tr><th colspan=\"2\">{content}</th></tr>");
        }
    }
}
```

This tag helper is asynchronous and overrides the ProcessAsync method so that it can access the existing content of the elements it transforms. The ProcessAsync method uses the properties of the TagHelperOuput object to generate a completely different element: the TagName property is used to specify a thead element, the TagMode property is used to specify that the element is written using start and end tags, the Attributes.SetAttribute method is used to define a class attribute, and the Content property is used to set the element content.

The existing content of the element is obtained through the asynchronous GetChildContentAsync method, which returns a TagHelperContent object. This is the same object that is returned by the TagHelperOutput.Content property and allows the content of the element to be inspected and changed using the same type, through the methods described in Table 25-6.

Table 25-6. *Useful TagHelperContent Methods*

Name	Description
GetContent()	This method returns the contents of the HTML element as a string.
SetContent(text)	This method sets the content of the output element. The string argument is encoded so that it is safe for inclusion in an HTML element.
SetHtmlContent(html)	This method sets the content of the output element. The string argument is assumed to be safely encoded. Use with caution.
Append(text)	This method safely encodes the specified string and adds it to the content of the output element.
AppendHtml(html)	This method adds the specified string to the content of the output element without performing any encoding. Use with caution.
Clear()	This method removes the content of the output element.

In Listing 25-13, the existing content of the element is read through the GetContent element and then set using the SetHtmlContent method. The effect is to wrap the existing content in the transformed element in tr and th elements.

Restart ASP.NET Core and navigate to http://localhost:5000/home/index/1, and you will see the effect of the tag helper, which is shown in Figure 25-6.

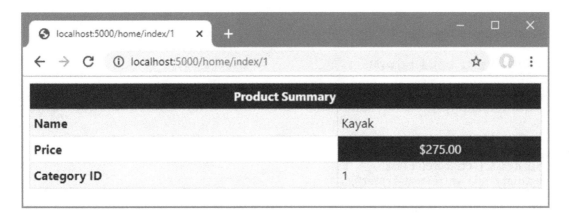

Figure 25-6. *Using a shorthand element*

The tag helper transforms this shorthand element:

```
...
<tablehead bg-color="dark">Product Summary</tablehead>
...
```

into these elements:

```
...
<thead class="bg-dark text-white text-center">
    <tr>
        <th colspan="2">Product Summary</th>
    </tr>
</thead>
...
```

Notice that the transformed elements do not include the bg-color attribute. Attributes matched to properties defined by the tag helper are removed from the output element and must be explicitly redefined if they are required.

Creating Elements Programmatically

When generating new HTML elements, you can use standard C# string formatting to create the content you require, which is the approach I took in Listing 25-13. This works, but it can be awkward and requires close attention to avoid typos. A more robust approach is to use the TagBuilder class, which is defined in the Microsoft.AspNetCore.Mvc.Rendering namespace and allows elements to be created in a more structured manner. The TagHelperContent methods described in Table 25-6 accept TagBuilder objects, which makes it easy to create HTML content in tag helpers, as shown in Listing 25-14.

Listing 25-14. Creating HTML Elements in the TableHeadTagHelper.cs File in the TagHelpers Folder

```
using Microsoft.AspNetCore.Razor.TagHelpers;
using System.Threading.Tasks;
using Microsoft.AspNetCore.Mvc.Rendering;

namespace WebApp.TagHelpers {

    [HtmlTargetElement("tablehead")]
    public class TableHeadTagHelper: TagHelper {

        public string BgColor { get; set; } = "light";

        public override async Task ProcessAsync(TagHelperContext context,
                TagHelperOutput output) {

            output.TagName = "thead";
            output.TagMode = TagMode.StartTagAndEndTag;
            output.Attributes.SetAttribute("class",
                $"bg-{BgColor} text-white text-center");

            string content = (await output.GetChildContentAsync()).GetContent();

            TagBuilder header = new TagBuilder("th");
            header.Attributes["colspan"] = "2";
            header.InnerHtml.Append(content);

            TagBuilder row = new TagBuilder("tr");
            row.InnerHtml.AppendHtml(header);

            output.Content.SetHtmlContent(row);
        }
    }
}
```

This example creates each new element using a TagBuilder object and composes them to produce the same HTML structure as the string-based version in Listing 25-13.

Prepending and Appending Content and Elements

The TagHelperOutput class provides four properties that make it easy to inject new content into a view so that it surrounds an element or the element's content, as described in Table 25-7. In the sections that follow, I explain how you can insert content around and inside the target element.

Table 25-7. *The TagHelperOutput Properties for Appending Context and Elements*

Name	Description
PreElement	This property is used to insert elements into the view before the target element.
PostElement	This property is used to insert elements into the view after the target element.
PreContent	This property is used to insert content into the target element, before any existing content.
PostContent	This property is used to insert content into the target element, after any existing content.

Inserting Content Around the Output Element

The first TagHelperOuput properties are PreElement and PostElement, which are used to insert elements into the view before and after the output element. To demonstrate the use of these properties, add a class file named ContentWrapperTagHelper.cs to the WebApp/TagHelpers folder with the content shown in Listing 25-15.

Listing 25-15. The Contents of the WrapperTagHelper.cs File in the TagHelpers Folder

```
using Microsoft.AspNetCore.Mvc.Rendering;
using Microsoft.AspNetCore.Razor.TagHelpers;

namespace WebApp.TagHelpers {

    [HtmlTargetElement("*", Attributes = "[wrap=true]")]
    public class ContentWrapperTagHelper: TagHelper {

        public override void Process(TagHelperContext context,
                TagHelperOutput output) {
            TagBuilder elem = new TagBuilder("div");
            elem.Attributes["class"] = "bg-primary text-white p-2 m-2";
            elem.InnerHtml.AppendHtml("Wrapper");

            output.PreElement.AppendHtml(elem);
            output.PostElement.AppendHtml(elem);
        }
    }
}
```

This tag helper transforms elements that have a wrap attribute whose value is true, which it does using the PreElement and PostElement properties to add a div element before and after the output element. Listing 25-16 adds an element to the Index view that is transformed by the tag helper.

Listing 25-16. Adding an Element in the Index.cshtml File in the Views/Index Folder

```
@model Product
@{
    Layout = "_SimpleLayout";
}
```

```
<div class="m-2" wrap="true">Inner Content</div>
```

```
<table class="table table-striped table-bordered table-sm">
    <tablehead bg-color="dark">Product Summary</tablehead>
    <tbody>
        <tr><th>Name</th><td>@Model.Name</td></tr>
        <tr>
            <th>Price</th>
            <td bg-color="dark">@Model.Price.ToString("c")</td>
        </tr>
```

```
        <tr><th>Category ID</th><td>@Model.CategoryId</td></tr>
    </tbody>
</table>
```

Restart ASP.NET Core and use a browser to request `http://localhost:5000/home/index/1`. The response includes the transformed element, as shown in Figure 25-7.

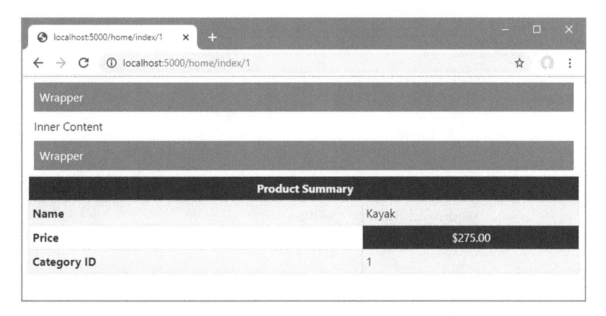

Figure 25-7. *Inserting content around the output element*

If you examine the HTML sent to the browser, you will see that this element:

```
...
<div class="m-2" wrap="true">Inner Content</div>
...
```

has been transformed into these elements:

```
...
<div class="bg-primary text-white p-2 m-2">Wrapper</div>
<div class="m-2" wrap="true">Inner Content</div>
<div class="bg-primary text-white p-2 m-2">Wrapper</div>
...
```

Notice that the wrap attribute has been left on the output element. This is because I didn't define a property in the tag helper class that corresponds to this attribute. If you want to prevent attributes from being included in the output, then define a property for them in the tag helper class, even if you don't use the attribute value.

Inserting Content Inside the Output Element

The PreContent and PostContent properties are used to insert content inside the output element, surrounding the original content. To demonstrate this feature, add a class file named HighlightTagHelper.cs to the TagHelpers folder and use it to define the tag helper shown in Listing 25-17.

Listing 25-17. The Contents of the HighlightTagHelper.cs File in the TagHelpers Folder

```
using Microsoft.AspNetCore.Razor.TagHelpers;

namespace WebApp.TagHelpers {

    [HtmlTargetElement("*", Attributes = "[highlight=true]")]
    public class HighlightTagHelper: TagHelper {

        public override void Process(TagHelperContext context,
                TagHelperOutput output) {

            output.PreContent.SetHtmlContent("<b><i>");
            output.PostContent.SetHtmlContent("</i></b>");
        }
    }
}
```

This tag helper inserts b and i elements around the output element's content. Listing 25-18 adds the wrap attribute to one of the table cells in the Index view.

Listing 25-18. Adding an Attribute in the Index.cshtml File in the Views/Home Folder

```
@model Product
@{
    Layout = "_SimpleLayout";
}

<div class="m-2" wrap="true">Inner Content</div>

<table class="table table-striped table-bordered table-sm">
    <tablehead bg-color="dark">Product Summary</tablehead>
    <tbody>
        <tr><th>Name</th><td highlight="true">@Model.Name</td></tr>
        <tr>
            <th>Price</th>
            <td bg-color="dark">@Model.Price.ToString("c")</td>
        </tr>
        <tr><th>Category ID</th><td>@Model.CategoryId</td></tr>
    </tbody>
</table>
```

Restart ASP.NET Core and use a browser to request http://localhost:5000/home/index/1. The response includes the transformed element, as shown in Figure 25-8.

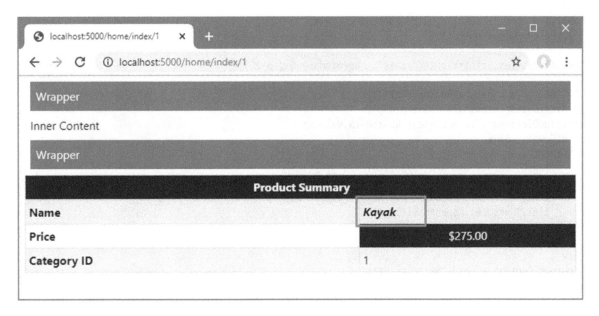

Figure 25-8. *Inserting content inside an element*

If you examine the HTML sent to the browser, you will see that this element:

```
...
<td highlight="true">@Model.Name</td>
...
```

has been transformed into these elements:

```
...
<td highlight="true"><b><i>Kayak</i></b></td>
...
```

Getting View Context Data

A common use for tag helpers is to transform elements so they contain details of the current request or the view model/ page model, which requires access to context data. To create this type of tag helper, add a file named RouteDataTagHelper.cs to the TagHelpers folder, with the content shown in Listing 25-19.

Listing 25-19. The Contents of the RouteDataTagHelper.cs File in the WebApps/TagHelpers Folder

```
using Microsoft.AspNetCore.Mvc.Rendering;
using Microsoft.AspNetCore.Mvc.ViewFeatures;
using Microsoft.AspNetCore.Razor.TagHelpers;
using Microsoft.AspNetCore.Routing;

namespace WebApp.TagHelpers {

    [HtmlTargetElement("div", Attributes="[route-data=true]")]
    public class RouteDataTagHelper: TagHelper {

        [ViewContext]
        [HtmlAttributeNotBound]
        public ViewContext Context { get; set; }
```

```
        public override void Process(TagHelperContext context,
                TagHelperOutput output) {

            output.Attributes.SetAttribute("class", "bg-primary m-2 p-2");

            TagBuilder list = new TagBuilder("ul");
            list.Attributes["class"] = "list-group";
            RouteValueDictionary rd = Context.RouteData.Values;
            if (rd.Count > 0) {
                foreach (var kvp in rd) {
                    TagBuilder item = new TagBuilder("li");
                    item.Attributes["class"] = "list-group-item";
                    item.InnerHtml.Append($"{kvp.Key}: {kvp.Value}");
                    list.InnerHtml.AppendHtml(item);
                }
                output.Content.AppendHtml(list);
            } else {
                output.Content.Append("No route data");
            }
        }
    }
}
```

The tag helper transforms div elements that have a route-data attribute whose value is true and populates the output element with a list of the segment variables obtained by the routing system.

To get the route data, I added a property called Context and decorated it with two attributes, like this:

```
...
[ViewContext]
[HtmlAttributeNotBound]
public ViewContext Context { get; set; }
...
```

The ViewContext attribute denotes that the value of this property should be assigned a ViewContext object when a new instance of the tag helper class is created, which provides details of the view that is being rendered, including the routing data, as described in Chapter 13.

The HtmlAttributeNotBound attribute prevents a value from being assigned to this property if there is a matching attribute defined on the div element. This is good practice, especially if you are writing tag helpers for other developers to use.

■ **Tip** Tag helpers can declare dependencies on services in their constructors, which are resolved using the dependency injection feature described in Chapter 14.

Listing 25-20 adds an element to the Home controller's Index view that will be transformed by the new tag helper.

Listing 25-20. Adding an Element in the Index.cshtml File in the Views/Home Folder

```
@model Product
@{
    Layout = "_SimpleLayout";
}

<div route-data="true"></div>

<table class="table table-striped table-bordered table-sm">
    <tablehead bg-color="dark">Product Summary</tablehead>
```

```
    <tbody>
        <tr><th>Name</th><td highlight="true">@Model.Name</td></tr>
        <tr>
            <th>Price</th>
            <td bg-color="dark">@Model.Price.ToString("c")</td>
        </tr>
        <tr><th>Category ID</th><td>@Model.CategoryId</td></tr>
    </tbody>
</table>
```

Restart ASP.NET Core and use a browser to request http://localhost:5000/home/index/1. The response will include a list of the segment variables the routing system has matched, as shown in Figure 25-9.

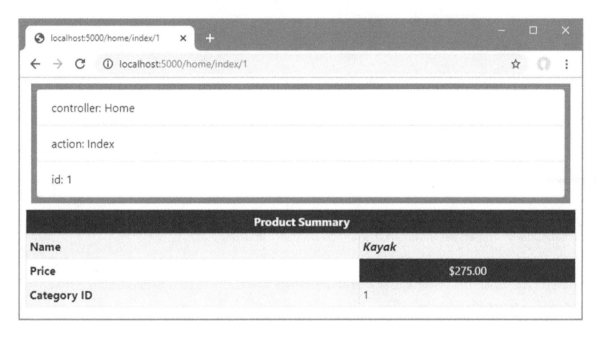

Figure 25-9. *Displaying context data with a tag helper*

Working with Model Expressions

Tag helpers can operate on the view model, tailoring the transformations they perform or the output they create. To see how this feature works, add a class file named ModelRowTagHelper.cs to the TagHelpers folder, with the code shown in Listing 25-21.

Listing 25-21. The Contents of the ModelRowTagHelper.cs File in the TagHelpers Folder

```
using Microsoft.AspNetCore.Mvc.Rendering;
using Microsoft.AspNetCore.Mvc.ViewFeatures;
using Microsoft.AspNetCore.Razor.TagHelpers;

namespace WebApp.TagHelpers {

    [HtmlTargetElement("tr", Attributes = "for")]
    public class ModelRowTagHelper : TagHelper {

        public string Format { get; set; }
        public ModelExpression For { get; set; }
```

```
        public override void Process(TagHelperContext context,
                TagHelperOutput output) {

            output.TagMode = TagMode.StartTagAndEndTag;

            TagBuilder th = new TagBuilder("th");
            th.InnerHtml.Append(For.Name);
            output.Content.AppendHtml(th);

            TagBuilder td = new TagBuilder("td");
            if (Format != null && For.Metadata.ModelType == typeof(decimal)) {
                td.InnerHtml.Append(((decimal)For.Model).ToString(Format));
            } else {
                td.InnerHtml.Append(For.Model.ToString());
            }
            output.Content.AppendHtml(td);
        }
    }
}
```

This tag helper transforms tr elements that have a for attribute. The important part of this tag helper is the type of the For property, which is used to receive the value of the for attribute.

```
...
public ModelExpression For { get; set; }
...
```

The ModelExpression class is used when you want to operate on part of the view model, which is most easily explained by jumping forward and showing how the tag helper is applied in the view, as shown in Listing 25-22.

■ **Note** The ModelExpression feature can be used only on view models or page models. It cannot be used on variables that are created within a view, such as with an @foreach expression.

Listing 25-22. Using the Tag Helper in the Index.cshtml File in the Views/Home Folder

```
@model Product
@{
    Layout = "_SimpleLayout";
}

<div route-data="true"></div>

<table class="table table-striped table-bordered table-sm">
    <tablehead bg-color="dark">Product Summary</tablehead>
    <tbody>
        <tr for="Name" />
        <tr for="Price" format="c" />
        <tr for="CategoryId" />
    </tbody>
</table>
```

The value of the for attribute is the name of a property defined by the view model class. When the tag helper is created, the type of the For property is detected and assigned a ModelExpression object that describes the selected property.

I am not going to describe the ModelExpression class in any detail because any introspection on types leads to endless lists of classes and properties. Further, ASP.NET Core provides a useful set of built-in tag helpers that use the view model to transform elements, as described in Chapter 26, which means you don't need to create your own.

For the example tag helper, I use three basic features that are worth describing. The first is to get the name of the model property so that I can include it in the output element, like this:

```
...
th.InnerHtml.Append(For.Name);
...
```

The Name property returns the name of the model property. The second feature is to get the type of the model property so that I can determine whether to format the value, like this:

```
...
if (Format != null && For.Metadata.ModelType == typeof(decimal)) {
...
```

The third feature is to get the value of the property so that it can be included in the response.

```
...
td.InnerHtml.Append(For.Model.ToString());
...
```

Restart ASP.NET Core and use a browser to request http://localhost:5000/home/index/2, and you will see the response shown in Figure 25-10.

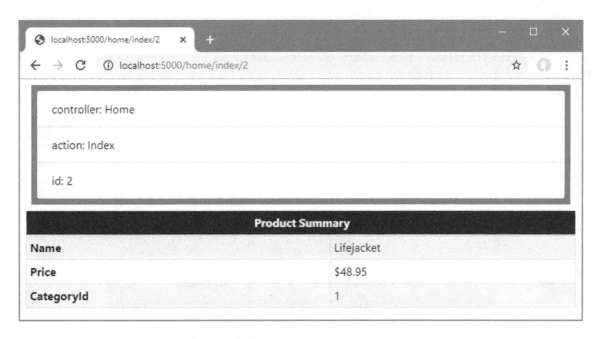

Figure 25-10. *Using the view model in a tag helper*

Working with the Page Model

Tag helpers with model expressions can be applied in Razor Pages, although the expression that selects the property must account for the way that the Model property returns the page model class. Listing 25-23 applies the tag helper to the Editor Razor Page, whose page model defines a Product property.

Listing 25-23. Applying a Tag Helper in the Editor.cshtml File in the Pages Folder

```
@page "{id:long}"
@model EditorModel
@{
    Layout = null;
}

<!DOCTYPE html>
<html>
<head>
    <link href="/lib/twitter-bootstrap/css/bootstrap.min.css" rel="stylesheet" />
</head>
<body>
    <div class="bg-primary text-white text-center m-2 p-2">Editor</div>
    <div class="m-2">
        <table class="table table-sm table-striped table-bordered">
            <tbody>
                <tr for="Product.Name" />
                <tr for="Product.Price" format="c" />
            </tbody>
        </table>
        <form method="post">
            @Html.AntiForgeryToken()
            <div class="form-group">
                <label>Price</label>
                <input name="price" class="form-control"
                        value="@Model.Product.Price" />
            </div>
            <button class="btn btn-primary" type="submit">Submit</button>
        </form>
    </div>
</body>
</html>
```

The value for the `for` attribute selects the nested properties through the `Product` property, which provides the tag helper with the `ModelExpression` it requires. Use a browser to request `http://localhost:5000/editor/1` to see the response from the page, which is shown on the left of Figure 25-11.

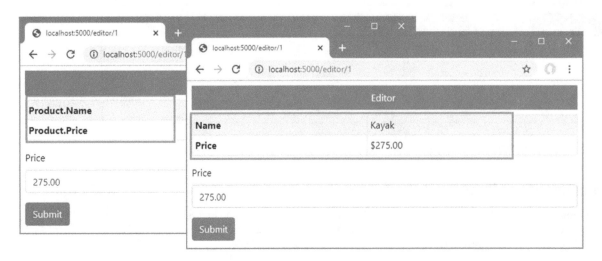

Figure 25-11. Using a model expression tag helper with a Razor Page

One consequence of the page model is that the ModelExpression.Name property will return Product.Name, for example, instead of just Name. Listing 25-24 updates the tag helper so that it will display just the last part of the model expression name.

■ **Note**   This example is intended to highlight the effect of the page model on model expressions. Instead of displaying just the last part of the name, a more flexible approach is to add support for another attribute that allows the display value to be overridden as needed.

Listing 25-24. Processing Names in the ModelRowTagHelper.cs File in the TagHelpers Folder

```
using Microsoft.AspNetCore.Mvc.Rendering;
using Microsoft.AspNetCore.Mvc.ViewFeatures;
using Microsoft.AspNetCore.Razor.TagHelpers;
using System.Linq;

namespace WebApp.TagHelpers {

    [HtmlTargetElement("tr", Attributes = "for")]
    public class ModelRowTagHelper : TagHelper {

        public string Format { get; set; }
        public ModelExpression For { get; set; }

        public override void Process(TagHelperContext context,
                TagHelperOutput output) {

            output.TagMode = TagMode.StartTagAndEndTag;

            TagBuilder th = new TagBuilder("th");
            th.InnerHtml.Append(For.Name.Split(".").Last());
            output.Content.AppendHtml(th);

            TagBuilder td = new TagBuilder("td");
            if (Format != null && For.Metadata.ModelType == typeof(decimal)) {
                td.InnerHtml.Append(((decimal)For.Model).ToString(Format));
            } else {
                td.InnerHtml.Append(For.Model.ToString());
            }
            output.Content.AppendHtml(td);
        }
    }
}
```

Restart ASP.NET Core and use a browser to request http://localhost:5000/editor/1; you will see the revised response, which is shown on the right of Figure 25-11.

Coordinating Between Tag Helpers

The TagHelperContext.Items property provides a dictionary used by tag helpers that operate on elements and those that operate on their descendants. To demonstrate the use of the Items collection, add a class file named CoordinatingTagHelpers.cs to the WebApp/TagHelpers folder and add the code shown in Listing 25-25.

Listing 25-25. The Contents of the CoordinatingTagHelpers.cs File in the TagHelpers Folder

```
using Microsoft.AspNetCore.Razor.TagHelpers;

namespace WebApp.TagHelpers {

    [HtmlTargetElement("tr", Attributes = "theme")]
    public class RowTagHelper: TagHelper {

        public string Theme { get; set; }

        public override void Process(TagHelperContext context,
                TagHelperOutput output) {
            context.Items["theme"] = Theme;
        }
    }

    [HtmlTargetElement("th")]
    [HtmlTargetElement("td")]
    public class CellTagHelper : TagHelper {

        public override void Process(TagHelperContext context,
                TagHelperOutput output) {

            if (context.Items.ContainsKey("theme")) {
                output.Attributes.SetAttribute("class",
                    $"bg-{context.Items["theme"]} text-white");
            }
        }
    }
}
```

The first tag helper operates on tr elements that have a theme attribute. Coordinating tag helpers can transform their own elements, but this example simply adds the value of the theme attribute to the Items dictionary so that it is available to tag helpers that operate on elements contained within the tr element. The second tag helper operates on th and td elements and uses the theme value from the Items dictionary to set the Bootstrap style for its output elements.

Listing 25-26 adds elements to the Home controller's Index view that apply the coordinating tag helpers.

■ **Note**   Notice that I have added the th and td elements that are transformed in Listing 25-26, instead of relying on a tag helper to generate them. Tag helpers are not applied to elements generated by other tag helpers and affect only the elements defined in the view.

Listing 25-26. Applying a Tag Helper in the Index.cshtml File in the Views/Home Folder

```
@model Product
@{
    Layout = "_SimpleLayout";
}

<table class="table table-striped table-bordered table-sm">
    <tablehead bg-color="dark">Product Summary</tablehead>
    <tbody>
        <tr theme="primary">
            <th>Name</th><td>@Model.Name</td>
        </tr>
```

```
        <tr theme="secondary">
            <th>Price</th><td>@Model.Price.ToString("c")</td>
        </tr>
        <tr theme="info">
            <th>Category</th><td>@Model.CategoryId</td>
        </tr>
    </tbody>
</table>
```

Restart ASP.NET Core and use a browser to request `http://localhost:5000/home`, which produces the response shown in Figure 25-12. The value of the `theme` element has been passed from one tag helper to another, and a color theme is applied without needing to define attributes on each of the elements that is transformed.

Figure 25-12. *Coordination between tag helpers*

Suppressing the Output Element

Tag helpers can be used to prevent an element from being included in the HTML response by calling the `SuppressOuput` method on the `TagHelperOutput` object that is received as an argument to the `Process` method. In Listing 25-27, I have added an element to the Home controller's Index view that should be displayed only if the `Price` property of the view model exceeds a specified value.

Listing 25-27. Adding an Element in the Index.cshtml File in the Views/Home Folder

```
@model Product
@{
    Layout = "_SimpleLayout";
}

<div show-when-gt="500" for="Price">
    <h5 class="bg-danger text-white text-center p-2">
        Warning: Expensive Item
    </h5>
</div>

<table class="table table-striped table-bordered table-sm">
    <tablehead bg-color="dark">Product Summary</tablehead>
    <tbody>
        <tr theme="primary">
            <th>Name</th><td>@Model.Name</td>
        </tr>
```

```
            <tr theme="secondary">
                <th>Price</th><td>@Model.Price.ToString("c")</td>
            </tr>
            <tr theme="info">
                <th>Category</th><td>@Model.CategoryId</td>
            </tr>
        </tbody>
</table>
```

The show-when-gt attribute specifies the value above which the div element should be displayed, and the for property selects the model property that will be inspected. To create the tag helper that will manage the elements, including the response, add a class file named SelectiveTagHelper.cs to the WebApp/TagHelpers folder with the code shown in Listing 25-28.

Listing 25-28. The Contents of the SelectiveTagHelper.cs File in the TagHelpers Folder

```
using Microsoft.AspNetCore.Mvc.ViewFeatures;
using Microsoft.AspNetCore.Razor.TagHelpers;

namespace WebApp.TagHelpers {

    [HtmlTargetElement("div", Attributes = "show-when-gt, for")]
    public class SelectiveTagHelper: TagHelper {

        public decimal ShowWhenGt { get; set; }
        public ModelExpression For { get; set; }

        public override void Process(TagHelperContext context,
                TagHelperOutput output) {

            if (For.Model.GetType() == typeof(decimal)
                    && (decimal)For.Model <= ShowWhenGt) {
                output.SuppressOutput();
            }
        }
    }
}
```

The tag helper uses the model expression to access the property and calls the SuppressOutput method unless the threshold is exceeded. To see the effect, restart ASP.NET Core and use a browser to request http://localhost:5000/home/index/1 and http://localhost:5000/home/index/5. The value for the Price property of the Product selected by the first URL is less than the threshold, so the element is suppressed. The value for the Price property of the Product selected by the second URL is more than the threshold, so the element is displayed. Figure 25-13 shows both responses.

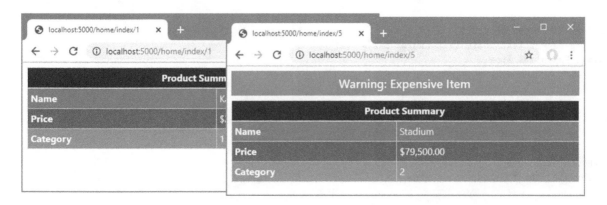

Figure 25-13. *Suppressing output elements*

Using Tag Helper Components

Tag helper components provide an alternative approach to applying tag helpers as services. This feature can be useful when you need to set up tag helpers to support another service or middleware component, which is typically the case for diagnostic tools or functionality that has both a client-side component and a server-side component, such as Blazor, which is described in Part 4. In the sections that follow, I show you how to create and apply tag helper components.

Creating a Tag Helper Component

Tag helper components are derived from the TagHelperComponent class, which provides a similar API to the TagHelper base class used in earlier examples. To create a tag helper component, add a class file called TimeTagHelperComponent.cs in the TagHelpers folder with the content shown in Listing 25-29.

Listing 25-29. The Contents of the TimeTagHelperComponent.cs File in the TagHelpers Folder

```
using Microsoft.AspNetCore.Mvc.Rendering;
using Microsoft.AspNetCore.Razor.TagHelpers;
using System;

namespace WebApp.TagHelpers {

    public class TimeTagHelperComponent: TagHelperComponent {

        public override void Process(TagHelperContext context,
                TagHelperOutput output) {

            string timestamp = DateTime.Now.ToLongTimeString();

            if (output.TagName == "body") {
                TagBuilder elem = new TagBuilder("div");
                elem.Attributes.Add("class", "bg-info text-white m-2 p-2");
                elem.InnerHtml.Append($"Time: {timestamp}");
                output.PreContent.AppendHtml(elem);
            }
        }
    }
}
```

Tag helper components do not specify the elements they transform, and the Process method is invoked for every element for which the tag helper component feature has been configured. By default, tag helper components are applied to transform head and body elements. This means that tag helper component classes must check the TagName property of the output element to ensure they perform only their intended transformations. The tag helper component in Listing 25-29 looks for body elements and uses the PreContent property to insert a div element containing a timestamp before the rest of the element's content.

■ **Tip**   I show you how to increase the range of elements handled by tag helper components in the next section.

Tag helper components are registered as services that implement the ITagHelperComponent interface, as shown in Listing 25-30.

Listing 25-30. Registering a Tag Helper Component in the Startup.cs File in the WebApp Folder

```
using Microsoft.AspNetCore.Builder;
using Microsoft.Extensions.DependencyInjection;
using Microsoft.Extensions.Configuration;
using Microsoft.EntityFrameworkCore;
using WebApp.Models;
using Microsoft.AspNetCore.Razor.TagHelpers;
using WebApp.TagHelpers;
```

```
namespace WebApp {
    public class Startup {

        public Startup(IConfiguration config) {
            Configuration = config;
        }

        public IConfiguration Configuration { get; set; }

        public void ConfigureServices(IServiceCollection services) {
            services.AddDbContext<DataContext>(opts => {
                opts.UseSqlServer(Configuration[
                    "ConnectionStrings:ProductConnection"]);
                opts.EnableSensitiveDataLogging(true);
            });
            services.AddControllersWithViews().AddRazorRuntimeCompilation();
            services.AddRazorPages().AddRazorRuntimeCompilation();
            services.AddSingleton<CitiesData>();
            services.AddTransient<ITagHelperComponent, TimeTagHelperComponent>();
        }

        public void Configure(IApplicationBuilder app, DataContext context) {
            app.UseDeveloperExceptionPage();
            app.UseStaticFiles();
            app.UseRouting();
            app.UseEndpoints(endpoints => {
                endpoints.MapControllers();
                endpoints.MapDefaultControllerRoute();
                endpoints.MapRazorPages();
            });
            SeedData.SeedDatabase(context);
        }
    }
}
```

The AddTransient method is used to ensure that each request is handled using its own instance of the tag helper component class. To see the effect of the tag helper component, restart ASP.NET Core and use a browser to request http://localhost:5000/ home. This response—and all other HTML responses from the application—contain the content generated by the tag helper component, as shown in Figure 25-14.

Figure 25-14. *Using a tag helper component*

Expanding Tag Helper Component Element Selection

By default, only the head and body elements are processed by the tag helper components, but additional elements can be selected by creating a class derived from the terribly named TagHelperComponentTagHelper class. Add a class file named TableFooterTagHelperComponent.cs to the TagHelpers folder and use it to define the classes shown in Listing 25-31.

Listing 25-31. The Contents of the TableFooterTagHelperComponent.cs File in the TagHelpers Folder

```
using Microsoft.AspNetCore.Mvc.Razor.TagHelpers;
using Microsoft.AspNetCore.Mvc.Rendering;
using Microsoft.AspNetCore.Razor.TagHelpers;
using Microsoft.Extensions.Logging;

namespace WebApp.TagHelpers {

    [HtmlTargetElement("table")]
    public class TableFooterSelector: TagHelperComponentTagHelper {

        public TableFooterSelector(ITagHelperComponentManager mgr,
            ILoggerFactory log): base(mgr, log) { }
    }

    public class TableFooterTagHelperComponent: TagHelperComponent {

        public override void Process(TagHelperContext context,
                TagHelperOutput output) {

            if (output.TagName == "table") {
                TagBuilder cell = new TagBuilder("td");
                cell.Attributes.Add("colspan", "2");
                cell.Attributes.Add("class", "bg-dark text-white text-center");
                cell.InnerHtml.Append("Table Footer");
                TagBuilder row = new TagBuilder("tr");
                row.InnerHtml.AppendHtml(cell);
                TagBuilder footer = new TagBuilder("tfoot");
                footer.InnerHtml.AppendHtml(row);
                output.PostContent.AppendHtml(footer);
            }
        }
    }
}
```

The TableFooterSelector class is derived from TagHelperComponentTagHelper, and it is decorated with the HtmlTargetElement attribute that expands the range of elements processed by the application's tag helper components. In this case, the attribute selects table elements.

The TableFooterTagHelperComponent class, defined in the same file, is a tag helper component that transforms table elements by adding a tfoot element, which represents a table footer.

■ **Caution**   Bear in mind that when you create a new TagHelperComponentTagHelper, all the tag helper components will receive the elements selected by the HtmlTargetAttribute element.

The tag helper component must be registered as a service to receive elements for transformation, but the tag helper component tag helper (which is one of the worst naming choices I have seen for some years) is discovered and applied automatically. Listing 25-32 adds the tag helper component service.

Listing 25-32. Registering a Tag Helper Component in the Startup.cs File in the WebApp Folder

```
...
public void ConfigureServices(IServiceCollection services) {
    services.AddDbContext<DataContext>(opts => {
        opts.UseSqlServer(Configuration[
            "ConnectionStrings:ProductConnection"]);
        opts.EnableSensitiveDataLogging(true);
    });
    services.AddControllersWithViews().AddRazorRuntimeCompilation();
    services.AddRazorPages().AddRazorRuntimeCompilation();
    services.AddSingleton<CitiesData>();
    services.AddTransient<ITagHelperComponent, TimeTagHelperComponent>();
    services.AddTransient<ITagHelperComponent, TableFooterTagHelperComponent>();
}
...
```

Restart ASP.NET Core and use a browser to request a URL that renders a table, such as http://localhost:5000/home or http://localhost:5000/cities. Each table will contain a table footer, as shown in Figure 25-15.

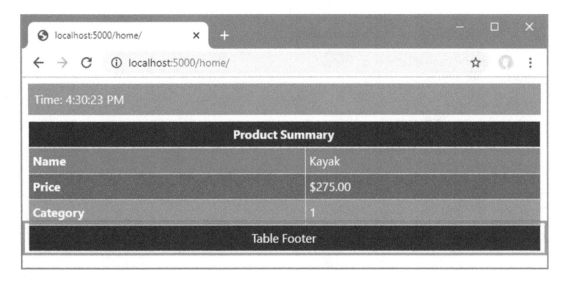

Figure 25-15. *Expanding tag helper component element selection*

Summary

In this chapter, I explained how tag helpers work and their role in transforming HTML elements in views and pages. I showed you how to create and apply tag helpers, how to control the elements that are selected for transformation, and how to use the advanced features to get specific results. I finished the chapter by explaining the tag helper component feature, which are defined as services. In the next chapter, I describe the built-in tag helpers that ASP.NET Core provides.

CHAPTER 26

■ ■ ■

Using the Built-in Tag Helpers

ASP.NET Core provides a set of built-in tag helpers that apply the most commonly required element transformations. In this chapter, I explain those tag helpers that deal with anchor, `script`, `link`, and image elements, as well as features for caching content and selecting content based on the environment. In Chapter 27, I describe the tag helpers that support HTML forms. Table 26-1 puts the built-in tag helpers in context.

Table 26-1. *Putting the Built-in Tag Helpers in Context*

Question	Answer
What are they?	The built-in tag helpers perform commonly required transformations on HTML elements.
Why are they useful?	Using the built-in tag helpers means you don't have to create custom helpers using the techniques in Chapter 25.
How are they used?	The tag helpers are applied using attributes on standard HTML elements or through custom HTML elements.
Are there any pitfalls or limitations?	No, these tag helpers are well-tested and easy to use. Unless you have unusual needs, using these tag helpers is preferable to custom implementation.
Are there any alternatives?	These tag helpers are optional, and their use is not required.

Table 26-2 summarizes the chapter.

Table 26-2. *Chapter Summary*

Problem	Solution	Listing
Creating elements that target endpoints	Use the anchor element tag helper attributes	7, 8
Including JavaScript files in a response	Use the JavaScript tag helper attributes	9–13
Including CSS files in a response	Use the CSS tag helper attributes	14, 15
Managing image caching	Use the image tag helper attributes	16
Caching sections of a view	Use the caching tag helper	17–21
Varying content based on the application environment	Use the environment tag helper	22

Preparing for This Chapter

This chapter uses the WebApp project from Chapter 25. To prepare for this chapter, comment out the statements that register the tag component helpers in the `Startup` class, as shown in Listing 26-1.

A. Freeman, *Pro ASP.NET Core 3*, https://doi.org/10.1007/978-1-4842-5440-0_26

■ **Tip** You can download the example project for this chapter—and for all the other chapters in this book—from `https://github.com/apress/pro-asp.net-core-3`. See Chapter 1 for how to get help if you have problems running the examples.

Listing 26-1. The Contents of the Startup.cs File in the WebApp Folder

```
using Microsoft.AspNetCore.Builder;
using Microsoft.Extensions.DependencyInjection;
using Microsoft.Extensions.Configuration;
using Microsoft.EntityFrameworkCore;
using WebApp.Models;
//using Microsoft.AspNetCore.Razor.TagHelpers;
//using WebApp.TagHelpers;

namespace WebApp {
    public class Startup {

        public Startup(IConfiguration config) {
            Configuration = config;
        }

        public IConfiguration Configuration { get; set; }

        public void ConfigureServices(IServiceCollection services) {
            services.AddDbContext<DataContext>(opts => {
                opts.UseSqlServer(Configuration[
                    "ConnectionStrings:ProductConnection"]);
                opts.EnableSensitiveDataLogging(true);
            });
            services.AddControllersWithViews().AddRazorRuntimeCompilation();
            services.AddRazorPages().AddRazorRuntimeCompilation();
            services.AddSingleton<CitiesData>();
            //services.AddTransient<ITagHelperComponent, TimeTagHelperComponent>();
            //services.AddTransient<ITagHelperComponent,
            //      TableFooterTagHelperComponent>();
        }

        public void Configure(IApplicationBuilder app, DataContext context) {
            app.UseDeveloperExceptionPage();
            app.UseStaticFiles();
            app.UseRouting();
            app.UseEndpoints(endpoints => {
                endpoints.MapControllers();
                endpoints.MapDefaultControllerRoute();
                endpoints.MapRazorPages();
            });
            SeedData.SeedDatabase(context);
        }
    }
}
```

Next, update the _RowPartial.cshtml partial view in the Views/Home folder, making the changes shown in Listing 26-2.

Listing 26-2. Making Changes in the _RowPartial.cshtml File in the Views/Home Folder

```
@model Product

<tr>
    <td>@Model.Name</td>
    <td>@Model.Price.ToString("c")</td>
    <td>@Model.CategoryId</td>
    <td>@Model.SupplierId</td>
    <td></td>
</tr>
```

Add the elements shown in Listing 26-3 to define additional columns in the table rendered in the Home controller's List view.

Listing 26-3. Adding Elements in the List.cshtml File in the Views/Home Folder

```
@model IEnumerable<Product>
@{ Layout = "_SimpleLayout"; }

<h6 class="bg-secondary text-white text-center m-2 p-2">Products</h6>
<div class="m-2">
    <table class="table table-sm table-striped table-bordered">
        <thead>
            <tr>
                <th>Name</th><th>Price</th>
                <th>Category</th><th>Supplier</th><th></th>
            </tr>
        </thead>
        <tbody>
            @foreach (Product p in Model) {
                <partial name="_RowPartial" model="p" />
            }
        </tbody>
    </table>
</div>
```

Adding an Image File

One of the tag helpers described in this chapter provides services for images. I created the wwwroot/images folder and added an image file called city.png. This is a public domain panorama of the New York City skyline, as shown in Figure 26-1.

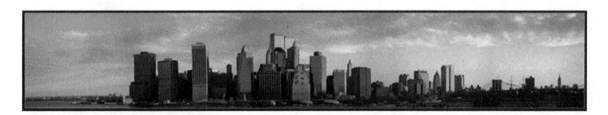

Figure 26-1. *Adding an image to the project*

This image file is included in the source code for this chapter, which is available in the GitHub repository for this book. You can substitute your own image if you don't want to download the example project.

645

Installing a Client-Side Package

Some of the examples in this chapter demonstrate the tag helper support for working with JavaScript files, for which I use the jQuery package. Use a PowerShell command prompt to run the command shown in Listing 26-4 in the project folder, which contains the WebApp.csproj file. If you are using Visual Studio, you can select Project ➤ Manage Client-Side Libraries to select the jQuery package.

Listing 26-4. Installing a Package

```
libman install jquery@3.4.1 -d wwwroot/lib/jquery
```

Dropping the Database

Open a new PowerShell command prompt, navigate to the folder that contains the WebApp.csproj file, and run the command shown in Listing 26-5 to drop the database.

Listing 26-5. Dropping the Database

```
dotnet ef database drop --force
```

Running the Example Application

Select Start Without Debugging or Run Without Debugging from the Debug menu or use the PowerShell command prompt to run the command shown in Listing 26-6.

Listing 26-6. Running the Example Application

```
dotnet run
```

Use a browser to request http://localhost:5000/Home/list, which will display a list of products, as shown in Figure 26-2.

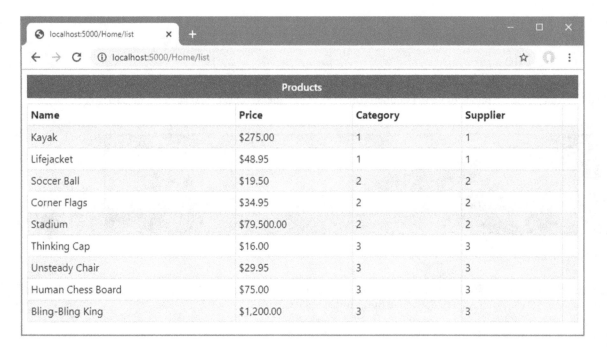

Figure 26-2. Running the example application

Enabling the Built-in Tag Helpers

The built-in tag helpers are all defined in the Microsoft.AspNetCore.Mvc.TagHelpers namespace and are enabled by adding an @addTagHelpers directive to individual views or pages or, as in the case of the example project, to the view imports file. Here is the required directive from the _ViewImports.cshtml file in the Views folder, which enables the built-in tag helpers for controller views:

```
@using WebApp.Models
@addTagHelper *, Microsoft.AspNetCore.Mvc.TagHelpers
@using WebApp.Components
@addTagHelper *, WebApp
```

Here is the corresponding directive in the _ViewImports.cshtml file in the Pages folder, which enables the built-in tag helpers for Razor Pages:

```
@namespace WebApp.Pages
@using WebApp.Models
@addTagHelper *, Microsoft.AspNetCore.Mvc.TagHelpers
@addTagHelper *, WebApp
```

These directives were added to the example project in Chapter 24 to enable the view components feature.

Transforming Anchor Elements

The a element is the basic tool for navigating around an application and sending GET requests to the application. The AnchorTagHelper class is used to transform the href attribute of a elements so they target URLs generated using the routing system, which means that hard-coded URLs are not required and a change in the routing configuration will be automatically reflected in the application's anchor elements. Table 26-3 describes the attributes the AnchorTagHelper class supports.

Table 26-3. *The Built-in Tag Helper Attributes for Anchor Elements*

Name	Description
asp-action	This attribute specifies the action method that the URL will target.
asp-controller	This attribute specifies the controller that the URL will target. If this attribute is omitted, then the URL will target the controller or page that rendered the current view.
asp-page	This attribute specifies the Razor Page that the URL will target.
asp-page-handler	This attribute specifies the Razor Page handler function that will process the request, as described in Chapter 23.
asp-fragment	This attribute is used to specify the URL fragment (which appears after the # character).
asp-host	This attribute specifies the name of the host that the URL will target.
asp-protocol	This attribute specifies the protocol that the URL will use.
asp-route	This attribute specifies the name of the route that will be used to generate the URL.
asp-route-*	Attributes whose name begins with asp-route- are used to specify additional values for the URL so that the asp-route-id attribute is used to provide a value for the id segment to the routing system.
asp-all-route-data	This attribute provides values used for routing as a single value, rather than using individual attributes.

The AnchorTagHelper is simple and predictable and makes it easy to generate URLs in a elements that use the application's routing configuration. Listing 26-7 adds an anchor element that uses attributes from the table to create a URL that targets another action defined by the Home controller.

Listing 26-7. Transforming an Element in the _RowPartial.cshtml File in the Views/Home Folder

```
@model Product

<tr>
    <td>@Model.Name</td>
    <td>@Model.Price.ToString("c")</td>
    <td>@Model.CategoryId</td>
    <td>@Model.SupplierId</td>
    <td>
        <a asp-action="index" asp-controller="home" asp-route-id="@Model.ProductId"
                class="btn btn-sm btn-info">
            Select
        </a>
    </td>
</tr>
```

The `asp-action` and `asp-controller` attributes specify the name of the action method and the controller that defines it. Values for segment variables are defined using `asp-route-[name]` attributes, such that the `asp-route-id` attribute provides a value for the `id` segment variable that is used to provide an argument for the action method selected by the `asp-action` attribute.

■ **Tip** The `class` attributes added to the anchor elements in Listing 26-7 apply Bootstrap CSS Framework styles that give the elements the appearance of buttons. This is not a requirement for using the tag helper.

To see the anchor element transformations, use a browser to request `http://localhost:5000/home/list`, which will produce the response shown in Figure 26-3.

Products				
Name	**Price**	**Category**	**Supplier**	
Kayak	$275.00	1	1	Select
Lifejacket	$48.95	1	1	Select
Soccer Ball	$19.50	2	2	Select
Corner Flags	$34.95	2	2	Select
Stadium	$79,500.00	2	2	Select
Thinking Cap	$16.00	3	3	Select
Unsteady Chair	$29.95	3	3	Select
Human Chess Board	$75.00	3	3	Select
Bling-Bling King	$1,200.00	3	3	Select

Figure 26-3. *Transforming anchor elements*

648

If you examine the Select anchor elements, you will see that each href attribute includes the ProductId value of the Product object it relates to, like this:

```
...
<a class="btn btn-sm btn-info" href="/Home/index/3">Select</a>
...
```

In this case, the value provided by the asp-route-id attribute means the default URL cannot be used, so the routing system has generated a URL that includes segments for the controller and action name, as well as a segment that will be used to provide a parameter to the action method. In both cases, since only an action method was specified, the URLs created by the tag helper target the controller that rendered the view. Clicking the anchor elements will send an HTTP GET request that targets the Home controller's Index method.

Using Anchor Elements for Razor Pages

The asp-page attribute is used to specify a Razor Page as the target for an anchor element's href attribute. The path to the page is prefixed with the / character, and values for route segments defined by the @page directive are defined using asp-route-[name] attributes. Listing 26-8 adds an anchor element that targets the List page defined in the Pages/Suppliers folder.

■ **Note** The asp-page-handler attribute can be used to specify the name of the page model handler method that will process the request.

Listing 26-8. Targeting a Razor Page in the List.cshtml File in the Views/Home Folder

```
@model IEnumerable<Product>
@{
    Layout = "_SimpleLayout";
}

<h6 class="bg-secondary text-white text-center m-2 p-2">Products</h6>
<div class="m-2">
    <table class="table table-sm table-striped table-bordered">
        <thead>
            <tr>
                <th>Name</th><th>Price</th>
                <th>Category</th><th>Supplier</th><th></th>
            </tr>
        </thead>
        <tbody>
            @foreach (Product p in Model) {
                <partial name="_RowPartial" model="p" />
            }
        </tbody>
    </table>
    <a asp-page="/suppliers/list" class="btn btn-secondary">Suppliers</a>
</div>
```

Use a browser to request http://localhost:5000/home/list, and you will see the anchor element, which is styled to appear as a button. If you examine the HTML sent to the client, you will see the anchor element has been transformed like this:

```
...
<a class="btn btn-secondary" href="/lists/suppliers">Suppliers</a>
...
```

This URL used in the href attribute reflects the @page directive, which has been used to override the default routing convention in this page. Click the element, and the browser will display the Razor Page, as shown in Figure 26-4.

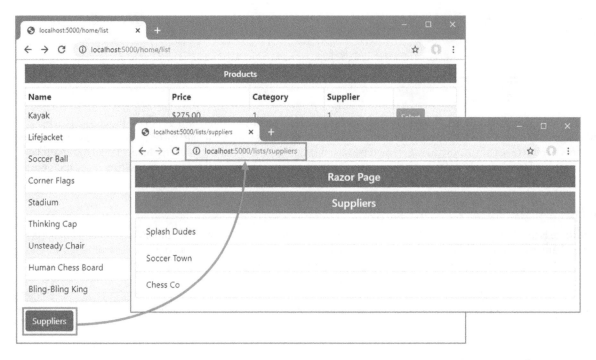

Figure 26-4. *Targeting a Razor Page with an anchor element*

GENERATING URLS (AND NOT LINKS)

The tag helper generates URLs only in anchor elements. If you need to generate a URL, rather than a link, then you can use the Url property, which is available in controllers, page models, and views. This property returns an object that implements the IUrlHelper interface, which provides a set of methods and extension methods that generate URLs. Here is a Razor fragment that generates a URL in a view:

```
...
<div>@Url.Page("/suppliers/list")</div>
...
```

This fragment produces a div element whose content is the URL that targets the /Suppliers/List Razor Page. The same interface is used in controllers or page model classes, such as with this statement:

```
...
string url = Url.Action("List", "Home");
...
```

The statement generates a URL that targets the List action on the Home controller and assigns it to the string variable named url.

Using the JavaScript and CSS Tag Helpers

ASP.NET Core provides tag helpers that are used to manage JavaScript files and CSS stylesheets through the script and link elements. As you will see in the sections that follow, these tag helpers are powerful and flexible but require close attention to avoid creating unexpected results.

Managing JavaScript Files

The ScriptTagHelper class is the built-in tag helper for script elements and is used to manage the inclusion of JavaScript files in views using the attributes described in Table 26-4, which I describe in the sections that follow.

650

Table 26-4. *The Built-in Tag Helper Attributes for script Elements*

Name	Description
asp-src-include	This attribute is used to specify JavaScript files that will be included in the view.
asp-src-exclude	This attribute is used to specify JavaScript files that will be excluded from the view.
asp-append-version	This attribute is used for cache busting, as described in the "Understanding Cache Busting" sidebar.
asp-fallback-src	This attribute is used to specify a fallback JavaScript file to use if there is a problem with a content delivery network.
asp-fallback-src-include	This attribute is used to select JavaScript files that will be used if there is a content delivery network problem.
asp-fallback-src-exclude	This attribute is used to exclude JavaScript files to present their use when there is a content delivery network problem.
asp-fallback-test	This attribute is used to specify a fragment of JavaScript that will be used to determine whether JavaScript code has been correctly loaded from a content delivery network.

Selecting JavaScript Files

The asp-src-include attribute is used to include JavaScript files in a view using globbing patterns. Globbing patterns support a set of wildcards that are used to match files, and Table 26-5 describes the most common globbing patterns.

Table 26-5. *Common Globbing Patterns*

Pattern	Example	Description
?	js/src?.js	This pattern matches any single character except /. The example matches any file contained in the js directory whose name is src, followed by any character, followed by .js, such as js/src1.js and js/srcX.js but not js/src123.js or js/mydir/src1.js.
*	js/*.js	This pattern matches any number of characters except /. The example matches any file contained in the js directory with the .js file extension, such as js/src1.js and js/src123.js but not js/mydir/src1.js.
**	js/**/*.js	This pattern matches any number of characters including /. The example matches any file with the .js extension that is contained within the js directory or any subdirectory, such as /js/src1.js and /js/mydir/src1.js.

Globbing is a useful way of ensuring that a view includes the JavaScript files that the application requires, even when the exact path to the file changes, which usually happens when the version number is included in the file name or when a package adds additional files.

Listing 26-9 uses the asp-src-include attribute to include all the JavaScript files in the wwwroot/lib/jquery folder, which is the location of the jQuery package installed with the command in Listing 26-4.

Listing 26-9. Selecting JS Files in the _SimpleLayout.cshtml File in the Views/Shared Folder

```
<!DOCTYPE html>
<html>
<head>
    <title>@ViewBag.Title</title>
    <link href="/lib/twitter-bootstrap/css/bootstrap.min.css" rel="stylesheet" />
    <script asp-src-include="lib/jquery/**/*.js"></script>
</head>
<body>
    <div class="m-2">
        @RenderBody()
    </div>
</body>
</html>
```

Patterns are evaluated within the wwwroot folder, and the pattern I used locates any file with the js file extension, regardless of its location within the wwwroot folder; this means that any JavaScript package added to the project will be included in the HTML sent to the client.

Use a browser to request http://localhost:5000/home/list and examine the HTML sent to the browser. You will see the single script element in the layout has been transformed into a script element for each JavaScript file, like this:

```
...
<head>
  <title></title>
  <link href="/lib/twitter-bootstrap/css/bootstrap.min.css" rel="stylesheet">
  <script src="/lib/jquery/core.js"></script>
  <script src="/lib/jquery/jquery.js"></script>
  <script src="/lib/jquery/jquery.min.js"></script>
  <script src="/lib/jquery/jquery.slim.js"></script>
  <script src="/lib/jquery/jquery.slim.min.js"></script>

</head>
...
```

If you are using Visual Studio, you may not have realized that the jQuery packages contain so many JavaScript files because Visual Studio hides them in the Solution Explorer. To reveal the full contents of the client-side package folders, you can either expand the individual nested entries in the Solution Explorer window or disable file nesting by clicking the button at the top of the Solution Explorer window, as shown in Figure 26-5. (Visual Studio Code does not nest files.)

Figure 26-5. *Disabling file nesting in the Visual Studio Solution Explorer*

UNDERSTANDING SOURCE MAPS

JavaScript files are minified to make them smaller, which means they can be delivered to the client faster and using less bandwidth. The minification process removes all the whitespace from the file and renames functions and variables so that meaningful names such as myHelpfullyNamedFunction will be represented by a smaller number of characters, such as x1. When using the browser's JavaScript debugger to track down problems in your minified code, names like x1 make it almost impossible to follow progress through the code.

The files that have the map file extension are *source maps*, which browsers use to help debug minified code by providing a map between the minified code and the developer-readable, unminified source file. When you open the browser's F12 developer tools, the browser will automatically request source maps and use them to help debug the application's client-side code.

Narrowing the Globbing Pattern

No application would require all the files selected by the pattern in Listing 26-9. Many packages include multiple JavaScript files that contain similar content, often removing less popular features to save bandwidth. The jQuery package includes the jquery.slim.js file, which contains the same code as the jquery.js file but without the features that handle asynchronous HTTP requests and animation effects. (There is also a core.js file, but this is included in the package by error and should be ignored.)

Each of these files has a counterpart with the min.js file extension, which denotes a minified file. Minification reduces the size of a JavaScript file by removing all whitespace and renaming functions and variables to use shorter names.

Only one JavaScript file is required for each package and if you only require the minified versions, which will be the case in most projects, then you can restrict the set of files that the globbing pattern matches, as shown in Listing 26-10.

Listing 26-10. Selecting Minified Files in the _SimpleLayout.cshtml File in the Views/Shared Folder

```
<!DOCTYPE html>
<html>
<head>
    <title>@ViewBag.Title</title>
    <link href="/lib/twitter-bootstrap/css/bootstrap.min.css" rel="stylesheet" />
    <script asp-src-include="lib/jquery**/*.min.js"></script>
</head>
<body>
    <div class="m-2">
        @RenderBody()
    </div>
</body>
</html>
```

Use a browser to request http://localhost:5000/home/list again and examine the HTML sent by the application. You will see that only the minified files have been selected.

```
...
<head>
  <title></title>
  <link href="/lib/twitter-bootstrap/css/bootstrap.min.css" rel="stylesheet">
  <script src="/lib/jquery/jquery.min.js"></script>
  <script src="/lib/jquery/jquery.slim.min.js"></script>
</head>
...
```

Narrowing the pattern for the JavaScript files has helped, but the browser will still end up with the normal and slim versions of jQuery and the bundled and unbundled versions of the Bootstrap JavaScript files. To narrow the selection further, I can include slim in the pattern, as shown in Listing 26-11.

Listing 26-11. Narrowing the Focus in the _SimpleLayout.cshtml File in the Views/Shared Folder

```
<!DOCTYPE html>
<html>
<head>
    <title>@ViewBag.Title</title>
    <link href="/lib/twitter-bootstrap/css/bootstrap.min.css" rel="stylesheet" />
    <script asp-src-include="lib/jquery**/*slim.min.js"></script>
</head>
<body>
    <div class="m-2">
        @RenderBody()
    </div>
</body>
</html>
```

Use the browser to request `http://localhost:5000/home/list` and examine the HTML the browser receives. The `script` element has been transformed like this:

```
...
<head>
  <title></title>
  <link href="/lib/twitter-bootstrap/css/bootstrap.min.css" rel="stylesheet">
  <script src="/lib/jquery/jquery.slim.min.js"></script>
</head>
...
```

Only one version of the jQuery file will be sent to the browser while preserving the flexibility for the location of the file.

Excluding Files

Narrowing the pattern for the JavaScript files helps when you want to select a file whose name contains a specific term, such as `slim`. It isn't helpful when the file you want doesn't have that term, such as when you want the full version of the minified file. Fortunately, you can use the `asp-src-exclude` attribute to remove files from the list matched by the `asp-src-include` attribute, as shown in Listing 26-12.

Listing 26-12. Excluding Files in the _SimpleLayout.cshtml File in the Views/Shared Folder

```
<!DOCTYPE html>
<html>
<head>
    <title>@ViewBag.Title</title>
    <link href="/lib/twitter-bootstrap/css/bootstrap.min.css" rel="stylesheet" />
    <script asp-src-include="/lib/jquery/**/*.min.js"
        asp-src-exclude="**.slim.**">
    </script>
</head>
<body>
    <div class="m-2">
        @RenderBody()
    </div>
</body>
</html>
```

If you use the browser to request `http://localhost:5000/home/list` and examine the HTML response, you will see that the `script` element links only to the full minified version of the jQuery library, like this:

```
...
<head>
    <title></title>
    <link href="/lib/twitter-bootstrap/css/bootstrap.min.css" rel="stylesheet">
    <script src="/lib/jquery/jquery.min.js"></script>
</head>
...
```

UNDERSTANDING CACHE BUSTING

Static content, such as images, CSS stylesheets, and JavaScript files, is often cached to stop requests for content that rarely changes from reaching the application servers. Caching can be done in different ways: the browser can be told to cache content by the server, the application can use cache servers to supplement the application servers, or the content can be distributed using a content delivery network. Not all caching will be under your control. Large corporations, for example, often install caches to reduce their bandwidth demands since a substantial percentage of requests tend to go to the same sites or applications.

One problem with caching is that clients don't immediately receive new versions of static files when you deploy them because their requests are still being serviced by previously cached content. Eventually, the cached content will expire, and the new content will be used, but that leaves a period where the dynamic content generated by the application's controllers is out of step with the static content being delivered by the caches. This can lead to layout problems or unexpected application behavior, depending on the content that has been updated.

Addressing this problem is called *cache busting*. The idea is to allow caches to handle static content but immediately reflect any changes that are made at the server. The tag helper classes support cache busting by adding a query string to the URLs for static content that includes a checksum that acts as a version number. For JavaScript files, for example, the ScriptTagHelper class supports cache busting through the asp-append-version attribute, like this:

```
...
<script asp-src-include="/lib/jquery/**/*.min.js"
    asp-src-exclude="**.slim.**" asp-append-version="true">
</script>
...
```

Enabling the cache busting feature produces an element like this in the HTML sent to the browser:

```
...
<script src="/lib/jquery/dist/jquery.min.js?v=3zRSQ1HF-ocUiVcdv9yKTXqM"></script>
...
```

The same version number will be used by the tag helper until you change the contents of the file, such as by updating a JavaScript library, at which point a different checksum will be calculated. The addition of the version number means that each time you change the file, the client will request a different URL, which caches treat as a request for new content that cannot be satisfied with the previously cached content and pass on to the application server. The content is then cached as normal until the next update, which produces another URL with a different version.

Working with Content Delivery Networks

Content delivery networks (CDNs) are used to offload requests for application content to servers that are closer to the user. Rather than requesting a JavaScript file from your servers, the browser requests it from a hostname that resolves to a geographically local server, which reduces the amount of time required to load files and reduces the amount of bandwidth you have to provision for your application. If you have a large, geographically disbursed set of users, then it can make commercial sense to sign up to a CDN, but even the smallest and simplest application can benefit from using the free CDNs operated by major technology companies to deliver common JavaScript packages, such as jQuery.

For this chapter, I am going to use CDNJS, which is the same CDN used by the Library Manager tool to install client-side packages in the ASP.NET Core project. You can search for packages at https://cdnjs.com; for jQuery 3.4.1, which is the package and version installed in Listing 26-4, there are six CDNJS URLs.

- https://cdnjs.cloudflare.com/ajax/libs/jquery/3.4.1/jquery.js
- https://cdnjs.cloudflare.com/ajax/libs/jquery/3.4.1/jquery.min.js
- https://cdnjs.cloudflare.com/ajax/libs/jquery/3.4.1/jquery.min.map
- https://cdnjs.cloudflare.com/ajax/libs/jquery/3.4.1/jquery.slim.js
- https://cdnjs.cloudflare.com/ajax/libs/jquery/3.4.1/jquery.slim.min.js
- https://cdnjs.cloudflare.com/ajax/libs/jquery/3.4.1/jquery.slim.min.map

These URLs provide the regular JavaScript file, the minified JavaScript file, and the source map for the minified file for both the full and slim versions of jQuery. (There is also a URL for the core.js file, but, as noted earlier, this file is not used and will be removed from future jQuery releases.)

The problem with CDNs is that they are not under your organization's control, and that means they can fail, leaving your application running but unable to work as expected because the CDN content isn't available. The ScriptTagHelper class provides the ability to fall back to local files when the CDN content cannot be loaded by the client, as shown in Listing 26-13.

Listing 26-13. Using CDN Fallback in the _SimpleLayout.cshtml File in the Views/Shared Folder

```
<!DOCTYPE html>
<html>
<head>
    <title>@ViewBag.Title</title>
    <link href="/lib/twitter-bootstrap/css/bootstrap.min.css" rel="stylesheet" />
    <script src="https://cdnjs.cloudflare.com/ajax/libs/jquery/3.4.1/jquery.min.js"
        asp-fallback-src="/lib/jquery/jquery.min.js"
        asp-fallback-test="window.jQuery">
    </script>
</head>
<body>
    <div class="m-2">
        @RenderBody()
    </div>
</body>
</html>
```

The src attribute is used to specify the CDN URL. The asp-fallback-src attribute is used to specify a local file that will be used if the CDN is unable to deliver the file specified by the regular src attribute. To figure out whether the CDN is working, the asp-fallback-test attribute is used to define a fragment of JavaScript that will be evaluated at the browser. If the fragment evaluates as false, then the fallback files will be requested.

■ **Tip** The asp-fallback-src-include and asp-fallback-src-exclude attributes can be used to select the local files with globbing patterns. However, given that CDN script elements select a single file, I recommend using the asp-fallback-src attribute to select the corresponding local file, as shown in the example.

Use a browser to request http://localhost:5000/home/list, and you will see that the HTML response contains two script elements, like this:

```
...
<head>
    <title></title>
    <link href="/lib/twitter-bootstrap/css/bootstrap.min.css" rel="stylesheet">
    <script src="https://cdnjs.cloudflare.com/ajax/libs/jquery/3.4.1/jquery.min.js"></script>
    <script>
        (window.jQuery||document.write("\u003Cscript
            src=\u0022/lib/jquery/jquery.min.js\u0022\u003E\u003C/script\u003E"));
    </script>
</head>
...
```

The first script element requests the JavaScript file from the CDN. The second script element evaluates the JavaScript fragment specified by the asp-fallback-test attribute, which checks to see whether the first script element has worked. If the fragment evaluates to true, then no action is taken because the CDN worked. If the fragment evaluates to false, a new script element is added to the HTML document that instructs the browser to load the JavaScript file from the fallback URL.

It is important to test your fallback settings because you won't find out if they fail until the CDN has stopped working and your users cannot access your application. The simplest way to check the fallback is to change the name of the file specified by the src attribute to something that you know doesn't exist (I append the word FAIL to the file name) and then look at the network requests that the browser makes using the F12 developer tools. You should see an error for the CDN file followed by a request for the fallback file.

■ **Caution** The CDN fallback feature relies on browsers loading and executing the contents of `script` elements synchronously and in the order in which they are defined. There are a number of techniques in use to speed up JavaScript loading and execution by making the process asynchronous, but these can lead to the fallback test being performed before the browser has retrieved a file from the CDN and executed its contents, resulting in requests for the fallback files even when the CDN is working perfectly and defeating the use of a CDN in the first place. Do not mix asynchronous script loading with the CDN fallback feature.

Managing CSS Stylesheets

The `LinkTagHelper` class is the built-in tag helper for `link` elements and is used to manage the inclusion of CSS style sheets in a view. This tag helper supports the attributes described in Table 26-6, which I demonstrate in the following sections.

Table 26-6. *The Built-in Tag Helper Attributes for link Elements*

Name	Description
asp-href-include	This attribute is used to select files for the href attribute of the output element.
asp-href-exclude	This attribute is used to exclude files from the href attribute of the output element.
asp-append-version	This attribute is used to enable cache busting, as described in the "Understanding Cache Busting" sidebar.
asp-fallback-href	This attribute is used to specify a fallback file if there is a problem with a CDN.
asp-fallback-href-include	This attribute is used to select files that will be used if there is a CDN problem.
asp-fallback-href-exclude	This attribute is used to exclude files from the set that will be used when there is a CDN problem.
asp-fallback-href-test-class	This attribute is used to specify the CSS class that will be used to test the CDN.
asp-fallback-href-test-property	This attribute is used to specify the CSS property that will be used to test the CDN.
asp-fallback-href-test-value	This attribute is used to specify the CSS value that will be used to test the CDN.

Selecting Stylesheets

The `LinkTagHelper` shares many features with the `ScriptTagHelper`, including support for globbing patterns to select or exclude CSS files so they do not have to be specified individually. Being able to accurately select CSS files is as important as it is for JavaScript files because stylesheets can come in regular and minified versions and support source maps. The popular Bootstrap package, which I have been using to style HTML elements throughout this book, includes its CSS stylesheets in the `wwwroot/lib/twitter-bootstrap/css` folder. These will be visible in Visual Studio Code, but you will have to expand each item in the Solution Explorer or disable nesting to see them in the Visual Studio Solution Explorer, as shown in Figure 26-6.

Figure 26-6. *The Bootstrap CSS files*

The bootstrap.css file is the regular stylesheet, the bootstrap.min.css file is the minified version, and the bootstrap.css.map file is a source map. The other files contain subsets of the CSS features to save bandwidth in applications that don't use them.

Listing 26-14 replaces the regular link element in the layout with one that uses the asp-href-include and asp-href-exclude attributes. (I removed the script element for jQuery, which is no longer required.)

Listing 26-14. Selecting a Stylesheet in the _SimpleLayout.cshtml File in the Views/Shared Folder

```
<!DOCTYPE html>
<html>
<head>
    <title>@ViewBag.Title</title>
    <link asp-href-include="/lib/twitter-bootstrap/css/*.min.css"
        asp-href-exclude="**/*-reboot*,**/*-grid*" rel="stylesheet" />
</head>
<body>
    <div class="m-2">
        @RenderBody()
    </div>
</body>
</html>
```

The same attention to detail is required as when selecting JavaScript files because it is easy to generate link elements for multiple versions of the same file or files that you don't want.

Working with Content Delivery Networks

The LinkTag helper class provides a set of attributes for falling back to local content when a CDN isn't available, although the process for testing to see whether a stylesheet has loaded is more complex than testing for a JavaScript file. Listing 26-15 uses the CDNJS URL for the Bootstrap CSS stylesheet.

Listing 26-15. Using a CDN for CSS in the _SimpleLayout.cshtml File in the Views/Home Folder

```html
<!DOCTYPE html>
<html>
<head>
    <title>@ViewBag.Title</title>
    <link href="https://cdnjs.cloudflare.com/ajax/libs/twitter-bootstrap/4.3.1/css/bootstrap.min.css"
        asp-fallback-href="/lib/twitter-bootstrap/css/bootstrap.min.css"
        asp-fallback-test-class="btn"
        asp-fallback-test-property="display"
        asp-fallback-test-value="inline-block"
        rel="stylesheet" />
</head>
<body>
    <div class="m-2">
        @RenderBody()
    </div>
</body>
</html>
```

The href attribute is used to specify the CDN URL, and I have used the asp-fallback-href attribute to select the file that will be used if the CDN is unavailable. Testing whether the CDN works, however, requires the use of three different attributes and an understanding of the CSS classes defined by the CSS stylesheet that is being used.

Use a browser to request http://localhost:5000/home/list and examine the HTML elements in the response. You will see that the link element from the layout has been transformed into three separate elements, like this:

```html
...
<head>
    <title></title>
    <link href="https://cdnjs.cloudflare.com/.../bootstrap.min.css" rel="stylesheet">
    <meta name="x-stylesheet-fallback-test" content="" class="btn">
    <script>
      ! function(a, b, c, d) {
        var e, f = document,
          g = f.getElementsByTagName("SCRIPT"),
          h = g[g.length1].previousElementSibling,
          i = f.defaultView && f.defaultView.getComputedStyle ?
          f.defaultView.getComputedStyle(h) : h.currentStyle;
        if (i && i[a] !== b)
          for (e = 0; e < c.length; e++)
            f.write('<link href="' + c[e] + '" ' + d + "/>")
      }("display", "inline-block", ["/lib/twitter-bootstrap/css/bootstrap.min.css"],
          "rel=\u0022stylesheet\u0022 ");
    </script>
</head>
...
```

To make the transformation easier to understand, I have formatted the JavaScript code and shortened the URL.

The first element is a regular link whose href attribute specifies the CDN file. The second element is a meta element, which specifies the class from the asp-fallback-test-class attribute in the view. I specified the btn class in the listing, which means that an element like this is added to the HTML sent to the browser:

```html
<meta name="x-stylesheet-fallback-test" content="" class="btn">
```

The CSS class that you specify must be defined in the stylesheet that will be loaded from the CDN. The btn class that I specified provides the basic formatting for Bootstrap button elements.

The asp-fallback-test-property attribute is used to specify a CSS property that is set when the CSS class is applied to an element, and the asp-fallback-test-value attribute is used to specify the value that it will be set to.

The script element created by the tag helper contains JavaScript code that adds an element to the specified class and then tests the value of the CSS property to determine whether the CDN stylesheet has been loaded. If not, a link element is created for the fallback file. The Bootstrap btn class sets the display property to inline-block, and this provides the test to see whether the browser has been able to load the Bootstrap stylesheet from the CDN.

■ Tip The easiest way to figure out how to test for third-party packages like Bootstrap is to use the browser's F12 developer tools. To determine the test in Listing 26-15, I assigned an element to the btn class and then inspected it in the browser, looking at the individual CSS properties that the class changes. I find this easier than trying to read through long and complex style sheets.

Working with Image Elements

The ImageTagHelper class is used to provide cache busting for images through the src attribute of img elements, allowing an application to take advantage of caching while ensuring that modifications to images are reflected immediately. The ImageTagHelper class operates in img elements that define the asp-append-version attribute, which is described in Table 26-7 for quick reference.

Table 26-7. *The Built-in Tag Helper Attribute for Image Elements*

Name	Description
asp-append-version	This attribute is used to enable cache busting, as described in the "Understanding Cache Busting" sidebar.

In Listing 26-16, I have added an img element to the shared layout for the city skyline image that I added to the project at the start of the chapter. I have also reset the link element to use a local file for brevity.

Listing 26-16. Adding an Image in the _SimpleLayout.cshtml File in the Views/Shared Folder

```
<!DOCTYPE html>
<html>
<head>
    <title>@ViewBag.Title</title>
    <link href="/lib/twitter-bootstrap/css/bootstrap.min.css" rel="stylesheet" />
</head>
<body>
    <div class="m-2">
        <img src="/images/city.png" asp-append-version="true" class="m-2" />
        @RenderBody()
    </div>
</body>
</html>
```

Use a browser to request http://localhost:5000/home/list, which will produce the response shown in Figure 26-7.

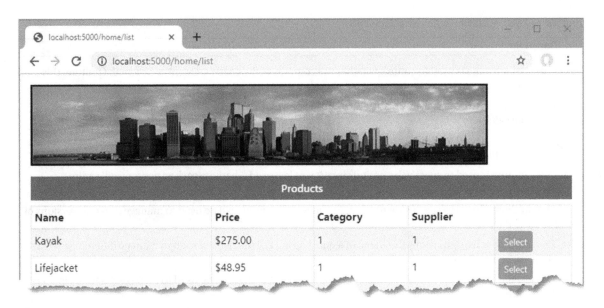

Figure 26-7. *Using an image*

Examine the HTML response, and you will see that the URL used to request the image file includes a version checksum, like this:

```
...
<img src="/images/city.png?v=KaMNDSZFAJufRcRDpKhOK_IIPNc7E" class="m-2">
...
```

The addition of the checksum ensures that any changes to the file will pass through any caches, avoiding stale content.

Using the Data Cache

The CacheTagHelper class allows fragments of content to be cached to speed up rendering of views or pages. The content to be cached is denoted using the cache element, which is configured using the attributes shown in Table 26-8.

■ **Note**   Caching is a useful tool for reusing sections of content so they don't have to be generated for every request. But using caching effectively requires careful thought and planning. While caching can improve the performance of an application, it can also create odd effects, such as users receiving stale content, multiple caches containing different versions of content, and update deployments that are broken because content cached from the previous version of the application is mixed with content from the new version. Don't enable caching unless you have a clearly defined performance problem to resolve, and make sure you understand the impact that caching will have.

Table 26-8. *The Built-in Tag Helper Attributes for cache Elements*

Name	Description
enabled	This bool attribute is used to control whether the contents of the cache element are cached. Omitting this attribute enables caching.
expires-on	This attribute is used to specify an absolute time at which the cached content will expire, expressed as a DateTime value.
expires-after	This attribute is used to specify a relative time at which the cached content will expire, expressed as a TimeSpan value.
expires-sliding	This attribute is used to specify the period since it was last used when the cached content will expire, expressed as a TimeSpan value.
vary-by-header	This attribute is used to specify the name of a request header that will be used to manage different versions of the cached content.
vary-by-query	This attribute is used to specify the name of a query string key that will be used to manage different versions of the cached content.
vary-by-route	This attribute is used to specify the name of a routing variable that will be used to manage different versions of the cached content.
vary-by-cookie	This attribute is used to specify the name of a cookie that will be used to manage different versions of the cached content.
vary-by-user	This bool attribute is used to specify whether the name of the authenticated user will be used to manage different versions of the cached content.
vary-by	This attribute is evaluated to provide a key used to manage different versions of the content.
priority	This attribute is used to specify a relative priority that will be taken into account when the memory cache runs out of space and purges unexpired cached content.

Listing 26-17 replaces the img element from the previous section with content that contains timestamps.

Listing 26-17. Caching Content in the _SimpleLayout.cshtml File in the Views/Shared Folder

```
<!DOCTYPE html>
<html>
<head>
    <title>@ViewBag.Title</title>
    <link href="/lib/twitter-bootstrap/css/bootstrap.min.css" rel="stylesheet" />
</head>
<body>
    <div class="m-2">
        <h6 class="bg-primary text-white m-2 p-2">
            Uncached timestamp: @DateTime.Now.ToLongTimeString()
        </h6>
        <cache>
            <h6 class="bg-primary text-white m-2 p-2">
                Cached timestamp: @DateTime.Now.ToLongTimeString()
            </h6>
        </cache>
        @RenderBody()
    </div>
</body>
</html>
```

The cache element is used to denote a region of content that should be cached and has been applied to one of the h6 elements that contains a timestamp. Use a browser to request http://localhost:5000/home/list, and both timestamps will be the same. Reload the browser, and you will see that the cached content is used for one of the h6 elements and the timestamp doesn't change, as shown in Figure 26-8.

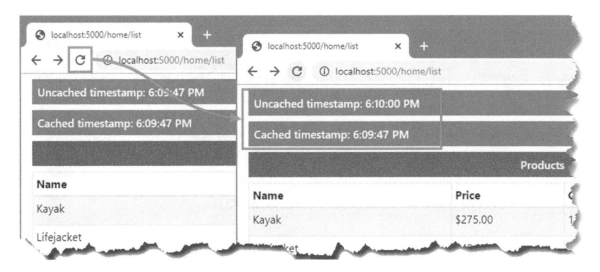

Figure 26-8. *Using the caching tag helper*

USING DISTRIBUTED CACHING FOR CONTENT

The cache used by the CacheTagHelper class is memory-based, which means that its capacity is limited by the available RAM and that each application server maintains a separate cache. Content will be ejected from the cache when there is a shortage of capacity available, and the entire contents are lost when the application is stopped or restarted.

The distributed-cache element can be used to store content in a shared cache, which ensures that all application servers use the same data and that the cache survives restarts. The distributed-cache element is configured with the same attributes as the cache element, as described in Table 26-8. See Chapter 17 for details of setting up a distributed cache.

Setting Cache Expiry

The expires-* attributes allow you to specify when cached content will expire, expressed either as an absolute time or a time relative to the current time, or to specify a duration during which the cached content isn't requested. In Listing 26-18, I have used the expires-after attribute to specify that the content should be cached for 15 seconds.

Listing 26-18. Setting Cache Expiry in the _SimpleLayout.cshtml File in the Views/Shared Folder

```
<!DOCTYPE html>
<html>
<head>
    <title>@ViewBag.Title</title>
    <link href="/lib/twitter-bootstrap/css/bootstrap.min.css" rel="stylesheet" />
</head>
<body>
    <div class="m-2">
        <h6 class="bg-primary text-white m-2 p-2">
            Uncached timestamp: @DateTime.Now.ToLongTimeString()
        </h6>
        <cache expires-after="@TimeSpan.FromSeconds(15)">
            <h6 class="bg-primary text-white m-2 p-2">
                Cached timestamp: @DateTime.Now.ToLongTimeString()
            </h6>
        </cache>
        @RenderBody()
```

```
        </div>
    </body>
</html>
```

Use a browser to request `http://localhost:5000/home/list` and then reload the page. After 15 seconds the cached content will expire, and a new section of content will be created.

Setting a Fixed Expiry Point

You can specify a fixed time at which cached content will expire using the `expires-on` attribute, which accepts a `DateTime` value, as shown in Listing 26-19.

Listing 26-19. Setting Cache Expiry in the _SimpleLayout.cshtml File in the Views/Shared Folder

```
<!DOCTYPE html>
<html>
<head>
    <title>@ViewBag.Title</title>
    <link href="/lib/twitter-bootstrap/css/bootstrap.min.css" rel="stylesheet" />
</head>
<body>
    <div class="m-2">
        <h6 class="bg-primary text-white m-2 p-2">
            Uncached timestamp: @DateTime.Now.ToLongTimeString()
        </h6>
        <cache expires-on="@DateTime.Parse("2100-01-01")">
            <h6 class="bg-primary text-white m-2 p-2">
                Cached timestamp: @DateTime.Now.ToLongTimeString()
            </h6>
        </cache>
        @RenderBody()
    </div>
</body>
</html>
```

I have specified that that data should be cached until the year 2100. This isn't a useful caching strategy since the application is likely to be restarted before the next century starts, but it does illustrate how you can specify a fixed point in the future rather than expressing the expiry point relative to the moment when the content is cached.

Setting a Last-Used Expiry Period

The `expires-sliding` attribute is used to specify a period after which content is expired if it hasn't been retrieved from the cache. In Listing 26-20, I have specified a sliding expiry of 10 seconds.

Listing 26-20. Using a Sliding Expiry in the _SimpleLayout.cshtml File in the Views/Shared Folder

```
<!DOCTYPE html>
<html>
<head>
    <title>@ViewBag.Title</title>
    <link href="/lib/twitter-bootstrap/css/bootstrap.min.css" rel="stylesheet" />
</head>
```

```
<body>
    <div class="m-2">
        <h6 class="bg-primary text-white m-2 p-2">
            Uncached timestamp: @DateTime.Now.ToLongTimeString()
        </h6>
        <cache expires-sliding="@TimeSpan.FromSeconds(10)">
            <h6 class="bg-primary text-white m-2 p-2">
                Cached timestamp: @DateTime.Now.ToLongTimeString()
            </h6>
        </cache>
        @RenderBody()
    </div>
</body>
</html>
```

You can see the effect of the express-sliding attribute by requesting http://localhost:5000/home/list and periodically reloading the page. If you reload the page within 10 seconds, the cached content will be used. If you wait longer than 10 seconds to reload the page, then the cached content will be discarded, the view component will be used to generate new content, and the process will begin anew.

Using Cache Variations

By default, all requests receive the same cached content. The CacheTagHelper class can maintain different versions of cached content and use them to satisfy different types of HTTP requests, specified using one of the attributes whose name begins with vary-by. Listing 26-21 shows the use of the vary-by-route attribute to create cache variations based on the action value matched by the routing system.

Listing 26-21. Creating a Variation in the _SimpleLayout.cshtml File in the Views/Shared Folder

```
<!DOCTYPE html>
<html>
<head>
    <title>@ViewBag.Title</title>
    <link href="/lib/twitter-bootstrap/css/bootstrap.min.css" rel="stylesheet" />
</head>
<body>
    <div class="m-2">
        <h6 class="bg-primary text-white m-2 p-2">
            Uncached timestamp: @DateTime.Now.ToLongTimeString()
        </h6>
        <cache expires-sliding="@TimeSpan.FromSeconds(10)" vary-by-route="action">
            <h6 class="bg-primary text-white m-2 p-2">
                Cached timestamp: @DateTime.Now.ToLongTimeString()
            </h6>
        </cache>
        @RenderBody()
    </div>
</body>
</html>
```

If you use two browser tabs to request http://localhost:5000/home/index and http://localhost:5000/home/list, you will see that each window receives its own cached content with its own expiration, since each request produces a different action routing value.

■ **Tip** If you are using Razor Pages, then you can achieve the same effect using page as the value matched by the routing system.

Using the Hosting Environment Tag Helper

The EnvironmentTagHelper class is applied to the custom environment element and determines whether a region of content is included in the HTML sent to the browser-based on the hosting environment, which I described in Chapters 15 and 16. The environment element relies on the names attribute, which I have described in Table 26-9.

Table 26-9. *The Built-in Tag Helper Attribute for environment Elements*

Name	Description
names	This attribute is used to specify a comma-separated list of hosting environment names for which the content contained within the environment element will be included in the HTML sent to the client.

In Listing 26-22, I have added environment elements to the shared layout including different content in the view for the development and production hosting environments.

Listing 26-22. Using environment in the _SimpleLayout.cshtml File in the Views/Shared Folder

```
<!DOCTYPE html>
<html>
<head>
    <title>@ViewBag.Title</title>
    <link href="/lib/twitter-bootstrap/css/bootstrap.min.css" rel="stylesheet" />
</head>
<body>
    <div class="m-2">
        <environment names="development">
            <h2 class="bg-info text-white m-2 p-2">This is Development</h2>
        </environment>
        <environment names="production">
            <h2 class="bg-danger text-white m-2 p-2">This is Production</h2>
        </environment>
        @RenderBody()
    </div>
</body>
</html>
```

The environment element checks the current hosting environment name and either includes the content it contains or omits it (the environment element itself is always omitted from the HTML sent to the client). Figure 26-9 shows the output for the development and production environments. (See Chapter 15 for details of how to set the environment.)

Figure 26-9. Managing content using the hosting environment

Summary

In this chapter, I described the basic built-in tag helpers and explained how they are used to transform anchor, link, script, and image elements. I also explained how to cache sections of content and how to render content based on the application's environment. In the next chapter, I describe the tag helpers that ASP.NET Core provides for working with HTML forms.

CHAPTER 27

■ ■ ■

Using the Forms Tag Helpers

In this chapter, I describe the built-in tag helpers that are used to create HTML forms. These tag helpers ensure forms are submitted to the correct action or page handler method and that elements accurately represent specific model properties. Table 27-1 puts the form tag helpers in context.

Table 27-1. *Putting Form Tag Helpers in Context*

Question	Answer
What are they?	These built-in tag helpers transform HTML form elements.
Why are they useful?	These tag helpers ensure that HTML forms reflect the application's routing configuration and data model.
How are they used?	Tag helpers are applied to HTML elements using asp-* attributes.
Are there any pitfalls or limitations?	These tag helpers are reliable and predictable and present no serious issues.
Are there any alternatives?	You don't have to use tag helpers and can define forms without them if you prefer.

Table 27-2 summarizes the chapter.

Table 27-2. *Chapter Summary*

Problem	Solution	Listing
Specifying how a form will be submitted	Use the form tag helper attributes	10–13
Transforming input elements	Use the input tag helper attributes	14–22
Transforming label elements	Use the label tag helper attributes	23
Populating select elements	Use the select tag helper attributes	24–26
Transforming text areas	Use the text area tag helper attributes	27
Protecting against cross-site request forgery	Enable the anti-forgery feature	28–32

Preparing for This Chapter

This chapter uses the WebApp project from Chapter 26. To prepare for this chapter, replace the contents of the _SimpleLayout. cshtml file in the Views/Shared folder with those shown in Listing 27-1.

■ **Tip** You can download the example project for this chapter—and for all the other chapters in this book—from https://github. com/apress/pro-asp.net-core-3. See Chapter 1 for how to get help if you have problems running the examples.

Listing 27-1. The Contents of the _SimpleLayout.cshtml File in the Views/Shared Folder

```
<!DOCTYPE html>
<html>
<head>
    <title>@ViewBag.Title</title>
    <link href="/lib/twitter-bootstrap/css/bootstrap.min.css" rel="stylesheet" />
</head>
<body>
    <div class="m-2">
        @RenderBody()
    </div>
</body>
</html>
```

This chapter uses controller views and Razor Pages to present similar content. To differentiate more readily between controllers and pages, add the route shown in Listing 27-2 to the Startup class.

Listing 27-2. Adding a Route in the Startup.cs File in the WebApp Folder

```
using Microsoft.AspNetCore.Builder;
using Microsoft.Extensions.DependencyInjection;
using Microsoft.Extensions.Configuration;
using Microsoft.EntityFrameworkCore;
using WebApp.Models;

namespace WebApp {
    public class Startup {

        public Startup(IConfiguration config) {
            Configuration = config;
        }

        public IConfiguration Configuration { get; set; }

        public void ConfigureServices(IServiceCollection services) {
            services.AddDbContext<DataContext>(opts => {
                opts.UseSqlServer(Configuration[
                    "ConnectionStrings:ProductConnection"]);
                opts.EnableSensitiveDataLogging(true);
            });
            services.AddControllersWithViews().AddRazorRuntimeCompilation();
            services.AddRazorPages().AddRazorRuntimeCompilation();
            services.AddSingleton<CitiesData>();
        }

        public void Configure(IApplicationBuilder app, DataContext context) {
            app.UseDeveloperExceptionPage();
            app.UseStaticFiles();
            app.UseRouting();
            app.UseEndpoints(endpoints => {
                endpoints.MapControllers();
                endpoints.MapControllerRoute("forms",
                    "controllers/{controller=Home}/{action=Index}/{id?}");
                endpoints.MapDefaultControllerRoute();
                endpoints.MapRazorPages();
            });
```

```
            SeedData.SeedDatabase(context);
        }
    }
}
```

The new route introduces a static path segment that makes it obvious that a URL targets a controller.

Dropping the Database

Open a new PowerShell command prompt, navigate to the folder that contains the WebApp.csproj file, and run the command shown in Listing 27-3 to drop the database.

Listing 27-3. Dropping the Database

```
dotnet ef database drop --force
```

Running the Example Application

Select Start Without Debugging or Run Without Debugging from the Debug menu or use the PowerShell command prompt to run the command shown in Listing 27-4.

Listing 27-4. Running the Example Application

```
dotnet run
```

Use a browser to request http://localhost:5000/controllers/home/list, which will display a list of products, as shown in Figure 27-1.

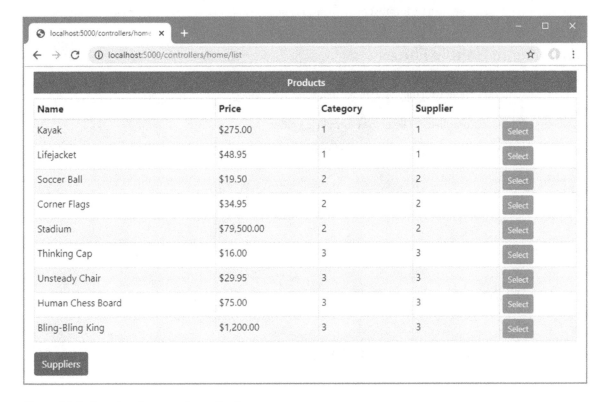

Figure 27-1. *Running the example application*

Understanding the Form Handling Pattern

Most HTML forms exist within a well-defined pattern, shown in Figure 27-2. First, the browser sends an HTTP GET request, which results in an HTML response containing a form, making it possible for the user to provide the application with data. The user clicks a button that submits the form data with an HTTP POST request, which allows the application to receive and process the user's data. Once the data has been processed, a response is sent that redirects the browser to a URL that provides confirmation of the user's actions.

Figure 27-2. *The HTML Post/Redirect/Get pattern*

This is known as the Post/Redirect/Get pattern, and the redirection is important because it means the user can click the browser's reload button without sending another POST request, which can lead to inadvertently repeating an operation.

In the sections that follow, I show how to follow the pattern with controllers and Razor Pages. I start with a basic implementation of the pattern and then demonstrate improvements using tag helpers and, in Chapter 28, the model binding feature.

Creating a Controller to Handle Forms

Controllers that handle forms are created by combining features described in earlier chapters. Add a class file named FormController.cs to the Controllers folder with the code shown in Listing 27-5.

Listing 27-5. The Contents of the FormController.cs File in the Controllers Folder

```
using Microsoft.AspNetCore.Mvc;
using System.Linq;
using System.Threading.Tasks;
using WebApp.Models;

namespace WebApp.Controllers {

    public class FormController : Controller {
        private DataContext context;

        public FormController(DataContext dbContext) {
            context = dbContext;
        }

        public async Task<IActionResult> Index(long id = 1) {
            return View("Form", await context.Products.FindAsync(id));
        }
```

```
[HttpPost]
public IActionResult SubmitForm() {
    foreach (string key in Request.Form.Keys
            .Where(k => !k.StartsWith("_"))) {
        TempData[key] = string.Join(", ", Request.Form[key]);
    }
    return RedirectToAction(nameof(Results));
}

public IActionResult Results() {
    return View(TempData);
}
    }
}
```

The Index action method selects a view named Form, which will render an HTML form to the user. When the user submits the form, it will be received by the SubmitForm action, which has been decorated with the HttpPost attribute so that it can only receive HTTP POST requests. This action method processes the HTML form data available through the HttpRequest.Form property so that it can be stored using the temp data feature. The temp data feature can be used to pass data from one request to another but can be used only to store simple data types. Each form data value is presented as a string array, which I convert to a single comma-separated string for storage. The browser is redirected to the Results action method, which selects the default view and provides the temp data as the view model.

■ **Tip** Only form data values whose name doesn't begin with an underscore are displayed. I explain why in the "Using the Anti-forgery Feature" section, later in this chapter.

To provide the controller with views, create the Views/Form folder and add to it a Razor view file named Form.cshtml with the content shown in Listing 27-6.

Listing 27-6. The Contents of the Form.cshtml File in the Views/Form Folder

```
@model Product
@{ Layout = "_SimpleLayout"; }

<h5 class="bg-primary text-white text-center p-2">HTML Form</h5>

<form action="/controllers/form/submitform" method="post">
    <div class="form-group">
        <label>Name</label>
        <input class="form-control" name="Name" value="@Model.Name" />
    </div>
    <button type="submit" class="btn btn-primary">Submit</button>
</form>
```

This view contains a simple HTML form that is configured to submit its data to the SubmitForm action method using a POST request. The form contains an input element whose value is set using a Razor expression. Next, add a Razor view named Results.cshtml to the Views/Forms folder with the content shown in Listing 27-7.

Listing 27-7. The Contents of the Results.cshtml File in the Views/Form Folder

```
@model TempDataDictionary
@{ Layout = "_SimpleLayout"; }

<table class="table table-striped table-bordered table-sm">
    <thead>
        <tr class="bg-primary text-white text-center">
            <th colspan="2">Form Data</th>
        </tr>
```

```
        </thead>
        <tbody>
            @foreach (string key in Model.Keys) {
                <tr>
                    <th>@key</th>
                    <td>@Model[key]</td>
                </tr>
            }
        </tbody>
    </table>
    <a class="btn btn-primary" asp-action="Index">Return</a>
```

This view displays the form data back to the user. I'll show you how to process form data in more useful ways in Chapter 31, but for this chapter the focus is on creating the forms, and seeing the data contained in the form is enough to get started.

Restart ASP.NET Core and use a browser to request `http://localhost:5000/controllers/form` to see the HTML form. Enter a value into the text field and click Submit to send a POST request, which will be handled by the `SubmitForm` action. The form data will be stored as temp data, and the browser will be redirected, producing the response shown in Figure 27-3.

Figure 27-3. *Using a controller to render and process an HTML form*

Creating a Razor Page to Handle Forms

The same pattern can be implemented using Razor Pages. One page is required to render and process the form data, and a second page displays the results. Add a Razor Page named `FormHandler.cshtml` to the `Pages` folder with the contents shown in Listing 27-8.

Listing 27-8. The Contents of the FormHandler.cshtml File in the Pages Folder

```
@page "/pages/form/{id:long?}"
@model FormHandlerModel
@using Microsoft.AspNetCore.Mvc.RazorPages

<div class="m-2">
    <h5 class="bg-primary text-white text-center p-2">HTML Form</h5>
    <form asp-page="FormHandler" method="post">
        <div class="form-group">
            <label>Name</label>
            <input class="form-control" name="Name" value="@Model.Product.Name" />
        </div>
        <button type="submit" class="btn btn-primary">Submit</button>
    </form>
</div>
```

```
@functions {

    [IgnoreAntiforgeryToken]
    public class FormHandlerModel : PageModel {
        private DataContext context;

        public FormHandlerModel(DataContext dbContext) {
            context = dbContext;
        }

        public Product Product { get; set; }

        public async Task OnGetAsync(long id = 1) {
            Product = await context.Products.FindAsync(id);
        }

        public IActionResult OnPost() {
            foreach (string key in Request.Form.Keys
                    .Where(k => !k.StartsWith("_"))) {
                TempData[key] = string.Join(", ", Request.Form[key]);
            }
            return RedirectToPage("FormResults");
        }
    }
}
```

The `OnGetAsync` handler methods retrieves a `Product` from the database, which is used by the view to set the value for the `input` element in the HTML form. The form is configured to send an HTTP POST request that will be processed by the `OnPost` handler method. The form data is stored as temp data, and the browser is sent a redirection to a form named `FormResults`. To create the page that the browser will be redirected to, add a Razor Page named `FormResults.cshtml` to the Pages folder with the content shown in Listing 27-9.

■ **Tip** The page model class in Listing 27-8 is decorated with the `IgnoreAntiforgeryToken` attribute, which is described in the "Using the Anti-forgery Feature" section.

Listing 27-9. The Contents of the FormResults.cshtml File in the Pages Folder

```
@page "/pages/results"

<div class="m-2">
    <table class="table table-striped table-bordered table-sm">
        <thead>
            <tr class="bg-primary text-white text-center">
                <th colspan="2">Form Data</th>
            </tr>
        </thead>
        <tbody>
            @foreach (string key in TempData.Keys) {
                <tr>
                    <th>@key</th>
                    <td>@TempData[key]</td>
                </tr>
            }
        </tbody>
    </table>
    <a class="btn btn-primary" asp-page="FormHandler">Return</a>
</div>
```

No code is required for this page, which accesses temp data directly and displays it in a table. Use a browser to navigate to http://localhost:5000/pages/form, enter a value into the text field, and click the Submit button. The form data will be processed by the OnPost method defined in Listing 27-9, and the browser will be redirected to /pages/results, which displays the form data, as shown in Figure 27-4.

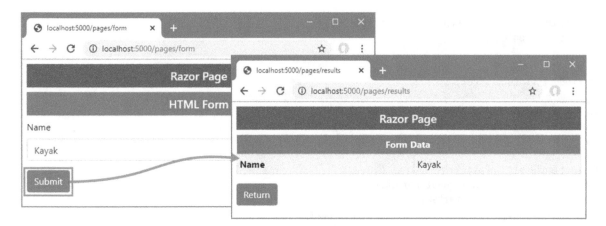

Figure 27-4. *Using Razor Pages to render and process an HTML form*

Using Tag Helpers to Improve HTML Forms

The examples in the previous section show the basic mechanisms for dealing with HTML forms, but ASP.NET Core includes tag helpers that transform form elements. In the sections that follow, I describe the tag helpers and demonstrate their use.

Working with Form Elements

The FormTagHelper class is the built-in tag helper for form elements and is used to manage the configuration of HTML forms so that they target the right action or page handler without the need to hard-code URLs. This tag helper supports the attributes described in Table 27-3.

Table 27-3. *The Built-in Tag Helper Attributes for Form Elements*

Name	Description
asp-controller	This attribute is used to specify the controller value to the routing system for the action attribute URL. If omitted, then the controller rendering the view will be used.
asp-action	This attribute is used to specify the action method for the action value to the routing system for the action attribute URL. If omitted, then the action rendering the view will be used.
asp-page	This attribute is used to specify the name of a Razor Page.
asp-page-handler	This attribute is used to specify the name of the handler method that will be used to process the request. You can see an example of this attribute in the SportsStore application in Chapter 9.
asp-route-*	Attributes whose name begins with asp-route- are used to specify additional values for the action attribute URL so that the asp-route-id attribute is used to provide a value for the id segment to the routing system.
asp-route	This attribute is used to specify the name of the route that will be used to generate the URL for the action attribute.
asp-antiforgery	This attribute controls whether anti-forgery information is added to the view, as described in the "Using the Anti-forgery Feature" section.
asp-fragment	This attribute specifies a fragment for the generated URL.

Setting the Form Target

The FormTagHelper transforms form elements so they target an action method or Razor Page without the need for hard-coded URLs. The attributes supported by this tag helper work in the same way as for anchor elements, described in Chapter 26, and use attributes to provide values that help generate URLs through the ASP.NET Core routing system. Listing 27-10 modifies the form element in the Form view to apply the tag helper.

■ **Note** If a form element is defined without a method attribute, then the tag helper will add one with the post value, meaning that the form will be submitted using an HTTP POST request. This can lead to surprising results if you omitted the method attribute because you expect the browser to follow the HTML5 specification and send the form using an HTTP GET request. It is a good idea to always specify the method attribute so that it is obvious how the form should be submitted.

Listing 27-10. Using a Tag Helper in the Form.cshtml File in the Views/Form Folder

```
@model Product
@{ Layout = "_SimpleLayout"; }

<h5 class="bg-primary text-white text-center p-2">HTML Form</h5>

<form asp-action="submitform" method="post">
    <div class="form-group">
        <label>Name</label>
        <input class="form-control" name="Name" value="@Model.Name" />
    </div>
    <button type="submit" class="btn btn-primary">Submit</button>
</form>
```

The asp-action attribute is used to specify the name of the action that will receive the HTTP request. The routing system is used to generate the URLs, just as for the anchor elements described in Chapter 26. The asp-controller attribute has not been used in Listing 27-10, which means the controller that rendered the view will be used in the URL.

The asp-page attribute is used to select a Razor Page as the target for the form, as shown in Listing 27-11.

Listing 27-11. Setting the Form Target in the FormHandler.cshtml File in the Pages Folder

```
...
<div class="m-2">
    <h5 class="bg-primary text-white text-center p-2">HTML Form</h5>
    <form asp-page="FormHandler" method="post">
        <div class="form-group">
            <label>Name</label>
            <input class="form-control" name="Name" value="@Model.Product.Name" />
        </div>
        <button type="submit" class="btn btn-primary">Submit</button>
    </form>
</div>
...
```

Use a browser to navigate to http://localhost:5000/controllers/form and examine the HTML received by the browser; you will see that the tag helper as added the action attribute to the form element like this:

```
...
<form method="post" action="controllers/Form/submitform">
...
```

This is the same URL that I defined statically when I created the view but with the advantage that changes to the routing configuration will be reflected automatically in the form URL. Request `http://localhost:5000/pages/form`, and you will see that the `form` element has been transformed to target the page URL, like this:

```
...
<form method="post" action="/pages/form">
...
```

Transforming Form Buttons

The buttons that send forms can be defined outside of the `form` element. In these situations, the button has a `form` attribute whose value corresponds to the `id` attribute of the form element it relates to and a `formaction` attribute that specifies the target URL for the form.

The tag helper will generate the `formaction` attribute through the `asp-action`, `asp-controller`, or `asp-page` attributes, as shown in Listing 27-12.

Listing 27-12. Transforming a Button in the Form.cshtml File in the Views/Form Folder

```
@model Product
@{ Layout = "_SimpleLayout"; }

<h5 class="bg-primary text-white text-center p-2">HTML Form</h5>

<form asp-action="submitform" method="post" id="htmlform">
    <div class="form-group">
        <label>Name</label>
        <input class="form-control" name="Name" value="@Model.Name" />
    </div>
    <button type="submit" class="btn btn-primary">Submit</button>
</form>

<button form="htmlform" asp-action="submitform" class="btn btn-primary mt-2">
    Sumit (Outside Form)
</button>
```

The value of the `id` attribute added to the `form` element is used by the `button` as the value of the `form` attribute, which tells the browser which form to submit when the button is clicked. The attributes described in Table 27-3 are used to identify the target for the form, and the tag helper will use the routing system to generate a URL when the view is rendered. Listing 27-13 applies the same technique to the Razor Page.

Listing 27-13. Transforming a Button in the FormHandler.cshtml File in the Pages Folder

```
...
<div class="m-2">
    <h5 class="bg-primary text-white text-center p-2">HTML Form</h5>
    <form asp-page="FormHandler" method="post" id="htmlform">
        <div class="form-group">
            <label>Name</label>
            <input class="form-control" name="Name" value="@Model.Product.Name" />
        </div>
        <button type="submit" class="btn btn-primary">Submit</button>
    </form>
    <button form="htmlform" asp-page="FormHandler" class="btn btn-primary mt-2">
        Sumit (Outside Form)
    </button>
</div>
...
```

Use a browser to request `http://localhost:5000/controllers/form` or `http://localhost:5000/pages/form` and inspect the HTML sent to the browser. You will see the `button` element outside of the form has been transformed like this:

```
...
<button form="htmlform" class="btn btn-primary mt-2"
        formaction="/controllers/Form/submitform">
    Sumit (Outside Form)
</button>
...
```

Clicking the button submits the form, just as for a button that is defined within the form element, as shown in Figure 27-5.

Figure 27-5. *Defining a button outside of a form element*

Working with input Elements

The `input` element is the backbone of HTML forms and provides the main means by which a user can provide an application with unstructured data. The `InputTagHelper` class is used to transform `input` elements so they reflect the data type and format of a view model property they are used to gather, using the attributes described in Table 27-4.

Table 27-4. *The Built-in Tag Helper Attributes for input Elements*

Name	Description
asp-for	This attribute is used to specify the view model property that the input element represents.
asp-format	This attribute is used to specify a format used for the value of the view model property that the input element represents.

The `asp-for` attribute is set to the name of a view model property, which is then used to set the `name`, `id`, `type`, and `value` attributes of the input element. Listing 27-14 modifies the input element in the controller view to use the `asp-for` attribute.

Listing 27-14. Configuring an input Element in the Form.cshtml File in the Views/Form Folder

```
@model Product
@{  Layout = "_SimpleLayout"; }

<h5 class="bg-primary text-white text-center p-2">HTML Form</h5>

<form asp-action="submitform" method="post" id="htmlform">
    <div class="form-group">
        <label>Name</label>
```

```
            <input class="form-control" asp-for="Name" />
        </div>
        <button type="submit" class="btn btn-primary">Submit</button>
</form>

<button form="htmlform" asp-action="submitform" class="btn btn-primary mt-2">
    Sumit (Outside Form)
</button>
```

This tag helper uses a model expression, described in Listing 27-14, which is why the value for the asp-for attribute is specified without the @ character. If you inspect the HTML the application returns when using a browser to request http://localhost:5000/controllers/form, you will see the tag helper has transformed the input element like this:

```
...
<div class="form-group">
    <label>Name</label>
    <input class="form-control" type="text" id="Name" name="Name" value="Kayak">
</div>
...
```

The values for the id and name attributes are obtained through the model expression, ensuring that you don't introduce typos when creating the form. The other attributes are more complex and are described in the sections that follow.

SELECTING MODEL PROPERTIES IN RAZOR PAGES

The asp-for attribute for this and the other tag helpers described in this chapter can be used for Razor Pages, but the value for the name and id attributes in the transformed element includes the name of the page model property. For example, this element selects the Name property through the page model's Product property:

```
...
<input class="form-control" asp-for="Product.Name" />
...
```

The transformed element will have the following id and name attributes:

```
...
<input class="form-control" type="text" id="Product_Name" name="Product.Name" >
...
```

This difference is important when using the model binding feature to receive form data, as described in Chapter 28.

Transforming the input Element type Attribute

The input element's type attribute tells the browser how to display the element and how it should restrict the values the user enters. The input element in Listing 27-14 is configured to the text type, which is the default input element type and offers no restrictions. Listing 27-15 adds another input element to the form, which will provide a more useful demonstration of how the type attribute is handled.

Listing 27-15. Adding an input Element in the Form.cshtml File in the Views/Form Folder

```
@model Product
@{ Layout = "_SimpleLayout"; }

<h5 class="bg-primary text-white text-center p-2">HTML Form</h5>

<form asp-action="submitform" method="post" id="htmlform">
    <div class="form-group">
        <label>Id</label>
        <input class="form-control" asp-for="ProductId" />
    </div>
```

```
    <div class="form-group">
        <label>Name</label>
        <input class="form-control" asp-for="Name" />
    </div>
    <button type="submit" class="btn btn-primary">Submit</button>
</form>

<button form="htmlform" asp-action="submitform" class="btn btn-primary mt-2">
    Sumit (Outside Form)
</button>
```

The new element uses the asp-for attribute to select the view model's ProductId property. Use a browser to request http://localhost:5000/controllers/form to see how the tag helper has transformed the element.

```
...
<div class="form-group">
    <label>Id</label>
    <input class="form-control" type="number" data-val="true"
        data-val-required="The ProductId field is required."
        id="ProductId" name="ProductId" value="1">
</div>
...
```

The value of the type attribute is determined by the type of the view model property specified by the asp-for attribute. The type of the ProductId property is the C# long type, which has led the tag helper to set the input element's type attribute to number, which restricts the element so it will accept only numeric characters. The data-val and data-val-required attributes are added to the input element to assist with validation, which is described in Chapter 29. Table 27-5 describes how different C# types are used to set the type attribute of input elements.

■ **Note**   There is latitude in how the type attribute is interpreted by browsers. Not all browsers respond to all the type values that are defined in the HTML5 specification, and when they do, there are differences in how they are implemented. The type attribute can be a useful hint for the kind of data that you are expecting in a form, but you should use the model validation feature to ensure that users provide usable data, as described in Chapter 29.

Table 27-5. *C# Property Types and the Input Type Elements They Generate*

C# Type	input Element type Attribute
byte, sbyte, int, uint, short, ushort, long, ulong	number
float, double, decimal	text, with additional attributes for model validation, as described in Chapter 29
bool	checkbox
string	text
DateTime	datetime

The float, double, and decimal types produce input elements whose type is text because not all browsers allow the full range of characters that can be used to express legal values of this type. To provide feedback to the user, the tag helper adds attributes to the input element that are used with the validation features described in Chapter 29.

You can override the default mappings shown in Table 27-5 by explicitly defining the type attribute on input elements. The tag helper won't override the value you define, which allows you to specify a type attribute value.

The drawback of this approach is that you must remember to set the type attribute in all the views where input elements are generated for a given model property. A more elegant—and reliable approach—is to apply one of the attributes described in Table 27-6 to the property in the C# model class.

> **Tip** The tag helper will set the `type` attribute of `input` elements to `text` if the model property isn't one of the types in Table 27-5 and has not been decorated with an attribute.

Table 27-6. *The Input Type Elements Attributes*

Attribute	input Element type Attribute
[HiddenInput]	hidden
[Text]	text
[Phone]	tel
[Url]	url
[EmailAddress]	email
[DataType(DataType.Password)]	password
[DataType(DataType.Time)]	time
[DataType(DataType.Date)]	date

Formatting input Element Values

When the action method provides the view with a view model object, the tag helper uses the value of the property given to the asp-for attribute to set the `input` element's value attribute. The `asp-format` attribute is used to specify how that data value is formatted. To demonstrate the default formatting, Listing 27-16 adds a new `input` element to the `Form` view.

Listing 27-16. Adding an Element in the Form.cshtml File in the Views/Form Folder

```
@model Product
@{ Layout = "_SimpleLayout"; }

<h5 class="bg-primary text-white text-center p-2">HTML Form</h5>

<form asp-action="submitform" method="post" id="htmlform">
    <div class="form-group">
        <label>Id</label>
        <input class="form-control" asp-for="ProductId" />
    </div>
    <div class="form-group">
        <label>Name</label>
        <input class="form-control" asp-for="Name" />
    </div>
    <div class="form-group">
        <label>Price</label>
        <input class="form-control" asp-for="Price" />
    </div>
    <button type="submit" class="btn btn-primary">Submit</button>
</form>

<button form="htmlform" asp-action="submitform" class="btn btn-primary mt-2">
    Sumit (Outside Form)
</button>
```

Use a browser to navigate to `http://localhost:5000/controllers/form/index/5` and examine the HTML the browser receives. By default, the `value` of the `input` element is set using the value of the model property, like this:

```
...
<input class="form-control" type="text" data-val="true"
    data-val-number="The field Price must be a number."
    data-val-required="The Price field is required."
    id="Price" name="Price" value="79500.00">
...
```

This format, with two decimal places, is how the value is stored in the database. In Chapter 26, I used the Column attribute to select a SQL type to store Price values, like this:

```
...
[Column(TypeName = "decimal(8, 2)")]
public decimal Price { get; set; }
...
```

This type specifies a maximum precision of eight digits, two of which will appear after the decimal place. This allows a maximum value of 999,999.99, which is enough to represent prices for most online stores. The asp-format attribute accepts a format string that will be passed to the standard C# string formatting system, as shown in Listing 27-17.

Listing 27-17. Formatting a Data Value in the Form.cshtml File in the Views/Form Folder

```
@model Product
@{ Layout = "_SimpleLayout"; }

<h5 class="bg-primary text-white text-center p-2">HTML Form</h5>

<form asp-action="submitform" method="post" id="htmlform">
    <div class="form-group">
        <label>Id</label>
        <input class="form-control" asp-for="ProductId" />
    </div>
    <div class="form-group">
        <label>Name</label>
        <input class="form-control" asp-for="Name" />
    </div>
    <div class="form-group">
        <label>Price</label>
        <input class="form-control" asp-for="Price" asp-format="{0:#,###.00}" />
    </div>
    <button type="submit" class="btn btn-primary">Submit</button>
</form>

<button form="htmlform" asp-action="submitform" class="btn btn-primary mt-2">
    Sumit (Outside Form)
</button>
```

The attribute value is used verbatim, which means you must include the curly brace characters and the 0: reference, as well as the format you require. Refresh the browser, and you will see that the value for the input element has been formatted, like this:

```
...
<input class="form-control" type="text" data-val="true"
    data-val-number="The field Price must be a number."
    data-val-required="The Price field is required."
    id="Price" name="Price" value="79,500.00">
...
```

This feature should be used with caution because you must ensure that the rest of the application is configured to support the format you use and that the format you create contains only legal characters for the input element type.

Applying Formatting via the Model Class

If you always want to use the same formatting for a model property, then you can decorate the C# class with the DisplayFormat attribute, which is defined in the System.ComponentModel.DataAnnotations namespace. The DisplayFormat attribute requires two arguments to format a data value: the DataFormatString argument specifies the formatting string, and setting the ApplyFormatInEditMode to true specifies that formatting should be used when values are being applied to elements used for editing, including the input element. Listing 27-18 applies the attribute to the Price property of the Product class, specifying a different formatting string from earlier examples.

Listing 27-18. Applying a Formatting Attribute to the Product.cs File in the Models Folder

```
using System.ComponentModel.DataAnnotations.Schema;
using System.ComponentModel.DataAnnotations;

namespace WebApp.Models {
    public class Product {

        public long ProductId { get; set; }

        public string Name { get; set; }

        [Column(TypeName = "decimal(8, 2)")]
        [DisplayFormat(DataFormatString = "{0:c2}", ApplyFormatInEditMode = true)]
        public decimal Price { get; set; }

        public long CategoryId { get; set; }
        public Category Category { get; set; }

        public long SupplierId { get; set; }
        public Supplier Supplier { get; set; }
    }
}
```

The asp-format attribute takes precedence over the DisplayFormat attribute, so I have removed the attribute from the view, as shown in Listing 27-19.

Listing 27-19. Removing an Attribute in the Form.cshtml File in the Views/Form Folder

```
@model Product
@{ Layout = "_SimpleLayout"; }

<h5 class="bg-primary text-white text-center p-2">HTML Form</h5>

<form asp-action="submitform" method="post" id="htmlform">
    <div class="form-group">
        <label>Id</label>
        <input class="form-control" asp-for="ProductId" />
    </div>
    <div class="form-group">
        <label>Name</label>
        <input class="form-control" asp-for="Name" />
    </div>
    <div class="form-group">
        <label>Price</label>
        <input class="form-control" asp-for="Price" />
    </div>
    <button type="submit" class="btn btn-primary">Submit</button>
</form>

<button form="htmlform" asp-action="submitform" class="btn btn-primary mt-2">
    Sumit (Outside Form)
</button>
```

Restart ASP.NET Core and use a browser to request `http://localhost:5000/controllers/form/index/5`, and you will see that the formatting string defined by the attribute has been applied, as shown in Figure 27-6.

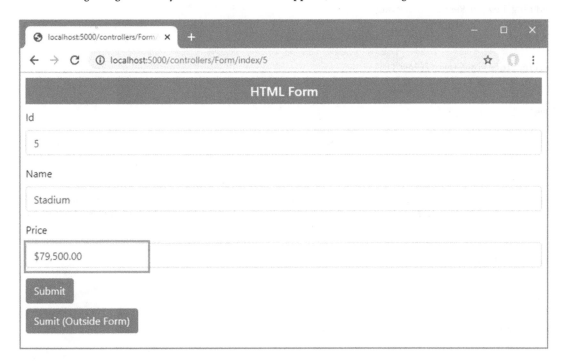

Figure 27-6. *Formatting data values*

I chose this format to demonstrate the way the formatting attribute works, but, as noted previously, care must be taken to ensure that the application is able to process the formatted values using the model binding and validation features described in Chapters 28 and 29.

Displaying Values from Related Data in input Elements

When using Entity Framework Core, you will often need to display data values that are obtained from related data, which is easily done using the `asp-for` attribute because a model expression allows the nested navigation properties to be selected. First, Listing 27-20 includes related data in the view model object provided to the view.

Listing 27-20. Including Related Data in the FormController.cs File in the Controllers Folder

```
using Microsoft.AspNetCore.Mvc;
using System.Linq;
using System.Threading.Tasks;
using WebApp.Models;
using Microsoft.EntityFrameworkCore;

namespace WebApp.Controllers {

    public class FormController : Controller {
        private DataContext context;

        public FormController(DataContext dbContext) {
            context = dbContext;
        }

        public async Task<IActionResult> Index(long id = 1) {
            return View("Form", await context.Products.Include(p => p.Category)
                .Include(p => p.Supplier).FirstAsync(p => p.ProductId == id));
        }
```

```
        [HttpPost]
        public IActionResult SubmitForm() {
            foreach (string key in Request.Form.Keys
                    .Where(k => !k.StartsWith("_"))) {
                TempData[key] = string.Join(", ", Request.Form[key]);
            }
            return RedirectToAction(nameof(Results));
        }

        public IActionResult Results() {
            return View(TempData);
        }
    }
}
```

Notice that I don't need to worry about dealing with circular references in the related data because the view model object isn't serialized. The circular reference issue is important only for web service controllers. In Listing 27-21, I have updated the Form view to include input elements that use the asp-for attribute to select related data.

Listing 27-21. Displaying Related Data in the Form.cshtml File in the Views/Form Folder

```
@model Product
@{ Layout = "_SimpleLayout"; }

<h5 class="bg-primary text-white text-center p-2">HTML Form</h5>

<form asp-action="submitform" method="post" id="htmlform">
    <div class="form-group">
        <label>Id</label>
        <input class="form-control" asp-for="ProductId" />
    </div>
    <div class="form-group">
        <label>Name</label>
        <input class="form-control" asp-for="Name" />
    </div>
    <div class="form-group">
        <label>Price</label>
        <input class="form-control" asp-for="Price" />
    </div>
    <div class="form-group">
        <label>Category</label>
        <input class="form-control" asp-for="Category.Name" />
    </div>
    <div class="form-group">
        <label>Supplier</label>
        <input class="form-control" asp-for="Supplier.Name" />
    </div>
    <button type="submit" class="btn btn-primary">Submit</button>
</form>

<button form="htmlform" asp-action="submitform" class="btn btn-primary mt-2">
    Sumit (Outside Form)
</button>
```

The value of the asp-for attribute is expressed relative to the view model object and can include nested properties, allowing me to select the Name properties of the related objects that Entity Framework Core has assigned to the Category and Supplier navigation properties. The same technique is used in Razor Pages, except that the properties are expressed relative to the page model object, as shown in Listing 27-22.

Listing 27-22. Displayed Related Data in the FormHandler.cshtml File in the Pages Folder

```
@page "/pages/form/{id:long?}"
@model FormHandlerModel
@using Microsoft.AspNetCore.Mvc.RazorPages
@using Microsoft.EntityFrameworkCore

<div class="m-2">
    <h5 class="bg-primary text-white text-center p-2">HTML Form</h5>
    <form asp-page="FormHandler" method="post" id="htmlform">
        <div class="form-group">
            <label>Name</label>
            <input class="form-control" asp-for="Product.Name" />
        </div>
        <div class="form-group">
            <label>Price</label>
            <input class="form-control" asp-for="Product.Price" />
        </div>
        <div class="form-group">
            <label>Category</label>
            <input class="form-control" asp-for="Product.Category.Name" />
        </div>
        <div class="form-group">
            <label>Supplier</label>
            <input class="form-control" asp-for="Product.Supplier.Name" />
        </div>
        <button type="submit" class="btn btn-primary">Submit</button>
    </form>
    <button form="htmlform" asp-page="FormHandler" class="btn btn-primary mt-2">
        Sumit (Outside Form)
    </button>
</div>

@functions {

    [IgnoreAntiforgeryToken]
    public class FormHandlerModel : PageModel {
        private DataContext context;

        public FormHandlerModel(DataContext dbContext) {
            context = dbContext;
        }

        public Product Product { get; set; }

        public async Task OnGetAsync(long id = 1) {
            Product = await context.Products.Include(p => p.Category)
                .Include(p => p.Supplier).FirstAsync(p => p.ProductId == id);
        }
```

```
        public IActionResult OnPost() {
            foreach (string key in Request.Form.Keys
                    .Where(k => !k.StartsWith("_"))) {
                TempData[key] = string.Join(", ", Request.Form[key]);
            }
            return RedirectToPage("FormResults");
        }
    }
}
```

To see the effect, restart ASP.NET Core so the changes to the controller take effect, and use a browser to request http://localhost:5000/controller/form, which produces the response shown on the left of Figure 27-7. Use the browser to request http://localhost:5000/pages/form, and you will see the same features used by the Razor Page, as shown on the right of Figure 27-7.

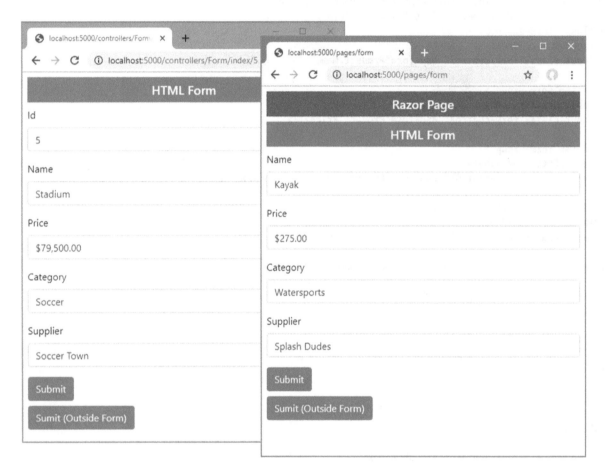

Figure 27-7. *Displaying related data*

Working with label Elements

The LabelTagHelper class is used to transform label elements so the for attribute is set consistently with the approach used to transform input elements. Table 27-7 describes the attribute supported by this tag helper.

Table 27-7. *The Built-in Tag Helper Attribute for label Elements*

Name	Description
asp-for	This attribute is used to specify the view model property that the label element describes.

The tag helper sets the content of the label element so that it contains the name of the selected view model property. The tag helper also sets the for attribute, which denotes an association with a specific input element. This aids users who rely on screen readers and allows an input element to gain the focus when its associated label is clicked.

Listing 27-23 applies the asp-for attribute to the Form view to associate each label element with the input element that represents the same view model property.

Listing 27-23. Transforming label Elements in the Form.cshtml File in the Views/Form Folder

```
@model Product
@{ Layout = "_SimpleLayout"; }

<h5 class="bg-primary text-white text-center p-2">HTML Form</h5>

<form asp-action="submitform" method="post" id="htmlform">
    <div class="form-group">
        <label asp-for="ProductId"></label>
        <input class="form-control" asp-for="ProductId" />
    </div>
    <div class="form-group">
        <label asp-for="Name"></label>
        <input class="form-control" asp-for="Name" />
    </div>
    <div class="form-group">
        <label asp-for="Price"></label>
        <input class="form-control" asp-for="Price" />
    </div>
    <div class="form-group">
        <label asp-for="Category.Name">Category</label>
        <input class="form-control" asp-for="Category.Name" />
    </div>
    <div class="form-group">
        <label asp-for="Supplier.Name">Supplier</label>
        <input class="form-control" asp-for="Supplier.Name" />
    </div>
    <button type="submit" class="btn btn-primary">Submit</button>
</form>

<button form="htmlform" asp-action="submitform" class="btn btn-primary mt-2">
    Sumit (Outside Form)
</button>
```

You can override the content for a label element by defining it yourself, which is what I have done for the related data properties in Listing 27-23. The tag helper would have set the content for both these label elements to be Name, which is not a useful description. Defining the element content means the for attribute will be applied, but a more useful name will be displayed to the user. Use a browser to request http://localhost:5000/controllers/form to see the names used for each element, as shown in Figure 27-8.

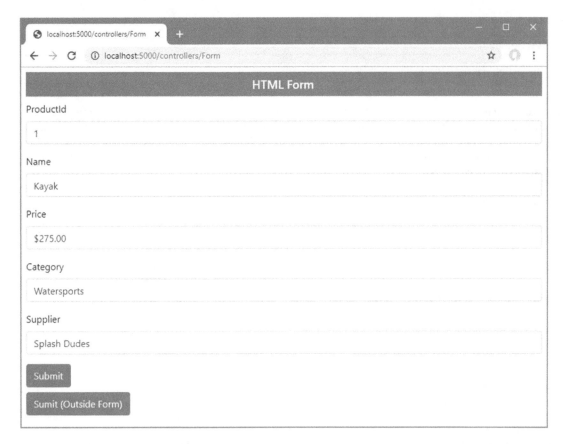

Figure 27-8. *Transforming label elements*

Working with Select and Option Elements

The select and option elements are used to provide the user with a fixed set of choices, rather than the open data entry that is possible with an input element. The SelectTagHelper is responsible for transforming select elements and supports the attributes described in Table 27-8.

Table 27-8. *The Built-in Tag Helper Attributes for select Elements*

Name	Description
asp-for	This attribute is used to specify the view or page model property that the select element represents.
asp-items	This attribute is used to specify a source of values for the option elements contained within the select element.

The asp-for attribute sets the value of the for and id attributes to reflect the model property that it receives. In Listing 27-24, I have replaced the input element for the category with a select element that presents the user with a fixed range of values.

Listing 27-24. Using a select Element in the Form.cshtml File in the Views/Form Folder

```
@model Product
@{ Layout = "_SimpleLayout"; }

<h5 class="bg-primary text-white text-center p-2">HTML Form</h5>

<form asp-action="submitform" method="post" id="htmlform">
    <div class="form-group">
        <label asp-for="ProductId"></label>
```

```
            <input class="form-control" asp-for="ProductId" />
        </div>
        <div class="form-group">
            <label asp-for="Name"></label>
            <input class="form-control" asp-for="Name" />
        </div>
        <div class="form-group">
            <label asp-for="Price"></label>
            <input class="form-control" asp-for="Price" />
        </div>
        <div class="form-group">
            <label asp-for="Category.Name">Category</label>
            <select class="form-control" asp-for="CategoryId">
                <option value="1">Watersports</option>
                <option value="2">Soccer</option>
                <option value="3">Chess</option>
            </select>
        </div>
        <div class="form-group">
            <label asp-for="Supplier.Name">Supplier</label>
            <input class="form-control" asp-for="Supplier.Name" />
        </div>
        <button type="submit" class="btn btn-primary">Submit</button>
</form>

<button form="htmlform" asp-action="submitform" class="btn btn-primary mt-2">
    Sumit (Outside Form)
</button>
```

I have manually populated the select element with option elements that provide a range of categories for the user to choose from. If you use a browser to request http://localhost:5000/controllers/form/index/5 and examine the HTML response, you will see that the tag helper has transformed the select element like this:

```
...
<div class="form-group">
    <label for="Category_Name">Category</label>
    <select class="form-control" data-val="true"
        data-val-required="The CategoryId field is required."
        id="CategoryId" name="CategoryId">
        <option value="1">Watersports</option>
        <option value="2" selected="selected">Soccer</option>
        <option value="3">Chess</option>
    </select>
</div>
...
```

Notice that selected attribute has been added to the option element that corresponds to the view model's CategoryId value, like this:

```
...
<option value="2" selected="selected">Soccer</option>
...
```

The task of selecting an option element is performed by the OptionTagHelper class, which receives instructions from the SelectTagHelper through the TagHelperContext.Items collection, described in Chapter 25. The result is that the select element displays the name of the category associated with the Product object's CategoryId value.

Populating a select Element

Explicitly defining the option elements for a select element is a useful approach for choices that always have the same possible values but doesn't help when you need to provide options that are taken from the data model or where you need the same set of options in multiple views and don't want to manually maintain duplicated content.

The asp-items attribute is used to provide the tag helper with a list sequence of SelectListItem objects for which option elements will be generated. Listing 27-25 modifies the Index action of the Form controller to provide the view with a sequence of SelectListItem objects through the view bag.

Listing 27-25. Providing a Data Sequence in the FormController.cs File in the Controllers Folder

```
using Microsoft.AspNetCore.Mvc;
using System.Linq;
using System.Threading.Tasks;
using WebApp.Models;
using Microsoft.EntityFrameworkCore;
using Microsoft.AspNetCore.Mvc.Rendering;

namespace WebApp.Controllers {

    public class FormController : Controller {
        private DataContext context;

        public FormController(DataContext dbContext) {
            context = dbContext;
        }

        public async Task<IActionResult> Index(long id = 1) {
            ViewBag.Categories
                = new SelectList(context.Categories, "CategoryId", "Name");
            return View("Form", await context.Products.Include(p => p.Category)
                .Include(p => p.Supplier).FirstAsync(p => p.ProductId == id));
        }

        [HttpPost]
        public IActionResult SubmitForm() {
            foreach (string key in Request.Form.Keys
                    .Where(k => !k.StartsWith("_"))) {
                TempData[key] = string.Join(", ", Request.Form[key]);
            }
            return RedirectToAction(nameof(Results));
        }

        public IActionResult Results() {
            return View(TempData);
        }
    }
}
```

SelectListItem objects can be created directly, but ASP.NET Core provides the SelectList class to adapt existing data sequences. In this case, I pass the sequence of Category objects obtained from the database to the SelectList constructor, along with the names of the properties that should be used as the values and labels for option elements. In Listing 27-26, I have updated the Form view to use the SelectList.

Listing 27-26. Using a SelectList in the Form.cshtml File in the Views/Form Folder

```
@model Product
@{  Layout = "_SimpleLayout"; }

<h5 class="bg-primary text-white text-center p-2">HTML Form</h5>

<form asp-action="submitform" method="post" id="htmlform">
    <div class="form-group">
        <label asp-for="ProductId"></label>
        <input class="form-control" asp-for="ProductId" />
    </div>
    <div class="form-group">
        <label asp-for="Name"></label>
        <input class="form-control" asp-for="Name" />
    </div>
    <div class="form-group">
        <label asp-for="Price"></label>
        <input class="form-control" asp-for="Price" />
    </div>
    <div class="form-group">
        <label asp-for="Category.Name">Category</label>
        <select class="form-control" asp-for="CategoryId"
            asp-items="@ViewBag.Categories">
        </select>
    </div>
    <div class="form-group">
        <label asp-for="Supplier.Name">Supplier</label>
        <input class="form-control" asp-for="Supplier.Name" />
    </div>
    <button type="submit" class="btn btn-primary">Submit</button>
</form>

<button form="htmlform" asp-action="submitform" class="btn btn-primary mt-2">
    Sumit (Outside Form)
</button>
```

Restart ASP.NET Core so the changes to the controller take effect and use a browser to request http://localhost:5000/
controllers/form/index/5. There is no visual change to the content presented to the user, but the option elements used to
populate the select element have been generated from the database, like this:

```
...
<div class="form-group">
    <label for="Category_Name">Category</label>
    <select class="form-control" data-val="true"
            data-val-required="The CategoryId field is required."
            id="CategoryId" name="CategoryId">
        <option value="1">Watersports</option>
        <option selected="selected" value="2">Soccer</option>
        <option value="3">Chess</option>
    </select>
</div>
...
```

This approach means that the options presented to the user will automatically reflect new categories added to the database.

Working with Text Areas

The textarea element is used to solicit a larger amount of text from the user and is typically used for unstructured data, such as notes or observations. The TextAreaTagHelper is responsible for transforming textarea elements and supports the single attribute described in Table 27-9.

Table 27-9. *The Built-in Tag Helper Attributes for TextArea Elements*

Name	Description
asp-for	This attribute is used to specify the view model property that the textarea element represents.

The TextAreaTagHelper is relatively simple, and the value provided for the asp-for attribute is used to set the id and name attributes on the textarea element. The value of the property selected by the asp-for attribute is used as the content for the textarea element. Listing 27-27 replaces the input element for the Supplier.Name property with a text area to which the asp-for attribute has been applied.

Listing 27-27. Using a Text Area in the Form.cshtml File in the Views/Form Folder

```
@model Product
@{ Layout = "_SimpleLayout"; }

<h5 class="bg-primary text-white text-center p-2">HTML Form</h5>

<form asp-action="submitform" method="post" id="htmlform">
    <div class="form-group">
        <label asp-for="ProductId"></label>
        <input class="form-control" asp-for="ProductId" />
    </div>
    <div class="form-group">
        <label asp-for="Name"></label>
        <input class="form-control" asp-for="Name" />
    </div>
    <div class="form-group">
        <label asp-for="Price"></label>
        <input class="form-control" asp-for="Price" />
    </div>
    <div class="form-group">
        <label asp-for="Category.Name">Category</label>
        <select class="form-control" asp-for="CategoryId"
            asp-items="@ViewBag.Categories">
        </select>
    </div>
    <div class="form-group">
        <label asp-for="Supplier.Name">Supplier</label>
        <textarea class="form-control" asp-for="Supplier.Name"></textarea>
    </div>
    <button type="submit" class="btn btn-primary">Submit</button>
</form>

<button form="htmlform" asp-action="submitform" class="btn btn-primary mt-2">
    Sumit (Outside Form)
</button>
```

Use a browser to request http://localhost:5000/controllers/form and examine the HTML received by the browser to see the transformation of the textarea element.

```
...
<div class="form-group">
    <label for="Supplier_Name">Supplier</label>
    <textarea class="form-control" id="Supplier_Name" name="Supplier.Name">
        Soccer Town
    </textarea>
</div>
...
```

The TextAreaTagHelper is relatively simple, but it provides consistency with the rest of the form element tag helpers that I have described in this chapter.

Using the Anti-forgery Feature

When I defined the controller action method and page handler methods that process form data, I filtered out form data whose name begins with an underscore, like this:

```
...
[HttpPost]
public IActionResult SubmitForm() {
    foreach (string key in Request.Form.Keys
            .Where(k => !k.StartsWith("_"))) {
        TempData[key] = string.Join(", ", Request.Form[key]);
    }
    return RedirectToAction(nameof(Results));
}
...
```

I applied this filter to hide a feature to focus on the values provided by the HTML elements in the form. Listing 27-28 removes the filter from the action method so that all the data received from the HTML form is stored in temp data.

Listing 27-28. Removing a Filter in the FormController.cs File in the Controllers Folder

```
...
[HttpPost]
public IActionResult SubmitForm() {
    foreach (string key in Request.Form.Keys) {
        TempData[key] = string.Join(", ", Request.Form[key]);
    }
    return RedirectToAction(nameof(Results));
}
...
```

Restart ASP.NET Core and use a browser to request http://localhost:5000/controllers. Click the Submit button to send the form to the application, and you will see a new item in the results, as shown in Figure 27-9.

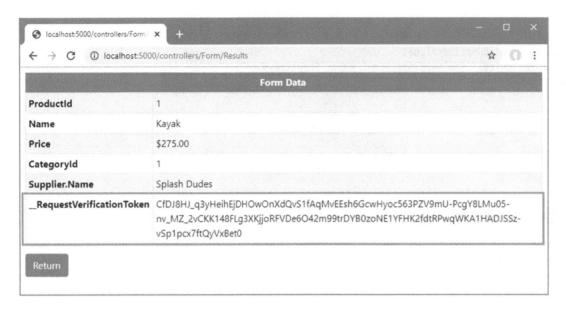

Figure 27-9. *Showing all form data*

The _RequestVerificationToken form value displayed in the results is a security feature that is applied by the FormTagHelper to guard against cross-site request forgery. Cross-site request forgery (CSRF) exploits web applications by taking advantage of the way that user requests are typically authenticated. Most web applications—including those created using ASP.NET Core—use cookies to identify which requests are related to a specific session, with which a user identity is usually associated.

CSRF—also known as *XSRF*—relies on the user visiting a malicious website after using your web application and without explicitly ending their session. The application still regards the user's session as being active, and the cookie that the browser has stored has not yet expired. The malicious site contains JavaScript code that sends a form request to your application to perform an operation without the user's consent—the exact nature of the operation will depend on the application being attacked. Since the JavaScript code is executed by the user's browser, the request to the application includes the session cookie, and the application performs the operation without the user's knowledge or consent.

■ **Tip** CSRF is described in detail at http://en.wikipedia.org/wiki/Cross-site_request_forgery.

If a form element doesn't contain an action attribute—because it is being generated from the routing system with the asp-controller, asp-action, and asp-page attributes—then the FormTagHelper class automatically enables an anti-CSRF feature, whereby a security token is added to the response as a cookie. A hidden input element containing the same security token is added to the HTML form, and it is this token that is shown in Figure 27-9.

Enabling the Anti-forgery Feature in a Controller

By default, controllers accept POST requests even when they don't contain the required security tokens. To enable the anti-forgery feature, an attribute is applied to the controller class, as shown in Listing 27-29.

Listing 27-29. Enabling the Anti-forgery Feature in the FormController.cs File in the Controllers Folder

```
using Microsoft.AspNetCore.Mvc;
using System.Linq;
using System.Threading.Tasks;
using WebApp.Models;
using Microsoft.EntityFrameworkCore;
using Microsoft.AspNetCore.Mvc.Rendering;
```

```
namespace WebApp.Controllers {

    [AutoValidateAntiforgeryToken]
    public class FormController : Controller {
        private DataContext context;

        public FormController(DataContext dbContext) {
            context = dbContext;
        }

        public async Task<IActionResult> Index(long id = 1) {
            ViewBag.Categories
                = new SelectList(context.Categories, "CategoryId", "Name");
            return View("Form", await context.Products.Include(p => p.Category)
                .Include(p => p.Supplier).FirstAsync(p => p.ProductId == id));
        }

        [HttpPost]
        public IActionResult SubmitForm() {
            foreach (string key in Request.Form.Keys) {
                TempData[key] = string.Join(", ", Request.Form[key]);
            }
            return RedirectToAction(nameof(Results));
        }

        public IActionResult Results() {
            return View(TempData);
        }
    }
}
```

Not all requests require an anti-forgery token, and the AutoValidateAntiforgeryToken ensures that checks are performed for all HTTP methods except GET, HEAD, OPTIONS, and TRACE.

■ **Tip** Two other attributes can be used to control token validation. The IgnoreValidationToken attribute suppresses validation for an action method or controller. The ValidateAntiForgeryToken attribute does the opposite and enforces validation, even for requests that would not normally require validation, such as HTTP GET requests. I recommend using the AutoValidateAntiforgeryToken attribute, as shown in the listing.

Testing the anti-CSRF feature is a little tricky. I do it by requesting the URL that contains the form (http://localhost:5000/controllers/forms for this example) and then using the browser's F12 developer tools to locate and remove the hidden input element from the form (or change the element's value). When I populate and submit the form, it is missing one part of the required data, and the request will fail.

Enabling the Anti-forgery Feature in a Razor Page

The anti-forgery feature is enabled by default in Razor Pages, which is why I applied the IgnoreAntiforgeryToken attribute to the page handler method in Listing 27-29 when I created the FormHandler page. Listing 27-30 removes the attribute to enable the validation feature.

Listing 27-30. Enabling Request Validation in the FormHandler.cshtml File in the Pages Folder

```
@page "/pages/form/{id:long?}"
@model FormHandlerModel
@using Microsoft.AspNetCore.Mvc.RazorPages
@using Microsoft.EntityFrameworkCore

<div class="m-2">
    <h5 class="bg-primary text-white text-center p-2">HTML Form</h5>
    <form asp-page="FormHandler" method="post" id="htmlform">
        <div class="form-group">
            <label>Name</label>
            <input class="form-control" asp-for="Product.Name" />
        </div>

        <div class="form-group">
            <label>Price</label>
            <input class="form-control" asp-for="Product.Price" />
        </div>
        <div class="form-group">
            <label>Category</label>
            <input class="form-control" asp-for="Product.Category.Name" />
        </div>
        <div class="form-group">
            <label>Supplier</label>
            <input class="form-control" asp-for="Product.Supplier.Name" />
        </div>
        <button type="submit" class="btn btn-primary">Submit</button>
    </form>
    <button form="htmlform" asp-page="FormHandler" class="btn btn-primary mt-2">
        Sumit (Outside Form)
    </button>
</div>

@functions {

    //[IgnoreAntiforgeryToken]
    public class FormHandlerModel : PageModel {
        private DataContext context;

        public FormHandlerModel(DataContext dbContext) {
            context = dbContext;
        }

        public Product Product { get; set; }

        public async Task OnGetAsync(long id = 1) {
            Product = await context.Products.Include(p => p.Category)
                .Include(p => p.Supplier).FirstAsync(p => p.ProductId == id);
        }

        public IActionResult OnPost() {
            foreach (string key in Request.Form.Keys
                    .Where(k => !k.StartsWith("_"))) {
                TempData[key] = string.Join(", ", Request.Form[key]);
            }
```

```
            return RedirectToPage("FormResults");
        }
    }
}
```

Testing the validation feature is done in the same way as for controllers and requires altering the HTML document using the browser's developer tools before submitting the form to the application.

Using Anti-forgery Tokens with JavaScript Clients

By default, the anti-forgery feature relies on the ASP.NET Core application being able to include an element in an HTML form that the browser sends back when the form is submitted. This doesn't work for JavaScript clients because the ASP.NET Core application provides data and not HTML, so there is no way to insert the hidden element and receive it in a future request.

For web services, the anti-forgery token can be sent as a JavaScript-readable cookie, which the JavaScript client code reads and includes as a header in its POST requests. Some JavaScript frameworks, such an Angular, will automatically detect the cookie and include a header in requests. For other frameworks and custom JavaScript code, additional work is required.

Listing 27-31 shows the changes required to the ASP.NET Core application to configure the anti-forgery feature for use with JavaScript clients.

Listing 27-31. Configuring the Anti-forgery Token in the Startup.cs File in the WebApp Folder

```
using Microsoft.AspNetCore.Builder;
using Microsoft.Extensions.DependencyInjection;
using Microsoft.Extensions.Configuration;
using Microsoft.EntityFrameworkCore;
using WebApp.Models;
using Microsoft.AspNetCore.Antiforgery;
using Microsoft.AspNetCore.Http;

namespace WebApp {
    public class Startup {

        public Startup(IConfiguration config) {
            Configuration = config;
        }

        public IConfiguration Configuration { get; set; }

        public void ConfigureServices(IServiceCollection services) {
            services.AddDbContext<DataContext>(opts => {
                opts.UseSqlServer(Configuration[
                    "ConnectionStrings:ProductConnection"]);
                opts.EnableSensitiveDataLogging(true);
            });
            services.AddControllersWithViews().AddRazorRuntimeCompilation();
            services.AddRazorPages().AddRazorRuntimeCompilation();
            services.AddSingleton<CitiesData>();

            services.Configure<AntiforgeryOptions>(opts => {
                opts.HeaderName = "X-XSRF-TOKEN";
            });
        }

        public void Configure(IApplicationBuilder app, DataContext context,
                IAntiforgery antiforgery) {
```

```
        app.UseRequestLocalization();

        app.UseDeveloperExceptionPage();
        app.UseStaticFiles();
        app.UseRouting();

        app.Use(async (context, next) => {
            if (!context.Request.Path.StartsWithSegments("/api")) {
                context.Response.Cookies.Append("XSRF-TOKEN",
                    antiforgery.GetAndStoreTokens(context).RequestToken,
                    new CookieOptions { HttpOnly = false });
            }
            await next();
        });

        app.UseEndpoints(endpoints => {
            endpoints.MapControllers();
            endpoints.MapControllerRoute("forms",
                "controllers/{controller=Home}/{action=Index}/{id?}");
            endpoints.MapDefaultControllerRoute();
            endpoints.MapRazorPages();
        });
        SeedData.SeedDatabase(context);
    }
  }
}
```

The options pattern is used to configure the anti-forgery feature, through the AntiforgeryOptions class. The HeaderName property is used to specify the name of a header through which anti-forgery tokens will be accepted, which is X-XSRF-TOKEN in this case.

A custom middleware component is required to set the cookie, which is named XSRF-TOKEN in this example. The value of the cookie is obtained through the IAntiForgery service and must be configured with the HttpOnly option set to false so that the browser will allow JavaScript code to read the cookie.

■ **Tip**   I have followed the names that are supported by Angular in this example. Other frameworks follow their own conventions but can usually be configured to use any set of cookie and header names.

To create a simple JavaScript client that uses the cookie and header, add a Razor Page named JavaScriptForm.cshtml to the Pages folder with the content shown in Listing 27-32.

Listing 27-32. The Contents of the JavaScriptForm.cshtml File in the Pages Folder

```
@page "/pages/jsform"

<script type="text/javascript">
    async function sendRequest() {
        const token = document.cookie
            .replace(/(?:(?:^|.*;\s*)XSRF-TOKEN\s*\=\s*([^;]*).*$)|^.*$/, "$1");

        let form = new FormData();
        form.append("name", "Paddle");
        form.append("price", 100);
        form.append("categoryId", 1);
        form.append("supplierId", 1);
```

```
        let response = await fetch("@Url.Page("FormHandler")", {
            method: "POST",
            headers: { "X-XSRF-TOKEN": token },
            body: form
        });
        document.getElementById("content").innerHTML = await response.text();
    }

    document.addEventListener("DOMContentLoaded",
        () => document.getElementById("submit").onclick = sendRequest);
</script>

<button class="btn btn-primary m-2" id="submit">Submit JavaScript Form</button>
<div id="content"></div>
```

The JavaScript code in this Razor Page responds to a button click by sending an HTTP POST request to the FormHandler Razor Page. The value of the XSRF-TOKEN cookie is read and included in the X-XSRF-TOKEN request header. The response from the FormHandler page is a redirection to the Results page, which the browser will follow automatically. The response from the Results page is read by the JavaScript code and inserted into an element so it can be displayed to the user. To test the JavaScript code, use a browser to request http://localhost:5000/pages/jsform and click the button. The JavaScript code will submit the form and display the response, as shown in Figure 27-10.

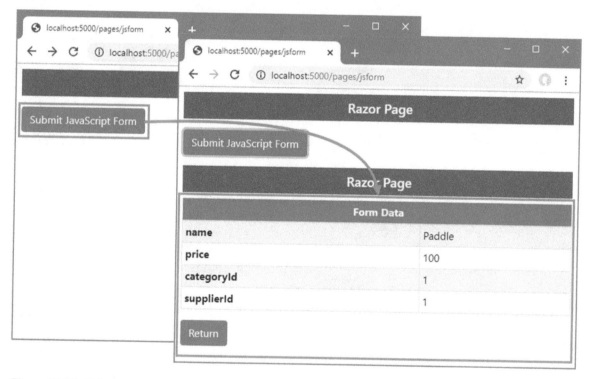

Figure 27-10. *Using a security token in JavaScript code*

Summary

In this chapter, I explained the features that ASP.NET Core provides for creating HTML forms. I showed you how tag helpers are used to select the form target and associate input, textarea, and select elements with view model or page model properties. In the next chapter, I describe the model binding feature, which extracts data from requests so that it can easily be consumed in action and handler methods.

CHAPTER 28

Using Model Binding

Model binding is the process of creating .NET objects using the values from the HTTP request to provide easy access to the data required by action methods and Razor Pages. In this chapter, I describe the way the model binding system works; show how it binds simple types, complex types, and collections; and demonstrate how you can take control of the process to specify which part of the request provides the data values your application requires. Table 28-1 puts model binding in context.

Table 28-1. *Putting Model Binding in Context*

Question	Answer
What is it?	Model binding is the process of creating the objects that action methods and page handlers require using data values obtained from the HTTP request.
Why is it useful?	Model binding lets controllers or page handlers declare method parameters or properties using C# types and automatically receive data from the request without having to inspect, parse, and process the data directly.
How is it used?	In its simplest form, methods declare parameters or classes define properties whose names are used to retrieve data values from the HTTP request. The part of the request used to obtain the data can be configured by applying attributes to the method parameters or properties.
Are there any pitfalls or limitations?	The main pitfall is getting data from the wrong part of the request. I explain the way that requests are searched for data in the "Understanding Model Binding" section, and the search locations can be specified explicitly using the attributes that I describe in the "Specifying a Model Binding Source" section.
Are there any alternatives?	Data can be obtained without model binding using context objects. However, the result is more complicated code that is hard to read and maintain.

Table 28-2 summarizes the chapter.

Table 28-2. *Chapter Summary*

Problem	Solution	Listing
Binding simple types	Define method parameters with primitive types	5–9
Binding complex types	Define method parameters with class types	10
Binding to a property	Use the BindProperty attribute	11, 12
Binding nested types	Ensure the form value types follow the dotted notation	13–17
Selecting properties for binding	Use the Bind and BindNever attributes	18–19
Binding collections	Follow the sequence binding conventions	20–25
Specifying the source for binding	Use one of the source attributes	26–31
Manually performing binding	Use the TryUpdateModel method	32

© Adam Freeman 2020
A. Freeman, *Pro ASP.NET Core 3*, https://doi.org/10.1007/978-1-4842-5440-0_28

Preparing for This Chapter

This chapter uses the WebApp project from Chapter 27. To prepare for this chapter, replace the contents of the Form.cshtml file in the Views/Form folder with the content shown in Listing 28-1.

■ **Tip** You can download the example project for this chapter—and for all the other chapters in this book—from https://github. com/apress/pro-asp.net-core-3. See Chapter 1 for how to get help if you have problems running the examples.

Listing 28-1. The Contents of the Form.cshtml File in the Views/Form Folder

```
@model Product
@{ Layout = "_SimpleLayout"; }

<h5 class="bg-primary text-white text-center p-2">HTML Form</h5>

<form asp-action="submitform" method="post" id="htmlform">
    <div class="form-group">
        <label asp-for="Name"></label>
        <input class="form-control" asp-for="Name" />
    </div>
    <div class="form-group">
        <label asp-for="Price"></label>
        <input class="form-control" asp-for="Price" />
    </div>
    <button type="submit" class="btn btn-primary">Submit</button>
</form>
```

Next, comment out the DisplayFormat attribute that has been applied to the Product model class, as shown in Listing 28-2.

Listing 28-2. Removing an Attribute in the Product.cs File in the Models Folder

```
using System.ComponentModel.DataAnnotations.Schema;
using System.ComponentModel.DataAnnotations;

namespace WebApp.Models {
    public class Product {

        public long ProductId { get; set; }

        public string Name { get; set; }

        [Column(TypeName = "decimal(8, 2)")]
        //[DisplayFormat(DataFormatString = "{0:c2}", ApplyFormatInEditMode = true)]
        public decimal Price { get; set; }

        public long CategoryId { get; set; }
        public Category Category { get; set; }

        public long SupplierId { get; set; }
        public Supplier Supplier { get; set; }
    }
}
```

Dropping the Database

Open a new PowerShell command prompt, navigate to the folder that contains the WebApp.csproj file, and run the command shown in Listing 28-3 to drop the database.

Listing 28-3. Dropping the Database

```
dotnet ef database drop --force
```

Running the Example Application

Select Start Without Debugging or Run Without Debugging from the Debug menu or use the PowerShell command prompt to run the command shown in Listing 28-4.

Listing 28-4. Running the Example Application

```
dotnet run
```

Use a browser to request http://localhost:5000/controllers/form, which will display an HTML form. Click the Submit button, and the form data will be displayed, as shown in Figure 28-1.

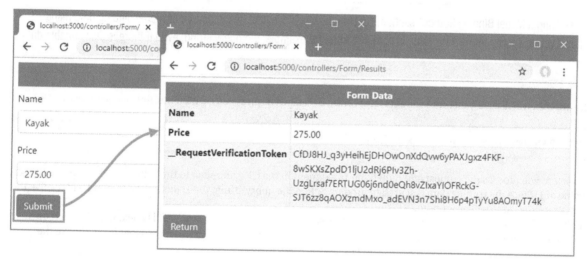

Figure 28-1. Running the example application

Understanding Model Binding

Model binding is an elegant bridge between the HTTP request and action or page handler methods. Most ASP.NET Core applications rely on model binding to some extent, including the example application for this chapter.

You can see model binding at work by using the browser to request http://localhost:5000/controllers/form/index/5. This URL contains the value of the ProductId property of the Product object that I want to view, like this:

```
http://localhost:5000/controllers/form/index/5
```

This part of the URL corresponds to the id segment variable defined by the controller routing pattern and matches the name of the parameter defined by the Form controller's Index action:

```
...
public async Task<IActionResult> Index(long id = 1) {
...
```

A value for the id parameter is required before the MVC Framework can invoke the action method, and finding a suitable value is the responsibility of the *model binding* system. The model binding system relies on *model binders*, which are components responsible for providing data values from one part of the request or application. The default model binders look for data values in these four places:

- Form data

- The request body (only for controllers decorated with ApiController)

- Routing segment variables

- Query strings

Each source of data is inspected in order until a value for the argument is found. There is no form data in the example application, so no value will be found there, and the Form controller isn't decorated with the ApiController attribute, so the request body won't be checked. The next step is to check the routing data, which contains a segment variable named id. This allows the model binding system to provide a value that allows the Index action method to be invoked. The search stops after a suitable data value has been found, which means that the query string isn't searched for a data value.

■ **Tip** In the "Specifying a Model Binding Source" section, I explain how you can specify the source of model binding data using attributes. This allows you to specify that a data value is obtained from, for example, the query string, even if there is also suitable data in the routing data.

Knowing the order in which data values are sought is important because a request can contain multiple values, like this URL:

```
http://localhost:5000/controllers/Form/Index/5?id=1
```

The routing system will process the request and match the id segment in the URL template to the value 3, and the query string contains an id value of 1. Since the routing data is searched for data before the query string, the Index action method will receive the value 3, and the query string value will be ignored.

On the other hand, if you request a URL that doesn't have an id segment, then the query string will be examined, which means that a URL like this one will also allow the model binding system to provide a value for the id argument so that it can invoke the Index method.

```
http://localhost:5000/controllers/Form/Index?id=4
```

You can see the effect of both these URLs in Figure 28-2.

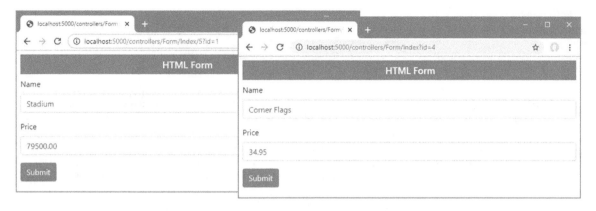

Figure 28-2. *The effect of model binding data source order*

Binding Simple Data Types

Request data values must be converted into C# values so they can be used to invoke action or page handler methods. *Simple types* are values that originate from one item of data in the request that can be parsed from a string. This includes numeric values, bool values, dates, and, of course, `string` values.

Data binding for simple types makes it easy to extract single data items from the request without having to work through the context data to find out where it is defined. Listing 28-5 adds parameters to the `SubmitForm` action method defined by the `Form` controller method so that the model binder will be used to provide `name` and `price` values.

Listing 28-5. Adding Method Parameters in the FormController.cs File in the Controllers Folder

```
using Microsoft.AspNetCore.Mvc;
using System.Linq;
using System.Threading.Tasks;
using WebApp.Models;
using Microsoft.EntityFrameworkCore;
using Microsoft.AspNetCore.Mvc.Rendering;

namespace WebApp.Controllers {

    [AutoValidateAntiforgeryToken]
    public class FormController : Controller {
        private DataContext context;

        public FormController(DataContext dbContext) {
            context = dbContext;
        }

        public async Task<IActionResult> Index(long id = 1) {
            ViewBag.Categories
                = new SelectList(context.Categories, "CategoryId", "Name");
            return View("Form", await context.Products.Include(p => p.Category)
                .Include(p => p.Supplier).FirstAsync(p => p.ProductId == id));
        }

        [HttpPost]
        public IActionResult SubmitForm(string name, decimal price) {
            TempData["name param"] = name;
            TempData["price param"] = price.ToString();
            return RedirectToAction(nameof(Results));
        }
```

```
        public IActionResult Results() {
            return View(TempData);
        }
    }
}
```

The model binding system will be used to obtain name and price values when ASP.NET Core receives a request that will be processed by the SubmitForm action method. The use of parameters simplifies the action method and takes care of converting the request data into C# data types so that the price value will be converted to the C# decimal type before the action method is invoked. (I had to convert the decimal back to a string to store it as temp data in this example. I demonstrate more useful ways of dealing with form data in Chapter 31.) Restart ASP.NET Core so the change to the controller takes effect and request http://localhost:5000/controllers/Form. Click the Submit button, and you will see the values that were extracted from the request by the model binding feature, as shown in Figure 28-3.

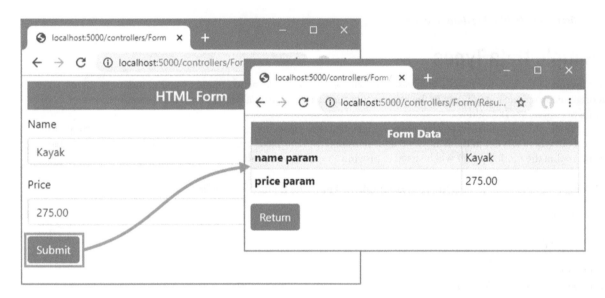

Figure 28-3. *Model binding for simple types*

Binding Simple Data Types in Razor Pages

Razor Pages can use model binding, but care must be taken to ensure that the value of the form element's name attribute matches the name of the handler method parameter, which may not be the case if the asp-for attribute has been used to select a nested property. To ensure the names match, the name attribute can be defined explicitly, as shown in Listing 28-6, which also simplifies the HTML form so that it matches the controller example.

Listing 28-6. Using Model Binding in the FormHandler.cshtml File in the Pages Folder

```
@page "/pages/form/{id:long?}"
@model FormHandlerModel
@using Microsoft.AspNetCore.Mvc.RazorPages
@using Microsoft.EntityFrameworkCore

<div class="m-2">
    <h5 class="bg-primary text-white text-center p-2">HTML Form</h5>
    <form asp-page="FormHandler" method="post" id="htmlform">
        <div class="form-group">
            <label>Name</label>
            <input class="form-control" asp-for="Product.Name" name="name"/>
        </div>
        <div class="form-group">
            <label>Price</label>
```

```
            <input class="form-control" asp-for="Product.Price" name="price" />
        </div>
        <button type="submit" class="btn btn-primary">Submit</button>
    </form>
</div>

@functions {

    public class FormHandlerModel : PageModel {
        private DataContext context;

        public FormHandlerModel(DataContext dbContext) {
            context = dbContext;
        }

        public Product Product { get; set; }

        public async Task OnGetAsync(long id = 1) {
            Product = await context.Products.Include(p => p.Category)
                .Include(p => p.Supplier).FirstAsync(p => p.ProductId == id);
        }

        public IActionResult OnPost(string name, decimal price) {
            TempData["name param"] = name;
            TempData["price param"] = price.ToString();
            return RedirectToPage("FormResults");
        }
    }
}
```

The tag helper would have set the name attributes of the input elements to Product.Name and Product.Price, which prevents the model binder from matching the values. Explicitly setting the name attribute overrides the tag helper and ensures the model binding process works correctly. Use a browser to request http://localhost:5000/pages/form and click the Submit button, and you will see the values found by the model binder, as shown in Figure 28-4.

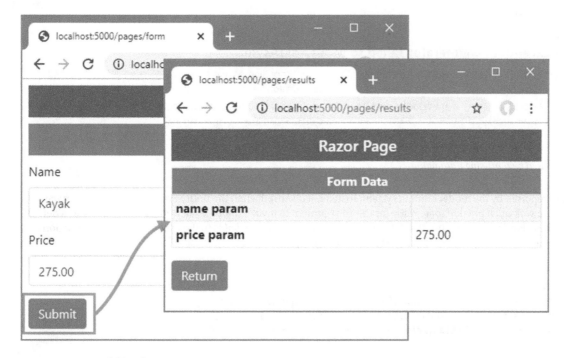

Figure 28-4. *Model binding in a Razor Page*

Understanding Default Binding Values

Model binding is a best-effort feature, which means the model binder will try to get values for method parameters but will still invoke the method if data values cannot be located. You can see how this works by removing the default value for the id parameter in the Form controller's Index action method, as shown in Listing 28-7.

Listing 28-7. Removing a Parameter in the FormController.cs File in the Controllers Folder

```
...
public async Task<IActionResult> Index(long id) {
    ViewBag.Categories
        = new SelectList(context.Categories, "CategoryId", "Name");
    return View("Form", await context.Products.Include(p => p.Category)
        .Include(p => p.Supplier).FirstAsync(p => p.ProductId == id));
}
...
```

Restart ASP.NET Core and request http://localhost:5000/controllers/Form. The URL doesn't contain a value that the model binder can use for the id parameter, and there is no query string or form data, but the method is still invoked, producing the error shown in Figure 28-5.

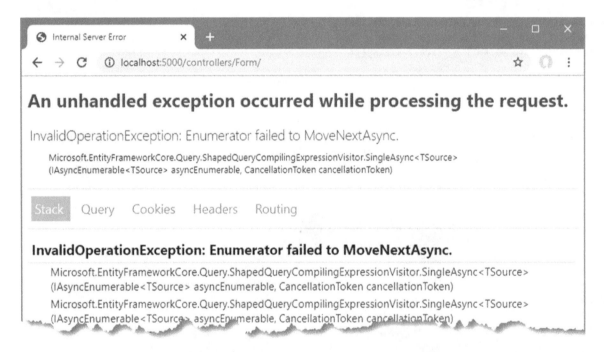

Figure 28-5. *An error caused by a missing data value*

This exception isn't reported by the model binding system. Instead, it occurred when the Entity Framework Core query was executed. The MVC Framework must provide *some* value for the id argument to invoke the Index action method, so it uses a default value and hopes for the best. For long arguments, the default value is 0, and this is what leads to the exception. The Index action method uses the id value as the key to query the database for a Product object, like this:

```
...
public async Task<IActionResult> Index(long id) {
    ViewBag.Categories = new SelectList(context.Categories, "CategoryId", "Name");
    return View("Form", await context.Products.Include(p => p.Category)
        .Include(p => p.Supplier).FirstAsync(p => p.ProductId == id));
}
...
```

When there is no value available for model binding, the action method tries to query the database with an id of zero. There is no such object, which causes the error shown in the figure when Entity Framework Core tries to process the result.

Applications must be written to cope with default argument values, which can be done in several ways. You can add fallback values to the routing URL patterns used by controllers (as shown in Chapter 21) or pages (as shown in Chapter 23). You can assign default values when defining the parameter in the action or page handler method, which is the approach that I have taken so far in this part of the book. Or you can simply write methods that accommodate the default values without causing an error, as shown in Listing 28-8.

Listing 28-8. Avoiding a Query Error in the FormController.cs File in the Controllers Folder

```
...
public async Task<IActionResult> Index(long id) {
    ViewBag.Categories = new SelectList(context.Categories, "CategoryId", "Name");
    return View("Form", await context.Products.Include(p => p.Category)
        .Include(p => p.Supplier).FirstOrDefaultAsync(p => p.ProductId == id));
}
...
```

The Entity Framework Core FirstOrDefaultAsync method will return null if there is no matching object in the database and won't attempt to load related data. The tag helpers cope with null values and display empty fields, which you can see by restarting ASP.NET Core and requesting http://localhost:5000/controllers/Form, which produces the result shown in Figure 28-6.

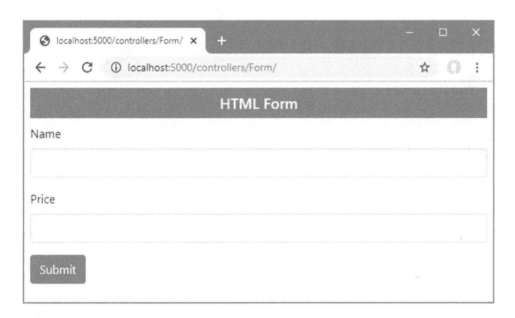

Figure 28-6. *Avoiding an error*

Some applications need to differentiate between a missing value and any value provided by the user. In these situations, a nullable parameter type can be used, as shown in Listing 28-9.

Listing 28-9. Using a Nullable Parameter in the FormController.cs File in the Controllers Folder

```
...
public async Task<IActionResult> Index(long? id) {
    ViewBag.Categories = new SelectList(context.Categories, "CategoryId", "Name");
    return View("Form", await context.Products.Include(p => p.Category)
        .Include(p => p.Supplier)
        .FirstOrDefaultAsync(p => id == null || p.ProductId == id));
}
...
```

The id parameter will be null only if the request doesn't contain a suitable value, which allows the expression passed to the FirstOrDefaultAsync method to default to the first object in the database when there is no value and to query for any other value. To see the effect, restart ASP.NET Core and request http://localhost:5000/controllers/Form and http://localhost:5000/controllers/Form/index/0. The first URL contains no id value, so the first object in the database is selected. The second URL provides an id value of zero, which doesn't correspond to any object in the database. Figure 28-7 shows both results.

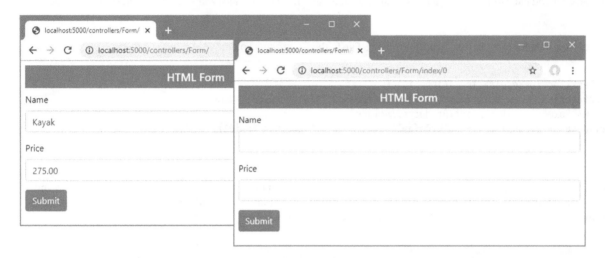

Figure 28-7. *Using a nullable type to determine whether a request contains a value*

Binding Complex Types

The model binding system shines when dealing with complex types, which are any type that cannot be parsed from a single string value. The model binding process inspects the complex type and performs the binding process on each of the public properties it defines. This means that instead of dealing with individual values such as name and price, I can use the binder to create complete Product objects, as shown in Listing 28-10.

Listing 28-10. Binding a Complex Type in the FormController.cs File in the Controllers Folder

```
using Microsoft.AspNetCore.Mvc;
using System.Linq;
using System.Threading.Tasks;
using WebApp.Models;
using Microsoft.EntityFrameworkCore;
using Microsoft.AspNetCore.Mvc.Rendering;

namespace WebApp.Controllers {

    [AutoValidateAntiforgeryToken]
    public class FormController : Controller {
        private DataContext context;

        public FormController(DataContext dbContext) {
            context = dbContext;
        }

        public async Task<IActionResult> Index(long? id) {
            ViewBag.Categories
                = new SelectList(context.Categories, "CategoryId", "Name");
            return View("Form", await context.Products.Include(p => p.Category)
                .Include(p => p.Supplier)
                .FirstOrDefaultAsync(p => id == null || p.ProductId == id));
        }
```

```
    [HttpPost]
    public IActionResult SubmitForm(Product product) {
        TempData["product"] = System.Text.Json.JsonSerializer.Serialize(product);
        return RedirectToAction(nameof(Results));
    }

    public IActionResult Results() {
        return View(TempData);
    }
    }
}
```

The listing changes the SubmitForm action method so that it defines a Product parameter. Before the action method is invoked, a new Product object is created, and the model binding process is applied to each of its public properties. The SubmitForm method is then invoked, using the Product object as its argument.

To see the model binding process, restart ASP.NET Core, navigate to http://localhost:5000/controllers/Form, and click the Submit button. The model binding process will extract the data values from the request and produce the result shown in Figure 28-8. The Product object created by the model binding process is serialized as JSON data so that it can be stored as temp data, making it easy to see the request data.

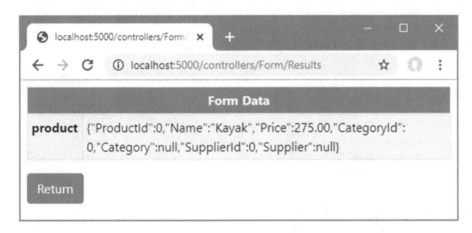

Figure 28-8. *Data binding a complex type*

The data binding process for complex types remains a best-effort feature, meaning that a value will be sought for each public property defined by the Product class, but missing values won't prevent the action method from being invoked. Instead, properties for which no value can be located will be left as the default value for the property type. The example provided values for the Name and Price properties, but the ProductId, CategoryId, and SupplierId properties are zero, and the Category and Supplier properties are null.

Binding to a Property

Using parameters for model binding doesn't fit with the Razor Pages development style because the parameters often duplicate properties defined by the page model class, as shown in Listing 28-11.

Listing 28-11. Binding a Complex Type in the FormHandler.cshtml File in the Pages Folder

```
...
@functions {

    public class FormHandlerModel : PageModel {
        private DataContext context;
```

```
        public FormHandlerModel(DataContext dbContext) {
            context = dbContext;
        }

        public Product Product { get; set; }

        public async Task OnGetAsync(long id = 1) {
            Product = await context.Products.Include(p => p.Category)
                .Include(p => p.Supplier).FirstAsync(p => p.ProductId == id);
        }

        public IActionResult OnPost(Product product) {
            TempData["product"] = System.Text.Json.JsonSerializer.Serialize(product);
            return RedirectToPage("FormResults");
        }
    }
}
...
```

This code works, but the OnPost handler method has its own version of the Product object, mirroring the property used by the OnGetAsync handler. A more elegant approach is to use the existing property for model binding, as shown in Listing 28-12.

Listing 28-12. Using a Property for Model Binding in the FormHandler.cshtml File in the Pages Folder

```
@page "/pages/form/{id:long?}"
@model FormHandlerModel
@using Microsoft.AspNetCore.Mvc.RazorPages
@using Microsoft.EntityFrameworkCore

<div class="m-2">
    <h5 class="bg-primary text-white text-center p-2">HTML Form</h5>
    <form asp-page="FormHandler" method="post" id="htmlform">
        <div class="form-group">
            <label>Name</label>
            <input class="form-control" asp-for="Product.Name" />
        </div>
        <div class="form-group">
            <label>Price</label>
            <input class="form-control" asp-for="Product.Price"  />
        </div>
        <button type="submit" class="btn btn-primary">Submit</button>
    </form>
</div>

@functions {

    public class FormHandlerModel : PageModel {
        private DataContext context;

        public FormHandlerModel(DataContext dbContext) {
            context = dbContext;
        }

        [BindProperty]
        public Product Product { get; set; }

        public async Task OnGetAsync(long id = 1) {
            Product = await context.Products.Include(p => p.Category)
```

714

```
                .Include(p => p.Supplier).FirstAsync(p => p.ProductId == id);
        }

        public IActionResult OnPost() {
            TempData["product"] = System.Text.Json.JsonSerializer.Serialize(Product);
            return RedirectToPage("FormResults");
        }
    }
}
```

Decorating a property with the BindProperty attribute indicates that its properties should be subject to the model binding process, which means the OnPost handler method can get the data it requires without declaring a parameter. When the BindProperty attribute is used, the model binder uses the property name when locating data values, so the explicit name attributes added to the input element are not required. By default, BindProperty won't bind data for GET requests, but this can be changed by setting the BindProperty attribute's SupportsGet argument to true.

■ **Note**   The BindProperties attribute can be applied to classes that require the model binding process for all the public properties they define, which can be more convenient than applying BindProperty to many individual properties. Decorate properties with the BindNever attribute to exclude them from model binding.

Binding Nested Complex Types

If a property that is subject to model binding is defined using a complex type, then the model binding process is repeated using the property name as a prefix. For example, the Product class defines the Category property, whose type is the complex Category type. Listing 28-13 adds elements to the HTML form to provide the model binder with values for the properties defined by the Category class.

Listing 28-13. Adding Nested Form Elements in the Form.cshtml File in the Views/Form Folder

```
@model Product
@{  Layout = "_SimpleLayout"; }

<h5 class="bg-primary text-white text-center p-2">HTML Form</h5>

<form asp-action="submitform" method="post" id="htmlform">
    <div class="form-group">
        <label asp-for="Name"></label>
        <input class="form-control" asp-for="Name" />
    </div>
    <div class="form-group">
        <label asp-for="Price"></label>
        <input class="form-control" asp-for="Price" />
    </div>
    <div class="form-group">
        <label>Category Name</label>
        <input class="form-control" name="Category.Name"
            value="@Model.Category.Name" />
    </div>
    <button type="submit" class="btn btn-primary">Submit</button>
</form>
```

The name attribute combines the property names, separated by periods. In this case, the element is for the Name property of the object assigned to the view model's Category property, so the name attribute is set to Category.Name. The input element tag helper will automatically use this format for the name attribute when the asp-for attribute is applied, as shown in Listing 28-14.

Listing 28-14. Using a Tag Helper in the Form.cshtml File in the Views/Form Folder

```
@model Product
@{ Layout = "_SimpleLayout"; }

<h5 class="bg-primary text-white text-center p-2">HTML Form</h5>

<form asp-action="submitform" method="post" id="htmlform">
    <div class="form-group">
        <label asp-for="Name"></label>
        <input class="form-control" asp-for="Name" />
    </div>
    <div class="form-group">
        <label asp-for="Price"></label>
        <input class="form-control" asp-for="Price" />
    </div>
    <div class="form-group">
        <label>Category Name</label>
        <input class="form-control" asp-for="Category.Name"  />
    </div>
    <button type="submit" class="btn btn-primary">Submit</button>
</form>
```

The tag helper is a more reliable method of creating elements for nested properties and avoids the risk of typos producing elements that are ignored by the model binding process. To see the effect of the new elements, request http://localhost:5000/controllers/Form and click the Submit button, which will produce the response shown in Figure 28-9.

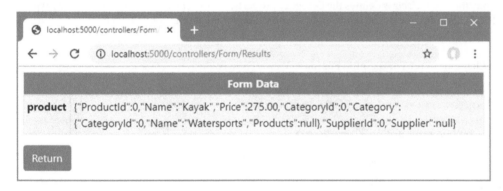

Figure 28-9. *Model binding a nested property*

During the model binding process, a new Category object is created and assigned to the Category property of the Product object. The model binder locates the value for the Category object's Name property, which can be seen in the figure, but there is no value for the CategoryId property, which is left as the default value.

Specifying Custom Prefixes for Nested Complex Types

There are occasions when the HTML you generate relates to one type of object but you want to bind it to another. This means that the prefixes containing the view won't correspond to the structure that the model binder is expecting, and your data won't be properly processed. Listing 28-15 demonstrates this problem by changing the type of the parameter defined by the controller's SubmitForm action method.

Listing 28-15. Changing a Parameter in the FormController.cs File in the Controllers Folder

```
...
[HttpPost]
public IActionResult SubmitForm(Category category) {
    TempData["category"] = System.Text.Json.JsonSerializer.Serialize(category);
    return RedirectToAction(nameof(Results));
}
...
```

The new parameter is a Category, but the model binding process won't be able to pick out the data values correctly, even though the form data sent by the Form view will contain a value for the Category object's Name property. Instead, the model binder will find the Name value for the Product object and use that instead, which you can see by restarting ASP.NET Core, requesting http://localhost:5000/controllers/Form, and submitting the form data, which will produce the first response shown in Figure 28-10.

This problem is solved by applying the Bind attribute to the parameter and using the Prefix argument to specify a prefix for the model binder, as shown in Listing 28-16.

Listing 28-16. Setting a Prefix in the FormController.cs File in the Controllers Folder

```
...
[HttpPost]
public IActionResult SubmitForm([Bind(Prefix ="Category")] Category category) {
    TempData["category"] = System.Text.Json.JsonSerializer.Serialize(category);
    return RedirectToAction(nameof(Results));
}
...
```

The syntax is awkward, but the attribute ensures the model binder can locate the data the action method requires. In this case, setting the prefix to Category ensures the correct data values are used to bind the Category parameter. Restart ASP.NET Core, request http://localhost:5000/controllers/form, and submit the form, which produces the second response shown in Figure 28-10.

Figure 28-10. *Specifying a model binding prefix*

When using the BindProperty attribute, the prefix is specified using the Name argument, as shown in Listing 28-17.

Listing 28-17. Specifying a Model Binding Prefix in the FormHandler.cshtml File in the Pages Folder

```
@page "/pages/form/{id:long?}"
@model FormHandlerModel
@using Microsoft.AspNetCore.Mvc.RazorPages
@using Microsoft.EntityFrameworkCore

<div class="m-2">
    <h5 class="bg-primary text-white text-center p-2">HTML Form</h5>
    <form asp-page="FormHandler" method="post" id="htmlform">
        <div class="form-group">
```

```
            <label>Name</label>
            <input class="form-control" asp-for="Product.Name" />
        </div>
        <div class="form-group">
            <label>Price</label>
            <input class="form-control" asp-for="Product.Price"  />
        </div>
        <div class="form-group">
            <label>Category Name</label>
            <input class="form-control" asp-for="Product.Category.Name"  />
        </div>
        <button type="submit" class="btn btn-primary">Submit</button>
    </form>
</div>

@functions {

    public class FormHandlerModel : PageModel {
        private DataContext context;

        public FormHandlerModel(DataContext dbContext) {
            context = dbContext;
        }

        [BindProperty]
        public Product Product { get; set; }

        [BindProperty(Name = "Product.Category")]
        public Category Category { get; set; }

        public async Task OnGetAsync(long id = 1) {
            Product = await context.Products.Include(p => p.Category)
                .Include(p => p.Supplier).FirstAsync(p => p.ProductId == id);
        }

        public IActionResult OnPost() {
            TempData["product"] = System.Text.Json.JsonSerializer.Serialize(Product);
            TempData["category"]
                = System.Text.Json.JsonSerializer.Serialize(Category);
            return RedirectToPage("FormResults");
        }
    }
}
```

This listing adds an input element that uses the asp-for attribute to select the Product.Category property. A page handler class defined a Category property that is decorated with the BindProperty attribute and configured with the Name argument. To see the result of the model binding process, use a browser to request http://localhost:5000/pages/form and click the Submit button. The model binding finds values for both the decorated properties, which produces the response shown in Figure 28-11.

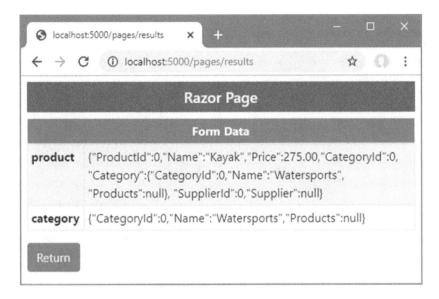

Figure 28-11. *Specifying a model binding prefix in a Razor Page*

Selectively Binding Properties

Some model classes define properties that are sensitive and for which the user should not be able to specify values. A user may be able to change the category for a Product object, for example, but should not be able to alter the price.

You might be tempted to simply create views that omit HTML elements for sensitive properties but that won't prevent malicious users from crafting HTTP requests that contain values anyway, which is known as an *over-binding attack*. To prevent the model binder from using values for sensitive properties, the list of properties that should be bound can be specified, as shown in Listing 28-18.

Listing 28-18. Selectively Binding Properties in the FormController.cs File in the Controllers Folder

```
using Microsoft.AspNetCore.Mvc;
using System.Linq;
using System.Threading.Tasks;
using WebApp.Models;
using Microsoft.EntityFrameworkCore;
using Microsoft.AspNetCore.Mvc.Rendering;

namespace WebApp.Controllers {

    [AutoValidateAntiforgeryToken]
    public class FormController : Controller {
        private DataContext context;

        public FormController(DataContext dbContext) {
            context = dbContext;
        }

        public async Task<IActionResult> Index(long? id) {
            ViewBag.Categories
                = new SelectList(context.Categories, "CategoryId", "Name");
            return View("Form", await context.Products.Include(p => p.Category)
                .Include(p => p.Supplier)
                .FirstOrDefaultAsync(p => id == null || p.ProductId == id));
        }
```

```
[HttpPost]
public IActionResult SubmitForm([Bind("Name", "Category")] Product product) {
    TempData["name"] = product.Name;
    TempData["price"] = product.Price.ToString();
    TempData["category name"] = product.Category.Name;
    return RedirectToAction(nameof(Results));
}

public IActionResult Results() {
    return View(TempData);
}
    }
}
```

I have returned to the Product type for the action method parameter, which has been decorated with the Bind attribute to specify the names of the properties that should be included in the model binding process. This example tells the model binding feature to look for values for the Name and Category properties, which excludes any other property from the process. Restart ASP.NET Core, navigate to http://localhost:5000/controller/Form, and submit the form. Even though the browser sends a value for the Price property as part of the HTTP POST request, it is ignored by the model binder, as shown in Figure 28-12.

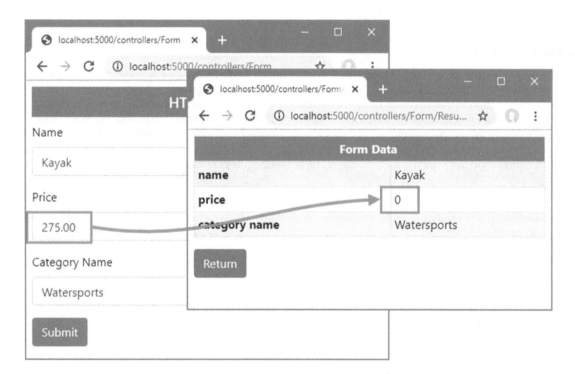

Figure 28-12. *Selectively binding properties*

Selectively Binding in the Model Class

If you are using Razor Pages or you want to use the same set of properties for model binding throughout the application, you can apply the BindNever attribute directly to the model class, as shown in Listing 28-19.

Listing 28-19. Decorating a Property in the Product.cs File in the Models Folder

```
using System.ComponentModel.DataAnnotations.Schema;
using System.ComponentModel.DataAnnotations;
using Microsoft.AspNetCore.Mvc.ModelBinding;
```

```
namespace WebApp.Models {
    public class Product {

        public long ProductId { get; set; }

        public string Name { get; set; }

        [Column(TypeName = "decimal(8, 2)")]
        [BindNever]
        public decimal Price { get; set; }

        public long CategoryId { get; set; }
        public Category Category { get; set; }

        public long SupplierId { get; set; }
        public Supplier Supplier { get; set; }
    }
}
```

The BindNever attribute excludes a property from the model binder, which has the same effect as omitting it from the list used in the previous section. To see the effect, restart ASP.NET Core so the change to the Product class takes effect, request http://localhost:5000/pages/form, and submit the form. Just as with the previous example, the model binder ignores the value for the Price property, as shown in Figure 28-13.

■ **Tip**   There is also a BindRequired attribute that tells the model binding process that a request must include a value for a property. If the request doesn't have a required value, then a model validation error is produced, as described in Chapter 29.

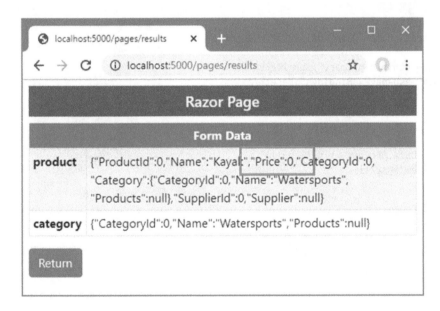

Figure 28-13. Excluding a property from model binding

Binding to Arrays and Collections

The model binding process has some nice features for binding request data to arrays and collections, which I demonstrate in the following sections.

Binding to Arrays

One elegant feature of the default model binder is how it supports arrays. To see how this feature works, add a Razor Page named Bindings.cshtml to the Pages folder with the content shown in Listing 28-20.

Listing 28-20. The Contents of the Bindings.cshtml File in the Pages Folder

```
@page "/pages/bindings"
@model BindingsModel
@using Microsoft.AspNetCore.Mvc
@using Microsoft.AspNetCore.Mvc.RazorPages

<div class="container-fluid">
    <div class="row">
        <div class="col">
            <form asp-page="Bindings" method="post">
                <div class="form-group">
                    <label>Value #1</label>
                    <input class="form-control" name="Data" value="Item 1" />
                </div>
                <div class="form-group">
                    <label>Value #2</label>
                    <input class="form-control" name="Data" value="Item 2" />
                </div>
                <div class="form-group">
                        <label>Value #3</label>
                    <input class="form-control" name="Data" value="Item 3" />
                </div>
                <button type="submit" class="btn btn-primary">Submit</button>
                <a class="btn btn-secondary" asp-page="Bindings">Reset</a>
            </form>
        </div>
        <div class="col">
            <ul class="list-group">
                @foreach (string s in Model.Data.Where(s => s != null)) {
                    <li class="list-group-item">@s</li>
                }
            </ul>
        </div>
    </div>
</div>

@functions {

    public class BindingsModel : PageModel {

        [BindProperty(Name = "Data")]
        public string[] Data { get; set; } = Array.Empty<string>();
    }
}
```

Model binding for an array requires setting the name attribute to the same value for all the elements that will provide an array value. This page displays three input elements, all of which have a name attribute value of Data. To allow the model binder to find the array values, I have decorated the page model's Data property with the BindProperty attribute and used the Name argument.

■ **Tip** Notice that the page model class in Listing 28-20 defines no handler methods. This is unusual, but it works because there is no explicit processing required for any requests since requests only provide values for and display the Data array.

When the HTML form is submitted, a new array is created and populated with the values from all three input elements, which are displayed to the user. To see the binding process, request http://localhost:5000/pages/bindings, edit the form fields, and click the Submit button. The contents of the Data array are displayed in a list using an @foreach expression, as shown in Figure 28-14.

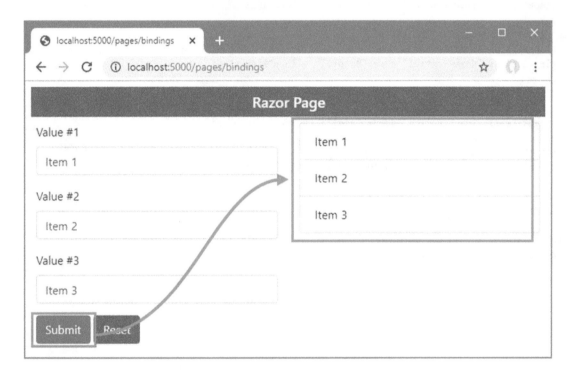

Figure 28-14. *Model binding for array values*

Notice that I filter out null values when displaying the array contents.

```
...
@foreach (string s in Model.Data.Where(s => s != null)) {
    <li class="list-group-item">@s</li>
}
...
```

Empty form fields produce null values in the array, which I don't want to show in the results. In Chapter 29, I show you how to ensure that values are provided for model binding properties.

Specifying Index Positions for Array Values

By default, arrays are populated in the order in which the form values are received from the browser, which will generally be the order in which the HTML elements are defined. The name attribute can be used to specify the position of values in the array if you need to override the default, as shown in Listing 28-21.

Listing 28-21. Specifying Array Position in the Bindings.cshtml File in the Pages Folder

```
@page "/pages/bindings"
@model BindingsModel
@using Microsoft.AspNetCore.Mvc
@using Microsoft.AspNetCore.Mvc.RazorPages

<div class="container-fluid">
    <div class="row">
        <div class="col">
            <form asp-page="Bindings" method="post">
                <div class="form-group">
                    <label>Value #1</label>
                    <input class="form-control" name="Data[1]" value="Item 1" />
                </div>
                <div class="form-group">
                    <label>Value #2</label>
                    <input class="form-control" name="Data[0]" value="Item 2" />
                </div>
                <div class="form-group">
                        <label>Value #3</label>
                    <input class="form-control" name="Data[2]" value="Item 3" />
                </div>
                <button type="submit" class="btn btn-primary">Submit</button>
                <a class="btn btn-secondary" asp-page="Bindings">Reset</a>
            </form>
        </div>
        <div class="col">
            <ul class="list-group">
                @foreach (string s in Model.Data.Where(s => s != null)) {
                    <li class="list-group-item">@s</li>
                }
            </ul>
        </div>
    </div>
</div>

@functions {

    public class BindingsModel : PageModel {

        [BindProperty(Name = "Data")]
        public string[] Data { get; set; } = Array.Empty<string>();
    }
}
```

The array index notation is used to specify the position of a value in the data-bound array. Use a browser to request http://localhost:5000/pages/bindings and submit the form, and you will see the items appear in the order dictated by the name attributes, as shown in Figure 28-15. The index notation must be applied to all the HTML elements that provide array values, and there must not be any gaps in the numbering sequence.

Figure 28-15. *Specifying array position*

Binding to Simple Collections

The model binding process can create collections as well as arrays. For sequence collections, such as lists and sets, only the type of the property or parameter that is used by the model binder is changed, as shown in Listing 28-22.

Listing 28-22. Binding to a List in the Bindings.cshtml File in the Pages Folder

```
@page "/pages/bindings"
@model BindingsModel
@using Microsoft.AspNetCore.Mvc
@using Microsoft.AspNetCore.Mvc.RazorPages

<div class="container-fluid">
    <div class="row">
        <div class="col">
            <form asp-page="Bindings" method="post">
                <div class="form-group">
                    <label>Value #1</label>
                    <input class="form-control" name="Data[1]" value="Item 1" />
                </div>
                <div class="form-group">
                    <label>Value #2</label>
                    <input class="form-control" name="Data[0]" value="Item 2" />
                </div>
                <div class="form-group">
                        <label>Value #3</label>
                    <input class="form-control" name="Data[2]" value="Item 3" />
                </div>
                <button type="submit" class="btn btn-primary">Submit</button>
                <a class="btn btn-secondary" asp-page="Bindings">Reset</a>
            </form>
        </div>
```

725

```
        <div class="col">
            <ul class="list-group">
                @foreach (string s in Model.Data.Where(s => s != null)) {
                    <li class="list-group-item">@s</li>
                }
            </ul>
        </div>
    </div>
</div>

@functions {

    public class BindingsModel : PageModel {

        [BindProperty(Name = "Data")]
        public SortedSet<string> Data { get; set; } = new SortedSet<string>();
    }
}
```

I changed the type of the Data property to SortedSet<string>. The model binding process will populate the set with the values from the input elements, which will be sorted alphabetically. I have left the index notation on the input element name attributes, but they have no effect since the collection class will sort its values alphabetically. To see the effect, use a browser to request http://localhost:5000/pages/bindings, edit the text fields, and click the Submit button. The model binding process will populate the sorted set with the form values, which will be presented in order, as shown in Figure 28-16.

Figure 28-16. *Model binding to a collection*

Binding to Dictionaries

For elements whose name attribute is expressed using the index notation, the model binder will use the index as the key when binding to a Dictionary, allowing a series of elements to be transformed into key/value pairs, as shown in Listing 28-23.

Listing 28-23. Binding to a Dictionary in the Bindings.cshtml File in the Pages Folder

```
@page "/pages/bindings"
@model BindingsModel
@using Microsoft.AspNetCore.Mvc
@using Microsoft.AspNetCore.Mvc.RazorPages

<div class="container-fluid">
    <div class="row">
        <div class="col">
            <form asp-page="Bindings" method="post">
                <div class="form-group">
                    <label>Value #1</label>
                    <input class="form-control" name="Data[first]" value="Item 1" />
                </div>
                <div class="form-group">
                    <label>Value #2</label>
                    <input class="form-control" name="Data[second]" value="Item 2" />
                </div>
                <div class="form-group">
                        <label>Value #3</label>
                    <input class="form-control" name="Data[third]" value="Item 3" />
                </div>
                <button type="submit" class="btn btn-primary">Submit</button>
                <a class="btn btn-secondary" asp-page="Bindings">Reset</a>
            </form>
        </div>
        <div class="col">
            <table class="table table-sm table-striped">
                <tbody>
                    @foreach (string key in Model.Data.Keys) {
                        <tr>
                            <th>@key</th><td>@Model.Data[key]</td>
                        </tr>
                    }
                </tbody>
            </table>
        </div>
    </div>
</div>

@functions {

    public class BindingsModel : PageModel {

        [BindProperty(Name = "Data")]
        public Dictionary<string, string> Data { get; set; }
            = new Dictionary<string, string>();
    }
}
```

All elements that provide values for the collection must share a common prefix, which is Data in this example, followed by the key value in square brackets. The keys for this example are the strings first, second, and third, and will be used as the keys for the content the user provides in the text fields. To see the binding process, request http://localhost:5000/pages/bindings, edit the text fields, and submit the form. The keys and values from the form data will be displayed in a table, as shown in Figure 28-17.

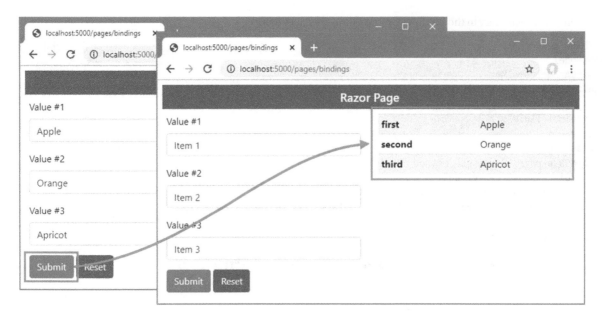

Figure 28-17. *Model binding to a dictionary*

Binding to Collections of Complex Types

The examples in this section have all been collections of simple types, but the same process can be used for complex types, too. To demonstrate, Listing 28-24 revises the Razor Page to gather details used to bind to an array of Product objects.

Listing 28-24. Binding to Complex Types in the Bindings.cshtml File in the Pages Folder

```
@page "/pages/bindings"
@model BindingsModel
@using Microsoft.AspNetCore.Mvc
@using Microsoft.AspNetCore.Mvc.RazorPages

<div class="container-fluid">
    <div class="row">
        <div class="col">
            <form asp-page="Bindings" method="post">
                @for (int i = 0; i < 2; i++) {
                    <div class="form-group">
                        <label>Name #@i</label>
                        <input class="form-control" name="Data[@i].Name"
                            value="Product-@i" />
                    </div>
                    <div class="form-group">
                        <label>Price #@i</label>
                        <input class="form-control" name="Data[@i].Price"
                            value="@(100 + i)" />
                    </div>
                }
                <button type="submit" class="btn btn-primary">Submit</button>
                <a class="btn btn-secondary" asp-page="Bindings">Reset</a>
            </form>
        </div>
    </div>
```

```
            <div class="col">
                <table class="table table-sm table-striped">
                    <tbody>
                        <tr><th>Name</th><th>Price</th></tr>
                        @foreach (Product p in Model.Data) {
                            <tr>
                                <td>@p.Name</td><td>@p.Price</td>
                            </tr>
                        }
                    </tbody>
                </table>
            </div>
        </div>
</div>

@functions {

    public class BindingsModel : PageModel {

        [BindProperty(Name = "Data")]
        public Product[] Data { get; set; } = Array.Empty<Product>();
    }
}
```

The name attributes for the input elements use the array notation, followed by a period, followed by the name of the complex type properties they represent. To define elements for the Name and Price properties, this requires elements like this:

```
...
<input class="form-control" name="Data[0].Name" />
...
<input class="form-control" name="Data[0].Price" />
...
```

During the binding process, the model binder will attempt to locate values for all the public properties defined by the target type, repeating the process for each set of values in the form data.

This example relies on model binding for the Price property defined by the Product class, which was excluded from the binding process with the BindNever attribute. Remove the attribute from the property, as shown in Listing 28-25.

Listing 28-25. Removing an Attribute in the Product.cs File in the Models Folder

```
using System.ComponentModel.DataAnnotations.Schema;
using System.ComponentModel.DataAnnotations;
using Microsoft.AspNetCore.Mvc.ModelBinding;

namespace WebApp.Models {
    public class Product {

        public long ProductId { get; set; }

        public string Name { get; set; }

        [Column(TypeName = "decimal(8, 2)")]
        //[BindNever]
        public decimal Price { get; set; }
```

```
        public long CategoryId { get; set; }
        public Category Category { get; set; }

        public long SupplierId { get; set; }
        public Supplier Supplier { get; set; }
    }
}
```

Restart ASP.NET Core so the change to the Product class takes effect and use a browser to request http://localhost:5000/pages/bindings. Enter names and prices into the text fields and submit the form, and you will see the details of the Product objects created from the data displayed in a table, as shown in Figure 28-18.

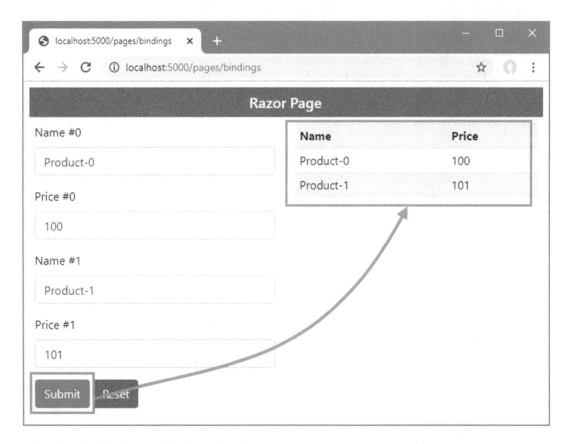

Figure 28-18. *Binding to a collection of complex types*

Specifying a Model Binding Source

As I explained at the start of the chapter, the default model binding process looks for data in four places: the form data values, the request body (for web service controllers only), the routing data, and the request query string.

The default search sequence isn't always helpful, either because you always want data to come from a specific part of the request or because you want to use a data source that isn't searched by default. The model binding feature includes a set of attributes used to override the default search behavior, as described in Table 28-3.

■ **Tip** There is also the FromService attribute, which doesn't get a value from the request, but through the dependency injection feature described in Chapter 14.

Table 28-3. *The Model Binding Source Attributes*

Name	Description
FromForm	This attribute is used to select form data as the source of binding data. The name of the parameter is used to locate a form value by default, but this can be changed using the Name property, which allows a different name to be specified.
FromRoute	This attribute is used to select the routing system as the source of binding data. The name of the parameter is used to locate a route data value by default, but this can be changed using the Name property, which allows a different name to be specified.
FromQuery	This attribute is used to select the query string as the source of binding data. The name of the parameter is used to locate a query string value by default, but this can be changed using the Name property, which allows a different query string key to be specified.
FromHeader	This attribute is used to select a request header as the source of binding data. The name of the parameter is used as the header name by default, but this can be changed using the Name property, which allows a different header name to be specified.
FromBody	This attribute is used to specify that the request body should be used as the source of binding data, which is required when you want to receive data from requests that are not form-encoded, such as in API controllers that provide web services.

The FromForm, FromRoute, and FromQuery attributes allow you to specify that the model binding data will be obtained from one of the standard locations but without the normal search sequence. Earlier in the chapter, I used this URL:

```
http://localhost:5000/controllers/Form/Index/5?id=1
```

This URL contains two possible values that can be used for the id parameter of the Index action method on the Form controller. The routing system will assign the final segment of the URL to a variable called id, which is defined in the default URL pattern for controllers, and the query string also contains an id value. The default search pattern means that the model binding data will be taken from the route data and the query string will be ignored.

In Listing 28-26, I have applied the FromQuery attribute to the id parameter defined by the Index action method, which overrides the default search sequence.

Listing 28-26. Selecting the Query String in the FormController.cs File in the Controllers Folder

```csharp
using Microsoft.AspNetCore.Mvc;
using System.Linq;
using System.Threading.Tasks;
using WebApp.Models;
using Microsoft.EntityFrameworkCore;
using Microsoft.AspNetCore.Mvc.Rendering;

namespace WebApp.Controllers {

    [AutoValidateAntiforgeryToken]
    public class FormController : Controller {
        private DataContext context;

        public FormController(DataContext dbContext) {
            context = dbContext;
        }
```

```
public async Task<IActionResult> Index([FromQuery] long? id) {
    ViewBag.Categories
        = new SelectList(context.Categories, "CategoryId", "Name");
    return View("Form", await context.Products.Include(p => p.Category)
        .Include(p => p.Supplier)
        .FirstOrDefaultAsync(p => id == null || p.ProductId == id));
}

[HttpPost]
public IActionResult SubmitForm([Bind("Name", "Category")] Product product) {
    TempData["name"] = product.Name;
    TempData["price"] = product.Price.ToString();
    TempData["category name"] = product.Category.Name;
    return RedirectToAction(nameof(Results));
}

public IActionResult Results() {
    return View(TempData);
}
    }
}
```

The attribute specifies the source for the model binding process, which you can see by restarting ASP.NET Core and using a browser to request http://localhost:5000/controllers/Form/Index/5?id=1. Instead of using the value that has been matched by the routing system, the query string will be used instead, producing the response shown in Figure 28-19. No other location will be used if the query string doesn't contain a suitable value for the model binding process.

▪ **Tip** You can still bind complex types when specifying a model binding source such as the query string. For each simple property in the parameter type, the model binding process will look for a query string key with the same name.

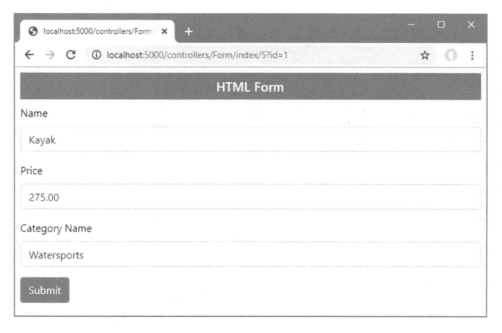

Figure 28-19. *Specifying a model binding data source*

Selecting a Binding Source for a Property

The same attributes can be used to model bind properties defined by a page model or a controller, as shown in Listing 28-27.

Listing 28-27. Selecting the Query String in the Bindings.cshtml File in the Pages Folder

```
...
@functions {

    public class BindingsModel : PageModel {

        //[BindProperty(Name = "Data")]
        [FromQuery(Name = "Data")]
        public Product[] Data { get; set; } = Array.Empty<Product>();
    }
}
...
```

The use of the FromQuery attribute means the query string is used as the source of values for the model binder as it creates the Product array, which you can see by requesting http://localhost:5000/pages/bindings?data[0].name=Skis&data[0].price=500, which produces the response shown in Figure 28-20.

■ **Note** In this example, I have used a GET request because it allows the query string to be easily set. Although it is harmless in such a simple example, care must be taken when sending GET requests that modify the state of the application. As noted previously, making changes in GET requests can lead to problems.

Figure 28-20. Specifying a model binding data source in a Razor Page

---

■ **Tip** Although it is rarely used, you can bind complex types using header values by applying the FromHeader attribute to the properties of a model class.

Using Headers for Model Binding

The FromHeader attribute allows HTTP request headers to be used as the source for binding data. In Listing 28-28, I have added a simple action method to the Form controller that defines a parameter that will be model bound from a standard HTTP request header.

Listing 28-28. Model Binding from a Header in the FormController.cs File in the Controllers Folder

```
using Microsoft.AspNetCore.Mvc;
using System.Linq;
using System.Threading.Tasks;
using WebApp.Models;
using Microsoft.EntityFrameworkCore;
using Microsoft.AspNetCore.Mvc.Rendering;

namespace WebApp.Controllers {

    [AutoValidateAntiforgeryToken]
    public class FormController : Controller {
        private DataContext context;

        // ...other action methods omitted for brevity...

        public string Header([FromHeader]string accept) {
            return $"Header: {accept}";
        }
    }
}
```

The Header action method defines an accept parameter, the value for which will be taken from the Accept header in the current request and returned as the method result. Restart ASP.NET Core and request http://localhost:5000/controllers/form/header, and you will see a result like this:

```
Header: text/html,application/xhtml+xml,application/xml;q=0.9,image/webp,
    image/apng,*/*;q=0.8,application/signed-exchange;v=b3
```

Not all HTTP header names can be easily selected by relying on the name of the action method parameter because the model binding system doesn't convert from C# naming conventions to those used by HTTP headers. In these situations, you must configure the FromHeader attribute using the Name property to specify the name of the header, as shown in Listing 28-29.

Listing 28-29. Selecting a Header by Name in the FormController.cs File in the Controllers Folder

```
using Microsoft.AspNetCore.Mvc;
using System.Linq;
using System.Threading.Tasks;
using WebApp.Models;
using Microsoft.EntityFrameworkCore;
using Microsoft.AspNetCore.Mvc.Rendering;

namespace WebApp.Controllers {

    [AutoValidateAntiforgeryToken]
    public class FormController : Controller {
        private DataContext context;

        // ...other action methods omitted for brevity...

        public string Header([FromHeader(Name = "Accept-Language")] string accept) {
            return $"Header: {accept}";
        }
    }
}
```

I can't use Accept-Language as the name of a C# parameter, and the model binder won't automatically convert a name like AcceptLanguage into Accept-Language so that it matches the header. Instead, I used the Name property to configure the attribute so that it matches the right header. If you restart ASP.NET Core and request http://localhost:5000/controllers/form/header, you will see a result like this, which will vary based on your locale settings:

```
Header: en-US;q=0.9,en;q=0.8
```

Using Request Bodies as Binding Sources

Not all data sent by clients is sent as form data, such as when a JavaScript client sends JSON data to an API controller. The FromBody attribute specifies that the request body should be decoded and used as a source of model binding data. In Listing 28-30, I have added a new action method to the Form controller with a parameter that is decorated with the FromBody attribute.

■ **Tip** The FromBody attribute isn't required for controllers that are decorated with the ApiController attribute.

Listing 28-30. Adding an Action Method in the FormController.cs File in the Controllers Folder

```
using Microsoft.AspNetCore.Mvc;
using System.Linq;
using System.Threading.Tasks;
using WebApp.Models;
using Microsoft.EntityFrameworkCore;
using Microsoft.AspNetCore.Mvc.Rendering;

namespace WebApp.Controllers {

    [AutoValidateAntiforgeryToken]
    public class FormController : Controller {
        private DataContext context;

        public FormController(DataContext dbContext) {
            context = dbContext;
        }

        // ...other action methods omitted for brevity...

        [HttpPost]
        [IgnoreAntiforgeryToken]
        public Product Body([FromBody] Product model) {
            return model;
        }
    }
}
```

To test the model binding process, restart ASP.NET Core, open a new PowerShell command prompt, and run the command in Listing 28-31 to send a request to the application.

■ **Note** I added the IgnoreAntiforgeryToken to the action method in Listing 28-31 because the request that I am going to send won't include an anti-forgery token, which I described in Chapter 27.

Listing 28-31. Sending a Request

```
Invoke-RestMethod http://localhost:5000/controllers/form/body -Method POST -Body  (@{ Name="Soccer Boots";
Price=89.99} | ConvertTo-Json) -ContentType "application/json"
```

The JSON-encoded request body is used to model bind the action method parameter, which produces the following response:

```
productId  : 0
name       : Soccer Boots
price      : 89.99
categoryId : 0
category   :
supplierId : 0
supplier   :
```

Manually Model Binding

Model binding is applied automatically when you define a parameter for an action or handler method or apply the `BindProperty` attribute. Automatic model binding works well if you can consistently follow the name conventions and you always want the process to be applied. If you need to take control of the binding process or you want to perform binding selectively, then you can perform model binding manually, as shown in Listing 28-32.

Listing 28-32. Manually Binding in the Bindings.cshtml File in the Pages Folder

```
@page "/pages/bindings"
@model BindingsModel
@using Microsoft.AspNetCore.Mvc
@using Microsoft.AspNetCore.Mvc.RazorPages

<div class="container-fluid">
    <div class="row">
        <div class="col">
            <form asp-page="Bindings" method="post">
                <div class="form-group">
                    <label>Name</label>
                    <input class="form-control" asp-for="Data.Name" />
                </div>
                <div class="form-group">
                    <label>Price</label>
                    <input class="form-control" asp-for="Data.Price"
                            value="@(Model.Data.Price + 1)" />
                </div>
                <div class="form-check m-2">
                    <input class="form-check-input" type="checkbox" name="bind"
                        value="true" checked />
                    <label class="form-check-label">Model Bind?</label>
                </div>
                <button type="submit" class="btn btn-primary">Submit</button>
                <a class="btn btn-secondary" asp-page="Bindings">Reset</a>
            </form>
        </div>
    </div>
```

```
        <div class="col">
            <table class="table table-sm table-striped">
                <tbody>
                    <tr><th>Name</th><th>Price</th></tr>
                    <tr>
                        <td>@Model.Data.Name</td><td>@Model.Data.Price</td>
                    </tr>
                </tbody>
            </table>
        </div>
    </div>
</div>

@functions {

    public class BindingsModel : PageModel {

        public Product Data { get; set; }
            = new Product() { Name = "Skis", Price = 500 };

        public async Task OnPostAsync([FromForm] bool bind) {
            if (bind) {
                await TryUpdateModelAsync<Product>(Data,
                    "data", p => p.Name, p => p.Price);
            }
        }
    }
}
```

Manual model binding is performed using the TryUpdateModelAsync method, which is provided by the PageModel and ControllerBase classes, which means it is available for both Razor Pages and MVC controllers.

This example mixes automatic and manual model binding. The OnPostAsync method uses automatic model binding to receive a value for its bind parameter, which has been decorated with the FromForm attribute. If the value of the parameter is true, the TryUpdateModelAsync method is used to apply model binding. The arguments to the TryUpdateModelAsync method are the object that will be model bound, the prefix for the values, and a series of expressions that select the properties that will be included in the process, although there are other versions of the TryUpdateModelAsync method available.

The result is that the model binding process for the Data property is performed only when the user checks the checkbox added to the form in Listing 28-32. If the checkbox is unchecked, then no model binding occurs, and the form data is ignored. To make it obvious when model binding is used, the value of the Price property is incremented when the form is rendered. To see the effect, request http://localhost:5000/pages/bindings and submit the form with the checkbox checked and then unchecked, as shown in Figure 28-21.

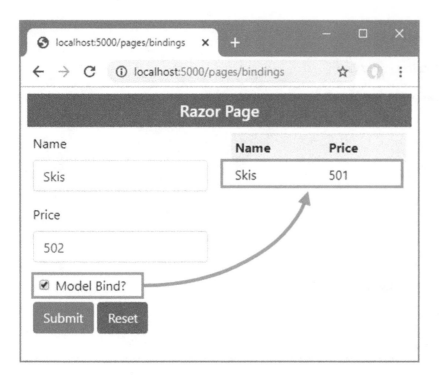

Figure 28-21. *Using manual model binding*

Summary

In this chapter, I introduced the model binding feature, which makes it easy to work with request data. I showed you how to use model binding with parameters and properties, how to bind simple and complex types, and the conventions required to bind to arrays and collections. I also explained how to control which part of the request is used for model binding and how to take control of when model binding is performed. In the next chapter, I describe the features that ASP.NET Core provides to validate form data.

CHAPTER 29

Using Model Validation

In the previous chapter, I showed you how the model binding process creates objects from HTTP requests. Throughout that chapter, I simply displayed the data that the application received. That's because the data that users provide should not be used until it has been inspected to ensure that the application is able to use it. The reality is that users will often enter data that isn't valid and cannot be used, which leads me to the topic of this chapter: *model validation.*

Model validation is the process of ensuring the data received by the application is suitable for binding to the model and, when this is not the case, providing useful information to the user that will help explain the problem.

The first part of the process, checking the data received, is one of the most important ways to preserve the integrity of an application's data. Rejecting data that cannot be used can prevent odd and unwanted states from arising in the application. The second part of the validation process is helping the user correct the problem and is equally important. Without the feedback needed to correct the problem, users become frustrated and confused. In public-facing applications, this means users will simply stop using the application. In corporate applications, this means the user's workflow will be hindered. Neither outcome is desirable, but fortunately, ASP.NET Core provides extensive support for model validation. Table 29-1 puts model validation in context.

Table 29-1. *Putting Model Validation in Context*

Question	Answer
What is it?	Model validation is the process of ensuring that the data provided in a request is valid for use in the application.
Why is it useful?	Users do not always enter valid data, and using it in the application can produce unexpected and undesirable errors.
How is it used?	Controllers and Razor Pages check the outcome of the validation process, and tag helpers are used to include validation feedback in views displayed to the user. Validation can be performed automatically during the model binding process and can be supplemented with custom validation.
Are there any pitfalls or limitations?	It is important to test the efficacy of your validation code to ensure that it covers the full range of values that the application can receive.
Are there any alternatives?	Model validation is optional, but it is a good idea to use it whenever using model binding.

Table 29-2 summarizes the chapter.

Table 29-2. *Chapter Summary*

Problem	Solution	Listing
Validating data	Manually use the ModelState features or apply validation attributes	5, 13–20
Displaying validation messages	Use the classes to which form elements are assigned and the validation tag helpers	6–12
Validating data before the form is submitted	Use client-side and remote validation	21–25

© Adam Freeman 2020
A. Freeman, *Pro ASP.NET Core 3*, https://doi.org/10.1007/978-1-4842-5440-0_29

Preparing for This Chapter

This chapter uses the WebApp project from Chapter 28. To prepare for this chapter, change the contents of the Form controller's Form view so it contains input elements for each of the properties defined by the Product class, excluding the navigation properties used by Entity Framework Core, as shown in Listing 29-1.

■ **Tip** You can download the example project for this chapter—and for all the other chapters in this book—from https://github. com/apress/pro-asp.net-core-3. See Chapter 1 for how to get help if you have problems running the examples.

Listing 29-1. Changing Elements in the Form.cshtml File in the Views/Form Folder

```
@model Product
@{ Layout = "_SimpleLayout"; }

<h5 class="bg-primary text-white text-center p-2">HTML Form</h5>

<form asp-action="submitform" method="post" id="htmlform">
    <div class="form-group">
        <label asp-for="Name"></label>
        <input class="form-control" asp-for="Name" />
    </div>
    <div class="form-group">
        <label asp-for="Price"></label>
        <input class="form-control" asp-for="Price" />
    </div>
    <div class="form-group">
        <label>CategoryId</label>
        <input class="form-control" asp-for="CategoryId" />
    </div>
    <div class="form-group">
        <label>SupplierId</label>
        <input class="form-control" asp-for="SupplierId" />
    </div>
    <button type="submit" class="btn btn-primary">Submit</button>
</form>
```

Replace the contents of the FormController.cs file with those shown in Listing 29-2, which adds support for displaying the properties defined in Listing 29-1 and removes model binding attributes and action methods that are no longer required.

Listing 29-2. Replacing the Contents of the FormController.cs File in the Controllers Folder

```
using Microsoft.AspNetCore.Mvc;
using System.Linq;
using System.Threading.Tasks;
using WebApp.Models;
using Microsoft.EntityFrameworkCore;

namespace WebApp.Controllers {

    [AutoValidateAntiforgeryToken]
    public class FormController : Controller {
        private DataContext context;

        public FormController(DataContext dbContext) {
            context = dbContext;
        }
```

```
public async Task<IActionResult> Index(long? id) {
    return View("Form", await context.Products
        .FirstOrDefaultAsync(p => id == null || p.ProductId == id));
}

[HttpPost]
public IActionResult SubmitForm(Product product) {
    TempData["name"] = product.Name;
    TempData["price"] = product.Price.ToString();
    TempData["categoryId"] = product.CategoryId.ToString();
    TempData["supplierId"] = product.SupplierId.ToString();
    return RedirectToAction(nameof(Results));
}

public IActionResult Results() {
    return View(TempData);
}
}
}
```

Dropping the Database

Open a new PowerShell command prompt, navigate to the folder that contains the WebApp.csproj file, and run the command shown in Listing 29-3 to drop the database.

Listing 29-3. Dropping the Database

```
dotnet ef database drop --force
```

Running the Example Application

Select Start Without Debugging or Run Without Debugging from the Debug menu or use the PowerShell command prompt to run the command shown in Listing 29-4.

Listing 29-4. Running the Example Application

```
dotnet run
```

Use a browser to request http://localhost:5000/controllers/Form, which will display an HTML form. Click the Submit button, and the form data will be displayed, as shown in Figure 29-1.

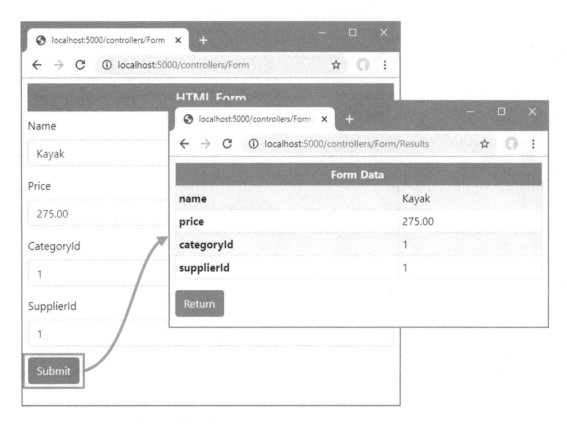

Figure 29-1. *Running the example application*

Understanding the Need for Model Validation

Model validation is the process of enforcing the requirements that an application has for the data it receives from clients. Without validation, an application will try to operate on any data it receives, which can lead to exceptions and unexpected behavior that appear immediately or long-term problems that appear gradually as the database is populated with bad, incomplete, or malicious data.

Currently, the action and handler methods that receive form data will accept any data that the user submits, which is why the examples just display the form data and don't store it in the database.

Most data values have constraints of some sort. This can involve requiring a value to be provided, requiring the value to be a specific type, and requiring the value to fall within a specific range.

As an example, before I can safely store a Product object in the database, for example, I need to make sure that the user provides values for the Name, Price, CategoryId, and SupplierId properties. The Name value can be any valid string, the Price property must be a valid currency amount, and the CategoryId and SupplierId properties must correspond to existing Supplier and Category products in the database. In the following sections, I demonstrate how model validation can be used to enforce these requirements by checking the data that the application receives and providing feedback to the user when the application cannot use the data the user has submitted.

Explicitly Validating Data in a Controller

The most direct way of validating data is to do so in an action or handler method, as shown in Listing 29-5, recording details of any problems so they can be displayed to the user.

Listing 29-5. Explicitly Validating Data in the FormController.cs File in the Controllers Folder

```
using Microsoft.AspNetCore.Mvc;
using System.Linq;
using System.Threading.Tasks;
using WebApp.Models;
```

```
using Microsoft.EntityFrameworkCore;
using Microsoft.AspNetCore.Mvc.ModelBinding;

namespace WebApp.Controllers {

    [AutoValidateAntiforgeryToken]
    public class FormController : Controller {
        private DataContext context;

        public FormController(DataContext dbContext) {
            context = dbContext;
        }

        public async Task<IActionResult> Index(long? id) {
            return View("Form", await context.Products
                .FirstOrDefaultAsync(p => id == null || p.ProductId == id));
        }

        [HttpPost]
        public IActionResult SubmitForm(Product product) {

            if (string.IsNullOrEmpty(product.Name)) {
                ModelState.AddModelError(nameof(Product.Name), "Enter a name");
            }

            if (ModelState.GetValidationState(nameof(Product.Price))
                    == ModelValidationState.Valid && product.Price < 1) {
                ModelState.AddModelError(nameof(Product.Price),
                    "Enter a positive price");
            }

            if (!context.Categories.Any(c => c.CategoryId == product.CategoryId)) {
                ModelState.AddModelError(nameof(Product.CategoryId),
                    "Enter an existing category ID");
            }

            if (!context.Suppliers.Any(s => s.SupplierId == product.SupplierId)) {
                ModelState.AddModelError(nameof(Product.SupplierId),
                    "Enter an existing supplier ID");
            }

            if (ModelState.IsValid) {
                TempData["name"] = product.Name;
                TempData["price"] = product.Price.ToString();
                TempData["categoryId"] = product.CategoryId.ToString();
                TempData["supplierId"] = product.SupplierId.ToString();
                return RedirectToAction(nameof(Results));
            } else {
                return View("Form");
            }
        }

        public IActionResult Results() {
            return View(TempData);
        }
    }
}
```

For each of the properties of the `Product` parameter created, I check to see the value provided by the user and record any errors I find using the `ModelStateDictionary` object that is returned by the `ModelState` property inherited from the `ControllerBase` class.

As its name suggests, the `ModelStateDictionary` class is a dictionary used to track details of the state of the model object, with an emphasis on validation errors. Table 29-3 describes the most important `ModelStateDictionary` members.

Table 29-3. *Selected ModelStateDictionary Members*

Name	Description
AddModelError(property, message)	This method is used to record a model validation error for the specified property.
GetValidationState(property)	This method is used to determine whether there are model validation errors for a specific property, expressed as a value from the `ModelValidationState` enumeration.
IsValid	This property returns `true` if all the model properties are valid and returns `false` otherwise.
Clear()	This property clears the validation state.

As an example of using the `ModelStateDictionary`, consider how the `Name` property was validated.

```
...
if (string.IsNullOrEmpty(product.Name)) {
    ModelState.AddModelError(nameof(Product.Name), "Enter a name");
}
...
```

One of the validation requirements for the `Product` class is to ensure the user provides a value for the `Name` property, so I use the static `string.IsNullOrEmpty` method to test the property value that the model binding process has extracted from the request. If the `Name` property is `null` or an empty string, then I know that the value cannot be used by the application, and I use the `ModelState.AddModelError` method to register a validation error, specifying the name of the property (`Name`) and a message that will be displayed to the user to explain the nature of the problem (`Enter a name`).

The `ModelStateDictionary` is also used during the model binding process to record any problems with finding and assigning values to model properties. The `GetValidationState` method is used to see whether there have been any errors recorded for a model property, either from the model binding process or because the `AddModelError` method has been called during explicit validation in the action method. The `GetValidationState` method returns a value from the `ModelValidationState` enumeration, which defines the values described in Table 29-4.

Table 29-4. *The ModelValidationState Values*

Name	Description
Unvalidated	This value means that no validation has been performed on the model property, usually because there was no value in the request that corresponded to the property name.
Valid	This value means that the request value associated with the property is valid.
Invalid	This value means that the request value associated with the property is invalid and should not be used.
Skipped	This value means that the model property has not been processed, which usually means that there have been so many validation errors that there is no point continuing to perform validation checks.

For the `Price` property, I check to see whether the model binding process has reported a problem parsing the value sent by the browser into a decimal value, like this:

```
...
if (ModelState.GetValidationState(nameof(Product.Price))
        == ModelValidationState.Valid && product.Price < 1) {
    ModelState.AddModelError(nameof(Product.Price), "Enter a positive price");
}
...
```

I want to make sure that the user provides a Price value that is equal to or greater than 1, but there is no point in recording an error about zero or negative values if the user has provided a value that the model binder cannot convert into a decimal value. I use the GetValidationState method to determine the validation status of the Price property before performing my own validation check.

After I have validated all the properties in the Product object, I check the ModelState.IsValid property to see whether there were errors. This method returns true if the Model.State.AddModelError method was called during the checks or if the model binder had any problems creating the object.

```
...
if (ModelState.IsValid) {
    TempData["name"] = product.Name;
    TempData["price"] = product.Price.ToString();
    TempData["categoryId"] = product.CategoryId.ToString();
    TempData["supplierId"] = product.SupplierId.ToString();
    return RedirectToAction(nameof(Results));
} else {
    return View("Form");
}
...
```

The Product object is valid if the IsValid property returns true, in which case the action method redirects the browser to the Results action, where the validated form values will be displayed. There is a validation problem if the IsValue property returns false, which is dealt with by calling the View method to render the Form view again.

Displaying Validation Errors to the User

It may seem odd to deal with a validation error by calling the View method, but the context data provided to the view contains details of the model validation errors; these details are used by the tag helper to transform the input elements.

To see how this works, restart ASP.NET Core so the changes to the controller take effect and use a browser to request http://localhost:5000/controllers/form. Clear the contents of the Name field and click the Submit button. There won't be any visible change in the content displayed by the browser, but if you examine the input element for the Name field, you will see the element has been transformed. Here is the input element before the form was submitted:

```
<input class="form-control" type="text" id="Name" name="Name" value="Kayak">
```

Here is the input element after the form has been submitted:

```
<input class="form-control input-validation-error" type="text" id="Name"
    name="Name" value="">
```

The tag helper adds elements whose values have failed validation to the input-validation-error class, which can then be styled to highlight the problem to the user.

You can do this by defining custom CSS styles in a stylesheet, but a little extra work is required if you want to use the built-in validation styles that CSS libraries like Bootstrap provides. The name of the class added to the input elements cannot be changed, which means that some JavaScript code is required to map between the name used by ASP.NET Core and the CSS error classes provided by Bootstrap.

■ **Tip** Using JavaScript code like this can be awkward, and it can be tempting to use custom CSS styles, even when working with a CSS library like Bootstrap. However, the colors used for validation classes in Bootstrap can be overridden by using themes or by customizing the package and defining your own styles, which means you have to ensure that any changes to the theme are matched by corresponding changes to any custom styles you define. Ideally, Microsoft will make the validation class names configurable in a future release of ASP.NET Core, but until then, using JavaScript to apply Bootstrap styles is a more robust approach than creating custom stylesheets.

To define the JavaScript code so that it can be used by both controllers and Razor Pages, use the Visual Studio JavaScript File template to add a file named _Validation.cshtml to the Views/Shared folder with the content shown in Listing 29-6. Visual Studio Code doesn't require templates, and you can just add a file named _Validation.cshtml in the Views/Shared folder with the code shown in the listing.

Listing 29-6. The Contents of the _Validation.cshtml File in the Views/Shared Folder

```
<script src="/lib/jquery/jquery.min.js"></script>
<script type="text/javascript">
    $(document).ready(function () {
        $("input.input-validation-error").addClass("is-invalid");
    });
</script>
```

I will use the new file as a partial view, which contains a script element that loads the jQuery library and contains a custom script that locates input elements that are members of the input-validation-error class and adds them to the is-invalid class (which Bootstrap uses to set the error color for form elements). Listing 29-7 uses the partial tag helper to incorporate the new partial view into the HTML form so that fields with validation errors are highlighted.

Listing 29-7. Including a Partial View in the Form.cshtml File in the Views/Form Folder

```
@model Product
@{ Layout = "_SimpleLayout"; }

<h5 class="bg-primary text-white text-center p-2">HTML Form</h5>

<partial name="_Validation" />

<form asp-action="submitform" method="post" id="htmlform">
    <div class="form-group">
        <label asp-for="Name"></label>
        <input class="form-control" asp-for="Name" />
    </div>
    <div class="form-group">
        <label asp-for="Price"></label>
        <input class="form-control" asp-for="Price" />
    </div>
    <div class="form-group">
        <label>CategoryId</label>
        <input class="form-control" asp-for="CategoryId"  />
    </div>
    <div class="form-group">
        <label>SupplierId</label>
        <input class="form-control" asp-for="SupplierId"  />
    </div>
    <button type="submit" class="btn btn-primary">Submit</button>
</form>
```

The jQuery code runs when the browser has finished parsing all the elements in the HTML document, and the effect is to highlight the input elements that have been assigned to the input-validaton-error class. You can see the effect by navigating to http://localhost:5000/controllers/form, clearing the contents of the Name field, and submitting the form, which produces the response shown in Figure 29-2.

Figure 29-2. *Highlighting a validation error*

The user will not be shown the Results view until the form is submitted with data that can be parsed by the model browser and that passes the explicit validation checks in the action method. Until that happens, submitting the form will cause the Form view to be rendered with the highlighted validation errors.

Displaying Validation Messages

The CSS classes that the tag helpers apply to input elements indicate that there are problems with a form field, but they do not tell the user what the problem is. Providing the user with more information requires the use of a different tag helper, which adds a summary of the problems to the view, as shown in Listing 29-8.

Listing 29-8. Displaying a Summary in the Form.cshtml File in the Views/Form Folder

```
@model Product
@{ Layout = "_SimpleLayout"; }

<h5 class="bg-primary text-white text-center p-2">HTML Form</h5>

<partial name="_Validation" />

<form asp-action="submitform" method="post" id="htmlform">
    <div asp-validation-summary="All" class="text-danger"></div>
    <div class="form-group">
        <label asp-for="Name"></label>
        <input class="form-control" asp-for="Name" />
    </div>
    <div class="form-group">
        <label asp-for="Price"></label>
        <input class="form-control" asp-for="Price" />
    </div>
    <div class="form-group">
        <label>CategoryId</label>
```

```
        <input class="form-control" asp-for="CategoryId" />
    </div>
    <div class="form-group">
        <label>SupplierId</label>
        <input class="form-control" asp-for="SupplierId" />
    </div>
    <button type="submit" class="btn btn-primary">Submit</button>
</form>
```

The ValidationSummaryTagHelper class detects the asp-validation-summary attribute on div elements and responds by adding messages that describe any validation errors that have been recorded. The value of the asp-validation-summary attribute is a value from the ValidationSummary enumeration, which defines the values shown in Table 29-5 and which I demonstrate shortly.

Table 29-5. *The ValidationSummary Values*

Name	Description
All	This value is used to display all the validation errors that have been recorded.
ModelOnly	This value is used to display only the validation errors for the entire model, excluding those that have been recorded for individual properties, as described in the "Displaying Model-Level Messages" section.
None	This value is used to disable the tag helper so that it does not transform the HTML element.

Presenting error messages helps the user understand why the form cannot be processed. As an example, try submitting the form with a negative value in the Price field, such as –10, and with a value that cannot be converted into a decimal value, such as **ten**. Each value results in a different error message, as shown in Figure 29-3.

Figure 29-3. *Displaying validation messages*

Configuring the Default Validation Error Messages

The model binding process performs its own validation when it tries to provide the data values required to invoke an action method, which is why you see a validation message when the Price value cannot be converted to a decimal, for example. Not all the validation messages produced by the model binder are helpful to the user, which you can see by clearing the Price field and submitting the form. The empty field produces the following message:

```
The value '' is invalid
```

This message is added to the ModelStateDictionary by the model binding process when it can't find a value for a property or does find a value but can't parse it. In this case, the error has arisen because the empty string sent in the form data can't be parsed into a decimal value for the Price property of the Product class.

The model binder has a set of predefined messages that it uses for validation errors. These can be replaced with custom messages using the methods defined by the DefaultModelBindingMessageProvider class, as described in Table 29-6.

Table 29-6. *The DefaultModelBindingMessageProvider Methods*

Name	Description
SetValueMustNotBeNullAccessor	The function assigned to this property is used to generate a validation error message when a value is null for a model property that is non-nullable.
SetMissingBindRequiredValueAccessor	The function assigned to this property is used to generate a validation error message when the request does not contain a value for a required property.
SetMissingKeyOrValueAccessor	The function assigned to this property is used to generate a validation error message when the data required for dictionary model object contains null keys or values.
SetAttemptedValueIsInvalidAccessor	The function assigned to this property is used to generate a validation error message when the model binding system cannot convert the data value into the required C# type.
SetUnknownValueIsInvalidAccessor	The function assigned to this property is used to generate a validation error message when the model binding system cannot convert the data value into the required C# type.
SetValueMustBeANumberAccessor	The function assigned to this property is used to generate a validation error message when the data value cannot be parsed into a C# numeric type.
SetValueIsInvalidAccessor	The function assigned to this property is used to generate a fallback validation error message that is used as a last resort.

Each of the methods described in the table accepts a function that is invoked to get the validation message to display to the user. These methods are applied through the options pattern in the Startup class, as shown in Listing 29-9, in which I have replaced the default message that is displayed when a value is null or cannot be converted.

Listing 29-9. Changing a Validation Message in the Startup.cs File in the WebApp Folder

```
using Microsoft.AspNetCore.Builder;
using Microsoft.Extensions.DependencyInjection;
using Microsoft.Extensions.Configuration;
using Microsoft.EntityFrameworkCore;
using WebApp.Models;
using Microsoft.AspNetCore.Antiforgery;
using Microsoft.AspNetCore.Http;
using Microsoft.AspNetCore.Mvc;

namespace WebApp {
    public class Startup {

        public Startup(IConfiguration config) {
            Configuration = config;
        }

        public IConfiguration Configuration { get; set; }

        public void ConfigureServices(IServiceCollection services) {
            services.AddDbContext<DataContext>(opts => {
                opts.UseSqlServer(Configuration[
                    "ConnectionStrings:ProductConnection"]);
                opts.EnableSensitiveDataLogging(true);
            });
```

```
            services.AddControllersWithViews().AddRazorRuntimeCompilation();
            services.AddRazorPages().AddRazorRuntimeCompilation();
            services.AddSingleton<CitiesData>();

            services.Configure<AntiforgeryOptions>(opts => {
                opts.HeaderName = "X-XSRF-TOKEN";
            });

            services.Configure<MvcOptions>(opts => opts.ModelBindingMessageProvider
                .SetValueMustNotBeNullAccessor(value => "Please enter a value"));
        }

        public void Configure(IApplicationBuilder app, DataContext context,
                IAntiforgery antiforgery) {

            app.UseRequestLocalization();

            app.UseDeveloperExceptionPage();
            app.UseStaticFiles();
            app.UseRouting();

            app.Use(async (context, next) => {
                if (!context.Request.Path.StartsWithSegments("/api")) {
                    context.Response.Cookies.Append("XSRF-TOKEN",
                        antiforgery.GetAndStoreTokens(context).RequestToken,
                        new CookieOptions { HttpOnly = false });
                }
                await next();
            });

            app.UseEndpoints(endpoints => {
                endpoints.MapControllers();
                endpoints.MapControllerRoute("forms",
                    "controllers/{controller=Home}/{action=Index}/{id?}");
                endpoints.MapDefaultControllerRoute();
                endpoints.MapRazorPages();
            });
            SeedData.SeedDatabase(context);
        }
    }
}
```

The function that you specify receives the value that the user has supplied, although that is not especially useful when dealing with null values. To see the custom message, restart ASP.NET Core, use the browser to request http://localhost:5000/controllers/form, and submit the form with an empty Price field. The response will include the custom error message, as shown in Figure 29-4.

Figure 29-4. *Changing the default validation messages*

Displaying Property-Level Validation Messages

Although the custom error message is more meaningful than the default one, it still isn't that helpful because it doesn't clearly indicate which field the problem relates to. For this kind of error, it is more useful to display the validation error messages alongside the HTML elements that contain the problem data. This can be done using the ValidationMessageTag tag helper, which looks for span elements that have the asp-validation-for attribute, which is used to specify the property for which error messages should be displayed.

In Listing 29-10, I have added property-level validation message elements for each of the input elements in the form.

Listing 29-10. Adding Property-Level Messages in the Form.cshtml File in the Views/Form Folder

```
@model Product
@{  Layout = "_SimpleLayout"; }

<h5 class="bg-primary text-white text-center p-2">HTML Form</h5>

<partial name="_Validation" />

<form asp-action="submitform" method="post" id="htmlform">
    <div asp-validation-summary="All" class="text-danger"></div>
    <div class="form-group">
        <label asp-for="Name"></label>
        <div><span asp-validation-for="Name" class="text-danger"></span></div>
        <input class="form-control" asp-for="Name" />
    </div>
    <div class="form-group">
        <label asp-for="Price"></label>
        <div><span asp-validation-for="Price" class="text-danger"></span></div>
        <input class="form-control" asp-for="Price" />
    </div>
    <div class="form-group">
        <label>CategoryId</label>
        <div><span asp-validation-for="CategoryId" class="text-danger"></span></div>
        <input class="form-control" asp-for="CategoryId"  />
    </div>
    <div class="form-group">
        <label>SupplierId</label>
```

```
        <div><span asp-validation-for="SupplierId" class="text-danger"></span></div>
        <input class="form-control" asp-for="SupplierId"  />
    </div>
    <button type="submit" class="btn btn-primary">Submit</button>
</form>
```

Since span elements are displayed inline, care must be taken to present the validation messages to make it obvious which element the message relates to. You can see the effect of the new validation messages by requesting http://localhost:5000/ controllers/form, clearing the Name and Price fields, and submitting the form. The response, shown in Figure 29-5, includes validation messages alongside the text fields.

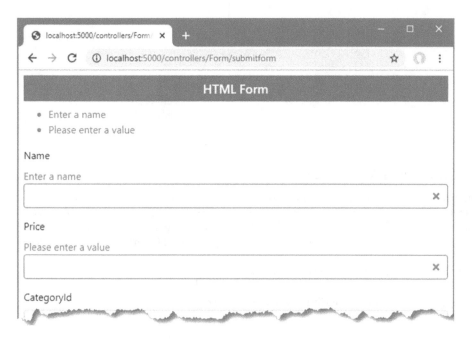

Figure 29-5. *Displaying property-level validation messages*

Displaying Model-Level Messages

It may seem that the validation summary message is superfluous because it duplicates the property-level messages. But the summary has a useful trick, which is the ability to display messages that apply to the entire model and not just individual properties. This means you can report errors that arise from a combination of individual properties, which would otherwise be hard to express with a property-level message.

In Listing 29-11, I have added a check to the FormController.SubmitForm action that records a validation error when the Price value exceeds 100 at the time that the Name value starts with Small.

Listing 29-11. Performing Model-Level Validation in the FormController.cs File in the Controllers Folder

```
...
[HttpPost]
public IActionResult SubmitForm(Product product) {

    if (string.IsNullOrEmpty(product.Name)) {
        ModelState.AddModelError(nameof(Product.Name), "Enter a name");
    }

    if (ModelState.GetValidationState(nameof(Product.Price))
            == ModelValidationState.Valid && product.Price < 1) {
        ModelState.AddModelError(nameof(Product.Price), "Enter a positive price");
    }
```

```
    if (ModelState.GetValidationState(nameof(Product.Name))
            == ModelValidationState.Valid
            && ModelState.GetValidationState(nameof(Product.Price))
            == ModelValidationState.Valid
            && product.Name.ToLower().StartsWith("small") && product.Price > 100) {
        ModelState.AddModelError("", "Small products cannot cost more than $100");
    }

    if (!context.Categories.Any(c => c.CategoryId == product.CategoryId)) {
        ModelState.AddModelError(nameof(Product.CategoryId),
            "Enter an existing category ID");
    }

    if (!context.Suppliers.Any(s => s.SupplierId == product.SupplierId)) {
        ModelState.AddModelError(nameof(Product.SupplierId),
            "Enter an existing supplier ID");
    }

    if (ModelState.IsValid) {
        TempData["name"] = product.Name;
        TempData["price"] = product.Price.ToString();
        TempData["categoryId"] = product.CategoryId.ToString();
        TempData["supplierId"] = product.SupplierId.ToString();
        return RedirectToAction(nameof(Results));
    } else {
        return View("Form");
    }
}
...
```

If the user enters a Name value that starts with Small and a Price value that is greater than 100, then a model-level validation error is recorded. I check for the combination of values only if there are no validation problems with the individual property values, which ensures the user doesn't get conflicting messages. Validation errors that relate to the entire model are recorded using the AddModelError with the empty string as the first argument.

Listing 29-12 changes the value of the asp-validation-summary attribute to ModelOnly, which excludes property-level errors, meaning that the summary will display only those errors that apply to the entire model.

Listing 29-12. Configuring the Validation Summary in the Form.cshtml File in the Views/Form Folder

```
@model Product
@{ Layout = "_SimpleLayout"; }

<h5 class="bg-primary text-white text-center p-2">HTML Form</h5>

<partial name="_Validation" />

<form asp-action="submitform" method="post" id="htmlform">
    <div asp-validation-summary="ModelOnly" class="text-danger"></div>
    <div class="form-group">
        <label asp-for="Name"></label>
        <div><span asp-validation-for="Name" class="text-danger"></span></div>
        <input class="form-control" asp-for="Name" />
    </div>
    <div class="form-group">
        <label asp-for="Price"></label>
        <div><span asp-validation-for="Price" class="text-danger"></span></div>
        <input class="form-control" asp-for="Price" />
    </div>
```

```
        <div class="form-group">
            <label>CategoryId</label>
            <div><span asp-validation-for="CategoryId" class="text-danger"></span></div>
            <input class="form-control" asp-for="CategoryId"  />
        </div>
        <div class="form-group">
            <label>SupplierId</label>
            <div><span asp-validation-for="SupplierId" class="text-danger"></span></div>
            <input class="form-control" asp-for="SupplierId"  />
        </div>
        <button type="submit" class="btn btn-primary">Submit</button>
</form>
```

Restart ASP.NET Core and request `http://localhost:5000/controllers/form`. Enter **Small Kayak** into the Name field and **150** into the Price field and submit the form. The response will include the model-level error message, as shown in Figure 29-6.

Figure 29-6. *Displaying a model-level validation message*

Explicitly Validating Data in a Razor Page

Razor Page validation relies on the features used in the controller in the previous section. Listing 29-13 adds explicit validation checks and error summaries to the FormHandler page.

Listing 29-13. Validating Data in the FormHandler.cshtml File in the Pages Folder

```
@page "/pages/form/{id:long?}"
@model FormHandlerModel
@using Microsoft.AspNetCore.Mvc.RazorPages
@using Microsoft.EntityFrameworkCore
@using Microsoft.AspNetCore.Mvc.ModelBinding

<partial name="_Validation" />

<div class="m-2">
    <h5 class="bg-primary text-white text-center p-2">HTML Form</h5>
    <form asp-page="FormHandler" method="post" id="htmlform">
        <div asp-validation-summary="ModelOnly" class="text-danger"></div>
        <div class="form-group">
            <label>Name</label>
            <div>
```

```
                <span asp-validation-for="Product.Name" class="text-danger">
                </span>
            </div>
            <input class="form-control" asp-for="Product.Name" />
        </div>
        <div class="form-group">
            <label>Price</label>
            <div>
                <span asp-validation-for="Product.Price" class="text-danger">
                </span>
            </div>
            <input class="form-control" asp-for="Product.Price"  />
        </div>
        <div class="form-group">
            <label>CategoryId</label>
            <div>
                <span asp-validation-for="Product.CategoryId" class="text-danger">
                </span>
            </div>
            <input class="form-control" asp-for="Product.CategoryId"  />
        </div>
        <div class="form-group">
            <label>SupplierId</label>
            <div>
                <span asp-validation-for="Product.SupplierId" class="text-danger">
                </span>
            </div>
            <input class="form-control" asp-for="Product.SupplierId"  />
        </div>
        <button type="submit" class="btn btn-primary">Submit</button>
    </form>
</div>

@functions {

    public class FormHandlerModel : PageModel {
        private DataContext context;

        public FormHandlerModel(DataContext dbContext) {
            context = dbContext;
        }

        [BindProperty]
        public Product Product { get; set; }

        //[BindProperty(Name = "Product.Category")]
        //public Category Category { get; set; }

        public async Task OnGetAsync(long id = 1) {
            Product = await context.Products.FirstAsync(p => p.ProductId == id);
        }

        public IActionResult OnPost() {

            if (string.IsNullOrEmpty(Product.Name)) {
                ModelState.AddModelError("Product.Name", "Enter a name");
            }
```

```
                    if (ModelState.GetValidationState("Product.Price")
                            == ModelValidationState.Valid && Product.Price < 1) {
                        ModelState.AddModelError("Product.Price", "Enter a positive price");
                    }

                    if (ModelState.GetValidationState("Product.Name")
                            == ModelValidationState.Valid
                        && ModelState.GetValidationState("Product.Price")
                            == ModelValidationState.Valid
                        && Product.Name.ToLower().StartsWith("small")
                        && Product.Price > 100) {
                            ModelState.AddModelError("",
                                "Small products cannot cost more than $100");
                    }

                    if (!context.Categories.Any(c => c.CategoryId == Product.CategoryId)) {
                        ModelState.AddModelError("Product.CategoryId",
                            "Enter an existing category ID");
                    }

                    if (!context.Suppliers.Any(s => s.SupplierId == Product.SupplierId)) {
                            ModelState.AddModelError("Product.SupplierId",
                                "Enter an existing supplier ID");
                    }

                    if (ModelState.IsValid) {
                        TempData["name"] = Product.Name;
                        TempData["price"] = Product.Price.ToString();
                        TempData["categoryId"] = Product.CategoryId.ToString();
                        TempData["supplierId"] = Product.SupplierId.ToString();
                        return RedirectToPage("FormResults");
                    } else {
                        return Page();
                    }
                }
            }
        }
}
```

The PageModel class defines a ModelState property that is the equivalent of the one I used in the controller and allows validation errors to be recorded. The process for validation is the same, but you must take care when recording errors to ensure the names match the pattern used by Razor Pages. When I recorded an error, I used the nameof keyword to select the property to which the error relates, like this:

```
...
ModelState.AddModelError(nameof(Product.Name), "Enter a name");
...
```

This is a common convention because it ensures that a typo won't cause errors to be recorded incorrectly. This expression won't work in the Razor Page, where the error must be recorded against Product.Name, rather than Name, to reflect that @Model expressions in Razor Pages return the page model object, like this:

```
...
ModelState.AddModelError("Product.Name", "Enter a name");
...
```

To test the validation process, use a browser to request `http://localhost:5000/pages/form` and submit the form with empty fields or with values that cannot be converted into the C# types required by the `Product` class. The error messages are displayed just as they are for controllers, as shown in Figure 29-7. (The values 1, 2, and 3 are valid for both the `CategoryId` and `SupplierId` fields.)

■ **Tip** The methods described in Table 29-6 that change the default validation messages affect Razor Pages as well as controllers.

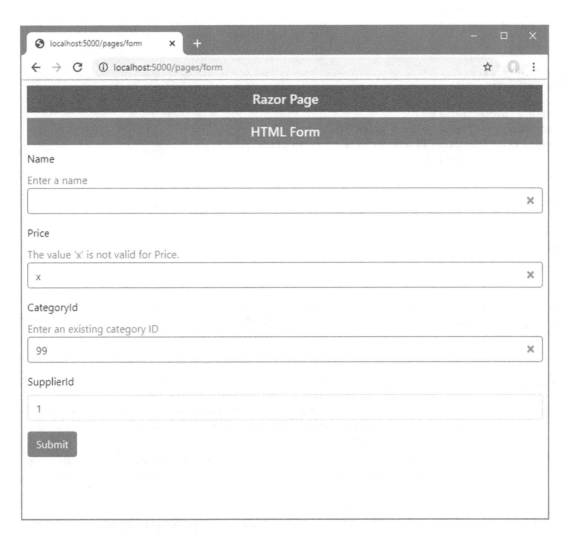

Figure 29-7. *Validating data in a Razor Page*

Specifying Validation Rules Using Metadata

One problem with putting validation logic into an action method is that it ends up being duplicated in every action or handler method that receives data from the user. To help reduce duplication, the validation process supports the use of attributes to express model validation rules directly in the model class, ensuring that the same set of validation rules will be applied regardless of which action method is used to process a request. In Listing 29-14, I have applied attributes to the `Product` class to describe the validation required for the `Name` and `Price` properties.

Listing 29-14. Applying Validation Attributes in the Product.cs File in the Models Folder

```
using System.ComponentModel.DataAnnotations.Schema;
using System.ComponentModel.DataAnnotations;
using Microsoft.AspNetCore.Mvc.ModelBinding;

namespace WebApp.Models {
    public class Product {

        public long ProductId { get; set; }

        [Required]
        [Display(Name = "Name")]
        public string Name { get; set; }

        [Column(TypeName = "decimal(8, 2)")]
        [Required(ErrorMessage = "Please enter a price")]
        [Range(1, 999999, ErrorMessage = "Please enter a positive price")]
        public decimal Price { get; set; }

        public long CategoryId { get; set; }
        public Category Category { get; set; }

        public long SupplierId { get; set; }
        public Supplier Supplier { get; set; }
    }
}
```

I used two validation attributes in the listing: Required and Range. The Required attribute specifies that it is a validation error if the user doesn't submit a value for a property. The Range attribute specifies a subset of acceptable values. Table 29-7 shows the set of built-in validation attributes available.

Table 29-7. *The Built-in Validation Attributes*

Attribute	Example	Description
Compare	[Compare ("OtherProperty")]	This attribute ensures that properties must have the same value, which is useful when you ask the user to provide the same information twice, such as an e-mail address or a password.
Range	[Range(10, 20)]	This attribute ensures that a numeric value (or any property type that implements IComparable) is not outside the range of specified minimum and maximum values. To specify a boundary on only one side, use a MinValue or MaxValue constant.
RegularExpression	[RegularExpression ("pattern")]	This attribute ensures that a string value matches the specified regular expression pattern. Note that the pattern must match the *entire* user-supplied value, not just a substring within it. By default, it matches case sensitively, but you can make it case insensitive by applying the (?i) modifier—that is, [RegularExpression("(?i)mypattern")].
Required	[Required]	This attribute ensures that the value is not empty or a string consisting only of spaces. If you want to treat whitespace as valid, use [Required(AllowEmptyStrings = true)].
StringLength	[StringLength(10)]	This attribute ensures that a string value is no longer than a specified maximum length. You can also specify a minimum length: [StringLength(10, MinimumLength=2)].

All the validation attributes support specifying a custom error message by setting a value for the ErrorMessage property, like this:

```
...
[Column(TypeName = "decimal(8, 2)")]
[Required(ErrorMessage = "Please enter a price")]
[Range(1, 999999, ErrorMessage = "Please enter a positive price")]
public decimal Price { get; set; }
...
```

If there is no custom error message, then the default messages will be used, but they tend to reveal details of the model class that will make no sense to the user unless you also use the Display attribute, like this:

```
...
[Required]
[Display(Name = "Name")]
public string Name { get; set; }
...
```

The default message generated by the Required attribute reflects the name specified with the Display attribute and so doesn't reveal the name of the property to the user.

VALIDATION WORK AROUNDS

Getting the validation results you require can take some care when using the validation attributes. For example, you cannot use the Required attribute if you want to ensure that a user has checked a checkbox because the browser will send a false value when the checkbox is unchecked, which will always pass the checks applied by the Required attribute. Instead, use the Range attribute and specify the minimum and maximum values as true, like this:

```
...
[Range(typeof(bool), "true", "true", ErrorMessage="You must check the box")]
...
```

If this sort of workaround feels uncomfortable, then you can create custom validation attributes, as described in the next section.

The use of the validation attributes on the Product class allows me to remove the explicit validation checks for the Name and Price properties, as shown in Listing 29-15.

Listing 29-15. Removing Explicit Validation in the FormController.cs File in the Controllers Folder

```
...
[HttpPost]
public IActionResult SubmitForm(Product product) {

    //if (string.IsNullOrEmpty(product.Name)) {
    //    ModelState.AddModelError(nameof(Product.Name), "Enter a name");
    //}

    //if (ModelState.GetValidationState(nameof(Product.Price))
    //        == ModelValidationState.Valid && product.Price < 1) {
    //    ModelState.AddModelError(nameof(Product.Price), "Enter a positive price");
    //}

    if (ModelState.GetValidationState(nameof(Product.Name))
            == ModelValidationState.Valid
            && ModelState.GetValidationState(nameof(Product.Price))
            == ModelValidationState.Valid
```

```
            && product.Name.ToLower().StartsWith("small") && product.Price > 100) {
        ModelState.AddModelError("", "Small products cannot cost more than $100");
    }

    if (!context.Categories.Any(c => c.CategoryId == product.CategoryId)) {
        ModelState.AddModelError(nameof(Product.CategoryId),
            "Enter an existing category ID");
    }

    if (!context.Suppliers.Any(s => s.SupplierId == product.SupplierId)) {
        ModelState.AddModelError(nameof(Product.SupplierId),
            "Enter an existing supplier ID");
    }

    if (ModelState.IsValid) {
        TempData["name"] = product.Name;
        TempData["price"] = product.Price.ToString();
        TempData["categoryId"] = product.CategoryId.ToString();
        TempData["supplierId"] = product.SupplierId.ToString();
        return RedirectToAction(nameof(Results));
    } else {
        return View("Form");
    }
}
...
```

The validation attributes are applied before the action method is called, which means that I can still rely on the model state to determine whether individual properties are valid when performing model-level validation. To see the validation attributes in action, restart ASP.NET Core MVC, request `http://localhost:5000/controllers/form`, clear the Name and Price fields, and submit the form. The response will include the validation errors produced by the attributes, as shown in Figure 29-8.

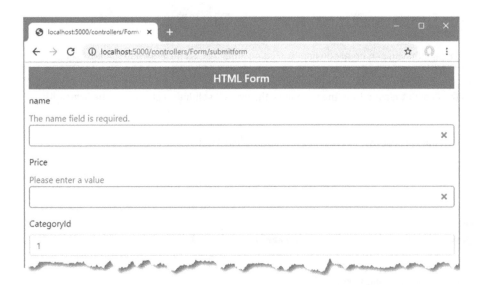

Figure 29-8. *Using validation attributes*

UNDERSTANDING WEB SERVICE CONTROLLER VALIDATION

Controllers that have been decorated with the `ApiController` attribute do not need to check the `ModelState.IsValid` property. Instead, the action method is invoked only if there are no validation errors, which means you can always rely on receiving validated objects through the model binding feature. If any validation errors are detected, then the request is terminated, and an error response is sent to the browser.

Creating a Custom Property Validation Attribute

The validation process can be extended by creating an attribute that extends the `ValidationAttribute` class. To demonstrate, I created the `WebApp/Validation` folder and added to it a class file named `PrimaryKeyAttribute.cs`, which I used to define the class shown in Listing 29-16.

Listing 29-16. The Contents of the PrimaryKeyAttribute.cs File in the Validation Folder

```
using Microsoft.EntityFrameworkCore;
using System;
using System.ComponentModel.DataAnnotations;

namespace WebApp.Validation {
    public class PrimaryKeyAttribute : ValidationAttribute {

        public Type ContextType { get; set; }

        public Type DataType { get; set; }

        protected override ValidationResult IsValid(object value,
                ValidationContext validationContext) {
            DbContext context
                = validationContext.GetService(ContextType) as DbContext;
            if (context.Find(DataType, value) == null) {
                return new ValidationResult(ErrorMessage
                    ?? "Enter an existing key value");
            } else {
                return ValidationResult.Success;
            }
        }
    }
}
```

Custom attributes override the `IsValid` method, which is called with the value to check, and a `ValidationContext` object that provides context about the validation process and provides access to the application's services through its `GetService` method.

In Listing 29-16, the custom attribute receives the type of an Entity Framework Core database context class and the type of a model class. In the `IsValid` method, the attribute obtains an instance of the context class and uses it to query the database to determine whether the value has been used as a primary key value.

REVALIDATING DATA

You may need to perform the validation process again if you modify the object received from the model binder. For these situations, use the `ModelState.Clear` method to clear any existing validation errors and call the `TryValidateModel` method.

Custom validation attributes can also be used to perform model-level validation. To demonstrate, I added a class file named `PhraseAndPriceAttribute.cs` to the `Validation` folder and used it to define the class shown in Listing 29-17.

Listing 29-17. The Contents of the PhraseAndPriceAttribute.cs File in the Validation Folder

```
using System;
using System.ComponentModel.DataAnnotations;
using WebApp.Models;

namespace WebApp.Validation {
    public class PhraseAndPriceAttribute: ValidationAttribute {

        public string Phrase { get; set; }

        public string Price { get; set; }

        protected override ValidationResult IsValid(object value,
                ValidationContext validationContext) {
            Product product = value as Product;
            if (product != null
                && product.Name.StartsWith(Phrase,
                    StringComparison.OrdinalIgnoreCase)
                && product.Price > decimal.Parse(Price)) {
                    return new ValidationResult(ErrorMessage
                        ?? $"{Phrase} products cannot cost more than ${Price}");
            }
            return ValidationResult.Success;
        }
    }
}
```

This attribute is configured with Phrase and Price properties, which are used in the IsValid method to check the Name and Price properties of the model object. Property-level custom validation attributes are applied directly to the properties they validate, and model-level attributes are applied to the entire class, as shown in Listing 29-18.

Listing 29-18. Applying Custom Validation Attributes in the Product.cs File in the Models Folder

```
using System.ComponentModel.DataAnnotations.Schema;
using System.ComponentModel.DataAnnotations;
using Microsoft.AspNetCore.Mvc.ModelBinding;
using WebApp.Validation;

namespace WebApp.Models {

    [PhraseAndPrice(Phrase ="Small", Price = "100")]
    public class Product {

        public long ProductId { get; set; }

        [Required]
        [Display(Name = "Name")]
        public string Name { get; set; }

        [Column(TypeName = "decimal(8, 2)")]
        [Required(ErrorMessage = "Please enter a price")]
        [Range(1, 999999, ErrorMessage = "Please enter a positive price")]
        public decimal Price { get; set; }

        [PrimaryKey(ContextType= typeof(DataContext), DataType = typeof(Category))]
        public long CategoryId { get; set; }
        public Category Category { get; set; }
```

```
    [PrimaryKey(ContextType = typeof(DataContext), DataType = typeof(Category))]
    public long SupplierId { get; set; }
    public Supplier Supplier { get; set; }
    }
}
```

The custom attributes allow the remaining explicit validation statements to be removed from the Form controller's action method, as shown in Listing 29-19.

Listing 29-19. Removing Explicit Validation in the FormController.cs File in the Controllers Folder

```
using Microsoft.AspNetCore.Mvc;
using System.Linq;
using System.Threading.Tasks;
using WebApp.Models;
using Microsoft.EntityFrameworkCore;
using Microsoft.AspNetCore.Mvc.ModelBinding;

namespace WebApp.Controllers {

    [AutoValidateAntiforgeryToken]
    public class FormController : Controller {
        private DataContext context;

        public FormController(DataContext dbContext) {
            context = dbContext;
        }

        public async Task<IActionResult> Index(long? id) {
            return View("Form", await context.Products
                .FirstOrDefaultAsync(p => id == null || p.ProductId == id));
        }

        [HttpPost]
        public IActionResult SubmitForm(Product product) {
            if (ModelState.IsValid) {
                TempData["name"] = product.Name;
                TempData["price"] = product.Price.ToString();
                TempData["categoryId"] = product.CategoryId.ToString();
                TempData["supplierId"] = product.SupplierId.ToString();
                return RedirectToAction(nameof(Results));
            } else {
                return View("Form");
            }
        }

        public IActionResult Results() {
            return View(TempData);
        }
    }
}
```

The validation attributes are applied automatically before the action method is invoked, which means that the validation outcome can be determined simply by reading the ModelState.IsValid property. The same simplification can be applied to the Razor Page, as shown in Listing 29-20.

Listing 29-20. Removing Explicit Validation in the FormHandler.cshtml File in the Pages Folder

```
...
@functions {

    public class FormHandlerModel : PageModel {
        private DataContext context;

        public FormHandlerModel(DataContext dbContext) {
            context = dbContext;
        }

        [BindProperty]
        public Product Product { get; set; }

        public async Task OnGetAsync(long id = 1) {
            Product = await context.Products.FirstAsync(p => p.ProductId == id);
        }

        public IActionResult OnPost() {
            if (ModelState.IsValid) {
                TempData["name"] = Product.Name;
                TempData["price"] = Product.Price.ToString();
                TempData["categoryId"] = Product.CategoryId.ToString();
                TempData["supplierId"] = Product.SupplierId.ToString();
                return RedirectToPage("FormResults");
            } else {
                return Page();
            }
        }
    }
}
...
```

Expressing the validation through the custom attributes removes the code duplication between the controller and the Razor Page and ensures that validation is applied consistently wherever model binding is used for Product objects. To test the validation attributes, restart ASP.NET Core and navigate to http://localhost:5000/controllers/form or http://localhost:5000/pages/form. Clear the form fields or enter bad key values and submit the form, and you will see the error messages produced by the attributes, some of which are shown in Figure 29-9. (The values 1, 2, and 3 are valid for both the CategoryId and SupplierId fields.)

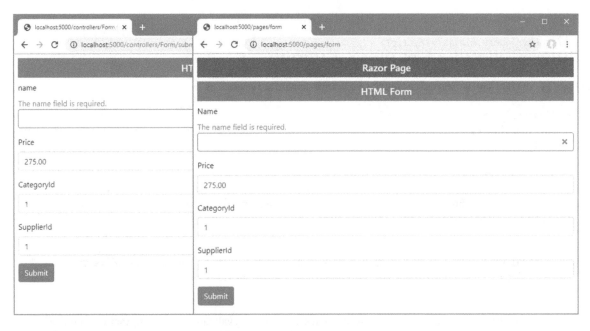

Figure 29-9. *Using custom validation attributes*

Performing Client-Side Validation

The validation techniques I have demonstrated so far have all been examples of *server-side validation*. This means the user submits their data to the server, and the server validates the data and sends back the results of the validation (either success in processing the data or a list of errors that need to be corrected).

In web applications, users typically expect immediate validation feedback—without having to submit anything to the server. This is known as *client-side validation* and is implemented using JavaScript. The data that the user has entered is validated before being sent to the server, providing the user with immediate feedback and an opportunity to correct any problems.

ASP.NET Core supports *unobtrusive client-side validation*. The term *unobtrusive* means that validation rules are expressed using attributes added to the HTML elements that views generate. These attributes are interpreted by a JavaScript library distributed by Microsoft that, in turn, configures the jQuery Validation library, which does the actual validation work. In the following sections, I will show you how the built-in validation support works and demonstrate how I can extend the functionality to provide custom client-side validation.

The first step is to install the JavaScript packages that deal with validation. Open a new PowerShell command prompt, navigate to the WebApp project folder, and run the command shown in Listing 29-21.

■ **Tip** The core jQuery command was added to the project in Chapter 26. Run the following command if you need to install it again:
`libman install jquery@3.4.1 -d wwwroot/lib/jquery`.

Listing 29-21. Installing the Validation Packages

```
libman install jquery-validate@1.19.1 -d wwwroot/lib/jquery-validate
libman install jquery-validation-unobtrusive@3.2.11 -d wwwroot/lib/jquery-validation-unobtrusive
```

Once the packages are installed, add the elements shown in Listing 29-22 to the _Validation.cshtml file in the Views/Shared folder, which provides a convenient way to introduce the validation alongside the existing jQuery code in the application.

■ **Tip** The elements must be defined in the order in which they are shown.

Listing 29-22. Adding Elements in the _Validation.cshtml File in the Views/Shared Folder

```
<script src="/lib/jquery/jquery.min.js"></script>
<script src="~/lib/jquery-validate/jquery.validate.min.js"></script>
<script
    src="~/lib/jquery-validation-unobtrusive/jquery.validate.unobtrusive.min.js">
</script>
<script type="text/javascript">
    $(document).ready(function () {
        $("input.input-validation-error").addClass("is-invalid");
    });
</script>
```

The tag helpers add `data-val*` attributes to `input` elements that describe validation constraints for fields. Here are the attributes added to the `input` element for the Name field, for example:

```
...
<input class="form-control valid" type="text" data-val="true" data-val-required="The name field is required."
id="Name" name="Name" value="Kayak" aria-describedby="Name-error" aria-invalid="false">
...
```

The unobtrusive validation JavaScript code looks for these attributes and performs validation in the browser when the user attempts to submit the form. The form won't be submitted, and an error will be displayed if there are validation problems. The data won't be sent to the application until there are no outstanding validation issues.

The JavaScript code looks for elements with the `data-val` attribute and performs local validation in the browser when the user submits the form, without sending an HTTP request to the server. You can see the effect by running the application and submitting the form while using the F12 tools to note that validation error messages are displayed even though no HTTP request is sent to the server.

AVOIDING CONFLICTS WITH BROWSER VALIDATION

Some of the current generation of HTML5 browsers support simple client-side validation based on the attributes applied to `input` elements. The general idea is that, say, an `input` element to which the `required` attribute has been applied, for example, will cause the browser to display a validation error when the user tries to submit the form without providing a value.

If you are generating form elements using tag helpers, as I have been doing in this chapter, then you won't have any problems with browser validation because the elements that are assigned `data` attributes are ignored by the browser.

However, you may run into problems if you are unable to completely control the markup in your application, something that often happens when you are passing on content generated elsewhere. The result is that the jQuery validation and the browser validation can both operate on the form, which is just confusing to the user. To avoid this problem, you can add the `novalidate` attribute to the `form` element to disable browser validation.

One of the nice client-side validation features is that the same attributes that specify validation rules are applied at the client *and* at the server. This means that data from browsers that do not support JavaScript are subject to the same validation as those that do, without requiring any additional effort.

To test the client-side validation feature, request `http://localhost:5000/controllers/form` or `http://localhost:5000/pages/form`, clear the Name field, and click the Submit button.

The error message looks like the ones generated by server-side validation, but if you enter text into the field, you will see the error message disappear immediately as the JavaScript code responds to the user interaction, as shown in Figure 29-10.

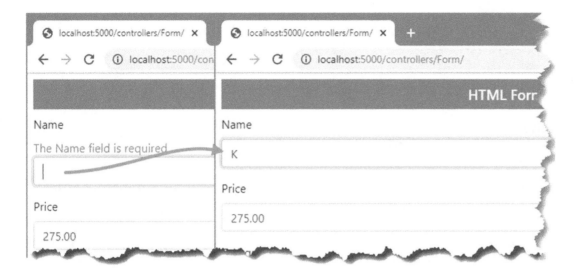

Figure 29-10. *Performing client-side validation*

EXTENDING CLIENT-SIDE VALIDATION

The client-side validation feature supports the built-in property-level attributes. The feature can be extended but requires fluency in JavaScript and requires working directly with the jQuery Validation package. See https://jqueryvalidation.org/documentation for details.

If you don't want to start writing JavaScript code, then you can follow the common pattern of using client-side validation for the built-in validation checks and server-side validation for custom validation.

Performing Remote Validation

Remote validation blurs the line between client- and server-side validation: the validation checks are enforced by the client-side JavaScript code, but the validation checking is performed by sending an asynchronous HTTP request to the application to test the value entered into the form by the user.

A common example of remote validation is to check whether a username is available in applications when such names must be unique, the user submits the data, and the client-side validation is performed. As part of this process, an asynchronous HTTP request is made to the server to validate the username that has been requested. If the username has been taken, a validation error is displayed so that the user can enter another value.

This may seem like regular server-side validation, but there are some benefits to this approach. First, only some properties will be remotely validated; the client-side validation benefits still apply to all the other data values that the user has entered. Second, the request is relatively lightweight and is focused on validation, rather than processing an entire model object.

The third difference is that the remote validation is performed in the background. The user doesn't have to click the submit button and then wait for a new view to be rendered and returned. It makes for a more responsive user experience, especially when there is a slow network between the browser and the server.

That said, remote validation is a compromise. It strikes a balance between client-side and server-side validation, but it does require requests to the application server, and it is not as quick to validate as normal client-side validation.

For the example application, I am going to use remote validation to ensure the user enters existing key values for the CategoryId and SupplierId properties. The first step is to create a web service controller whose action methods will perform the validation checks. I added a class file named ValidationController.cs to the Controllers folder with the code shown in Listing 29-23.

Listing 29-23. The Contents of the ValidationController.cs File in the Controllers Folder

```
using Microsoft.AspNetCore.Mvc;
using WebApp.Models;

namespace WebApp.Controllers {

    [ApiController]
    [Route("api/[controller]")]
    public class ValidationController: ControllerBase {
        private DataContext dataContext;

        public ValidationController(DataContext context) {
            dataContext = context;
        }

        [HttpGet("categorykey")]
        public bool CategoryKey(string categoryId) {
            long keyVal;
            return long.TryParse(categoryId, out keyVal)
                && dataContext.Categories.Find(keyVal) != null;
        }

        [HttpGet("supplierkey")]
        public bool SupplierKey(string supplierId) {
            long keyVal;
            return long.TryParse(supplierId, out keyVal)
                && dataContext.Suppliers.Find(keyVal) != null;
        }
    }
}
```

Validation action methods must define a parameter whose name matches the field they will validate, which allows the model binding process to extract the value to test from the request query string. The response from the action method must be JSON and can be only true or false, indicating whether a value is acceptable. The action methods in Listing 29-23 receive candidate values and check they have been used as database keys for Category or Supplier objects.

■ **Tip**   I could have taken advantage of model binding so that the parameter to the action methods would be converted to a `long` value, but doing so would mean that the validation method wouldn't be called if the user entered a value that cannot be converted to the `long` type. If the model binder cannot convert a value, then the MVC Framework is unable to invoke the action method and validation can't be performed. As a rule, the best approach to remote validation is to accept a `string` parameter in the action method and perform any type conversion, parsing, or model binding explicitly.

To use the remote validation method, I apply the Remote attribute to the CategoryId and SupplierId properties in the Product class, as shown in Listing 29-24.

Listing 29-24. Using the Remote Attribute in the Product.cs File in the Models Folder

```
using System.ComponentModel.DataAnnotations.Schema;
using System.ComponentModel.DataAnnotations;
using Microsoft.AspNetCore.Mvc.ModelBinding;
using WebApp.Validation;
using Microsoft.AspNetCore.Mvc;
```

```
namespace WebApp.Models {

    [PhraseAndPrice(Phrase ="Small", Price = "100")]
    public class Product {

        public long ProductId { get; set; }

        [Required]
        [Display(Name = "Name")]
        public string Name { get; set; }

        [Column(TypeName = "decimal(8, 2)")]
        [Required(ErrorMessage = "Please enter a price")]
        [Range(1, 999999, ErrorMessage = "Please enter a positive price")]
        public decimal Price { get; set; }

        [PrimaryKey(ContextType= typeof(DataContext),
            DataType = typeof(Category))]
        [Remote("CategoryKey", "Validation", ErrorMessage = "Enter an existing key")]
        public long CategoryId { get; set; }
        public Category Category { get; set; }

        [PrimaryKey(ContextType = typeof(DataContext),
            DataType = typeof(Category))]
        [Remote("SupplierKey", "Validation", ErrorMessage = "Enter an existing key")]
        public long SupplierId { get; set; }
        public Supplier Supplier { get; set; }
    }
}
```

The arguments to the Remote attribute specify the name of the validation controller and its action method. I have also used the optional ErrorMessage argument to specify the error message that will be displayed when validation fails. To see the remote validation, restart ASP.NET Core and navigate to http://localhost:5000/controllers/form, enter an invalid key value, and submit the form. You will see an error message, and the value of the input element will be validated after each key press, as shown in Figure 29-11. (Only the values 1, 2, and 3 are valid for both the CategoryId and SupplierId fields.)

Figure 29-11. *Performing remote validation*

■ **Caution**　The validation action method will be called when the user first submits the form and again each time the data is edited. For text input elements, every keystroke will lead to a call to the server. For some applications, this can be a significant number of requests and must be accounted for when specifying the server capacity and bandwidth that an application requires in production. Also, you might choose *not* to use remote validation for properties that are expensive to validate (the example repeatedly queries the database for key values, which may not be sensible for all applications or databases).

Performing Remote Validation in Razor Pages

Remote validation works in Razor Pages, but attention must be paid to the names used in the asynchronous HTTP request used to validate values. For the controller example in the previous section, the browser will send requests to URLs like this:

```
http://localhost:5000/api/Validation/categorykey?CategoryId=1
```

But for the example Razor Page, the URL will be like this, reflecting the use of the page model:

```
http://localhost:5000/api/Validation/categorykey?Product.CategoryId=1
```

The way I prefer to address this difference is by adding parameters to the validation action methods that will accept both types of request, which is easy to do using the model binding features described in previous chapters, as shown in Listing 29-25.

Listing 29-25. Adding Parameters in the ValidationController.cs File in the Controllers Folder

```
using Microsoft.AspNetCore.Mvc;
using WebApp.Models;

namespace WebApp.Controllers {

    [ApiController]
    [Route("api/[controller]")]
    public class ValidationController: ControllerBase {
        private DataContext dataContext;

        public ValidationController(DataContext context) {
            dataContext = context;
        }

        [HttpGet("categorykey")]
        public bool CategoryKey(string categoryId, [FromQuery] KeyTarget target) {
            long keyVal;
            return long.TryParse(categoryId ?? target.CategoryId, out keyVal)
                && dataContext.Categories.Find(keyVal) != null;
        }

        [HttpGet("supplierkey")]
        public bool SupplierKey(string supplierId, [FromQuery] KeyTarget target) {
            long keyVal;
            return long.TryParse(supplierId ?? target.SupplierId, out keyVal)
                && dataContext.Suppliers.Find(keyVal) != null;
        }
    }
```

```
    [Bind(Prefix = "Product")]
    public class KeyTarget {
        public string CategoryId { get; set; }
        public string SupplierId{ get; set; }
    }
}
```

The KeyTarget class is configured to bind to the Product part of the request, with properties that will match the two types of remote validation request. Each action method has been given a KeyTarget parameter, which is used if no value is received for existing parameters. This allows the same action method to accommodate both types of request, which you can see by restarting ASP.NET Core, navigating to http://localhost:5000/pages/form, entering a nonexistent key value, and clicking the Submit button, which will produce the response shown in Figure 29-12.

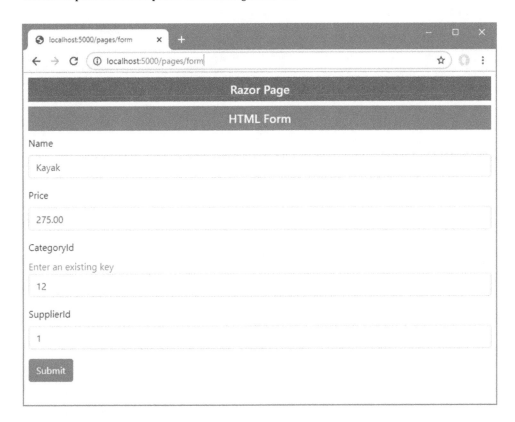

Figure 29-12. *Performing remote validation using a Razor Page*

Summary

In this chapter, I described the ASP.NET Core data validation features. I explained how to explicitly perform validation, how to use attributes to describe validation constraints, and how to validate individual properties and entire objects. I showed you how to display validation messages to the user and how to improve the user's experience of validation with client-side and remote validation. In the next chapter, I describe the ASP.NET Core filters feature.

CHAPTER 30

Using Filters

Filters inject extra logic into request processing. Filters are like middleware that is applied to a single endpoint, which can be an action or a page handler method, and they provide an elegant way to manage a specific set of requests. In this chapter, I explain how filters work, describe the different types of filter that ASP.NET Core supports, and demonstrate the use of custom filters and the filters provided by ASP.NET Core. Table 30-1 summarizes the chapter.

Table 30-1. *Chapter Summary*

Problem	Solution	Listing
Implementing a security policy	Use an authorization filter	15, 16
Implementing a resource policy, such as caching	Use a resource filter	17–19
Altering the request or response for an action method	Use an action filter	20–23
Altering the request or response for a page handler method	Use a page filter	24–26
Inspecting or altering the result produced by an endpoint	Use a result filter	27–29
Inspecting or altering uncaught exceptions	Use an exception filter	30–31
Altering the filter lifecycle	Use a filter factory or define a service	32–35
Applying filters throughout an application	Use a global filter	36, 37
Changing the order in which filters are applied	Implement the IOrderedFilter interface	38–42

Preparing for This Chapter

This chapter uses the WebApp project from Chapter 29. To prepare for this chapter, open a new PowerShell command prompt, navigate to the WebApp project folder, and run the command shown in Listing 30-1 to remove the files that are no longer required.

Listing 30-1. Removing Files from the Project

```
Remove-Item -Path Controllers,Views,Pages -Recurse -Exclude _*,Shared
```

This command removes the controllers, views, and Razor Pages, leaving behind the shared layouts, data model, and configuration files.

■ **Tip** You can download the example project for this chapter—and for all the other chapters in this book—from https://github.com/apress/pro-asp.net-core-3. See Chapter 1 for how to get help if you have problems running the examples.

Create the WebApp/Controllers folder and add a class file named HomeController.cs to the Controllers folder with the code shown in Listing 30-2.

Listing 30-2. The Contents of the HomeController.cs File in the Controllers Folder

```
using Microsoft.AspNetCore.Mvc;

namespace WebApp.Controllers {

    public class HomeController : Controller {

        public IActionResult Index() {
            return View("Message",
                "This is the Index action on the Home controller");
        }
    }
}
```

The action method renders a view called Message and passes a string as the view data. I added a Razor view named Message.cshtml with the content shown in Listing 30-3.

Listing 30-3. The Contents of the Message.cshtml File in the Views/Shared Folder

```
@{ Layout = "_SimpleLayout"; }

@if (Model is string) {
    @Model
} else if (Model is IDictionary<string, string>) {
    var dict = Model as IDictionary<string, string>;
    <table class="table table-sm table-striped table-bordered">
        <thead><tr><th>Name</th><th>Value</th></tr></thead>
        <tbody>
            @foreach (var kvp in dict) {
                <tr><td>@kvp.Key</td><td>@kvp.Value</td></tr>
            }
        </tbody>
    </table>
}
```

Add a Razor Page named Message.cshtml to the Pages folder and add the content shown in Listing 30-4.

Listing 30-4. The Contents of the Message.cshtml File in the Pages Folder

```
@page "/pages/message"
@model MessageModel
@using Microsoft.AspNetCore.Mvc.RazorPages
@using System.Collections.Generic

@if (Model.Message is string) {
    @Model.Message
} else if (Model.Message is IDictionary<string, string>) {
    var dict = Model.Message as IDictionary<string, string>;
    <table class="table table-sm table-striped table-bordered">
        <thead><tr><th>Name</th><th>Value</th></tr></thead>
        <tbody>
            @foreach (var kvp in dict) {
                <tr><td>@kvp.Key</td><td>@kvp.Value</td></tr>
            }
        </tbody>
```

```
        </table>
}

@functions {
    public class MessageModel : PageModel {

        public object Message { get; set; } = "This is the Message Razor Page";
    }
}
```

Enabling HTTPS Connections

Some of the examples in this chapter require the use of SSL. Add the configuration entries shown in Listing 30-5 to the launchSettings.json file in the Properties folder to enable SSL and set the port to 44350.

Listing 30-5. Enabling HTTPS in the launchSettings.json File in the Properties Folder

```
{
  "iisSettings": {
    "windowsAuthentication": false,
    "anonymousAuthentication": true,
    "iisExpress": {
      "applicationUrl": "http://localhost:5000",
      "sslPort": 44350
    }
  },
  "profiles": {
    "IIS Express": {
      "commandName": "IISExpress",
      "launchBrowser": true,
      "environmentVariables": {
        "ASPNETCORE_ENVIRONMENT": "Development"
      }
    },
    "WebApp": {
      "commandName": "Project",
      "launchBrowser": true,
      "environmentVariables": {
        "ASPNETCORE_ENVIRONMENT": "Development"
      },
      "applicationUrl": "http://localhost:5000;https://localhost:44350"
    }
  }
}
```

The .NET Core runtime includes a test certificate that is used for HTTPS requests. Run the commands shown in Listing 30-6 in the WebApp folder to regenerate and trust the test certificate.

Listing 30-6. Regenerating the Development Certificates

```
dotnet dev-certs https --clean

dotnet dev-certs https --trust
```

Click Yes to the prompts to delete the existing certificate that has already been trusted and click Yes to trust the new certificate, as shown in Figure 30-1.

Figure 30-1. *Regenerating the HTTPS certificate*

Dropping the Database

Open a new PowerShell command prompt, navigate to the folder that contains the WebApp.csproj file, and run the command shown in Listing 30-7 to drop the database.

Listing 30-7. Dropping the Database

```
dotnet ef database drop --force
```

Running the Example Application

Select Start Without Debugging or Run Without Debugging from the Debug menu or use the PowerShell command prompt to run the command shown in Listing 30-8.

Listing 30-8. Running the Example Application

```
dotnet run
```

Use a browser to request http://localhost:5000 and https://localhost:44350. Both URLs will be handled by the Index action defined by the Home controller, producing the responses shown in Figure 30-2.

Figure 30-2. *Responses from the Home controller*

Request `http://localhost:5000/pages/message` and `https://localhost:44350/pages/message` to see the response from the Message Razor Page, delivered over HTTP and HTTPS, as shown in Figure 30-3.

Figure 30-3. *Responses from the Message Razor Page*

Using Filters

Filters allow logic that would otherwise be applied in a middleware component or action method to be defined in a class where it can be easily reused.

Imagine that you want to enforce HTTPS requests for some action methods. In Chapter 16, I showed you how this can be done in middleware by reading the IsHttps property of the HttpRequest object. The problem with this approach is that the middleware would have to understand the configuration of the routing system to know how to intercept requests for specific action methods. A more focused approach would be to read the HttpRequest.IsHttps property within action methods, as shown in Listing 30-9.

Listing 30-9. Selectively Enforcing HTTPS in the HomeController.cs File in the Controllers Folder

```
using Microsoft.AspNetCore.Mvc;
using Microsoft.AspNetCore.Http;

namespace WebApp.Controllers {

    public class HomeController : Controller {

        public IActionResult Index() {
            if (Request.IsHttps) {
                return View("Message",
                    "This is the Index action on the Home controller");
            } else {
                return new StatusCodeResult(StatusCodes.Status403Forbidden);
            }
        }
    }
}
```

Restart ASP.NET Core and request `http://localhost:5000`. This method now requires HTTPS, and you will see an error response. Request `https://localhost:44350`, and you will see the message output. Figure 30-4 shows both responses.

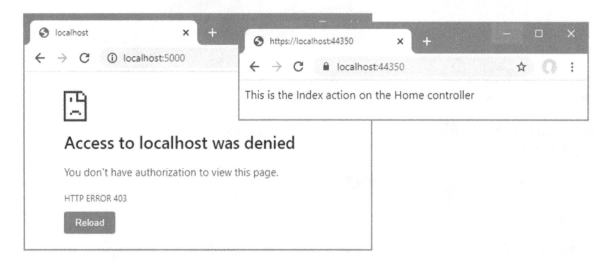

Figure 30-4. *Enforcing HTTPS in an action method*

■ **Tip**   Clear your browser's history if you don't get the results you expect from the examples in this section. Browsers will often refuse to send requests to servers that have previously generated HTTPS errors, which is a good security practice but can be frustrating during development.

This approach works but has problems. The first problem is that the action method contains code that is more about implementing a security policy than about handling the request. A more serious problem is that including the HTTP-detecting code within the action method doesn't scale well and must be duplicated in every action method in the controller, as shown in Listing 30-10.

Listing 30-10. Adding Action Methods in the HomeController.cs File in the Controllers Folder

```
using Microsoft.AspNetCore.Mvc;
using Microsoft.AspNetCore.Http;

namespace WebApp.Controllers {

    public class HomeController : Controller {

        public IActionResult Index() {
            if (Request.IsHttps) {
                return View("Message",
                    "This is the Index action on the Home controller");
            } else {
                return new StatusCodeResult(StatusCodes.Status403Forbidden);
            }
        }

        public IActionResult Secure() {
            if (Request.IsHttps) {
                return View("Message",
                    "This is the Secure action on the Home controller");
```

```
        } else {
            return new StatusCodeResult(StatusCodes.Status403Forbidden);
        }
    }
}
}
```

I must remember to implement the same check in every action method in every controller for which I want to require HTTPS. The code to implement the security policy is a substantial part of the—admittedly simple—controller, which makes the controller harder to understand, and it is only a matter of time before I forget to add it to a new action method, creating a hole in my security policy.

This is the type of problem that filters address. Listing 30-11 replaces my checks for HTTPS and implements a filter instead.

Listing 30-11. Applying a Filter in the HomeController.cs File in the Controllers Folder

```
using Microsoft.AspNetCore.Mvc;
using Microsoft.AspNetCore.Http;

namespace WebApp.Controllers {

    public class HomeController : Controller {

        [RequireHttps]
        public IActionResult Index() {
            return View("Message",
                "This is the Index action on the Home controller");
        }

        [RequireHttps]
        public IActionResult Secure() {
            return View("Message",
                "This is the Secure action on the Home controller");
        }
    }
}
```

The RequireHttps attribute applies one of the built-in filters provided by ASP.NET Core. This filter restricts access to action methods so that only HTTPS requests are supported and allows me to remove the security code from each method and focus on handling the successful requests.

■ **Note** The RequireHttps filter doesn't work the same way as my custom code. For GET requests, the RequireHttps attribute redirects the client to the originally requested URL, but it does so by using the https scheme so that a request to http:// localhost:5000 will be redirected to https://localhost:5000. This makes sense for most deployed applications but not during development because HTTP and HTTPS are on different local ports. The RequireHttpsAttribute class defines a protected method called HandleNonHttpsRequest that you can override to change the behavior. Alternatively, I re-create the original functionality from scratch in the "Understanding Authorization Filters" section.

I must still remember to apply the RequireHttps attribute to each action method, which means that I might forget. But filters have a useful trick: applying the attribute to a controller class has the same effect as applying it to each individual action method, as shown in Listing 30-12.

Listing 30-12. Applying a Filter to All Actions in the HomeController.cs File in the Controllers Folder

```
using Microsoft.AspNetCore.Mvc;
using Microsoft.AspNetCore.Http;

namespace WebApp.Controllers {

    [RequireHttps]
    public class HomeController : Controller {

        public IActionResult Index() {
            return View("Message",
                "This is the Index action on the Home controller");
        }

        public IActionResult Secure() {
            return View("Message",
                "This is the Secure action on the Home controller");
        }
    }
}
```

Filters can be applied with differing levels of granularity. If you want to restrict access to some actions but not others, then you can apply the RequireHttps attribute to just those methods. If you want to protect all the action methods, including any that you add to the controller in the future, then the RequireHttps attribute can be applied to the class. If you want to apply a filter to every action in an application, then you can use *global filters*, which I describe later in this chapter.

Using Filters in Razor Pages

Filters can also be used in Razor Pages. To implement the HTTPS-only policy in the Message Razor Pages, for example, I would have to add a handler method that inspects the connection, as shown in Listing 30-13.

Listing 30-13. Checking Connections in the Message.cshtml File in the Pages Folder

```
@page "/pages/message"
@model MessageModel
@using Microsoft.AspNetCore.Mvc.RazorPages
@using System.Collections.Generic
@using Microsoft.AspNetCore.Http

@if (Model.Message is string) {
    @Model.Message
} else if (Model.Message is IDictionary<string, string>) {
    var dict = Model.Message as IDictionary<string, string>;
    <table class="table table-sm table-striped table-bordered">
        <thead><tr><th>Name</th><th>Value</th></tr></thead>
        <tbody>
            @foreach (var kvp in dict) {
                <tr><td>@kvp.Key</td><td>@kvp.Value</td></tr>
            }
        </tbody>
    </table>
}
```

```
@functions {

    public class MessageModel : PageModel {

        public object Message { get; set; } = "This is the Message Razor Page";

        public IActionResult OnGet() {
            if (!Request.IsHttps) {
                return new StatusCodeResult(StatusCodes.Status403Forbidden);
            } else {
                return Page();
            }
        }
    }
}
```

The handler method works, but it is awkward and presents the same problems encountered with action methods. When using filters in Razor Pages, the attribute can be applied to the handler method or, as shown in Listing 30-14, to the entire class.

Listing 30-14. Applying a Filter in the Message.cshtml File in the Pages Folder

```
@page "/pages/message"
@model MessageModel
@using Microsoft.AspNetCore.Mvc.RazorPages
@using System.Collections.Generic
@using Microsoft.AspNetCore.Http

@if (Model.Message is string) {
    @Model.Message
} else if (Model.Message is IDictionary<string, string>) {
    var dict = Model.Message as IDictionary<string, string>;
    <table class="table table-sm table-striped table-bordered">
        <thead><tr><th>Name</th><th>Value</th></tr></thead>
        <tbody>
            @foreach (var kvp in dict) {
                <tr><td>@kvp.Key</td><td>@kvp.Value</td></tr>
            }
        </tbody>
    </table>
}

@functions {

    [RequireHttps]
    public class MessageModel : PageModel {

        public object Message { get; set; } = "This is the Message Razor Page";
    }
}
```

You will see a normal response if you request https://localhost:44350/pages/message. If you request the regular HTTP URL, http://localhost:5000/pages/messages, the filter will redirect the request, and you will see an error (as noted earlier, the RequireHttps filter redirects the browser to a port that is not enabled in the example application).

Understanding Filters

ASP.NET Core supports different types of filters, each of which is intended for a different purpose. Table 30-2 describes the filter categories.

Table 30-2. *The Filter Types*

Name	Description
Authorization filters	This type of filter is used to apply the application's authorization policy.
Resource filters	This type of filter is used to intercept requests, typically to implement features such as caching.
Action filters	This type of filter is used to modify the request before it is received by an action method or to modify the action result after it has been produced. This type of filter can be applied only to controllers and actions.
Page filters	This type of filter is used to modify the request before it is received by a Razor Page handler method or to modify the action result after it has been produced. This type of filter can be applied only to Razor Pages.
Result filters	This type of filter is used to alter the action result before it is executed or to modify the result after execution.
Exception filters	This type of filter is used to handle exceptions that occur during the execution of the action method or page handler.

Filters have their own pipeline and are executed in a specific order, as shown in Figure 30-5.

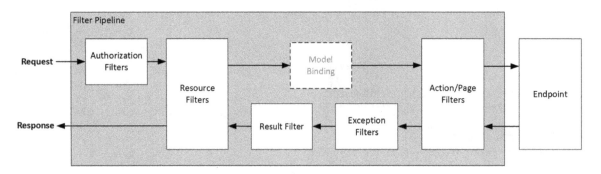

Figure 30-5. *The filter pipeline*

Filters can short-circuit the filter pipeline to prevent a request from being forwarded to the next filter. For example, an authorization filter can short-circuit the pipeline and return an error response if the user is unauthenticated. The resource, action, and page filters are able to inspect the request before and after it has been handled by the endpoint, allowing these types of filter to short-circuit the pipeline; to alter the request before it is handled; or to alter the response. (I have simplified the flow of filters in Figure 30-5. Page filters run before and after the model binding process, as described in the "Understanding Page Filters" section.)

Each type of filter is implemented using interfaces defined by ASP.NET Core, which also provides base classes that make it easy to apply some types of filters as attributes. I describe each interface and the attribute classes in the sections that follow, but they are shown in Table 30-3 for quick reference.

Table 30-3. *The Filter Types, Interfaces, and Attribute Base Classes*

Filter Type	Interfaces	Attribute Class
Authorization filters	`IAuthorizationFilter` `IAsyncAuthorizationFilter`	No attribute class is provided.
Resource filters	`IResourceFilter` `IAsyncResourceFilter`	No attribute class is provided.
Action filters	`IActionFilter` `IAsyncActionFilter`	`ActionFilterAttribute`
Page filters	`IPageFilter` `IAsyncPageFilter`	No attribute class is provided.

Result filters	`IResultFilter`
	`IAsyncResultFilter`
	`IAlwaysRunResultFilter`
	`IAsyncAlwaysRunResultFilter`
		`ResultFilterAttribute`

Exception Filters	`IExceptionFilter` `IAsyncExceptionFilter`	`ExceptionFilterAttribute`

Creating Custom Filters

Filters implement the `IFilterMetadata` interface, which is in the `Microsoft.AspNetCore.Mvc.Filters` namespace. Here is the interface:

```
namespace Microsoft.AspNetCore.Mvc.Filters {
    public interface IFilterMetadata { }
}
```

The interface is empty and doesn't require a filter to implement any specific behaviors. This is because each of the categories of filter described in the previous section works in a different way. Filters are provided with context data in the form of a `FilterContext` object. For convenience, Table 30-4 describes the properties that `FilterContext` provides.

Table 30-4. *The FilterContext Properties*

Name	Description
`ActionDescriptor`	This property returns an `ActionDescriptor` object, which describes the action method.
`HttpContext`	This property returns an `HttpContext` object, which provides details of the HTTP request and the HTTP response that will be sent in return.
`ModelState`	This property returns a `ModelStateDictionary` object, which is used to validate data sent by the client.
`RouteData`	This property returns a `RouteData` object that describes the way that the routing system has processed the request.
`Filters`	This property returns a list of filters that have been applied to the action method, expressed as an `IList<IFilterMetadata>`.

Understanding Authorization Filters

Authorization filters are used to implement an application's security policy. Authorization filters are executed before other types of filter and before the endpoint handles the request. Here is the definition of the `IAuthorizationFilter` interface:

```
namespace Microsoft.AspNetCore.Mvc.Filters {

    public interface IAuthorizationFilter : IFilterMetadata {

        void OnAuthorization(AuthorizationFilterContext context);
    }
}
```

The OnAuthorization method is called to provide the filter with the opportunity to authorize the request. For asynchronous authorization filters, here is the definition of the IAsyncAuthorizationFilter interface:

```
using System.Threading.Tasks;

namespace Microsoft.AspNetCore.Mvc.Filters {

    public interface IAsyncAuthorizationFilter : IFilterMetadata {

        Task OnAuthorizationAsync(AuthorizationFilterContext context);
    }
}
```

The OnAuthorizationAsync method is called so that the filter can authorize the request. Whichever interface is used, the filter receives context data describing the request through an AuthorizationFilterContext object, which is derived from the FilterContext class and adds one important property, as described in Table 30-5.

Table 30-5. *The AuthorizationFilterContext Property*

Name	Description
Result	This IActionResult property is set by authorization filters when the request doesn't comply with the application's authorization policy. If this property is set, then ASP.NET Core executes the IActionResult instead of invoking the endpoint.

Creating an Authorization Filter

To demonstrate how authorization filters work, I created a Filters folder in the example project, added a class file called HttpsOnlyAttribute.cs, and used it to define the filter shown in Listing 30-15.

Listing 30-15. The Contents of the HttpsOnlyAttribute.cs File in the Filters Folder

```
using System;
using Microsoft.AspNetCore.Http;
using Microsoft.AspNetCore.Mvc;
using Microsoft.AspNetCore.Mvc.Filters;

namespace WebApp.Filters {
    public class HttpsOnlyAttribute : Attribute, IAuthorizationFilter {

        public void OnAuthorization(AuthorizationFilterContext context) {
            if (!context.HttpContext.Request.IsHttps) {
                context.Result =
                    new StatusCodeResult(StatusCodes.Status403Forbidden);
            }
        }
    }
}
```

An authorization filter does nothing if a request complies with the authorization policy and inaction allows ASP.NET Core to move on to the next filter and, eventually, to execute the endpoint. If there is a problem, the filter sets the Result property of the AuthorizationFilterContext object that is passed to the OnAuthorization method. This prevents further execution from happening and provides a result to return to the client. In the listing, the HttpsOnlyAttribute class inspects the IsHttps property of the HttpRequest context object and sets the Result property to interrupt execution if the request has been made without HTTPS. Authorization filters can be applied to controllers, action methods, and Razor Pages. Listing 30-16 applies the new filter to the Home controller.

Listing 30-16. Applying a Custom Filter in the HomeController.cs File in the Controllers Folder

```
using Microsoft.AspNetCore.Mvc;
using Microsoft.AspNetCore.Http;
using WebApp.Filters;

namespace WebApp.Controllers {

    [HttpsOnly]
    public class HomeController : Controller {

        public IActionResult Index() {
            return View("Message",
                "This is the Index action on the Home controller");
        }

        public IActionResult Secure() {
            return View("Message",
                "This is the Secure action on the Home controller");
        }
    }
}
```

This filter re-creates the functionality that I included in the action methods in Listing 30-10. This is less useful in real projects than doing a redirection like the built-in RequireHttps filter because users won't understand the meaning of a 403 status code, but it does provide a useful example of how authorization filters work. Restart ASP.NET Core and request http://localhost:5000, and you will see the effect of the filter, as shown in Figure 30-6. Request https://localhost:44350, and you will receive the response from the action method, also shown in the figure.

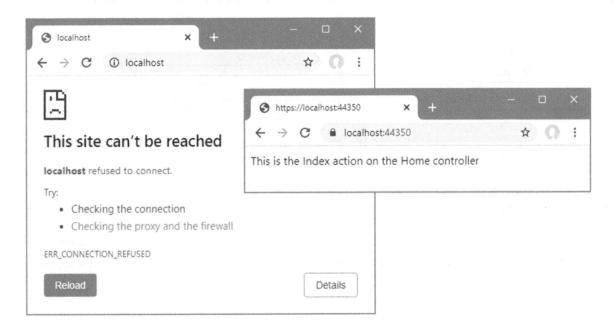

Figure 30-6. Applying a custom authorization filter

Understanding Resource Filters

Resource filters are executed twice for each request: before the ASP.NET Core model binding process and again before the action result is processed to generate the result. Here is the definition of the IResourceFilter interface:

```
namespace Microsoft.AspNetCore.Mvc.Filters {
    public interface IResourceFilter : IFilterMetadata {

        void OnResourceExecuting(ResourceExecutingContext context);

        void OnResourceExecuted(ResourceExecutedContext context);
    }
}
```

The OnResourceExecuting method is called when a request is being processed, and the OnResourceExecuted method is called after the endpoint has handled the request but before the action result is executed. For asynchronous resource filters, here is the definition of the IAsyncResourceFilter interface:

```
namespace Microsoft.AspNetCore.Mvc.Filters {
    public interface IAsyncResourceFilter : IFilterMetadata {

        Task OnResourceExecutionAsync(ResourceExecutingContext context,
            ResourceExecutionDelegate next);
    }
}
```

This interface defines a single method that receives a context object and a delegate to invoke. The resource filter is able to inspect the request before invoking the delegate and inspect the response before it is executed. The OnResourceExecuting method is provided with context using the ResourceExecutingContext class, which defines the property shown in Table 30-6 in addition to those defined by the FilterContext class.

Table 30-6. *The Property Defined by the ResourceExecutingContext Class*

Name	Description
Result	This IActionResult property is used to provide a result to short-circuit the pipeline.

The OnResourceExecuted method is provided with context using the ResourceExecutedContext class, which defines the properties shown in Table 30-7, in addition to those defined by the FilterContext class.

Table 30-7. *The Properties Defined by the ResourceExecutedContext Class*

Name	Description
Result	This IActionResult property provides the action result that will be used to produce a response.
ValueProviderFactories	This property returns an IList<IValueProviderFactory>, which provides access to the objects that provide values for the model binding process.

Creating a Resource Filter

Resource filters are usually used where it is possible to short-circuit the pipeline and provide a response early, such as when implementing data caching. To create a simple caching filter, add a class file called SimpleCacheAttribute.cs to the Filters folder with the code shown in Listing 30-17.

FILTERS AND DEPENDENCY INJECTION

Filters that are applied as attributes cannot declare dependencies in their constructors unless they implement the IFilterFactory interface and take responsibility for creating instances directly, as explained in the "Creating Filter Factories" section later in this chapter.

Listing 30-17. The Contents of the SimpleCacheAttribute.cs File in the Filters Folder

```
using Microsoft.AspNetCore.Http;
using Microsoft.AspNetCore.Mvc;
using Microsoft.AspNetCore.Mvc.Filters;
using System;
using System.Collections.Generic;

namespace WebApp.Filters {

    public class SimpleCacheAttribute : Attribute, IResourceFilter {
        private Dictionary<PathString, IActionResult> CachedResponses
            = new Dictionary<PathString, IActionResult>();

        public void OnResourceExecuting(ResourceExecutingContext context) {
            PathString path = context.HttpContext.Request.Path;
            if (CachedResponses.ContainsKey(path)) {
                context.Result = CachedResponses[path];
                CachedResponses.Remove(path);

            }
        }

        public void OnResourceExecuted(ResourceExecutedContext context) {
            CachedResponses.Add(context.HttpContext.Request.Path, context.Result);
        }
    }
}
```

This filter isn't an especially useful cache, but it does show how a resource filter works. The OnResourceExecuting method provides the filter with the opportunity to short-circuit the pipeline by setting the context object's Result property to a previously cached action result. If a value is assigned to the Result property, then the filter pipeline is short-circuited, and the action result is executed to produce the response for the client. Cached action results are used only once and then discarded from the cache. If no value is assigned to the Result property, then the request passes to the next step in the pipeline, which may be another filter or the endpoint.

The OnResourceExecuted method provides the filter with the action results that are produced when the pipeline is not short-circuited. In this case, the filter caches the action result so that it can be used for subsequent requests. Resource filters can be applied to controllers, action methods, and Razor Pages. Listing 30-18 applies the custom resource filter to the Message Razor Page and adds a timestamp that will help determine when an action result is cached.

Listing 30-18. Applying a Resource Filter in the Message.cshtml File in the Pages Folder

```
@page "/pages/message"
@model MessageModel
@using Microsoft.AspNetCore.Mvc.RazorPages
@using System.Collections.Generic
@using Microsoft.AspNetCore.Http
@using WebApp.Filters
```

```
@if (Model.Message is string) {
    @Model.Message
} else if (Model.Message is IDictionary<string, string>) {
    var dict = Model.Message as IDictionary<string, string>;
    <table class="table table-sm table-striped table-bordered">
        <thead><tr><th>Name</th><th>Value</th></tr></thead>
        <tbody>
            @foreach (var kvp in dict) {
                <tr><td>@kvp.Key</td><td>@kvp.Value</td></tr>
            }
        </tbody>
    </table>
}

@functions {

    [RequireHttps]
    [SimpleCache]
    public class MessageModel : PageModel {

        public object Message { get; set; } =
            $"{DateTime.Now.ToLongTimeString()}: This is the Message Razor Page";
    }
}
```

To see the effect of the resource filter, restart ASP.NET Core and request https://localhost:44350/pages/message. Since this is the first request for the path, there will be no cached result, and the request will be forwarded along the pipeline. As the response is processed, the resource filter will cache the action result for future use. Reload the browser to repeat the request, and you will see the same timestamp, indicating that the cached action result has been used. The cached item is removed when it is used, which means that reloading the browser will generate a response with a fresh timestamp, as shown in Figure 30-7.

Figure 30-7. *Using a resource filter*

Creating an Asynchronous Resource Filter

The interface for asynchronous resource filters uses a single method that receives a delegate used to forward the request along the filter pipeline. Listing 30-19 reimplements the caching filter from the previous example so that it implements the IAsyncResourceFilter interface.

Listing 30-19. Creating an Asynchronous Filter in the SimpleCacheAttribute.cs File in the Filters Folder

```
using Microsoft.AspNetCore.Http;
using Microsoft.AspNetCore.Mvc;
using Microsoft.AspNetCore.Mvc.Filters;
using System;
using System.Collections.Generic;
using System.Threading.Tasks;
```

```
namespace WebApp.Filters {

    public class SimpleCacheAttribute : Attribute, IAsyncResourceFilter {
        private Dictionary<PathString, IActionResult> CachedResponses
            = new Dictionary<PathString, IActionResult>();

        public async Task OnResourceExecutionAsync(ResourceExecutingContext context,
                ResourceExecutionDelegate next) {
            PathString path = context.HttpContext.Request.Path;
            if (CachedResponses.ContainsKey(path)) {
                context.Result = CachedResponses[path];
                CachedResponses.Remove(path);
            } else {
                ResourceExecutedContext execContext = await next();
                CachedResponses.Add(context.HttpContext.Request.Path,
                    execContext.Result);
            }
        }
    }
}
```

The OnResourceExecutionAsync method receives a ResourceExecutingContext object, which is used to determine whether the pipeline can be short-circuited. If it cannot, the delegate is invoked without arguments and asynchronously produces a ResourceExecutedContext object when the request has been handled and is making its way back along the pipeline. Restart ASP. NET Core and repeat the requests described in the previous section, and you will see the same caching behavior, as shown in Figure 30-7.

■ **Caution**   It is important not to confuse the two context objects. The action result produced by the endpoint is available only in the context object that is returned by the delegate.

Understanding Action Filters

Like resource filters, action filters are executed twice. The difference is that action filters are executed after the model binding process, whereas resource filters are executed before model binding. This means that resource filters can short-circuit the pipeline and minimize the work that ASP.NET Core does on the request. Action filters are used when model binding is required, which means they are used for tasks such as altering the model or enforcing validation. Action filters can be applied only to controllers and action methods, unlike resource filters, which can also be used with Razor Pages. (The Razor Pages equivalent to action filters is the page filter, described in the "Understanding Page Filters" section.) Here is the IActionFilter interface:

```
namespace Microsoft.AspNetCore.Mvc.Filters {

    public interface IActionFilter : IFilterMetadata {

        void OnActionExecuting(ActionExecutingContext context);

        void OnActionExecuted(ActionExecutedContext context);
    }
}
```

When an action filter has been applied to an action method, the OnActionExecuting method is called just before the action method is invoked, and the OnActionExecuted method is called just after. Action filters are provided with context data through two different context classes: ActionExecutingContext for the OnActionExecuting method and ActionExecutedContext for the OnActionExecuted method.

The ActionExecutingContext class, which is used to describe an action that is about to be invoked, defines the properties described in Table 30-8, in addition to the FilterContext properties.

Table 30-8. *The ActionExecutingContext Property*

Name	Description
Controller	This property returns the controller whose action method is about to be invoked. (Details of the action method are available through the ActionDescriptor property inherited from the base classes.)
ActionArguments	This property returns a dictionary of the arguments that will be passed to the action method, indexed by name. The filter can insert, remove, or change the arguments.
Result	If the filter assigns an IActionResult to this property, then the pipeline will be short-circuited, and the action result will be used to generate the response to the client without invoking the action method.

The ActionExecutedContext class is used to represent an action that has been executed and defines the properties described in Table 30-9, in addition to the FilterContext properties.

Table 30-9. *The ActionExecutedContext Properties*

Name	Description
Controller	This property returns the Controller object whose action method will be invoked.
Canceled	This bool property is set to true if another action filter has short-circuited the pipeline by assigning an action result to the Result property of the ActionExecutingContext object.
Exception	This property contains any Exception that was thrown by the action method.
ExceptionDispatchInfo	This method returns an ExceptionDispatchInfo object that contains the stack trace details of any exception thrown by the action method.
ExceptionHandled	Setting this property to true indicates that the filter has handled the exception, which will not be propagated any further.
Result	This property returns the IActionResult produced by the action method. The filter can change or replace the action result if required.

Asynchronous action filters are implemented using the IAsyncActionFilter interface.

```
namespace Microsoft.AspNetCore.Mvc.Filters {

    public interface IAsyncActionFilter : IFilterMetadata {

        Task OnActionExecutionAsync(ActionExecutingContext context,
            ActionExecutionDelegate next);
    }
}
```

This interface follows the same pattern as the IAsyncResourceFilter interface described earlier in the chapter. The OnActionExecutionAsync method is provided with an ActionExecutingContext object and a delegate. The ActionExecutingContext object describes the request before it is received by the action method. The filter can short-circuit the pipeline by assigning a value to the ActionExecutingContext.Result property or pass it along by invoking the delegate. The delegate asynchronously produces an ActionExecutedContext object that describes the result from the action method.

Creating an Action Filter

Add a class file called ChangeArgAttribute.cs to the Filters folder and use it to define the action filter shown in Listing 30-20.

Listing 30-20. The Contents of the ChangeArgAttribute.cs File in the Filters Folder

```
using Microsoft.AspNetCore.Mvc.Filters;
using System;
using System.Threading.Tasks;

namespace WebApp.Filters {
    public class ChangeArgAttribute : Attribute, IAsyncActionFilter {

        public async Task OnActionExecutionAsync(ActionExecutingContext context,
                ActionExecutionDelegate next) {

            if (context.ActionArguments.ContainsKey("message1")) {
                context.ActionArguments["message1"] = "New message";
            }
            await next();
        }
    }
}
```

The filter looks for an action argument named message1 and changes the value that will be used to invoke the action method. The values that will be used for the action method arguments are determined by the model binding process. Listing 30-21 adds an action method to the Home controller and applies the new filter.

Listing 30-21. Applying a Filter in the HomeController.cs File in the Controllers Folder

```
using Microsoft.AspNetCore.Mvc;
using Microsoft.AspNetCore.Http;
using WebApp.Filters;

namespace WebApp.Controllers {

    [HttpsOnly]
    public class HomeController : Controller {

        public IActionResult Index() {
            return View("Message",
                "This is the Index action on the Home controller");
        }

        public IActionResult Secure() {
            return View("Message",
                "This is the Secure action on the Home controller");
        }

        [ChangeArg]
        public IActionResult Messages(string message1, string message2 = "None") {
            return View("Message", $"{message1}, {message2}");
        }
    }
}
```

Restart ASP.NET Core and request `https://localhost:44350/home/messages?message1=hello&message2=world`. The model binding process will locate values for the parameters defined by the action method from the query string. One of those values is then modified by the action filter, producing the response shown in Figure 30-8.

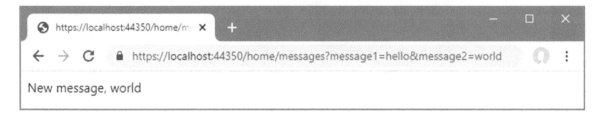

Figure 30-8. *Using an action filter*

Implementing an Action Filter Using the Attribute Base Class

Action attributes can also be implemented by deriving from the `ActionFilterAttribute` class, which extends `Attribute` and inherits both the `IActionFilter` and `IAsyncActionFilter` interfaces so that implementation classes override just the methods they require. In Listing 30-22, I have reimplemented the `ChangeArg` filter so that it is derived from `ActionFilterAttribute`.

Listing 30-22. Using a Filter Base Class in the ChangeArgsAttribute.cs File in the Filters Folder

```
using Microsoft.AspNetCore.Mvc.Filters;
using System;
using System.Threading.Tasks;

namespace WebApp.Filters {
    public class ChangeArgAttribute : ActionFilterAttribute {

        public override async Task OnActionExecutionAsync(
            ActionExecutingContext context,
                ActionExecutionDelegate next) {

            if (context.ActionArguments.ContainsKey("message1")) {
                context.ActionArguments["message1"] = "New message";
            }
            await next();
        }
    }
}
```

This attribute behaves in just the same way as the earlier implementation, and the use of the base class is a matter of preference. Restart ASP.NET Core and request `https://localhost:44350/home/messages?message1=hello&message2=world`, and you will see the response shown in Figure 30-8.

Using the Controller Filter Methods

The `Controller` class, which is the base for controllers that render Razor views, implements the `IActionFilter` and `IAsyncActionFilter` interfaces, which means you can define functionality and apply it to the actions defined by a controller and any derived controllers. Listing 30-23 implements the `ChangeArg` filter functionality directly in the `HomeController` class.

Listing 30-23. Using Action Filter Methods in the HomeController.cs File in the Controllers Folder

```
using Microsoft.AspNetCore.Mvc;
using Microsoft.AspNetCore.Http;
using WebApp.Filters;
using Microsoft.AspNetCore.Mvc.Filters;

namespace WebApp.Controllers {

    [HttpsOnly]
    public class HomeController : Controller {

        public IActionResult Index() {
            return View("Message",
                "This is the Index action on the Home controller");
        }

        public IActionResult Secure() {
            return View("Message",
                "This is the Secure action on the Home controller");
        }

        //[ChangeArg]
        public IActionResult Messages(string message1, string message2 = "None") {
            return View("Message", $"{message1}, {message2}");
        }

        public override void OnActionExecuting(ActionExecutingContext context) {
            if (context.ActionArguments.ContainsKey("message1")) {
                context.ActionArguments["message1"] = "New message";
            }
        }
    }
}
```

The Home controller overrides the Controller implementation of the OnActionExecuting method and uses it to modify the arguments that will be passed to the execution method.

Restart ASP.NET Core and request https://localhost:44350/home/messages?message1=hello&message2=world, and you will see the response shown in Figure 30-8.

Understanding Page Filters

Page filters are the Razor Page equivalent of action filters. Here is the IPageFilter interface, which is implemented by synchronous page filters:

```
namespace Microsoft.AspNetCore.Mvc.Filters {

    public interface IPageFilter : IFilterMetadata {

        void OnPageHandlerSelected(PageHandlerSelectedContext context);

        void OnPageHandlerExecuting(PageHandlerExecutingContext context);

        void OnPageHandlerExecuted(PageHandlerExecutedContext context);
    }
}
```

793

The OnPageHandlerSelected method is invoked after ASP.NET Core has selected the page handler method but before model binding has been performed, which means the arguments for the handler method have not been determined. This method receives context through the PageHandlerSelectedContext class, which defines the properties shown in Table 30-10, in addition to those defined by the FilterContext class. This method cannot be used to short-circuit the pipeline, but it can alter the handler method that will receive the request.

Table 30-10. *The PageHandlerSelectedContext Properties*

Name	Description
ActionDescriptor	This property returns the description of the Razor Page.
HandlerMethod	This property returns a HandlerMethodDescriptor object that describes the selected handler method.
HandlerInstance	This property returns the instance of the Razor Page that will handle the request.

The OnPageHandlerExecuting method is called after the model binding process has completed but before the page handler method is invoked. This method receives context through the PageHandlerExecutingContext class, which defines the properties shown in Table 30-11.

Table 30-11. *The PageHandlerExecutingContext Properties*

Name	Description
HandlerArguments	This property returns a dictionary containing the page handler arguments, indexed by name.
Result	The filter can short-circuit the pipeline by assigning an IActionResult object to this property.

The OnPageHandlerExecuted method is called after the page handler method has been invoked but before the action result is processed to create a response. This method receives context through the PageHandlerExecutedContext class, which defines the properties shown in Table 30-12 in addition to the PageHandlerSelectedContext properties.

Table 30-12. *The PageHandlerExecutedContext Properties*

Name	Description
Canceled	This property returns true if another filter short-circuited the filter pipeline.
Exception	This property returns an exception if one was thrown by the page handler method.
ExceptionHandled	This property is set to true to indicate that an exception thrown by the page handler has been handled by the filter.
Result	This property returns the action result that will be used to create a response for the client.

Asynchronous page filters are created by implementing the IAsyncPageFilter interface, which is defined like this:

```
namespace Microsoft.AspNetCore.Mvc.Filters {
    public interface IAsyncPageFilter : IFilterMetadata {

        Task OnPageHandlerSelectionAsync(PageHandlerSelectedContext context);

        Task OnPageHandlerExecutionAsync(PageHandlerExecutingContext context,
            PageHandlerExecutionDelegate next);
    }
}
```

The OnPageHandlerSelectionAsync is called after the handler method is selected and is equivalent to the synchronous OnPageHandlerSelected method. The OnPageHandlerExecutionAsync is provided with a PageHandlerExecutingContext object that allows it to short-circuit the pipeline and a delegate that is invoked to pass on the request. The delegate produces a PageHandlerExecutedContext object that can be used to inspect or alter the action result produced by the handler method.

Creating a Page Filter

To create a page filter, add a class file named ChangePageArgs.cs to the Filters folder and use it to define the class shown in Listing 30-24.

Listing 30-24. The Contents of the ChangePageArgs.cs File in the Filters Folder

```
using Microsoft.AspNetCore.Mvc.Filters;
using System;

namespace WebApp.Filters {
    public class ChangePageArgs : Attribute, IPageFilter {

        public void OnPageHandlerSelected(PageHandlerSelectedContext context) {
            // do nothing
        }

        public void OnPageHandlerExecuting(PageHandlerExecutingContext context) {
            if (context.HandlerArguments.ContainsKey("message1")) {
                context.HandlerArguments["message1"] = "New message";
            }
        }

        public void OnPageHandlerExecuted(PageHandlerExecutedContext context) {
            // do nothing
        }
    }
}
```

The page filter in Listing 30-24 performs the same task as the action filter I created in the previous section. In Listing 30-25, I have modified the Message Razor Page to define a handler method and have applied the page filter. Page filters can be applied to individual handler methods or, as in the listing, to the page model class, in which case the filter is used for all handler methods. (I also disabled the SimpleCache filter in Listing 30-25. Resource filters can work alongside page filters. I disabled this filter because caching responses makes some of the examples more difficult to follow.)

Listing 30-25. Using a Page Filter in the Message.cshtml File in the Pages Folder

```
@page "/pages/message"
@model MessageModel
@using Microsoft.AspNetCore.Mvc.RazorPages
@using System.Collections.Generic
@using Microsoft.AspNetCore.Http
@using WebApp.Filters

@if (Model.Message is string) {
    @Model.Message
} else if (Model.Message is IDictionary<string, string>) {
    var dict = Model.Message as IDictionary<string, string>;
    <table class="table table-sm table-striped table-bordered">
        <thead><tr><th>Name</th><th>Value</th></tr></thead>
        <tbody>
```

```
        @foreach (var kvp in dict) {
            <tr><td>@kvp.Key</td><td>@kvp.Value</td></tr>
        }
    </tbody>
</table>
}

@functions {

    [RequireHttps]
    //[SimpleCache]
    [ChangePageArgs]
    public class MessageModel : PageModel {

        public object Message { get; set; } =
            $"{DateTime.Now.ToLongTimeString()}: This is the Message Razor Page";

        public void OnGet(string message1, string message2) {
            Message = $"{message1}, {message2}";
        }
    }
}
```

Restart ASP.NET Core and request `https://localhost:44350/pages/message?message1=hello&message2=world`. The page filter will replace the value of the `message1` argument for the `OnGet` handler method, which produces the response shown in Figure 30-9.

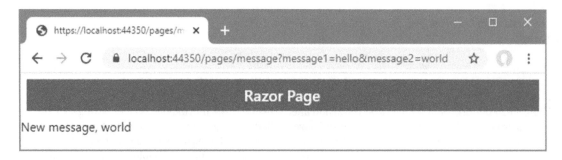

Figure 30-9. *Using a page filter*

Using the Page Model Filter Methods

The `PageModel` class, which is used as the base for page model classes, implements the `IPageFilter` and `IAsyncPageFilter` interfaces, which means you can add filter functionality directly to a page model, as shown in Listing 30-26.

Listing 30-26. Using the PageModel Filter Methods in the Message.cshtml File in the Pages Folder

```
@page "/pages/message"
@model MessageModel
@using Microsoft.AspNetCore.Mvc.RazorPages
@using System.Collections.Generic
@using Microsoft.AspNetCore.Http
@using WebApp.Filters
@using Microsoft.AspNetCore.Mvc.Filters
```

```
@if (Model.Message is string) {
    @Model.Message
} else if (Model.Message is IDictionary<string, string>) {
    var dict = Model.Message as IDictionary<string, string>;
    <table class="table table-sm table-striped table-bordered">
        <thead><tr><th>Name</th><th>Value</th></tr></thead>
        <tbody>
            @foreach (var kvp in dict) {
                <tr><td>@kvp.Key</td><td>@kvp.Value</td></tr>
            }
        </tbody>
    </table>
}

@functions {

    [RequireHttps]
    //[SimpleCache]
    //[ChangePageArgs]
    public class MessageModel : PageModel {

        public object Message { get; set; } =
            $"{DateTime.Now.ToLongTimeString()}: This is the Message Razor Page";

        public void OnGet(string message1, string message2) {
            Message = $"{message1}, {message2}";
        }

        public override void OnPageHandlerExecuting(
                PageHandlerExecutingContext context) {
            if (context.HandlerArguments.ContainsKey("message1")) {
                context.HandlerArguments["message1"] = "New message";
            }
        }
    }
}
```

Request https://localhost:44350/pages/message?message1=hello&message2=world. The method implemented by the page model class in Listing 30-26 will produce the same result as shown in Figure 30-9.

Understanding Result Filters

Result filters are executed before and after an action result is used to generate a response, allowing responses to be modified after they have been handled by the endpoint. Here is the definition of the IResultFilter interface:

```
namespace Microsoft.AspNetCore.Mvc.Filters {
    public interface IResultFilter : IFilterMetadata {

        void OnResultExecuting(ResultExecutingContext context);

        void OnResultExecuted(ResultExecutedContext context);
    }
}
```

The OnResultExecuting method is called after the endpoint has produced an action result. This method receives context through the ResultExecutingContext class, which defines the properties described in Table 30-13, in addition to those defined by the FilterContext class.

Table 30-13. *The ResultExecutingContext Class Properties*

Name	Description
Result	This property returns the action result produced by the endpoint.
ValueProviderFactories	This property returns an IList<IValueProviderFactory>, which provides access to the objects that provide values for the model binding process.

The OnResultExecuted method is called after the action result has been executed to generate the response for the client. This method receives context through the ResultExecutedContext class, which defines the properties shown in Table 30-14, in addition to those it inherits from the FilterContext class.

Table 30-14. *The ResultExecutedContext Class*

Name	Description
Canceled	This property returns true if another filter short-circuited the filter pipeline.
Controller	This property returns the object that contains the endpoint.
Exception	This property returns an exception if one was thrown by the page handler method.
ExceptionHandled	This property is set to true to indicate that an exception thrown by the page handler has been handled by the filter.
Result	This property returns the action result that will be used to create a response for the client. This property is read-only.

Asynchronous result filters implement the IAsyncResultFilter interface, which is defined like this:

```
namespace Microsoft.AspNetCore.Mvc.Filters {

    public interface IAsyncResultFilter : IFilterMetadata {

        Task OnResultExecutionAsync(ResultExecutingContext context,
            ResultExecutionDelegate next);
    }
}
```

This interface follows the pattern established by the other filter types. The OnResultExecutionAsync method is invoked with a context object whose Result property can be used to alter the response and a delegate that will forward the response along the pipeline.

Understanding Always-Run Result Filters

Filters that implement the IResultFilter and IAsyncResultFilter interfaces are used only when a request is handled normally by the endpoint. They are not used if another filter short-circuits the pipeline or if there is an exception. Filters that need to inspect or alter the response, even when the pipeline is short-circuited, can implement the IAlwaysRunResultFilter or IAsyncAlwaysRunResultFilter interface. These interfaces derived from IResultFilter and IAsyncResultFilter but define no new features. Instead, ASP.NET Core detects the always-run interfaces and always applies the filters.

Creating a Result Filter

Add a class file named ResultDiagnosticsAttribute.cs to the Filters folder and use it to define the filter shown in Listing 30-27.

798

Listing 30-27. The Contents of the ResultDiagnosticsAttribute.cs File in the Filters Folder

```
using Microsoft.AspNetCore.Mvc;
using Microsoft.AspNetCore.Mvc.Filters;
using Microsoft.AspNetCore.Mvc.ModelBinding;
using Microsoft.AspNetCore.Mvc.RazorPages;
using Microsoft.AspNetCore.Mvc.ViewFeatures;
using System;
using System.Collections.Generic;
using System.Threading.Tasks;

namespace WebApp.Filters {

    public class ResultDiagnosticsAttribute : Attribute, IAsyncResultFilter {

        public async Task OnResultExecutionAsync(
                ResultExecutingContext context, ResultExecutionDelegate next) {

            if (context.HttpContext.Request.Query.ContainsKey("diag")) {
                Dictionary<string, string> diagData =
                    new Dictionary<string, string> {
                        {"Result type", context.Result.GetType().Name }
                    };
                if (context.Result is ViewResult vr) {
                    diagData["View Name"] = vr.ViewName;
                    diagData["Model Type"] = vr.ViewData.Model.GetType().Name;
                    diagData["Model Data"] = vr.ViewData.Model.ToString();
                } else if (context.Result is PageResult pr) {
                    diagData["Model Type"] = pr.Model.GetType().Name;
                    diagData["Model Data"] = pr.ViewData.Model.ToString();
                }
                context.Result = new ViewResult() {
                    ViewName = "/Views/Shared/Message.cshtml",
                    ViewData = new ViewDataDictionary(
                                    new EmptyModelMetadataProvider(),
                                    new ModelStateDictionary()) {
                        Model = diagData
                    }
                };
            }
            await next();
        }
    }
}
```

This filter examines the request to see whether it contains a query string parameter named diag. If it does, then the filter creates a result that displays diagnostic information instead of the output produced by the endpoint. The filter in Listing 30-27 will work with the actions defined by the Home controller or the Message Razor Page. Listing 30-28 applies the result filter to the Home controller.

■ **Tip** Notice that I use a fully qualified name for the view when I create the action result in Listing 30-27. This avoids a problem with filters applied to Razor Pages, where ASP.NET Core tries to execute the new result as a Razor Page and throws an exception about the model type.

Listing 30-28. Applying a Result Filter in the HomeController.cs File in the Controllers Folder

```
using Microsoft.AspNetCore.Mvc;
using Microsoft.AspNetCore.Http;
using WebApp.Filters;
using Microsoft.AspNetCore.Mvc.Filters;

namespace WebApp.Controllers {

    [HttpsOnly]
    [ResultDiagnostics]
    public class HomeController : Controller {

        public IActionResult Index() {
            return View("Message",
                "This is the Index action on the Home controller");
        }

        public IActionResult Secure() {
            return View("Message",
                "This is the Secure action on the Home controller");
        }

        //[ChangeArg]
        public IActionResult Messages(string message1, string message2 = "None") {
            return View("Message", $"{message1}, {message2}");
        }

        public override void OnActionExecuting(ActionExecutingContext context) {
            if (context.ActionArguments.ContainsKey("message1")) {
                context.ActionArguments["message1"] = "New message";
            }
        }
    }
}
```

Restart ASP.NET Core and request `https://localhost:44350/?diag`. The query string parameter will be detected by the filter, which will generate the diagnostic information shown in Figure 30-10.

Name	Value
Result type	ViewResult
View Name	Message
Model Type	String
Model Data	This is the Index action on the Home controller

Figure 30-10. *Using a result filter*

Implementing a Result Filter Using the Attribute Base Class

The ResultFilterAttribute class is derived from Attribute and implements the IResultFilter and IAsyncResultFilter interfaces and can be used as the base class for result filters, as shown in Listing 30-29. There is no attribute base class for the always-run interfaces.

Listing 30-29. Using the Attribute Base Class in the ResultDiagnosticsAttribute.cs File in the Filters Folder

```
using Microsoft.AspNetCore.Mvc;
using Microsoft.AspNetCore.Mvc.Filters;
using Microsoft.AspNetCore.Mvc.ModelBinding;
using Microsoft.AspNetCore.Mvc.RazorPages;
using Microsoft.AspNetCore.Mvc.ViewFeatures;
using System;
using System.Collections.Generic;
using System.Threading.Tasks;

namespace WebApp.Filters {

    public class ResultDiagnosticsAttribute : ResultFilterAttribute {

        public override async Task OnResultExecutionAsync(
                ResultExecutingContext context, ResultExecutionDelegate next) {

            if (context.HttpContext.Request.Query.ContainsKey("diag")) {
                Dictionary<string, string> diagData =
                    new Dictionary<string, string> {
                        {"Result type", context.Result.GetType().Name }
                    };
                if (context.Result is ViewResult vr) {
                    diagData["View Name"] = vr.ViewName;
                    diagData["Model Type"] = vr.ViewData.Model.GetType().Name;
                    diagData["Model Data"] = vr.ViewData.Model.ToString();
                } else if (context.Result is PageResult pr) {
                    diagData["Model Type"] = pr.Model.GetType().Name;
                    diagData["Model Data"] = pr.ViewData.Model.ToString();
                }
                context.Result = new ViewResult() {
                    ViewName = "/Views/Shared/Message.cshtml",
                    ViewData = new ViewDataDictionary(
                                        new EmptyModelMetadataProvider(),
                                        new ModelStateDictionary()) {
                        Model = diagData
                    }
                };
            }
            await next();
        }
    }
}
```

Restart ASP.NET Core and request https://localhost:44350/?diag. The filter will produce the output shown in Figure 30-10.

Understanding Exception Filters

Exception filters allow you to respond to exceptions without having to write `try...catch` blocks in every action method. Exception filters can be applied to controller classes, action methods, page model classes, or handler methods. They are invoked when an exception is not handled by the endpoint or by the action, page, and result filters that have been applied to the endpoint. (Action, page, and result filters can deal with an unhandled exception by setting the `ExceptionHandled` property of their context objects to true.) Exception filters implement the `IExceptionFilter` interface, which is defined as follows:

```
namespace Microsoft.AspNetCore.Mvc.Filters {

    public interface IExceptionFilter : IFilterMetadata {

        void OnException(ExceptionContext context);
    }
}
```

The `OnException` method is called if an unhandled exception is encountered. The `IAsyncExceptionFilter` interface can be used to create asynchronous exception filters. Here is the definition of the asynchronous interface:

```
using System.Threading.Tasks;

namespace Microsoft.AspNetCore.Mvc.Filters {

    public interface IAsyncExceptionFilter : IFilterMetadata {

        Task OnExceptionAsync(ExceptionContext context);
    }
}
```

The `OnExceptionAsync` method is the asynchronous counterpart to the `OnException` method from the `IExceptionFilter` interface and is called when there is an unhandled exception. For both interfaces, context data is provided through the `ExceptionContext` class, which is derived from `FilterContext` and defines the additional properties shown in Table 30-15.

Table 30-15. *The ExceptionContext Properties*

Name	Description
Exception	This property contains any Exception that was thrown.
ExceptionHandled	This bool property is used to indicate if the exception has been handled.
Result	This property sets the IActionResult that will be used to generate the response.

Creating an Exception Filter

Exception filters can be created by implementing one of the filter interfaces or by deriving from the `ExceptionFilterAttribute` class, which is derived from `Attribute` and implements both the `IExceptionFilter` and `IAsyncException` filters. The most common use for an exception filter is to present a custom error page for a specific exception type in order to provide the user with more useful information than the standard error-handling capabilities can provide.

To create an exception filter, add a class file named `RangeExceptionAttribute.cs` to the `Filters` folder with the code shown in Listing 30-30.

Listing 30-30. The Contents of the RangeExceptionAttribute.cs File in the Filters Folder

```
using Microsoft.AspNetCore.Mvc;
using Microsoft.AspNetCore.Mvc.Filters;
using Microsoft.AspNetCore.Mvc.ModelBinding;
using Microsoft.AspNetCore.Mvc.ViewFeatures;
using System;
```

```
namespace WebApp.Filters {
    public class RangeExceptionAttribute : ExceptionFilterAttribute {

        public override void OnException(ExceptionContext context) {
            if (context.Exception is ArgumentOutOfRangeException) {
                context.Result = new ViewResult() {
                    ViewName = "/Views/Shared/Message.cshtml",
                    ViewData = new ViewDataDictionary(
                        new EmptyModelMetadataProvider(),
                        new ModelStateDictionary()) {
                        Model = @"The data received by the
                                    application cannot be processed"
                    }
                };
            }
        }
    }
}
```

This filter uses the ExceptionContext object to get the type of the unhandled exception and, if the type is ArgumentOutOfRangeException, creates an action result that displays a message to the user. Listing 30-31 adds an action method to the Home controller to which I have applied the exception filter.

Listing 30-31. Applying an Exception Filter in the HomeController.cs File in the Controllers Folder

```
using Microsoft.AspNetCore.Mvc;
using Microsoft.AspNetCore.Http;
using WebApp.Filters;
using Microsoft.AspNetCore.Mvc.Filters;
using System;

namespace WebApp.Controllers {

    [HttpsOnly]
    [ResultDiagnostics]
    public class HomeController : Controller {

        public IActionResult Index() {
            return View("Message",
                "This is the Index action on the Home controller");
        }

        public IActionResult Secure() {
            return View("Message",
                "This is the Secure action on the Home controller");
        }

        //[ChangeArg]
        public IActionResult Messages(string message1, string message2 = "None") {
            return View("Message", $"{message1}, {message2}");
        }

        public override void OnActionExecuting(ActionExecutingContext context) {
            if (context.ActionArguments.ContainsKey("message1")) {
                context.ActionArguments["message1"] = "New message";
            }
        }
```

```
        [RangeException]
        public ViewResult GenerateException(int? id) {
            if (id == null) {
                throw new ArgumentNullException(nameof(id));
            } else if (id > 10) {
                throw new ArgumentOutOfRangeException(nameof(id));
            } else {
                return View("Message", $"The value is {id}");
            }
        }
    }
}
```

The GenerateException action method relies on the default routing pattern to receive a nullable int value from the request URL. The action method throws an ArgumentNullException if there is no matching URL segment and throws an ArgumentOutOfRangeException if its value is greater than 50. If there is a value and it is in range, then the action method returns a ViewResult.

Restart ASP.NET Core and request https://localhost:44350/Home/GenerateException/100. The final segment will exceed the range expected by the action method, which will throw the exception type that is handled by the filter, producing the result shown in Figure 30-11. If you request /Home/GenerateException, then the exception thrown by the action method won't be handled by the filter, and the default error handling will be used.

Figure 30-11. *Using an exception filter*

Managing the Filter Lifecycle

By default, ASP.NET Core manages the filter objects it creates and will reuse them for subsequent requests. This isn't always the desired behavior, and in the sections that follow, I describe different ways to take control of how filters are created. To create a filter that will show the lifecycle, add a class file called GuidResponseAttribute.cs to the Filters folder, and use it to define the filter shown in Listing 30-32.

Listing 30-32. The Contents of the GuidResponseAttribute.cs File in the Filters Folder

```
using Microsoft.AspNetCore.Mvc;
using Microsoft.AspNetCore.Mvc.Filters;
using Microsoft.AspNetCore.Mvc.ModelBinding;
using Microsoft.AspNetCore.Mvc.ViewFeatures;
using System;
using System.Collections.Generic;
using System.Threading.Tasks;
```

```
namespace WebApp.Filters {

    [AttributeUsage(AttributeTargets.Method | AttributeTargets.Class,
        AllowMultiple = true)]
    public class GuidResponseAttribute : Attribute, IAsyncAlwaysRunResultFilter {
        private int counter = 0;
        private string guid = Guid.NewGuid().ToString();

        public async Task OnResultExecutionAsync(ResultExecutingContext context,
            ResultExecutionDelegate next) {

            Dictionary<string, string> resultData;
            if (context.Result is ViewResult vr
                && vr.ViewData.Model is Dictionary<string, string> data) {
                    resultData = data;
            } else {
                resultData = new Dictionary<string, string>();
                context.Result = new ViewResult() {
                    ViewName = "/Views/Shared/Message.cshtml",
                    ViewData = new ViewDataDictionary(
                                    new EmptyModelMetadataProvider(),
                                    new ModelStateDictionary()) {
                        Model = resultData
                    }
                };
            }
            while (resultData.ContainsKey($"Counter_{counter}")) {
                counter++;
            }
            resultData[$"Counter_{counter}"] = guid;
            await next();
        }
    }
}
```

This result filter replaces the action result produced by the endpoint with one that will render the Message view and display a unique GUID value. The filter is configured so that it can be applied more than once to the same target and will add a new message if a filter earlier in the pipeline has created a suitable result. Listing 30-33 applies the filter twice to the Home controller. (I have also removed all but one of the action methods for brevity.)

Listing 30-33. Applying a Filter in the HomeController.cs File in the Controllers Folder

```
using Microsoft.AspNetCore.Mvc;
using Microsoft.AspNetCore.Http;
using WebApp.Filters;
using Microsoft.AspNetCore.Mvc.Filters;
using System;

namespace WebApp.Controllers {

    [HttpsOnly]
    [ResultDiagnostics]
    [GuidResponse]
    [GuidResponse]
    public class HomeController : Controller {
```

```
    public IActionResult Index() {
        return View("Message",
            "This is the Index action on the Home controller");
    }
  }
}
```

To confirm that the filter is being reused, restart ASP.NET Core and request https://localhost:44350/?diag. The response will contain GUID values from the two GuidResponse filter attributes. Two instances of the filter have been created to handle the request. Reload the browser, and you will see the same GUID values displayed, indicating that the filter objects created to handle the first request have been reused (Figure 30-12).

Figure 30-12. *Demonstrating filter reuse*

Creating Filter Factories

Filters can implement the IFilterFactory interface to take responsibility for creating instances of filters and specify whether those instances can be reused. The IFilterFactory interface defines the members described in Table 30-16.

Table 30-16. *The IFilterFactory Members*

Name	Description
IsReusable	This bool property indicates whether instances of the filter can be reused.
CreateInstance(servicePr ovider)	This method is invoked to create new instances of the filter and is provided with an IServiceProvider object.

Listing 30-34 implements the IFilterFactory interface and returns false for the IsReusable property, which prevents the filter from being reused.

Listing 30-34. Implementing an Interface in the GuidResponseAttribute.cs File in the Filters Folder

```
using Microsoft.AspNetCore.Mvc;
using Microsoft.AspNetCore.Mvc.Filters;
using Microsoft.AspNetCore.Mvc.ModelBinding;
using Microsoft.AspNetCore.Mvc.ViewFeatures;
using System;
using System.Collections.Generic;
using System.Threading.Tasks;
using Microsoft.Extensions.DependencyInjection;
```

```
namespace WebApp.Filters {

    [AttributeUsage(AttributeTargets.Method | AttributeTargets.Class,
        AllowMultiple = true)]
    public class GuidResponseAttribute : Attribute,
            IAsyncAlwaysRunResultFilter, IFilterFactory {
        private int counter = 0;
        private string guid = Guid.NewGuid().ToString();

        public bool IsReusable => false;

        public IFilterMetadata CreateInstance(IServiceProvider serviceProvider) {
            return ActivatorUtilities
                .GetServiceOrCreateInstance<GuidResponseAttribute>(serviceProvider);
        }

        public async Task OnResultExecutionAsync(ResultExecutingContext context,
            ResultExecutionDelegate next) {

            Dictionary<string, string> resultData;
            if (context.Result is ViewResult vr
                && vr.ViewData.Model is Dictionary<string, string> data) {
                    resultData = data;
            } else {
                resultData = new Dictionary<string, string>();
                context.Result = new ViewResult() {
                    ViewName = "/Views/Shared/Message.cshtml",
                    ViewData = new ViewDataDictionary(
                                    new EmptyModelMetadataProvider(),
                                    new ModelStateDictionary()) {
                        Model = resultData
                    }
                };
            }
            while (resultData.ContainsKey($"Counter_{counter}")) {
                counter++;
            }
            resultData[$"Counter_{counter}"] = guid;
            await next();
        }
    }
}
```

I create new filter objects using the GetServiceOrCreateInstance method, defined by the ActivatorUtilities class in the Microsoft.Extensions.DependencyInjection namespace. Although you can use the new keyword to create a filter, this approach will resolve any dependencies on services that are declared through the filter's constructor.

To see the effect of implementing the IFilterFactory interface, restart ASP.NET Core and request https://localhost:44350/?diag. Reload the browser, and each time the request is handled, new filters will be created, and new GUIDs will be displayed, as shown in Figure 30-13.

Figure 30-13. *Preventing filter reuse*

Using Dependency Injection Scopes to Manage Filter Lifecycles

Filters can be registered as services, which allows their lifecycle to be controlled through dependency injection, which I described in Chapter 14. Listing 30-35 registers the GuidResponse filter as a scoped service.

Listing 30-35. Creating a Filter Service in the Startup.cs File in the WebApp Folder

```
using Microsoft.AspNetCore.Builder;
using Microsoft.Extensions.DependencyInjection;
using Microsoft.Extensions.Configuration;
using Microsoft.EntityFrameworkCore;
using WebApp.Models;
using Microsoft.AspNetCore.Antiforgery;
using Microsoft.AspNetCore.Http;
using Microsoft.AspNetCore.Mvc;
using WebApp.Filters;

namespace WebApp {
    public class Startup {

        public Startup(IConfiguration config) {
            Configuration = config;
        }

        public IConfiguration Configuration { get; set; }

        public void ConfigureServices(IServiceCollection services) {
            services.AddDbContext<DataContext>(opts => {
                opts.UseSqlServer(Configuration[
                    "ConnectionStrings:ProductConnection"]);
                opts.EnableSensitiveDataLogging(true);
            });
            services.AddControllersWithViews().AddRazorRuntimeCompilation();
            services.AddRazorPages().AddRazorRuntimeCompilation();
            services.AddSingleton<CitiesData>();

            services.Configure<AntiforgeryOptions>(opts => {
                opts.HeaderName = "X-XSRF-TOKEN";
            });
```

```
        services.Configure<MvcOptions>(opts => opts.ModelBindingMessageProvider
            .SetValueMustNotBeNullAccessor(value => "Please enter a value"));

        services.AddScoped<GuidResponseAttribute>();
    }

    public void Configure(IApplicationBuilder app, DataContext context,
            IAntiforgery antiforgery) {

        // ...statements omitted for brevity...
    }
}
}
```

By default, ASP.NET Core creates a scope for each request, which means that a single instance of the filter will be created for each request. To see the effect, restart ASP.NET Core and request `https://localhost:44350/?diag`. Both attributes applied to the Home controller are processed using the same instance of the filter, which means that both GUIDs in the response are the same. Reload the browser; a new scope will be created, and a new filter object will be used, as shown in Figure 30-14.

Figure 30-14. *Using dependency injection to manage filters*

USING FILTERS AS SERVICES WITHOUT THE IFILTERFACTORY INTERFACE

The change in lifecycle took effect immediately in this example because I used the `ActivatorUtilities.` `GetServiceOrCreateInstance` method to create the filter object when I implemented the `IFilterFactory` interface. This method will check to see whether there is a service available for the requested type before invoking its constructor. If you want to use filters as services without implementing `IFilterFactory` and using `ActivatorUtilities`, you can apply the filter using the `ServiceFilter` attribute, like this:

```
...
[ServiceFilter(typeof(GuidResponseAttribute))]
...
```

ASP.NET Core will create the filter object from the service and apply it to the request. Filters that are applied in this way do not have to be derived from the `Attribute` class.

Creating Global Filters

Global filters are applied to every request that ASP.NET Core handles, which means they don't have to be applied to individual controllers or Razor Pages. Any filter can be used as a global filter; however, action filters will be applied to requests only where the endpoint is an action method, and page filters will be applied to requests only where the endpoint is a Razor Page.

Global filters are set up using the options pattern in the Startup class, as shown in Listing 30-36.

Listing 30-36. Creating a Global Filter in the Startup.cs File in the WebApp Folder

```
...
public void ConfigureServices(IServiceCollection services) {
    services.AddDbContext<DataContext>(opts => {
        opts.UseSqlServer(Configuration[
            "ConnectionStrings:ProductConnection"]);
        opts.EnableSensitiveDataLogging(true);
    });
    services.AddControllersWithViews().AddRazorRuntimeCompilation();
    services.AddRazorPages().AddRazorRuntimeCompilation();
    services.AddSingleton<CitiesData>();

    services.Configure<AntiforgeryOptions>(opts => {
        opts.HeaderName = "X-XSRF-TOKEN";
    });

    services.Configure<MvcOptions>(opts => opts.ModelBindingMessageProvider
        .SetValueMustNotBeNullAccessor(value => "Please enter a value"));

    services.AddScoped<GuidResponseAttribute>();
    services.Configure<MvcOptions>(opts => opts.Filters.Add<HttpsOnlyAttribute>());
}
...
```

The MvcOptions.Filters property returns a collection to which filters are added to apply them globally, either using the Add<T> method or using the AddService<T> method for filters that are also services. There is also an Add method without a generic type argument that can be used to register a specific object as a global filter.

The statement in Listing 30-36 registers the HttpsOnly filter I created earlier in the chapter, which means that it no longer needs to be applied directly to individual controllers or Razor Pages, so Listing 30-37 removes the filter from the Home controller.

■ **Note** Notice that I have disabled the GuidResponse filter in Listing 30-37. This is an always-run result filter and will replace the result generated by the global filter.

Listing 30-37. Removing a Filter in the HomeController.cs File in the Controllers Folder

```
using Microsoft.AspNetCore.Mvc;
using Microsoft.AspNetCore.Http;
using WebApp.Filters;
using Microsoft.AspNetCore.Mvc.Filters;
using System;

namespace WebApp.Controllers {

    //[HttpsOnly]
    [ResultDiagnostics]
    //[GuidResponse]
    //[GuidResponse]
```

```
public class HomeController : Controller {

    public IActionResult Index() {
        return View("Message",
            "This is the Index action on the Home controller");
    }
}
}
```

Restart ASP.NET Core and request http://localhost:5000 to confirm that the HTTPS-only policy is being applied even though the attribute is no longer used to decorate the controller. The global authorization filter will short-circuit the filter pipeline and produce the response shown in Figure 30-15.

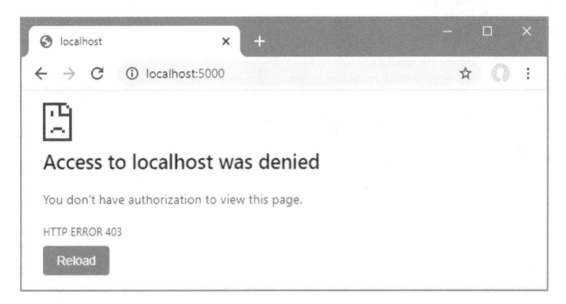

Figure 30-15. *Using a global filter*

Understanding and Changing Filter Order

Filters run in a specific sequence: authorization, resource, action, or page, and then result. But if there are multiple filters of a given type, then the order in which they are applied is driven by the scope through which the filters have been applied.

To demonstrate how this works, add a class file named MessageAttribute.cs to the Filters folder and use it to define the filter shown in Listing 30-38.

Listing 30-38. The Contents of the MessageAttribute.cs File in the Filters Folder

```
using Microsoft.AspNetCore.Mvc;
using Microsoft.AspNetCore.Mvc.Filters;
using Microsoft.AspNetCore.Mvc.ModelBinding;
using Microsoft.AspNetCore.Mvc.ViewFeatures;
using System;
using System.Collections.Generic;
using System.Threading.Tasks;
```

```
namespace WebApp.Filters {

    [AttributeUsage(AttributeTargets.Method | AttributeTargets.Class,
        AllowMultiple = true)]
    public class MessageAttribute : Attribute, IAsyncAlwaysRunResultFilter {
        private int counter = 0;
        private string msg;

        public MessageAttribute(string message) => msg = message;

        public async Task OnResultExecutionAsync(ResultExecutingContext context,
                ResultExecutionDelegate next) {
            Dictionary<string, string> resultData;
            if (context.Result is ViewResult vr
                && vr.ViewData.Model is Dictionary<string, string> data) {
                resultData = data;
            } else {
                resultData = new Dictionary<string, string>();
                context.Result = new ViewResult() {
                    ViewName = "/Views/Shared/Message.cshtml",
                    ViewData = new ViewDataDictionary(
                                    new EmptyModelMetadataProvider(),
                                    new ModelStateDictionary()) {
                        Model = resultData
                    }
                };
            }
            while (resultData.ContainsKey($"Message_{counter}")) {
                counter++;
            }
            resultData[$"Message_{counter}"] = msg;
            await next();
        }
    }
}
```

This result filter uses techniques shown in earlier examples to replace the result from the endpoint and allows multiple filters to build up a series of messages that will be displayed to the user. Listing 30-39 applies several instances of the Message filter to the Home controller.

Listing 30-39. Applying a Filter in the HomeController.cs File in the Controllers Folder

```
using Microsoft.AspNetCore.Mvc;
using Microsoft.AspNetCore.Http;
using WebApp.Filters;
using Microsoft.AspNetCore.Mvc.Filters;
using System;

namespace WebApp.Controllers {

    [Message("This is the controller-scoped filter")]
    public class HomeController : Controller {

        [Message("This is the first action-scoped filter")]
        [Message("This is the second action-scoped filter")]
        public IActionResult Index() {
            return View("Message",
```

```
            "This is the Index action on the Home controller");
        }
    }
}
```

Listing 30-40 registers the Message filter globally.

Listing 30-40. Creating a Global Filter in the Startup.cs File in the WebApp Folder

```
...
public void ConfigureServices(IServiceCollection services) {
    services.AddDbContext<DataContext>(opts => {
        opts.UseSqlServer(Configuration[
            "ConnectionStrings:ProductConnection"]);
        opts.EnableSensitiveDataLogging(true);
    });
    services.AddControllersWithViews().AddRazorRuntimeCompilation();
    services.AddRazorPages().AddRazorRuntimeCompilation();
    services.AddSingleton<CitiesData>();

    services.Configure<AntiforgeryOptions>(opts => {
        opts.HeaderName = "X-XSRF-TOKEN";
    });

    services.Configure<MvcOptions>(opts => opts.ModelBindingMessageProvider
        .SetValueMustNotBeNullAccessor(value => "Please enter a value"));

    services.AddScoped<GuidResponseAttribute>();
    services.Configure<MvcOptions>(opts => {
        opts.Filters.Add<HttpsOnlyAttribute>();
        opts.Filters.Add(new MessageAttribute("This is the globally-scoped filter"));
    });
}
...
```

There are four instances of the same filter. To see the order in which they are applied, restart ASP.NET Core and request https://localhost:44350, which will produce the response shown in Figure 30-16.

Name	Value
Message_0	This is the globally-scoped filter
Message_1	This is the controller-scoped filter
Message_2	This is the first action-scoped filter
Message_3	This is the second action-scoped filter

Figure 30-16. *Applying the same filter in different scopes*

By default, ASP.NET Core runs global filters, then filters applied to controllers or page model classes, and finally filters applied to action or handler methods.

Changing Filter Order

The default order can be changed by implementing the IOrderedFilter interface, which ASP.NET Core looks for when it is working out how to sequence filters. Here is the definition of the interface:

```
namespace Microsoft.AspNetCore.Mvc.Filters {

    public interface IOrderedFilter : IFilterMetadata {
        int Order { get; }
    }
}
```

The Order property returns an int value, and filters with low values are applied before those with higher Order values. In Listing 30-41, I have implemented the interface in the Message filter and defined a constructor argument that will allow the value for the Order property to be specified when the filter is applied.

Listing 30-41. Adding Ordering Support in the MessageAttribute.cs File in the Filters Folder

```
using Microsoft.AspNetCore.Mvc;
using Microsoft.AspNetCore.Mvc.Filters;
using Microsoft.AspNetCore.Mvc.ModelBinding;
using Microsoft.AspNetCore.Mvc.ViewFeatures;
using System;
using System.Collections.Generic;
using System.Threading.Tasks;

namespace WebApp.Filters {

    [AttributeUsage(AttributeTargets.Method | AttributeTargets.Class,
        AllowMultiple = true)]
    public class MessageAttribute : Attribute, IAsyncAlwaysRunResultFilter,
            IOrderedFilter {
        private int counter = 0;
        private string msg;

        public MessageAttribute(string message) => msg = message;

        public int Order { get; set; }

        public async Task OnResultExecutionAsync(ResultExecutingContext context,
                ResultExecutionDelegate next) {

            // ...statements omitted for brevity...
        }
    }
}
```

In Listing 30-42, I have used the constructor argument to change the order in which the filters are applied.

Listing 30-42. Setting Filter Order in the HomeController.cs File in the Controllers Folder

```
using Microsoft.AspNetCore.Mvc;
using Microsoft.AspNetCore.Http;
using WebApp.Filters;
```

```
using Microsoft.AspNetCore.Mvc.Filters;
using System;

namespace WebApp.Controllers {

    [Message("This is the controller-scoped filter", Order = 10)]
    public class HomeController : Controller {

        [Message("This is the first action-scoped filter", Order = 1)]
        [Message("This is the second action-scoped filter", Order = -1)]
        public IActionResult Index() {
            return View("Message",
                "This is the Index action on the Home controller");
        }
    }
}
```

Order values can be negative, which is a helpful way of ensuring that a filter is applied before any global filters with the default order (although you can also set the order when creating global filters, too). Restart ASP.NET Core and request https://localhost:44350 to see the new filter order, which is shown in Figure 30-17.

Figure 30-17. *Changing filter order*

Summary

In this chapter, I described the ASP.NET Core filter feature and explained how it can be used to alter requests and results for specific endpoints. I described the different types of filters and demonstrated how to create and apply each of them. I also showed you how to manage the lifecycle of filters and control the order in which they are executed. In the next chapter, I show you how to combine the features described in this part of the book to create form applications.

CHAPTER 31

Creating Form Applications

The previous chapters have focused on individual features that deal with one aspect of HTML forms, and it can sometimes be difficult to see how they fit together to perform common tasks. In this chapter, I go through the process of creating controllers, views, and Razor Pages that support an application with create, read, update, and delete (CRUD) functionality. There are no new features described in this chapter, and the objective is to demonstrate how features such as tag helpers, model binding, and model validation can be used in conjunction with Entity Framework Core.

Preparing for This Chapter

This chapter uses the WebApp project from Chapter 30. To prepare for this chapter, replace the contents of the HomeController.cs file in the Controllers folder with those shown in Listing 31-1.

Tip   You can download the example project for this chapter—and for all the other chapters in this book—from https://github.com/apress/pro-asp.net-core-3. See Chapter 1 for how to get help if you have problems running the examples.

Listing 31-1. The Contents of the HomeController.cs File in the Controllers Folder

```
using Microsoft.AspNetCore.Mvc;
using Microsoft.EntityFrameworkCore;
using System.Collections.Generic;
using System.Threading.Tasks;
using WebApp.Models;

namespace WebApp.Controllers {

    [AutoValidateAntiforgeryToken]
    public class HomeController : Controller {
        private DataContext context;

        private IEnumerable<Category> Categories => context.Categories;
        private IEnumerable<Supplier> Suppliers => context.Suppliers;

        public HomeController(DataContext data) {
            context = data;
        }

        public IActionResult Index() {
            return View(context.Products.
                Include(p => p.Category).Include(p => p.Supplier));
        }
    }
}
```

Create the Views/HomeIndex.cshtml,

Listing 31-2. The Contents of the Index.cshtml File in the Views/Home Folder

```
@model IEnumerable<Product>
@{ Layout = "_SimpleLayout"; }

<h4 class="bg-primary text-white text-center p-2">Products</h4>
<table class="table table-sm table-bordered table-striped">
    <thead>
        <tr>
            <th>ID</th><th>Name</th><th>Price</th><th>Category</th><th></th>
        </tr>
    </thead>
    <tbody>
        @foreach (Product p in Model) {
            <tr>
                <td>@p.ProductId</td>
                <td>@p.Name</td>
                <td>@p.Price</td>
                <td>@p.Category.Name</td>
                <td class="text-center">
                    <a asp-action="Details" asp-route-id="@p.ProductId"
                        class="btn btn-sm btn-info">Details</a>
                    <a asp-action="Edit" asp-route-id="@p.ProductId"
                        class="btn btn-sm btn-warning">Edit</a>
                    <a asp-action="Delete" asp-route-id="@p.ProductId"
                        class="btn btn-sm btn-danger">Delete</a>
                </td>
            </tr>
        }
    </tbody>
</table>
<a asp-action="Create" class="btn btn-primary">Create</a>
```

Next, update the Product class as shown in Listing 31-3 to change the validation constraints to remove the model-level checking and disable remote validation.

Listing 31-3. Changing Validation in the Product.cs File in the Models Folder

```
using System.ComponentModel.DataAnnotations.Schema;
using System.ComponentModel.DataAnnotations;
using Microsoft.AspNetCore.Mvc.ModelBinding;
using WebApp.Validation;
using Microsoft.AspNetCore.Mvc;

namespace WebApp.Models {

    //[PhraseAndPrice(Phrase = "Small", Price = "100")]
    public class Product {

        public long ProductId { get; set; }

        [Required]
        [Display(Name = "Name")]
        public string Name { get; set; }
```

```
    [Column(TypeName = "decimal(8, 2)")]
    [Required(ErrorMessage = "Please enter a price")]
    [Range(1, 999999, ErrorMessage = "Please enter a positive price")]
    public decimal Price { get; set; }

    [PrimaryKey(ContextType = typeof(DataContext),
        DataType = typeof(Category))]
    //[Remote("CategoryKey", "Validation",
    //      ErrorMessage = "Enter an existing key")]
    public long CategoryId { get; set; }
    public Category Category { get; set; }

    [PrimaryKey(ContextType = typeof(DataContext),
        DataType = typeof(Category))]
    //[Remote("SupplierKey", "Validation",
    //      ErrorMessage = "Enter an existing key")]
    public long SupplierId { get; set; }
    public Supplier Supplier { get; set; }
    }
}
```

Finally, disable the global filters in the Startup class, as shown in Listing 31-4.

Listing 31-4. Disabling Filters in the Startup.cs File in the WebApp Folder

```
...
public void ConfigureServices(IServiceCollection services) {
    services.AddDbContext<DataContext>(opts => {
        opts.UseSqlServer(Configuration[
            "ConnectionStrings:ProductConnection"]);
        opts.EnableSensitiveDataLogging(true);
    });
    services.AddControllersWithViews().AddRazorRuntimeCompilation();
    services.AddRazorPages().AddRazorRuntimeCompilation();
    services.AddSingleton<CitiesData>();

    services.Configure<AntiforgeryOptions>(opts => {
        opts.HeaderName = "X-XSRF-TOKEN";
    });

    services.Configure<MvcOptions>(opts => opts.ModelBindingMessageProvider
        .SetValueMustNotBeNullAccessor(value => "Please enter a value"));

    services.AddScoped<GuidResponseAttribute>();
    //services.Configure<MvcOptions>(opts => {
    //    opts.Filters.Add<HttpsOnlyAttribute>();
    //    opts.Filters.Add(new MessageAttribute(
    //        "This is the globally-scoped filter"));
    //});
}
...
```

Dropping the Database

Open a new PowerShell command prompt, navigate to the folder that contains the WebApp.csproj file, and run the command shown in Listing 31-5 to drop the database.

Listing 31-5. Dropping the Database

```
dotnet ef database drop --force
```

Running the Example Application

Select Start Without Debugging or Run Without Debugging from the Debug menu or use the PowerShell command prompt to run the command shown in Listing 31-6.

Listing 31-6. Running the Example Application

```
dotnet run
```

Use a browser to request http://localhost:5000/controllers, which will display a list of products, as shown in Figure 31-1. There are anchor elements styled to appear as buttons, but these will not work until later when I add the features to create, edit, and delete objects.

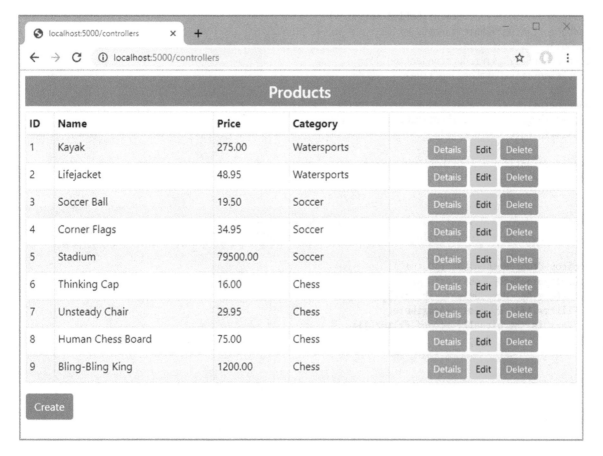

Figure 31-1. Running the example application

Creating an MVC Forms Application

In the sections that follow, I show you how to perform the core data operations using MVC controllers and views. Later in the chapter, I create the same functionality using Razor Pages.

Preparing the View Model and the View

I am going to define a single form that will be used for multiple operations, configured through its view model class. To create the view model class, add a Class File named `ProductViewModel.cs` to the `Models` folder and add the code shown in Listing 31-7.

Listing 31-7. The Contents of the ProductViewModel.cs File in the Models Folder

```
using System.Collections.Generic;
using System.Linq;

namespace WebApp.Models {

    public class ProductViewModel {
        public Product Product { get; set; }
        public string Action { get; set; } = "Create";
        public bool ReadOnly { get; set; } = false;
        public string Theme { get; set; } = "primary";
        public bool ShowAction { get; set; } = true;
        public IEnumerable<Category> Categories { get; set; }
            = Enumerable.Empty<Category>();
        public IEnumerable<Supplier> Suppliers { get; set; }
            = Enumerable.Empty<Supplier>();
    }
}
```

This class will allow the controller to pass data and display settings to its view. The `Product` property provides the data to display, and the `Categories` and `Suppliers` properties provide access to the `Category` and `Suppliers` objects when they are required. The other properties configure aspects of how the content is presented to the user: the `Action` property specifies the name of the action method for the current task, the `ReadOnly` property specifies whether the user can edit the data, the `Theme` property specifies the Bootstrap theme for the content, and the `ShowAction` property is used to control the visibility of the button that submits the form.

To create the view that will allow the user to interact with the application's data, add a Razor View named `ProductEditor.cshtml` to the `Views/Home` folder with the content shown in Listing 31-8.

Listing 31-8. The Contents of the ProductEditor.cshtml File in the Views/Home Folder

```
@model ProductViewModel
@{ Layout = "_SimpleLayout"; }

<partial name="_Validation" />

<h5 class="bg-@Model.Theme text-white text-center p-2">@Model.Action</h5>

<form asp-action="@Model.Action" method="post">
    <div class="form-group">
        <label asp-for="Product.ProductId"></label>
        <input class="form-control" asp-for="Product.ProductId" readonly />
    </div>
    <div class="form-group">
        <label asp-for="Product.Name"></label>
```

```
        <div>
            <span asp-validation-for="Product.Name" class="text-danger"></span>
        </div>
        <input class="form-control" asp-for="Product.Name"
            readonly="@Model.ReadOnly" />
    </div>
    <div class="form-group">
        <label asp-for="Product.Price"></label>
        <div>
            <span asp-validation-for="Product.Price" class="text-danger"></span>
        </div>
        <input class="form-control" asp-for="Product.Price"
            readonly="@Model.ReadOnly" />
    </div>
    <div class="form-group">
        <label asp-for="Product.CategoryId">Category</label>
        <div>
            <span asp-validation-for="Product.CategoryId" class="text-danger"></span>
        </div>
        <select asp-for="Product.CategoryId" class="form-control"
            disabled="@Model.ReadOnly"
            asp-items="@(new SelectList(Model.Categories,
                "CategoryId", "Name"))">
            <option value="" disabled selected>Choose a Category</option>
        </select>
    </div>
    <div class="form-group">
        <label asp-for="Product.SupplierId">Supplier</label>
        <div>
            <span asp-validation-for="Product.SupplierId" class="text-danger"></span>
        </div>
        <select asp-for="Product.SupplierId" class="form-control"
            disabled="@Model.ReadOnly"
            asp-items="@(new SelectList(Model.Suppliers,
                "SupplierId", "Name"))">
            <option value="" disabled selected>Choose a Supplier</option>
        </select>
    </div>
    @if (Model.ShowAction) {
        <button class="btn btn-@Model.Theme" type="submit">@Model.Action</button>
    }
    <a class="btn btn-secondary" asp-action="Index">Back</a>
</form>
```

This view can look complicated, but it combines only the features you have seen in earlier chapters and will become clearer once you see it in action. The model for this view is a ProductViewModel object, which provides both the data that is displayed to the user and some direction about how that data should be presented.

For each of the properties defined by the Product class, the view contains a set of elements: a label element that describes the property, an input or select element that allows the value to be edited, and a span element that will display validation messages. Each of the elements is configured with the asp-for attribute, which ensures tag helpers will transform the elements for each property. There are div elements to define the view structure, and all the elements are members of Bootstrap CSS classes to style the form.

Reading Data

The simplest operation is reading data from the database and presenting it to the user. In most applications, this will allow the user to see additional details that are not present in the list view. Each task performed by the application will require a different set of ProductViewModel properties. To manage these combinations, add a class file named ViewModelFactory.cs to the Models folder with the code shown in Listing 31-9.

Listing 31-9. The Contents of the ViewModelFactory.cs File in the Models Folder

```
using System.Collections.Generic;
using System.Linq;

namespace WebApp.Models {

    public static class ViewModelFactory {

        public static ProductViewModel Details(Product p) {
            return new ProductViewModel {
                Product = p, Action = "Details",
                ReadOnly = true, Theme = "info", ShowAction = false,
                Categories = p == null ? Enumerable.Empty<Category>()
                    : new List<Category> { p.Category },
                Suppliers = p == null ? Enumerable.Empty<Supplier>()
                    : new List<Supplier> { p.Supplier},
            };
        }
    }
}
```

The Details method produces a ProductViewModel object configured for viewing an object. When the user views the details, the category and supplier details will be read-only, which means that I need to provide only the current category and supplier information.

Next, add an action method to the Home controller that uses the ViewModelFactory.Details method to create a ProductViewModel object and display it to the user with the ProductEditor view, as shown in Listing 31-10.

Listing 31-10. Adding an Action Method in the HomeController.cs File in the Controllers Folder

```
using Microsoft.AspNetCore.Mvc;
using Microsoft.EntityFrameworkCore;
using System.Collections.Generic;
using System.Threading.Tasks;
using WebApp.Models;

namespace WebApp.Controllers {

    [AutoValidateAntiforgeryToken]
    public class HomeController : Controller {
        private DataContext context;

        private IEnumerable<Category> Categories => context.Categories;
        private IEnumerable<Supplier> Suppliers => context.Suppliers;

        public HomeController(DataContext data) {
            context = data;
        }

        public IActionResult Index() {
            return View(context.Products.
                Include(p => p.Category).Include(p => p.Supplier));
        }

        public async Task<IActionResult> Details(long id) {
            Product p = await context.Products.
                Include(p => p.Category).Include(p => p.Supplier)
                .FirstOrDefaultAsync(p => p.ProductId == id);
```

```
            ProductViewModel model = ViewModelFactory.Details(p);
            return View("ProductEditor", model);
        }
    }
}
```

The action method uses the id parameter, which will be model bound from the routing data, to query the database and passes the Product object to the ViewModelFactory.Details method. Most of the operations are going to require the Category and Supplier data, so I have added properties that provide direct access to the data.

To test the details feature, restart ASP.NET Core and request http://localhost:5000/controllers. Click one of the Details buttons, and you will see the selected object presented in read-only form using the ProductEditor view, as shown in Figure 31-2.

Figure 31-2. *Viewing data*

If the user navigates to a URL that doesn't correspond to an object in the database, such as http://localhost:5000/controllers/Home/Details/100, for example, then an empty form will be displayed.

Creating Data

Creating data relies on model binding to get the form data from the request and relies on validation to ensure the data can be stored in the database. The first step is to add a factory method that will create the view model object for creating data, as shown in Listing 31-11.

Listing 31-11. Adding a Method in the ViewModelFactory.cs File in the Models Folder

```
using System.Collections.Generic;
using System.Linq;

namespace WebApp.Models {
```

```
public static class ViewModelFactory {

    public static ProductViewModel Details(Product p) {
        return new ProductViewModel {
            Product = p, Action = "Details",
            ReadOnly = true, Theme = "info", ShowAction = false,
            Categories = p == null ? Enumerable.Empty<Category>()
                : new List<Category> { p.Category },
            Suppliers = p == null ? Enumerable.Empty<Supplier>()
                : new List<Supplier> { p.Supplier},
        };
    }

    public static ProductViewModel Create(Product product,
        IEnumerable<Category> categories, IEnumerable<Supplier> suppliers) {
        return new ProductViewModel {
            Product = product, Categories = categories, Suppliers = suppliers
        };
    }
}
}
```

The defaults I used for the ProductViewModel properties were set for creating data, so the Create method in Listing 31-11 sets only the Product, Categories, and Suppliers properties. Listing 31-12 adds the action methods that will create data to the Home controller.

Listing 31-12. Adding Actions in the HomeController.cs File in the Controllers Folder

```
using Microsoft.AspNetCore.Mvc;
using Microsoft.EntityFrameworkCore;
using System.Collections.Generic;
using System.Threading.Tasks;
using WebApp.Models;

namespace WebApp.Controllers {

    [AutoValidateAntiforgeryToken]
    public class HomeController : Controller {
        private DataContext context;

        private IEnumerable<Category> Categories => context.Categories;
        private IEnumerable<Supplier> Suppliers => context.Suppliers;

        public HomeController(DataContext data) {
            context = data;
        }

        public IActionResult Index() {
            return View(context.Products.
                Include(p => p.Category).Include(p => p.Supplier));
        }

        public async Task<IActionResult> Details(long id) {
            Product p = await context.Products.
                Include(p => p.Category).Include(p => p.Supplier)
                .FirstOrDefaultAsync(p => p.ProductId == id);
            ProductViewModel model = ViewModelFactory.Details(p);
            return View("ProductEditor", model);
        }
```

```
        public IActionResult Create() {
            return View("ProductEditor",
                ViewModelFactory.Create(new Product(), Categories, Suppliers));
        }

        [HttpPost]
        public async Task<IActionResult> Create([FromForm] Product product) {
            if (ModelState.IsValid) {
                product.ProductId = default;
                product.Category = default;
                product.Supplier = default;
                context.Products.Add(product);
                await context.SaveChangesAsync();
                return RedirectToAction(nameof(Index));
            }
            return View("ProductEditor",
                ViewModelFactory.Create(product, Categories, Suppliers));
        }
    }
}
```

There are two Create methods, which are differentiated by the HttpPost attribute and method parameters. HTTP GET requests will be handled by the first method, which selects the ProductEditor view and provides it with a ProductViewModel object. When the user submits the form, it will be received by the second method, which relies on model binding to receive the data and model validation to ensure the data is valid.

If the data passes validation, then I prepare the object for storage in the database by resetting three properties, like this:

```
...
product.ProductId = default;
product.Category = default;
product.Supplier = default;
...
```

Entity Framework Core configures the database so that primary keys are allocated by the database server when new data is stored. If you attempt to store an object and provide a ProductId value other than zero, then an exception will be thrown.

I reset the Category and Supplier properties to prevent Entity Framework Core from trying to deal with related data when storing an object. Entity Framework Core is capable of processing related data, but it can produce unexpected outcomes. (I show you how to create related data in the "Creating New Related Data Objects" section, later in this chapter.)

Notice I call the View method with arguments when validation fails, like this:

```
...
return View("ProductEditor",
    ViewModelFactory.Create(product, Categories, Suppliers));
...
```

I do this because the view model object expected by the view isn't the same data type that I have extracted from the request using model binding. Instead, I create a new view model object that incorporates the model bound data and passes this to the View method.

Restart ASP.NET Core, request http://localhost:5000/controllers, and click Create. Fill out the form and click the Create button to submit the data. The new object will be stored in the database and displayed when the browser is redirected to the Index action, as shown in Figure 31-3.

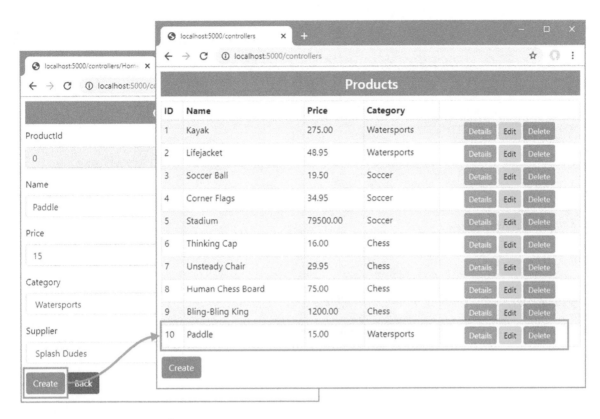

Figure 31-3. *Creating a new object*

Notice that select elements allow the user to select the values for the CategoryId and SupplierId properties, using the category and supplier names, like this:

```
...
<select asp-for="Product.SupplierId" class="form-control" disabled="@Model.ReadOnly"
        asp-items="@(new SelectList(Model.Suppliers, "SupplierId", "Name"))">
    <option value="" disabled selected>Choose a Supplier</option>
</select>
...
```

In Chapter 30, I used input elements to allow the value of these properties to be set directly, but that was because I wanted to demonstrate different types of validation. In real applications, it is a good idea to provide the user with restricted choices when the application already has the data it expects the user to choose from. Making the user enter a valid primary key, for example, makes no sense in a real project because the application can easily provide the user with a list of those keys to choose from, as shown in Figure 31-4.

■ **Tip** I show you different techniques for creating related data in the "Creating New Related Data Objects" section.

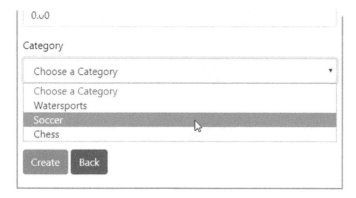

Figure 31-4. *Presenting the user with a choice*

Editing Data

The process for editing data is similar to creating data. The first step is to add a new method to the view model factory that will configure the way the data is presented to the user, as shown in Listing 31-13.

Listing 31-13. Adding a Method in the ViewModelFactory.cs File in the Models Folder

```
using System.Collections.Generic;
using System.Linq;

namespace WebApp.Models {

    public static class ViewModelFactory {

        public static ProductViewModel Details(Product p) {
            return new ProductViewModel {
                Product = p, Action = "Details",
                ReadOnly = true, Theme = "info", ShowAction = false,
                Categories = p == null ? Enumerable.Empty<Category>()
                    : new List<Category> { p.Category },
                Suppliers = p == null ? Enumerable.Empty<Supplier>()
                    : new List<Supplier> { p.Supplier},
            };
        }

        public static ProductViewModel Create(Product product,
                IEnumerable<Category> categories, IEnumerable<Supplier> suppliers) {
            return new ProductViewModel {
                Product = product, Categories = categories, Suppliers = suppliers
            };
        }

        public static ProductViewModel Edit(Product product,
                IEnumerable<Category> categories, IEnumerable<Supplier> suppliers) {
            return new ProductViewModel {
                Product = product, Categories = categories, Suppliers = suppliers,
                Theme = "warning", Action = "Edit"
            };
        }
    }
}
```

The next step is to add the action methods to the Home controller that will display the current properties of a Product object to the user and receive the changes the user makes, as shown in Listing 31-14.

Listing 31-14. Adding Action Methods in the HomeController.cs File in the Controllers Folder

```
using Microsoft.AspNetCore.Mvc;
using Microsoft.EntityFrameworkCore;
using System.Collections.Generic;
using System.Threading.Tasks;
using WebApp.Models;

namespace WebApp.Controllers {

    [AutoValidateAntiforgeryToken]
    public class HomeController : Controller {
        private DataContext context;

        private IEnumerable<Category> Categories => context.Categories;
        private IEnumerable<Supplier> Suppliers => context.Suppliers;

        public HomeController(DataContext data) {
            context = data;
        }

        // ...other action methods omitted for brevity...

        public async Task<IActionResult> Edit(long id) {
            Product p = await context.Products.FindAsync(id);
            ProductViewModel model = ViewModelFactory.Edit(p, Categories, Suppliers);
            return View("ProductEditor", model);
        }

        [HttpPost]
        public async Task<IActionResult> Edit([FromForm]Product product) {
            if (ModelState.IsValid) {
                product.Category = default;
                product.Supplier = default;
                context.Products.Update(product);
                await context.SaveChangesAsync();
                return RedirectToAction(nameof(Index));
            }
            return View("ProductEditor",
                ViewModelFactory.Edit(product, Categories, Suppliers));
        }
    }
}
```

To see the editing feature at work, restart ASP.NET Core, navigate to http://localhost:5000/controllers, and click one of the Edit buttons. Change one or more property values and submit the form. The changes will be stored in the database and reflected in the list displayed when the browser is redirected to the Index action, as shown in Figure 31-5.

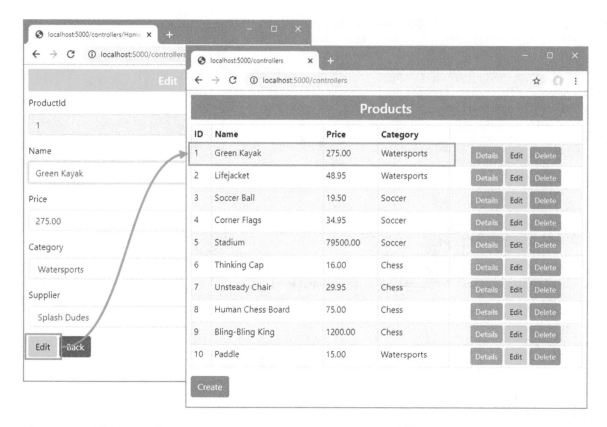

Figure 31-5. *Editing a product*

Notice that the `ProductId` property cannot be changed. Attempting to change the primary key of an object should be avoided because it interferes with the Entity Framework Core understanding of the identity of its objects. If you can't avoid changing the primary key, then the safest approach is to delete the existing object and store a new one.

Deleting Data

The final basic operation is removing objects from the database. By now the pattern will be clear, and the first step is to add a method to create a view model object to determine how the data is presented to the user, as shown in Listing 31-15.

Listing 31-15. Adding a Method in the ViewModelFactory.cs File in the Models Folder

```
using System.Collections.Generic;
using System.Linq;

namespace WebApp.Models {

    public static class ViewModelFactory {

        // ...other methods omitted for brevity...

        public static ProductViewModel Delete(Product p,
                IEnumerable<Category> categories, IEnumerable<Supplier> suppliers) {
            return new ProductViewModel {
                Product = p, Action = "Delete",
                ReadOnly = true, Theme = "danger",
```

```
                Categories = categories, Suppliers = suppliers
            };
        }
    }
}
```

Listing 31-16 adds the action methods to the Home controller that will respond to the GET request by displaying the selected object and the POST request to remove that object from the database.

Listing 31-16. Adding Action Methods in the HomeController.cs File in the Controllers Folder

```
using Microsoft.AspNetCore.Mvc;
using Microsoft.EntityFrameworkCore;
using System.Collections.Generic;
using System.Threading.Tasks;
using WebApp.Models;

namespace WebApp.Controllers {

    [AutoValidateAntiforgeryToken]
    public class HomeController : Controller {
        private DataContext context;

        private IEnumerable<Category> Categories => context.Categories;
        private IEnumerable<Supplier> Suppliers => context.Suppliers;

        public HomeController(DataContext data) {
            context = data;
        }

        // ...other action methods removed for brevity...

        public async Task<IActionResult> Delete(long id) {
            ProductViewModel model = ViewModelFactory.Delete(
                await context.Products.FindAsync(id), Categories, Suppliers);
            return View("ProductEditor", model);
        }

        [HttpPost]
        public async Task<IActionResult> Delete(Product product) {
            context.Products.Remove(product);
            await context.SaveChangesAsync();
            return RedirectToAction(nameof(Index));
        }
    }
}
```

The model binding process creates a Product object from the form data, which is passed to Entity Framework Core to remove from the database. Once the data has been removed from the database, the browser is redirected to the Index action, as shown in Figure 31-6.

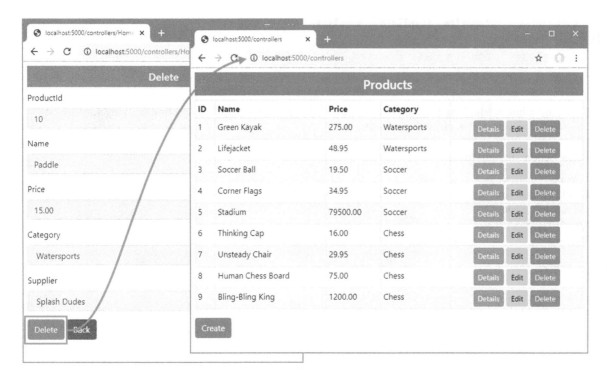

Figure 31-6. *Deleting data*

Creating a Razor Pages Forms Application

Working with Razor Forms relies on similar techniques as the controller examples, albeit broken up into smaller chunks of functionality. As you will see, the main difficulty is preserving the modular nature of Razor Pages without duplicating code and markup. The first step is to create the Razor Page that will display the list of Product objects and provide the links to the other operations. Add a Razor Page named Index.cshtml to the Pages folder with the content shown in Listing 31-17.

Listing 31-17. The Contents of the Index.cshtml File in the Pages Folder

```
@page "/pages/{id:long?}"
@model IndexModel
@using Microsoft.AspNetCore.Mvc.RazorPages
@using Microsoft.EntityFrameworkCore

<div class="m-2">
    <h4 class="bg-primary text-white text-center p-2">Products</h4>
    <table class="table table-sm table-bordered table-striped">
        <thead>
            <tr>
                <th>ID</th><th>Name</th><th>Price</th><th>Category</th><th></th>
            </tr>
        </thead>
        <tbody>
            @foreach (Product p in Model.Products) {
```

```
                <tr>
                    <td>@p.ProductId</td>
                    <td>@p.Name</td>
                    <td>@p.Price</td>
                    <td>@p.Category.Name</td>
                    <td class="text-center">
                        <a asp-page="Details" asp-route-id="@p.ProductId"
                            class="btn btn-sm btn-info">Details</a>
                        <a asp-page="Edit" asp-route-id="@p.ProductId"
                            class="btn btn-sm btn-warning">Edit</a>
                        <a asp-page="Delete" asp-route-id="@p.ProductId"
                            class="btn btn-sm btn-danger">Delete</a>
                    </td>
                </tr>
            }
        </tbody>
    </table>
    <a asp-page="Create" class="btn btn-primary">Create</a>
</div>

@functions {

    public class IndexModel: PageModel {
        private DataContext context;

        public IndexModel(DataContext dbContext) {
            context = dbContext;
        }

        public IEnumerable<Product> Products { get; set; }

        public void OnGetAsync(long id = 1) {
            Products = context.Products
                .Include(p => p.Category).Include(p => p.Supplier);
        }
    }
}
```

This view part of the page displays a table populated with the details of the Product objects obtained from the database by the page model. Use a browser to request http://localhost:5000/pages, and you will see the response shown in Figure 31-7. Alongside the details of the Product objects, the page displays anchor elements that navigate to other Razor Pages, which I define in the sections that follow.

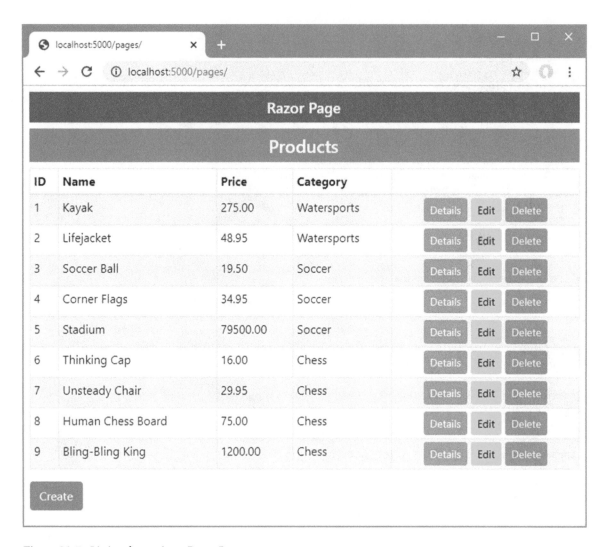

Figure 31-7. *Listing data using a Razor Page*

Creating Common Functionality

I don't want to duplicate the same HTML form and supporting code in each of the pages required by the example application. Instead, I am going to define a partial view that defines the HTML form and a base class that defines the common code required by the page model classes. For the partial view, a Razor View named _ProductEditor.cshtml to the Pages folder with the content shown in Listing 31-18.

USING MULTIPLE PAGE

The asp-page-handler attribute can be used to specify the name of a handler method, which allows a Razor Page to be used for more than one operation. I don't like this feature because the result is too close to a standard MVC controller and undermines the self-contained and modular aspects of Razor Page development that I like.

The approach I prefer is, of course, the one that I have taken in this chapter, which is to consolidate common content in partial views and a shared base class. Either approach works, and I recommend you try both to see which suits you and your project.

Listing 31-18. The Contents of the _ProductEditor.cshtml File in the Pages Folder

```
@model ProductViewModel

<partial name="_Validation" />

<h5 class="bg-@Model.Theme text-white text-center p-2">@Model.Action</h5>

<form asp-page="@Model.Action" method="post">
    <div class="form-group">
        <label asp-for="Product.ProductId"></label>
        <input class="form-control" asp-for="Product.ProductId" readonly />
    </div>
    <div class="form-group">
        <label asp-for="Product.Name"></label>
        <div>
            <span asp-validation-for="Product.Name" class="text-danger"></span>
        </div>
        <input class="form-control" asp-for="Product.Name"
                readonly="@Model.ReadOnly" />
    </div>
    <div class="form-group">
        <label asp-for="Product.Price"></label>
        <div>
            <span asp-validation-for="Product.Price" class="text-danger"></span>
        </div>
        <input class="form-control" asp-for="Product.Price"
                readonly="@Model.ReadOnly" />
    </div>
    <div class="form-group">
        <label asp-for="Product.CategoryId">Category</label>
        <div>
            <span asp-validation-for="Product.CategoryId" class="text-danger"></span>
        </div>
        <select asp-for="Product.CategoryId" class="form-control"
                disabled="@Model.ReadOnly"

                asp-items="@(new SelectList(Model.Categories,
                    "CategoryId", "Name"))">
            <option value="" disabled selected>Choose a Category</option>
        </select>
    </div>
    <div class="form-group">
        <label asp-for="Product.SupplierId">Supplier</label>
        <div>
            <span asp-validation-for="Product.SupplierId" class="text-danger"></span>
        </div>
        <select asp-for="Product.SupplierId" class="form-control"
                disabled="@Model.ReadOnly"
                asp-items="@(new SelectList(Model.Suppliers,
                    "SupplierId", "Name"))">
            <option value="" disabled selected>Choose a Supplier</option>
        </select>
    </div>
    @if (Model.ShowAction) {
        <button class="btn btn-@Model.Theme" type="submit">@Model.Action</button>
    }
    <a class="btn btn-secondary" asp-page="Index">Back</a>
</form>
```

The partial view uses the `ProductViewModel` class as its model type and relies on the built-in tag helpers to present `input` and `select` elements for the properties defined by the `Product` class. This is the same content used earlier in the chapter, except with the `asp-action` attribute replaced with `asp-page` to specify the target for the `form` and `anchor` elements.

To define the page model base class, add a class file named `EditorPageModel.cs` to the `Pages` folder and use it to define the class shown in Listing 31-19.

Listing 31-19. The Contents of the EditorPageModel.cs File in the Pages Folder

```
using Microsoft.AspNetCore.Mvc.RazorPages;
using System.Collections.Generic;
using WebApp.Models;

namespace WebApp.Pages {

    public class EditorPageModel : PageModel {

        public EditorPageModel(DataContext dbContext) {
            DataContext = dbContext;
        }

        public DataContext DataContext { get; set; }

        public IEnumerable<Category> Categories => DataContext.Categories;
        public IEnumerable<Supplier> Suppliers => DataContext.Suppliers;

        public ProductViewModel ViewModel { get; set; }
    }
}
```

The properties defined by this class are simple, but they will help simplify the page model classes of the Razor Pages that handle each operation.

All the Razor Pages required for this example depend on the same namespaces. Add the expressions shown in Listing 31-20 to the `_ViewImports.cshtml` file in the Pages folder to avoid duplicate expressions in the individual pages.

■ **Tip** Make sure you alter the `_ViewImports.cshtml` file in the `Pages` folder and not the file with the same name in the `Views` folder.

Listing 31-20. Adding Namespaces in the _ViewImports.cshtml File in the Pages Folder

```
@namespace WebApp.Pages
@using WebApp.Models
@addTagHelper *, Microsoft.AspNetCore.Mvc.TagHelpers
@addTagHelper *, WebApp
@using Microsoft.AspNetCore.Mvc.RazorPages
@using Microsoft.EntityFrameworkCore
@using WebApp.Pages
@using System.Text.Json
@using Microsoft.AspNetCore.Http
```

Defining Pages for the CRUD Operations

With the partial view and shared base class in place, the pages that handle individual operations are simple. Add a Razor Page named `Details.cshtml` to the Pages folder with the code and content shown in Listing 31-21.

Listing 31-21. The Contents of the Details.cshtml File in the Pages Folder

```
@page "/pages/details/{id}"
@model DetailsModel

<div class="m-2">
    <partial name="_ProductEditor" model="@Model.ViewModel" />
</div>

@functions {

    public class DetailsModel: EditorPageModel {

        public DetailsModel(DataContext dbContext): base(dbContext) {}

        public async Task OnGetAsync(long id) {
            Product p = await DataContext.Products.
                Include(p => p.Category).Include(p => p.Supplier)
                .FirstOrDefaultAsync(p => p.ProductId == id);
            ViewModel = ViewModelFactory.Details(p);
        }
    }
}
```

The constructor receives an Entity Framework Core context object, which it passes to the base class. The handler method responds to requests by querying the database and using the response to create a ProductViewModel object using the ViewModelFactory class.

Add a Razor Page named Create.cshtml to the Pages folder with the code and content shown in Listing 31-22.

■ **Tip**   Using a partial view means that the asp-for attributes set element names without an additional prefix. This allows me to use the FromForm attribute for model binding without using the Name argument.

Listing 31-22. The Contents of the Create.cshtml File in the Pages Folder

```
@page "/pages/create"
@model CreateModel

<div class="m-2">
    <partial name="_ProductEditor" model="@Model.ViewModel" />
</div>

@functions {

    public class CreateModel: EditorPageModel {

        public CreateModel(DataContext dbContext): base(dbContext) {}

        public void OnGet() {
            ViewModel = ViewModelFactory.Create(new Product(),
                Categories, Suppliers);
        }
```

```
    public async Task<IActionResult> OnPostAsync([FromForm]Product product) {
        if (ModelState.IsValid) {
            product.ProductId = default;
            product.Category = default;
            product.Supplier = default;
            DataContext.Products.Add(product);
            await DataContext.SaveChangesAsync();
            return RedirectToPage(nameof(Index));
        }
        ViewModel = ViewModelFactory.Create(product, Categories, Suppliers);
        return Page();
    }
}
}
```

Add a Razor Page named Edit.cshtml to the Pages folder with the code and content shown in Listing 31-23.

Listing 31-23. The Contents of the Edit.cshtml File in the Pages Folder

```
@page "/pages/edit/{id}"
@model EditModel

<div class="m-2">
    <partial name="_ProductEditor" model="@Model.ViewModel" />
</div>

@functions {

    public class EditModel: EditorPageModel {

        public EditModel(DataContext dbContext): base(dbContext) {}

        public async Task OnGetAsync(long id) {
            Product p = await this.DataContext.Products.FindAsync(id);
            ViewModel = ViewModelFactory.Edit(p, Categories, Suppliers);
        }

        public async Task<IActionResult> OnPostAsync([FromForm]Product product) {
            if (ModelState.IsValid) {
                product.Category = default;
                product.Supplier = default;
                DataContext.Products.Update(product);
                await DataContext.SaveChangesAsync();
                return RedirectToPage(nameof(Index));
            }
            ViewModel = ViewModelFactory.Edit(product, Categories, Suppliers);
            return Page();
        }
    }
}
```

Add a Razor Page named Delete.cshtml to the Pages folder with the code and content shown in Listing 31-24.

Listing 31-24. The Contents of the Delete.cshtml File in the Pages Folder

```
@page "/pages/delete/{id}"
@model DeleteModel

<div class="m-2">
    <partial name="_ProductEditor" model="@Model.ViewModel" />
</div>

@functions {

    public class DeleteModel: EditorPageModel {

        public DeleteModel(DataContext dbContext): base(dbContext) {}

        public async Task OnGetAsync(long id) {
            ViewModel = ViewModelFactory.Delete(
                await DataContext.Products.FindAsync(id), Categories, Suppliers);
        }

        public async Task<IActionResult> OnPostAsync([FromForm]Product product) {
            DataContext.Products.Remove(product);
            await DataContext.SaveChangesAsync();
            return RedirectToPage(nameof(Index));
        }
    }
}
```

Restart ASP.NET Core and navigate to `http://localhost:5000/pages`, and you will be able to click the links to view, create, edit, and remove data, as shown in Figure 31-8.

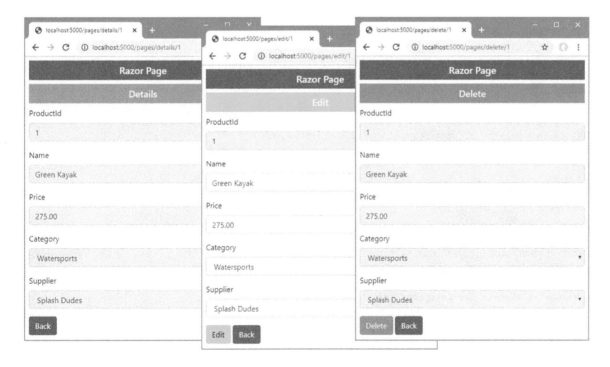

Figure 31-8. Using Razor Pages

Creating New Related Data Objects

Some applications will need to allow the user to create new related data so that, for example, a new Category can be created along with a Product in that Category. There are two ways to approach this problem, as described in the sections that follow.

Providing the Related Data in the Same Request

The first approach is to ask the user to provide the data required to create the related data in the same form. For the example application, this means collecting details for a Category object in the same form that the user enters the values for the Product object.

This can be a useful approach for simple data types, where only a small amount of data is required to create the related object but is not well suited for types with many properties.

I prefer to define the HTML elements for the related data type in their own partial view. Add a Razor View named _CategoryEditor.cshtml to the Pages folder with the content shown in Listing 31-25.

Listing 31-25. The Contents of the _CategoryEditor.cshtml File in the Pages Folder

```
@model Product
<script type="text/javascript">
    $(document).ready(() => {
        const catGroup = $("#categoryGroup").hide();
        $("select[name='Product.CategoryId']").on("change", (event) =>
            event.target.value === "-1" ? catGroup.show() : catGroup.hide());
    });
</script>

<div class="form-group bg-info p-1" id="categoryGroup">
    <label class="text-white" asp-for="Category.Name">
        New Category Name
    </label>
    <input class="form-control" asp-for="Category.Name" value="" />
</div>
```

The Category type requires only one property, which the user will provide using a standard input element. The script element in the partial view contains jQuery code that hides the new elements until the user selects an option element that sets a value of -1 for the Product.CategoryId property. (Using JavaScript is entirely optional, but it helps to emphasize the purpose of the new elements.)

Listing 31-26 adds the partial view to the editor, along with the option element that will display the elements for creating a new Category object.

Listing 31-26. Adding Elements in the _ProductEditor.cshtml File in the Pages Folder

```
...
<div class="form-group">
    <label asp-for="Product.CategoryId">Category</label>
    <div>
        <span asp-validation-for="Product.CategoryId" class="text-danger"></span>
    </div>
    <select asp-for="Product.CategoryId" class="form-control"
            disabled="@Model.ReadOnly" asp-items="@(new SelectList(Model.Categories,
                "CategoryId", "Name"))">
        <option value="-1">Create New Category...</option>
        <option value="" disabled selected>Choose a Category</option>
    </select>
</div>
```

```
<partial name="_CategoryEditor" for="Product" />
<div class="form-group">
    <label asp-for="Product.SupplierId">Supplier</label>
    <div><span asp-validation-for="Product.SupplierId" class="text-danger"></span></div>
    <select asp-for="Product.SupplierId" class="form-control" disabled="@Model.ReadOnly"
            asp-items="@(new SelectList(Model.Suppliers,
                "SupplierId", "Name"))">
        <option value="" disabled selected>Choose a Supplier</option>
    </select>
</div>
...
```

I need the new functionality in multiple pages, so to avoid code duplication, I have added a method that handles the related data to the page model base class, as shown in Listing 31-27.

Listing 31-27. Adding a Method in the EditorPageModel.cs File in the Pages Folder

```
using Microsoft.AspNetCore.Mvc.RazorPages;
using System.Collections.Generic;
using WebApp.Models;
using System.Threading.Tasks;

namespace WebApp.Pages {

    public class EditorPageModel : PageModel {

        public EditorPageModel(DataContext dbContext) {
            DataContext = dbContext;
        }

        public DataContext DataContext { get; set; }

        public IEnumerable<Category> Categories => DataContext.Categories;
        public IEnumerable<Supplier> Suppliers => DataContext.Suppliers;

        public ProductViewModel ViewModel { get; set; }

        protected async Task CheckNewCategory(Product product) {
            if (product.CategoryId == -1
                    && !string.IsNullOrEmpty(product.Category?.Name)) {
                DataContext.Categories.Add(product.Category);
                await DataContext.SaveChangesAsync();
                product.CategoryId = product.Category.CategoryId;
                ModelState.Clear();
                TryValidateModel(product);
            }
        }
    }
}
```

The new code creates a Category object using the data received from the user and stores it in the database. The database server assigns a primary key to the new object, which Entity Framework Core uses to update the Category object. This allows me to update the CategoryId property of the Product object and then re-validate the model data, knowing that the value assigned to the CategoryId property will pass validation because it corresponds to the newly allocated key. To integrate the new functionality into the Create page, add the statement shown in Listing 31-28.

Listing 31-28. Adding a Statement in the Create.cshtml File in the Pages Folder

```
...
public async Task<IActionResult> OnPostAsync([FromForm]Product product) {
    await CheckNewCategory(product);
    if (ModelState.IsValid) {
        product.ProductId = default;
        product.Category = default;
        product.Supplier = default;
        DataContext.Products.Add(product);
        await DataContext.SaveChangesAsync();
        return RedirectToPage(nameof(Index));
    }
    ViewModel = ViewModelFactory.Create(product, Categories, Suppliers);
    return Page();
}
...
```

Add the same statement to the handler method in the Edit page, as shown in Listing 31-29.

Listing 31-29. Adding a Statement in the Edit.cshtml File in the Pages Folder

```
...
public async Task<IActionResult> OnPostAsync([FromForm]Product product) {
    await CheckNewCategory(product);
    if (ModelState.IsValid) {
        product.Category = default;
        product.Supplier = default;
        DataContext.Products.Update(product);
        await DataContext.SaveChangesAsync();
        return RedirectToPage(nameof(Index));
    }
    ViewModel = ViewModelFactory.Edit(product, Categories, Suppliers);
    return Page();
}
...
```

Restart ASP.NET Core so the page model base class is recompiled and use a browser to request http://localhost:5000/pages/ edit/1. Click the Category select element and choose Create New Category from the list of options. Enter a new category name into the input element and click the Edit button. When the request is processed, a new Category object will be stored in the database and associated with the Product object, as shown in Figure 31-9.

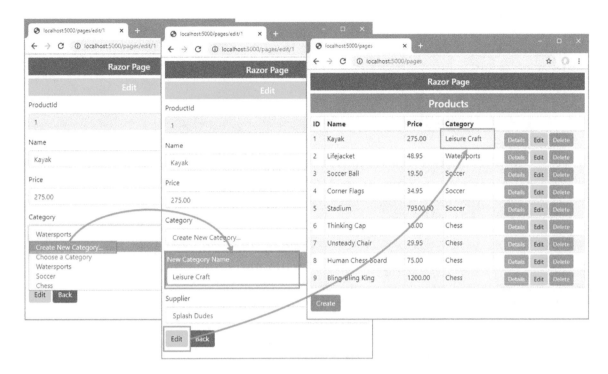

Figure 31-9. *Creating related data*

Breaking Out to Create New Data

For related data types that have their own complex creation process, adding elements to the main form can be overwhelming to the user; a better approach is to navigate away from the main form to another controller or page, let the user create the new object, and then return to complete the original task. I will demonstrate this technique for the creation of Supplier objects, even though the Supplier type is simple and requires only two values from the user.

To create a form that will let the user create Supplier objects, add a Razor Page named SupplierBreakOut.cshtml to the Pages folder with the content shown in Listing 31-30.

Listing 31-30. The Contents of the SupplierBreakOut.cshtml File in the Pages Folder

```
@page "/pages/supplier"
@model SupplierPageModel

<div class="m-2">
    <h5 class="bg-secondary text-white text-center p-2">New Supplier</h5>
    <form asp-page="SupplierBreakOut" method="post">
        <div class="form-group">
            <label asp-for="Supplier.Name"></label>
            <input class="form-control" asp-for="Supplier.Name" />
        </div>
        <div class="form-group">
            <label asp-for="Supplier.City"></label>
            <input class="form-control" asp-for="Supplier.City" />
        </div>
        <button class="btn btn-secondary" type="submit">Create</button>
        <a class="btn btn-outline-secondary"
                asp-page="@Model.ReturnPage" asp-route-id="@Model.ProductId">
            Cancel
        </a>
    </form>
</div>
```

```
@functions {

    public class SupplierPageModel: PageModel {
        private DataContext context;

        public SupplierPageModel(DataContext dbContext) {
            context = dbContext;
        }

        [BindProperty]
        public Supplier Supplier { get; set; }

        public string ReturnPage { get; set; }
        public string ProductId { get; set; }

        public void OnGet([FromQuery(Name="Product")] Product product,
                string returnPage) {
            TempData["product"] = Serialize(product);
            TempData["returnAction"] = ReturnPage = returnPage;
            TempData["productId"] = ProductId = product.ProductId.ToString();
        }

        public async Task<IActionResult> OnPostAsync() {
            context.Suppliers.Add(Supplier);
            await context.SaveChangesAsync();
            Product product = Deserialize(TempData["product"] as string);
            product.SupplierId = Supplier.SupplierId;
            TempData["product"] = Serialize(product);
            string id = TempData["productId"] as string;
            return RedirectToPage(TempData["returnAction"] as string,
                new { id = id });
        }

        private string Serialize(Product p) => JsonSerializer.Serialize(p);
        private Product Deserialize(string json) =>
            JsonSerializer.Deserialize<Product>(json);
    }
}
```

The user will navigate to this page using a GET request that will contain the details of the Product the user has provided and the name of the page that the user should be returned to. This data is stored using the temp data feature.

This page presents the user with a form containing fields for the Name and City properties required to create a new Supplier object. When the form is submitted, the POST handler method stores a new Supplier object and uses the key assigned by the database server to update the Product object, which is then stored as temp data again. The user is redirected back to the page from which they arrived.

Listing 31-31 adds elements to the _ProductEditor partial view that will allow the user to navigate to the new page.

Listing 31-31. Adding Elements in the _ProductEditor.cshtml File in the Pages Folder

```
...
<partial name="_CategoryEditor" for="Product" />

<div class="form-group">
    <label asp-for="Product.SupplierId">
        Supplier
        @if (!Model.ReadOnly) {
            <input type="hidden" name="returnPage" value="@Model.Action" />
            <button class="btn btn-sm btn-outline-primary ml-3"
```

```
                    asp-page="SupplierBreakOut" formmethod="get" formnovalidate>
                Create New Supplier
            </button>
        }
    </label>
    <div>
        <span asp-validation-for="Product.SupplierId" class="text-danger"></span>
    </div>
    <select asp-for="Product.SupplierId" class="form-control"
        disabled="@Model.ReadOnly" asp-items="@(new SelectList(Model.Suppliers,
                "SupplierId", "Name"))">
        <option value="" disabled selected>Choose a Supplier</option>
    </select>
</div>
...
```

The new elements add a hidden input element that captures the page to return to and a button element that submits the form data to the SupplierBreakOut page using a GET request, which means the form values will be encoded in the query string (and is the reason I used the FromQuery attribute in Listing 31-30). Listing 31-32 shows the change required to the Create page to add support for retrieving the temp data and using it to populate the Product form.

Listing 31-32. Retrieving Data in the Create.cshtml File in the Pages Folder

```
@page "/pages/create"
@model CreateModel

<div class="m-2">
    <partial name="_ProductEditor" model="@Model.ViewModel" />
</div>

@functions {

    public class CreateModel: EditorPageModel {

        public CreateModel(DataContext dbContext): base(dbContext) {}

        public void OnGet() {
            Product p = TempData.ContainsKey("product")
                ? JsonSerializer.Deserialize<Product>(TempData["product"] as string)
                : new Product();
            ViewModel = ViewModelFactory.Create(p, Categories, Suppliers);
        }

        public async Task<IActionResult> OnPostAsync([FromForm]Product product) {
            await CheckNewCategory(product);
            if (ModelState.IsValid) {
                product.ProductId = default;
                product.Category = default;
                product.Supplier = default;
                DataContext.Products.Add(product);
                await DataContext.SaveChangesAsync();
                return RedirectToPage(nameof(Index));
            }
            ViewModel = ViewModelFactory.Create(product, Categories, Suppliers);
            return Page();
        }
    }
}
```

845

A similar change is required in the Edit page, as shown in Listing 31-33. (The other pages do not require a change since the breakout is required only when the user is able to create or edit Product data.)

Listing 31-33. Retrieving Data in the Edit.cshtml File in the Pages Folder

```
@page "/pages/edit/{id}"
@model EditModel

<div class="m-2">
    <partial name="_ProductEditor" model="@Model.ViewModel" />
</div>

@functions {

    public class EditModel: EditorPageModel {

        public EditModel(DataContext dbContext): base(dbContext) {}

        public async Task OnGetAsync(long id) {
            Product p = TempData.ContainsKey("product")
                ? JsonSerializer.Deserialize<Product>(TempData["product"] as string)
                : await this.DataContext.Products.FindAsync(id);
            ViewModel = ViewModelFactory.Edit(p, Categories, Suppliers);
        }

        public async Task<IActionResult> OnPostAsync([FromForm]Product product) {
            await CheckNewCategory(product);
            if (ModelState.IsValid) {
                product.Category = default;
                product.Supplier = default;
                DataContext.Products.Update(product);
                await DataContext.SaveChangesAsync();
                return RedirectToPage(nameof(Index));
            }
            ViewModel = ViewModelFactory.Edit(product, Categories, Suppliers);
            return Page();
        }
    }
}
```

The effect is that the user is presented with a Create New Supplier button, which sends the browser to a form that can be used to create a Supplier object. Once the Supplier has been stored in the database, the browser is sent back to the originating page, and the form is populated with the data the user had entered, and the Supplier select element is set to the newly created object, as shown in Figure 31-10.

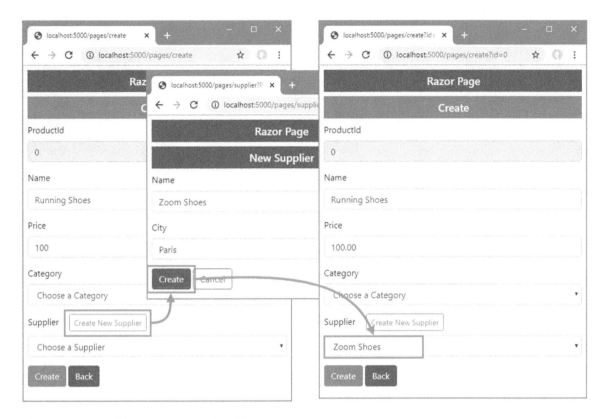

Figure 31-10. *Breaking out to create related data*

Summary

In this chapter, I demonstrated how the features described in earlier chapters can be combined with Entity Framework Core to create, read, update, and delete data. In Part 4, I describe some of the advanced features that ASP.NET Core provides.

PART IV

■ ■ ■

Advanced ASP.NET Core Features

CHAPTER 32

Creating the Example Project

In this chapter, you will create the example project used throughout this part of the book. The project contains a data model that is displayed using simple controllers and Razor Pages.

Creating the Project

Open a new PowerShell command prompt from the Windows Start menu and run the commands shown in Listing 32-1.

■ **Tip** You can download the example project for this chapter—and for all the other chapters in this book—from `https://github.com/apress/pro-asp.net-core-3`. See Chapter 1 for how to get help if you have problems running the examples.

Listing 32-1. Creating the Project

```
dotnet new globaljson --sdk-version 3.1.101 --output Advanced
dotnet new web --no-https --output Advanced --framework netcoreapp3.1
dotnet new sln -o Advanced

dotnet sln Advanced add Advanced
```

If you are using Visual Studio, open the Advanced.sln file in the Advanced folder. Select Project ➤ Platform Properties, navigate to the Debug page, and change the App URL field to **http://localhost:5000**, as shown in Figure 32-1. This changes the port that will be used to receive HTTP requests. Select File ➤ Save All to save the configuration changes.

© Adam Freeman 2020
A. Freeman, *Pro ASP.NET Core 3*, https://doi.org/10.1007/978-1-4842-5440-0_32

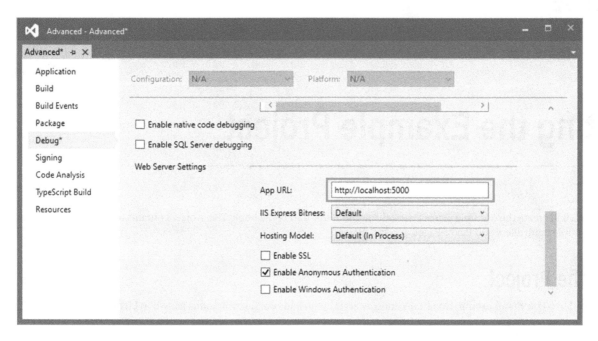

Figure 32-1. *Changing the HTTP port*

If you are using Visual Studio Code, open the Advanced folder. Click the Yes button when prompted to add the assets required for building and debugging the project, as shown in Figure 32-2.

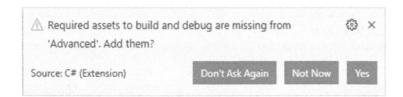

Figure 32-2. *Adding project assets*

Adding NuGet Packages to the Project

The data model will use Entity Framework Core to store and query data in a SQL Server LocalDB database. To add the NuGet packages for Entity Framework Core, use a PowerShell command prompt to run the commands shown in Listing 32-2 in the Advanced project folder.

Listing 32-2. Adding Packages to the Project

```
dotnet add package Microsoft.EntityFrameworkCore.Design --version 3.1.1
dotnet add package Microsoft.EntityFrameworkCore.SqlServer --version 3.1.1
```

If you are using Visual Studio, you can add the packages by selecting Project ➤ Manage NuGet Packages. Take care to choose the correct version of the packages to add to the project.

If you have not followed the examples in earlier chapters, you will need to install the global tool package that is used to create and manage Entity Framework Core migrations. Run the commands shown in Listing 32-3 to remove any existing version of the package and install the version required for this book.

Listing 32-3. Installing a Global Tool Package

```
dotne.t tool uninstall --global dotnet-ef
dotnet tool install --global dotnet-ef --version 3.1.1
```

Adding a Data Model

The data model for this application will consist of three classes, representing people, the department in which they work, and their location. Create a Models folder and add to it a class file named Person.cs with the code in Listing 32-4.

Listing 32-4. The Contents of the Person.cs File in the Models Folder

```
using System.Collections.Generic;

namespace Advanced.Models {

    public class Person {

        public long PersonId { get; set; }
        public string Firstname { get; set; }
        public string Surname { get; set; }
        public long DepartmentId { get; set; }
        public long LocationId { get; set; }

        public Department Department {get; set; }
        public Location Location { get; set; }
    }
}
```

Add a class file named Department.cs to the Models folder and use it to define the class shown in Listing 32-5.

Listing 32-5. The Contents of the Department.cs File in the Models Folder

```
using System.Collections.Generic;

namespace Advanced.Models {
    public class Department {

        public long Departmentid { get; set; }
        public string Name { get; set; }

        public IEnumerable<Person> People { get; set; }
    }
}
```

Add a class file named Location.cs to the Models folder and use it to define the class shown in Listing 32-6.

Listing 32-6. The Contents of the Location.cs File in the Models Folder

```
using System.Collections.Generic;

namespace Advanced.Models {
    public class Location {

        public long LocationId { get; set; }
        public string City { get; set; }
        public string State { get; set; }
```

```
            public IEnumerable<Person> People { get; set; }
        }
    }
```

Each of the three data model classes defines a key property whose value will be allocated by the database when new objects are stored and defines foreign key properties that define the relationships between the classes. These are supplemented by navigation properties that will be used with the Entity Framework Core Include method to incorporate related data into queries.

To create the Entity Framework Core context class that will provide access to the database, add a file called DataContext.cs to the Models folder and add the code shown in Listing 32-7.

Listing 32-7. The Contents of the DataContext.cs File in the Models Folder

```
using Microsoft.EntityFrameworkCore;

namespace Advanced.Models {
    public class DataContext: DbContext {

        public DataContext(DbContextOptions<DataContext> opts)
            : base(opts) { }

        public DbSet<Person> People { get; set; }
        public DbSet<Department> Departments { get; set; }
        public DbSet<Location> Locations { get; set; }
    }
}
```

The context class defines properties that will be used to query the database for Person, Department, and Location data.

Preparing the Seed Data

Add a class called SeedData.cs to the Models folder and add the code shown in Listing 32-8 to define the seed data that will be used to populate the database.

Listing 32-8. The Contents of the SeedData.cs File in the Models Folder

```
using Microsoft.EntityFrameworkCore;
using System.Linq;

namespace Advanced.Models {
    public static class SeedData {

        public static void SeedDatabase(DataContext context) {
            context.Database.Migrate();
            if (context.People.Count() == 0 && context.Departments.Count() == 0 &&
                context.Locations.Count() == 0) {

                Department d1 = new Department { Name = "Sales" };
                Department d2 = new Department { Name = "Development" };
                Department d3 = new Department { Name = "Support" };
                Department d4 = new Department { Name = "Facilities" };

                context.Departments.AddRange(d1, d2, d3, d4);
                context.SaveChanges();

                Location l1 = new Location { City = "Oakland", State = "CA" };
                Location l2 = new Location { City = "San Jose", State = "CA" };
```

```
            Location l3 = new Location { City = "New York", State = "NY" };
            context.Locations.AddRange(l1, l2, l3);

            context.People.AddRange(
                new Person {
                    Firstname = "Francesca", Surname = "Jacobs",
                    Department = d2, Location = l1
                },
                new Person {
                    Firstname = "Charles", Surname = "Fuentes",
                    Department = d2, Location = l3
                },
                new Person {
                    Firstname = "Bright", Surname = "Becker",
                    Department = d4, Location = l1
                },
                new Person {
                    Firstname = "Murphy", Surname = "Lara",
                    Department = d1, Location = l3
                },
                new Person {
                    Firstname = "Beasley", Surname = "Hoffman",
                    Department = d4, Location = l3
                },
                new Person {
                    Firstname = "Marks", Surname = "Hays",
                    Department = d4, Location = l1
                },
                new Person {
                    Firstname = "Underwood", Surname = "Trujillo",
                    Department = d2, Location = l1
                },
                new Person {
                    Firstname = "Randall", Surname = "Lloyd",
                    Department = d3, Location = l2
                },
                new Person {
                    Firstname = "Guzman", Surname = "Case",
                    Department = d2, Location = l2
                });
            context.SaveChanges();
        }
      }
    }
}
```

The static SeedDatabase method ensures that all pending migrations have been applied to the database. If the database is empty, it is seeded with data. Entity Framework Core will take care of mapping the objects into the tables in the database, and the key properties will be assigned automatically when the data is stored.

Configuring Entity Framework Core Services and Middleware

Make the changes to the `Startup` class shown in Listing 32-9, which configure Entity Framework Core and set up the `DataContext` services that will be used throughout this part of the book to access the database.

Listing 32-9. Preparing Services and Middleware in the Startup.cs File in the Advanced Folder

```
using System;
using System.Collections.Generic;
using System.Linq;
using System.Threading.Tasks;
using Microsoft.AspNetCore.Builder;
using Microsoft.AspNetCore.Hosting;
using Microsoft.AspNetCore.Http;
using Microsoft.Extensions.DependencyInjection;
using Microsoft.Extensions.Hosting;
using Microsoft.Extensions.Configuration;
using Microsoft.EntityFrameworkCore;
using Advanced.Models;

namespace Advanced {
    public class Startup {

        public Startup(IConfiguration config) {
            Configuration = config;
        }

        public IConfiguration Configuration { get; set; }

        public void ConfigureServices(IServiceCollection services) {
            services.AddDbContext<DataContext>(opts => {
                opts.UseSqlServer(Configuration[
                    "ConnectionStrings:PeopleConnection"]);
                opts.EnableSensitiveDataLogging(true);
            });
        }

        public void Configure(IApplicationBuilder app, DataContext context) {

            app.UseDeveloperExceptionPage();
            app.UseRouting();

            app.UseEndpoints(endpoints => {
                endpoints.MapGet("/", async context => {
                    await context.Response.WriteAsync("Hello World!");
                });
            });

            SeedData.SeedDatabase(context);
        }
    }
}
```

To define the connection string that will be used for the application's data, add the configuration settings shown in Listing 32-10 in the appsettings.json file. The connection string should be entered on a single line.

Listing 32-10. Defining a Connection String in the appsettings.json File in the Advanced Folder

```
{
  "Logging": {
    "LogLevel": {
      "Default": "Information",
      "Microsoft": "Warning",
      "Microsoft.Hosting.Lifetime": "Information",
      "Microsoft.EntityFrameworkCore": "Information"
    }
  },
  "AllowedHosts": "*",
  "ConnectionStrings": {
    "PeopleConnection": "Server=(localdb)\\MSSQLLocalDB;Database=People;MultipleActiveResultSets=True"
  }
}
```

In addition to the connection string, Listing 32-10 increases the logging detail for Entity Framework Core so that the SQL queries sent to the database are logged.

Creating and Applying the Migration

To create the migration that will set up the database schema, use a PowerShell command prompt to run the command shown in Listing 32-11 in the Advanced project folder.

Listing 32-11. Creating an Entity Framework Core Migration

```
dotnet ef migrations add Initial
```

Once the migration has been created, apply it to the database using the command shown in Listing 32-12.

Listing 32-12. Applying the Migration to the Database

```
dotnet ef database update
```

The logging messages displayed by the application will show the SQL commands that are sent to the database.

■ **Note** If you need to reset the database, then run the dotnet ef database drop --force command and then the command in Listing 32-12.

Adding the Bootstrap CSS Framework

Following the pattern established in earlier chapters, I will use the Bootstrap CSS framework to style the HTML elements produced by the example application. To install the Bootstrap package, run the commands shown in Listing 32-13 in the Advanced project folder. These commands rely on the Library Manager package.

Listing 32-13. Installing the Bootstrap CSS Framework

```
libman init -p cdnjs
libman install twitter-bootstrap@4.3.1 -d wwwroot/lib/twitter-bootstrap
```

If you are using Visual Studio, you can install client-side packages by right-clicking the Advanced project item in the Solution Explorer and selecting Add ➤ Client-Side Library from the popup menu.

Configuring the Services and Middleware

I am going to enable runtime Razor view compilation in this project. Run the command shown in Listing 32-14 in the Advanced project folder to install the package that will provide the runtime compilation service.

Listing 32-14. Adding a Package to the Example Project

```
dotnet add package Microsoft.AspNetCore.Mvc.Razor.RuntimeCompilation --version 3.1.1
```

The example application in this part of the book will respond to requests using both MVC controllers and Razor Pages. Add the statements shown in Listing 32-15 to the Startup class to configure the services and middleware the application will use.

Listing 32-15. Adding Services and Middleware in the Startup.cs File in the Advanced Folder

```
using System;
using System.Collections.Generic;
using System.Linq;
using System.Threading.Tasks;
using Microsoft.AspNetCore.Builder;
using Microsoft.AspNetCore.Hosting;
using Microsoft.AspNetCore.Http;
using Microsoft.Extensions.DependencyInjection;
using Microsoft.Extensions.Hosting;
using Microsoft.Extensions.Configuration;
using Microsoft.EntityFrameworkCore;
using Advanced.Models;

namespace Advanced {
    public class Startup {

        public Startup(IConfiguration config) {
            Configuration = config;
        }

        public IConfiguration Configuration { get; set; }

        public void ConfigureServices(IServiceCollection services) {
            services.AddDbContext<DataContext>(opts => {
                opts.UseSqlServer(Configuration[
                    "ConnectionStrings:PeopleConnection"]);
                opts.EnableSensitiveDataLogging(true);
            });
            services.AddControllersWithViews().AddRazorRuntimeCompilation();
            services.AddRazorPages().AddRazorRuntimeCompilation();
        }

        public void Configure(IApplicationBuilder app, DataContext context) {

            app.UseDeveloperExceptionPage();
            app.UseStaticFiles();
            app.UseRouting();
```

```
        app.UseEndpoints(endpoints => {
            endpoints.MapControllerRoute("controllers",
                "controllers/{controller=Home}/{action=Index}/{id?}");
            endpoints.MapDefaultControllerRoute();
            endpoints.MapRazorPages();
        });

        SeedData.SeedDatabase(context);
    }
}
}
```

In addition to the default controller route, I have added a route that matches URL paths that begin with controllers, which will make it easier to follow the examples in later chapters as they switch between controllers and Razor Pages. This is the same convention I adopted in earlier chapters, and I will route URL paths beginning with /pages to Razor Pages.

Creating a Controller and View

To display the application's data using a controller, create a folder named Controllers in the Advanced project folder and add to it a class file named HomeController.cs, with the content shown in Listing 32-16.

Listing 32-16. The Contents of the HomeController.cs File in the Controllers Folder

```
using Advanced.Models;
using Microsoft.AspNetCore.Mvc;
using Microsoft.EntityFrameworkCore;
using System.Collections.Generic;
using System.Linq;

namespace Advanced.Controllers {
    public class HomeController : Controller {
        private DataContext context;

        public HomeController(DataContext dbContext) {
            context = dbContext;
        }

        public IActionResult Index([FromQuery] string selectedCity) {
            return View(new PeopleListViewModel {
                People = context.People
                    .Include(p => p.Department).Include(p => p.Location),
                Cities = context.Locations.Select(l => l.City).Distinct(),
                SelectedCity = selectedCity
            });
        }
    }

    public class PeopleListViewModel {
        public IEnumerable<Person> People { get; set; }
        public IEnumerable<string> Cities { get; set; }
        public string SelectedCity { get; set; }

        public string GetClass(string city) =>
            SelectedCity == city ? "bg-info text-white" : "";
    }
}
```

To provide the controller with a view, create the Views/Home folder and add to it a Razor View named Index.cshtml with the content shown in Listing 32-17.

Listing 32-17. The Contents of the Index.cshtml File in the Views/Home Folder

```
@model PeopleListViewModel

<h4 class="bg-primary text-white text-center p-2">People</h4>

<table class="table table-sm table-bordered table-striped">
    <thead>
        <tr>
            <th>ID</th><th>Name</th><th>Dept</th><th>Location</th>
        </tr>
    </thead>
    <tbody>
        @foreach (Person p in Model.People) {
            <tr class="@Model.GetClass(p.Location.City)">
                <td>@p.PersonId</td>
                <td>@p.Surname, @p.Firstname</td>
                <td>@p.Department.Name</td>
                <td>@p.Location.City, @p.Location.State</td>
            </tr>
        }
    </tbody>
</table>

<form asp-action="Index" method="get">
    <div class="form-group">
        <label for="selectedCity">City</label>
        <select name="selectedCity" class="form-control">
            <option disabled selected>Select City</option>
            @foreach (string city in Model.Cities) {
                <option selected="@(city == Model.SelectedCity)">
                    @city
                </option>
            }
        </select>
    </div>
    <button class="btn btn-primary" type="submit">Select</button>
</form>
```

To enable tag helpers and add the namespaces that will be available by default in views, add a Razor View Imports file named _ViewImports.cshtml to the Views folder with the content shown in Listing 32-18.

Listing 32-18. The Contents of the _ViewImports.cshtml File in the Views Folder

```
@addTagHelper *, Microsoft.AspNetCore.Mvc.TagHelpers
@using Advanced.Models
@using Advanced.Controllers
```

To specify the default layout for controller views, add a Razor View Start start file named _ViewStart.cshtml to the Views folder with the content shown in Listing 32-19.

Listing 32-19. The Contents of the _ViewStart.cshtml File in the Views Folder

```
@{
    Layout = "_Layout";
}
```

To create the layout, create the Views/Shared folder and add to it a Razor Layout named _Layout.cshtml with the content shown in Listing 32-20.

Listing 32-20. The Contents of the _Layout.cshtml File in the Views/Shared Folder

```html
<!DOCTYPE html>
<html>
<head>
    <title>@ViewBag.Title</title>
    <link href="/lib/twitter-bootstrap/css/bootstrap.min.css" rel="stylesheet" />
</head>
<body>
    <div class="m-2">
        @RenderBody()
    </div>
</body>
</html>
```

Creating a Razor Page

To display the application's data using a Razor Page, create the Pages folder and add to it a Razor Page named Index.cshtml with the content shown in Listing 32-21.

Listing 32-21. The Contents of the Index.cshtml File in the Pages Folder

```html
@page "/pages"
@model IndexModel

<h4 class="bg-primary text-white text-center p-2">People</h4>

<table class="table table-sm table-bordered table-striped">
    <thead>
        <tr>
            <th>ID</th><th>Name</th><th>Dept</th><th>Location</th>
        </tr>
    </thead>
    <tbody>
        @foreach (Person p in Model.People) {
            <tr class="@Model.GetClass(p.Location.City)">
                <td>@p.PersonId</td>
                <td>@p.Surname, @p.Firstname</td>
                <td>@p.Department.Name</td>
                <td>@p.Location.City, @p.Location.State</td>
            </tr>
        }
    </tbody>
</table>

<form asp-page="Index" method="get">
    <div class="form-group">
        <label for="selectedCity">City</label>
        <select name="selectedCity" class="form-control">
            <option disabled selected>Select City</option>
            @foreach (string city in Model.Cities) {
                <option selected="@(city == Model.SelectedCity)">
                    @city
                </option>
            }
```

```
        </select>
    </div>
    <button class="btn btn-primary" type="submit">Select</button>
</form>

@functions {

    public class IndexModel: PageModel {
        private DataContext context;

        public IndexModel(DataContext dbContext) {
            context = dbContext;
        }

        public IEnumerable<Person> People { get; set; }

        public IEnumerable<string> Cities { get; set; }

        [FromQuery]
        public string SelectedCity { get; set; }

        public void OnGet() {
            People = context.People.Include(p => p.Department)
                .Include(p => p.Location);
            Cities = context.Locations.Select(l => l.City).Distinct();
        }

        public string GetClass(string city) =>
            SelectedCity == city ? "bg-info text-white" : "";
    }
}
```

To enable tag helpers and add the namespaces that will be available by default in the view section of the Razor Pages, add a Razor view imports file named _ViewImports.cshtml to the Pages folder with the content shown in Listing 32-22.

Listing 32-22. The Contents of the _ViewImports.cshtml File in the Pages Folder

```
@addTagHelper *, Microsoft.AspNetCore.Mvc.TagHelpers
@using Advanced.Models
@using Microsoft.AspNetCore.Mvc.RazorPages
@using Microsoft.EntityFrameworkCore
```

To specify the default layout for Razor Pages, add a Razor View Start file named _ViewStart.cshtml to the Pages folder with the content shown in Listing 32-23.

Listing 32-23. The Contents of the _ViewStart.cshtml File in the Pages Folder

```
@{
    Layout = "_Layout";
}
```

To create the layout, add a Razor Layout named _Layout.cshtml to the Pages folder with the content shown in Listing 32-24.

Listing 32-24. The Contents of the _Layout.cshtml File in the Pages Folder

```
<!DOCTYPE html>
<html>
<head>
    <title>@ViewBag.Title</title>
```

```
        <link href="/lib/twitter-bootstrap/css/bootstrap.min.css" rel="stylesheet" />
</head>
<body>
    <div class="m-2">
        <h5 class="bg-secondary text-white text-center p-2">Razor Page</h5>
        @RenderBody()
    </div>
</body>
</html>
```

Running the Example Application

Start the application, either by selecting Start Without Debugging or Run Without Debugging from the Debug menu or by running the command shown in Listing 32-25 in the Advanced project folder.

Listing 32-25. Running the Example Application

```
dotnet run
```

Use a browser to request http://localhost:5000/controllers and http://localhost:5000/pages. Select a city using the select element and click the Select button to highlight rows in the table, as shown in Figure 32-3.

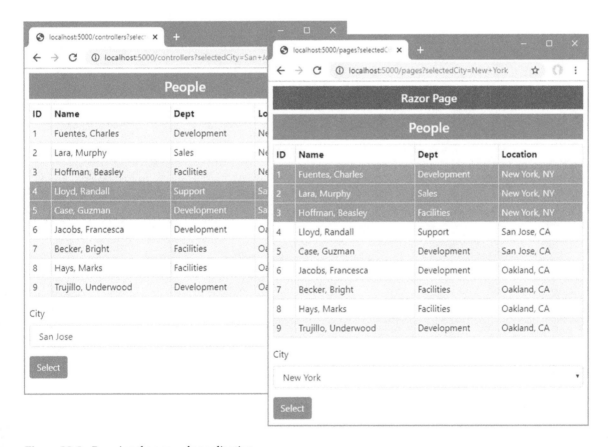

Figure 32-3. Running the example application

Summary

In this chapter, I showed how to create the example application that is used throughout this part of the book. The project was created with the Empty template, and it contains a data model that relies on Entity Framework Core and handles requests using a controller and a Razor Page. In the next chapter, I introduce Blazor, which is a new addition to ASP.NET Core.

■ ■ ■

CHAPTER 33

Using Blazor Server, Part 1

Blazor is a new addition to ASP.NET Core that adds client-side interactivity to web applications. There are two varieties of Blazor, and in this chapter, I focus on Blazor Server. I explain the problem it solves and how it works. I show you how to configure an ASP. NET Core application to use Blazor Server and describe the basic features available when using Razor Components, which are the building blocks for Blazor Server projects. I describe more advanced Blazor Server features in Chapters 34–36, and in Chapter 37, I describe Blazor WebAssembly, which is the other variety of Blazor. Table 33-1 puts Blazor Server in context.

Table 33-1. *Putting Blazor Server in Context*

Question	Answer
What is it?	Blazor Server uses JavaScript to receive browser events, which are forwarded to ASP.NET Core and evaluated using C# code. The effect of the event on the state of the application is sent back to the browser and displayed to the user.
Why is it useful?	Blazor Server can produce a richer and more responsive user experience compared to standard web applications.
How is it used?	The building block for Blazor Server is the Razor Component, which uses a syntax similar to Razor Pages. The view section of the Razor Component contains special attributes that specify how the application will respond to user interaction.
Are there any pitfalls or limitations?	Blazor Server relies on a persistent HTTP connection to the server and cannot function when that connection is interrupted. Blazor Server is not supported by older browsers.
Are there any alternatives?	The features described in Part 3 of this book can be used to create web applications that work broadly but that offer a less responsive experience. You could also consider a client-side JavaScript framework, such as Angular, React, or Vue.js.

Table 33-2 summarizes the chapter.

Table 33-2. *Chapter Summary*

Problem	Solution	Listing
Configuring Blazor	Use the AddServerSideBlazor and MapBlazorHub methods to set up the required services and middleware and configure the JavaScript file	3–6
Creating a Blazor Component	Create a .blazor file and use it to define code and markup	7
Applying a component	Use a component element	8, 9
Handling events	Use an attribute to specify the method or expression that will handle an event	10–15
Creating a two-way relationship with an element	Create a data binding	16–20
Defining the code separately from the markup	Use a code-behind class	21–23
Defining a component without declarative markup	Use a Razor Component class	24, 25

© Adam Freeman 2020

A. Freeman, *Pro ASP.NET Core 3*, https://doi.org/10.1007/978-1-4842-5440-0_33

Preparing for This Chapter

This chapter uses the Advanced project from Chapter 32. No changes are required to prepare for this chapter.

■ **Tip** You can download the example project for this chapter—and for all the other chapters in this book—from `https://github.com/apress/pro-asp.net-core-3`. See Chapter 1 for how to get help if you have problems running the examples.

Open a new PowerShell command prompt, navigate to the folder that contains the `Advanced.csproj` file, and run the command shown in Listing 33-1 to drop the database.

Listing 33-1. Dropping the Database

```
dotnet ef database drop --force
```

Select Start Without Debugging or Run Without Debugging from the Debug menu or use the PowerShell command prompt to run the command shown in Listing 33-2.

Listing 33-2. Running the Example Application

```
dotnet run
```

Use a browser to request `http://localhost:5000/controllers`, which will display a list of data items. Pick a city from the drop-down list and click the Select button to highlight elements, as shown in Figure 33-1.

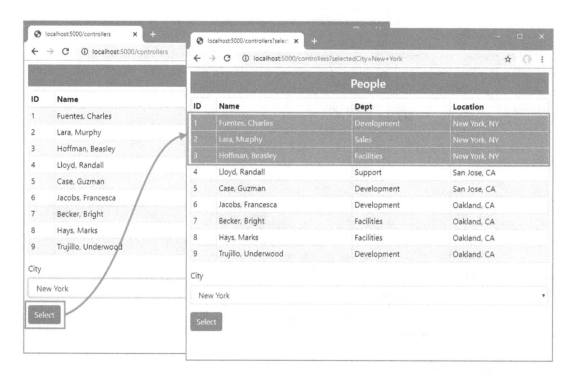

Figure 33-1. *Running the example application*

Understanding Blazor Server

Consider what happens when you choose a city and click the Select button presented by the example application. The browser sends an HTTP GET request that submits a form, which is received by either an action method or a handler method, depending on whether you use the controller or Razor Page. The action or handler renders its view, which sends a new HTML document that reflects the selection to the browser, as illustrated by Figure 33-2.

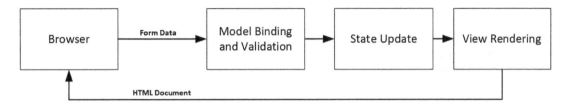

Figure 33-2. *Interacting with the example application*

This cycle is effective but can be inefficient. Each time the Submit button is clicked, the browser sends a new HTTP request to ASP.NET Core. Each request contains a complete set of HTTP headers that describe the request and the types of responses the browser is willing to receive. In its response, the server includes HTTP headers that describe the response and includes a complete HTML document for the browser to display.

The amount of data sent by the example application is about 3KB on my system, and almost all of it is duplicated between requests. The browser only wants to tell the server which city has been selected, and the server only wants to indicate which table rows should be highlighted; however, each HTTP request is self-contained, so the browser must parse a complete HTML document each time. The root issue that every interaction is the same: send a request and get a complete HTML document in return.

Blazor takes a different approach. A JavaScript library is included in the HTML document that is sent to the browser. When the JavaScript code is executed, it opens an HTTP connection back to the server and leaves it open, ready for user interaction. When the user picks a value using the select element, for example, details of the selection are sent to the server, which responds with just the changes to apply to the existing HTML, as shown in Figure 33-3.

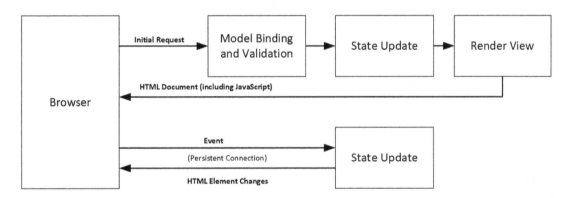

Figure 33-3. *Interacting with Blazor*

The persistent HTTP connection minimizes the delay, and replying with just the differences reduces the amount of data sent between the browser and the server.

Understanding the Blazor Server Advantages

The biggest attraction of Blazor is that it is based on Razor Pages written in C#. This means you can increase efficiency and responsiveness without having to learn a new framework, such as Angular or React, and a new language, such as TypeScript or JavaScript. Blazor is nicely integrated into the rest of ASP.NET Core and is built on features described in earlier chapters, which makes it easy to use (especially when compared to a framework like Angular, which has a dizzyingly steep learning curve).

Understanding the Blazor Server Disadvantages

Blazor requires a modern browser to establish and maintain its persistent HTTP connection. And, because of this connection, applications that use Blazor stop working if the connection is lost, which makes them unsuitable for offline use, where connectivity cannot be relied on or where connections are slow. These issues are addressed by Blazor WebAssembly, described in Chapter 36, but, as I explain, this has its own set of limitations.

Choosing Between Blazor Server and Angular/React/Vue.js

Decisions between Blazor and one of the JavaScript frameworks should be driven by the development team's experience and the users' expected connectivity. If you have no JavaScript expertise and have not used one of the JavaScript frameworks, then you should use Blazor, but only if you can rely on good connectivity and modern browsers. This makes Blazor a good choice for line-of-business applications, for example, where the browser demographic and network quality can be determined in advance.

If you have JavaScript experience and you are writing a public-facing application, then you should use one of the JavaScript frameworks because you won't be able to make assumptions about browsers or network quality. (It doesn't matter which framework you choose—I have written books about Angular, React, and View, and they are all excellent. My advice for choosing a framework is to create a simple app in each of them and pick the one whose development model appeals to you the most.)

If you are writing a public-facing application and you don't have JavaScript experience, then you have two choices. The safest option is to stick to the ASP.NET Core features described in earlier chapters and accept the inefficiencies this can bring. This isn't a terrible choice to make, and you can still produce top-quality applications. A more demanding choice is to learn TypeScript or JavaScript and one Angular, React, or Vue.js—but don't underestimate the amount of time it takes to master JavaScript or the complexity of these frameworks.

Getting Started with Blazor

The best way to get started with Blazor is to jump right in. In the sections that follow, I configure the application to enable Blazor and re-create the functionality offered by the controller and Razor Page. After that, I'll go right back to basics and explain how Razor Components work and the different features they offer.

Configuring ASP.NET Core for Blazor Server

Preparation is required before Blazor can be used. The first step is to add the services and middleware to the Startup class, as shown in Listing 33-3.

Listing 33-3. Adding Services and Middleware in the Startup.cs File in the Advanced Folder

```
using System;
using System.Collections.Generic;
using System.Linq;
using System.Threading.Tasks;
using Microsoft.AspNetCore.Builder;
using Microsoft.AspNetCore.Hosting;
using Microsoft.AspNetCore.Http;
using Microsoft.Extensions.DependencyInjection;
using Microsoft.Extensions.Hosting;
using Microsoft.Extensions.Configuration;
using Microsoft.EntityFrameworkCore;
using Advanced.Models;

namespace Advanced {
    public class Startup {

        public Startup(IConfiguration config) {
            Configuration = config;
        }
```

```
        public IConfiguration Configuration { get; set; }

        public void ConfigureServices(IServiceCollection services) {
            services.AddDbContext<DataContext>(opts => {
                opts.UseSqlServer(Configuration[
                    "ConnectionStrings:PeopleConnection"]);
                opts.EnableSensitiveDataLogging(true);
            });
            services.AddControllersWithViews().AddRazorRuntimeCompilation();
            services.AddRazorPages().AddRazorRuntimeCompilation();
            services.AddServerSideBlazor();
        }

        public void Configure(IApplicationBuilder app, DataContext context) {

            app.UseDeveloperExceptionPage();
            app.UseStaticFiles();
            app.UseRouting();

            app.UseEndpoints(endpoints => {
                endpoints.MapControllerRoute("controllers",
                    "controllers/{controller=Home}/{action=Index}/{id?}");
                endpoints.MapDefaultControllerRoute();
                endpoints.MapRazorPages();
                endpoints.MapBlazorHub();
            });

            SeedData.SeedDatabase(context);
        }
    }
}
```

The "hub" in the MapBlazorHub method relates to SignalR, which is the part of ASP.NET Core that handles the persistent HTTP request. I don't describe SignalR in this book because it is rarely used directly, but it can be useful if you need ongoing communication between clients and the server. See https://docs.microsoft.com/en-gb/aspnet/core/signalr for details. For this book—and most ASP.NET Core applications—it is enough to know that SignalR is used to manage the connections that Blazor relies on.

Adding the Blazor JavaScript File to the Layout

Blazor relies on JavaScript code to communicate with the ASP.NET Core server. Add the elements shown in Listing 33-4 to the _Layout.cshtml file in the Views/Shared folder to add the JavaScript file to the layout used by controller views.

Listing 33-4. Adding Elements in the _Layout.cshtml File in the Views/Shared Folder

```
<!DOCTYPE html>
<html>
<head>
    <title>@ViewBag.Title</title>
    <link href="/lib/twitter-bootstrap/css/bootstrap.min.css" rel="stylesheet" />
    <base href="~/" />
</head>
<body>
    <div class="m-2">
        @RenderBody()
    </div>
    <script src="_framework/blazor.server.js"></script>
</body>
</html>
```

The `script` element specifies the name of the JavaScript file, and requests for it are intercepted by the middleware added to the request pipeline in Listing 33-3 so that no additional package is required to add the JavaScript code to the project. The `base` element must also be added to specify the root URL for the application. The same elements must be added to the layout used by Razor Pages, as shown in Listing 33-5.

Listing 33-5. Adding Elements in the _Layout.cshtml File in the Pages Folder

```
<!DOCTYPE html>
<html>
<head>
    <title>@ViewBag.Title</title>
    <link href="/lib/twitter-bootstrap/css/bootstrap.min.css" rel="stylesheet" />
    <base href="~/" />
</head>
<body>
    <div class="m-2">
        <h5 class="bg-secondary text-white text-center p-2">Razor Page</h5>
        @RenderBody()
    </div>
    <script src="_framework/blazor.server.js"></script>
</body>
</html>
```

Creating the Blazor Imports File

Blazor requires its own imports file to specify the namespaces that it uses. It is easy to forget to add this file to a project, but, without it, Blazor will silently fail. Add a file named `_Imports.razor` to the Advanced folder with the content shown in Listing 33-6. (If you are using Visual Studio, you can use the Razor View Imports template to create this file, but ensure you use the `.razor` file extension.)

Listing 33-6. The Contents of the _Imports.razor File in the Advanced Folder

```
@using Microsoft.AspNetCore.Components
@using Microsoft.AspNetCore.Components.Forms
@using Microsoft.AspNetCore.Components.Routing
@using Microsoft.AspNetCore.Components.Web
@using Microsoft.JSInterop
@using Microsoft.EntityFrameworkCore
@using Advanced.Models
```

The first five `@using` expressions are for the namespaces required for Blazor. The last two expressions are for convenience in the examples that follow because they will allow me to use Entity Framework Core and the classes in the `Models` namespace.

Creating a Razor Component

There is a clash in terminology: the technology is *Blazor*, but the key building block is called a *Razor Component*. Razor Components are defined in files with the `.razor` extension and must begin with a capital letter. Components can be defined anywhere, but they are usually grouped together to help keep the project organized. Create a `Blazor` folder in the `Advanced` folder and add to it a Razor Component named `PeopleList.razor` with the content shown in Listing 33-7.

Listing 33-7. The Contents of the PeopleList.razor File in the Blazor Folder

```
<table class="table table-sm table-bordered table-striped">
    <thead>
        <tr>
            <th>ID</th><th>Name</th><th>Dept</th><th>Location</th>
        </tr>
    </thead>
    <tbody>
```

```
        @foreach (Person p in People) {
            <tr class="@GetClass(p.Location.City)">
                <td>@p.PersonId</td>
                <td>@p.Surname, @p.Firstname</td>
                <td>@p.Department.Name</td>
                <td>@p.Location.City, @p.Location.State</td>
            </tr>
        }
    </tbody>
</table>

<div class="form-group">
    <label for="city">City</label>
    <select name="city" class="form-control" @bind="SelectedCity">
        <option disabled selected>Select City</option>
        @foreach (string city in Cities) {
            <option value="@city" selected="@(city == SelectedCity)">
                @city
            </option>
        }
    </select>
</div>

@code {

    [Inject]
    public DataContext Context { get; set; }

    public IEnumerable<Person> People =>
        Context.People.Include(p => p.Department).Include(p => p.Location);

    public IEnumerable<string> Cities => Context.Locations.Select(l => l.City);

    public string SelectedCity { get; set; }

    public string GetClass(string city) =>
        SelectedCity == city ? "bg-info text-white" : "";
}
```

Razor Components are similar to Razor Pages. The view section relies on the Razor features you have seen in earlier chapters, with @ expressions to insert data values into the component's HTML or to generate elements for objects in a sequence, like this:

```
...
@foreach (string city in Cities) {
    <option value="@city" selected="@(city == SelectedCity)">
}
...
```

This @foreach expression generates option elements for each value in the Cities sequence and is identical to the equivalent expression in the controller view and Razor Page created in Chapter 32.

Although Razor Components look familiar, there are some important differences. The first is that there is no page model class and no @model expression. The properties and methods that support a component's HTML are defined directly in an @code expression, which is the counterpart to the Razor Page @functions expression. To define the property that will provide the view section with Person objects, for example, I just define a People property in the @code section, like this:

```
...
public IEnumerable<Person> People =>
    Context.People.Include(p => p.Department).Include(p => p.Location);
...
```

And, because there is no page model class, there is no constructor through which to declare service dependencies. Instead, the dependency injection sets the values of properties that have been decorated with the Inject attribute, like this:

```
...
[Inject]
public DataContext Context { get; set; }
...
```

The most significant difference is the use of a special attribute on the select element.

```
...
<select name="city" class="form-control" @bind="SelectedCity">
    <option disabled selected>Select City</option>
...
```

This Blazor attribute creates a data binding between the value of the select element and the SelectedCity property defined in the @code section.

I describe data bindings in more detail in the "Working with Data Bindings" section, but for now, it is enough to know that the value of the SelectedCity will be updated when the user changes the value of the select element.

Using a Razor Component

Razor components are delivered to the browser as part of a Razor Page or a controller view. Listing 33-8 shows how to use a Razor Component in a controller view.

Listing 33-8. Using a Razor Component in the Index.cshtml File in the Views/Home Folder

```
@model PeopleListViewModel

<h4 class="bg-primary text-white text-center p-2">People</h4>

<component type="typeof(Advanced.Blazor.PeopleList)" render-mode="Server" />
```

Razor Components are applied using the component element, for which there is a tag helper. The component element is configured using the type and render-mode attributes. The type attribute is used to specify the Razor Component. Razor Components are compiled into classes just like controller views and Razor Pages. The PeopleList component is defined in the Blazor folder in the Advanced project, so the type will be Advanced.Blazor.PeopleList, like this:

```
...
<component type="typeof(Advanced.Blazor.PeopleList)" render-mode="Server" />
...
```

The render-mode attribute is used to select how content is produced by the component, using a value from the RenderMode enum, described in Table 33-3.

Table 33-3. *The RenderMode Values*

Name	Description
Static	The Razor Component renders its view section as static HTML with no client-side support.
Server	The HTML document is sent to the browser with a placeholder for the component. The HTML displayed by the component is sent to the browser over the persistent HTTP connection and displayed to the user.
ServerPrerendered	The view section of the component is included in the HTML and displayed to the user immediately. The HTML content is sent again over the persistent HTTP connection.

For most applications, the Server option is a good choice. The ServerPrerendered includes a static rendition of the Razor Component's view section in the HTML document sent to the browser. This acts as placeholder content so that the user isn't presented with an empty browser window while the JavaScript code is loaded and executed. Once the persistent HTTP connection has been established, the placeholder content is deleted and replaced with a dynamic version sent by Blazor. The idea of showing static content to the user is a good one, but it can be confusing because the HTML elements are not wired up to the server-side part of the application, and any interaction from the user either doesn't work or will be discarded once the live content arrives.

To see Blazor in action, restart ASP.NET Core and use a browser to request http://localhost:5000/controllers. No form submission is required when using Blazor because the data binding will respond as soon as the select element's value is changed, as shown in Figure 33-4.

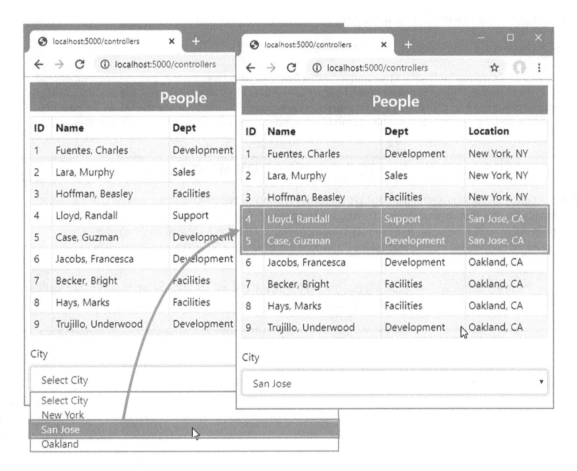

Figure 33-4. *Using a Razor Component*

When you use the select element, the value you choose is sent over the persistent HTTP connection to the ASP.NET Core server, which updates the Razor Component's SelectedCity property and rerenders the HTML content. A set of updates is sent to the JavaScript code, which updates the table.

Razor Components can also be used in Razor Pages. Add a Razor Page named `Blazor.cshtml` to the `Pages` folder and add the content shown in Listing 33-9.

Listing 33-9. The Contents of the Blazor.cshtml File in the Pages Folder

```
@page "/pages/blazor"

<script type="text/javascript">
    window.addEventListener("DOMContentLoaded", () => {
        document.getElementById("markElems").addEventListener("click", () => {
            document.querySelectorAll("td:first-child")
                .forEach(elem => {
                    elem.innerText = `M:${elem.innerText}`
                    elem.classList.add("border", "border-dark");
                });
        });
    });
</script>

<h4 class="bg-primary text-white text-center p-2">Blazor People</h4>

<button id="markElems" class="btn btn-outline-primary mb-2">Mark Elements</button>

<component type="typeof(Advanced.Blazor.PeopleList)" render-mode="Server" />
```

The Razor Page in Listing 33-9 contains additional JavaScript code that helps demonstrate that only changes are sent, instead of an entirely new HTML table. Restart ASP.NET Core and request `http://localhost:5000/pages/blazor`. Click the Mark Elements button, and the cells in the ID column will be changed to display different content and a border. Now use the `select` element to pick a different city, and you will see that the elements in the table are modified without being deleted, as shown in Figure 33-5.

UNDERSTANDING BLAZOR CONNECTION MESSAGES

When you stop ASP.NET Core, you will see an error message in the browser window, which indicates the connection to the server has been lost and prevents the user from interacting with the displayed component. Blazor will attempt to reconnect and pick up where it left off when the disconnection is caused by temporary network issues, but it won't be able to do so when the server has been stopped or restarted because the context data for the connection has been lost; you will have to explicitly request a new URL.

There is a default reload link in the connection message, but that goes to the default URL for the website, which isn't useful for this book where I direct you to specific URLs to see the effect of examples. See Chapter 34 for details of how to configure the connection messages.

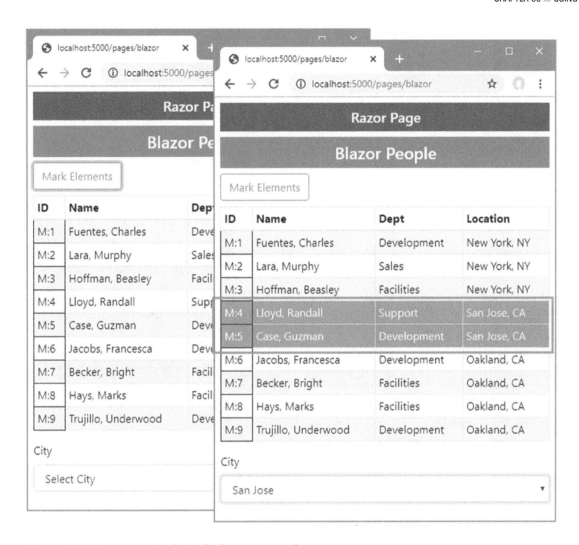

Figure 33-5. *Demonstrating that only changes are used*

Understanding the Basic Razor Component Features

Now that I have demonstrated how Blazor can be used and how it works, it is time to go back to the basics and introduce the features that Razor Components offer. Although the example in the previous section showed how standard ASP.NET Core features can be reproduced using Blazor, there is a much wider set of features available.

Understanding Blazor Events and Data Bindings

Events allow a Razor Component to respond to user interaction, and Blazor uses the persistent HTTP connection to send details of the event to the server where it can be processed. To see Blazor events in action, add a Razor Component named Events.razor to the Blazor folder with the content shown in Listing 33-10.

Listing 33-10. The Contents of the Events.razor File in the Blazor Folder

```
<div class="m-2 p-2 border">
    <button class="btn btn-primary" @onclick="IncrementCounter">Increment</button>
    <span class="p-2">Counter Value: @Counter</span>
</div>
```

```
@code {
    public int Counter { get; set; } = 1;

    public void IncrementCounter(MouseEventArgs e) {
        Counter++;
    }
}
```

You register a handler for an event by adding an attribute to an HTML element, where the attribute name is @on, followed by the event name. In the example, I have set up a handler for the click events generated by a button element, like this:

```
...
<button class="btn btn-primary" @onclick="IncrementCounter">Increment</button>
...
```

The value assigned to the attribute is the name of the method that will be invoked when the event is triggered. The method can define an optional parameter that is either an instance of the EventArgs class or a class derived from EventArgs that provides additional information about the event.

For the onclick event, the handler method receives a MouseEventArgs object, which provides additional details, such as the screen coordinates of the click. Table 33-4 lists the event description events and the events for which they are used.

Table 33-4. *The EventArgs Classes and the Events They Represent*

Class	Events
ChangeEventArgs	onchange, oninput
ClipboardEventArgs	oncopy, oncut, onpaste
DragEventArgs	ondrag, ondragend, ondragenter, ondragleave, ondragover, ondragstart, ondrop
ErrorEventArgs	onerror
FocusEventArgs	onblur, onfocus, onfocusin, onfocusout
KeyboardEventArgs	onkeydown, onkeypress, onkeyup
MouseEventArgs	onclick, oncontextmenu, ondblclick, onmousedown, onmousemove, onmouseout, onmouseover, onmouseup, onmousewheel, onwheel
PointerEventArgs	ongotpointercapture, onlostpointercapture, onpointercancel, onpointerdown, onpointerenter, onpointerleave, onpointermove, onpointerout, onpointerover, onpointerup
ProgressEventArgs	onabort, onload, onloadend, onloadstart, onprogress, ontimeout
TouchEventArgs	ontouchcancel, ontouchend, ontouchenter, ontouchleave, ontouchmove, ontouchstart
EventArgs	onactivate, onbeforeactivate, onbeforecopy, onbeforecut, onbeforedeactivate, onbeforepaste, oncanplay, oncanplaythrough, oncuechange, ondeactivate, ondurationchange, onemptied, onended, onfullscreenchange, onfullscreenerror, oninvalid, onloadeddata, onloadedmetadata, onpause, onplay, onplaying, onpointerlockchange, onpointerlockerror, onratechange, onreadystatechange, onreset, onscroll, onseeked, onseeking, onselect, onselectionchange, onselectstart, onstalled, onstop, onsubmit, onsuspend, ontimeupdate, onvolumechange, onwaiting

The Blazor JavaScript code receives the event when it is triggered and forwards it to the server over the persistent HTTP connection. The handler method is invoked, and the state of the component is updated. Any changes to the content produced by the component's view section will be sent back to the JavaScript code, which will update the content displayed by the browser.

In the example, the click event will be handled by the IncrementCounter method, which changes the value of the Counter property. The value of the Counter property is included in the HTML rendered by the component, so Blazor sends the changes to the browser so that the JavaScript code can update the HTML elements displayed to the user. To display the Events component, replace the contents of the Blazor.cshtml file in the Pages folder, as shown in Listing 33-11.

Listing 33-11. Using a New Component in the Blazor.cshtml File in the Pages Folder

```
@page "/pages/blazor"

<h4 class="bg-primary text-white text-center p-2">Events</h4>

<component type="typeof(Advanced.Blazor.Events)" render-mode="Server" />
```

Listing 33-11 changes the `type` attribute of the component element and removes the custom JavaScript and the `button` element I used to mark elements in the previous example. Restart ASP.NET Core and request `http://localhost:5000/pages/blazor` to see the new component. Click the Increment button, and the `click` event will be received by the Blazor JavaScript code and sent to the server for processing by the `IncrementCounter` method, as shown in Figure 33-6.

Figure 33-6. *Handling an event*

Handling Events from Multiple Elements

To avoid code duplication, elements from multiple elements can be received by a single handler method, as shown in Listing 33-12.

Listing 33-12. Handling Events in the Events.razor File in the Blazor Folder

```
<div class="m-2 p-2 border">
    <button class="btn btn-primary" @onclick="@(e => IncrementCounter(e, 0))">
        Increment Counter #1
    </button>
    <span class="p-2">Counter Value: @Counter[0]</span>
</div>

<div class="m-2 p-2 border">
    <button class="btn btn-primary" @onclick="@(e => IncrementCounter(e, 1))">
        Increment Counter #2
    </button>
    <span class="p-2">Counter Value: @Counter[1]</span>
</div>

@code {
    public int[] Counter { get; set; } = new int[] { 1, 1 };

    public void IncrementCounter(MouseEventArgs e, int index) {
        Counter[index]++;
    }
}
```

Blazor event attributes can be used with lambda functions that receive the EventArgs object and invoke a handler method with additional arguments. In this example, I have added an index parameter to the IncrementCounter method, which is used to determine which counter value should be updated. The value for the argument is defined in the @onclick attribute, like this:

```
...
<button class="btn btn-primary" @onclick="@(e => IncrementCounter(e, 0))">
...
```

This technique can also be used when elements are generated programmatically, as shown in Listing 33-13. In this example, I use an @for expression to generate elements and use the loop variable as the argument to the handler method. I have also removed the EventArgs parameter from the handler method, which isn't being used.

AVOIDING THE HANDLER METHOD NAME PITFALL

The most common mistake when specifying an event handler method is to include parentheses, like this:

```
...
<button class="btn btn-primary" @onclick="IncrementCounter()">
...
```

The error message this produces will depend on the event handler method. You may see a warning telling you a formal parameter is missing or that void cannot be converted to an EventCallback. When specifying a handler method, you must specify just the event name, like this:

```
...
<button class="btn btn-primary" @onclick="IncrementCounter">
...
```

You can specify the method name as a Razor expression, like this:

```
...
<button class="btn btn-primary" @onclick="@IncrementCounter">
...
```

Some developers find this easier to parse, but the result is the same. A different set of rules applies when using a lambda function, which must be defined within a Razor expression, like this:

```
...
<button class="btn btn-primary" @onclick="@( ... )">
...
```

Within the Razor expression, the lambda function is defined as it would be in a C# class, which means defining the parameters, followed by the "goes to" arrow, followed by the function body, like this:

```
...
<button class="btn btn-primary" @onclick="@((e) => HandleEvent(e, local))">
...
```

If you don't need to use the EventArgs object, then you can omit the parameter from the lambda function, like this:

```
...
<button class="btn btn-primary" @onclick="@(() => IncrementCounter(local))">
...
```

You will quickly become used to these rules as you start to work with Blazor, even if they seem inconsistent at first.

Listing 33-13. Generating Elements in the Events.razor File in the Blazor Folder

```
@for (int i = 0; i < ElementCount; i++) {
    int local = i;
    <div class="m-2 p-2 border">
        <button class="btn btn-primary" @onclick="@(() => IncrementCounter(local))">
            Increment Counter #@(i + 1)
        </button>
        <span class="p-2">Counter Value: @GetCounter(i)</span>
    </div>
}

@code {
    public int ElementCount { get; set; } = 4;

    public Dictionary<int, int> Counters { get; } = new Dictionary<int, int>();

    public int GetCounter(int index) =>
        Counters.ContainsKey(index) ? Counters[index] : 0;

    public void IncrementCounter(int index)  =>
        Counters[index] = GetCounter(index) + 1;
}
```

The important point to understand about event handlers is that the @onclick lambda function isn't evaluated until the server receives the click event from the browser. This means care must be taken not to use the loop variable i as the argument to the IncrementCounter method because it will always be the final value produced by the loop, which would be 4 in this case. Instead, you must capture the loop variable in a local variable, like this:

```
...
int local = i;
...
```

The local variable is then used as the argument to the event handler method in the attribute, like this:

```
...
<button class="btn btn-primary" @onclick="@(() => IncrementCounter(local))">
...
```

The local variable fixes the value for the lambda function for each of the generated elements. Restart ASP.NET Core and use a browser to request http://localhost:5000/pages/blazor, which will produce the response shown in Figure 33-7. The click events produced by all the button elements are handled by the same method, but the argument provided by the lambda function ensures that the correct counter is updated.

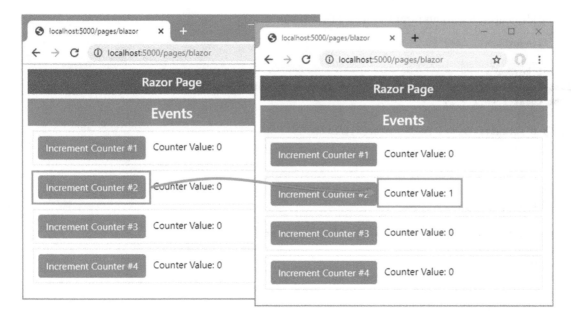

Figure 33-7. *Handling events from multiple elements*

Processing Events Without a Handler Method

Simple event handling can be done directly in a lambda function, without using a handler method, as shown in Listing 33-14.

Listing 33-14. Handling Events in the Events.razor File in the Blazor Folder

```
@for (int i = 0; i < ElementCount; i++) {
    int local = i;
    <div class="m-2 p-2 border">
        <button class="btn btn-primary" @onclick="@(() => IncrementCounter(local))">
            Increment Counter #@(i + 1)
        </button>
        <button class="btn btn-info" @onclick="@(() => Counters.Remove(local))">
            Reset
        </button>
        <span class="p-2">Counter Value: @GetCounter(i)</span>
    </div>
}

@code {
    public int ElementCount { get; set; } = 4;

    public Dictionary<int, int> Counters { get; } = new Dictionary<int, int>();

    public int GetCounter(int index) =>
        Counters.ContainsKey(index) ? Counters[index] : 0;

    public void IncrementCounter(int index)  =>
        Counters[index] = GetCounter(index) + 1;
}
```

Complex handlers should be defined as methods, but this approach is more concise for simple handlers. Restart ASP.NET Core and request http://localhost:5000/pages/blazor. The Reset buttons remove values from the Counters collection without relying on a method in the @code section of the component, as shown in Figure 33-8.

Figure 33-8. *Handling events in a lambda expression*

Preventing Default Events and Event Propagation

Blazor provides two attributes that alter the default behavior of events in the browser, as described in Table 33-5. These attributes, where the name of the event is followed by a colon and then a keyword, are known as *parameters*.

Table 33-5. *The Event Configuration Parameters*

Name	Description
@on{event}:preventDefault	This parameter determines whether the default event for an element is triggered.
@on{event}:stopPropagation	This parameter determines whether an event is propagated to its ancestor elements.

Listing 33-15 demonstrates what these parameters do and why they are useful.

Listing 33-15. Overriding Event Defaults in the Events.razor File in the Blazor Folder

```
<form action="/pages/blazor" method="get">
    @for (int i = 0; i < ElementCount; i++) {
        int local = i;
        <div class="m-2 p-2 border">
            <button class="btn btn-primary"
                @onclick="@(() => IncrementCounter(local))"
                @onclick:preventDefault="EnableEventParams">
                    Increment Counter #@(i + 1)
            </button>
            <button class="btn btn-info" @onclick="@(() => Counters.Remove(local))">
                    Reset
            </button>
            <span class="p-2">Counter Value: @GetCounter(i)</span>
        </div>
    }
</form>
```

881

```
<div class="m-2" @onclick="@(() => IncrementCounter(1))">
    <button class="btn btn-primary" @onclick="@(() => IncrementCounter(0))"
            @onclick:stopPropagation="EnableEventParams">Propagation Test</button>
</div>

<div class="form-check m-2">
    <input class="form-check-input" type="checkbox"
            @onchange="@(() => EnableEventParams = !EnableEventParams)" />
    <label class="form-check-label">Enable Event Parameters</label>
</div>

@code {
    public int ElementCount { get; set; } = 4;

    public Dictionary<int, int> Counters { get; } = new Dictionary<int, int>();

    public int GetCounter(int index) =>
        Counters.ContainsKey(index) ? Counters[index] : 0;

    public void IncrementCounter(int index)  =>
        Counters[index] = GetCounter(index) + 1;

    public bool EnableEventParams { get; set; } = false;
}
```

This example creates two situations in which the default behavior of events in the browser can cause problems. The first is caused by adding a form element. By default, button elements contained in a form will submit that form when they are clicked, even when the @onclick attribute is present. This means that whenever one of the Increment Counter buttons is clicked, the browser will send the form data to the ASP.NET Core server, which will respond with the contents of the Blazor.cshtml Razor Page.

The second problem is demonstrated by an element whose parent also defines an event handler, like this:

```
...
<div class="m-2" @onclick="@(() => IncrementCounter(1))">
    <button class="btn btn-primary" @onclick="@(() => IncrementCounter(0))"
...
```

Events go through a well-defined lifecycle in the browser, which includes being passed up the chain of ancestor elements. In the example, this means clicking the button will cause two counters to be updated, once by the @onclick handler for the button element and once by the @onclick handler for the enclosing div element.

To see these problems, restart ASP.NET Core and request http://localhost:5000/pages/blazor. Click an Increment Counter button; you will see that the form is submitted and the page is essentially reloaded. Click the Propagation Test button, and you will see that two counters are updated. Figure 33-9 shows both problems.

Figure 33-9. *Problems caused by the default behavior of events in the browser*

The checkbox in Listing 33-15 toggles the property that applies the parameters described in Table 33-5, with the effect that the form isn't submitted and only the handler on the button element receives the event. To see the effect, check the checkbox and then click an Increment Counter button and the Propagation Test buttons, which produces the result shown in Figure 33-10.

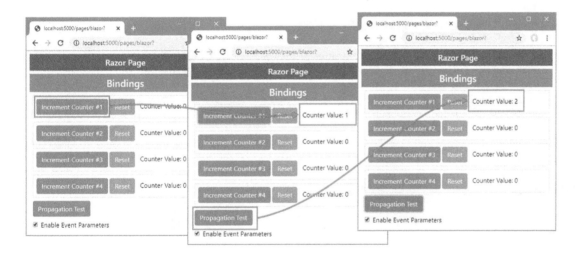

Figure 33-10. *Overriding the default behavior of events in the browser*

Working with Data Bindings

Event handlers and Razor expressions can be used to create a two-way relationship between an HTML element and a C# value, which is useful for elements that allow users to make changes, such as input and select elements. Add a Razor Component named Bindings.razor to the Blazor folder with the content shown in Listing 33-16.

Listing 33-16. The Contents of the Bindings.razor File in the Blazor Folder

```
<div class="form-group">
    <label>City:</label>
    <input class="form-control" value="@City" @onchange="UpdateCity" />
</div>
<div class="p-2 mb-2">City Value: @City</div>
```

```
<button class="btn btn-primary" @onclick="@(() => City = "Paris")">Paris</button>
<button class="btn btn-primary" @onclick="@(() => City = "Chicago")">Chicago</button>

@code {

    public string City { get; set; } = "London";

    public void UpdateCity(ChangeEventArgs e) {
        City = e.Value as string;
    }
}
```

The @onchange attribute registers the UpdateCity method as a handler for the change event from the input element. The events are described using the ChangeEventArgs class, which provides a Value property. Each time a change event is received, the City property is updated with the contents of the input element.

The input element's value attribute creates a relationship in the other direction so that when the value of the City property changes, so does the element's value attribute, which changes the text displayed to the user. To apply the new Razor Component, change the component attribute in the Razor Page, as shown in Listing 33-17.

Listing 33-17. Using a Razor Component in the Blazor.cshtml File in the Pages Folder

```
@page "/pages/blazor"

<h4 class="bg-primary text-white text-center p-2">Events</h4>

<component type="typeof(Advanced.Blazor.Bindings)" render-mode="Server" />
```

To see both parts of the relationship defined by the binding in Listing 33-16, restart ASP.NET Core, navigate to http://localhost:5000/pages/blazor, and edit the content of the input element. The change event is triggered only when the input element loses the focus, so once you have finished editing, press the Tab key or click outside of the input element; you will see the value you entered displayed through the Razor expression in the div element, as shown on the left of Figure 33-11. Click one of the buttons, and the City property will be changed to Paris or Chicago, and the selected value will be displayed by both the div element and the input element, as shown on the right of the figure.

Two-way relationships involving the change event can be expressed as data bindings, which allows both the value and the event to be configured with a single attribute, as shown in Listing 33-18.

Figure 33-11. *Creating a two-way relationship between an element and a property*

Listing 33-18. Using a Data Binding in the Bindings.razor File in the Blazor Folder

```
<div class="form-group">
    <label>City:</label>
    <input class="form-control" @bind="City" />
</div>
<div class="p-2 mb-2">City Value: @City</div>
<button class="btn btn-primary" @onclick="@(() => City = "Paris")">Paris</button>
<button class="btn btn-primary" @onclick="@(() => City = "Chicago")">Chicago</button>

@code {

    public string City { get; set; } = "London";

    //public void UpdateCity(ChangeEventArgs e) {
    //    City = e.Value as string;
    //}
}
```

The @bind attribute is used to specify the property that will be updated when the change event is triggered and that will update the value attribute when it changes. The effect in Listing 33-18 is the same as Listing 33-16 but expressed more concisely and without the need for a handler method or a lambda function to update the property.

Changing the Binding Event

By default, the change event is used in bindings, which provides reasonable responsiveness for the user without requiring too many updates from the server. The event used in a binding can be changed by using the attributes described in Table 33-6.

These attributes are used instead of @bind, as shown in Listing 33-19, but can be used only with events that are represented with the ChangeEventArgs class. This means that only the onchange and oninput events can be used, at least in the current release.

Table 33-6. The Binding Attributes for Specifying an Event

Attribute	Description
@bind-value	This attribute is used to select the property for the data binding.
@bind-value:event	This attribute is used to select the event for the data binding.

Listing 33-19. Specifying an Event for a Binding in the Bindings.razor File in the Blazor Folder

```
<div class="form-group">
    <label>City:</label>
    <input class="form-control" @bind-value="City" @bind-value:event="oninput"  />
</div>
<div class="p-2 mb-2">City Value: @City</div>
<button class="btn btn-primary" @onclick="@(() => City = "Paris")">Paris</button>
<button class="btn btn-primary" @onclick="@(() => City = "Chicago")">Chicago</button>

@code {
    public string City { get; set; } = "London";
}
```

This combination of attributes creates a binding for the City property that is updated when the oninput event is triggered, which happens after every keystroke, rather than only when the input element loses the focus. To see the effect, restart ASP.NET Core, navigate to http://localhost:5000/pages/blazor, and start typing into the input element. The City property will be updated after every keystroke, as shown in Figure 33-12.

Creating DateTime Bindings

Blazor has special support for creating bindings for DateTime properties, allowing them to be expressed using a specific culture or a format string. This feature is applied using the parameters described in Table 33-7.

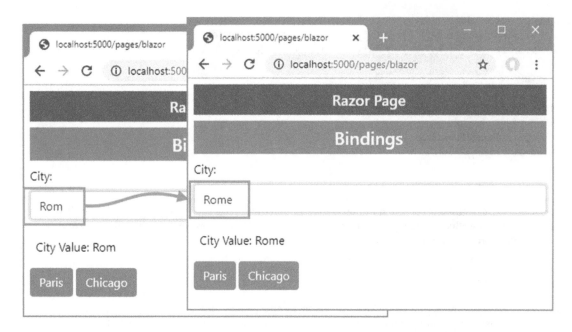

Figure 33-12. *Changing the event in a data binding*

■ **Tip** If you have used the @bind-value and @bind-value:event attributes to select an event, then you must use the @bind-value:culture and @bind-value:format parameters instead.

Table 33-7. *The DateTime Parameters*

Name	Description
@bind:culture	This attribute is used to select a CultureInfo object that will be used to format the DateTime value.
@bind:format	This attribute is used to specify a data formatting string that will be used to format the DateTime value.

Listing 33-20 shows the use of these attributes with a DateTime property.

■ **Note** The formatting strings used in these examples are described at https://docs.microsoft.com/en-us/dotnet/api/system.datetime?view=netcore-3.1.

Listing 33-20. Using a DateTime Property in the Bindings.razor File in the Blazor Folder

```
@using System.Globalization

<div class="form-group">
    <label>City:</label>
    <input class="form-control" @bind-value="City" @bind-value:event="oninput"  />
</div>
<div class="p-2 mb-2">City Value: @City</div>
<button class="btn btn-primary" @onclick="@(() => City = "Paris")">Paris</button>
<button class="btn btn-primary" @onclick="@(() => City = "Chicago")">Chicago</button>

<div class="form-group mt-2">
    <label>Time:</label>
    <input class="form-control my-1" @bind="Time" @bind:culture="Culture"
        @bind:format="MMM-dd" />
    <input class="form-control my-1" @bind="Time" @bind:culture="Culture" />
    <input class="form-control" type="date" @bind="Time" />
</div>
<div class="p-2 mb-2">Time Value: @Time</div>

<div class="form-group">
    <label>Culture:</label>
    <select class="form-control" @bind="Culture">
        <option value="@CultureInfo.GetCultureInfo("en-us")">en-US</option>
        <option value="@CultureInfo.GetCultureInfo("en-gb")">en-GB</option>
        <option value="@CultureInfo.GetCultureInfo("fr-fr")">fr-FR</option>
    </select>
</div>

@code {
    public string City { get; set; } = "London";

    public DateTime Time { get; set; } = DateTime.Parse("2050/01/20 09:50");

    public CultureInfo Culture { get; set; } = CultureInfo.GetCultureInfo("en-us");
}
```

There are three input elements that are used to display the same DataTime value, two of which have been configured using the attributes from Table 33-7. The first element has been configured with a culture and a format string, like this:

```
...
<input class="form-control my-1" @bind="Time" @bind:culture="Culture"
        @bind:format="MMM-dd" />
...
```

The DateTime property is displayed using the culture picked in the select element and with a format string that displays an abbreviated month name and the numeric date. The second input element specifies just a culture, which means the default formatting string will be used.

```
...
<input class="form-control my-1" @bind="Time" @bind:culture="Culture" />
...
```

To see how dates are displayed, restart ASP.NET Core, request http://localhost:5000/pages/blazor, and use the select element to pick different culture settings. The settings available represent English as it is used in the United States, English as it used in the United Kingdom, and French as it is used in France. Figure 33-13 shows the formatting each produces.

The initial locale in this example is en-US. When you switch to en-GB, the order in which the month and date appear changes. When you switch to en-FR, the abbreviated month name changes.

887

Figure 33-13. *Formatting DateTime values*

LETTING THE BROWSER FORMAT DATES

Notice that the value displayed by the third `input` element in Listing 33-20 doesn't change, regardless of the locale you choose. This `input` element has neither of the attributes described in Table 33-7 but does have its `type` attribute set to `date`, like this:

```
...
<input class="form-control" type="date" @bind="Time" />
...
```

You should not specify a culture or a format string when setting the type attribute to `date`, `datetime-local`, `month`, or `time`, because Blazor will automatically format date values into a culture-neutral format that the browser translates into the user's locale. Figure 33-11 shows how the date is formatted in the `en-US` locale but the user will see the date expressed in their local convention.

Using Class Files to Define Components

If you don't like the mix of code and markup that Razor Components support, you can use C# class files to define part, or all, of the component.

Using a Code-Behind Class

The @code section of a Razor Component can be defined in a separate class file, known as a *code-behind class* or *code-behind file*. Code-behind classes for Razor Components are defined as `partial` classes with the same name as the component they provide code for.

Add a Razor Component named `Split.razor` to the `Blazor` folder with the content shown in Listing 33-21.

Listing 33-21. The Contents of the Split.razor File in the Blazor Folder

```
<ul class="list-group">
    @foreach (string name in Names) {
        <li class="list-group-item">@name</li>
    }
</ul>
```

This file contains only HTML content and Razor expressions and renders a list of names that it expects to receive through a Names property. To provide the component with its code, add a class file named Split.razor.cs to the Blazor folder and use it to define the partial class shown in Listing 33-22.

Listing 33-22. The Contents of the Split.razor.cs File in the Blazor Folder

```
using Advanced.Models;
using Microsoft.AspNetCore.Components;
using System.Collections.Generic;
using System.Linq;

namespace Advanced.Blazor {

    public partial class Split {

        [Inject]
        public DataContext Context { get; set; }

        public IEnumerable<string> Names => Context.People.Select(p => p.Firstname);
    }
}
```

The partial class must be defined in the same namespace as its Razor Component and have the same name. For this example, that means the namespace is Advanced.Blazor, and the class name is Splt. Code-behind classes do not define constructors and receive services using the Inject attribute. Listing 33-23 applies the new component.

Listing 33-23. Applying a New Component in the Blazor.cshtml File in the Pages Folder

```
@page "/pages/blazor"

<h4 class="bg-primary text-white text-center p-2">Code-Behind</h4>

<component type="typeof(Advanced.Blazor.Split)" render-mode="Server" />
```

Restart ASP.NET Core and request http://localhost:5000/pages/blazor, and you will see the response shown in Figure 33-14.

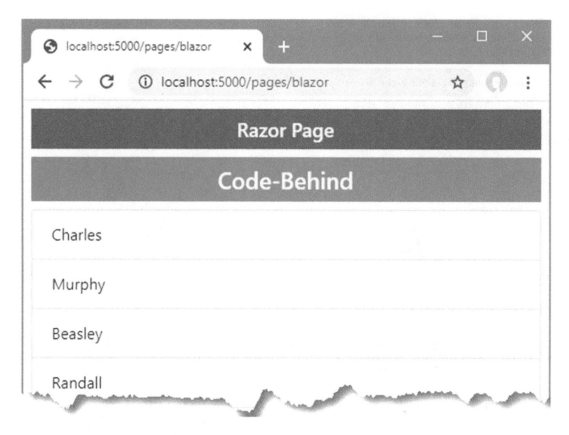

Figure 33-14. *Using a code-behind class to define a Razor Component*

Defining a Razor Component Class

Razor Components can be defined entirely in a class file, although this can be less expressive than using Razor expressions. Add a class file named CodeOnly.cs to the Blazor folder and use it to define the class shown in Listing 33-24.

Listing 33-24. The Contents of the CodeOnly.cs File in the Blazor Folder

```
using Advanced.Models;
using Microsoft.AspNetCore.Components;
using Microsoft.AspNetCore.Components.Rendering;
using Microsoft.AspNetCore.Components.Web;
using System.Collections.Generic;
using System.Linq;

namespace Advanced.Blazor {

    public class CodeOnly : ComponentBase {

        [Inject]
        public DataContext Context { get; set; }

        public IEnumerable<string> Names => Context.People.Select(p => p.Firstname);

        public bool Ascending { get; set; } = false;

        protected override void BuildRenderTree(RenderTreeBuilder builder) {
            IEnumerable<string> data = Ascending
                ? Names.OrderBy(n => n) : Names.OrderByDescending(n => n);
```

```
        builder.OpenElement(1, "button");
        builder.AddAttribute(2, "class", "btn btn-primary mb-2");
        builder.AddAttribute(3, "onclick",
            EventCallback.Factory.Create<MouseEventArgs>(this,
                () => Ascending = !Ascending));
        builder.AddContent(4, new MarkupString("Toggle"));
        builder.CloseElement();

        builder.OpenElement(5, "ul");
        builder.AddAttribute(6, "class", "list-group");
        foreach (string name in data) {
            builder.OpenElement(7, "li");
            builder.AddAttribute(8, "class", "list-group-item");
            builder.AddContent(9, new MarkupString(name));
            builder.CloseElement();
        }
        builder.CloseElement();
    }
  }
}
```

The base class for components is ComponentBase. The content that would normally be expressed as annotated HTML elements is created by overriding the BuildRenderTree method and using the RenderTreeBuilder parameter. Creating content can be awkward because each element is created and configured using multiple code statements, and each statement must have a sequence number that the compiler uses to match up code and content. The OpenElement method starts a new element, which is configured using the AddElement and AddContent methods and then completed with the CloseElement method. All the features available in regular Razor Components are available, including events and bindings, which are set up by adding attributes to elements, just as if they were defined literally in a .razor file. The component in Listing 33-24 displays a list of sorted names, with the sort direction altered when a button element is clicked. Listing 33-25 applies the component so that it will be displayed to the user.

Listing 33-25. Applying a New Component in the Blazor.cshtml File in the Pages Folder

```
@page "/pages/blazor"

<h4 class="bg-primary text-white text-center p-2">Class Only</h4>

<component type="typeof(Advanced.Blazor.CodeOnly)" render-mode="Server" />
```

Restart ASP.NET Core and request http://localhost:5000/pages/blazor to see the content produced by the class-based Razor Component. When you click the button, the sort direction of the names in the list is changed, as shown in Figure 33-15.

Figure 33-15. *Defining a component entirely in code*

Summary

In this chapter, I introduced Blazor Server, explained the problem it solves, and described the advantages and disadvantages it presents. I showed you how to configure an ASP.NET Core application to enable Blazor Server and showed you the basic features that are available when using Razor Components, which are the Blazor building blocks. In the next chapter, I continue to describe the features provided by Blazor.

CHAPTER 34

Using Blazor Server, Part 2

In this chapter, I continue to describe Blazor Server, focusing on the way that Razor Components can be used together to create more complex features. Table 34-1 summarizes the chapter.

Table 34-1. *Chapter Summary*

Problem	Solution	Listing
Creating complex features using Blazor	Combine components to reduce duplication	3, 4
Configuring a component	Use the Parameter attribute to receive a value from an attribute	5–10
Defining custom events and bindings	Use EventCallbacks to receive the handler for the event and follow the convention to create bindings	11–14
Displaying child content in a component	Use a RenderFragment named ChildContent	15, 16
Creating templates	Use named RenderFragment properties	17, 25
Distributing configuration settings widely	Use a cascading parameter	26, 27
Responding to connection errors	Use the connection element and classes	28, 29
Responding to unhandled errors	Use the error element and classes	30, 31

Preparing for This Chapter

This chapter uses the Advanced project from Chapter 33. No changes are required to prepare for this chapter.

Tip You can download the example project for this chapter—and for all the other chapters in this book—from https://github.com/apress/pro-asp.net-core-3. See Chapter 1 for how to get help if you have problems running the examples.

Open a new PowerShell command prompt, navigate to the folder that contains the Advanced.csproj file, and run the command shown in Listing 34-1 to drop the database.

Listing 34-1. Dropping the Database

```
dotnet ef database drop --force
```

Select Start Without Debugging or Run Without Debugging from the Debug menu or use the PowerShell command prompt to run the command shown in Listing 34-2.

Listing 34-2. Running the Example Application

```
dotnet run
```

Use a browser to request `http://localhost:5000/controllers`, which will display a list of data items. Request `http://localhost:5000/pages/blazor`, and you will see the component from Chapter 33 I used to demonstrate data bindings. Figure 34-1 shows both responses.

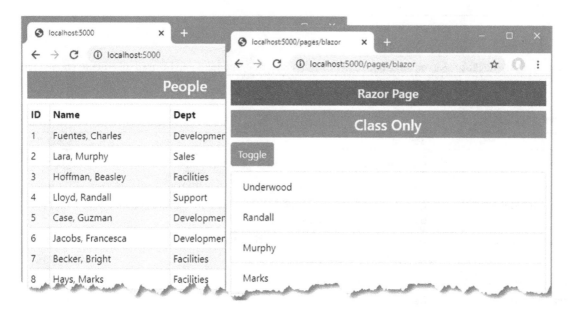

Figure 34-1. *Running the example application*

Combining Components

Blazor components can be combined to create more complex features. In the sections that follow, I show you how multiple components can be used together and how components can communicate. To get started, add a Razor Component named `SelectFilter.razor` to the `Blazor` folder with the content shown in Listing 34-3.

Listing 34-3. The Contents of the SelectFilter.razor File in the Blazor Folder

```
<div class="form-group">
    <label for="select-@Title">@Title</label>
    <select name="select-@Title" class="form-control" @bind="SelectedValue">
        <option disabled selected>Select @Title</option>
        @foreach (string val in Values) {
            <option value="@val" selected="@(val == SelectedValue)">
                @val
            </option>
        }
    </select>
</div>

@code {
```

```
    public IEnumerable<string> Values { get; set; } = Enumerable.Empty<string>();

    public string SelectedValue { get; set; }

    public string Title { get; set; } = "Placeholder";
}
```

The component renders a select element that will allow the user to choose a city. In Listing 34-4, I have applied the SelectFilter component, replacing the existing select element.

Listing 34-4. Applying a Component in the PeopleList.razor File in the Blazor Folder

```
<table class="table table-sm table-bordered table-striped">
    <thead><tr><th>ID</th><th>Name</th><th>Dept</th><th>Location</th></tr></thead>
    <tbody>
        @foreach (Person p in People) {
            <tr class="@GetClass(p.Location.City)">
                <td>@p.PersonId</td>
                <td>@p.Surname, @p.Firstname</td>
                <td>@p.Department.Name</td>
                <td>@p.Location.City, @p.Location.State</td>
            </tr>
        }
    </tbody>
</table>

<SelectFilter />

@code {

    [Inject]
    public DataContext Context { get; set; }

    public IEnumerable<Person> People =>
        Context.People.Include(p => p.Department).Include(p => p.Location);

    public IEnumerable<string> Cities => Context.Locations.Select(l => l.City);

    public string SelectedCity { get; set; }

    public string GetClass(string city) =>
        SelectedCity == city ? "bg-info text-white" : "";
}
```

When a component is added to the content rendered by a controller view or Razor Page, the component element is used, as shown in Chapter 33. When a component is added to the content rendered by another component, then the name of the component is used as an element instead. In this case, I am adding the SelectFilter component to the content rendered by the PeopleList component, which I do with a SelectFilter element. It is important to pay close attention to the capitalization, which must match exactly.

When combining components, the effect is that one component delegates responsibility for part of its layout to another. In this case, I have removed the select element that the PeopleList component used to present the user with a choice of cities and replaced it with the SelectFilter component, which will provide the same feature. The components form a parent/child relationship; the PeopleList component is the parent, and the SelectFilter component is the child.

Additional work is required before everything is properly integrated, but you can see that adding the SelectFilter element displays the SelectFilter component by restarting ASP.NET Core and requesting http://localhost:5000/controllers, which produces the response shown in Figure 34-2.

Figure 34-2. *Adding one component to the content rendered by another*

Configuring Components with Attributes

My goal with the SelectList component is to create a general-purpose feature that I can use throughout the application, configuring the values it displays each time it is used. Razor Components are configured using attributes added to the HTML element that applies them. The values assigned to the HTML element attributes are assigned to the component's C# properties. The Parameter attribute is applied to the C# properties that a component allows to be configured, as shown in Listing 34-5.

Listing 34-5. Declaring Configurable Properties in the SelectFilter.razor File in the Blazor Folder

```
<div class="form-group">
    <label for="select-@Title">@Title</label>
    <select name="select-@Title" class="form-control" @bind="SelectedValue">
        <option disabled selected>Select @Title</option>
        @foreach (string val in Values) {
            <option value="@val" selected="@(val == SelectedValue)">
                @val
            </option>
        }
    </select>
</div>

@code {

    [Parameter]
    public IEnumerable<string> Values { get; set; } = Enumerable.Empty<string>();

    public string SelectedValue { get; set; }

    [Parameter]
    public string Title { get; set; } = "Placeholder";
}
```

Components can be selective about the properties they allow to be configured. In this case, the Parameter attribute has been applied to two of the properties defined by the SelectFilter component. In Listing 34-6, I have modified the element the PeopleList component uses to apply the SelectFilter component to add configuration attributes.

Listing 34-6. Configuring a Component in the PeopleList.razor File in the Blazor Folder

```
<table class="table table-sm table-bordered table-striped">
    <thead><tr><th>ID</th><th>Name</th><th>Dept</th><th>Location</th></tr></thead>
    <tbody>
        @foreach (Person p in People) {
```

```
            <tr class="@GetClass(p.Location.City)">
                <td>@p.PersonId</td>
                <td>@p.Surname, @p.Firstname</td>
                <td>@p.Department.Name</td>
                <td>@p.Location.City, @p.Location.State</td>
            </tr>
        }
    </tbody>
</table>
```

```
<SelectFilter values="@Cities" title="City" />
```

```
@code {

    [Inject]
    public DataContext Context { get; set; }

    public IEnumerable<Person> People =>
        Context.People.Include(p => p.Department).Include(p => p.Location);

    public IEnumerable<string> Cities => Context.Locations.Select(l => l.City);

    public string SelectedCity { get; set; }

    public string GetClass(string city) =>
        SelectedCity == city ? "bg-info text-white" : "";
}
```

For each property that should be configured, an attribute of the same name is added to the parent's HTML element. The attribute values can be fixed values, such as the City string assigned to the title attribute, or Razor expressions, such as @Cities, which assigns the sequence of objects from the Cities property to the values attribute.

Setting and Receiving Bulk Configuration Settings

Defining individual properties to receive values can be error-prone if there are many configuration settings, especially if those values are being received by a component so they can be passed on, either to a child component or to a regular HTML element. In these situations, a single property can be designated to receive any attribute values that have not been matched by other properties, which can then be applied as a set, as shown in Listing 34-7.

Listing 34-7. Receiving Bulk Attributes in the SelectFilter.razor File in the Blazor Folder

```
<div class="form-group">
    <label for="select-@Title">@Title</label>
    <select name="select-@Title" class="form-control"
            @bind="SelectedValue" @attributes="Attrs">
        <option disabled selected>Select @Title</option>
        @foreach (string val in Values) {
            <option value="@val" selected="@(val == SelectedValue)">
                @val
            </option>
        }
    </select>
</div>
```

```
@code {
```

897

```
    [Parameter]
    public IEnumerable<string> Values { get; set; } = Enumerable.Empty<string>();

    public string SelectedValue { get; set; }

    [Parameter]
    public string Title { get; set; } = "Placeholder";

    [Parameter(CaptureUnmatchedValues = true)]
    public Dictionary<string, object> Attrs { get; set; }
}
```

Setting the Parameter attribute's CaptureUnmatchedValues argument to true identifies a property as the catchall for attributes that are not otherwise matched. The type of the property must be Dictionary<string, object>, which allows the attribute names and values to be represented.

Properties whose type is Dictionary<string, object> can be applied to elements using the @attribute expression, like this:

```
...
<select name="select-@Title" class="form-control" @bind="SelectedValue"
    @attributes="Attrs">
...
```

This is known as *attribute splatting*, and it allows a set of attributes to be applied in one go. The effect of the changes in Listing 34-7 means that the SelectFilter component will receive the Values and Title attribute values and that any other attributes will be assigned to the Attrs property and passed on to the select element. Listing 34-8 adds some attributes to demonstrate the effect.

Listing 34-8. Adding Element Attributes in the PeopleList.razor File in the Blazor Folder

```
<table class="table table-sm table-bordered table-striped">
    <thead><tr><th>ID</th><th>Name</th><th>Dept</th><th>Location</th></tr></thead>
    <tbody>
        @foreach (Person p in People) {
            <tr class="@GetClass(p.Location.City)">
                <td>@p.PersonId</td>
                <td>@p.Surname, @p.Firstname</td>
                <td>@p.Department.Name</td>
                <td>@p.Location.City, @p.Location.State</td>
            </tr>
        }
    </tbody>
</table>

<SelectFilter values="@Cities" title="City" autofocus="true" name="city"
    required="true" />

@code {

    // ...statements omitted for brevity...
}
```

Restart ASP.NET Core and navigate to http://localhost:5000/controllers. The attributes passed on to the select element do not affect appearance, but if you right-click the select element and select Inspect from the popup menu, you will see the attributes added to the SelectFilter element in the PeopleList component have been added to the element rendered by the SelectFilter component, like this:

```
...
<select class="form-control" autofocus="true" name="city" required="true">
...
```

Configuring a Component in a Controller View or Razor Page

Attributes are also used to configure components when they are applied using the component element. In Listing 34-9, I have added properties to the PeopleList component that specify how many items from the database should be displayed and a string value that will be passed on to the SelectFilter component.

Listing 34-9. Adding Configuration Properties in the PeopleList.razor File in the Blazor Folder

```
<table class="table table-sm table-bordered table-striped">
    <thead><tr><th>ID</th><th>Name</th><th>Dept</th><th>Location</th></tr></thead>
    <tbody>
        @foreach (Person p in People) {
            <tr class="@GetClass(p.Location.City)">
                <td>@p.PersonId</td>
                <td>@p.Surname, @p.Firstname</td>
                <td>@p.Department.Name</td>
                <td>@p.Location.City, @p.Location.State</td>
            </tr>
        }
    </tbody>
</table>

<SelectFilter values="@Cities" title="@SelectTitle" />

@code {

    [Inject]
    public DataContext Context { get; set; }

    public IEnumerable<Person> People => Context.People.Include(p => p.Department)
            .Include(p => p.Location).Take(ItemCount);

    public IEnumerable<string> Cities => Context.Locations.Select(l => l.City);

    public string SelectedCity { get; set; }

    public string GetClass(string city) =>
        SelectedCity == city ? "bg-info text-white" : "";

    [Parameter]
    public int ItemCount { get; set; } = 4;

    [Parameter]
    public string SelectTitle { get; set; }
}
```

Values for the C# properties are provided by adding attributes whose name begins with param-, followed by the property name, to the component element, as shown in Listing 34-10.

Listing 34-10. Adding Configuration Attributes in the Index.cshtml File in the Views/Home Folder

```
@model PeopleListViewModel

<h4 class="bg-primary text-white text-center p-2">People</h4>

<component type="typeof(Advanced.Blazor.PeopleList)" render-mode="Server"
        param-itemcount="5" param-selecttitle="@("Location")" />
```

The param-itemcount attribute provides a value for the ItemCount property, and the param-selecttitle attribute provides a value for the SelectTitle property.

When using the component element, attributes values that can be parsed into numeric or bool values are handled as literal values and not Razor expressions, which is why I am able to specify the value for the ItemCount property as 4. Other values are assumed to be Razor expressions and not literal values, even though they are not prefixed with @. This oddity means that since I want to specify the value for the SelectTitle property as a literal string, I need a Razor expression, like this:

```
...
<component type="typeof(Advanced.Blazor.PeopleList)" render-mode="Server"
        param-itemcount="5" param-selecttitle="@("Location")" />
...
```

To see the effect of the configuration attributes, restart ASP.NET Core and request http://localhost:5000/controllers, which will produce the response shown in Figure 34-3.

Figure 34-3. *Configuring components with attributes*

Creating Custom Events and Bindings

The SelectFilter component receives its data values from its parent component, but it has no way to indicate when the user makes a selection. For this, I need to create a custom event for which the parent component can register a handler method, just as it would for events from regular HTML elements. Listing 34-11 adds a custom event to the SelectFilter component.

Listing 34-11. Creating an Event in the SelectFilter.razor File in the Blazor Folder

```
<div class="form-group">
    <label for="select-@Title">@Title</label>
    <select name="select-@Title" class="form-control"
            @onchange="HandleSelect" value="@SelectedValue">
        <option disabled selected>Select @Title</option>
        @foreach (string val in Values) {
            <option value="@val" selected="@(val == SelectedValue)">
                @val
            </option>
        }
    </select>
</div>

@code {

    [Parameter]
    public IEnumerable<string> Values { get; set; } = Enumerable.Empty<string>();

    public string SelectedValue { get; set; }

    [Parameter]
    public string Title { get; set; } = "Placeholder";

    [Parameter(CaptureUnmatchedValues = true)]
    public Dictionary<string, object> Attrs { get; set; }

    [Parameter]
    public EventCallback<string> CustomEvent { get; set; }

    public async Task HandleSelect(ChangeEventArgs e) {
        SelectedValue = e.Value as string;
        await CustomEvent.InvokeAsync(SelectedValue);
    }
}
```

The custom event is defined by adding a property whose type is EventCallback<T>. The generic type argument is the type that will be received by the parent's event handler and is string in this case. I have changed the select element so the @onchange attribute registers the HandleSelect method when the select element triggers its onchange event.

The HandleSelect method updates the SelectedValue property and triggers the custom event by invoking the EventCallback<T>.InvokeAsync method, like this:

```
...
await CustomEvent.InvokeAsync(SelectedValue);
...
```

The argument to the InvokeAsync method is used to trigger the event using the value received from the ChangeEventArgs object that was received from the select element. Listing 34-12 changes the PeopleList component so that it receives the custom event emitted by the SelectList component.

Listing 34-12. Handling an Event in the PeopleList.razor File in the Blazor Folder

```
<table class="table table-sm table-bordered table-striped">
    <thead><tr><th>ID</th><th>Name</th><th>Dept</th><th>Location</th></tr></thead>
    <tbody>
        @foreach (Person p in People) {
            <tr class="@GetClass(p.Location.City)">
                <td>@p.PersonId</td>
                <td>@p.Surname, @p.Firstname</td>
                <td>@p.Department.Name</td>
                <td>@p.Location.City, @p.Location.State</td>
            </tr>
        }
    </tbody>
</table>

<SelectFilter values="@Cities" title="@SelectTitle" CustomEvent="@HandleCustom" />

@code {

    [Inject]
    public DataContext Context { get; set; }

    public IEnumerable<Person> People => Context.People.Include(p => p.Department)
            .Include(p => p.Location).Take(ItemCount);

    public IEnumerable<string> Cities => Context.Locations.Select(l => l.City);

    public string SelectedCity { get; set; }

    public string GetClass(string city) =>
        SelectedCity as string == city ? "bg-info text-white" : "";

    [Parameter]
    public int ItemCount { get; set; } = 4;

    [Parameter]
    public string SelectTitle { get; set; }

    public void HandleCustom(string newValue) {
        SelectedCity = newValue;
    }
}
```

To set up the event handler, an attribute is added to the element that applies the child component using the name of its EventCallback<T> property. The value of the attribute is a Razor expression that selects a method that receives a parameter of type T.

Restart ASP.NET Core, request http://localhost:5000/controllers, and select a value from the list of cities. The custom event completes the relationship between the parent and child components. The parent configures the child through its attributes to specify the title and the list of data values that will be presented to the user. The child component uses a custom event to tell the parent when the user selects a value, allowing the parent to highlight the corresponding rows in its HTML table, as shown in Figure 34-4.

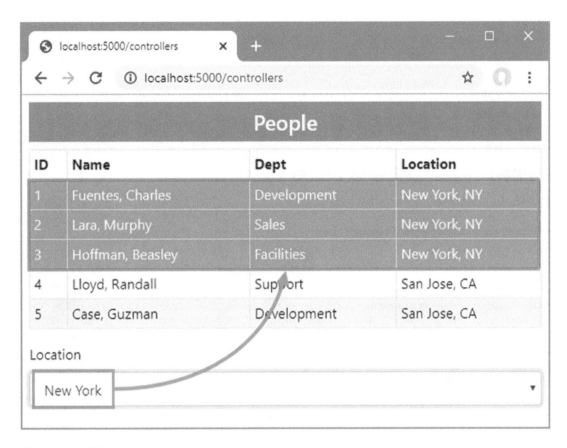

Figure 34-4. *Using a custom event*

Creating a Custom Binding

A parent component can create a binding on a child component if it defines a pair of properties, one of which is assigned a data value and the other of which is a custom event. The names of the property are important: the name of the event property must be the same as the data property plus the word Changed. Listing 34-13 updates the SelectFilter component so it presents the properties required for the binding.

Listing 34-13. Preparing for Custom Binding in the SelectFilter.razor File in the Blazor Folder

```
<div class="form-group">
    <label for="select-@Title">@Title</label>
    <select name="select-@Title" class="form-control"
            @onchange="HandleSelect" value="@SelectedValue">
        <option disabled selected>Select @Title</option>
        @foreach (string val in Values) {
            <option value="@val" selected="@(val == SelectedValue)">
                @val
            </option>
        }
    </select>
</div>

@code {

    [Parameter]
    public IEnumerable<string> Values { get; set; } = Enumerable.Empty<string>();
```

903

```
[Parameter]
public string SelectedValue { get; set; }

[Parameter]
public string Title { get; set; } = "Placeholder";

[Parameter(CaptureUnmatchedValues = true)]
public Dictionary<string, object> Attrs { get; set; }

[Parameter]
public EventCallback<string> SelectedValueChanged { get; set; }

public async Task HandleSelect(ChangeEventArgs e) {
    SelectedValue = e.Value as string;
    await SelectedValueChanged.InvokeAsync(SelectedValue);
}
}
```

Notice that the Parameter attribute must be applied to both the SelectedValue and SelectedValueChanged properties. If either attribute is omitted, the data binding won't work as expected.

The parent component binds to the child with the @bind-<name> attribute, where <name> corresponds to the property defined by the child component. In this example, the name of the child component's property is SelectedValue, and the parent can create a binding using @bind-SelectedValue, as shown in Listing 34-14.

Listing 34-14. Using a Custom Binding in the PeopleList.razor File in the Blazor Folder

```
<table class="table table-sm table-bordered table-striped">
    <thead><tr><th>ID</th><th>Name</th><th>Dept</th><th>Location</th></tr></thead>
    <tbody>
        @foreach (Person p in People) {
            <tr class="@GetClass(p.Location.City)">
                <td>@p.PersonId</td>
                <td>@p.Surname, @p.Firstname</td>
                <td>@p.Department.Name</td>
                <td>@p.Location.City, @p.Location.State</td>
            </tr>
        }
    </tbody>
</table>

<SelectFilter values="@Cities" title="@SelectTitle"
    @bind-SelectedValue="SelectedCity" />

<button class="btn btn-primary"
    @onclick="@(() => SelectedCity = "San Jose")">
        Change
</button>

@code {

    [Inject]
    public DataContext Context { get; set; }

    public IEnumerable<Person> People => Context.People.Include(p => p.Department)
            .Include(p => p.Location).Take(ItemCount);

    public IEnumerable<string> Cities => Context.Locations.Select(l => l.City);
```

```
public string SelectedCity { get; set; }

public string GetClass(string city) =>
    SelectedCity as string == city ? "bg-info text-white" : "";

[Parameter]
public int ItemCount { get; set; } = 4;

[Parameter]
public string SelectTitle { get; set; }

//public void HandleCustom(string newValue) {
//    SelectedCity = newValue;
//}
}
```

Restart ASP.NET Core, request `http://localhost:5000/controllers`, and select New York from the list of cities. The custom binding will cause the value chosen in the `select` element to be reflected by the highlighting in the table. Click the Change button to test the binding in the other direction, and you will see the highlighted city change, as shown in Figure 34-5.

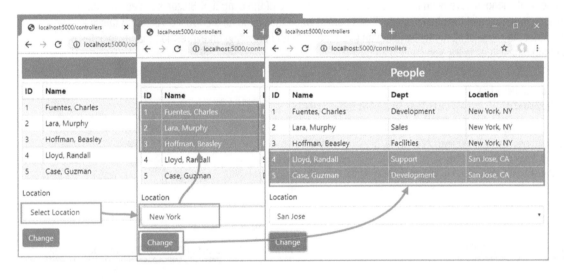

Figure 34-5. *Using a custom binding*

Displaying Child Content in a Component

Components that display child content act as wrappers around elements provided by their parents. To see how child content is managed, add a Razor Component named ThemeWrapper.razor to the Blazor folder with the content shown in Listing 34-15.

Listing 34-15. The Contents of the ThemeWrapper.razor File in the Blazor Folder

```
<div class="p-2 bg-@Theme border text-white">
    <h5 class="text-center">@Title</h5>
    @ChildContent
</div>

@code {
    [Parameter]
    public string Theme { get; set; }
```

```
    [Parameter]
    public string Title { get; set; }

    [Parameter]
    public RenderFragment ChildContent { get; set; }
}
```

To receive child content, a component defines a property named ChildContent whose type is RenderFragment and that has been decorated with the Parameter attribute. The @ChildContent expression includes the child content in the component's HTML output. The component in the listing wraps its child content in a div element that is styled using a Bootstrap theme color and that displays a title. The name of the theme color and the text of the title are also received as parameters.

RESTRICTING ELEMENT REUSE

When updating the content presented to the user, Blazor will reuse elements if it can because creating new elements is a relatively expensive operation. This is particularly true when displaying elements for a sequence of values, such as with @for or @foreach expressions. If the sequence changes, Blazor will reuse the elements it created for the old data values to display the new data.

This can cause problems if changes have been made to the elements outside of the control of Blazor, such as with custom JavaScript code. Blazor isn't aware of the changes, which will persist when the elements are reused. Although this is a rare situation, you can restrict the reuse of elements by using an @key attribute and providing an expression that associates the element with one of the data values in the sequence, like this:

```
...
@foreach (Person p in People) {
    <tr @key="p.PersonId" class="@GetClass(p.Location.City)">

        <td>@p.PersonId</td>
        <td>@p.Surname, @p.Firstname</td>
        <td>@p.Department.Name</td>
        <td>@p.Location.City, @p.Location.State</td>
    </tr>
}
...
```

Blazor will reuse an element only if there is a data item that has the same key. For other values, new elements will be created.

Child content is defined by adding HTML elements between the start and end tags when applying the component, as shown in Listing 34-16.

Listing 34-16. Defining Child Content in the PeopleList.razor File in the Blazor Folder

```
<table class="table table-sm table-bordered table-striped">
    <thead><tr><th>ID</th><th>Name</th><th>Dept</th><th>Location</th></tr></thead>
    <tbody>
        @foreach (Person p in People) {
            <tr class="@GetClass(p.Location.City)">
                <td>@p.PersonId</td>
                <td>@p.Surname, @p.Firstname</td>
                <td>@p.Department.Name</td>
                <td>@p.Location.City, @p.Location.State</td>
            </tr>
        }
    </tbody>
</table>
```

```
<ThemeWrapper Theme="info" Title="Location Selector">
    <SelectFilter values="@Cities" title="@SelectTitle"
        @bind-SelectedValue="SelectedCity" />
    <button class="btn btn-primary"
        @onclick="@(() => SelectedCity = "San Jose")">
            Change
    </button>
</ThemeWrapper>

@code {

    // ...statements omitted for brevity...
}
```

No additional attributes are required to configure the child content, which is processed and assigned to the `ChildContent` property automatically. To see how the `ThemeWrapper` component presents its child content, restart ASP.NET Core and request `http://localhost:5000/controllers`. You will see the configuration attributes that selected the theme and the title text used to produce the response shown in Figure 34-6.

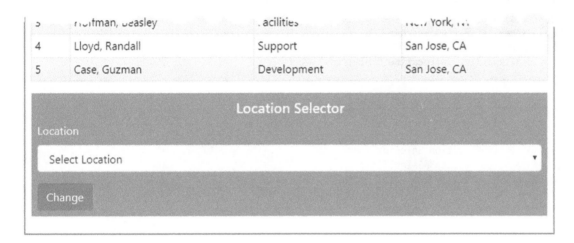

Figure 34-6. *Using child content*

Creating Template Components

Template components bring more structure to the presentation of child content, allowing multiple sections of content to be displayed. Template components are a good way of consolidating features that are used throughout an application to prevent the duplication of code and content.

To see how this works, add a Razor Component named `TableTemplate.razor` to the `Blazor` folder with the content shown in Listing 34-17.

Listing 34-17. The Contents of the TableTemplate.razor File in the Blazor Folder

```
<table class="table table-sm table-bordered table-striped">
    @if (Header != null) {
        <thead>@Header</thead>
    }
    <tbody>@Body</tbody>
</table>

@code {
    [Parameter]
    public RenderFragment Header { get; set; }
```

907

```
    [Parameter]
    public RenderFragment Body { get; set; }
}
```

The component defines a RenderFragment property for each region of child content it supports. The TableTemplate component defines two RenderFragment properties, named Header and Body, which represent the content sections of a table. Each region of child content is rendered using a Razor expression, @Header and @Body, and you can check to see whether content has been provided for a specific section by checking to see whether the property value is null, which this component does for the Header section.

When using a template component, the content for each region is enclosed in an HTML element whose tag matches the name of the corresponding RenderFragment property, as shown in Listing 34-18.

Listing 34-18. Applying a Template Component in the PeopleList.razor File in the Blazor Folder

```
<TableTemplate>
    <Header>
        <tr><th>ID</th><th>Name</th><th>Dept</th><th>Location</th></tr>
    </Header>
    <Body>
        @foreach (Person p in People) {
            <tr class="@GetClass(p.Location.City)">
                <td>@p.PersonId</td>
                <td>@p.Surname, @p.Firstname</td>
                <td>@p.Department.Name</td>
                <td>@p.Location.City, @p.Location.State</td>
            </tr>
        }
    </Body>
</TableTemplate>

<ThemeWrapper Theme="info" Title="Location Selector">
    <SelectFilter values="@Cities" title="@SelectTitle"
        @bind-SelectedValue="SelectedCity" />
    <button class="btn btn-primary"
        @onclick="@(() => SelectedCity = "San Jose")">
            Change
    </button>
</ThemeWrapper>

@code {

    // ...statements omitted for brevity...
}
```

The child content is structured into sections that correspond to the template component's properties, Header and Body, which leaves the TableTemplate component responsible for the table structure and the PeopleList component responsible for providing the detail. Restart ASP.NET Core and request http://localhost:5000/controllers, and you will see the output produced by the template component, as shown in Figure 34-7.

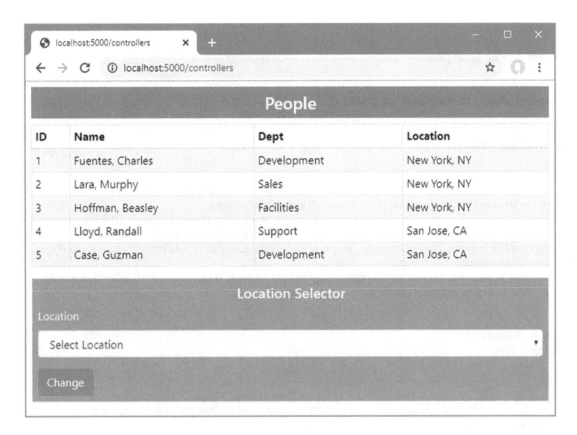

Figure 34-7. *Using a template component*

Using Generic Type Parameters in Template Components

The template component I created in the previous section is useful, in the sense that it provides a consistent representation of a table that I can use throughout the example application. But it is also limited because it relies on the parent component to take responsibility for generating the rows for the table body. The template component doesn't have any insight into the content it presents, which means it cannot do anything with that content other than display it.

Template components can be made data-aware with the use of a generic type parameter, which allows the parent component to provide a sequence of data objects and a template for presenting them. The template component becomes responsible for generating the content for each data object and, consequently, can provide more useful functionality. As a demonstration, I am going to add support to the template component for selecting how many table rows are displayed and for selecting table rows. The first step is to add a generic type parameter to the component and use it to render the content for the table body, as shown in Listing 34-19.

Listing 34-19. Adding a Generic Type Parameter in the TableTemplate.razor File in the Blazor Folder

```
@typeparam RowType

<table class="table table-sm table-bordered table-striped">
    @if (Header != null) {
        <thead>@Header</thead>
    }
    <tbody>
        @foreach (RowType item in RowData) {
            <tr>@RowTemplate(item)</tr>
        }
    </tbody>
</table>
```

909

```
@code {
    [Parameter]
    public RenderFragment Header { get; set; }

    [Parameter]
    public RenderFragment<RowType> RowTemplate{ get; set; }

    [Parameter]
    public IEnumerable<RowType> RowData { get; set; }
}
```

The generic type parameter is specified using the @typeparam attribute, and, in this case, I have given the parameter the name RowType because it will refer to the data type for which the component will generate table rows.

The data the component will process is received by adding a property whose type is a sequence of objects of the generic type. I have named the property RowData, and its type is IEnumerable<RowType>. The content the component will display for each object is received using a RenderFragment<T> property. I have named this property RowTemplate, and its type is RenderFragment<RowType>, reflecting the name I selected for the generic type parameter.

When a component receives a content section through a RenderFragment<T> property, it can render it for a single object by invoking the section as a method and using the object as the argument, like this:

```
...
@foreach (RowType item in RowData) {
    <tr>@RowTemplate(item)</tr>
}
...
```

This fragment of code enumerates the RowType objects in the RowData sequence and renders the content section received through the RowTemplate property for each of them.

Using a Generic Template Component

I have simplified the PeopleList component so it only uses the template component to produce a table of Person objects, and I have removed earlier features, as shown in Listing 34-20.

Listing 34-20. Using a Generic Template Component in the PeopleList.razor File in the Blazor Folder

```
<TableTemplate RowType="Person" RowData="People">
    <Header>
        <tr><th>ID</th><th>Name</th><th>Dept</th><th>Location</th></tr>
    </Header>
    <RowTemplate Context="p">
        <td>@p.PersonId</td>
        <td>@p.Surname, @p.Firstname</td>
        <td>@p.Department.Name</td>
        <td>@p.Location.City, @p.Location.State</td>
    </RowTemplate>
</TableTemplate>

@code {

    [Inject]
    public DataContext Context { get; set; }

    public IEnumerable<Person> People => Context.People
            .Include(p => p.Department)
            .Include(p => p.Location);
}
```

The RowType attribute is used to specify the value for the generic type argument. The RowData attribute specifies the data the template component will process.

The RowTemplate element denotes the elements that will be produced for each data object. When defining a content section for a RenderFragment<T> property, the Context attribute is used to assign a name to the current object being processed. In this case, the Context attribute is used to assign the name p to the current object, which is then referred to in the Razor expressions used to populate the content section's elements.

The overall effect is that the template component is configured to display Person objects. The component will generate a table row for each Person, which will contain td elements whose content is set using the current Person object's properties.

Since I removed properties that were decorated with the Parameter attribute in Listing 34-20, I need to remove the corresponding attributes from the element that applies the PepleList component, as shown in Listing 34-21.

Listing 34-21. Removing Attributes in the Index.cshtml File in the Views/Home Folder

```
@model PeopleListViewModel

<h4 class="bg-primary text-white text-center p-2">People</h4>

<component type="typeof(Advanced.Blazor.PeopleList)" render-mode="Server" />
```

To see the generic template component, restart ASP.NET Core and request http://localhost:5000/controllers. The data and content sections provided by the PeopleList component have been used by the TableTemplate component to produce the table shown in Figure 34-8.

Figure 34-8. *Using a generic template component*

Adding Features to the Generic Template Component

This may feel like a step backward, but, as you will see, giving the template component insight into the data it handles sets the foundation for adding features, as shown in Listing 34-22.

Listing 34-22. Adding a Feature in the TableTemplate.razor File in the Blazor Folder

```
@typeparam RowType

<div class="container-fluid">
    <div class="row">
        <div class="col">
            <SelectFilter Title="@("Sort")" Values="@SortDirectionChoices"
                @bind-SelectedValue="SortDirectionSelection" />
        </div>
        <div class="col">
            <SelectFilter Title="@("Highlight")" Values="@HighlightChoices()"
                @bind-SelectedValue="HighlightSelection" />
        </div>
    </div>
</div>

<table class="table table-sm table-bordered table-striped">
    @if (Header != null) {
        <thead>@Header</thead>
    }
    <tbody>
        @foreach (RowType item in SortedData()) {
            <tr class="@IsHighlighted(item)">@RowTemplate(item)</tr>
        }
    </tbody>
</table>

@code {
    [Parameter]
    public RenderFragment Header { get; set; }

    [Parameter]
    public RenderFragment<RowType> RowTemplate{ get; set; }

    [Parameter]
    public IEnumerable<RowType> RowData { get; set; }

    [Parameter]
    public Func<RowType, string> Highlight { get; set; }

    public IEnumerable<string> HighlightChoices() =>
        RowData.Select(item => Highlight(item)).Distinct();

    public string HighlightSelection { get; set; }

    public string IsHighlighted(RowType item) =>
        Highlight(item) == HighlightSelection ? "bg-dark text-white": "";

    [Parameter]
    public Func<RowType, string> SortDirection { get; set; }

    public string[] SortDirectionChoices =
        new string[] { "Ascending", "Descending" };

    public string SortDirectionSelection{ get; set; } = "Ascending";
```

```
    public IEnumerable<RowType> SortedData() =>
        SortDirectionSelection == "Ascending"
            ? RowData.OrderBy(SortDirection)
            : RowData.OrderByDescending(SortDirection);
}
```

The changes present the user with two select elements that are presented using the SelectFilter component created earlier in the chapter. These new elements allow the user to sort the data in ascending and descending order and to select a value used to highlight rows in the table. The parent component provides additional parameters that give the template component functions that select the properties used for sorting and highlighting, as shown in Listing 34-23.

Listing 34-23. Configuring Template Component Features in the PeopleList.razor File in the Blazor Folder

```
<TableTemplate RowType="Person" RowData="People"
        Highlight="@(p => p.Location.City)" SortDirection="@(p => p.Surname)">
    <Header>
        <tr><th>ID</th><th>Name</th><th>Dept</th><th>Location</th></tr>
    </Header>
    <RowTemplate Context="p">
        <td>@p.PersonId</td>
        <td>@p.Surname, @p.Firstname</td>
        <td>@p.Department.Name</td>
        <td>@p.Location.City, @p.Location.State</td>
    </RowTemplate>
</TableTemplate>

@code {

    [Inject]
    public DataContext Context { get; set; }

    public IEnumerable<Person> People => Context.People
            .Include(p => p.Department)
            .Include(p => p.Location);
}
```

The Highlight attribute provides the template component with a function that selects the property used for highlighting table rows, and the SortDirection attribute provides a function that selects a property used for sorting. To see the effect, restart ASP.NET Core and request http://localhost:5000/controllers. The response will contain the new select elements, which can be used to change the sort order or select a city for filtering, as shown in Figure 34-9.

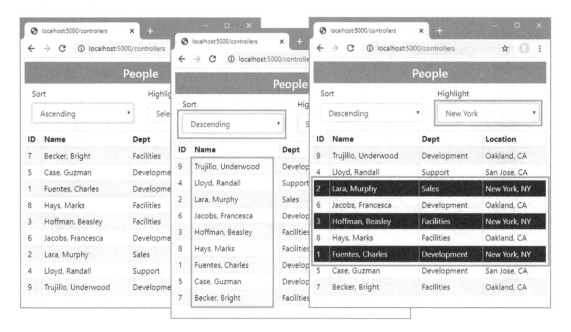

Figure 34-9 *Adding features to a template component*

Reusing a Generic Template Component

The features added to the template component all relied on the generic type parameter, which allows the component to modify the content it presents without being tied to a specific class. The result is a component that can be used to display, sort, and highlight any data type wherever a table is required. Add a Razor Component named DepartmentList.razor to the Blazor folder with the content shown in Listing 34-24.

Listing 34-24. The Contents of the DepartmentList.razor File in the Blazor Folder

```
<TableTemplate RowType="Department" RowData="Departments"
    Highlight="@(d => d.Name)"
    SortDirection="@(d => d.Name)">
    <Header>
        <tr><th>ID</th><th>Name</th><th>People</th><th>Locations</th></tr>
    </Header>
    <RowTemplate Context="d">
        <td>@d.Departmentid</td>
        <td>@d.Name</td>
        <td>@(String.Join(", ", d.People.Select(p => p.Surname)))</td>
        <td>
            @(String.Join(", ", d.People.Select(p => p.Location.City).Distinct()))
        </td>
    </RowTemplate>
</TableTemplate>

@code {

    [Inject]
    public DataContext Context { get; set; }

    public IEnumerable<Department> Departments => Context.Departments
            .Include(d => d.People).ThenInclude(p => p.Location);
}
```

The TableTemplate component is used to present the user with a list of the Department objects in the database, along with details of the related Person and Location objects, which are queried with the Entity Framework Core Include and ThenInclude methods. Listing 34-25 changes the Razor Component displayed by the Razor Page named Blazor.

Listing 34-25. Changing the Component in the Blazor.cshtml File in the Pages Folder

```
@page "/pages/blazor"

<h4 class="bg-primary text-white text-center p-2">Departments</h4>

<component type="typeof(Advanced.Blazor.DepartmentList)" render-mode="Server" />
```

Restart ASP.NET Core and request http://localhost:5000/pages/blazor. The response will be presented using the templated component, as shown in Figure 34-10.

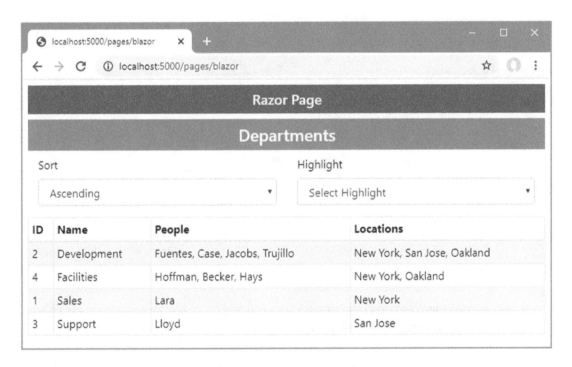

Figure 34-10. *Reusing a generic template component*

Cascading Parameters

As the number of components increases, it can be useful for a component to provide configuration data to descendants deep in the hierarchy of components. This can be done by having each component in the chain receive the data and pass it on to all of its children, but that is error-prone and requires every component to participate in the process, even if none of its descendants uses the data it passes on.

Blazor provides a solution to this problem by supporting *cascading parameters*, in which a component provides data values that are available directly to any of its descendants, without being relayed by intermediate components. Cascading parameters are defined using the CascadingValue component, which is used to wrap a section of content, as shown in Listing 34-26.

Listing 34-26. Creating a Cascading Parameter in the DepartmentList.razor File in the Blazor Folder

```
<CascadingValue Name="BgTheme" Value="Theme" IsFixed="false" >
    <TableTemplate RowType="Department" RowData="Departments"
        Highlight="@(d => d.Name)"
        SortDirection="@(d => d.Name)">
        <Header>
```

915

```
                <tr><th>ID</th><th>Name</th><th>People</th><th>Locations</th></tr>
            </Header>
            <RowTemplate Context="d">
                <td>@d.Departmentid</td>
                <td>@d.Name</td>
                <td>@(String.Join(", ", d.People.Select(p => p.Surname)))</td>
                <td>
                    @(String.Join(", ",
                        d.People.Select(p => p.Location.City).Distinct()))
                </td>
            </RowTemplate>
        </TableTemplate>
</CascadingValue>

<SelectFilter Title="@("Theme")" Values="Themes" @bind-SelectedValue="Theme" />

@code {

    [Inject]
    public DataContext Context { get; set; }

    public IEnumerable<Department> Departments => Context.Departments
            .Include(d => d.People).ThenInclude(p => p.Location);

    public string Theme { get; set; } = "info";
    public string[] Themes = new string[] { "primary", "info", "success" };
}
```

The CascadingValue element makes a value available to the components it encompasses and their descendants. The Name attribute specifies the name of the parameter, the Value attribute specifies the value, and the isFixed attribute is used to specify whether the value will change. The CascadingValue element has been used in Listing 34-26 to create a cascading parameter named BgTheme, whose value is set by an instance of the SelectFilter component that presents the user with a selection of Bootstrap CSS theme names.

■ **Tip** Each CascadingValue element creates one cascading parameter. If you need to pass on multiple values, then you can nest the CascadingValue or create a simple parameter that provides multiple settings through a dictionary.

Cascading parameters are received directly by the components that require them with the CascadingParameter attribute, as shown in Listing 34-27.

Listing 34-27. Receiving a Cascading Parameter in the SelectFilter.razor File in the Blazor Folder

```
<div class="form-group p-2 bg-@Theme @TextColor()">
    <label for="select-@Title">@Title</label>
    <select name="select-@Title" class="form-control"
            @onchange="HandleSelect" value="@SelectedValue">
        <option disabled selected>Select @Title</option>
        @foreach (string val in Values) {
            <option value="@val" selected="@(val == SelectedValue)">
                @val
            </option>
        }
    </select>
</div>
```

```
@code {

    [Parameter]
    public IEnumerable<string> Values { get; set; } = Enumerable.Empty<string>();

    [Parameter]
    public string SelectedValue { get; set; }

    [Parameter]
    public string Title { get; set; } = "Placeholder";

    [Parameter(CaptureUnmatchedValues = true)]
    public Dictionary<string, object> Attrs { get; set; }

    [Parameter]
    public EventCallback<string> SelectedValueChanged { get; set; }

    public async Task HandleSelect(ChangeEventArgs e) {
        SelectedValue = e.Value as string;
        await SelectedValueChanged.InvokeAsync(SelectedValue);
    }

    [CascadingParameter(Name ="BgTheme")]
    public string Theme { get; set; }

    public string TextColor() => Theme == null ? "" : "text-white";
}
```

The CascadingParameter attribute's Name argument is used to specify the name of the cascading parameter. The BgTheme parameter defined in Listing 34-26 is received by the Theme property in Listing 34-27 and used to set the background for the component. Restart ASP.NET Core and request http://localhost:5000/pages/blazor, which produces the response shown in Figure 34-11.

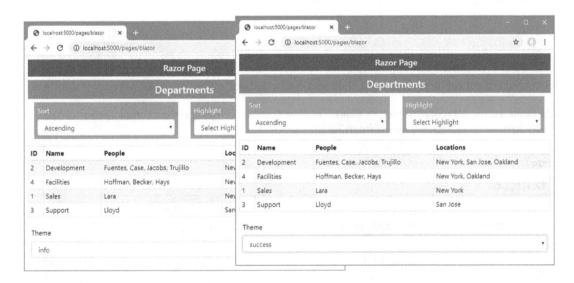

Figure 34-11. *Using a cascading parameter*

There are three instances of the SelectFilter component used in this example, but only two of them are within the hierarchy contained by the CascadingValue element. The other instance is defined outside of the CascadingValue element and does not receive the cascading value.

Handling Errors

In the following sections, I describe the features Blazor provides for dealing with connection errors and unhandled application errors.

Handling Connection Errors

Blazor relies on its persistent HTTP connection between the browser and the ASP.NET Core server. The application cannot function when the connection is disrupted, and a modal error message is displayed that prevents the user from interacting with components.

Blazor allows the connection errors to be customized by defining an element with a specific id, as shown in Listing 34-28.

Listing 34-28. Defining a Connection Error Element in the Blazor.cshtml File in the Pages Folder

```
@page "/pages/blazor"

<h4 class="bg-primary text-white text-center p-2">Departments</h4>

<link rel="stylesheet" href="connectionErrors.css" />

<div id="components-reconnect-modal"
    class="h4 bg-dark text-white text-center my-2 p-2 components-reconnect-hide">
    Blazor Connection Lost
    <div class="reconnect">
        Trying to reconnect...
    </div>
    <div class="failed">
        Reconnection Failed.
        <button class="btn btn-light" onclick="window.Blazor.reconnect()">
            Reconnect
        </button>
    </div>
    <div class="rejected">
        Reconnection Rejected.
        <button class="btn btn-light" onclick="location.reload()">
            Reload
        </button>
    </div>
</div>

<component type="typeof(Advanced.Blazor.DepartmentList)" render-mode="Server" />
```

The id attribute of the custom error element must be components-reconnect-modal. When there is a connection error, Blazor locates this element and adds it to one of four classes, described in Table 34-2.

Table 34-2. The Connection Error Classes

Name	Description
components-reconnect-show	The element is added to this class when the connection has been lost and Blazor is attempting a reconnection. The error message should be displayed to the user, and interaction with the Blazor content should be prevented.
components-reconnect-hide	The element is added to this class if the connection is reestablished. The error message should be hidden, and interaction should be permitted.
components-reconnect-failed	The element is added to this class if Blazor reconnection fails. The user can be presented with a button that invokes window.Blazor.reconnect() to attempt reconnection again.
components-reconnect-rejected	The element is added to this class if Blazor is able to reach the server, but the user's connection state has been lost. This typically happens when the server has been restarted. The user can be presented with a button that invokes location.reload() to reload the application and try again.

The element isn't added to any of these classes initially, so I have explicitly added it to the components-reconnect-hide class so that it isn't visible until a problem occurs.

I want to present specific messages to the user for each of the conditions that can arise during reconnection. To this end, I added elements that display a message for each condition. To manage their visibility, add a CSS Stylesheet named connectionErrors.css to the wwwroot folder and use it to define the styles shown in Listing 34-29.

Listing 34-29. The Contents of the connectionErrors.css File in the wwwroot Folder

```
#components-reconnect-modal {
    position: fixed; top: 0; right: 0; bottom: 0;
    left: 0; z-index: 1000; overflow: hidden; opacity: 0.9;
}

.components-reconnect-hide { display: none; }
.components-reconnect-show { display: block; }

.components-reconnect-show > .reconnect { display: block; }
.components-reconnect-show > .failed,
.components-reconnect-show > .rejected {
    display: none;
}

.components-reconnect-failed > .failed {
    display: block;
}
.components-reconnect-failed > .reconnect,
.components-reconnect-failed > .rejected {
    display: none;
}

.components-reconnect-rejected > .rejected {
    display: block;
}
.components-reconnect-rejected > .reconnect,
.components-reconnect-rejected > .failed {
    display: none;
}
```

These styles show the components-reconnect-modal element as a modal item, with its visibility determined by the components-reconnect-hide and components-reconnect-show classes. The visibility of the specific messages is toggled based on the application of the classes in Table 34-2.

To see the effect, restart ASP.NET Core and request http://localhost:5000/pages/blazor. Wait until the component is displayed and then stop the ASP.NET Core server. You will see an initial error message as Blazor attempts to reconnect. After a few seconds, you will see the message that indicates that reconnection has failed.

Restart ASP.NET Core and request http://localhost:5000/pages/blazor. Wait until the component is displayed and then restart ASP.NET Core. This time Blazor will be able to connect to the server, but the connection will be rejected because the server restart has caused the connection state to be lost. Figure 34-12 shows both sequences of error messages.

■ **Tip** It is not possible to test successful connection recovery with just the browser because there is no way to interrupt the persistent HTTP connection. I use the excellent Fiddler proxy, https://www.telerik.com/fiddler, which allows me to terminate the connection without stopping the ASP.NET Core server.

Figure 34-12. *Handling connection errors*

Handling Uncaught Application Errors

Blazor does not respond well to uncaught application errors, which are almost always treated as terminal. To see the default error behavior, add the elements shown in Listing 34-30 to the DepartmentList component.

Listing 34-30. Adding Elements in the DepartmentList.razor File in the Blazor Folder

```
<CascadingValue Name="BgTheme" Value="Theme" IsFixed="false" >
    <TableTemplate RowType="Department" RowData="Departments"
        Highlight="@(d => d.Name)"
        SortDirection="@(d => d.Name)">
        <Header>
            <tr><th>ID</th><th>Name</th><th>People</th><th>Locations</th></tr>
        </Header>
        <RowTemplate Context="d">
            <td>@d.Departmentid</td>
            <td>@d.Name</td>
            <td>@(String.Join(", ", d.People.Select(p => p.Surname)))</td>
            <td>
                @(String.Join(", ",
                    d.People.Select(p => p.Location.City).Distinct()))
            </td>
        </RowTemplate>
    </TableTemplate>
</CascadingValue>

<SelectFilter Title="@("Theme")" Values="Themes" @bind-SelectedValue="Theme" />

<button class="btn btn-danger" @onclick="@(() => throw new Exception())">
    Error
</button>

@code {

    // ...statements omitted for brevity...
}
```

Restart ASP.NET Core, request `http://localhost:5000/pages/blazor`, and click the Error button. There is no visible change in the browser, but the exception thrown at the server when the button was clicked has proved fatal: the user can still choose values using the select elements because these are presented by the browser, but the event handlers that respond to selections no longer work, and the application is essentially dead.

When there is an unhandled application error, Blazor looks for an element whose `id` is `blazor-error-ui` and sets its CSS `display` property to `block`. Listing 34-31 adds an element with this `id` to the `Blazor.cshtml` file styled to present a useful message.

Listing 34-31. Adding an Error Element in the Blazor.cshtml File in the Pages Folder

```
@page "/pages/blazor"

<h4 class="bg-primary text-white text-center p-2">Departments</h4>

<link rel="stylesheet" href="connectionErrors.css" />

<div id="components-reconnect-modal"
    class="h4 bg-dark text-white text-center my-2 p-2 components-reconnect-hide">
    Blazor Connection Lost
    <div class="reconnect">
        Trying to reconnect...
    </div>
    <div class="failed">
        Reconnection Failed.
        <button class="btn btn-light" onclick="window.Blazor.reconnect()">
            Reconnect
        </button>
    </div>
    <div class="rejected">
        Reconnection Rejected.
        <button class="btn btn-light" onclick="location.reload()">
            Reload
        </button>
    </div>
</div>

<div id="blazor-error-ui"
    class="text-center bg-danger h6 text-white p-2 fixed-top w-100"
    style="display:none">
    An error has occurred. This application will not respond until reloaded.
    <button class="btn btn-sm btn-primary" onclick="location.reload()">
        Reload
    </button>
</div>

<component type="typeof(Advanced.Blazor.DepartmentList)" render-mode="Server" />
```

When the element is shown, the user will be presented with a warning and a button that reloads the browser. To see the effect, restart ASP.NET Core, request `http://localhost:5000/pages/blazor`, and click the Error button, which will display the message shown in Figure 34-13.

Figure 34-13. *Displaying an error message*

Summary

In this chapter, I showed you how to combine Razor Components to create more complex features. I showed you how to create parent/child relationships between components, how to configure components with attributes, and how to create custom events to signal when important changes occur. I also showed you how a component can receive content from its parent and how to generate content consistently using template components, which can be defined with one or more generic type parameters. I finished the chapter by demonstrating how Blazor applications can react to connection and application errors. In the next chapter, I describe the advanced features that Blazor provides.

CHAPTER 35

■ ■ ■

Advanced Blazor Features

In this chapter, I explain how Blazor supports URL routing so that multiple components can be displayed through a single request. I show you how to set up the routing system, how to define routes, and how to create common content in a layout.

This chapter also covers the component lifecycle, which allows components to participate actively in the Blazor environment, which is especially important once you start using the URL routing feature. Finally, this chapter explains the different ways that components can interact outside of the parent/child relationships described in earlier chapters. Table 35-1 puts these features in context.

Table 35-1. *Putting Blazor Routing and Lifecycle Component Interactions in Context*

Question	Answer
What are they?	The routing feature allows components to respond to changes in the URL without requiring a new HTTP connection. The lifecycle feature allows components to define methods that are invoked as the application executes, and the interaction features provide useful ways of communicating between components and with other JavaScript code.
Why are they useful?	These features allow the creation of complex applications that take advantage of the Blazor architecture.
How are they used?	URL routing is set up using built-in components and configured using @page directives. The lifecycle features are used by overriding methods in a component's @code section. The interaction features are used in different ways depending on what a component is interacting with.
Are there any pitfalls or limitations?	These are advanced features that must be used with care, especially when creating interactions outside of Blazor.
Are there any alternatives?	All of the features described in this chapter are optional, but it is hard to create complex applications without them.

Table 35-2 summarizes the chapter.

Table 35-2. *Chapter Summary*

Problem	Solution	Listing
Selecting components based on the current URL	Use URL routing	6–12
Defining content that will be used by multiple components	Use a layout	13, 14
Responding to the stages of the component's lifecycle	Implement the lifecycle notification methods	15–17
Coordinating the activities of multiple components	Retain references with the @ref expression	18–19
Coordinating with code outside of Blazor	Use the interoperability features	20–35

© Adam Freeman 2020
A. Freeman, *Pro ASP.NET Core 3*, https://doi.org/10.1007/978-1-4842-5440-0_35

Preparing for This Chapter

This chapter uses the Advanced project from Chapter 35. No changes are required for this chapter.

■ **Tip** You can download the example project for this chapter—and for all the other chapters in this book—from https://github.com/apress/pro-asp.net-core-3. See Chapter 1 for how to get help if you have problems running the examples.

Open a new PowerShell command prompt, navigate to the folder that contains the Advanced.csproj file, and run the command shown in Listing 35-1 to drop the database.

Listing 35-1. Dropping the Database

```
dotnet ef database drop --force
```

Select Start Without Debugging or Run Without Debugging from the Debug menu or use the PowerShell command prompt to run the command shown in Listing 35-2.

Listing 35-2. Running the Example Application

```
dotnet run
```

Use a browser to request http://localhost:5000/controllers, which will display a list of data items. Request http://localhost:5000/pages/blazor, and you will see the component from Chapter 34 that I used to demonstrate bindings. Figure 35-1 shows both responses.

Figure 35-1. *Running the example application*

Using Component Routing

Blazor includes support for selecting the components to display to the user based on the ASP.NET Core routing system so that the application responds to changes in the URL by displaying different Razor Components. To get started, add a Razor Component named Routed.razor to the Blazor folder with the content shown in Listing 35-3.

Listing 35-3. The Contents of the Routed.razor File in the Blazor Folder

```
<Router AppAssembly="typeof(Startup).Assembly">
    <Found>
        <RouteView RouteData="@context" />
    </Found>
    <NotFound>
        <h4 class="bg-danger text-white text-center p-2">
            No Matching Route Found
        </h4>
    </NotFound>
</Router>
```

The Router component is included with ASP.NET Core and provides the link between Blazor and the ASP.NET Core routing features. Router is a generic template component that defines Found and NotFound sections.

The Router component requires the AppAssembly attribute, which specifies the .NET assembly to use. For most projects this is the current assembly, which is specified like this:

```
...
<Router AppAssembly="typeof(Startup).Assembly">
...
```

The type of the Router component's Found property is RenderFragment<RouteData>, which is passed on to the RouteView component through its RouteData property, like this:

```
...
<Found>
    <RouteView RouteData="@context" />
</Found>
...
```

The RouteView component is responsible for displaying the component matched by the current route and, as I explain shortly, for displaying common content through layouts. The type of the NotFound property is RenderFragment, without a generic type argument, and displays a section of content when no component can be found for the current route.

Preparing the Razor Page

Individual components can be displayed in existing controller views and Razor Pages, as previous chapters have shown. But when using component routing, it is preferable to create a set of URLs that are distinct to working with Blazor because the way that URLs are supported is limited and leads to tortured workarounds. Add a Razor Page named _Host.cshtml to the Pages folder and add the content shown in Listing 35-4.

Listing 35-4. The Contents of the _Host.cshtml File in the Pages Folder

```
@page "/"
@{ Layout = null; }

<!DOCTYPE html>
<html>
<head>
    <title>@ViewBag.Title</title>
    <link href="/lib/twitter-bootstrap/css/bootstrap.min.css" rel="stylesheet" />
    <base href="~/" />
</head>
<body>
```

```
    <div class="m-2">
        <component type="typeof(Advanced.Blazor.Routed)" render-mode="Server" />
    </div>
    <script src="_framework/blazor.server.js"></script>
</body>
</html>
```

This page contains a `component` element that applies the `Routed` component defined in Listing 35-4 and a `script` element for the Blazor JavaScript code. There is also a `link` element for the Bootstrap CSS stylesheet. Alter the configuration for the example application to use the _Host.cshtml file as a fallback when requests are not matched by the existing URL routes, as shown in Listing 35-5.

Listing 35-5. Adding the Fallback in the Startup.cs File in the Advanced Folder

```
...
public void Configure(IApplicationBuilder app, DataContext context) {

    app.UseDeveloperExceptionPage();
    app.UseStaticFiles();
    app.UseRouting();

    app.UseEndpoints(endpoints => {
        endpoints.MapControllerRoute("controllers",
            "controllers/{controller=Home}/{action=Index}/{id?}");
        endpoints.MapDefaultControllerRoute();
        endpoints.MapRazorPages();
        endpoints.MapBlazorHub();
        endpoints.MapFallbackToPage("/_Host");
    });

    SeedData.SeedDatabase(context);
}
...
```

The `MapFallbackToPage` method configures the routing system to use the _Host page as a last resort for unmatched requests.

Adding Routes to Components

Components declare the URLs for which they should be displayed using @page directives. Listing 35-6 adds the @page directive to the `PeopleList` component.

Listing 35-6. Adding a Directive in the PeopleList.razor File in the Blazor Folder

```
@page "/people"

<TableTemplate RowType="Person" RowData="People"
        Highlight="@(p => p.Location.City)" SortDirection="@(p => p.Surname)">
    <Header>
        <tr><th>ID</th><th>Name</th><th>Dept</th><th>Location</th></tr>
    </Header>
    <RowTemplate Context="p">
        <td>@p.PersonId</td>
        <td>@p.Surname, @p.Firstname</td>
        <td>@p.Department.Name</td>
        <td>@p.Location.City, @p.Location.State</td>
    </RowTemplate>
</TableTemplate>

@code {
```

```
    [Inject]
    public DataContext Context { get; set; }

    public IEnumerable<Person> People => Context.People
            .Include(p => p.Department)
            .Include(p => p.Location);
}
```

The directive in Listing 35-6 means the PeopleList component will be displayed for the http://localhost:5000/people URL. Components can declare support for more than one route using multiple @page directives. Listing 35-7 adds @page directives to the DepartmentList component to support two URLs.

Listing 35-7. Adding a Directive in the DepartmentList.razor File in the Blazor Folder

```
@page "/departments"
@page "/depts"

<CascadingValue Name="BgTheme" Value="Theme" IsFixed="false" >
    <TableTemplate RowType="Department" RowData="Departments"
        Highlight="@(d => d.Name)"
        SortDirection="@(d => d.Name)">
        <Header>
            <tr><th>ID</th><th>Name</th><th>People</th><th>Locations</th></tr>
        </Header>
        <RowTemplate Context="d">
            <td>@d.Departmentid</td>
            <td>@d.Name</td>
            <td>@(String.Join(", ", d.People.Select(p => p.Surname)))</td>
            <td>
                @(String.Join(", ",
                    d.People.Select(p => p.Location.City).Distinct()))
            </td>
        </RowTemplate>
    </TableTemplate>
</CascadingValue>

<SelectFilter Title="@("Theme")" Values="Themes" @bind-SelectedValue="Theme" />

<button class="btn btn-danger" @onclick="@(() => throw new Exception())">
    Error
</button>

@code {

    [Inject]
    public DataContext Context { get; set; }

    public IEnumerable<Department> Departments => Context.Departments
            .Include(d => d.People).ThenInclude(p => p.Location);

    public string Theme { get; set; } = "info";
    public string[] Themes = new string[] { "primary", "info", "success" };
}
```

Most of the routing pattern features described in Chapter 13 can be used in @page expressions, except catchall segment variables and optional segment variables. Using two @page expressions, one with a segment variable, can be used to re-create the optional variable feature, as demonstrated in Chapter 36, where I show you how to implement a CRUD application using Blazor.

To see the basic Razor Component routing feature at work, restart ASP.NET Core and request http://localhost:5000/people and http://localhost:5000/depts. Each URL displays one of the components in the application, as shown in Figure 35-2.

Figure 35-2. *Enabling Razor Component routing in the example application*

Setting a Default Component Route

The configuration change in Listing 35-5 set up the fallback route for requests in the Startup class. A corresponding route is required in one of the application's components to identify the component that should be displayed for the application's default URL, http://localhost:5000, as shown in Listing 35-8.

Listing 35-8. Defining the Default Route in the PeopleList.razor File in the Blazor Folder

```
@page "/"
@page "/people"

<TableTemplate RowType="Person" RowData="People"
        Highlight="@(p => p.Location.City)" SortDirection="@(p => p.Surname)">
    <Header>
        <tr><th>ID</th><th>Name</th><th>Dept</th><th>Location</th></tr>
    </Header>
    <RowTemplate Context="p">
        <td>@p.PersonId</td>
        <td>@p.Surname, @p.Firstname</td>
        <td>@p.Department.Name</td>
        <td>@p.Location.City, @p.Location.State</td>
    </RowTemplate>
</TableTemplate>

@code {

    [Inject]
    public DataContext Context { get; set; }

    public IEnumerable<Person> People => Context.People
            .Include(p => p.Department)
            .Include(p => p.Location);
}
```

Restart ASP.NET Core and request http://localhost:5000, and you will see the content produced by the PeopleList component, as shown in Figure 35-3.

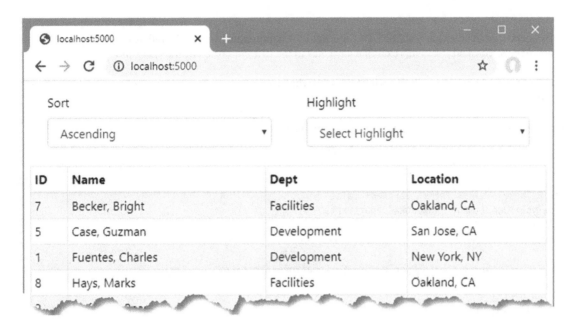

Figure 35-3. *Displaying a component for the default URL*

Navigating Between Routed Components

The basic routing configuration is in place, but it may not be obvious why using routes offers any advantages over the independent components demonstrated in earlier chapters. Improvements come through the NavLink component, which renders anchor elements that are wired into the routing system. Listing 35-9 adds NavLink to the PeopleList component.

Listing 35-9. Adding Navigation in the PeopleList.razor File in the Blazor Folder

```
@page "/"
@page "/people"

<TableTemplate RowType="Person" RowData="People"
        Highlight="@(p => p.Location.City)" SortDirection="@(p => p.Surname)">
    <Header>
        <tr><th>ID</th><th>Name</th><th>Dept</th><th>Location</th></tr>
    </Header>
    <RowTemplate Context="p">
        <td>@p.PersonId</td>
        <td>@p.Surname, @p.Firstname</td>
        <td>@p.Department.Name</td>
        <td>@p.Location.City, @p.Location.State</td>
    </RowTemplate>
</TableTemplate>

<NavLink class="btn btn-primary" href="/depts">Departments</NavLink>

@code {

    [Inject]
    public DataContext Context { get; set; }
```

```
public IEnumerable<Person> People => Context.People
        .Include(p => p.Department)
        .Include(p => p.Location);
}
```

Unlike the anchor elements used in other parts of ASP.NET Core, Navlink components are configured using URLs and not component, page, or action names. The NavLink in this example navigates to the URL supported by the @page directive of the DepartmentList component.

Navigation can also be performed programmatically, which is useful when a component responds to an event and then needs to navigate to a different URL, as shown in Listing 35-10.

Listing 35-10. Navigating Programmatically in the DepartmentList.razor File in the Blazor Folder

```
@page "/departments"
@page "/depts"

<CascadingValue Name="BgTheme" Value="Theme" IsFixed="false" >
    <TableTemplate RowType="Department" RowData="Departments"
        Highlight="@(d => d.Name)"
        SortDirection="@(d => d.Name)">
        <Header>
            <tr><th>ID</th><th>Name</th><th>People</th><th>Locations</th></tr>
        </Header>
        <RowTemplate Context="d">
            <td>@d.Departmentid</td>
            <td>@d.Name</td>
            <td>@(String.Join(", ", d.People.Select(p => p.Surname)))</td>
            <td>
                @(String.Join(", ",
                    d.People.Select(p => p.Location.City).Distinct()))
            </td>
        </RowTemplate>
    </TableTemplate>
</CascadingValue>

<SelectFilter Title="@("Theme")" Values="Themes" @bind-SelectedValue="Theme" />

<button class="btn btn-primary" @onclick="HandleClick">People</button>

@code {

    [Inject]
    public DataContext Context { get; set; }

    public IEnumerable<Department> Departments => Context.Departments
            .Include(d => d.People).ThenInclude(p => p.Location);

    public string Theme { get; set; } = "info";
    public string[] Themes = new string[] { "primary", "info", "success" };

    [Inject]
    public NavigationManager NavManager { get; set; }

    public void HandleClick() => NavManager.NavigateTo("/people");
}
```

The NavigationManager class provides programmatic access to navigation. Table 35-3 describes the most important members provided by the NavigationManager class.

Table 35-3. *Useful NavigationManager Members*

Name	Description
NavigateTo(url)	This method navigates to the specified URL without sending a new HTTP request.
ToAbsoluteUri(path)	This method converts a relative path to a complete URL.
ToBaseRelativePath(url)	This method gets a relative path from a complete URL.
LocationChanged	This event is triggered when the location changes.
Uri	This property returns the current URL.

The NavigationManager class is provided as a service and is received by Razor Components using the Inject attribute, which provides access to the dependency injection features described in Chapter 14.

The NavigationManager.NavigateTo method navigates to a URL and is used in this example to navigate to the /people URL, which will be handled by the PeopleList component.

To see why routing and navigation are important, restart ASP.NET Core and request http://localhost:5000/people. Click the Departments link, which is styled as a button, and the DepartmentList component will be displayed. Click the People link, and you will return to the PeopleList component, as shown in Figure 35-4.

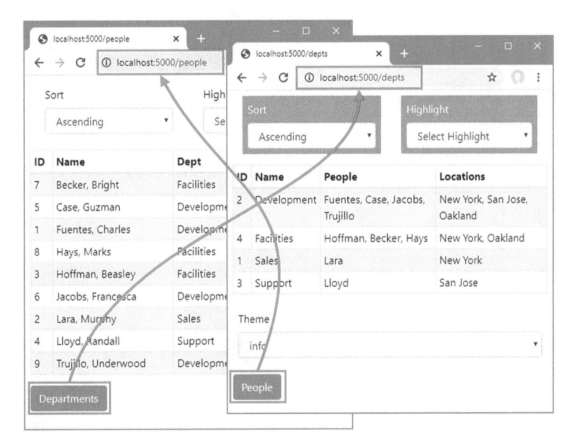

Figure 35-4. *Navigating between routed components*

If you perform this sequence with the F12 developer tools open, you will see that the transition from one component to the next is done without needing a separate HTTP request, even though the URL displayed by the browser changes. Blazor delivers the content rendered by each component over the persistent HTTP connection that is established when the first component is displayed and uses a JavaScript API to navigate without loading a new HTML document.

■ **Tip** The NavigationManager.NavigateTo method accepts an optional argument that, when true, forces the browser to send a new HTTP request and reload the HTML document.

Receiving Routing Data

Components can receive segment variables by decorating a property with the Parameter attribute. To demonstrate, add a Razor Component named PersonDisplay.razor to the Blazor folder with the content shown in Listing 35-11.

Listing 35-11. The Contents of the PersonDisplay.razor in the Blazor Folder

```
@page "/person"
@page "/person/{id:long}"

<h5>Editor for Person: @Id</h5>

<NavLink class="btn btn-primary" href="/people">Return</NavLink>

@code {

    [Parameter]
    public long Id { get; set; }
}
```

This component doesn't do anything other than displaying the value it receives from the routing data until I add features later in the chapter. The @page expression includes a segment variable named id, whose type is specified as long. The component receives the value assigned to the segment variable by defining a property with the same name and decorating it with the Parameter attribute.

■ **Tip** If you don't specify a type for segment variables in the @page expression, then you must set the type of the property to be string.

Listing 35-12 uses the NavLink component to create navigation links for each of the Person objects displayed by the PeopleList component.

Listing 35-12. Adding Navigation Links in the PeopleList.razor File in the Blazor Folder

```
@page "/"
@page "/people"

<TableTemplate RowType="Person" RowData="People"
        Highlight="@(p => p.Location.City)" SortDirection="@(p => p.Surname)">
    <Header>
        <tr><th>ID</th><th>Name</th><th>Dept</th><th>Location</th>
            <td></td>
        </tr>
    </Header>
    <RowTemplate Context="p">
        <td>@p.PersonId</td>
        <td>@p.Surname, @p.Firstname</td>
        <td>@p.Department.Name</td>
        <td>@p.Location.City, @p.Location.State</td>
        <td>
            <NavLink class="btn btn-sm btn-info" href="@GetEditUrl(p.PersonId)">
                Edit
            </NavLink>
```

```
        </td>
     </RowTemplate>
</TableTemplate>

<NavLink class="btn btn-primary" href="/depts">Departments</NavLink>

@code {

    [Inject]
    public DataContext Context { get; set; }

    public IEnumerable<Person> People => Context.People
            .Include(p => p.Department)
            .Include(p => p.Location);

    public string GetEditUrl(long id) => $"/person/{id}";
}
```

Razor Components do no support mixing static content and Razor expressions in attribute values. Instead, I have defined the GetEditUrl method to generate the navigation URLs for each Person object, which is called to produce the value for the NavLink href attributes.

Restart ASP.NET Core, request http://localhost:5000/people, and click one of the Edit buttons. The browser will navigate to the new URL without reloading the HTML document and display the placeholder content generated by the PersonDisplay component, as shown in Figure 35-5, which shows how a component can receive data from the routing system.

Figure 35-5. Receiving data from the routing system in a Razor Component

Defining Common Content Using Layouts

Layouts are template components that provide common content for Razor Components. To create a layout, add a Razor Component called NavLayout.razor to the Blazor folder and add the content shown in Listing 35-13.

Listing 35-13. The Contents of the NavLayout.razor File in the Blazor Folder

```
@inherits LayoutComponentBase

<div class="container-fluid">
    <div class="row">
        <div class="col-3">
            @foreach (string key in NavLinks.Keys) {
                <NavLink class="btn btn-outline-primary btn-block"
                        href="@NavLinks[key]"
                        ActiveClass="btn-primary text-white"
                        Match="NavLinkMatch.Prefix">
```

```
                    @key
                </NavLink>
            }
        </div>
        <div class="col">
            @Body
        </div>
    </div>
</div>

@code {

    public Dictionary<string, string> NavLinks
        = new Dictionary<string, string> {
            {"People", "/people" },
            {"Departments", "/depts" },
            {"Details", "/person" }
        };
}
```

Layouts use @inherits expression to specify the LayoutComponentBase class as the base for the class generated from the Razor Component. The LayoutComponentBase class defines a RenderFragment class named Body that is used to specify the content from components within the common content displayed by the layout. In this example, the layout component creates a grid layout that displays a set of NavLink components for each of the components in the application. The NavLink components are configured with two new attributes, described in Table 35-4.

Table 35-4. *The NavLink Configuration Attributes*

Name	Description
ActiveClass	This attribute specifies one or more CSS classes that the anchor element rendered by the NavLink component will be added to when the current URL matches the href attribute value.
Match	This attribute specifies how the current URL is matched to the href attribute, using a value from the NavLinkMatch enum. The values are Prefix, which considers a match if the href matches the start of the URL, and All, which requires the entire URL to be the same.

The NavLink components are configured to use Prefix matching and to add the anchor elements they render to the Bootstrap btn-primary and text-white classes when there is a match.

Applying a Layout

There are three ways that a layout can be applied. A component can select its own layout using an @layout expression. A parent can use a layout for its child components by wrapping them in the built-in LayoutView component. A layout can be applied to all components by setting the DefaultLayout attribute of the RouteView component, as shown in Listing 35-14.

Listing 35-14. Applying a Layout in the Routed.razor File in the Blazor Folder

```
<Router AppAssembly="typeof(Startup).Assembly">
    <Found>
        <RouteView RouteData="@context" DefaultLayout="typeof(NavLayout)" />
    </Found>
    <NotFound>
        <h4 class="bg-danger text-white text-center p-2">
            Not Matching Route Found
        </h4>
    </NotFound>
</Router>
```

Restart ASP.NET Core and request `http://localhost:5000/people`. The layout will be displayed with the content rendered by the `PeopleList` component. The navigation buttons on the left side of the layout can be used to navigate through the application, as shown in Figure 35-6.

Figure 35-6. *Using a layout component*

■ **Note** If you request `http://localhost:5000`, you will see the content from the `PeopleList` component, but the corresponding navigation button will not be highlighted. I show you how to resolve this problem in the next section.

Understanding the Component Lifecycle Methods

Razor Components have a well-defined lifecycle, which is represented with methods that components can implement to receive notifications of key transitions. Table 35-5 describes the lifecycle methods.

Table 35-5. *The Razor Component Lifecycle Methods*

Name	Description
OnInitialized() OnInitializedAsync()	These methods are invoked when the component is first initialized.
OnParametersSet() OnParametersSetAsync()	These methods are invoked after the values for properties decorated with the `Parameter` attribute have been applied.
ShouldRender()	This method is called before the component's content is rendered to update the content presented to the user. If the method returns `false`, the component's content will not be rendered, and the update is suppressed. This method does not suppress the initial rendering for the component.
OnAfterRender(first) OnAfterRenderAsync(first)	This method is invoked after the component's content is rendered. The `bool` parameter is `true` when Blazor performs the initial render for the component.

Using either the `OnInitialized` or `OnParameterSet` method is useful for setting the initial state of the component. The layout defined in the previous section doesn't deal with the default URL because the `NavLink` component matches only a single URL. The same issue exists for the `DepartmentList` component, which can be requested using the `/departments` and `/depts` paths.

UNDERSTANDING LIFECYCLES FOR ROUTED COMPONENTS

When using URL routing, components can be removed from the display when the URL changes. Components can implement the `System.IDisposable` interface, and Blazor will call the method when the component is removed.

Creating a component that matches multiple URLs requires the use of lifecycle methods. To understand why, add a Razor Component named MultiNavLink.razor to the Blazor folder with the content shown in Listing 35-15.

Listing 35-15. The Contents of the MultiNavLink.razor File in the Blazor Folder

```
<a class="@ComputedClass" @onclick="HandleClick"   href="">
    @ChildContent
</a>

@code {

    [Inject]
    public NavigationManager NavManager { get; set; }

    [Parameter]
    public IEnumerable<string> Href { get; set; }

    [Parameter]
    public string Class { get; set; }

    [Parameter]
    public string ActiveClass { get; set; }

    [Parameter]
    public NavLinkMatch? Match { get; set; }

    public NavLinkMatch ComputedMatch { get =>
            Match ?? (Href.Count() == 1 ? NavLinkMatch.Prefix : NavLinkMatch.All); }

    [Parameter]
    public RenderFragment ChildContent { get; set; }

    public string ComputedClass { get; set; }

    public void HandleClick() {
        NavManager.NavigateTo(Href.First());
    }

    private void CheckMatch(string currentUrl) {
        string path = NavManager.ToBaseRelativePath(currentUrl);
        path = path.EndsWith("/") ? path.Substring(0, path.Length - 1) : path;
        bool match = Href.Any(href => ComputedMatch == NavLinkMatch.All
                ? path == href : path.StartsWith(href));
        ComputedClass = match ? $"{Class} {ActiveClass}" : Class;
    }

    protected override void OnParametersSet() {
        ComputedClass = Class;
        NavManager.LocationChanged += (sender, arg) => CheckMatch(arg.Location);
        Href = Href.Select(h => h.StartsWith("/") ? h.Substring(1) : h);
        CheckMatch(NavManager.Uri);
    }
}
```

This component works in the same way as a regular NavLink but accepts an array of paths to match. The component relies on the OnParametersSet lifecycle method because some initial setup is required that cannot be performed until after values have been assigned to the properties decorated with the Parameter attribute, such as extracting the individual paths.

This component responds to changes in the current URL by listening for the LocationChanged event defined by the NavigationManager class. The event's Location property provides the component with the current URL, which is used to alter the classes for the anchor element. Listing 35-16 applies the new component in the layout.

■ **Tip**   Notice that I have removed the Match attribute in Listing 35-14. The new component supports this attribute but defaults to matching based on the number of paths that it receives through the href attribute.

Listing 35-16. Applying a New Component in the NavLayout.razor File in the Blazor Folder

```
@inherits LayoutComponentBase

<div class="container-fluid">
    <div class="row">
        <div class="col-3">
            @foreach (string key in NavLinks.Keys) {
                <MultiNavLink class="btn btn-outline-primary btn-block"
                        href="@NavLinks[key]" ActiveClass="btn-primary text-white">
                    @key
                </MultiNavLink>
            }
        </div>
        <div class="col">
            @Body
        </div>
    </div>
</div>

@code {

    public Dictionary<string, string[]> NavLinks
        = new Dictionary<string, string[]> {
            {"People", new string[] {"/people", "/" } },
            {"Departments", new string[] {"/depts", "/departments" } },
            {"Details", new string[] { "/person" } }
        };
}
```

Restart ASP.NET Core and request http://localhost:5000 and http://localhost:5000/departments. Both URLs are recognized, and the corresponding navigation buttons are highlighted, as shown in Figure 35-7.

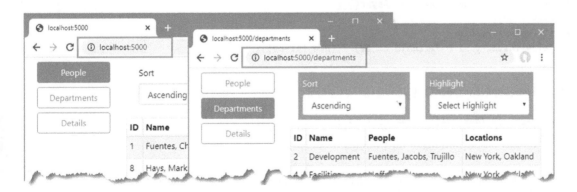

Figure 35-7. Using the lifecycle methods

937

Using the Lifecycle Methods for Asynchronous Tasks

The lifecycle methods are also useful for performing tasks that may complete after the initial content from the component has been rendered, such as querying the database. Listing 35-17 replaces the placeholder content in the PersonDisplay component and uses the lifecycle methods to query the database using values received as parameters.

Listing 35-17. Querying for Data in the PersonDisplay.razor File in the Blazor Folder

```
@page "/person"
@page "/person/{id:long}"

@if (Person == null) {
    <h5 class="bg-info text-white text-center p-2">Loading...</h5>
} else {
    <table class="table table-striped table-bordered">
        <tbody>
            <tr><th>Id</th><td>@Person.PersonId</td></tr>
            <tr><th>Surname</th><td>@Person.Surname</td></tr>
            <tr><th>Firstname</th><td>@Person.Firstname</td></tr>
        </tbody>
    </table>
}

<button class="btn btn-outline-primary" @onclick="@(() => HandleClick(false))">
    Previous
</button>
<button class="btn btn-outline-primary" @onclick="@(() => HandleClick(true))">
    Next
</button>

@code {

    [Inject]
    public DataContext Context { get; set; }

    [Inject]
    public NavigationManager NavManager { get; set; }

    [Parameter]
    public long Id { get; set; } = 0;

    public Person Person { get; set; }

    protected async override Task OnParametersSetAsync() {
        await Task.Delay(1000);
        Person = await Context.People
            .FirstOrDefaultAsync(p => p.PersonId == Id) ?? new Person();
    }

    public void HandleClick(bool increment) {
        Person = null;
        NavManager.NavigateTo($"/person/{(increment ? Id + 1 : Id -1)}");
    }
}
```

The component can't query the database until the parameter values have been set and so the value of the Person property is obtained in the OnParametersSetAsync method. Since the database is running alongside the ASP.NET Core server, I have added a one-second delay before querying the database to help emphasize the way the component works.

The value of the Person property is null until the query has completed, at which point it will be either an object representing the query result or a new Person object if the query doesn't produce a result. A loading message is displayed while the Person object is null.

Restart ASP.NET Core and request http://localhost:5000. Click one of the Edit buttons presented in the table, and the PersonDisplay component will display a summary of the data. Click the Previous and Next buttons to query for the objects with the adjacent primary key values, producing the results shown in Figure 35-8.

Figure 35-8. *Performing asynchronous tasks in a component*

Notice that Blazor doesn't wait for the Task performed in the OnParametersSetAsync method to complete before displaying content to the user, which is why a loading message is useful when the Person property is null. Once the Task is complete and a value has been assigned to the Person property, the component's view is automatically re-rendered, and the changes are sent to the browser over the persistent HTTP connection to be displayed to the user.

Managing Component Interaction

Most components work together through parameters and events, allowing the user's interaction to drive changes in the application. Blazor also provides advanced options for managing interaction with components, which I describe in the following sections.

Using References to Child Components

A parent component can obtain a reference to a child component and use it to consume the properties and methods it defines. In preparation, Listing 35-18 adds a disabled state to the MultiNavLink component.

Listing 35-18. Adding a Feature in the MultiNavLink.razor File in the Blazor Folder

```
<a class="@ComputedClass" @onclick="HandleClick"  href="">
    @if (Enabled) {
        @ChildContent
    } else {
        @("Disabled")
    }
</a>

@code {

    [Inject]
    public NavigationManager NavManager { get; set; }

    [Parameter]
    public IEnumerable<string> Href { get; set; }
```

```
[Parameter]
public string Class { get; set; }

[Parameter]
public string ActiveClass { get; set; }

[Parameter]
public string DisabledClasses { get; set; }

[Parameter]
public NavLinkMatch? Match { get; set; }

public NavLinkMatch ComputedMatch { get =>
        Match ?? (Href.Count() == 1 ? NavLinkMatch.Prefix : NavLinkMatch.All); }

[Parameter]
public RenderFragment ChildContent { get; set; }

public string ComputedClass { get; set; }

public void HandleClick() {
    NavManager.NavigateTo(Href.First());
}

private void CheckMatch(string currentUrl) {
    string path = NavManager.ToBaseRelativePath(currentUrl);
    path = path.EndsWith("/") ? path.Substring(0, path.Length - 1) : path;
    bool match = Href.Any(href => ComputedMatch == NavLinkMatch.All
            ? path == href : path.StartsWith(href));
    if (!Enabled) {
        ComputedClass = DisabledClasses;
    } else {
        ComputedClass = match ? $"{Class} {ActiveClass}" : Class;
    }
}

protected override void OnParametersSet() {
    ComputedClass = Class;
    NavManager.LocationChanged += (sender, arg) => CheckMatch(arg.Location);
    Href = Href.Select(h => h.StartsWith("/") ? h.Substring(1) : h);
    CheckMatch(NavManager.Uri);
}

private bool Enabled { get; set; } = true;

public void SetEnabled(bool enabled) {
    Enabled = enabled;
    CheckMatch(NavManager.Uri);
}
}
```

In Listing 35-19, I have updated the shared layout so that it retains references to the MultiNavLink components and a button that toggles their Enabled property value.

Listing 35-19. Retaining References in the NavLayout.razor File in the Blazor Folder

```
@inherits LayoutComponentBase

<div class="container-fluid">
    <div class="row">
        <div class="col-3">
            @foreach (string key in NavLinks.Keys) {
                <MultiNavLink class="btn btn-outline-primary btn-block"
                        href="@NavLinks[key]"
                        ActiveClass="btn-primary text-white"
                        DisabledClasses="btn btn-dark text-light btn-block disabled"
                        @ref="Refs[key]">
                    @key
                </MultiNavLink>
            }
            <button class="btn btn-secondary btn-block mt-5 " @onclick="ToggleLinks">
                Toggle Links
            </button>
        </div>
        <div class="col">
            @Body
        </div>
    </div>
</div>

@code {

    public Dictionary<string, string[]> NavLinks
        = new Dictionary<string, string[]> {
            {"People", new string[] {"/people", "/" } },
            {"Departments", new string[] {"/depts", "/departments" } },
            {"Details", new string[] { "/person" } }
        };

    public Dictionary<string, MultiNavLink> Refs
        = new Dictionary<string, MultiNavLink>();

    private bool LinksEnabled = true;

    public void ToggleLinks() {
        LinksEnabled = !LinksEnabled;
        foreach (MultiNavLink link in Refs.Values) {
            link.SetEnabled(LinksEnabled);
        }
    }
}
```

References to components are created by adding an @ref attribute and specifying the name of a field or property to which the component should be assigned. Since the MultiNavLink components are created in a @foreach loop driven by a Dictionary, the simplest way to retain references is also in a Dictionary, like this:

```
...
<MultiNavLink class="btn btn-outline-primary btn-block"
    href="@NavLinks[key]" ActiveClass="btn-primary text-white"
    DisabledClasses="btn btn-dark text-light btn-block disabled"
    @ref="Refs[key]">
...
```

As each `MultiNavLink` component is created, it is added to the `Refs` dictionary. Razor Components are compiled into standard C# classes, which means that a collection of `MultiNavLink` components is a collection of `MultiNavlink` objects.

```
...
public Dictionary<string, MultiNavLink> Refs
        = new Dictionary<string, MultiNavLink>();
...
```

Restart ASP.NET Core, request http://localhost:5000, and click the Toggle Links button. The event handler invokes the `ToggleLinks` method, which sets the value of the `Enabled` property for each of the `MultiNavLink` components, as shown in Figure 35-9.

■ **Caution** References can be used only after the component's content has been rendered and the `OnAfterRender/OnAfterRenderAsync` lifecycle methods have been invoked. This makes references ideal for use in event handlers but not the earlier lifecycle methods.

Figure 35-9. *Retaining references to components*

Interacting with Components from Other Code

Components can be used by other code in the ASP.NET Core application, allowing a richer interaction between parts of complex projects. Listing 35-20 alters the method in the `MultiNavLink` component so it can be invoked by other parts of the ASP.NET Core application to enable and disable navigation.

Listing 35-20. Replacing a Method in the MultiNavLink.razor File in the Blazor Folder

```
<a class="@ComputedClass" @onclick="HandleClick"  href="">
    @if (Enabled) {
        @ChildContent
    } else {
        @("Disabled")
    }
</a>

@code {

    // ...other properties and methods omitted for brevity...

    public void SetEnabled(bool enabled) {
        InvokeAsync(() => {
            Enabled = enabled;
            CheckMatch(NavManager.Uri);
```

```
        StateHasChanged();
    });
  }
}
```

Razor Components provide two methods that are used in code that is invoked outside of the Blazor environment, as described in Table 35-6.

Table 35-6. *The Razor Component External Invocation Methods*

Name	Description
InvokeAsync(func)	This method is used to execute a function inside the Blazor environment.
StateHasChanged()	This method is called when a change occurs outside of the normal lifecycle, as shown in the next section.

The InvokeAsync method is used to invoke a function within the Blazor environment, ensuring that changes are processed correctly. The StateHasChanged method is invoked when all the changes have been applied, triggering a Blazor update and ensuring changes are reflected in the component's output.

To create a service that will be available throughout the application, create the Advanced/Services folder and add to it a class file named ToggleService.cs, with the code shown in Listing 35-21.

Listing 35-21. The Contents of the ToggleService.cs File in the Services Folder

```
using Advanced.Blazor;
using System.Collections.Generic;

namespace Advanced.Services {
    public class ToggleService {
        private List<MultiNavLink> components = new List<MultiNavLink>();
        private bool enabled = true;

        public void EnrolComponents(IEnumerable<MultiNavLink> comps) {
            components.AddRange(comps);
        }

        public bool ToggleComponents() {
            enabled = !enabled;
            components.ForEach(c => c.SetEnabled(enabled));
            return enabled;
        }
    }
}
```

This service managed a collection of components and invokes the SetEnabled method on all of them when its ToggleComponents method is called. There is nothing specific to Blazor in this service, which relies on the C# classes that are produced when Razor Component files are compiled. Listing 35-22 updates the application configuration to configure the ToggleService class as a singleton service.

Listing 35-22. Configuring a Service in the Startup.cs File in the Advanced Folder

```
...
public void ConfigureServices(IServiceCollection services) {
    services.AddDbContext<DataContext>(opts => {
        opts.UseSqlServer(Configuration[
            "ConnectionStrings:PeopleConnection"]);
        opts.EnableSensitiveDataLogging(true);
    });
    services.AddControllersWithViews().AddRazorRuntimeCompilation();
```

```
    services.AddRazorPages().AddRazorRuntimeCompilation();
    services.AddServerSideBlazor();
    services.AddSingleton<Services.ToggleService>();
}
...
```

Listing 35-23 updates the Blazor layout so that references to the MultiNavLink components are retained and registered with the new service.

Listing 35-23. Using the Service in the NavLayout.razor File in the Blazor Folder

```
@inherits LayoutComponentBase
@using Advanced.Services

<div class="container-fluid">
    <div class="row">
        <div class="col-3">
            @foreach (string key in NavLinks.Keys) {
                <MultiNavLink class="btn btn-outline-primary btn-block"
                        href="@NavLinks[key]"
                        ActiveClass="btn-primary text-white"
                        DisabledClasses="btn btn-dark text-light btn-block disabled"
                        @ref="Refs[key]">
                    @key
                </MultiNavLink>
            }
            <button class="btn btn-secondary btn-block mt-5 " @onclick="ToggleLinks">
                Toggle Links
            </button>
        </div>
        <div class="col">
            @Body
        </div>
    </div>
</div>

@code {

    [Inject]
    public ToggleService Toggler { get; set; }

    public Dictionary<string, string[]> NavLinks
        = new Dictionary<string, string[]> {
            {"People", new string[] {"/people", "/" } },
            {"Departments", new string[] {"/depts", "/departments" } },
            {"Details", new string[] { "/person" } }
        };

    public Dictionary<string, MultiNavLink> Refs
        = new Dictionary<string, MultiNavLink>();

    protected override void OnAfterRender(bool firstRender) {
        if (firstRender) {
            Toggler.EnrolComponents(Refs.Values);
        }
    }
}
```

```
    public void ToggleLinks() {
        Toggler.ToggleComponents();
    }
}
```

As noted in the previous section, component references are not available until after the content has been rendered. Listing 35-23 uses the OnAfterRender lifecycle method to register the component references with the service, which is received via dependency injection.

The final step is to use the service from a different part of the ASP.NET Core application. Listing 35-24 adds a simple action method to the Home controller that invokes the ToggleService.ToggleComponents method every time it handles a request.

Listing 35-24. Adding an Action Method in the HomeController.cs File in the Controllers Folder

```
using Advanced.Models;
using Microsoft.AspNetCore.Mvc;
using Microsoft.EntityFrameworkCore;
using System.Collections.Generic;
using System.Linq;
using Advanced.Services;

namespace Advanced.Controllers {
    public class HomeController : Controller {
        private DataContext context;
        private ToggleService toggleService;

        public HomeController(DataContext dbContext, ToggleService ts) {
            context = dbContext;
            toggleService = ts;
        }

        public IActionResult Index([FromQuery] string selectedCity) {
            return View(new PeopleListViewModel {
                People = context.People
                    .Include(p => p.Department).Include(p => p.Location),
                Cities = context.Locations.Select(l => l.City).Distinct(),
                SelectedCity = selectedCity
            });
        }

        public string Toggle() => $"Enabled: { toggleService.ToggleComponents() }";
    }

    public class PeopleListViewModel {
        public IEnumerable<Person> People { get; set; }
        public IEnumerable<string> Cities { get; set; }
        public string SelectedCity { get; set; }

        public string GetClass(string city) =>
            SelectedCity == city ? "bg-info text-white" : "";
    }
}
```

Restart ASP.NET Core and request http://localhost:5000. Open a separate browser window and request http://localhost:5000/controllers/home/toggle. When the second request is processed by the ASP.NET Core application, the action method will use the service, which toggles the state of the navigation button. Each time you request /controllers/home/toggle, the state of the navigation buttons will change, as shown in Figure 35-10.

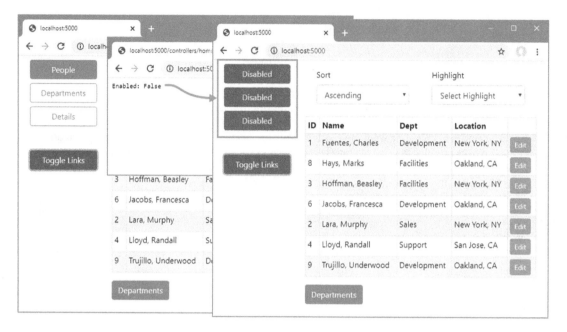

Figure 35-10. *Invoking component methods*

Interacting with Components Using JavaScript

Blazor provides a range of tools for interaction between JavaScript and server-side C# code, as described in the following sections.

Invoking a JavaScript Function from a Component

To prepare for these examples, add a JavaScript file named `interop.js` to the `wwwroot` folder and add the code shown in Listing 35-25.

Listing 35-25. The Contents of the interop.js File in the wwwroot Folder

```
function addTableRows(colCount) {
    let elem = document.querySelector("tbody");
    let row = document.createElement("tr");
    elem.append(row);
    for (let i = 0; i < colCount; i++) {
        let cell = document.createElement("td");
        cell.innerText = "New Elements"
        row.append(cell);
    }
}
```

The JavaScript code uses the API provided by the browser to locate a tbody element, which denotes the body of a table and adds a new row containing the number of cells specified by the function parameter.

To incorporate the JavaScript file into the application, add the element shown in Listing 35-26 to the _Host Razor Page, which was configured as the fallback page that delivers the Blazor application to the browser.

Listing 35-26. Adding an Element in the _Host.cshtml File in the Pages Folder

```
@page "/"
@{ Layout = null; }

<!DOCTYPE html>
<html>
```

```
<head>
    <title>@ViewBag.Title</title>
    <link href="/lib/twitter-bootstrap/css/bootstrap.min.css" rel="stylesheet" />
    <base href="~/" />
</head>
<body>
    <div class="m-2">
        <component type="typeof(Advanced.Blazor.Routed)" render-mode="Server" />
    </div>
    <script src="_framework/blazor.server.js"></script>
    <script src="~/interop.js"></script>
</body>
</html>
```

Listing 35-27 revises the PersonDisplay component so that it renders a button that invokes the JavaScript function when the onclick event is triggered. I have also removed the delay that I added earlier to demonstrate the use of the component lifecycle methods.

Listing 35-27. Invoking a JavaScript Function in the PersonDisplay.razor File in the Blazor Folder

```
@page "/person"
@page "/person/{id:long}"

@if (Person == null) {
    <h5 class="bg-info text-white text-center p-2">Loading...</h5>
} else {
    <table class="table table-striped table-bordered">
        <tbody>
            <tr><th>Id</th><td>@Person.PersonId</td></tr>
            <tr><th>Surname</th><td>@Person.Surname</td></tr>
            <tr><th>Firstname</th><td>@Person.Firstname</td></tr>
        </tbody>
    </table>
}

<button class="btn btn-outline-primary" @onclick="@HandleClick">
    Invoke JS Function
</button>

@code {

    [Inject]
    public DataContext Context { get; set; }

    [Inject]
    public NavigationManager NavManager { get; set; }

    [Inject]
    public IJSRuntime JSRuntime { get; set; }

    [Parameter]
    public long Id { get; set; } = 0;

    public Person Person { get; set; }

    protected async override Task OnParametersSetAsync() {
        //await Task.Delay(1000);
        Person = await Context.People
            .FirstOrDefaultAsync(p => p.PersonId == Id) ?? new Person();
    }
```

```
    public async Task HandleClick() {
        await JSRuntime.InvokeVoidAsync("addTableRows", 2);
    }
}
```

Invoking a JavaScript function is done through the IJSRuntime interface, which components receive through dependency injection. The service is created automatically as part of the Blazor configuration and provides the methods described in Table 35-7.

Table 35-7. *The IJSRuntime Methods*

Name	Description
InvokeAsync<T>(name, args)	This method invokes the specified function with the arguments provided. The result type is specified by the generic type parameter.
InvokeVoidAsync(name, args)	This method invokes a function that doesn't produce a result.

In Listing 35-27, I use the InvokeVoidAsync method to invoke the addTableRows JavaScript function, providing a value for the function parameter. Restart ASP.NET Core, navigate to http://localhost:5000/person/1, and click the Invoke JS Function button. Blazor will invoke the JavaScript function, which adds a row to the end of the table, as shown in Figure 35-11.

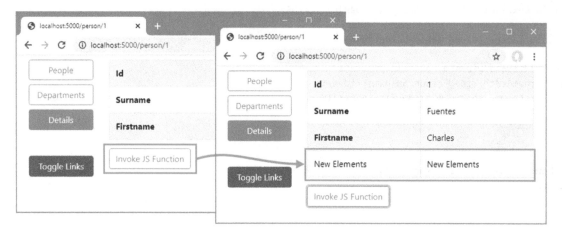

Figure 35-11. *Invoking a JavaScript function*

Retaining References to HTML Elements

Razor Components can retain references to the HTML elements they create and pass those references to JavaScript code. Listing 35-28 changes the JavaScript function from the previous example so that it operates on an HTML element it receives through a parameter.

Listing 35-28. Defining a Parameter in the interop.js File in the wwwroot Folder

```
function addTableRows(colCount, elem) {
    //let elem = document.querySelector("tbody");
    let row = document.createElement("tr");
    elem.parentNode.insertBefore(row, elem);
    for (let i = 0; i < colCount; i++) {
        let cell = document.createElement("td");
        cell.innerText = "New Elements"
        row.append(cell);
    }
}
```

In Listing 35-29, the PersonDisplay component retains a reference to one of the HTML elements it creates and passes it as an argument to the JavaScript function.

Listing 35-29. Retaining a Reference in the PersonDisplay.razor File in the Blazor Folder

```
@page "/person"
@page "/person/{id:long}"

@if (Person == null) {
    <h5 class="bg-info text-white text-center p-2">Loading...</h5>
} else {
    <table class="table table-striped table-bordered">
        <tbody>
            <tr><th>Id</th><td>@Person.PersonId</td></tr>
            <tr @ref="RowReference"><th>Surname</th><td>@Person.Surname</td></tr>
            <tr><th>Firstname</th><td>@Person.Firstname</td></tr>
        </tbody>
    </table>
}

<button class="btn btn-outline-primary" @onclick="@HandleClick">
    Invoke JS Function
</button>

@code {

    [Inject]
    public DataContext Context { get; set; }

    [Inject]
    public NavigationManager NavManager { get; set; }

    [Inject]
    public IJSRuntime JSRuntime { get; set; }

    [Parameter]
    public long Id { get; set; } = 0;

    public Person Person { get; set; }

    protected async override Task OnParametersSetAsync() {
        //await Task.Delay(1000);
        Person = await Context.People
            .FirstOrDefaultAsync(p => p.PersonId == Id) ?? new Person();
    }

    public ElementReference RowReference { get; set; }

    public async Task HandleClick() {
        await JSRuntime.InvokeVoidAsync("addTableRows", 2, RowReference);
    }
}
```

The @ref attribute assigns the HTML element to a property, whose type must be ElementReference. Restart ASP.NET Core, request http://localhost:5000/person/1, and click the Invoke JS Function button. The value of the ElementReference property is passed as an argument to the JavaScript function through the InvokeVoidAsync method, producing the result shown in Figure 35-12.

■ **Note**   The only use for a reference to a regular HTML element is to pass it to a JavaScript function. Use the binding and event features described in earlier chapters to interact with the elements rendered by a component.

Figure 35-12. *Retaining a reference to an HTML element*

Invoking a Component Method from JavaScript

The basic approach for invoking a C# method from JavaScript is to use a static method. Listing 35-30 adds a static method to the MultiNavLink component that changes the enabled state.

Listing 35-30. Introducing Static Members in the MultiNavLink.razor File in the Blazor Folder

```
<a class="@ComputedClass" @onclick="HandleClick"  href="">
    @if (Enabled) {
        @ChildContent
    } else {
        @("Disabled")
    }
</a>

@code {

    // ...other methods and properties omitted for brevity...

    [JSInvokable]
    public static void ToggleEnabled() => ToggleEvent.Invoke(null, new EventArgs());

    private static event EventHandler ToggleEvent;

    protected override void OnInitialized() {
        ToggleEvent += (sender, args) => SetEnabled(!Enabled);
    }
}
```

Static methods must be decorated with the JSInvokable attribute before they can be invoked from JavaScript code. The main limitation of using static methods is that it makes it difficult to update individual components, so I have defined a static event that each instance of the component will handle. The event is named ToggleEvent, and it is triggered by the static method that will be called from JavaScript. To listen for the event, I have used the OnInitialized lifecycle event. When the event is received, the enabled state of the component is toggled through the instance method SetEnabled, which uses the InvokeAsync and StateHasChanged methods required when a change is made outside of Blazor.

Listing 35-31 adds a function to the JavaScript file that creates a button element that invokes the static C# method when it is clicked.

Listing 35-31. Adding a Function in the interop.js File in the wwwroot Folder

```
function addTableRows(colCount, elem) {
    //let elem = document.querySelector("tbody");
    let row = document.createElement("tr");
    elem.parentNode.insertBefore(row, elem);
    for (let i = 0; i < colCount; i++) {
        let cell = document.createElement("td");
        cell.innerText = "New Elements";
        row.append(cell);
    }
}

function createToggleButton() {
    let sibling = document.querySelector("button:last-of-type");
    let button = document.createElement("button");
    button.classList.add("btn", "btn-secondary", "btn-block");
    button.innerText = "JS Toggle";
    sibling.parentNode.insertBefore(button, sibling.nextSibling);
    button.onclick = () => DotNet.invokeMethodAsync("Advanced", "ToggleEnabled");
}
```

The new function locates one of the existing button elements and adds a new button after it. When the button is clicked, the component method is invoked, like this:

```
...
button.onclick = () => DotNet.invokeMethodAsync("Advanced", "ToggleEnabled");
...
```

It is important to pay close attention to the capitalization of the JavaScript function used to C# methods: it is DotNet, followed by a period, followed by invokeMethodAsync, with a lowercase i. The arguments are the name of the assembly and the name of the static method. (The name of the component is not required.)

The button element that the function in Listing 35-31 looks for isn't available until after Blazor has rendered content for the user. For this reason, Listing 35-32 adds a statement to the OnAfterRenderAsync method defined by the NavLayout component to invoke the JavaScript function only when the content has been rendered. (The NavLayout component is the parent to the MultiNavLink components that will be affected when the static method is invoked and allows me to ensure the JavaScript function is invoked only once.)

Listing 35-32. Invoking a JavaScript Function in the NavLayout.razor File in the Blazor Folder

```
...
@code {

    [Inject]
    public IJSRuntime JSRuntime { get; set; }

    [Inject]
    public ToggleService Toggler { get; set; }

    public Dictionary<string, string[]> NavLinks
        = new Dictionary<string, string[]> {
            {"People", new string[] {"/people", "/" } },
            {"Departments", new string[] {"/depts", "/departments" } },
            {"Details", new string[] { "/person" } }
        };
```

```
    public Dictionary<string, MultiNavLink> Refs
        = new Dictionary<string, MultiNavLink>();

    protected async override Task OnAfterRenderAsync(bool firstRender) {
        if (firstRender) {
            Toggler.EnrolComponents(Refs.Values);
            await JSRuntime.InvokeVoidAsync("createToggleButton");
        }
    }

    public void ToggleLinks() {
        Toggler.ToggleComponents();
    }
}
...
```

Restart ASP.NET Core and request http://localhost:5000. Once Blazor has rendered its content, the JavaScript function will be called and creates a new button. Clicking the button invokes the static method, which triggers the event that toggles the state of the navigation buttons and causes a Blazor update, as shown in Figure 35-13.

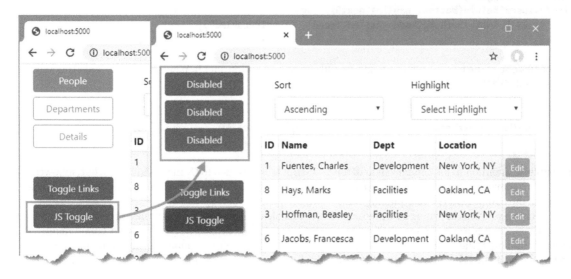

Figure 35-13. *Invoking a component method from JavaScript*

Invoking an Instance Method from a JavaScript Function

Part of the complexity in the previous example comes from responding to a static method to update the Razor Component objects. An alternative approach is to provide the JavaScript code with a reference to an instance method, which it can then invoke directly.

The first step is to add the JSInvokable attribute to the method that the JavaScript code will invoke. I am going to invoke the ToggleComponents methods defined by the ToggleService class, as shown in Listing 35-33.

Listing 35-33. Applying an Attribute in the ToggleService.cs File in the Services Folder

```
using Advanced.Blazor;
using System.Collections.Generic;
using Microsoft.JSInterop;

namespace Advanced.Services {
    public class ToggleService {
        private List<MultiNavLink> components = new List<MultiNavLink>();
        private bool enabled = true;
```

```
public void EnrolComponents(IEnumerable<MultiNavLink> comps) {
    components.AddRange(comps);
}

[JSInvokable]
public bool ToggleComponents() {
    enabled = !enabled;
    components.ForEach(c => c.SetEnabled(enabled));
    return enabled;
}
    }
}
```

The next step is to provide the JavaScript function with a reference to the object whose method will be invoked, as shown in Listing 35-34.

Listing 35-34. Providing an Instance in the NavLayout.razor File in the Blazor Folder

```
...
protected async override Task OnAfterRenderAsync(bool firstRender) {
    if (firstRender) {
        Toggler.EnrolComponents(Refs.Values);
        await JSRuntime.InvokeVoidAsync("createToggleButton",
            DotNetObjectReference.Create(Toggler));
    }
}
...
```

The DotNetObjectReference.Create method creates a reference to an object, which is passed to the JavaScript function as an argument using the JSRuntime.InvokeVoidAsync method. The final step is to receive the object reference in JavaScript and invoke its method when the button element is clicked, as shown in Listing 35-35.

Listing 35-35. Invoking a C# Method in the interop.js File in the wwwroot Folder

```
function addTableRows(colCount, elem) {
    //let elem = document.querySelector("tbody");
    let row = document.createElement("tr");
    elem.parentNode.insertBefore(row, elem);
    for (let i = 0; i < colCount; i++) {
        let cell = document.createElement("td");
        cell.innerText = "New Elements"
        row.append(cell);
    }
}

function createToggleButton(toggleServiceRef) {
    let sibling = document.querySelector("button:last-of-type");
    let button = document.createElement("button");
    button.classList.add("btn", "btn-secondary", "btn-block");
    button.innerText = "JS Toggle";
    sibling.parentNode.insertBefore(button, sibling.nextSibling);
    button.onclick = () => toggleServiceRef.invokeMethodAsync("ToggleComponents");
}
```

The JavaScript function receives the reference to the C# object as a parameter and invokes its methods using invokeMethodAsync, specifying the name of the method as the argument. (Arguments to the method can also be provided but are not required in this example.)

Restart ASP.NET Core, request `http://localhost:5000`, and click the JS Toggle button. The result is the same as shown in Figure 35-13, but the change in the components is managed through the `ToggleService` object.

Summary

In this chapter, I explained how components can be combined with routing to alter the content displayed to the user based on the current URL. I described the component lifecycle and the methods it can implement for each stage in the process, and I finished this chapter by explaining the different ways that component methods can be invoked from outside of Blazor, including interoperability with JavaScript. In the next chapter, I describe the features that Blazor provides for HTML forms.

■ ■ ■

CHAPTER 36

Blazor Forms and Data

In this chapter, I describe the features that Blazor provides for dealing with HTML forms, including support for data validation. I describe the built-in components that Blazor provides and show you how they are used. In this chapter, I also explain how the Blazor model can cause unexpected results with Entity Framework Core and show you how to address these issues. I finish the chapter by creating a simple form application for creating, reading, updating, and deleting data (the CRUD operations) and explain how to extend the Blazor form features to improve the user's experience. Table 36-1 puts the Blazor form features in context.

Table 36-1. *Putting Blazor Form Features in Context*

Question	Answer
What are they?	Blazor provides a set of built-in components that present the user with a form that can be easily validated.
Why are they useful?	Forms remain one of the core building blocks of web applications, and these components provide functionality that will be required in most projects.
How are they used?	The EditForm component is used as a parent for individual form field components.
Are there any pitfalls or limitations?	There can be issues with the way that Entity Framework Core and Blazor work together, and these become especially apparent when using forms.
Are there any alternatives?	You could create your own form components and validation features, although the features described in this chapter are suitable for most projects and, as I demonstrate, can be easily extended.

Table 36-2 summarizes the chapter.

Table 36-2. *Chapter Summary*

Problem	Solution	Listing
Creating an HTML form	Use the EditForm and Input* components	7–9, 13
Validating data	Use the standard validation attributes and the events emitted by the EditForm component	10–12
Discarding unsaved data	Explicitly release the data or create new scopes for components	14–16
Avoiding repeatedly querying the database	Manage query execution explicitly	17–19

Preparing for This Chapter

This chapter uses the Advanced project from Chapter 35. To prepare for this chapter, create the Blazor/Forms folder and add to it a Razor Component named EmptyLayout.razor with the content shown in Listing 36-1. I will use this component as the main layout for this chapter.

▮ **Tip** You can download the example project for this chapter—and for all the other chapters in this book—from `https://github.com/apress/pro-asp.net-core-3`. See Chapter 1 for how to get help if you have problems running the examples.

Listing 36-1. The Contents of the EmptyLayout.razor File in the Blazor/Forms Folder

```
@inherits LayoutComponentBase
<div class="m-2">
    @Body
</div>
```

Add a `RazorComponent` named `FormSpy.razor` to the `Blazor/Forms` folder with the content shown in Listing 36-2. This is a component I will use to display form elements alongside the values that are being edited.

Listing 36-2. The Contents of the FormSpy.razor File in the Blazor/Forms Folder

```
<div class="container-fluid no-gutters">
    <div class="row">
        <div class="col">
            @ChildContent
        </div>
        <div class="col">
            <table class="table table-sm table-striped table-bordered">
                <thead>
                    <tr><th colspan="2" class="text-center">Data Summary</th></tr>
                </thead>
                <tbody>
                    <tr><th>ID</th><td>@PersonData?.PersonId</td></tr>
                    <tr><th>Firstname</th><td>@PersonData?.Firstname</td></tr>
                    <tr><th>Surname</th><td>@PersonData?.Surname</td></tr>
                    <tr><th>Dept ID</th><td>@PersonData?.DepartmentId</td></tr>
                    <tr><th>Location ID</th><td>@PersonData?.LocationId</td></tr>
                </tbody>
            </table>
        </div>
    </div>
</div>

@code {

    [Parameter]
    public RenderFragment ChildContent { get; set; }

    [Parameter]
    public Person PersonData { get; set; }
}
```

Next, add a component named `Editor.razor` to the `Blazor/Forms` folder and add the content shown in Listing 36-3. This component will be used to edit existing `Person` objects and to create new ones.

▮ **Caution** Do not use the `Editor` and `List` components in real projects until you have read the rest of the chapter. I have included common pitfalls that I explain later in the chapter.

Listing 36-3. The Contents of the Editor.razor File in the Blazor/Forms Folder

```
@page "/forms/edit/{id:long}"
@layout EmptyLayout

<h4 class="bg-primary text-center text-white p-2">Edit</h4>

<FormSpy PersonData="PersonData">
    <h4 class="text-center">Form Placeholder</h4>
    <div class="text-center">
        <NavLink class="btn btn-secondary" href="/forms">Back</NavLink>
    </div>
</FormSpy>

@code {

    [Inject]
    public NavigationManager NavManager { get; set; }

    [Inject]
    DataContext Context { get; set; }

    [Parameter]
    public long Id { get; set; }

    public Person PersonData { get; set; } = new Person();

    protected async override Task OnParametersSetAsync() {
        PersonData = await Context.People.FindAsync(Id);
    }
}
```

The component in Listing 36-3 uses an @layout expression to override the default layout and select EmptyLayout. The side-by-side layout is used to present the PersonTable component alongside a placeholder, which is where I will add a form.

Finally, create a component named List.razor in the Blazor/Forms folder and add the content shown in Listing 36-4 to define a component that will present the user with a list of Person objects, presented as a table.

Listing 36-4. The Contents of the List.razor File in the Blazor/Forms Folder

```
@page "/forms"
@page "/forms/list"
@layout EmptyLayout

<h5 class="bg-primary text-white text-center p-2">People</h5>

<table class="table table-sm table-striped table-bordered">
    <thead>
        <tr>
            <th>ID</th><th>Name</th><th>Dept</th><th>Location</th><th></th>
        </tr>
    </thead>
    <tbody>
        @if (People.Count() == 0) {
            <tr><th colspan="5" class="p-4 text-center">Loading Data...</th></tr>
        } else {
            @foreach (Person p in People) {
                <tr>
```

```
                    <td>@p.PersonId</td>
                    <td>@p.Surname, @p.Firstname</td>
                    <td>@p.Department.Name</td>
                    <td>@p.Location.City</td>
                    <td>
                        <NavLink class="btn btn-sm btn-warning"
                            href="@GetEditUrl(p.PersonId)">
                            Edit
                        </NavLink>
                    </td>
                </tr>
            }
        }
    </tbody>
</table>

@code {

    [Inject]
    public DataContext Context { get; set; }

    public IEnumerable<Person> People { get; set; } = Enumerable.Empty<Person>();

    protected override void OnInitialized() {
        People = Context.People.Include(p => p.Department).Include(p => p.Location);
    }

    string GetEditUrl(long id) => $"/forms/edit/{id}";
}
```

Dropping the Database and Running the Application

Open a new PowerShell command prompt, navigate to the folder that contains the Advanced.csproj file, and run the command shown in Listing 36-5 to drop the database.

Listing 36-5. Dropping the Database

```
dotnet ef database drop --force
```

Select Start Without Debugging or Run Without Debugging from the Debug menu or use the PowerShell command prompt to run the command shown in Listing 36-6.

Listing 36-6. Running the Example Application

```
dotnet run
```

Use a browser to request http://localhost:5000/forms, which will produce a data table. Click one of the Edit buttons, and you will see a placeholder for the form and a summary showing the current property values of the selected Person object, as shown in Figure 36-1.

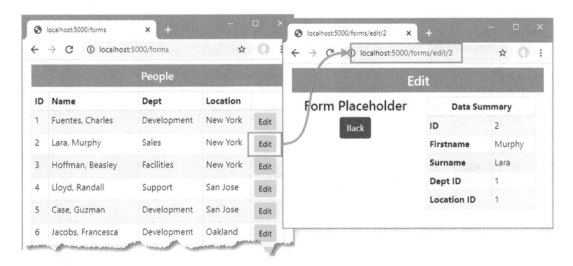

Figure 36-1. *Running the example application*

Using the Blazor Form Components

Blazor provides a set of built-in components that are used to render form elements, ensuring that the server-side component properties are updated after user interaction and integrating validation. Table 36-3 describes the components that Blazor provides.

Table 36-3. *The Bazor Form Components*

Name	Description
EditForm	This component renders a form element that is wired up for data validation.
InputText	This component renders an input element that is bound to a C# string property.
InputCheckbox	This component renders an input element whose type attribute is checkbox and that is bound to a C# bool property.
InputDate	This component renders an input element those type attribute is date and that is bound to a C# DateTime or DateTimeOffset property.
InputNumber	This component renders an input element those type attribute is number and that is bound to a C# int, long, float, double, or decimal value.
InputTextArea	This component renders a textarea component that is bound to a C# string property.

The EditForm component must be used for any of the other components to work. In Listing 36-7, I have added an EditForm, along with InputText components that represent two of the properties defined by the Person class.

Listing 36-7. Using Form Components in the Editor.razor File in the Blazor/Forms Folder

```
@page "/forms/edit/{id:long}"
@layout EmptyLayout

<h4 class="bg-primary text-center text-white p-2">Edit</h4>

<FormSpy PersonData="PersonData">
    <EditForm Model="PersonData">
        <div class="form-group">
            <label>Person ID</label>
            <InputNumber class="form-control"
                @bind-Value="PersonData.PersonId" disabled />
        </div>
```

```
        <div class="form-group">
            <label>Firstname</label>
            <InputText class="form-control" @bind-Value="PersonData.Firstname" />
        </div>
        <div class="form-group">
            <label>Surname</label>
            <InputText class="form-control" @bind-Value="PersonData.Surname" />
        </div>
        <div class="form-group">
            <label>Dept ID</label>
            <InputNumber class="form-control"
                @bind-Value="PersonData.DepartmentId" />
        </div>
        <div class="text-center">
            <NavLink class="btn btn-secondary" href="/forms">Back</NavLink>
        </div>
    </EditForm>
</FormSpy>

@code {

    // ...statements omitted for brevity...
}
```

The EditForm component renders a form element and provides the foundation for the validation features described in the "Validating Form Data" section. The Model attribute is used to provide the EditForm with the object that the form is used to edit and validate.

The components in Table 36-3 whose names begin with Input are used to display an input or textarea element for a single model property. These components define a custom binding named Value that is associated with the model property using the @bind-Value attribute. The property-level components must be matched to the type of the property they present to the user. It is for this reason that I have used the InputText component for the Firstname and Surname properties of the Person class, while the InputNumber component is used for the PersonId and DepartmentId properties. If you use a property-level component with a model property of the wrong type, you will receive an error when the component attempts to parse a value entered into the HTML element.

Restart ASP.NET Core and request http://localhost:5000/forms/edit/2, and you will see the three input elements displayed. Edit the values and move the focus by pressing the Tab key, and you will see the summary data on the right of the window update, as shown in Figure 36-2. The built-in form components support attribute splatting, which is why the disabled attribute applied to the InputNumber component for the PersonId property has been applied to the input element.

Figure 36-2. *Using the Blazor form elements*

960

Creating Custom Form Components

Blazor provides built-in components for only input and textarea elements. Fortunately, creating a custom component that integrates into the Blazor form features is a simple process. Add a Razor Component named CustomSelect.razor to the Blazor/Forms folder and use it to define the component shown in Listing 36-8.

Listing 36-8. The Contents of the CustomSelect.razor File in the Blazor/Forms Folder

```
@typeparam TValue
@inherits InputBase<TValue>

<select class="form-control @CssClass" value="@CurrentValueAsString"
        @onchange="@(ev => CurrentValueAsString = ev.Value as string)">
    @ChildContent
    @foreach (KeyValuePair<string, TValue> kvp in Values) {
        <option value="@kvp.Value">@kvp.Key</option>
    }
</select>

@code {

    [Parameter]
    public RenderFragment ChildContent { get; set; }

    [Parameter]
    public IDictionary<string, TValue> Values { get; set; }

    [Parameter]
    public Func<string, TValue> Parser { get; set; }

    protected override bool TryParseValueFromString(string value, out TValue result,
            out string validationErrorMessage) {
        try {
            result = Parser(value);
            validationErrorMessage = null;
            return true;
        } catch {
            result = default(TValue);
            validationErrorMessage = "The value is not valid";
            return false;
        }
    }
}
```

The base class for form components is InputBase<TValue>, where the generic type argument is the model property type the component represents. The base class takes care of most of the work and provides the CurrentValueAsString property, which is used to provide the current value in event handlers when the user selects a new value, like this:

```
...
<select class="form-control @CssClass" value="@CurrentValueAsString"
        @onchange="@(ev => CurrentValueAsString = ev.Value as string)">
...
```

In preparation for data validation, which I describe in the next section, this component includes the value of the CssClass property in the select element's class attribute, like this:

```
...
<select class="form-control @CssClass" value="@CurrentValueAsString"
        @onchange="@(ev => CurrentValueAsString = ev.Value as string)">
...
```

961

The abstract TryParseValueFromString method has to be implemented so that the base class is able to map between string values used by HTML elements and the corresponding value for the C# model property. I don't want to implement my custom select element to any specific C# data type, so I have used an @typeparam expression to define a generic type parameter. The Values property is used to receive a dictionary mapping string values that will be displayed to the user and TValue values that will be used as C# values. The method receives two out parameters that are used to set the parsed value and a parser validation error message that will be displayed to the user if there is a problem. Since I am working with generic types, the Parser property receives a function that is invoked to parse a string value into a TValue value.

Listing 36-9 applies the new form component so the user can select values for the DepartmentId and LocationId properties defined by the Person class.

Listing 36-9. Using a Custom Form Element in the Editor.razor File in the Blazor/Forms Folder

```
@page "/forms/edit/{id:long}"
@layout EmptyLayout

<h4 class="bg-primary text-center text-white p-2">Edit</h4>

<FormSpy PersonData="PersonData">

    <EditForm Model="PersonData">
        <div class="form-group">
            <label>Firstname</label>
            <InputText class="form-control" @bind-Value="PersonData.Firstname" />
        </div>
        <div class="form-group">
            <label>Surname</label>
            <InputText class="form-control" @bind-Value="PersonData.Surname" />
        </div>
        <div class="form-group">
            <label>Dept ID</label>
            <CustomSelect TValue="long" Values="Departments"
                          Parser="@(str => long.Parse(str))"
                          @bind-Value="PersonData.DepartmentId">
                <option selected disabled value="0">Choose a Department</option>
            </CustomSelect>
        </div>
        <div class="form-group">
            <label>Location ID</label>
            <CustomSelect TValue="long" Values="Locations"
                          Parser="@(str => long.Parse(str))"
                          @bind-Value="PersonData.LocationId">
                <option selected disabled value="0">Choose a Location</option>
            </CustomSelect>
        </div>
        <div class="text-center">
            <NavLink class="btn btn-secondary" href="/forms">Back</NavLink>
        </div>
    </EditForm>
</FormSpy>

@code {

    [Inject]
    public NavigationManager NavManager { get; set; }

    [Inject]
    DataContext Context { get; set; }
```

```
[Parameter]
public long Id { get; set; }

public Person PersonData { get; set; } = new Person();

public IDictionary<string, long> Departments { get; set; }
    = new Dictionary<string, long>();
public IDictionary<string, long> Locations { get; set; }
    = new Dictionary<string, long>();

protected async override Task OnParametersSetAsync() {
    PersonData = await Context.People.FindAsync(Id);
    Departments = await Context.Departments
        .ToDictionaryAsync(d => d.Name, d => d.Departmentid);
    Locations = await Context.Locations
        .ToDictionaryAsync(l => $"{l.City}, {l.State}", l => l.LocationId);
    }
}
```

I use the Entity Framework Core ToDictionaryAsync method to create collections of values and labels from the Department and Location data and use them to configure the CustomSelect components. Restart ASP.NET Core and request http://localhost:5000/forms/edit/2; you will see the select elements shown in Figure 36-3. When you pick a new value, the CustomSelect component will update the CurrentValueAsString property, which will result in a call to the TryParseValueFromString method, with the result used to update the Value binding.

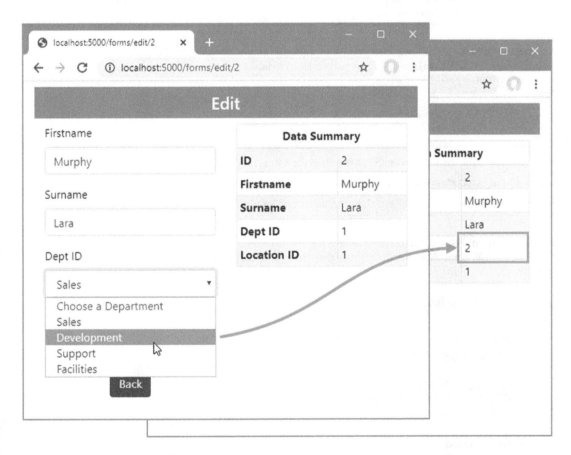

Figure 36-3. *Using a custom form element*

Validating Form Data

Blazor provides components that perform validation using the standard attributes. Table 36-4 describes the validation components.

Table 36-4. *The Blazor Validation Components*

Name	Description
DataAnnotationsValidator	This component integrates the validation attributes applied to the model class into the Blazor form features.
ValidationMessage	This component displays validation error messages for a single property.
ValidationSummary	This component displays validation error messages for the entire model object.

The validation components generate elements assigned to classes, described in Table 36-5, which can be styled with CSS to draw the user's attention.

Table 36-5. *The Classes Used by the Blazor Validation Components*

Name	Description
validation-errors	The ValidationSummary component generates a ul element that is assigned to this class and is the top-level container for the summary of validation messages.
validation-message	The ValidationSummary component populates its ul element with li elements assigned to this class for each validation message. The ValidationMessage component renders a div element assigned to this class for its property-level messages.

The Blazor Input* components add the HTML elements they generate to the classes described in Table 36-6 to indicate validation status. This includes the InputBase<TValue> class from which I derived the CustomSelect component and is the purpose of the CssClass property in Listing 36-8.

Table 36-6. *The Validation Classes Added to Form Elements*

Name	Description
modified	Elements are added to this class once the user has edited the value.
valid	Elements are added to this class if the value they contain passes validation.
invalid	Elements are added to this class if the value they contain fails validation.

This combination of components and classes can be confusing at first, but the key is to start by defining the CSS styles you require based on the classes in Tables 36-5 and 36-6. Add a CSS Stylesheet named blazorValidation.css to the wwwroot folder with the content shown in Listing 36-10.

Listing 36-10. The Contents of the blazorValidation.css File in the wwwroot Folder

```
.validation-errors {
    background-color: rgb(220, 53, 69); color: white; padding: 8px;
    text-align: center; font-size: 16px; font-weight: 500;
}
div.validation-message { color: rgb(220, 53, 69); font-weight: 500 }
.modified.valid { border: solid 3px rgb(40, 167, 69); }
.modified.invalid { border: solid 3px rgb(220, 53, 69); }
```

These styles format error messages in red and apply a red or green border to individual form elements. Listing 36-11 imports the CSS stylesheet and applies the Blazor validation components.

Listing 36-11. Applying Validation Components in the Editor.razor File in the Blazor/Forms Folder

```
@page "/forms/edit/{id:long}"
@layout EmptyLayout

<link href="/blazorValidation.css" rel="stylesheet" />
<h4 class="bg-primary text-center text-white p-2">Edit</h4>

<FormSpy PersonData="PersonData">
    <EditForm Model="PersonData">
        <DataAnnotationsValidator />
        <ValidationSummary />
        <div class="form-group">
            <label>Firstname</label>
            <ValidationMessage For="@(() => PersonData.Firstname)" />
            <InputText class="form-control" @bind-Value="PersonData.Firstname" />
        </div>
        <div class="form-group">
            <label>Surname</label>
            <ValidationMessage For="@(() => PersonData.Surname)" />
            <InputText class="form-control" @bind-Value="PersonData.Surname" />
        </div>
        <div class="form-group">
            <label>Dept ID</label>
            <ValidationMessage For="@(() => PersonData.DepartmentId)" />
            <CustomSelect TValue="long" Values="Departments"
                          Parser="@(str => long.Parse(str))"
                          @bind-Value="PersonData.DepartmentId">
                <option selected disabled value="0">Choose a Department</option>
            </CustomSelect>
        </div>
        <div class="form-group">
            <label>Location ID</label>
            <ValidationMessage For="@(() => PersonData.LocationId)" />
            <CustomSelect TValue="long" Values="Locations"
                          Parser="@(str => long.Parse(str))"
                          @bind-Value="PersonData.LocationId">
                <option selected disabled value="0">Choose a Location</option>
            </CustomSelect>
        </div>
        <div class="text-center">
            <NavLink class="btn btn-secondary" href="/forms">Back</NavLink>
        </div>
    </EditForm>
</FormSpy>

@code {

    // ...statements omitted for brevity...
}
```

The DataAnnotationsValidator and ValidationSummary components are applied without any configuration attributes. The ValidationMessage attribute is configured using the For attribute, which receives a function that returns the property the component represents. For example, here is the expression that selects the Firstname property:

```
...
<ValidationMessage For="@(() => PersonData.Firstname)" />
...
```

The expression defines no parameters and selects the property from the object used for the Model attribute of the EditForm component and not the model type. For this example, this means the expression operates on the PersonData object and not the Person class.

■ **Tip** Blazor isn't always able to determine the type of the property for the ValidationMessage component. If you receive an exception, then you can add a TValue attribute to set the type explicitly. For example, if the type of the property the ValidationMessage represents is long, then add a TValue="long" attribute.

The final step for enabling data validation is to apply attributes to the model class, as shown in Listing 36-12.

Listing 36-12. Applying Validation Attributes in the Person.cs File in the Models Folder

```
using System.Collections.Generic;
using System.ComponentModel.DataAnnotations;

namespace Advanced.Models {

    public class Person {

        public long PersonId { get; set; }

        [Required(ErrorMessage = "A firstname is required")]
        [MinLength(3, ErrorMessage = "Firstnames must be 3 or more characters")]
        public string Firstname { get; set; }

        [Required(ErrorMessage = "A surname is required")]
        [MinLength(3, ErrorMessage = "Surnames must be 3 or more characters")]
        public string Surname { get; set; }

        [Required]
        [Range(1, long.MaxValue,
            ErrorMessage = "A department must be selected")]
        public long DepartmentId { get; set; }

        [Required]
        [Range(1, long.MaxValue,
            ErrorMessage = "A location must be selected")]
        public long LocationId { get; set; }

        public Department Department { get; set; }
        public Location Location { get; set; }
    }
}
```

To see the effect of the validation components, restart ASP.NET Core and request http://localhost:5000/forms/edit/2. Clear the Firstname field and move the focus by pressing the Tab key or clicking on another field. As the focus changes, validation is performed, and error messages will be displayed. The Editor component shows both summary and per-property messages, so you will see the same error message shown twice. Delete all but the first two characters from the Surname field, and a second validation message will be displayed when you change the focus, as shown in Figure 36-4. (There is validation support for the other properties, too, but the select element doesn't allow the user to select an invalid valid. If you change a value, the select element will be decorated with a green border to indicate a valid selection, but you won't be able to see an invalid response until I demonstrate how the form components can be used to create new data objects.)

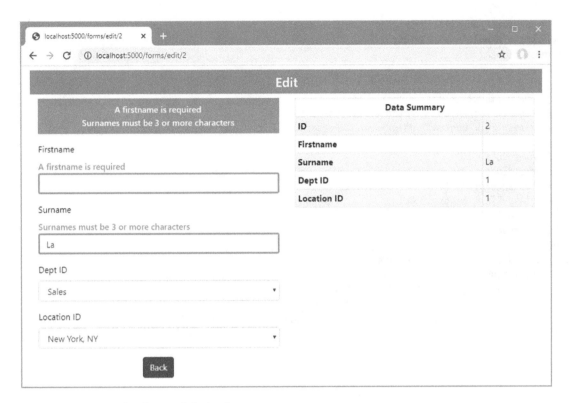

Figure 36-4. *Using the Blazor validation features*

Handling Form Events

The EditForm component defines events that allow an application to respond to user action, as described in Table 36-7.

Table 36-7. *The EditForm Events*

Name	Description
OnValidSubmit	This event is triggered when the form is submitted and the form data passes validation.
OnInvalidSubmit	This event is triggered when the form is submitted and the form data fails validation.
OnSubmit	This event is triggered when the form is submitted and before validation is performed.

These events are triggered by adding a conventional submit button within the content contained by the EditForm component. The EditForm component handles the onsubmit event sent by the form element it renders, applies validation, and triggers the events described in the table. Listing 36-13 adds a submit button to the Editor component and handles the EditForm events.

Listing 36-13. Handling EditForm Events in the Editor.razor File in the Blazor/Forms Folder

```
@page "/forms/edit/{id:long}"
@layout EmptyLayout

<link href="/blazorValidation.css" rel="stylesheet" />

<h4 class="bg-primary text-center text-white p-2">Edit</h4>
<h6 class="bg-info text-center text-white p-2">@FormSubmitMessage</h6>

<FormSpy PersonData="PersonData">
```

```
    <EditForm Model="PersonData" OnValidSubmit="HandleValidSubmit"
            OnInvalidSubmit="HandleInvalidSubmit">
        <DataAnnotationsValidator />
        <ValidationSummary />
        <div class="form-group">
            <label>Firstname</label>
            <ValidationMessage For="@(() => PersonData.Firstname)" />
            <InputText class="form-control" @bind-Value="PersonData.Firstname" />
        </div>
        <div class="form-group">
            <label>Surname</label>
            <ValidationMessage For="@(() => PersonData.Surname)" />
            <InputText class="form-control" @bind-Value="PersonData.Surname" />
        </div>
        <div class="form-group">
            <label>Dept ID</label>
            <ValidationMessage For="@(() => PersonData.DepartmentId)" />
            <CustomSelect TValue="long" Values="Departments"
                        Parser="@(str => long.Parse(str))"
                        @bind-Value="PersonData.DepartmentId">
                <option selected disabled value="0">Choose a Department</option>
            </CustomSelect>
        </div>
        <div class="form-group">
            <label>Location ID</label>
            <ValidationMessage For="@(() => PersonData.LocationId)" />
            <CustomSelect TValue="long" Values="Locations"
                        Parser="@(str => long.Parse(str))"
                        @bind-Value="PersonData.LocationId">
                <option selected disabled value="0">Choose a Location</option>
            </CustomSelect>
        </div>
        <div class="text-center">
            <button type="submit" class="btn btn-primary">Submit</button>
            <NavLink class="btn btn-secondary" href="/forms">Back</NavLink>
        </div>
    </EditForm>
</FormSpy>

@code {

    // ...other statements omitted for brevity...

    public string FormSubmitMessage { get; set; } = "Form Data Not Submitted";
    public void HandleValidSubmit() => FormSubmitMessage = "Valid Data Submitted";
    public void HandleInvalidSubmit() =>
        FormSubmitMessage = "Invalid Data Submitted";
}
```

Restart ASP.NET Core and request http://localhost:5000/forms/edit/2. Clear the Firstname field, and click the Submit button. In addition to the validation error, you will see a message indicating that the form was submitted with invalid data. Enter a name into the field and click Submit again, and the message will change, as shown in Figure 36-5.

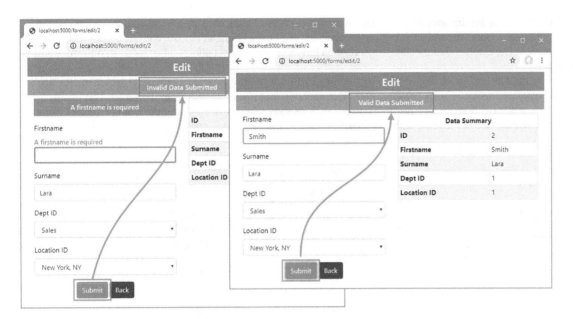

Figure 36-5. *Handling EditForm events*

Using Entity Framework Core with Blazor

The Blazor model changes the way that Entity Framework Core behaves, which can lead to unexpected results if you are used to writing conventional ASP.NET Core applications. In the sections that follow, I explain the issues and how to avoid the problems that can arise.

Understanding the Entity Framework Core Context Scope Issue

To see the first issue, request `http://localhost:5000/forms/edit/2`, clear the Firstname field, and change the contents of the Surname field to **La**. Neither of these values passes validation, and you will see error messages as you move between the form elements. Click the Back button, and you will see that the data table reflects the changes you made, as shown in Figure 36-6, even though they were not valid.

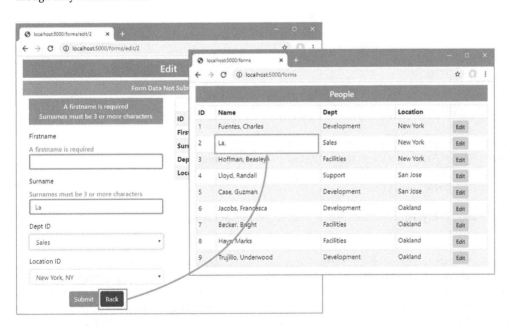

Figure 36-6. *The effect of editing data*

In a conventional ASP.NET Core application, written using controllers or Razor Pages, clicking a button triggers a new HTTP request. Each request is handled in isolation, and each request receives its own Entity Framework Core context object, which is configured as a scoped service. The result is that the data created when handling one request affects other requests only once it has been written to the database.

In a Blazor application, the routing system responds to URL changes without sending new HTTP requests, which means that multiple components are displayed using only the persistent HTTP connection that Blazor maintains to the server. This results in a single dependency injection scope being shared by multiple components, as shown in Figure 36-7, and the changes made by one component will affect other components even if the changes are not written to the database.

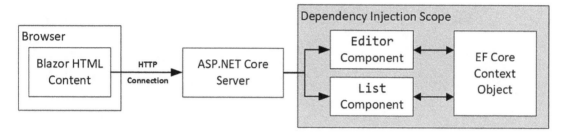

Figure 36-7. *The use of an Entity Framework Core context in a Blazor application*

Entity Framework Core is trying to be helpful, and this approach allows complex data operations to be performed over time before being stored (or discarded). Unfortunately, much like the helpful approach Entity Framework Core takes to dealing with related data, which I described in Chapter 35, it presents a pitfall for the unwary developer who expects components to handle data like the rest of ASP.NET Core.

Discarding Unsaved Data Changes

If sharing a context between components is appealing, which it will be for some applications, then you can embrace the approach and ensure that components discard any changes when they are destroyed, as shown in Listing 36-14.

Listing 36-14. Discarding Unsaved Data Changes in the Editor.razor File in the Blazor/Forms Folder

```
@page "/forms/edit/{id:long}"
@layout EmptyLayout
@implements IDisposable

<!-- ...elements omitted for brevity... -->

@code {

    // ...statements omitted for brevity...

    public string FormSubmitMessage { get; set; } = "Form Data Not Submitted";
    public void HandleValidSubmit() => FormSubmitMessage = "Valid Data Submitted";
    public void HandleInvalidSubmit() =>
        FormSubmitMessage = "Invalid Data Submitted";

    public void Dispose() => Context.Entry(PersonData).State = EntityState.Detached;
}
```

As I noted in Chapter 35, components can implement the System.IDisposable interface, and the Dispose method will be invoked when the component is about to be destroyed, which happens when navigation to another component occurs. In Listing 36-14, the implementation of the Dispose method tells Entity Framework Core to disregard the PersonData object, which means it won't be used to satisfy future requests. To see the effect, restart ASP.NET Core, request http://localhost:5000/forms/edit/2, clear the Firstname field, and click the Back button. The modified Person object is disregarded when Entity Framework Core provides the List component with its data, as shown in Figure 36-8.

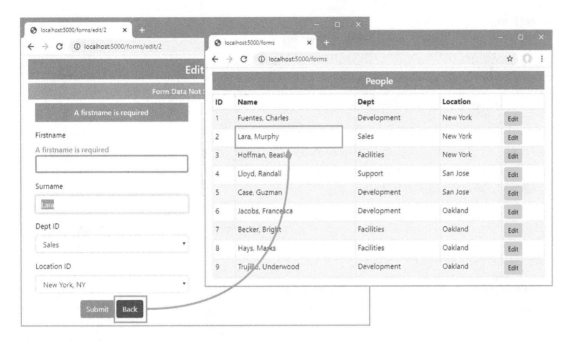

Figure 36-8. *Discarding data objects*

Creating New Dependency Injection Scopes

You must create new dependency injection scopes if you want to preserve the model used by the rest of ASP.NET Core and have each component receive its own Entity Framework Core context object. This is done by using the @inherits expression to set the base class for the component to OwningComponentBase or OwningComponentBase<T>.

The OwningComponentCase class defines a ScopedServices property that is inherited by the component and that provides an IServiceProvider object that can be used to obtain services that are created in a scope that is specific to the component's lifecycle and will not be shared with any other component, as shown in Listing 36-15.

Listing 36-15. Using a New Scope in the Editor.razor File in the Blazor/Forms Folder

```
@page "/forms/edit/{id:long}"
@layout EmptyLayout
@inherits OwningComponentBase
@using Microsoft.Extensions.DependencyInjection

<link href="/blazorValidation.css" rel="stylesheet" />

<h4 class="bg-primary text-center text-white p-2">Edit</h4>
<h6 class="bg-info text-center text-white p-2">@FormSubmitMessage</h6>

<!-- ...elements omitted for brevity... -->

@code {

    [Inject]
    public NavigationManager NavManager { get; set; }

    //[Inject]
    DataContext Context => ScopedServices.GetService<DataContext>();

    [Parameter]
    public long Id { get; set; }

    // ...statements omitted for brevity...
```

971

```
//public void Dispose() =>
//        Context.Entry(PersonData).State = EntityState.Detached;
}
```

In the listing, I commented out the Inject attribute and set the value of the Context property by obtaining a DataContext service. The Microsoft.Extensions.DependencyInjection namespace contains extension methods that make it easier to obtain services from an IServiceProvider object, as described in Chapter 14.

■ **Note** Changing the base class doesn't affect services that are received using the Inject attribute, which will still be obtained within the request scope. Each service that you require in the dedicated component's scope must be obtained through the ScopedServices property, and the Inject attribute should not be applied to that property.

The OwningComponentBase<T> class defines an additional convenience property that provides access to a scoped service of type T and that can be useful if a component requires only a single scoped service, as shown in Listing 36-16 (although further services can still be obtained through the ScopedServices property).

Listing 36-16. Using the Typed Base Class in the Editor.razor File in the Blazor/Forms Folder

```
@page "/forms/edit/{id:long}"
@layout EmptyLayout
@inherits OwningComponentBase<DataContext>

<link href="/blazorValidation.css" rel="stylesheet" />

<h4 class="bg-primary text-center text-white p-2">Edit</h4>
<h6 class="bg-info text-center text-white p-2">@FormSubmitMessage</h6>

<!-- ...elements omitted for brevity... -->

@code {

    [Inject]
    public NavigationManager NavManager { get; set; }

    //[Inject]
    DataContext Context => Service;

    // ...statements omitted for brevity...
}
```

The scoped service is available through a property named Service. In this example, I specified DataContext as the type argument for the base class.

Regardless of which base class is used, the result is that the Editor component has its own dependency injection scope and its own DataContext object. The List component has not been modified, so it will receive the request-scoped DataContext object, as shown in Figure 36-9.

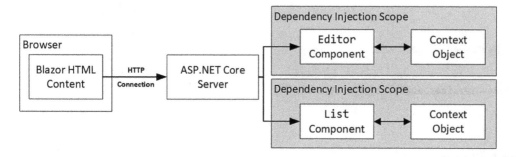

Figure 36-9. Using scoped services for components

Restart ASP.NET Core, navigate to `http://localhost:5000/forms/edit/2`, clear the Firstname field, and click the Back button. The changes made by the Editor component are not saved to the database, and since the Editor component's data context is separate from the one used by the List component, the edited data is discarded, producing the same response as shown in Figure 36-8.

Understanding the Repeated Query Issue

Blazor responds to changes in state as efficiently as possible but still has to render a component's content to determine the changes that should be sent to the browser.

One consequence of the way that Blazor works is that it can lead to a sharp increase in the number of queries sent to the database. To demonstrate the issue, Listing 36-17 adds a button that increments a counter to the List component.

Listing 36-17. Adding a Button in the List.razor File in the Blazor/Forms Folder

```
@page "/forms"
@page "/forms/list"
@layout EmptyLayout

<h5 class="bg-primary text-white text-center p-2">People</h5>

<table class="table table-sm table-striped table-bordered">
    <thead>
        <tr>
            <th>ID</th><th>Name</th><th>Dept</th><th>Location</th><th></th>
        </tr>
    </thead>
    <tbody>
        @if  (People.Count() == 0) {
            <tr><th colspan="5" class="p-4 text-center">Loading Data...</th></tr>
        } else {
            @foreach (Person p in People) {
                <tr>
                    <td>@p.PersonId</td>
                    <td>@p.Surname, @p.Firstname</td>
                    <td>@p.Department.Name</td>
                    <td>@p.Location.City</td>
                    <td>
                        <NavLink class="btn btn-sm btn-warning"
                                href="@GetEditUrl(p.PersonId)">
                            Edit
                        </NavLink>
                    </td>
                </tr>
            }
        }
    </tbody>
</table>

<button class="btn btn-primary" @onclick="@(() => Counter++)">Increment</button>
<span class="h5">Counter: @Counter</span>

@code {

    [Inject]
    public DataContext Context { get; set; }

    public IEnumerable<Person> People { get; set; } = Enumerable.Empty<Person>();
```

```
    protected override void OnInitialized() {
        People = Context.People.Include(p => p.Department).Include(p => p.Location);
    }

    string GetEditUrl(long id) => $"/forms/edit/{id}";

    public int Counter { get; set; } = 0;
}
```

Restart ASP.NET Core and request http://localhost:5000/forms. Click the button and watch the output from the ASP. NET Core server. Each time you click the button, the event handler is invoked, and a new database query is sent to the database, producing logging messages like these:

```
...
info: Microsoft.EntityFrameworkCore.Database.Command[20101]
      Executed DbCommand (1ms) [Parameters=[], CommandType='Text',
      CommandTimeout='30']
  SELECT [p].[PersonId], [p].[DepartmentId], [p].[Firstname], [p].[LocationId],
      [p].[Surname], [d].[Departmentid], [d].[Name], [l].[LocationId], [l].[City],
      [l].[State]
    FROM [People] AS [p]
    INNER JOIN [Departments] AS [d] ON [p].[DepartmentId] = [d].[Departmentid]
    INNER JOIN [Locations] AS [l] ON [p].[LocationId] = [l].[LocationId]
info: Microsoft.EntityFrameworkCore.Database.Command[20101]
      Executed DbCommand (0ms) [Parameters=[], CommandType='Text',
      CommandTimeout='30']
  SELECT [p].[PersonId], [p].[DepartmentId], [p].[Firstname], [p].[LocationId],
      [p].[Surname], [d].[Departmentid], [d].[Name], [l].[LocationId], [l].[City],
      [l].[State]
    FROM [People] AS [p]
    INNER JOIN [Departments] AS [d] ON [p].[DepartmentId] = [d].[Departmentid]
    INNER JOIN [Locations] AS [l] ON [p].[LocationId] = [l].[LocationId]
...
```

Each time the component is rendered, Entity Framework Core sends two identical requests to the database, even when the Increment button is clicked where no data operations are performed.

This issue can arise whenever Entity Framework Core is used and is exacerbated by Blazor. Although it is common practice to assign database queries to IEnumerable<T> properties, doing so masks an important aspect of Entity Framework Core, which is that its LINQ expressions are expressions of queries and not results, and each time the property is read, a new query is sent to the database. The value of the People property is read twice by the List component: once by the Count property to determine whether the data has loaded and once by the @foreach expression to generate the rows for the HTML table. When the user clicks the Increment button, Blazor renders the List component again to figure out what has changed, which causes the People property to be read twice more, producing two additional database queries.

Blazor and Entity Framework Core are both working the way they should. Blazor must rerender the component's output to figure out what HTML changes need to be sent to the browser. It has no way of knowing what effect clicking the button has until after it has rendered the elements and evaluated all the Razor expressions. Entity Framework Core is executing its query each time the property is read, ensuring that the application always has fresh data.

This combination of features presents two issues. The first is that needless queries are sent to the database, which can increase the capacity required by an application (although not always because database servers are adept at handling queries).

The second issue is that changes to the database will be reflected in the content presented to the user after they make an unrelated interaction. If another user adds a Person object to the database, for example, it will appear in the table the next time the user clicks the Increment button. Users expect applications to reflect only their actions, and unexpected changes are confusing and distracting.

Managing Queries in a Component

The interaction between Blazor and Entity Framework Core won't be a problem for all projects, but, if it is, then the best approach is to query the database once and requery only for operations where the user might expect an update to occur. Some applications may need to present the user with an explicit option to reload the data, especially for applications where updates are likely to occur that the user will want to see, as shown in Listing 36-18.

Listing 36-18. Controlling Queries in the List.razor File in the Blazor/Forms Folder

```
@page "/forms"
@layout EmptyLayout

<h5 class="bg-primary text-white text-center p-2">People</h5>

<table class="table table-sm table-striped table-bordered">
    <thead>
        <tr>
            <th>ID</th><th>Name</th><th>Dept</th><th>Location</th><th></th>
        </tr>
    </thead>
    <tbody>
        @if  (People.Count() == 0) {
            <tr><th colspan="5" class="p-4 text-center">Loading Data...</th></tr>
        } else {
            @foreach (Person p in People) {
                <tr>
                    <td>@p.PersonId</td>
                    <td>@p.Surname, @p.Firstname</td>
                    <td>@p.Department.Name</td>
                    <td>@p.Location.City</td>
                    <td></td>
                </tr>
            }
        }
    </tbody>
</table>

<button class="btn btn-danger" @onclick="UpdateData">Update</button>

<button class="btn btn-primary" @onclick="@(() => Counter++)">Increment</button>
<span class="h5">Counter: @Counter</span>

@code {

    [Inject]
    public DataContext Context { get; set; }

    public IEnumerable<Person> People { get; set; } = Enumerable.Empty<Person>();

    protected async override Task OnInitializedAsync() {
        await UpdateData();
    }

    private async Task UpdateData() =>
        People = await Context.People.Include(p => p.Department)
            .Include(p => p.Location).ToListAsync<Person>();

    public int Counter { get; set; } = 0;
}
```

The UpdateData method performs the same query but applies the ToListAsync method, which forces evaluation of the Entity Framework Core query. The results are assigned to the People property and can be read repeatedly without triggering additional queries. To give the user control over the data, I added a button that invokes the UpdateData method when it is clicked. Restart ASP. NET Core, request http://localhost:5000/forms, and click the Increment button. Monitor the output from the ASP.NET Core server, and you will see that there is a query made only when the component is initialized. To explicitly trigger a query, click the Update button.

Some operations may require a new query, which is easy to perform. To demonstrate, Listing 36-19 adds a sort operation to the List component, which is implemented both with and without a new query.

Listing 36-19. Adding Operations to the List.razor File in the Blazor/Forms Folder

```
@page "/forms"
@page "/forms/list"
@layout EmptyLayout

<h5 class="bg-primary text-white text-center p-2">People</h5>

<table class="table table-sm table-striped table-bordered">
    <thead>
        <tr>
            <th>ID</th><th>Name</th><th>Dept</th><th>Location</th><th></th>
        </tr>
    </thead>
    <tbody>
        @if  (People.Count() == 0) {
            <tr><th colspan="5" class="p-4 text-center">Loading Data...</th></tr>
        } else {
            @foreach (Person p in People) {
                <tr>
                    <td>@p.PersonId</td>
                    <td>@p.Surname, @p.Firstname</td>
                    <td>@p.Department.Name</td>
                    <td>@p.Location.City</td>
                    <td>
                        <NavLink class="btn btn-sm btn-warning"
                                href="@GetEditUrl(p.PersonId)">
                            Edit
                        </NavLink>
                    </td>
                </tr>
            }
        }
    </tbody>
</table>

<button class="btn btn-danger" @onclick="@(() => UpdateData())">Update</button>
<button class="btn btn-info" @onclick="SortWithQuery">Sort (With Query)</button>
<button class="btn btn-info" @onclick="SortWithoutQuery">Sort (No Query)</button>
<button class="btn btn-primary" @onclick="@(() => Counter++)">Increment</button>
<span class="h5">Counter: @Counter</span>

@code {

    [Inject]
    public DataContext Context { get; set; }

    public IEnumerable<Person> People { get; set; } = Enumerable.Empty<Person>();

    protected async override Task OnInitializedAsync() {
        await UpdateData();
    }

    private IQueryable<Person> Query => Context.People.Include(p => p.Department)
            .Include(p => p.Location);
```

```
private async Task UpdateData(IQueryable<Person> query = null) =>
    People = await (query ?? Query).ToListAsync<Person>();

public async Task SortWithQuery() {
    await UpdateData(Query.OrderBy(p => p.Surname));
}

public void SortWithoutQuery() {
    People = People.OrderBy(p => p.Firstname).ToList<Person>();
}

string GetEditUrl(long id) => $"/forms/edit/{id}";

public int Counter { get; set; } = 0;
}
```

Entity Framework Core queries are expressed as IQueryable<T> objects, allowing the query to be composed with additional LINQ methods before it is dispatched to the database server. The new operations in the example both use the LINQ OrderBy method, but one applies this to the IQueryable<T>, which is then evaluated to send the query with the ToListAsync method. The other operation applies the OrderBy method to the existing result data, sorting it without sending a new query. To see both operations, restart ASP.NET Core, request http://localhost:5000/forms, and click the Sort buttons, as shown in Figure 36-10. When the Sort (With Query) button is clicked, you will see a log message indicating that a query has been sent to the database.

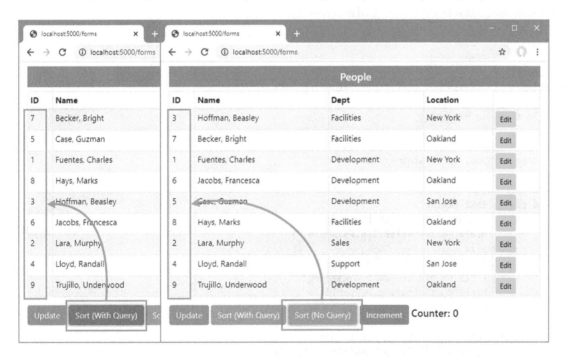

Figure 36-10. *Managing component queries*

AVOIDING THE OVERLAPPING QUERY PITFALL

You may encounter an exception telling you that "a second operation started on this context before a previous operation completed." This happens when a child component uses the OnParametersSetAsync method to perform an asynchronous Entity Framework Core query and a change in the parent's data triggers a second call to OnParametersSetAsync before the query is complete. The second method call starts a duplicate query that causes the exception. This problem can be resolved by performing the Entity Framework Core query synchronously. You can see an example in Listing 36-12, where I perform queries synchronously because the parent component will trigger an update when it receives its data.

Performing Create, Read, Update, and Delete Operations

To show how the features described in previous sections fit together, I am going to create a simple application that allows the user to perform CRUD operations on `Person` objects.

Creating the List Component

The `List` component contains the basic functionality I require. Listing 36-20 removes some of the features from earlier sections that are no longer required and adds buttons that allow the user to navigate to other functions.

Listing 36-20. Preparing the Component in the List.razor File in the Blazor/Forms Folder

```
@page "/forms"
@page "/forms/list"
@layout EmptyLayout
@inherits OwningComponentBase<DataContext>


<h5 class="bg-primary text-white text-center p-2">People</h5>

<table class="table table-sm table-striped table-bordered">
    <thead>
        <tr>
            <th>ID</th><th>Name</th><th>Dept</th><th>Location</th><th></th>
        </tr>
    </thead>
    <tbody>
        @if  (People.Count() == 0) {
            <tr><th colspan="5" class="p-4 text-center">Loading Data...</th></tr>
        } else {
            @foreach (Person p in People) {
                <tr>
                    <td>@p.PersonId</td>
                    <td>@p.Surname, @p.Firstname</td>
                    <td>@p.Department.Name</td>
                    <td>@p.Location.City</td>
                    <td class="text-center">
                        <NavLink class="btn btn-sm btn-info"
                                href="@GetDetailsUrl(p.PersonId)">
                            Details
                        </NavLink>
                        <NavLink class="btn btn-sm btn-warning"
                                href="@GetEditUrl(p.PersonId)">
                            Edit
                        </NavLink>
                        <button class="btn btn-sm btn-danger"
                                @onclick="@(() => HandleDelete(p))">
                            Delete
                        </button>
                    </td>
                </tr>
            }
        }
    </tbody>
</table>

<NavLink class="btn btn-primary" href="/forms/create">Create</NavLink>
```

```
@code {

    public DataContext Context => Service;

    public IEnumerable<Person> People { get; set; } = Enumerable.Empty<Person>();

    protected async override Task OnInitializedAsync() {
        await UpdateData();
    }

    private IQueryable<Person> Query => Context.People.Include(p => p.Department)
            .Include(p => p.Location);

    private async Task UpdateData(IQueryable<Person> query = null) =>
        People = await (query ?? Query).ToListAsync<Person>();

    string GetEditUrl(long id) => $"/forms/edit/{id}";
    string GetDetailsUrl(long id) => $"/forms/details/{id}";

    public async Task HandleDelete(Person p) {
        Context.Remove(p);
        await Context.SaveChangesAsync();
        await UpdateData();
    }
}
}
```

The operations for creating, viewing, and editing objects navigate to other URLs, but the delete operations are performed by the List component, taking care to reload the data after the changes have been saved to reflect the change to the user.

Creating the Details Component

The details component displays a read-only view of the data, which doesn't require the Blazor form features or present any issues with Entity Framework Core. Add a Blazor Component named Details.razor to the Blazor/Forms folder with the content shown in Listing 36-21.

Listing 36-21. The Contents of the Details.razor File in the Blazor/Forms Folder

```
@page "/forms/details/{id:long}"
@layout EmptyLayout
@inherits OwningComponentBase<DataContext>

<h4 class="bg-info text-center text-white p-2">Details</h4>

<div class="form-group">
    <label>ID</label>
    <input class="form-control" value="@PersonData.PersonId" disabled />
</div>
<div class="form-group">
    <label>Firstname</label>
    <input class="form-control" value="@PersonData.Firstname" disabled />
</div>
<div class="form-group">
    <label>Surname</label>
    <input class="form-control" value="@PersonData.Surname" disabled />
</div>
```

```
<div class="form-group">
    <label>Department</label>
    <input class="form-control" value="@PersonData.Department?.Name" disabled />
</div>
<div class="form-group">
    <label>Location</label>
    <input class="form-control"
            value="@($"{PersonData.Location?.City}, {PersonData.Location?.State}")"
            disabled />
</div>
<div class="text-center">
    <NavLink class="btn btn-info" href="@EditUrl">Edit</NavLink>
    <NavLink class="btn btn-secondary" href="/forms">Back</NavLink>
</div>

@code {

    [Inject]
    public NavigationManager NavManager { get; set; }

    DataContext Context => Service;

    [Parameter]
    public long Id { get; set; }

    public Person PersonData { get; set; } = new Person();

    protected async override Task OnParametersSetAsync() {
        PersonData = await Context.People.Include(p => p.Department)
            .Include(p => p.Location).FirstOrDefaultAsync(p => p.PersonId == Id);
    }

    public string EditUrl => $"/forms/edit/{Id}";
}
```

All the input elements displayed by this component are disabled, which means there is no need to handle events or process user input.

Creating the Editor Component

The remaining features will be handled by the Editor component. Listing 36-22 removes the features from earlier examples that are no longer required and adds support for creating and editing objects, including persisting the data.

Listing 36-22. Adding Application Features in the Editor.razor File in the Forms/Blazor Folder

```
@page "/forms/edit/{id:long}"
@page "/forms/create"
@layout EmptyLayout
@inherits OwningComponentBase<DataContext>

<link href="/blazorValidation.css" rel="stylesheet" />

<h4 class="bg-@Theme text-center text-white p-2">@Mode</h4>

<EditForm Model="PersonData" OnValidSubmit="HandleValidSubmit">
    <DataAnnotationsValidator />
```

```
    @if (Mode == "Edit") {
        <div class="form-group">
            <label>ID</label>
            <InputNumber class="form-control"
                @bind-Value="PersonData.PersonId" readonly />
        </div>
    }
    <div class="form-group">
        <label>Firstname</label>
        <ValidationMessage For="@(() => PersonData.Firstname)" />
        <InputText class="form-control" @bind-Value="PersonData.Firstname" />
    </div>
    <div class="form-group">
        <label>Surname</label>
        <ValidationMessage For="@(() => PersonData.Surname)" />
        <InputText class="form-control" @bind-Value="PersonData.Surname" />
    </div>
    <div class="form-group">
        <label>Deptartment</label>
        <ValidationMessage For="@(() => PersonData.DepartmentId)" />
        <CustomSelect TValue="long" Values="Departments"
                      Parser="@(str => long.Parse(str))"
                      @bind-Value="PersonData.DepartmentId">
            <option selected disabled value="0">Choose a Department</option>
        </CustomSelect>
    </div>
    <div class="form-group">
        <label>Location</label>
        <ValidationMessage For="@(() => PersonData.LocationId)" />
        <CustomSelect TValue="long" Values="Locations"
                      Parser="@(str => long.Parse(str))"
                      @bind-Value="PersonData.LocationId">
            <option selected disabled value="0">Choose a Location</option>
        </CustomSelect>
    </div>
    <div class="text-center">
        <button type="submit" class="btn btn-@Theme">Save</button>
        <NavLink class="btn btn-secondary" href="/forms">Back</NavLink>
    </div>
</EditForm>

@code {

    [Inject]
    public NavigationManager NavManager { get; set; }

    DataContext Context => Service;

    [Parameter]
    public long Id { get; set; }

    public Person PersonData { get; set; } = new Person();

    public IDictionary<string, long> Departments { get; set; }
        = new Dictionary<string, long>();
    public IDictionary<string, long> Locations { get; set; }
        = new Dictionary<string, long>();
```

```
protected async override Task OnParametersSetAsync() {
    if (Mode == "Edit") {
        PersonData = await Context.People.FindAsync(Id);
    }
    Departments = await Context.Departments
        .ToDictionaryAsync(d => d.Name, d => d.Departmentid);
    Locations = await Context.Locations
        .ToDictionaryAsync(l => $"{l.City}, {l.State}", l => l.LocationId);
}

public string Theme => Id == 0 ? "primary" : "warning";
public string Mode => Id == 0 ? "Create" : "Edit";

public async Task HandleValidSubmit()  {
    if (Mode== "Create") {
        Context.Add(PersonData);
    }
    await Context.SaveChangesAsync();
    NavManager.NavigateTo("/forms");
}
}
```

I added support for a new URL and used Bootstrap CSS themes to differentiate between creating a new object and editing an existing one. I removed the validation summary so that only property-level validation messages are displayed and added support for storing the data through Entity Framework Core. Unlike form applications created using controllers or Razor Pages, I don't have to deal with model binding because Blazor lets me work directly with the object that Entity Framework Core produces from the initial database query. Restart ASP.NET Core and request http://localhost:5000/forms. You will see the list of Person objects shown in Figure 36-11, and clicking the Create, Details, Edit, and Delete buttons will allow you to work with the data in the database.

■ **Tip** Open a command prompt and run dotnet ef database drop --force in the Advanced project folder if you need to reset the database to undo the changes you have made. The database will be seeded again when you restart ASP.NET Core, and you will see the data shown in the figure.

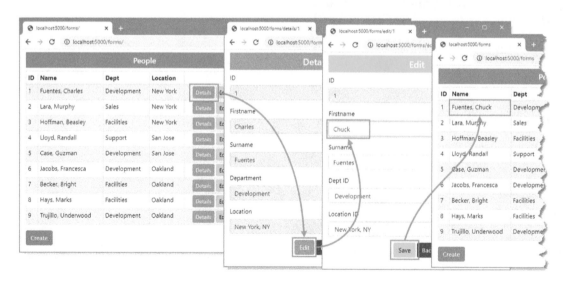

Figure 36-11. Using Blazor to work with data

Extending the Blazor Form Features

The Blazor form features are effective but have the rough edges that are always found in new technology. I expect future releases to round out the feature set, but, in the meantime, Blazor makes it easy to enhance the way that forms work. The EditForm component defines a cascading EditContext object that provides access to form validation and makes it easy to create custom form components through the events, properties, and methods described in Table 36-8.

Table 36-8. *The EditContext Features*

Name	Description
OnFieldChanged	This event is triggered when any of the form fields are modified.
OnValidationRequested	This event is triggered when validation is required and can be used to create custom validation processes.
OnValidationStateChanged	This event is triggered when the validation state of the overall form changes.
Model	This property returns the value passed to the EditForm component's Model property.
Field(name)	This method is used to get a FieldIdentifier object that describes a single field.
IsModified()	This method returns true if any of the form fields have been modified.
IsModified(field)	This method returns true if the field specified by the FieldIdentifier argument has been modified.
GetValidationMessages()	This method returns a sequence containing the validation error messages for the entire form.
GetValidationMessages(field)	This method returns a sequence containing the validation error messages for a single field, using a FieldIdentifer object obtained from the Field method.
MarkAsUnmodified()	This method marks the form as unmodified.
MarkAsUnmodified(field)	This method marks a specific field as unmodified, using a FieldIdentifer object obtained from the Field method.
NotifyValidationStateChanged()	This method is used to indicate a change in validation status.
NotifyFieldChanged(field)	This method is used to indicate when a field has changed, using a FieldIdentifer object obtained from the Field method.
Validate()	This method performs validation on the form, returning true if all the form fields pass validation and false otherwise.

Creating a Custom Validation Constraint

You can create components that apply custom validation constraints if the built-in validation attributes are not sufficient. This type of component doesn't render its own content, and it is more easily defined as a class. Add a class file named DeptStateValidator. cs to the Blazor/Forms folder and use it to define the component class shown in Listing 36-23.

Listing 36-23. The Contents of the DeptStateValidator.cs File in the Blazor/Forms Folder

```
using Advanced.Models;
using Microsoft.AspNetCore.Components;
using Microsoft.AspNetCore.Components.Forms;
using System.Collections.Generic;
using System.Linq;

namespace Advanced.Blazor.Forms {

    public class DeptStateValidator: OwningComponentBase<DataContext> {

        public DataContext Context => Service;
```

983

```
        [Parameter]
        public long DepartmentId { get; set; }

        [Parameter]
        public string State { get; set; }

        [CascadingParameter]
        public EditContext CurrentEditContext { get; set; }

        private string DeptName { get; set; }
        private IDictionary<long, string> LocationStates { get; set; }

        protected override void OnInitialized() {
            ValidationMessageStore store =
                new ValidationMessageStore(CurrentEditContext);
            CurrentEditContext.OnFieldChanged += (sender, args) => {
                string name = args.FieldIdentifier.FieldName;
                if (name == "DepartmentId" || name == "LocationId") {
                    Validate(CurrentEditContext.Model as Person, store);
                }
            };
        }

        protected override void OnParametersSet() {
            DeptName = Context.Departments.Find(DepartmentId).Name;
            LocationStates = Context.Locations
                .ToDictionary(l => l.LocationId, l => l.State);
        }

        private void Validate(Person model, ValidationMessageStore store) {

            if (model.DepartmentId == DepartmentId &&
                (!LocationStates.ContainsKey(model.LocationId) ||
                    LocationStates[model.LocationId] != State)) {
                store.Add(CurrentEditContext.Field("LocationId"),
                    $"{DeptName} staff must be in: {State}");
            } else {
                store.Clear();
            }
            CurrentEditContext.NotifyValidationStateChanged();
        }
    }
}
```

This component enforces a restriction on the state in which departments can be defined so that, for example, locations in California are the valid options only when the Development department has been chosen, and any other locations will produce a validation error.

The component has its own scoped DataContext object, which it receives by using OwningComponentBase<T> as its base class. The parent component provides values for the DepartmentId and State properties, which are used to enforce the validation rule. The cascading EditContext property is received from the EditForm component and provides access to the features described in Table 36-8.

When the component is initialized, a new ValidationMessageStore is created. This object is used to register validation error messages and accepts the EditContext object as its constructor argument, like this:

```
...
ValidationMessageStore store = new ValidationMessageStore(CurrentEditContext);
...
```

984

Blazor takes care of processing the messages added to the store, and the custom validation component only needs to decide which messages are required, which is handled by the Validate method. This method checks the DepartmentId and LocationId properties to make sure that the combination is allowed. If there is an issue, then a new validation message is added to the store, like this:

```
...
store.Add(CurrentEditContext.Field("LocationId"),
    $"{DeptName} staff must be in: {State}");
...
```

The arguments to the Add method are a FieldIdentifier that identifies the field the error relates to and the validation message. If there are no validation errors, then the message store's Clear method is called, which will ensure that any stale messages that have been previously generated by the component are no longer displayed.

The Validation method is called by the handler for the OnFieldChanged event, which allows the component to respond whenever the user makes a change.

```
...
CurrentEditContext.OnFieldChanged += (sender, args) => {
    string name = args.FieldIdentifier.FieldName;
    if (name == "DepartmentId" || name == "LocationId") {
        Validate(CurrentEditContext.Model as Person, store);
     }
};
...
```

The handler receives a FieldChangeEventArgs object, which defines a FieldIdentifer property that indicates which field has been modified. Listing 36-24 applies the new validation to the Editor component.

Listing 36-24. Applying a Validation Component in the Editor.razor File in the Blazor/Forms Folder

```
@page "/forms/edit/{id:long}"
@page "/forms/create"
@layout EmptyLayout
@inherits OwningComponentBase<DataContext>

<link href="/blazorValidation.css" rel="stylesheet" />

<h4 class="bg-@Theme text-center text-white p-2">@Mode</h4>

<EditForm Model="PersonData" OnValidSubmit="HandleValidSubmit">
    <DataAnnotationsValidator />
    <DeptStateValidator DepartmentId="2" State="CA" />

    <!-- ...elements omitted for brevity... -->

</EditForm>

@code {

    // ...statements omitted for brevity...
}
```

The DepartmentId and State attributes specify the restriction that only locations in California can be selected for the Development department. Restart ASP.NET Core and request http://localhost:5000/forms/edit/2. Choose Development for the Department field, and you will see a validation error because the location for this Person is New York. This error will remain visible until you select a location in California or change the department, as shown in Figure 36-12.

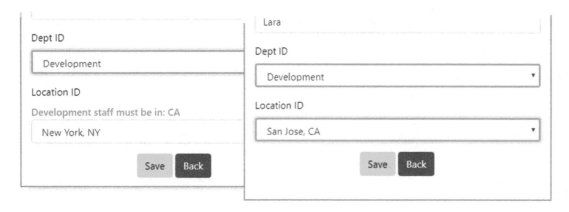

Figure 36-12. *Creating a custom validation component*

Creating a Valid-Only Submit Button Component

To finish this chapter, I am going to create a component that will render a submit button for the form that is enabled only when the data is valid. Add a Razor Component named ValidButton.razor to the Forms/Blazor folder with the contents shown in Listing 36-25.

Listing 36-25. The Contents of the ValidButton.razor File in the Forms/Blazor Folder

```
<button class="@ButtonClass" @attributes="Attributes" disabled="@Disabled">
    @ChildContent
</button>

@code {

    [Parameter]
    public RenderFragment ChildContent { get; set; }

    [Parameter]
    public string BtnTheme { get; set; }

    [Parameter]
    public string DisabledClass { get; set;} = "btn-outline-dark disabled";

    [Parameter(CaptureUnmatchedValues = true)]
    public IDictionary<string, object> Attributes { get; set; }

    [CascadingParameter]
    public EditContext CurrentEditContext { get; set; }

    public bool Disabled { get; set; }

    public string ButtonClass =>
        Disabled ? $"btn btn-{BtnTheme} {DisabledClass}" : $"btn btn-{BtnTheme}";

    protected override void OnInitialized() {
        SetButtonState();
        CurrentEditContext.OnValidationStateChanged +=
            (sender, args) => SetButtonState();
        CurrentEditContext.Validate();
    }
```

```
        public void SetButtonState() {
            Disabled = CurrentEditContext.GetValidationMessages().Any();
        }
    }
}
```

This component responds to the OnValidationStateChanged method, which is triggered when the validation state of the form changes. There is no EditContext property that details the validation state, so the best way to see if there are any validation issues is to see whether there are any validation messages. If there are, there are validation issues. If there are no validation messages, the form is valid. To ensure the button state is displayed correctly, the Validation method is called so that a validation check is performed as soon as the component is initialized.

Listing 36-26 uses the new component to replace the conventional button in the Editor component.

Listing 36-26. Applying a Component in the Editor.razor File in the Blazor/Forms Folder

```
...
<div class="text-center">
    <ValidButton type="submit" BtnTheme="@Theme">Save</ValidButton>
    <NavLink class="btn btn-secondary" href="/forms">Back</NavLink>
</div>
...
```

Restart ASP.NET Core and request http://localhost:5000/forms/create; you will see the validation messages displayed for each form element, with the Save button disabled. The button will be enabled once each validation issue has been resolved, as shown in Figure 36-13.

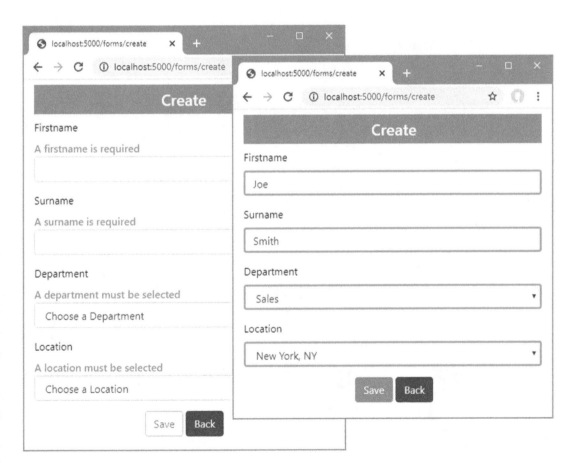

Figure 36-13. Creating a custom form button

Summary

In this chapter, I described Blazor form features and showed you how they can be used to create forms that validate data. I also explained how the interactions between Entity Framework Core and Blazor can cause unexpected results and how these can be resolved by creating dependency injection scopes and managing how queries are executed. In the next chapter, I describe Blazor WebAssembly, which executes Razor Components entirely in the browser.

CHAPTER 37

■ ■ ■

Using Blazor Web Assembly

In this chapter, I demonstrate the use of Blazor WebAssembly, which is an implementation of Blazor written for WebAssembly.

WebAssembly is a virtual machine running inside the browser. High-level languages are compiled into low-level language-neutral assembler format that can be executed at close to native performance. WebAssembly provides access to the APIs available to JavaScript applications, which means that WebAssembly applications can access the domain object model, use cascading style sheets, and initiate asynchronous HTTP requests.

Blazor WebAssembly, as its name suggests, is an implementation of Blazor that runs in the WebAssembly virtual machine. Blazor WebAssembly breaks the dependency on the server and executes the Blazor application entirely in the browser. The result is a true client-side application, with access to all the same features of Blazor Server but without the need for a persistent HTTP connection.

It is early days for both WebAssembly and Blazor WebAssembly, and there are some serious restrictions, at least for now. WebAssembly is a new technology and is supported only by the latest browser versions. You will not be able to use WebAssembly if your project needs to support legacy browsers—or even older versions of modern browsers. Blazor WebAssembly is still in preview, which means that the current implementation is unsupported, has some rough edges, and is not supported for production use. The final release is subject to change, and you will find the current tools and runtime are not as mature as their Blazor Server equivalents.

Even allowing for its preview status, Blazor WebAssembly isn't without its drawbacks. Blazor WebAssembly relies on an implementation of the .NET Core runtime that was written for WebAssembly. To run a Blazor WebAssembly application, the browser must download the .NET Core runtime, the .NET assemblies the application requires, and the application code. At the time of writing, this means that browsers must download about 5MB of data before an application can start. I expect that production releases will reduce the amount of data required, but that magnitude of data will make Blazor WebAssembly unsuitable for some projects. And Blazor WebAssembly applications are restricted to the set of APIs the browser provides, which means that not all .NET features can be used in a WebAssembly application. This doesn't disadvantage Blazor when compared to client-side frameworks like Angular, but it does mean that features such as Entity Framework Core are not available because browsers restrict WebAssembly applications to making HTTP requests.

Still, despite the limitations of Blazor WebAssembly, it is an exciting technology, and it offers the promise of being able to write true client-side applications using C# and ASP.NET Core, without the need for a JavaScript framework. Table 37-1 puts Blazor WebAssembly in context.

■ **Caution** I have written this chapter because Blazor WebAssembly shows the future of ASP.NET Core. But Blazor WebAssembly is not ready for production, and you should not use it in real projects.

Table 37-1. *Putting Blazor WebAssembly in Context*

Question	Answer
What is it?	Blazor WebAssembly is an implementation of Blazor that runs in the browser using WebAssembly.
Why is it useful?	Blazor WebAssembly allows client-side applications to be written in C# without server-side execution or the persistent HTTP connection required by Blazor Server.
How is it used?	Blazor components are added to a project that is dedicated to Blazor WebAssembly.
Are there any pitfalls or limitations?	Not all browsers support WebAssembly. A larger download is required to provide the browser with the code it requires, and not all ASP.NET Core features are available in Blazor WebAssembly components.
Are there any alternatives?	Blazor WebAssembly is the only combination of true client-side applications written using ASP.NET Core. Blazor Server can be used if server-side support is acceptable; otherwise, a JavaScript framework, such as Angular, React, or Vue.js, should be used.

© Adam Freeman 2020
A. Freeman, *Pro ASP.NET Core 3*, https://doi.org/10.1007/978-1-4842-5440-0_37

Preparing for This Chapter

This chapter uses the Advanced project from Chapter 26. To prepare for this chapter, add a class file named `DataController.cs` to the `Controllers` folder and use it to define the web service controller shown in Listing 37-1.

■ **Tip** You can download the example project for this chapter—and for all the other chapters in this book—from `https://github.com/apress/pro-asp.net-core-3`. See Chapter 1 for how to get help if you have problems running the examples.

Listing 37-1. The Contents of the DataController.cs File in the Controllers Folder

```csharp
using Advanced.Models;
using Microsoft.AspNetCore.Mvc;
using Microsoft.EntityFrameworkCore;
using System.Collections.Generic;
using System.Threading.Tasks;

namespace Advanced.Controllers {

    [ApiController]
    [Route("/api/people")]
    public class DataController : ControllerBase {
        private DataContext context;

        public DataController(DataContext ctx) {
            context = ctx;
        }

        [HttpGet]
        public IEnumerable<Person> GetAll() {
            IEnumerable<Person> people
                = context.People.Include(p => p.Department).Include(p => p.Location);
            foreach (Person p in people) {
                p.Department.People = null;
                p.Location.People = null;
            }
            return people;
        }

        [HttpGet("{id}")]
        public async Task<Person> GetDetails(long id) {
            Person p = await context.People.Include(p => p.Department)
                .Include(p => p.Location).FirstAsync(p => p.PersonId == id);
            p.Department.People = null;
            p.Location.People = null;
            return p;
        }

        [HttpPost]
        public async Task Save([FromBody]Person p) {
            await context.People.AddAsync(p);
            await context.SaveChangesAsync();
        }
```

```
[HttpPut]
public async Task Update([FromBody]Person p) {
    context.Update(p);
    await context.SaveChangesAsync();
}

[HttpDelete("{id}")]
public async Task Delete(long id) {
    context.People.Remove(new Person() { PersonId = id });
    await context.SaveChangesAsync();
}

[HttpGet("/api/locations")]
public IAsyncEnumerable<Location> GetLocations() => context.Locations;
[HttpGet("/api/departments")]
public IAsyncEnumerable<Department> GetDepts() => context.Departments;
    }
}
```

This controller provides actions that allow Person objects to be created, read, updated, and deleted. I have also added actions that return the Location and Department objects. I usually create separate controllers for each type of data, but these actions are required only in support of the Person features, so I have combined all the operations into a single controller.

Dropping the Database and Running the Application

Open a new PowerShell command prompt, navigate to the folder that contains the Advanced.csproj file, and run the command shown in Listing 37-2 to drop the database.

Listing 37-2. Dropping the Database

```
dotnet ef database drop --force
```

Select Start Without Debugging or Run Without Debugging from the Debug menu or use the PowerShell command prompt to run the command shown in Listing 37-3.

Listing 37-3. Running the Example Application

```
dotnet run
```

Use a browser to request http://localhost:5000/api/people, which will produce a JSON representation of the Person objects from the database, as shown in Figure 37-1.

Figure 37-1. *Running the example application*

Setting Up Blazor WebAssembly

Blazor WebAssembly requires a separate project so that Razor Components can be compiled ready to be executed by the browser. The compiled components can be delivered to the browser by a standard ASP.NET Core server, which can also provide data through web services. To make it easy for the Blazor WebAssembly components to consume the data provided by the ASP.NET Core server, a third project is required that contains those items that are shared between them.

The process for creating the three projects is involved, partly because I am going to move some of the existing classes from the Advanced project into the data model project. Although it is possible to perform some of the steps using the Visual Studio wizards, I have set out the steps using the command-line tools to minimize errors.

■ **Note** If you have problems following the steps, you can download all three projects from the GitHub repository for this book, at https://github.com/apress/pro-asp.net-core-3.

Creating the Shared Project

Make sure Visual Studio or Visual Studio Code is closed before you start. Open a new PowerShell command prompt and navigate to the Advanced project folder, which is the one that contains the Advanced.csproj file, and run the commands shown in Listing 37-4.

Listing 37-4. Preparing the Project for Blazor

```
dotnet new classlib -o ../DataModel -f netstandard2.1
dotnet add ../DataModel package System.ComponentModel.Annotations --version 4.7.0
Move-Item -Path @("Models/Person.cs", "Models/Location.cs", "Models/Department.cs") ../DataModel
```

These commands create a new project named DataModel. They install the System.ComponentModel.Annotations package (which contains the attributes used for data validation) and move the data model classes to the new project.

Creating the Blazor WebAssembly Project

I usually prefer to start with an empty project and add the packages and configuration files that the application requires, but Blazor WebAssembly is still experimental, and its project structure and dependencies are likely to change; therefore, there will be no advantage in understanding how a Blazor WebAssembly project works until the technology stabilizes. Instead, I am going to create the Blazor WebAssembly using the template provided by Microsoft. The Blazor WebAssembly template isn't included in the standard .NET Core template library, so the first step is to use a PowerShell command prompt to run the command shown in Listing 37-5 to install the template.

■ **Tip** You need to run this command only the first time you create a Blazor WebAssembly project. Once the template is installed, you can skip this step and jump to the command shown in Listing 37-6.

Listing 37-5. Installing the Blazor WebAssembly Project Template

```
dotnet new -i Microsoft.AspNetCore.Blazor.Templates::3.1.0-preview4.19579.2
```

The output from this command is confusing and can leave you with the impression that the installation has failed. The command shows a list of the installed templates, and you will know the command has succeeded if you see this entry in the list:

```
...
Blazor WebAssembly App    blazorwasm    [C#]    Web/Blazor/WebAssembly
...
```

Next, use the PowerShell command prompt to run the commands shown in Listing 37-6 from within the Advanced project folder (the folder that contains the Advanced.csproj file).

Listing 37-6. Creating the Blazor WebAssembly Project

```
dotnet new blazorwasm -o ../BlazorWebAssembly
dotnet add ../BlazorWebAssembly reference ../DataModel
```

These commands create a Blazor WebAssembly project named BlazorWebAssembly and add a reference to the DataModel project, which makes the Person, Department, and Location classes available.

Preparing the ASP.NET Core Project

Use the PowerShell command prompt to run the commands shown in Listing 37-7 in the Advanced project folder.

Listing 37-7. Preparing the Advanced Project

```
dotnet add reference ../DataModel ../BlazorWebAssembly

dotnet add package Microsoft.AspNetCore.Blazor.Server --version 3.1.0-preview4.19579.2
```

These commands create references to the other projects so that the data model classes and the components in the Blazor WebAssembly project can be used.

Adding the Solution References

Run the command shown in Listing 37-8 in the Advanced folder to add references to the new project to the solution file.

Listing 37-8. Adding Solution References

```
dotnet sln add ../DataModel ../BlazorWebAssembly
```

Opening the Projects

Once you have set up all three projects, start Visual Studio or Visual Studio Code. If you are using Visual Studio, open the Advanced.sln file in the Advanced folder. All three projects are open for editing, as shown in Figure 37-2. If you are using Visual Studio Code, open the folder that contains all three projects, as shown in Figure 37-2.

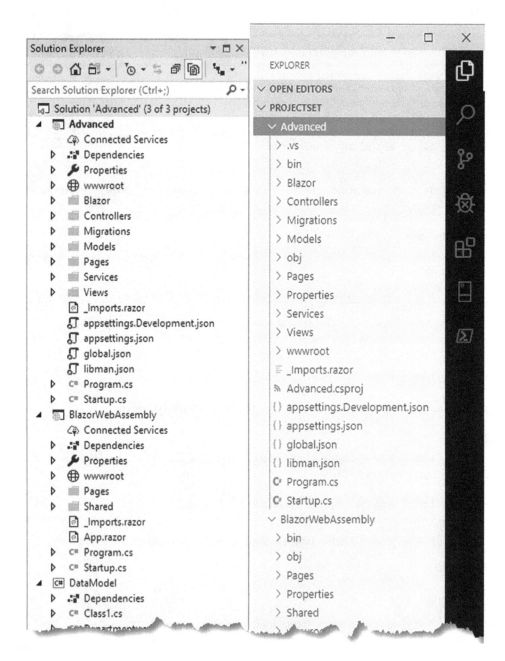

Figure 37-2. *Opening the three projects*

Completing the Blazor WebAssembly Configuration

The next step is to configure the ASP.NET Core project so that it can deliver the contents of the Blazor WebAssembly project to clients. Add the statements shown in Listing 37-9 to the Startup.cs file in the Advanced folder.

■ **Caution** It is important to pay close attention to which files you are editing. Files with the same name exist in multiple projects, and if you don't follow the examples closely, you won't end up with a working application. Future versions of Blazor may be easier to work with, but for the moment, the details are important.

Listing 37-9. Configuring the Application in the Startup.cs File in the Advanced Project

```
using System;
using System.Collections.Generic;
using System.Linq;
using System.Threading.Tasks;
using Microsoft.AspNetCore.Builder;
using Microsoft.AspNetCore.Hosting;
using Microsoft.AspNetCore.Http;
using Microsoft.Extensions.DependencyInjection;
using Microsoft.Extensions.Hosting;
using Microsoft.Extensions.Configuration;
using Microsoft.EntityFrameworkCore;
using Advanced.Models;
using Microsoft.AspNetCore.ResponseCompression;

namespace Advanced {
    public class Startup {

        public Startup(IConfiguration config) {
            Configuration = config;
        }

        public IConfiguration Configuration { get; set; }

        public void ConfigureServices(IServiceCollection services) {
            services.AddDbContext<DataContext>(opts => {
                opts.UseSqlServer(Configuration[
                    "ConnectionStrings:PeopleConnection"]);
                opts.EnableSensitiveDataLogging(true);
            });
            services.AddControllersWithViews().AddRazorRuntimeCompilation();
            services.AddRazorPages().AddRazorRuntimeCompilation();
            services.AddServerSideBlazor();
            services.AddSingleton<Services.ToggleService>();

            services.AddResponseCompression(opts => {
                opts.MimeTypes = ResponseCompressionDefaults.MimeTypes.Concat(
                    new[] { "application/octet-stream" });
            });
        }

        public void Configure(IApplicationBuilder app, DataContext context) {

            app.UseDeveloperExceptionPage();
            app.UseStaticFiles();
            app.UseRouting();

            app.UseEndpoints(endpoints => {
                endpoints.MapControllerRoute("controllers",
                    "controllers/{controller=Home}/{action=Index}/{id?}");
```

```
                endpoints.MapDefaultControllerRoute();
                endpoints.MapRazorPages();
                endpoints.MapBlazorHub();

                endpoints.MapFallbackToClientSideBlazor<BlazorWebAssembly.Startup>
                    ("/webassembly/{*path:nonfile}", "index.html");

                endpoints.MapFallbackToPage("/_Host");
            });

            app.Map("/webassembly", opts =>
                opts.UseClientSideBlazorFiles<BlazorWebAssembly.Startup>());

            SeedData.SeedDatabase(context);
        }
    }
}
```

These statements enable response compression, which Blazor WebAssembly requires, and configure the ASP.NET Core request pipeline so that requests for /webassembly are handled by Blazor WebAssembly using the contents of the BlazorWebAssembly project.

Setting the Base URL

The final step is to modify the HTML file that will be used to respond to requests for the /webassembly URL. Apply the change shown in Listing 37-10 to the index.html file in the wwwroot folder of the BlazorWebAssembly folder.

▪ **Caution**   Make sure there are forward-slash (/) characters before and after webassembly in the href attribute of the base element. If you omit either character, then Blazor WebAssembly will not work.

Listing 37-10. Setting the URL in the index.html File in the wwwroot Folder of the BlazorWebAssembly Project

```html
<!DOCTYPE html>
<html>

<head>
    <meta charset="utf-8" />
    <meta name="viewport" content="width=device-width" />
    <title>BlazorWebAssembly</title>
    <base href="/webassembly/" />
    <link href="css/bootstrap/bootstrap.min.css" rel="stylesheet" />
    <link href="css/site.css" rel="stylesheet" />
</head>

<body>
    <app>Loading...</app>

    <div id="blazor-error-ui">
        An unhandled error has occurred.
        <a href="" class="reload">Reload</a>
        <a class="dismiss">x</a>
    </div>
    <script src="_framework/blazor.webassembly.js"></script>
</body>

</html>
```

The base element sets the URL from which all relative URLs in the document are defined and is required for the correct operation of the Blazor WebAssembly routing system.

Testing the Placeholder Components

Start ASP.NET Core by selecting Start Without Debugging or Run Without Debugging from the Debug menu. If you prefer to use the command prompt, run the command shown in Listing 37-11 in the Advanced project folder.

Listing 37-11. Running the Example Application

```
dotnet run
```

Use a browser to request `http://localhost:5000/webassembly`, and you will see the placeholder content added by the template used to create the BlazorWebAssembly project.

Using the PowerShell command prompt, run the following commands from within the Advanced project folder. Click the Counter and Fetch Data links, and you will see different content displayed, as shown in Figure 37-3.

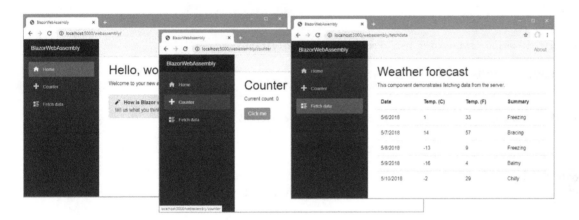

Figure 37-3. The Blazor WebAssembly placeholder content

Creating a Blazor WebAssembly Component

Blazor WebAssembly uses the same approach as Blazor Server, relying on components as building blocks for applications, connected through the routing system, and displaying common content through layouts. In this section, I show how to create a Razor Component that works with Blazor WebAssembly, and then I'll re-create the simple forms application from Chapter 36.

Importing the Data Model Namespace

The components I will create in this chapter all use the classes in the shared DataModel project. Rather than add @using expressions to each component, add the namespace for the data model classes to the _Imports.razor file in the root folder of the BlazorWebAssembly project, as shown in Listing 37-12.

Listing 37-12. Adding a Namespace in the _Imports.razor File in the BlazorWebAssembly Project

```
@using System.Net.Http
@using Microsoft.AspNetCore.Components.Forms
@using Microsoft.AspNetCore.Components.Routing
@using Microsoft.AspNetCore.Components.Web
@using Microsoft.JSInterop
```

```
@using BlazorWebAssembly
@using BlazorWebAssembly.Shared
@using Advanced.Models
```

Notice that although I moved the model classes to the DataModel project, I have specified the Advanced.Models namespace. This is because the class files I moved all have namespace declarations that specify Advanced.Models, which means that moving the files hasn't changed the namespace in which the classes exist.

Creating a Component

In earlier chapters, I defined my Razor Components in a Blazor folder to keep the new content separate from the other parts of ASP. NET Core. There is only Blazor content in the BlazorWebAssembly project, so I am going to follow the convention adopted by the project template and use the Pages and Shared folders.

Add a Razor Component named List.razor to the Pages folder of the BlazorWebAssembly project and add the content shown in Listing 37-13.

Listing 37-13. The Contents of the List.razor File in the Pages Folder of the BlazorWebAssembly Project

```
@page "/forms"
@page "/forms/list"

<h5 class="bg-primary text-white text-center p-2">People (WebAssembly)</h5>

<table class="table table-sm table-striped table-bordered">
    <thead>
        <tr>
            <th>ID</th><th>Name</th><th>Dept</th><th>Location</th><th></th>
        </tr>
    </thead>
    <tbody>
        @if  (People.Count() == 0) {
            <tr><th colspan="5" class="p-4 text-center">Loading Data...</th></tr>
        } else {
            @foreach (Person p in People) {
                <tr>
                    <td>@p.PersonId</td>
                    <td>@p.Surname, @p.Firstname</td>
                    <td>@p.Department.Name</td>
                    <td>@p.Location.City</td>
                    <td class="text-center">
                        <NavLink class="btn btn-sm btn-info"
                                href="@GetDetailsUrl(p.PersonId)">
                            Details
                        </NavLink>
                        <NavLink class="btn btn-sm btn-warning"
                                href="@GetEditUrl(p.PersonId)">
                            Edit
                        </NavLink>
                        <button class="btn btn-sm btn-danger"
                                @onclick="@(() => HandleDelete(p))">
                            Delete
                        </button>
                    </td>
                </tr>
            }
        }
    </tbody>
</table>
```

```
<NavLink class="btn btn-primary" href="forms/create">Create</NavLink>

@code {

    [Inject]
    public HttpClient Http { get; set; }

    public Person[] People { get; set; } = Array.Empty<Person>();

    protected async override Task OnInitializedAsync() {
        await UpdateData();
    }

    private async Task UpdateData() {
        People = await Http.GetJsonAsync<Person[]>("/api/people");
    }

    string GetEditUrl(long id) => $"forms/edit/{id}";
    string GetDetailsUrl(long id) => $"forms/details/{id}";

    public async Task HandleDelete(Person p) {
        HttpResponseMessage resp =
            await Http.DeleteAsync($"/api/people/{p.PersonId}");
        if (resp.IsSuccessStatusCode) {
            await UpdateData();
        }
    }
}
}
```

If you compare this component with the Blazor Server equivalent from Chapter 36, you will see that they are largely the same. Both types of Blazor use the same set of core features, which is why the content uses the same Razor directives, handles events with the @onclick attributes, and uses the same @code section for C# statements. A Blazor WebAssembly component is compiled into a C# class, just like its Blazor Server counterpart. The key difference is, of course, that the C# class that is generated is executed in the browser—and that's the reason for the differences from the component in Chapter 36.

Navigating in a Blazor WebAssembly Component

Notice that the URLs that are used for navigation are expressed without a leading forward-slash character, like this:

```
...
<NavLink class="btn btn-primary" href="forms/create">Create</NavLink>
...
```

The root URL for the application was specified using the base element in Listing 37-13, and using relative URLs ensures that navigation is performed relative to the root. In this case, the relative forms/create URL is combined with the /webassembly/ root specified by the base element, and navigation will be to /webassembly/forms/create. Including a leading forward slash would navigate to /forms/create instead, which is outside the set of URLs that are being managed by the Blazor WebAssembly part of the application. This change is required only for navigation URLs. URLs specified with the @page directive, for example, are not affected.

Getting Data in a Blazor WebAssembly Component

The biggest change is that Blazor WebAssembly can't use Entity Framework Core. Although the runtime may be able to execute the Entity Framework Core classes, the browser restricts WebAssembly applications to HTTP requests, preventing the use of SQL. To get data, Blazor WebAssembly applications consume web services, which is why I added the API controller to the Advanced project at the start of the chapter.

As part of the Blazor WebAssembly application startup, a service is created for the HttpClient class, which components can receive using the standard dependency injection features. The List component receives an HttpClient component through a property that has been decorated with the Inject attribute, like this:

```
...
[Inject]
public HttpClient Http { get; set; }
...
```

The HttpClient class provides the methods described in Table 37-2 to send HTTP requests.

Table 37-2. *The Methods Defined by the HttpClient Class*

Name	Description
GetAsync(url)	This method sends an HTTP GET request.
PostAsync(url, data)	This method sends an HTTP POST request.
PutAsync(url, data)	This method sends an HTTP PUT request.
PatchAync(url, data)	This method sends an HTTP PATCH request.
DeleteAsync(url)	This method sends an HTTP DELETE request.
SendAsync(request)	This method sends an HTTP, configured using an HttpRequestMessage object.

The methods in Table 37-2 return a Task<HttpResponseMessage> result, which describes the response received from the HTTP server to the asynchronous request. Table 37-3 shows the most useful HttpResponseMessage properties.

Table 37-3. *Useful HttpClient Properties*

Name	Description
Content	This property returns the content returned by the server.
HttpResponseHeaders	This property returns the response headers.
StatusCode	This property returns the response status code.
IsSuccessStatusCode	This property returns true if the response status code is between 200 and 299, indicating a successful request.

The List component uses the DeleteAsync methods to ask the web service to delete objects when the user clicks a Delete button.

```
...
HttpResponseMessage resp =
    await Http.DeleteAsync($"/api/people/{p.PersonId}");
    if (resp.IsSuccessStatusCode) {
        await UpdateData();
    }
}
...
```

These methods are useful when you don't need to work with the data the web service sends back, such as in this situation where I check to see only if the DELETE request has been successful. Notice that I specify the path for the request URL only when using the HttpClient service because the web service is available using the same scheme, host, and port as the application.

For operations where the web service returns data, the extension methods for the HttpClient class described in Table 37-4 are more useful. These methods serialize data into JSON so it can be sent to the server and parse JSON responses into C# objects. For requests that return no result, the generic type argument can be omitted.

Table 37-4. *The HttpClient Extension Methods*

Name	Description
GetJsonAsync<T>(url)	This method sends an HTTP GET request and parses the response to type T.
PostJsonAsync<T>(url, data)	This method sends an HTTP POST request and parses the response to type T.
PutJsonAsync<T>(url, data)	This method sends an HTTP PUT request and parses the response to type T.
SendJsonAsync<T>(method, url, data)	This method sends an HTTP request using the specified method and parses the response to type T.

The List component uses the GetJsonAsync<T> method to request data from the web service.

```
...
private async Task UpdateData() {
    People = await Http.GetJsonAsync<Person[]>("/api/people");
}
...
```

Setting the generic type argument to Person[] tells HttpClient to parse the response into an array of Person objects.

■ **Note** The HttpClient class doesn't present any scope or lifecycle issues and sends requests only when one of the methods described in Table 37-2 or Table 37-4 is invoked. Some thought is required, however, about when to request new data. In this example, I requery the web service after an object has been deleted, rather than simply remove the object from the data that was requested when the component was initialized. This may not be suitable for all applications because it will reflect any changes to the database that have been made by other users.

Creating a Layout

The template used to create the Blazor WebAssembly project includes a layout that presents the navigation features for the placeholder content. I don't want these navigation features, so the first step is to create a new layout. Add a Razor Component named EmptyLayout.razor in the Shared folder of the BlazorWebAssembly project with the content shown in Listing 37-14.

Listing 37-14. The EmptyLayout.razor File in the Shared Folder of the BlazorWebAssembly Project

```
@inherits LayoutComponentBase

<div class="m-2">
    @Body
</div>
```

I could apply the new layout with @layout expressions, as I did in Chapter 36, but I am going to use this layout as the default by changing the routing configuration, which is defined in the App.razor file in the BlazorWebAssembly project, as shown in Listing 37-15.

Listing 37-15. Applying the Layout in the App.razor File in the BlazorWebAssembly Project

```
<Router AppAssembly="@typeof(Program).Assembly">
    <Found Context="routeData">
        <RouteView RouteData="@routeData" DefaultLayout="@typeof(EmptyLayout)" />
    </Found>
```

```
    <NotFound>
        <LayoutView Layout="@typeof(EmptyLayout)">
            <p>Sorry, there's nothing at this address.</p>
        </LayoutView>
    </NotFound>
</Router>
```

Chapter 35 describes the Router, RouteView, Found, and NotFound components.

Defining CSS Styles

The template created the Blazor WebAssembly project with its own copy of the Bootstrap CSS framework and with an additional stylesheet that combines the styles required to configure the Blazor WebAssembly error and validation elements and manage the layout of the application. Replace the link elements in the HTML file as shown in Listing 37-16 and apply styles directly to the error element. This has the effect of removing the styles used by the Microsoft layout and using the Bootstrap CSS stylesheet that was added to the Advanced project.

Listing 37-16. Modifying the index.html File in the wwwroot Folder in the BlazorWebAssembly Project

```
<!DOCTYPE html>
<html>

<head>
    <meta charset="utf-8" />
    <meta name="viewport" content="width=device-width" />
    <title>BlazorWebAssembly</title>
    <base href="/webassembly/" />
    <link href="/lib/twitter-bootstrap/css/bootstrap.min.css" rel="stylesheet" />
</head>

<body>
    <app>Loading...</app>

    <div id="blazor-error-ui"
            class="text-center bg-danger h6 text-white p-2 fixed-top w-100"
            style="display:none">
        An unhandled error has occurred.
        <a href="" class="reload">Reload</a>
        <a class="dismiss">x</a>
    </div>
    <script src="_framework/blazor.webassembly.js"></script>
</body>

</html>
```

To see the new component, restart ASP.NET Core and request http://localhost:5000/webassembly/forms, which will produce the response shown in Figure 37-4.

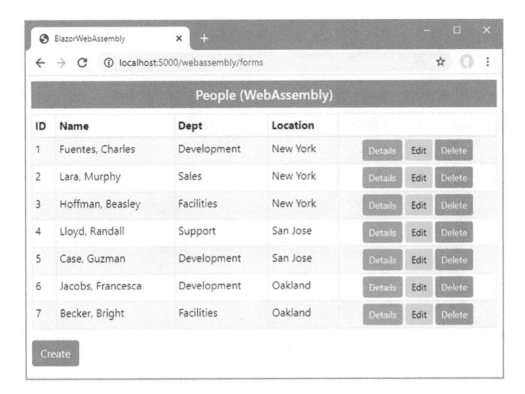

Figure 37-4. *A Blazor WebAssembly component*

Blazor WebAssembly components follow the standard Blazor lifecycle, and the component displays the data it receives from the web service.

Completing the Blazor WebAssembly Form Application

Only the Delete button displayed by the List component works currently. In the sections that follow, I complete the Blazor WebAssembly form application by creating additional components.

Creating the Details Component

Add a Razor Component named Details.razor to the Pages folder of the BlazorWebAssembly project with the content shown in Listing 37-17.

Listing 37-17. The Contents of the Details.razor File in the Pages Folder of the BlazorWebAssembly Project

```
@page "/forms/details/{id:long}"

<h4 class="bg-info text-center text-white p-2">Details (WebAssembly)</h4>

<div class="form-group">
    <label>ID</label>
    <input class="form-control" value="@PersonData.PersonId" disabled />
</div>
<div class="form-group">
    <label>Firstname</label>
    <input class="form-control" value="@PersonData.Firstname" disabled />
</div>
<div class="form-group">
    <label>Surname</label>
    <input class="form-control" value="@PersonData.Surname" disabled />
</div>
```

```
<div class="form-group">
    <label>Department</label>
    <input class="form-control" value="@PersonData.Department?.Name" disabled />
</div>
<div class="form-group">
    <label>Location</label>
    <input class="form-control"
           value="@($"{PersonData.Location?.City}, {PersonData.Location?.State}")"
           disabled />
</div>
<div class="text-center">
    <NavLink class="btn btn-info" href="@EditUrl">Edit</NavLink>
    <NavLink class="btn btn-secondary" href="forms">Back</NavLink>
</div>

@code {

    [Inject]
    public NavigationManager NavManager { get; set; }

    [Inject]
    public HttpClient Http { get; set; }

    [Parameter]
    public long Id { get; set; }

    public Person PersonData { get; set; } = new Person();

    protected async override Task OnParametersSetAsync() {
        PersonData = await Http.GetJsonAsync<Person>($"/api/people/{Id}");
    }

    public string EditUrl => $"forms/edit/{Id}";
}
```

The Details component has only two differences from its Blazor Server counterpart, following the pattern established by the List component: the data is obtained through the HttpClient service, and navigation targets are expressed using relative URLs. In all other regards, such as obtaining parameters from routing data, Blazor WebAssembly works just the same way as Blazor Server.

Creating the Editor Component

To complete the forms application, add a Razor Component named Editor.razor to the Pages folder of the BlazorWebAssembly project with the content shown in Listing 37-18.

Listing 37-18. The Contents of the Editor.razor File in the Pages Folder of the BlazorWebAssembly Project

```
@page "/forms/edit/{id:long}"
@page "/forms/create"

<link href="/blazorValidation.css" rel="stylesheet" />

<h4 class="bg-@Theme text-center text-white p-2">@Mode (WebAssembly)</h4>

<EditForm Model="PersonData" OnValidSubmit="HandleValidSubmit">
    <DataAnnotationsValidator />
    @if (Mode == "Edit") {
        <div class="form-group">
            <label>ID</label>
```

```
                <InputNumber class="form-control"
                    @bind-Value="PersonData.PersonId" readonly />
            </div>
        }
        <div class="form-group">
            <label>Firstname</label>
            <ValidationMessage For="@(() => PersonData.Firstname)" />
            <InputText class="form-control" @bind-Value="PersonData.Firstname" />
        </div>
        <div class="form-group">
            <label>Surname</label>
            <ValidationMessage For="@(() => PersonData.Surname)" />
            <InputText class="form-control" @bind-Value="PersonData.Surname" />
        </div>
        <div class="form-group">
            <label>Department</label>
            <ValidationMessage For="@(() => PersonData.DepartmentId)" />
            <select @bind="PersonData.DepartmentId" class="form-control">
                <option selected disabled value="0">Choose a Department</option>
                @foreach (var kvp in Departments) {
                    <option value="@kvp.Value">@kvp.Key</option>
                }
            </select>
        </div>
        <div class="form-group">
            <label>Location</label>
            <ValidationMessage For="@(() => PersonData.LocationId)" />
            <select @bind="PersonData.LocationId" class="form-control">
                <option selected disabled value="0">Choose a Location</option>
                @foreach (var kvp in Locations) {
                    <option value="@kvp.Value">@kvp.Key</option>
                }
            </select>
        </div>
        <div class="text-center">
            <button type="submit" class="btn btn-@Theme">Save</button>
            <NavLink class="btn btn-secondary" href="forms">Back</NavLink>
        </div>
</EditForm>

@code {

    [Inject]
    public HttpClient Http { get; set; }

    [Inject]
    public NavigationManager NavManager { get; set; }

    [Parameter]
    public long Id { get; set; }

    public Person PersonData { get; set; } = new Person();

    public IDictionary<string, long> Departments { get; set; }
        = new Dictionary<string, long>();
    public IDictionary<string, long> Locations { get; set; }
        = new Dictionary<string, long>();
```

```
protected async override Task OnParametersSetAsync() {
    if (Mode == "Edit") {
        PersonData = await Http.GetJsonAsync<Person>($"/api/people/{Id}");
    }
    Departments = (await Http.GetJsonAsync<Department[]>("/api/departments"))
        .ToDictionary(d => d.Name, d => d.Departmentid);
    Locations = (await Http.GetJsonAsync<Location[]>("/api/locations"))
        .ToDictionary(l => $"{l.City}, {l.State}", l => l.LocationId);
}

public string Theme => Id == 0 ? "primary" : "warning";
public string Mode => Id == 0 ? "Create" : "Edit";

public async Task HandleValidSubmit()  {
    await Http.SendJsonAsync(Mode == "Create" ? HttpMethod.Post : HttpMethod.Put,
        "/api/people", PersonData);
    NavManager.NavigateTo("forms");
}
}s
```

This component uses the Blazor form features described in Chapter 36 but uses HTTP requests to read and write data to the web service created at the start of the chapter. The GetJsonAsync<T> method is used to read data from the web service, and the SendJsonAsync method is used to send either POST or PUT requests when the user submits the form.

Notice that I have not used the custom select component or validation components I created in Chapter 36. Sharing components between projects—especially when Blazor WebAssembly is introduced after development has started—is awkward. I expect the process to improve in future releases, but for this chapter, I have simply done without the features. As a consequence, the select elements do not trigger validation when a value is selected, the submit button isn't automatically disabled, and there are no restrictions on the combination of department and location.

Restart ASP.NET Core and request http://localhost:5000/webassembly/forms, and you will see the Blazor WebAssembly version of the form application. Click the Details button for the first item in the table, and you will see the fields for the selected object. Click the Edit button, and you will be presented with an editable form. Make a change and click the Save button, and the changes will be sent to the web service and displayed in the data table, as shown in Figure 37-5.

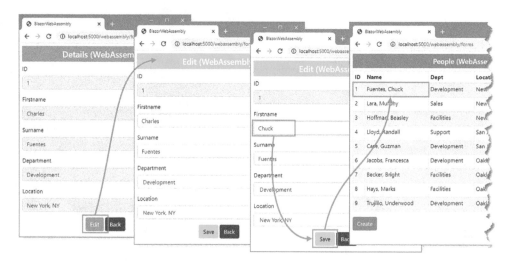

Figure 37-5. *The completed Blazor WebAssembly form application*

Summary

In this chapter, I described Blazor WebAssembly, showed you how to add it to a project, and demonstrated how it is similar—although not identical—to the Blazor Server described in earlier chapters. In the next chapter, I explain how to use ASP.NET Core Identity to secure an application.

CHAPTER 38

▪ ▪ ▪

Using ASP.NET Core Identity

ASP.NET Core Identity is an API from Microsoft to manage users in ASP.NET Core applications and includes support for integrating authentication and authorization into the request pipeline.

ASP.NET Core Identity is a toolkit with which you create the authorization and authentication features an application requires. There are endless integration options for features such as two-factor authentication, federation, single sign-on, and account self-service. There are options that are useful only in large corporate environments or when using cloud-hosted user management.

ASP.NET Core Identity has evolved into its own framework and is too large for me to cover in detail in this book. Instead, I have focused on the parts of the Identity API that intersect with web application development, much as I have done with Entity Framework Core. In this chapter, I show you how to add ASP.NET Core Identity to a project and explain how to consume the ASP.NET Core Identity API to create tools to perform basic user and role management. In Chapter 39, I show you how to use ASP.NET Core Identity to authenticate users and perform authorization. Table 38-1 puts ASP.NET Core Identity in context.

Table 38-1. *Putting ASP.NET Core Identity in Context*

Question	Answer
What is it?	ASP.NET Core Identity is an API for managing users.
Why is it useful?	Most applications have some features that should not be available to all users. ASP.NET Core Identity provides features to allow users to authenticate themselves and gain access to restricted features.
How is it used?	ASP.NET Core Identity is added to projects as a package and stores its data in a database using Entity Framework Core. Management of users is performed through a well-defined API, and its features are applied as attributes, as I describe in Chapter 39.
Are there any pitfalls or limitations?	ASP.NET Core Identity is complex and provides support for a wide range of authentication, authorization, and management models. It can be difficult to understand all the options, and documentation can be sparse.
Are there any alternatives?	There is no sensible alternative to ASP.NET Core Identity if a project needs to restrict access to features.

Table 38-2 summarizes the chapter.

Table 38-2. *Chapter Summary*

Problem	Solution	Listing
Preparing the application for Identity	Create the context class and use it to prepare a migration that is applied to the database	4–7
Managing user accounts	Use the UserManager<T> class	8–12, 15, 16
Setting a username and password policy	Use the options pattern to configure Identity	13, 14
Managing roles	Use the RoleManager<T> class to manage the roles and the UserManager<T> class to assign users to roles	17–20

© Adam Freeman 2020
A. Freeman, *Pro ASP.NET Core 3*, https://doi.org/10.1007/978-1-4842-5440-0_38

Preparing for This Chapter

This chapter uses the Advanced, DataModel, and BlazorWebAssembly projects from Chapter 37. If you are using Visual Studio, open the Advanced.sln file you created in the previous chapter to open all three projects. If you are using Visual Studio Code, open the folder that contains the three projects.

▓ **Tip** You can download the example project for this chapter—and for all the other chapters in this book—from https://github.com/apress/pro-asp.net-core-3. See Chapter 1 for how to get help if you have problems running the examples.

Open a new PowerShell command prompt, navigate to the folder that contains the Advanced.csproj file, and run the command shown in Listing 38-1 to drop the database.

Listing 38-1. Dropping the Database

```
dotnet ef database drop --force
```

Select Start Without Debugging or Run Without Debugging from the Debug menu or use the PowerShell command prompt to run the command shown in Listing 38-2.

Listing 38-2. Running the Example Application

```
dotnet run
```

Use a browser to request http://localhost:5000, which will produce the response shown in Figure 38-1.

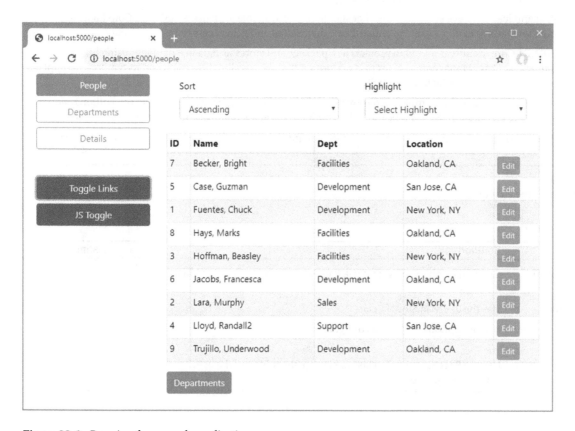

Figure 38-1. *Running the example application*

Preparing the Project for ASP.NET Core Identity

The process for setting up ASP.NET Core Identity requires adding a package to the project, configuring the application, and preparing the database. To get started, use a PowerShell command prompt to run the command shown in Listing 38-3 in the Advanced project folder, which installs the ASP.NET Core Identity package. If you are using Visual Studio, you can install the package by selecting Project ➤ Manage NuGet Packages.

Listing 38-3. Installing ASP.NET Core Identity Packages

```
dotnet add package Microsoft.AspNetCore.Identity.EntityFrameworkCore --version 3.1.1
```

Preparing the ASP.NET Core Identity Database

ASP.NET Identity requires a database, which is managed through Entity Framework Core. To create the Entity Framework Core context class that will provide access to the Identity data, add a class file named IdentityContext.cs to the Advanced/Models folder with the code shown in Listing 38-4.

Listing 38-4. The Contents of the IdentityContext.cs File in the Models Folder of the Advanced Project

```
using Microsoft.AspNetCore.Identity;
using Microsoft.AspNetCore.Identity.EntityFrameworkCore;
using Microsoft.EntityFrameworkCore;

namespace Advanced.Models {
    public class IdentityContext: IdentityDbContext<IdentityUser> {

        public IdentityContext(DbContextOptions<IdentityContext> options)
            : base(options) { }
    }
}
```

The ASP.NET Core Identity package includes the IdentityDbContext<T> class, which is used to create an Entity Framework Core context class. The generic type argument T is used to specify the class that will represent users in the database. You can create custom user classes, but I have used the basic class, called IdentityUser, which provides the core Identity features.

■ **Note** Don't worry if the classes used in Listing 38-4 don't make sense. If you are unfamiliar with Entity Framework Core, then I suggest you treat the class as a black box. Changes are rarely required once the building blocks for ASP.NET Core Identity have been set up, and you can copy the files from this chapter into your own projects.

Configuring the Database Connection String

A connection string is required to tell ASP.NET Core Identity where it should store its data. In Listing 38-5, I added a connection string to the appsettings.json file, alongside the one used for the application data.

Listing 38-5. Adding a Connection String in the appsettings.json File in the Advanced Project

```
{
  "Logging": {
    "LogLevel": {
      "Default": "Information",
      "Microsoft": "Warning",
      "Microsoft.Hosting.Lifetime": "Information",
```

```
        "Microsoft.EntityFrameworkCore": "Information"
      }
    },
  "AllowedHosts": "*",
  "ConnectionStrings": {
    "PeopleConnection": "Server=(localdb)\\MSSQLLocalDB;Database=People;MultipleActiveResultSets=True",
    "IdentityConnection": "Server=(localdb)\\MSSQLLocalDB;Database=Identity;MultipleActiveResultSets=True"
  }
}
```

The connection string specifies a LocalDB database named Identity.

■ **Note** The width of the printed page doesn't allow for sensible formatting of the connection string, which must appear in a single unbroken line. When you add the connection string to your own project, make sure that it is on a single line.

Configuring the Application

The next step is to configure ASP.NET Core so the Identity database context is set up as a service, as shown in Listing 38-6.

Listing 38-6. Configuring Identity in the Startup.cs File in the Advanced Project

```
using System;
using System.Collections.Generic;
using System.Linq;
using System.Threading.Tasks;
using Microsoft.AspNetCore.Builder;
using Microsoft.AspNetCore.Hosting;
using Microsoft.AspNetCore.Http;
using Microsoft.Extensions.DependencyInjection;
using Microsoft.Extensions.Hosting;
using Microsoft.Extensions.Configuration;
using Microsoft.EntityFrameworkCore;
using Advanced.Models;
using Microsoft.AspNetCore.ResponseCompression;
using Microsoft.AspNetCore.Identity;

namespace Advanced {
    public class Startup {

        public Startup(IConfiguration config) {
            Configuration = config;
        }

        public IConfiguration Configuration { get; set; }

        public void ConfigureServices(IServiceCollection services) {
            services.AddDbContext<DataContext>(opts => {
                opts.UseSqlServer(Configuration[
                    "ConnectionStrings:PeopleConnection"]);
                opts.EnableSensitiveDataLogging(true);
            });
            services.AddControllersWithViews().AddRazorRuntimeCompilation();
            services.AddRazorPages().AddRazorRuntimeCompilation();
            services.AddServerSideBlazor();
            services.AddSingleton<Services.ToggleService>();
```

```
        services.AddResponseCompression(opts => {
            opts.MimeTypes = ResponseCompressionDefaults.MimeTypes.Concat(
                new[] { "application/octet-stream" });
        });

        services.AddDbContext<IdentityContext>(opts =>
            opts.UseSqlServer(Configuration[
                "ConnectionStrings:IdentityConnection"]));
        services.AddIdentity<IdentityUser, IdentityRole>()
            .AddEntityFrameworkStores<IdentityContext>();
    }

    public void Configure(IApplicationBuilder app, DataContext context) {

        app.UseDeveloperExceptionPage();
        app.UseStaticFiles();
        app.UseRouting();

        app.UseEndpoints(endpoints => {
            endpoints.MapControllerRoute("controllers",
                "controllers/{controller=Home}/{action=Index}/{id?}");
            endpoints.MapDefaultControllerRoute();
            endpoints.MapRazorPages();
            endpoints.MapBlazorHub();

            endpoints.MapFallbackToClientSideBlazor<BlazorWebAssembly.Startup>
                ("/webassembly/{*path:nonfile}", "index.html");

            endpoints.MapFallbackToPage("/_Host");
        });

        app.Map("/webassembly", opts =>
            opts.UseClientSideBlazorFiles<BlazorWebAssembly.Startup>());

        SeedData.SeedDatabase(context);
    }
}
}
```

Creating and Applying the Identity Database Migration

The remaining step is to create the Entity Framework Core database migration and apply it to create the database. Open a new PowerShell window, navigate to the Advanced project folder, and run the commands shown in Listing 38-7.

Listing 38-7. Creating and Applying the Database Migration

```
dotnet ef migrations add --context IdentityContext Initial
dotnet ef database update --context IdentityContext
```

As I explained in earlier chapters, Entity Framework Core manages changes to database schemas through a feature called *migrations*. Now that there are two database context classes in the project, the Entity Framework Core tools require the --context argument to determine which context class is being used. The commands in Listing 38-7 create a migration that contains the ASP. NET Core Identity schema and apply it to the database.

RESETTING THE ASP.NET CORE IDENTITY DATABASE

If you need to reset the database, run the `dotnet ef database drop --force --context IdentityContext` command in the Advanced folder and then run the `dotnet ef database update --context IdentityContext` command. This will delete the existing database and create a new—and empty—replacement. Do not use these commands on production systems because you will delete user credentials. If you need to reset the main database, then run the `dotnet ef database drop --force --context DataContext` command, followed by `dotnet ef database update --context DataContext`.

Creating User Management Tools

In this section, I am going to create the tools that manage users through ASP.NET Core Identity. Users are managed through the UserManager<T> class, where T is the class chosen to represent users in the database. When I created the Entity Framework Core context class, I specified IdentityUser as the class to represent users in the database. This is the built-in class that is provided by ASP.NET Core Identity, and it provides the core features that are required by most applications. Table 38-3 describes the most useful IdentityUser properties. (There are additional properties defined by the IdentityUser class, but these are the ones required by most applications and are the ones I use in this book.)

SCAFFOLDING THE IDENTITY MANAGEMENT TOOLS

Microsoft provides a tool that will generate a set of Razor Pages for user management. The tool adds generic content—known as *scaffolding*—from templates to a project, which you then tailor to the application. I am not a fan of scaffolding or templates, and this is not an exception. The Microsoft Identity templates are well thought out, but they are of limited use because they focus on self-management, allowing users to create accounts, change passwords, and so on, without administrator intervention. You can adapt the templates to restrict the range of tasks that users perform, but the premise behind the features remains the same.

If you are writing the type of application where users manage their own credentials, then the scaffolding option may be worth considering and is described at `https://docs.microsoft.com/en-us/aspnet/core/security/authentication/scaffold-identity`. For all other approaches, the user management API provided by ASP.NET Core Identity should be used.

Table 38-3. *Useful IdentityUser Properties*

Name	Description
Id	This property contains the unique ID for the user.
UserName	This property returns the user's username.
Email	This property contains the user's e-mail address.

Table 38-4 describes the UserManagement<T> members I use in this section to manage users.

Table 38-4. *Useful UserManager<T> Members*

Name	Description
Users	This property returns a sequence containing the users stored in the database.
FindByIdAsync(id)	This method queries the database for the user object with the specified ID.
CreateAsync(user, password)	This method stores a new user in the database using the specified password.
UpdateAsync(user)	This method modifies an existing user in the database.
DeleteAsync(user)	This method removes the specified user from the database.

Preparing for User Management Tools

In preparation for creating the management tools, add the expressions shown in Listing 38-8 to the _ViewImports.cshtml file in the Pages folder of the Advanced project.

Listing 38-8. Adding Expressions in the _ViewImports.cshtml File in the Pages Folder of the Advanced Project

```
@addTagHelper *, Microsoft.AspNetCore.Mvc.TagHelpers
@using Advanced.Models
@using Microsoft.AspNetCore.Mvc.RazorPages
@using Microsoft.EntityFrameworkCore
@using System.ComponentModel.DataAnnotations
@using Microsoft.AspNetCore.Identity
@using Advanced.Pages
```

Next, create the Pages/Users folder in the Advanced project and add to it a Razor Layout named _Layout.cshtml to the Pages/Users folder with the content shown in Listing 38-9.

Listing 38-9. The _Layout.cshtml File in the Pages/Users Folder in the Advanced Project

```
<!DOCTYPE html>
<html>
<head>
    <title>Identity</title>
    <link href="/lib/twitter-bootstrap/css/bootstrap.min.css" rel="stylesheet" />
</head>
<body>
    <div class="m-2">
        <h5 class="bg-info text-white text-center p-2">User Administration</h5>
        @RenderBody()
    </div>
</body>
</html>
```

Add a class file named AdminPageModel.cs to the Pages folder and use it to define the class shown in Listing 38-10.

Listing 38-10. The AdminPageModel.cs File in the Pages Folder in the Advanced Project

```
using Microsoft.AspNetCore.Mvc.RazorPages;

namespace Advanced.Pages {
    public class AdminPageModel: PageModel {

    }
}
```

This class will be the base for the page model classes defined in this section. As you will see in Chapter 39, a common base class is useful when it comes to securing the application.

Enumerating User Accounts

Although the database is currently empty, I am going to start by creating a Razor Page that will enumerate user accounts. Add a Razor Page named List.cshtml to the Pages/Users folder in the Advanced project with the content shown in Listing 38-11.

Listing 38-11. The Contents of the List.cshtml File in the Pages/Users Folder in the Advanced Project

```
@page
@model ListModel

<table class="table table-sm table-bordered">
    <tr><th>ID</th><th>Name</th><th>Email</th><th></th></tr>
    @if (Model.Users.Count() == 0) {
        <tr><td colspan="4" class="text-center">No User Accounts</td></tr>
    } else {
        foreach (IdentityUser user in Model.Users) {
            <tr>
                <td>@user.Id</td>
                <td>@user.UserName</td>
                <td>@user.Email</td>
                <td class="text-center">
                    <form asp-page="List" method="post">
                        <input type="hidden" name="Id" value="@user.Id" />
                        <a class="btn btn-sm btn-warning" asp-page="Editor"
                            asp-route-id="@user.Id" asp-route-mode="edit">Edit</a>
                        <button type="submit" class="btn btn-sm btn-danger">
                            Delete
                        </button>
                    </form>
                </td>
            </tr>
        }
    }
</table>

<a class="btn btn-primary" asp-page="create">Create</a>

@functions {

    public class ListModel : AdminPageModel {
        public UserManager<IdentityUser> UserManager;

        public ListModel(UserManager<IdentityUser> userManager) {
            UserManager = userManager;
        }

        public IEnumerable<IdentityUser> Users { get; set; }

        public void OnGet() {
            Users = UserManager.Users;
        }
    }
}
```

The UserManager<IdentityUser> class is set up as a service so that it can be consumed via dependency injection. The Users property returns a collection of IdentityUser objects, which can be used to enumerate the user accounts. This Razor Page displays the users in a table, with buttons that allow each user to be edited or deleted, although this won't be visible initially because a placeholder message is shown when there are no user objects to display. There is a button that navigates to a Razor Page named Create, which I define in the next section.

Restart ASP.NET and request http://localhost:5000/users/list to see the (currently empty) data table, which is shown in Figure 38-2.

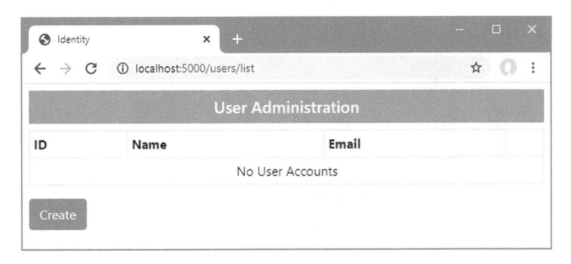

Figure 38-2. *Enumerating users*

Creating Users

Add a Razor Page named Create.cshtml to the Pages/Users folder with the content shown in Listing 38-12.

Listing 38-12. The Contents of the Create.cshtml File in the Pages/Users Folder of the Advanced Project

```
@page
@model CreateModel

<h5 class="bg-primary text-white text-center p-2">Create User</h5>
<form method="post">
    <div asp-validation-summary="All" class="text-danger"></div>
    <div class="form-group">
        <label>User Name</label>
        <input name="UserName" class="form-control" value="@Model.UserName" />
    </div>
    <div class="form-group">
        <label>Email</label>
        <input name="Email" class="form-control" value="@Model.Email" />
    </div>
    <div class="form-group">
        <label>Password</label>
        <input name="Password" class="form-control" value="@Model.Password" />
    </div>
    <button type="submit" class="btn btn-primary">Submit</button>
    <a class="btn btn-secondary" asp-page="list">Back</a>
</form>

@functions {

    public class CreateModel : AdminPageModel {
        public UserManager<IdentityUser> UserManager;

        public CreateModel(UserManager<IdentityUser> usrManager) {
            UserManager = usrManager;
        }
```

```
        [BindProperty][Required]
        public string UserName { get; set; }

        [BindProperty][Required][EmailAddress]
        public string Email { get; set; }

        [BindProperty][Required]
        public string Password { get; set; }

        public async Task<IActionResult> OnPostAsync() {
            if (ModelState.IsValid) {
                IdentityUser user =
                    new IdentityUser { UserName = UserName, Email = Email };
                IdentityResult result =
                    await UserManager.CreateAsync(user, Password);
                if (result.Succeeded) {
                    return RedirectToPage("List");
                }
                foreach (IdentityError err in result.Errors) {
                    ModelState.AddModelError("", err.Description);
                }
            }
            return Page();
        }
    }
}
```

Even though ASP.NET Core Identity data is stored using Entity Framework Core, you don't work directly with the database context class. Instead, data is managed through the methods provided by the UserManager<T> class. New users are created using the CreateAsync method, which accepts an IdentityUser object and a password string as arguments.

This Razor Page defines three properties that are subject to model binding. The UserName and Email properties are used to configure the IdentityUser object, which is combined with the value bound to the Password property to call the CreateAsync method. These properties are configured with validation attributes, which ensure that values are supplied and that the Email property is a formatted e-mail address.

The result of the CreateAsync method is a Task<IdentityResult> object, which indicates the outcome of the create operation, using the properties described in Table 38-5.

Table 38-5. *The Properties Defined by the IdentityResult Class*

Name	Description
Succeeded	Returns true if the operation succeeded.
Errors	Returns a sequence of IdentityError objects that describe the errors encountered while attempting the operation. Each IdentityError object provides a Description property that summarizes the problem.

I inspect the Succeeded property to determine whether a new user has been created in the database. If the Succeeded property is true, then the client is redirected to the List page so that the list of users is displayed, reflecting the new addition.

```
...
if (result.Succeeded) {
    return RedirectToPage("List");
}
foreach (IdentityError err in result.Errors) {
    ModelState.AddModelError("", err.Description);
}
...
```

If the Succeeded property is false, then the sequence of IdentityError objects provided by the Errors property is enumerated, with the Description property used to create a model-level validation error using the ModelState.AddModelError method.

To test the ability to create a new user account, restart ASP.NET Core and request http://localhost:5000/users/list. Click the Create button and fill in the form with the values shown in Table 38-6.

■ **Tip** There are domains reserved for testing, including example.com. You can see a complete list at https://tools.ietf.org/html/rfc2606.

Table 38-6. *The Values for Creating an Example User*

Field	Description
Name	Joe
Email	*joe@example.com*
Password	Secret123$

Once you have entered the values, click the Submit button. ASP.NET Core Identity will create the user in the database, and the browser will be redirected, as shown in Figure 38-3. (You will see a different ID value because IDs are randomly generated for each user.)

■ **Note** I used a regular input element for the Password field to make it easier to follow the examples in this chapter. For real projects, it is a good idea to set the input element's type attribute to password so that the characters entered cannot be seen.

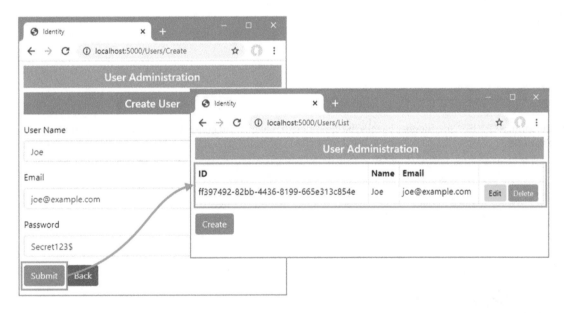

Figure 38-3. *Creating a new user*

Click the Create button again and enter the same details into the form, using the values in Table 38-6. This time you will see an error reported through the model validation summary when you click the Create button, as shown in Figure 38-4. This is an example of an error returned through the IdentityResult object produced by the CreateAsync method.

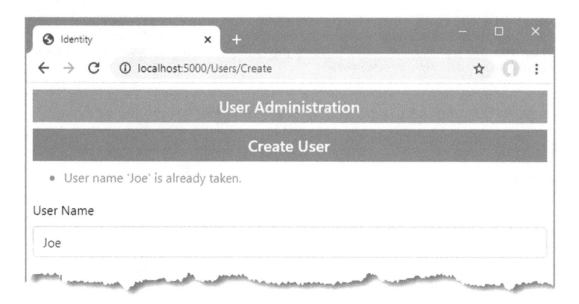

Figure 38-4. *An error when creating a new user*

Validating Passwords

One of the most common requirements, especially for corporate applications, is to enforce a password policy. You can see the default policy by navigating to `http://localhost:5000/Users/Create` and filling out the form with the data shown in Table 38-7.

Table 38-7. *The Values for Creating an Example User*

Field	Description
Name	Alice
Email	alice@example.com
Password	secret

When you submit the form, ASP.NET Core Identity checks the candidate password and generates errors if it doesn't match the password, as shown in Figure 38-5.

Figure 38-5. *Password validation errors*

The password validation rules are configured using the options pattern, as shown in Listing 38-13.

Listing 38-13. Configuring Password Validation in the Startup.cs File in the Advanced Project

```
...
public void ConfigureServices(IServiceCollection services) {
    services.AddDbContext<DataContext>(opts => {
        opts.UseSqlServer(Configuration[
            "ConnectionStrings:PeopleConnection"]);
        opts.EnableSensitiveDataLogging(true);
    });
    services.AddControllersWithViews().AddRazorRuntimeCompilation();
    services.AddRazorPages().AddRazorRuntimeCompilation();
    services.AddServerSideBlazor();
    services.AddSingleton<Services.ToggleService>();

    services.AddResponseCompression(opts => {
        opts.MimeTypes = ResponseCompressionDefaults.MimeTypes.Concat(
            new[] { "application/octet-stream" });
    });

    services.AddDbContext<IdentityContext>(opts =>
        opts.UseSqlServer(Configuration["ConnectionStrings:IdentityConnection"]));
    services.AddIdentity<IdentityUser, IdentityRole>()
        .AddEntityFrameworkStores<IdentityContext>();

    services.Configure<IdentityOptions>(opts => {
        opts.Password.RequiredLength = 6;
        opts.Password.RequireNonAlphanumeric = false;
        opts.Password.RequireLowercase = false;
        opts.Password.RequireUppercase = false;
```

```
        opts.Password.RequireDigit = false;
    });
}
...
```

ASP.NET Core Identity is configured using the IdentityOptions class, whose Password property returns a PasswordOptions class that configures password validation using the properties described in Table 38-8.

Table 38-8. *The PasswordOptions Properties*

Name	Description
RequiredLength	This int property is used to specify the minimum length for passwords.
RequireNonAlphanumeric	Setting this bool property to true requires passwords to contain at least one character that is not a letter or a digit.
RequireLowercase	Setting this bool property to true requires passwords to contain at least one lowercase character.
RequireUppercase	Setting this bool property to true requires passwords to contain at least one uppercase character.
RequireDigit	Setting this bool property to true requires passwords to contain at least one numeric character.

In the listing, I specified that passwords must have a minimum length of six characters and disabled the other constraints. This isn't something that you should do without careful consideration in a real project, but it allows for an effective demonstration. Restart ASP.NET Core, request http://localhost:5000/users/create, and fill out the form using the details from Table 38-7. When you click the Submit button, the password will be accepted by the new validation rules, and a new user will be created, as shown in Figure 38-6.

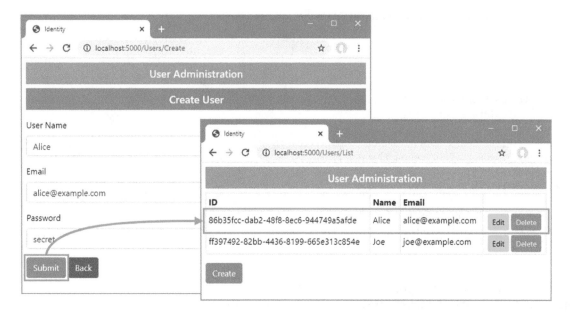

Figure 38-6. *Changing the password validation rules*

Validating User Details

Validation is also performed on usernames and e-mail addresses when accounts are created. To see how validation is applied, request http://localhost:5000/users/create and fill out the form using the values shown in Table 38-9.

Table 38-9. *The Values for Creating an Example User*

Field	Description
Name	Bob!
Email	alice@example.com
Password	secret

Click the Submit button, and you will see the error message shown in Figure 38-7.

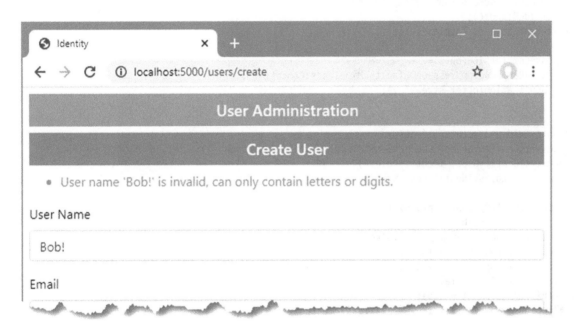

Figure 38-7. *A user details validation error*

Validation can be configured with the options pattern, using the User property defined by the IdentityOptions class. This class returns a UserOptions class, whose properties are described in Table 38-10.

Table 38-10. *The UserOptions Properties*

Name	Description
AllowedUserNameCharacters	This string property contains all the legal characters that can be used in a username. The default value specifies a–z, A–Z, and 0–9 and the hyphen, period, underscore, and @ characters. This property is not a regular expression, and every legal character must be specified explicitly in the string.
RequireUniqueEmail	Setting this bool property to true requires new accounts to specify e-mail addresses that have not been used previously.

In Listing 38-14, I have changed the configuration of the application so that unique e-mail addresses are required and so that only lowercase alphabetic characters are allowed in usernames.

Listing 38-14. Changing the User Validation Settings in the Startup.cs File in the Advanced Project

```
...
public void ConfigureServices(IServiceCollection services) {
    services.AddDbContext<DataContext>(opts => {
        opts.UseSqlServer(Configuration[
            "ConnectionStrings:PeopleConnection"]);
        opts.EnableSensitiveDataLogging(true);
    });
    services.AddControllersWithViews().AddRazorRuntimeCompilation();
    services.AddRazorPages().AddRazorRuntimeCompilation();
    services.AddServerSideBlazor();
    services.AddSingleton<Services.ToggleService>();

    services.AddResponseCompression(opts => {
        opts.MimeTypes = ResponseCompressionDefaults.MimeTypes.Concat(
            new[] { "application/octet-stream" });
    });

    services.AddDbContext<IdentityContext>(opts =>
        opts.UseSqlServer(Configuration["ConnectionStrings:IdentityConnection"]));
    services.AddIdentity<IdentityUser, IdentityRole>()
        .AddEntityFrameworkStores<IdentityContext>();

    services.Configure<IdentityOptions>(opts => {
        opts.Password.RequiredLength = 6;
        opts.Password.RequireNonAlphanumeric = false;
        opts.Password.RequireLowercase = false;
        opts.Password.RequireUppercase = false;
        opts.Password.RequireDigit = false;
        opts.User.RequireUniqueEmail = true;
        opts.User.AllowedUserNameCharacters = "abcdefghijklmnopqrstuvwxyz";
    });
}
...
```

Restart ASP.NET Core, request http://localhost:5000/users/create, and fill out the form with the values in Table 38-9. Click the Submit button, and you will see that the e-mail address now causes an error. The username still contains illegal characters and is also flagged as an error, as shown in Figure 38-8.

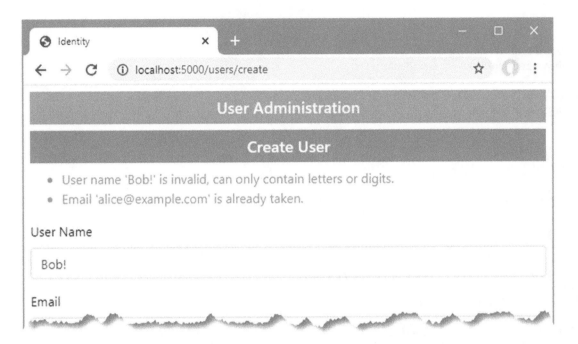

Figure 38-8. *Validating user detail*

Editing Users

To add support for editing users, add a Razor Page named `Editor.cshtml` to the `Pages/Users` folder of the Advanced project with the content shown in Listing 38-15.

Listing 38-15. The Contents of the Editor.cshtml File in the Pages/Users Folder of the Advanced Project

```
@page "{id}"
@model EditorModel

<h5 class="bg-warning text-white text-center p-2">Edit User</h5>
<form method="post">
    <div asp-validation-summary="All" class="text-danger"></div>
    <div class="form-group">
        <label>ID</label>
        <input name="Id" class="form-control" value="@Model.Id" disabled />
        <input name="Id" type="hidden" value="@Model.Id" />
    </div>
    <div class="form-group">
        <label>User Name</label>
        <input name="UserName" class="form-control" value="@Model.UserName" />
    </div>
    <div class="form-group">
        <label>Email</label>
        <input name="Email" class="form-control" value="@Model.Email" />
    </div>
    <div class="form-group">
        <label>New Password</label>
        <input name="Password" class="form-control" value="@Model.Password" />
    </div>
    <button type="submit" class="btn btn-warning">Submit</button>
    <a class="btn btn-secondary" asp-page="list">Back</a>
</form>
```

1023

```
@functions {

    public class EditorModel : AdminPageModel {
        public UserManager<IdentityUser> UserManager;

        public EditorModel(UserManager<IdentityUser> usrManager) {
            UserManager = usrManager;
        }

        [BindProperty][Required]
        public string Id { get; set; }

        [BindProperty][Required]
        public string UserName { get; set; }

        [BindProperty][Required][EmailAddress]
        public string Email { get; set; }

        [BindProperty]
        public string Password { get; set; }

        public async Task OnGetAsync(string id) {
            IdentityUser user = await UserManager.FindByIdAsync(id);
            Id = user.Id; UserName = user.UserName; Email = user.Email;
        }

        public async Task<IActionResult> OnPostAsync() {
            if (ModelState.IsValid) {
                IdentityUser user = await UserManager.FindByIdAsync(Id);
                user.UserName = UserName;
                user.Email = Email;
                IdentityResult result = await UserManager.UpdateAsync(user);
                if (result.Succeeded && !String.IsNullOrEmpty(Password)) {
                    await UserManager.RemovePasswordAsync(user);
                    result = await UserManager.AddPasswordAsync(user, Password);
                }
                if (result.Succeeded) {
                    return RedirectToPage("List");
                }
                foreach (IdentityError err in result.Errors) {
                    ModelState.AddModelError("", err.Description);
                }
            }
            return Page();
        }
    }
}
```

The Editor page uses the UserManager<T>.FindByIdAsync method to locate the user, querying the database with the id value received through the routing system and received as an argument to the OnGetAsync method. The values from the IdentityUser object returned by the query are used to populate the properties that are displayed by the view part of the page, ensuring that the values are not lost if the page is redisplayed due to validation errors.

When the user submits the form, the FindByIdAsync method is used to query the database for the IdentityUser object, which is updated with the UserName and Email values provided in the form. Passwords required a different approach and must be removed from the user object before a new password is assigned, like this:

```
...
await UserManager.RemovePasswordAsync(user);
result = await UserManager.AddPasswordAsync(user, Password);
...
```

The Editor page changes the password only if the form contains a Password value and if the updates for the UserName and Email fields have been successful. Errors from ASP.NET Core Identity are presented as validation messages, and the browser is redirected to the List page after a successful update. Request http://localhost:5000/Users/List, click the Edit button for Joe, and change the UserName field to **bob**, with all lowercase characters. Click the Submit button, and you will see the change reflected in the list of users, as shown in Figure 38-9.

■ **Note**   You will see an error if you click the Edit button for the Alice account and click Submit without making changes. This is because the account was created before the validation policy was changed. ASP.NET Core Identity applies validation checks for updates, leading to the odd situation where the data in the database can be read—and used—but must be changed for the user to be updated.

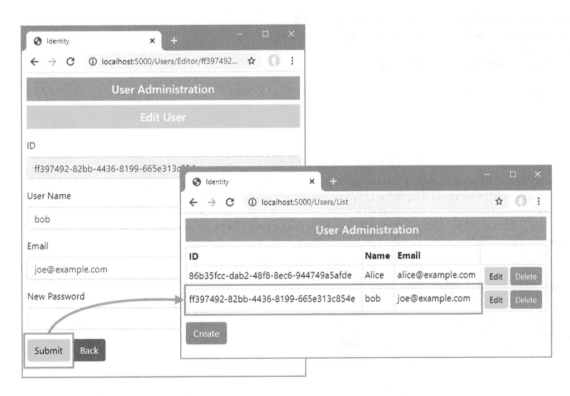

Figure 38-9. *Editing a user*

Deleting Users

The last feature I need for my basic user management application is the ability to delete users, as shown in Listing 38-16.

Listing 38-16. Deleting Users in the List.cshtml File in the Pages/Users Folder in the Advanced Project

```
...
@functions {

    public class ListModel : AdminPageModel {
        public UserManager<IdentityUser> UserManager;

        public ListModel(UserManager<IdentityUser> userManager) {
            UserManager = userManager;
        }

        public IEnumerable<IdentityUser> Users { get; set; }

        public void OnGet() {
            Users = UserManager.Users;
        }

        public async Task<IActionResult> OnPostAsync(string id) {
            IdentityUser user = await UserManager.FindByIdAsync(id);
            if (user != null) {
                await UserManager.DeleteAsync(user);
            }
            return RedirectToPage();
        }
    }
}
...
```

The List page already displays a Delete button for each user in the data table, which submits a POST request containing the Id value for the IdentityUser object to be removed. The OnPostAsync method receives the Id value and uses it to query Identity using the FindByIdAsync method, passing the object that is returned to the DeleteAsync method, which deletes it from the database. To check the delete functionality, request http://localhost:5000/Users/List and click Delete for the Alice account. The user object will be removed, as shown in Figure 38-10.

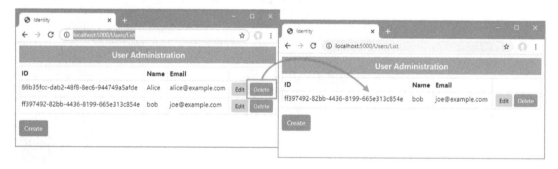

Figure 38-10. Deleting a user

Creating Role Management Tools

Some applications enforce only two levels of authorization: authenticated users are allowed access to all the application's features, while unauthenticated users have less—or no—access. The SportsStore application in Part 1 followed this approach: there was one user, and once authenticated, they had access to all the application's features, including administration tools, while unauthenticated users were restricted to the public store features.

ASP.NET Core Identity supports *roles* for applications that require more granular authorization. Users are assigned to one or more roles, and their membership of those roles determines which features are accessible. In the sections that follow, I show you how to build tools to create and manage roles.

Roles are managed through the RoleManager<T> class, where T is the representation of roles in the database. When I configured ASP.NET Core Identity at the start of the chapter, I selected IdentityRole, which is the built-in class that Identity provides to describe a role, which means that I will be using the RoleManager<IdentityRole> class in these examples. The RoleManager<T> class defines the methods and properties shown in Table 38-11 that allow roles to be created and managed.

Table 38-11. *The Members Defined by the RoleManager<T> Class*

Name	Description
CreateAsync(role)	Creates a new role
DeleteAsync(role)	Deletes the specified role
FindByIdAsync(id)	Finds a role by its ID
FindByNameAsync(name)	Finds a role by its name
RoleExistsAsync(name)	Returns true if a role with the specified name exists
UpdateAsync(role)	Stores changes to the specified role
Roles	Returns an enumeration of the roles that have been defined

Table 38-12 describes the key properties defined by the IdentityRole class.

Table 38-12. *Useful IdentityRole Properties*

Name	Description
Id	This property contains the unique ID for the role.
Name	This property returns the role name.

Although roles are managed through the RoleManager<T> class, membership of roles is managed through the methods provided by UserManager<T> described in Table 38-13.

Table 38-13. *The UserManager<T> Methods for Managing Role Membership*

Name	Description
AddToRoleAsync(user, role)	This method adds a user to a role.
RemoveFromRoleAsync(user, role)	This method removes a user from a role.
GetRolesAsync(user)	This method returns the roles for which the user is a member.
GetUsersInRoleAsync(role)	This method returns users who are members of the specified role.
IsInRoleAsync(user, role)	This method returns true if the user is a member of the specified role.

Preparing for Role Management Tools

To prepare for the role management tools, create the Pages/Roles folder in the Advanced project and add to it a Razor layout named _Layout.cshtml with the content shown in Listing 38-17.

Listing 38-17. The Contents of the _Layout.cshtml File in the Pages/Roles Folder in the Advanced Project

```
<!DOCTYPE html>
<html>
<head>
    <title>Identity</title>
    <link href="/lib/twitter-bootstrap/css/bootstrap.min.css" rel="stylesheet" />
</head>
<body>
    <div class="m-2">
        <h5 class="bg-secondary text-white text-center p-2">Role Administration</h5>
        @RenderBody()
    </div>
</body>
</html>
```

This layout will ensure there is an obvious difference between the user and role management tools.

Enumerating and Deleting Roles

Add a Razor Page named List.cshtml to the Pages/Roles folder in the Advanced project with the content shown in Listing 38-18.

Listing 38-18. The Contents of the List.cshtml File in the Pages/Roles Folder in the Advanced Project

```
@page
@model ListModel

<table class="table table-sm table-bordered">
    <tr><th>ID</th><th>Name</th><th>Members</th><th></th></tr>
    @if (Model.Roles.Count() == 0) {
        <tr><td colspan="4" class="text-center">No Roles</td></tr>
    } else {
        foreach (IdentityRole role in Model.Roles) {
            <tr>
                <td>@role.Id</td>
                <td>@role.Name</td>
                <td>@(await Model.GetMembersString(role.Name))</td>
                <td class="text-center">
                    <form asp-page="List" method="post">
                        <input type="hidden" name="Id" value="@role.Id" />
                        <a class="btn btn-sm btn-warning" asp-page="Editor"
                            asp-route-id="@role.Id" asp-route-mode="edit">Edit</a>
                        <button type="submit" class="btn btn-sm btn-danger">
                            Delete
                        </button>
                    </form>
                </td>
            </tr>
        }
    }
</table>
<a class="btn btn-primary" asp-page="create">Create</a>

@functions {

    public class ListModel : AdminPageModel {
        public UserManager<IdentityUser> UserManager;
        public RoleManager<IdentityRole> RoleManager;
```

```
        public ListModel(UserManager<IdentityUser> userManager,
                RoleManager<IdentityRole> roleManager) {
            UserManager = userManager;
            RoleManager = roleManager;
        }

        public IEnumerable<IdentityRole> Roles { get; set; }

        public void OnGet() {
            Roles = RoleManager.Roles;
        }

        public async Task<string> GetMembersString(string role) {
            IEnumerable<IdentityUser> users
                = (await UserManager.GetUsersInRoleAsync(role));
            string result = users.Count() == 0
                ? "No members"
                : string.Join(", ", users.Take(3).Select(u => u.UserName).ToArray());
            return users.Count() > 3 ? $"{result}, (plus others)" : result;
        }

        public async Task<IActionResult> OnPostAsync(string id) {
            IdentityRole role = await RoleManager.FindByIdAsync(id);
            await RoleManager.DeleteAsync(role);
            return RedirectToPage();
        }
    }
}
```

The roles are enumerated, along with the names of up to three of the role members or a placeholder message if there are no members. There is also a Create button, and each role is presented with Edit and Delete buttons, following the same pattern I used for the user management tools.

The Delete button sends a POST request back to the Razor Page. The OnPostAsync method uses the FindByIdAsync method to retrieve the role object, which is passed to the DeleteAsync method to remove it from the database.

Creating Roles

Add a Razor Page named Create.cshtml in the Pages/Roles folder in the Advanced project with the contents shown in Listing 38-19.

Listing 38-19. The Contents of the Create.cshtml File in the Pages/Roles Folder in the Advanced Project

```
@page
@model CreateModel

<h5 class="bg-primary text-white text-center p-2">Create Role</h5>
<form method="post">
    <div asp-validation-summary="All" class="text-danger"></div>
    <div class="form-group">
        <label>Role Name</label>
        <input name="Name" class="form-control" value="@Model.Name" />
    </div>
    <button type="submit" class="btn btn-primary">Submit</button>
    <a class="btn btn-secondary" asp-page="list">Back</a>
</form>
```

```
@functions {

    public class CreateModel : AdminPageModel {
        public RoleManager<IdentityRole> RoleManager;

        public CreateModel(UserManager<IdentityUser> userManager,
                RoleManager<IdentityRole> roleManager) {
            RoleManager = roleManager;
        }

        [BindProperty][Required]
        public string Name { get; set; }

        public async Task<IActionResult> OnPostAsync() {
            if (ModelState.IsValid) {
                IdentityRole role = new IdentityRole { Name = Name };
                IdentityResult result = await RoleManager.CreateAsync(role);
                if (result.Succeeded) {
                    return RedirectToPage("List");
                }
                foreach (IdentityError err in result.Errors) {
                    ModelState.AddModelError("", err.Description);
                }
            }
            return Page();
        }
    }
}
```

The user is presented with a form containing an input element to specify the name of the new role. When the form is submitted, the OnPostAsync method creates a new IdentityRole object and passes it to the CreateAsync method.

Assigning Role Membership

To add support for managing role memberships, add a Razor Page named Editor.cshtml to the Pages/Roles folder in the Advanced project, with the content shown in Listing 38-20.

Listing 38-20. The Contents of the Editor.cshtml File in the Pages/Roles Folder in the Advanced Project

```
@page "{id}"
@model EditorModel

<h5 class="bg-primary text-white text-center p-2">Edit Role: @Model.Role.Name</h5>

<form method="post">
    <input type="hidden" name="rolename" value="@Model.Role.Name" />
    <div asp-validation-summary="All" class="text-danger"></div>
    <h5 class="bg-secondary text-white p-2">Members</h5>
    <table class="table table-sm table-striped table-bordered">
        <thead><tr><th>User</th><th>Email</th><th></th></tr></thead>
        <tbody>
            @if ((await Model.Members()).Count() == 0) {
                <tr><td colspan="3" class="text-center">No members</td></tr>
            }
```

```
            @foreach (IdentityUser user in await Model.Members()) {
                <tr>
                    <td>@user.UserName</td>
                    <td>@user.Email</td>
                    <td>
                        <button asp-route-userid="@user.Id"
                                class="btn btn-primary btn-sm" type="submit">
                            Change
                        </button>
                    </td>
                </tr>
            }
        </tbody>
    </table>

    <h5 class="bg-secondary text-white p-2">Non-Members</h5>
    <table class="table table-sm table-striped table-bordered">
        <thead><tr><th>User</th><th>Email</th><th></th></tr></thead>
        <tbody>
            @if ((await Model.NonMembers()).Count() == 0) {
                <tr><td colspan="3" class="text-center">No non-members</td></tr>
            }
            @foreach (IdentityUser user in await Model.NonMembers()) {
                <tr>
                    <td>@user.UserName</td>
                    <td>@user.Email</td>
                    <td>
                        <button asp-route-userid="@user.Id"
                            class="btn btn-primary btn-sm" type="submit">
                                Change
                        </button>
                    </td>
                </tr>
            }
        </tbody>
    </table>
</form>

<a class="btn btn-secondary" asp-page="list">Back</a>

@functions {

    public class EditorModel : AdminPageModel {
        public UserManager<IdentityUser> UserManager;
        public RoleManager<IdentityRole> RoleManager;

        public EditorModel(UserManager<IdentityUser> userManager,
                RoleManager<IdentityRole> roleManager) {
            UserManager = userManager;
            RoleManager = roleManager;
        }

        public IdentityRole Role { get; set; }

        public Task<IList<IdentityUser>> Members() =>
                UserManager.GetUsersInRoleAsync(Role.Name);
```

```
    public async Task<IEnumerable<IdentityUser>> NonMembers() =>
            UserManager.Users.ToList().Except(await Members());

    public async Task OnGetAsync(string id) {
        Role = await RoleManager.FindByIdAsync(id);
    }

    public async Task<IActionResult> OnPostAsync(string userid,
            string rolename) {
        Role = await RoleManager.FindByNameAsync(rolename);
        IdentityUser user = await UserManager.FindByIdAsync(userid);
        IdentityResult result;
        if (await UserManager.IsInRoleAsync(user, rolename)) {
            result = await UserManager.RemoveFromRoleAsync(user, rolename);
        } else {
            result = await UserManager.AddToRoleAsync(user, rolename);
        }
        if (result.Succeeded) {
            return RedirectToPage();
        } else {
            foreach (IdentityError err in result.Errors) {
                ModelState.AddModelError("", err.Description);
            }
            return Page();
        }
    }
}
}
```

The user is presented with a table showing the users who are members of the role and with a table showing nonmembers. Each row contains a Change button that submits the form. The OnPostAsync method uses the UserManager.FindByIdAsync method to retrieve the user object from the database. The IsInRoleAsync method is used to determine whether the user is a member of the role, and the AddToRoleAsync and RemoveFromRoleAsync methods are used to add and remove the user, respectively.

Restart ASP.NET Core and request http://localhost:5000/roles/list. The list will be empty because there are no roles in the database. Click the Create button, enter **Admins** into the text field, and click the Submit button to create a new role. Once the role has been created, click the Edit button, and you will see the list of users who can be added to the role. Clicking the Change button will move the user in and out of the role. Click back, and the list will be updated to show the users who are members of the role, as shown in Figure 38-11.

■ **Caution**   ASP.NET Core Identity revalidates user details when changing role assignments, which will result in an error if you try to modify a user whose details do not match the current restrictions, which happens when restrictions are introduced after the application has been deployed and the database is already populated with users created under the old roles. It is for this reason that the Razor Page in Listing 38-20 checks the result from the operations to add or remove users from a role and displays any errors as validation messages.

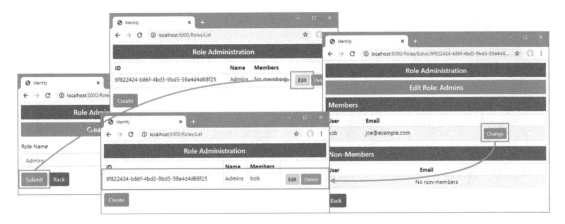

Figure 38-11. *Managing roles*

Summary

In this chapter, I showed you how to add ASP.NET Core Identity to a project and prepare its database to store users and roles. I described the basic ASP.NET Core Identity API and showed you how it can be used to create tools to manage users and roles. In the next chapter, I show you how to apply ASP.NET Core Identity to control access to controllers, Razor Pages, Blazor applications, and web services.

CHAPTER 39

Applying ASP.NET Core Identity

In this chapter, I explain how ASP.NET Core Identity is applied to authenticate users and authorize access to application features. I create the features required for users to establish their identity, explain how access to endpoints can be controlled, and demonstrate the security features that Blazor provides. I also show two different ways to authenticate web service clients. Table 39-1 summarizes the chapter.

Table 39-1. *Chapter Summary*

Problem	Solution	Listing
Authenticating users	Use the SignInManager<T> class to validate the credentials users provide and use the built-in middleware to trigger authentication	3–18
Restricting access to endpoints	Use the Authorize attribute and the built-in middleware to control access	9–13
Restricting access to Blazor components	Use the Authorize attribute and the built-in Razor Components to control access	14–17
Restricting access to web services	Use cookie authentication or bearer tokens	18–30

Preparing for This Chapter

This chapter uses the projects from Chapter 38. To prepare for this chapter, I am going to reset both the application data and ASP.NET Core Identity databases and create new users and roles. Open a new command prompt and run the commands shown in Listing 39-1 in the Advanced project folder, which contains the Advanced.csproj file. These commands remove the existing databases and re-create them.

■ **Tip**   You can download the example project for this chapter—and for all the other chapters in this book—from https://github.com/apress/pro-asp.net-core-3. See Chapter 1 for how to get help if you have problems running the examples.

Listing 39-1. Re-creating the Project Databases

```
dotnet ef database drop --force --context DataContext
dotnet ef database drop --force --context IdentityContext
dotnet ef database update --context DataContext
dotnet ef database update --context IdentityContext
```

Now that the application contains multiple database context classes, the Entity Framework Core commands require the --context argument to select the context that a command applies to.

Select Start Without Debugging or Run Without Debugging from the Debug menu or use the PowerShell command prompt to run the command shown in Listing 39-2.

Listing 39-2. Running the Example Application

```
dotnet run
```

Use a browser to request http://localhost:5000/home/index, which will produce the response shown in Figure 39-1.

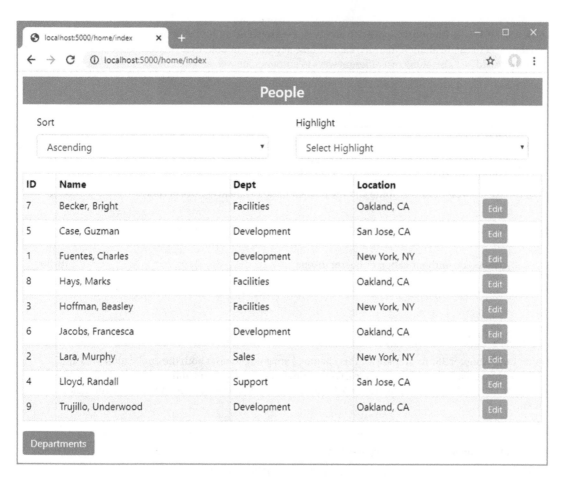

Figure 39-1. *Running the example application*

The main application database is automatically reseeded when the application starts. There is no seed data for the ASP.NET Core Identity database. Request http://localhost:5000/users/list and http://localhost:5000/roles/list, and you will see the responses in Figure 39-2, which show the database is empty.

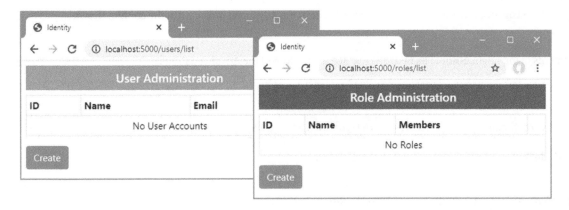

Figure 39-2. *The empty ASP.NET Core Identity database*

Authenticating Users

In the sections that follow, I show you how to add authentication features to the example project so that users can present their credentials and establish their identity to the application.

AUTHENTICATION VS. AUTHORIZATION

It is important to understand the difference between authentication and authorization when working with ASP.NET Core Identity. *Authentication*, often referred to as *AuthN*, is the process of establishing the identity of a user, which the user does by presenting their credentials to the application. In the case of the example application, those credentials are a username and a password. The username is public information, but the password is known only by the user, and when the correct password is presented, the application is able to authenticate the user.

Authorization, often referred to as *AuthZ*, is the process of granting access to application features based on a user's identity. Authorization can be performed only when a user has been authenticated because an application has to know the identity of a user before deciding whether they are entitled to use a specific feature.

Creating the Login Feature

To enforce a security policy, the application must allow users to authenticate themselves, which is done using the ASP.NET Core Identity API. Create the Pages/Account folder and add to it a Razor Page named _Layout.cshtml with the content shown in Listing 39-3. This layout will provide common content for authentication features.

Listing 39-3. The Contents of the _Layout.cshtml File in the Pages/Account Folder in the Advanced Project

```
<!DOCTYPE html>
<html>
<head>
    <title>Identity</title>
    <link href="/lib/twitter-bootstrap/css/bootstrap.min.css" rel="stylesheet" />
</head>
<body>
    <div class="m-2">
        @RenderBody()
    </div>
</body>
</html>
```

Add a Razor Page named Login.cshtml to the Pages/Account folder in the Advanced project with the content shown in Listing 39-4.

Listing 39-4. The Contents of the Login.cshtml File in the Pages/Account Folder of the Advanced Project

```
@page
@model LoginModel

<div class="bg-primary text-center text-white p-2"><h4>Log In</h4></div>

<div class="m-1 text-danger" asp-validation-summary="All"></div>

<form method="post">
    <input type="hidden" name="returnUrl" value="@Model.ReturnUrl" />
    <div class="form-group">
        <label>UserName</label>
        <input class="form-control" asp-for="UserName" />
    </div>
    <div class="form-group">
        <label>Password</label>
        <input asp-for="Password" type="password" class="form-control" />
    </div>
    <button class="btn btn-primary" type="submit">Log In</button>
</form>

@functions {

    public class LoginModel : PageModel {
        private SignInManager<IdentityUser> signInManager;

        public LoginModel(SignInManager<IdentityUser> signinMgr) {
            signInManager = signinMgr;
        }

        [BindProperty] [Required]
        public string UserName { get; set; }

        [BindProperty] [Required]
        public string Password { get; set; }

        [BindProperty(SupportsGet = true)]
        public string ReturnUrl { get; set; }

        public async Task<IActionResult> OnPostAsync() {
            if (ModelState.IsValid) {
                Microsoft.AspNetCore.Identity.SignInResult result =
                    await signInManager.PasswordSignInAsync(UserName, Password,
                        false, false);
                if (result.Succeeded) {
                    return Redirect(ReturnUrl ?? "/");
                }
                ModelState.AddModelError("", "Invalid username or password");
            }
            return Page();
        }
    }
}
```

ASP.NET Core Identity provides the SigninManager<T> class to manage logins, where the generic type argument T is the class that represents users in the application, which is IdentityUser for the example application. Table 39-2 describes the SigninManager<T> members I use in this chapter.

Table 39-2. *Useful SigninManager<T> Members*

Name	Description
PasswordSignInAsync(name, password, persist, lockout)	This method attempts authentication using the specified username and password. The persist argument determines whether a successful authentication produces a cookie that persists after the browser is closed. The lockout argument determines whether the account should be locked if authentication fails.
SignOutAsync()	This method signs out the user.

The Razor Page presents the user with a form that collects a username and a password, which are used to perform authentication with the PasswordSignInAsync method, like this:

```
...
Microsoft.AspNetCore.Identity.SignInResult result =
    await signInManager.PasswordSignInAsync(UserName, Password, false, false);
...
```

The result from the PasswordSignInAsync methods is a SignInResult object, which defines a Suceeded property that is true if the authentication is successful. (There is also a SignInResult class defined in the Microsoft.AspNetCore.Mvc namespace, which is why I used a fully qualified class name in the listing.)

Authentication in an ASP.NET Core application is usually triggered when the user tries to access an endpoint that requires authorization, and it is convention to return the user to that endpoint if authentication is successful, which is why the Login page defines a ReturnUrl property that is used in a redirection if the user has provided valid credentials.

```
...
if (result.Succeeded) {
    return Redirect(ReturnUrl ?? "/");
}
...
```

If the user hasn't provided valid credentials, then a validation message is shown, and the page is redisplayed.

PROTECTING THE AUTHENTICATION COOKIE

The authentication cookie contains the user's identity, and ASP.NET Core trusts that requests containing the cookie originate from the authenticated user. This means you should use HTTPS for production applications that use ASP.NET Core Identity to prevent the cookie from being intercepted by an intermediary. See Part 2 for details of enabling HTTPS in ASP.NET Core.

Inspecting the ASP.NET Core Identity Cookie

When a user is authenticated, a cookie is added to the response so that subsequent requests can be identified as being already authenticated. Add a Razor Page named Details.cshtml to the Pages/Account folder of the Advanced project with the content shown in Listing 39-5, which displays the cookie when it is present.

Listing 39-5. The Contents of the Details.cshtml File in the Pages/Account Folder of the Advanced Folder

```
@page
@model DetailsModel

<table class="table table-sm table-bordered">
    <tbody>
        @if (Model.Cookie == null) {
            <tr><th class="text-center">No Identity Cookie</th></tr>
        } else {
            <tr>
                <th>Cookie</th>
                <td class="text-break">@Model.Cookie</td>
            </tr>
        }
    </tbody>
</table>

@functions {

    public class DetailsModel : PageModel {

        public string Cookie { get; set; }

        public void OnGet() {
            Cookie = Request.Cookies[".AspNetCore.Identity.Application"];
        }
    }
}
```

The name used for the ASP.NET Core Identity cookie is `.AspNetCore.Identity.Application`, and this page retrieves the cookie from the request and displays its value or a placeholder message if there is no cookie.

Creating a Sign-Out Page

It is important to give users the ability to sign out so they can explicitly delete the cookie, especially if public machines may be used to access the application. Add a Razor Page named `Logout.cshtml` to the Pages/Account folder of the Advanced folder with the content shown in Listing 39-6.

Listing 39-6. The Contents of the Logout.cshtml File in the Pages/Account Folder in the Advanced Project

```
@page
@model LogoutModel

<div class="bg-primary text-center text-white p-2"><h4>Log Out</h4></div>
<div class="m-2">
    <h6>You are logged out</h6>
    <a asp-page="Login" class="btn btn-secondary">OK</a>
</div>

@functions {

    public class LogoutModel : PageModel {
        private SignInManager<IdentityUser> signInManager;

        public LogoutModel(SignInManager<IdentityUser> signInMgr) {
            signInManager = signInMgr;
        }
```

```
        public async Task OnGetAsync() {
            await signInManager.SignOutAsync();
        }
    }
}
```

This page calls the SignOutAsync method described in Table 39-2 to sign the application out of the application. The ASP.NET Core Identity cookie will be deleted so that the browser will not include it in future requests (and invalidated the cookie, so that requests will not be treated as authenticated even if the cookie is used again anyway).

Testing the Authentication Feature

Restart ASP.NET Core and request http://localhost:5000/users/list. Click the Create button and fill out the form using the data shown in Table 39-3. Click the Submit button to submit the form and create the user account.

Table 39-3. *The Data Values to Create a User*

Field	Description
UserName	bob
Email	bob@example.com
Password	secret

Navigate to http://localhost:5000/account/login and authenticate using the username and password from Table 39-3. No return URL has been specified, and you will be redirected to the root URL once you have been authenticated. Request http://localhost:5000/account/details, and you will see the ASP.NET Core Identity cookie. Request http://localhost:5000/account/logout to log out of the application and return to http://localhost:5000/account/details to confirm that the cookie has been deleted, as shown in Figure 39-3.

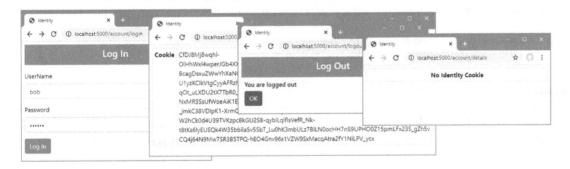

Figure 39-3. *Authenticating a user*

Enabling the Identity Authentication Middleware

ASP.NET Core Identity provides a middleware component that detects the cookie created by the SignInManager<T> class and populates the HttpContex object with details of the authenticated user. This provides endpoints with details about the user without needing to be aware of the authentication process or having to deal directly with the cookie created by the authentication process. Listing 39-7 adds the authentication middleware to the example application's request pipeline.

Listing 39-7. Enabling Middleware in the Startup.cs File in the Advanced Folder

```
...
public void Configure(IApplicationBuilder app, DataContext context) {

    app.UseDeveloperExceptionPage();
    app.UseStaticFiles();
    app.UseRouting();

    app.UseAuthentication();

    app.UseEndpoints(endpoints => {
        endpoints.MapControllerRoute("controllers",
            "controllers/{controller=Home}/{action=Index}/{id?}");
        endpoints.MapDefaultControllerRoute();
        endpoints.MapRazorPages();
        endpoints.MapBlazorHub();

        endpoints.MapFallbackToClientSideBlazor<BlazorWebAssembly.Startup>
            ("/webassembly/{*path:nonfile}", "index.html");

        endpoints.MapFallbackToPage("/_Host");
    });

    app.Map("/webassembly", opts =>
        opts.UseClientSideBlazorFiles<BlazorWebAssembly.Startup>());

    SeedData.SeedDatabase(context);
}
...
```

The middleware sets the value of the HttpContext.User property to a ClaimsPrincipal object. *Claims* are pieces of information about a user and details of the source of that information, providing a general-purpose approach to describing the information known about a user.

The ClaimsPrincipal class is part of .NET Core and isn't directly useful in most ASP.NET Core applications, but there are two nested properties that are useful in most applications, as described in Table 39-4.

Table 39-4. Useful Nested ClaimsPrincipal Properties

Name	Description
ClaimsPrincipal.Identity.Name	This property returns the username, which will be null if there is no user associated with the request.
ClaimsPrincipal.Identity. IsAuthenticated	This property returns true if the user associated with the request has been authenticated.

The username provided through the ClaimsPrincipal object can be used to obtain the ASP.NET Core Identity user object, as shown in Listing 39-8.

Listing 39-8. User Details in the Details.cshtml File in the Pages/Account Folder of the Advanced Project

```
@page
@model DetailsModel

<table class="table table-sm table-bordered">
    <tbody>
        @if (Model.IdentityUser == null) {
            <tr><th class="text-center">No User</th></tr>
```

```
    } else {
        <tr><th>Name</th><td>@Model.IdentityUser.UserName</td></tr>
        <tr><th>Email</th><td>@Model.IdentityUser.Email</td></tr>
    }
    </tbody>
</table>

@functions {

    public class DetailsModel : PageModel {
        private UserManager<IdentityUser> userManager;

        public DetailsModel(UserManager<IdentityUser> manager) {
            userManager = manager;
        }

        public IdentityUser IdentityUser { get; set; }

        public async Task OnGetAsync() {
            if (User.Identity.IsAuthenticated) {
                IdentityUser = await userManager.FindByNameAsync(User.Identity.Name);
            }
        }
    }
}
```

The HttpContext.User property can be accessed through the User convenience property defined by the PageModel and ControllerBase classes. This Razor Page confirms that there is an authenticated user associated with the request and gets the IdentityUser object that describes the user.

Restart ASP.NET Core, request http://localhost:5000/account/login, and authenticate using the details in Table 39-3. Request http://localhost:5000/account/details, and you will see how the ASP.NET Core Identity middleware enabled in Listing 39-7 has processed the cookie to associate user details with the request, as shown in Figure 39-4.

CONSIDERING TWO-FACTOR AUTHENTICATION

I have performed single-factor authentication in this chapter, which is where the user is able to authenticate using a single piece of information known to them in advance: the password.

ASP.NET Core Identity also supports two-factor authentication, where the user needs something extra, usually something that is given to the user at the moment they want to authenticate. The most common examples are a value from a hardware token or smartphone app or an authentication code that is sent as an e-mail or text message. (Strictly speaking, the two factors can be anything, including fingerprints, iris scans, and voice recognition, although these are options that are rarely required for most web applications.)

Security is increased because an attacker needs to know the user's password *and* have access to whatever provides the second factor, such as an e-mail account or cell phone.

I don't show two-factor authentication in the book for two reasons. The first is that it requires a lot of preparatory work, such as setting up the infrastructure that distributes the second-factor e-mails and texts and implementing the validation logic, all of which is beyond the scope of this book.

The second reason is that two-factor authentication forces the user to remember to jump through an additional hoop to authenticate, such as remembering their phone or keeping a security token nearby, something that isn't always appropriate for web applications. I carried a hardware token of one sort or another for more than a decade in various jobs, and I lost count of the number of times that I couldn't log in to an employer's system because I left the token at home. If you are considering two-factor authentication, then I recommend using one of the many hosted providers that will take care of distributing and managing the second factors for you.

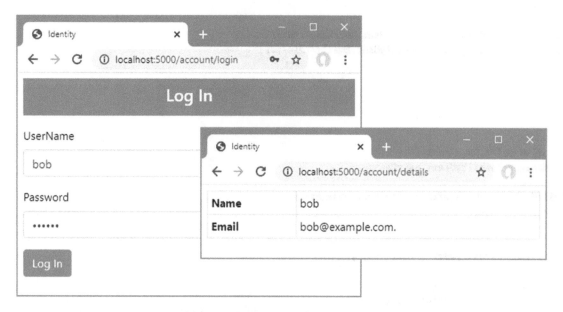

Figure 39-4. *Getting details of an authenticated user*

Authorizing Access to Endpoints

Once an application has an authentication feature, user identities can be used to restrict access to endpoints. In the sections that follow, I explain the process for enabling authorization and demonstrate how an authorization policy can be defined.

Applying the Authorization Attribute

The Authorize attribute is used to restrict access to an endpoint and can be applied to individual action or page handler methods or to controller or page model classes, in which case the policy applies to all the methods defined by the class. I want to restrict access to the user and role administration tools created in Chapter 38. When there are multiple Razor Pages or controllers for which the same authorization policy is required, it is a good idea to define a common base class to which the Authorize attribute can be applied because it ensures that you won't accidentally omit the attribute and allow unauthorized access. It is for this reason that I defined the AdminPageModel class and used it as the base for all the administration tool page models in Chapter 38. Listing 39-9 applies the Authorize attribute to the AdminPageModel class to create the authorization policy.

Listing 39-9. Applying an Attribute in the AdminPageModel.cs File in the Pages Folder in the Advanced Project

```
using Microsoft.AspNetCore.Mvc.RazorPages;
using Microsoft.AspNetCore.Authorization;

namespace Advanced.Pages {

    [Authorize(Roles="Admins")]
    public class AdminPageModel : PageModel {

    }
}
```

The Authorize attribute can be applied without arguments, which restricts access to any authenticated user. The Roles argument is used to further restrict access to users who are members of specific roles, which are expressed as a comma-separated list. The attribute in this listing restricts access to users assigned to the Admins role. The authorization restrictions are inherited, which means that applying the attribute to the base class restricts access to all the Razor Pages created to manage users and roles in Chapter 38.

■ **Note** If you want to restrict access to most, but not all, of the action methods in a controller, then you can apply the `Authorize` attribute to the controller class and the `AllowAnonymous` attribute to just the action methods for which authenticated access is required.

Enabling the Authorization Middleware

The authorization policy is enforced by a middleware component, which must be added to the application's request pipeline, as shown in Listing 39-10.

Listing 39-10. Adding Middleware in the Startup.cs File in the Advanced Project

```
...
public void Configure(IApplicationBuilder app, DataContext context) {

    app.UseDeveloperExceptionPage();
    app.UseStaticFiles();
    app.UseRouting();

    app.UseAuthentication();
    app.UseAuthorization();

    app.UseEndpoints(endpoints => {
        endpoints.MapControllerRoute("controllers",
            "controllers/{controller=Home}/{action=Index}/{id?}");
        endpoints.MapDefaultControllerRoute();
        endpoints.MapRazorPages();
        endpoints.MapBlazorHub();

        endpoints.MapFallbackToClientSideBlazor<BlazorWebAssembly.Startup>
            ("/webassembly/{*path:nonfile}", "index.html");

        endpoints.MapFallbackToPage("/_Host");
    });

    app.Map("/webassembly", opts =>
        opts.UseClientSideBlazorFiles<BlazorWebAssembly.Startup>());

    SeedData.SeedDatabase(context);
}
...
```

The `UseAuthorization` method must be called between the `UseRouting` and `UseEndpoints` methods and after the `UseAuthentication` method has been called. This ensures that the authorization component can access the user data and inspect the authorization policy after the endpoint has been selected but before the request is handled.

Creating the Access Denied Endpoint

The application must deal with two different types of authorization failure. If no user has been authenticated when a restricted endpoint is requested, then the authorization middleware will return a challenge response, which will trigger a redirection to the login page so the user can present their credentials and prove they should be able to access the endpoint.

But if an authenticated user requests a restricted endpoint and doesn't pass the authorization checks, then an access denied response is generated so the application can display a suitable warning to the user. Add a Razor Page named `AccessDenied.cshtml` to the `Pages/Account` folder of the Advanced folder with the content shown in Listing 39-11.

Listing 39-11. The AccessDenied.cshtml File in the Pages/Account Folder of the Advanced Project

```
@page

<h4 class="bg-danger text-white text-center p-2">Access Denied</h4>

<div class="m-2">
    <h6>You are not authorized for this URL</h6>
    <a class="btn btn-outline-danger" href="/">OK</a>
    <a class="btn btn-outline-secondary" asp-page="Logout">Logout</a>
</div>
```

This page displays a warning message to the user, with a button that navigates to the root URL. There is typically little the user can do to resolve authorization failures without administrative intervention, and my preference is to keep the access denied response as simple as possible.

Creating the Seed Data

In Listing 39-9, I restricted access to the user and role administration tools, so they can be accessed only by users in the Admin role. There is no such role in the database, which creates a problem: I am locked out of the administration tools because there is no authorized account that will let me create the role.

I could have created an administration user and role before applying the Authorize attribute, but that complicates deploying the application, when making code changes should be avoided. Instead, I am going to create seed data for ASP.NET Core Identity to ensure there will always be at least one account that can be used to access the user and role management tools. Add a class file named IdentitySeedData.cs to the Models folder in the Advanced project and use it to define the class shown in Listing 39-12.

Listing 39-12. The Contents of the IdentitySeedData.cs File in the Models Folder of the Advanced Project

```
using System;
using System.Threading.Tasks;
using Microsoft.AspNetCore.Identity;
using Microsoft.Extensions.Configuration;
using Microsoft.Extensions.DependencyInjection;

namespace Advanced.Models {
    public class IdentitySeedData {

        public static void CreateAdminAccount(IServiceProvider serviceProvider,
                IConfiguration configuration) {
            CreateAdminAccountAsync(serviceProvider, configuration).Wait();
        }

        public static async Task CreateAdminAccountAsync(IServiceProvider
                serviceProvider, IConfiguration configuration) {

            serviceProvider = serviceProvider.CreateScope().ServiceProvider;

            UserManager<IdentityUser> userManager =
                serviceProvider.GetRequiredService<UserManager<IdentityUser>>();
            RoleManager<IdentityRole> roleManager =
                serviceProvider.GetRequiredService<RoleManager<IdentityRole>>();

            string username = configuration["Data:AdminUser:Name"] ?? "admin";
            string email
                = configuration["Data:AdminUser:Email"] ?? "admin@example.com";
            string password = configuration["Data:AdminUser:Password"] ?? "secret";
            string role = configuration["Data:AdminUser:Role"] ?? "Admins";
```

```
            if (await userManager.FindByNameAsync(username) == null) {
                if (await roleManager.FindByNameAsync(role) == null) {
                    await roleManager.CreateAsync(new IdentityRole(role));
                }

                IdentityUser user = new IdentityUser {
                    UserName = username,
                    Email = email
                };

                IdentityResult result = await userManager
                    .CreateAsync(user, password);
                if (result.Succeeded) {
                    await userManager.AddToRoleAsync(user, role);
                }
            }
        }
    }
}
```

The UserManager<T> and RoleManager<T> services are scoped, which means I need to create a new scope before requesting the services since the seeding will be done when the application starts. The seeding code creates a user account that is assigned to a role. The values for the seed data are read from the application's configuration with fallback values, making it easy to configure the seeded account without needing a code change. Listing 39-13 adds a statement to the Startup class so that the database is seeded when the application starts.

▪ **Caution** Putting passwords in code files or plain-text configuration files means you must make it part of your deployment process to change the default account's password when you deploy the application and initialize a new database for the first time. You can also use the user secrets feature to keep sensitive data outside of the project.

Listing 39-13. Seeding Identity in the Startup.cs File in the Advanced Project

```
...
public void Configure(IApplicationBuilder app, DataContext context) {

    app.UseDeveloperExceptionPage();
    app.UseStaticFiles();
    app.UseRouting();

    app.UseAuthentication();
    app.UseAuthorization();

    app.UseEndpoints(endpoints => {
        endpoints.MapControllerRoute("controllers",
            "controllers/{controller=Home}/{action=Index}/{id?}");
        endpoints.MapDefaultControllerRoute();
        endpoints.MapRazorPages();
        endpoints.MapBlazorHub();

        endpoints.MapFallbackToClientSideBlazor<BlazorWebAssembly.Startup>
            ("/webassembly/{*path:nonfile}", "index.html");

        endpoints.MapFallbackToPage("/_Host");
    });
```

```
    app.Map("/webassembly", opts =>
        opts.UseClientSideBlazorFiles<BlazorWebAssembly.Startup>());

    SeedData.SeedDatabase(context);
    IdentitySeedData.CreateAdminAccount(app.ApplicationServices, Configuration);
}
...
```

Testing the Authentication Sequence

Restart ASP.NET Core and request http://localhost:5000/account/logout to ensure that no user is logged in to the application. Without logging in, request http://localhost:5000/users/list. The endpoint that will be selected to handle the request requires authentication, and the login prompt will be shown since there is no authenticated user associated with the request. Authenticate with the username bob and the password secret. This user doesn't have access to the restricted endpoint, and the access denied response will be shown, as illustrated by Figure 39-5.

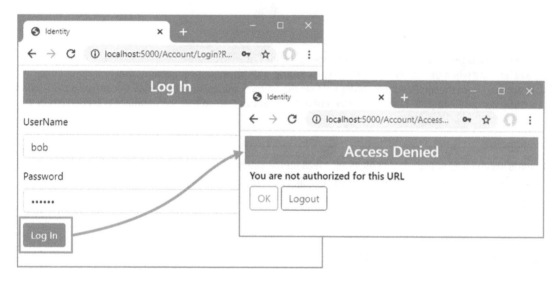

Figure 39-5. *A user without authorization*

Click the Logout button and request http://localhost:5000/users/list again, which will lead to the login prompt being displayed. Authenticate with the username admin and the password secret. This is the user account created by the seed data and that is a member of the role specified by the Authorize attribute. The user passes the authorization check, and the requested Razor Page is displayed, as shown in Figure 39-6.

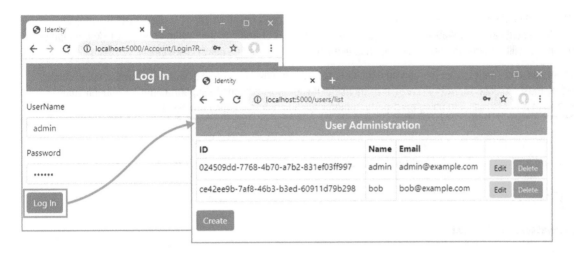

Figure 39-6. *A user with authorization*

CHANGING THE AUTHORIZATION URLS

The /Account/Login and /Account/AccessDenied URLs are the defaults used by ASP.NET Core authorization files. These can be changed in the Startup class using the options pattern, like this:

```
...
services.Configure<CookieAuthenticationOptions>(
        IdentityConstants.ApplicationScheme,
    opts => {
        opts.LoginPath = "/Authenticate";
        opts.AccessDeniedPath = "/NotAllowed";
    });
...
```

Configuration is performed using the CookieAuthenticationOptions class, defined in the Microsoft.AspNetCore.Authentication.Cookies namespace. The LoginPath property is used to specify the path to which browsers will be redirected when an unauthenticated user attempts to access a restricted endpoint. The AccessDeniedPath property is used to specify the path when an authenticated user attempts to access a restricted endpoint and does not have authorization.

Authorizing Access to Blazor Applications

The simplest way to protect Blazor applications is to restrict access to the action method or Razor Page that acts as the entry point. In Listing 39-14, I added the Authorize attribute to the page model class for the _Host page, which is the entry point for the Blazor application in the example project.

UNDERSTANDING OAUTH AND IDENTITYSERVER

If you read the Microsoft documentation, you will be left with the impression that you need to use a third-party server called IdentityServer (http://identityserver.io) to authenticate web services.

IdentityServer is a high-quality open source package that provides authentication and authorization services, with paid-for options for add-ons and support. IdentityServer provides support for OAuth, which is a standard for managing authentication and authorization and provides packages for a range of client-side frameworks.

What the Microsoft documentation is saying—albeit awkwardly—is that Microsoft has used IdentityServer in the project templates that include authentication for web services. If you create an Angular or React project using an ASP.NET Core template provided by Microsoft, you will find that the authentication has been implemented using IdentityServer.

Authentication is complex, and IdentityServer can be difficult to set up correctly. I like IdentityServer, but it is not essential and is not required by most projects. IdentityServer may be useful if your project needs to support complex authentication scenarios, but my advice is not to rush into using third-party authentication servers until they are essential.

Listing 39-14. Applying an Attribute in the _Host.cshtml File in the Pages Folder of the Advanced Project

```
@page "/"
@{ Layout = null; }
@model HostModel
@using Microsoft.AspNetCore.Authorization

<!DOCTYPE html>
<html>
<head>
    <title>@ViewBag.Title</title>
    <link href="/lib/twitter-bootstrap/css/bootstrap.min.css" rel="stylesheet" />
    <base href="~/" />
</head>
<body>
    <div class="m-2">
        <component type="typeof(Advanced.Blazor.Routed)" render-mode="Server" />
    </div>
    <script src="_framework/blazor.server.js"></script>
    <script src="~/interop.js"></script>
</body>
</html>

@functions {

    [Authorize]
    public class HostModel : PageModel {}
}
```

This has the effect of preventing unauthenticated users from accessing the Blazor application. Request http://localhost:5000/account/logout to ensure the browser doesn't have an authentication cookie and then request http://localhost:5000. This request will be handled by the _Host page, but the authorization middleware will trigger the redirection to the login prompt. Authenticate with the username bob and the password secret, and you will be granted access to the Blazor application, as shown in Figure 39-7.

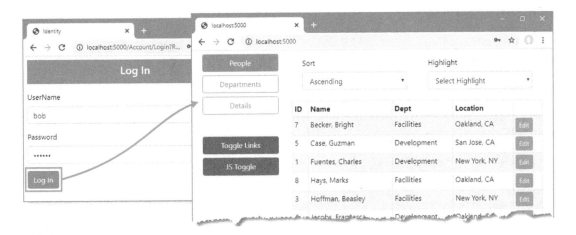

Figure 39-7. *Restricting access to the Blazor endpoint*

Performing Authorization in Blazor Components

Restricting access to the endpoint is an effective technique, but it applies the same level of authorization to all the Blazor functionality. For applications that require more granular restrictions, Blazor provides the AuthorizeRouteView component, which allows different content to be displayed for authorized and unauthorized when components are managed using URL routing. Listing 39-15 adds the AuthorizeRouteView to the routing component in the example application.

Listing 39-15. Adding a Component in the Routed.razor File in the Blazor Folder of the Advanced Project

```
@using Microsoft.AspNetCore.Components.Authorization

<Router AppAssembly="typeof(Startup).Assembly">
    <Found>
        <AuthorizeRouteView RouteData="@context" DefaultLayout="typeof(NavLayout)">
            <NotAuthorized Context="authContext">
                <h4 class="bg-danger text-white text-center p-2">Not Authorized </h4>
                <div class="text-center">
                    You may need to log in as a different user
                </div>
            </NotAuthorized>
        </AuthorizeRouteView>
    </Found>
    <NotFound>
        <h4 class="bg-danger text-white text-center p-2">
            Not Matching Route Found
        </h4>
    </NotFound>
</Router>
```

The NotAuthorized section is used to define the content that will be presented to users when they attempt to access a restricted resource. To demonstrate this feature, I am going to restrict access to the DepartmentList component to users assigned to the Admins role, as shown in Listing 39-16.

Listing 39-16. Restricting Access in the DepartmentList.cshtml File in the Blazor Folder in the Advanced Project

```
@page "/departments"
@page "/depts"
@using Microsoft.AspNetCore.Authorization
@attribute [Authorize(Roles = "Admins")]
```

```
<CascadingValue Name="BgTheme" Value="Theme" IsFixed="false" >
    <TableTemplate RowType="Department" RowData="Departments"
        Highlight="@(d => d.Name)"
        SortDirection="@(d => d.Name)">
        <Header>
            <tr><th>ID</th><th>Name</th><th>People</th><th>Locations</th></tr>
        </Header>
        <RowTemplate Context="d">
            <td>@d.Departmentid</td>
            <td>@d.Name</td>
            <td>@(String.Join(", ", d.People.Select(p => p.Surname)))</td>
            <td>
                @(String.Join(", ",
                    d.People.Select(p => p.Location.City).Distinct()))
            </td>
        </RowTemplate>
    </TableTemplate>
</CascadingValue>

<SelectFilter Title="@("Theme")" Values="Themes" @bind-SelectedValue="Theme" />

<button class="btn btn-primary" @onclick="HandleClick">People</button>

@code {

    [Inject]
    public DataContext Context { get; set; }

    public IEnumerable<Department> Departments => Context.Departments
            .Include(d => d.People).ThenInclude(p => p.Location);

    public string Theme { get; set; } = "info";
    public string[] Themes = new string[] { "primary", "info", "success" };

    [Inject]
    public NavigationManager NavManager { get; set; }

    public void HandleClick() => NavManager.NavigateTo("/people");
}
```

I have used the @attribute directive to apply the Authorize attribute to the component. Restart ASP.NET Core and request http://localhost:5000/account/logout to remove the authentication cookie and then request http://localhost:5000. When prompted, authenticate with the username bob and the password secret. You will see the Blazor application, but when you click the Departments button, you will see the authorization content defined in Listing 39-15, as shown in Figure 39-8. Log out again and log in as admin with the password secret, and you will be able to use the restricted component.

Figure 39-8. *Using authorization in a Blazor application*

Displaying Content to Authorized Users

The AuthorizeView component is used to restrict access to sections of content rendered by a component. In Listing 39-17, I have changed the authorization for the DepartmentList component so that any authenticated user can access the page and use the AuthorizeView component so that the contents of the Locations column in the table is shown only to users assigned to the Admins group.

Listing 39-17. Selective Content in the DepartmentList.razor File in the Blazor Folder in the Advanced Project

```
@page "/departments"
@page "/depts"
@using Microsoft.AspNetCore.Authorization
@using Microsoft.AspNetCore.Components.Authorization
@attribute [Authorize]

<CascadingValue Name="BgTheme" Value="Theme" IsFixed="false" >
    <TableTemplate RowType="Department" RowData="Departments"
        Highlight="@(d => d.Name)"
        SortDirection="@(d => d.Name)">
        <Header>
            <tr><th>ID</th><th>Name</th><th>People</th><th>Locations</th></tr>
        </Header>
        <RowTemplate Context="d">
            <td>@d.Departmentid</td>
            <td>@d.Name</td>
            <td>@(String.Join(", ", d.People.Select(p => p.Surname)))</td>
            <td>
                <AuthorizeView Roles="Admins">
                    <Authorized>
                        @(String.Join(", ",
                            d.People.Select(p => p.Location.City).Distinct()))
                    </Authorized>
                    <NotAuthorized>
                        (Not authorized)
                    </NotAuthorized>
                </AuthorizeView>
            </td>
        </RowTemplate>
    </TableTemplate>
</CascadingValue>
```

1053

```
<SelectFilter Title="@("Theme")" Values="Themes" @bind-SelectedValue="Theme" />

<button class="btn btn-primary" @onclick="HandleClick">People</button>

@code {

    // ...statements omitted for brevity...
}
```

The AuthorizeView component is configured with the Roles property, which accepts a comma-separated list of authorized roles. The Authorized section contains the content that will be shown to authorized users. The NotAuthorized section contains the content that will be shown to unauthorized users.

■ **Tip** You can omit the NotAuthorized section if you don't need to show content to unauthorized users.

Restart ASP.NET Core and authenticate as bob, with password secret, before requesting http://localhost:5000/depts. This user is not authorized to see the contents of the Locations column, as shown in Figure 39-9. Authenticate as admin, with password secret, and request http://localhost:5000/depts again. This time the user is a member of the Admins role and passes the authorization checks, also shown in Figure 39-9.

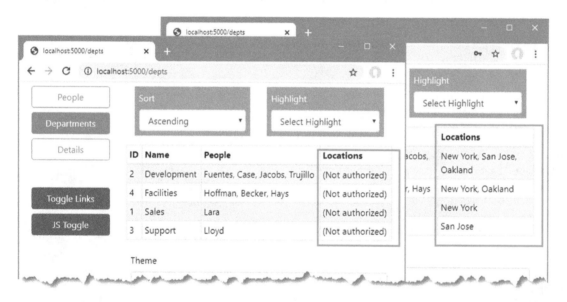

Figure 39-9. *Selectively displaying content based on authorization*

Authenticating and Authorizing Web Services

The authorization process in the previous section relies on being able to redirect the client to a URL that allows the user to enter their credentials. A different approach is required when adding authentication and authorization to a web service because there is no option to present the user with an HTML form to collect their credentials. The first step in adding support for web services authentication is to disable the redirections so that the client will receive HTTP error responses when attempting to request an endpoint that requires authentication. Add a class file named CookieAuthenticationExtensions.cs to the Advanced folder and use it to define the extension method shown in Listing 39-18.

Listing 39-18. The Contents of the CookieAuthenticationExtensions.cs File in the Advanced Folder

```
using System;
using System.Collections.Generic;
using System.Linq;
using System.Linq.Expressions;
using System.Threading.Tasks;

namespace Microsoft.AspNetCore.Authentication.Cookies {
    public static class CookieAuthenticationExtensions {

        public static void DisableRedirectForPath(
            this CookieAuthenticationEvents events,
            Expression<Func<CookieAuthenticationEvents,
                Func<RedirectContext<CookieAuthenticationOptions>, Task>>> expr,
            string path, int statuscode) {

            string propertyName = ((MemberExpression)expr.Body).Member.Name;
            var oldHandler = expr.Compile().Invoke(events);

            Func<RedirectContext<CookieAuthenticationOptions>, Task> newHandler
                    = context => {
                if (context.Request.Path.StartsWithSegments(path)) {
                    context.Response.StatusCode = statuscode;
                } else {
                    oldHandler(context);
                }
                return Task.CompletedTask;
            };

            typeof(CookieAuthenticationEvents).GetProperty(propertyName)
                .SetValue(events, newHandler);
        }
    }
}
```

This code is hard to follow. ASP.NET Core provides the CookieAuthenticationOptions class, which is used to configure cookie-based authentication. The CookieAuthenticationOptions.Events property returns a CookieAuthenticationEvents object, which is used to set the handlers for the events triggered by the authentication system, including the redirections that occur when the user requests unauthorized content. The extension methods in Listing 39-18 replaces the default handler for an event with one that performs redirection only if the request doesn't start with a specified path string. Listing 39-19 uses the extension method to replace the OnRedirectToLogin and OnRedirectToAccessDenied handlers so that redirections are not performed when the request path starts with /api.

Listing 39-19. Preventing Redirection in the Startup.cs File in the Advanced Folder

```
using System;
using System.Collections.Generic;
using System.Linq;
using System.Threading.Tasks;
using Microsoft.AspNetCore.Builder;
using Microsoft.AspNetCore.Hosting;
using Microsoft.AspNetCore.Http;
using Microsoft.Extensions.DependencyInjection;
using Microsoft.Extensions.Hosting;
using Microsoft.Extensions.Configuration;
using Microsoft.EntityFrameworkCore;
using Advanced.Models;
```

```
using Microsoft.AspNetCore.ResponseCompression;
using Microsoft.AspNetCore.Identity;
using Microsoft.AspNetCore.Authentication.Cookies;

namespace Advanced {
    public class Startup {

        public Startup(IConfiguration config) {
            Configuration = config;
        }

        public IConfiguration Configuration { get; set; }

        public void ConfigureServices(IServiceCollection services) {
            services.AddDbContext<DataContext>(opts => {
                opts.UseSqlServer(Configuration[
                    "ConnectionStrings:PeopleConnection"]);
                opts.EnableSensitiveDataLogging(true);
            });
            services.AddControllersWithViews().AddRazorRuntimeCompilation();
            services.AddRazorPages().AddRazorRuntimeCompilation();
            services.AddServerSideBlazor();
            services.AddSingleton<Services.ToggleService>();

            services.AddResponseCompression(opts => {
                opts.MimeTypes = ResponseCompressionDefaults.MimeTypes.Concat(
                    new[] { "application/octet-stream" });
            });

            services.AddDbContext<IdentityContext>(opts =>
                opts.UseSqlServer(Configuration[
                    "ConnectionStrings:IdentityConnection"]));
            services.AddIdentity<IdentityUser, IdentityRole>()
                .AddEntityFrameworkStores<IdentityContext>();

            services.Configure<IdentityOptions>(opts => {
                opts.Password.RequiredLength = 6;
                opts.Password.RequireNonAlphanumeric = false;
                opts.Password.RequireLowercase = false;
                opts.Password.RequireUppercase = false;
                opts.Password.RequireDigit = false;
                opts.User.RequireUniqueEmail = true;
                opts.User.AllowedUserNameCharacters = "abcdefghijklmnopqrstuvwxyz";
            });

            services.AddAuthentication(opts => {
                opts.DefaultScheme =
                    CookieAuthenticationDefaults.AuthenticationScheme;
                opts.DefaultChallengeScheme =
                    CookieAuthenticationDefaults.AuthenticationScheme;
            }).AddCookie(opts => {
                opts.Events.DisableRedirectForPath(e => e.OnRedirectToLogin,
                    "/api", StatusCodes.Status401Unauthorized);
                opts.Events.DisableRedirectForPath(e => e.OnRedirectToAccessDenied,
                    "/api", StatusCodes.Status403Forbidden);
            });
        }
```

```
    public void Configure(IApplicationBuilder app, DataContext context) {

        // ...statements omitted for brevity...
    }
  }
}
```

The AddAuthentication method is used to select cookie-based authentication and is chained with the AddCookie method to replace the event handlers that would otherwise trigger redirections.

Building a Simple JavaScript Client

To demonstrate how to perform authentication with web services, I am going to create a simple JavaScript client that will consume data from the Data controller in the example project.

■ **Tip** You don't have to be familiar with JavaScript to follow the examples in this part of the chapter. It is the server-side code that is important and the way it supports authentication by the client so that it can access the web service.

Add an HTML Page called webclient.html to the wwwroot folder of the Advanced project with the elements shown in Listing 39-20.

Listing 39-20. The Contents of the webclient.html File in the wwwroot Folder of the Advanced Project

```
<!DOCTYPE html>
<html>
<head>
    <title>Web Service Authentication</title>
    <link href="/lib/twitter-bootstrap/css/bootstrap.min.css" rel="stylesheet" />
    <script type="text/javascript" src="webclient.js"></script>
</head>
<body>
    <div id="controls" class="m-2"></div>
    <div id="data" class="m-2 p-2">
        No data
    </div>
</body>
</html>
```

Add a JavaScript file named webclient.js to the wwwroot of the Advanced project with the content shown in Listing 39-21.

Listing 39-21. The Contents of the webclient.js File in the wwwroot Folder of the Advanced Project

```
const username = "bob";
const password = "secret";

window.addEventListener("DOMContentLoaded", () => {
    const controlDiv = document.getElementById("controls");
    createButton(controlDiv, "Get Data", getData);
    createButton(controlDiv, "Log In", login);
    createButton(controlDiv, "Log Out", logout);
});

function login() {
    // do nothing
}
```

```javascript
function logout() {
    // do nothing
}

async function getData() {
    let response = await fetch("/api/people");
    if (response.ok) {
        let jsonData = await response.json();
        displayData(...jsonData.map(item => `${item.surname}, ${item.firstname}`));
    } else {
        displayData(`Error: ${response.status}: ${response.statusText}`);
    }
}

function displayData(...items) {
    const dataDiv = document.getElementById("data");
    dataDiv.innerHTML = "";
    items.forEach(item => {
        const itemDiv = document.createElement("div");
        itemDiv.innerText = item;
        itemDiv.style.wordWrap = "break-word";
        dataDiv.appendChild(itemDiv);
    })
}

function createButton(parent, label, handler) {
    const button = document.createElement("button");
    button.classList.add("btn", "btn-primary", "m-2");
    button.innerText = label;
    button.onclick = handler;
    parent.appendChild(button);
}
```

This code presents the user with Get Data and Log In and Log Out buttons. Clicking the Get Data button sends an HTTP request using the Fetch API, processes the JSON result, and displays a list of names. The other buttons do nothing, but I'll use them in later examples to authenticate with the ASP.NET Core application using the hardwired credentials in the JavaScript code.

▪ **Caution**   This is just a simple client to demonstrate server-side authentication features. If you need to write a JavaScript client, then consider a framework such as Angular or React. Regardless of how you build your clients, do not include hardwired credentials in the JavaScript files.

Request http://localhost:5000/webclient.html, and click the Get Data button. The JavaScript client will send an HTTP request to the Data controller and display the results, as shown in Figure 39-10.

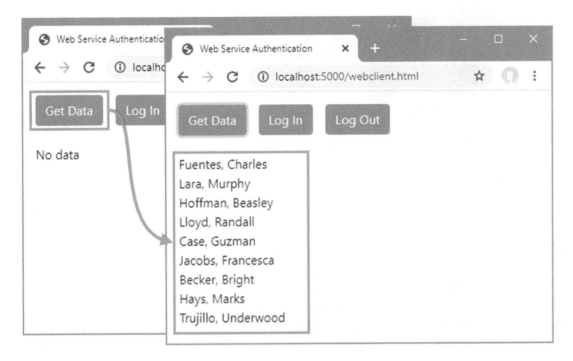

Figure 39-10. *A simple web client*

Restricting Access to the Web Service

The standard authorization features are used to restrict access to web service endpoints, and in Listing 39-22, I have applied the Authorize attribute to the DataController class.

Listing 39-22. Applying an Attribute in the DataController.cs File in the Controllers Folder of the Advanced Project

```
using Advanced.Models;
using Microsoft.AspNetCore.Mvc;
using Microsoft.EntityFrameworkCore;
using System.Collections.Generic;
using System.Threading.Tasks;
using Microsoft.AspNetCore.Authorization;

namespace Advanced.Controllers {

    [ApiController]
    [Route("/api/people")]
    [Authorize]
    public class DataController : ControllerBase {
        private DataContext context;

        // ...methods omitted for brevity...
    }
}
```

Restart ASP.NET Core and request http://localhost:5000/account/logout to ensure that the JavaScript client doesn't use an authentication cookie from a previous example. Request http://localhost:5000/webclient.html to load the JavaScript client and click the Get Data button to send the HTTP request. The server will respond with a 401 Unauthorized response, as shown in Figure 39-11.

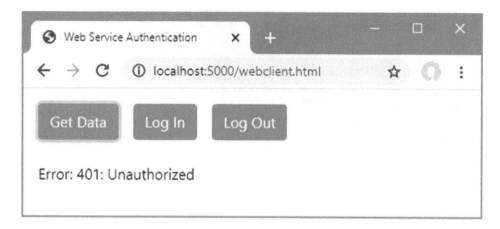

Figure 39-11. *An unauthorized request*

Using Cookie Authentication

The simplest way to implement authentication is to rely on the standard ASP.NET Core cookies demonstrated in previous sections. Add a class file named `ApiAccountController.cs` to the `Controllers` folder of the `Advanced` project and use it to define the controller shown in Listing 39-23.

Listing 39-23. The Contents of the ApiAccountController.cs File in the Controllers Folder of the Advanced Project

```csharp
using Microsoft.AspNetCore.Authorization;
using Microsoft.AspNetCore.Identity;
using Microsoft.AspNetCore.Mvc;
using System.ComponentModel.DataAnnotations;
using System.Threading.Tasks;

namespace Advanced.Controllers {

    [ApiController]
    [Route("/api/account")]
    public class ApiAccountController : ControllerBase {
        private SignInManager<IdentityUser> signinManager;

        public ApiAccountController(SignInManager<IdentityUser> mgr) {
            signinManager = mgr;
        }

        [HttpPost("login")]
        public async Task<IActionResult> Login([FromBody]Credentials creds) {
            Microsoft.AspNetCore.Identity.SignInResult result
                = await signinManager.PasswordSignInAsync(creds.Username,
                    creds.Password, false, false);
            if (result.Succeeded) {
                return Ok();
            }
            return Unauthorized();
        }

        [HttpPost("logout")]
        public async Task<IActionResult> Logout() {
            await signinManager.SignOutAsync();
            return Ok();
        }
```

```
        public class Credentials {
            [Required]
            public string Username { get; set; }
            [Required]
            public string Password { get; set; }
        }
    }
}
```

This web service controller defines actions that allow clients to log in and log out. The response for a successful authentication request will contain a cookie that the browser will automatically include in requests made by the JavaScript client.

Listing 39-24 adds support to the simple JavaScript client for authenticating using the action methods defined in Listing 39-23.

Listing 39-24. Adding Authentication in the webclient.js File in the wwwroot Folder of the Advanced Project

```javascript
const username = "bob";
const password = "secret";

window.addEventListener("DOMContentLoaded", () => {
    const controlDiv = document.getElementById("controls");
    createButton(controlDiv, "Get Data", getData);
    createButton(controlDiv, "Log In", login);
    createButton(controlDiv, "Log Out", logout);
});

async function login() {
    let response = await fetch("/api/account/login", {
        method: "POST",
        headers: { "Content-Type": "application/json" },
        body: JSON.stringify({ username: username, password: password })
    });
    if (response.ok) {
        displayData("Logged in");
    } else {
        displayData(`Error: ${response.status}: ${response.statusText}`);
    }
}

async function logout() {
    let response = await fetch("/api/account/logout", {
        method: "POST"
    });
    if (response.ok) {
        displayData("Logged out");
    } else {
        displayData(`Error: ${response.status}: ${response.statusText}`);
    }
}

async function getData() {
    let response = await fetch("/api/people");
    if (response.ok) {
        let jsonData = await response.json();
        displayData(...jsonData.map(item => `${item.surname}, ${item.firstname}`));
    } else {
        displayData(`Error: ${response.status}: ${response.statusText}`);
    }
}
```

```
function displayData(...items) {
    const dataDiv = document.getElementById("data");
    dataDiv.innerHTML = "";
    items.forEach(item => {
        const itemDiv = document.createElement("div");
        itemDiv.innerText = item;
        itemDiv.style.wordWrap = "break-word";
        dataDiv.appendChild(itemDiv);
    })
}

function createButton(parent, label, handler) {
    const button = document.createElement("button");
    button.classList.add("btn", "btn-primary",  "m-2");
    button.innerText = label;
    button.onclick = handler;
    parent.appendChild(button);
}
```

Restart ASP.NET Core, request `http://localhost:5000/webclient.html`, and click the Login In button. Wait for the message confirming authentication and then click the Get Data button. The browser includes the authentication cookie, and the request passes the authorization checks. Click the Log Out button and then click Get Data again. No cookie is used, and the request fails. Figure 39-12 shows both requests.

Figure 39-12. *Using cookie authentication*

Using Bearer Token Authentication

Not all web services will be able to rely on cookies because not all clients can use then. An alternative is to use a bearer token, which is a string that clients are given and is included in the requests they send to the web service. Clients don't understand the meaning of the token—which is said to be *opaque*—and just use whatever token the server provides.

I am going to demonstrate authentication using a JSON Web Token (JWT), which provides the client with an encrypted token that contains the authenticated username. The client is unable to decrypt or modify the token, but when it is included in a request, the ASP.NET Core server decrypts the token and uses the name it contains as the identity of the user. The JWT format is described in detail at `https://tools.ietf.org/html/rfc7519`.

■ **Caution** ASP.NET Core will trust that any request that includes the token originates from the authenticated user. Just as when using cookies, production applications should use HTTPS to prevent tokens from being intercepted and reused.

Preparing the Application

Open a new PowerShell command prompt, navigate to the Advanced project folder, and run the commands shown in Listing 39-25 to add the packages for JWT to the project.

Listing 39-25. Installing the NuGet Package

```
dotnet add package System.IdentityModel.Tokens.Jwt --version 5.6.0
dotnet add package Microsoft.AspNetCore.Authentication.JwtBearer --version 3.1.1
```

JWT requires a key that is used to encrypt and decrypt tokens. Add the configuration setting shown in Listing 39-26 to the appsettings.json file. If you use JWT in a real application, ensure you change the key.

Listing 39-26. Adding a Setting in the appsettings.json File in the Advanced Project

```
{
  "Logging": {
    "LogLevel": {
      "Default": "Information",
      "Microsoft": "Warning",
      "Microsoft.Hosting.Lifetime": "Information",
      "Microsoft.EntityFrameworkCore": "Information",
      "Microsoft.AspNetCore.Authentication": "Debug"

    }
  },
  "AllowedHosts": "*",
  "ConnectionStrings": {
    "PeopleConnection": "Server=(localdb)\\MSSQLLocalDB;Database=People;MultipleActiveResultSets=True",
    "IdentityConnection": "Server=(localdb)\\MSSQLLocalDB;Database=Identity;MultipleActiveResultSets=True"
  },
  "jwtSecret": "apress_jwt_secret"
}
```

Creating Tokens

The client will send an HTTP request that contains user credentials and will receive a JWT in response. Listing 39-27 adds an action method to the ApiAccount controller that receives the credentials, validates them, and generates tokens.

Listing 39-27. Generating Tokens in the ApiAccountController.cs File in the Controllers Folder of the Advanced Project

```
using Microsoft.AspNetCore.Authorization;
using Microsoft.AspNetCore.Identity;
using Microsoft.AspNetCore.Mvc;
using System.ComponentModel.DataAnnotations;
using System.Threading.Tasks;
using Microsoft.IdentityModel.Tokens;
using System.IdentityModel.Tokens.Jwt;
using System.Text;
using System.Security.Claims;
using System;
using Microsoft.Extensions.Configuration;
```

```
namespace Advanced.Controllers {

    [ApiController]
    [Route("/api/account")]
    public class ApiAccountController : ControllerBase {
        private SignInManager<IdentityUser> signinManager;
        private UserManager<IdentityUser> userManager;
        private IConfiguration configuration;

        public ApiAccountController(SignInManager<IdentityUser> mgr,
                UserManager<IdentityUser> usermgr, IConfiguration config) {
            signinManager = mgr;
            userManager = usermgr;
            configuration = config;
        }

        [HttpPost("login")]
        public async Task<IActionResult> Login([FromBody]Credentials creds) {
            Microsoft.AspNetCore.Identity.SignInResult result
                = await signinManager.PasswordSignInAsync(creds.Username,
                    creds.Password, false, false);
            if (result.Succeeded) {
                return Ok();
            }
            return Unauthorized();
        }

        [HttpPost("logout")]
        public async Task<IActionResult> Logout() {
            await signinManager.SignOutAsync();
            return Ok();
        }

        [HttpPost("token")]
        public async Task<IActionResult> Token([FromBody]Credentials creds) {
            if (await CheckPassword(creds)) {
                JwtSecurityTokenHandler handler = new JwtSecurityTokenHandler();
                byte[] secret = Encoding.ASCII.GetBytes(configuration["jwtSecret"]);
                SecurityTokenDescriptor descriptor = new SecurityTokenDescriptor {
                    Subject = new ClaimsIdentity(new Claim[] {
                        new Claim(ClaimTypes.Name, creds.Username)
                    }),
                    Expires = DateTime.UtcNow.AddHours(24),
                    SigningCredentials = new SigningCredentials(
                        new SymmetricSecurityKey(secret),
                            SecurityAlgorithms.HmacSha256Signature)
                };
                SecurityToken token = handler.CreateToken(descriptor);
                return Ok(new {
                    success = true,
                    token = handler.WriteToken(token)
                });
            }
            return Unauthorized();
        }
```

```
        private async Task<bool> CheckPassword(Credentials creds) {
            IdentityUser user = await userManager.FindByNameAsync(creds.Username);
            if (user != null) {
                foreach (IPasswordValidator<IdentityUser> v in
                        userManager.PasswordValidators) {
                    if ((await v.ValidateAsync(userManager, user,
                            creds.Password)).Succeeded) {
                        return true;
                    }
                }
            }
            return false;
        }

        public class Credentials {
            [Required]
            public string Username { get; set; }
            [Required]
            public string Password { get; set; }
        }
    }
}
```

The UserManager<T> class defines a PasswordValidators property that returns a sequence of objects that implement the IPasswordValidator<T> interface. When the Token action method is invoked, it passes the credentials to the CheckPassword method, which enumerates the IPasswordValidator<T> objects to invoke the ValidateAsync method on each of them. If the password is validated by any of the validators, then the Token method creates a token.

The JWT specification defines a general-purpose token that can be used more broadly than identifying users in HTTP requests, and many of the options that are available are not required for this example. The token that is created in Listing 39-27 contains a payload like this:

```
...
{
  "unique_name": "bob",
  "nbf": 1579765454,
  "exp": 1579851854,
  "iat": 1579765454
}
...
```

The unique_name property contains the name of the user and is used to authenticate requests that contain the token. The other payload properties are timestamps, which I do not use.

The payload is encrypted using the key defined in Listing 39-27 and returned to the client as a JSON-encoded response that looks like this:

```
...
{
    "success":true,
    "token":"eyJhbGciOiJIUzI1NiIsInR5cCI6IkpXVCJ9..."
}
...
```

I have shown just the first part of the token because they are long strings and it is the structure of the response that is important. The client receives the token and includes it in future requests using the Authorization header, like this:

```
...
Authorization: Bearer eyJhbGciOiJIUzI1NiIsInR5cCI6IkpXVCJ9
...
```

The server receives the token, decrypts it using the key, and authenticates the request using the value of the unique_name property from the token payload. No further validation is performed, and requests with a valid token will be authenticated using whatever username is contained in the payload.

Authenticating with Tokens

The next step is to configure the application to receive and validate the tokens, as shown in Listing 39-28.

Listing 39-28. Authenticating Tokens in the Startup.cs File in the Advanced Project

```
using System;
using System.Collections.Generic;
using System.Linq;
using System.Threading.Tasks;
using Microsoft.AspNetCore.Builder;
using Microsoft.AspNetCore.Hosting;
using Microsoft.AspNetCore.Http;
using Microsoft.Extensions.DependencyInjection;
using Microsoft.Extensions.Hosting;
using Microsoft.Extensions.Configuration;
using Microsoft.EntityFrameworkCore;
using Advanced.Models;
using Microsoft.AspNetCore.ResponseCompression;
using Microsoft.AspNetCore.Identity;
using Microsoft.AspNetCore.Authentication.Cookies;
using Microsoft.IdentityModel.Tokens;
using System.Text;
using System.Security.Claims;
using Microsoft.AspNetCore.Authentication.JwtBearer;

namespace Advanced {
    public class Startup {

        public Startup(IConfiguration config) {
            Configuration = config;
        }

        public IConfiguration Configuration { get; set; }

        public void ConfigureServices(IServiceCollection services) {
            services.AddDbContext<DataContext>(opts => {
                opts.UseSqlServer(Configuration[
                    "ConnectionStrings:PeopleConnection"]);
                opts.EnableSensitiveDataLogging(true);
            });
            services.AddControllersWithViews().AddRazorRuntimeCompilation();
            services.AddRazorPages().AddRazorRuntimeCompilation();
            services.AddServerSideBlazor();
            services.AddSingleton<Services.ToggleService>();

            services.AddResponseCompression(opts => {
                opts.MimeTypes = ResponseCompressionDefaults.MimeTypes.Concat(
                    new[] { "application/octet-stream" });
            });
```

```
        services.AddDbContext<IdentityContext>(opts =>
            opts.UseSqlServer(Configuration[
                "ConnectionStrings:IdentityConnection"]));

        services.AddIdentity<IdentityUser, IdentityRole>()
            .AddEntityFrameworkStores<IdentityContext>();

        services.Configure<IdentityOptions>(opts => {
            opts.Password.RequiredLength = 6;
            opts.Password.RequireNonAlphanumeric = false;
            opts.Password.RequireLowercase = false;
            opts.Password.RequireUppercase = false;
            opts.Password.RequireDigit = false;
            opts.User.RequireUniqueEmail = true;
            opts.User.AllowedUserNameCharacters = "abcdefghijklmnopqrstuvwxyz";
        });

        services.AddAuthentication(opts => {
            opts.DefaultScheme =
                CookieAuthenticationDefaults.AuthenticationScheme;
            opts.DefaultChallengeScheme =
                CookieAuthenticationDefaults.AuthenticationScheme;
        }).AddCookie(opts => {
            opts.Events.DisableRedirectForPath(e => e.OnRedirectToLogin,
                "/api", StatusCodes.Status401Unauthorized);
            opts.Events.DisableRedirectForPath(e => e.OnRedirectToAccessDenied,
                "/api", StatusCodes.Status403Forbidden);
        }).AddJwtBearer(opts => {
            opts.RequireHttpsMetadata = false;
            opts.SaveToken = true;
            opts.TokenValidationParameters = new TokenValidationParameters {
                ValidateIssuerSigningKey = true,
                IssuerSigningKey = new SymmetricSecurityKey(
                    Encoding.ASCII.GetBytes(Configuration["jwtSecret"])),
                ValidateAudience = false,
                ValidateIssuer = false
            };
            opts.Events = new JwtBearerEvents {
                OnTokenValidated = async ctx => {
                    var usrmgr = ctx.HttpContext.RequestServices
                        .GetRequiredService<UserManager<IdentityUser>>();
                    var signinmgr = ctx.HttpContext.RequestServices
                        .GetRequiredService<SignInManager<IdentityUser>>();
                    string username =
                        ctx.Principal.FindFirst(ClaimTypes.Name)?.Value;
                    IdentityUser idUser = await usrmgr.FindByNameAsync(username);
                    ctx.Principal =
                        await signinmgr.CreateUserPrincipalAsync(idUser);
                }
            };
        });
    }

    public void Configure(IApplicationBuilder app, DataContext context) {

        // ...statements omitted for brevity...
    }
  }
}
```

The AddJwtBearer adds support for JWT to the authentication system and provides the settings required to decrypt tokens. I have added a handler for the OnTokenValidated event, which is triggered when a token is validated so that I can query the user database and associate the IdentityUser object with the request. This acts as a bridge between the JWT tokens and the ASP.NET Core Identity data, ensuring that features like role-based authorization work seamlessly.

Restricting Access with Tokens

To allow a restricted endpoint to be accessed with tokens, I have modified the Authorize attribute applied to the Data controller, as shown in Listing 39-29.

Listing 39-29. Enabling Tokens in the DataController.cs File in the Controllers Folder of the Advanced Project

```
using Advanced.Models;
using Microsoft.AspNetCore.Mvc;
using Microsoft.EntityFrameworkCore;
using System.Collections.Generic;
using System.Threading.Tasks;
using Microsoft.AspNetCore.Authorization;

namespace Advanced.Controllers {

    [ApiController]
    [Route("/api/people")]
    [Authorize(AuthenticationSchemes = "Identity.Application, Bearer")]
    public class DataController : ControllerBase {
        private DataContext context;

        // ...methods omitted for brevity...
    }
}
```

The AuthenticationSchemes argument is used to specify the types of authentication that can be used to authorize access to the controller. In this case, I have specified that the default cookie authentication and the new bearer tokens can be used.

Using Tokens to Request Data

The final step is to update the JavaScript client so that it obtains a token and includes it in requests for data, as shown in Listing 39-30.

Listing 39-30. Using Tokens in the webclient.js File in the wwwroot Folder of the Advanced Project

```
const username = "bob";
const password = "secret";
let token;

window.addEventListener("DOMContentLoaded", () => {
    const controlDiv = document.getElementById("controls");
    createButton(controlDiv, "Get Data", getData);
    createButton(controlDiv, "Log In", login);
    createButton(controlDiv, "Log Out", logout);
});

async function login() {
    let response = await fetch("/api/account/token", {
        method: "POST",
        headers: { "Content-Type": "application/json" },
        body: JSON.stringify({ username: username, password: password })
    });
```

```
        if (response.ok) {
            token = (await response.json()).token;
            displayData("Logged in", token);
        } else {
            displayData(`Error: ${response.status}: ${response.statusText}`);
        }
}

async function logout() {
    token = "";
    displayData("Logged out");
}

async function getData() {
    let response = await fetch("/api/people", {
        headers: { "Authorization": `Bearer ${token}` }
    });
    if (response.ok) {
        let jsonData = await response.json();
        displayData(...jsonData.map(item => `${item.surname}, ${item.firstname}`));
    } else {
        displayData(`Error: ${response.status}: ${response.statusText}`);
    }
}

function displayData(...items) {
    const dataDiv = document.getElementById("data");
    dataDiv.innerHTML = "";
    items.forEach(item => {
        const itemDiv = document.createElement("div");
        itemDiv.innerText = item;
        itemDiv.style.wordWrap = "break-word";
        dataDiv.appendChild(itemDiv);
    })
}

function createButton(parent, label, handler) {
    const button = document.createElement("button");
    button.classList.add("btn", "btn-primary",  "m-2");
    button.innerText = label;
    button.onclick = handler;
    parent.appendChild(button);
}
```

The client receives the authentication response and assigns the token so it can be used by the GetData method, which sets the Authorization header. Notice that no logout request is required, and the variable used to store the token is simply reset when the user clicks the Log Out button.

▪ **Caution**   It is easy to end up authenticating with a cookie when attempting to test tokens. Make sure you clear your browser cookies before testing this feature to ensure that cookies from previous tests are not used.

Restart ASP.NET Core and request http://localhost:5000/webclient.html. Click the Log In button, and a token will be generated and displayed. Click the Get Data button, and the token will be sent to the server and used to authenticate the user, producing the results shown in Figure 39-13.

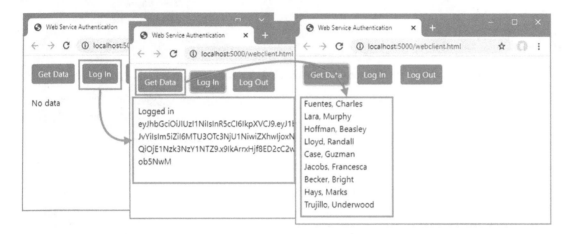

Figure 39-13. *Using a token for authentication*

Summary

In this chapter, I showed you how to apply authentication and authorization in an ASP.NET Core application. I explained the process for authenticating users and restricting access to endpoints. I explained how users are authorized in Blazor applications, and I demonstrated how web service clients can be authenticated using cookies and bearer tokens.

That's all I have to teach you about ASP.NET Core. I can only hope that you have enjoyed reading this book as much as I enjoyed writing it, and I wish you every success in your ASP.NET Core projects.

Index

© Adam Freeman 2020
A. Freeman, *Pro ASP.NET Core 3*, https://doi.org/10.1007/978-1-4842-5440-0

▓ W, X, Y, Z